Gender Identity
and the Law

Gender Identity and the Law

David B. Cruz
Newton Professor of Constitutional Law
USC Gould School of Law

Jillian T. Weiss
Special Co-Counsel to Outten & Golden, LLP
LGBTQ Practice Group

CAROLINA ACADEMIC PRESS
Durham, North Carolina

ISBN   978-1-5310-1587-9
e-ISBN   978-1-5310-1588-6
LCCN   2020946870

Carolina Academic Press
700 Kent Street
Durham, North Carolina 27701
Telephone (919) 489-7486
Fax (919) 493-5668
www.cap-press.com

Printed in the United States of America

For J.C., and trans youth everywhere, with the hope that this book may in some measure help make your journey easier

—DBC

Contents

Table of Cases

Introduction

Over the past decades, a framework has begun to emerge in U.S. law regarding gender identity and expression, shaping the rights of millions of people who are transgender or "trans," used here to include gender non-conforming, nonbinary, and other related categories. Having evolved from a patchwork quilt of statutory laws, administrative regulations and policies, and judicial opinions, the emergent framework contains many tensions and inconsistencies yet to be resolved.

The authors of this casebook bring distinct perspectives from within the LGBTQ+ community. David Cruz is Newton Professor of Constitutional Law at the University of Southern California Gould School of Law, a cisgender, out gay Latino, who has written extensively on U.S. constitutional law and sex, gender, and sexual orientation law. He first taught a course on gender identity and the law in 2010. Jillian Weiss, a transgender woman, has a practice primarily representing transgender clients in employment discrimination matters. She is also a retired Professor of Law and Society from Ramapo College of New Jersey and former executive director of the Transgender Legal Defense and Education Fund, and she has widely published in the area of transgender rights.

This casebook is designed to provide students a comprehensive understanding of the decades-long revolution in law and society regarding the concepts of gender identity and expression that affect trans individuals in many related contexts. A background chapter explains the modern conceptions of gender identity and expression, and their relation to traditional notions of sex and gender, that have driven extensive legal developments resulting in hundreds of decisions in areas of law commonly considered unrelated. The book invites students to examine these concepts in a range of contexts nearly as broad as the lives we all live, including government identification, parenting and youth care, schools, employment, disability, healthcare, housing, public accommodations, immigration, and incarceration. It encourages students to analyze how these varied areas are or should be understood as interrelated and integrated, and what they mean for traditional legal and social understandings of sex and gender.

This book enables examination of its topics from the standpoint of trans persons, foregrounding their lived experience and the discriminatory effects of transphobia, transmisogyny, and transmasculine erasure. This stands in distinction to approaches that theorize transgender people's experiences of law as fundamentally outgrowths of gender or sexual orientation biases. This focus enables students to theorize the legal wrongs against trans persons as wrongs qua wrongs against their lived identities, understanding them as trespasses against their right to live in their chosen gender, rather than merely as sequelae of incorrect stereotypes of their gender assigned at birth. At the same time, the advances in the social statuses and legal rights of trans people are inseparable from "gender" issues and issues of sex, gender, sex roles, and sex stereotyping.

Students should carry away from a course taught from this casebook an understanding of how gendered our law is, how entrenched gender identity biases are, and ways in which the law has been used to lessen the oppressions experienced by trans people. This book's role is not only to facilitate teaching the specifics of this area of law, but to show new lawyers how effective the law can be in combatting social ills as well as ways in which it is less effective or ill-suited to the task of social change. It shines an analytic spotlight on a population subject to numerous social harms in which law has sometimes been complicit and whom increasingly law is developing to protect. It is our hope this will inspire a new generation of lawyers to pursue justice for trans people.

In editing materials for this book, the authors have omitted footnotes without indication; preserved original footnote numbering for those sources where footnotes were retained; used lowercase letters for footnotes we have authored; omitted citations and sometimes parentheticals without indication; and altered citations' formats (e.g., reporters, short form vs. long form) and omitted pinpoint citations generally without indication. Although not entirely consistently in this first edition, the authors tried to indicate with "[*sic*]" when opinions first use terminology that is today widely regarded as derogatory or outdated; we have also albeit incompletely tried to list the movement organizations that have litigated so many of the cases presented. The undercompensated and sometimes unsung efforts of dedicated movement lawyers have been key to the evolution in the law examined in this text.

This book has been a labor of love—a great labor—over many years, and we are profoundly grateful that it has come to fruition. We are thankful that Erwin Chemerinsky put us in touch with Carol McGeehan at Carolina Academic Press, which has been excited about and critical to this book—and we thank Carol, Keith Sipe, Scott Sipe, Ryland Bowman, Jennifer Hill, and everyone at CAP who touched this project. Jillian Weiss would like to thank David Cruz, who has spent so many years in pursuit of justice for trans people, for which she is personally grateful. Having talked together about co-authoring such a casebook for over a decade, it is David's mastery of the subject matter, dedication, and tireless enthusiasm in the face of many distractions that made this very timely book happen. David Cruz would like to thank Jillian Weiss, whose legal scholarship on transgender issues, advocacy, and life lived out loud and proud have inspired him for decades. He would not have attempted this project without her. He gives special thanks to law professors Dean Spade and Janet Halley for sharing their transgender law course materials with him when he was preparing to teach his first class in this area, as well as to Alex Bastian, Mark Ohl, and Tina Sohaili, the intrepid USC Gould School of Law students who showed up at 8:00 a.m. for this new course, whose weekly insights about the material helped influence his thinking about the field, and whose discussions of RuPaul's Drag Race helped ensure the course never lost touch with the culture that has been changing in ways necessary to allow gender identity and expression law to develop in the more open and inclusive ways as so much of it has. A legion of student research assistants have helped with trans law research, including (with profound apologies to anyone inadvertently omitted) Alex Bastian, Emily Cronin, Edward Demirjian, Nicholas Duncan, George Ellis, Robina Gallagher, Kate Im, John Korevec, Sabrina Kumre, Tiffany Li, Abby Lu, Mack Matthews, Chris McElwain, Melissa Mende, Paul Moura, Jacob Ordos, Gus Paras, Brett Pugliese, Eric Remijan, Christina Roberto, Gabriela Rodriguez, Matthew Schuman, Travis Schumer, Melissa Shinto, Jessica Bromall Sparkman, Kerry Sparks, Queenie Sun, Christina Tapia, Jill Vander Borght, Helen You, and especially Ryan Gorman, whose work for this book was instrumental in helping the authors bring it to completion. The brilliant and talented USC Gould School of Law librarians particularly including Judy Davis, Diana Jaque, Paul Moorman, Brian Raphael, and Karen Skinner have helped with research over many years. Kathleen Perrin, founder and president of Equality Case Files, has selflessly brought her expertise to bear to provide David research on trans legal issues, often on very short time frames. The USC Gould School of Law and its Deans Scott Bice (who hired David), Matt Spitzer (under whom he earned tenure following selfless mentoring by Mary Dudziak and Jody Armour), Ed McCaffery, Bob Rasmussen, and Andrew Guzman (under whom David became the Newton Professor of Constitutional Law, for which he is also grateful to the late Mr. and Dr. Newton) provided economic and other support for his scholarship on LGBTQ+ issues starting at a time when those were much less recognized as worthwhile areas of scholarly inquiry. David owes a special debt to his assistant and dear friend Katie Waitman, whose great talents, sound judgment, and tremendous labors, from the earliest phases of the project to the very end, have made this casebook possible and much better than it would otherwise have been. David also thanks his family, including especially his parents Sue (who passed during the completion of this book) and Nick, for their support and sacrifices. Finally syntactically but first and foremost substantively, David thanks his husband and partner of decades Steve Greene, for encouraging him to go to law school and to pursue his commitment to justice for LGBTQ+ people, for putting up with the long hours David put in on this book everywhere including with his laptop on his lap in the car every week for well over a year, and for unflagging love and support.

Gender Identity
and the Law

Chapter 1

A Survey of Sex/Gender Variation

This chapter of the casebook focuses on historical, scientific, and sociological information about sex, gender, gender identity, gender performativity, and related notions relevant to the study of law's engagement with transgender, gender nonconforming, and nonbinary persons.

A. From the Ancients Through Early Moderns

Gender variation is found throughout history across cultures. What follows is a discussion of some of these gender variations. Understanding them is important because they demonstrate that gender is not solely a product of biology, and that gender variance is a human trait not solely a product of culture. In addition, premodern cultures did not always see a sharp distinction between gender expression or identity and sexual orientation.

Many pre-modern cultures incorporated differences in gender expression and identity. In the pre-colonial Americas, the *ninauposkitzipxpe* were a third gender in the North Piegan tribe of the Blackfoot Confederacy in northern Montana and Southern Alberta, Canada. Its meaning is generally translated as "manly-hearted woman." It referred to a person assigned female at birth who was not restricted by social constraints of other women, though they did not necessarily dress in a masculine mode. The Incas had *chuqui chinchay*, a dual-gendered god, whose adherents were considered a third gender and wore androgynous clothing.

Europeans generally saw people with these alternate genders as "sodomites" and interpreted them in that light. Caution must be exercised with these and all non-Western identities to avoid cultural misappropriation. Modern discussions of American Indian "two-spirit" identities sometimes incorrectly conflate traditions of different Native American tribes, and also wrongly analogize them to contemporary conceptions of "transgender" identities found in the global North. Terms such as "*berdache*," a pejorative word for two-spirit people meaning catamite, created by European conquerors, have been used by modern Westerners who were unaware of the impropriety of the term.

In pre-colonial African civilizations, the Kingdom of Dahomey had the *mino*, female warriors. They were unmarried and childless women who were thought to have masculine traits. The Bangala people's shamans would dress in women's clothing in order the gain the ability to solve crimes such as murder. The Ankole people elected a woman to dress as a man and thereby become an oracle to the god Mukasa. Among the Sakalavas in Madagascar, feminine boys were raised as girls. The Antandroy and Hova called their gender crossers "*sekrata*." They wore their hair long and in decorative knots, sported pierced ears, and wore bracelets on their arms, wrists and ankles.

In the Fertile Crescent, Asia Minor, and Central Asia, gender variations took various forms as well. In Assyria, there were religious acolytes who often wore female clothing and used female symbols. In ancient India, the *hijra* were a caste of third-gender people, generally assigned male at birth, who lived in a female role. The *hijra* traditions are still active in modern India and Pakistan. During the Mamluk Sultanate, children assigned female at birth who had masculine traits were raised as boys and as adults were understood to be men. The *köçek* were people assigned male at birth who lived as women. Many of them were dancers, and today there is a *köçek* folkloric dance tradition. The Chukchi of Siberia had a tradition of "soft men," highly respected shamans, assigned male at birth, who assumed female sex roles, using female hairstyles and some female clothing.

Because pre-modern cultures did not necessarily define gender variance in the ways in which it is understood today in Western cultures, European colonial invaders generally completely misunderstood the cultures of colonized people. This often resulted in violence by the colonizers, who considered same-sex relationships to be deserving of serious violence and death. The early modern European understanding of gender variance, discussed below, must be understood in this light.[a]

The Construction of Homosexuality[*]

Early texts, including Greek and Roman sources, speak of same-sex desire but do not categorize persons solely by the sex of their partners. There was no single identity that linked all men who engaged in same-sex acts. Indeed, adult patrician males were expected to have sex with both boys and women, who were passive and expected to be so. Homosexual behavior was not limited to some subculture that had distinct tastes for men only. Significantly, as mirrored in the distaste for effeminacy of much of modern gay male and patriarchal culture, and the separation of gay

---

a. For further information about historical sex/gender variation around the world, see, for example, Oscar Lewis, *Manly-Hearted Women Among the North Piegan*, 43.2 Amer. Anthropologist 173 (1941); Walter L. Williams, The Spirit and the Flesh: Sexual Diversity in American Indian Culture (1992); Jean E. Balestrery, Intersecting Discourses on Race and Sexuality: Compounded Colonization Among LGBTTQ American Indians/Alaska Natives, 59 J. Homosexuality 633 (2012); Ed Butts, Bodyguards! From Gladiators to the Secret Service (2012); *Global Terms*, Digital Transgender Archives, https://www.digitaltransgenderarchive.net/learn/terms (last visited July 14, 2020); *A Map of Gender Diverse Cultures*, PBS, Aug. 11, 2015, http://www.pbs.org/independentlens/content/two-spirits_map-html/ (last visited July 14, 2020).

* This section is excerpted with minor alterations from Jillian T. Weiss, GL vs. BT: *The Archaeology of Biphobia and Transphobia Within the U.S. Gay and Lesbian Community*, 3.3–4 J. Bisexuality 25, p.35–p.37 (2004).

culture from what we now call "transgender" culture, Greek texts satirized effeminate males, and both literary and legal texts suggested it was unmanly behavior to accept a passive role in sexual intercourse after passing a certain age. Also in keeping with patriarchal culture, women were believed not to have sexual feelings, and with the exception of the poetry of Sappho, little was written or understood about female same-sex acts. They were assumed not to exist; their various forms were secret and did not inform the public perceptions of same-sex relations.

By the fourth century, the male same-sex acts that had been so public were forced to go underground, creating a tension between secret identity and public identity, between "passing" or "assimilating" (as a non-sodomite or non-homosexual) versus being open about one's sexuality, either to potential partners or to the public, by declaration or behavioral style. Those who wished to engage in such practices risked strong social condemnation and severe judicial punishment. In keeping with earlier ideas, it was believed that any man who was led astray, rather than a distinct subgroup of men who had inclinations towards men only, could indulge in same-sex behavior. However, there is evidence that, beginning in the twelfth century, this belief began to change, and the contrasting belief that there was a certain type of man who engaged exclusively in same-sex behaviors slowly began to arise. Those who engaged in same-sex behaviors were beginning to be designated as "sodomites." Nonetheless, it was "passive" homosexuals who received the brunt of the condemnation, leaving in place an ethic in favor of the masculine. Passing as the opposite sex occurred fairly frequently, however, and while it was also forbidden, it was rarely punished, as it was not considered, in and of itself, a sexual crime. It does not appear that there was any necessary linkage in the public mind between cross-dressing and sodomy until the eighteenth century.

By the eighteenth century, the public understanding was that same-sex acts were connected with effeminacy and cross-dressing, that those who engaged in same-sex acts did so exclusively, that same-sex acts were confined to a specific group of people, and that the propensity towards such acts was inborn. Despite this linkage between male same-sex behavior and effeminacy in the public mind, most men who engaged in same-sex behavior rejected effeminate practices and role-playing. The public conception of homosexuality coincided with a growing concern with effeminacy that appeared in England in the eighteenth century. Boys typically wore girls' clothing until they were sent away to boarding school. Men's clothing was frilly in the Elizabethan Age. However, clothing became more sharply differentiated from the 1770s on. There were diatribes against fops and dandies. By the nineteenth century, men no longer dared embrace in public or shed tears. Concerns about effeminacy periodically boiled over during the ensuing years with regularity.

The nineteenth century scientific crusaders, Karl Heinrich Ulrichs and Magnus Hirschfeld, furthered the linkage between homosexuality and gender by theorizing homosexual men as "hermaphrodites of the mind," with male bodies and female souls, though not without opposition. In 1910, Hirschfeld coined the term "transvestite" to refer to one who prefers to wear the clothing of the opposite sex, to distinguish it and separate it from the phenomenon of homosexuality. Hirschfeld first mentioned "psychic transsexualism" in passing in 1923, but the term was not widely accepted until popularized by Dr. Harry Benjamin in the 1960s.

Thus, from the nineteenth century unitary conception of homosexuality there developed two concepts: "sexual orientation" (sexual object choice) and "gender identity" (sexual self- identification as male or female). This scientific rationalism and medicalization of homosexuality confirmed it as a unitary, monolithic phenomenon. This created a monosexist "homosexual identity" (one committed to the superiority of exclusively same-sex orientations over a bisexual orientation) and a corresponding tension between, on the one hand, identification as homosexual, and on the other, passing as heterosexual and/or engaging in heterosexual relationships.

B. Nineteenth and Twentieth Century Normalization and Medicalization

The understanding of "transgender" identity, as it is understood in the global North today, is a product of the thinking that originated in pre-modern times. It is generally accepted among modern health professionals and scientists that gender identity and expression are not solely products of biology and are distinct from (though culturally related to) sexual orientation. However, one cannot appreciate the patchwork of legal frameworks governing transgender people today without knowing the intertwined history of gender variance, sexual orientation, beliefs in biological origins, and changing scientific understandings.

The Meaning of "Transgender"*
A. Defining "Transgender"

As with so many words defining matters touched by social change, the term "transgender" has come to mean something different from what it originally described. When it was originally created in the 1980s (as "transgenderist"), it referred to those who lived in a sex role different from their sex assigned at birth, but who did not opt for medical or surgical intervention. In other words, transgender described someone who retained his or her original anatomy, but who used gender expressions, such as dress, grooming, and voice, to live in a different sex role. It was coined in distinct opposition to the term "transsexual," which at that time referred to someone who sought medical and surgical intervention to achieve sex reassignment. While to the uninitiated these terms might seem similar, the natures of these identities are quite distinct. In order to determine their relationship with

---

* This section is excerpted with minor alterations from Jillian T. Weiss, *Transgender Identity, Textualism, and the Supreme Court: What Is the Plain Meaning of Sex in Title VII of the Civil Rights Act of 1964?*, 18 Temp. Pol. & Civ. Rts. L. Rev. 573, p.581–p.590 (2008).

the term "sex" as used in Title VII, it is imperative to understand their significant differences in connotation, which requires a brief history of their etymology.

1. Homosexuals and Transvestites

In 1864, the German sex researcher Karl Heinrich Ulrichs created the term "urning" to refer to men who constituted a "third sex." In prior centuries, it was believed that anyone could be led astray, rather than a distinct subgroup of people who had inclinations towards same-sex relations.[b] Ulrichs, who considered himself an urning, theorized that these men were similar to hermaphrodites,[56] though in a psychological, rather than physical sense. In 1868, Hungarian writer Karl-Maria Kertbeny, who disagreed with Ulrichs' theory, coined the term "homosexual" to refer to men who had the inborn and unchangeable desire for same-sex romantic partners. While Ulrichs' term cast a wider net, Kertbeny's narrower term became the preferred one. In 1910, Dr. Magnus Hirschfeld, a German sex researcher, came up with a different term, "transvestism," to distinguish men who crossdressed in female clothing from homosexuals. Hirschfeld's group of transvestites consisted of both males and females, with heterosexual, homosexual, bisexual, and asexual orientations. These identities, as conceived at that time, could be diagramed as follows:

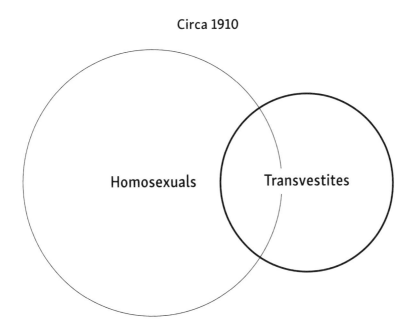

Circa 1910

Homosexuals   Transvestites

---

b. *Cf.* Eve Kosofsky Sedgwick, Epistemology of the Closet 1 (1990) (distinguishing "minoritizing" and "universalizing" conceptions of same-sex desire).

56. "Hermaphrodite" refers to an organism having both male and female reproductive organs. As applied to humans, the term "intersex" is preferred, as the term "hermaphrodite" has become associated with sensationalism.

2. Transvestites and Transsexuals

While transvestism was a phenomenon primarily defined by clothing choice, it was clear to Hirschfeld at the time he coined the term that those defined as transvestites had different meanings attached to their crossdressing. Some did so for pleasure (both erotic and non-erotic), to attract romantic partners, or for work (as female impersonators in the theater, as women engaged in male occupations, or as prostitutes). Others, however, felt that their clothing choices were dictated by their inner cross-gender identity. Hirschfeld first mentioned "psychological transsexualism" ("*seelischer transsexualismus*") in 1923. This new term did not refer to medical or surgical intervention because there were no such techniques available at that time.[65] Rather, this new term allowed identification of a sub-group that wore their gendered identity not only on the outside, but also on the inside. There were other subgroups within the transvestite category, but the scientific community did not distinguish them. These subgroups were known by various informal names in different communities, such as drag queens (in the gay community) and two-spirit people (in certain Native American tribes). There were and are dozens of such informal groupings. The term "transsexual" did not become widely used, however, until popularized by the books of Dr. Harry Benjamin and Christine Jorgensen in the 1960s. The new term's place in the taxonomy could be diagrammed as follows:

Circa 1965

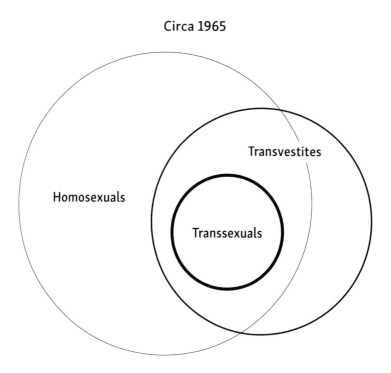

---

65. The first identifiable sex reassignment surgery took place in 1930, which Hirschfeld supervised. It is clear, however, that Hirschfeld did not consider such surgical intervention critical to the identity. Such surgeries did not become generally available until the late 1960s.

3. Transsexuals and Transgenders

The preceding diagram quickly became inaccurate because of a series of developments. When the story of Christine Jorgensen was published in 1951, debates began about whether she was properly classified as homosexual or transsexual. In the first case study of Jorgensen, published in 1951 by her endocrinologist, he referred to her "homosexual tendencies." Jorgensen herself, however, specifically distinguished her condition from homosexuality, referring to the prevalent theory of transsexuality as a mistake of nature in which a woman is trapped in a man's body. She took pains to distinguish her situation from "a much more horrible illness of the mind. One which, although very common, is not as yet accepted as a true illness, with the necessity for great understanding." This "horrible illness of the mind" is likely a reference to homosexuality. In this way, Jorgensen, and many transsexuals [*sic*] of the time, attempted to avoid the severe mid-century stigma of homosexuality. Jorgensen's endocrinologist later changed his mind, deciding that Jorgensen's condition differed fundamentally from homosexuality. Many other prominent scientists and doctors agreed, provoking intense controversy.

Jorgensen's story and the writings of Dr. Harry Benjamin suggested that the transsexual label should be reserved for those who wanted surgical intervention to assist them in sex reassignment. The placement of this label in the taxonomy caused some confusion. Some continued to see this group as a subset of the homosexual group, while others considered it a severe form of transvestism. The vast majority of transsexual people not only *desired* to reassign their sex, but also considered themselves *members* of that new sex. Therefore, even if their sex assigned at birth was the same as that of their romantic partners, their new sex was now the opposite of that of their romantic partners, making them heterosexuals. Thus, in order to correctly understand the meaning of the transsexual identity, the transsexual group must be separated from the homosexual group. At the same time, however, it must be recognized that many transsexuals prefer romantic partners of their "new" sex.

There were also many people who had intense cross-gender feelings, so much so that they lived in the opposite sex role in a more permanent way, but did not desire sex reassignment surgery. The latter group specifically disavowed the transsexual's persistent desire to change physical sex characteristics. Nor would it be accurate to say that they dressed in the clothing of the opposite sex occasionally for personal enjoyment. The term "transgender" was coined by Virginia Prince in the 1970s as a demarcation of a space separate from the transsexual category, though its popular usage did not adhere to this fine distinction. People began to use transgender to refer to all types of cross-gender behavior. This broader use of the term gained substantial ground in the academic world, when feminist scholars began to take the theoretical stance that greater social acceptance of deviations from traditional gender roles was an important goal. The use of the term transgender began to gain a connotation of political unity among people with types of cross-gender behavior previously seen as separate and unrelated.

Further complicating the picture, a subgroup of transvestites emerged who were not homosexuals and wished to mark a separate identity outside of homosexual transvestites. This group, known as crossdressers, contains self-proclaimed heterosexual males, sometimes with girlfriends and wives, who occasionally dress in female clothing, mostly in private or in private groups.

. . . .

Today, "transgender" has taken on a different usage—as an umbrella term to denote transsexuals, transvestites, crossdressers, and anyone else whose gender identity or gender expression varies from the dimorphic norm. Although, typically, male and female biological attributes go with certain distinct gender attributes, the correspondence is not certain. Some people have nontraditional gender identity or expression—male biological attributes are combined with "female" gender attributes, or female biological attributes are combined with "male" gender attributes.[97] The most widely known transgender identity/expression is that of post-operative transsexuals, who live in the opposite sex role from that of their birth and have received surgical and medical intervention to change their anatomical configuration to match that of the opposite sex. Many people think of this identity when they hear the word transgender. This is, however, only one of many transgender identities. An employee's gender identity categorization has become an issue when trying to decide whether a transgender employee is covered by Title VII of the Civil Rights Act of 1964.

Although many of the cases addressing nontraditional gender identities use medical terms, such as transsexual and transvestite, these terms presume a set of relationships between sex and gender that are not inherent in Title VII analysis. The statute specifically refers to discrimination "because of . . . sex," not "because of transsexuality." The important issue for an employee seeking redress is whether sex is involved, not whether they are classified as a transsexual or a transvestite. Many assume that there is a precise line marked by surgery dividing transvestite and transsexual. This is incorrect. Many of those who are classified as male-to-female transvestites have breast augmentation and facial feminization surgery. Many of those who are classified as female-to-male transsexuals do not have phalloplasty. The genitalia of a transgender person may or may not correspond to their gender. The actual state of the genitalia of a transgender person is, however, rarely at issue in the employment setting because employee genitalia are rarely uncovered. This is crucial to Title VII analysis because it demonstrates that employers generally do not know the anatomical sex of their transgender employees. Rather, they presume their sex from their gendered appearance, and this sex-derived presumption leads to the dismissal.

---

97. I refer to "male" and "female" gender attributes in quotes, as these attributes are not intrinsically male or female, but are typically found in biological males or biological females.

It should be noted that transgender identity or expression is different from issues of the sexual orientation of lesbians, gays, and bisexuals. Transgender refers to "gender identity or expression," meaning "our own deeply held conviction and deeply felt inner awareness that we belong to one gender or the other." Transgender also refers to "gender expression," the behavioral and social expressions traditionally engaged in by persons of a particular gender. Transgender self-identification and self-expression do not correspond to the physical body in the usual way. In contrast, lesbian, gay, and bisexual individuals who are not transgender identify and express themselves as male or female according to their physical anatomy. The distinguishing characteristic of lesbian, gay, and bisexual identity is attraction to sex partners with the same anatomy (although bisexuals are also attracted to the opposite sex). In contrast to laws protecting transgender people, which often refer to "gender identity or expression," laws protecting lesbians, gays, and bisexuals refer to "sexual orientation," which defines the sex of the individuals to whom one is emotionally and erotically attracted.

C. Non-European Gender Variance[*]

The discussion of gender variance in pre-modern cultures in Section A of this chapter provides some illumination of the origins of modern understandings of gender. The caveat discussed at the end of that section regarding cultural misappropriation applies here as well. It is particularly important to understand that the modern U.S. understanding of transgender identity is not necessarily mappable to non-European gender variances. Gender, gender identity, and gender expression are not solely products of biology but are influenced by culture. Therefore, various cultures have both distinct and overlapping understandings of these. Because the United States is largely a nation of immigrants, with a continued strong influx from other countries around the globe, these different conceptions are often present in our discussions of gender, often without acknowledgment of their very different meanings. This can create problems for lawyers without knowledge of these issues in attempting to understand the needs of clients.

Different societies have different names referring to transgender people, as well as different social locations for them. In many countries (and in many languages), the term "transgender" does not exist or is largely unrecognized. The older terms "transsexual" and "transvestite" are instead sometimes used. Other terms, such as "*hijra*" (India and Pakistan) or "*kathoey*" (Thailand), are used, with varying degrees of acceptance and pejorativeness. In such places, these terms are used to

---

* Some of the material in this section is drawn from Jillian T. Weiss, *Teaching Transgender Issues: Global Social Movements Based on Gender Identity*, Ch. 2, *in* A Twenty-First Century Approach to Teaching Social Justice: Educating for Both Advocacy and Action, 358 Counterpoints 27 (2009).

describe a wide variety of gender variance, and do not have the narrowed meanings found in the United States (where "transsexual" commonly describes only those who have or plan to have genital surgery and "transvestite" primarily those heterosexuals who cross-dress in private). For example, there is a term "*transgenero*" in Spanish, but many Spanish speakers do not recognize the term. Instead, they respond to "*transsexualismo*" or "*travesti*," neither of which is completely synonymous with their English cognates, "transsexuality and "transvestite," and both are often defined by inclusion of elements of what is considered "sexual orientation" in the United States. In some cultures, transsexuals consider themselves "gay" or "homosexual," whereas other cultures have a sharply defined distinction between transgender and gay identities. These differing language elements reflect more than simple linguistic differences—they show significant social and political differences in the understanding and inclusion of gender-variant citizens.

A detailed archive of the cultural and linguistic differences across the world regarding gender non-conformity can be found at *Global Terms*, Digital Transgender Archive, https://www.digitaltransgenderarchive.net/learn/terms (last visited Feb. 27, 2020). In the following discussion, examples of these differences from the Digital Transgender Archive and PBS's *A Map of Gender-Diverse Cultures*, Aug. 11, 2015, https://www.pbs.org/independentlens/content/two-spirits_map -html/ (last visited July 14, 2020) are described with some quotation.

In parts of South America, the term *travesti* refers to a person who was assigned male at birth, has a feminine gender identity, and whose romantic partners are generally masculine men. Their identities often include "feminine dress, language, and social and sexual roles." However, many *travestis* identify as gay or homosexual rather than identifying as women, and they "rarely seek genital surgery" (although some seek hormone or silicone treatment). Because of rampant discrimination, many *travestis* are in the occupations of sex worker or hairdresser. In recent years, violence against *travestis* has skyrocketed.

In North America, the Dominican Republic has a long tradition surrounding one type of people born with an intersex trait. They are assigned female at birth and generally raised as girls. They experience a male puberty, however, because of undescended testicles that become manifest at that time. Most of these individuals live as a third gender called *guevedoche* ("testicles at 12") or *machi-embra* ("man-woman"). They have social roles distinct from those of men and women.

Native American cultures, although negatively influenced in some cases by settler societies, continue to have a vibrant tradition of gender variance. *Winkte* is a Lakota word for two-spirit people. The *winkte* "are assigned male at birth but assume many traditional women's roles" (*e.g.*, cooking and childcare). They also play key roles in "rituals and serving as the keeper of the tribe's oral traditions." *Nadleehi* is a Navajo term that refers to a person assigned male at birth who "embodies both the masculine and feminine spirit." Similarly, the Navajo term *dilbaa* refers to a person assigned female at birth who is masculine. *Nadleehi* and *dilbaa* are each considered to embody both genders simultaneously. They are held in high regard and often assume roles as healers. The Zuni people use the word *lhamana* to describe a person who embodies both genders simultaneously. *Lhamana* "play a key role in society as mediators, priests, and artists," and they engage in both "traditional women's work" (*e.g.*, pottery, crafts) and "traditional men's work" (*e.g.*, hunting).

In Europe, Italy has a particularly rich history of gender variance. The term *femminiello*, which translates literally as "little man-woman," refers to people assigned male at birth but who live as women, mostly in Naples and surrounding areas. Although European society generally looked down on similar identities, the *femminiello's* station in society is traditionally considered a respected one. Many *femminielli* do not wish to be called "transgender" or "transsexual," finding those terms alien to their culture. They have many ancient ceremonies, which are in some ways a kind of theater, such as the Marriage of Zeza, a marriage festival, the "Death of Carnival," an ersatz funeral, and the Figliata, a simulated birth. These have complex meaning and symbols, and merit in-depth study to understand their significance. To call these *femminielli* "transgender" is to misidentify and perhaps misunderstand them.

Gender variance also has a long history in Africa. Among the Maale people of southern Ethiopia, *ashtime* referred to eunuchs who lived in the ruler's palace, performing traditionally female duties in lieu of women who were forbidden from entering. The term is now often used to refer to any gender non-conforming male. *Mashoga* is a Swahili term that may refer to gay men, as well as people assigned male at birth who assert a female gender. They "characteristically wear both men and women's clothing," but in a different style from others. They often are asked to participate in wedding ceremonies. Last, the *xanith* of Oman have a non-binary gender. While they take on female roles, they often have male names and are referred to with male grammar. They are accorded the rights of men, including the right to testify in court, attend the mosque with men, and be employed.

South Asian cultures also have their own history of gender variance. In India, Pakistan, and Bangladesh, *hijras* have a female gender identity. Many *hijras* understand themselves as a third gender. Due to prejudice, *hijras* are marginalized. Continuing attempts to eliminate discrimination have achieved little success. The British had tried to eliminate *hijras*, including them in the Criminal Tribes Act 1871, which required them to register with the authorities. Decriminalization occurred in 1952.

The term *meti* refers to a third gender in Nepal. They are assigned male at birth but assume a female gender identity. *Metis* are subject to violence and prejudice, and most make their living as sex workers. In Thailand, transgender women are referred to as *sago*. The term *kathoey*, loosely translated as "lady-boy," is considered pejorative. According to Thai tradition, kathoeys "are known as being born male but 'having a female heart.'"

Malaysian *acault* are people assigned male at birth who live as women and "often serve as spirit mediums in the indigenous animistic belief system." Indonesian *waria* are assigned male at birth but live on a "continuum of gender identity." The

Bugi people of southern Sulawesi recognize three non-traditional genders: *calabai*, *calalai*, and *bissu*. *Calabai* are people assigned male at birth who live as women. *Calalai* are people assigned female at birth who live as men. *Bissu* is a non-binary category, "either encompassing all genders or none at all." And in the Philippines, *bakla* refers to various sexual orientations and gender identities but most often specifically denotes a person assigned male at birth who "assumes the dress, mannerisms, and social roles of a woman."

In Australia, the terms *sistergirl* and *brotherboy* describe certain indigenous transgender individuals. These individuals were well integrated into society prior to colonization. The Maori *whakawahine* are people assigned male at birth who "prefer the company of women and take up traditionally feminine occupations such as weaving." *Wakatane* are people assigned female at birth who pursue "traditionally male roles" (*e.g.*, warrior, physical labor). There are similar third gender traditions in Samoa (*fa'afafine*), Hawai'i (*mahu*), and Tonga (*fakaleiti*).

These are but a sampling of various non-European identities around the world. They contrast sharply with the modern European assumption that there are only two sexes that conform rigidly to assignment at birth. This brief survey provides contrasting context for many of the early cases presented in this book that express incredulity at the idea that a person can deviate from their sex assigned at birth. Of course, with colonization came Christian priests and missionaries, who often viewed the indigenous cultures as inferior and undesirable, to be inveighed against and eliminated. Colonized people were taught to be ashamed of their cultures and to aspire to European mores, particularly with regard to the more aggressive forms of masculinity prevalent among eighteenth and nineteenth century colonizers. This has resulted in some holding the historically uninformed belief that being lesbigay or transgender is a European importation. In fact, a great many cultures have traditionally understood gender variation as a typical feature of human life.

D. Sex and Gender Under Women's and Homophile Movements

The second wave of feminism, beginning in the 1950s, and the "homophile" movements, beginning around the same time, were both promoting the idea that women, and gay and lesbian people, are entitled to equal rights with men and heterosexually identified persons. These movements felt it was to their benefit to rebut the often-leveled charge that they were advocating the end of gender or promoting the feminization of men. Each consequently engaged in an aggressive campaign of demonstrating their buy-in to the prevailing concepts of gender by repudiating those within their groups perceived to be gender non-conforming and thus gender-disruptive. The early second wave feminist movement attacked "the lavender menace," referring to lesbians who sought to participate in the movement. The early homophile movement attacked gender non-conforming gay and lesbian and transsexual people. The following article excerpt explores the reaction of the early gay equality movements to transgender people.

The History of Transphobia[*]

When the story of Christine Jorgensen was published in 1951, debates began amongst these groups as to the proper response. In the first case study of Jorgensen, published in 1951 by her endocrinologist, he referred to her "homosexual tendencies." Jorgensen herself, however, specifically distinguished her condition from homosexuality, referring to the prevalent theory of transsexuality as "nature's mistake," in which a woman is trapped in a man's body. She takes pains to distinguish her situation from "a much more horrible illness of the mind. One that, although very common, is not as yet accepted as a true illness, with the necessity for great understanding." This "horrible illness of the mind" is a reference to homosexuality. In this way, she attempts to avoid the severe mid-century stigma of homosexuality, as did many transsexual people of the time. Jorgensen's endocrinologist later changed his mind, deciding that Jorgensen's condition differed fundamentally from homosexuality, and many other prominent scientists and doctors agreed, provoking intense controversy. The importance of this controversy can only be understood in reference to the extreme intensity and pervasive ubiquity of the stigma of homosexuality up to the 1950s. Such prejudice provokes compassion for Jorgensen's attempts to distinguish herself from homosexuality, and empathy for those who saw her as an opportunist who condemned homosexuals in order to earn the acceptance of straight society.

There was a vigorous debate in the U.S. homophile movement of the 1950s as to whether homosexuals should embrace Jorgensen. Some gay men and lesbians denounced those who felt themselves to be of the opposite sex, criticizing them for acting like "freaks," bringing disrepute to those gays and lesbians trying to live quietly within heterosexual society. Such attitudes were prevalent within the gay and lesbian community at the time. Meyerowitz relates one such debate from 1953:

> In 1953, for example, ONE magazine published a debate among its readers as to whether gay men should denounce Jorgensen. In the opening salvo, the author Jeff Winters accused Jorgensen of a "sweeping disservice" to gay men. "As far as the public knows," Winters wrote, "you were merely another unhappy homosexual who decided to get drastic about it." For Winters, Jorgensen's story simply confirmed the false belief that all men attracted to other men must be basically feminine, which, he said, *they are not.* Jorgensen's precedent, he thought, encouraged the "reasoning" that led "to legal limitations upon the homosexual, mandatory injections, psychiatric

---

* This section is excerpted with minor alterations from Jillian T. Weiss, *GL v. BT: The Archaeology of Biphobia and Transphobia Within the U.S. Gay and Lesbian Community*, 3.3–4 J. Bisexuality 25, p.38–p.42 (2004).

treatment—and worse." In the not-so-distant past, scientists had experimented with castrating gay men.

Meyerowitz portrays the tension between homosexuals and transsexuals as based upon the tension between passing and openness, what she terms "gender transgression," suggesting that it may have derived from class differences and differing class tolerances for "swish" and "butch." She notes that some gays and lesbians associated gender transgression with undignified and low-class behavior, while "fairies" and "butches" were more readily accepted in working class communities. She also relates a survey from the 1960s that found that more than two-thirds of a sample of almost 300 gays and lesbians in the homophile movement considered those who asked for sex-change surgery to be "severely neurotic."

Kay Brown of Transhistory.org ("Transsexual, Transgender and Intersex History") has set forth a long chronology of the ejection of those whom we now know as "transgender" from gay organizations starting in the 1970s, and the following material is drawn from her website. [http://www.transhistory.org/history/index.html] She notes that transgender people played pivotal roles in gay organizations of the late 1960s and early 1970s, including the Gay Liberation Front and the Gay Activists Alliance ("GAA"). While the original goals included complete acceptance of sexual diversity and expression, by the early 70s the gay men's community returned to the assimilationist strategy as the lesbians turned to separatism and radical feminism. There seemed to be no room for transgender people in either camp. For example, in 1971 the GAA wrote and introduced a bill to the New York City Council to protect homosexuals from discrimination. The bill did not include any explicit protection for transsexuals.

In early 1970's, Beth Elliott, a founder and active member of a number of gay and lesbian organizations, was Vice-President of the San Francisco chapter of the Daughters of Bilitis. Brown describes the events as follows:

> Late in [Elliott's] term of office her transgender status became a point of contention at the West Coast Lesbian Conference, where she was outed and vilified for being an MTF transsexual. The complaint was that Beth Elliott had insinuated herself into a position of power over women as a patriarchal man, a propagandist ploy that was to become common when attacking other transgender people. At the conference she was forced to stop her music concert due to the catcalls from the audience by women that knew nothing more about her than that she was transsexual. She was required to sit through a popular vote of the attendees to determine whether they would let her finish her set. In the weeks and months to follow she was further vilified and even betrayed by women who had once called her friend. [The treatment she received led her to become "stealth" for many years after.]

In 1973, during a gay rally, a well-known transgender activist was followed on the stage by a lesbian separatist who denounced transgender women as men who, by "impersonating women," were exploiting women for profit. Later in the 70s, lesbian separatists made an issue of the presence of lesbian-identified transsexual women in their movement. Central to the conflict was a transsexual recording engineer working at Olivia Records. Lesbian separatists threatened a boycott of Olivia products and concerts.[c] On the edge of profitability, the company eventually fired the engineer. Attempts to exclude transsexuals also characterized the 1977 San Francisco Gay Pride Parade.

Two years later, Janice Raymond, a lesbian academic, wrote *The Transsexual Empire*, a book based on her doctoral dissertation. Raymond argued that the phenomenon of transsexuality was created by fetishistic males who sought to escape into a faux stereotypical femininity, with the connivance of male doctors who thought that femaleness could be medically created and homosexuality medically vitiated. Although "male to constructed female" transsexuals claimed to be against the stereotyped gender system by virtue of their escape from stereotypical masculinity, they in fact added force to the binary system by merely escaping from one stereotype to another, or at most mixing together different stereotypes, rather than advocating true gender freedom. They were not political radicals, as they claimed, but reactionaries seeking to preserve a stereotypical gender system that was already dramatically changing due to the political action of 60s and 70s feminists and gays. Transsexuals were, according to Raymond, sheep in wolves' clothing.[d]

Henry Rubin argues that the creation of a separate transsexual identity and community emerges in the 1970s in the U.S., when it was made repeatedly clear that butch lesbians were no longer welcome within the lesbian feminist movement.

The blatant lack of regard for transgender identities can also be found in gay rewriting of history. For example, Dr. Alan L. Hart was born October 4, 1890 as a female named Alberta Lucille Hart. After graduating from the University of Oregon Medical College in 1917, Hart consistently presented a male persona to the world for four and a half decades until his death in 1962. In the 1920s, Hart consulted a psychiatrist, underwent a hysterectomy and changed his name to Alan L. Hart. The majority of Hart's biographers insist upon viewing the doctor as a woman in disguise, without regard for Hart's self-identification as a man, medical treatment, and legal documentation.

In his 1976 book, *Gay American History,* for example, Professor Jonathan Ned Katz categorized Hart as "clearly a lesbian, a woman-loving woman [who] illustrates only too well one extreme to which an intelligent, aspiring Lesbian in early twentieth-century America might be driven by her own and her doctor's acceptance of society's condemnation of women-loving women." [Margaret Deirdre]

---

c. Sandy Stone, *The Empire Strikes Back: A Posttranssexual Manifesto, in* Body Guards: The Cultural Politics of Gender Ambiguity (Julia Epstein & Kristina Straub, eds., 1991).

d. For a more recent example of such trans exclusive radical feminism or "TERF," as it is sometimes called, see Sheila Jeffreys, Gender Hurts: A Feminist Analysis of the Politics of Transgenderism (2014).

O'Hartigan refers to Pat Califia's statement that "Katz's book is unfortunately tainted with a heavy dose of transphobia." She also brings up Katz's footnote in his *Gay/Lesbian Almanac* about an unpublished paper: *"Transsexualism": Today's Quack Medicine: An Issue for Every Body,* and notes his statement "An historical study needs to be made of the medical and autobiographical literature on 'transsexualism'; it will, I think, reveal the fundamentally sexist nature of the concept and of the associated medical treatments." O'Hartigan also sets forth, disapprovingly, an explanation for referring to Hart as female by [transgender woman] Susan Stryker: "As an historian favoring 'social construction' approaches to questions of identity, I have reservations about using the word 'transsexual' to refer to people before the mid-20th century who identify in a profound, ongoing manner with a gender that they were not assigned to at birth."

It is against this backdrop that, in the early 1990's, the term "transgender," a neologism with an unclear meaning, began to be included in the GLB coalition. The term was used as an umbrella term referring to transvestites, crossdressers, transsexuals, and other gender-variant people, who seemed to have similar and interlocking interests with gay men and lesbian women, and who had caught the imagination of the public through sympathetic portrayals of transsexuals such as Christine Jorgensen, Renee Richards and Wendy Williams. Originally, the term "transgender" was intended by its coiner to refer only to certain non-operative transsexuals, but later mutated to refer to anyone whose gender performance varied from the norm. This more open meaning, however, conflicted with the goals of the coalition builders, which was to capture public sympathy by appealing to an image of homosexuals as people "just like" the majority of U.S. voters, middle class people (or people with middle class yearnings), who held steady jobs, had long, loving relationships with partners of the same sex, and who wanted the same lives that the majority of U.S. voters wanted. As a result, some gays find themselves agreeing with straights who see in transgender people an assault on normative reality, as in the following diatribe thinly veiled as humor:

> There's something a little annoying about transgendered people insisting that they be called whatever sex they want to be called . . . Like so many transgendered people, Califia is like a bush resenting the grass for not calling it a tree. Well, if you've got bush and no trunk, are you really a tree? Before all the MTF (male-to-female) transgendered people flick their compact mirrors shut and take up their pitchforks (with matching handbags, of course), I'd like to point out that there's a reality that exists outside of ourselves. If you wear brown and insist that I call it red because you say so, then you're asking me to skew an objective reality to your liking. Enrolling people into in an illusion unsupported by facts seems manipulative to me . . . So for all the Pattys, Pats and Patricks out there, you go boys/girls/TBA. Just don't back over us with your whoop-ass mobile because we didn't get your pronoun right.

> . . . .

Chapter 2

Conceptualizing Sex/Gender

Sex—here referring to a classification of persons, rather than to activities regarded as erotic—is not nearly as simple as many people commonly believe and law often presupposes. Although it is quite reasonably contestable, as this chapter illustrates, the male/female dichotomy is widely naturalized. "Socially, people treat persons as male or female based on presumptions about how male and female persons look and act, and often on the unverifiable belief that God or Nature created humans as two mutually exclusive, exhaustive types." David B. Cruz, *Disestablishing Sex and Gender*, 90 CALIF. L. REV. 997, 1055 (2002). As one of this casebook's authors has argued:

> States (and individuals) generally act as though they believe that people can be divided into two classes, male and female, that stand in a relationship of opposition to one another (hence "the opposite sex"), that are mutually exclusive . . . , and that are exhaustive (you must be in . . . one of these sex groups). Though they should not, the seeming naturalness and utter familiarity of this common taxonomic scheme of sex identity sometimes lead one to overlook the human agency that state actors are exercising when they make determinations of sex identity. Biology does not so neatly partition humankind. People are marked by tremendous biological, anatomical, hormonal, and even genetic variation.

David B. Cruz, *Sexual Judgments: Full Faith and Credit and the Relational Character of Legal Sex*, 46 HARV. C.R.-C.L. L. REV. 51, 64–65 (2011). Hence, as Prof. Cruz concludes, "gender is ideological, for it is a way of imposing order on, and making sense of, the world; it is a matter of belief. . . ." David B. Cruz, *Getting Sex "Right": Heteronormativity and Biologism in Trans and Intersex Marriage Litigation and Scholarship*, 18 DUKE J. GENDER L. & POL'Y 203, 215 (2010).

Section A of this chapter presents factual information about the variety of bodily characteristics that human societies have coded as male or female. It emphasizes modern medicine's appreciation of the many "components" that may go into determining a person's sex. And it discusses how societies have treated sex, transgender persons, and intersex persons (also described as persons with intersex conditions), who might not so easily be located in taxonomic schemes that try to provide simple criteria for sorting humans into male and female as two mutually exclusive, exhaustive, permanent classes. Section B then takes up questions of the protection that law might offer persons with intersex conditions from the sorts of painful, often unsuccessful surgeries frequently performed upon intersex newborns or infants when their genitalia do not clearly conform to envisioned binary standards of "proper" male or female anatomy.

A. Scientific/Medical Conceptions of Sex/Gender

Modern science and modern medicine recognize numerous "sex markers," or "components" of sex, including but not limited to chromosomes and genitalia. For many people these may consistently point toward female or toward male. But there can be (and is, to a greater extent than most people probably recognize) inconsistency between different sex markers, and even individual sex markers might be ambiguous and by themselves not clearly suggest a person is female or male. While in the past people with such conditions may have been referred to as "hermaphrodites," that is widely regarded as pejorative today; "intersex" may be the preferred term today (though some use "differences of sex development" to describe such conditions). For a fairly comprehensive academic study of the legal treatment of people with intersex conditions, see Julie A. Greenberg, Intersexuality and the Law: Why Sex Matters (2012). This book builds upon an earlier, trail blazing, and frequently judicially cited law journal article of Professor Greenberg's, Julie A. Greenberg, *Defining Male and Female: Intersexuality and the Collision Between Law and Biology*, 41 Ariz. L. Rev. 265 (1999).

Note also that, while intersex people often have a binary gender identity (as male or female), there is today increasing recognition of people with nonbinary gender identities. As Professor Jessica Clarke has explained:

> People with nonbinary gender identities do not exclusively identify as men or women. The term "gender identity" generally refers to a person's internal sense of whether they are a man or a woman while "sex" refers to "bodily characteristics" or the male or female designation ascribed to an infant at birth. . . . [N]ot all nonbinary people identify as transgender, and many transgender people identify as men or women. Nonbinary gender identity is not the same thing as intersex variation. "'Intersex' refers to people who are born with any of a range of sex characteristics that may not fit a doctor's notions of binary 'male' or 'female' bodies." While some nonbinary people have intersex variations, not all do, and many people with intersex variations have male or female gender identities.

Jessica A. Clarke, *They, Them, and Theirs*, 132 Harv. L. Rev. 894, 897–98 (2019).

Human Sex Development

In re Heilig involved an unopposed petition filed by a transgender woman seeking a court order both changing her legal name to Janet Heilig Wright from the conventionally male name she had been assigned at birth and declaring her "sexual identity" designation to be female. The trial court granted the name change but denied the request to declare Wright's sex changed, on the independent grounds that sex was at some level unchangeable and that it lacked authority to issue such a declaration. The intermediate appellate court affirmed, but the state high court (the "Court of Appeals") concluded that the state courts did have such equitable authority. It vacated the judgment below and directed the petition be sent back to the trial court for determination whether Ms. Wright was entitled to such a declaration. The case is summarized in Chapter 16, Note, *infra* at p. 1111. What follows is the court's discussion of the medical literature on sex development, with references to transgender persons and to persons with intersex conditions.

In re Heilig

816 A.2d 68 (Md. 2003)

[Ms. Wright was represented by transgender attorneys/scholars/activists Alyson Dodi Meiselman and (now Judge) Phyllis Randolph Frye.]

Argued before BELL, C.J., ELDRIDGE, RAKER, WILNER, CATHELL, HARRELL, and BATTAGLIA, JJ.

WILNER, Judge.

. . . .

Background

Perhaps because there was no opposition to the petition, the factual evidence in support of petitioner's request for a legal determination of gender change was rather skimpy. . . .

The hearing conducted by the Circuit Court dealt entirely with the issue of jurisdiction. No inquiry was made as to whether petitioner had undergone any sex reassignment surgery, whether and to what extent the hormonal therapy noted by Dr. Dempsey was permanent and irreversible, or what, if any, criteria had been generally accepted in the medical or legal community for determining when, if ever, a complete, permanent, and irreversible gender change has occurred. Although it seems clear from our research that this issue has been considered by courts and legislatures in other States and countries and by various non-judicial agencies, no evidence of the type just noted was presented to the Circuit Court. . . .

Discussion
Transsexualism: Medical Aspects

One of the dominant themes of transsexualism,[3] which, to some extent, is reflected in the two letters and the Standards offered by petitioner [*i.e.*, the Standards of Care

---

3. Several different terms have been used, and misused, in describing persons whose sexual identity is inconsistent with their assigned gender. We shall use the term "transsexual," notwithstanding that it, too, has been defined in different ways. STEDMAN'S MEDICAL DICTIONARY 1865 (27th ed. 2000) defines a "transsexual," in relevant part, as "[a] person with the external genitalia

of the Harry Benjamin International Gender Dysphoria Association [now, World Professional Association for Transgender Health or WPATH—Eds.], is the belief that sex/gender is not, in all instances, a binary concept—all male or all female. *See* Leslie Pearlman, *Transsexualism as Metaphor: The Collision of Sex and Gender*, 43 Buffalo L. Rev. 835 (1995); Julie A. Greenberg, *Defining Male and Female: Intersexuality and the Collision Between Law and Biology*, 41 Ariz. L. Rev. 265, 275–76 (1999). Transsexuals, as petitioner claims to be, seek to achieve recognition of the view that a person's gender/sex is determined by his or her personal sexual identity rather than by physical characteristics alone.[4] Sex reassignment surgery, under that view, merely harmonizes a person's physical characteristics with that identity. *See M.T. v. J.T.*, 355 A.2d 204 (N.J. Super. Ct. App. Div. 1976) ("In this case the transsexual's gender and genitalia are no longer discordant; they have been harmonized through medical treatment. Plaintiff has become physically and psychologically unified and fully capable of sexual activity consistent with her reconciled sexual attributes of gender and anatomy.").

This Opinion is not intended to be a medical text. Apart from our own incompetence to write such a text, it appears that some of the concepts that underlie the views espoused by transsexuals who seek recognition of gender change are the subject of debate, in both the medical and legal communities. The literature, in both communities, is extensive and daunting, and, unguided by expert testimony, there is no way that we could evaluate it properly. It is, however, necessary to understand those underlying concepts in order to determine what gender is and whether, or how, it may be changed.

---

and secondary sexual characteristics of one sex, but whose personal identification and psychosocial configuration is that of the opposite sex." That definition, in the context before us in this case, may be too limiting, at least with respect to persons who, as a result of hormone therapy and sex reassignment surgery, have brought their genitalia and some secondary sexual characteristics into conformity with their personal identification. Persons who have undergone those procedures may no longer regard themselves as transsexual but as having achieved a consistent gender. That, however, is the issue. See Lori Johnson, *The Legal Status of Post-Operative Transsexuals*, 2 Health L.J. 159 (1994). For pure convenience and without implying anything substantive, we shall use the term as descriptive of the person both before and after any medical procedures. Transsexualism has also been referred to as gender dysphoria. It is a condition to be distinguished from transvestism (crossdressing) and homosexuality (sexual attraction to persons of one's own gender).

    4. In the context before us, the terms "sex" and "gender" are not necessarily synonymous for all purposes, and, indeed, the perceived distinctions between them, to some extent, lie at the core of transsexualism. The term "sex" is often used to denote anatomical or biological sex, whereas "gender" refers to a person's psychosexual individuality or identity. *See* Jerold Taitz, *Judicial Determination of the Sexual Identity of Post-Operative Transsexuals: A New Form of Sex Discrimination*, 13 Am. J.L. & Med. 53 (1987); Laura Hermer, *Paradigms Revised: Intersex Children, Bioethics & the Law*, 11 Ann. Health L. 195 (2002); *see also* Pearlman, *supra*, 43 Buffalo L. Rev. at 835; Francisco Valdes, *Queers, Sissies, Dykes, and Tomboys: Deconstructing the Conflation of "Sex," "Gender," and "Sexual Orientation" in Euro-American Law and Society*, 83 Calif. L. Rev. 3 (1995). Much of the debate concerns whether "gender," which takes greater account of psychological factors, is the more relevant concept deserving of legal recognition. The source material uses both terms, and, without implying anything of substance, we shall use the terms interchangeably.

There is a recognized medical viewpoint that gender is not determined by any single criterion, but that the following seven factors may be relevant:

(1) Internal morphologic sex (seminal vesicles/prostate or vagina/uterus/fallopian tubes);

(2) External morphologic sex (genitalia);

(3) Gonadal sex (testes or ovaries);

(4) Chromosomal sex (presence or absence of Y chromosome);

(5) Hormonal sex (predominance of androgens or estrogens);

(6) Phenotypic sex (secondary sex characteristics, *e.g.* facial hair, breasts, body type); and

(7) Personal sexual identity.

See Greenberg (citing John Money, Sex Errors of the Body and Related Syndromes: A Guide to Counseling Children, Adolescents and Their Families (2d ed. 1994)); *In re Estate of Gardiner*, 22 P.3d 1086 (Kan. App. 2001) (citing Greenberg); *Maffei v. Kolaeton Indus.*, 164 Misc. 2d 547, 626 N.Y.S.2d 391 (N.Y. Sup. Ct. 1995); *compare Corbett v. Corbett*, [1970] 2 All E.R. 33, 2 W.L.R. 1306 (Probate, Divorce, and Admiralty Div. 1970) (stressing, for purposes of determining the validity of a marriage, only the chromosomal, gonadal, and genital factors); *Attorney General v. Otahuhu Family Court*, [1995] 1 N.Z.L.R. 603 (High Court Wellington, N.Z. 1994) (stressing importance as well of psychological and social aspects of gender); Stedman's Medical Dictionary 1626 (27th ed. 2000) (defining "sex").

Blackburn notes that the initial development of a fetus is asexual. Susan Tucker Blackburn, Maternal, Fetal, & Neonatal Physiology: a Clinical Perspective 19–24 (2d ed. 2002). The fetus first forms rudimentary sexual organs—gonads, genital ridge, and internal duct system—that later develop into sexually differentiated organs: testes or ovaries, penis/scrotum or clitoris/labia, and fallopian tubes or seminal vesicles/vas deferens, respectively. This initial differentiation, according to Blackburn, is governed by the presence or absence of a Y chromosome inherited from the father. If present, the Y chromosome triggers the development of testes, which begin to produce male hormones that influence much of the fetus's further sexual development. Those hormones cause the development of male genitalia and inhibit the development of the fetus's primitive fallopian tube system. If the Y chromosome is not present, the fetus continues on what has been characterized as the "default" path of sexual development. The gonads develop into ovaries, and, freed from the inhibiting influence of male hormones, the fetus's primordial duct system develops into fallopian tubes and a uterus.

Most often, it appears, a fetus's sexual development is uneventful, and, because all of the sexual features are consistent and indicate one gender or the other, the person becomes easily identifiable as either male or female. When this development is changed or interrupted, however, the situation may become less clear, and people may be born with sexual features that are either ambiguous (consistent with either sex) or incongruent (seemingly inconsistent with their "assigned" sex). *See generally* Alice Domurat Dreger, Hermaphrodites and the Medical Invention of Sex 35–40 (1998) (summarizing varieties of sexual ambiguity); Blackburn (discussing physiological anomalies in fetal sexual development); Greenberg; Claude J. Migeon & Amy B. Wisniewski, *Sexual Differentiation: From Genes to Gender*, 50 Horm. Res. 245 (1998); Selma Feldman Witchel & Peter A. Lee, *Ambiguous Genitalia, in* Pediatric Endocrinology 2d 111 (Mark A. Sperling ed., 2002); Alan J. Schafer & Peter N. Goodfellow, *Sex Determination in Humans*, 18 Bioessays 955 (1996); John Money & Anke A. Ehrhardt, Man & Woman, Boy & Girl: Gender Identity from Conception to Maturity 1–21 (1996).

Individuals who have biological features that are ambiguous or incongruent are sometimes denoted as intersexed or hermaphroditic.[5] *See* Greenberg (summarizing plethora of medical conditions where factors contributing to sex determinations are ambiguous or incongruent). The variety of intersexed conditions encompasses virtually every permutation of variance among the seven factors considered in determining gender. These various ambiguities, moreover, may occur both within a specific factor (*e.g.*, ambiguous, unclassifiable genitalia) or between two or more different factors (*e.g.*, chromosomal sex is incongruent with morphological sex).

Generally, these conditions are classified into three "theoretical types": male pseudohermaphroditism, female pseudohermaphroditism, and true hermaphroditism. The true hermaphrodite consists of an individual with at least some ovarian tissue and some testicular tissue, and is the most rare. Female pseudohermaphrodites often have XX chromosomes and ovaries, but exhibit "masculinized" external genitalia. The "masculinization" of the genitalia can take many forms, including the enlargement of the clitoris or swelling of the labia (thus resembling a scrotum).

Male pseudohermaphroditism describes an individual who is chromosomally male (XY) and has testes, but who also has external genitalia that have become feminized. In one condition, called androgen insensitivity syndrome (AIS), the feminization of the genitalia is the result of the body's inability to respond to the developmental influences of androgen. Without the effects of the male hormone, the genitalia develop along the "default" path of femininity. This process continues through puberty, resulting in a person with (undescended) testes and male chromosomes who is very feminine. Because the condition may be detectable only upon an internal examination, it is often undiagnosed until puberty, when the presumed woman fails to menstruate.

A condition that produces similar results is known as 5-alpha-reductase deficiency (5AR). Like AIS, the individual with 5AR deficiency has testes but fails to respond to androgen in the womb, resulting in feminine external genitalia.

---

5. Although these terms too are sometimes given distinct meanings within the medical literature, the distinction is unimportant for the purposes of this case. We shall use the terms interchangeably.

With the onset of puberty, however, the individual does begin to respond to the increased production of testosterone, and the body begins to masculinize. The individual grows tall and muscular, begins to grow facial hair, and the genitals become more masculine. Some of these types of ambiguities, as noted above, may go largely unnoticed by the individual manifesting them, and may go undiagnosed for years.

In other cases, the individual's sexual ambiguity may be the result of a mistaken "sex assignment" at birth. The official designation of a person as male or female usually occurs at or immediately after birth, and is often based on the appearance of the external genitalia. *See* William Reiner, *To Be Male or Female—That is the Question*, 151 Archives Ped. & Adolescent Med. 224 (1997); Milton Diamond & H. Keith Sigmundson, *Sex Reassignment at Birth*, 151 Archives Ped. & Adolescent Med. 298 (1997); Fayek Ghabrial & Saa M. Girgis, *Reorientation of Sex: Report of Two Cases*, 7 Int'l J. Fertility 249 (1962). Sometimes, when the genitalia are abnormal, doctors have erred in determining the baby's sex, mistaking an enlarged clitoris for a small penis, or vice versa. The criteria for determining sex at birth, one researcher has argued, are simply too rudimentary to be entirely accurate. [Reiner] notes that,

> Past clinical decisions about gender identity and sex reassignment when genitalia are greatly abnormal have by necessity occurred in a relative vacuum because of inadequate scientific data. Clinical decisions have been constructed largely on the predicted adequacy of the genitalia for adult sexual function. But the human may not be so easily deconstructed. Sex chromosome anomalies, gender identity disorder, genital malformations, metabolic adrenal or testicular errors—these conditions imply a sexual plasticity of great complexity.

In the past, it was not uncommon, if a doctor examining the neonatal child observed what appeared to be ambiguous genitalia and concluded that the genitalia so observed would be incapable of functioning in the male capacity, for the doctor to recommend that the child be surgically altered and raised as a girl. *See* Kenneth I. Glassberg, *Gender Assignment and the Pediatric Urologist*, 161 J. Urology 1308 (1999). It was previously believed that a person was psychosexually neutral at birth, and that subsequent psychosexual development was dependent on the appearance of the genitals. Thus, it was assumed, the altered male would psychologically respond, adapt to the new genitalia, and develop into a functional and healthy female.

That view appears no longer to be generally accepted. Individuals who have undergone such surgical alterations as a result of abnormal genitalia often have rejected their "assigned" gender and ultimately request that the alterations be surgically negated so that they may assume their original gender. Diamond and Sigmundson, *supra*, at 303 ("there is no known case where a 46-chromosome, XY male, unequivocally so at birth, has ever easily and fully accepted an imposed life as an androphilic female regardless of physical and medical intervention."). In this regard, the medical community seems to have concluded that human brains are not psychosexually neutral at birth but are "predisposed and biased to interact with environmental, familial, and social forces in either a male or female mode." *Id.*[6]

The medical community's experience with patients born with ambiguous genitalia has led many researchers to believe that the brain "differentiates" in utero to one gender or the other and that, once the child's brain has differentiated, that child cannot be made into a person of the other gender simply through surgical alterations. Some scientists have argued that such medical developments now offer a robust biological explanation of transsexualism—that the brain has differentiated to one sex while the rest of the body has differentiated to another. *See* Frank P.M. Kruijver et al., *Male-to-Female Transsexuals Have Female Neuron Numbers in a Limbic Nucleus*, 85 J. Clin. Endocrinology & Metabolism 2034 (2000); *see also* discussion in *Bellinger v. Bellinger*, [2001] EWCA Civ. 1140, [2002] Fam. 150 (C.A. 2001).

Transsexualism was once regarded as a form of sexual or psychological deviance and, in some quarters, is still considered so today. *See, e.g., Hartin v. Bureau of Records*, 75 Misc.2d 229, 347 N.Y.S.2d 515, 518 (N.Y. Sup. Ct. 1973) (where the New York Board of Health described sex reassignment surgery as "an experimental form of psychotherapy by which mutilating surgery is conducted on a person with the intent of setting his mind at ease, and that nonetheless, does not change the body cells governing sexuality."); *Corbett v. Corbett* (finding litigant's transsexualism to be a "psychological abnormality"); *Maggert v. Hanks*, 131 F.3d 670, 671 (7th Cir. 1997) (in describing transsexual wishing to undergo sex reassignment surgery, court observed that "[s]omeone eager to undergo this mutilation is plainly suffering from a profound psychiatric disorder.").

Recent studies have suggested that this condition may be associated with certain conditions in the womb and certain processes in the developing pre-natal brain. As noted, there is evidence suggesting that the brain differentiates into "male" and "female" brains, just as the fetus's rudimentary sex organs differentiate into "male" and "female" genitalia. *See* Diamond & Sigmundson. These studies, the authors assert, "clearly support the paradigm that in transsexuals sexual differentiation of the brain and genitals may go into opposite directions and point to a neurobiological

---

6. As a result of this more recent experience and knowledge, doctors and clinicians seem now to be more skeptical about surgical alteration of ambiguous genitalia in very young children. Some doctors and advocates have proposed a moratorium on all surgical reconstruction prior to the patient becoming capable of consenting. *See* Milton Diamond, *Pediatric Management of Ambiguous and Traumatized Genitalia*, 162 J. Urology 1021 (1999). Others argue that surgical alteration of the genitalia should be an absolute last resort, performed only if all available alternatives fail. *See* Glassberg, 161 J. Urology at 1309; Melissa Hendricks, *Into the Hands of Babes*, Johns Hopkins Magazine, Sept. 2000, available at http://www.jhu.edu/~jhumag/0900web/babes/html (quoting William Reiner, head of Johns Hopkins Gender Identity and Psychosexual Disorders Clinic); *see also* Hazel Glenn Beh & Milton Diamond, *An Emerging Ethical and Medical Dilemma: Should Physicians Perform Sex Assignment Surgery on Infants with Ambiguous Genitalia*, 7 Mich. J. Gender & L. 1 (2000); Hermer, 11 Ann. Health L. at 197–98.

basis of gender identity disorder." *Id.*; *see also* Kruijver et al.; *see also* Jiang-Ning Zhou et al., *A Sex Difference in the Human Brain and its Relation to Transsexuality*, 378 NATURE 68 (1995). Researchers theorize that the developing brain may differentiate in response to hormonal levels in the womb — "intrauterine androgen exposure." This hypothesis has been tested with animals. *See* John Money, *The Concept of Gender Identity Disorder in Childhood and Adolescence After 39 Years*, 20 J. SEX & MARITAL THERAPY 163 (1994). Research has indicated, for instance, that the sexual differentiation of primates may be manipulated by controlling prenatal hormone exposure. *See* Robert W. Goy et al., *Behavioral Masculinization Is Independent of Genital Masculinization in Prenatally Androgenized Female Rhesus Macaques*, 22 HORMONES & BEHAVIOR 552 (1988). Such experimental results have been cited by at least one court. *See Doe v. McConn*, 489 F. Supp. 76 (S.D. Tex. 1980) (describing the results of experiments discussed above).

The studies imply that transsexualism may be more similar to other physiological conditions of sexual ambiguity, such as androgen insensitivity syndrome, than to purely psychological disorders. Reiner posits:

> What can be stated is that the absence of prenatal androgen exposure, whether a child is XX, XO, has an androgen insensitivity syndrome, and so on, may render the brain to the default, or female, position. Within the potential for transformation from the default brain to the virilized brain is the opportunity for errors of incomplete or improperly timed androgen exposure. Such errors, in addition to acquired, sometimes iatrogenic, post-natal injuries . . . may lead to the misassignment or reassignment of sex at birth from the genetic sex.

The ultimate conclusion of such studies, which, as noted, is the central point sought to be made by transsexuals, is that the preeminent factor in determining gender is the individual's own sexual identity as it has developed in the brain. Reiner continues:

> In the end it is only the children themselves who can and must identify who and what they are. It is for us as clinicians and researchers to listen and to learn. Clinical decisions must ultimately be based not on anatomical predictions, nor on the 'correctness' of sexual function, for this is neither a question of morality nor of social consequence, but on that path most appropriate to the likeliest psychosexual developmental pattern of the child. In other words, the organ that appears to be critical to psychosexual development and adaptation is not the external genitalia, but the brain.

Regardless of its cause, the accounts from transsexuals themselves are startlingly consistent. *See, e.g., Gardiner*; *Littleton v. Prange*, 9 S.W.3d 223, 224 (Tex. Ct. App. 1999); *M.T. v. J.T.* They grow up believing that they are not the sex that their body indicates they are. They believe that they have mistakenly grown up with the wrong genitalia. These disconcerting feelings often begin early in childhood, as early as three or four years. *See, e.g., Littleton*; *M.T.* (where the expert witness testified that "[t]here was . . . 'very little disagreement' on the fact that gender identity generally is established 'very, very firmly, almost immediately, by the age of 3 to 4 years.'"); *McConn* ("Most, if not all, specialists in gender identity are agreed that the transsexual condition establishes itself very early, before the child is capable of elective choice in the matter"). These individuals often rebel against any attempt to impose social gender expectations that are inconsistent with what they believe they are — they may refuse to wear the "appropriate" clothes and refuse to participate in activities associated with their assigned gender. That kind of behavior has become one of the determining factors for a diagnosis of gender identity disorder.

A transsexual wishing to transition to a different gender has limited options. *See* Harry Benjamin International Gender Dysphoria Association, Standards of Care for Gender Identity Disorders (5th ed. 1998). Generally, the options consist of psychotherapy, living as a person of the desired sex, hormonal treatment, and sex reassignment surgery. Although psychotherapy may help the transsexual deal with the psychological difficulties of transsexualism, courts have recognized that psychotherapy is not a "cure" for transsexualism. *McConn*. Because transsexualism is universally recognized as inherent, rather than chosen, psychotherapy will never succeed in "curing" the patient:

> Most, if not all, specialists in gender identity are agreed that the transsexual condition establishes itself very early, before the child is capable of elective choice in the matter, probably in the first two years of life; some say even earlier, before birth during the fetal period. These findings indicate that the transsexual has not made a choice to be as he is, but rather that the choice has been made for him through many causes preceding and beyond his control. Consequently, it has been found that attempts to treat the true adult transsexual psychotherapeutically have consistently met with failure.

McConn.

Hormonal treatment has been shown to be more effective, and, for the male-to-female transsexual, results in breast growth, feminine body fat distribution, a decrease in body hair, and softening of the skin. Although most of these effects are reversible upon termination of the treatment, the individual's breast growth may not reverse entirely. Hormonal treatment for female-to-male transsexuals results in deepening of the voice, enlargement of the clitoris, breast atrophy, increased upper body strength, weight gain, increased facial and body hair, baldness, increased sexual arousal, and decreased hip fat.

Surgical options for the male-to-female transsexual include orchiectomy (removal of gonads), vaginoplasty (construction of vagina), and mammoplasty (construction of breasts). Jerold Taitz, *Judicial Determination of the Sexual Identity of Post-Operative Transsexuals: A New Form of Sex Discrimination*, 13 Am. J.L. & Med. 53 (1987). Some patients elect to undergo additional cosmetic surgeries to enhance other secondary sex features, such as facial structure or voice tone. Surgical options for the female-to-male transsexual include mastectomy, hysterectomy, vaginectomy, and phalloplasty. As most health insurance companies currently exclude coverage for transsexual treatment, the out-of-pocket cost is often prohibitively expensive. One commentator has asserted that a male-to-female operation costs an average of $37,000, whereas the average female-to-male operation costs $77,000. Aaron C. McKee, *The American Dream—2.5 Kids and a White Picket Fence: The Need for Federal Legislation to Protect the Insurance Rights of Infertile Couples*, 41 Washburn L.J. 191 (2001). Another estimate describes the cost as "easily reach[ing] $100,000." *Maggert*. Contributing to the much higher cost of female-to-male sex reassignment surgery is the increased technical difficulty of phalloplasty, estimates for which range from $30,000 to $150,000. *See* Shana Brown, *Sex Changes and "Opposite Sex" Marriage: Applying the Full Faith and Credit Clause to Compel Interstate Recognition of Transgendered Persons' Amended Legal Sex for Marital Purposes*, 38 San Diego L. Rev. 1113 (2001); Patricia A. Cain, *Stories From the Gender Garden: Transsexuals and Anti-Discrimination Law*, 75 Denv. U. L. Rev. 1321 (1998). The procedure may require several operations.

Estimates of the number of intersexed individuals vary considerably, from 1 per 37,000 people to 1 per 2,000 to as high as 3 per 2,000. It seems to be a guess, although Dreger suggests that "the frequency of births in which the child exhibits a condition which today could count as 'intersexual' or 'sexually ambiguous' is significantly higher than most people outside the medical field (and many inside) assume it is."

In reviewing the medical literature, we have avoided making pronouncements of our own, but have simply recounted some of the assertions and conclusions that appear in that literature—assertions and conclusions which, when presented in the form of testimony in court, have evoked differing responses from the courts, both in the United States and elsewhere. Notwithstanding that this remains an evolving field, in which final conclusions as to some aspects may be premature, the current medical thinking does seem to support at least these relevant propositions: (1) that external genitalia are not the sole medically recognized determinant of gender; (2) that the medically recognized determinants of gender may sometimes be either ambiguous or incongruent; (3) that due to mistaken assumptions made by physicians of an infant's ambiguous external genitalia at or shortly after birth, some people are mislabeled at that time as male or female and thereafter carry an official gender status that is medically incorrect; (4) that at least some of the medically recognized determinants of gender are subject to being altered in such a way as to make them inconsistent with the individual's officially declared gender and consistent with the opposite gender; and (5) whether or not a person's psychological gender identity is physiologically based, it has received recognition as one of the determinants of gender and plays a powerful role in the person's psychic makeup and adaptation.

For our purposes, the relevance of these propositions lies in the facts that (1) gender itself is a fact that may be established by medical and other evidence, (2) it may be, or possibly may become, other than what is recorded on the person's birth certificate, and (3) a person has a deep personal, social, and economic interest in having the official designation of his or her gender match what, in fact, it always was or possibly has become.[7] The issue then becomes the circumstances under which a court may declare one's gender to be other than what is officially recorded and the criteria to be used in making any such declaration.

. . . .

Discussion

1. While the Maryland Court of Appeals uses "hermaphroditic" and "intersexed" interchangeably, many people with intersex conditions and allies consider "hermaphrodite"/"hermaphroditic" to be archaic and pejorative, and today "intersex" is used more than "intersexed," with phrases such as "intersex persons," "persons with an intersex condition," and "differences of sex development" (an alternative to the more normative, medical phrase "disorders of sex development") (each abbreviated DSD) becoming increasingly common. Indeed, it should be noted that the "disorders of sex development" phraseology "created a division between those [intersex activists] who were willing to accept DSD terminology and work with medical professionals, and those who preferred intersex." Maayan Sudai, *Revisiting the Limits of Professional Autonomy: The Intersex Rights Movement's Path to De-Medicalization*, 41 Harv. J.L. & Gender 1, 12 (2018). As Maayan Sudai, now an assistant professor of law at the University of Haifa, recounts:

> Those who adhered to the intersex terminology claimed that the term "DSD" pathologized intersex while violating the movement's original core principle: namely, that intersex requires neither medical intervention nor a "cure." Although prominent figures in the movement endorsed DSD terminology for mostly pragmatic reasons, in particular a desire to facilitate dialogue between activists and medical professionals, . . . the use of DSD language was hotly contested and highly divisive.

Id. at 12–13.

2. The court reports that "[e]stimates of the number of intersexed individuals vary considerably, from 1 per 37,000 people to 1 per 2,000 to as high as 3 per 2,000." An incidence rate for intersexuality depends upon the definition adopted, and some estimates are even higher than *Heilig* suggests. Using a definition encompassing any "individual who deviates from the Platonic ideal of physical dimorphism at the chromosomal, genital, gonadal, or hormonal levels," Anne Fausto-Sterling and co-authors estimate 1.7% of the world population to be intersex. Melanie Blackless, Anthony Charuvastra, Amanda Derryck, Anne Fausto-Sterling, Karl Lauzanne, & Ellen Lee, *How Sexually Dimorphic Are We? Review and Synthesis*, 12 Am. J. Human Biology 151 (2000). One researcher has reported that one in 300 persons are born with genital

---

7. Indeed, that interest has received recognition as a "right" under the European Convention for the Protection of Human Rights and Fundamental Freedoms. *See Goodwin v. United Kingdom*, [2002] 2 FCR 577, 67 BMLR 199 (European Court of Human Rights (Grand Chamber) 2002).

"abnormalities," with one in 4,500 people born having genitalia sufficiently ambiguous to preclude assigning a sex immediately upon birth. Kate Davies, *Disorders of Sex Development — Ambiguous Genitalia*, 32 J. PEDIATRIC NURSING 463 (2016).

3. Does the information the court notes about physical and genetic variation among human beings call into question the notion that sex is binary? If it does, what sorts of repercussions should that understanding have for law in a variety of settings?

Gender and Genitals: Constructs of Sex and Gender[*]
Ruth Hubbard

. . . . I would like to take the opportunity . . . to discuss some recent insights into the way the social and biological sciences have constructed sex and gender. In so doing, I accept the usual distinction between these concepts by which sex — whether we are male or female, men or women — is defined in terms of chromosomes (XX or XY), gonads (ovaries or testes), and genitals (the presence of a vagina or a penis — or, more usually, merely the presence or absence of a penis). Gender, specified as masculine or feminine, denotes the psychosocial attributes and behaviors people develop as a result of what society expects of them, depending on whether they were born female or male. However, as [Suzanne J.] Kessler and [Wendy] McKenna and Barbara Fried have pointed out, the concepts of sex and gender are often overlapping and blurred, not only in ordinary speech but also in the scientific literature. . . .

. . . . [Many] manifestations we decide to designate as natural are shaped, or at least affected, by cultural factors, while biology — genes, hormones, and such — affects manifestations we choose to attribute to nurture. In general, what we attribute to nature is no more immune from change than what we attribute to socialization. In fact, in our technological and medicalized era, supposed biological factors often are easier to manipulate than are the forces thought to reflect cultural institutions and traditions or deeply held beliefs. . . .

Sex is usually assigned when an infant is born by looking to see whether it has a penis. If it does, it's a boy; if it doesn't, it's a girl. Gender develops over time and the lore generally accepted in the social science literature is that, in order to develop a coherent gender identity and psychic health, children should know that they are a girl or a boy by the time their language abilities are at the appropriate stage, about age two or two and a half.

Embedded and unquestioned in this developmental formulation from sex to gender is the binary paradigm that, biologically speaking, there are only two kinds of people — women and men — so, two sexes, and that people who belong to one or the other, through socialization and experience, come to emphasize the characteristics appropriate to the corresponding gender. Let us now look at this situation in greater detail.

---

[*] Excerpted from Ruth Hubbard, *Gender and Genitals: Constructs of Sex and Gender*, 14 SOC. TEXT 157 (1996). Reprinted by permission of Elijah Wald.

When it comes to sex, the Western assumption that there are only two sexes probably derives from our culture's close coupling between sex and procreation. That coupling, if it does not grow out of the teachings of Western religions, is surely reinforced by them. Yet, this binary concept does not reflect biological reality. Biologist Anne Fausto-Sterling estimates that approximately 1 or 2 percent of children are born with mixed or ambiguous sex characteristics, though, for obvious reasons, it is difficult to be sure of the numbers. . . .

. . . . [In] several villages in the Dominican Republic a certain number of children who are chromosomally XY and who develop embryonic testes (so, "male") manifest a genetic variation in which the transformation of their testosterone into dihydrotestosterone (DHT) is impeded. Since DHT is the form of testosterone that ordinarily serves to masculinize the external genitalia in XY embryos, these children are born looking like girls and are therefore said to be socialized like girls. However, at puberty their testosterone shows its effects: their testes descend into what have hitherto been thought to be labia, their voice deepens and their clitoris is transformed into a penis. The U.S. biomedical scientists who first described this situation reported that, though these children have been raised as females, most of them accept their transformation and have it accepted by their society. They were said to change not only their sex but their gender identity—in other words, to become biological and social males.

In fact, there is a good deal of debate about this situation. The original team of U.S. scientists seems to have been entirely unaware of their own enculturation in the binary paradigms of sex and gender and apparently did not ask any questions about how the people among whom this phenomenon occurs thought about sex differences, the immutability of sex, or the relationship between sex and gender.

The fact is that the villagers have special terms for these individuals. They call them *guevedoche* (balls at twelve) or *machihembra* (male female). This suggests that they do not regard such persons as either female or male, but as a third category, a third sex. The attempt to describe the Dominican Republic system in terms of our own binary sex/gender systems has been criticized by the anthropologist Gilbert Herdt. He notes that unfortunately the lack of self-awareness of the biomedical researchers may have distorted the Dominican villagers' viewpoint sufficiently to make it impossible to reconstruct the way they conceptualized this situation before the American researchers arrived on the scene and how they coded it in terms of either sex or gender, if this distinction is at all valid in their setting.

. . . .

In our own culture, before sex was medicalized, people who were obviously intermediate in their anatomy or physiological functions had closeted lives whenever possible. If their indeterminate status became known, they lived more or less miserable lives because intermediate forms are not accepted in the West. In the last few decades, in conformity with the binary paradigm, medical interventions have been developed to try to "correct" the genitals of infants who manifest any form of sex ambiguity. . . .

A rule that appears to operate in such medical sex reconstructions—or rather constructions—is to concentrate on the appearance of the external genitalia and to make them look as unequivocally male or female as possible. . . .

Another rule is for the physicians to emphasize that, from the start, the infant has been of the sex they have decided to assign it to. The ambiguity is made to appear as a minor mistake of nature that modern medical methods can readily right. Therefore, the physicians try to determine as quickly as possible which sex assignment is technically most feasible and to stick with that decision. If they must revise their assessment, every effort is made to say that the baby all along was the sex to which it is being definitively assigned and that the physicians initially made a mistake. The goal is to make the parents feel sure of their child's intrinsic male- or femaleness as soon as possible so that they can act on this conviction in the way they raise her or him from earliest infancy, and not jeopardize the growing child's gender identity.

In this way, as Suzanne Kessler points out, "the belief that gender consists of two exclusive types is maintained and perpetuated by the medical community in the face of incontrovertible physical evidence that this is not mandated by biology." In other words, our gender dichotomy does not flow "naturally" from the biological dichotomy of the two sexes. The absolute dichotomy of the sexes into males and females, women and men, is itself socially constructed, and the fact that we insist on sex being binary and permanent for life feeds into the notion that, for people to be "normal," their gender must also be binary and must match their genital sex. Where ambiguities exist, whatever their nature, the external genitalia are taken to be what counts for gender socialization and development.

. . . . Some transgender theorists and activists have begun to insist that the binary model is hopelessly flawed and needs to be abandoned. They argue not only for an increased fluidity, but want to have gender unhooked from genitals and speak of a "rainbow" of gender. There is no good reason, they say, why the accident of being born with a penis or a vagina should prevent one from fully experiencing what life is as a woman or man.

Not surprisingly, transgender activists and theorists want to have their decisions about gender demedicalized and hence want to abolish psychiatric categories such as "gender identity disorders" or "gender dysphoria." On the other hand, many of them would like to ease access to hormones and surgery so as to make it less difficult for people to transform their anatomies in ways that blur their sex/gender or change it.

. . . . Accounts by or about some of the newer transgenderists place less emphasis on actual surgical transformations of the genitals than used to be true and concentrate more on other satisfactions associated with becoming a transperson. . . .

As a result of greater openness, the demographics have begun to look different. The fact that most of the earlier public transsexuals had been born male gave the appearance that many fewer born women than men wanted to change their sex. Now, however, about the same number of women and men approach medical providers about a sex change. And among the female-to-male transpersons, for whom the techniques of genital reconstruction are fairly inadequate, genitals are assigned even lower priority. . . .

To the extent that transgenderism is becoming just another way in which people construct a gender identity and gender transformations become more acceptable and easier to achieve, the changes need no longer involve the agonies experienced by people who had to overcome society's and their own sense that they were disgusting freaks. At the same time, surgical transformations, though still important, are becoming more optional and less central to the transgender experience. As people can come out of the closet, they find it easier to think about what they really need or want, and sometimes that is a public persona (or range of personae) rather than a more private, genital transformation.

The question for social and natural scientists to ponder is how to reconcile these newer ways of looking at sex and gender with the barrage of sex differences research that claims to "prove" that there are clear-cut differences between women's and men's learning styles, mathematical abilities, brain structures and functions, and so on.

. . . [To] understand both the motivation and the results of this research, we have to bear in mind that most Western scientists come to sex differences research imbued with the binary male/female model. If this binary model is their theoretical starting point, the scientists must begin their investigations by identifying the significant attributes that distinguish the two groups. When they find (as they must) that women and men overlap so widely as to be virtually indistinguishable on a specific criterion, they must go on to look for other criteria and to concentrate on whatever differences they unearth. Small wonder they come to highlight characteristics that fit in with their difference-paradigm while ignoring the overlaps that contradict it. And so, the dichotomization into two and only two sexes or genders gets superimposed on a heterogeneous mix of bodies, feelings, and minds.

. . . .

The time is ripe for physicians and scientists also to remove their binary spectacles and, rather than explore what it means to be "male" or "female," look into what it means to be neither or both, which is what most of us are. All of us, female or male, are very much alike and also very different from each other. Major scientific distortions have resulted from ignoring similarities and overlaps in the effort to group differences by sex or gender. A paradigm that stresses fluidity will generate quite different questions and hence come up with different descriptions and analyses than those derived from the binary view. Social and natural scientists need to move on and explore the implications of the emerging paradigm of a continuum, or rainbow, for the study of sex and gender.

Discussion

1. In what way or ways, if any, might a society's recognition of a "third sex" category be superior to binary sex conceptualizations criticized by the late Dr. Hubbard? Unless a given society's "third sex" refers to everyone who does not fully fall within a binary endpoint of male or female, what challenges might its recognition create?

2. How might law move to implement a conception of sex/gender as a continuum rather than a binary or dichotomy?

———————

Foundational, critical research on intersex persons and their treatment by medicine was conducted by Suzanne Kessler. For Professor Kessler's first, pathbreaking article on the topic, see Suzanne J. Kessler, *The Medical Construction of Gender: Case Management of Intersexed Infants*, 16 Signs: J. Women in Culture & Soc'y 3 (1990). Maayan Sudai identifies this as the first study "to expose the sexist views that pervade the medical treatment of intersex children." Maayan Sudai, *Revisiting the Limits of Professional Autonomy: The Intersex Rights Movement's Path to De-Medicalization*, 41 Harv. J.L. & Gender 1, 15 (2018). What follow are excerpts from her subsequent, book-length treatment of the issues.

Lessons from the Intersexed[*]
Suzanne J. Kessler

Physicians. . . . have considerable leeway in assigning gender, and their decisions are influenced by cultural as well as medical factors. What is the relationship between the physician as discoverer and the physician as determiner of gender? . . . . I am arguing that the peculiar balance of discovery and determination throughout treatment permits physicians to handle very problematic cases of gender in the most unproblematic of ways.

This balance relies fundamentally on a particular conception of "natural." Although the "deformity" of intersexed genitals would be immutable were it not for medical interference, physicians do not consider it natural. Instead, they think of, and speak of, the surgical/hormonal alteration of such "deformities" as natural because such intervention returns the body to what it ought to have been if events had taken their typical course. The nonnormative is converted into the normative, and the normative state is considered natural. The genital ambiguity is remedied to conform to a "natural," that is, culturally indisputable gender dichotomy. . . . Language and imagery help create and maintain a specific view of what is natural about the two genders, and I would argue, about the very idea of gender—that it consists of two exclusive types: female and male. [This belief] is maintained and

———————

[*] Excerpts from Suzanne J. Kessler, Lessons from the Intersexed 30–33, 44–46 (1998). © 1998 by Suzanne J. Kessler.

perpetuated by the medical community in the face of incontrovertible physical evidence that this is not mandated by biology.

The lay conception of human anatomy and physiology assumes a concordance among clearly dimorphic gender markers—chromosomes, genitals, gonads, hormones—but physicians understand that concordance and dimorphism do not always exist. Their understanding of biology's complexity, however, does not inform their understanding of gender's complexity. . . . If physicians recognized that implicit in their management of gender is the notion that finally, and always, people construct gender, as well as the social systems that are grounded in gender-based concepts, the possibilities for real societal transformations would be unlimited. Unfortunately, ... [t]heir "understanding" that particular genders are medically (re)constructed in these cases does not lead them to see that gender is *always* constructed. Accepting genital ambiguity as a natural option would require that physicians also acknowledge that genital ambiguity is "corrected," not because it is threatening to the infant's life but because it is threatening to the infant's culture. Rather than admit to their role in perpetuating gender, physicians "psychologize" the issue by talking about the parents' anxiety and humiliation in being confronted with an anomalous infant. They talk as though they have no choice but to respond to the parents' pressure for a resolution of psychological discomfort and as though they have no choice but to use medical technology in the service of a two-gender culture. Neither the psychology nor the technology is doubted, since both shield physicians from responsibility. . . . Most people assume that the boundary between "female" and "male" is clear. But is the boundary between female and male genitals so obvious that when physicians encounter a "problem" genital they know it? . . . .

Obstetricians. . . . seem to know ambiguity when they see it. In the medical literature on intersexuality, . . . the phrase[] "ambiguous genitals" is used freely with no apparent need to define what "ambiguous" means in this context. . . . It is not uncommon to read statements like, "Their [intersexed] external genitals look much more like a clitoris and labia than a penis or scrotum." . . . .

Ambiguity is at least partially determined by factors such as who is looking, why they are looking, and how hard they are looking. [P]hysicians are cautioned about using testosterone in "treating [an] infant or young boy with a normal-size penis which *appears* [my emphasis] small because it is partially buried in the prepubic fat pad." How hard one "looks" at genitals and what one "sees" is not constrained by the optic nerve but by ideology. . . . Not all parts of "male" genitals are equally important. The cultural meaning of the penis so overshadows the scrotum (fused or not and filled or not) as a gender marker, that scrotal "imperfection" is generally irrelevant. A writer who interviewed Roger Gorski, a physician/researcher at the University of California, Los Angeles, reported that Gorski showed him a close-up photograph of a child's genitals and asked, "What sex is it?" The writer, seeing a penis "plain as day," said confidently that it was a boy. "Gorski's eyebrows shot up. 'Where are the testicles?' he asked. I looked closer. Oops." Gorski was using the photograph to show how the genitals of a genetic female with CAH can be affected, but the example illustrates as well how the average (nonmedical) person, even one who is interviewing a doctor about genitals and gender, can accept a missing scrotum as reasonable.

What one sees when one looks at a clitoris betrays as much about the viewer's assumptions as about the clitoris. One urologist, who was adamant about the need to reduce a girl's larger-than-typical clitoris, told a reporter that he worried about the effects on her when the girl's parents and caregivers saw her spend her early life with *a big huge phallus in the lower end of the abdomen.* [T]his "enormity" is likely to be about an inch in length. The atypical clitoris, as it is photographed for medical texts (brightly lit in a tight "close-up," with the labia held wide apart), is more conspicuous than it might otherwise seem—certainly more than it is in almost all real-life circumstances.

The fact that "looking" matters is supported by the invention of a surgical technique that involves recessing the enlarged clitoris beneath the labia so that it can no longer be seen. [One] problem with this technique is that the "buried" clitoris swells during sexual arousal and produces a painful erection. At what cost is the clitoris required to be an internal organ? In older drawings of the female organs, the clitoris is portrayed as internal, like the bladder, uterus, and cervix. More recent sketches treat it as an external part of the genitals. Clitorises are not protruding more than they used to. Rather, public discussions of female sexuality in the last thirty years have helped evolve a public meaning for the clitoris.

Labia, in contrast, do not (yet) have much of a public role in Western cultures. The less delineated and meaningful a body part is, the more variability is tolerated. . . .

How much of [a quoted surgeon's] deemphasis of the labia minora is due to current surgical limitations, and how much to the assumption "out of sight, out of mind," is left to speculation. It is obvious, though, that looking at labia in this way, much like an everyday person, and not as someone with stringent "ideals," promotes a degree of tolerance not extended to other genital parts but that might serve as a model for how to think about them. . . .

––––––––––––

Discussion

1. If we accept Suzanne Kessler's conclusion that "[t]he belief that gender consists of two exclusive types is maintained and perpetuated by the medical community in the face of incontrovertible physical evidence that this is not mandated by biology[,]" what can be done to try to change that ideological production?

2. If Dr. Kessler is right "that genital ambiguity is 'corrected,' not because it is threatening to the infant's life but because it is threatening to the infant's culture[,]" what ramifications might that have for efforts to eliminate "normalizing" surgeries on intersex infants and children?

3. For a critique of "genital exceptionalism"—"the importance that society places on genitalia as the determinative variable in establishing an individual's

gender, regardless of the individual's identity and gender performance"—in law for "assum[ing] a strict binary view of gender," "treat[ing] non-normative genitalia with contempt," and having "negative, destructive" effects particularly on "transgender and intersex communities," as seen for example "in the absence of legal prohibitions on performing genital-normalizing surgery on infant and minor intersex children," see Lindsey M. Walker, *Genital Exceptionalism Has No Place in the Law: Improving Transgender and Intersex Rights in the 21st Century*, 97 Wash. U. L. Rev. 245 (2019).

B. Legal Protections for Persons with Intersex Conditions

Reading Guide for M.C. v. Aaronson *Complaint*

1. The litigation culminating in an appellate decision represents one effort to secure monetary redress for harms suffered by M.C., an intersex boy who was subjected to "sex assignment surgery" as an infant. Note how the Preliminary Statement in M.C.'s complaint seeks to establish a narrative framing of the dispute.

2. M.C. is suing under a federal statute, 42 U.S.C. §1983, for money damages for violation of his constitutional rights. Which of his constitutional rights does M.C. allege were violated? Note that the Counts in his complaint identify what each defendant allegedly did unlawfully but do not provide detailed argument (*e.g.*, with case citations) as to why their actions were unlawful. A complaint is unlike a brief in that respect, and only has to put the defendants on notice as to the general nature of the claims against them.

M.C., A Minor By and Through His Parents Pamela Crawford and John Mark Crawford v. Dr. Ian Aaronson, Dr. James Amrhein, Dr. Yawappiagyei-Dankah, Kim Aydlette, Meredith Williams, Candice "Candi" Davis, Mary Searcy, and Doe #1, Doe #2, and Doe #3, Unknown South Carolina Department of Social Services Employees

No. 2:13-CV-01303, 2013 WL 1961775 (D.S.C. May 14, 2013)

Complaint

. . . .

I. Preliminary Statement

1. This lawsuit challenges the decision by government officials and doctors to perform an irreversible, painful, and medically unnecessary sex assignment surgery on a sixteen-month-old child in state custody. Defendants performed this surgery for the purpose of "assigning" the child the female gender despite their own conclusion that he "was a true hermaphrodite but that there was no compelling reason that she should either be male or female."

2. Plaintiff M.C. is currently eight years old. When M.C. was an infant, the South

Carolina Department of Social Services ("SCDSS") took him into state care and custody because M.C.'s biological mother was deemed unfit and M.C.'s father was deemed to have abandoned him. M.C.'s biological parents' rights were ultimately terminated.

3. At birth, M.C. was identified as a male based on his external genitalia. Shortly after birth, however, M.C.'s doctors discovered that M.C. had "ambiguous genitals" and both male and female internal reproductive structures. As his medical records repeatedly indicated, M.C.'s doctors determined that he could be raised as either a boy or a girl.

4. Despite not knowing whether M.C. would ultimately grow up to be a man or a woman, and whether he would elect to have any genital surgery, Defendants, who include doctors at a state hospital and SCDSS officials, decided to remove M.C.'s healthy genital tissue and radically restructure his reproductive organs in order to make his body appear to be female.

5. Defendant doctors Aaronson, Amrhein, and Appiagyei-Dankah were primarily responsible for M.C.'s treatment during the time he was in the care of SCDSS. Despite the fact that M.C.'s condition did not threaten his health, the defendant doctors planned and decided to perform a "feminizing-genitoplasty" on the sixteen-month-old M.C. During this surgery, Dr. Aaronson cut off M.C.'s phallus to reduce it to the size of a clitoris, removed one of M.C.'s testicles, excised all testicular tissue from M.C.'s second gonad, and constructed labia for M.C. The surgery eliminated M.C.'s potential to procreate as a male and caused a significant and permanent impairment of sexual function.

6. M.C. was just under sixteen months old at the time of the surgery. The defendant doctors knew that sex assignment surgeries on infants with conditions like M.C.'s pose a significant risk of imposing a gender that is ultimately rejected by the patient. Indeed, one of the doctor defendants who performed the surgery on M.C. had previously published an article in a medical journal wherein he recognized that "carrying out a feminizing-genitoplasty on an infant who might eventually identify herself as a boy would be catastrophic."

7. Since a young age, M.C. has shown strong signs of developing a male gender. He is currently living as a boy. His interests, manner and play, and refusal to be identified as a girl indicate that M.C.'s gender has developed as male. Indeed, M.C. is living as a boy with the support of his family, friends, school, religious leaders, and pediatrician.

8. Defendants' decision to perform irreversible, invasive, and painful sex assignment surgery was unnecessary to M.C.'s medical well-being. Medical authority recognizes that children like M.C. may be assigned a gender of rearing independent of any surgery, meaning M.C. could have been raised as a girl or a boy until he was old enough for his gender identity to emerge. At that point, M.C. and his guardians could have made appropriate decisions regarding medical treatment—including whether to have any surgery at all.

9. Defendants usurped these intimate and profound decisions from M.C. when he was barely older than an infant, knowing that surgically mis-assigning M.C.'s sex would lead to disastrous results. Unfortunately, medical technology has not devised a way to replace what M.C. has lost.

10. By their actions, Defendants also interfered with M.C's future ability to form intimate, procreative relationships, choices central to his personal dignity and autonomy. Defendants decided to perform grossly invasive, painful, and irreversible feminizing-genitoplasty surgery on him, despite the fact that such surgery often sterilizes the individual, in many cases leaves the individual with limited or absent sexual response, and impairs the individual's ability to function sexually as the person might have chosen without surgery. Defendants' actions constituted an egregious, arbitrary, and enduring invasion of M.C.'s bodily integrity.

11. Despite the fact that M.C. could have been raised as either a boy or a girl, Defendants rushed to perform a medically unnecessary, painful, and irreversible sex-assignment surgery on a sixteen-month-old child. Defendants permanently changed M.C.'s body, disregarding his physical and psychological well-being and causing M.C. irreparable injury.

12. Acting under color of state law, Defendants violated M.C.'s substantive and procedural due process rights, including his fundamental rights to bodily integrity, procreation, liberty, and privacy, as guaranteed under the United States Constitution. Through this suit, M.C., by and through his parents and legal guardians Pamela and John Mark Crawford, seeks to vindicate his rights and requests relief in the form of compensatory and punitive damages, as well as attorneys' fees and costs.

II. Jurisdiction and Venue

13. This action arises under 42 U.S.C. § 1983.

14. This Court has jurisdiction under 28 U.S.C. § 1331, which confers original jurisdiction on federal district courts in suits to redress the deprivation of rights and privileges and immunities secured by the laws and Constitution of the United States, in this case the Fourteenth Amendment.

15. Venue is proper in this District and the Charleston Division pursuant to 28 U.S.C. Section 1391(b)(2) and L.R. 3.01(A)(1) because a substantial part of the transactions or occurrences underlying Plaintiffs' claims occurred within the Charleston Division of this District, including a substantial part of the medical decision-making and the procedures which underlie Plaintiffs' claims.

III. Parties

16. Plaintiff M.C. is an eight-year-old child and a current resident of Richland County, South Carolina. He was born on XX/XX/2004 in Greenville, South Carolina.

17. Pamela Crawford ("Pam") and John Mark Crawford ("Mark") are M.C.'s adoptive parents and legal guardians. They took custody of M.C. in August of 2006 and formally adopted M.C. on December 11, 2006. They are current residents

of Richland County, South Carolina. They bring this action in their representative capacity for the benefit of their son, M.C., and hereby apply to this Court for appointment as next friends or guardians ad litem of M.C. for the purposes of this action.

18. Defendant Ian Aaronson, upon information and belief, is, or was at all relevant times hereto, a pediatric urologist and employee of the Medical University of South Carolina ("MUSC"), a medical facility located in Charleston County, South Carolina. MUSC is an agency of the state of South Carolina. Defendant Aaronson is a resident of and/or maintains a medical practice in Charleston, South Carolina. At all relevant times, MUSC provided medical treatment to M.C. pursuant to the state's responsibility for his well-being and care. At all relevant times, Defendant Aaronson provided medical care to M.C. pursuant to the state's responsibility for the well-being and care of M.C. At all relevant times, Defendant Aaronson was acting under color of state law. He is sued in his individual capacity.

19. Defendant James Amrhein, upon information and belief, is, or was at all relevant times hereto, a pediatric endocrinologist and employee of Greenville Hospital System, d/b/a Greenville Memorial Hospital (hereinafter "Greenville Hospital"), a municipal hospital located in Greenville County, South Carolina. . . . Defendant Amrhein is a resident of and/or maintains a medical practice in Greenville County, South Carolina. At all relevant times, Greenville Hospital provided medical treatment to M.C. pursuant to the state's responsibility for his well-being and care. Defendant Amrhein became involved in M.C.'s case in or about February 2005 and was the primary doctor at Greenville Hospital overseeing M.C.'s treatment. At all relevant times, Defendant Amrhein provided medical treatment to M.C. pursuant to the state's responsibility for the well-being and care of M.C. Defendant Amrhein remained involved in treatment-related decisions at least through the sex-assignment surgery performed on M.C. in April 2006. At all relevant times, Defendant Amrhein was acting under color of state law. He is sued in his individual capacity.

20. Defendant Yaw Appiagyei-Dankah, upon information and belief, is, or was at all relevant times hereto, a pediatric endocrinologist and employee of MUSC, with its hospital facility located in County of Charleston, State of South Carolina. At all relevant times, Defendant Appiagyei-Dankah was a resident of and/or maintained a medical practice in Charleston County, South Carolina. MUSC is an agency of the State of South Carolina. At all relevant times, MUSC provided medical treatment to M.C. pursuant to the state's responsibility for his well-being and care. Defendant Appiagyei-Dankah became involved in M.C.'s case in or about January of 2006. At all relevant times, Defendant Appiagyei-Dankah provided medical treatment to M.C. pursuant to the state's responsibility for the well-being and care of M.C. Defendant Appiagyei-Dankah remained involved in treatment-related decisions at least through the sex-assignment surgery performed on M.C. in April 2006. At all relevant times, defendant Appiagyei-Dankah was acting under color of state law. He is sued in his individual capacity.

21. Defendant Kim Aydlette was the Director of the South Carolina Department of Social Services from 2003 through at least August of 2006. SCDSS is an agency of the state of South Carolina, with offices located statewide and its main office in Columbia, Richland County, South Carolina. SCDSS is charged with protecting the safety and well-being of children, who, like M.C, are entrusted to its care and custody. SCDSS retained legal custody of M.C. and had the authority to make all medical decisions for M.C. from February 16, 2005, the date of the ex parte order removing M.C. from his biological parents, until December 11, 2006, the date that he was adopted, and at all times relevant to the claims in this case. Defendant Aydlette was statutorily "vested with the duty and authority to oversee, manage, and control the operation, administration, and organization of the department, subject only to the laws of this State and the United States." S.C. Code Ann. § 43-1-50 (1993). Pursuant to SCDSS policy, any significant medical decision for a child in SCDSS custody required Defendant Aydlette's authorization. She is sued in her individual capacity.

22. Defendant Meredith Williams was a SCDSS employee supervising M.C.'s case. She was responsible for the oversight of M.C.'s case, including his safety and well-being while he was in state custody. She participated in making and carrying out the treatment plan that caused M.C.'s sex assignment surgery. Upon information and belief, she instructed M.C.'s foster mother to physically deliver him to the hospital to undergo the sex assignment surgery. She is sued in her individual capacity.

23. Defendant Candice "Candi" Davis was a SCDSS employee assigned to M.C.'s case and was his adoption caseworker. She was responsible for the oversight of M.C.'s case, including his safety and well-being while he was in state custody. She participated in making and carrying out the treatment plan that caused M.C.'s sex assignment surgery. Upon information and belief, she instructed M.C.'s foster mother to physically deliver him to the hospital to undergo the sex assignment surgery. She is sued in her individual capacity.

24. Defendant Mary Searcy was a SCDSS employee involved in M.C.'s case and responsible for his safety and well-being while he was in state custody. On or about April 17 and 18, 2006, she provided the necessary SCDSS consent for M.C.'s sex assignment surgery. She is sued in her individual capacity.

25. Defendant Doe #1 is or was at all relevant times hereto, a caseworker for, and employee of, SCDSS. Upon information and belief, at all relevant times, Defendant Doe #1 was entrusted with M.C.'s well-being and care while M.C. was in state custody and participated in making and carrying out the treatment plan that caused M.C.'s sex assignment surgery. Defendant Doe #1 is the unnamed SCDSS case worker recorded in M.C.'s medical records as having met with Defendant Appiagyei-Dankah on January 18, 2006. Doe #1's name is currently unknown to Plaintiff. Defendant Doe #1 is sued in his or her individual capacity.

26. Defendant Doe #2 is or was at all relevant times hereto, a caseworker for, and employee of, SCDSS. At all relevant times, Defendant Doe #2 was entrusted

with M.C.'s well-being and care while M.C. was in state custody and participated in making and carrying out the treatment plan that caused M.C.'s sex assignment surgery. Defendant Doe #2 is the unnamed SCDSS case worker recorded in M.C.'s medical records as having met with Defendant Aaronson on January 18, 2006. Doe #2's name is currently unknown to Plaintiff. Defendant Doe #2 is sued in his or her individual capacity.

27. Defendant Doe #3 is or was at all relevant times hereto, a caseworker for, and employee of, SCDSS. At all relevant times, Defendant Doe #3 was entrusted with M.C.'s well-being and care while M.C. was in state custody and participated in making and carrying out the treatment plan that caused M.C.'s sex assignment surgery. Defendant Doe #3 is the unnamed SCDSS case worker recorded in M.C.'s medical records as having met with Defendant Aaronson on February 27, 2006. Doe #3's identity is currently unknown to Plaintiff. Defendant Doe #3 is sued in his or her individual capacity.

28. The Defendants identified in paragraphs 21–27 above are collectively identified in this Complaint as "Defendant SCDSS Officials."

IV. Background on Differences of Sexual Development

29. Moments after a child is born, a physician visually identifies the newborn's genitalia and records the newborn's sex as "male" or "female" on that basis. Biological sex is determined by a number of different physiological factors, including chromosomes, gonads, hormones, and genitalia, although it is commonly generally understood to be as simple as the appearance of the external genitals. Usually a determination of an infant's biological sex is uneventful. Eventually, children develop a gender identity, meaning that their brains identify with a particular gender — a sense of who they are inside.

30. The combined trajectory of biological sex and gender identity is commonly assumed, yet accepted medical standards recognize that gender identity develops independently from external genitalia or other markers of biological sex. There is no definitive consensus on what determines gender identity beyond the fact that this determination occurs within an individual's brain. Gender identity develops over time — the physical aspects visible at birth are not determinative.

31. An estimated one in 2,000 babies is born with reproductive or sexual anatomy that does not fit typical definitions of male or female — a higher incidence than Down syndrome or cystic fibrosis. These infants' physiology is not easily classifiable as male or female. The chromosomes, gonads, internal reproductive system and/or genitalia develop in an atypical pattern. The conditions that cause these variations are sometimes grouped under the terms "intersex" or "DSD" (Differences/Disorders of Sex Development). The medical condition M.C. was born with is ovotesticular DSD, also referred to in medical literature and M.C.'s records as "true hermaphroditism."

32. When a child is born with mixed or ambiguous markers of biological sex, standard medical practice is to assign a sex that is most likely to match the child's gender identity. However, with many intersex conditions, including ovotesticular

DSD, it is impossible to predict with certainty what gender identity will develop. Current standards of care regard the initial sex assignment as provisional, and recommend correcting the sex designation later if the prediction of future gender identity turns out to be incorrect. Recognizing that sex assignment presents a life-changing decision, doctors have typically suggested that adults seeking sex assignment surgery undergo psychotherapy beforehand so that these individuals are both psychologically and practically prepared for this profound step.

33. Irreversible surgical alteration of the genitals and reproductive organs of infants born with intersex conditions, undertaken to create a more typically male or typically female appearance, may reduce or eliminate reproductive capacity and almost always result in significant reduction of sexual function. Sometimes, individuals subjected to childhood sex assignment surgery end up identifying with a gender that does not correspond to the surgical assignment. Even in circumstances where the individual ultimately identifies with the gender the doctors attempted to assign, they have been forced to undergo an extraordinarily invasive, nonconsensual genital restructuring. Current standards of care recognize that children with intersex conditions can be raised as boys or girls without early genital surgery, and that surgery may be postponed until the gender identity has emerged and the patient can decide whether to undergo procedures that risk infertility and the elimination of sexual sensation.

V. Factual Background
Social Services Takes Custody of M.C. Shortly After His Birth

34. M.C. was born on XX/XX/2004, ... weighing less than two pounds at birth. . . .

35. Due to medical complications concerning M.C.'s premature birth and acid reflux (unrelated to his intersex condition), he remained in the hospital for approximately two and a half months after birth.

36. Shortly after M.C.'s birth, SCDSS began an investigation into possible neglect by M.C.'s biological parents. According to a December 7, 2004 SCDSS report, M.C.'s biological mother . . . was difficult to reach by telephone to obtain consent for medical procedures. SCDSS notes indicate that SCDSS officials believed that both biological parents posed substantial risk of physically neglecting M.C.

37. On February 8, 2005, M.C. was released from the hospital into his biological parents' care. Just one week later, his biological parents notified SCDSS that they wanted to relinquish their parental rights. M.C.'s biological parents had earlier given SCDSS written permission to access his medical records.

38. SCDSS then pursued an ex parte order to remove M.C. from the custody of his biological parents. On February 16, 2005, a court ordered that custody of M.C. be placed with SCDSS. About six months later, SCDSS filed a termination of parental rights complaint. The court terminated M.C.'s biological parents' parental rights on September 9, 2006.

39. Until his adoption in 2006, M.C. lived with two different foster families. Pursuant to state law, however, SCDSS retained legal custody of M.C. while he was in foster care. SCDSS officials made decisions whether to authorize medical treatment, including the sex assignment surgery, prepared paperwork necessary to implement the sex assignment treatment plan, and instructed the foster family at the time to deliver M.C. to the hospital at which the sex assignment surgery was performed. SCDSS retained the authority to make all medical decisions for M.C. from February 16, 2005, the date of the ex parte order removing M.C. from his biological parents, until December 11, 2006, the date that he was adopted.

M.C.'s Diagnosis of Ovotesticular DSD

40. M.C. was born with a condition called ovotesticular DSD (Difference/Disorder of Sex Development). Previously referred to as "true hermaphroditism," ovotesticular DSD is characterized by the presence of both ovarian and testicular tissue.

41. M.C.'s doctors identified him as male in both the labor and delivery summary and the newborn identification form. He was born with a testicle, an ovotestis (a gonad with both ovarian and testicular tissue), and other male and female internal reproductive structures. The medical record of M.C. at birth noted that his "phallus was rather large," measuring approximately 1.5 to 2 centimeters in length. Routine blood tests indicated that M.C.'s testosterone levels were "extremely elevated." Subsequent medical records note that the M.C. was born with small vaginal opening below a "significant" phallus, with a "scrotalized" labia.

42. For most of M.C.'s first year of life, his doctors were not certain of his sex. In his early medical records, the medical professionals treating him referred to him sometimes as male and sometimes as female. They performed multiple tests to determine hormone levels and the presence of internal sex organs. On April 26, 2005, when M.C. was about six months old, Dr. Michael Gauderer performed surgery on M.C. related to M.C.'s acid reflux condition at Greenville Hospital. During the surgery, Dr. Gauderer performed exploratory surgery to inspect M.C.'s internal sex organs. His medical report indicates that M.C. had "ambiguous" genitalia, and that one gonad most closely resembled an ovary and the other gonad most closely resembled a testis.

43. In a letter to M.C.'s pediatrician dated October 5, 2005, Defendant Amrhein, who had become involved in M.C.'s case earlier that February, described M.C.'s DSD as "confusing." In the letter, he noted that M.C. had a vagina and perhaps a uterus, but that M.C. also had "a 3.0 cm well-developed phallus" and "scrotalized labia," and that M.C.'s testosterone levels were "extremely elevated." Defendant Amrhein noted that despite his intersex condition, M.C. "continue[d] to do well with no specific concerns or problems."

44. On October 11, 2005, Dr. Gauderer performed a second surgery on M.C. at Greenville Hospital. He biopsied M.C.'s internal sex organs, and attempted to rearrange M.C.'s reproductive organs by moving the ovotestis up into the abdominal cavity and the testicle down into the labia majora. The notes from that surgery

indicated that M.C. had a "short vagina, absent uterus, normal infantile left testis, and a right ovotestis."

Defendant Doctors' Decision to Perform Medically Unnecessary Sex Assignment Surgery on M.C.

45. Following the biopsy performed by Dr. Gauderer, Defendant Amrhein wrote to M.C.'s pediatrician, stating that in his opinion, M.C. was a "true hermaphrodite." Defendant Amrhein further opined that a decision needed to be made regarding M.C.'s gender of rearing and "surgical correction." Having decided that M.C. needed "surgical correction," Defendant Amrhein referred his case to [Defendant] Aaronson, the surgeon who ultimately performed the sex assignment surgery, and Defendant Appiagyei-Dankah, a pediatric endocrinologist at MUSC. Defendant Aaronson, Appiagyei-Dankah, and Amrhein collaborated to ultimately decide to perform the sex assignment surgery. At no time did any doctor request an ethics consult to determine whether the surgery was in M.C.'s best interest.

46. Over the next six months, from January to May 2006, Defendants Aaronson and Appiagyei-Dankah examined M.C. at MUSC several times and discussed his condition amongst themselves, sometimes with involvement of SCDSS employees. Having examined M.C., Defendants Aaronson, Appiagyei-Dankah, and Amrhein all concurred that there was no compelling biological reason to raise M.C. as either male or female. This view is noted in the following medical records:

a. January 18, 2006: "Due to the nature of [M.C.'s] external genital anatomy, either sex of rearing is possible with appropriate surgery." [Defendant Appiagyei-Dankah's progress notes].

b. January 18, 2006: "I was . . . able to reassure both her social worker and adoptive [*sic*] mother that as far as the external genitalia are concerned, this can be corrected surgically so that the baby looks either a normal boy or girl" [Letter from Defendant Aaronson to Defendant Amrhein].

c. February 27, 2006: "[C]urrently she could be potentially raised, surgically reconstructed, and treated to be male or female." [Defendant Appiagyei-Dankah's progress notes].

d. February 27, 2006: "[M]y bias at the moment is towards female, although I have raised the possibility, because of the substantial virilization of the external genitalia, that there may have been sufficient testosterone imprinting to question ultimate gender identity." [Defendant Appiagyei-Dankah's progress notes].

e. December 27, 2006: "Dr. Appiagyei noted that this was a case of 'true hermaphroditism' and he ordered additional lab work. Dr. Aaronson concurred that this was a true hermaphrodite but that there was no compelling reason that she should be either male or female—the decision was made to raise her as female. On April 17th, 2006 she had preoperative lab work and was admitted for surgery on April 18th, 2006." [Developmental Pediatric Evaluation].

47. Defendant Aaronson's notes indicate that he was aware that M.C.'s exposure to high levels of testosterone ("testosterone imprinting") could affect M.C.'s ultimate gender identification. In a letter to Defendant Amrhein, which copied Defendant Appiagyei-Dankah, Defendant Aaronson stated that "because of the substantial virilization of the external genitalia, that there may have been testosterone imprinting to question ultimate gender identity." Defendant Aaronson was also aware that the effects of performing irreversible feminizing surgery on a child who might ultimately identify as a boy would be devastating. In fact, Defendant Aaronson had earlier published an article in a medical journal where he recognized that "carrying out a feminizing genitoplasty on an infant who might eventually identify herself as a boy would be catastrophic."[1]

48. No medical standard exists to determine the gender of a child with M.C.'s condition, particularly at such an early age. Defendants Amrhein, Aaronson, and Appiagyei-Dankah knew they could not predict whether the child's gender would develop as male or female.

49. Despite knowing that they could assign M.C. a gender of rearing and postpone surgery, and that they could not reasonably predict whether M.C. would ultimately identify as a man or a woman, Defendants Aaronson, Appiagyi-Dankah, and Amrhein formed the treatment team that ultimately urged SCDSS officials that M.C. undergo sex assignment surgery in order to make his body appear female. The recommendation to SCDSS officials that they authorize sex assignment surgery was made jointly by Defendants Aaronson, Appiagyei-Dankah, and Amrhein, with each doctor contributing based on his area of specialization.

50. In urging that sex assignment surgery for M.C., Defendants Aaronson, Appiagyei-Dankah, and Amrhein knew of the irreversible nature of the surgery and its severe risks, which include complete loss of sexual function, scarring, loss of male fertility, gender misassignment, and lifetime psychological distress.

Medically Unnecessary Sex Assignment Surgery is Performed on M.C.

51. On April 18, 2006, with SCDSS authorization, Defendant Aaronson surgically removed the majority of M.C.'s phallus, calling it a "reduction clitoroplasty." He also removed M.C.'s one functioning testicle and most, if not all, of the testicular tissue in M.C.'s other gonad.

52. There was no medical necessity to perform sex assignment surgery on M.C. as a sixteen-month-old child. There was no medical reason why surgery could not be postponed until M.C.'s gender emerged. M.C.'s condition had no negative impact on his physical well-being at the time and M.C. could have been raised as female or male without immediate genital surgery. Defendants' actions caused emotional trauma, stress, physical pain and confinement, and loss of bodily integrity, permanently

---

1. Ian A. Aaronson, *The Investigation and Management of the Infant with Ambiguous Genitalia: A Surgeon's Perspective*, 31 CURR. PROBL. PEDIAT. 168 (2001).

impacted M.C.'s potential to function sexually and permanently destroyed M.C.'s potential male reproductive function.

53. Defendants Aaronson, Amrhein, and Appiagyei-Dankah's actions deprived M.C. of the opportunity to delay the decision regarding which sexual surgeries to have until after M.C.'s dominant gender characteristics emerged. They deprived M.C. of the ability to make the very personal decision of which genital surgeries, if any, he wanted.

54. At no relevant time did Defendants Aaronson, Appiagyei-Dankah, and Amrhein request or initiate a hearing before taking action to terminate M.C.'s protected liberty interests in bodily integrity, privacy, and procreation. Defendants Aaronson, Appiagyei-Dankah, and Amrhein knew no such hearing had taken place prior to the decision to proceed with the sex assignment surgery.

Defendant South Carolina Department of Social Services Officials Authorize M.C.'s Unnecessary Sex Assignment Surgery

55. SCDSS retained custody of M.C. and had the authority to make all medical decisions for him from February 16, 2005, the date of the ex-parte order removing him from his biological parents, until December 11, 2006, the date that he was adopted.

56. Defendant Meredith Williams, Defendant Mary Searcy, Defendant Candice "Candi" Davis, and Defendants Doe #1, Doe #2, and Doe #3, the SCDSS employees responsible for M.C's care and well-being, attended M.C.'s medical appointments at various points during the time when it was decided that M.C. undergo sex assignment surgery.

57. Defendants Williams and Davis, along with Defendants Does #1, #2, and #3 received multiple communications from the defendant doctors regarding the recommended sex assignment treatment plan for M.C. Upon information and belief, Defendant Williams, Defendant Davis, Defendant Doe #1, Defendant Doe #2, and Defendant Doe #3 participated in making the decision to authorize the sex assignment surgery and to implement the sex assignment treatment plan, coordinated the logistical steps needed to implement the plan (including, but not limited to, coordinating transport and M.C.'s appointment times with the foster mother, and the completion of necessary paperwork) and provided the requisite "Checklist of Necessary Information" that described the sex assignment surgery to be approved by Defendant Aydlette.

58. As part of the implementation, Defendants Davis and Williams directed M.C.'s foster parents to deliver M.C. to the hospital for the sex assignment surgery.

59. SCDSS authorization for the sex assignment surgery was given to Defendant Aaronson's surgical nurse via telephone, by SCDSS social worker Defendant Mary Searcy.

60. Defendants Williams, Davis, Searcy, Doe #1, Doe #2, and Doe #3 knew that the proposed treatment plan was a sex assignment surgery, and that it included the

removal of healthy genital tissue that could result in sterilization. At no relevant time did Defendants Davis, Williams, Searcy, Doe #1, Doe #2, or Doe #3 request or initiate a hearing before taking action to terminate M.C.'s protected liberty interests in bodily integrity, privacy, and procreation. Defendants Davis, Williams, Searcy, Doe #1, Doe #2, and Doe #3 knew no such hearing had taken place prior to the decision to proceed with the sex assignment surgery.

61. SCDSS policy, effective September 2, 2003, required Defendant Aydlette's signature for any "major surgery" requiring in-patient hospitalization. Among other items in a "Check List of Necessary Information" to be attached to the request for consent included the following:

a. "Nature of the proposed medical procedure (in non-medical English);"

b. "Significant risks presented by the procedure;"

c. "Why the doctor believes the procedure is needed, and the anticipated result of the procedure;" and

d. "Physician's/hospital's consent forms (if applicable)."

Upon information and belief, Defendant Aydlette signed the request for consent, thus allowing the surgery. In signing, Defendant Aydlette was aware of the nature of the surgery, including that the elimination of male sexual and reproductive ability and removal of reproductive organs and would terminate and severely interfere with M.C.'s protected liberty interests in procreation, privacy, and bodily integrity. Despite this, Defendant Aydlette did not request or initiate notice or a hearing before taking action to terminate M.C.'s protected liberty interests in bodily integrity, privacy, and procreation. Defendant Aydlette knew no such hearing had taken place prior to the decision to proceed with the sex assignment surgery.

62. The Defendant SCDSS Officials' actions deprived M.C. of the opportunity to delay the decision regarding which sexual surgeries to have until after M.C.'s dominant gender characteristics emerged. They deprived M.C. of the ability to make the very personal decision of which genital surgeries, if any, he wanted.

63. The Defendant SCDSS Officials subjected M.C., or permitted M.C. to be subjected to, a painful and medically unnecessary sex assignment surgery that altered M.C.'s body and permanently limited M.C.'s ability to procreate and function sexually.

M.C.'s Current Situation

64. In June 2006, two months after the sex assignment surgery, Pam Crawford and Mark Crawford saw M.C.'s profile on the State of South Carolina's child adoption website. Mrs. Crawford expressed her interest in adopting M.C. and learned about his condition. Based on her familiarity with the negative effects of these surgeries through the experience of a childhood friend, Mrs. Crawford called the agency and clearly expressed the family's desire not to subject M.C. to unnecessary sex assignment surgery. Unfortunately, the surgery had already been completed. Mr. and Mrs. Crawford gained custody of M.C. in August 2006, and legally adopted him on December 11, 2006.

65. Mr. and Mrs. Crawford initially raised M.C. as a female in accordance with the gender of rearing. However, he has always shown strong signs of developing a male gender. His interests, manner and play, and refusal to be identified as a girl indicate that M.C.'s gender has developed as male. Indeed, M.C. is living as a boy with the support of his family, friends, school, religious leaders, and pediatrician.

VI. Causes of Action
Count One:
Fourteenth Amendment Substantive Due Process; 42 U.S.C. § 1983

(as against Defendant Doctors Aaronson, Amrhein, Appiagyei-Dankah, and Defendant Meredith Williams, Defendant Mary Searcy, Defendant Candice "Candi" Davis, Defendant Kim Aydlette, and Defendants Doe #1, Doe #2, and Doe #3)

66. Plaintiff incorporates all preceding paragraphs of the Complaint as if fully stated herein.

67. The Fourteenth Amendment to the United States Constitution provides that no State shall "deprive any person of life, liberty, or property without due process of law."

68. On April 18, 2006, Defendant Aaronson surgically removed the majority of M.C.'s phallus, calling it a "reduction clitoroplasty." He also removed M.C.'s one functioning testicle and most, if not all, of the testicular tissue in M.C.'s other gonad.

69. Throughout M.C.'s time under the care of SCDSS, Defendant Aaronson, Defendant Amrhein, and Defendant Appiagyei-Dankah developed a treatment plan for M.C.'s care relating to his intersex condition. Defendants Amrhein and Appiagyei-Dankah were pediatric endocrinologists and Defendant Aaronson a pediatric urologist. Each examined M.C. and, with each contributing recommendations and observations according to each doctor's area of medical expertise, worked with the other two to determine M.C.'s course of treatment.

70. The decision to assign the female sex and to recommend the sex assignment surgery was made jointly between Defendant Aaronson, Defendant Amrhein, and Defendant Appiagyei-Dankah, and all three urged SCDSS officials to approve the surgery.

71. Given that the removal of M.C.'s phallus and potential sterilization was not medically necessary, caused significant physical pain, imposed unreasonable risks of future physical and mental pain and suffering, and deprived M.C. of the opportunity to make his own deeply intimate decisions about whether to undergo genital surgery, if any, when he reached maturity, Defendants Aaronson, Amrhein, and Appiagyei-Dankah's actions were an intentional and egregious invasion of M.C.'s rights to bodily integrity, privacy, and procreation that shock the conscience. In taking these actions, Defendants Aaronson, Amrhein, and Appiagyei-Dankah acted unreasonably and inflicted harm on M.C. without justification.

72. Defendants Aaronson, Amrhein, and Appiagyei-Dankah acted under color of state law and unreasonably violated Plaintiff's substantive due process rights to

bodily integrity, privacy, procreation, and liberty, in violation of the Fourteenth Amendment of the United States Constitution.

73. Defendant Kim Aydlette, upon information and belief, signed the medical consent form required under SCDSS policy in order for surgery to be performed on M.C. Authorizing a procedure that removed M.C.'s phallus and removed his male reproductive ability was an intentional and egregious invasion of M.C.'s rights to bodily integrity, privacy, and procreation that shocks the conscience. In taking this action, Defendant Aydlette acted unreasonably and inflicted harm upon M.C. without justification.

74. Defendant Aydlette acted under color of state law when she knowingly permitted medically unnecessary sex assignment surgery on M.C., a child entrusted to her care and custody, violating Plaintiff's substantive due rights to bodily integrity, procreation, privacy and liberty, in violation of the Fourteenth Amendment of the United States Constitution.

75. Defendant Meredith Williams, Defendant Mary Searcy, Defendant Candice "Candi" Davis, Defendant Doe #1, Defendant Doe #2, and Defendant Doe #3 were responsible for M.C., including his safety and well-being, while M.C. was in state custody. Defendant Williams, Defendant Davis, Defendant Doe #1, Defendant Doe #2, and Defendant Doe #3 participated in making and carrying out the treatment plan that caused M.C.'s sex assignment surgery. Defendant Searcy provided SCDSS consent over the phone to enable the sex assignment surgery to take place.

76. Implementing and consenting to the treatment plan for a surgery that ultimately removed M.C.'s phallus and potentially sterilized him was an intentional and egregious invasion of M.C.'s rights to bodily integrity, privacy, and procreation that shocks the conscience. In taking these actions, Defendants Williams, Davis, Searcy, Doe #1, Doe #2, and Doe #3 acted unreasonably and inflicted harm upon M.C. without justification.

77. By participating in and implementing the treatment plan for medically unnecessary sex assignment surgery, Defendants Williams, Davis, Searcy, Doe #1, Doe #2, and Doe #3 acted under color of state law and unreasonably violated Plaintiff's substantive due rights to bodily integrity, procreation, privacy, and liberty, in violation of the Fourteenth Amendment of the United States Constitution.

Count Two:
Fourteenth Amendment Procedural Due Process; 42 U.S.C. § 1983

(as against Defendant Doctors Aaronson, Amrhein, Appiagyei-Dankah, and Defendant Meredith Williams, Defendant Mary Searcy, and Defendant Candice "Candi" Davis, Defendant Kim Aydlette, and Other Unknown SCDSS Employees)

. . . .

80. Knowing that their plan of treatment, including the sex assignment surgery, would result in the elimination of M.C.'s male reproductive capacity and sexual function, Defendant Aaronson, Defendant Amrhein, and Defendant Appiagyei-Dankah

did not request, initiate, or inquire about a pre-deprivation hearing before taking action to terminate M.C.'s protected liberty interests in bodily integrity, privacy, and procreation. They knew that no hearing had taken place at the time the surgery was performed.

81. There was no compelling reason, medical or otherwise, to perform the surgery that resulted in the removal of M.C.'s phallus and corresponding potential sterilization, causing significant physical pain, imposing unreasonable risks of future physical and mental pain and suffering, and depriving M.C. of the opportunity to make his own deeply intimate decisions about whether to undergo genital surgery, if any, when he reached maturity,

82. In choosing to perform the surgery and potential sterilization without requesting, initiating, or inquiring as to a pre-deprivation hearing, Defendants Aaronson, Amrhein, and Appiagyei-Dankah acted under color of state law and unreasonably violated Plaintiff's procedural due process rights to bodily integrity, privacy, procreation, and liberty, in violation of the Fourteenth Amendment of the United States Constitution.

83. Defendants Aaronson, Amrhein, and Appiagyei-Dankah's violations of M.C.'s Fourteenth Amendment rights to procedural due process were without reasonable justification and were not in service of any legitimate government interest.

84. Defendant Aydlette, upon information and belief, signed the medical consent form required under SCDSS policy in order for surgery to be performed on M.C. At no time did Defendant Aydlette request, initiate, or inquire about a pre-deprivation hearing before taking action to terminate M.C.'s protected liberty interests in bodily integrity, privacy, and procreation. Defendant Aydlette knew that no such hearing had taken place at the time she authorized the surgery.

85. By authorizing the procedure that removed M.C.'s phallus and potentially sterilized him without first initiating, requesting, or inquiring about a hearing, Defendant Aydlette acted unreasonably, without any justification, and not in service of any legitimate government interest.

86. Defendant Aydlette acted unreasonably and under color of state law when she knowingly permitted medically unnecessary sex assignment surgery on M.C. to take place without a pre-deprivation hearing, violating Plaintiff's Fourteenth Amendment rights to procedural due process.

87. Defendant Meredith Williams, Defendant Mary Searcy, Defendant Candice "Candi" Davis, and Defendants Doe #1, Doe #2, and Doe #3 were responsible for M.C., including his safety and well-being, while M.C. was in state custody. Defendants Williams, Davis, Doe #1, Doe #2, and Doe #3 participated in making and implementing the treatment plan that caused M.C.'s sex assignment surgery. Defendant Searcy provided the oral consent, over the phone, on the date of the surgery. In taking these actions, neither Defendants Williams, Searcy, Davis, Doe #1, Doe #2, nor Doe #3 requested, initiated, or inquired as to a pre-deprivation hearing before

taking action to terminate M.C.'s protected liberty interests in bodily integrity, privacy, and procreation. Defendants Williams, Searcy, Davis, Doe #1, Doe #2, and Doe #3 knew no such hearing had been held prior to the sex assignment surgery.

88. By knowingly permitting medically unnecessary sex assignment surgery on M.C. to take place without a pre-deprivation hearing, Defendants Williams, Searcy, Davis, Doe #1, Doe #2, and Doe #3 violated Plaintiff's procedural due rights to bodily integrity, procreation, privacy, and liberty, in violation of the Fourteenth Amendment of the United States Constitution.

89. In violating M.C.'s Fourteenth Amendment rights to procedural due process, all Defendant SCDSS Officials acted unreasonably and inflicted harm upon M.C. without justification.

Prayer for Relief

WHEREFORE, Plaintiff M.C. respectfully prays that this Court enter judgment in his favor and against Defendants, providing the following relief:

90. A declaration that Defendants have violated M.C.'s rights.

91. Compensatory damages in an amount to be determined at trial adequate to compensate the plaintiff for his harms and losses, together with an award of punitive damages in an amount to be determined at trial.

92. For interest, where appropriate, on any damages awarded to Plaintiff.

93. Attorneys' fees, expenses, and costs incurred in the prosecution of this action pursuant to, inter alia, 42 U.S.C. § 1988 and other applicable laws.

94. For any other relief as the Court deems just and proper.

Dated: May 14, 2013

Respectfully submitted,

/s/ [Signed by M.C.'s counsel, including private counsel as well as attorneys from Advocates for Informed Choice (now known as interAct: Advocates for Intersex Youth) and the Southern Poverty Law Center]

Discussion

Note that this legal complaint advances what has been characterized as a "patient-centered" model of the appropriate care for intersex infants, prioritizing patients' right to self-determination and eventual decision by the person with differences of sex development as to how their body will be treated, as distinguished from an older "concealment-centered model" that seeks to conform an infant to societal binary gender expectations by "normalizing" external genitalia, with a physician deciding based on medical tests and physical appearance which gender to assign and surgical interventions to perform upon the child. *See, e.g.*, Nikki Burrill & Valita Fredland, *The Forgotten Patient: A Health Provider's Guide to Providing Comprehensive*

Care for Transgender Patients, 9 Ind. Health L. Rev. 69 (2012). What legal and/or other social changes might be necessary for a patient-centered model to replace the long-dominant concealment-centered model of care for intersex people?

Reading Guide for M.C. ex rel Crawford v. Amrhein

1. The litigation here represents an effort to secure monetary redress for harms suffered by M.C., an intersex boy who was subjected to "sex assignment surgery" as an infant. 42 U.S.C. § 1983 is a federal statute authorizing suits against individuals and local government entities for violations of federal constitutional rights (and some federal statutory rights) conducted by people/entities acting "under color of" state law. In cases where individual defendants are sued in their "individual capacity" or "personal capacity" for money damages to come from their assets, they may raise a defense of "qualified immunity," which will preclude monetary liability unless the rights they are alleged to have violated were "clearly established" at the time of their allegedly unlawful actions.

2. M.C. argued that the defendants violated his substantive constitutional rights protected by the Due Process Clause of the Fourteenth Amendment. What three substantive due process rights does M.C. contend the defendants violated? What reasons for each does the court of appeals give for concluding that even if the defendants' actions were as alleged in M.C.'s complaint, the defendants were nonetheless entitled to qualified immunity? M.C. also argued that he was unconstitutionally denied a hearing before he was subject to the surgery that ensured his sterilization. What reasons does the court give for holding that M.C.'s right to such a hearing was not clearly established and thus qualified immunity precluded liability?

M.C., A Minor By and Through His Parents Pamela Crawford and John Mark Crawford v. Dr. James Amrhein

598 Fed. Appx. 143 (4th Cir. 2015)

[M.C. was represented by private counsel, Advocates for Informed Choice (now, interAct: Advocates for Intersex Youth), and the Southern Poverty Law Center. He was supported by amici AIS-DSD Support Group, The Program for the Study of Reproductive Justice—Information Society Project at the Yale Law School, and Constitutional Scholars.]

Before Motz and Diaz, Circuit Judges, and Davis, Senior Circuit Judge.

Opinion

Diaz, Circuit Judge:

In April 2006, a doctor performed sex assignment surgery on sixteen-month-old M.C., who was in the legal custody of the South Carolina Department of Social Services and had been diagnosed at birth with an intersex condition. Four months after the surgery, Pamela and Mark Crawford took custody of M.C. before adopting him in December 2006. The Crawfords filed this 42 U.S.C. § 1983 action on M.C.'s behalf, against the officials and doctors who played a part in the decision to have M.C. undergo the surgery. The district court denied the officials' and doctors' motions to dismiss based on qualified immunity. Because we find that no then-extant precedent gave fair warning to those involved in the decision regarding M.C.'s surgery that they were violating his clearly established constitutional rights, we reverse.

I

In our de novo review of a denial of a motion to dismiss based on qualified immunity, we take "as true the facts as alleged in the complaint, and view those facts in the light most favorable to the nonmoving party." We draw the following facts from M.C.'s complaint.

M.C. was born with ovotesticular difference/disorder of sex development (DSD). Ovotesticular DSD is an intersex condition where the individual has ovarian and testicular tissue. Hospital records first identified M.C. as male, but treating physicians later sometimes referred to M.C. as female. Through tests, examinations, and surgery, doctors determined that M.C. had "extremely elevated" testosterone levels and that his genitalia consisted of a testicle, an ovotestis with ovarian and testicular tissue, a phallus, scrotalized labia, a short vagina, and no uterus.

In February 2005, M.C. was placed in the custody of the South Carolina Department of Social Services ("SCDSS") until December 2006, when the Crawfords adopted him. Before the adoption, SCDSS had was authorized to make medical decisions for M.C.

After many examinations, tests, two surgeries, and numerous consultations among SCDSS officials and doctors over the course of a year, Drs. James Amrhein, Yaw Appiagyei-Dankah, and Ian Aaronson recommended that M.C. have sex assignment surgery. According to M.C., the doctors recommended the "irreversible, invasive, and painful" surgery despite "no compelling biological reason to raise M.C. as either male or female." The doctors also knew that they could "assign M.C. a gender of rearing and postpone surgery" and that the surgery carried risks of "complete loss of sexual function, scarring, loss of male fertility, gender misassignment, and lifetime psychological distress." In short, M.C. alleges that the surgery was medically unnecessary.

In April 2006, with consent from SCDSS, Dr. Aaronson performed a feminizing genitoplasty on sixteen-month-old M.C. This surgery involved removing most of M.C.'s phallus, his testicle, and the testicular tissue in his ovotestis.

After adopting M.C., the Crawfords originally raised him as a girl, consistent with the sex assignment surgery. But as M.C. grew older, it became clear that he identified as male, and he is now living as a boy.

M.C., by and through the Crawfords, filed a § 1983 lawsuit against the three doctors and seven SCDSS officials who played a part in the decision to perform the sex assignment surgery. He alleged Fourteenth Amendment substantive and procedural due process violations. The district court denied the defendants' motions to dismiss on qualified immunity grounds. The court concluded that M.C. had pleaded sufficient facts to support his contention that the defendants "violated his clearly established constitutional right to procreation." The defendants appealed. . . .

II

A

To avoid dismissal of a complaint after a qualified immunity defense is raised, a plaintiff must allege sufficient facts to "make out a violation of a constitutional right" and the court must find that this right "was clearly established at the time of" the alleged violation. *Pearson v. Callahan*, 555 U.S. 223 (2009). Courts are "permitted to exercise their sound discretion in deciding which of the two prongs of the qualified immunity analysis should be addressed first in light of the circumstances in the particular case at hand."

The right at issue must be defined "at a high level of particularity." *Bland v. Roberts*, 730 F.3d 368 (4th Cir. 2013). "This is not to say that an official action is protected by qualified immunity unless the very action in question has previously been held unlawful, but it is to say that in the light of pre-existing law the unlawfulness must be apparent." *Anderson v. Creighton*, 483 U.S. 635 (1987).

To be clearly established, "[t]he contours of the right must be sufficiently clear that a reasonable official would understand that what he is doing violates that right." *Id.* The law can be clearly established "even in novel factual circumstances" so long as officials had "fair notice" that their conduct violated a constitutional right. *Hope v. Pelzer*, 536 U.S. 730 (2002).

The "salient question" before us is "whether the state of the law in [2006] gave [the defendants] fair warning that their alleged treatment of [M.C.] was unconstitutional." *Id.* Because we find that the alleged rights at issue in this case were not clearly established at the time of M.C.'s 2006 sex assignment surgery, we need not reach the question of whether M.C. alleged sufficient facts to show that the surgery violated his constitutional rights.

B

We first consider M.C.'s contention, accepted by the district court, that the defendants had fair warning that the sex assignment surgery violated his constitutional right to reproduction. In support of this proposition, M.C. draws our attention to three cases: *Planned Parenthood of Southeastern Pennsylvania v. Casey*, 505 U.S. 833 (1992); *Skinner v. Oklahoma ex rel. Williamson*, 316 U.S. 535 (1942); and *Avery v. County of Burke*, 660 F.2d 111 (4th Cir. 1981). Although we acknowledge the broad statements in these cases about reproductive rights, we cannot say that a reasonable official would understand them as clearly establishing an infant's constitutional right to delay sex assignment surgery.

In *Casey*, the Supreme Court reaffirmed the three-part essential holding of *Roe v. Wade*, 410 U.S. 113 (1973), recognizing "the right of the woman to choose to have an abortion before viability and to obtain it without undue interference from the

State"; confirming "the State's power to restrict abortions after fetal viability, if the law contains exceptions for pregnancies which endanger the woman's life or health"; and establishing "the principle that the State has legitimate interests from the outset of the pregnancy in protecting the health of the woman and the life of the fetus that may become a child." *Casey*.

Skinner involved Oklahoma's statutory scheme to sterilize inmates classified as habitual criminals. In finding the scheme unconstitutional, the Court focused its analysis on how the law "la[id] an unequal hand on those who ha[d] committed intrinsically the same quality of offense and sterilize[d] one and not the other." The Court gave the example that the sterilization law did not apply to embezzlers but did apply to those who committed grand larceny.

In *Avery*, we considered the case of a fifteen-year-old girl who was misdiagnosed with sickle cell trait and then counseled by state actors to be sterilized. Relying on their advice, "Avery and her mother consented to the sterilization," but later tests showed that she did not have sickle cell trait. Avery claimed "that she was wrongfully sterilized" because of the misdiagnosis and "because sterilization is not medically recommended or proper, even when there has been a correct diagnosis of [sickle cell] trait." She sued the individuals who recommended sterilization and their employers, the local county and its Board of Health and Board of Social Services.

Concluding that "[t]he county and the boards may be liable under § 1983 if their policies or customs actually caused Avery's injuries," we found that summary judgment in favor of the local government entities was improper because a genuine issue existed as to whether the county health boards' failure to implement policies for counseling and sterilizing people with sickle cell trait amounted to a tacit authorization or deliberate indifference to Avery's right of procreation.[3]

Relying on the principles gleaned from these cases, the district court concluded that the defendants violated M.C.'s clearly established "right to procreation." We think, however, that this frames the right too broadly for purposes of assessing the defendants' entitlement to qualified immunity. *See, e.g., Winfield v. Bass*, 106 F.3d 525 (4th Cir. 1997) (en banc) (holding that the district court erred in defining the right at an inappropriate "degree of abstraction" and instead considering whether a much more factually detailed right was clearly established).

In our view, the alleged right at issue is that of an infant to delay medically unnecessary sex assignment surgery. By "medically unnecessary," we mean that no imminent threat to M.C.'s health or life required state officials to consent to the surgery, or doctors to perform it. Viewed in that light, we do not think that *Casey, Skinner*, or *Avery* put reasonable officials on notice that they were violating M.C.'s constitutional rights. As we have repeatedly emphasized, "[o]fficials are not liable for bad guesses in gray areas; they are liable for transgressing bright lines." *Maciariello v.*

---

3. Notably, however, *Avery* made no mention of the merits of the claim against the individual defendants.

Sumner, 973 F.2d 295 (4th Cir. 1992). We hold that the defendants did not transgress such a bright line in this case.

C

Although not reached by the district court, M.C. also contends that the defendants had fair warning that the sex assignment surgery violated his constitutional rights to bodily integrity and privacy. For the right to bodily integrity, M.C. points us to *Winston v. Lee*, 470 U.S. 753 (1985), and *Rochin v. California*, 342 U.S. 165 (1952). For the right to privacy, M.C. relies on *Lawrence v. Texas*, 539 U.S. 558 (2003). We find these cases too dissimilar to give the defendants fair notice of the alleged constitutional violation.

Lee and *Rochin* involved medical procedures to secure evidence against individuals suspected of committing a crime. In *Lee*, the Court disapproved of a compelled surgical procedure to extract a bullet that could connect Lee to a robbery. The Court in *Rochin* found shocking and unconstitutional three police officers' struggle to open Rochin's mouth to extract the capsules he had swallowed and, when that method proved unsuccessful, forced stomach pumping to retrieve the capsules. Neither of these cases, however, gave the defendants fair notice that they were violating M.C.'s right to bodily integrity by performing sex assignment surgery that M.C. contends was medically unnecessary.

As for *Lawrence*, that case struck down "a Texas statute making it a crime for two persons of the same sex to engage in certain intimate sexual conduct." We do not think that a case barring a criminal prosecution based on intimate, private sexual conduct between consenting adults gave the defendants fair notice that they could not perform sex assignment surgery on M.C. because it might impact his future sexual autonomy.

D

M.C. also alleges that the defendants violated his clearly established procedural due process rights by not seeking a "pre-deprivation hearing" "in which a neutral fact finder could weigh the risks and purported benefits of early [sex assignment] surgery, as well as the possibility of postponement or alternatives to surgery." In so alleging, he equates the sex assignment surgery to forced sterilization. To support his argument, M.C. relies on *Buck v. Bell*, 274 U.S. 200 (1927); a concurring opinion in *Skinner*; and numerous state statutes and cases requiring a court hearing "before an individual incapable of consent can be sterilized." Appellee's Br.

We find, however, that reasonable officials in 2006 did not have fair warning that they were violating M.C.'s clearly established rights by not seeking a hearing before performing, or consenting to, the sex assignment surgery. M.C.'s citations to state statutes and cases are unpersuasive because many postdate 2006, when the surgery took place, and all come from outside South Carolina, where the surgery took place.

Moreover, *Buck* and *Skinner* involved intentional, certain sterilization "of mental defectives" committed to state institutions and "habitual criminal[s]," respectively.

In stark contrast, the complaint in this case alleges that the sex assignment surgery was performed on an infant with "ambiguous genitals" and that such surgery "*may* reduce or eliminate reproductive capacity." J.A. (emphasis added). And although M.C.'s brief describes the surgery as "fertility-destroying" and a "surgical[] castrat[ion]," the complaint more cautiously describes the surgery as a "potential" sterilization, with "loss of male fertility" as one of the "risks."

While it is true that "the very action in question" need not have "previously been held unlawful" for an official to be stripped of qualified immunity, the unlawfulness must nonetheless "be apparent" "in the light of pre-existing law." *Anderson.* We conclude that the authority on which M.C. relies did not make it apparent that the defendants acted unlawfully by not seeking a hearing before the surgery.

III

Our core inquiry is whether a reasonable official in 2006 would have fair warning from then-existing precedent that performing sex assignment surgery on sixteen-month-old M.C. violated a clearly established constitutional right. In concluding that these officials did not have fair warning, we do not mean to diminish the severe harm that M.C. claims to have suffered. While M.C. may well have a remedy under state law, we hold that qualified immunity bars his federal constitutional claims because the defendants did not violate M.C.'s clearly established rights.

We therefore reverse the district court's denial of the defendants' motions to dismiss and remand with instructions to dismiss the complaint.

Reversed and remanded with instructions.

———————

Discussion

1. If, as alleged in M.C.'s complaint, there was no medical need requiring that M.C. receive surgery as an infant, what might have led the medical and social work professionals involved to subject him to it? Be aware that "defenders of the medical approach [to intersex conditions] assert that general satisfaction rates from early normalization surgeries are high. They argue that 'surgery is done because it is thought to result in better psychological outcomes for the child than leaving the genitalia unaltered,' and because 'it is generally felt that surgery that is performed for cosmetic reasons in the first year of life relieves parental distress and improves attachment between the child and the parents.'" Maayan Sudai, *Revisiting the Limits of Professional Autonomy: The Intersex Rights Movement's Path to De-Medicalization*, 41 Harv. J.L. & Gender 1, 8–9 (2018). "However, such statements are controversial, even among medical professionals, and recent studies published in medical journals have urged the medical community to reexamine findings and approaches." *Id.* at 9.

2. Note that in deciding what rules of law were clearly established, the court of appeals ignores the clearly stated rationales of cases expressly protecting, for example, a "right to procreate," instead distinguishing them based on their factual

contexts. Why might it have adopted such an approach to determining whether cases at the time gave the defendants "fair notice" that their conduct was unconstitutional? (Should it matter that the vast majority of governmental employees exercising discretion are indemnified by their employers for the performance of their official duties?)

Reading Guide for Crawford v. Medical University of South Carolina

1. The litigation here represents an effort to secure monetary redress for harms suffered by M.C., an intersex boy who was subjected to "sex assignment surgery" as an infant. The settlement below was approved subsequently to the federal Court of Appeals decision in *M.C. v. Amrhein, supra*.

2. Which defendants are covered by this settlement? What claims are the plaintiffs settling with them? What does the settlement agreement provide the plaintiffs? Looking at the complaint in *M.C. v. Aaronson, supra*, can you determine against which defendants the plaintiffs still have claims after this settlement agreement?

Pamela and John Mark Crawford, as Parents of M.C. Crawford, a Minor, v. Medical University of South Carolina, South Carolina Department of Social Services and Greenville Hospital System

No. 2013-CP-4002877, 2016 WL 4539816 (S.C. Ct. Com. Pl. July 28, 2016)

Order Approving Settlement on Behalf of a Minor

DeAndrea Gist Benjamin, Judge.

This matter is before the Court upon the Petition of Pamela Crawford and John Mark Crawford, as Parents and Guardians Ad Litem of M.C, a minor child, for approval of a settlement involving a minor. In support of this Petition, Petitioners would show that:

I

This Court finds that Petitioners are the adoptive parents and Guardians Ad Litem of M.C., a minor. The Court further finds that this action arises out of injuries allegedly sustained by M.C. as a result of medical treatment provided by physicians employed by the Medical University of South Carolina ("MUSC") and Greenville Hospital System, also known as Greenville Health System (GHS), while M.C. was in the custody of the South Carolina Department of Social Services (DSS). Petitioners allege that a sex assignment was performed without MUSC and GHS first obtaining informed consent. Petitioners bring this Petition pursuant to Section 62-5-433 of the 1976 Code of Laws of South Carolina, seeking approval from this Court of the settlement proposed in this Petition.

II

M.C. was born in . . . 2004 in Greenville, South Carolina with an intersex condition known as True Hermaphroditism or Ovotesticular Difference/Disorder of Sexual Development ("Ovotesticular DSD"). This condition is characterized by the presence of both testicular and ovarian tissue and aspects of both male and female genitalia. Three months after M.C. was born, he was taken into custody by DSS, which maintained legal custody of M.C. until his adoption by the Crawfords in December 2006.

Soon after M.C.'s birth, and continuing for a little more than a year, a pediatric endocrinologist employed by the Greenville Hospital System ("GHS"), performed a thorough diagnostic workup on M.C., ultimately diagnosing M.C. with ambiguous genitalia. In December of 2005, this doctor referred M.C. to physicians at MUSC for a second opinion regarding decisions on sex of rearing and sex of assignment. Following the referral to MUSC, M.C. was seen by a pediatric endocrinologist and a pediatric urologist employed by MUSC. On April 18, 2006, M.C. underwent a surgical procedure known as a feminizing genitoplasty at MUSC. The surgery was performed by the MUSC pediatric urologist.

III

Plaintiffs allege that the injuries suffered by M.C. were caused and brought about by the negligent acts of his physicians at MUSC and GHS in failing to obtain informed consent for the sex assignment, and that DSS acted in a grossly negligent manner in authorizing and enabling this treatment. Defendant Greenville Hospital System denies any liability in this matter. Specifically, GHS denies that it had an obligation to obtain informed consent for a procedure it did not perform.

IV

Plaintiffs allege that M.C. has incurred medical bills, pain and suffering, psychological damages, and permanent impairment. Plaintiffs agree that any medical liens as a result of M.C.'s treatment and care are the responsibility of Plaintiffs and will be paid out of the proceeds of this settlement.

V

At the time of this event, Defendant was self-insured in the amount of $1.2 million, the limits of the statutory caps contained in the South Carolina Tort Claims Act.

VI

Petitioners have sought and obtained an offer of peaceful settlement of this matter, whereby the Petitioners, for the benefit of M.C, in consideration of (1) the sum of Twenty Thousand, and NO/100 ($20,000.00) Dollars and (2) an agreement on the part of GHS to implement and/or retain certain policies and procedures, will execute a Release of the Greenville Hospital System and its employees and agents for alleged damages incurred by M.C, including all claims arising under the facts alleged in the complaint.

VII

Petitioners' attorneys have been advancing costs to litigate this case. Their agreements with Petitioners provide for reimbursement of expenses to be incurred in litigating this case against the remaining Defendants through trial. Petitioners therefore request that the Court approve such use, with the proceeds of this settlement to be held in escrow until the conclusion of this case (by virtue of a trial verdict or settlement or otherwise) as to all Defendants.

VIII

The Petitioners request specific approval to execute all appropriate papers to consummate this settlement, including any releases, stipulations of dismissal, and/or other documents in consummation of this settlement.

IX

After conducting a hearing on Plaintiffs' Petition on [x date], this Court finds: (1) this settlement offer, as well as the proposed distribution by Petitioner, are reasonable and appropriate under the circumstances; (2) Petitioners and their attorney have complied with Section 15-51-41 et. seq., S.C. Code of Laws, 1976, as amended, and (3) that their attorney has appropriately filed the required attorney's certification. After having given careful consideration to Plaintiffs' petition, and after having fully considered the argument provided at the settlement hearing in this matter as to the facts and circumstances surrounding the injuries suffered by M.C., the Court is satisfied that the proposal on behalf of Defendant GHS to settle all claims that may have arisen against it as a result of GHS' actions and omissions and the injuries alleged by M.C. in this action, is fair and reasonable and is in the best interest of M.C.

X

Wherefore, this Court approves the proposed settlement and authorizes Petitioners as parents and natural guardians of M.C. to enter and exchange for the consideration outlined in this Petition a Release running to and releasing the Greenville Hospital System, its employees and agents and their heirs, administrators, executors, personal representatives, predecessors, successors, assignees, employees, agents, affiliates, servants, subsidiaries, officers, directors, parents, and stockholders from all claims and demands of whatsoever nature or kind for damages arising out of the injuries suffered by M.C. allegedly as a result of the care and treatment provided by the Greenville Hospital System, and as described in Paragraph II of this Order.

And it is so ordered.

<<signature>>

The Honorable DeAndrea Gist Benjamin

Presiding Judge

Columbia, South Carolina

7-28, 2016

We Consent:

<<signature>>

[Attorneys for GHS and for Pamela & John Mark Crawford, as parents and guardians of minor M.C.]

———————

Discussion

1. Why might the plaintiffs have settled for what seems like such a small amount in light of what was done to M.C.?

2. Looking at the complaint in *M.C. v. Aaronson*, *supra*, can you determine against which defendants the plaintiffs still have claims after this settlement agreement?

3. The plaintiffs settled their litigation with the remaining defendants just short of a year after the settlement approval above for a payment of $270,000 to purchase an annuity worth $440,000 in sixteen years. The defendants admitted no wrongdoing. $15,000 of the earlier $20,000 settlement (above) was to be used by the plaintiffs to reimburse their attorneys for costs they incurred in the litigation. *See* Azeen Gorayshi, *A Landmark Suit About an Intersex Baby's Genital Surgery Just Settled for $440,000*, BuzzFeed News (July 26, 2017, updated July 27, 2017), https://www.buzzfeednews.com/article/azeenghorayshi/intersex-surgery-lawsuit-settles; Order Approving Settlement on Behalf of a Minor, *Pamela and Mark Crawford as parents of M.C. Crawford, a minor, v. Medical University of South Carolina, South Carolina Department of Social Services and Greenville Hospital System*, C.A. No. 13-CP-40-02877 (S.C. Ct. Com. Pl. July 24, 2017), https://assets.documentcloud.org/documents/3901419/Final-Settlement.pdf.

4. As this book goes to press, Dana Zzyym is suing to require the U.S. Department of State to provide a passport with a non-binary gender marker. Zzyym is an intersex person who identifies as nonbinary, neither male nor female. Thus far, however, the State Department has refused to issue a passport unless Zzyym selects "male" or "female." This litigation is presented in Chapter 16, Section C, *infra*.

5. In her important book *Intersexuality and the Law*, Julie Greenberg examines "three potential legal frameworks effectively employed by other progressive social justice movements—human rights, disability rights, and sex discrimination—that may help the intersex movement accomplish its goals" through litigation. Julie A. Greenberg, Intersexuality and the Law: Why Sex Matters 106 (2012). After surveying advantages and disadvantages to each approach for use in the U.S., she adds that "[b]ecause some courts may be unwilling to apply sex discrimination prohibitions to claims brought by people with an intersex condition, the intersex movement may want to encourage legislatures to adopt statutes that specifically protect the intersex community." *Id.* at 125. Professor Greenberg concludes, however, that such lobbying efforts might not hold great promise due to "the small size of the intersex community and the limited funds available to intersex advocacy groups."

Id. at 126. Greenberg concludes on the basis of *Price Waterhouse v. Hopkins*, 490 U.S. 228 (1989), and subsequent lower court decisions taking expansive views of sex discrimination under Title VII of the Civil Rights Act of 1964, that sex discrimination proscriptions could protect intersex infants from genital surgeries intended to make their bodies "conform to sex and gender norms." *Id.* at 124. With the Supreme Court's decision in *Bostock v. Clayton County, Georgia*, 140 S. Ct. 1731 (2020), Chapter 5, Section D, *infra*, adopting a broad view of the meaning of sex discrimination (in the context of Title VII), prospects of such results seem enhanced. For a critical though ultimately approbative review of Greenberg's book, see Kai Haswell, Intersexuality and the Law: Why Sex Matters *by Julie A. Greenberg. New York: New York University Press, 2012*, 28 Berkeley J. Gender L. & Just. 293 (2013).

6. Are law suits an effective tactic for pursuing "the de-medicalization of intersexuality," a project of moving society to "view intersex as biological or human variance instead of a pathology"? Maayan Sudai, *Revisiting the Limits of Professional Autonomy: The Intersex Rights Movement's Path to De-Medicalization*, 41 Harv. J.L. & Gender 1, 9 (2018). In contrast to lawsuits, Professor Sudai has concluded that "[m]edical activism has proven effective at giving intersex patients more representation in biomedical policy-making bodies," and has "managed to gradually generate more progressive guidelines and develop incremental changes in professional consensus regarding the appropriate standard of care for intersex people." *Id.* at 53. At the same time, she argues it has led to greater normative cooptation, with continued "acceptance of intersexuality as pathological and a subject of normalization." Legal activism making various sorts of rights claims, however, has not had "the same de-radicalizing effects for the intersex movement." And "[i]ntersex activists have used different legal mechanisms to politicize and problematize the standard of care in a way that has ignited public discussion and triggered a rethinking about the way intersexuality is conceptualized, both among the lay public and within the medical profession." *Id.*

Chapter 3

Anti-"Cross-Dressing" Laws

Particularly in parts of the United States, there is a long history of bans on "cross-dressing," wearing clothing conventionally associated with a sex other than one's own. Legal scholar Bill Eskridge has noted that "[a]lthough cross-dressing ordinances originated in the pre-Civil War period, they became widespread only in the period between the Civil War and World War I." Professor Eskridge notes the adoption of such laws in Columbus, OH (1848); Springfield, IL (1856); Charleston, SC (1858); Kansas City, MO (1860); Houston, TX (1861); Toledo, OH (1862); St. Louis, MO (1864); San Francisco, CA (1866); Atlanta, GA (1873); Minneapolis, MN (1877); Oakland, CA (1879); Nashville, TN (1881); San Jose, CA (1882); Sioux City, IA (1882); Sioux Falls, SD (1882); Tucson, AZ (1883); Peoria, IL (1884); Butte, MT (1885); Denver, CO (1886); Salt Lake City, UT (1888); Los Angeles, CA (1889); Santa Barbara, CA (1890); Omaha, NE (1890); Cedar Rapids, IA (1906); Memphis, TN (1909); and Dallas, TX (1911). William N. Eskridge, Jr., *Law and the Construction of the Closet: American Regulation of Same-Sex Intimacy*, 1880–1946, 82 Iowa L. Rev. 1007, 1040 (1997). "Most of these laws are no longer on the books, and the laws that remain are rarely enforced." Jeffery Kosbie, *(No) State Interests in Regulating Gender: How Suppression of Gender Nonconformity Violates Freedom of Speech*, 19 Wm. & Mary J. Women & L. 187, 190 (2013).

Eskridge endorses the view of law professor Nan Hunter that these laws were largely aimed at preventing gender fraud, people misrepresenting their gender to others. He also argues, however, that some such laws were negative responses to feminist demands for complete equality with men including sartorial equality (to wit, the right to wear trousers). Eskridge also contends that preventing sexual deviancy and targeting mental illness were other purposes of cross-dressing bans. Although these laws have in history been enforced against both women and men, the majority of judicial opinions addressing their constitutionality in recent decades, as this chapter reflects, have involved transgender women, people assigned male at birth who seek to live consistently with their female gender identity. Jeffery Kosbie suggests that laws banning "cross-dressing" "vividly illustrate how the state targets conduct in order to suppress a message of gender nonconformity." Kosbie, *supra*.

In addition, note that criminal bans on "cross-dressing" are far from the only way that gendered regulation of attire is effected. Dress codes may specify what clothing is acceptable for men and specify different clothing that is for women. See, for example, *Jespersen v. Harrah's Operating Co.*, 392 F.3d 1076 (9th Cir. 2004), *aff'd*, 444 F.3d 1104 (9th Cir. 2006), discussed in *Schroer v. Billington* (*Schroer III*), 577 F.

Supp. 2d 293 (D.D.C. 2008), in Chapter 5, Section D, *infra*. Employers might fire workers for cross-dressing even away from the workplace. *See Oiler v. Winn-Dixie La., Inc.*, No. 00-3114, Section "I," 2002 WL 31098541, 2002 U.S. Dist. LEXIS 17417 (E.D. La. Sept. 16, 2002), *infra* Chapter 14. Courts may restrict parental visitation if a parent (usually one regarded as male) cross-dresses. *See, e.g., In re Marriage of B., a/k/a B. (Anonymous) v. B. (Anonymous)*, 585 N.Y.S.2d 65, 184 A.D.2d 609 (App. Div. 1992), *infra* Chapter 8. And, as Chapter 1, Section D, *supra*, notes, gay and lesbian people have an assimilationist history (and ongoing practice in some quarters) of repudiating people including transgender people who do not conform to "mainstream" notions of gender propriety. *See also, e.g.*, Jessi Gan, *"Still at the Back of the Bus": Sylvia Rivera's Struggle, in* THE TRANSGENDER STUDIES READER 2 pp. 291–301 (Susan Stryker and Aren Z. Aizura eds., 2013).

Reading Guide for Columbus v. Zanders

1. Criminal defendant Zanders challenged the constitutionality of Columbus, Ohio's criminal ban on cross-dressing, contending that it violated a number of constitutional rights. Which ones?

2. The court analyzes the constitutionality of the statute by asking whether it "bear[s] a real and substantial relation to the public health, safety, morals, or general welfare." This language of statutory fit to broad public purposes was formerly used by the Supreme Court to describe rational basis review. Today, cases holding laws unconstitutional for failing to meet that standard are often thought to have applied a less deferential standard than contemporary "rational basis review," which asks whether a law or government action is rationally related to a legitimate governmental purpose. Does the *Zanders* court conclude that the challenged law passes or fails the level of scrutiny the court applies, and why?

3. The court also considers Zanders's additional argument that the statute cannot be applied to Zanders "as a transsexual." Does the court accept or reject that argument and why?

City of Columbus v. Zanders

266 N.E.2d 602 (Ohio Mun. Ct. 1970)

JENKINS, Judge.

Defendant herein was arrested, charged and tried under Section 2343.04 of the Columbus Municipal Code which reads as follows:

> No person shall appear upon any public street or other public place in a state of nudity or in a dress not belonging to his or her sex, or in an indecent or lewd dress.

[D]efendant was apprehended wearing woman's clothing and make-up and impersonating a female in violation of the aforementioned ordinance.

Dr. Byron Stinson, chairman of the Department of Psychiatry Transsexual Protocol Committee of the Ohio State University Hospital, testified that he has had contact with and examined the defendant, as have two other members of his staff, for a period of a year and a half, including a period of six weeks as an in-patient in Upham Hall for a study for a prospective transsexual operation.

The results of the psychiatric examinations, the social and emotional testing, indicate strongly that the defendant was a true transsexual; he scoring [*sic*] very high on the feminine scale. The doctor indicated that he was a prime candidate for transsexual surgery.

The doctor revealed further that the defendant feels as a female, has no emotional investment in this male sex organs and he feels that he is a female trapped in a male body belonging to someone else. His attraction sensually is to males without the desire for the abnormal sexual contact of a homosexual, and dressing as a woman does not engender any erotic sexual stimulations but, on the contrary, causes him to feel natural and normal.

The testimony of the doctor indicated quite clearly that he and his staff approached his problem with extreme caution. . . . They plan to keep the defendant on female hormones for a period of six months and it is desirable that defendant dress and otherwise identify as a woman for a period of a year before submitting to surgery.

At the time of arrest defendant had been on female hormones for a period of a month and, as the doctor indicated, in the defendant this matter of dressing as a woman is a compulsion. The matter of his being transformed into a woman is a matter of psychotherapy.

The experience of Johns Hopkins University with some 2,000 patients indicated that the change made for better psychological emotional and social adjustment in these people.

Defendant's counsel argue that the ordinance in question is contrary to the guarantees of the United States Constitution being a deprivation of a right of expression guaranteed by the First Amendment, a deprivation of the right of privacy guaranteed by the Fourth Amendment, a deprivation of due process guaranteed by the Fifth Amendment and constitutes cruel and unusual punishment contrary to the Eighth Amendment as applied to the due process clause of the Fourteenth Amendment. . . .

The question then presents itself, does Section 2343.04 of the Columbus City Code bear a real and substantial relation to the public health, safety, morals or general welfare? Is there a public need for such regulation?

The law in this area has been well stated by the Ohio Supreme Court when it held that "Laws or ordinances passed by virtue of the police power which limit or abrogate constitutionally guaranteed rights must not be arbitrary, discriminatory, capricious or unreasonable and must bear a real and substantial relation to the object sought to be obtained, namely, the health, safety, morals or general welfare of the public." *Cincinnati v. Correll*, 49 N.E.2d 412 (Ohio 1943).

Defendant asks this court to declare the ordinance unconstitutional inasmuch as it prevents him from "doing his own thing" in the vernacular of the "Pepsi generation." It is apparent in this day and age that the entire philosophic concept of public morals, religion, ethical values, and rules of decency has undergone a substantial change. We are not unmindful of the early critics of the Puritan Ethic, and the wit and humor of Artemus Ward who stated, "The Puritans nobly fled from a land of despotism to a land of freedom, where they could not only enjoy their own religion, but could prevent everybody else from enjoying his." In spite of changing times and morals, common sense and experience discloses that this ordinance has a real and substantial relation to the public safety and general welfare. There are numerous subjects who would want to change their sex identity in order to perpetrate crimes of homicide, rape, robbery, assault, etc. We hold, therefore, that Section 2343.04 of the Columbus City Code has a real and substantial relation to the public safety and is therefore constitutional and a valid exercise of the police power.

We next consider defendant's argument that the provisions of this ordinance must not be applied to him by reason of his medical and psychological problem as a transsexual. We believe this to be a case of first impression within this state.

Attention is invited to an outstanding article by Dr. Harry Benjamin of New York who wrote in the AMERICAN JOURNAL OF PSYCHOTHERAPY 1963, at pages 460, 461, 462 and 465.

[Lengthy quotations omitted.]

See also *Female Psychosexual Inversion: Transsexualism* by Dr. I. B. Pauly, presented at the 11th annual meeting of the American Psychiatric Association May 19, 1963, and *Transvestism* by Dr. C. Hamburger and others in *Journal of the American Medical Association* 152:391-1953.

It is apparent from the medical authorities cited that the true transsexual suffers from a mental defect over which he has little practical control. In the instant case defendant's course of conduct in dressing and posing as a female is more the result of an irresistible impulse or a loss of will power than a deliberate act or violation of the provisions of the ordinance in question. In this area the American Law Institute has long urged a uniform adoption by the states of Section 401 of the Model Penal Code, which reads:

> A person is not responsible for criminal conduct if at the time of such conduct as a result of mental defect he lacks substantial capacity either to appreciate the wrongfulness of his conduct or to conform his conduct to the requirements of law.

An accused is not criminally responsible if his unlawful act is the product of a mental disease or a mental defect. Criminal responsibility attaches to those who, of their own free will and with evil intent (sometimes called mens rea), commit acts which violate the law. On the facts of this case we cannot hold defendant criminally liable and therefore the charges brought against him are hereby dismissed.

. . . .

Case dismissed.

Discussion

1. It is a commonplace that courts will avoid constitutional questions when there is a reasonable interpretation of a challenged statute that would resolve the case; that is often referred to as the canon of constitutional avoidance. Given that, why might the court have analyzed the issues in the order in which it did?

2. Consider the court's basis for holding that Zanders could not be held criminally liable for violating Columbus's ban on cross-dressing. While this holding spared Zanders the consequences of a criminal conviction, what negative effects (on Zanders or society more generally) might the court's reasoning have? Lee Clark, a transgender scholar, has argued that the case "forced assimilation, imposed the gender binary, and pathologized our humanness." Lee Clark, *The Pressures of Passing, Reinforced by Precedent*, 22 CUNY L. Rev. F. 17, 23 (2019). Are there ways to protect transgender persons from such laws without compromising their agency in the fashion that the court, at least arguably, did here?

3. The court's approach can be understood as an example of the "medicalization" of trans identity. For an examination of some of the many issues implicated by that conceptualization, see *infra* Chapter 14.

Reading Guide for Cincinnati v. Adams

1. Why might Cincinnati have enacted this criminal ban on cross-dressing? What generalizations about cross-dressers or transgender persons might lie behind the ban? How does the court frame the first issue in *City of Cincinnati v. Adams*? What kind of evidence did the court wish to see on that point?

2. What is Adams's second constitutional attack on the city's anti-cross-dressing law? With respect to that argument, what applications does the court see as problematic? Why might the court be concerned about whether the city's law reaches that far?

3. From the existence of what other criminal laws does the court take comfort in holding the ban on cross-dressing unconstitutional? Why does the court take those laws to be relevant?

City of Cincinnati v. Adams A.K.A. Harris

330 N.E.2d 463 (Ohio Mun. Ct. 1974)

GORMAN, Judge.

This matter is before the court upon defendant's motion to dismiss the complaint on grounds that Section 909-5 of the Cincinnati Municipal Code, under which he is charged, violates defendant's right of freedom of expression guaranteed by the First and Fourteenth Amendments to the United States Constitution and is also unconstitutionally vague. Section 909-5 provides as follows:

> No person within the city of Cincinnati shall appear in a dress or costume not customarily worn by his or her sex, or in a disguise when such dress, apparel, or disguise is worn with the intent of committing any indecent or immoral act or of violating any ordinance of the city of Cincinnati or law of the state of Ohio.

> All of the surrounding circumstances and behavior of the individual charged with the violation of this section may be considered as relevant in regard to showing the existence of the required intent.

> Whoever violates this section shall be guilty of dressing for illegal or immoral purposes, a misdemeanor of the fourth degree.

On February 2, 1974 the defendant was standing in a parking lot dressed in a blouse, brassiere and woman's [*sic*] slacks. He wore a woman's wig and earrings and carried a purse. Police had this area under surveillance due to complaints from residents concerning soliciting prostitutes in this neighborhood. An undercover police cadet approached the defendant in the parking lot, and a discussion ensued in which defendant asked if the cadet wanted a date. Some discussion relative to money followed, but this topic changed to other unrelated subjects. When he was leaving the parking lot, police officers arrested the defendant and filed the complaint now before the court which alleges that defendant "with intent to commit an immoral act * * * did appear in a disguise, contrary to and in violation of Section 909-5 * * *."

. . . .

We are called upon in this case to determine whether a transvestite's mode of dress is an expression protected by the First Amendment. Freedom of expression is not limited exclusively to speech. Expression may encompass certain forms of conduct illustrative of " * * * ideas for the bringing about of political and social changes desired by the people," *Roth v. United States*, 354 U.S. 476, 484 (1957). Conduct protected by the First and Fourteenth Amendments may include one's manner of dress or his personal grooming if truly representative of a philosophy, an idealism, or a point of view. *Schneider v. Ohio Youth Comm.*, 287 N.E.2d 633 (Ohio Ct. App. 1972).

The Supreme Court, however, in *United States v. O'Brien*, 391 U.S. 367, 376 (1968), renounced the view that all conduct is deemed to be speech merely because it is intended to be communicative. . . . .

Whether specific types of dress or grooming are equivalent to an expression is the subject of a conflict in authority. First and Fourteenth Amendment guarantees were extended to protesting students wearing black armbands in *Tinker v. Des Moines Community School District*, 393 U.S. 503 (1969) to members of a group dressed as brown shirts in *Kalemba v. Turk*, 353 F. Supp. 1101 (N.D. Ohio 1973), and to one who wore a jacket bearing a four-letter word in *Cohen v. California*, 403 U.S. 15 (1971). In sustaining school or government dress codes, however, long hair was held not to be an expression in *Jackson v. Dorrier*, 424 F.2d 213 (6th Cir. 1970), and in *Schneider*.

At the hearing on the motion to dismiss, the defendant did not offer any evidence other than to examine the cadet and arresting officers. In absence of evidence supporting his contention that his costume represented a philosophy or ideal, we cannot conclude in this case that defendant's conduct is an expression within the contemplation of the First Amendment. To be sure, the police power does not confer power upon government to prohibit a man from making a fool of himself, but we agree with those authorities that have held that the legislative body can prohibit cross-dressing when it is associated with criminal misconduct and bears a reasonable relation to the public health, safety, morals and welfare. *Columbus v. Zanders*, 266 N.E.2d 602 (Ohio Mun. Ct. 1970); *People v. Simmons*, 79 Misc. 2d 249, 357 N.Y.S.2d 362 (Crim. Ct. 1974).

We agree, however, that this ordinance is unconstitutionally vague and violates the defendant's right to due process guaranteed by the Fourteenth Amendment. Although city council is empowered to prohibit certain forms of dress, Section 909-5 is valid only if it provides ascertainable standards of conduct, *Coates v. Cincinnati*, 402 U.S. 611 (1971). Such standards are inadequate if they fail[]

> * * * to give a person of ordinary intelligence fair notice that his contemplated conduct is forbidden by the statute. The underlying principle is that no man shall be held criminally responsible for conduct which he could not reasonably understand to be proscribed.

United States v. Harriss, 347 U.S. 612 (1954).

Whether apparel is proscribed by Section 909-5 depends essentially upon the definition of the words, "not customarily worn." *Webster's Third New International Dictionary* defines "custom" as, "a form or course of action characteristically repeated under like circumstances: a usage or practice that is common to many or to a particular place or class or is habitual with an individual." Not only does Section 909-5, limit one's dress in public, but its prohibitions reach into the privacy of one's home. It goes so far as to bring under suspect the woman who wears one of her husband's old shirts to paint lawn furniture, the trick or treater, the guests at a masquerade party, or the entertainer. Such a standard is purely subjective and materially fluctuates from person to person. Additionally, the element of an intent to commit an "indecent" or "immoral" act, while so dressed, represents an unascertainable standard. Both terms lack the precise definition necessary to withstand strict construction of a criminal ordinance, *Cincinnati v. Wayne*, 261 N.E.2d 131 (Ohio Ct. App. 1970). Such a prohibition depends upon one's moral philosophy and can, for example, include a female Christian Scientist wearing a tie and pants suit who enters a physician's office seeking treatment.

Obviously, these imprecise terms render Section 909-5 unconstitutionally vague for the same reasons that the Cincinnati prowling ordinance, Section 901-P10, C.M.C., was declared void, *Cincinnati v. Taylor*, 303 N.E.2d 886 (Ohio 1973). In the *Taylor* case an ordinance which prohibited prowling "* * * under circumstances which warrant a reasonable man to believe that the safety of persons or security of property in the surrounding area is threatened," was declared void as lacking adequate standards. The Ohio Supreme Court said:

> * * * Such boundless discretion granted by the ordinance encourages arbitrary and capricious enforcement of the law. It provides a convenient instrument for "harsh and discriminatory enforcement by prosecuting officials, against particular groups deemed to merit their displeasure * * *." *Thornhill v. Alabama*, 310 U.S. 88 (1940).

City council's effort to thwart criminal schemes before they mature into an attempt is, indeed, commendable although the propriety of criminalizing cross-dressing in view of contemporary clothing and hair styles common to both sexes is debatable, *Simmons*. Particularly apparent is the fact that absent this ordinance the conduct of a transvestite remains subject to statutes or ordinances prohibiting soliciting (R.C. 2907.24), importuning (R.C. 2907.07), pandering obscenity (R.C. 2907.32), public indecency (R.C. 2907.02), trespassing (R.C. 2911.21) or soliciting rides or hitchhiking (R.C. 4511.51).

Because Section 909-5 fails to provide adequate standards for the average person or for law enforcement officials, it is unconstitutional on its face and void, *Cincinnati v. Taylor*. Accordingly, defendant's motion to dismiss is granted and the defendant is hereby discharged.

Motion to dismiss granted.

———————

Discussion

1. The court rejects the defendant's claim that Cincinnati's cross-dressing ban implicates expression protected by the First Amendment. (Professor Franke has argued that "[i]n so doing, the court ignored the obvious: that an overarching ideology or philosophy was necessary to justify the norm of certain clothing belonging to one or another sex." Katherine M. Franke, *The Central Mistake of Sex Discrimination Law: The Disaggregation of Sex from Gender*, 144 U. Pa. L. Rev. 1, 67 (1995).) Should this be considered a holding (ordinarily understood to encompass reasoning necessary to a court's decision) or dictum? In deciding, note that the court accepts the defendant's vagueness/due process challenge.

Jeffery Kosbie has argued that the city's action here indeed violated Adams's First Amendment rights: "Adams was not arrested merely because he disguised his identity. The particular city ordinance did not prohibit all disguises. Adams was arrested because he wore particular clothes. Adams wore clothes that communicated a gender. . . . Adams could only be arrested under this law for communicating gender nonconformity. Adams's arrest suppressed his communication of a message." Jeffery Kosbie, *(No) State Interests in Regulating Gender: How Suppression of Gender Nonconformity Violates Freedom of Speech*, 19 WM. & MARY J. WOMEN & L. 187, 189 (2013).

What advantages or disadvantages might a free-expression challenge to a cross-dressing ban have relative to challenges grounded in statutory or constitutional anti-discrimination law?

2. Suppose the city council of Cincinnati remained convinced of the importance of its ban on cross-dressing. First, setting aside the court's reasoning about the "indecent or immoral act" portion of the statute, try to rewrite the statute to remedy the vagueness problem. Can you do so? Does your revision create any potential equal protection problems? (Consider the Supreme Court's understanding of the kinds of conduct that count as sex discrimination in *Bostock v. Clayton County, Georgia*, 140 S. Ct. 1731 (2020), Chapter 5, Section D, *infra*.) Second, can you rewrite the "indecent or immoral act" purpose language to make it more specific and give the constitutionally required warning of what is prohibited? How would law enforcement officers determine whether someone was cross-dressing with such a purpose?

Note on the Intermediate Appellate Decision in
City of Chicago v. Wilson

In a decision subsequently overturned by the state supreme court in the next main case, *City of Chicago v. Wilson*, 357 N.E.2d 1337 (Ill. Ct. App. 1976), the Appellate Court of Illinois upheld the conviction of two defendants for violating Section 192-8 of the Municipal Code of the City of Chicago, which specified:

> Any person who shall appear in a public place in a state of nudity, or in a dress not belonging to his or her sex, with intent to conceal his or her sex, or in an indecent or lewd dress, or who shall make any indecent exposure of his or her person, shall be fined not less than $20.00 nor more than $500.00 for each offense.

The defendants, who had male genitalia and one of whom had "small breasts," testified that they were undergoing psychiatric treatment in preparation for "a sex change operation."

The appellate court suggested that "the language of the ordinance suggests it was enacted not to regulate the manner in which one may dress. Rather, it appears to prohibit conduct of a homosexual nature which is offensive to the general populace."

(Is this a fair interpretation of the statutory language? What presuppositions about lesbigay people does it appear to make?) "If a state may prohibit homosexual activity between consenting adults in private," the court reasoned, citing the Supreme Court's summary affirmance of the constitutionality of Virginia's sodomy law in *Doe v. Commonwealth's Attorney*, 425 U.S. 901 (1976), "it is clear that it may also prohibit the offensive display of homosexual conduct in public" in order to protect community morals. The court thought that a contrary ruling here, "[allowing] a disguising of the sexes[,] would hinder the detection of crime, would render uncertain the traditional separation of the sexes in public facilities, and would allow males to more easily victimize females, particularly in public ladies' facilities where vulnerability to attack is already too great." Acknowledging the necessity of the defendants' dress as preparatory for surgery, the court nonetheless believed "their appearance in public dressed as females in an attempt to hide their true sex has . . . the same negative effect on the public morality and safety which has been prohibited by the Chicago City Council. Should the Council wish to create an exception in the ordinance based on the hardship alleged by the defendants, it may do so but it is not within our authority to judicially create such an exception."

The court rejected the defendants' free expression claim, incorrectly asserting without citation that the First Amendment "does not protect conduct." It rejected their vagueness and overbreadth challenge to the ordinance (which had invoked unisex clothing, Halloween costumes, theatrical performances, and kilts) on the ground that these defendants had the specific intent to conceal their sex, dismissing any difficult questions about the ordinance's applicability in other cases as "marginal offenses." Finally, the court rejected the defendants' arguments that the law violated the Equal Protection Clause because it believed that "the State does have an interest in maintaining the integrity of the sexes," and because it concluded somewhat opaquely that "there has been no arbitrary, sex based classification created; the classification which is the subject of this action is gender itself."

Reading Guide for the State Supreme Court Decision in Chicago v. Wilson

1. On appeal from the decision discussed in the preceding note, does the state supreme court in *City of Chicago v. Wilson* hold the challenged law unconstitutional on its face, so that it cannot be used thereafter to prosecute anyone, or does it only hold the challenged law unconstitutional as applied to the appellants (the criminal defendants below)?

2. What level of constitutional scrutiny might the court implicitly use to hold Chicago's criminal ban on cross-dressing unconstitutional in *Wilson*? (Consider what the court says about the state of the record and what the city has or has not justified.) To what potential "crimes in washrooms" may Chicago be alluding, and what is its likely argument that there is a rational basis for the statute?

City of Chicago v. Wallace Wilson et al.

389 N.E.2d 522 (Ill. 1978)

THOMAS J. MORAN, Justice.

Following a bench trial in the circuit court of Cook County, the defendants, Wallace Wilson and Kim Kimberley, were convicted of having violated section 192-8 of the Municipal Code of the city of Chicago (Code), which prohibits a person from wearing clothing of the opposite sex with the intent to conceal his or her sex. Defendant Wilson was wearing a black knee-length dress, a fur coat, nylon stockings and a black wig. Defendant Kimberley had a bouffant hair style and was wearing a pants suit, high-heeled shoes and cosmetic makeup. Defendants were taken to the police station and were required to pose for pictures in various stages of undress. Both defendants were wearing brassieres and garter belts; both had male genitals.

At trial, the defendants testified that they were transsexuals, and were, at the time of their arrests, undergoing psychiatric therapy in preparation for a sex reassignment operation. As part of this therapy, both defendants stated, they were required to wear female clothing and to adopt a female life-style. Kimberley stated that he had explained this to the police at the time of his arrest. Both defendants said they had been transsexuals all of their lives and thought of themselves as females. . . .

Section 192-8 of the Code provides:

> "Any person who shall appear in a public place * * * in a dress not belonging to his or her sex, with intent to conceal his or her sex, * * * shall be fined not less than twenty dollars nor more than five hundred dollars for each offense."

The existence of unspecified constitutionally protected freedoms cannot be doubted. *E.g., Roe v. Wade*, 410 U.S. 113, 152–54 (1973); *Griswold v. Connecticut*, 381 U.S. 479 (1965).

In *Kelley v. Johnson*, 425 U.S. 238 (1976), the Supreme Court was confronted with the question of whether one's choice of appearance was constitutionally protected from governmental infringement. At issue was an order promulgated by [the] commissioner of police for Suffolk County, New York, [establishing] hair-grooming standards for male members of the police force. The court acknowledged that the due process clause of the fourteenth amendment "affords not only a procedural guarantee against deprivation of 'liberty,' but likewise protects substantive aspects of liberty against unconstitutional restrictions by the State." The court observed, however, that its prior cases offered little, if any, guidance on whether the citizenry at large has some sort of liberty interest in matters of personal appearance. It assumed for purposes of its opinion that such did exist.

In determining the scope of that interest and the justification that would warrant its infringement, the court distinguished claims asserted by individuals of a uniformed police department from claims by the citizenry at large, noting that the distinction was "highly significant." . . . . After analyzing the need for uniformity and discipline within the ranks of the police department, the court concluded that the challenged order was rationally related to two legitimate objectives: first, "to make police officers readily recognizable to the members of the public," and second, to foster the "esprit de corps which such similarity is felt to inculcate within the police force itself." Mr. Justice Powell, who specially concurred, noted that "[w]hen the State has an interest in regulating one's personal appearance * * * there must be a weighing of the degree of infringement of the individual's liberty interest against the need for the regulation."

This court has long recognized restrictions on the State's power to regulate matters pertinent to one's choice of a life-style which has not been demonstrated to be harmful to society's health, safety or welfare. *E.g., People v. Fries,* 250 N.E.2d 149 (Ill. 1969) (statute requiring the wearing of a motorcycle helmet held invalid); *City of Chicago v. Drake Hotel Co.,* 113 N.E. 718 (Ill. 1916) (ordinance prohibiting public dancing in restaurants held invalid).

The notion that the State can regulate one's personal appearance, unconfined by any constitutional strictures whatsoever, is fundamentally inconsistent with "values of privacy, self-identity, autonomy, and personal integrity that * * * the Constitution was designed to protect." *Kelley v. Johnson,* 425 U.S. 238, 251 (1976) (Marshall, J., dissenting).

. . . .With the exception of one [lower court] decision all of the cases subsequent to *Kelley* have involved regulations set in the context of an organized governmental activity. Such circumstance is distinguished from that in which a regulation, as here, controls the dress of the citizens at large. This distinction, as noted in *Kelley,* is "highly significant."

Even though one's choice of appearance is not considered a "fundamental" right (*Richards v. Thurston,* 424 F.2d 1281, 1284–85 (1st Cir. 1970)), the State is not relieved from showing some justification for its intrusion.

In this court, the city has asserted four reasons for the total ban against cross-dressing in public: (1) to protect citizens from being misled or defrauded; (2) to aid in the description and detection of criminals; (3) to prevent crimes in washrooms; and (4) to prevent inherently antisocial conduct which is contrary to the accepted norms of our society. The record, however, contains no evidence to support these reasons.

If we assume that the ordinance is, in part, directed toward curbing criminal activity, the city has failed to demonstrate any justification for infringing upon the defendants' choice of public dress under the circumstances of this case.

Both defendants testified that they are transsexuals and were, at the time of their arrest, undergoing psychiatric therapy in preparation for a sex-reassignment operation. Neither of the defendants was engaged in deviate sexual conduct or any other criminal activity. Absent evidence to the contrary, we cannot assume that individuals who cross-dress for purposes of therapy are prone to commit crimes.

The city's fourth reason (as noted above) for prohibiting the defendants' choice of public dress is apparently directed at protecting the public morals. In its brief, however, the city has not articulated the manner in which the ordinance is designed to protect the public morals. It is presumably believed that cross-dressing in public is offensive to the general public's aesthetic preference. There is no evidence, however, that cross-dressing, when done as a part of a preoperative therapy program or otherwise, is, in and of itself, harmful to society. In this case, the aesthetic preference of society must be balanced against the individual's well-being.

Through the enactment of section 17(1)(d) of the Vital Records Act (Ill. Rev. Stat. 1977, ch. 1111/2, par. 73-17(1)(d)), which authorizes the issuance of a new certificate of birth following sex-reassignment surgery, the legislature has implicitly recognized the necessity and validity of such surgery. It would be inconsistent to permit sex-reassignment surgery yet, at the same time, impede the necessary therapy in preparation for such surgery. Individuals contemplating such surgery should, in consultation with their doctors, be entitled to pursue the therapy necessary to insure the correctness of their decision.

Inasmuch as the city has offered no evidence to substantiate its reasons for infringing on the defendants' choice of dress under the circumstances of this case, we do not find the ordinance invalid on its face; however, we do find that section 192-8 as applied to the defendants is an unconstitutional infringement of their liberty interest.

Judgments reversed; cause remanded, with directions.

Ward, Chief Justice, dissenting:

The majority states that it does not find the ordinance to be unconstitutional on its face, but it concludes that the ordinance was unconstitutional as applied to these defendants. That conclusion is founded on the premise that the defendants' conduct was part of a psychiatrically prescribed program to prepare them for sex-reassignment surgery. The only testimony in support of the defendants' claim was that of the defendants themselves. [The] defendant Wilson, on cross-examination, testified that he didn't know what sex-reassignment surgery would involve and said he did not know the doctor who would perform it.

The majority ignores a basic consideration that the credibility to be given the defendants' testimony was for the trial judge. . . .

Underwood and Ryan, JJ., join in this dissent.

Discussion

1. Years after *Chicago v. Wilson*, the U.S. Court of Appeals for the Eleventh Circuit noted that "[a]lthough a few courts in the late 1960's and early 1970's held motorcycle helmet laws unconstitutional, each of these cases has been reversed or overruled. Courts in subsequent cases have uniformly upheld the provisions." *Picou*

v. Gillum, 874 F.2d 1519 (11th Cir. 1989) (footnotes omitted). How could this observation be used to challenge the conclusion in *Wilson*?

2. The court does not directly explain the city's protecting-against-misleading-or-fraud justification. What is the nature of the "fraud" to which the city alludes, and what negative stereotypes regarding trans people might it invoke?

3. Given that the Illinois Supreme Court did not hold the ordinance unconstitutional on its face but only as applied to the particular arrests before it in *Wilson*, what might its reasoning suggest about the kinds of circumstances and evidence this court may require in future cases for those who cross-dress to secure similar constitutional protection? Is the dissent right to protest the assumptions made by the majority opinion? What is the effect of this "medicalization" of trans lives on trans people? How might requiring medical treatment, supervision, or "vouchesafing" for the bona fides of a person's trans identity discriminate against low-income transgender communities? How would such medical treatment/supervision requirements affect police officers, who are expected to enforce constitutionally valid criminal laws?

4. Transgender scholar Katrina Rose has criticized Justice Ward's dissent:

> At least two problems exist with Justice Ward's line of reasoning. First, the Court of Appeals had essentially viewed violation of the ordinance as a strict liability crime. Under that view, what would be the point of a psychiatrist's testimony? Second, Ward focused on the defendant's lack of knowledge concerning both the genital surgery procedure itself as well as who would perform it. Many otherwise intelligent adults would likely flunk tests on genital physiology as well as the specifics of any particular type of surgery. Why should a transsexual be any different regarding SRS [*i.e.*, sex reassignment surgery]? After all, as a prerequisite for surgery, a transsexual is required to be diagnosed with GID, not licensed to make such a diagnosis.

Katrina C. Rose, *The Transsexual and the Damage Done: The Fourth Court of Appeals Opens Pandora's Box by Closing the Door on Transsexuals' Right to Marry*, 9 Law & Sexuality 1, 37 (2000).

Reading Guide for Doe v. McConn

1. The plaintiffs in *Doe v. McConn* were eight residents of Houston, Texas, who were transsexual persons, primarily or perhaps exclusively transsexual women, proceeding pseudonymously "to insulate themselves from possible harassment, to protect their privacy, and to protect themselves from prosecution resulting from this action." They were all "fully diagnosed transsexuals who, as of the commencement of this cause of action, had not undergone sexual reassignment surgery." Also suing was Dr. Maxwell, a psychiatrist who treated transsexual persons including four of his co-plaintiffs. "The Defendants [were] past and present City of Houston officials charged with the responsibility of promulgating and/or enforcing" the challenged

municipal law criminalizing cross-dressing. *Doe v. McConn*, 489 F. Supp. 76 (S.D. Tex. 1980).

2. The opinion in *Doe v. McConn* uses antiquated terminology ("homosexuality, transvestism, and transsexualism") generally replaced in contemporary professional usage by terms such as "sexual orientation," "gender identity," and "gender dysphoria." What function does the emphasis on the need for a "trained psychiatrist" to distinguish among "common areas of concern" of the populations discussed serve in this opinion?

3. What constitutional right does the court hold the cross-dressing ban violated? How, according to the court, does it violate that right? Whose constitutional right does the court conclude the law violated?

Jane Doe 1 et al. v. McConn et al.; M.B. v. City of Houston

489 F. Supp. 76 (S.D. Tex. 1980)

NORMAN W. BLACK, District Judge.

Statement of Case

These are consolidated actions wherein Plaintiffs allege that § 28-42.4 of the Code of Ordinances of the City of Houston constitutes a deprivation, under color of state law, of rights, privileges, and immunities secured to them by the First, Fourth, Fifth, Eighth, Ninth, Tenth and Fourteenth Amendments to the Constitution and the laws of the United States.

Findings of Fact

Transsexualism is a rare syndrome of gender identity disturbance which appears to occur more frequently in male than in female subjects. The cause of this syndrome is unknown. . . . Treatment of this condition in adults by psychotherapy alone has been futile. Administration of hormones of the opposite sex followed by sex-conversion operations has resulted in better emotional and social adjustment by the transsexual individual in the majority of cases. Prior to undergoing surgery, the patient is required to be seen by a team of specialists in physical and psychological medicine over an extensive period of time, generally one to two years.

. . . . The patient is treated with heterotypic sex hormones and is required to live, dress, and become rehabilitated in the cross-gender role.

There is a resemblance between homosexuality, transvestism, and transsexualism, with observable common areas of concern, but essential distinctions become apparent to the trained psychiatrist. Most transvestites cross-dress, or employ the imagery of cross-dressing, in order to achieve sexual satisfaction. The effeminate homosexual occasionally may cross-dress, but he does not share the transvestite's compulsion to do so. Although he plays the feminine role with his male partner, he has no compelling desire to be a woman.

. . . .

The criteria for diagnosis are by no means absolute, and research is proceeding with the purpose of further refining the distinctions between the various gender identity syndromes. To date, it is generally agreed that the common requirement of a pre-operative period of six to twenty-four months of living and working in the gender role of choice provides the best index of judgment for eliminating non-transsexuals.

Most, if not all, specialists in gender identity are agreed that the transsexual condition establishes itself very early, before the child is capable of elective choice in the matter, probably in the first two years of life; some say even earlier, before birth during the fetal period. These findings indicate that the transsexual has not made a choice to be as he is, but rather that the choice has been made for him through many causes preceding and beyond his control. Consequently, it has been found that attempts to treat the true adult transsexual psychotherapeutically have consistently met with failure.

Yet, some sort of treatment is urgently indicated, for in many instances his suffering is so intense that suicide and self-mutilation are not uncommon.

Although the causes of the transsexual condition are not yet understood, extensive research in recent years has indicated some possible biological and psychological factors which might render one individual more vulnerable than another to develop in this way. Experiments with animals suggest that the altering of hormone balances, during certain limited, critical pre-natal periods, will affect those areas of the brain that regulate masculine and feminine behavior. In fact, cross-dressing is mandatory, as surgery will generally not be performed unless cross-dressing has occurred for a minimum specified period of time.

The policies and procedures of the Defendants make it illegal for the transsexual Plaintiffs to appear in public areas in women's clothing. Said policies and procedures directly inhibit the treatment of the transsexual Plaintiffs and their reassignment. Defendants have arrested and prosecuted certain of the Plaintiffs, pursuant to § 28-42.4 of the Code of Ordinances of the City of Houston which states:

> It shall be unlawful for any person to appear on any public street, sidewalk, alley, or other public thoroughfare dressed with the designed intent to disguise his or her true sex as that of the opposite sex.

In determining whether or not a person is dressing as that of the opposite sex, the person is required to disrobe. There is no exception or defense under the ordinance for transsexuals, including those under a doctor's care. The ordinance has been regularly enforced; for the year 1977, 53 persons were arrested in accordance with it.

Plaintiff Maxwell is a practicing psychiatrist. He counsels . . . transsexual patients, including four of the transsexual Plaintiffs here, in conjunction with and prior to surgery to be performed at the University of Texas Medical Branch. His prescribed treatment, required for adequate sexual integration, is thwarted by the Ordinance in direct contravention of medical and psychological indications.

Defendants have not submitted evidence of a state interest in the enforcement of the Ordinance in question. In fact, the City of Houston presently has in force Section 24-42.6 of the Code of Ordinances to prevent crimes in washrooms, which states:

> It shall be unlawful for any person to knowingly and intentionally enter any public restroom designated for the exclusive use of the sex opposite to his or hers without the permission of the owner, tenant, manager, lessees or other person in charge of the premises, in a manner calculated to cause a disturbance.

Conclusions of Law

We find that the Ordinance, as applied to individuals undergoing psychiatric therapy in preparation for sex-reassignment surgery, is unconstitutional.

The Fourteenth Amendment affords not only a procedural guarantee against the deprivation of liberty, but also protects substantive aspects of this interest against unconstitutional restrictions by the States. See *Kelley v. Johnson*, 425 U.S. 238, 244 (1976). In *Kelley*, the Supreme Court assumed, without deciding, that individuals have "some sort of 'liberty' interest within the Fourteenth Amendment in matters of personal appearance." Justice Powell's concurring opinion in *Kelley* is the view shared by this Court, that "no negative implication" as to the more general liberty interest in personal appearance is to be drawn from the *Kelley* majority opinion. "The notion that the state can regulate one's personal appearance, nonconfined by any constitutional strictures whatsoever, is fundamentally inconsistent with 'values of privacy, self-identity, autonomy, and personal integrity that . . . the Constitution was designed to protect.'" *City of Chicago v. Wilson*, 389 N.E.2d 522 (Ill. 1978), citing *Kelley v. Johnson* (Marshall, J., dissenting). Moreover, the Supreme Court has recognized a constitutionally-derived right to control one's own body. *See Roe v. Wade*, 410 U.S. 113 (1973); *Griswold v. Connecticut*, 381 U.S. 479 (1965).

The Court must consider the constitutional importance of the affected individual interests and the need for regulation. In their Answer to the Complaint, Defendants state: "The Constitutional infringements, if any exist, are so insignificant as to be outweighed by the public's desire and the police department's need to know someone's true sexual identity."

Defendants, however, have no concrete evidence to justify their intrusion under the circumstances herein. Moreover, this Court cannot perceive of any reasons for infringing on Plaintiffs' constitutional rights under these circumstances.

Since the challenged Ordinance fails to pass even a minimal degree of scrutiny, there is no need to determine which standard of scrutiny is appropriate.

Accordingly, the Ordinance, as applied herein, is unconstitutional.

———————

Discussion

1. What function does the court's reasoning about choice and control play in finding a constitutional liberty interest? Gender identity includes not only those with transsexual and cisgender identities, but also non-binary people, who identify as neither male nor female and often prefer they/them pronouns. Some nonbinary individuals opt for surgery. How does this interact with the court's reasoning regarding choice and control?

2. The court emphasizes the lengthy and serious nature of the medical treatment. What is the importance of this to the judge? An alternative medical protocol that has recently emerged, called the "informed consent model," requires only that the client be informed of the risks of hormones and surgery and does not depend on lengthy testing and professional medical permissions. This informed consent model of care allows transgender patients to "access desired health interventions such as hormone treatments and surgeries without undergoing a mental health intervention or referral from a mental health specialist." Sarah L. Schulz, *The Informed Consent Model of Transgender Care: An Alternative to the Diagnosis of Gender Dysphoria*, 1 J. HUMANISTIC PSYCHOL. 72, 83 (2018). By not requiring a mental health diagnosis—as is required under the dominant approach thus far, sometimes called a "gatekeeping" model of transgender care—the informed consent model "promotes a departure from the use of the diagnosis of gender dysphoria as a prerequisite for accessing transition services and . . . attempts to impact the way that transgender individuals experience and access health care by removing the psychotherapy/gatekeeping requirement." *Id.* How would the new informed consent model affect the court's reasoning?

3. The court refers to a Houston criminal ordinance 24-42.6 restricting use of restrooms designated for the "opposite" sex, apparently to justify the court's decision. What, though, is the connection between the ban on cross-dressing and the limitation on restroom use? Is the judge saying that his decision is valid because transsexual women would at any rate not be allowed in women's restrooms, or that, if they were to use a women's restroom, other users would be protected against "disturbance," or is the connection something else entirely? Might the court's reasoning rest on a sense of the governmental interests involved in restroom or cross-dressing regulations? Under this restroom statute, what restrooms should transgender women use, and what conduct would involve "disturbance"? See Chapter 5, Section E, *infra*, for discussion of restrictions on restroom use in workplaces and Chapter 13, *infra*, for discussion of restrictions on restroom use in schools.

Reading Guide for Muhamad Juzaili bin Mohd Khamis v. State Government of Negeri Sembilan

1. The following case allows you to look comparatively at the judicial treatment of the constitutionality of laws prohibiting cross-dressing. It is a decision from the Court of Appeal of Malaysia, the penultimate appellate court in that nation's judicial system. That decision was subsequently voided by the Federal Court of Malaysia

on the technical ground (not based on the merits of the constitutional rights claims) that the plaintiffs did not follow the correct specific procedures for bringing their claims before the High Court and the Court of Appeal. *See* Tamir Moustafa, *The Judicialization of Religion*, 52 Law & Soc'y Rev. 685, 703 (2018) (citing *State Government of Negeri Sembilan & Ors. v. Muhammad Juzaili Bin Mohd Khamis & Ors.* [2015] MLJU 597).

2. What (Malaysian) constitutional rights do the appellants contend the ban on cross-dressing violates? Which, if any, of those rights does the court agree are violated, and why? In addition to Malaysian Court cases (from the Malayan Law Journal (MLJ) or Current Law Journal (CLJ)), upon what sources does the court draw? What is the court's ultimate holding, and what remedy, if any, does it adopt?

Muhamad Juzaili Bin Mohd Khamis & Ors. v. State Government of Negeri Sembilan & Ors.
Court of Appeal (Putrajaya)
2 JANUARY 2015
CIVIL APPEAL NO N-01 498 11 OF 2012
[2015] 3 MLJ 513

Full Judgment of the Court

Mohd Hishamudin JCA [Judge of the Court of Appeal]:

Introduction

This appeal is against the decision of the High Court of Seremban of 11 October 2012 that had dismissed the appellants' application for judicial review.

The application for judicial review is for a declaration that §66 of the Syariah Criminal Enactment 1992 (Negeri Sembilan) is void by reason of being inconsistent with [Articles 5(1), 8(1), 8(2), 9(2), and 10(1)(a)] of the Federal Constitution. . . .

. . . .

Background Facts

The three appellants are Muslim men. Medically, however, they are not normal males. This is because they have a medical condition called "Gender Identity Disorder" ("GID"). Because of this medical condition, since a young age the appellants have been expressing themselves as women and showing the mannerisms of the feminine gender such as wearing women's clothes and using makeups. Indeed, they feel natural being such.

That the appellants are sufferers of GID is confirmed by a psychiatrist from the Kuala Lumpur Hospital; as well as by a psychologist. The evidence of these experts remains unrebutted.

In 1992 the Legislature of the State of Negeri Sembilan enacted the Syariah Criminal Enactment 1992 (Negeri Sembilan). Section 66 of this Enactment makes it an offence for any Muslim male person to do any of the following in a public place: to wear a woman's attire, or to pose as a woman. Those convicted can be liable to a fine not exceeding RM1,000 or to imprisonment for a term not exceeding six months or to both. This section makes no exception for sufferers of GID like the appellants. No explanation has been given by the state for this unfortunate omission.

Hence, as a consequence, the appellants have been repeatedly detained, arrested, and prosecuted by the religious authority of Negeri Sembilan acting pursuant to §66 for cross-dressing.

The injustice and humiliation that they are subject to moved them to apply to the court for this declaration.

Their application involves the interpretation of the Federal Constitution; and we pause for a moment here to reiterate that only the superior civil courts established under Part IX (The Judiciary) of the Federal Constitution have the jurisdiction to determine disputes on the interpretation of the provisions of the Federal Constitution. In *Latifah bte Mat Zin v. Rosmawati bte Sharibun & Anor.* [2007] 5 MLJ 101; [2007] 5 CLJ 253 . . . the Federal Court reminds us[:] "Interpretation of the Federal Constitution is a matter for this court, not the syariah court. . . ."

Gender Identity: Medical Evidence
Diagnosis of the appellants by psychiatrist Dr. Ang Jin Kiat

The appellants had been medically examined by one Dr Ang Jin Kiat, a psychiatrist from the Kuala Lumpur Hospital, a government hospital.

Dr. Ang's medical reports confirm that the appellants suffer from a medical condition known as [GID]. According to Dr. Ang's reports, the "desire to dress as a female and to be recognized as a female is in keeping with this condition" and there is no "scientifically proven pharmacological treatment or psychological therapy." In other words, cross-dressing is intrinsic to the appellants' nature; and that this abnormal condition is incurable.

Dr. Ang Jin Kiat's medical reports are unrebutted by the respondents.

Consultant psychiatrist's opinion by Dr. Deva Dass

Dr. Deva Dass, a Consultant Psychiatrist, by an affidavit, provides further opinion on GID. Dr. Deva Dass states that GID is also referred to as "Transsexualism." and those who suffer from it are called "Transsexuals." He states that GID is not a preference and is ineradicable, and that wearing clothing of the opposite sex occurs among sufferers of GID.

. . . .

According to Dr. Dass:

> The sufferer from this anomaly feels he should have been the other gender "a female spirit trapped in a male body" and is quite unconvinced by scientific tests that show him to be indisputably male.

Clinical Psychologist's Report

Besides the two psychiatrists' evidence/reports above, the appellants have also tendered a report by one Ms. Vizla Kumaresan; a clinical psychologist.

The report confirms that the appellants psychologically identify themselves as women.

Likewise, Ms. Kumaresan's psychological reports, exhibited in the respective affidavits of the appellants, have not been rebutted by the respondents.

Sociologist's Evidence

In further support of the appellants' case, affidavits are also filed by one Professor Teh Yik Koon, a renowned Malaysian sociologist, explaining that a law like § 66 has adverse effects on transsexuals and on Malaysian society. In the expert opinion of the learned professor:

. . . .

. . . . Based on my experiences with the transsexual community in Malaysia, the research findings in my Book and from my study of gender issues as a sociologist, it is my opinion that, in Malaysia, a law like section 66 of the Syariah Criminal (Negeri Sembilan) Enactment 1992 which criminalizes any male person who in any public place merely wears a woman's attire or poses as a woman:

I. Stigmatizes transsexuals as deviants and in doing so:

(a) strips them of their value and worth as members of our society.

(b) affects their ability to freely engage in decent and productive work, and this results in them pursuing sex work as a source of income.

(c) affects the ability for transsexuals to move freely and reside within the borders of Negeri Sembilan without fear of persecution.

(d) affects their well-being, self-confidence and self-empowerment.

(e) impedes awareness-raising among members of society on the problems and troubles faced by transsexuals and how society can play a part in helping them.

II. Adversely affects society by depriving it of an entire class of individuals, that is transsexuals, who could contribute to well-being.

III. Infringes the privacy of transsexuals by preventing them making decisions and choices regarding their own bodies.

IV. Infringes the ability for transsexuals to express their identity through speech, deportment, dress and bodily characteristics.

What the Appellants' Evidence Established

The evidence furnished by the appellants, therefore, establish that GID is an attribute of the appellants' nature that they did not choose and cannot change;

and that much harm would be caused to them should they be punished for merely exhibiting a manifestation of GID ie cross-dressing.

. . . .

Section 66 of the Syariah Criminal Enactment 1992 (Negeri Sembilan)

Section 66 is a state enacted Islamic law [that] was passed by the State Legislative Assembly of Negeri Sembilan on 3 August 1992 and came into force on 1 June 1993. Section 66 reads:

. . . .

English Version

Any male person who, in any public place wears a woman's attire or poses as a woman shall be guilty of an offence and shall be liable on conviction to a fine not exceeding one thousand ringgit or to imprisonment for a term not exceeding six months or to both.

Mufti's Opinion

The state in response to the appellants' constitutional challenge, have filed an affidavit by the learned Mufti of the State of Negeri Sembilan. In his affidavit the learned Mufti opines that the prohibition of a male Muslim dressing or posing as a woman is a precept of Islam. . . .

The Mufti's opinion is tendered to explain that the offence prescribed by § 66 is in accordance with the precepts of Islam.

[Whether] or not § 66 is consistent with the precepts of Islam is not in issue in the present case. Indeed, this is conceded by Mr. Aston Paiva, learned counsel for the appellants.

But Mr. Paiva makes a pertinent point, and that is that, the Mufti's opinion, remarkably, fails to address the issue that is crucial for the purpose of the present constitutional challenge: what is the position in Islam as to the appropriate dress code for male Muslims who are sufferers of GID, like the appellants?

Whether Section 66 Is in Breach of Art. 5(1) of the Federal Constitution

Article 5(1) of the Federal Constitution guarantees that no person shall be deprived of his life and personal liberty save in accordance with law. . . .

The Federal Court . . . in *Sivarasa Rasiah v. Badan Peguam Malaysia & Anor.* [2010] 2 MLJ 333; [2010] 3 CLJ 507 has held that:

(i) other freedoms may be found embedded in the "life" and "personal liberty" limbs of Art. 5(1);

(ii) "in accordance with law" in Art. 5(1) refers to a law that is fair and just and not merely any enacted law however arbitrary or unjust it may be; and

(iii) when a law is challenged as violating a fundamental right under Art. 5(1), Art. 8(1) will at once be engaged.

Infringement of the Right to Live with Dignity

In *Lembaga Tatatertib Perkhidmatan Awam, Hospital Besar Pulau Pinang & Anor. v. Utra Badi a/l K Perumal* [2000] 3 MLJ 281; [2000] 3 CLJ 224 Gopal Sri Ram JCA (as he then was) in delivering the decision of the Court of Appeal . . . explained that the word "life" in Art. 5(1) includes the right to live with dignity. In his words:

> . . . it is the fundamental right of every person within the shores of Malaysia to live with common human dignity.

The learned judge quotes . . . the Indian Supreme Court case of *Francis Coralie Mullin v. Union of India* (1981) AIR 746 at p. 753:

> . . . We think that the right to life includes the right to live with human dignity and all that goes along with it namely, the bare necessaries of life such as adequate nutrition, clothing and shelter over the head and facilities for reading, writing and expressing oneself in diverse forms, freely moving about and commingling with fellow human beings.

Section 66 prohibits the appellants and all other male Muslim sufferers of GID from cross-dressing, and punishes them for any breach of the prohibition. Learned counsel for the appellants argues that the profound effect of § 66 is that the appellants and other GID sufferers are perpetually at risk of arrest and prosecution simply because they express themselves in a way which is part of their experience of being human. The very core identity of the appellants is criminalised solely on account of their gender identity. Learned counsel submitted that § 66 is irreconcilable with the existence of the appellants and all other GID sufferers. A more disturbing effect of § 66 is that it builds insecurity and vulnerability into the lives of the appellants and other Muslim male persons with GID. The existence of a law that punishes the gender expression of transsexuals, degrades and devalues persons with GID in our society. As such, § 66 directly affects the appellants' right to live with dignity, guaranteed by Art. 5(1), by depriving them of their value and worth as members of our society.

We find merit in this argument. As long as § 66 is in force the appellants will continue to live in uncertainty, misery and indignity. They now come before this court in the hope that they may be able to live with dignity and be treated as equal citizens of this nation.

We, therefore, hold that § 66 is inconsistent with Art. 5(1) of the Federal Constitution in that the section deprives the appellants of their right to live with dignity.

Therefore, § 66 is unconstitutional and void.

Infringement of Right to Livelihood/Work

There is yet another reason as to why § 66 is inconsistent with Art. 5(1). It has also been established by judicial authorities that the word "life" in Art. 5(1) means more than mere animal existence: it also includes such rights as livelihood and the quality of life. In *Tan Tek Seng v. Suruhanjaya Perkhidmatan Pendidikan & Anor.* [1996] 1 MLJ 261 . . . the Court of Appeal . . . said:

> Adopting the approach that commends itself to me, I have reached the conclusion that the expression 'life' appearing in Art. 5(1) does not refer to mere existence. It incorporates all those facets that are an integral part of life itself and those matters which go to form the quality of life. Of these are the right to seek and be engaged in lawful and gainful employment and to receive those benefits that our society has to offer to its members. It includes the right to live in a reasonably healthy and pollution free environment.

The above principle was approved by the Federal Court in *Lee Kwan Woh v. Public Prosecutor* [2009] 5 MLJ 301; [2009] 5 CLJ 631 . . . :

> When Art. 5(1) is read prismatically and in the light of Art. 8(1), the concepts of 'life' and 'personal liberty' housed in the former are found to contain in them other rights. Thus, 'life' means more than mere animal existence and includes such rights as livelihood and the quality of life (*see Tan Tek Seng*'s case).

The effect of § 66 is that it prohibits the appellants and other sufferers of GID who cross-dress from moving in public places to reach their respective places of work.

The appellants submit that § 66 has the inevitable effect of rendering their right to livelihood/work illusory, for they will never be able to leave their homes, cross-dressed, to go to their respective places of work without being exposed to being arrested and punished under § 66. Section 66 is therefore inconsistent with Art. 5(1).

Whether § 66 Contravenes Art. 8(1) of the Federal Constitution

Article 8(1) of the Federal Constitution guarantees equality before the law and equal protection of the law. This article provides:

Equality

8(1) All persons are equal before the law and entitled to the equal protection of the law.

In the present appeal, the object of § 66 is to prohibit all male Muslims from cross-dressing or appearing as a woman in a public place. But the appellants are male Muslims suffering from gender identity disorder (GID), where the desire to dress as a female and to be recognised as a female is part of the said medical condition; and that there is no scientifically proven pharmacological treatment or psychological therapy for such medical condition.

In this appeal, we accept the appellants' argument that they, as male Muslims suffering from GID, are in a different situation as compared to normal male Muslims. They and the normal male Muslims are not under like circumstances and are thus unequals. Being unequals, the appellants should not be treated similarly as the normal male Muslims. Yet § 66 provides for equal treatment. It does not provide for any exception for sufferers of GID like the appellants. The state, although does not dispute the existence of sufferers of GID among male Muslims such as the appellants, yet does not explain for such a serious legislative omission. In other words, the state and the impugned section simply ignore GID sufferers such as the appellants, and unfairly subject them to the enforcement of the law. As a consequence, §66 places the GID sufferers in an untenable and horrible situation. They could not dress in public in the way that is natural to them. They will commit the crime of offending §66 the very moment they leave their homes to attend to the basic needs of life, to earn a living, or to socialise; and be liable to arrest, detention and prosecution. This is degrading, oppressive and inhuman. Thus the inclusion of persons suffering from GID in the §66 prohibition discriminates against them. Therefore, §66 is inconsistent with Art. 8(1) of the Federal Constitution as it is discriminatory and oppressive, and denies the appellants the equal protection of the law.

The Indian Supreme Court has in a number of cases laid down the proposition that Art. 14 of the Indian Constitution (our Art. 8(1)) guarantees that unequal objects, transactions or persons should not be treated equally. Just as a difference in treatment of persons similarly situate leads to discrimination, so also discrimination can arise if persons who are unequals, that is to say, are differently placed, are treated similarly. In *Venkateshwara Theatre v. State of Andhra Pradesh & Ors.* [1993] 3 SCR 616 at p.637A the Supreme Court of India held:

> Just as a difference in treatment of persons similarly situate leads to discrimination, so also discrimination can arise if persons who are unequals, *i.e.* differently placed, are treated similarly. In such a case failure on the part of the legislature to classify the persons who are dissimilar in separate categories and applying the same law, irrespective of the differences, brings about the same consequences as in a case where the law makes a distinction between persons who are similarly placed. A law providing for equal treatment of unequal objects, transactions or persons would be condemned as discriminatory if there is absence of rational relation to the object intended to be achieved by the law.

Section 66 is therefore unconstitutional as it offends Art. 8(1) of the Federal Constitution, and is therefore void.

Whether §66 Contravenes Art. 8(2) of the Federal Constitution

Article 8(2) of the Federal Constitution states that in any law there shall be no discrimination against citizens on the ground of gender. The article reads:

> (2) Except as expressly authorized by this Constitution, there shall be no discrimination against citizens on ground only of religion, race, descent, place of birth or gender in any law or in the appointment to any office or employment under a public authority or in the administration of any law relating to the acquisition, holding or disposition of property or the establishment or carrying on of any trade, business, profession, vocation or employment.

It is submitted by learned counsel for the appellants that § 66 is inconsistent with Art. 8(2). The appellants are male Muslims. Section 66 only prohibits male Muslims from cross-dressing or from posing as a woman in public. But this section does not prohibit female Muslims from cross-dressing as a man or from posing as a man in public. It is argued that § 66 thus subjects male Muslim persons like the appellants to an unfavourable bias vis-à-vis female Muslim persons. Therefore, § 66 is discriminatory on the ground of gender, and is inconsistent with Art. 8(2).

With respect, we find that there is merit in this argument. We therefore rule that § 66 also violates Art. 8(2) of the Federal Constitution and is void.

. . . .

Whether § 66 is Inconsistent with Art. 9(2) of the Federal Constitution

Article 9(2) of the Federal Constitution guarantees freedom of movement within the Federation. It provides:

Prohibition of banishment or excluded from the Federation

9. (1) . . .

(2) Subject to Clause (3) and to any law relating to the security of the Federation or any part thereof, public order, public health, or the punishment of offenders, every citizen has the right to move freely throughout the Federation and to reside in any part thereof.

Section 66 is explicit in criminalising any Muslim man who in any public place wears a woman's attire or poses as a woman.

Thus, § 66 cannot be said to merely *restrict* the appellants' freedom of movement. The impact of § 66 is more severe than that: it has the effect of *denying* the appellants and sufferers of GID of the right to move freely in public places. In effect, the appellants and other male Muslim sufferers of GID will never be able to leave their homes and move freely in the State of Negeri Sembilan without being exposed to being arrested and punished under § 66. In other words, § 66 *denies* the appellants and other male Muslim sufferers of GID of their right to freedom of movement.

As such, we accept the argument that § 66 is inconsistent with Art. 9(2) of the Federal Constitution.

However, even if we were to regard § 66 as a restriction and not as a denial of the right to move freely within the country, still, such restriction, according to judicial authorities (*see Sivarasa Rasiah*; *Dr. Mohd Nasir bin Hashim v. Menteri Dalam Negeri Malaysia* [2006] 6 MLJ 213; [2007] 1 CLJ 19; and *Muhammad Hilman bin Idham & Ors. v. Kerajaan Malaysia & Ors.* [2011] 6 MLJ 507; [2011] 9 CLJ 50), must be subject to the test of reasonableness. However, we hold that § 66 is an unreasonable restriction of the appellants' right to freedom of movement and hence unconstitutional as being inconsistent with Art. 9(2) of the Federal Constitution.

Whether § 66 is in Breach of Art. 10(2) of the Federal Constitution

Article 10(1)(a) of the Federal Constitution guarantees freedom of expression. It provides:

Freedom of Speech, Assembly and Association

10. (1) Subject to Clauses (2), (3) and (4)

(a) every citizen has the right to freedom of speech and expression;

. . .

(2) Parliament may by law impose—

(a) on the rights conferred by paragraph (a) of Clause (1), such restrictions as it deems necessary or expedient in the interest of the security of the Federation or any part thereof, friendly relations with other countries, public order or morality and restrictions designed to protect the privileges of Parliament or of any Legislative Assembly or to provide against contempt of court, defamation, or incitement to any offence.

A person's dress, attire or articles of clothing are a form of expression, which in our view, is guaranteed under Art. 10(1)(a).

Professor Shad Saleem Faruqi in his book *Document of Destiny, the Constitution of the Federation of Malaysia*, expresses the view that even "symbolic speech" like the manner of one's dressing and grooming can be treated as part of one's freedom of expression.

We find support for the above view from the landmark American Supreme Court case of *Tinker v. Des Moines Independent Community School District*, 393 US 503 (1969). In *Tinker*, it was held that a school regulation which prohibited students from wearing black armbands to silently protest against the United States Government's policy in Vietnam was violative of the First Amendment to the United States Constitution, which guaranteed free speech.

Section 66 directly affects the appellants' right to freedom of expression, in that they are prohibited from wearing the attire and articles of clothing of their choice.

Article 10(2)(a) states that only Parliament may restrict freedom of expression in limited situations; and so long as such restrictions are reasonable.

The State Legislative Assemblies in Malaysia (and this includes the State Legislature of Negeri Sembilan) have no power to restrict freedom of speech and expression. Only Parliament has such power. This is confirmed by the Supreme Court in *Dewan Undangan Negeri Kelantan & Anor. v. Nordin bin Salleh & Anor.* [1992] 1 MLJ 697; [1992] 1 CLJ (Rep) 72:

Next it must be observed that Art. 10(2) of the Federal Constitution provides that only Parliament may by law impose those restrictions referred to in arts 10(2), (3) and (4) of the Federal Constitution. Therefore even if any such restriction purported to have been imposed by the Constitution of the State of Kelantan was valid, and it is not, it is clear that the restriction could not be imposed by a law passed by any State Legislature. That would be another ground why Article XXXIA of the Constitution of Kelantan should be invalidated.

Section 66 is a state law that criminalises any male Muslim who wears a woman's attire or who poses as a woman in a public place. Hence, §66 is unconstitutional since it is a law purporting to restrict freedom of speech and expression but it is a law not made by Parliament.

Moreover, any restriction on freedom of expression must be reasonable. . . . *Sivarasa Rasiah*.

Clearly, the restriction imposed on the appellants and other GID sufferers by §66 is unreasonable. Thus, also from the aspect of reasonableness, §66 is unconstitutional.

National Legal Services Authority v. Union of India and Others

We accept the submission of learned counsel for the appellants that the issues in the Indian Supreme Court case of *National Legal Services Authority v. Union of India and others* [2014] 3 MLJ 595 are directly on point with most of the issues herein. [In it] the Indian Supreme Court . . . decided on a writ petition filed by the National Legal Services Authority on behalf of the transgender community of India . . . , who sought a legal declaration of their gender identity than the one assigned to them, male or female, at the time of birth; and their prayer is that non-recognition of their gender identity violates Art. 14 (our Art. 8(1)) and Art. 21 (our Art. 5(1)) of the Constitution of India.

[The] Indian Supreme Court. . . . explores a myriad of international human rights conventions and norms, case laws on transsexuals, and legislation in other countries on transgenders and ruled as follows:

> . . . any international convention not inconsistent with the fundamental rights and in harmony with its spirit must be read into those provisions . . . of the Constitution to enlarge the meaning and content thereof and to promote the object of constitutional guarantee.

The court considers the stigmatisation and discrimination faced by transgenders in society and ruled as follows:

> (a) that the word "sex" in Art. 15 (our Art. 8(2)) of the Indian Constitution includes "gender identity";

> (b) that the guarantee under Art. 19(1)(a) (our Art. 10(1)(a)) of the Indian Constitution includes the right to expression of one's gender through dress, and that '[n]o restriction can be placed on one's personal appearance or choice of dressing . . ."; and

(c) that Art. 21 (our Art. 5(1)) protects the dignity of human life and one's right to privacy, and that "[r]ecognition of one's gender identity lies at the heart of the fundamental right to dignity.

The Indian Supreme Court, in granting the appropriate directions (at para [129] of the judgment), held:

> discrimination on the basis of . . . gender identity includes any discrimination, exclusion, restriction or preference, which has the effect of nullifying or transposing equality by the law or the equal protection of laws guaranteed under our Constitution.

In this appeal, in arriving at our decision we are much guided by the above learned and inspiring judgment of the Indian Supreme Court. In particular, we adopt the following passages in the judgment:

Article 19(1)(a) and Transgenders

Article 19(1) of the Constitution guarantees certain fundamental rights, subject to the power of the State to impose restrictions from exercise of those rights. The rights conferred by Article 19 are not available to any person who is not a citizen of India. Article 19(1) guarantees those great basic rights which are recognized and guaranteed as the natural rights inherent in the status of the citizen of a free country. Article 19(1)(a) of the Constitution states that all citizens shall have the right to freedom of speech and expression, which includes one's right to expression of his self-identified gender. Self-identified gender can be expressed through dress, words, action or behavior or any other form. No restriction can be placed on one's personal appearance or choice of dressing, subject to the restrictions contained in Article 19(2) of the Constitution.

We may, in this connection, refer to few judgments of the US Supreme Courts on the rights of TG's freedom of expression. The Supreme Court of the State of Illinois in *City of Chicago v. Wilson et al.*, [389 N.E.2d 522 (Ill. 1978),] struck down the municipal law prohibiting cross-dressing, and held as follows—

> the notion that the State can regulate one's personal appearance, unconfined by any constitutional strictures whatsoever, is fundamentally inconsistent with 'values of privacy, self-identify, autonomy and personal integrity that . . . the Constitution was designed to protect.'

In *Doe v. Yunits et al.* [No. 00-1060-A, 2000 WL 33162199 (Mass. Super. Ct. Oct. 11, 2000), Chapter 13, *infra*], the Superior Court of Massachusetts upheld the right of a person to wear school dress that matches her gender identity as part of protected speech and expression and observed as follows:

> by dressing in clothing and accessories traditionally associated with the female gender, she is expressing her identification with the gender. In

additional, plaintiff's ability to express herself and her gender identity through dress is important for her health and well-being. Therefore, plaintiff's expression is not merely a personal preference but a necessary symbol of her identity.

Principles referred to above clearly indicate that the freedom of expression guaranteed under Article 19(1)(a) includes the freedom to express one's chosen gender identity through varied ways and means by way of expression, speech, mannerism, clothing, etc.

Gender identity, therefore, lies at the core of one's personal identity, gender expression and presentation and, therefore, it will have to be protected under Article 19(1)(a) of the Constitution of India. A transgender's [*sic*] personality could be expressed by the transgender's behavior and presentation. State cannot prohibit, restrict or interfere with a transgender's expression of such personality, which reflects that inherent personality. Often the State and its authorities either due to ignorance or otherwise fail to digest the innate character and identity of such persons. We, therefore, hold that values of privacy, self-identity, autonomy and personal integrity are fundamental rights guaranteed to members of the transgender community under Article 19(1)(a) of the Constitution of India and the State is bound to protect and recognize those rights.

Article 21 and the Transgenders

Article 21 of the Constitution of India reads as follows:

> 21. Protection of life and personal liberty—No person shall be deprived of his life or personal liberty except according to procedure established by law.

Article 21 is the heart and soul of the Indian Constitution, which speaks of the rights to life and personal liberty. Right to life is one of the basic fundamental rights and not even the State has the authority to violate or take away that right. Article 21 takes all those aspects of life which go to make a person's life meaningful. Article 21 protects the dignity of human life, one's personal autonomy, one's right to privacy, etc. Right to dignity has been recognized to be an essential part of the right to life and accrues to all persons on account of being humans. In *Francis Coralie Mullin v. Administrator, Union Territory of Delhi* (1981) 1 SCC 608 (paras 7 and 8), this Court held that the right to dignity forms an essential part of our constitutional culture which seeks to ensure the full development and evolution of persons and includes 'expressing oneself in diverse forms, freely moving about and mixing and comingling with fellow human beings'. Recognition of one's gender identity lies at the heart of the fundamental right to dignity. Gender, as already indicated, constitutes the core of one's sense of being as well as an integral part of a person's identity. Legal recognition of gender identity is, therefore, part of right to dignity and freedom guaranteed under our Constitution.

. . . .

Conclusion

We hold that § 66 is invalid as being unconstitutional. It is inconsistent with Art. 5(1), Art. 8(1) and (2), Art. 9(2), and Art. 10(1)(a) of the Federal Constitution.

The appeal is allowed.

We, therefore, grant the declaration sought in prayer B(1) of the judicial review application but in the following terms: that § 66 of the Syariah Criminal Enactment 1992 (Enactment 4 of 1992) of Negeri Sembilan is inconsistent with Art. 5(1), Art. 8(1) and (2), Art. 9(2), and Art. 10(1)(a); and is therefore void.

The appellants' counsel not asking for costs.

Appeal allowed; application for judicial review granted; each party to bear own costs.

Discussion

1. Although much of the court's reasoning relies on the particular circumstances of people who might in the West be described as transgender women, not all of its arguments appear so limited. If the State of Negeri Sembilan were to reenact section 66 with an exception for transgender persons, which, if any, of the constitutional rights violations the court found would be eliminated? Which, if any, of the violations would remain? What if the Parliament of Malaysia enacted the equivalent of section 66 with an exception for transgender persons—would that be constitutional under the court's reasoning? Should all people assigned male at birth have constitutionally protected freedom to dress as they wish, even if that means dressing in clothing commonly worn by people assigned female at birth, or is such constitutional freedom properly limited to a subset of the population with a certain gender identity? (Should the answer to that depend on which constitution of which country is being interpreted?) How can gendered restrictions on "cross-dressing" be understood as anything other than discriminatory on the basis of sex, potentially in violation of constitutional and human rights guarantees of equality? *Cf. Bostock v. Clayton County, Georgia*, 140 S. Ct. 1731 (2020), Chapter 5, Section D, *infra*, (reasoning, in cases under Title VII of the Civil Rights Act of 1964, that penalizing a person for conduct tolerated of a member of a different sex constitutes sex discrimination).

2. Although the U.S. Supreme Court often states that it will not decide more issues than are necessary to resolve a case, many other courts in the world do not follow this approach (sometimes termed "judicial minimalism," *see, e.g.*, CASS R. SUN-STEIN, ONE CASE AT A TIME: JUDICIAL MINIMALISM ON THE SUPREME COURT (Harv. U. Press 2001)). Here, the court ruled that section 66 violated many constitutional

guarantees (how many?) and determined that each violation of these guarantees rendered the provision void. What advantages might such an approach to adjudication have? What disadvantages?

3. The court finds a violation of transgender persons' right to freedom of movement because the statute effectively bans them from moving freely in public spaces in attire consistent with their gender identity. Recent legislative attempts in the U.S. to ban transgender people from using restrooms consistent with their gender identity have similarly been criticized as efforts to exclude transgender people from public life. *See, e.g.,* HEATH FOGG DAVIS, BEYOND TRANS: DOES GENDER MATTER? 57 (2017) ("What the authors of [North Carolina's 'bathroom bill'] HB2 were really saying to transgender people was, 'We don't want to *see* you in public restrooms because we don't want to see you in public.'"); Stephen Rushin & Jenny Carroll, *Bathroom Laws as Status Crimes,* 86 FORDHAM L. REV. 101, 113 & n.90 (citing, *inter alia,* TIMOTHY WANG ET AL., CTR. FOR AM. PROGRESS, STATE ANTI-TRANSGENDER BATHROOM BILLS THREATEN TRANSGENDER PEOPLE'S HEALTH AND PARTICIPATION IN PUBLIC LIFE 1 (2016), http://fenwayhealth.org/wp-content/uploads/2015 /12/COM-2485-Transgender-Bathroom-Bill-Brief_v8-pages.pdf [https://perma.cc /9PKA-FNTN]); Alex Chen, *The Design of Segregated Public Bathrooms: Victorian, Jim Crow, Trans, and Disability,* MEDIUM, http:// https://medium.com/@thetutting-tutor/the-design-of-segregated-public-bathrooms-victorian-jim-crow-trans-and -disability-33c632ad9d7a (last visited Mar. 22, 2019). Like cross-dressing bans, such restroom restrictions allocate rights expressly based on people's sex and so should be understood as discriminating on the basis of sex and thus subject to heightened equal protection scrutiny when governmentally imposed. (Although the Court in *Bostock, supra,* expressly disclaimed reaching the lawfulness of sex-discriminatory dress codes or sex-segregated restrooms under Title VII, the dissent thought the majority's reasoning could extend so far.)

What though of facially sex-neutral laws that might be used in ways that limit trans people's "ability to participate fully in public life," Rushin & Carroll, *supra,* at 113? Despite its characterization by some opponents as "a discriminatory law that targets transgender women of color," Matt Tracy, *Repeal of Walking While Trans Ban Clinches State Senate Votes,* GAY CITY NEWS, June 10, 2020, https://www .gaycitynews.com/repeal-of-walking-while-trans-ban-clinches-state-senate-votes/, New York's state law criminalizing "loitering for the purpose of engaging in a prostitution offense" does not expressly single out transgender people but applies broadly to "any person," and, unlike cross-dressing bans or restroom restrictions, is not defined in terms of gender-specific practices. *See* N.Y. PENAL LAW § 240.37. Hence, it would appear difficult to bring a successful challenge based on the ground that the loitering-for-prostitution law discriminatorily classifies on the basis of sex. The basis for characterizing the law as a "walking while trans ban" is that it is claimed to give "police officers . . . a green light to stop transgender women of color and arrest them for baseless reasons like walking down the street in certain clothing." Tracy, *supra.* In 2019 as part of a settlement of a suit challenging it, "the NYPD updated its patrol guide to stop targeting people on the basis of 'gender, gender identity, clothing, and location.'" Matt Tracy, *Sex Work Decrim Advocates Now Focused on "Walking While Trans" Repeal*, GAY CITY NEWS, Jan. 31, 2020, https://www.gaycitynews.com/sex-work-decrim-advocates-now-focused-on-walking-while-trans-repeal/. The Legal Aid Society "noted in a June 6 release that it had clients who were arrested simply for wearing a 'short dress,' 'a skirt and high heels,' 'tight black pants,' or 'a black dress.' Women were also stopped for simply standing outside or walking from a subway or grocery store back to their home." Matt Tracy, *NYPD Loosens Enforcement of Loitering Law*, GAY CITY NEWS, June 13, 2019, https://www.gaycitynews.com/nypd-loosens-enforcement-of-loitering-law/. "The patrol guide now states that those factors 'are not sufficient alone or together to establish probable cause,' and cops will be required to provide more details and specificity when recording observations." *Id.*

Other than legislative reform, what possible legal challenges might be brought against facially-sex-neutral loitering laws used to target transgender women of color?

Chapter 4

Youth in Out-of-Home Care

Not all minors live in homes with their birth or adoptive parents. For a variety of reasons, including rejection by their families, many live in foster care of some sort or other, which is broadly defined in federal regulations as "24-hour substitute care for children placed away from their parents or guardians and for whom the State agency has placement and care responsibility. This includes, but is not limited to, placements in foster family homes, foster homes of relatives, group homes, emergency shelters, residential facilities, child care institutions, and preadoptive homes." 45 C.F.R. § 1355.20. LGBTQ youth may be disproportionately represented in such out-of-home care. For example, based on one of the first surveys to explore directly the presence of sexual minorities in foster care, the Williams Institute has estimated that in Los Angeles "there are between 1.5 to 2 times as many LGBTQ youth living in foster care as LGBTQ youth estimated to be living outside of foster care." BIANCA D.M. WILSON ET AL., SEXUAL AND GENDER MINORITY YOUTH IN FOSTER CARE: ASSESSING DISPROPORTIONALITY AND DISPARITIES IN LOS ANGELES 6 (2014). The estimates in this study were that 5.6% of the foster youth population in L.A. identified as transgender, whereas only 2.25% of the general youth population did. The study further found that

> LGBTQ youth have a higher average number of foster care placements and are more likely to be living in a group home. They also reported being treated less well by the child welfare system, were more likely to have been hospitalized for emotional reasons at some point in their lifetime, and were more likely to have been homeless at some point in their life. The significance of these findings is supported by previous scholarship that has linked multiple placements, mental health concerns, homelessness, and placements in group homes are barriers to permanency faced by all youth, and LGBTQ youth in particular.

The finding that trans youth may not be treated well in out-of-home care is regrettably reflected in some of the reported litigation. In the next case, for example, New York City's agency in charge of foster care insisted on classifying a transgender girl as a boy for purposes of placement in a single-sex group home and then refused to let her wear skirts or dresses.

Reading Guide for Doe v. Bell

1. Note that this case is somewhat dated both in terminology and in substance. Linguistically, today, the phrase "transgendered person" is disfavored, as "transgender" is itself considered an adjective, rather than a verb; on such an understanding, referring to a "gayed person" would likewise be disfavored. Also, most within the trans and ally community would think it proper for a young person who lives as a female to be referred to as a "transgender girl," rather than a "transgender boy," in order to respect the person's gender identity.

Substantively, the court relied on the now superseded fourth edition of the American Psychiatric Association's *Diagnostic and Statistical Manual of Mental Disorders* ("DSM"). In its fifth edition (DSM-V™), it has eliminated the use of the diagnosis "gender identity disorder," with its rigid categorization of stereotypically masculine and feminine behaviors and requirement of clinically significant distress. "Gender dysphoria" is a new diagnosis, which emphasizes incongruence between internal and external perceptions of gender, permitting a more nuanced understanding of gender differences. *See* Chapter 14, *infra*.

2. What had New York's highest court (the Court of Appeals) previously held sufficient to show someone had a disability within the meaning of the New York State Human Rights Law ("NYSHRL")? Why does the trial court here (the Supreme Court, counterintuitively) conclude that Jean Doe has a statutory "disability"?

3. The agency and other governmental defendants here had refused to let Jean Doe wear skirts or dresses in the group facility in which the state had placed her, enforcing its dress code policy despite her gender identity disorder (*see* note 1 above). Why does the court conclude that this action did not discriminate against Doe on the basis of her disability? What other requirement of the NYSHRL does the court nonetheless conclude the defendants did violate? Why does the court reject the defendants' safety justification for its policy?

Doe v. Bell

194 Misc. 2d 774, 754 N.Y.S.2d 846 (Sup. Ct. 2003)

Louise Gruner Gans, J.

Petitioner Jean Doe, a 17-year-old biological male,[1] who has been diagnosed with gender identity disorder (GID) brings this CPLR article 78 petition seeking an order barring respondents, New York City Administration for Children's Services and Commissioner William Bell (collectively hereinafter ACS), from preventing Doe from keeping and wearing skirts and dresses at the Atlantic Transitional Foster Facility, the all-male ACS-operated, 24 bed, congregate foster care facility in which

---

1. Although biologically male, Doe identifies as a woman. Based on this identity, the parties have used feminine pronouns to refer to her. The Court does so as well.

she lives.[2] Doe contends that by denying her the right to wear such feminine clothing consistent with her gender identity, Atlantic Transitional's policy constitutes
unlawful disability and sex discrimination in contravention of the New York State
Human Rights Law (Executive Law § 291 et seq.), and violates Doe's constitutional
right to freedom of expression.

Facts

Jean Doe is a 17-year-old teenager, who albeit with some interruptions, has been
in foster care since age nine. Born a male, she identifies as a female. She experiences
an intense need to wear women's clothing and act as a woman. She feels uncomfortable dressing as a male, finding such dress awkward and alienating. Indeed, Doe has
run away from prior foster care placements in which she was forced to dress like
a man. This condition is known as gender identity disorder or GID. The American Psychiatric Association's Diagnostic and Statistical Manual of Mental
Disorders (4th ed. 1994) (DSM-IV) recognizes GID as a mental disorder. According to the DSM-IV, there are three components of GID: (i) "a strong and persistent
cross-gender identification, which is the desire to be, or the insistence that one is,
of the other sex"; (ii) "[t]here must also be evidence of that persistent discomfort
about one's assigned sex or a sense of inappropriateness in the gender role of that
sex"; and (iii) "clinically significant distress or impairment in social, occupational,
or other important areas of functioning." Doe's insistence on dressing in feminine
clothing is a characteristic of persons with GID. As noted in the DSM-IV, "[i]n boys,
the cross-gender identification is manifested by a marked preoccupation with traditionally feminine activities. They may have a preference for dressing in girls' or
women's clothes. . . ." Dr. Spritz, a psychiatrist who had treated Doe, testified that
she had diagnosed Doe with GID based on Doe's self-identification as a woman and
desire to wear women's clothing, her discomfort in being forced to wear male clothing, and the distress she experienced when forced to do so.

Dr. Spritz testified that the treatment plan for Jean Doe called for Doe to dress
according to her identity as a woman, including "wearing girls' clothing, accessories, and makeup, and sometimes other items to make [herself] look . . . more feminine, such as breast enhancers." Dr. Spritz explained the reason for such treatment:
"[t]he goal is to facilitate acceptance of the gender identity of a transgendered person by allowing her to dress in a manner consistent with her internal identity. . . .
Research has found that forcing youths with GID to dress in conflict with their
identity, though it may be in harmony with their biological attributes, causes significant anxiety, psychological harm, and antisocial behavior." Her opinion was sec-
onded by Gerald P. Mallon, Ph.D., a Professor at the Hunter College School of Social

---

2. Atlantic Transitional is an all-male congregate care facility used by ACS for short-term placement of boys in foster care aged 15–21. Generally, boys will stay at Atlantic Transitional only for
a period of 30–40 days or until a permanent placement is found. Where there are difficulties in
finding a suitable permanent placement, as has been the case with Jean Doe, a resident may stay at
Atlantic Transitional for a longer period.

Work and founder of the Green Chimneys Children's Services Program for, inter alia, transgendered youth, who expressed the opinion that "[t]he proper course of treatment for transgendered boys is to allow them to wear feminine clothing in an integrated environment."

Since the time of Jean Doe's second admission to Atlantic Transitional in January 2002, respondents have restricted the kinds of clothing she may wear. In March 2002, Wayne Antoine, director of Atlantic Transitional, issued a memorandum to the staff explaining that Jean Doe was not permitted "to wear 'female attire' in the facility. He can wear it only if he is walking directly out of the facility. If he returns to the facility, he must be escorted to his room so he can remove the female attire."[4] Later that month, after petitioner's counsel complained to ACS that Ms. Doe was being denied the right to dress in a feminine manner, ACS, by letter from its legal counsel unit . . . , refused to take any action to alter the Atlantic Transitional policy. ACS determined that because of its need to protect "the safety and welfare of the resident children, [Ms. Doe] is not permitted to dress in female clothing at his current group home." ACS noted that it had previously placed Ms. Doe in two group homes for gay, lesbian, bisexual, and transgendered youth, both of which permitted her to wear women's clothing, but that Doe had been discharged from both of these facilities for misconduct.

Mr. Antoine issued a memorandum announcing new written dress standards for residents of Atlantic Transitional. It stated that residents "must wear pants, or in warm weather, loose-fitting shorts that extend at least to mid-thigh. Shirts (or blouses) must also be worn at all times and must not expose the chest or midriff." [That] July 18 memorandum further prohibits Atlantic residents from wearing "clothing that is sexually provocative, that is, excessively short or tight fitting, or which is see thru." As part of the standards, "[r]esidents who wish to wear female attire may do so as long as the above guidelines are respected. Female attire that does not conform to the policy may only be worn by a resident when leaving facility premises. Residents whose attire does not conform to these guidelines must be immediately sent to their rooms to change." Thus, residents at Atlantic Transitional are not permitted to wear skirts or dresses at the facility. At the same time, Atlantic Transitional has continued to permit Jean Doe to wear scarves, "nails," breast enhancers and brassieres, hair weaves (a kind of hair lengthening hairpiece), and makeup.

Discussion

The New York State Human Rights Law (Executive Law § 296(18)(2)) provides that it is "an unlawful discriminatory practice for the owner, lessee, sub-lessee, assignee, or managing agent of, or other person having the right of ownership of or possession of or the right to rent or lease housing accommodations . . . [t]o refuse

---

4. Respondents do not dispute that the memorandum concerned Jean Doe and the clothing she would be permitted to wear in the Atlantic Transitional facility.

to make reasonable accommodations in rules, policies, practices, or services, when such accommodations may be necessary to afford said person with a disability equal opportunity to use and enjoy a dwelling."

A. Is Jean Doe Disabled Under the State Human Rights Law?

Under the State Human Rights Law, the term "disability" is broadly defined. Disability "means (a) a physical, mental or medical impairment resulting from anatomical, physiological, genetic or neurological conditions which prevents the exercise of a normal bodily function or is demonstrable by medically accepted clinical or laboratory diagnostic techniques. . . ." Executive Law § 292(21). Doe argues that, under this broad definition, she is a person with a disability, namely, GID. The court agrees.

In *State Div. of Human Rights v. Xerox Corp.*, 65 N.Y.2d 213, 480 N.E.2d (N.Y. 1985), the Court of Appeals held that an obese employee was a disabled employee who could not be terminated based on her disability under the State Human Rights Law. In rejecting the employer's argument that an employee could not be considered disabled under the State Human Rights Law absent a showing that her impairment limited his or her ability to perform particular activities, the Court of Appeals focused on New York's broad statutory definition of disability:

> [The employer's] arguments might have some force under typical disability or handicap statutes narrowly defining the terms in the ordinary sense to include only physical or mental conditions which limit the ability to perform certain activities. . . . However in New York, the term "disability" is more broadly defined. The statute provides that disabilities are not limited to physical or mental impairments but may also include "medical impairments." In addition, to qualify as a disability, the condition may manifest itself in one of two ways: (1) by preventing the exercise of a normal bodily function or (2) by being "demonstrable by medically accepted clinical or diagnostic techniques. . . ." Fairly read, the statute covers a range of conditions varying in degree from those involving a loss of a bodily function to those which are merely diagnosable medical anomalies which impair bodily integrity and thus may lead to more serious conditions in the future.

Based on this definition, the Court of Appeals held that the Commissioner of the State Division of Human Rights "could find that the complainant's obese condition itself, which was clinically diagnosed, . . . constituted an impairment and therefore a disability within the contemplation of the statute." *See also Reeves v. Johnson Controls World Servs.*, 140 F.3d 144 (2d Cir. 1998) (holding that, under *Xerox*, plaintiff's panic disorder was a disability under the State Human Rights Law) ("[*Xerox*'s] literal reading of the statute . . . treats a medically diagnosable impairment as necessarily a disability for purposes of the NYHRL. 'Thus, an individual can be disabled under the [NYHRL] if his or her impairment is demonstrable by medically accepted techniques; it is not required that the impairment substantially limit that individual's normal activities.'").

. . . . Doe's disorder has been clinically diagnosed by Dr. Spritz, as well as by Dr. Levin of the Family Court Mental Health Services, using the medically accepted standards set forth in the DSM-IV. No more is required for Doe to be protected from discrimination under the State Human Rights Law. . . .

B. Does Atlantic Transitional's Dress Policy Discriminate Against Jean Doe?

Doe argues that the dress code barring her from wearing feminine clothing, such as dresses and skirts, violates the State Human Rights Law because (i) it discriminates against her based on disability, and (ii) the city failed to make reasonable accommodations for Doe's disability.

Doe's first argument is without merit. There is nothing in the Atlantic Transitional policy that discriminates against Doe or other persons with disabilities based on her disability. The policy is neutral on its face and applies to all persons at the facility who wish to wear feminine clothing, whether or not they suffer from GID. The policy does not target persons who have GID and there is nothing in the record to suggest that the dress policy was promulgated to subject persons with disabilities to adverse treatment.

The State Human Rights Law, of course, is not simply a prohibition on discriminatory actions taken because of a person's disability. Quite the contrary, the State Human Rights Law, like federal disability discrimination statutes, requires covered entities to provide to persons with disabilities reasonable accommodations not offered to other persons in order to ensure that persons with disabilities enjoy equality of opportunity.

. . . .

Accordingly, the question is whether the city discriminated against Jean Doe by failing to accommodate her disability by exempting her from Atlantic Transitional's dress policy forbidding the wearing of dresses and skirts within the facility. In other words, does this case fall within the duty to provide reasonable accommodations . . . ?

The text of the State Human Rights Law sheds considerable light on the meaning of the duty to provide reasonable accommodations in rules, procedures, and policies. First, a covered entity has an obligation to provide reasonable accommodations in the rules, procedures, and practices of a housing facility "when such accommodations may be necessary to afford said person with a disability equal opportunity to use and enjoy a dwelling." Executive Law § 296(18)(2). Thus, persons with disabilities are entitled to accommodations from generally applicable rules that limit their ability to enjoy the use of a dwelling on the same terms as nondisabled persons. For example, in [*Ocean Gate Associates Starrett Sys., Inc. v. Dopico*, 109 Misc. 2d 774, 441 N.Y.S.2d 34 (Civ. Ct. 1981)], the reasonable accommodation [permitting a service dog] ensured that a disabled tenant would not be victimized because of the individual's disability. Thus, by providing disabled persons with the right to have a dog, the accommodation sought to grant wheelchair bound disabled tenants the security enjoyed by nondisabled tenants.

Section 292(21-e) further defines the term "reasonable accommodation." That section provides that "reasonable accommodation" means "actions taken which permit an employee, prospective employee or member with a disability to perform in a reasonable manner the activities involved in the job or occupation sought or held . . . ; provided, however, that such actions do not impose an undue hardship on the business, program or enterprise of the entity from which the action is requested." Executive Law § 292(21-e). This section tells us that a covered entity need not offer all accommodations sought by an individual with a disability. If the proposed accommodation would pose an undue hardship on the entity or is otherwise unreasonable, no liability arises from the failure to provide it.

. . . .

Based on the record before the court, the court concludes that exempting Jean Doe from the Atlantic Transitional dress policy is a reasonable accommodation. The record establishes that, because of her GID and the treatment she has been receiving for her condition, Jean Doe needs to be able to wear feminine clothing, including dresses and skirts now banned under the ACS-approved dress policy. The evidence before the court establishes that, because of her disability, Jean Doe experiences significant emotional distress if denied the right to wear such feminine clothing. Indeed, the treatment she has received for her GID calls for her to wear feminine clothing, including dresses and skirts. Granting her an exemption from the dress policy avoids this psychological distress. Moreover, it allows Ms. Doe the equal opportunity to use and enjoy the facilities at Atlantic Transitional—a right that would be denied to her if forced to endure psychological distress as a result of the ACS' dress policy. As in *Dopico*, because of this particularized showing of need, the exemption is a reasonable one.

The only difference between this case and *Dopico* is that Doe seeks an accommodation because the ACS dress policy conflicts with her GID and the psychological treatment she is receiving, whereas the tenant in *Dopico* needed an accommodation because the no pet clause conflicted with the tenant's physical limitations, depriving the tenant of the security a guard dog could bring. That *Dopico* involved a physical disability and this case a mental disability is, of course, of no moment. The State Human Rights Law protects both kinds of disabilities and requires the provision of reasonable accommodations to both physically and emotionally disabled persons.

ACS concedes that the State Human Rights Law applies to the policies it enacts for the foster care residents in its custody, but denies any failure to make a required reasonable accommodation. It makes three separate arguments in an attempt to avoid the conclusion that it failed to make a reasonable accommodation to Jean Doe's disability.

[The court first rejected the claim that ACS was ignorant of Doe's disability as contrary to the evidence before it.]

Second, ACS argues that it has provided a limited accommodation to Jean Doe, permitting her to wear certain feminine clothing, *i.e.*, blouses, makeup, and augmented breasts, and that any broader accommodation would be unreasonable because it would jeopardize the safety of the residents and staff of Atlantic Transitional. In short, ACS asserts that Ms. Doe's request to wear the range of feminine clothing at the facility would not be a reasonable accommodation because it would threaten the safety and security of the institution.[8]

It is, of course, well established that a disabled person is not entitled to an accommodation that would jeopardize the health and well-being of others. *Cf. Chevron U.S.A. Inc. v Echazabal*, 536 U.S. 73 (2002) (upholding regulation authorizing refusal to hire disabled employee where worker's disability on the job would pose a direct threat to himself and others). At the same time, courts must be wary of adverse treatment visited on persons with disabilities based on a need to protect others from them, lest overbroad generalizations about a disability be used as justification for discrimination.

In *School Board of Nassau County, Fla. v. Arline*, 480 U.S. 273 (1987), the Supreme Court. . . . directed lower courts to make an individualized inquiry to determine whether a disabled person posed a direct threat to others. "Such an inquiry is essential if [the federal Rehabilitation Act] is to achieve its goal of protecting handicapped individuals from deprivations based on prejudice, stereotypes, or unfounded fear, while giving appropriate weight to such legitimate concerns of grantees as avoiding exposing others to significant health and safety risks."

ACS asserts that its dress policy is necessary to protect the safety of residents and staff. According to Dr. Antoine, it was necessary to restrict the kind of dress worn by Jean Doe because a male in feminine clothing creates a "sexual dynamic . . . that can lead to unsafe and emotionally harmful sexual behavior." Further, at the facility, "there are many boys who are not emotionally mature and who feel confused or threatened by the presence of a transgendered boy among them and are prone to act out when Jean is nearby."

The court is not persuaded that Mr. Antoine's concerns render the accommodation sought by Jean Doe an unreasonable one. The premise of respondents' argument is that cross-dressing by a resident can lead to unsafe sexual behavior and other inappropriate conduct. But respondents permit Jean Doe to wear a number of different kinds of feminine clothing without jeopardizing the safety of the facility and its residents. As respondents freely admit, Jean Doe is allowed to wear fake breasts, makeup, women's blouses, scarves, nails, hair weaves and other female clothing while at Atlantic Transitional. Respondents cannot explain why she may safely wear these feminine items of clothing and accessories, but may not wear skirts or dresses without endangering the safety of the facility and its residents.[9] "As

---

8. Respondents frame this argument in terms of the reasonableness of Doe's accommodation. They do not argue that the accommodation, if reasonable, would pose an undue burden.

9. Moreover, the altercations involving Jean Doe of which ACS complains occurred when she was not wearing a skirt or dress. The problems presented by Jean Doe's deportment are separate from her dress. *See Doe v. Yunits*, No. 00-1060-A, 2000 WL 33162199 (Mass. Super. Ct.)[, Chapter 13 *infra*].

a means of pursuing the objective of [safety] that respondents now articulate, the [dress policy] is so woefully underinclusive as to render belief in that purpose a challenge to the credulous." *Republican Party of Minn. v. White*, 536 U.S. 765 (2002). There is simply no rational basis for treating dresses and skirts differently than the other feminine accoutrements which Jean Doe may now wear. In these circumstances, the city's purported safety concerns provide no basis for rejecting Doe's accommodation as unreasonable.[10]

Third, respondents point to the fact that the city previously placed Doe in foster care facilities designed for gay, lesbian, bisexual, and transgendered youth—facilities in which there were no restrictions on Doe's right to dress in a feminine manner—and that Doe was ejected from these facilities because of her own misconduct. Respondents claim that because Doe was ejected from these facilities, she should not be heard to complain about Atlantic Transitional's dress policy. The court disagrees. The ACS' obligation to act in a nondiscriminatory fashion is not satisfied merely by providing a small number of facilities at which children with GID are assured nondiscriminatory treatment. At each and every facility run and operated by the ACS, it must comply with the Human Rights Law's mandate to provide reasonable accommodations to persons with disabilities. That Doe engaged in misconduct that led to her expulsion from the foster care facilities designed for gay, lesbian, bisexual, and transgendered youth gives ACS no license to discriminate against her by denying her a reasonable accommodation.

Accordingly, the court finds that respondents have refused to accommodate reasonably Doe's GID in violation of the New York State Human Rights Law. Doe is therefore entitled to relief in the form of an exemption from respondents' dress policy, to the extent it bars her from wearing skirts and dresses at the Atlantic Transitional congregate foster care facility. Because the court finds that Doe is entitled to relief on her disability discrimination claim, the court need not reach her alternative bases for relief.

Accordingly, the petition of Jean Doe is granted. . . .

---

10. To support their argument that their dress policy does not offend the State Human Rights Law, the city relies on . . . *Matter of Custodio v Popolizio*, 139 Misc. 2d 391 (Sup. Ct. 1987). . . . In *Custodio*, . . . [b]ecause the city could deny housing to a tenant who caused substantial disturbance to others, the court held that the city was entitled to information regarding the proposed tenant's disability to determine if the tenant could meet the standards of conduct reasonably required of tenants. These cases are inapposite here. Although the city does point out that Ms. Doe caused some disturbances at Atlantic Transitional, the city does not seek to exclude Ms. Doe from housing. The question here is whether the city can restrict Jean Doe's wearing of certain feminine clothing based on its claim that such clothing will jeopardize the institutional safety of Atlantic Transitional. For the reasons explained above, the city's safety justification fails because there is no rational distinction, in terms of institutional safety, between the feminine clothing permitted and that banned under the city's policy.

Discussion

1. The court holds that ACS may not deny Ms. Doe the use of skirts and dresses based on the propensity of others to become disruptive in response. What regulations, if any, may ACS impose regarding the wearing of female clothing in its "all-male" group home? If ACS had not let anyone in its boys' group homes wear any "female" clothing (how would it write such a rule?), how might that have affected the court's reasoning? What if ACS also adopted such a broader rule for its group homes for LGBT youth? Consider whether a rule requiring residents of group homes for boys to wear "male" clothing and a rule requiring residents of group homes for girls to wear "female" clothing would discriminate on the basis of sex under the rationale of the Supreme Court in *Bostock v. Clayton County, Georgia*, 140 S. Ct. 1731 (2020), Chapter 5, Section D, *infra*. *Bostock* adopted a but-for view of sex discrimination under Title VII of the Civil Rights Act of 1964, reasoning that an employer who tolerates a behavior or trait in workers of one sex but would not tolerate it in works of a different sex has engaged in discrimination "because of" sex.

2. While the diagnostic change mentioned in point 1 of the Reading Guide for this case was largely welcomed by the transgender and therapeutic communities, can an argument be made that the new diagnosis no longer fits within the definition of disability and the protection of the disability discrimination law?

3. Do the facts indicate that the rule against skirts was created in response to and for the purpose of regulating Jean Doe's attire, although it was phrased as a generally applicable rule in the July 18 memorandum? Had ACS appealed the court's judgment against it, would Doe's counsel have been well advised to include an argument that the generally applicable rule was discriminatory in intent and/or effect, and how likely would such an argument be to prevail?

4. Disability statutes include the concept of reasonable accommodation, which anti-discrimination statutes reaching other forms of discrimination (save some forbidding religious discrimination) generally do not include. How does that affect the efficacy of disability statutes as compared to other anti-discrimination statutes? For an argument that constitutional rights under the First Amendment and the Equal Protection Clause mean that "minors in group foster homes cannot legally be forced to wear traditionally gender-conforming clothing or otherwise perform traditional gender roles, regardless of their biological sex," see Christine L. Olson, *Transgender Foster Youth: A Forced Identity*, 19 Tex. J. Women & L. 25, 28 (2009).

The same year *Doe v. Bell* was decided, "California passed a state law—the first of its kind in the country—that prohibited discrimination in the foster care system on the basis of sexual orientation and gender identity. . . ." Rudy Estrada & Jody Marksamer, *Lesbian, Gay, Bisexual, and Transgender Young People in State Custody: Making the Child Welfare and Juvenile Justice Systems Safe for All Youth Through Litigation, Advocacy, and Education*, 79 Temp. L. Rev. 415, 416 (2006) (citing Foster Care Anti-Discrimination Act of 2003, 2003 Cal. Legis. Serv. 331 (West) (codified as amended at Cal. Health & Safety Code §§ 1522.41, 1529.2, 1563 (West

Supp. 2006) and Cal. Welf. & Inst. Code §§ 16001.9, 16003, 160013 (West Supp. 2006)). (For assessment of "the strengths and shortcomings" of the California law, see Larisa Maxwell, *Fostering Care for All: Towards Meaningful Legislation to Protect LGBTQ Youth in Foster Care*, 1 Tex. A&M L. Rev. 209 (2013).) Estrada and Marksamer also discuss initiatives of Lambda Legal and of the National Center for Lesbian Rights to improve the treatment of LGBT youth in out-of-home care. *Id.* at 436–38. How might you lobby your state or local legislative and administrative bodies to adopt similar laws and policies?

Reading Guide for Duronslet v. County of Los Angeles

1. The next case involves a transgender girl who was detained by the Los Angeles County Department of Children's and Family Services in connection with a juvenile dependency case and made to use the "boys' side" of the facility where she was kept; her suit seeks compensation for the infringement of various rights she argues that conduct violated. The court describes the transgender plaintiff Genevieve as "biologically male." This may seem like a statement about anatomy and physiology—does it imply any proposition about the relationship (or lack thereof) between gender identity and anatomy/physiology? If so, ought that proposition be reevaluated in light of scientific studies in recent years regarding genetic origins and brain structure differences (see, for example, the discussion in *In re Heilig*, 816 A.2d 68 (Md. 2003), *supra* Chapter 2)? Also, note that the court's use of the terms "transgenderism" and "transsexualism" is currently disfavored because those terms suggest that gender identity is a belief or creed, similar to other "isms," rather than an innate identity.

2. Why does the court dismiss Genevieve's claim that the defendants discriminated against her on the basis of her gender identity in violation of California's Unruh Civil Rights Act?

3. Why does the court dismiss her claim that the defendants committed the tort of intentional infliction of emotional distress against her? Which element or elements does the court hold the plaintiff failed adequately to plead sufficient supporting facts? Are the court's pronouncements about the relevance of the number of times the plaintiff was forced to use male restrooms and sleeping facilities consistent?

4. Why does the court deny the defendants' motion to dismiss Genevieve's due process claim?

5. What level of equal protection scrutiny, if any, does the court determine applies to Genevieve's equal protection claim? Why does the court deny the defendants' motion to dismiss that claim?

Genevieve Duronslet v. County of Los Angeles

266 F. Supp. 3d 1213 (C.D. Cal. 2017)

[Lambda Legal filed an amicus brief supporting the plaintiff's opposition to the defendants' motion to dismiss.]

Otis D. Wright, II, United States District Judge

I. Introduction

Plaintiff Genevieve Duronslet is a transgender minor who is biologically male but who identifies as female. In October 2015, the Los Angeles County Department of Child and Family Services ("DCFS") detained Plaintiff in connection with a juvenile dependency case. During her detention, DCFS personnel allegedly forced Plaintiff to use male restroom facilities and to sleep on the "boy's side" of the DCFS Welcome Center, even though they "knew or should have known" that Plaintiff identified as female. Plaintiff alleges that DCFS staff were acting pursuant to an official policy or practice that treats transgender detainees according to their birth-assigned gender rather than their gender identity. Plaintiff subsequently filed suit against Defendant County of Los Angeles, alleging: (1) violation of the California Unruh Civil Rights Act; (2) intentional infliction of emotional distress; (3) violation of the federal Due Process Clause; and (4) violation of the federal Equal Protection Clause. The County has moved to dismiss all of Plaintiff's claims. For the reasons discussed below, the Court GRANTS IN PART and DENIES IN PART the County's Motion.

. . . .

III. Discussion

A. Unruh Civil Rights Act

The County argues that there are insufficient facts to infer that DCFS personnel intentionally discriminated against Plaintiff. Because Plaintiff is required to plausibly allege intentional discrimination to state a claim under the Unruh Civil Rights Act, the County argues, Plaintiff's claim must be dismissed. The Court agrees.

The Unruh Civil Rights Act provides as follows:

> All persons within the jurisdiction of this state are free and equal, and no matter what their sex . . . are entitled to the full and equal accommodations, advantages, facilities, privileges, or services in all business establishments of every kind whatsoever.

Cal. Civ. Code § 51(b); *see also id.* § 52(a) ("Whoever denies, aids or incites a denial, or makes any discrimination or distinction contrary to Section 51 . . . is liable for each and every offense. . . ."). The Act defines "sex" discrimination to include discrimination based on gender identity. *Id.* § 51(e)(5). "[A] plaintiff seeking to establish a case under the Unruh Act must plead and prove intentional discrimination." *Harris v. Capital Growth Investors XIV*, 805 P.2d 873 (Cal. 1991). Facts showing that a facially neutral policy has a disparate impact on a protected class "may be probative of intentional discrimination," but is alone insufficient to establish liability. *Id.*

In federal court, a plaintiff cannot plead discriminatory intent merely by making a conclusory allegation to that effect. *Ashcroft v. Iqbal*, 556 U.S. 662 (2009). Rather, the complaint must include some factual context that gives rise to a plausible inference of discriminatory intent.

Plaintiff has not met that standard here. To show that the County intended to discriminate against her based on her transgender status, Plaintiff must plausibly allege that the County knew of her transgender status. While Plaintiff makes the conclusory assertion that the County "knew or should have known" that she was transgender, there are insufficient underlying facts showing how or why the County knew or should have known this. The only allegation potentially supporting such an inference is Plaintiff's repeated insistence that she was "forced" to use male facilities, which suggests that she first requested to use female facilities. However, this does not necessarily mean that she informed them of her transgender status or that they otherwise must have drawn the conclusion that she is transgender. Thus, the Court dismisses this claim with leave to amend to cure this deficiency.

B. Intentional Infliction of Emotional Distress

. . . .

2. Merits

The County next argues that its alleged conduct was not "extreme and outrageous" as a matter of law, that Plaintiff has failed to allege intentional or reckless conduct by the County, and that Plaintiff has not suffered "severe emotional distress" as a matter of law.

"A cause of action for intentional infliction of emotional distress exists when there is (1) extreme and outrageous conduct by the defendant with the intention of causing, or reckless disregard of the probability of causing, emotional distress; (2) the plaintiff's suffering severe or extreme emotional distress; and (3) actual and proximate causation of the emotional distress by the defendant's outrageous conduct." *Hughes v. Pair*, 209 P.3d 963 (Cal. 2009).

i. Intentional/Reckless Conduct

To recover under a theory of intentional infliction of emotional distress, "[t]he defendant must have engaged in 'conduct intended to inflict injury or engaged in with the realization that injury will result.'" *Potter v. Firestone Tire & Rubber Co.*, 863 P.2d 795 (Cal. 1993). As previously noted, Plaintiff has not plausibly alleged that DCFS personnel knew or should have known that she was transgender. Without this, Plaintiff also cannot plausibly allege that the County intended to cause her emotional distress — or that they acted with reckless disregard for the probability of causing her emotional distress — by forcing her to use male restroom and sleeping facilities. The Court therefore dismisses this claim but grants leave to amend to cure this deficiency.

ii. Extreme and Outrageous Conduct

"A defendant's conduct is 'outrageous' when it is so extreme as to exceed all bounds of that usually tolerated in a civilized community." *Hughes*. "Behavior may be considered outrageous if a defendant (1) abuses a relation or position which gives him power to damage the plaintiff's interest; (2) knows the plaintiff is susceptible to injuries through mental distress; or (3) acts intentionally or unreasonably with the recognition that the acts are likely to result in illness through mental distress." *Molko v. Holy Spirit Assn.*, 762 P.2d 46 (Cal. 1988). However, outrageous conduct does not include "mere insults, indignities, threats, annoyances, petty oppressions, or other trivialities." *Hughes*. Whether conduct is "extreme and outrageous" is a question of fact for a jury to resolve unless reasonable minds could not differ on the issue. *Molko*.

Plaintiff's current allegations are insufficient to show that the County's conduct was extreme and outrageous. First, as previously noted, Plaintiff has not plausibly alleged that the County knew or should have known of Plaintiff's transgender status. Without this, all that Plaintiff has plausibly alleged is that the County required a biologically male minor to use male restroom and sleeping facilities. This in and of itself is not "extreme and outrageous." Second, as the County points out, it is unclear how many times DCFS personnel required Plaintiff to use the male facilities, whether they did so despite observing a negative reaction from Plaintiff, or what other facts may exist demonstrating the outrageousness of their conduct. These facts might make the difference between culpable conduct and conduct that, while unfair and inconsiderate, does not "exceed all bounds of that usually tolerated in a civilized community." *Hughes*. The Court will therefore dismiss this claim with leave to amend to provide more facts in support of this claim.

However, to provide further guidance to the parties on this element, the Court also addresses the County's remaining arguments. The County cites *Hughes* for the proposition that forcing minors to use restroom and sleeping facilities that do not comport with their gender identity is not extreme and outrageous as a matter of law. The Court fails to see any similarity between this case and *Hughes*. In *Hughes*, the court held that sexual comments made to the plaintiff by her ex-husband during two encounters did not constitute extreme and outrageous conduct. The County suggests that its alleged conduct is less egregious than the conduct in *Hughes*, but it does not identify any meaningful similarities between the two situations. Indeed, if anything, the conduct here is more egregious than in *Hughes* due to the existence of an adult-minor caregiver relationship between Plaintiff and the County, and the susceptibility of transgender teens in foster care to emotional distress. . . . Given this, it is far from certain that the County's conduct would not be extreme and outrageous as a matter of law even if there was only a single instance where the DCFS knowingly forced Plaintiff to use facilities that did not comport with her gender identity.

iii. Severe Emotional Distress

"With respect to the requirement that the plaintiff show severe emotional distress, this court has set a high bar. Severe emotional distress means emotional distress of such substantial quality or enduring quality that no reasonable person in civilized society should be expected to endure it." *Hughes*; *see also id.* (allegation that the plaintiff suffered "discomfort, worry, anxiety, upset stomach, concern, and agitation" insufficient). Plaintiff also fails to satisfy this element. As the County notes, Plaintiff alleges only that she suffered "shock, embarrassment, and emotional distress" as a result of the County's conduct. Under *Hughes*, this is insufficient. While the Court is cognizant of the severe emotional distress that a transgender teen could suffer by being forced to use facilities that do not comport with their gender identity, there are simply insufficient allegations to conclude that such is the case here. The Court therefore dismisses the claim on this basis but grants leave to cure this deficiency.

C. Due Process

The County argues that there are insufficient facts to establish that the County has a policy or practice of treating transgender detainees according to their birth-assigned gender rather than their gender identity. The Court disagrees.

Federal law, unlike state law, does not hold a public entity vicariously liable for constitutional violations committed by its employees. 42 U.S.C. § 1983; *Monell v. Dep't of Soc. Servs. of City of N.Y.*, 436 U.S. 658 (1978). "Instead, it is when execution of a government's policy or custom, whether made by its lawmakers or by those whose edicts or acts may fairly be said to represent official policy, inflicts the injury that the government as an entity is responsible under § 1983." *Id.* "Official municipal policy includes the decisions of a government's lawmakers, the acts of its policymaking officials, and practices so persistent and widespread as to practically have the force of law." *Connick v. Thompson*, 563 U.S. 51 (2011).

Plaintiff alleges, upon information and belief, "that the actions of Defendants . . . w[ere] the result of policies and procedures as well as customs and practices on the part of the [County] which precludes [*sic* — Eds.] detainees and persons under the supervision of the DCFS to be treated [according to] their assigned sex at birth rather than [their] gender identity, regardless of the individual circumstances and the fact that said actions are known to cause extreme emotional distress to persons in the position of Plaintiff." The Court finds this allegation sufficient at the pleading stage. First, assuming that the DCFS was aware of Plaintiff's transgender status, its treatment of Plaintiff itself gives rise to an inference (albeit a weak one) that the County has such a policy or practice, and that DCFS personnel were acting pursuant to that policy or practice. Second, courts have permitted plaintiffs to plead ultimate facts solely on information and belief where the underlying evidence is "peculiarly in the defendant's possession and control." *Arista Records, LLC v. Doe 3*, 604 F.3d 110 (2d Cir. 2010); *see also GCIU-Emp'r Ret. Fund v. Quad/Graphics, Inc.*, No. 216-CV-00100-ODW-AFMX, 2016 WL 3027336, at *3 (C.D. Cal. May 26, 2016) (collecting cases). Here, any evidence regarding the policies, customs, and practices of the County certainly falls into the category of evidence that is "peculiarly in [its] possession and control." The Court thus denies the County's Motion with respect to Plaintiff's Due Process claim.

D. Equal Protection

Finally, the County argues that Plaintiff has not alleged sufficient facts show-ing that DCFS personnel deprived her of equal protection of the law. The County argues that rational basis review applies to discrimination claims against transgen-der persons, and that Plaintiff's allegations do not establish that a policy of requir-ing transgender minors to use facilities that align with their birth-assigned gender rather than their gender identity is not rationally related to a legitimate government interest. Plaintiff and her supporting amicus argue that transgender discrimination claims should be evaluated under strict scrutiny or at least intermediate scrutiny, but that in any event Plaintiff pleads sufficient facts to establish that the County's policy would not survive under even rational basis review.

"The Equal Protection Clause of the Fourteenth Amendment commands that no State shall 'deny to any person within its jurisdiction the equal protection of the laws,' which is essentially a direction that all persons similarly situated should be treated alike." *City of Cleburne, Tex. v. Cleburne Living Ctr.*, 473 U.S. 432 (1985). "However, courts must balance this mandate with the 'practical necessity that most legislation classifies for one purpose or another, with resulting disadvantage to vari-ous groups or persons.'" *Golinski v. U.S. Office of Pers. Mgmt.*, 824 F. Supp. 2d 968, 981 (N.D. Cal. 2012) (quoting *Romer v. Evans*, 517 U.S. 620 (1996)). "[T]o reconcile the promise of equal protection with the reality of lawmaking, courts apply the most searching constitutional scrutiny to those laws that burden a fundamental right or target a suspect class, such as those based on race, national origin, sex or religion." *Id.* Laws that do not burden a protected class or infringe on a constitutionally pro-tected fundamental right, on the other hand, are subject to rational basis review. *Id.*

In determining the level of scrutiny to apply, the Supreme Court has considered several factors, including: "(1) the history of invidious discrimination against the class burdened by the legislation; (2) whether the characteristics that distinguish the class indicate a typical class member's ability to contribute to society; (3) whether the distinguishing characteristics are 'immutable' or beyond the class members' control; and (4) the political power of the subject class." *Id.*; *see also Windsor v. United States*, 699 F.3d 169 (2d Cir. 2012), *aff'd*, 570 U.S. 744 (2013) (collecting cases); *Whitewood v. Wolf*, 992 F. Supp. 2d 410 (M.D. Pa. 2014) (collecting cases); *Varnum v. Brien*, 763 N.W.2d 862, 887 (Iowa 2009) (collecting cases). The Court has also considered trends in Congressional legislation regarding the class at issue. *Frontiero v. Richardson*, 411 U.S. 677 (1973).

The County points to *Holloway v. Arthur Andersen & Co.*, 566 F.2d 659 (9th Cir. 1977), for the proposition that transgender discrimination is subject to rational basis review.[5] In *Holloway*, an employer terminated a transgender employee based on

---

5. In its reply, the County does not further reference *Holloway* or even continue arguing that transgender discrimination claims are subject to rational basis review. Nonetheless, because it is an open question whether *Holloway* still sets the level of scrutiny for transgender discrimination claims, the Court will address the issue.

her transgender status, and the employee brought suit against her former employer for "sex" discrimination under Title VII, 42 U.S.C. § 2000e. The Ninth Circuit held that "sex" discrimination only encompassed discrimination based one's anatomical gender, and not discrimination based on a change in one's gender or gender identity. *Id.*; *see also id.* ("Holloway has not claimed to have [been] treated discriminatorily because she is male or female, but rather because she is a transsexual who chose to change her sex. This type of claim is not actionable under Title VII. . . ."). The court also rejected the employee's contention that Congress's exclusion of transgender persons from Title VII protection violated the Equal Protection Clause. In doing so, the court held that rational basis review applied to transgender discrimination claims under the Equal Protection Clause because "transsexuals are not necessarily a 'discrete and insular minority'" and because it "ha[d] [not] been established that transsexuality is an 'immutable characteristic determined solely by the accident of birth' like race or national origin."

Over twenty years later, the Ninth Circuit held that *Holloway*'s interpretation of "sex" discrimination had been effectively overruled by the "logic and language" of subsequent Supreme Court cases. *Schwenk v. Hartford*, 204 F.3d 1187 (9th Cir. 2000). The Supreme Court held in *Price Waterhouse v. Hopkins*, 490 U.S. 228 (1989), that Title VII "barred not just discrimination based on the fact that Hopkins was a woman, but also discrimination based on the fact that she failed 'to act like a woman'—that is, to conform to socially-constructed gender expectations." *Schwenk*. Thus, *Schwenk* held, "sex" discrimination under Title VII included discrimination on the basis of a change in one's gender identity. *Schwenk* further noted that Title VII's protections paralleled those of the Gender Motivated Violence Act, and thus "gender"-motivated violence under the latter Act included violence motivated by gender identity.

Although *Schwenk* did not directly address *Holloway*'s Equal Protection holding, at least one district court has held that *Schwenk*'s reasoning effectively overruled *Holloway* on that issue as well. *Norsworthy v. Beard*, 87 F. Supp. 3d 1104 (N.D. Cal. 2015). The Court ultimately agrees that *Holloway* does not require it to apply rational basis review here. First, the change in judicial approach to federal sex discrimination statutes since *Holloway* requires a fresh examination of the appropriate level of scrutiny for transgender discrimination claims under the Equal Protection Clause. *See Frontiero* (trends in federal discrimination statutes relevant to determining the level of scrutiny under the Equal Protection Clause). Second, *Holloway* itself appeared to accept that future developments in our understanding of transgenderism would require such a reexamination. That is, the court noted that there was substantial uncertainty among experts surrounding the "origin and development of transsexualism," and appeared to limit its factual determinations accordingly, *see id.* (holding that transgender persons were not "necessarily" a discrete and insular minority and that it "ha[d] [not] been established" that transgenderism was an immutable characteristic). We are now forty years past *Holloway*. Thus, it would not be inconsistent with *Holloway* for this Court to conclude, based on an adequately developed factual record, that our current understanding of transgenderism requires the application of heightened scrutiny.

Beyond this, however, the Court finds it premature to determine either the level of scrutiny to apply or whether the County's policy can withstand such scrutiny. Both are fact-dependent inquiries that are unsuitable for resolution at the pleading stage. *See Golinski* (relying extensively on the factual record in determining the level of scrutiny and applying strict scrutiny); *Latta v. Otter*, 19 F. Supp. 3d 1054 (D. Idaho) (converting motion to dismiss into motion for summary judgment before addressing level of scrutiny), *aff'd*, 771 F.3d 456 (9th Cir. 2014). Indeed, in making their respective arguments concerning the level of scrutiny and the legitimacy of the government's justifications, both the County and Plaintiff's supporting amicus rely heavily on statistics and facts that are neither in the complaint nor supported by documents subject to judicial notice. For now, it is enough for the Court to conclude that Plaintiff has plausibly established that some form of heightened scrutiny might apply to her Equal Protection claim, which shifts the burden to the County to justify its conduct. *United States v. Virginia*, 518 U.S. 515 (1996). And because a plaintiff need not allege facts negating issues on which the defendant carries the burden of proof, *see ASARCO, LLC v. Union Pac. R. Co.*, 765 F.3d 999, 1004 (9th Cir. 2014), Plaintiff need not allege any additional facts to state an Equal Protection claim.

IV. Conclusion

For the reasons discussed above, the Court GRANTS IN PART and DENIES IN PART the County's Motion. Plaintiff must file an amended complaint within 14 days that cures these deficiencies. The County's response to Plaintiff's amended complaint shall be due 14 days thereafter.

IT IS SO ORDERED.

Discussion

1. On a motion to dismiss, where all reasonable inferences are to be drawn in favor of the party opposing the motion, why should the court insist Genevieve establish that her evidence "necessarily" shows the defendants knew she was transgender? What kind of facts could Genevieve have pleaded to show that the staff knew or should have known that she is transgender and female?

2. What type of evidence would show that the staff had the "realization that injury would result"? Is the "reckless disregard" standard that the court references different from this?

3. If the pleadings specified that staff had required a "biologically female" girl to sleep with boys and use boys' bathrooms and dressing rooms, could such conduct not be extreme and outrageous as a matter of law? Is this an apt comparison to the court's reasoning?

4. Why does the court presume that ACS knew of plaintiff's transgender status for purposes of determining whether a county custom or policy supported liability on the plaintiff's due process claim but not for the preceding causes of action?

Under federal pleading standards, plaintiff must plead facts that, if proven, show the plaintiff has a plausible claim. To establish a due process or equal protection violation under even the lowest level of constitutional scrutiny that might apply, "rational basis review," the plaintiff could have, but did not, plead facts showing that the alleged policy was unrelated to a legitimate government interest. There were also no facts pleaded regarding the constitutional level of scrutiny. (To be fair to the plaintiff, she began the action in state court, which had different pleading standards, and the case was removed to federal court by the defendant.) In its equal protection analysis the court skirts the plausibility standard by placing the burden of proof on the defendant. (In its due process analysis the court only addresses causation, not the question of justification.) While the court acknowledges that it is "inappropriate" to determine the level of constitutional scrutiny at this pleading stage, it holds that the burden of proof shifts to defendant because the plaintiff has "plausibly established" that some form of heightened scrutiny "might apply." Is the court's reasoning internally inconsistent?

5. Under established equal protection precedents, discrimination on the basis of sex is subject to intermediate scrutiny. *United States v. Virginia*, 518 U.S. 515 (1996). If anti-transgender discrimination necessarily involves sex discrimination for purposes of the Equal Protection Clause, then anti-transgender discrimination would necessarily receive at least intermediate scrutiny as a form of sex discrimination. A six-member majority of the Supreme Court held that discrimination on the basis of transgender status necessarily involves discrimination on the basis of sex for purposes of Title VII of the Civil Rights Act of 1964. *See Bostock v. Clayton County, Georgia*, 140 S. Ct. 1731 (2020), Chapter 5, Section D, *infra*. Is there any reason to think that that reasoning should not apply under the Equal Protection Clause as well?

The next two decisions address efforts by transgender youth in the New York City foster care system to secure transition-related medical procedures. As you read them, contemplate why they reach different results.

Reading Guide for Mariah L. v. Administration for Children's Services

1. Note that this case is typically cited as *Brian L. v. Administration for Children's Services*. But the youth went by Mariah L., which also appeared in the official caption of the case.

Note also that in the following case the court refers to the term "sex reassignment surgery," which is sometimes abbreviated SRS. SRS refers to several medical procedures that may be used to reassign primary and secondary sexual characteristics, including genital, chest, and facial characteristics. The term has fallen out of favor in recent years in the U.S. trans community, although it is still often used in the medical community. Terms increasingly used include gender reassignment surgery, gender affirmation surgery, and gender confirmation surgery. Within the trans community and among allies and people who provide medical care for trans people in the United States today, the term "sex change" is often considered derogatory and sometimes considered inaccurate. The philosophical question of whether sex and/or gender are being reassigned or affirmed is a controversial one.

2. The appeals court here states that gender identity disorder refers to "a disjunction between an individual's sexual organs and sexual identity." (The court uses the term "sexual identity," an ambiguous term that may refer to one's identification with a sex, such as male, or one's identification with a sexuality, such as gay. In this context, the term "gender identity" was most likely intended.) This notion of disjunction implies that certain sexual organs normally correlate with a certain sexual or gender identity. If this implication were to be incorrect, how might this affect the court's reasoning?

Note also that the American Psychiatric Association has replaced the diagnosis "gender identity disorder" with "gender dysphoria," with the intent of differentiating between a trans person who is well-adjusted to their gender and others who are experiencing clinically significant distress because of their gender. The APA's *Diagnostic and Statistical Manual of Mental Disorders* (5th ed.) is designed to provide guidance to mental health professionals in differential diagnosis. It does not distinguish between distress from incongruence between assigned sex and gender identity and distress caused by social prejudice. Perhaps it is not possible or desirable to create a sharp line between the two.

3. The appeals court rejects the argument that the agency must arrange surgery for Mariah L. because of the New York City Rules & Regulations requirement that the Administration for Children's Services ("ACS") "must provide or arrange for such follow-up care" as required by the physician. 18 NYCRR 441.22(g). The regulation requires agencies to provide "periodic individualized medical examinations" on a regular basis. For what reason does the court conclude that the regulation does not apply, and why does it alternatively hold that even if the regulation did apply it would not have authorized the courts to order ACS to arrange for Mariah's surgery?

In re Brian L., Also Known as Mariah L. v. Administration for Children's Services

51 A.D.3d 488 (N.Y. App. Div. 2008)

[A great many amici participated in this case including but not limited to the following organizations: the American Civil Liberties Union; Gay & Lesbian Advocates & Defenders; The National Center for Lesbian Rights; The National Center for Transgender Equality; The New York Civil Liberties Union; The Transgender Law and Policy Institute; The Association of Gay and Lesbian Psychiatrists; Hispanic AIDS Forum; The World Professional Association for Transgender Health, Inc.;

Children's Law Center for Los Angeles; The Youth Law Center, San Francisco, CA; and Suffolk University Law School, Child Advocacy Clinic.]

Andria, J.P., Friedman, Sweeny, McGuire, JJ.

. . . .

Petitioner [Mariah L.] was born a biological male but at some point during adolescence was diagnosed with gender identity disorder (GID), "which the American Psychiatric Association characterizes as a disjunction between an individual's sexual organs and sexual identity." *Smith v. City of Salem, Ohio*, 378 F.3d 566, 568 (6th Cir. 2004), citing American Psychiatric Association, Diagnostic and Statistical Manual of Mental Disorders 576–582 (4th ed. 2000 [text revision]). Petitioner began receiving mental health and medical care for GID, including psychological and psychiatric treatment and hormone therapy aimed at developing secondary female sex characteristics. [The Administration for Children's Services ("ACS")] was responsible for arranging and paying for petitioner's medical care since she was in foster care between 1995 and April 2006.

In December 2005, petitioner, through her former law guardian, made a motion in Family Court seeking to compel ACS to provide her with all medical treatment recommended by her doctors for GID, including sex reassignment surgery, which for male-to-female individuals "'involves the removal of the external male sexual organs and the construction of an artificial vagina by plastic surgery. It is supplemented by hormone treatments that facilitate the change in secondary sex characteristics,' such as breast development" . . . .

The motion was supported by the written reports of a psychologist, a psychotherapist and two medical doctors, each of whom had evaluated petitioner to determine whether she was a suitable candidate and ready for sex reassignment surgery. . . .

ACS opposed the motion on the ground that it was only permitted to pay for medical treatments approved by Medicaid law and that Medicaid law prohibited payment for sex reassignment surgery. No evidence was submitted in support of the agency's opposition. Family Court granted the motion and directed ACS to arrange for petitioner to have the surgery, and ACS appealed.

Upon remand, ACS supplemented the record before Family Court with the affidavit of Pratt, its assistant commissioner in charge of matters related to the provision of medical services to foster children under ACS' care. Pratt explained that petitioner was a foster child who received medical care pursuant to article 5, title 11 of the Social Services Law, the state Medicaid law, and that "her [medical] coverage is defined by and limited by the Medicaid statute and regulations." Pratt further explained [*sic*—Eds.] that state Medicaid law prohibited ACS from paying for sex reassignment surgery.

Pratt stated that, even assuming that ACS could legally pay for the surgery, it would not do so as a matter of discretion, because petitioner had not satisfied certain eligibility requirements for sex reassignment surgery [the *Standards of Care* for

GID published by the Harry Benjamin International Gender Dysphoria Associa-tion [now, the World Professional Association for Transgender Health — Eds.] ("the Harry Benjamin standards"). Specifically, petitioner did not have a psychological evaluation and psychotherapy if required or recommended, and she lacked demon-strable knowledge of costs, procedures, complications of various surgical procedures and an awareness of different competent surgeons. Pratt also stated that petitioner had not evinced that she was ready for the surgery under the criteria set forth in the Harry Benjamin standards; petitioner, according to Pratt, did not demonstrate that she had a stable, enduring and comfortable gender identity, and she did not show progress in dealing with work, family and interpersonal issues. Pratt averred, based upon multiple conversations with petitioner and information imparted to her by foster care staff, that petitioner "simply has not demonstrated the kind of seri-ous, thoughtful, and committed approach that would, as a matter of basic logic, be expected of anyone appropriately planning for this type of fundamental and serious surgical process. Rather, she has behaved in a manner that is indecisive, unstable, and self-defeating, and has been all but impossible to engage in meaningful plan-ning on this or any other vital issue."

. . . .

While [under the court's earlier statutory analysis, omitted from this opinion here — Eds.,] ACS has a duty to provide necessary medical and surgical care to all of the children in its care and must, if necessary, pay for that care, the question remains whether ACS can be judicially compelled to pay for petitioner's sex reassignment surgery. ACS' position is that Family Court does not have the power to order ACS to arrange for the surgery and that Family Court's order encroaches upon ACS' authority to provide medical and surgical care to children under ACS' care. Thus, ACS asserts that it has discretion to determine whether a particular medical treat-ment is necessary and that this determination may not be disturbed unless it lacks a rational basis. Citing Pratt's affidavit, ACS urges that its decision not to arrange for petitioner's sex reassignment surgery has a rational basis. Petitioner argues that ACS has an obligation under Social Services Law §398(6)(c) to arrange for her to have the surgery, that ACS failed to articulate a reasonable basis for its decision not to arrange it, and, thus, Family Court had the authority to order ACS to do so.

Petitioner identifies two provisions of the Family Court Act that authorize Family Court to direct ACS to provide services to a person in foster care, Family Court Act §255 and §1015-a. Family Court Act §255 states, in pertinent part, that:

> It is hereby made the duty of, and the family court or a judge thereof may order, any state, county, municipal and school district officer and employee to render such assistance and cooperation as shall be within his [or her] legal authority, as may be required, to further the objects of this act. . . . It is hereby made the duty of and the family court or judge thereof may order, any agency or other institution to render such information, assistance and cooperation as shall be within its legal authority concerning a child who

is or shall be under its care, treatment, supervision or custody as may be required to further the objects of this act.

In *Matter of Lorie C.*, 400 N.E.2d 336 (N.Y. 1980), the Court of Appeals [New York's highest court—Eds.] discussed the scope of Family Court's authority to direct governmental agencies to act under Family Court Act § 255 . . . . Noting that Social Services Law § 398(6)(h) provided commissioners of public welfare with the responsibility to supervise certain classes of children until they become 21 years old, are discharged or are adopted, the Court concluded that the plan set forth in Family Court's order [in that case directing the department of social services and the probation department setting standards and procedures for placement of children in foster homes and directing those departments to implement and follow that plan] impermissibly treaded upon the department of social services' statutory authority. [T]he Court observed that "courts do not normally have overview of the lawful acts of appointive and elective officials involving questions of judgment, discretion, allocation of resources and priorities," and that "it is a fundamental of the doctrine of distribution of powers that each department should be free from interference."

. . . .

Petitioner's assertion that 18 NYCRR 441.22, when read in conjunction with Social Services Law § 398(6)(c), imposes upon ACS "an unqualified and nondiscretionary obligation" to arrange for her to have sex reassignment surgery, such that Family Court had the authority under Family Court Act § 255 to order ACS to arrange for the surgery, is without merit.

Subdivision (a) of section 441.22 states that "[e]ach authorized agency [such as ACS] is responsible for providing comprehensive medical and health services for every foster child in its care." Subdivision (f) of that section directs that children in foster care must have "periodic individualized medical examinations" and sets forth the intervals at which such examinations must take place. . . . Paragraph (2) of subdivision (f) states that the examinations must include [certain specified assessments or diagnostics]. . . .

Subdivision (g) of 441.22, the linchpin of petitioner's argument, provides that "[w]hen the medical examination indicates a condition requiring follow-up care as determined by the child's physician, the agency responsible for the child's care must provide or arrange for such follow-up care as recommended by the child's physician."

Subdivision (g) does not apply to petitioner's situation. That subdivision applies "[w]hen *the medical examination* indicates a condition requiring follow-up care as determined by the child's physician" (emphasis added). "[T]he medical examination" is a reference to one of the periodic medical examinations required by subdivision (f) . . . . Here, however, a periodic medical examination did not indicate a condition requiring follow-up care. Rather, in 2004 ACS arranged for petitioner to be evaluated by Rachlin, a psychologist, because petitioner had expressed an interest in having sex reassignment surgery; petitioner was subsequently evaluated by Wheeler, a psychotherapist, and Drs. Kreditor and Bartalos.

Even assuming that section 441.22(g) is applicable (*i.e.*, a periodic medical examination indicated that petitioner required follow-up care and petitioner's physician recommended a specific course of action), it could not be given the effect petitioner urges. As discussed above, the Legislature conferred upon commissioners of public welfare and city public welfare officers, including the Commissioner of ACS, the authority and responsibility to provide necessary medical and surgical care to children under their care (Social Services Law § 398(6)(c); *see Arlene L.*, 187 Misc. 2d 356, 722 N.Y.S.2d 712 (Fam. Ct. 2001)). Thus, a regulation cannot restrict or impair those officers' authority (*see Weiss v. City of New York*, 731 N.E.2d 594 (N.Y. 2000) ("It is a fundamental principle of administrative law that an agency cannot promulgate rules or regulations that contravene the will of the Legislature"); *Finger Lakes Racing Assn. v. New York State Racing & Wagering Bd.*, 382 N.E.2d 1131 (N.Y. 1978) ("Of course, the Board is without power to promulgate rules in contravention of the will of the Legislature. Administrative agencies can only promulgate rules to further the implementation of the law as it exists; they have no authority to create a rule out of harmony with the statute"). As section 441.22(g) would be "out of harmony" with Social Services Law § 398(6)(c) to the extent the regulation purported to substitute the discretion of a foster child's physician for that of the public officer charged with responsibility for ensuring that the child receives necessary medical and surgical care, the statute prevails and the regulation does not require the public officer to provide or arrange for whatever follow-up care may be recommended by the child's physician, *see Weiss*).

. . . .

Lastly, while the parties devote extensive attention to the question of whether ACS' refusal to arrange for the surgery was arbitrary and capricious, *i.e.*, did not have a rational basis, that question is not a proper subject of this proceeding. To obtain review of the determination of an administrative agency made in the absence of a hearing required by law, a party must commence a CPLR article 78 proceeding seeking mandamus to review. *See* CPLR 7801. An article 78 proceeding must be commenced in Supreme Court; it cannot be prosecuted in Family Court. Thus, Family Court does not have subject matter jurisdiction to review ACS' refusal to arrange for petitioner to have sex reassignment surgery.[6] Rather, this proceeding involves the question of whether Family Court has the power to order ACS to arrange for petitioner to have the surgery, a question that is separate and distinct from whether that court has the jurisdiction to review an administrative determination of ACS.

---

6. While neither of the parties raise the issue of whether Family Court lacked subject matter jurisdiction to review the administrative determination of ACS, we may reach it on our own volition.

Accordingly, we reverse the order directing ACS to arrange for petitioner to have sex reassignment surgery, deny petitioner's motion, grant ACS' cross motion and dismiss the proceeding.

———————

Discussion

1. The Court states that Mariah was "born a biological male." Given the scientific studies noted elsewhere in this book regarding the brain structures and genetics of some people with trans identities, what might the statement mean, and what evidence would be needed to prove its truth with respect to a particular individual? What does the court mean by the adjective "biological"?

2. Assistant Commissioner Pratt asserted that the petitioner should not be permitted sex reassignment surgery because she had not had a psychological evaluation and psychotherapy; lacked knowledge of various relevant factors; lacked a sufficiently stable gender identity; had not shown sufficient progress in dealing with interrelational issues; did not have a serious, thoughtful, and committed approach to surgery in the eyes of her foster care staff; behaved indecisively, unstably, and self-defeatingly; and could not be engaged in meaningful planning. To what extent do these assertions indicate a "gatekeeping" approach to transgender care? *See* Sarah L. Schulz, *The Informed Consent Model of Transgender Care: An Alternative to the Diagnosis of Gender Dysphoria*, 1 J. HUMANISTIC PSYCHOL. 72, 83 (2018); *see also* Chapter 3, *supra* at p. 82 (contrasting informed consent model and gatekeeping model of access to gender-affirming medical care). How would the arguments about Mariah L's mindset (such as her alleged lack of a "sufficiently stable" gender identity, the claimed knowledge of "relevant" factors, and other psychologically-based arguments) be evaluated under the gatekeeper model of trans care, or conversely, under the informed consent model? Would or should arguments about a person's mindset be considered reasonable in the context of other types of medically necessary surgery? Should the New York Administration for Children's Services adopt the informed consent model (*i.e.*, not require mental health treatment as a prerequisite to delivering sex reassignment surgery)?

3. How could the court have interpreted 18 NYCRR 441.22(g) differently to apply here and require ACS to arrange for Mariah's surgery? How might the court have interpreted New York law to allow it to so order ACS? Why might the court not have adopted these interpretations?

4. The Court holds that the New York Department of Social Services could not enforce a regulation binding local agencies to provide care as prescribed by a physician, because the statute gives commissioners of public welfare both the duty and the authority to provide medical care. Does it seem surprising to interpret a statute requiring physician-ordered medical care to mean that the agency has discretion to deny it? Since those in foster care are wards of the state, is there any constitutional provision that might be invoked if serious medical needs are ignored? If a juvenile is

incarcerated, would there be other constitutional arguments in favor of their receiving sex reassignment surgery?

5. Assistant Commissioner Pratt argued that the ACS decision not to arrange for surgery had a rational basis because of her affidavit, although nothing in the court's opinion indicates that she was a physician or psychologist, and her assessment of Mariah L.'s medical needs appears to contradict the affidavits submitted by Mariah's treating physicians and psychologists. The court decided that the proper way under New York law to address this question of the rationality of ACS's refusal was by a mandamus proceeding, which in New York is called an "Article 78" proceeding. New York's highest court has ruled that "if a determination is rational it must be sustained even if the court concludes that another result would also have been rational." *Madison Cty. Indus. Dev. Agency v. Authorities Budget Office*, 123 N.E.2d 239 (NY 2019). Given that many highly-regarded attorneys filed in support of the petitioner, why might Mariah L.'s counsel not have brought an Article 78 proceeding in the first place? What would have been the result had they argued constitutional principles of equal protection and due process?

Reading Guide for D.F. v. Carrion

1. At one level, the issue in this case is whether the New York City foster care system is required to pay for transition-related medical care including genital reconstruction surgery for D.F., a young transgender woman who is in foster care and who understands the risk and wishes to give her informed consent to those procedures. What law provides the basic obligation for that foster care system to pay for D.F.'s care? (Why were there not other sources of payment legally available from the state of New York?)

2. For what reason did the city's Administration for Children's Services ("ACS") deny D.F.'s request for medical care? What reason does the court find facially legitimate?

3. What standard of review does the court apply in assessing the decision of ACS? For what reasons does it conclude that ACS's refusal to provide the transition care D.F. sought failed that standard of review despite the facially legitimate reason ACS had offered?

Matter of D.F. v. Gladys Carrion

43 Misc. 3d 746, 986 N.Y.S.2d 769 (Sup. Ct. 2014)

PETER H. MOULTON, J.

. . . .

Background

Petitioner's assigned sex at birth was male but she has for a number of years identified as female. She is currently twenty years old. She has been diagnosed with gender dysphoria, which refers to an individual's distress arising from incongruence between her experienced or expressed gender and the gender she was assigned at birth. Among other diagnostic criteria, a person with gender dysphoria has strong desires to be rid of her own sex characteristics and to adopt the sex characteristics of the opposite gender (or of some alternate gender different from one's assigned gender).[7]

[New York City's Administration for Children's Services, or "ACS"] does not contest petitioner's gender dysphoria diagnosis.

A. Petitioner's Entry into Foster Care and Identification as Transgender

Petitioner and her sister entered foster care after ACS filed a petition of neglect against their parents in 2009. . . .

. . . Family Court placed petitioner in Green Chimneys Gramercy Residence, a group home for lesbian, gay, bisexual, transgender and questioning ("LGBTQ") youth. When petitioner entered foster care, she disclosed that she was transgender and began to request that her caregivers assist her in changing her legal status and her appearance to conform to her identity as a female. She successfully brought a petition in Civil Court to change her name. She changed her gender marker on her Social Security and New York State identification cards from "male" to "female."

In August 2011, with the assistance of staff at her residential placement, petitioner began to explore the possibility of engaging in hormone therapy at the Callen-Lorde Community Health Center, where she attended the Health Outreach to Teens Clinic ("HOTT Clinic"). Under the supervision of physicians at the HOTT Clinic, petitioner began taking orally administered hormones. After discussions with physicians at the HOTT Clinic, in which she was instructed on the proper method to self-inject hormone treatments, she began administering the injections to herself using aseptic techniques. [Hormone] therapy has been adopted by ACS as part of her Family Assessment and Service Plan.

While she regularly availed herself of the health services at Callen-Lorde, petitioner was frequently absent without leave from Green Chimneys. These absences totaled more than 300 days over a four year period. She also missed numerous appointments with Green Chimneys' Psychologist Dr. Jordan Conrad. In July 2013, after the Green Chimneys facility closed, petitioner moved into a new residence for LGBTQ youth run by SCO Family of Services ("SCO"). She has also been chronically absent from this new placement, and resides mostly at a friend's house in Queens. Petitioner avers that SCO is considering certifying this home as a Foster Home.

It is unclear why petitioner was absent so often from two residences designed for LGBTQ youth, and petitioner does not submit an affidavit explaining the absences. However, despite her absences from Green Chimneys, Dr. Conrad

---

7. The diagnosis is described in full at *Diagnostic and Statistical Manual of Mental Disorders, Fifth Edition* 451–459 (2013).

submitted letters in support of petitioner's applications to ACS for gender affirming procedures and therapies. Petitioner made these two applications pursuant to ACS' Policy Number 2010/04 which is entitled "Provision of Non-Medicaid Reimbursable Treatment or Services for Youth in Foster Care" (referred to herein as the "NMR Policy"). It is ACS' denial of petitioner's second application that is the subject of this proceeding.

The NMR Policy is discussed below.

B. ACS' NMR Policy

ACS is required to provide "necessary medical or surgical care" for all children in foster care. Social Services Law § 398(6)(c); 18 NYCRR § 441.22. Section 398(6)(c) requires ACS to provide necessary medical or surgical care in a suitable hospital, sanatorium, preventorium or other institution or in his own home for any child needing such care and pay for such care from public funds, if necessary. However, in the case of a child or minor who is eligible to receive care as medical assistance for needy persons pursuant to [the Medicaid Statute], such care shall be provided pursuant to the provisions of [the Medicaid Statute].

New York State Medicaid excludes coverage of costs relating to "care, services, drugs or supplies for the purpose of gender reassignment (also known as transsexual surgery) or any care, services, drugs, or supplies intended to promote such treatment." 14 NYCRR § 505.2(1). In *Matter of Brian L. v. Administration for Children's Servs.*, 51 A.D.3d 488 (N.Y. App. Div. 2008), the First Department held that ACS has a duty to "provide necessary medical care and must, if necessary, pay for that care" where Medicaid does not provide reimbursement.

On June 7, 2010, ACS instituted the NMR Policy to provide a procedure for review of requests for payment of medically necessary treatment not covered by Medicaid. The NMR policy, and a subsequent memorandum dated January 29, 2013, entitled "NMR Guidance for Trans-Related Healthcare" ("NMR Guidance") provide that a Foster Care Agency must first determine if there are other sources of funds, such as family and friends, that could pay for the requested procedures. If it determines that there are no such sources of financial support, the Agency then submits to ACS various forms and statements from medical professionals concerning, *inter alia*, the need for the requested therapies and procedures. Applications for certain types of procedures, including surgeries, are submitted to the "ACS Health Review Committee." The ACS Health Review Committee reviews the materials and then makes a recommendation to the ACS Deputy Commissioner who has been delegated the responsibility of final decision-maker. The NMR Policy provides that the ACS Health Review Committee has the discretion to consult with "specialist(s) from the field(s) in which a particular type of treatment or care is being requested."

Both the NMR Policy and the NMR Guidance provide that decisions concerning heath care for transgender people in ACS' care shall be made according to the standards of care established by the World Professional Association for Transgender

Health ("the WPATH standards of care").[8] Pursuant to the NMR Guidance, an application for gender affirming treatment and procedures must be "demonstrated to be effective based on current medical and mental health standards" as measured by the WPATH standards of care.

C. Petitioner's Two Applications Pursuant to the NMR Policy

On May 2, 2012, Green Chimneys submitted to ACS a written request for payment on petitioner's behalf for breast augmentation, tracheal shaving, and laser hair removal. The request was subsequently augmented with additional information sought by ACS. These materials included letters from Dr. Daniel Garza, a psychiatrist at the HOTT Clinic, Dr. Paul Weiss, the surgeon who would perform the requested procedures, Dr. Conrad, the psychologist at Green Chimneys, and Dr. Carmen Alonso, a psychiatrist also associated with Green Chimneys. Dr. Alonso's report summarizes the reasons that the procedures are necessary:

> [Petitioner] meets criteria for diagnosis of gender identity disorder (GID), including a diagnosis of true transsexualism. She has demonstrated the desire and [sic] to live and be accepted as a female, in addition to a desire to make her body as congruent as possible with her preferred female identity, through hormone replacement for over two years. . . . She has successfully lived and gone to school within her desired female gender role full-time for two years (real life experience) without returning to her original gender.

Petitioner's first application was submitted to the ACS Health Review Committee, which approved the request in its entirety. In its recommendation, the Health Review Committee noted petitioner's repeated absences from her residence, but nonetheless recommended that ACS approve the procedures.

Petitioner's first application was denied by Deputy Commissioner Benita Miller in a letter dated July 11, 2013. The denial was based on petitioner's alleged failure to receive "ongoing psychiatric care." In addition the letter invoked petitioner's frequent absences from Green Chimneys, and her "history of missing health appointments at the Gramercy Residence." The letter also noted that petitioner had requested other surgeries since submitting her initial application, but that she had not embodied these requests in a new NMR Policy application. Petitioner sought a fair hearing review of the denial of her first application. The hearing officer held that the Deputy Commissioner's decision was final and unreviewable. Petitioner. . . . now focuses her challenge to the Deputy Commissioner's denial of petitioner's second application, which is described below.

Petitioner submitted her second application on July 18, 2013, which requested five procedures: 1) full sexual reassignment surgery, 2) facial feminization, 3) tracheal shaving, 4) breast augmentation and 5) laser hair removal. The second application

---

8. World Professional Association for Transgender Health, Standards of Care for the Health of Transsexual, Transgender, and Gender Nonconforming People, 7th Version.

relied on the materials included in the first application and included, *inter alia*, new letters from both Dr. Garza and Dr. Alonso. Dr. Garza notes that hormone treatment is "insufficient to [petitioner's] ultimate goals," and states that the proposed procedures "would serve a therapeutic purpose and improve her well-being." Dr. Alonso states:

> [Petitioner's] clinically relevant distress causing impaired ability to function in social, school or work-related situations as a result of her preoccupation with non-identification with her gender assigned at birth (Gender Dysphoria) will only be significantly resolved by undergoing her desired gender-affirming healthcare procedures.

Both doctors found that petitioner understood the risks of gender confirmation surgery and was able to provide informed consent. The total cost of all five procedures, based on the quotes submitted with the two applications, would be approximately $46,000.

ACS did not submit the second request to the ACS Health Review Committee. The reasons for this departure from the procedures set forth in the NMR Policy and Guidance are not clearly explained in respondent's papers. The Answer to the Petition states only that the second application was not submitted to the Committee because "it was submitted so closely in time to ACS's denial of the First Request and essentially repeated the First Request with added requests for two additional procedures."

Instead, ACS consulted with an independent specialist, Dr. John Steever. Dr. Steever is an Assistant Professor of Pediatrics and Adolescent Medicine at the Icahn School of Medicine at Mount Sinai. He has long focused on the health issues facing LGBTQ youth. As an attending physician at Mount Sinai's Transgender Health Program he has seen more than 75 patients from ages 9 to 22 for transrelated health services since 2005.

Dr. Steever reviewed petitioner's health records and certain foster care records. He did not meet with petitioner in conducting his review, although the opportunity was provided to him. Dr. Steever has reiterated through ACS' counsel and through an affidavit submitted in this proceeding that he does not need to meet with petitioner in order to render his opinion. Instead, relying solely on petitioner's records, Dr. Steever concluded that it was in petitioner's best interest to defer the requested procedures. He based this conclusion on petitioner's "poor adherence to ACS recommendations and programs." Specifically, Dr. Steever found that petitioner's chronic absences without leave from her residence, and failure to consistently meet with the therapist at her residence, placed her health and safety at risk. He also noted that petitioner missed a court appearance in her name change proceeding. Based on her absences, and failure to follow through on agency directions, Dr. Steever opined that petitioner might fail to follow directions concerning her post-operative care, which could potentially result in infections, unnecessary scarring, urinary problems, and sexual sensation problems.

While Dr. Steever agrees that petitioner has been correctly diagnosed with gender dysphoria, he states in his affidavit that the procedures sought by petitioner are not "emergent in nature" (*i.e.*, not necessary to address emergencies) and that they can be deferred until such time as the patient can comply with the necessary follow-up care. He does not address how a transgender young adult, aging out of foster care with no family support and few apparent prospects for employment, might pay for these procedures.

Deputy Commissioner Miller denied the second application in a letter dated October 15, 2013. The letter explicitly relies on the analysis and conclusion of Dr. Steever.

Discussion

It is well-settled that "[j]udicial review of an administrative determination is confined to the facts and record adduced before the agency." *Matter of Yarbough v. Franco*, 740 N.E.2d 224 (N.Y. 2000). The reviewing court may not substitute its judgment for that of the agency's [*sic*], and the decision will be upheld if it is supported by any rational basis. The First Department has held that ACS' denial of trans-related health care to people in its care is to be judged by whether the denial was arbitrary and capricious. *Brian L.*

It is important to make clear that ACS' denial is not based on any dispute about petitioner's diagnosis of gender dysphoria, or that surgery is a medically accepted means of treating gender dysphoria. While not all transgender people seek surgery to align their appearance more closely with their gender identity, various surgeries are established treatments for people with gender dysphoria. New York Courts have long understood that such treatment is not the equivalent of elective plastic surgery. Rather, the proposed treatment is therapeutic, designed to address a particular diagnosis. ACS' denial is also not based on some specious supposition that petitioner is "going through a phase" and that she may change her mind about wanting irreversible gender affirming surgeries. Her consistency since coming out as transgender, and the opinions of psychiatrists who have treated her, foreclose that argument.

ACS' denial here was based on Dr. Steever's assessment that petitioner may not be capable "at this time" of following the necessary post-operative steps to ensure a healthy recovery from the five procedures sought by petitioner. It is unclear from respondent's papers what post-operative protocol is required by one of the procedures, laser hair removal. The remaining four procedures clearly require that a patient attend to certain post-operative procedures. This is particularly the case with respect to sexual reassignment surgery.

This reason for denial has facial validity. A doctor, one with evident expertise with transgender patients, states that post-operative wound care is important. This is an assertion which appears unassailable, and which is not disputed by petitioner.

However, the decision is nonetheless arbitrary and capricious for several reasons.

The decision rests on the premise that has no foundation in the record: that petitioner's chronic absences without leave from her group homes, and her failure to consistently participate in programs at those group homes, are indicators that she will not participate in necessary post-operative care. The mental health professionals who supported petitioner's applications all knew of her chronic absences, yet all stated that she needed the surgeries and procedures in question. None of them questioned whether petitioner would follow through with post-operative care. These physicians had direct evidence of petitioner's capacity and willingness to engage in the tasks that are required by her transition. Her medical records show that petitioner has demonstrated commitment and maturity in dealing with her health care, both trans-related and non-trans-related. Her consistency in following protocols for hormone therapy is noted above. She has repeatedly and consistently tested negative for STDs and HIV. There is no indication that she has participated in negative behaviors such as drug or alcohol abuse. It is arbitrary and capricious for an agency to render a decision unsupported by the record before it.

Additionally, the decision is arbitrary and capricious because ACS did not follow its own procedures in reaching the decision. The WPATH standards of care, which ACS purports to follow in the NMR Policy and Guidance, states that "[g]enital and breast/chest surgeries as medically necessary treatments for gender dysphoria are to be undertaken after assessment of the patient by qualified mental health professionals." Petitioner has undergone such assessments, and the mental health professionals in question agree that she should undergo the surgeries requested. Dr. Steever, while he may be an experienced clinician, is a pediatrician, not a mental health professional.

It was also a deviation from the WPATH standards of care for ACS to follow the recommendation of a physician who had not met with petitioner. The WPATH standards of care set forth "Tasks Related to Assessment and Referral" to be followed by mental health professionals working with transgender patients. All of these tasks involve actually treating a patient by meeting with her. Only by meeting with a patient as many times as necessary to render a diagnosis and determine appropriate treatment can a mental health professional refer the patient for a range of potential treatments including hormone therapy and surgery. The doctors who met with petitioner multiple times were able to make that assessment. The doctor upon whom ACS relied did not meet once with petitioner.

ACS also failed to follow its own procedures by failing to refer petitioner's second application to the ACS Health Review Committee. . . . The first application was submitted to the ACS Health Review Committee, and the Committee recommended payment for all the procedures requested. For unexplained reasons, the second application was not given to the ACS Health Review Committee despite the mandatory language in the NMR Policy. The Deputy Commissioner sought "additional clinical advice" not from the Committee, as provided in the NMR Policy, but from Dr. Steever.

An agency's failure to follow its own procedures or rules in rendering a decision is arbitrary and capricious. *E.g. Gilman v. New York State Div. of Housing and Community Renewal*, 782 N.E.2d 1137 (N.Y. 2002).

Apart from ACS' failure to follow its own procedures, the NMR Policy and Guidance contain a fundamental flaw: they give complete discretion to the relevant Deputy Commissioner to approve or disapprove gender affirming surgeries and procedures. This discretion is unlimited. It is true that the NMR Policy enumerates five criteria that an applicant must satisfy before ACS will pay for a treatment.[5] Presumably, these five criteria are meant to determine when a procedure is "necessary medical or surgical care" that must be paid for by ACS pursuant to Social Services Law § 398(6)(c). However, even where a petitioner meets all five criteria, the Deputy Commissioner may deny the request for treatment. The Deputy Commissioner may thus determine what medical or surgical care is "necessary" without having to justify his or her decision by reference to any specified set of criteria. This procedure allows ACS to deny payment for medically necessary care, in derogation of its duty under Social Services Law § 398(6)(c). The adoption of a procedure allowing for unfettered discretion in agency decision making is arbitrary and capricious. *See Matter of Nicholas v. Kahn*, 389 N.E.2d 1086 (N.Y. 1979).

. . . .

Finally, the NMR Policy and Guidance do not address at all an important economic factor that intersects with the clinical decision to withhold care. As discussed above, Dr. Steever judged that petitioner's gender dysphoria did not require treatment with the requested procedures "at this time" because she might not follow necessary post-operative protocols. The implication of this temporal limitation, which was adopted by the Deputy Commissioner in her denial, is that petitioner may, at some later time, be ready for post-operative protocols and, therefore, be ready for the surgery.

ACS' denial of the requested surgeries and procedures "at this time" thus completely ignores another factor: petitioner's almost certain inability to pay for these surgeries and procedures. Once she ages out of foster care, petitioner's chances of raising the money necessary to pay for these procedures appear to be nil. Certainly for the near future her inability to pay for the procedures is clear. She has yet to complete her GED. She is estranged from her family. She faces a transphobic society that discriminates against transgender people in employment, housing and the distribution of other opportunities and resources. While there are increasing legal protections for transgender people in some jurisdictions via statute, court decisions, and executive orders, most jurisdictions do not have anti-discrimination laws that explicitly cover transgender people.

---

5. The five criteria, in summary, are 1) the treatment must be supported by a statement from a qualified medical or mental health professional, 2) the treatment is expected to relieve substantial psychological and/or physical distress, 3) the proposed treatment is demonstrated to be effective based on current medical standards, 4) there is significant benefit to the child/youth, as documented by a qualified medical or mental health professional stating the risks and benefits of the proposed procedure and 5) Medicaid Funding is unavailable.

The inability to pay for gender affirming surgeries and procedures after foster care is not a factor that should trump clinical factors, but it certainly should not be absent from ACS' decision making. Payment by ACS for necessary medical procedures may be a transgender youth's only chance to achieve congruence between her gender identity and her physical appearance. Accordingly, ACS' omission of this factor from its NMR Policy and Guidance is arbitrary and capricious.

Conclusion

For the reasons stated, it is ORDERED AND ADJUDGED that the decision of respondent Administration for Children's Services dated October 15, 2013 is annulled; and it is further ORDERED AND ADJUDGED that Administration for Children's Services shall take all steps necessary to pay for the procedures specified in petitioner's application dated July 18, 2013. This constitutes the Decision, Order and Judgment of the Court.

Discussion

1. The court's argument in *D.F.* took note of the fact that because D.F. was approaching age 21, she would soon "age out" of the foster care system and no longer be entitled to the medical care it provides to youth in the system. Was that a legally proper factor for the court to consider? Were its other arguments sufficient to establish the illegality of the agency's denial of care even without that factor?

2. Why does D.F. succeed in her suit seeking transition-related care while Mariah L. in *Brian L. v. Administration for Children's Services, supra,* which the court here purports to follow, was unsuccessful? What might other transgender youth in New York City's foster care system do to try to secure transition-related care? What might ACS do to try to forestall having to provide such care to other trans youth in the future?

3. Note that in one sense the basic dispute here was over *who would have to pay* for D.F.'s transition-related medical care. In that respect, *D.F. v. Carrion* is like many of the suits by incarcerated persons seeking access to transition-related medical care. *See* Chapter 12, Section A, Subsection 2, *infra.*

4. Agreeing with Dr. Ryan, Caitlin Ryan, *Generating a Revolution in Prevention, Wellness, and Care for LGBT Children and Youth*, 23 TEMP. POL. & CIV. RTS. L. REV. 331, 342 (2014), Professor Fedders has argued that work for justice for LGBT youth "must move beyond protection from har[m] and toward promotion of well-being." Barbara Fedders, *LGBT Youth in the Child Welfare and Juvenile Justice Systems: Charting a Way Forward*, 23 TEMP. POL. & CIV. RTS. L. REV. 431, 444 (2014). After canvassing reasons why LGBT youth enter the child welfare and juvenile justice systems, *id.* at 432–36, and significant advances thus far, *id.* at 437–44, Fedders calls for "a more radical, liberatory path forward," *id.* at 444, with a "focus on helping *all* youth move beyond rigid, stereotype-inducing, restrictive gender norms and oppressive sexuality mores to obtain healthier concepts of gender and sexual

orientation." *Id.* This would lead to fewer youth entering these systems in the first place, instead living healthy, happy lives in their homes. What policies would you recommend to "meet [unaccepting] families where they are—in other words, . . . to understand the religious or cultural norms from which these families are operating as we seek to work on the confusion and hostility they may feel with regard to their LGBT children"? *Id.* at 445.

Chapter 5

Employee Rights Under Civil Rights Laws and the Constitution

In order to subsist in most economies, people need income, and for most adults, that requires employment. Even for people who might have government support or independent wealth, employment can help somewhat with one's sense of independence, perhaps with living a life of dignity. *See, e.g.,* Christopher A. Bracey, *Getting Back to Basics: Some Thoughts on Dignity, Materialism, and a Culture of Racial Equality*, 26 CHICANA/O-LATINA/O L. REV. 15, 32 (2006) ("If we understand that ability to work and reap the fruits of one's labor is an important freedom, then a dignity-centered approach [to race jurisprudence] might ask what preconditions need to be in place in order for all citizens, regardless of race, to exercise this basic freedom on an equal basis."). Even aside from the debates over work and dignity, when people have trouble securing and maintaining employment the negative consequences can be devastating. Many transgender persons in the United States have experienced employment discrimination. The 2015 U.S. Transgender Survey is "the largest survey examining the experiences of transgender people in the United States, with 27,715 respondents from all fifty states, the District of Columbia, American Samoa, Guam, Puerto Rico, and U.S. military bases overseas." SANDY E. JAMES ET AL., THE REPORT OF THE 2015 U.S. TRANSGENDER SURVEY 4 (2016). Almost 30% of the respondents were living in poverty, more than double the rate in the entire U.S. population. *Id.* at 5. The unemployment rate of the respondents was triple that of the U.S. population, 15% compared to 5%, respectively, at the time of the survey, "with Middle Eastern, American Indian, multiracial, Latino/a, and Black respondents experiencing higher rates of unemployment." *Id.* at 5, 12.

In particular:

* One in six (16%) respondents who have ever been employed—or 13% of all respondents in the sample—reported losing a job because of their gender identity or expression in their lifetime.

* 27% of those who held or applied for a job during [the year before the survey]—19% of all respondents—reported being fired, denied a promotion, or not being hired for a job they applied for because of their gender identity or expression.

* Fifteen percent (15%) of respondents who had a job in the past year were verbally harassed, physically attacked, and/or sexually assaulted at work because of their gender identity or expression.

* Nearly one-quarter (23%) of those who had a job in the past year reported other forms of mistreatment based on their gender identity or expression during that year, such as being forced to use a restroom that did not match their gender identity, being told to present in the wrong gender in order to keep their job, or having a boss or coworker share private information about their transgender status with others without their permission.

* Overall, 30% of respondents who had a job in the past year reported being fired, denied a promotion, or experiencing some other form of mistreatment related to their gender identity or expression.

* More than three-quarters (77%) of respondents who had a job in the past year took steps to avoid mistreatment in the workplace, such as hiding or delaying their gender transition or quitting their job.

Id. at 12–13. (For another large-scale academic study, see Genny Beemyn & Susan Rankin, The Lives of Transgender People (2011) (analyzing online survey completed by 3,474 respondents, 419 of whom also participated in detailed follow-up interviews).)

Part of the problem transgender people face in employment is that there is a norm in U.S. law of employment-at-will—the idea that an employment contract between an employer and an employee ordinarily allows either to terminate the employment relationship whenever they might choose, that is, at will. This norm is limited in numerous ways by statutory and judicially recognized exceptions at the local, state, and federal level. If a nondiscrimination law forbids discrimination on specified grounds, that will override the employment-at-will norm. As of January 28, 2016, at least 225 cities and counties expressly forbade governmental or private employers to discriminate on the basis of gender identity. Human Rights Campaign, *Cities and Counties with Non-Discrimination Ordinances that Include Gender Identity*, http://www .hrc.org/resources/cities-and-counties-with-non-discrimination-ordinances-that -include-gender. As of 2015, only a minority of states (19), plus the District of Columbia and Puerto Rico, expressly prohibited gender identity discrimination in employment by governmental and private employers. National Center for Transgender Equality, *Know Your Rights: Employment (General)*, http://www.transequality .org/know-your-rights/employment-general.

At the federal level, no statute currently expressly forbids employment discrimination on the basis of gender identity or expression. Executive orders issued by the President prohibit certain employers who contract with the federal government from discriminating on various grounds including gender identity, and the primary federal employment nondiscrimination law, Title VII of the Civil Rights Act of 1964, prohibits discrimination "because of," "based on," or "on account of" sex. 42 U.S.C. § 2000e-2(a) (2012); *id.* at §§ 2000e-3(b), 2000e-16(a); *id.* at § 2000e-5(g)(2)

(A) (referring to 42 U.S.C. § 2000e-3(a)). This chapter extensively treats the evolution of that ban's applicability, or lack thereof, to anti-transgender discrimination, as well as other issues of employment discrimination against transgender persons. In *Bostock v. Clayton County, Georgia*, 140 S. Ct. 1731 (2020), Section D, *infra*, less than a month before the 56th anniversary of that law, a 6–3 majority of the Supreme Court for the first time reached the merits of a worker's suit alleging that sexual orientation or gender identity discrimination violated Title VII's ban on sex discrimination. Cementing a judicial trend, *Bostock* held that discrimination against a worker because of their "homosexuality" or their "transgender status" is, necessarily, sex discrimination under Title VII. This decision is likely to revolutionize the legal protection of transgender people in a variety contexts, and this chapter provides an in-depth study of the half-century evolution in the application (some might say, the meaning) of Title VII sex discrimination law. In addition, see Chapter 14, *infra* for discussion of the use of laws forbidding disability discrimination to protect transgender workers.

A. Early Judicial Approaches to Anti-Transgender Discrimination

Note on Holloway v. Arthur Andersen *and* Sommers v. Budget Marketing

A decade after the Civil Rights Act of 1964 was enacted, the federal courts began to consider, and reject, claims that the ban on sex discrimination in Title VII of the act forbade employers to discriminate against employees because they are transgender. *See, e.g., Voyles v. Ralph K. Davies Medical Center*, 403 F. Supp. 456 (N.D. Cal. 1975); *Grossman v. Bernards Township Board of Education*, 11 Emp. Prac. Dec. (CCH) P 10,686 (D.N.J. 1975), *aff'd mem.*, 538 F.2d 319 (3d Cir. 1976), *cert. denied*, 429 U.S. 897 (1976). The first published appellate opinions also rejected the transgender plaintiffs' interpretation of Title VII.

Holloway v. Arthur Andersen & Co., 566 F.2d 659 (9th Cir. 1977), affirmed the dismissal of a claim brought by Ramona Holloway (who had been identified male at birth) when she was fired after she had started transitioning on the job at an accounting firm, presenting as a woman. By a 2–1 vote, the U.S. Court of Appeals held that Title VII should be given its "plain meaning," that "Congress had only the traditional notions of 'sex' in mind" when it passed Title VII, that Congress's failure to pass later bills amending Title VII to ban discrimination on the basis of "sexual preference" confirmed the narrowness of its intent, and that Congress's purpose in forbidding sex discrimination in Title VII was simply assuring equal treatment of men and women. As the court characterized the suit, "Holloway has not claimed to have [been] treated discriminatorily because she is male or female, but rather because she is a transsexual [*sic*] who chose to change her sex. This type of claim," the majority concluded, "is not actionable under Title VII and," the majority continued in what may not be a holding (because Ms. Holloway only brought a claim under Title VII, not under the Constitution), "is certainly not in violation of the doctrines of Due Process and Equal Protection." One judge dissented, believing that the ban on sex discrimination encompassed discrimination both because one *is* a woman and because one *becomes* a woman.

Five years later, the U.S. Court of Appeals for the Eighth Circuit agreed with *Holloway* in *Sommers v. Budget Marketing, Inc.*, 667 F.2d 748 (8th Cir. 1982). Transgender woman Audra Sommers identified herself as a woman when she applied to Budget Marketing; she was subsequently fired for allegedly "misrepresenting" her sex, which the company claimed was disruptive because several other women employees threatened to quit if Sommers were allowed to use women's restrooms. The court of appeals affirmed the district court's dismissal of Sommers's sex discrimination claim under Title VII and held that the statute's ban on sex discrimination did not reach discrimination against a person because of her transsexuality. Echoing *Holloway*, the *Sommers* court said "sex" should be given its plain meaning, that the limited legislative history of Title VII showed no "intention to include transsexualism in Title VII," and that the statutory provision's "main thrust" was to equalize employment opportunities for women. Also like *Holloway*, the court in *Sommers* believed that subsequent congressional rejection of proposed amendments to reach "sexual preference" confirmed the narrowness of the term "sex" in Title VII.[a]

Almost two years later, U.S. District Judge John F. Grady reached a contrary conclusion in *Ulane v. Eastern Airlines, Inc.*, 581 F. Supp. 821 (1983). Transgender woman Karen Ulane's victory was, however, short-lived, as a panel of the Court of Appeals for the Seventh Circuit reversed. *Ulane v. Eastern Airlines, Inc.*, 742 F.2d 1081 (7th Cir. 1984). The opinions from the conflicting decisions in her case follow.

Reading Guide for Ulane v. Eastern Airlines *(district court opinion)*

1. How does Judge Grady deal with the fact that bills to amend Title VII to prohibit discrimination based on "sexual preference" repeatedly were introduced in Congress but not adopted?

2. How does the opinion deal with the ostensible lack of any legislative history specifying that Congress intended the term "sex" in Title VII to include transsexual persons? How does it go about defining "sex" in the statute?

3. What evidence does the court rely on to conclude that Eastern Airlines fired Karen Ulane because of her sex? On what grounds does the court reject the airline's

---

a. Ms. Sommers also lost a state law disability discrimination lawsuit she brought against Budget Marketing. *Sommers v. Iowa Civil Rights Comm'n*, 337 N.W.2d 470 (Iowa 1983) (holding that "transsexualism" was not a "disability" under Iowa Civil Rights Act), discussed in a note in Chapter 14, *infra*, at p. 963. Decades later the statute at issue there was amended to forbid gender identity discrimination. *See* 2007 Iowa Acts ch. 191, employment provision codified at Iowa Code § 216.6.

various allegedly nondiscriminatory reasons for the termination? In particular, what comparisons does the court draw between Ulane and other employees?

4. What were Ulane's two theories of how Eastern Airlines had unlawfully discriminated against her based on her sex? What does Judge Grady ultimate rule on each of the two counts?

Karen Frances Ulane v. Eastern Airlines, Inc.

581 F. Supp. 821 (N.D. Ill. 1983)

GRADY, District Judge.

Transcript of Proceedings

* * * *

THE COURT: I will give you my findings of fact and conclusions of law.

The threshold issue before the Court is whether Title VII of the Civil Rights Act of 1964 applies to transsexuals [*sic*]. The statutory language in Title 42, Section 2000e-2(a) provides that:

> "It shall be an unlawful employment practice for an employer to fail or refuse to hire or to discharge any individual or otherwise to discriminate against any individual with respect to his compensation, terms, conditions or privileges of employment because of such individual's race, color, religion, sex, or national origin."

So the specific question before the Court is whether the phrase, "because of the individual's sex," encompasses a person such as the plaintiff who alleges that she is a transsexual [*sic*] or, alternatively, that having gone through sex reassignment surgery, she is now no longer a man but a woman.

The legislative history of the statute. . . . is summarized in the case of *Holloway v. Arthur Andersen & Company* (9th Cir. 1977) . . . . The Court there said:

> "There is a dearth of legislative history on Section 2000e-2(a)(1) . . . . The major concern of Congress at the time the Act was promulgated was race discrimination. Sex as a basis of discrimination was added as a floor amendment one day before the House approved Title VII and without prior hearing or debate."

[Those] who argue that the legislative history indicates a lack of intention on the part of Congress that the Act would apply to transsexuals cite the unsuccessful attempts to amend Title VII in later years to include protection for homosexuals [*sic*] and transvestites [*sic*]. I think that argument is invalid. There is in the record before us evidence which makes quite clear that there is a distinction between homosexuals and transvestites on the one hand and transsexuals on the other.

Homosexuals and transvestites are not persons who have sexual identity problems. They are content with the sex into which they were born. Transsexuals, on the other hand, are persons with a problem relating to their very sexual identity as a man or a woman. I believe on that basis the situation of a transsexual is distinguishable.

[There] is no settled definition in the medical community as to what we mean by sex.

[Plaintiff's] witness, Dr. Green, and other witnesses as well emphasized that sexual identity is in part a psychological question. That is to say, it is a question of one's own self-perception: How does one perceive oneself in terms of maleness or femaleness? It is also a social matter: How does society perceive the individual?

[Title] VII is a remedial statute which is to be liberally construed. . . . The only defense witness I can recall who argued with or contradicted the proposition that sex is at least in part a question of self-perception and a societal perception was Dr. Wise. He stated flatly that sex is chromosomal. That creates a dispute in the evidence, . . . which I resolve against the defendant because I do not feel comfortable relying upon the testimony of Dr. Wise. He was a remarkable witness. He stated that the plaintiff is beyond a shadow of a doubt a transvestite. This is a man of science who had never seen the plaintiff, who knew very little about her, who had not even read all of the records pertaining to her, who had read very few of the recent records which seemed to me to be very important, who had read some of the literature in the field but stated that he disagreed with other literature even though he had not read it, and who stated that he knows beyond a shadow of a doubt—those are his exact words—that this plaintiff is a transvestite and not a transsexual.

I have been listening to witnesses for many years, and I have never heard an expert witness state that he was sure of anything beyond a shadow of a doubt. That was typical of Dr. Wise's testimony. That is the most egregious example that I can think of from his testimony, but it is by no means atypical of the tenor of his testimony.

[I] attach no weight whatever to his testimony. . . .

. . . . Plaintiff has under the laws of the State of Illinois been issued a new birth certificate with a sex designation of female. This is a statute that was enacted by the people of the State of Illinois. This to me is pretty strong evidence of a social policy in this area.

[I] find by the greater weight of the evidence that sex is not a cut-and-dried matter of chromosomes, and that while there may be some argument about the matter in the medical community, the evidence in this record satisfies me that the term, "sex," as used in any scientific sense and as used in the statute can be and should be reasonably interpreted to include among its denotations the question of sexual identity and that, therefore, transsexuals are protected by Title VII.

[Congress] never intended anything one way or the other on the question of whether the term, "sex," would include transsexuals. The matter simply was not thought of. It was not discussed. . . . [The] term, "sex," literally applies to transsexuals and . . . it applies scientifically to transsexuals. . . .

[I] turn now to . . . whether the plaintiff is a transsexual. The defendant argues that she is not . . . , that instead she is a transvestite. If that is true, she is not protected by the statute.

There are a number of things which persuade me that the plaintiff is a transsexual. She was found to be such by the unanimous decision of the Gender Identity Board of the University of Chicago Medical School. [I] am disinclined to overrule that finding on the basis of the testimony I have heard from defendants' witnesses.

I found Dr. Berger a very credible witness. . . . He was perhaps primarily in charge of her case. There is no doubt whatever in Dr. Berger's mind that plaintiff was and is a transsexual. I believe that he is eminently qualified to make that determination. Plaintiff meets the criteria of the [American Psychiatric Association's *Diagnostic and Statistical Manual of Mental Disorders*, 3d ed.] DSM III, the recognized definitional standard for judging transsexuality.

[I] find that she was and is a transsexual.

[Another] factor which I think is relevant is how plaintiff appears to other people. I have the psychiatric reports and the testimony of the various psychiatrists as to how plaintiff appears to them. She appears to them to be a woman. She conducts herself as a woman. She dresses as a woman. There is nothing flamboyant, nothing freakish, about the plaintiff. It would take an extremely practiced eye, it seems to me, to detect any difference between the plaintiff and the biological woman. My observation of her in this courtroom and on the witness stand leads me to concur with those witnesses who have said that she appears to be a biological woman. That, I think, has a bearing on the likelihood of her successful post-operative course.

It also has a bearing . . . on the question of whether she is a transsexual in the first place. There has been no reversion to any masculine behavior that we have any knowledge of. . . .

[Another] question is whether the plaintiff was discharged because of her transsexuality, which is another way of asking whether she was discharged because of her sex. The question, of course, is not whether sex was the sole cause of her discharge. The question is whether it was a motivating factor but for which she would not have been fired. There may have been other causes. [But] assuming there were, if she would not have been fired but for her transsexuality, the statute has been violated.

[T]he transsexual surgery [*sic*] is what triggered the firing. . . . Plaintiff had been employed by Eastern as an airline pilot for 12 years and had performed successfully. . . .

The first inkling of any discharge was when she had this surgery. So that differentiates this case from the usual Title VII case where the defendant says there were many things in the background of this employee which explain the discharge other than race or sex or whatever might be involved. Here there is not anything in the background other than the matters which first arose when plaintiff had the sex reassignment surgery.

The second unusual feature of this case is that the discharge was managed and coordinated by the defendant's legal department, which carefully drafted the two discharge letters in an obvious attempt to avoid liability under the sex discrimination law. You had here a filtering process that you do not ordinarily have when a disciplinary action is taken against an employee. . . .

[The court turned to the first discharge letter Eastern sent, dated April 24th, 1981. It listed five allegedly independently sufficient reasons for Ulane's termination.

(1) Eastern claimed that keeping Ulane on as a pilot was inconsistent with the safety considerations underlying the so-called coordinated crew concept it followed. On this point the court held that Eastern failed even to articulate a nondiscriminatory ground for the firing, seeking refuge behind nonexplanatory buzz words, never seeking the facts of the situation, and presenting testimony of a pilot who further admitted that he would have no problem if female hormones were all Ulane was taking.

(2) Eastern said it fired Ulane because her first class medical certificate was not unconditional or unrestricted. The court concluded this reason was pretextual because Eastern accepted substantively identical certificates for alcoholic pilots and had not changed its mind about Ulane even after she obtained an unrestricted certificate, instead presenting a witness who insisted that the FAA was wrong to grant her that.

(3) Eastern claimed that Ulane's sex confirmation surgery did not change her underlying transsexuality. The court found this reason to be pretextual, first, because it failed to explain how surgery would have made Ulane *less* safe than in preceding years where she was transsexual but flew; second, because Eastern made utterly no attempt to find out whether Ulane herself presented safety concerns, instead categorizing all transsexual persons as potentially unsafe due to its willful ignorance, an attitude the court believed Title VII sought to eliminate; and third, because of the contempt for transsexual persons manifest in Eastern's witnesses and in particular resentment in aviation-connected witnesses of "the intrusion of a transsexual in the aviation field."

(4) Eastern claimed that keeping Ulane on would undermine "their efforts to assure the public that airline travel is safe." The court rejected this argument as it had rejected the substantive safety argument, and the court found that it too was pretextual and echoed earlier anti-civil rights arguments that tried to blame the public for an employer's discriminatory choices.

(5) Eastern told Ulane that "[t]o the extent the operation and the counseling you have undergone have been successful in changing your essential nature from male to female, it has changed you from the person Eastern has hired into a different person. Eastern would not have hired you had it known you contemplated or might in the future contemplate such an action." This, the court held, was an admission of sex-based discrimination; inconsistent with Eastern's position that Ulane has not changed sex; and pretextual.

The court found that both individually and in combination these arguments were pretextual, and that Ulane was really fired because Eastern thought its public image would be tarnished if it had a transsexual pilot.]

[The court found that Eastern's second discharge letter, dated March 25, 1982, was not in retaliation for having contested her termination but was an attempt to bolster the case for discharge. The court concluded, however, that none of its four articulated reasons constituted a non-discriminatory reason for firing Ulane that was not pretextual.]

I find in summary that all of the reasons advanced by Eastern for the discharge of the plaintiff were pretextual and were not advanced in good faith.

I further find that but for being a transsexual and but for having had the transsexual surgery, the sex reassignment surgery, and adopting the life style of a woman, the plaintiff would not have been discharged.

I further find that the plaintiff was in almost every instance subjected to discriminatory and disparate treatment for conduct which was in almost every instance, if not every instance, far less serious than that of male alcoholics whose conduct was excused by Eastern.

I turn now to the second general question, and that is whether, assuming a sex-based series of decisions on the part of Eastern, those decisions can be justified as bona fide occupational qualifications; that is, can Eastern justify the proposition that not being a transsexual and not having transsexual surgery is a bona fide occupational qualification?

In order to prevail on that theory, on which Eastern has the burden of proof, Eastern would have to prove . . . "that the challenged [sex] qualification is reasonably related to the essential operation of its business and that either there is a factual basis for believing that all or substantially all [transsexuals] would be unable to effectively perform the duties of [a pilot] or that it is impossible or impracticable to determine job fitness on an individualized basis."

Eastern has proved neither of these propositions. The evidence, on the contrary, proves that neither of these propositions is true.

I am satisfied from this evidence that. . . . it cannot be said with any rationality that all transsexuals are unsafe airline pilots.

Neither can it be said with any rationality that it is impossible to make this determination of whether or not a safety hazard is really involved on an individualized basis. Eastern never attempted to do anything on an individualized basis and instead attempted to justify its discrimination against the plaintiff by resort to an indefensible generalization about all transsexuals. . . .

I am going to enter judgment for the plaintiff, and the question is on what counts and against which defendants. Count I alleges that plaintiff was discharged because she is a woman. Count II alleges that she was discharged because she is a transsexual.

[I] believe that these are truly alternate theories and that it cannot be both ways. It has got to be one or the other. The evidence much more clearly establishes in my opinion that transsexuals are entitled to protection under the act than it does that an operated [*sic*] transsexual is now a woman. While I would not argue with the latter proposition, the former seems to me more strongly supported by this record.

Accordingly, I am going to enter judgment against the defendants and in favor of the plaintiff on Count II, the transsexual count. In doing so, I do not mean to imply that if Count I were the only count I would not enter judgment for plaintiff on that count. I say that because one never knows "beyond a shadow of a doubt" what the Appellate Courts might do, and in the event the finding on Count II should be reversed, I would want plaintiff to be in the position of arguing alternatively that the judgment should be affirmed on Count I because upon remand in such a situation, I would enter judgment for plaintiff on Count I on the basis of the record that has already been made here. . . .

[I] . . . declare that the plaintiff is entitled to reinstatement with full seniority from the date of her discharge, all employment benefits that she would otherwise have received had she not been discharged, full back pay, and her reasonable attorneys' fees. What remains to be determined is the amount of the back pay and, of course, the amount of these benefits and her place on the roster, the possible question of mitigation of damages, all of which, it seems to me, will be fairly simple.

* * * *

Memorandum Opinion [February 8, 1984]

In my oral findings of fact and conclusions of law announced from the bench on December 28, 1983, I expressed an intention to find in favor of the plaintiff on Count II (discrimination against a transsexual) and against the plaintiff on Count I (discrimination against a female). It seemed to me that plaintiff had made a much better case that she is a transsexual than that she is a female. Upon further reflection, I think plaintiff may have made an equally good case on Count I. *See M.T. v. J.T.,* 355 A.2d 204 (N.J. App. Div.); *In Re Anonymous,* 57 Misc. 2d 813, 293 N.Y.S.2d 834 (Civ. Ct. 1968); *The Law and Transsexualism: A Faltering Response to a Conceptual Dilemma,* 7 Conn. L. Rev. 288 (1975); *Comment, Transsexualism, Sex Reassignment Surgery, and the Law,* 56 Cornell L. Rev. 963 (1971); *Comment, Transsexuals in Limbo: The Search for a Legal Definition of Sex,* 31 Md. L. Rev. 236 (1971). . . .

Accordingly, the judgment will be in favor of plaintiff on both Counts I and II of the complaint.

Supplemental Findings [March 6, 1984]

Plaintiff has moved . . . for clarification of the court's rulings in regard to Count I. . . . She asks for an indication that the findings supporting the conclusion that plaintiff is a transsexual also support a finding that she is a female and, further, that the findings as to sexual discrimination be made expressly applicable to Count I as well as to Count II.

The basic question in this case is whether plaintiff was discharged because of her sex within the meaning of Title VII. I found that, whether plaintiff be regarded as a transsexual or as a female, she was discharged by Eastern Airlines because of her sex. On the question of plaintiff's exact sexual status, I was satisfied from the evidence that she is a transsexual and so found. If Title VII protects transsexuals, then plaintiff is entitled to the relief awarded. On the other hand, if on appeal Title VII is held not to apply to transsexuals, then plaintiff should have a ruling on her alternative position that she is a female. As an alternative to my finding that plaintiff is a transsexual, I find that plaintiff's post operative legal status is that of a female. If on the evidence presented in this case the choices were limited to male or female, I would and do find that the evidence clearly predominates in favor of the conclusion that plaintiff is a female, not a male. All of the evidence which supports the view that plaintiff is a transsexual also supports the finding that she is a female.

It was and is my intention that all of my findings and conclusions concerning sexual discrimination against the plaintiff by Eastern Airlines, Inc. apply with equal force whether plaintiff be regarded as a transsexual or a female.

———————

Discussion

1. In light of Judge Grady's treatment of the evidence in this case, what would you have advised an employer to do or not to do (prior to the Supreme Court's decision in *Bostock v. Clayton County, Georgia*, 140 S. Ct. 1731 (2020), Section D, *infra*, at p. 244), if an employee transitions, in order to avoid violating Title VII?

2. Note Judge Grady's conclusion about the "literal" meaning of "sex." On this approach, is there any anti-transgender discrimination that would fall outside the protection of Title VII? And now after *Bostock*, *infra*, is *any* anti-transgender discrimination *not* sex discrimination under Title VII?

Reading Guide for Ulane v. Eastern Airlines *(court of appeals opinion)*

1. What language in the next opinion can be read as suggesting that the judges on the court of appeals did not believe that Karen Ulane was a woman?

2. The court of appeals reversed the district court, remanding the case for the district court to enter judgment in favor of Eastern Airlines on Count I of Karen Ulane's suit against Eastern Airlines (discrimination against her as a woman) and for it to dismiss Count II (discrimination against her because she was transsexual). The opinion of the court of appeals characterizes its ruling on Count II in different ways. What were they? In light of the opinion's reasoning and the way that Title VII protects employees against discrimination, which seems the best way to describe the holding?

3. In addressing Count II, the court of appeals deems the district court's definition of "sex" in Title VII to be "broad." In what sense might it have been "broad"?

The court of appeals says that it must interpret the statute in accord with Congress's intent. What other two "maxims" or principles of statutory construction does the court note? What does the court say about the legislative history of Title VII? What does it say about actions of subsequent Congresses? What institutional advantages does the court say Congress enjoys relative to the courts when it comes to determining whether Title VII protects transsexual persons from employment discrimination? Are those persuasive here?

4. What reasons does the court of appeals give for ruling in Eastern Airlines' favor on Count I?

Karen Frances Ulane v. Eastern Airlines, Inc.

742 F.2d 1081 (7th Cir. 1984)

HARLINGTON WOOD, Jr., Circuit Judge.

Plaintiff, as Kenneth Ulane, was hired in 1968 as a pilot for defendant, Eastern Air Lines, Inc., but was fired as Karen Frances Ulane in 1981. Ulane filed a timely charge of sex discrimination with the Equal Employment Opportunity Commission, which subsequently issued a right to sue letter. This suit followed. . . . The judge ruled in favor of Ulane on both counts after a bench trial. The court awarded her[2] reinstatement as a flying officer with full seniority and back pay, and attorneys' fees. This certified appeal followed[.]

Factual Background

Counsel for Ulane opens [sic] their brief by explaining: "This is a Title VII case brought by a pilot who was fired by Eastern Airlines for no reason other than the fact that she ceased being a male and became a female." That explanation may give some cause to pause, but this briefly is the story.

Ulane became a licensed pilot in 1964, serving in the United States Army from that time until 1968 with a record of combat missions in Vietnam for which Ulane received the Air Medal with eight clusters. Upon discharge in 1968, Ulane began flying for Eastern. With Eastern, Ulane progressed from Second to First Officer, and also served as a flight instructor, logging over 8,000 flight hours.

Ulane was diagnosed a transsexual[3] [sic] in 1979. She explains that although embodied as a male, from early childhood she felt like a female. Ulane first sought

---

2. Since Ulane considers herself to be female, and appears in public as female, we will use feminine pronouns in referring to her.

3. Transsexualism is a condition that exists when a physiologically normal person (i.e., not a hermaphrodite — a person whose sex is not clearly defined due to a congenital condition) experiences discomfort or discontent about nature's choice of his or her particular sex and prefers to be the other sex. This discomfort is generally accompanied by a desire to utilize hormonal, surgical, and civil procedures to allow the individual to live in his or her preferred sex role. The diagnosis is appropriate only if the discomfort has been continuous for at least two years, and is not due to another mental disorder, such as schizophrenia. See Testimony of Dr. Richard Green, expert

psychiatric and medical assistance in 1968 while in the military. Later, Ulane began taking female hormones as part of her treatment, and eventually developed breasts from the hormones. In 1980, she underwent "sex reassignment surgery."[4] After the surgery, Illinois issued a revised birth certificate indicating Ulane was female, and the FAA certified her for flight status as a female. Ulane's own physician explained, however, that the operation would not create a biological female in the sense that Ulane would "have a uterus and ovaries and be able to bear babies." Ulane's chromosomes,[5] all concede, are unaffected by the hormones and surgery. Ulane, however, claims that the lack of change in her chromosomes is irrelevant.[6] Eastern was not aware of Ulane's transsexuality, her hormone treatments, or her psychiatric counseling until she attempted to return to work after her reassignment surgery. Eastern knew Ulane only as one of its male pilots.

---

witness for plaintiff, trial transcript; *see generally* American Psychiatric Association, *Diagnostic and Statistical Manual of Mental Disorders* § 302.5x (3d ed. 1980); Edgerton, Langman, Schmidt & Sheppe, *Psychological Considerations of Gender Reassignment Surgery,* 9 CLINICS IN PLASTIC SURGERY 355, 357 (1982); Comment, *The Law and Transsexualism: A Faltering Response to a Conceptual Dilemma,* 7 CONN. L. REV. 288, 288 n. 1 (1975); Comment, *Transsexualism, Sex Reassignment Surgery, and the Law,* 56 CORNELL L. REV. 963, 963 n. 1 (1971).

To be distinguished are homosexuals [*sic*], who are sexually attracted to persons of the same sex, and transvestites [*sic*], who are generally male heterosexuals [*sic*] who cross-dress, *i.e.,* dress as females, for sexual arousal rather than social comfort; both homosexuals and transvestites are content with the sex into which they were born. *See Diagnostic and Statistical Manual of Mental Disorders* § 302.30 . . . .

4. Sex reassignment surgery for male-to-female transsexuals "involves the removal of the external male sexual organs and the construction of an artificial vagina by plastic surgery. It is supplemented by hormone treatments that facilitate the change in secondary sex characteristics," such as breast development. Comment, 56 CORNELL L. REV., *supra* note 3; *see also* Jones, *Operative Treatment of the Male Transsexual,* in TRANSSEXUALISM AND SEX REASSIGNMENT 313, 314–16 (R. Green & J. Money eds. 1969); Stoller, *Near Miss: "Sex Change" Treatment and Its Evaluation,* in EATING, SLEEPING, AND SEXUALITY 258, 259 (M. Zales ed. 1982); Shaw, *Sex-change Capital: Surgeon is Town's Top Draw,* CHICAGO TRIBUNE, Aug. 14, 1984, § 5, at 1, 3, col. 3.

5. The normal individual has 46 chromosomes, two of which designate sex. An XX configuration denotes female; XY denotes male. These chromosome patterns cannot be surgically altered. Wise, *Transsexualism: A Clinical Approach to Gender Dysphoria,* 1983 MEDIC. TRIAL TECH. Q. 167, 170.

6. Biologically, sex is defined by chromosomes, internal and external genitalia, hormones, and gonads. Wise, *supra* note 5, at 169. Chromosomal sex cannot be changed, and a uterus and ovaries cannot be constructed. This leads some in the medical profession to conclude that hormone treatments and sex reassignment surgery can alter the evident makeup of an individual, but cannot change the individual's innate sex. *See, e.g.,* Wise, *supra* note 5; Stoller, *supra* note 4; Comment, CORNELL L. REV., *supra* note 3. Others disagree, arguing that one must look beyond chromosomes when determining an individual's sex and consider factors such as psychological sex or assumed sex role. Comment, 7 CONN. L. REV., *supra* note 3 (psychological sex may be most important factor); Comment, CORNELL L. REV., *supra* note 3. These individuals conclude that post-operative male-to-female transsexuals do in fact qualify as females and are not merely "facsimiles." *E.g.,* Testimony of Dr. Richard Green, expert witness for plaintiff, trial transcript.

Legal Issues

A. Title VII and Ulane as a Transsexual.

The district judge first found under Count II that Eastern discharged Ulane because she was a transsexual, and that Title VII prohibits discrimination on this basis.[7] While we do not condone discrimination in any form,[8] we are constrained to hold that Title VII does not protect transsexuals [*sic*], and that the district court's order on this count therefore must be reversed for lack of jurisdiction.

Section 2000e-2(a)(1) provides in part that:

(a) It shall be an unlawful employment practice for an employer—

(1) to . . . discharge any individual . . . because of such individual's . . . sex. . . .

Other courts have held that the term "sex" as used in the statute is not synonymous with "sexual preference." *See, e.g., Sommers v. Budget Marketing, Inc.,* 667 F.2d 748 (8th Cir. 1982) (per curiam); *De Santis v. Pacific Telephone & Telegraph Co.,* 608 F.2d 327 (9th Cir. 1979); *Smith v. Liberty Mutual Insurance Co.,* 569 F.2d 325 (5th Cir. 1978); *Holloway v. Arthur Andersen & Co.,* 566 F.2d 659 (9th Cir. 1977); *Voyles v. Ralph K. Davies Medical Center,* 403 F. Supp. 456, 457 (N.D. Cal. 1975), *aff'd mem.,* 570 F.2d 354 (9th Cir. 1978). The district court recognized this, and agreed that homosexuals and transvestites do not enjoy Title VII protection, but distinguished transsexuals as persons who, unlike homosexuals and transvestites, have sexual *identity* problems; the judge agreed that the term "sex" does not comprehend "sexual preference," but held that it does comprehend "sexual identity." The district judge based this holding on his finding that "sex is not a cut-and-dried matter of chromosomes," but is in part a psychological question—a question of self-perception; and in part a social matter—a question of how society perceives the individual.[9] The district judge further supported his broad view of Title VII's coverage by recognizing Title VII as a remedial statute to be liberally construed. He concluded that it is reasonable to hold that the statutory word "sex" literally and scientifically applies to transsexuals even if it does not apply to homosexuals or transvestites. We must disagree.

---

7. Not all of the experts who testified agreed that Ulane is a transsexual. (Although doctors attempt to perform sex reassignment surgery only on transsexuals—as opposed, for example, on transvestites or schizophrenics [*sic*] [—]that an individual has undergone such surgery is not determinative of whether he or she is a true transsexual. *See supra* note 3 and sources cited therein.) If Ulane is not a transsexual, then she is a transvestite. Even in the trial judge's view, transvestites are not covered by Title VII.

8. Eastern presented a substantial amount of testimony and evidence at trial to prove that Ulane's discharge was not due to discrimination against her either as a transsexual or as a female, but we need not reach that issue.

9. The judge did recognize that there may be some argument in the medical community about the definition of sex that he adopted. *See, e.g., supra* notes 5 & 6.

Even though Title VII is a remedial statute, and even though some may define "sex" in such a way as to mean an individual's "sexual identity," our responsibility is to interpret this congressional legislation and determine what Congress intended when it decided to outlaw discrimination based on sex. The district judge did recognize that Congress manifested an intention to exclude homosexuals from Title VII coverage. . . . While we recognize distinctions among homosexuals, transvestites, and transsexuals, we believe that the same reasons for holding that the first two groups do not enjoy Title VII coverage apply with equal force to deny protection for transsexuals.

It is a maxim of statutory construction that, unless otherwise defined, words should be given their ordinary, common meaning. *Perrin v. United States,* 444 U.S. 37 (1979). The phrase in Title VII prohibiting discrimination based on sex, in its plain meaning, implies that it is unlawful to discriminate against women because they are women and against men because they are men. The words of Title VII do not outlaw discrimination against a person who has a sexual identity disorder, *i.e.,* a person born with a male body who believes himself to be female, or a person born with a female body who believes herself to be male; a prohibition against discrimination based on an individual's sex is not synonymous with a prohibition against discrimination based on an individual's sexual identity disorder or discontent with the sex into which they were born. The dearth of legislative history on section 2000e-2(a)(1) strongly reinforces the view that that section means nothing more than its plain language implies.

When Congress enacted the Civil Rights Act of 1964 it was primarily concerned with race discrimination. "Sex as a basis of discrimination was added as a floor amendment one day before the House approved Title VII, without prior hearing or debate." *Holloway v. Arthur Andersen & Co.,* 566 F.2d 659 (9th Cir. 1977); *Developments in the Law—Employment Discrimination and Title VII of the Civil Rights Act of 1964,* 84 HARV. L. REV. 1109 (1971). This sex amendment was the gambit of a congressman seeking to scuttle adoption of the Civil Rights Act. The ploy failed and sex discrimination was abruptly added to the statute's prohibition against race discrimination.

The total lack of legislative history supporting the sex amendment coupled with the circumstances of the amendment's adoption clearly indicates that Congress never considered nor intended that this 1964 legislation apply to anything other than the traditional concept of sex. Had Congress intended more, surely the legislative history would have at least mentioned its intended broad coverage of homosexuals, transvestites, or transsexuals, and would no doubt have sparked an interesting debate. There is not the slightest suggestion in the legislative record to support an all-encompassing interpretation.

Members of Congress have, moreover, on a number of occasions, attempted to amend Title VII to prohibit discrimination based upon "affectional [*sic*—Eds.] or sexual orientation." Each of these attempts has failed. While the proposed amendments were directed toward homosexuals, their rejection strongly indicates that the phrase in the Civil Rights Act prohibiting discrimination on the basis of sex should be given a narrow, traditional interpretation, which would also exclude transsexuals. Furthermore, Congress has continued to reject these amendments even after courts have specifically held that Title VII does not protect transsexuals from discrimination[.]

Although the maxim that remedial statutes should be liberally construed is well recognized, that concept has reasonable bounds beyond which a court cannot go without transgressing the prerogatives of Congress. [For] us to now hold that Title VII protects transsexuals would take us out of the realm of interpreting and reviewing and into the realm of legislating. *See Gunnison v. Commissioner*, 461 F.2d 496 (7th Cir. 1972) (it is for the legislature, not the courts, to expand the class of people protected by a statute). This we must not and will not do.

Congress has a right to deliberate on whether it wants such a broad sweeping of the untraditional and unusual within the term "sex" as used in Title VII. Only Congress can consider all the ramifications to society of such a broad view. We do not believe that the interpretation of the word "sex" as used in the statute is a mere matter of expert medical testimony or the credibility of witnesses produced in court. Congress may, at some future time, have some interest in testimony of that type, but it does not control our interpretation of Title VII based on the legislative history or lack thereof. If Congress believes that transsexuals should enjoy the protection of Title VII, it may so provide. Until that time, however, we decline in [*sic*] behalf of the Congress to judicially expand the definition of sex as used in Title VII beyond its common and traditional interpretation.

Our view of the application of Title VII to this type of case is not an original one. *Sommers*, and *Holloway*, the only two circuit court cases we found that have specifically addressed the issue, both held that discrimination against transsexuals does not fall within the ambit of Title VII. . . . We agree with the Eighth and Ninth Circuits that if the term "sex" as it is used in Title VII is to mean more than biological male or biological female, the new definition must come from Congress.

B. Title VII and Ulane as a Female.

The trial judge originally found only that Eastern had discriminated against Ulane under Count II as a transsexual. The judge subsequently amended his findings to hold that Ulane is also female and has been discriminated against on this basis. Even if we accept the district judge's holding that Ulane is female, he made no factual findings necessary to support his conclusion that Eastern discriminated against her on this basis. All the district judge said was that his previous "findings and conclusions concerning sexual discrimination against the plaintiff by Eastern Airlines, Inc. apply with equal force whether plaintiff be regarded as a transsexual or a female." This is insufficient to support a finding that Ulane was discriminated against because she is *female* since the district judge's previous findings all centered around his conclusion that Eastern did not want "[a] *transsexual* in the cockpit" (emphasis added).

Ulane is entitled to any personal belief about her sexual identity she desires. After the surgery, hormones, appearance changes, and a new Illinois birth certificate and FAA pilot's certificate, it may be that society, as the trial judge found, considers Ulane to be female. But even if one believes that a woman can be so easily created from what remains of a man, that does not decide this case. If Eastern had considered Ulane to be female and had discriminated against her because she was female (*i.e.*, Eastern treated females less favorably than males), then the argument might be made that Title VII applied, . . . but that is not this case. It is clear from the evidence that if Eastern did discriminate against Ulane, it was not because she is female, but because Ulane is a transsexual[10]—a biological male who takes female hormones, cross-dresses, and has surgically altered parts of her body to make it appear to be female.

Since Ulane was not discriminated against as a female, and since Title VII is not so expansive in scope as to prohibit discrimination against transsexuals, we reverse the order of the trial court and remand for entry of judgment in favor of Eastern on Count I and dismissal of Count II.

REVERSED.

Discussion

1. The appellate opinion in *Ulane* relied on a presumed intent of Congress in 1964, assuming a narrow ordinary, common, or usual definition of "sex" rather than focusing more broadly on what it linguistically or logically means to "discriminate" "based on" "sex." In ruling that Title VII's ban on sex discrimination proscribes discrimination because of an employee's "transgender status" in *Bostock v. Clayton County, Georgia*, 140 S. Ct. 1731 (2020), Section D, *infra*, at p. 244, the Supreme Court more than three and a half decades later adopted a an approach to the statutory text that was largely unconcerned by what Congress may have intended the statute to do.

2. The court of appeals' rendition of the legislative history of Title VII's ban on sex discrimination reflected and entrenched the conventional narrative on the issue. A substantial body of legal scholarship, however, shows *Ulane*'s claim of "total lack" of legislative history mistaken and misleading. *See, e.g.*, Robert C. Bird, *More Than a Congressional Joke: A Fresh Look at the Legislative History of Sex Discrimination of the 1964 Civil Rights Act*, 3 WM. & MARY J. WOMEN & L. 137 (1997) (arguing that "the sex discrimination provision was the result of complex political struggles involving racial issues, presidential politics, and competing factions of the women's rights movement" and concluding that "feminists who strongly supported the inclusion of sex as a protected class spoke out in favor of the provision and secured its passage

---

10. Because of our holding in section A, however, we need not and do not decide whether Eastern did actually discriminate against Ulane because of her transsexuality.

into law"); Arianne Renan Barzilay, *Parenting Title VII: Rethinking the History of the Sex Discrimination Prohibition*, 28 Yale J.L. & Feminism 55, 59 & nn.10–11 (2016) (describing and citing scholarship showing "that the inclusion of 'sex' in Title VII was more than a fluke or a joke perpetrated by Southern segregationists"). Indeed, Cary Franklin has argued at length that "the 'traditional concept' of sex discrimination, as articulated by courts, is an 'invented tradition.'" Cary Franklin, *Inventing the "Traditional Concept" of Sex Discrimination*, 125 Harv. L. Rev. 1307, 1312 (2012). "Courts claimed that their narrowly circumscribed definition of sex discrimination was deeply rooted in history, but in fact, it was quite new. It did not express a historical fact. It made a normative claim . . . about the limits of Title VII's prohibition of sex discrimination." *Id.*

3. Suppose a firm at which you were working prior to *Bostock*, in a federal Circuit that has no appellate precedent agreeing or disagreeing with the ultimate ruling in *Ulane*, has a transgender woman client who believes she was fired after she began transitioning on the job. What arguments could you make in court to try to persuade a judge to follow the district court's approach to Title VII in *Ulane* rather than the court of appeals' approach? Alternatively, if your firm in such a Circuit were engaged to defend an employer against a claim that it violated Title VII by discharging an employee because she began transitioning on the job, what arguments could you make in court to try to persuade a judge to follow the court of appeals' approach?

4. As the Supreme Court implicitly recognized in *Bostock*, various aspects of the court of appeals ruling in *Ulane* are at least in tension with a range of Supreme Court precedents, some decided before *Ulane*. In 1978, the Supreme Court had decided *Los Angeles Department of Water & Power v. Manhart*, 435 U.S. 702. There, it declared of Title VII that "[i]n forbidding employers to discriminate against individuals because of their sex, Congress intended to strike at *the entire spectrum* of disparate treatment of men and women resulting from sex stereotypes." *Id.* at 707 n.13 (emphasis added). This could be interpreted to include stereotypes about whether a man must always have been regarded as a man. In 1983, the Supreme Court decided *Newport News Shipbuilding & Dry Dock Co. v. EEOC*, 462 U.S. 669. There, as the Equal Employment Opportunity Commission later noted in *Macy v. Holder*, No. 0120120821, at *10 (E.E.O.C. Apr. 20, 2012), Section D, *infra* at p.228, the Supreme Court "reject[ed] the argument that discrimination against men does not violate Title VII despite the fact that discrimination against women was plainly the principal problem that Title VII's prohibition of sex discrimination was enacted to combat." The year after the circuit court's ruling in *Ulane*, the Supreme Court decided *Pension Benefit Guarantee Corp. v. LTV Corp.*, 496 U.S. 633 (1990). In *Pension Benefit Guarantee Corp.*, the Court explained that

> subsequent legislative history is a hazardous basis for inferring the intent of an earlier Congress. It is a particularly dangerous ground on which to rest an interpretation of a prior statute when it concerns . . . a proposal that does not become law. Congressional inaction lacks persuasive significance

> because several equally tenable inferences may be drawn from such inaction, including the inference that the existing legislation already incorporated the offered change.

Id. at 650 (internal citations and quotation marks omitted).

5. The circuit court reversed the district court's finding that Eastern Airlines had discriminated against Ms. Ulane because she was a woman, holding that conclusion to be unsupported by the evidence. Contrast this with the more recent treatment of the plaintiff's claim in *Cummings v. Greater Cleveland Regional Transit Authority*, 88 F. Supp. 3d 812 (N.D. Ohio 2015). There, Noel Cummings, a transgender African American woman, sued her employer for discriminating against her based on her race, gender, and gender identity. The agency argued that the court should dismiss her claims that she was discriminated against as a woman because she was identified as male at birth. The district court rejected this argument, holding that at the motion to dismiss stage Ms. Cummings's allegations that she "identifie[d] and consider[ed] herself a female," was female from "a biological standpoint," and had a valid (out-of-state) birth certificate identifying her as female were sufficient to allow her to claim that she had been discriminated against as a female.

6. The court of appeals ruling in *Ulane* has been the subject of substantial and ongoing criticism in legal scholarship. For a sample, see M. Dru Levasseur, *Gender Identity Defines Sex: Updating the Law to Reflect Modern Medical Science Is Key to Transgender Rights*, 39 Vt. L. Rev. 943, 973 (2015) (criticizing *Ulane* appellate opinion for "reveal[ing] a deep lack of understanding of who transgender people are"); David B. Cruz, *Acknowledging the Gender in Anti-Transgender Discrimination*, 32 Law & Ineq. 257 (2014) (arguing that *Ulane*'s reasoning "fails"); Demoya Gordon, Comment, *Transgender Legal Advocacy: What Do Feminist Legal Theories Have to Offer?*, 97 Cal. L. Rev. 1719, 1757 (2009) (criticizing Seventh Circuit panel for its "adherence to conventional understandings of sex and gender—which are but one possible approach to understanding these concepts—[as] not reflect[ing] the lived reality and experiences of thousands of individuals"); Kevin Schwin, Note, *Toward a Plain Meaning Approach to Title VII: Employment Discrimination Protection of Transsexuals*, 57 Clev. St. L. Rev. 645, 660 (2009) ("reasoning is hardly persuasive"); Julie A. Greenberg, *Defining Male and Female: Intersexuality and the Collision Between Law and Biology*, 41 Ariz. L. Rev. 265, 321 n.445 (1999) ("The court's characterization of the discrimination in this case as being based upon 'a change of sex' rather than discrimination based upon sex is inconsistent with the Title VII cases based upon religious discrimination"); Kristine Holt, Comment, *Reevaluating Holloway: Title VII, Equal Protection, and the Evolution of a Transgender Jurisprudence*, 70 Temp. L. Rev. 283, 317 (1997) ("specious" reasoning); D. Douglas Cotton, Note, Ulane v. Eastern Airlines*: Title VII and Transsexualism*, 80 Nw. U. L. Rev. 1037, 1065 (1986) ("misinterpreted congressional intent"); Richard Green, *Spelling "Relief" for Transsexuals: Employment Discrimination and the Criteria of Sex*, 4 Yale L. & Pol'y Rev. 125 (1985) ("the reasoning of the court ignores the behavioral science data").

B. Supreme Court Turning Points

Decades before the Supreme Court resolved much of the issue in *Bostock v. Clayton County, Georgia*, 140 S. Ct. 1731 (2020), Section D, *infra*, two key Supreme Court cases seem to have provided litigants and lower courts with important interpretive resources for rejecting the narrow reading of Title VII's ban on sex discrimination in cases such as *Ulane*. The first, *Price Waterhouse v. Hopkins*, 490 U.S. 228 (1989), made clear that sex discrimination based on gender stereotyping was within the scope of Title VII. The second, *Oncale v. Sundowner Offshore Services*, 523 U.S. 75 (1998), showed that the Court deemed the text of Title VII more important than the intent or expectations of the 1964 Congress in determining the scope of the statute. Both of those principles offered help to transgender plaintiffs seeking to use Title VII to protect them against anti-transgender employment discrimination. Georgetown law professor Chai Feldblum thus argued in 2000 that these "cases are creating a new momentum in sex discrimination law" and "changing the approach of courts to sex discrimination and gender non-conformity." Chair R. Feldblum, *Gay People, Trans People, Women: Is It All About Gender?*, 17 N.Y.L. Sch. J. Hum. Rts. 623, 642 (2000).

Reading Guide for Price Waterhouse v. Hopkins

1. Justice Brennan's opinion for a plurality of the Justices in *Price Waterhouse* is widely taken to explicate the holding of the Court, even though Justices White and O'Connor did not join it, instead concurring only in the judgment or outcome of the case. (Justice O'Connor's concurrence does not disagree with the stereotyping discussions in the plurality opinion; it disagreed on more technical "burden of proof" issues.) What use does the plurality opinion make of the text of Title VII? (Note the opinion's reliance not just on "sex" but also on "gender.") What does it have to say about congressional intent?

2. What does the plurality opinion say employers may not do when it comes to an employee's (or applicant's) sex? See especially sections II.A and C of the opinion. Although the Court does not use this terminology, note that "descriptive stereotypes" are stereotypes about how a group of people *are*, and "prescriptive stereotypes" are stereotypes about how a group of people *ought* to be. *See, e.g.*, Brian Soucek, *Perceived Homosexuals: Looking Gay Enough for Title VII*, 63 Am. U. L. Rev. 715, 762 n.303 (2014).

3. According to the Justices who together constitute the majority, what about the treatment of Ann Hopkins by Price Waterhouse shows sex discrimination?

Price Waterhouse v. Hopkins

490 U.S. 228 (1989)

Justice BRENNAN announced the judgment of the Court and delivered an opinion, in which Justice MARSHALL, Justice BLACKMUN, and Justice STEVENS join.

. . . .

[When] the partners in her office . . . refused to repropose her for partnership, [senior manager Ann Hopkins] sued Price Waterhouse under Title VII of the Civil Rights Act of 1964, 42 U.S.C. § 2000e *et seq.,* charging that the firm had discriminated against her on the basis of sex in its decisions regarding partnership. . . .

I

At Price Waterhouse, a nationwide professional accounting partnership, a senior manager becomes a candidate for partnership when the partners in her local office submit her name as a candidate. All of the other partners in the firm are then invited to submit written comments on each candidate—either on a "long" or a "short" form, depending on the partner's degree of exposure to the candidate. Not every partner in the firm submits comments on every candidate. After reviewing the comments and interviewing the partners who submitted them, the firm's Admissions Committee makes a recommendation to the Policy Board. This recommendation will be either that the firm accept the candidate for partnership, put her application on "hold," or deny her the promotion outright. The Policy Board then decides whether to submit the candidate's name to the entire partnership for a vote, to "hold" her candidacy, or to reject her. The recommendation of the Admissions Committee, and the decision of the Policy Board, are not controlled by fixed guidelines: a certain number of positive comments from partners will not guarantee a candidate's admission to the partnership, nor will a specific quantity of negative comments necessarily defeat her application. Price Waterhouse places no limit on the number of persons whom it will admit to the partnership in any given year.

Ann Hopkins had worked at Price Waterhouse's Office of Government Services in Washington, D.C., for five years when the partners in that office proposed her as a candidate for partnership [in 1982]. Of the 662 partners at the firm at that time, 7 were women. Of the 88 persons proposed for partnership that year, only 1—Hopkins—was a woman. Forty-seven of these candidates were admitted to the partnership, 21 were rejected, and 20—including Hopkins—were "held" for reconsideration the following year. Thirteen of the 32 partners who had submitted comments on Hopkins supported her bid for partnership. Three partners recommended that her candidacy be placed on hold, eight stated that they did not have an informed opinion about her, and eight recommended that she be denied partnership.

In a jointly prepared statement supporting her candidacy, the partners in Hopkins' office showcased her successful 2-year effort to secure a $25 million contract with the Department of State, labeling it "an outstanding performance" and one that Hopkins carried out "virtually at the partner level." Despite Price Waterhouse's attempt at trial to minimize her contribution to this project, Judge Gesell specifically found that Hopkins had "played a key role in Price Waterhouse's successful effort to win a multi-million dollar contract with the Department of State." Indeed, he went on, "[n]one of the other partnership candidates at Price Waterhouse that year had a comparable record in terms of successfully securing major contracts for the partnership."

The partners in Hopkins' office praised her character as well as her accomplishments, describing her in their joint statement as "an outstanding professional" who had a "deft touch," a "strong character, independence and integrity." Clients appear to have agreed with these assessments. At trial, one official from the State Department described her as "extremely competent, intelligent," "strong and forthright, very productive, energetic and creative." Another high-ranking official praised Hopkins' decisiveness, broadmindedness, and "intellectual clarity"; she was, in his words, "a stimulating conversationalist." Evaluations such as these led Judge Gesell to conclude that Hopkins "had no difficulty dealing with clients and her clients appear to have been very pleased with her work" and that she "was generally viewed as a highly competent project leader who worked long hours, pushed vigorously to meet deadlines and demanded much from the multidisciplinary staffs with which she worked."

On too many occasions, however, Hopkins' aggressiveness apparently spilled over into abrasiveness. Staff members seem to have borne the brunt of Hopkins' brusqueness. Long before her bid for partnership, partners evaluating her work had counseled her to improve her relations with staff members. Although later evaluations indicate an improvement, Hopkins' perceived shortcomings in this important area eventually doomed her bid for partnership. Virtually all of the partners' negative remarks about Hopkins — even those of partners supporting her — had to do with her "interpersonal skills." Both "[s]upporters and opponents of her candidacy," stressed Judge Gesell, "indicated that she was sometimes overly aggressive, unduly harsh, difficult to work with and impatient with staff."

There were clear signs, though, that some of the partners reacted negatively to Hopkins' personality because she was a woman. One partner described her as "macho"; another suggested that she "overcompensated for being a woman"; a third advised her to take "a course at charm school." Several partners criticized her use of profanity; in response, one partner suggested that those partners objected to her swearing only "because it's a lady using foul language." Another supporter explained that Hopkins "ha[d] matured from a tough-talking somewhat masculine hard-nosed [manager] to an authoritative, formidable, but much more appealing lady [partner] candidate." But it was the man who, as Judge Gesell found, bore responsibility for explaining to Hopkins the reasons for the Policy Board's decision to place her candidacy on hold who delivered the *coup de grace:* in order to improve her chances for partnership, Thomas Beyer advised, Hopkins should "walk more femininely, talk more femininely, dress more femininely, wear make-up, have her hair styled, and wear jewelry."

Dr. Susan Fiske, a social psychologist and Associate Professor of Psychology at Carnegie-Mellon University, testified at trial that the partnership selection process at Price Waterhouse was likely influenced by sex stereotyping. Her testimony focused not only on the overtly sex-based comments of partners but also on gender-neutral remarks, made by partners who knew Hopkins only slightly, that were intensely critical of her. One partner, for example, baldly stated that Hopkins was "universally disliked" by staff, and another described her as "consistently annoying and irritating"; yet these were people who had had very little contact with Hopkins. According to Fiske, Hopkins' uniqueness (as the only woman in the pool of candidates) and the subjectivity of the evaluations made it likely that sharply critical remarks such as these were the product of sex stereotyping—although Fiske admitted that she could not say with certainty whether any particular comment was the result of stereotyping. Fiske based her opinion on a review of the submitted comments, explaining that it was commonly accepted practice for social psychologists to reach this kind of conclusion without having met any of the people involved in the decisionmaking process.

In previous years, other female candidates for partnership also had been evaluated in sex-based terms. As a general matter, Judge Gesell concluded, "[c]andidates were viewed favorably if partners believed they maintained their femin[in]ity while becoming effective professional managers"; in this environment, "[t]o be identified as a 'women's lib[b]er' was regarded as [a] negative comment." In fact, the judge found that in previous years "[o]ne partner repeatedly commented that he could not consider any woman seriously as a partnership candidate and believed that women were not even capable of functioning as senior managers—yet the firm took no action to discourage his comments and recorded his vote in the overall summary of the evaluations."

Judge Gesell found that Price Waterhouse legitimately emphasized interpersonal skills in its partnership decisions, and also found that the firm had not fabricated its complaints about Hopkins' interpersonal skills as a pretext for discrimination. Moreover, he concluded, the firm did not give decisive emphasis to such traits only because Hopkins was a woman; although there were male candidates who lacked these skills but who were admitted to partnership, the judge found that these candidates possessed other, positive traits that Hopkins lacked.

The judge went on to decide, however, that some of the partners' remarks about Hopkins stemmed from an impermissibly cabined view of the proper behavior of women, and that Price Waterhouse had done nothing to disavow reliance on such comments. He held that Price Waterhouse had unlawfully discriminated against Hopkins on the basis of sex by consciously giving credence and effect to partners' comments that resulted from sex stereotyping. Noting that Price Waterhouse could avoid equitable relief by proving by clear and convincing evidence that it would have placed Hopkins' candidacy on hold even absent this discrimination, the judge decided that the firm had not carried this heavy burden. . . .

II

The specification of the standard of causation under Title VII is a decision about the kind of conduct that violates that statute. . . .

A

In passing Title VII, Congress made the simple but momentous announcement that sex, race, religion, and national origin are not relevant to the selection, evaluation, or compensation of employees. . . .

[I]n now-familiar language, the statute forbids an employer to "fail or refuse to hire or to discharge any individual, or otherwise to discriminate with respect to his compensation, terms, conditions, or privileges of employment," or to "limit, segregate, or classify his employees or applicants for employment in any way which would deprive or tend to deprive any individual of employment opportunities or otherwise adversely affect his status as an employee, *because of* such individual's . . . sex." 42 U.S.C. §§ 2000e-2(a)(1), (2) (emphasis added). We take these words to mean that gender must be irrelevant to employment decisions. . . .

[T]he critical inquiry, the one commanded by the words of § 703(a)(1), is whether gender was a factor in the employment decision *at the moment it was made*. . . .

[W]e need not leave our common sense at the doorstep when we interpret a statute. [W]e conclude . . . that Congress meant to obligate [a plaintiff] to prove that the employer relied upon sex-based considerations in coming to its decision.

[W]hile an employer may not take gender into account in making an employment decision (except in those very narrow circumstances in which gender is a [bona fide occupational qualification] [(]BFOQ), it is free to decide against a woman for other reasons. We think these principles require that, once a plaintiff in a Title VII case shows that gender played a motivating part in an employment decision, the defendant may avoid a finding of liability only by proving that it would have made the same decision even if it had not allowed gender to play such a role. This balance of burdens is the direct result of Title VII's balance of rights. . . .

C

In saying that gender played a motivating part in an employment decision, we mean that, if we asked the employer at the moment of the decision what its reasons were and if we received a truthful response, one of those reasons would be that the applicant or employee was a woman. In the specific context of sex stereotyping, an employer who acts on the basis of a belief that a woman cannot be aggressive, or that she must not be, has acted on the basis of gender.

Although the parties do not overtly dispute this last proposition, the placement by Price Waterhouse of "sex stereotyping" in quotation marks throughout its brief seems to us an insinuation either that such stereotyping was not present in this case or that it lacks legal relevance. We reject both possibilities. As to the existence of sex stereotyping in this case, we are not inclined to quarrel with the District Court's conclusion that a number of the partners' comments showed sex stereotyping at work. As for the legal relevance of sex stereotyping, we are beyond the day when an employer could evaluate employees by assuming or insisting that they matched the stereotype associated with their group, for "'[i]n forbidding employers to discriminate against individuals because of their sex, Congress intended to strike at the entire spectrum of disparate treatment of men and women resulting from sex stereotypes.'" *Los Angeles Dept. of Water and Power v. Manhart* (1978). An employer who objects to aggressiveness in women but whose positions require this trait places women in an intolerable and impermissible catch 22: out of a job if they behave aggressively and out of a job if they do not. Title VII lifts women out of this bind.

Remarks at work that are based on sex stereotypes do not inevitably prove that gender played a part in a particular employment decision. The plaintiff must show that the employer actually relied on her gender in making its decision. In making this showing, stereotyped remarks can certainly be *evidence* that gender played a part. In any event, the stereotyping in this case did not simply consist of stray remarks. On the contrary, Hopkins proved that Price Waterhouse invited partners to submit comments; that some of the comments stemmed from sex stereotypes; that an important part of the Policy Board's decision on Hopkins was an assessment of the submitted comments; and that Price Waterhouse in no way disclaimed reliance on the sex-linked evaluations. This is not, as Price Waterhouse suggests, "discrimination in the air"; rather, it is, as Hopkins puts it, "discrimination brought to ground and visited upon" an employee. By focusing on Hopkins' specific proof, however, we do not suggest a limitation on the possible ways of proving that stereotyping played a motivating role in an employment decision, and we refrain from deciding here which specific facts, "standing alone," would or would not establish a plaintiff's case, since such a decision is unnecessary in this case.

As to the employer's proof, in most cases, the employer should be able to present some objective evidence as to its probable decision in the absence of an impermissible motive.[11] Moreover, proving "'that the same decision would have been justified . . . is not the same as proving that the same decision would have been made.'" An employer may not, in other words, prevail in a mixed-motives case by offering a legitimate and sufficient reason for its decision if that reason did not motivate it at the time of the decision. Finally, an employer may not meet its burden in such a case by merely showing that at the time of the decision it was motivated only in part by a legitimate reason. The very premise of a mixed-motives case is that a legitimate reason was present, and indeed, in this case, Price Waterhouse already has made this showing by convincing Judge Gesell that Hopkins' interpersonal problems were a legitimate concern. The employer instead must show that its legitimate reason, standing alone, would have induced it to make the same decision.

---

11. Justice WHITE's suggestion that the employer's own testimony as to the probable decision in the absence of discrimination is due special credence where the court has, contrary to the employer's testimony, found that an illegitimate factor played a part in the decision, is baffling.

III

[In this Part of the opinion, the plurality concludes that to escape liability under Title VII an employer who has allowed a discriminatory impulse to play a motivating part in an employment decision must prove by a preponderance of the evidence that it would have made the same decision in the absence of discrimination.] [W]e shall remand this case so that that determination can be made.

IV

The District Court found that sex stereotyping "was permitted to play a part" in the evaluation of Hopkins as a candidate for partnership. Price Waterhouse disputes both that stereotyping occurred and that it played any part in the decision to place Hopkins' candidacy on hold. In the firm's view, in other words, the District Court's factual conclusions are clearly erroneous. We do not agree. In finding that some of the partners' comments reflected sex stereotyping, the District Court relied in part on Dr. Fiske's expert testimony. Without directly impugning Dr. Fiske's credentials or qualifications, Price Waterhouse insinuates that a social psychologist is unable to identify sex stereotyping in evaluations without investigating whether those evaluations have a basis in reality. This argument comes too late. At trial, counsel for Price Waterhouse twice assured the court that he did not question Dr. Fiske's expertise and failed to challenge the legitimacy of her discipline. Without contradiction from Price Waterhouse, Fiske testified that she discerned sex stereotyping in the partners' evaluations of Hopkins and she further explained that it was part of her business to identify stereotyping in written documents. We are not inclined to accept petitioner's belated and unsubstantiated characterization of Dr. Fiske's testimony as "gossamer evidence" based only on "intuitive hunches" and of her detection of sex stereotyping as "intuitively divined." Nor are we disposed to adopt the dissent's dismissive attitude toward Dr. Fiske's field of study and toward her own professional integrity.

Indeed, we are tempted to say that Dr. Fiske's expert testimony was merely icing on Hopkins' cake. It takes no special training to discern sex stereotyping in a description of an aggressive female employee as requiring "a course at charm school." Nor, turning to Thomas Beyer's memorable advice to Hopkins, does it require expertise in psychology to know that, if an employee's flawed "interpersonal skills" can be corrected by a soft-hued suit or a new shade of lipstick, perhaps it is the employee's sex and not her interpersonal skills that has drawn the criticism.

Price Waterhouse also charges that Hopkins produced no evidence that sex stereotyping played a role in the decision to place her candidacy on hold. As we have stressed, however, Hopkins showed that the partnership solicited evaluations from all of the firm's partners; that it generally relied very heavily on such evaluations in making its decision; that some of the partners' comments were the product of stereotyping; and that the firm in no way disclaimed reliance on those particular comments, either in Hopkins' case or in the past. Certainly a plausible—and, one might say, inevitable—conclusion to draw from this set of circumstances is that the Policy Board in making its decision did in fact take into account all of the partners' comments, including the comments that were motivated by stereotypical notions about women's proper deportment.

[N]or is the finding that sex stereotyping played a part in the Policy Board's decision undermined by the fact that many of the suspect comments were made by supporters rather than detractors of Hopkins. A negative comment, even when made in the context of a generally favorable review, nevertheless may influence the decisionmaker to think less highly of the candidate; the Policy Board, in fact, did not simply tally the "yeses" and "noes" regarding a candidate, but carefully reviewed the content of the submitted comments. The additional suggestion that the comments were made by "persons outside the decisionmaking chain"—and therefore could not have harmed Hopkins—simply ignores the critical role that partners' comments played in the Policy Board's partnership decisions.

Price Waterhouse appears to think that we cannot affirm the factual findings of the trial court without deciding that, instead of being overbearing and aggressive and curt, Hopkins is, in fact, kind and considerate and patient. If this is indeed its impression, petitioner misunderstands the theory on which Hopkins prevailed. The District Judge acknowledged that Hopkins' conduct justified complaints about her behavior as a senior manager. But he also concluded that the reactions of at least some of the partners were reactions to her as a *woman* manager. Where an evaluation is based on a subjective assessment of a person's strengths and weaknesses, it is simply not true that each evaluator will focus on, or even mention, the same weaknesses. Thus, even if we knew that Hopkins had "personality problems," this would not tell us that the partners who cast their evaluations of Hopkins in sex-based terms would have criticized her as sharply (or criticized her at all) if she had been a man. It is not our job to review the evidence and decide that the negative reactions to Hopkins were based on reality; our perception of Hopkins' character is irrelevant. We sit not to determine whether Ms. Hopkins is nice, but to decide whether the partners reacted negatively to her personality because she is a woman.

V

We hold that when a plaintiff in a Title VII case proves that her gender played a motivating part in an employment decision, the defendant may avoid a finding of liability only by proving by a preponderance of the evidence that it would have made the same decision even if it had not taken the plaintiff's gender into account. Because the courts below erred by deciding that the defendant must make this proof by clear and convincing evidence, we reverse the Court of Appeals' judgment against Price Waterhouse on liability and remand the case to that court for further proceedings. *It is so ordered.*

Justice WHITE, concurring in the judgment.

[Justice White concurred to emphasize that "Hopkins was not required to prove that the illegitimate factor was the only, principal, or true reason for petitioner's action. Rather, as Justice O'CONNOR states, her burden was to show that the unlawful motive was a *substantial* factor in the adverse employment action. The District Court . . . so found, and I agree that the finding was supported by the record."]

Justice O'CONNOR, concurring in the judgment.

[Justice O'Connor wrote separately to address the substantive requirement of causation under the statute and the majority's "broad statements regarding the applicability of the allocation of the burden of proof applied in this case."]

I

[Here Justice O'Connor argued in favor of reading Title VII as requiring but-for causation, but still shifting the burden of proof to an employer as the plurality did.]

II

[I]n this case, the District Court found that a number of the evaluations of Ann Hopkins submitted by partners in the firm overtly referred to her failure to conform to certain gender stereotypes as a factor militating against her election to the partnership The District Court further found that these evaluations were given "great weight" by the decisionmakers at Price Waterhouse. In addition, the District Court found that the partner responsible for informing Hopkins of the factors which caused her candidacy to be placed on hold, indicated that her "professional" problems would be solved if she would "walk more femininely, talk more femininely, wear make-up, have her hair styled, and wear jewelry." As the Court of Appeals characterized it, Ann Hopkins proved that Price Waterhouse "permitt[ed] stereotypical attitudes towards women to play a significant, though unquantifiable, role in its decision not to invite her to become a partner."

At this point Ann Hopkins had taken her proof as far as it could go. She had proved discriminatory input into the decisional process, and had proved that participants in the process considered her failure to conform to the stereotypes credited by a number of the decisionmakers had been a substantial factor in the decision. It is as if Ann Hopkins were sitting in the hall outside the room where partnership decisions were being made. As the partners filed in to consider her candidacy, she heard several of them make sexist remarks in discussing her suitability for partnership. As the decisionmakers exited the room, she was *told* by one of those privy to the decisionmaking process that her gender was a major reason for the rejection of her partnership bid. [O]ne would be hard pressed to think of a situation where it would be more appropriate to require the defendant to show that its decision would have been justified by wholly legitimate concerns. . . .

Justice Kennedy, with whom the Chief Justice and Justice Scalia join, dissenting.

[The dissent discussed at length the standard of proof and burden-shifting rules under Title VII. It then disparaged Ann Hopkins's expert witness Dr. Susan Fiske, whose testimony the dissent grudgingly conceded it was bound to accept following Price Waterhouse's acceptance of it at trial.]

. . . . I think it important to stress that Title VII creates no independent cause of action for sex stereotyping. Evidence of use by decisionmakers of sex stereotypes is, of course, quite relevant to the question of discriminatory intent. The ultimate question, however, is whether discrimination caused the plaintiff's harm. . . .

. . . . In this case, Hopkins plainly presented a strong case both of her own professional qualifications and of the presence of discrimination in Price Waterhouse's partnership process. Had the District Court found on this record that sex discrimination caused the adverse decision, I doubt it would have been reversible error. That decision was for the finder of fact, however, and the District Court made plain that sex discrimination was not a but-for cause of the decision to place Hopkins' partnership candidacy on hold. . . . I would remand the case for entry of judgment in favor of Price Waterhouse.

Discussion

1. *Price Waterhouse* recognizes that "Title VII does identify one circumstance in which an employer may take gender into account in making an employment decision, namely, when gender is a 'bona fide occupational qualification [(BFOQ)] reasonably necessary to the normal operation of th[e] particular business or enterprise.' 42 U.S.C. §2000e-2(e)." (This BFOQ provision also applies to religion and national origin, but not to race or color.) Other than "the special context of affirmative action," 490 U.S. 228, 239 (1989), then, the plurality opinion in *Price Waterhouse* says, "an employer may not take gender into account in making an employment decision (except in those very narrow circumstances in which gender is a [bona fide occupational qualification] [(]BFOQ)." In *Dothard v. Rawlinson*, the Court insisted "that the BFOQ exception was in fact meant to be an extremely narrow exception to the general prohibition of discrimination on the basis of sex." Note also that the BFOQ provision is limited in its scope; although it sometimes allows employers to use sex in the hiring or assigning of employees to certain positions, it does not apply to Title VII's ban on "discriminat[ing] against any individual with respect to his [or her] compensation, terms, conditions, or privileges of employment." 42 U.S.C. §2000e-2(e). *See* David B. Cruz, *Making Up Women: Casinos, Cosmetics, and Title VII*, 5 Nev. L.J. 240, 244–245 (2004).

2. The Civil Rights Act of 1991 codified the motivating factor test of the *Price Waterhouse* plurality opinion (rather than the concurrers' "substantial motivating

factor" proposal), but it changes Title VII as interpreted in the plurality, such that now an adverse employment action taken based on a forbidden criterion violates Title VII even if an employer were to prove that it would have taken the same action without reliance on the unlawful criterion. That kind of proof now may, at most, serve to limit statutory remedies available to an employment discrimination plaintiff. Pub. L. No. 102-166, § 107, 105 Stat. 1075–1076 (1991). In *Bostock v. Clayton County, Georgia*, 140 S. Ct. 1731 (2020), Section D, *infra*, the Supreme Court recognized that establishing that sex was a "motivating factor" of an employer's adverse decision remains an option for employees to establish a violation of Title VII even as the Court held that proving but-for causation — showing that had the worker's sex been different the employer would not have subjected them to the adverse restriction — is generally what Title VII means by discrimination "because of" sex.

3. Reconsider the facts of *Ulane, supra*. If Karen Ulane were suing Eastern Airlines after *Price Waterhouse* (but before *Bostock*), what in the reasoning of *Price Waterhouse* could Ulane's counsel rely on to support her contention that Eastern Airlines violated her right to be free of sex discrimination in employment?

4. Note that *Price Waterhouse* reads Title VII to forbid both descriptive and prescriptive stereotypes: "In the specific context of sex stereotyping, an employer who acts on the basis of a belief that a woman cannot be aggressive, or that she must not be, has acted on the basis of gender. . . . As for the legal relevance of sex stereotyping, we are beyond the day when an employer could evaluate employees by assuming or insisting that they matched the stereotype associated with their group. . . ."

In *Jameka K. Evans v. Georgia Regional Hospital et al.*, 850 F.3d 1248 (11th Cir. 2017), a divided court of appeals (2–1) rejected the argument that Title VII's ban on sex discrimination categorically forbade sexual orientation discrimination. Circuit Judge William Pryor wrote a concurring opinion attempting to harmonize his position that sexual orientation discrimination does not necessarily involve discrimination based on gender nonconformity with his earlier vote in *Glenn v. Brumby*, 663 F.3d 1312 (11th Cir. 2011) (presented *infra* at p. 185), that anti-transgender discrimination there constituted sex discrimination in violation of the Equal Protection Clause.

Besides setting up an arguably false dichotomy between actions based on sex and actions based on sexual orientation, *see, e.g., Evans*, 850 F.3d at 1259, Judge Pryor was at pains to limit the sweep of *Price Waterhouse*. On his reading, "*Price Waterhouse* and *Glenn* concerned claims that an employee's *behavior*, not status alone, deviated from a gender stereotype held by an employer." *Id.* (emphasis in original).

Dissenting Circuit Judge Robin Stacie Rosenbaum strongly disagreed. On the facts, she insisted that *Glenn* understood Vandy Beth Glenn to have been fired "solely for *being* transsexual—that is, for failing to conform to her employer's view of what a birth-assigned male should *be*." *Id.* at 1255 (emphases added). As for Pryor's reasoning, Rosenbaum argued that he invoked "an artificial line between discrimination because an employee has not behaved in a way that the employer thinks a person of that gender should, on the one hand, and discrimination because an employee is not the way that the employer thinks a person of that gender should be, on the other. As a matter of logic, no basis exists for this arbitrary line." *Id.* at 1266.

Is there any language in *Price Waterhouse* that supports this status/conduct limitation on the reach of its anti-sex-stereotyping principle? For one (sophisticated) examination of status/conduct distinctions in sexual orientation contexts out of a large literature, see Janet E. Halley, Romer *v.* Hardwick, 68 U. Colo. L. Rev. 429 (1997).

The Supreme Court ultimately rejected a reading of Title VII sex discrimination doctrine that would limit it to discriminatory treatments based on "*behavior*, not status alone" (to quote Judge Pryor), holding in *Bostock v. Clayton County, Georgia*, 140 S. Ct. 1731 (2020), Section D, *infra*, that "[a]n employer who fires an individual *for being* homosexual or transgender fires that person for traits or actions it would not have questioned in members of a different sex. Sex plays a necessary and undisguisable role in the decision, exactly what Title VII forbids." (emphasis added). The majority did not, however, engage with the reasoning of *Price Waterhouse*, although the dissent found "unpersuasive" the litigants' and amici's argument "that discrimination because of sexual orientation or gender identity violates Title VII because it constitutes prohibited discrimination on the basis of sex stereotypes."

5. The scholarly literature on *Price Waterhouse* is mammoth. For a small sample, see Mary Anne Case, *Legal Protections for the "Personal Best" of Each Employee: Title VII's Prohibition on Sex Discrimination, The Legacy of* Price Waterhouse v. Hopkins, *and the Prospect of ENDA*, 66 Stan. L. Rev. 1333 (2014); Alexandra Fiona McSpedon, Note, *Employer Perceptions of Trans Women's Sex and Behavior in Title VII Sex Stereotyping Claims: The Case for Reading* Price Waterhouse *as a Blanket Prohibition of Gender Policing by Employers*, 35 Cardozo L. Rev. 2505 (2014); Zachary R. Herz, Note, Price's *Progress: Sex Stereotyping and Its Potential for Antidiscrimination Law*, 124 Yale L.J. 396 (2014); Kimberly A. Yuracko, *Soul of a Woman: The Sex Stereotyping Prohibition at Work*, 161 U. Pa. L. Rev. 757 (2013); Chair R. Feldblum, *Gay People, Trans People, Women: Is It All About Gender?*, 17 N.Y.L. Sch. J. Hum. Rts. 623, 642 (2000); Jennifer L. Levi, *Paving the Road: A Charles Hamilton Houston Approach to Securing Trans Rights*, 7 Wm. & Mary J. Women & L. 5 (2000); Mary Anne C. Case, *Disaggregating Gender from Sex and Sexual Orientation: The Effeminate Man in the Law and Feminist Jurisprudence*, 105 Yale L.J. 1 (1995); Katherine M. Franke, *The Central Mistake of Sex Discrimination Law: The Disaggregation of Sex from Gender*, 144 U. Pa. L. Rev. 1 (1995); Francisco Valdes, *Queers, Sissies, Dykes, and Tomboys:*

Deconstructing the Conflation of "Sex," "Gender," and "Sexual Orientation" in Euro-American Law and Society, 83 Cal. L. Rev. 1 (1995).

Reading Guide for Oncale v. Sundowner Offshore Services

1. After sustained feminist campaigning and litigation, the Supreme Court embraced the view that sexual harassment can be a form of sex discrimination prohibited by Title VII. *See Meritor Savings Bank v. Vinson*, 477 U.S. 57 (1986). As noted in *Meritor*, the EEOC had issued Guidelines in 1980 specifying that "sexual harassment" is a form of sex discrimination. These included "[u]nwelcome sexual advances, requests for sexual favors, and other verbal or physical conduct of a sexual nature." 29 C.F.R. § 1604.11(a) (1985). The Guidelines recognized that the sexually harassing conduct could be linked to a condition of employment or promotion, called quid pro quo (Latin: "this for that") sexual harassment. They also recognized that the conduct also violated Title VII even if not linked to an economic quid pro quo, if it "has the purpose or effect of unreasonably interfering with an individual's work performance or creating an intimidating, hostile, or offensive working environment." *Meritor* approved the EEOC approach, but added requirements that the harassment must be "sufficiently severe or pervasive to alter the conditions of [the victim's] employment and create an abusive working environment." *Meritor* also held that sexual conduct may be unwelcome, and thus constitute sexual harassment, even if an employee's involvement in it was not involuntary. Because many lower courts had held that Title VII's ban on sex discrimination did not prohibit sexual orientation discrimination (which generally took the form of anti-lesbigay discrimination), *see* Discussion, note 2, *infra* at pp. 240–42, questions arose whether Title VII prohibited harassment of an employee by supervisors or co-employees of the same sex. This is the question that the Supreme Court took up in *Oncale v. Sundowner Offshore Services, Inc.*, 523 U.S. 75 (1998).

2. How does Justice Scalia's opinion for the Court treat the statutory text of Title VII? How did it treat the intent of Congress in 1964 when it enacted Title VII? Did he maintain that Congress intended to forbid same-sex sexual harassment?

3. The Court's opinion offers a few ways in which a plaintiff might attempt to satisfy the requirements of Title VII to challenge sexual harassment by someone of the same sex. Are these suggestions sound? (Are there any potential pitfalls to its partial reliance on "common sense"?) Are the Court's suggestions exhaustive, that is, are they the exclusive routes to establishing Title VII liability?

Joseph Oncale v. Sundowner Offshore Services, Inc.

523 U.S. 75 (1998)

Justice Scalia delivered the opinion of the Court.

This case presents the question whether workplace harassment can violate Title VII's prohibition against "discriminat[ion] . . . because of . . . sex," 42 U.S.C. § 2000e–2(a)(1), when the harasser and the harassed employee are of the same sex.

I

[P]etitioner Joseph Oncale. . . . was working for respondent Sundowner Offshore Services, Inc., on a Chevron U.S.A., Inc., oil platform in the Gulf of Mexico. He was employed as a roustabout on an eight-man crew which included respondents John Lyons, Danny Pippen, and Brandon Johnson. Lyons, the crane operator, and Pippen, the driller, had supervisory authority. [Oncale alleges that the harassment included Pippen and Johnson restraining him while Lyons placed his penis on Oncale's neck, on one occasion, and on another occasion on Oncale's arm; threats of rape by Lyons and Pippen; and the use of force by Lyons to push a bar of soap into Oncale's anus while Pippen restrained Oncale as he was showering on Sundowner premises.]

Oncale's complaints to supervisory personnel produced no remedial action; in fact, the company's Safety Compliance Clerk . . . told Oncale that Lyons and Pippen "picked [on] him all the time too," and called him a name suggesting homosexuality. Oncale eventually quit—asking that his pink slip reflect that he "voluntarily left due to sexual harassment and verbal abuse." When asked at his deposition why he left Sundowner, Oncale stated: "I felt that if I didn't leave my job, that I would be raped or forced to have sex."

Oncale filed a complaint against Sundowner in the United States District Court for the Eastern District of Louisiana, alleging that he was discriminated against in his employment because of his sex. Relying on the Fifth Circuit's decision in *Garcia v. Elf Atochem North America*, the District Court held that "Mr. Oncale, a male, has no cause of action under Title VII for harassment by male co-workers." On appeal, a panel of the Fifth Circuit concluded that *Garcia* was binding Circuit precedent, and affirmed. We granted certiorari.

II

Title VII of the Civil Rights Act of 1964 provides, in relevant part, that "[i]t shall be an unlawful employment practice for an employer . . . to discriminate against any individual with respect to his compensation, terms, conditions, or privileges of employment, because of such individual's race, color, religion, sex, or national origin." We have held that this not only covers "terms" and "conditions" in the narrow contractual sense, but "evinces a congressional intent to strike at the entire spectrum of disparate treatment of men and women in employment." *Meritor Savings Bank, FSB v. Vinson*, 477 U.S. 57 (1986). "When the workplace is permeated with discriminatory intimidation, ridicule, and insult that is sufficiently severe or pervasive to alter the conditions of the victim's employment and create an abusive working environment, Title VII is violated." *Harris v. Forklift Systems, Inc.*, 510 U.S. 17 (1993).

Title VII's prohibition of discrimination "because of . . . sex" protects men as well as women, *Newport News Shipbuilding & Dry Dock Co. v. EEOC*, 462 U.S. 669 (1983), and in the related context of racial discrimination in the workplace we have rejected any conclusive presumption that an employer will not discriminate against members of his own race. "Because of the many facets of human motivation, it would be unwise to presume as a matter of law that human beings of one definable group will not discriminate against other members of their group." *Castaneda v. Partida*, 430 U.S. 482 (1977). In *Johnson v. Transportation Agency, Santa Clara Cnty.*, 480 U.S. 616 (1987), a male employee claimed that his employer discriminated against him because of his sex when it preferred a female employee for promotion. Although we ultimately rejected the claim on other grounds, we did not consider it significant that the supervisor who made that decision was also a man. If our precedents leave any doubt on the question, we hold today that nothing in Title VII necessarily bars a claim of discrimination "because of . . . sex" merely because the plaintiff and the defendant (or the person charged with acting on behalf of the defendant) are of the same sex.

Courts have had little trouble with that principle in cases like *Johnson*, where an employee claims to have been passed over for a job or promotion. But when the issue arises in the context of a "hostile environment" sexual harassment claim, the state and federal courts have taken a bewildering variety of stances. Some, like the Fifth Circuit in this case, have held that same-sex sexual harassment claims are never cognizable under Title VII. Other decisions say that such claims are actionable only if the plaintiff can prove that the harasser is homosexual (and thus presumably motivated by sexual desire). Still others suggest that workplace harassment that is sexual in content is always actionable, regardless of the harasser's sex, sexual orientation, or motivations.

We see no justification in the statutory language or our precedents for a categorical rule excluding same-sex harassment claims from the coverage of Title VII. As some courts have observed, male-on-male sexual harassment in the workplace was assuredly not the principal evil Congress was concerned with when it enacted Title VII. But statutory prohibitions often go beyond the principal evil to cover reasonably comparable evils, and it is ultimately the provisions of our laws rather than the principal concerns of our legislators by which we are governed. Title VII prohibits "discriminat[ion] . . . because of . . . sex" in the "terms" or "conditions" of employment. Our holding that this includes sexual harassment must extend to sexual harassment of any kind that meets the statutory requirements.

Respondents and their *amici* contend that recognizing liability for same-sex harassment will transform Title VII into a general civility code for the American workplace. But that risk is no greater for same-sex than for opposite-sex harassment, and is adequately met by careful attention to the requirements of the statute.

Title VII does not prohibit all verbal or physical harassment in the workplace; it is directed only at "*discriminat[ion]* . . . because of . . . sex." We have never held that workplace harassment, even harassment between men and women, is automatically discrimination because of sex merely because the words used have sexual content or connotations. "The critical issue, Title VII's text indicates, is whether members of one sex are exposed to disadvantageous terms or conditions of employment to which members of the other sex are not exposed." *Harris* (Ginsburg, J., concurring).

Courts and juries have found the inference of discrimination easy to draw in most male-female sexual harassment situations, because the challenged conduct typically involves explicit or implicit proposals of sexual activity; it is reasonable to assume those proposals would not have been made to someone of the same sex. The same chain of inference would be available to a plaintiff alleging same-sex harassment, if there were credible evidence that the harasser was homosexual. But harassing conduct need not be motivated by sexual desire to support an inference of discrimination on the basis of sex. A trier of fact might reasonably find such discrimination, for example, if a female victim is harassed in such sex-specific and derogatory terms by another woman as to make it clear that the harasser is motivated by general hostility to the presence of women in the workplace. A same-sex harassment plaintiff may also, of course, offer direct comparative evidence about how the alleged harasser treated members of both sexes in a mixed-sex workplace. Whatever evidentiary route the plaintiff chooses to follow, he or she must always prove that the conduct at issue was not merely tinged with offensive sexual connotations, but actually constituted "*discrimina[tion]* . . . because of . . . sex."

And there is another requirement that prevents Title VII from expanding into a general civility code: As we emphasized in *Meritor* and *Harris*, the statute does not reach genuine but innocuous differences in the ways men and women routinely interact with members of the same sex and of the opposite sex. The prohibition of harassment on the basis of sex requires neither asexuality nor androgyny in the workplace; it forbids only behavior so objectively offensive as to alter the "conditions" of the victim's employment. "Conduct that is not severe or pervasive enough to create an objectively hostile or abusive work environment—an environment that a reasonable person would find hostile or abusive—is beyond Title VII's purview." *Harris*. We have always regarded that requirement as crucial, and as sufficient to ensure that courts and juries do not mistake ordinary socializing in the workplace—such as male-on-male horseplay or intersexual flirtation—for discriminatory "conditions of employment."

We have emphasized, moreover, that the objective severity of harassment should be judged from the perspective of a reasonable person in the plaintiff's position, considering "all the circumstances." *Harris*. In same-sex (as in all) harassment cases, that inquiry requires careful consideration of the social context in which particular behavior occurs and is experienced by its target. A professional football player's working environment is not severely or pervasively abusive, for example, if the coach smacks him on the buttocks as he heads onto the field—even if the same behavior would reasonably be experienced as abusive by the coach's secretary (male or female) back at the office. The real social impact of workplace behavior often depends on a constellation of surrounding circumstances, expectations, and relationships which are not fully captured by a simple recitation of the words used or the physical acts performed. Common sense, and an appropriate sensitivity to social context, will enable courts and juries to distinguish between simple teasing or roughhousing among members of the same sex, and conduct which a reasonable person in the plaintiff's position would find severely hostile or abusive.

III

Because we conclude that sex discrimination consisting of same-sex sexual harassment is actionable under Title VII, the judgment of the Court of Appeals for the Fifth Circuit is reversed, and the case is remanded for further proceedings consistent with this opinion.

It is so ordered.

[A concurring statement by Justice Thomas is omitted.]

Discussion

1. Was the Court right to prioritize the text of Title VII over the intent or expectations of its congressional drafters? For an influential article arguing that statutes should "be interpreted . . . in light of their present societal, political, and legal context," see William N. Eskridge, Jr., *Dynamic Statutory Interpretation*, 135 U. Pa. L. Rev. 1479 (1987). For a strong defense of applying such an evolutionary interpretive approach to adapt laws to apply to gay men and lesbians in a wide range of legal contexts, see Heidi A. Sorensen, Note, *A New Gay Rights Agenda? Dynamic Statutory Interpretation and Sexual Orientation Discrimination*, 81 Geo. L.J. 2105 (1993). For a similar, textualist argument that Title VII's ban on sex discrimination forbids anti-transgender discrimination, building from *Oncale* and *Price Waterhouse* and relying on evolution in the common meaning of "sex" since 1964, see Jillian Todd Weiss, *Transgender Identity, Textualism, and the Supreme Court: What Is the "Plain Meaning" of "Sex" in Title VII of the Civil Rights Act of 1964?*, 18 Temple Pol. & C.R. L. Rev. 574 (2009).

2. The Supreme Court addressed whether Title VII's ban on sex discrimination is violated when an employer fires workers because of their sexual orientation or transgender status—holding that it is—in *Bostock v. Clayton County, Georgia*, 140 S. Ct. 1731 (2020). In its analysis, the Court's opinion seemingly rejected a dynamic mode of statutory interpretation, insisting that the words of the statute must be interpreted as they would have been understood when Title VII was enacted in 1964, although the dissent believed the majority not to have done that. *Bostock* is presented in Section D, *infra*.

C. Sex Stereotyping

By ruling that Title VII did not simply forbid discrimination against women as a class or discrimination against men as a class, but forbade any sex discrimination based on sex stereotyping, *Price Waterhouse* cleared the way for courts to hold that anti-transgender discrimination did in fact constitute sex discrimination under Title VII, *pace Ulane*. Courts did not immediately take up that invitation. In the first reported post-*Price Waterhouse* case presenting a claim that anti-transgender discrimination violated Title VII, *Dobre v. National Railroad Passenger Corporation* ("*Amtrak*"), 850 F. Supp. 284 (E.D. Pa. 1993), the district court rejected transgender woman Andria Adams Dobre's Title VII claim against her employer for discriminating against her after she started her transition and informed her employer of it. The district court adhered to *Ulane*'s position on Title VII without even mentioning *Price Waterhouse* in its opinion. Some subsequent opinions did the same. *See, e.g., James v. Ranch Mart Hardware, Inc.*, No. 94-2235-KHV, 1994 WL 731517 (D. Kan. Dec. 23, 1994), and 881 F. Supp. 478 (D. Kansas 1995); *Cox v. Denny's, Inc.*, No. 98-1085-CIV-J-16B, 1999 WL 1317785 (M.D. Fla. Dec. 22, 1999). In one case at the start of the new millennium, *Broadus v. State Farm Ins. Co.*, No. 98-4254CVC-SOWECF, 2000 WL 1585257 (W.D. Mo. Oct. 11, 2000), the court held that transgender man Kylar Broadus's Title VII sex stereotyping harassment claim failed because he had not established that his treatment by his supervisor was sufficiently severe and pervasive to amount to a discriminatory hostile environment. The district judge acknowledged *Price Waterhouse* but did not resolve whether, after that Supreme Court decision, anti-transgender discrimination and harassment violated Title VII, merely assuming for sake of argument that it did without further analysis. (For first person discussion of Broadus's case and the emergence of sex stereotyping as a route to protection for transgender employees, see Kylar W. Broadus, *The Evolution of Employment Discrimination Protection for Transgender People, in* Paisley Currah, Richard M. Juang, and Shannon Price Minter, Transgender Rights 93–101 (Minneapolis, MN: Univ. of Minnesota Press 2006).)

Note on Early Sex Stereotyping Rulings

The first signs of success of the sex-stereotyping argument against anti-transgender discrimination came in statutory bans on sex discrimination other than Title VII and Title VII cases not involving transgender plaintiffs. In 2000, the U.S. Court of Appeals for the Ninth Circuit upheld a transgender woman inmate's right to sue for sexual assault under the Gender Motivated Violence Act in *Schwenk v. Hartford*, 204 F.3d 1187 (9th Cir. 2000). Transgender woman Crystal Schwenk, an inmate in a men's prison, alleged that a guard subjected her to an escalating series of unwelcome sexual advances and harassment that culminated in a sexual assault. She sued, relying in part on the Gender Motivated Violence Act (GMVA or Act), which provides a cause of action for victims of "crime[s] of violence committed because of gender or on the basis of gender, and due, at least in part, to an animus based on the victim's gender." 42 U.S.C. § 13981(c)." Following *Price Waterhouse*'s treatment of Title VII and the codification thereof in the Civil Rights Act of 1991, Pub.L. No. 102-166, 105 Stat. 1071 § 107(a), codified at 42 U.S.C.A. § 2000e-2(m), the court in *Schwenk* ruled that gender need only be a motivating factor for liability under the GMVA. Recognizing that some courts had treated transsexual persons as outside the protection of Title VII's ban on sex discrimination, the court concluded that "[t]he initial judicial approach taken in cases such as *Holloway* [*see* Note, *supra*, and *Ulane*, *supra*] has been overruled by the logic and language of *Price Water-house*." The court of appeals explained that "[w]hat matters, for purposes of this part of the *Price Waterhouse* analysis, is that in the mind of the perpetrator the discrimination is related to the sex of the victim: here, for example, the perpetrator's actions stem from the fact that he believed that the victim was a man who 'failed to act like' one." (While many subsequent cases quote or discuss *Schwenk*, be aware that the Supreme Court subsequently held the GMVA not to be within Congress's constitutional authority to enact. *See* Note on *Schwenk v. Hartford*, Chapter 12, Section A, Subsection 1, *infra*.)

The same year as *Schwenk*, the Court of Appeals for the First Circuit ruled in favor of a transgender woman who had been labeled male at birth and named Lucas Rosa, *see* Katharine M. Franke, Lucas Rosa v. Park West Bank and Trust Company, 7 Mich. J. Gender & L. 141, 143 & n.1 (2001), in *Rosa v. Park West Bank & Trust Co.*, 214 F.3d 213 (1st Cir. 2000). The bank had refused to give a credit application to Rosa unless she returned home and changed from the conventionally female attire she was wearing to more conventionally male apparel. Rosa sued under the federal Equal Credit Opportunity Act (ECOA), 15 U.S.C. §§ 1691-1691f, which bans discrimination "with respect to any aspect of a credit transaction[,] on the basis of race, color, religion, national origin, sex or marital status, or age." 15 U.S.C. § 1691(a). The district court granted the bank's motion to dismiss, but the Court of Appeals reversed. After noting that it relies on Title VII case law for guidance in ECOA cases, including *Price Waterhouse* and *Oncale*, the court held that if the proof ended up showing "that Rosa did not receive the loan application because he was a man, whereas a similarly situated woman would have received the loan application[,]" that would establish unlawful sex discrimination.

The gender stereotyping theory of *Price Waterhouse* first proved expansive in cases under Title VII itself outside the context of transgender workers. The year following *Schwenk* and *Rosa*, the U.S. Court of Appeals for the Ninth Circuit decided *Nichols v. Azteca Restaurant Enterprises, Inc.*, 256 F.3d 864 (9th Cir. 2001). Host and food server Antonio Sanchez "was subjected to a relentless campaign of insults, name-calling, and vulgarities. . . . Male co-workers . . . taunted him in Spanish and English as, among other things, a 'faggot' and a 'fucking female whore.'" He complained repeatedly to the company and was eventually terminated. He sued under Title VII, arguing that the harassment was "because of" sex and his termination in retaliation for his complaints. The Court of Appeals concluded that the sexual harassment was "because of" Sanchez's sex. Citing *Schwenk*, the opinion agreed with him that *Price Waterhouse*, which used Title VII to protect a woman perceived as too masculine, also protects "a man who is discriminated against for acting too feminine." As the court explained:

> At its essence, the systematic abuse directed at Sanchez reflected a belief that Sanchez did not act as a man should act. Sanchez was attacked for walking and carrying his tray "like a woman" — *i.e.*, for having feminine mannerisms. Sanchez was derided for not having sexual intercourse with a waitress who was his friend. Sanchez's male co-workers and one of his supervisors repeatedly reminded Sanchez that he did not conform to their gender-based stereotypes, referring to him as "she" and "her." And, the most vulgar name-calling directed at Sanchez was cast in female terms. We conclude that this verbal abuse was closely linked to gender.

Four months later, a federal district court ruled that a transgender woman could pursue a claim for sex discrimination under Title VII based on the sex stereotyping reasoning of *Price Waterhouse. See Doe v. United Consumer Fin. Servs.*, 2001 WL 34350174, 2001 U.S. Dist. LEXIS 25509 (N.D. Ohio Nov. 9, 2001). The federal Courts of Appeals began to weigh in on the relevance of sex stereotyping to antitransgender discrimination in a published opinion about three years later.

Reading Guide for Smith v. City of Salem

1. The core of the analysis in *Smith v. City of Salem* is the sex stereotyping reasoning in Part II.A.1 of the opinion. How does the court describe the anti-transgender actions that would violate Title VII as sex stereotyping? Is there *any* anti-transgender discrimination that would not involve sex stereotyping? The first opinion issued by the Sixth Circuit Court of Appeals in *Smith*, 369 F.3d 912 (6th Cir. June 1, 2004), seemed to answer that question in the negative. The relevant paragraph, 369 F.3d at 921–22, however, was subsequently deleted by the court, *see* 378 F.3d 566, 575 (6th Cir. Aug. 5, 2004), as noted by Anna Kirkland, *What's at Stake in Transgender Discrimination as Sex Discrimination*, 32 Signs 83 (2006). The court's original discussion is presented in a Note, *infra* at p. 195.

2. What *evidence* of sex discrimination predicated upon sex stereotyping does the court hold Jimmie Smith alleged in her complaint?

3. How does *Smith* treat the viability of *Ulane v. Eastern Airlines* as precedent?

Smith v. City of Salem, Ohio

378 F.3d 566 (6th Cir. 2004), superseding 369 F.3d 912 (June 1, 2004)

[Jimmie Smith was represented on the briefing by private counsel including Randi A. Barnabee.]

Before COLE and GILMAN, Circuit Judges; SCHWARZER, Senior District Judge.*

Amended Opinion

COLE, Circuit Judge.

. . . .

I. Background

[According to the complaint filed in federal court by transgender woman Jimmie L. Smith, Smith was a lieutenant in the fire department of the city of Salem, Ohio. Smith, "biologically and by birth a male," was transsexual and had been diagnosed with Gender Identity Disorder ("GID"), which the American Psychiatric Association described as a disjunction between an individual's sexual organs and sexual identity. AMERICAN PSYCHIATRIC ASSOCIATION, DIAGNOSTIC AND STATISTICAL MANUAL OF MENTAL DISORDERS 576–582 (4th ed. [text revision] 2000). After receiving the diagnosis, Smith began "expressing a more feminine appearance on a full-time basis"—including at work—in accordance with international medical protocols for treating GID. Soon thereafter, Smith's co-workers began questioning her—in the litigation Smith's counsel, opposing counsel, and the courts used male pronouns for Smith, which will be retained here where the opinion is quoted—about her appearance and commenting that her appearance and mannerisms were not "masculine enough." "In order to have Smith's immediate supervisor, Defendant Thomas Eastek, be able to respond to her co-workers, Smith informed Eastek about her diagnosis and treatment, indicating that it likely would eventually include 'complete physical transformation from male to female,' and offering to answer any questions Eastek might have concerning her appearance and manner."

[After Eastek broke his promise to Smith of confidentiality and promptly told Defendant Walter Greenamyer, Chief of the Fire Department, about Smith's behavior and GID, Greenamyer met with the Law Director for the City, intending to use Smith's transsexualism and its manifestations to terminate her employment. They arranged an April 18, 2001 meeting of the City's executive body to discuss Smith and devise a plan for terminating her employment; they did not comply with the state law procedural requirements to hold such a meeting. Also present was Salem Safety Director Henry L. Willard, deceased by the time of the Sixth Circuit decision here, who was never a named defendant in this action. During the meeting, the defendants agreed to arrange for the Salem Civil Service Commission to require

---

* The Honorable William W. Schwarzer, Senior United States District Judge for the Northern District of California, sitting by designation.

Smith to undergo three separate psychological evaluations with physicians of the City's choosing. They hoped Smith would either resign or refuse to comply, in which case they planned to fire Smith for insubordination. Willard, who remained silent during the meeting, telephoned Smith afterwards to inform her of the plan, calling Defendants' scheme a "witch hunt."

[Two days later Smith's counsel telephoned one defendant to advise him of Smith's legal representation and the potential legal consequences for the City if it followed through on the plan. Two more days later, Smith received a "right to sue" letter from the U.S. Equal Employment Opportunity Commission. Four days after that, on April 26, 2001, Chief Greenamyer suspended Smith for one 24-hour shift, based on an alleged infraction of a City and/or Fire Department policy.

At a subsequent appeal before the Salem Civil Service Commission, Smith argued the suspension was a result of selective enforcement in retaliation for her having obtained a lawyer in response to Defendants' plan to fire Smith. Smith tried to present testimony from witnesses regarding the April 18, 2001 meeting, but the Commission refused to allow any such testimony, despite the fact that Ohio law permitted Smith to introduce evidence of disparate treatment and selective enforcement in her hearing before the Commission.]

The Commission ultimately upheld Smith's suspension. Smith appealed to the Columbiana County Court of Common Pleas, which reversed the suspension, finding that "[b]ecause the regulation [that Smith was alleged to have violated] was not effective[,] [Smith] could not be charged with violation of it."

Smith then filed suit in the federal district court. In his complaint, he [*sic*] asserted claims of sex discrimination and retaliation under Title VII [of the Civil Rights Act of 1964, 42 U.S.C. § 2000e *et seq.*], along with claims pursuant to 42 U.S.C. § 1983 and state law claims of invasion of privacy and civil conspiracy. [The district court dismissed the federal claims, granting judgment on the pleadings to the defendants.] The district judge also dismissed the state law claims without prejudice, having declined to exercise supplemental jurisdiction over them. . . .

II. Analysis

On appeal, Smith contends that the district court erred in holding that: (1) he failed to state a claim of sex stereotyping; (2) Title VII protection is unavailable to transsexuals [*sic*]; (3) even if he had stated a claim of sex stereotyping, he failed to demonstrate that he suffered an adverse employment action; and (4) he failed to state a claim based on the deprivation of a constitutional or federal statutory right, pursuant to 42 U.S.C. § 1983. . . .

A. Title VII

The parties disagree over two issues pertaining to Smith's Title VII claims: (1) whether Smith properly alleged a claim of sex stereotyping, in violation of the Supreme Court's pronouncements in *Price Waterhouse v. Hopkins,* 490 U.S. 228 (1989); and (2) whether Smith alleged that he suffered an adverse employment action.

[We] affirmatively find that Smith has made out a *prima facie* case for both claims. To establish a *prima facie* case of employment discrimination pursuant to Title VII, Smith must show that: (1) he is a member of a protected class; (2) he suffered an adverse employment action; (3) he was qualified for the position in question; and (4) he was treated differently from similarly situated individuals outside of his protected class. *Perry v. McGinnis,* 209 F.3d 597 (6th Cir. 2000). Smith is a member of a protected class. His complaint asserts that he is a male with Gender Identity Disorder, and Title VII's prohibition of discrimination "because of . . . sex" protects men as well as women. *Newport News Shipbuilding and Dry Dock Co. v. E.E.O.C.,* 462 U.S. 669 (1983). The complaint also alleges both that Smith was qualified for the position in question — he had been a lieutenant in the Fire Department for seven years without any negative incidents — and that he would not have been treated differently, on account of his non-masculine behavior and GID, had he been a woman instead of a man.

To establish a *prima facie* case of retaliation pursuant to Title VII, a plaintiff must show that: (1) he engaged in an activity protected by Title VII; (2) the defendant knew he engaged in this protected activity; (3) thereafter, the defendant took an employment action adverse to him; and (4) there was a causal connection between the protected activity and the adverse employment action. *DiCarlo v. Potter,* 358 F.3d 408 (6th Cir. 2004). Smith's complaint satisfies the first two requirements by explaining how he sought legal counsel after learning of the Salem executive body's April 18, 2001 meeting concerning his employment; how his attorney [advised] Defendants of Smith's representation; and how Smith filed a complaint with the EEOC concerning Defendants' meeting and intended actions. ["Although] no one factor is dispositive in establishing a causal connection, evidence . . . that the adverse action was taken shortly after the plaintiff's exercise of protected rights is relevant to causation." *Nguyen v. City of Cleveland,* 229 F.3d 559 (6th Cir. 2000); *see also . . . Miller v. Fairchild Indus., Inc.,* 797 F.2d 727 (9th Cir. 1986) ("Causation sufficient to establish a prima facie case of unlawful retaliation may be inferred from the proximity in time between the protected action and the allegedly retaliatory discharge"). Here, Smith was suspended . . . just days after he engaged in protected activity by receiving his "right to sue" letter from the EEOC, which occurred four days before the suspension, and by his attorney contacting Mayor DeJane, which occurred six days before the suspension. The temporal proximity between the events is significant enough to constitute direct evidence of a causal connection for the purpose of satisfying Smith's burden of demonstrating a *prima facie* case.

We turn now to examining whether Smith properly alleged a claim of sex stereotyping, in violation of the Supreme Court's pronouncements in *Price Waterhouse v. Hopkins,* and whether Smith alleged that he suffered an adverse employment action.

1. Sex Stereotyping

Title VII . . . provides, in relevant part, that "[i]t shall be an unlawful employment practice for an employer . . . to discriminate against any individual with respect to his compensation, terms, conditions, or privileges of employment because of such individual's race, color, religion, sex, or national origin." 42 U.S.C. § 2000e-2(a).

In his complaint, Smith asserts Title VII claims of retaliation and employment discrimination "because of . . . sex." The district court dismissed Smith's Title VII claims on the ground that he failed to state a claim for sex stereotyping pursuant to *Price Waterhouse*. The district court implied that Smith's claim was disingenuous, stating that he merely "invokes the term-of-art created by *Price Waterhouse,* that is, 'sex-stereotyping,'" as an end run around his "real" claim, which, the district court stated, was "based upon his transsexuality." The district court then held that "Title VII does not prohibit discrimination based on an individual's transsexualism."

Relying on *Price Waterhouse*—which held that Title VII's prohibition of discrimination "because of . . . sex" bars gender discrimination, including discrimination based on sex stereotypes—Smith contends on appeal that he was a victim of discrimination "because of . . . sex" both because of his gender non-conforming conduct and, more generally, because of his identification as a transsexual [*sic*].

We first address whether Smith has stated a claim for relief, pursuant to *Price Waterhouse*'s prohibition of sex stereotyping, based on his gender non-conforming behavior and appearance. In *Price Waterhouse,* the plaintiff, a female senior manager in an accounting firm, was denied partnership in the firm, in part, because she was considered "macho." She was advised that she could improve her chances for partnership if she were to take "a course at charm school," "walk more femininely, talk more femininely, dress more femininely, wear make-up, have her hair styled, and wear jewelry." Six members of the Court agreed that such comments bespoke gender discrimination, holding that Title VII barred not just discrimination because Hopkins was a woman, but also sex stereotyping—that is, discrimination because she failed to *act* like a woman. *Id.* (plurality opinion of four Justices); *id.* (White, J., concurring); *id.* (O'Connor, J., concurring) (accepting plurality's sex stereotyping analysis and characterizing the "failure to conform to [gender] stereotypes" as a discriminatory criterion; concurring separately to clarify the separate issues of causation and allocation of the burden of proof). . . . The Supreme Court made clear that in the context of Title VII, discrimination because of "sex" includes gender discrimination: "In the context of sex stereotyping, an employer who acts on the basis of a belief that a woman cannot be aggressive, or that she must not be, has acted on the basis of gender." *Price Waterhouse.* The Court emphasized that "we are beyond the day when an employer could evaluate employees by assuming or insisting that they matched the stereotype associated with their group."

 Smith contends that the same theory of sex stereotyping applies here. His complaint sets forth the conduct and mannerisms which, he alleges, did not conform with his employers' and co-workers' sex stereotypes of how a man should look and behave. Smith's complaint states that, after being diagnosed with GID, he began to express a more feminine appearance and manner on a regular basis, including at work. The complaint states that his co-workers began commenting on his appearance and mannerisms as not being masculine enough; and that his supervisors at the Fire Department and other municipal agents knew about this allegedly unmasculine conduct and appearance. The complaint then describes a high-level meeting among Smith's supervisors and other municipal officials regarding his employment. Defendants allegedly schemed to compel Smith's resignation by forcing him to undergo multiple psychological evaluations of his gender non-conforming behavior. The complaint makes clear that these meetings took place soon after Smith assumed a more feminine appearance and manner and after his conversation about this with Eastek. In addition, the complaint alleges that Smith was suspended for twenty-four hours for allegedly violating an unenacted municipal policy, and that the suspension was ordered in retaliation for his pursuing legal remedies after he had been informed about Defendants' plan to intimidate him into resigning. In short, Smith claims that the discrimination he experienced was based on his failure to conform to sex stereotypes by expressing less masculine, and more feminine mannerisms and appearance.

Having alleged that his failure to conform to sex stereotypes concerning how a man should look and behave was the driving force behind Defendants' actions, Smith has sufficiently pleaded claims of sex stereotyping and gender discrimination.

In so holding, we find that the district court erred in relying on a series of pre-*Price Waterhouse* cases from other federal appellate courts holding that transsexuals, as a class, are not entitled to Title VII protection because "Congress had a narrow view of sex in mind" and "never considered nor intended that [Title VII] apply to anything other than the traditional concept of sex." *Ulane v. Eastern Airlines, Inc.,* 742 F.2d 1081 (7th Cir. 1984); *see also Holloway v. Arthur Andersen & Co.,* 566 F.2d 659 (9th Cir. 1977) (refusing to extend protection of Title VII to transsexuals because discrimination against transsexuals is based on "gender" rather than "sex"). It is true that, in the past, federal appellate courts regarded Title VII as barring discrimination based only on "sex" (referring to an individual's anatomical and biological characteristics), but not on "gender" (referring to socially-constructed norms associated with a person's sex). *See, e.g., Ulane* (construing "sex" in Title VII narrowly to mean only anatomical sex rather than gender); *Sommers v. Budget Mktg., Inc.,* 667 F.2d 748 (8th Cir. 1982) (holding that transsexuals are not protected by Title VII because the "plain meaning" must be ascribed to the term "sex" in the absence of clear congressional intent to do otherwise); *Holloway* (refusing to extend protection of Title VII to transsexuals because discrimination against transsexualism is based on "gender" rather than "sex;" and "sex" should be given its traditional definition based on the anatomical characteristics dividing "organisms" and "living beings" into male and female). In this earlier jurisprudence, male-to-female transsexuals (who were the plaintiffs in *Ulane, Sommers,* and *Holloway*)—as biological males whose outward behavior and emotional identity did not conform to socially-prescribed expectations of masculinity—were denied Title VII protection by courts because they were considered victims of "gender" rather than "sex" discrimination.

However, the approach in *Holloway, Sommers,* and *Ulane*—and by the district court in this case—has been eviscerated by *Price Waterhouse. See Schwenk v. Hartford,* 204 F.3d 1187 (9th Cir. 2000) ("The initial judicial approach taken in cases such as *Holloway* [and *Ulane*] has been overruled by the logic and language of *Price Waterhouse*"). By holding that Title VII protected a woman who failed to conform to social expectations concerning how a woman should look and behave, the Supreme Court established that Title VII's reference to "sex" encompasses both the biological differences between men and women, and gender discrimination, that is, discrimination based on a failure to conform to stereotypical gender norms. *See Price Waterhouse*; *see also Schwenk* (stating that Title VII encompasses instances in which "the perpetrator's actions stem from the fact that he believed that the victim was a man who 'failed to act like' one" and that "sex" under Title VII encompasses both the anatomical differences between men and women and gender); *Rene v. MGM Grand Hotel, Inc.*, 305 F.3d 1061 (9th Cir. 2002) (en banc) (Pregerson, J., concurring) (noting that the Ninth Circuit had previously found that "same-sex gender stereotyping of the sort suffered by [Medina] Rene — *i.e.* gender stereotyping of a male gay employee by his male co-workers" constituted actionable harassment under Title VII and concluding that "[t]he repeated testimony that his co-workers treated Rene, in a variety of ways, 'like a woman' constitutes ample evidence of gender stereotyping"); *Bibby v. Philadelphia Coca Cola Bottling Co.*, 260 F.3d 257 (3d Cir. 2001) (stating that a plaintiff may be able to prove a claim of sex discrimination by showing that the "harasser's conduct was motivated by a belief that the victim did not conform to the stereotypes of his or her gender"); *Nichols v. Azteca Rest. Enters., Inc.*, 256 F.3d 86 (9th Cir. 2001) (holding that harassment "based upon the perception that [the plaintiff] is effeminate" is discrimination because of sex, in violation of Title VII), *overruling DeSantis v. Pac. Tel. & Tel. Co., Inc.*, 608 F.2d 327 (9th Cir. 1979); *Doe v. Belleville*, 119 F.3d 563 (7th Cir. 1997) (holding that "Title VII does not permit an employee to be treated adversely because his or her appearance or conduct does not conform to stereotypical gender roles" and explaining that "a man who is harassed because his voice is soft, his physique is slight, his hair long, or because in some other respect he exhibits his masculinity in a way that does not meet his coworkers' idea of how men are to appear and behave, is harassed 'because of his sex'"), *vacated and remanded on other grounds*, 523 U.S. 1001 (1998).

After *Price Waterhouse*, an employer who discriminates against women because, for instance, they do not wear dresses or makeup, is engaging in sex discrimination because the discrimination would not occur but for the victim's sex. It follows that employers who discriminate against men because they *do* wear dresses and makeup, or otherwise act femininely, are also engaging in sex discrimination, because the discrimination would not occur but for the victim's sex. *See, e.g., Nichols* (Title VII sex discrimination and hostile work environment claim upheld where plaintiff's male co-workers and supervisors repeatedly referred to him as "she" and "her" and where co-workers mocked him for walking and carrying his serving tray "like a woman"); *Higgins v. New Balance Athletic Shoe, Inc.*, 194 F.3d 252 (1st Cir. 1999) ("[J]ust as a woman can ground an action on a claim that men discriminated against her because she did not meet stereotyped expectations of femininity, a man can ground a claim on evidence that other men discriminated against him because he did not meet stereotypical expectations of masculinity" (internal citation omitted)); *see also Rosa v. Park West Bank & Trust Co.*, 214 F.3d 213 (1st Cir. 2000) (applying *Price Waterhouse* and Title VII jurisprudence to an Equal Credit Opportunity Act claim and reinstating claim on behalf of biologically male plaintiff who alleged that he was denied an opportunity to apply for a loan because was dressed in "traditionally feminine attire").

Yet some courts have held that this latter form of discrimination is of a different and somehow more permissible kind. For instance, the man who acts in ways typically associated with women is not described as engaging in the same activity as a woman who acts in ways typically associated with women, but is instead described as engaging in the different activity of being a transsexual (or in some instances, a homosexual [*sic*] or transvestite). Discrimination against the transsexual is then found not to be discrimination "because of . . . sex," but rather, discrimination against the plaintiff's unprotected status or mode of self-identification. In other words, these courts superimpose classifications such as "transsexual" on a plaintiff, and then legitimize discrimination based on the plaintiff's gender non-conformity by formalizing the non-conformity into an ostensibly unprotected classification. *See, e.g., Dillon v. Frank*, No. 90-2290, 1992 WL 5436 (6th Cir. Jan. 15, 1992).

[Such] analyses cannot be reconciled with *Price Waterhouse*, which does not make Title VII protection against sex stereotyping conditional or provide any reason to exclude Title VII coverage for non sex-stereotypical behavior simply because the person is a transsexual. As such, discrimination against a plaintiff who is a transsexual — and therefore fails to act and/or identify with his or her gender — is no different from the discrimination directed against Ann Hopkins in *Price Waterhouse*, who, in sex-stereotypical terms, did not act like a woman. Sex stereotyping based on a person's gender non-conforming behavior is impermissible discrimination, irrespective of the cause of that behavior; a label, such as "transsexual," is not fatal to a sex discrimination claim where the victim has suffered discrimination because of his or her gender non-conformity. Accordingly, we hold that Smith has stated a claim for relief pursuant to Title VII's prohibition of sex discrimination.

Finally, we note that, in its opinion, the district court repeatedly places the term "sex stereotyping" in quotation marks and refers to it as a "term of art" used by Smith to disingenuously plead discrimination because of transsexualism. Similarly, Defendants refer to sex stereotyping as "the *Price Waterhouse* loophole." These characterizations are almost identical to the treatment that Price Waterhouse itself gave sex stereotyping in its briefs to the U.S. Supreme Court. As we do now, the Supreme Court noted the practice with disfavor, stating:

> In the specific context of sex stereotyping, an employer who acts on the basis of a belief that a woman cannot be aggressive, or that she must not be, has acted on the basis of gender. Although the parties do not overtly dispute this last proposition, the placement by Price Waterhouse of "sex stereotyping" in quotation marks throughout its brief seems to us an insinuation

either that such stereotyping was not present in this case or that it lacks legal relevance. We reject both possibilities.

Price Waterhouse.

2. Adverse Employment Action

Despite having dismissed Smith's Title VII claim for failure to state a claim of sex stereotyping—a finding we have just rejected—the district court nevertheless addressed the merits of Smith's Title VII claims *arguendo*. [Common] to both the employment discrimination and retaliation claims is a showing of an adverse employment action, which is defined as a "materially adverse change in the terms and conditions of [plaintiff's] employment." *Hollins v. Atlantic Co.*, 188 F.3d 652 (6th Cir. 1999). [Examples] of adverse employment actions include firing, failing to promote, reassignment with significantly different responsibilities, a material loss of benefits, suspensions, and other indices unique to a particular situation. Here, the Fire Department suspended Smith for twenty-four hours. Because Smith works in twenty-four hour shifts, that twenty-four hour suspension was the equivalent of three eight-hour days for the average worker, or, approximately 60% of a forty-hour work week. Pursuant to the liberal notice pleading requirements set forth in [Federal Rule of Civil Procedure 8], this allegation, at this phase of the litigation, is sufficient to satisfy the adverse employment requirement of both an employment discrimination and retaliation claim pursuant to Title VII.

It is irrelevant that Smith's suspension was ultimately reversed by the Court of Common Pleas after he challenged the suspension's legality. In [*White v. Burlington Northern & Sante Fe Ry. Co.*, 364 F.3d 789 (6th Cir. 2004) (en banc)], this Court recently joined the majority of other circuits in rejecting the "ultimate employment decision" standard whereby a negative employment action is not considered an "adverse employment action" for Title VII purposes when the decision is subsequently reversed by the employer, putting the plaintiff in the position he would have been in absent the negative action. Even if the "ultimate employment decision" standard were still viable, the district court erred in concluding that, because the Court of Common Pleas overturned the suspension, it was not an adverse employment action. There is no legal authority for the proposition that reversal by a *judicial* body—as opposed to the employer—declassifies a suspension as an adverse employment action.

Accordingly, Smith has stated an adverse employment action and, therefore, satisfied all of the elements necessary to allege a *prima facie* case of employment discrimination and retaliation pursuant to Title VII. We therefore reverse the district court's grant of judgment on the pleadings to Defendants with respect to those claims.

B. 42 U.S.C. § 1983 Claims

The district court also dismissed Smith's claims pursuant to 42 U.S.C. § 1983 on the ground that he failed to state a claim based on the deprivation of a constitutional or federal statutory right.

42 U.S.C. § 1983 provides a civil cause of action for individuals who are deprived of any rights, privileges, or immunities secured by the Constitution or federal laws by those acting under color of state law. Smith has stated a claim for relief pursuant to § 1983 in connection with his sex-based claim of employment discrimination. Individuals have a right, protected by the Equal Protection clause of the Fourteenth Amendment, to be free from discrimination on the basis of sex in public employment. *Davis v. Passman,* 442 U.S. 22 (1979). To make out such a claim, a plaintiff must prove that he suffered purposeful or intentional discrimination on the basis of gender. *Vill. of Arlington Heights v. Metro. Hous. Dev. Corp.,* 429 U.S. 252 (1977). As this Court has noted several times, "the showing a plaintiff must make to recover on a disparate treatment claim under Title VII mirrors that which must be made to recover on an equal protection claim under section § 1983." The facts Smith has alleged to support his claims of gender discrimination pursuant to Title VII easily constitute a claim of sex discrimination grounded in the Equal Protection Clause of the Constitution, pursuant to § 1983. *See Back v. Hastings on Hudson Union Free Sch. Dist.,* 365 F.3d 107 (2d Cir. 2004) (holding that claims premised on *Price Waterhouse* sex stereotyping theory sufficiently constitute claim of sex discrimination pursuant to § 1983).

[Because] Smith's sex discrimination claim so thoroughly and obviously sounds in a constitutional claim of equal protection, Defendants had fair notice of his claim and the ground upon which it rests. As such, we hold that Smith has satisfied the liberal notice pleading requirements set forth in Fed. R. Civ. P. 8 with respect to his claim of sex discrimination, grounded in an alleged equal protection violation, and we therefore reverse the district court's grant of judgment on the pleadings dismissing Smith's § 1983 claim.

In his appellate brief, Smith also contends that his complaint alleges a violation of his constitutional right to due process, based on the City's failure to comply with the state statutory and administrative procedures that an Ohio municipality must follow when taking official employment action against a public employee. . . .

However, it is well-settled that state law does not ordinarily define the parameters of due process for Fourteenth Amendment purposes, and that state law, by itself, cannot be the basis for a federal constitutional violation. Neither Smith's complaint nor his brief specifies what deprivation of property or liberty allegedly stemmed from the City's failure to comply with state procedural and administrative rules concerning his employment. Accordingly, he has failed to state a federal due process violation pursuant to § 1983. . . .

III. Conclusion

Because Smith has successfully stated claims for relief pursuant to both Title VII and 42 U.S.C. § 1983, the judgment of the district court is REVERSED and this case is REMANDED to the district court for further proceedings consistent with this opinion.

Discussion

1. Jimmie Smith's attorney Randi Barnabee is also a transgender woman who specializes in transgender-related discrimination issues. She also represented the plaintiffs in *Doe v. United Consumer Financial Services*, 2001 WL 34350174, 2001 U.S.LEXIS 25509 (N.D. Ohio Nov. 9, 2001) (holding that transgender woman Jane Doe could state a claim for sex discrimination based on *Price Waterhouse* and sex stereotyping); *Selena D. Johnson v. Fresh Mark, Inc.*, 337 F. Supp. 2d 996 (2003) (rejecting claims by a transgender woman who had not had genital reconstruction surgeries and was fired after refusing to use men's restrooms); and *Julie Nemecek v. Spring Arbor University*, filed in 2003 after Nemecek informed her employer that she was transgender and intended to transition, and settled in 2007, *see, e.g.*, Jim Larkin, *Understanding, acceptance sought for transgendered*, FLINT. J. (MICH.), 1 Religion Today section (Mar. 7, 2009), available at 2009 WLNR 4563736. Why might Ms. Barnabee and her client Ms. Smith have decided to identify Smith as a biological male and refer to her with male pronouns in the litigation?

2. Note *Smith*'s conclusion that "the approach in *Holloway, Sommers*, and *Ulane*—and by the district court in this case—has been eviscerated by *Price Waterhouse*." Litigators and courts have frequently quoted this line. Is it accurate on your reading of *Price Waterhouse*?

3. *Smith* quotes Sixth Circuit precedent stating that "the showing a plaintiff must make to recover on a disparate treatment claim under Title VII mirrors that which must be made to recover on an equal protection claim under section § 1983." Other courts have said the same. This, however, is not quite accurate. Except when sex is a bona fide occupational qualification (BFOQ) for a particular job under Title VII, or under a proper affirmative action program, sex discrimination will be unlawful under that statute. With respect to the Equal Protection Clause, however, sex discrimination will not be held unconstitutional where it satisfies "intermediate scrutiny," that is, where the sex discrimination is held to be in the service of an "important" governmental interest and the discrimination is "substantially related" to that interest. Courts generally have not analyzed and *held* that the BFOQ standard and intermediate scrutiny are coextensive.

Note on Barnes v. City of Cincinnati

The year after *Smith v. City of Salem*, the U.S. Court of Appeals for the Sixth Circuit in *Barnes v. City of Cincinnati*, 401 F. 3d 729 (6th Cir. 2005), upheld a jury verdict in a transgender police officer's Title VII suit. Philecia Barnes was a Black transgender woman presenting as a male at work as a police officer for Cincinnati but living as a woman off duty. After approximately 17 years on the force, Barnes passed an exam for promotion to sergeant and was placed in that position in a probationary period. At that time she "had a French manicure, had arched eyebrows and came to work with makeup or lipstick on [her] face on some occasions." The department subjected Barnes to operational restrictions including being required to wear a microphone at all times and subjected her to a specially devised evaluation program during the probationary period that was not used for any other sergeants. "[O]ne of Barnes's reviewing sergeants, [Sergeant Ford,] testified that Barnes was improving over the course of the training and that Barnes was placed in the special program to 'target him [*sic*] for failure.'"

The department's "Col. Twitty told Barnes he [*sic*] did not appear to be 'masculine,' and that he [*sic*] needed to stop wearing makeup and act more masculine prior to Barnes's promotion. Col. Twitty stated the objective of such statements was to correct Barnes's 'grooming deficiencies.' Col. Twitty also stated that the decision to fail Barnes from probation had nothing to do with Barnes's transsexual characteristics. However, Sergeant Ford warned Barnes that he heard rumors that Barnes was going to fail probation because Barnes had not been acting masculine enough." The evidence at trial showed that "Barnes's scores on the sergeant evaluation tests were higher than at least one other probationary sergeant. Barnes was the only person to be put in a Sergeant Field Training Program and the only one to fail probation between 1993 and 2000." Barnes sued for sex discrimination under Title VII and the Equal Protection Clause of the Constitution, relying on a sex stereotyping theory. She prevailed in a jury trial, and the city appealed to the U.S. Court of Appeals for the Sixth Circuit. The court of appeals affirmed in a unanimous panel opinion by Judge David W. McKeague (United States District Judge for the Western District of Michigan, sitting by designation).

Relying on *Smith*, the court of appeals held that "[b]y alleging that his failure to conform to sex stereotypes concerning how a man should look and behave was the driving force behind defendant's actions, Smith stated a claim for relief pursuant to Title VII's prohibition of sex discrimination." Moreover, invoking the standard of review on appeal, the court held that there was sufficient evidence for a reasonable jury to conclude that in fact Cincinnati had discriminated against Barnes "for his failure to conform to sex stereotypes." (Barnes's counsel presented Barnes as a gender-nonconforming male — how they believed the city perceived Barnes — in the litigation.) The court also accepted the trial court's jury instructions, which made it clear that "the plaintiff . . . presented enough evidence for a reasonable jury to find by a preponderance of the evidence that sex was a motivating factor in the decision to demote plaintiff."

Reading Guide for Glenn v. Brumby

1. In the wake of the Supreme Court's decision in *Price-Waterhouse v. Hopkins* (1989), making clear that Title VII's ban on sex discrimination forbids reliance on gender stereotypes, something that also offends the Equal Protection Clause, many courts have used Title VII precedents to inform Equal Protection Clause analysis and vice versa. Be careful to follow how *Glenn v. Brumby*, 663 F.3d 1312 (11th Cir. 2011), does so, as the structure of its analysis is a little underspecified: Part I of the opinion addresses the legal standard for sex discrimination reachable by the Equal Protection Clause; the "first inquiry" of Part II addresses the factual claim of whether the defendant in fact engaged in such sex discrimination; the rest of Part

II addresses whether any such sex discrimination might have been legally justified under the form of heightened scrutiny applicable to sex discrimination (and, if such discrimination were only motivated by gender stereotypes, what would be insufficient justification).

2. Note the court's reliance in *Glenn v. Brumby* on *Price Waterhouse* and in particular on that decision's condemnation of both descriptive stereotypes about what people of a particular sex *are* like and prescriptive stereotypes about what people of a particular sex *should be* like. Is the *Glenn* court persuasive in its articulation of how some or all anti-transgender discrimination is based on sex/gender stereotypes? Is its rejection of contrary precedent in footnote 5 persuasive?

3. What are the *Glenn* court's evidentiary grounds for concluding that the defendant in fact discriminated against the plaintiff on the basis of sex/gender stereotypes? Is the court's conclusion on this point persuasive? Was the court right to have rejected the defendant's articulated concern about the plaintiff's bathroom usage as insufficient to render his discrimination lawful?

Vandiver Elizabeth Glenn v. Sewell R. Brumby

663 F.3d 1312 (11th Cir. 2011)

[Plaintiff Vandy Beth Glenn was represented by Lambda Legal.]

Before BARKETT, PRYOR and KRAVITCH, Circuit Judges.

BARKETT, Circuit Judge:

Sewell R. Brumby appeals from an adverse summary judgment in favor of Vandiver Elizabeth Glenn on her complaint seeking declaratory and injunctive relief pursuant to 42 U.S.C. § 1983 for alleged violations of her rights under the Equal Protection Clause[.] Glenn claimed that Brumby fired her from her job as an editor in the Georgia General Assembly's Office of Legislative Counsel ("OLC") because of sex discrimination, thus violating the Equal Protection Clause. The district court granted summary judgment in Glenn's favor on this claim.

Glenn also claimed that her constitutional rights were violated because Brumby terminated her employment due to her medical condition, known as Gender Identity Disorder ("GID"). The district court ruled against Glenn on this claim, granting summary judgment to Brumby. Brumby appeals the district court's sex-discrimination ruling, and Glenn cross-appeals the ruling on her medical condition claim.

[Glenn] was born a biological male. Since puberty, Glenn has felt that she is a woman, and in 2005, she was diagnosed with GID, a diagnosis listed in the American Psychiatric Association's Diagnostic and Statistical Manual of Mental Disorders.

Starting in 2005, Glenn began to take steps to transition from male to female under the supervision of health care providers. This process included living as a woman outside of the workplace, which is a prerequisite to sex reassignment surgery. In October 2005, then known as Glenn Morrison and presenting as a man, Glenn was hired as an editor by the Georgia General Assembly's OLC. Sewell Brumby is the head of the OLC and is responsible for OLC personnel decisions, including the decision to fire Glenn.

In 2006, Glenn informed her direct supervisor, Beth Yinger, that she was a transsexual [*sic*] and was in the process of becoming a woman. On Halloween in 2006, when OLC employees were permitted to come to work wearing costumes, Glenn came to work presenting as a woman. When Brumby saw her, he told her that her appearance was not appropriate and asked her to leave the office. Brumby deemed her appearance inappropriate "[b]ecause he was a man dressed as a woman and made up as a woman." Brumby stated that "it's unsettling to think of someone dressed in women's clothing with male sexual organs inside that clothing," and that a male in women's clothing is "unnatural." Following this incident, Brumby met with Yinger to discuss Glenn's appearance on Halloween of 2006 and was informed by Yinger that Glenn intended to undergo a gender transition.

In the fall of 2007, Glenn informed Yinger that she was ready to proceed with gender transition and would begin coming to work as a woman and was also changing her legal name. Yinger notified Brumby, who subsequently terminated Glenn because "Glenn's intended gender transition was inappropriate, that it would be disruptive, that some people would view it as a moral issue, and that it would make Glenn's coworkers uncomfortable."

Glenn sued, alleging two claims of discrimination under the Equal Protection Clause. First, Glenn alleged that Brumby "discriminat[ed] against her because of her sex, including her female gender identity and her failure to conform to the sex stereotypes associated with the sex Defendant[] perceived her to be." Second, Glenn alleged that Brumby "discriminat[ed] against her because of her medical condition, GID[,]" because "[r]eceiving necessary treatment for a medical condition is an integral component of living with such a condition, and blocking that treatment is a form of discrimination based on the underlying medical condition."

[W]e first address Glenn's sex discrimination claim.

I. Equal Protection and Sex Stereotyping

[The] Equal Protection Clause requires the State to treat all persons similarly situated alike or, conversely, to avoid all classifications that are "arbitrary or irrational" and those that reflect "a bare . . . desire to harm a politically unpopular group." *City of Cleburne v. Cleburne Living Ctr., Inc.* (1985). States are presumed to act lawfully, and therefore state action is generally upheld if it is rationally related to a legitimate governmental purpose. *Id.* However, more than a rational basis is required in certain circumstances. In describing generally the contours of the Equal Protection Clause, the Supreme Court noted its application to this issue, referencing both gender and sex, using the terms interchangeably:

> Legislative classifications based on gender also call for a heightened standard of review. That factor generally provides no sensible ground for differential treatment. [W]hat differentiates sex from such nonsuspect statuses as

intelligence or physical disability . . . is that the sex characteristic frequently bears no relation to ability to perform or contribute to society. Rather than resting on meaningful considerations, statutes distributing benefits and burdens between the sexes in different ways very likely reflect outmoded notions of the relative capabilities of men and women. A gender classification fails unless it is substantially related to a sufficiently important governmental interest.

Id. In *United States v. Virginia*, 518 U.S. 515 (1996), the Supreme Court reaffirmed its prior holdings that sex-based discrimination is subject to intermediate scrutiny[4] under the Equal Protection Clause. This standard requires the government to show that its "gender classification . . . is substantially related to a sufficiently important government interest." *Cleburne.* Moreover, this test requires a "genuine" justification, not one that is "hypothesized or invented *post hoc* in response to litigation." In *Virginia*, the state's policy of excluding women from the Virginia Military Institute failed this test because the state could not rely on generalizations about different aptitudes of males and females to support the exclusion of women. "State actors controlling gates to opportunity, we have instructed, may not exclude qualified individuals based on 'fixed notions concerning the roles and abilities of males and females.'" *Id.* (quoting *Mississippi Univ. for Women v. Hogan*, 455 U.S. 935 (1982)).

The question here is whether discriminating against someone on the basis of his or her gender non-conformity constitutes sex-based discrimination under the Equal Protection Clause. For the reasons discussed below, we hold that it does.

In *Price Waterhouse v. Hopkins*, 490 U.S. 228 (1989), the Supreme Court held that discrimination on the basis of gender stereotype is sex-based discrimination. In that case, the Court considered allegations that a senior manager at Price Waterhouse was denied partnership in the firm because she was considered "macho," and "overcompensated for being a woman." Six members of the Supreme Court agreed that such comments were indicative of gender discrimination and held that Title VII barred not just discrimination because of biological sex, but also gender stereotyping — failing to act and appear according to expectations defined by gender. *Id.* (plurality opinion); *id.* (White, J., concurring); *id.* (O'Connor, J., concurring). The Court noted that "[a]s for the legal relevance of sex stereotyping, we are beyond the day when an employer could evaluate employees by assuming or insisting that they matched the stereotypes associated with their group. . . ."

---

4. The Court has established two standards of review of legislative classifications under the Equal Protection Clause — rational basis scrutiny and heightened scrutiny. *See Clark v. Jeter*, 486 U.S. 456 (1988). Rational basis scrutiny sets the minimum requirement that all classifications must be "rationally related to a legitimate governmental purpose." Heightened scrutiny is comprised of intermediate scrutiny and strict scrutiny. *Id.* Intermediate scrutiny applies to classifications based on sex or illegitimacy and requires that government action be "substantially related to an important governmental objective." Strict scrutiny is the most exacting form of review and it applies to classifications pertaining to race or national origin and to those affecting certain fundamental rights.

A person is defined as transgender precisely because of the perception that his or her behavior transgresses gender stereotypes. "[T]he very acts that define transgender people as transgender are those that contradict stereotypes of gender-appropriate appearance and behavior." Ilona M. Turner, *Sex Stereotyping Per Se: Transgender Employees and Title VII*, 95 Calif. L. Rev. 561, 563 (2007); *see also* Taylor Fl[y]nn, *Transforming the Debate: Why We Need to Include Transgender Rights in the Struggles for Sex and Sexual Orientation Equality*, 101 Colum. L. Rev. 392, 392 (2001) (defining transgender persons as those whose "appearance, behavior, or other personal characteristics differ from traditional gender norms"). There is thus a congruence between discriminating against transgender and transsexual individuals and discrimination on the basis of gender-based behavioral norms.

Accordingly, discrimination against a transgender individual because of her gender-nonconformity is sex discrimination, whether it's described as being on the basis of sex or gender. Indeed, several circuits have so held. For example, in *Schwenk v. Hartford*, 204 F.3d 118 (9th Cir. 2000), the Ninth Circuit concluded that a male-to-female transgender plaintiff who was singled out for harassment because he presented and defined himself as a woman had stated an actionable claim for sex discrimination under the Gender Motivated Violence Act because "the perpetrator's actions stem from the fact that he believed that the victim was a man who 'failed to act like one.'" The First Circuit echoed this reasoning in *Rosa v. Park West Bank & Trust Co.*, 214 F.3d 213 (1st Cir. 2000), where it held that a transgender plaintiff stated a claim by alleging that he "did not receive [a] loan application because he was a man, whereas a similarly situated woman would have received [a] loan application. That is, the Bank . . . treat[s] . . . a woman who dresses like a man differently than a man who dresses like a woman." These instances of discrimination against plaintiffs because they fail to act according to socially prescribed gender roles constitute discrimination under Title VII according to the rationale of *Price Waterhouse*.

The Sixth Circuit likewise recognized that discrimination against a transgender individual because of his or her gender non-conformity is gender stereotyping prohibited by Title VII and the Equal Protection Clause. *See Smith v. City of Salem*, 378 F.3d 566 (6th Cir. 2004). The court concluded that a transsexual firefighter could not be suspended because of "his transsexualism and its manifestations," because to do so was discrimination against him "based on his failure to conform to sex stereotypes by expressing less masculine, and more feminine mannerisms and appearance." *Id.*; *see Barnes v. City of Cincinnati*, 401 F.3d 729 (6th Cir. 2005) (holding that transsexual plaintiff stated a claim for sex discrimination "by alleging discrimination . . . for his failure to conform to sex stereotypes").

District courts have recognized as well that sex discrimination includes discrimination against transgender persons because of their failure to comply with stereotypical gender norms. *See Lopez v. River Oaks Imaging & Diagnostic Group, Inc.*, 542 F. Supp. 2d 653 (S.D. Tex. 2008) ("Title VII and *Price Waterhouse* . . . do not make any distinction between a transgendered litigant who fails to conform to traditional gender stereotypes and [a] 'macho' female who . . . is perceived by others to be in nonconformity with traditional gender stereotypes"); *Schroer v. Billington*, 424 F. Supp. 2d 203 (D.D.C. 2006) ("[I]t may be time to revisit [the] conclusion . . . that discrimination against transsexuals [*sic*—Eds.] *because they are transsexuals* is literally discrimination because of sex") (internal quotation marks and ellipsis omitted); *Mitchell v. Axcan Scandipharm*, 2006 WL 456173, 2006 U.S. Dist. LEXIS 6521 (W.D. Pa. Feb. 21, 2006) (holding that a transgender plaintiff may state a claim for sex discrimination by "showing that his failure to conform to sex stereotypes of how a man should look and behave was the catalyst behind defendant's actions"); *Kastl v. Maricopa Cnty. Comm. College Dist.*, 2004 WL 2008954, 2004 U.S. Dist. LEXIS 29825, (D. Ariz. June 3, 2004), *aff'd* 325 Fed. Appx. 492 (9th Cir. 2009) ("[N]either a woman with male genitalia nor a man with stereotypically female anatomy, such as breasts, may be deprived of a benefit or privilege of employment by reason of that nonconforming trait"); *Tronetti v. Healthnet Lakeshore Hosp.*, 2003 WL 22757935, 2003 U.S. Dist. LEXIS 23757 (W.D.N.Y. Sept. 26, 2003) (holding transsexual plaintiff may state a claim under Title VII "based on the alleged discrimination for failing to 'act like a man'").[5]

---

5. Prior to the Supreme Court's decision in *Price Waterhouse*, several courts concluded that Title VII afforded no protection to transgender victims of sex discrimination. *See, e.g., Ulane v. E. Airlines, Inc.*, 742 F.2d 1081 (7th Cir. 1984) (concluding that discrimination against plaintiff was "not because she is female, but because she is transsexual"); *Sommers v. Budget Mktg., Inc.*, 667 F.2d 748 (8th Cir. 1982) (rejecting transgender plaintiff's claim as falling outside "the traditional definition" of sex under Title VII); *Holloway v. Arthur Andersen & Co.*, 566 F.2d 659 (9th Cir. 1977) ("Congress has not shown any intent other than to restrict the term 'sex' to its traditional meaning"); *Voyles v. Ralph K. Davies Med. Ctr.*, 403 F. Supp. 456 (N.D. Cal. 1975) (holding that Title VII was not intended to "embrace 'transsexual' discrimination [*sic*—Eds.]"). However, since the decision in *Price Waterhouse*, federal courts have recognized with near-total uniformity that "the approach in *Holloway*, *Sommers*, and *Ulane* . . . has been eviscerated" by *Price Waterhouse*'s holding that "Title VII's reference to 'sex' encompasses both the biological differences between men and women, and gender discrimination, that is, discrimination based on a failure to conform to stereotypical gender norms." *Smith*; *see also Schwenk* ("The initial judicial approach taken in cases such as *Holloway* has been overruled by the logic and language of *Price Waterhouse*"); *Rosa* (affirming that transgender plaintiffs may claim sex discrimination based on their non-conformity with gender stereotype); *see generally* Demoya R. Gordon, *Transgender Legal Advocacy: What do Feminist Legal Theories Have to Offer?*, 97 Calif. L. Rev. 1719 (2009) (reviewing history of transgender discrimination in Title VII cases). *But see Creed v. Family Express Corp.*, No. 3:06-CV-465, 2009 WL 35237, 2009 U.S. Dist. LEXIS 237 (N.D. In. Jan. 5, 2009) (permitting employer to fire transgender employee based on . . . failure to conform to dress code and grooming policy); *Etsitty v. Utah Trans. Auth.*, No. 2:04-CV-616, 2005 WL 1505610, 2005 U.S. Dist. LEXIS 12634 (D. Utah June 24, 2005), *aff'd* 502 F.3d 1215 (10th Cir. 2007) (concluding that *Price Waterhouse* is inapplicable to transsexuals [*sic*—Eds.]); *Oiler v. Winn-Dixie La., Inc.*, 2002 WL 31098541, 2002 U.S. Dist. LEXIS 17417 (E.D. La. Sept. 16, 2002) (distinguishing *Price Waterhouse* on the basis that "[t]he plaintiff in that case may not have behaved as the partners thought a woman should have, but she never pretended to be a man . . ."). The pre-*Price Waterhouse* cases' reliance on the presumed intent of Title VII's drafters is also inconsistent with *Oncale v. Sundowner Offshore Services, Inc.*, where the Supreme Court held that original legislative intent must not be given controlling weight in interpreting Title VII. *See* 523 U.S. 75 (1998) ("[S]tatutory prohibitions [such as Title VII] often go beyond the principal evil

All persons, whether transgender or not, are protected from discrimination on the basis of gender stereotype. For example, courts have held that plaintiffs cannot be discriminated against for wearing jewelry that was considered too effeminate,[6] carrying a serving tray too gracefully,[7] or taking too active a role in child-rearing.[8] An individual cannot be punished because of his or her perceived gender-nonconformity. Because these protections are afforded to everyone, they cannot be denied to a transgender individual. The nature of the discrimination is the same; it may differ in degree but not in kind, and discrimination on this basis is a form of sex-based discrimination that is subject to heightened scrutiny under the Equal Protection Clause. Ever since the Supreme Court began to apply heightened scrutiny to sex-based classifications, its consistent purpose has been to eliminate discrimination on the basis of gender stereotypes.

In *Frontiero v. Richardson*, the Court struck down legislation requiring only female service members to prove that their spouses depended upon them financially in order to receive certain benefits for married couples. *See* 411 U.S. 677 (1973) (plurality opinion). The plurality applied heightened scrutiny to sex-based classifications by referring to the pervasiveness of gender stereotypes, *see id.* (noting a tradition of "'romantic paternalism'" that "put women[] not on a pedestal, but in a cage"), and held that gender-based classifications are "inherently suspect," because they are often animated by "stereotyped distinctions between the sexes." Two years later, the Court applied this heightened level of scrutiny to a Utah statute setting a lower age of majority for women and concluded that the statute could not be sustained by the stereotypical assumption that women tend to marry earlier than men. *See Stanton v. Stanton* (1975). The Court again rejected gender stereotypes, holding that "'old notions'" about men and women's behavior provided no support for the

---

to cover reasonably comparable evils, and it is ultimately the provisions of our laws rather than the principal concerns of our legislators by which we are governed").

6. [T]he Seventh Circuit held that a young man who was taunted by co-workers for wearing an earring and who was repeatedly asked whether he was "a boy or a girl" clearly stated a Title VII sexual harassment claim by alleging that "the way in which he projected the sexual aspect of his personality (and by that we mean his gender) did not conform to his coworkers' view of appropriate masculine behavior." *Doe v. City of Belleville*, 119 F.3d 563 (7th Cir. 1997), *vacated on other grounds by* 523 U.S. 1001 (1998).

7. In *Nichols v. Azteca Restaurant Enterprises*, the Ninth Circuit held that a waiter who was harassed by his co-workers for carrying a serving tray "like a woman" stated a claim for sexual harassment under Title VII because his antagonists were animated by his gender-nonconforming behavior. 256 F.3d 864 (9th Cir. 2001).

8. In *Knussman v. Maryland*, the Fourth Circuit upheld liability under the Equal Protection Clause against an employer who prohibited an employee, the father of a newborn, from taking statutory leave as a "primary care giver" under the Family Medical Leave Act. 272 F.3d 625 (4th Cir. 2001). The employer's rationale was that a father cannot act as primary caregiver because "God made women to have babies and, unless [the employee] could have a baby, there is no way he could be primary care giver." The court held that the employer's "irrebuttable presumption" that a father cannot act as the primary caregiver was incompatible with precedent prohibiting an individual's role in parenting to be limited based solely on gender.

State's classification. That same year, the Court confronted a provision of the Social Security Act that allowed certain benefits to widows while denying them to widowers. *See Weinberger v. Wiesenfeld*, 410 U.S. 636 (1975). The Court again used heightened scrutiny to strike at gender stereotype, concluding that "the Constitution also forbids gender-based differentiation" premised on the stereotypical assumption that a husband's income is always more important to the wife than is the wife's to the husband.

In each of these foundational cases, the Court concluded that discriminatory state action could not stand on the basis of gender stereotypes. *See also Craig v. Boren*, 429 U.S. 190 (1976) (explaining that "the weak congruence between gender and the characteristic or trait that gender purported to represent" necessitated applying heightened scrutiny); *Orr v. Orr*, 440 U.S. 268 (1979) ("Legislative classifications which distribute benefits and burdens on the basis of gender carry the risk of reinforcing stereotypes about the 'proper place' of women. . . ."). The Court's more recent cases reiterate that the Equal Protection Clause does not tolerate gender stereotypes. *See Hogan* (explaining that "the purpose" of heightened scrutiny is to ensure that sex-based classifications rest upon "reasoned analysis rather than . . . traditional, often inaccurate, assumptions about the proper roles of men and women"); *see also Virginia* ("[The government] must not rely on overbroad generalizations about the different talents, capacities, or preferences of males and females"); *cf. Nevada Dep't of Human Res. v. Hibbs*, 538 U.S. 721 (2003) (holding that Congress may enact remedial measures under Section Five of the Fourteenth Amendment to counteract sex-based stereotypes).[9] Accordingly, governmental acts based upon gender stereotypes—which presume that men and women's appearance and behavior will be determined by their sex—must be subjected to heightened scrutiny because they embody "the very stereotype the law condemns." *J.E.B. v. Alabama ex rel. T.B.*, 511 U.S. 127 (1994) (declaring unconstitutional a government attorney's use of peremptory juror strikes based on the presumption that potential jurors' views would correspond to their sexes).

We conclude that a government agent violates the Equal Protection Clause's prohibition of sex-based discrimination when he or she fires a transgender or transsexual employee because of his or her gender non-conformity.

---

9. The Court's reasoning has indicated that governmental reliance on gender-based stereotypes is dispositive in its equal protection analysis even in cases that uphold the government's challenged action under heightened scrutiny. In *Nguyen v. INS*, the Court concluded that an immigration statute burdening unwed fathers and mothers unequally survived intermediate scrutiny because the statute did *not* rely on gender stereotype. 533 U.S. 53, 68 (2001). The dissent disagreed, concluding that the statute was fatally flawed because it relied on stereotypes about the relative parenting abilities of fathers and mothers. *See* 533 U.S. at 74 (O'Connor, J., dissenting). Thus, both majority and dissent viewed the statute's reliance on gender-based stereotypes as determinative of its validity.

II. Glenn's Termination

We now turn to whether Glenn was fired on the basis of gender stereotyping. The first inquiry is whether Brumby acted on the basis of Glenn's gender-nonconformity. *See Vill. of Arlington Heights v. Metro. Hous. Dev. Corp.*, 429 U.S. 252 (1977) (requiring proof of discriminatory intent). If so, we must then apply heightened scrutiny to decide whether that action was substantially related to a sufficiently important governmental interest.

A plaintiff can show discriminatory intent through direct or circumstantial evidence. In this case, Brumby testified at his deposition that he fired Glenn because he considered it "inappropriate" for her to appear at work dressed as a woman and that he found it "unsettling" and "unnatural" that Glenn would appear wearing women's clothing. Brumby testified that his decision to dismiss Glenn was based on his perception of Glenn as "a man dressed as a woman and made up as a woman," and Brumby admitted that his decision to fire Glenn was based on "the sheer fact of the transition." Brumby's testimony provides ample direct evidence to support the district court's conclusion that Brumby acted on the basis of Glenn's gender non-conformity.

[W]e must, under heightened scrutiny, consider whether Brumby succeeded in showing an "exceedingly persuasive justification," *Virginia*, that is, that there was a "sufficiently important governmental interest" for his discriminatory conduct, *Cleburne*. This burden "is demanding and it rests entirely on the State." *Virginia*. The defendant's burden cannot be met by relying on a justification that is "hypothesized or invented post hoc in response to litigation." *Id.*

On appeal, Brumby advances only one putative justification for Glenn's firing: his purported concern that other women might object to Glenn's restroom use. However, Brumby presented insufficient evidence to show that he was actually motivated by concern over litigation regarding Glenn's restroom use. To support the justification that he now argues, Brumby points to a single statement in his deposition where he referred to a speculative concern about lawsuits arising if Glenn used the women's restroom. The district court recognized that this single reference, based on speculation, was overwhelmingly contradicted by specific evidence of Brumby's intent, and we agree. Indeed, Brumby testified that he viewed the possibility of a lawsuit by a co-worker if Glenn were retained as unlikely and the record indicates that the OLC, where Glenn worked, had only single-occupancy restrooms. Brumby advanced this argument before the district court only as a *conceivable* explanation for his decision to fire Glenn under rational basis review. The fact that such a hypothetical justification may have been sufficient to withstand rational-basis scrutiny, however, is wholly irrelevant to the heightened scrutiny analysis that is required here.

Brumby has advanced no other reason that could qualify as a governmental purpose, much less an "important" governmental purpose, and even less than that, a "sufficiently important governmental purpose" that was achieved by firing Glenn because of her gender non-conformity. *Cleburne*.

We therefore AFFIRM the judgment of the district court granting summary judgment in favor of Glenn on her sex-discrimination claim. In light of this decision, which provides Glenn with all the relief that she seeks, there is no need to address Glenn's cross-appeal.

AFFIRMED

Discussion

1. In footnote 4 the court uses "heightened scrutiny" to mean "either intermediate scrutiny or strict scrutiny." Be aware that "heightened scrutiny" is often used more specifically as a synonym just for intermediate scrutiny. It will generally be necessary to look to context to determine the sense in which a given author has used "heightened scrutiny."

2. Does *Glenn* in fact hold that anti-transgender is *always* a form of sex discrimination? Note first how the court identifies what "[t]he question here is," *supra* at p. 187. Next, consider the relevance of how the court says "[a] person is defined as transgender," the "congruence" it says follows from that, and its formulation in the following paragraph of what reads like a holding, *id.* See also the court's formulation of the Sixth Circuit Court of Appeals holding in *Smith v. City of Salem*, *supra* at p. 174; Note, *infra*, at p. 195, and its description of various district court holdings, *id.* Finally, look at the court's framing of its legal conclusion at the end of Part I of the opinion.

3. Recall that Eleventh Circuit Judge William Pryor attempted to distinguish the panel opinion in *Glenn v. Brumby*, accepting transgender woman Vandy Beth Glenn's sex stereotyping claim, from the later panel opinion in *Jameka Evans v. Georgia Regional Hospital et al.*, 850 F.3d 1248 (11th Cir. 2017), rejecting a lesbian plaintiff's similar attempt to sue under Title VII in reliance on *Price Waterhouse* and sex stereotyping. See Discussion, note 4, *supra* at p. 164. (Three-judge panels cannot overrule earlier panel decisions from the same circuit, so distinguishing two cases can be important if they seem to be in tension.) What language in *Glenn*, if any, supports limiting the holding to sex/gender stereotypes about a person's behavior alone? What language, if any, supports reading the holding to reach sex/gender stereotypes about a person's status? Which do you think is the best reading of *Glenn*?

4. Not all legal scholars have been sanguine about using Title VII's sex stereotyping approach to reach anti-transgender discrimination. One of this casebook's editors has argued, however, that many of their "concerns would be misplaced or lack force as a reason to reject the sex stereotyping or other broad understandings of forbidden sex discrimination, and, accordingly, they should not forestall courts from interpreting Title VII to forbid anti-trans discrimination. . . ." David B. Cruz, *Acknowledging the Gender in Anti-Transgender Discrimination*, 32 LAW & INEQUALITY 257, 274 (2014).

Some scholars object to certain trans-protective positions on the ground that those arguments are not consistent with lower court decisions about the reach of Title VII's ban on sex discrimination. [However, the] decisions upholding various forms of sex discrimination by employers that these scholars see as in tension or inconsistent with the logic of the plain reading of Title VII are not appropriate interpretations of Title VII's ban on sex discrimination. The poor reasoning of many of the cases addressing transgender plaintiffs suing under Title VII makes "fit with lower court case law" a particularly inapt standard by which to judge theories about the statute's scope. . . .

Another common complaint about approaches to Title VII—particularly reliance on the notion of sex stereotyping—that would hold anti-trans discrimination unlawful, is that the protection offered is incomplete or under-inclusive. . . . But these are problems with Title VII or with law generally—there are always problems outside the scope of a statute or its implementation. Perhaps Title VII might profitably be expanded to provide workers more protection. But that is not a reason to shrink from applying Title VII as it stands now categorically to prohibit discrimination by covered employers that can be proven to turn on the employee's transgender status, transition, or gender expression.

Another set of concerns about Title VII protection from anti-transgender discrimination centers on stereotypes: the fear that such protection reinforces gender norms or, contrarily but sometimes held by the same critics, do not allow gender norms enough latitude. . . . But these authors overstate what a court must do to rule for a transgender plaintiff. [The] doctrine does not actually confine protection to a limited class of persons and so does not require courts to decide the sex/gender class to which a plaintiff belongs. Disparate treatment doctrine asks about whether an employer took an action because of an employee's sex, a question answerable by reference to the employer's beliefs about the plaintiff's sex. "What matters . . . is that in the mind of the perpetrator the discrimination is related to the sex of the victim." "The critical inquiry," *Price Waterhouse* explained, "the one commanded by the words of [Title VII], is whether gender was a factor in the employment decision at the moment it was made." And so generally Title VII is violated when an "employer relie[s] upon sex-based considerations in coming to its decision."

Conversely, some scholars—indeed, some of the same scholars who complain that acknowledging the gender discrimination in anti-transgender discrimination reinforces sex stereotypes—fret that doing so does not leave employers sufficient latitude to require their employees to conform to gender norms. . . . But [even if robust application of sex stereotyping theory would reduce employers' freedom to impose different dress codes on people of different sexes,] their "reduced" freedom would be formally equal, so employers would not be able to use market leverage to reinforce a normative view of sex difference, which would be a good thing. Gender nonconformers would gain freedom from being sartorially marked as one sex, in at least this context, if people of all sexes have to be allowed to wear the same things. All persons would remain free to adhere to whatever gendered dress conventions they wish outside the workplace.

. . . . Title VII does not ban oppressive stereotypes; it bans sex discrimination, including that based on sex or gender stereotypes, whether or not someone deems it oppressive. The further problem with [the] suggestion that social or cultural approbation of gender norms is "meaningful" and should be protected is that this would allow imposition/unequal constraints on freedom justified by majority comfort. If there really is a social or cultural norm supporting a particular gender practice, its devotees should be comfortable enough to trust in its survival absent legal coercion of dissenters. If, conversely, the norm would be imperiled if it were not mandatory (enforced by laws and/or economic power), that should be sufficient evidence at a minimum to establish a prima facie case that the norm is unjustly denying persons equal liberty.

Id. at 275–81 (footnotes omitted).

D. Categorical Sex Discrimination

Title VII doctrine regarding anti-transgender discrimination continued to evolve in the lower courts after the emergence of the sex-stereotyping approach. In particular, there began to emerge a position that anti-trans discrimination is always or by definition a form of sex discrimination and thus generally prohibited by Title VII, a position the Supreme Court adopted in 2020 in *Bostock v. Clayton County, Georgia*, 140 S. Ct. 1731 (2020), *infra*. This section explores that development.

Note on Smith v. City of Salem

In *Smith v. City of Salem*, 369 F.3d 912 (6th Cir.), *superseded by* 378 F.3d 566 (6th Cir. 2004), *supra* Section C, the panel opinion originally reasoned more categorically in terms suggesting that anti-transgender discrimination is always a form of sex discrimination. In both the original and the revised opinion, the court of appeals rejected the district court's attempt to distinguish transgender woman Jimmie Smith's gender nonconformity from that of Ann Hopkins, the successful, not very feminine plaintiff in *Price Waterhouse v. Hopkins* (1989). The court of appeals held that the basis of someone's gender nonconformity was irrelevant under Title VII:

> Sex stereotyping based on a person's gender non-conforming behavior is impermissible discrimination, irrespective of the cause of that behavior; a label, such as "transsexual," is not fatal to a sex discrimination claim where

the victim has suffered discrimination because of his or her gender non-conformity. Accordingly, we hold that Smith has stated a claim for relief pursuant to Title VII's prohibition of sex discrimination.

369 F.3d at 921, 378 F.3d at 575.

The opinion as originally issued, however, did not stop there. Its next paragraph clarified its broad understanding of sex stereotyping under Title VII:

> Even if Smith had alleged discrimination based only on his self-identification as a transsexual—as opposed to his specific appearance and behavior—this claim too is actionable pursuant to Title VII. By definition, transsexuals are individuals who fail to conform to stereotypes about how those assigned a particular sex at birth should act, dress, and self-identify. Ergo, identification as a transsexual is the statement or admission that one wishes to be the opposite sex or does not relate to one's birth sex. Such an admission—for instance the admission by a man that he self-identifies as a woman and/or that he wishes to be a woman—itself violates the prevalent sex stereotype that a man should perceive himself as a man. Discrimination based on transsexualism is rooted in the insistence that sex (organs) and gender (social classification of a person as belonging to one sex or the other) coincide. This is the very essence of sex stereotyping. Accordingly, to the extent that Smith also alleges discrimination based solely on his identification as a transsexual, he has alleged a claim of sex stereotyping pursuant to Title VII. As noted above, Smith's birth sex is male and this is the basis for his protected class status under Title VII even under this formulation of his claim.

369 F.3d at 921–22. Hence, in the Sixth Circuit panel's original view, sex stereotyping was not limited to discrimination based on appearance and behavior but encompassed discrimination based on anatomy and/or identity as well.

This paragraph was removed by the panel judges when they issued a revised opinion two months later. In so doing, they may have avoided a rehearing en banc by the full complement of Sixth Circuit judges. *See generally, e.g.,* Anna Kirkland, *What's at Stake in Transgender Discrimination as Sex Discrimination*, 32 Signs: J. of Women in Culture & Soc'y 83, 96–100 (2006). It is possible that some other judges on the court had concerns that the ultimately expurgated paragraph went too far in condemning sex stereotypes and would be applicable as well to claims that sexual orientation-based discrimination is also sex discrimination forbidden by Title VII, an interpretation rejected in holdings or dicta by a great deal of lower court case law at that time. It is also possible that some other judges objected to the original paragraph as dicta, language purporting to resolve issues not before the court. Its initial sentence's use of the subjunctive tense contributes to that impression: "Even if Smith had alleged. . . ." That makes it sound like a counter-factual, a classic instance of dictum. The paragraph thus may have put off some of the panel's colleagues at the outset, and they might not have been reassured when finally at the end the opinion reformulates its discussion as addressing something "to the extent that Smith also alleges discrimination." Scholars and litigants might never know.

Diane Schroer and the Library of Congress

Litigation between transgender woman Diane Schroer (represented by the American Civil Liberties Union) and the Library of Congress in the U.S. District Court for the District of Columbia, resulting in three published opinions, represents important steps on the path to categorical coverage of anti-transgender discrimination under Title VII.

Schroer I

In *Schroer v. Billington*, 424 F. Supp. 2d 203 (D.D.C. 2006) (*Schroer I*), the district court ruled on a pre-discovery motion to dismiss filed by the defendants. Reading *Price Waterhouse* narrowly, the court rejected Ms. Schroer's sex stereotyping claim. *Schroer I* opined that *Price Waterhouse*'s discussion of sex stereotyping "meant no more than that: *disparate treatment* of men and women by sex stereotype violates Title VII. Adverse action taken on the basis of an employer's gender stereotype that does not impose unequal burdens on men and women or disadvantage one or the other does not state a claim under Title VII." Relying in part on lower court cases upholding different dress codes for male and female employees, the district court concluded that "[t]o the extent that Title VII after *Price Waterhouse* prohibits sex stereotyping alone, it does so to allow women such as Ms. Hopkins to express their individual female identities without being punished for being 'macho,' or for men to express their individual male identities without reprisal for being perceived as effeminate." The district court thought there was a difference in kind, "not simply one of degree," "between 'macho' women or effeminate men, whether transsexual or not, and persons such as Schroer whose adoption of a name and choice of clothing is part of an intentional presentation of herself as a person of a different sex than that of her birth." "Protection against sex stereotyping is different, not in degree, but in kind, from protecting men, whether effeminate or not, who seek to present themselves as women, or women, whether masculine or not, who present themselves as men." In reaching this conclusion, the court relied on the American Psychiatric Association's definition of "gender identity," which distinguishes that diagnosis from "a child's nonconformity to stereotypic sex-role behavior." Allowing that "[a] transsexual plaintiff might successfully state a *Price Waterhouse*-type claim if the claim is that he or she has been discriminated against because of a failure to act or appear masculine or feminine enough for an employer," the district court insisted that "such a claim must actually arise from the employee's appearance or conduct and the employer's stereotypical perceptions. Such a claim is not stated here, where the complaint alleges that Schroer's non-selection was the direct result of her disclosure of her gender dysphoria and of her intention to begin presenting herself as a woman, or her display of photographs of herself in feminine attire, or both." Why isn't a negative reaction to pictures of someone the employer had believed to be male appearing in feminine attire discrimination based on "the employee's appearance or conduct and the employer's stereotypical perceptions"? (The district court revised its reasoning on this point in *Schroer III* (*infra* at p. 199).)

The district court wrote with disfavor of lower court decisions that seem to treat *Price Waterhouse* as irrelevant to whether or how Title VII's ban on sex discrimination protects transsexual persons. Those opinions, the court observed, relied on *Ulane v. Eastern Airlines, Inc.*, 742 F.2d 1081, 1085 (7th Cir. 1984) (*supra* at p. 146), but that opinion's approach to statutory interpretation "perhaps persuasive when written, ha[s] lost [its] power after twenty years of changing jurisprudence," the *Schroer* court wrote, citing *Oncale v. Sundowner Offshore Services, Inc.*, 523 U.S. 75 (1998) (*supra* at p. 167). *Schroer I* suggested that "it may be time to revisit [District] Judge Grady's conclusion in [the trial court ruling in *Ulane*] that discrimination against transsexuals [*sic* *because they are transsexuals* is 'literally' discrimination 'because of . . . sex.'" However, *Schroer* did not so rule because, to do so, the judge thought, "[a] factual record is required, one that reflects the scientific basis of sexual identity in general, and gender dysphoria in particular."

Schroer II

Following denial of the pre-discovery motion to dismiss, Diane Schroer's counsel amended her complaint, and the following year the Library of Congress moved to dismiss the amended complaint for failure to state a claim or, in the alternative, for judgment in its favor on the pleadings. The district court denied the motion to dismiss in *Schroer v. Billington*, 525 F. Supp. 2d 58 (D.D.C. 2007) (*Schroer II*), concluding that Schroer's amended complaint "stated a Title VII claim based on a sex stereotyping theory." The court therefore did not decide whether or not to accept Schroer's argument that "discrimination against transsexuals because they are transsexuals is 'literally' discrimination 'because of . . . sex.'" The court rejected Schroer's constitutional claim that the Library of Congress violated her "constitutionally protected liberty interest in making medical decisions without penalty by the government in the absence of constitutionally sufficient justification." The court concluded that Schroer had not established that she had any such fundamental right under the Due Process Clause because she had not shown that her claimed right "to take 'the medically appropriate steps to bring her body into conformity with her gender identity'" was "either deeply rooted in this country's history or implicit to the concept of ordered liberty." The court also rejected an argument Schroer brought seeking equitable relief under the Library of Congress Act, concluding that the doctrine of "non-statutory review" would not let her pursue that extraordinary relief where the discrimination she faced could be fully remedied under Title VII.

Reading Guide for Schroer v. Billington *(D.D.C. 2008)* (Schroer III*)

1. Under Title VII as it stands now and at the time *Schroer (III)* was decided, if "sex" was a "motivating factor" behind an adverse employment action, the employer's action was unlawful, even if there were other reasons for the decision in addition to sex. (Establishing "but-for" causation requires more and is another route to

employer liability under Title VII.) Thus, the district court's opinion in Part I of the "Analysis" section below need only have shown that the Library of Congress's alleged nondiscriminatory reasons were not the only reasons for rejecting Diane Schroer and that sex was amongst its reasons. Nonetheless, the district court's opinion (following the bench trial) seems to go further and conclude in Part I of the "Analysis" section that the Library's reasons were all pretextual or false. Does the evidence recounted by the court support that conclusion? (Note that had this decision been appealed, the reviewing court would have deferentially asked of the judge's factual conclusions only whether they were "clearly erroneous," although the trial court's legal conclusions—which appear to include at least some of the considerations addressed in Part I.C—would have been reviewed "de novo" without deference.)

2. Was the district court's argument in Part II.A of its analysis that the Library of Congress discriminated against Diane Schroer based on sex stereotyping adequately supported by the evidence recounted?

3. Does the district court's invocation in Part II.A of its analysis of the idea of "an inherently gender-nonconforming transsexual" person mean that *any* anti-transgender discrimination will always be based upon sex and hence generally forbidden under Title VII? Part II.B of its analysis is sometimes cited for the proposition that the court held that "gender identity is a component of sex." This language appears *infra* at p. 209. Is this the best reading of Part II.B (and in particular its discussion of the scientific evidence presented by the parties)? What other arguments does the court make in II.B to support its seeming conclusion that anti-transgender discrimination is categorically a form of sex discrimination under Title VII?

Diane J. Schroer v. James H. Billington, Librarian of Congress (Schroer III)

577 F. Supp. 2d 293 (D.D.C. 2008)

[Diane Schroer was represented by the Capital Area ACLU and the national ACLU LGBT Project.]

Findings of Fact and Conclusions of Law

JAMES ROBERTSON, District Judge.

Diane Schroer claims that she was denied employment by the Librarian of Congress because of sex, in violation of Title VII of the Civil Rights Act of 1964, 42 U.S.C. § 2000e-2(a)(1). Evidence was taken in a bench trial on August 19–22, 2008.

Facts

Diane Schroer is a [transgender woman]. [Before] she changed her legal name or began presenting as a woman, Schroer applied for the position of Specialist in Terrorism and International Crime with the Congressional Research Service (CRS) at the Library of Congress. The terrorism specialist provides expert policy analysis to congressional committees, members of Congress and their staffs. The position requires a security clearance. Schroer was well qualified for the job. She is a graduate of both the National War College and the Army Command and General Staff College, and she holds masters degrees in history and international relations. During Schroer's twenty-five years of service in the U.S. Armed Forces, she held important command and staff positions in the Armored Calvary, Airborne, Special Forces and Special Operations Units, and in combat operations in Haiti and Rwanda. Before her retirement from the military in January 2004, Schroer was a Colonel assigned to the U.S. Special Operations Command, serving as the director of a 120-person classified organization that tracked and targeted high-threat international terrorist organizations. In this position, Colonel Schroer analyzed sensitive intelligence reports, planned a range of classified and conventional operations, and regularly briefed senior military and government officials, including the Vice President, the Secretary of Defense, and the Chairman of the Joint Chiefs of Staff. At the time of her military retirement, Schroer held a Top Secret, Sensitive Compartmented Information security clearance, and had done so on a continuous basis since 1987. After her retirement, Schroer joined a private consulting firm, Benchmark International, where, when she applied for the CRS position, she was working as a program manager on an infrastructure security project for the National Guard.

When Schroer applied for the terrorism specialist position, she had been diagnosed with gender identity disorder and was working with a licensed clinical social worker . . . to develop a medically appropriate plan for transitioning from male to female. The transitioning process was guided by a set of treatment protocols formulated by the leading organization for the study and treatment of gender identity disorders, the Harry Benjamin International Gender Dysphoria Association [now, the World Professional Association for Transgender Health (WPATH)—Eds.]. Because she had not yet begun presenting herself as a woman on a full-time basis, however, she applied for the position as "David J. Schroer," her legal name at the time. In October 2004, two months after submitting her application, Schroer was invited to interview with three members of the CRS staff—Charlotte Preece, Steve Bowman, and Francis Miko. Preece, the Assistant Director for Foreign Affairs, Defense and Trade, was the selecting official for the position. Schroer attended the interview dressed in traditionally masculine attire—a sport coat and slacks with a shirt and tie.

Schroer received the highest interview score of all eighteen candidates. In early December, Preece called Schroer, told her that she was on the shortlist of applicants still in the running, and asked for several writing samples and an updated list of references. After receiving these updated materials, the members of the selection committee unanimously recommended that Schroer be offered the job. In mid-December, Preece called Schroer [and] offered her the job. . . . Schroer accepted the offer, and Preece began to fill out the paperwork necessary to finalize the hire.

Before Preece had completed and submitted these documents, Schroer asked her to lunch on December 20, 2004. Schroer's intention was to tell Preece about her transsexuality. She was about to begin the phase of her gender transition during which she would be dressing in traditionally feminine clothing and presenting as a woman on a full-time basis. She believed that starting work at CRS as a woman would be less disruptive than if she started as a man and later began presenting as a woman.

When Schroer went to the Library for this lunch date, she was dressed in traditionally masculine attire. . . . As they were sitting down to lunch, Preece stated that they were excited to have Schroer join CRS because she was "significantly better than the other candidates." Schroer asked why that was so, and Preece explained that her skills, her operational experience, her ability creatively to answer questions, and her contacts in the military and in defense industries made her application superior.

About a half hour into their lunch, Schroer told Preece that she needed to discuss a "personal matter." She began by asking Preece if she knew what "transgender" meant. Preece responded that she did, and Schroer went on to explain that she was transgender, that she would be transitioning from male to female, and that she would be starting work as "Diane." Preece's first reaction was to ask, "Why in the world would you want to do that?" Schroer explained that she did not see being transgender as a choice and that it was something she had lived with her entire life. Preece then asked her a series of questions, starting with whether she needed to change Schroer's name on the hiring documentation. Schroer responded that she did not because her legal name, at that point, was still David. Schroer went on to explain the Harry Benjamin Standards of Care and her own medical process for transitioning. She told Preece that she planned to have facial feminization surgery in early January and assured her that recovery from this surgery was quick and would pose no problem for a mid-January start date. In the context of explaining the Benjamin [now, WPATH — Eds.] Standards of Care, Schroer explained that she would be living full-time as a woman for at least a year before having sex reassignment surgery. Such surgery, Schroer explained, could normally be accomplished during a two-week vacation period and would not interfere with the requirements of the job.

Preece then raised the issue of Schroer's security clearance, asking what name ought to appear on hiring documents. Schroer responded that she had several transgender friends who had retained their clearances while transitioning and said that she did not think it would be an issue in her case. Schroer also mentioned that her therapist would be available to answer any questions or provide additional background as needed. Because Schroer expected that there might be some concern about her appearance when presenting as a woman, she showed Preece three photographs of herself, wearing traditionally feminine professional attire. Although Preece did not say it to Schroer, her reaction on seeing these photos was that Schroer looked like "a man dressed in women's clothing." Preece did not ask Schroer whether she had told her references or anyone at Benchmark of her transition.

Although Schroer initially thought that her conversation with Preece had gone well, she thought it "ominous" that Preece ended it by stating "Well, you've given me a lot to think about. I'll be in touch."

Preece did not finish Schroer's hiring memorandum when she returned to the Library after lunch.[1] Instead, she went to speak with Cynthia Wilkins, the personnel security officer for the Library of Congress. Preece . . . asked [Wilkins] what impact [Schroer's planned transition] might have on the candidate's ability to get a security clearance. Wilkins did not know and said that she would have to look into the applicable regulations. Preece told Wilkins that the candidate was a 25-year military veteran. She did not recall whether or not she mentioned that Schroer currently held a security clearance. . . .

Preece testified that at this point, without waiting to hear more from Wilkins, she was leaning against hiring Schroer. She said that Schroer's transition raised five concerns for her. First, she was concerned about Schroer's ability to maintain her contacts within the military. Specifically, Preece thought that some of Schroer's contacts would no longer want to associate with her because she is transgender. At no point after learning of Schroer's transition, however, did Preece discuss the continuing viability of her contacts with Schroer, nor did she raise this concern with any of Schroer's references, all of whom in fact knew that she was transitioning. Second, Preece was concerned with Schroer's credibility when testifying before Congress. When CRS specialists testify before Congress, they typically provide Members with brief biographical statements to give them credibility. Preece was concerned "that everyone would know that [Schroer] had transitioned from male to female because only a man could have her military experiences." Preece thought that this would be an obstacle to Schroer's effectiveness. Third, Preece testified that she was concerned with Schroer's trustworthiness because she had not been up front about her transition from the beginning of the interview process. Preece did not, however, raise this concern to Schroer during their lunch. Fourth, Preece thought that Schroer's transition might distract her from her job. Although Preece seems to have connected this concern to Schroer's surgeries, she did not ask for additional information about them or otherwise discuss the issue further with Schroer. Finally, Preece was concerned with Schroer's ability to maintain her security clearance. In Preece's mind, "David Schroer" had a security clearance, but "Diane Schroer" did not. Even before speaking with Wilkins, Preece "strongly suspected" that David's clearance simply would not apply to Diane. She had this concern, but she did not ask Schroer for any information on the people she knew who had undergone gender transitions while retaining their clearances.

After her lunch with Schroer, Preece also relayed the details of her conversation to a number of other officials at CRS, including Daniel Mulholland, the Director of

---

1. Her partial, draft memorandum had begun:
   I recommend Mr. David Schroer for the position of Specialist in Terrorism and International Crime in the Foreign Affairs, Defense, and Trade Division of the Congressional Research Service. His qualifications and experience make[] him the best qualified candidate from among the other 8 applicants on the final referral list.
Mr. Schroer has extensive experience as a practitioner and strategic planner in counterterrorism. Since 1986 he was involved in leading counterterrorism and counter-insurgency operations around the world.

CRS, and Gary Pagliano, one of the defense section heads, whose reaction was to ask Preece if she had a good second candidate for the job. Later the same afternoon, Preece received an email from one of the Library's lawyers, setting up a meeting for the next morning to discuss the terrorism specialist position. That evening, as Preece thought about the issue, she was puzzled by the idea that "someone [could] go [] through the experience of Special Forces [and] decide that he wants to become a woman." Schroer's background in the Special Forces made it harder for Preece to think of Schroer as undergoing a gender transition.

The next morning, . . . Preece met with Kent Ronhovde, the Director of the Library of Congress, Wilkins, and two other members of the CRS staff from workforce development. Preece described her lunch conversation with Schroer and stated that Schroer had been, but no longer was, her first choice for the position. As Preece recalls the meeting, Wilkins stated that she was unable to say one way or another whether Diane Schroer would be able to get a security clearance. Preece testified that Wilkins proposed that Schroer would have to a have a "psychological fitness for duty examination," after which the Library would have to decide whether to initiate a full background investigation. Wilkins testified that she was not familiar with such an "examination" and likely would not have used such a phrase, but she confirmed that she told the meeting that she would not approve a waiver for Schroer so that she could start working before the clearance process was complete. Wilkins made this decision without having viewed Schroer's application, her resume, or her clearance status and history. Preece understood the substance of Wilkins' comments to be that David's security clearance was not relevant to Diane, and that Diane would need a separate clearance. She assumed that that process could take up to a year.

At no point during the meeting did Preece express a continuing interest in hiring Schroer. She did not suggest that Wilkins pull and review David Schroer's security file to confirm her own assumption that the security clearance process would be a lengthy one. No one in the meeting asked whether the organization currently holding Schroer's clearance knew of her transition. There was no discussion of whether anyone else at the Library had dealt with a similar situation.

By the end of the meeting, Preece had made up her mind that she no longer wanted to recommend Schroer for the terrorism specialist position. Preece testified that the security clearance was the critical, deciding factor because of "how long it would take." She also testified, however, that she would have leaned against hiring Schroer even if she had no concerns regarding the security clearance, because her second candidate, John Rollins, presented "fewer complications"—because, unlike Schroer, he was not transitioning from male to female.

Later that day, Preece circulated a draft of what she proposed to tell Schroer to those who had participated in the meeting. The email stated:

> David. I'm calling to let you know that I am not going forward with my recommendation to hire you for the terrorism position. In light of what you told me yesterday, I feel that you are putting me and CRS in an awkward

> position for a number of reasons as you go through this transition period. I am primarily concerned that you could not likely be brought on in a timeframe that is needed for me to fill the position. Our Personnel Security Office has told me that the background investigation process that will be required for you to start work could be lengthy. I am also concerned that the past contacts I had counted on you to bring to the position may not now be as fruitful as they were in the past. Finally I have concerns that the transition that you are in the process of might divert your full attention away from the mission of CRS.
>
> I could be wrong on any one of these complicated factors, but taken together I do not have a high enough degree of confidence to recommend you for the position. Having said that, I very much appreciate your candor and your courage. I wish you the best and want to let you know that you should feel free to[] apply for future positions at the Library.

Preece was then called into the General Counsel's office for a meeting at eleven o'clock. Afterward, Preece circulated a revised email with the header "Draft per discussion with General Coun[sel]." It read:

> David, Given the level and the complexities of the position, I don't think this is a good fit. This has been a difficult decision, but given the immediate needs of Congress, I've decided not to go forward with the recommendation.
>
> (Listen. If needed say) That's all I'm prepared to say at this time.

Later that same afternoon, Preece called Schroer to rescind the job offer. She said, "Well, after a long and sleepless night, based on our conversation yesterday, I've determined that you are not a good fit, not what we want." Schroer replied that she was very disappointed. Preece ended the conversation by thanking Schroer for her honesty. Preece then called John Rollins, who had a lower total interview score than Schroer, and offered him the position. He accepted.

Since January 2005, Schroer has lived full-time as a woman. She has changed her legal name to Diane Schroer and obtained a Virginia driver's license and a United States Uniformed Services card reflecting her name change and gender transition.

Analysis

It is unlawful for an employer "to fail or refuse to hire or to discharge any individual, or otherwise to discriminate against any individual with respect to his compensation, terms, conditions, or privileges of employment, because of such individual's race, color, religion, sex, or national origin." 42 U.S.C. § 2000e-2(a)(1). The "ultimate question" in every Title VII case is whether the plaintiff has proved that the defendant intentionally discriminated against her because of a protected characteristic. *St. Mary's Honor Ctr. v. Hicks*, 509 U.S. 502 (1993). The Library argues that it had a number of non-discriminatory reasons for refusing to hire Schroer. . . . The Library also argues that a hiring decision based on transsexuality is not unlawful discrimination under Title VII.

After hearing the evidence presented at trial, I conclude that Schroer was discriminated against because of sex in violation of Title VII. The reasons for that conclusion are set forth below, in two parts. First, I explain why, as a factual matter, several of the Library's stated reasons for refusing to hire Schroer were not its "true reasons, but were . . . pretext[s] for discrimination," *Tex. Dep't of Cmty. Affairs v. Burdine*, 450 U.S. 248, 253 (1981). Second, I explain why the Library's conduct, whether viewed as sex stereotyping or as discrimination literally "because of . . . sex," violated Title VII.

I

None of the five assertedly legitimate reasons that the Library has given for refusing to hire Schroer withstands scrutiny.

A. Security Clearance Concerns were Pretextual

Preece has claimed that her primary concern was Schroer's ability to receive a security clearance in a timely manner. It is uncontested that the ability to maintain or receive security clearance is a requirement for the terrorism specialist position. In light of the inquiry that the Library actually made into Schroer's clearance history and the specific facts affecting her case, however, I conclude that this issue was a pretext for discrimination. Kenneth Lopez, the Library's Director of Security and Emergency Preparedness, and Wilkins' supervisor, ... explained that, in appropriate circumstances, the Library recognizes as a matter of reciprocity the security clearance held by an individual at a prior government agency. The three general requirements for reciprocity are that the previous investigation was undertaken in a timely manner, that the investigation had an adequate scope,[2] and that there has not been a significant break in service. When new information that might raise security concerns about a candidate otherwise eligible for reciprocity is raised, the Library evaluates that information before making a decision as to whether to grant reciprocity. That there is new information does not necessarily mean that a new, full-scale investigation is needed.

When the candidate does not have a valid, prior clearance, the Library may nonetheless grant a waiver so that the person may start work, conditionally employed, before the security investigation has been completed. A waiver is not needed for someone holding a current clearance of appropriate scope.

Although Preece knew that Schroer held a security clearance, she did not provide Wilkins with any of the information that might have been needed to see whether reciprocity would apply. Wilkins had the ability to access Schroer's entire security file, but she did not do so—because she was not asked to.

---

2. "Scope" goes to the thoroughness of the prior investigation based on the level of clearance. Someone who holds only a "Secret" level clearance will not have had as thorough an investigation as someone holding a "Top Secret" clearance.

Without any specific information about Schroer—including whether she might have already addressed any issues arising out of her gender transition with the current holder of her security clearance (Benchmark)—Wilkins performed the most general kind of research. She looked into the Adjudication Guidelines and the Adjudication Desk Reference for information about transsexuality and found two potentially relevant guidelines.[3] The first was the sexual behavior guideline, which provides that sexual behavior that causes an individual to be vulnerable to blackmail or coercion may be cause for a security concern. Wilkins acknowledged, however, that an individual who has disclosed her transsexuality would not present blackmail concerns. The other potentially relevant guideline deals with security concerns raised by emotional, mental or personality disorders. Psychological disorders, including gender identity disorder, are not *per se* disqualifying but are to be evaluated as part of the person's entire background. Lopez testified when an employee discloses such a disorder, the proper procedure is for the personnel security officer to consult with the Library's Health Services. After interviewing the candidate and, potentially, his or her mental health providers, a Health Services officer determines whether or not the information raises a security concern. For an individual already holding a clearance, if Health Services is satisfied that the disorder raises no security concerns, the personnel security office proceeds to grant reciprocity.

The Library made no effort to determine whether Schroer's previous clearance would receive reciprocal recognition or to determine whether the agency previously holding Schroer's clearance already knew of, and had already investigated any concerns related to Schroer's gender identity disorder. Wilkins stated that she would not approve a waiver without determining whether reciprocity might apply, and therefore without determining whether a waiver actually would have been required. Without being given a concrete time frame by Wilkins, and without speaking to anyone in Health Services, Preece simply "assumed" that it would take a year before Schroer would be fully cleared. This assumption was connected to no specific information about Schroer or her clearance history, and was not informed by the Library's own procedures for adjudicating possible security issues arising from a psychological disorder.[4]

The Library's statements about the time pressures that they were operating under to fill the position with someone with a full security clearance, as opposed to a provisional waiver, are not credible. The terrorism specialist opening was first posted in August. Schroer was not interviewed until October and did not receive

---

3. Wilkins testified that these guidelines and reference materials implement Executive Order 10450, 18 Fed. Reg. 2489 (1953), and Executive Order 12968, 60 Fed. Reg. 40245 (1995).

4. The Library has never argued that Title VII's jurisdictional exemption regarding security clearances, 42 U.S.C. § 2000e-2(g), applies in this case, and, unlike in *Department of Navy v. Egan*, 484 U.S. 518 (1988), Schroer is not challenging the denial of a security clearance. She asserts, rather, that the Library's failure to follow its own procedures establishes pretext.

an offer until mid-December. The person who previously held the job, Audrey Cronin, worked for six months during 2003 before receiving her clearance. Cronin's first performance evaluation, completed after eight months on the job, in no way reflected that her work had been impaired by the fact that she had lacked a clearance during three quarters of the period under evaluation. John Rollins, who ultimately filled the position denied to Schroer, did not receive his final clearance until "several months" after he began working at CRS.

B. Trustworthiness and Distraction Concerns were Pretextual

The Library's professed concerns with Schroer's trustworthiness and ability to focus on the job were also pretextual. At trial, the Library conceded as undisputed that Schroer "had no other co-morbidities or stressors that would have prevented her from performing the duties of the terrorism specialist, or that would have presented any issue regarding her stability, judgment, reliability or ability to safeguard classified information." Preece's stated concern with Schroer's trustworthiness was belied by the fact that she thanked Schroer for her honesty in the course of rescinding the job offer. If Preece had really been concerned with Schroer's ability to focus on her work responsibilities, she could have raised the matter directly and asked Schroer additional questions about her planned surgeries, asked her current employer and references about Schroer's ability to focus, or spoken with Schroer's therapist, as Schroer had offered. Preece did none of those things.

C. Credibility and Contacts Concerns were Facially Discriminatory

The Library's final two proffered legitimate non-discriminatory reasons—that Schroer might lack credibility with Members of Congress, and that she might be unable to maintain contacts in the military—were explicitly based on her gender non-conformity and her transition from male to female and are facially discriminatory as a matter of law. Deference to the real or presumed biases of others is discrimination, no less than if an employer acts on behalf of his own prejudices. *See Williams v. Trans World Airlines, Inc.*, 660 F.2d 1267 (8th Cir.1981) (firing employee in response to racially charged, unverified customer complaint is direct evidence of racial discrimination by employer); *cf. Fernandez v. Wynn Oil Co.*, 653 F.2d 1273 (9th Cir. 1981) ("stereotypic impressions of male and female roles do not qualify gender as a [bona fide occupational qualification]"); *Diaz v. Pan American World Airways, Inc.*, 442 F.2d 385 (5th Cir.1971) (same). In any event, the Library made no effort to discern if its concern was actually a reasonable one, as it easily could have done by contacting any of the high-ranking military officials that Schroer listed as references.

II.

Schroer contends that the Library's decision not to hire her is sex discrimination banned by Title VII, advancing two legal theories. The first is unlawful discrimination based on her failure to conform with sex stereotypes. The second is that discrimination on the basis of gender identity is literally discrimination "because of . . . sex."

A. Sex Stereotyping

Plaintiff's sex stereotyping theory is grounded in the Supreme Court's decision in *Price Waterhouse v. Hopkins,* 490 U.S. 228 (1989) [*supra* at p. 154]. . . . After *Price Waterhouse,* numerous federal courts have concluded that punishing employees for failure to conform to sex stereotypes is actionable sex discrimination under Title VII. [Eds.: citations and parentheticals omitted.]

Following this line of cases, the Sixth Circuit has held that discrimination against transsexuals [*sic*] is a form of sex stereotyping prohibited by *Price Waterhouse* itself. . . . *Smith v. Salem,* 378 F.3d 566 (6th Cir. 2004) [*supra* at p. 174]; *see also Barnes v. City of Cincinnati,* 401 F.3d 729 (6th Cir. 2005) [*see supra* at p. 184]. In my 2006 memorandum denying the Library's motion to dismiss, in this case, I expressed reservations about the Sixth Circuit's broad reading of *Price Waterhouse.* . . . I held that what *Price Waterhouse* actually recognized was a Title VII action for *disparate treatment,* as between men and women, based on sex stereotyping. Accordingly, I concluded that "[a]dverse action taken on the basis of an employer's gender stereotype that does not impose unequal burdens on men and women does not state a claim under Title VII." While I agreed with the Sixth Circuit that a plaintiff's transsexuality is not a bar to a sex stereotyping claim, I took the position that "such a claim must actually arise from the employee's appearance or conduct and the employer's stereotypical perceptions." In other words, "a *Price-Waterhouse* claim could not be supported by facts showing that [an adverse employment action] resulted *solely* from [the plaintiff's] disclosure of her gender dysphoria." *Schroer v. Billington,* 525 F. Supp. 2d 58, 63 (D.D.C. 2007).

That was before the development of the factual record that is now before me.

My conclusion about a disparate treatment requirement relied heavily on the panel decision in *Jespersen v. Harrah's Operating Co.,* 392 F.3d 1076 (9th Cir. 2004). That decision was later affirmed *en banc. Jespersen v. Harrah's Operating Co.,* 444 F.3d 1104 (9th Cir. 2006). The defendant in *Jespersen* had instituted a company-wide "Personal Best" grooming policy, which, in addition to gender-neutral standards of fitness and professionalism, required women to wear stockings and colored nail polish, to wear their hair "teased, curled, or styled," and to wear make-up. The policy also prohibited men from wearing makeup, nail polish, or long hair. Plaintiff Darlene Jespersen was fired for refusing to wear makeup, which she testified made "her feel sick, degraded, exposed and violated," "forced [] to be feminine," and "dolled up" like a sexual object. Despite the subjective, gender-related toll that the policy exacted from Jespersen, the Ninth Circuit held that firing her for non-compliance with the policy did not violate Title VII, since, in that court's judgment, the "Personal Best" policy imposed equally burdensome, although gender-differentiated, standards on men and women.

In her post-trial briefing, Schroer convincingly argues that *Jespersen's* disparate treatment requirement ought not apply in this case. Unlike *Jespersen,* this case does not involve a generally applicable, gender-specific policy, requiring proof that the policy itself imposed unequal burdens on men and women. Instead, Schroer argues that her *direct evidence* that the Library's hiring decision was motivated by sex stereotypical views renders proof of disparate treatment unnecessary.[5]

Schroer's case indeed rests on direct evidence, and compelling evidence, that the Library's hiring decision was infected by sex stereotypes. [Preece], the decisionmaker, admitted that when she viewed the photographs of Schroer in traditionally feminine attire, with a feminine hairstyle and makeup, she saw a man in women's clothing. In conversations Preece had with colleagues at the Library after her lunch with Schroer, she repeatedly mentioned these photographs. Preece testified that her difficulty comprehending Schroer's decision to undergo a gender transition was heightened because she viewed David Schroer not just as a man, but, in light of her Special Forces background, as a particularly masculine kind of man. Preece's perception of David Schroer as especially masculine made it all the more difficult for her to visualize Diane Schroer as anyone other than a man in a dress. Preece admitted that she believed that others at CRS, as well as Members of Congress and their staffs, would not take Diane Schroer seriously because they, too, would view her as a man in women's clothing.

[Ultimately,] I do not think that it matters for purposes of Title VII liability whether the Library withdrew its offer of employment because it perceived Schroer to be an insufficiently masculine man, an insufficiently feminine woman, or an inherently gender-nonconforming transsexual [*sic*]. One or more of Preece's comments could be parsed in each of these three ways. While I would therefore conclude that Schroer is entitled to judgment based on a *Price Waterhouse*-type claim for sex stereotyping, I also conclude that she is entitled to judgment based on the language of the statute itself.

B. Discrimination Because of Sex

Schroer's second legal theory is that, because gender identity is a component of sex, discrimination on the basis of gender identity is sex discrimination. In support of this contention, Schroer adduced the testimony of Dr. Walter Bockting, a tenured associate professor at the University of Minnesota Medical School who specializes in gender identity disorders. [He] testified that it has long been accepted in the relevant scientific community that there are nine factors that constitute a person's sex. One of these factors is gender identity, which [he] defined as one's personal sense of being male or female.[7]

---

5. For example, in *Oncale v. Sundowner Offshore Services, Inc.*, the male plaintiff complaining of sexual harassment in violation of Title VII had been "forcibly subjected to sex-related, humiliating actions" and had been "physically assaulted . . . in a sexual manner" by other male co-workers. 523 U.S. 75 (1998). The Supreme Court did not require Oncale to show that he had been treated worse than women would have been treated, but only that "he suffered discrimination *in comparison to other men*." *Rene v. MGM Grand Hotel, Inc.*, 305 F.3d 1061 (9th Cir. 2002) (en banc) (emphasis in original).

7. The other eight factors, according to Dr. Bockting, are chromosomal sex, hypothalamic sex, fetal hormonal sex, pubertal hormonal sex, sex of assignment and rearing, internal morphological sex, external morphological sex, and gonads.

The Library adduced the testimony of Dr. Chester Schmidt, a professor of psychiatry at the Johns Hopkins University School of Medicine and also an expert in gender identity disorders. Dr. Schmidt disagreed with Dr. Bockting's view of the prevailing scientific consensus and testified that he and his colleagues regard gender identity as a component of "sexuality" rather than "sex." According to Dr. Schmidt, "sex" is made up of a number of facets, each of which has a determined biologic etiology. Dr. Schmidt does not believe that gender identity has a single, fixed etiology.

The testimony of both experts — on the science of gender identity and the relationship between intersex conditions and transsexuality — was impressive. Resolving the dispute between Dr. Schmidt and Dr. Bockting as to the proper scientific definition of sex, however, is not within this Court's competence. More importantly (because courts render opinions about scientific controversies with some regularity), deciding whether Dr. Bockting or Dr. Schmidt is right turns out to be unnecessary.

The evidence establishes that the Library was enthusiastic about hiring David Schroer — until she disclosed her transsexuality. The Library revoked the offer when it learned that a man named David intended to become, legally, culturally, and physically, a woman named Diane. This was discrimination "because of . . . sex."

Analysis "must begin . . . with the language of the statute itself" and "[i]n this case it is also where the inquiry should end, for where, as here, the statute's language is plain, 'the sole function of the courts is to enforce it according to its terms.'" *United States v. Ron Pair Enters.*, 489 U.S. 235 (1989) (quoting *Caminetti v. United States,* 242 U.S. 470 (1917)).

Imagine that an employee is fired because she converts from Christianity to Judaism. Imagine too that her employer testifies that he harbors no bias toward either Christians or Jews but only "converts." That would be a clear case of discrimination "because of religion." No court would take seriously the notion that "converts" are not covered by the statute. Discrimination "because of religion" easily encompasses discrimination because of a *change* of religion. But in cases where the plaintiff has changed her sex, and faces discrimination because of the decision to stop presenting as a man and to start appearing as a woman, courts have traditionally carved such persons out of the statute by concluding that "transsexuality" is unprotected by Title VII. In other words, courts have allowed their focus on the label "transsexual" to blind them to the statutory language itself.

In *Ulane v. Eastern Airlines* [*supra* at p. 146], the Seventh Circuit held that discrimination based on sex means only that "it is unlawful to discriminate against women because they are women and against men because they are men." The Court reasoned that the statute's legislative history "clearly indicates that Congress never considered nor intended that [Title VII] apply to anything other than the traditional concept of sex." The Ninth Circuit took a similar approach, holding that Title VII did not extend protection to transsexuals because Congress's "manifest purpose" in enacting the statute was only "to ensure that men and women are treated equally."

Holloway v. Arthur Andersen & Co. (9th Cir. 1977) [*see supra* at p. 137]. More recently, the Tenth Circuit has also held that because "sex" under Title VII means nothing more than "male and female," the statute only extends protection to transsexual employees "if they are discriminated against because they are male or because they are female." *Etsitty v. Utah Transit Authority,* 502 F.3d 1215 (10th Cir. 2005).

The decisions holding that Title VII only prohibits discrimination against men because they are men, and discrimination against women because they are women, represent an elevation of "judge-supposed legislative intent over clear statutory text." *Zuni Pub. Sch. Dist. No. 89 v. Dep't of Educ.,* 550 U.S. 81 (2007) (Scalia, J., dissenting).[8] In their holdings that discrimination based on changing one's sex is not discrimination because of sex, *Ulane, Holloway,* and *Etsitty* essentially reason "that a thing may be within the letter of the statute and yet not within the statute, because not within its spirit, nor within the intention of its makers." *Church of the Holy Trinity v. United States,* 143 U.S. 457 (1892). This is no longer a tenable approach to statutory construction. *See Public Citizen v. United States Dep't of Justice,* 491 U.S. 440, 473 (1989) (Kennedy, J., concurring). Supreme Court decisions subsequent to *Ulane* and *Holloway* have applied Title VII in ways Congress could not have contemplated. As Justice Scalia wrote for a unanimous court:

> Male-on-male sexual harassment in the workplace was assuredly not the principal evil Congress was concerned with when it enacted Title VII. But statutory prohibitions often go beyond the principal evil to cover reasonably comparable evils, and it is ultimately the provisions of our laws rather than the principal concerns of our legislators by which we are governed.

Oncale[, *supra* at p. 168.]

For Diane Schroer to prevail on the facts of her case, however, it is not necessary to draw sweeping conclusions about the reach of Title VII. Even if the decisions that define the word "sex" in Title VII as referring only to anatomical or chromosomal sex are still good law—after that approach "has been eviscerated by *Price Waterhouse,*" *Smith,* 378 F.3d at 573—the Library's refusal to hire Schroer after being advised that she planned to change her anatomical sex by undergoing sex reassignment surgery was *literally* discrimination "because of . . . sex."

In 2007, a bill that would have banned employment discrimination on the basis of sexual orientation and gender identity was introduced in the House of Representatives. *See* H.R. 2015, 110 Cong., 1st Sess. (2007). Two alternate bills were later introduced: one that banned discrimination only on the basis of sexual orientation, H.R. 3685, 110 Cong., 1st Sess. (2007), and another that banned only gender

---

8. Discrimination because of race has never been limited only to discrimination for being one race or another. Instead, courts have recognized that Title VII's prohibition against race discrimination protects employees from being discriminated against because of an interracial marriage, or based on friendships that cross racial lines. *See, e.g., McGinest v. GTE Serv. Corp.,* 360 F.3d 1103, 1118 (9th Cir. 2004).

identity discrimination, H.R. 3686, 110 Cong., 1st Sess. (2007). None of those bills was enacted.

The Library asserts that the introduction and non-passage of H.R.2015 and H.R. 3686 shows that transsexuals are not currently covered by Title VII and also that Congress is content with the status quo. However, as Schroer points out, another reasonable interpretation of that legislative non-history is that some Members of Congress believe that the *Ulane* court and others have interpreted "sex" in an unduly narrow manner, that Title VII means what it says, and that the statute requires, not amendment, but only correct interpretation. As the Supreme Court has explained,

> [S]ubsequent legislative history is a hazardous basis for inferring the intent of an earlier Congress. It is a particularly dangerous ground on which to rest an interpretation of a prior statute when it concerns, as it does here, a proposal that does not become law. Congressional inaction lacks persuasive significance because several equally tenable inferences may be drawn from such inaction, including the inference that the existing legislation already incorporated the offered change.

Pension Ben. Guar. Corp. v. LTV Corp., 496 U.S. 633, 650 (1990).

Conclusion

In refusing to hire Diane Schroer because her appearance and background did not comport with the decisionmaker's sex stereotypes about how men and women should act and appear, and in response to Schroer's decision to transition, legally, culturally, and physically, from male to female, the Library of Congress violated Title VII's prohibition on sex discrimination. The Clerk is directed to set a conference to discuss and schedule the remedial phase of this case.

Discussion

1. Should we read *Schroer* as holding that anti-transgender discrimination is always sex discrimination within the meaning of Title VII?

2. If you were in-house counsel advising an employer who came to you with concerns about potentially hiring a transgender applicant after *Schroer* and before *Bostock v. Clayton County, Georgia*, 140. S. Ct. (2020), *infra*, at p.244, what advice would you provide?

3. Consider the ethical and strategic issues addressed by one of Diane Schroer's counsel, Sharon McGowan (at the time of the ACLU LGBT Project, subsequently of the Civil Rights Division at the Department of Justice, and as of the date of this publication the Chief Strategy Officer and Legal Director of Lambda Legal), in the excerpts from her article below.

Reading Guide for McGowan,
Reflections on *Schroer v. Billington*

1. As you read, consider the range of potential arguments that a transgender individual could raise for a sex discrimination claim under Title VII. What argument did Ms. McGowan and the ACLU ultimately emphasize for Ms. Schroer? Why did they choose this argumentative approach? How does the court respond to this argument?

2. How do the rules of professional responsibility shape McGowan's approach in the case?

3. McGowan concludes that her arguments in the case "had a positive influence . . . in terms of affirming the autonomy and integrity of [her] client." As you read, consider the steps that McGowan took to achieve this outcome.

Working with Clients to Develop Compatible Visions of What It Means to "Win" A Case: Reflections on Schroer v. Billington[*]

Sharon M. McGowan

"I haven't gone through all this only to have a court vindicate my rights as a gender non-conforming man." I remember quite vividly the day that Diane Schroer expressed this sentiment to me. It was April 2005, and she and I had not yet signed a retainer agreement establishing the contours of a legal relationship that has lasted over four years. Perhaps more than any other conversation that we had over the course of her employment discrimination case against the Library of Congress ("Library"), this statement from Ms. Schroer illustrated how much more can be at stake for a client, and particularly for a transgender[3] client like Ms. Schroer, than simply winning or losing a legal claim. Some of the more challenging issues in the case, which I initially viewed as merely litigation strategy concerns, involved for Ms. Schroer fundamental questions about how her lawyer would present her life experience and, to some extent, defend the validity of her very identity to a court.

In this article, I recount my experience representing a transgender client, Diane Schroer, in her employment discrimination case against the Library. In doing so, I hope to illustrate practical and ethical questions and challenges that can arise in any kind of litigation. For example, do the lawyer and the client have compatible visions of what it means to "win" the case, and what steps does the lawyer need to take at various points during the litigation to ensure that the lawyer's actions are

---

[*] Excerpted with author's permission from 45 *Harvard Civil Rights-Civil Liberties Law Review* 205 (2010), Copyright © 2010 the President and Fellows of Harvard College; Sharon M. McGowan.

3. For purposes of this article, I shall use the terms Gender Identity Disorder, gender dysphoria, and transsexuality interchangeably, unless otherwise indicated, to describe the experience of having a gender identity different from the sex assigned to an individual at birth. [relocated footnote—Eds.]

consistent with this vision? How and when can a lawyer protect a client's privacy when engaging in high profile litigation? How should a lawyer respond when the court poses what seems to be the wrong question and suggests that the answer may be dispositive of the case? When should an advocate bring a claim that has a high risk of producing bad law not only in her own case but also for future litigants based on her belief that, even in losing the claim, benefits might accrue to her client?

. . . .

I. Background

. . . .

Ms. Schroer was devastated by [the] news [of Charlotte Preece's change of mind]. In anticipation of beginning with the Library, Ms. Schroer severed professional ties with her previous employer and disclosed her plan to transition to personal and professional contacts. After the Library rescinded the job offer, Ms. Schroer struggled to find work and had many sleepless nights worrying about how she would sustain herself. Although friends referred work to her, the projects were either unfulfilling or presented no opportunity for professional development. More demoralizing, though, was the fact that Ms. Schroer, a highly independent and self-sufficient person, was reduced to relying on her friends for work so that she could survive.

[Ms.] Schroer experienced a period of tremendous despair, during which time she had grave doubts about her ability to live a meaningful and successful life. As the court later acknowledged, it "cast doubt on the viability of living an open and productive life as a woman." Her stress manifested itself in ways that were physically painful as well as psychologically taxing.

. . . .

II. Key Pre-Litigation Questions

As an impact litigation organization, the ACLU looks for cases that are factually "clean" and have a significant likelihood of producing a favorable ruling on an important legal issue. At this stage, we only had Ms. Schroer's version of the events, but from what she told us, it appeared to be a straightforward case of discrimination due to the fact that Ms. Schroer was transgender. Everyone at the Project recognized how unfairly the Library had treated Ms. Schroer, but that fact alone did not mean that we would bring a case on her behalf. We would need to address a number of important questions before we could agree to represent her.

A. Assessing the Strength of Our Title VII Claim

[B]y the mid-1980s, a lawyer investigating the issue might have reasonably believed that transgender individuals who suffered discrimination due to their gender identity or transgender status had no claim under Title VII.

In 2003, the legal landscape changed significantly. In *Smith v. City of Salem* [*supra* at p. 174], the Sixth Circuit overruled a trial court decision to dismiss the complaint of a transgender fire fighter who claimed that his [*sic*] employer discriminated against him because of his failure to conform to social stereotypes associated with men. The court's ruling rested on the Supreme Court's 1989 decision in *Price Waterhouse v. Hopkins* [*supra* at p. 155] .... A second case from the Sixth Circuit, *Barnes v. City of Cincinnati*, [*see supra* at p. 183] confirmed that the sex stereotyping theory was a viable legal claim that transgender individuals could use to challenge adverse employment actions based on their gender nonconformity.

1. How Applicable and Helpful Were Existing Sex Stereotyping Precedents?

[T]hese Sixth Circuit decisions did not guarantee success in our case. First, as decisions from another circuit, neither *Smith* nor *Barnes* would bind a federal district court in the District of Columbia. Second, and more importantly, there were factual differences between our case and the *Smith* and *Barnes* cases. Specifically, in both *Smith* and *Barnes*, the plaintiffs were transgender women in the early stages of their gender transition. They had begun to exhibit more feminine characteristics, but were still presenting themselves as male in the workplace. By contrast, Ms. Schroer was not someone who experienced discrimination when she began gradually exhibiting more feminine features. Rather, she presented photographs of herself dressed as a woman to her employer and explained that she wanted to begin work as Diane rather than David, with a presentation that was consistent with the social conventions associated with women's professional attire. In other words, Ms. Schroer was not gradually departing from male stereotypes in terms of her appearance. Hers was not a case of a man growing his hair or fingernails "too long," or speaking in an increasingly feminine manner. Rather, from the employer's perspective, Ms. Schroer was a man one day, and a woman the next. We believed that the decision maker's discomfort with this transition by Ms. Schroer almost certainly stemmed, at least in part, from the decision maker's stereotypical beliefs about who is a man and who is a woman. It was nevertheless unclear to us whether these factual differences between our case and those earlier decisions would preclude us from convincing a court that what happened to Ms. Schroer was sex stereotyping just as it had been in *Smith* and *Barnes*.

Another fundamental question dealt with Ms. Schroer's personal identity. *Smith* and *Barnes* were both transgender women, but their complaints alleged that they were discriminated against because they were men who failed to conform to gender stereotypes associated with men. Framing their allegations in this manner was strategically sound in light of rulings in cases like *Rosa v. Park West Bank & Trust Co.* [*supra* at p. 172], in which the First Circuit Court of Appeals, applying *Price Waterhouse* to another remedial statute—the Equal Credit Opportunity Act—ruled that a man denied a credit application because he was dressed in traditionally feminine attire stated a claim of sex discrimination. Like the plaintiffs in *Smith* and *Barnes*, Rosa alleged that the bank discriminated against him by refusing to give him a credit application for failure to act and dress in a manner consistent with social norms and stereotypes associated with men.

We knew that the lawyers who had litigated these prior cases were deeply committed to promoting the rights of transgender people, and that they had framed their cases in the way most likely to fit within the *Price Waterhouse* theory. Nevertheless, arguing that Ms. Schroer was a man who failed to conform to social stereotypes associated with men felt uncomfortable to many of us at the Project, myself included. It felt as though we would be disavowing Ms. Schroer's identity as a woman, and accepting society's discriminatory conception that transgender women are just men who want to dress as women. Using a different framework for our case than was deployed in these previous cases, however, was an untested strategy.

Before filing a complaint, two important and interrelated questions had to be resolved. First, for purposes of pleading the elements of our Title VII claim, we needed to decide to which "protected class" we would allege that Ms. Schroer belonged. Second, and perhaps more importantly, who would make the final decision if Ms. Schroer reached a different conclusion than we did about the best course to pursue?

2. What Gender Is Your Client for Purposes of Litigation and Who Decides?

The Model Rules of Professional Conduct delineate decisions that are "client" decisions, and those that are "lawyer" decisions.[27] With respect to certain decisions, the line is easy to discern. For example, whether to accept a settlement offer or whether to testify are two examples of clear "client" decisions.

The rule also authorizes lawyers to "take such action on behalf of the client as is impliedly authorized to carry out the representation." In other words, the lawyer does not need to confer with the client prior to making many decisions related to the litigation of a case. The lawyer does not, however, have a blank check once the retainer is signed. The rules impose a duty upon the lawyer to "reasonably consult with the client about the means by which the client's objectives are to be accomplished," as well as to "explain a matter to the extent reasonably necessary to permit the client to make informed decisions regarding the representation."[30] A lawyer must discuss with the client not only the "objectives of [the] representation," but also the "means by which they are to be pursued."[31]

What constitutes a "reasonable" level of consultation about "the means by which the client's objectives are to be accomplished" can vary from client to client. The appropriate level will depend on a variety of factors, including, for example, the client's educational background and comprehension. A client's desire and ability to engage actively in these decisions may also depend on her emotional state and the

---

27. See MODEL RULES OF PROF'L CONDUCT R. 1.2(a) (1983) ("Subject to paragraphs (c) and (d), a lawyer shall abide by a client's decisions concerning the objectives of representation and, as required by Rule 1.4, shall consult with the client as to the means by which they are to be pursued. A lawyer may take such action on behalf of the client as is impliedly authorized to carry out the representation. A lawyer shall abide by a client's decision whether to settle a matter. In a criminal case, the lawyer shall abide by the client's decision, after consultation with the lawyer, as to a plea to be entered, whether to waive jury trial and whether the client will testify.").

30. MODEL RULES OF PROF'L CONDUCT R. 1.4(a)(2) & (b).

31. MODEL RULES OF PROF'L CONDUCT R. 1.2(a).

other challenges she is facing at the time of the litigation. Undoubtedly, many clients want their lawyer to frame a case in whatever way the lawyer thinks will maximize their chances of success and either do not want or do not feel competent to offer their opinion about the best strategy.

In our case, by contrast, Ms. Schroer had both the capacity and the desire to engage in a relatively sophisticated conversation about important strategic decisions that we faced, and could weigh the advantages and disadvantages associated with the different ways in which we could frame her sex stereotyping claim. What I perhaps underestimated was how much I would come to value her feedback during moments like this in the litigation. Instead of simply fulfilling my obligation to keep my client informed, these conversations were extremely helpful to me in thinking through our arguments. Yet, it became clearer to me over time that how we presented Ms. Schroer's life and identity to the court was more than just a strategic question. For her, it was also a highly personal matter implicating fundamental issues of identity and integrity. For these reasons, regardless of whether or not the letter of the rule required us to consult with Ms. Schroer regarding how we would frame our sex stereotyping claim in our pleadings, this decision was simply too important for us to make it without her input.

[I]n April 2005, Ms. Schroer and I met for the first time.

Upon meeting Ms. Schroer, I was struck by her calm and quiet demeanor. When I explained that the ACLU looks for cases that have the potential to serve as vehicles for public education, I wondered whether Ms. Schroer would decide that the exposure attendant with being an ACLU client was not something for which she was willing to volunteer. Even so, I hoped and suspected that Ms. Schroer would recognize that her life story, and particularly her extraordinary military background, was rather unique, and that it could potentially change people's attitudes and opinions both about who transgender people are and about the rampant discrimination they face. Ms. Schroer's willingness to consider litigation with us also seemed to me to be heightened by the fact that the discriminating party in this case was the federal government. To Ms. Schroer, the Library's actions felt more like a breach of trust in light of her decades of service and dedication in the military, and thus stung in a more painful way than if the employer had been a private sector entity.

. . . .

Before Ms. Schroer could decide whether she was willing to have the ACLU represent her, it was critical to discuss how we might frame a sex stereotyping claim. I explained that the only successful cases until that point had described the transgender female plaintiff as a gender nonconforming man. I also acknowledged that she might find it distasteful to file a complaint in federal court describing herself as a gender nonconforming man. Not surprisingly, Ms. Schroer indicated that she was not interested in making her life an open book by filing a lawsuit with the ACLU if the best case scenario was a court ruling that vindicated the right of a gender nonconforming man to be free of discrimination. In her view, she had decided to transition — and thereby risk discrimination by actors like the Library — precisely so that she could finally live her life as a woman, and it was her female identity that she wanted a court to affirm.

I explained that another option available to us, one that to my knowledge had never been employed successfully, was to plead in the complaint that Ms. Schroer was a woman, but that the employer had perceived Ms. Schroer to be a man at the time of her application for the position. From this premise, we would build our argument that the Library's actions were the product of impermissible sex stereotyping. In addition to being untested, however, this approach carried with it other risks that became clearer to me over time.

One case that seemed to support this strategy was *Kastl v. Maricopa County Community College District*.[32] In June 2004, a federal district court in Arizona rejected a motion to dismiss a Title VII and Title IX claim brought by a transgender woman who alleged that her employer's requirement that she use men's restroom facilities until she could provide proof of genital surgery, and her subsequent termination for failure to abide with that requirement, constituted discrimination because of her failure to conform to sex stereotypes. Of particular interest to us was that Kastl alleged that she was a "biological female incorrectly assigned to the male sex at birth." The court denied the defendant's motion to dismiss her Title VII claim, ruling that, unless an employer could prove that the presence or absence of certain anatomy (typically associated with a particular sex) is a bona fide occupational qualification ("BFOQ") for a position, adverse action against an employee for his or her failure to have anatomy that is stereotypically associated with a particular sex is a form of sex discrimination forbidden by Title VII.

As it turned out, this ruling in *Kastl*, which gave us such cause for optimism, did not reveal the complicated procedural maneuvering that preceded it, and in August 2006, the district court granted defendant's motion for summary judgment. . . . .

[Kastl had] filed an amended complaint in which she alleged that she was a "biological female." Specifically, she asserted that she "was raised as a male and lived as a male until her biological sex was correctly determined to be female." It was this complaint that produced the favorable motion to dismiss ruling upon which we intended to rely in our briefing. On a Rule 12(b)(6) motion, the court insisted, all of plaintiff's allegations — including her allegation that she was biologically female — would be accepted as true, and requiring a female to use male restroom facilities would state a claim of discrimination under Title VII and Title IX.

The proceedings in *Kastl* then took what I viewed as a disturbing turn that I recognized could have serious implications for our case. During discovery, the defendant insisted upon testing every allegation in Kastl's complaint, including the

---

32. No. Civ.02-1531PHX-SRB, 2004 WL 2008954, at *9–10 (D. Ariz. June 3, 2004) (order granting in part and denying in part defendant's motion to dismiss).

allegation that she was a "biological female." Consequently, the defendant demanded that Kastl submit to an independent medical examination (IME), including a blood draw, so that the defendant could conduct chromosomal testing to determine whether she was, in fact, a biological female. Kastl refused to submit voluntarily to a blood draw, which triggered a motion to compel from the defendant and a motion for a protective order from the plaintiff. The court agreed with the defendant's position that Kastl placed her biological sex "in controversy," and ordered her to submit to a blood draw.

The results of the chromosomal testing indicated that Kastl's chromosomal makeup was the XY pattern typically associated with males. Based on this evidence, and the fact that Kastl had male genitalia and was incapable of producing female hormones, the defendant moved for summary judgment, arguing that Kastl could not make out a prima facie case under Title VII because she was unable, in the face of this evidence, to establish that she was a biological woman, meaning—in the defendant's view—that she was not a member of a protected class. The district court agreed and granted the defendant's motion. The comments in the footnotes of the court's ruling on summary judgment suggest that the court might have been open to considering Kastl's argument that sex was more than merely a matter of chromosomes, genitalia, and hormones, and that her sex was, in fact, female, if Kastl had produced any scientific evidence in admissible form. Specifically, the court remarked upon Kastl's failure to demonstrate the existence of a disputed issue of material fact regarding whether she was a biological female during the events in the case, and noted that it was not inclined to reach out and create a disputed issue in light of the lack of any expert testimony or other admissible evidence from Kastl on the issue.

Had we known more about the procedural history of the Kastl case when considering our pleading options in 2005, we likely would have had greater reservations about alleging in our complaint that Ms. Schroer was a woman. On the other hand, at the time that we were making these key decisions, we were equally unaware that, in a 2001 case from Australia, a family court judge had ruled that a transgender man's legal sex was male (for purposes of assessing whether he was validly married to his wife), based on the kind of scientific evidence that Kastl had indicated that she would provide in support of her claims.[48]

[In] Spring 2005, . . . when we were weighing our options in Ms. Schroer's case, we did not have the benefit of any of this information. As a result, we were not

---

48. *Re Kevin* (2001) 165 F.L.R. 404 (Austl.) (Chisholm, J.), *aff'd sub nom., Attorney-Gen. for The Commonwealth v. "Kevin and Jennifer" and Human Rights and Equal Opportunity Comm'n* (2003) 172 F.L.R. 300 (Full Court of the Family Court of Australia affirming that post-operative transgender person (female to male) was a man at the time of his marriage). Particularly in the realm of transgender rights, advocates should remember that international tribunals, including national courts (*e.g.*, Canada, Australia) and regional human rights tribunals (*e.g.*, European Court of Justice, European Court of Human Rights), are sources of authority that, while not controlling, can often be directly on point, and thus highly persuasive to a decision-maker who is not overtly hostile to foreign law. . . . .

thinking about our case as an opportunity to litigate the questions of what criteria should be used to determine a person's sex or to litigate the etiology of gender identity and transsexuality. Instead, we focused on surviving a motion to dismiss our Title VII sex stereotyping claim without having to concede that Ms. Schroer was a "gender nonconforming man."

We attempted to avoid this difficulty by alleging that Ms. Schroer had a female gender identity, and thus was a woman, but that she had likely been perceived to be a man by the hiring official at the time of her application based on her traditionally male name and appearance. We then alleged that the hiring official's decision was based either on Ms. Schroer's failure to conform with social stereotypes associated with women or her failure to conform with social stereotypes associated with men, or some combination of the two. As we had not yet had the chance to depose any Library employees involved in the decision to rescind Ms. Schroer's offer, we could not provide further detail about the particular ways in which Ms. Schroer's failure to conform to traditional sex stereotypes had influenced the Library's decision. But we felt confident that our sex stereotyping allegations covered all of the possible iterations, and thus would be sufficient to survive a motion to dismiss. Once discovery began, we believed that depositions of the decision maker(s) would reveal how sex stereotyping had operated in this case.

B. Beyond Sex Stereotyping: Weighing the Risks and Benefits of Raising Other Potential Legal Claims

Although sex stereotyping was a sound theory for our Title VII claim, we had lingering concerns that a court viewing transgender issues only through this lens might not gain a sufficient understanding of what it meant to be transgender. Consequently, we began considering other claims that might provide us with a better vehicle for describing the experience of being transgender to a court with little or no familiarity with the concepts of gender identity, gender transition, and transsexuality beyond the negative images that appear in mainstream media. As we explored other options, however, it was evident that they came with significant political baggage.

. . . .

2. Framing the Decision to Undertake a Gender Transition as an Exercise of Constitutionally Protected Liberty

In mulling over this question, we recalled how, in numerous past transgender cases that we at the ACLU considered, the problems faced by the transgender employee related less to whether an employer was treating men and women differently in ways that were legally impermissible, and more to whether the employer respected the gender identity of the employee when deciding which gender's rules applied. Gendered dress codes and access to sex-segregated facilities like restrooms are two examples of where this issue might arise in the workplace. Unlike pure animus-driven cases of employment termination or denial of access to housing or public accommodations, which we thought of as "equality" claims, these cases involved the right of transgender people to define who they were and how they would live their lives—issues that were grounded in constitutional guarantees of autonomy and liberty as much, if not more than, equality principles.

From this point of departure, ... we looked to the liberty and autonomy guarantees encompassed by the Due Process Clause in an attempt not only to explain to the court what it meant for an individual to be transgender, but also to convey the gravity of the decision to transition from living as the gender assigned to a person at birth to the gender that was consistent with the person's gender identity.

. . . .

3. Defending Our Substantive Due Process Claim

. . . .

[The] court's recognition that Ms. Schroer's case involved her right to define herself as a woman, and live as a woman, appeared to present an obstacle in terms of our ability to convince the court that this case also involved impermissible sex stereotyping. As the court noted in its [2006] decision, Ms. Schroer was not someone who was simply looking to deviate from social stereotypes associated with masculinity. Rather, she identified as, and wished to live as, a woman. In many ways, she sought to embrace the social stereotypes associated with femininity. The court's recognition that Ms. Schroer was not simply a gender nonconforming man led to a dismissal without prejudice of our sex stereotyping claim. It appeared to us that the court believed that an employer's discomfort with someone who is transgender precluded an argument that the employer's actions were also motivated by impermissible considerations about proper behavior, conduct and appearance by men and women based on sex stereotypes.

Fortunately, in the course of discovery, we obtained statements from individuals involved in the Library's decision-making process that demonstrated how sex stereotyping influenced its decision, and therefore, we were able to amend our complaint to resuscitate those claims.[101] But at that first critical stage in the case, the court focused on the fact that Ms. Schroer lost her position with the Library because of her intention to live as a woman. Because none of the adverse Title VII decisions from the 1970s and 1980s involving transgender litigants was decided in the D.C. Circuit, none of them bound our court in terms of answering the question whether

---

101. Specifically, the decisionmaker stated that when she saw the photos of Ms. Schroer in female attire, in her view, Ms. Schroer looked like a man in a dress. The decision-maker also said that she did not believe that Ms. Schroer would be credible testifying before Congress because people would think that experiences on Ms. Schroer's resume were only experiences that a man could have. Statements like these, we argued, demonstrated that the Library's decisions had been based on impermissible sex stereotypes, even though there were certain ways Ms. Schroer was being penalized for being perceived as a man who did not conform to male stereotypes based on her appearance, and in other ways was suffering because she would be perceived as a woman who did not conform to female stereotypes in terms of her background and experience. The court recognized that these allegations were sufficient to state a claim of sex stereotyping, *Schroer v. Billington*, 525 F. Supp. 2d 58 (D.D.C. 2007), and once these allegations were proven at trial, that they were sufficient to sustain a finding of liability under Title VII. *Schroer v. Billington*, 577 F. Supp. 2d 293 (D.D.C. 2008).

discrimination against someone because of their gender identity or transsexuality was discrimination because of sex. Free from the constraints of any adverse precedent, the court asked the parties to build a record "that reflect[ed] the scientific basis of sexual identity in general, and gender dysphoria in particular" so that he could consider this question with the benefit of a fuller record.[102]

III. Mid-Litigation Decisions

We were pleased to survive the government's motion to dismiss, but knew that we were still in a very tenuous position. Although we were excited that the court was open to hearing evidence about the nature of gender identity, we were somewhat surprised by how the court framed the question. As mentioned previously, we did not anticipate the extent to which this case would involve litigation over issues of the etiology of gender identity and GID, but these were questions with which we now needed to grapple.

. . . .

B. Answering the Question of Whether Gender Identity is Part of One's "Biological Sex"

. . . .

Ultimately, . . . we tried to signal to the court that it did not need to reach the question of whether or not gender identity was part of one's biological sex. Rather, we sought to create a safety valve by reiterating to the court that, whether there is a known definitive biological determinant of gender identity or not, as a matter both of law and of scientific fact, one's gender identity is part of one's sex.

To some extent, this litigation position was in tension with our own client's views on the subject. Throughout the litigation, Ms. Schroer would share with me news reports about scientific research developments in the field of sexual differentiation of the brain. I would share these reports with Dr. Bockting to determine whether we could use these studies and reports to bolster our arguments, but in most cases, the stories were either reiterating the findings of reports we had already included in our presentation to the court or were describing hypotheses that were still being tested with the necessary degree of scientific rigor. Ultimately, however, Ms. Schroer agreed with our view that any positive ruling from the court that hinged on the verifiability of particular scientific truths could be vulnerable on appeal and therefore did not object to the strategy we adopted in our post-trial briefing.

In its ruling after trial, the court acknowledged the extensive expert testimony about the origins of gender identity and Gender Identity Disorder, but determined that it could rule on the legal issues presented in the case without deciding between the experts on the questions of etiology that the court itself had posed. The court concluded that the Library violated Title VII using straightforward statutory interpretation principles by analogizing our case to a case of religious discrimination. . . .

---

102. *Schroer v. Billington*, 424 F. Supp. 2d 203 (D.D.C. 2006).

The ruling was clear, easy to follow, and did not require the court to take a position on whether or not gender identity is part of one's biological sex.

The decision of the court to avoid this question was undoubtedly good for the case, and good for Ms. Schroer. Throughout the litigation, we recognized that any favorable decision for our client from the trial court might result in an appeal, and as we discussed with Ms. Schroer, a ruling that hinged on a determination by the court that gender identity was part of a person's biological sex might have felt like an especially "appealable" issue. Moreover, although the court's resolution of the factual dispute over whether gender identity was part of one's biological sex is the kind of finding that should generally be treated with deference by an appellate panel, the relevance of the answer to that scientific question to the question of whether gender identity was part of sex for purposes of Title VII remained a legal question, and thus would not be entitled to deference on appeal.

Therefore, from our perspective, the court's decision not to opine on whether gender identity was part of one's biological sex took one potential appealable issue out of the mix. The fact that the court based its Title VII ruling on both the sex stereotyping and "change of sex" theories gave us even greater confidence that we could defend this ruling for our client on appeal if necessary.

IV. Post-Litigation Reflections

Even after securing an outstanding result for our client, there are always "what if?" moments at the end of litigation. In this section, I explore two questions that linger in my mind about this case and that I expect to encounter again in future cases involving transgender clients.

A. Should We Have Pushed the Court to Rule that Gender Identity is Part of Sex?

Although I am comfortable that we made the right decision in terms of our case, and in defending the interests of our client, by signaling to the court that it need not rule on the question of whether gender identity is part of a person's biological sex, I still cannot help but wonder whether we lost an opportunity to secure a legal ruling on that question that would have been tremendously useful in later advocacy efforts.

My residual doubts were heightened somewhat after meeting Rachael Wallbank, an outstanding lawyer from Australia, during the 2009 biennial conference of the World Professional Association [for] Transgender Health in Oslo, Norway. Wallbank litigated the *Kevin* case, which involved the validity of the marriage of a couple involving a transgender husband and nontransgender wife, before an Australian family court judge.

I was especially excited to meet her because she had presented evidence similar to the evidence we had presented in *Schroer*, but secured the result that had eluded us. In her case, the state argued that a person's legal sex was determined by their chromosomal makeup, but their argument was a purely legal one. . . . Unlike in our case, the state did not put forth any expert testimony to contradict the testimony from Wallbank's experts that an individual's gender identity was a product of a person's "brain sex." After hearing all of the testimony, the judge concluded that, on balance, it was more likely than not that gender identity is a product of biological influences, including brain development, and that transsexuality was a natural variation of gender that, like intersexuality, demonstrated that gender was a spectrum rather than a rigid binary. While the court's determination that Kevin's legal sex was male "[did] not depend on this factual finding," the court offered an extensive analysis about the scientific support for the argument that gender identity was a part of one's biological sex.

. . . .

The significance of such findings by a court becomes clear when you examine the ways in which transgender people continue to suffer discrimination in their daily lives. Even in jurisdictions where gender identity discrimination is explicitly prohibited by the law, courts have sua sponte crafted exceptions to these laws with respect to gender-segregated facilities such as restrooms. The courts reason that, whereas discrimination against someone in terms of hiring and firing is proscribed by gender identity provisions, it is not gender identity discrimination to restrict an individual's access to the facility that corresponds with his or her "biological sex." For example, in *Goins v. West Group*,[142] a transgender woman sued her employer when it refused to allow her to use the female restroom at her place of employment. Minnesota law contained an explicit prohibition on discrimination due to gender identity and expression as part of its prohibition on sexual orientation discrimination. Nevertheless, the court found that the employer's refusal to allow a transgender woman to use the gender-identity appropriate restroom did not violate the state's prohibition on discrimination due to gender identity. The court found nothing wrong with an employer's designation of restrooms based on "biological sex," and ruled that, unless a transgender woman could prove that she was a member of that "biological sex," it was not discrimination for an employer to deny her access to the women's restroom.

. . . .

If advocates had a definitive legal ruling making clear that gender identity is part of what constitutes a person's biological sex, it seems like it would—or at least should—be much more difficult to restrict the access of transgender people to gender-identity appropriate facilities simply by characterizing access restrictions as neutral rules reflecting an irrefutable biological truth about sex. I am not naïve enough to believe that a ruling in our case that gender identity is part of one's biological sex would be a panacea for discrimination against transgender people in terms of their access to sex-segregated facilities. I suspect, however, that such a ruling would have been a powerful tool in our arsenal for combating the kinds of discrimination that most regularly interfere with transgender people's ability to participate meaningfully in society.

---

142. 635 N.W.2d 717 (Minn. 2001).

I recognize, of course, the limitations of relying on biological arguments to advance claims to equality, liberty, and basic human dignity. As discussed in the context of the debate over whether there is a biological or genetic explanation for a same-sex sexual orientation, framing the discussion about the source of one's gender identity in biological terms can create the impression that the claim to equality derives from a person's "innocence" with respect to the underlying condition that is triggering discrimination by third parties. Furthermore, there are many people for whom the question of gender identity is more complicated than whether they "feel like a man" or "feel like a woman" "on the inside." For them, their identity is more complicated than our current binary structure can accommodate. Until our society recognizes that its division of the world into a male-female binary simply does not reflect the range of experiences in the world, we will need to find ways to affirm the dignity and humanity of people for whom the options of male and female are neither descriptively accurate nor normatively affirming. Nevertheless, I believe that there can, and should, be a way to debunk the primacy given to certain biological manifestations of sex and gender, particularly chromosomes and genitalia, and legal advocacy regarding this issue must continue to be one option that we explore in order to achieve that goal.

. . . .

Conclusion

Many lawyers go through an entire career without having the opportunity to represent a client like Diane Schroer. Even fewer are lucky enough to have an amazing client with a compelling story at a time when society and the law (in that order) are prepared to revisit an injustice that has been left unaddressed for many years. In our case, we attempted to breathe life into old claims that had been left for dead, and tried to think about transgender civil rights issues in new ways that would promote the equality, liberty, and dignity of a group of people whom society has all but stripped of their humanity and their hope. Overall, I believe that we succeeded, but not without experiencing a few bumps along the way. By describing the challenges that we encountered and by sharing our experience in grappling with these challenges, I hope that future advocates for transgender clients will be able to learn from and either avoid or successfully navigate the pitfalls that we encountered along the way.

The challenges that we experienced, however, are in no way unique to working with transgender clients, and I hope that this article will assist advocates both in terms of developing their client relationships and choosing litigation strategy, and preferably in that order. In terms of specific strategic decisions that we made, the risks we took in terms of framing our client's gender and in presenting a novel claim about the constitutional interests implicated by our client's decision to transition were, in my view, risks worth taking. Although we do not yet know what the fallout will be from our negative due process ruling, I continue to believe that presenting the arguments had a positive influence on the case overall in terms of affirming the autonomy and integrity of our client, and highlighting the important values at stake in the case.

Although all lawyers have a duty of care to their clients, this case reaffirmed to me that lawyers have a special duty of care to their transgender clients to preserve, as much as possible, their privacy and dignity, especially around personal transition-related decisions. Yet this case demonstrated to me just how difficult it can be to police that line between public and private. This is especially true where part of your litigation strategy involves providing information to the court in an effort to explain that embarking upon a gender transition, or making other decisions with the goal of bringing one's outward presentation into conformity with an inner truth, are decisions that implicate the most fundamental constitutional values of autonomy, self-definition, and liberty, and that transgender people should be able to make such decisions without undue government interference.

I will continue to search for opportunities to make the argument that gender identity should be considered just as much a part of a person's biological sex as one's chromosomes or genitals, although I recognize that there are both litigation and societal risks associated with relying on biological truths as a basis for asserting claims of equality, liberty, and autonomy. For this reason, I equally look forward to more conversations with my colleagues about how we, as litigators, can find ways to convince courts that employers and businesses should not be given license to restrict the access of transgender people to important social structures like restrooms simply by couching their rules in the language of "biological sex."

Finally and most importantly, my hope is that all lawyers, and particularly those who work with transgender people, will agree about the need to explore the kinds of issues described in this article to ensure that both lawyer and client have the same vision of what it means "to win" the case.

Discussion

1. Sharon McGowan states that if she had known more about the *Kastl* case when considering strategies for her client, she "would have had greater reservations about alleging . . . that Ms. Schroer was a woman." In the *Kastl* case, the court granted summary judgment against a transgender female plaintiff because the plaintiff, who alleged she was a "biological female," had failed to materially dispute the evidence that her "biological" sex was male (XY chromosomal makeup, male genitalia, and lack of female hormones). Do you agree with the courts' grant of summary judgment in the *Kastl* case? Is it appropriate to limit one's understanding of an individual's "biological" sex to chromosomal makeup, genitalia, and/or hormones? (Consider the many factors that can inform medical understandings of "sex" addressed in Chapter 2, *see, e.g. In re Heilig*, Chapter 2, Section A, *supra* at p. 21.) Might a court today be more receptive to labeling a transgender woman as a "biological" female, given more widespread acceptance of the role of gender identity in determining

one's sex? Also, consider that Title VII of the Civil Rights Act of 1964 and numerous other anti-discrimination statutes protect against discrimination based on "sex," not expressly "biological sex." What are the consequences of interpolating the modifier "biological" into our reading of anti-discrimination statutes?

2. Despite McGowan's concerns over alleging that Ms. Schroer was a woman, the court ultimately ruled in favor of Ms. Schroer without "deciding between the experts on the questions of etiology [of gender identity]." Instead, the court analogized Ms. Schroer's case to a case of "religious discrimination." Is it proper to analogize cases of anti-transgender discrimination to cases of religious discrimination? What differences might there be (or might some argue there are) between "change of religion" and "change of sex"? Do religion-gender identity comparisons subvert the legitimacy of transgender identity in any way? Are there any advantages to arguing that gender identity is akin to a belief system as opposed to a "biological" component of sex?

3. McGowan discusses the positive and negative aspects of a hypothetical precedent establishing that gender identity is a constituent part of "sex" within the meaning of Title VII (or perhaps other legal provisions as well). She considers how such a precedent might allow for successful future claims for access to sex-segregated facilities (*e.g.*, restrooms), but may also lead to a doctrine that transgender individuals must be "innocent" or non-volitional to have valid sex discrimination claims based on the sex associated with their gender identities. Do you think the benefits of incorporating gender identity into our legal understanding of "sex" outweigh the costs? Should we instead incorporate gender identity as a separate protected class into our anti-discrimination statutes? Would the latter better serve the non-cisgender community as a whole, including gender non-conforming individuals who do not identify with either side of the traditional gender binary?

Note on Glenn v. Brumby

In *Glenn v. Brumby*, 663 F.3d 1312, 1318 (11th Cir. 2011), Section C, *supra* at p. 185, the U.S. Court of Appeals for the Eleventh Circuit came close to expressly holding that discrimination against persons because they are transgender is categorically sex discrimination, though its ultimate conclusions are ever so slightly hedged: "There is thus a congruence between discriminating against transgender and transsexual individuals and discrimination on the basis of gender-based behavioral norms." "[D]iscrimination against a transgender individual *because of her gender-nonconformity* is sex discrimination, whether it's described as being on the basis of sex or gender" (emphasis added). "The Sixth Circuit likewise recognized that discrimination against a transgender individual *because of his or her gender non-conformity* is gender stereotyping prohibited by Title VII and the Equal Protection Clause" (emphasis added). "[S]ex discrimination includes discrimination against transgender persons because of their failure to comply with stereotypical gender norms." "We conclude that a government agent violates the Equal Protection Clause's prohibition of sex-based discrimination when he or she fires a transgender or transsexual employee *because of his or her gender non-conformity*" (emphasis added). On the other hand, the court's discussion of how transgender persons are defined might suggest that any discrimination against people because they are transgender is based on sex/gender stereotypes. As a practical matter, there could be little difference at the end of the day between the approach of *Glenn v. Brumby* and a categorical holding that anti-transgender discrimination is sex discrimination, though getting to that conclusion under non-categorical approaches could increase litigation costs and time.

Reading Guide for Macy v. Holder

1. In *Macy v. Holder*, No. 0120120821, 2012 WL 1435995 (E.E.O.C. Apr 20, 2012), the Equal Employment Opportunity Commission ("EEOC" or "Commission") adopted the position that anti-transgender discrimination is always a form of sex discrimination within the meaning of Title VII. Note the different ways the plaintiff, transgender woman Mia Macy, characterized the discrimination she alleged against her. The Commission held that each was prohibited by Title VII. Is the Commission's argument on each persuasive? (Should it matter which formulation a plaintiff alleges?)

2. What lessons does the Commission draw from *Price Waterhouse v. Hopkins* (*supra* at p. 155)? How convincing/persuasive is its interpretation of that decision? How does the Commission interpret the Eleventh Circuit's decision in *Glenn v. Brumby* (*supra* at p. 185) as regards anti-transgender discrimination and sex stereotyping? Is that a fair reading of that decision?

Mia Macy v. Eric Holder, Attorney General, Department of Justice (Bureau of Alcohol, Tobacco, Firearms and Explosives)

EEOC DOC 0120120821, 2012 WL 1435995 (Apr 20, 2012)

Decision

On December 9, 2011, Complainant filed an appeal concerning her equal employment opportunity (EEO) complaint alleging employment discrimination in violation of Title VII of the Civil Rights Act of 1964 (Title VII), as amended, 42 U.S.C. § 2000e et seq. For the following reasons, the Commission finds that the Complainant's complaint of discrimination based on gender identity, change of sex, and/or transgender status is cognizable under Title VII and remands the complaint to the Agency for further processing.

Background[1]

Complainant, a transgender woman, was a police detective in Phoenix, Arizona. In December 2010 she decided to relocate to San Francisco for family reasons.

---

1. The facts in this section are taken from the EEO Counselor's Report and the formal complaint of discrimination. Because this decision addresses a jurisdictional issue, we offer no position on the facts themselves and thus no position on whether unlawful discrimination occurred in this case.

According to her formal complaint, Complainant was still known as a male at that time, having not yet made the transition to being a female.

Complainant's supervisor in Phoenix told her that the Bureau of Alcohol, Tobacco, Firearms and Explosives (Agency) had a position open at its Walnut Creek crime laboratory for which the Complainant was qualified. Complainant is trained and certified as a National Integrated Ballistic Information Network (NIBIN) operator and a BrassTrax ballistics investigator.

Complainant discussed the position with the Director of the Walnut Creek lab by telephone, in either December 2010 or January 2011, while still presenting as a man. According to Complainant, the telephone conversation covered her experience, credentials, salary and benefits. Complainant further asserts that, following the conversation, the Director told her she would be able to have the position assuming no problems arose during her background check. The Director also told her that the position would be filled as a civilian contractor through an outside company.

Complainant states that she talked again with the Director in January 2011 and asked that he check on the status of the position. According to Complainant in her formal complaint, the Director did so and reasserted that the job was hers pending completion of the background check. Complainant asserts, as evidence of her impending hire, that Aspen of DC ("Aspen"), the contractor responsible for filling the position, contacted her to begin the necessary paperwork and that an investigator from the Agency was assigned to do her background check.[3]

On March 29, 2011, Complainant informed Aspen via email that she was in the process of transitioning from male to female and she requested that Aspen inform the Director of the Walnut Creek lab of this change. According to Complainant, on April 3, 2011, Aspen informed Complainant that the Agency had been informed of her change in name and gender. Five days later, on April 8, 2011, Complainant received an email from the contractor's Director of Operations stating that, due to federal budget reductions, the position at Walnut Creek was no longer available.

According to Complainant, she was concerned about this quick change in events and on May 10, 2011, she contacted an agency EEO counselor to discuss her concerns. She states that the counselor told her that the position at Walnut Creek had not been cut but, rather, that someone else had been hired for the position. Complainant further states that the counselor told her that the Agency had decided to take the other individual because that person was farthest along in the background investigation. Complainant claims that this was a pretextual explanation because

---

3. On March 28, 2011, Complainant received an e-mail from the contractor asking her to fill out an application packet for the position. It is unclear how far the background investigation had proceeded prior to Complainant notifying the contractor of her gender change, but e-mails included in the record indicate that the Agency's Personnel Security Branch had received Complainant's completed security package, that Complainant had been interviewed by a security investigator, and that the investigator had contacted Complainant on March 31, 2011 and had indicated that he "hope[d] to finish your investigation the first of next week."

the background investigation had been proceeding on her as well. Complainant believes she was incorrectly informed that the position had been cut because the Agency did not want to hire her because she is transgender.

The EEO counselor's report indicates that Complainant alleged that she had been discriminated against based on sex, and had specifically described her claim of discrimination as "change in gender (from male to female)."

On June 13, 2011, Complainant filed her formal EEO complaint with the Agency. On her formal complaint form, Complainant checked off "sex" and the box "female," and then typed in "gender identity" and "sex stereotyping" as the basis of her complaint. In the narrative accompanying her complaint, Complainant stated that she was discriminated against on the basis of "my sex, gender identity (transgender woman) and on the basis of sex stereotyping."

On October 26, 2011, the Agency issued Complainant a Letter of Acceptance, stating that the "claim alleged and being accepted and referred for investigation is the following: Whether you were discriminated against based on your gender identity sex (female) stereotyping when on May 5, 2011, you learned that you were not hired as a Contractor for the position of [NIBIN] Ballistics Forensic Technician in the Walnut Creek Lab, San Francisco Field Office." The letter went on to state, however, that "since claims of discrimination on the basis of gender identity stereotyping cannot be adjudicated before the [EEOC], your claims will be processed according to Department of Justice policy." The letter provided that if Complainant did not agree with how the Agency had identified her claim, she should contact the EEO office within 15 days.

The Department of Justice has one system for adjudicating claims of sex discrimination under Title VII and a separate system for adjudicating complaints of sexual orientation and gender identity discrimination by its employees. This separate process does not include the same rights offered under Title VII and the EEOC regulations set forth under 29 C.F.R. Part 1614. *See* Department of Justice Order 1200.1, Chapter 4-1, B.7.j, found at http:// www.justice.gov/jmd/ps/chpt4-1.html (last accessed on March 30, 2012). While such complaints are processed utilizing the same EEO complaint process and time frames—including an ADR program, an EEO investigation and issuance of a final Agency decision—the Department of Justice process allows for fewer remedies and does not include the right to request a hearing before an EEOC Administrative Judge or the right to appeal the final Agency decision to the Commission.

On November 8, 2011, Complainant's attorney contacted the Agency by letter to explain that the claims that Complainant had set forth in the formal complaint had not been correctly identified by the Agency. The letter explained that the claim as identified by the Agency was both incomplete and confusing. The letter noted that "[Complainant] is a transgender woman who was discriminated against during the hiring process for a job with [the Agency]," and that the discrimination against Complainant was based on "separate and related" factors, including on the basis of sex, sex stereotyping, sex due to gender transition/change of sex, and sex due to gender identity. Thus, Complainant disagreed with the Agency's contention that her claim in its entirety could not be adjudicated through the Title VII and EEOC process simply because of how she had stated the alleged bases of discrimination.

On November 18, 2011, the Agency issued a correction to its Letter of Acceptance in response to Complainant's November 8, 2011 letter. In this letter, the Agency stated that it was accepting the complaint "on the basis of sex (female) and gender identity stereotyping." However, the Agency again stated that it would process only her claim "based on sex (female)" under Title VII and the EEOC's Part 1614 regulations. Her claim based on "gender identity stereotyping" would be processed instead under the Agency's "policy and practice," including the issuance of a final Agency decision from the Agency's Complaint Adjudication Office.

Contentions on Appeal

On December 6, 2011, Complainant, through counsel, submitted a Notice of Appeal to the Commission asking that it adjudicate the claim that she was discriminated against on the basis of "sex stereotyping, sex discrimination based gender transition/change of sex, and sex discrimination based gender identity" when she was denied the position as an NIBIN ballistics technician.

Complainant argues that EEOC has jurisdiction over her entire claim. She further asserts that the Agency's "reclassification" of her claim of discrimination into two separate claims of discrimination—one "based on sex (female) under Title VII" which the Agency will investigate under Title VII and the EEOC's Part 1614 regulations, and a separate claim of discrimination based on "gender identity stereotyping" which the Agency will investigate under a separate process designated for such claims—is a "de facto dismissal" of her Title VII claim of discrimination based on gender identity and transgender status.

In response to Complainant's appeal, the Agency sent a letter to the Commission on January 11, 2012, arguing that Complainant's appeal was "premature" because the Agency had accepted a claim designated as discrimination "based on sex (female)."

In response to the Agency's January 11, 2012 letter, Complainant wrote to the Agency on February 8, 2012, stating that, in light of how the Agency was characterizing her claim, she wished to withdraw her claim of "discrimination based on sex (female)," as characterized by the Agency, and to pursue solely the Agency's dismissal of her complaint of discrimination based on her gender identity, change of sex and/or transgender status. In a letter to the Commission dated February 9, 2012, Complainant explained that she had withdrawn the claim "based on sex (female)" as the Agency had characterized it, in order to remove any possible procedural claim that her appeal to the Commission was premature.

Complainant reiterates her contention that the Agency mischaracterized her claim and asks the Commission to rule on her appeal that the Agency should investigate, under Title VII and the EEOC's Part 1614 regulations, her claim of discriminatory failure to hire based on her gender identity, change of sex, and/or transgender status.

Analysis and Findings

The narrative accompanying Complainant's complaint makes clear that she believes she was not hired for the position as a result of making her transgender status known. As already noted, Complainant stated that she was discriminated against on the basis of "my sex, gender identity (transgender woman) and on the basis of sex stereotyping." In response to her complaint, the Agency stated that claims of gender identity discrimination "cannot be adjudicated before the [EEOC]." *See* Agency Letters of October 26, 2011 and November 18, 2011. Although it is possible that the Agency would have fully addressed her claims under that portion of her complaint accepted under the 1614 process, the Agency's communications prompted in Complainant a reasonable belief that the Agency viewed the gender identity discrimination she alleged as outside the scope of Title VII's sex discrimination prohibitions. Based on these communications, Complainant believed that her complaint would not be investigated effectively by the Agency, and she filed the instant appeal.

EEOC Regulation 29 C.F.R. § 1614.107(b) provides that where an agency decides that some, but not all, of the claims in a complaint should be dismissed, it must notify the complainant of its determination. However, this determination is not appealable until final action is taken on the remainder of the complaint. In apparent recognition of the operation of § 1614.107(b), Complainant withdrew the accepted portion of her complaint from the 1614 process so that the constructive dismissal of her gender identity discrimination claim would be a final decision and the matter ripe for appeal.

In the interest of resolving the confusion regarding a recurring legal issue that is demonstrated by this complaint's procedural history, as well as to ensure efficient use of resources, we accept this appeal for adjudication. Moreover, EEOC's responsibilities under Executive Order 12067 for enforcing all Federal EEO laws and leading the Federal government's efforts to eradicate workplace discrimination, require, among other things, that EEOC ensure that uniform standards be implemented defining the nature of employment discrimination under the statutes we enforce. Executive Order 12067, 43 F.R. 28967, § l-301(a) (June 30, 1978). To that end, the Commission hereby clarifies that claims of discrimination based on transgender status, also referred to as claims of discrimination based on gender identity, are cognizable under Title VII's sex discrimination prohibition, and may therefore be processed under Part 1614 of EEOC's federal sector EEO complaints process.

We find that the Agency mistakenly separated Complainant's complaint into separate claims: one described as discrimination based on "sex" (which the Agency accepted for processing under Title VII) and others that were alternatively described by Complainant as "sex stereotyping," "gender transition/change of sex," and "gender identity" (Complainant Letter of Nov. 8, 2011); by the Agency as "gender identity stereotyping" (Agency Letter Nov. 18, 2011); and finally by Complainant as "gender identity, change of sex and/or transgender status" (Complainant Letter Feb. 8, 2012). While Complainant could have chosen to avail herself of the Agency's administrative procedures for discrimination based on gender identity, she clearly expressed her desire to have her claims investigated through the 1614 process, and this desire should have been honored. Each of the formulations of Complainant's claims are simply different ways of stating the same claim of discrimination "based on . . . sex," a claim cognizable under Title VII.

Title VII states that, except as otherwise specifically provided, "[a]ll personnel actions affecting [federal] employees or applicants for employment . . . shall be made free from any discrimination *based on . . . sex. . . .*"42 U.S.C. § 2000e-16(a) (emphasis added). *Cf.* 42 U.S.C. §§ 2000e-2(a)(1), (2) (it is unlawful for a covered employer to "fail or refuse to hire or to discharge any individual, or otherwise to discriminate with respect to his compensation, terms, conditions, or privileges of employment," or to "limit, segregate, or classify his employees or applicants for employment in any way which would deprive or tend to deprive any individual of employment opportunities or otherwise adversely affect his status as an employee, *because of such individual's . . . sex*") (emphasis added).

As used in Title VII, the term "sex" "encompasses both sex — that is, the biological differences between men and women — and gender." *See Schwenk v. Hartford*, 204 F.3d 1187, 1202 (9th Cir. 2000); *see also Smith v. City of Salem*, 378 F.3d 566, 572 (6th Cir. 2004) ("The Supreme Court made clear that in the context of Title VII, discrimination because of 'sex' includes gender discrimination."). As the Eleventh Circuit noted in *Glenn v. Brumby*, 663 F.3d 1312, 1316 (11th Cir. 2011), six members of the Supreme Court in *Price Waterhouse* agreed that Title VII barred "not just discrimination because of biological sex, but also gender stereotyping — failing to act and appear according to expectations defined by gender." As such, the terms "gender" and "sex" are often used interchangeably to describe the discrimination prohibited by Title VII. *See, e.g., Price Waterhouse v. Hopkins*, 490 U.S. 228, 239 (1989) (emphasis added) ("Congress' intent to forbid employers to take *gender* into account in making employment decisions appears on the face of the statute").

That Title VII's prohibition on sex discrimination proscribes gender discrimination, and not just discrimination on the basis of biological sex, is important. If Title VII proscribed only discrimination on the basis of biological sex, the only prohibited gender-based disparate treatment would be when an employer prefers a man over a woman, or vice versa. But the statute's protections sweep far broader than that, in part because the term "gender" encompasses not only a person's biological sex but also the cultural and social aspects associated with masculinity and femininity.

In *Price Waterhouse*, the employer refused to make a female senior manager, Hopkins, a partner at least in part because she did not act as some of the partners thought a woman should act. She was informed, for example, that to improve her chances for partnership she should "walk more femininely, talk more femininely, dress more femininely, wear make-up, have her hair styled, and wear jewelry." The Court concluded that discrimination for failing to conform with gender-based expectations violates Title VII, holding that "[i]n the specific context of sex stereotyping, an employer who acts on the basis of a belief that a woman cannot be aggressive, or that she must not be, has acted on the basis of gender."

Although the partners at Price Waterhouse discriminated against Ms. Hopkins for failing to conform to stereotypical gender norms, gender discrimination occurs any time an employer treats an employee differently for failing to conform to any gender-based expectations or norms. "What matters, for purposes of . . . the *Price Waterhouse* analysis, is that in the mind of the perpetrator the discrimination is related to the sex of the victim." *Schwenk*; *see also Price Waterhouse* (noting the illegitimacy of allowing "sex-linked evaluations to play a part in the [employer's] decision-making process").

"Title VII does identify one circumstance in which an employer may take gender into account in making an employment decision, namely, when gender is a 'bona fide occupational qualification [(BFOQ)] reasonably necessary to the normal operation of th[e] particular business or enterprise.'" *Price Waterhouse* (quoting 42 U.S.C. § 2000e-2(e)). Even then, "the [BFOQ] exception was in fact meant to be an extremely narrow exception to the general prohibition of discrimination on the basis of sex.'" *See Phillips v. Martin Marietta Corp.*, 400 U.S. 542, 544 (1971) (Marshall, J., concurring). "The only plausible inference to draw from this provision is that, in all other circumstances, a person's gender may not be considered in making decisions that affect her." *Price Waterhouse.*[4]

When an employer discriminates against someone because the person is transgender, the employer has engaged in disparate treatment "related to the sex of the victim." *See Schwenk.* This is true regardless of whether an employer discriminates against an employee because the individual has expressed his or her gender in a non-stereotypical fashion, because the employer is uncomfortable with the fact that the person has transitioned or is in the process of transitioning from one gender to another, or because the employer simply does not like that the person is identifying as a transgender person. In each of these circumstances, the employer is making a gender-based evaluation, thus violating the Supreme Court's admonition that "an employer may not take gender into account in making an employment decision." *Price Waterhouse.*

Since *Price Waterhouse*, courts have widely recognized the availability of the sex stereotyping theory as a valid method of establishing discrimination "on the basis of sex" in many scenarios involving individuals who act or appear in gender-nonconforming ways.[5] And since *Price Waterhouse*, courts also have widely recog-

---

4. There are other, limited instances in which gender may be taken into account, such as is in the context of a valid affirmative action plan, *see Johnson v. Santa Clara County Transportation Agency*, 480 U.S. 616 (1987), or relatedly, as part of a settlement of a pattern or practice claim.

5. *See, e.g., Lewis v. Heartland Inns of Am., L.L.C.*, 591 F.3d 1033, 1041 (8th Cir. 2010) (concluding that evidence that a female "tomboyish" plaintiff had been fired for not having the "Midwestern girl look" suggested "her employer found her unsuited for her job . . . because her appearance did not comport with its preferred feminine stereotype"); *Prowel v. Wise Business Forms, Inc.*, 579 F.3d 285 (3rd Cir. 2009) (an effeminate gay man who did not conform to his employer's vision of how a man should look, speak, and act provided sufficient evidence of gender stereotyping harassment under Title VII); *Medina v. Income Support Div.*, 413 F.3d 1131, 1135 (10th Cir. 2005) (involving a

nized the availability of the sex stereotyping theory as a valid method of establishing discrimination "on the basis of sex" in scenarios involving transgender individuals.

For example, in *Schwenk v. Hartford*, a prison guard had sexually assaulted a pre-operative male-to-female transgender prisoner, and the prisoner sued, alleging that the guard had violated the Gender Motivated Violence Act (GMVA), 42 U.S.C. § 13981. The U.S. Court of Appeals for the Ninth Circuit found that the guard had known that the prisoner "considered herself a transsexual and that she planned to seek sex reassignment surgery in the future." According to the court, the guard had targeted the transgender prisoner "only after he discovered that she considered herself female[,]" and the guard was "motivated, at least in part, by [her] gender"—that is, "by her assumption of a feminine rather than a typically masculine appearance or demeanor." On these facts, the Ninth Circuit readily concluded that the guard's attack constituted discrimination because of gender within the meaning of both the GMVA and Title VII.

The court relied on *Price Waterhouse*, reasoning that it stood for the proposition that discrimination based on sex includes discrimination based on a failure "to conform to socially-constructed gender expectations." Accordingly, the Ninth Circuit concluded, discrimination against transgender females—*i.e.*, "as anatomical males whose *outward behavior and inward identity* [do] not meet social definitions of masculinity"—is actionable discrimination "because of sex." *Id.* (emphasis added); *cf. Rosa v. Park W. Bank & Trust Co.*, 214 F.3d 213 (1st Cir. 2000) (finding that under *Price Waterhouse*, a bank's refusal to give a loan application to a biologically-male plaintiff dressed in "traditionally feminine attire" because his "attire did not accord with his male gender" stated a claim of illegal sex discrimination in violation of the Equal Credit Opportunity Act, 15 U.S.C. §§ 1691–1691f).

---

heterosexual female who alleged that her lesbian supervisor discriminated against her on the basis of sex, and finding that "a plaintiff may satisfy her evidentiary burden [under Title VII] by showing that the harasser was acting to punish the plaintiff's noncompliance with gender stereotypes"); *Nichols v. Azteca Rest. Enters.*, 256 F.3d 864, 874–75 (9th Cir. 2001) (concluding that a male plaintiff stated a Title VII claim when he was discriminated against "for walking and carrying his tray 'like a woman'—*i.e.*, for having feminine mannerisms"); *Simonton v. Runyon*, 232 F.3d 33, 37 (2d Cir. 2000) (indicating that a gay man would have a viable Title VII claim if "the abuse he suffered was discrimination based on sexual stereotypes, which may be cognizable as discrimination based on sex"); *Higgins v. New Balance Athletic Shoe, Inc.*, 194 F.3d 252, 261 n.4 (1st Cir. 1999) (analyzing a gay plaintiff's claim that his co-workers harassed him by "mocking his supposedly effeminate characteristics" and acknowledging that "just as a woman can ground an action on a claim that men discriminated against her because she did not meet stereotyped expectations of femininity . . . a man can ground a claim on evidence that other men discriminated against him because he did not meet stereotypical expectations of masculinity"); *Doe by Doe v. City of Belleville*, 119 F.3d 563, 580–81 (7th Cir. 1997) (involving a heterosexual male who was harassed by other heterosexual males, and concluding that "a man who is harassed because his voice is soft, his physique is slight, his hair is long, or because in some other respect he . . . does not meet his coworkers' idea of how men are to appear and behave, is harassed 'because of his sex'"), *vacated and remanded on other grounds*, 523 U.S. 1001 (1998).

Similarly, in *Smith v. City of Salem*, the plaintiff was "biologically and by birth male." However, Smith was diagnosed with Gender Identity Disorder (GID), and began to present at work as a female (in accordance with medical protocols for treatment of GID). Smith's co-workers began commenting that her appearance and mannerisms were "not masculine enough." Smith's employer later subjected her to numerous psychological evaluations, and ultimately suspended her. Smith filed suit under Title VII alleging that her employer had discriminated against her because of sex, "both because of [her] *gender non-conforming conduct* and, more generally, because of [her] *identification* as a transsexual." (emphasis added).

The district court rejected Smith's efforts to prove her case using a sex-stereotyping theory, concluding that it was really an attempt to challenge discrimination based on "transsexuality." The U.S. Court of Appeals for the Sixth Circuit reversed, stating that the district court's conclusion:

> cannot be reconciled with *Price Waterhouse*, which does not make Title VII protection against sex stereotyping conditional or provide any reason to exclude Title VII coverage for non sex-stereotypical behavior simply because the person is a transsexual. As such, discrimination against a plaintiff who is a transsexual—and therefore fails to act and/or identify with his or her gender—is no different from the discrimination directed against [the plaintiff] in *Price Waterhouse* who, in sex-stereotypical terms, did not act like a woman. Sex stereotyping based on a person's gender non-conforming behavior is impermissible discrimination, irrespective of the cause of that behavior; a label, such as "transsexual" is not fatal to a sex discrimination claim where the victim has suffered discrimination because of his or her gender non-conformity. Accordingly, we hold that Smith has stated a claim for relief pursuant to Title VII's prohibition of sex discrimination.[6]

Finally, as the Eleventh Circuit suggested in *Glenn v. Brumby*, 663 F.3d 1312 (11th Cir. 2011), consideration of gender stereotypes will inherently be part of what drives discrimination against a transgendered individual. In that case, the employer testified at his deposition that it had fired Vandiver Elizabeth Glenn, a transgender woman, because he considered it "inappropriate" for her to appear at work dressed as a woman and that he found it "unsettling" and "unnatural" that she would appear wearing women's clothing. The firing supervisor further testified that his decision to dismiss Glenn was based on his perception of Glenn as "a man dressed as a woman and made up as a woman," and admitted that his decision to fire her was based on "the sheer fact of the transition." According to the Eleventh Circuit, this testimony "provides ample direct evidence" to support the conclusion that the

---

6. *See also Barnes v. City of Cincinnati*, 401 F.3d 729, 741 (6th Cir. 2005) (affirming a jury award in favor of a pre-operative transgender female, ruling that "a claim for sex discrimination under Title VII . . . can properly lie where the claim is based on 'sexual stereotypes'" and that the "district court therefore did not err when it instructed the jury that it could find discrimination based on 'sexual stereotypes'").

employer acted on the basis of the plaintiff's gender non-conformity and therefore granted summary judgment to her.

In setting forth its legal reasoning, the Eleventh Circuit explained:

> A person is defined as transgender precisely because of the perception that his or her behavior transgresses gender stereotypes. "[T]he very acts that define transgender people as transgender are those that contradict stereotypes of gender-appropriate appearance and behavior." Ilona M. Turner, *Sex Stereotyping Per Se: Transgender Employees and Title VII*, 95 Cal. L. Rev. 561, 563 (2007); *see also* Taylor Flynn, *Transforming the Debate: Why We Need to Include Transgender Rights in the Struggles for Sex and Sexual Orientation Equality,* 101 Colum. L. Rev. 392, 392 (2001) (defining transgender persons as those whose "appearance, behavior, or other personal characteristics differ from traditional gender norms"). There is thus a congruence between discriminating against transgender and transsexual individuals and discrimination on the basis of gender-based behavioral norms.

Accordingly, discrimination against a transgender individual because of her gendernonconformity is sex discrimination, whether it's described as being on the basis of sex or gender. *Glenn v. Brumby*, 663 F.3d 1312 (11th Cir. 2011).[7]

There has likewise been a steady stream of district court decisions recognizing that discrimination against transgender individuals on the basis of sex stereotyping constitutes discrimination because of sex. Most notably, in *Schroer v. Billington*, the Library of Congress rescinded an offer of employment it had extended to a transgender job applicant after the applicant informed the Library's hiring officials that she intended to undergo a gender transition. The U.S. District Court for the District of Columbia entered judgment in favor of the plaintiff on her Title VII sex discrimination claim. According to the district court, it did not matter "for purposes of Title VII liability whether the Library withdrew its offer of employment because it perceived Schroer to be an insufficiently masculine man, an insufficiently feminine woman, or an inherently gender-nonconforming transsexual. In any case, Schroer was "entitled to judgment based on a *Price-Waterhouse*-type claim for sex stereotyping. . . ."[8]

---

7. *But see Etsitty v. Utah Trans. Auth.*, No. 2:04-CV-616, 2005 WL 1505610, at *4–5 (D. Utah June 24, 2005) (concluding that *Price Waterhouse* is inapplicable to transsexuals), *aff'd on other grounds*, 502 F.3d 1215 (10th Cir. 2007).

8. The district court in *Schroer* also concluded that discrimination against a transgender individual on the basis of an intended, ongoing, or completed gender transition is "*literally* discrimination 'because of . . . sex.'" *Schroer*; *see also id.* (analogizing to cases involving discrimination based on an employee's religious conversion, which undeniably constitutes discrimination "because of . . . religion" under Title VII). For other district court cases using sex stereotyping as grounds for establishing coverage of transgender individuals under Title VII, *see Michaels v. Akal Security, Inc.*, No. 09-cv-1300, 2010 WL 2573988, at * 4 (D. Colo. June 24, 2010); *Lopez v. River Oaks Imaging & Diag. Group, Inc.*, 542 F. Supp. 2d 653, 660 (S.D. Tex. 2008); *Mitchell v. Axcan Scandipharm, Inc.*,

To be sure, the members of Congress that enacted Title VII in 1964 and amended it in 1972 were likely not considering the problems of discrimination that were faced by transgender individuals. But as the Supreme Court recognized in *Oncale v. Sundowner Offshore Services, Inc.*:

> [S]tatutory prohibitions often go beyond the principal evil [they were passed to combat] to cover reasonably comparable evils, and it is ultimately the provisions of our laws rather than the principal concerns of our legislators by which we are governed. Title VII prohibits "discrimination . . . because of . . . sex" in . . . employment. [This] . . . must extend to [sex-based discrimination] of any kind that meets the statutory requirements.

[See] also Newport News, 462 U.S. at 679–81 (rejecting the argument that discrimination against men does not violate Title VII despite the fact that discrimination against women was plainly the principal problem that Title VII's prohibition of sex discrimination was enacted to combat).

Although most courts have found protection for transgender people under Title VII under a theory of gender stereotyping, evidence of gender stereotyping is simply one means of proving sex discrimination. Title VII prohibits discrimination based on sex whether motivated by hostility,[9] by a desire to protect people of a certain gender,[10] by assumptions that disadvantage men,[11] by gender stereotypes,[12] or by the desire to accommodate other people's prejudices or discomfort.[13] While evidence that an employer has acted based on stereotypes about how men or women should act is certainly one means of demonstrating disparate treatment based on sex, "sex stereotyping" is not itself an independent cause of action. As the *Price Waterhouse* Court noted, while "stereotyped remarks can certainly be *evidence* that gender played a part" in an adverse employment action, the central question is always

---

No. Vic. A. 05-243, 2006 WL 456173 (W.D. Pa. Feb. 17, 2006); *Tronetti v. TLC HealthNet Lakeshore Hosp.*, No. 03-CV-0375E(SC), 2003 WL 22757935 (W.D.N.Y. Sept. 26, 2003).

   9. *See Meritor Savings Bank, FSB v. Vinson*, 477 U.S. 57 (1986) (recognizing that sexual harassment is actionable discrimination "because of sex"); *Oncale v. Sundowner Offshore Servs., Inc.*, 523 U.S. 75 (1998) ("A trier of fact might reasonably find such discrimination, for example, if a female victim is harassed in such sex-specific and derogatory terms by another woman as to make it clear that the harasser is motivated by general hostility to the presence of women in the workplace").

   10. *See Int'l Union v. Johnson Controls*, 499 U.S. 187 (1991) (policy barring all female employees except those who were infertile from working in jobs that exposed them to lead was facially discriminatory on the basis of sex).

   11. *See, e.g., Newport News* (providing different insurance coverage to male and female employees violates Title VII even though women are treated better).

   12. *See, e.g., Price Waterhouse.*

   13. *See, e.g., Chaney v. Plainfield Healthcare Ctr.*, 612 F.3d 908 (7th Cir. 2010) (concluding that "assignment sheet that unambiguously, and daily, reminded [the plaintiff, a black nurse,] and her co-workers that certain residents preferred no black" nurses created a hostile work environment); *Fernandez v. Wynn Oil Co.*, 653 F.2d 1273 (9th Cir. 1981) (a female employee could not lawfully be fired because her employer's foreign clients would only work with males); *Diaz v. Pan American World Airways, Inc.*, 442 F.2d 385 (5th Cir. 1971) (rejecting customer preference for female flight attendants as justification for discrimination against male applicants).

whether the "employer actually relied on [the employee's] gender in making its decision." (emphasis in original).

Thus, a transgender person who has experienced discrimination based on his or her gender identity may establish a prima facie case of sex discrimination through any number of different formulations. These different formulations are not, however, different claims of discrimination that can be separated out and investigated within different systems. Rather, they are simply different ways of describing sex discrimination.

For example, Complainant could establish a case of sex discrimination under a theory of gender stereotyping by showing that she did not get the job as an NIBIN ballistics technician at Walnut Creek because the employer believed that biological men should consistently present as men and wear male clothing.

Alternatively, if Complainant can prove that the reason that she did not get the job at Walnut Creek is that the Director was willing to hire her when he thought she was a man, but was not willing to hire her once he found out that she was now a woman—she will have proven that the Director discriminated on the basis of sex. Under this theory, there would actually be no need, for purposes of establishing coverage under Title VII, for Complainant to compile any evidence that the Director was engaging in gender stereotyping.

In this respect, gender is no different from religion. Assume that an employee considers herself Christian and identifies as such. But assume that an employer finds out that the employee's parents are Muslim, believes that the employee should therefore be Muslim, and terminates the employee on that basis. No one would doubt that such an employer discriminated on the basis of religion. There would be no need for the employee who experienced the adverse employment action to demonstrate that the employer acted on the basis of some religious stereotype— although, clearly, discomfort with the choice made by the employee with regard to religion would presumably be at the root of the employer's actions. But for purposes of establishing a prima facie case that Title VII has been violated, the employee simply must demonstrate that the employer impermissibly used religion in making its employment decision.

The District Court in *Schroer* provided reasoning along similar lines:

> Imagine that an employee is fired because she converts from Christianity to Judaism. Imagine too that her employer testifies that he harbors no bias toward either Christians or Jews but only 'converts.' That would be a clear case of discrimination 'because of religion.' No court would take seriously the notion that 'converts' are not covered by the statute. Discrimination "because of religion" easily encompasses discrimination because of a change of religion.

Applying Title VII in this manner does not create a new "class" of people covered under Title VII—for example, the "class" of people who have converted from Islam to Christianity or from Christianity to Judaism. Rather, it would simply be the result of applying the plain language of a statute prohibiting discrimination on the basis of religion to practical situations in which such characteristics are unlawfully taken into account. *See Brumby*, 663 F.3d at 1318–19 (noting that "all persons, whether transgender or not" are protected from discrimination and "[a]n individual cannot be punished because of his or her perceived gender non-conformity").

Thus, we conclude that intentional discrimination against a transgender individual because that person is transgender is, by definition, discrimination "based on . . . sex," and such discrimination therefore violates Title VII.[14]

Conclusion

Accordingly, the Agency's final decision declining to process Complainant's entire complaint within the Part 1614 EEO complaints process is REVERSED. The complaint is hereby REMANDED to the Agency for further processing in accordance with this decision. . . .

Discussion

1. Note that *Macy* does not resolve any factual disputes about the actual reasons for which Mia Macy was denied employment by the agency. The EEOC's decision rather establishes a rule of law applicable to federal employees (or applicants) in every U.S. jurisdiction. If an agency denies employment to a person because she (for example) is transgender, perhaps disagreeing with the Commission's interpretation of Title VII, that person could appeal that adverse employment decision to the Commission. Under *Macy*, the agency would lose that appeal, and it would have no right to seek judicial review of the Commission's decision. An aggrieved employee (or applicants), however, would have the right to seek judicial review of an adverse EEOC decision. Judicial review of agency employee or applicant discrimination claims is thus asymmetric, skewed in favor of vindicating claimants.

2. Three years after *Macy*, the EEOC took the position in an agency adjudication that sexual orientation discrimination, like anti-transgender discrimination, is always sex discrimination under Title VII. *See Baldwin v. Anthony Foxx, Secretary, Dep't of Transportation (Federal Aviation Administration), Agency*, Appeal

---

14. The Commission previously took this position in an amicus brief docketed with the district court in the Western District of Texas on Oct. 17, 2011, where it explained that "[i]t is the position of the EEOC that disparate treatment of an employee because he or she is transgender is discrimination "because of . . . sex" under Title VII." EEOC Amicus Brief in *Pacheco* v. *Freedom Buick GMC Truck*, No. 07-116 (W.D. Tex. Oct. 17, 2011), Dkt. No. 30, at page 1, 2011 WL 5410751. With this decision, we expressly overturn, in light of the recent developments in the caselaw described above, any contrary earlier decisions from the Commission. *See, e.g., Jennifer Casoni v. United States Postal Service*, EEOC DOC 01840104 (Sept. 28, 1984), 1984 WL 485399; *Campbell v. Dep't of Agriculture*, EEOC Appeal No. 01931703 (July 21, 1994), 1994 WL 652840; *Kowalczyk v. Dep't of Veterans Affairs*, EEOC Appeal No. 01942053 (March 14, 1996), 1996 WL 124832.

No. 0120133080, 2015 WL 4397641 (E.E.O.C. July 16, 2015). The Commission explained:

> Title VII's prohibition of sex discrimination means that employers may not "rel[y] upon sex-based considerations" or take gender into account when making employment decisions. *See Price Waterhouse v. Hopkins*, 490 U.S. 228 (1989); *Macy v. Dep't of Justice*, EEOC Appeal No. 0120120821, 2012 WL 1435995 (EEOC Apr. 20, 2012) (quoting *Price Waterhouse*). . . .
>
> Discrimination on the basis of sexual orientation is premised on sex-based preferences, assumptions, expectations, stereotypes, or norms. "Sexual orientation" as a concept cannot be defined or understood without reference to sex. A man is referred to as "gay" if he is physically and/or emotionally attracted to other men. A woman is referred to as "lesbian" if she is physically and/or emotionally attracted to other women. Someone is referred to as "heterosexual" or "straight" if he or she is physically and/or emotionally attracted to someone of the opposite-sex. . . .
>
> Sexual orientation discrimination is sex discrimination because it necessarily entails treating an employee less favorably because of the employee's sex. For example, assume that an employer suspends a lesbian employee for displaying a photo of her female spouse on her desk, but does not suspend a male employee for displaying a photo of his female spouse on his desk. The lesbian employee in that example can allege that her employer took an adverse action against her that the employer would not have taken had she been male. That is a legitimate claim under Title VII that sex was unlawfully taken into account in the adverse employment action. . . .
>
> Sexual orientation discrimination is also sex discrimination because it is associational discrimination on the basis of sex. That is, an employee alleging discrimination on the basis of sexual orientation is alleging that his or her employer took his or her sex into account by treating him or her differently for associating with a person of the same sex. For example, a gay man who alleges that his employer took an adverse employment action against him because he associated with or dated men states a claim of sex discrimination under Title VII; the fact that the employee is a man instead of a woman motivated the employer's discrimination against him. . . .
>
> Sexual orientation discrimination also is sex discrimination because it necessarily involves discrimination based on gender stereotypes. . . .

Foxx.

Some lower courts agreed with this conclusion and these arguments. *See, e.g., Zarda v. Altitude Express, Inc.*, 883 F.3d 100 (2d Cir. 2018) (en banc), *aff'd sub nom. Bostock v. Clayton County, Georgia*, 140 S. Ct. 1731 (2020), *infra*. In *Gerald Lynn Bostock v. Clayton County, Georgia*, 723 F. Appx. 964 (11th Cir. 2018),, rev'd, 140 S. Ct. 1731 (2020), *infra*, the U.S. Court of Appeals for the Eleventh Circuit followed

Jameka K. Evans v. Georgia Regional Hospital et al., 850 F.3d 1248 (11th Cir. 2017), and rejected the argument that Title VII's ban on sex discrimination categorically forbade sexual orientation discrimination, (Some judges also relied on old precedent to reject *Foxx*'s interpretation. *See, e.g., Wittmer v. Phillips 66 Co.*, 915 F. 3d 328, 338 (CA5 2019) (Ho, J., concurring in his own panel opinion).) The losing parties in *Zarda* and *Bostock* sought certiorari, which the Supreme Court granted; the Court consolidated the two cases and heard oral argument on October 8, 2019 — the same day it heard argument on whether anti-transgender discrimination is sex discrimination under Title VII, in the appeal of the case *EEOC v. R.G. & G.R. Harris Funeral Homes, Inc.*, 884 F.3d 560 (6th Cir. 2018). Ruling in one combined opinion for those three cases, on June 15, 2020, the Supreme Court held 6–3 that employers who fire employees because of their sexual orientation or transgender status categorically violate Title VII's ban on sex discrimination. *Bostock v. Clayton County, Georgia*, 140 S. Ct. 1731 (2020).

Reading Guide for Bostock v. Clayton County

1. How does the majority say courts must interpret federal statutes such as Title VII of the Civil Rights Act of 1964, which forbids covered employers to discriminate on the basis of race, color, religion, national origin, or sex? Does either of the two dissenting opinions disagree with the majority's articulated approach to statutory interpretation? What reasons do any of the opinions give for approaching statutory interpretation the way they specify? What reasons do the dissents offer for their conclusion that the majority opinion is not interpreting but instead "updating" Title VII?

2. How does the Court define the meaning of "sex" in title VII? Does either of the two dissenting opinions disagree with that definition? Note that the utility or accuracy of the phrase "biological sex," used extensively in Justice Alito's dissent in this case, is contested. Dru Levasseur, formerly the Transgender Rights Project National Director for Lambda Legal, has criticized what he terms "the 'biological sex' misnomer." M. Dru Levasseur, *Gender Identity Defines Sex: Updating the Law to Reflect Modern Medical Science Is Key to Transgender Rights*, 39 Vt. L. Rev. 943, 977 (2015). He observes that "[w]hen it comes to interpreting sex in the discrimination context, many courts have reverted back to the notion of sex as a biologically fixed truth, determined by genital characteristics, and somehow separate from . . . gender identity." *Id.* One alternative for characterizing the sex assigned a person at birth, generally based on external physical anatomy, would be to use the phrase "physical sex," which in its narrowness may avoid broader scientistic connotations (rejected by much of modern medicine) such as there supposedly being one unique bodily determinant of a person's sex or gender identity's ostensibly being irrelevant to one's sex. This description of sex as "physical" was used (though not necessarily for these reasons) by conservative Supreme Court Justice Antonin Scalia, for example in *J.E.B. v. Alabama ex rel. T.B.*, where he wrote that "[t]he word 'gender' has acquired the new and useful connotation of cultural or attitudinal characteristics

(as opposed to physical characteristics) distinctive to the sexes. That is to say, gender is to sex as feminine is to female and masculine is to male." 511 U.S. 127, 157 n.1 (1994) (Scalia, J., dissenting).

3. How does the Court define "because of" in the statute? What does Justice Alito's dissent say about that causation standard?

4. When the Court starts explaining why intentional discrimination on the basis of sexual orientation or transgender status necessarily involves intentional discrimination on the basis of sex, what are the different phrasings the majority opinion uses to describe the relationship between (discrimination based on) sexual orientation or gender identity and (discrimination based on) sex? Why does Justice Alito's dissent object to those formulations?

5. The majority and Justice Alito's dissent disagree over the significance of the Court's hypothetical about two employees who bring their spouse to an office holiday party. What does each think it does or doesn't show? They also disagree about the significance of a hypothetical form that asks applicants to check one box if they are "black or Catholic." What does each think this hypothetical does or doesn't show? What does the Court think its hypothetical about "1950s gender roles" shows? What do the dissenters argue their hypotheticals about four different employees show?

6. In what ways does the Court think *Phillips v. Martin Marietta Corp.,* 400 U.S. 542 (1971) (per curiam), *Los Angeles Dept. of Water and Power v. Manhart*, 435 U.S. 702 (1978), and *Oncale v. Sundowner Offshore Services, Inc.*, 523 U.S. 75 (1998), support its conclusion here? For what reasons does Alito argue those precedents do not support the majority?

7. What does the majority say about the possible distinction between legislative intent and expected applications? What note of caution does the majority sound about possible interpretive "objections about unexpected applications"? To what in the dissent is it likely responding? In discussing canons of interpretation at different points, what does the majority say about doughnut holes and about elephants?

8. The dissenters insist that sex, sexual orientation, and gender identity are "separate concepts" and that discrimination based on the latter two need not entail discrimination based on the first. How do they try to establish that latter claim? How does Alito's dissent try to counter the sex stereotyping approach of *Price Waterhouse*? How does it try to counter the interracial association parallel?

9. How do the dissenters argue that the "ordinary" meaning of "discrimination because of sex" and thus the meaning of Title VII do not extend to discrimination because of someone's sexual orientation or gender identity? What do they contend is the significance of Congress's record regarding Title VII in the decades after its adoption in 1964? What potential ramifications of the Court's ruling do the dissenters identify and how do they argue those are relevant? How does the majority respond to those potential-consequences claims? What contentions do the dissenters make about democracy?

Bostock v. Clayton County, Georgia

140 S.Ct. 1731 (2020)

Justice GORSUCH delivered the opinion of the Court.

. . . . In our time, few pieces of federal legislation rank in significance with the Civil Rights Act of 1964. There, in Title VII, Congress outlawed discrimination in the workplace on the basis of race, color, religion, sex, or national origin. Today, we must decide whether an employer can fire someone simply for being homosexual or transgender. The answer is clear. An employer who fires an individual for being homosexual or transgender fires that person for traits or actions it would not have questioned in members of a different sex. Sex plays a necessary and undisguisable role in the decision, exactly what Title VII forbids.

Those who adopted the Civil Rights Act might not have anticipated their work would lead to this particular result. Likely, they weren't thinking about many of the Act's consequences that have become apparent over the years, including its prohibition against discrimination on the basis of motherhood or its ban on the sexual harassment of male employees. But the limits of the drafters' imagination supply no reason to ignore the law's demands. When the express terms of a statute give us one answer and extratextual considerations suggest another, it's no contest. Only the written word is the law, and all persons are entitled to its benefit.

I

. . . . Each of the three cases before us started the same way: An employer fired a long-time employee shortly after the employee revealed that he or she is homosexual or transgender—and allegedly for no reason other than the employee's homosexuality or transgender status.

Gerald Bostock worked for Clayton County, Georgia, as a child welfare advocate. Under his leadership, the county won national awards for its work. After a decade with the county, Mr. Bostock began participating in a gay recreational softball league. Not long after that, influential members of the community allegedly made disparaging comments about Mr. Bostock's sexual orientation and participation in the league. Soon, he was fired for conduct "unbecoming" a county employee.

Donald Zarda worked as a skydiving instructor at Altitude Express in New York. After several seasons with the company, Mr. Zarda mentioned that he was gay and, days later, was fired.

Aimee Stephens worked at R.G. & G.R. Harris Funeral Homes in Garden City, Michigan. When she got the job, Ms. Stephens presented as a male. But two years into her service with the company, she began treatment for despair and loneliness. Ultimately, clinicians diagnosed her with gender dysphoria and recommended that she begin living as a woman. In her sixth year with the company, Ms. Stephens wrote a letter to her employer explaining that she planned to "live and work full-time as a woman" after she returned from an upcoming vacation. The funeral home fired her before she left, telling her "this is not going to work out."

. . . . Each employee brought suit under Title VII alleging unlawful discrimination on the basis of sex. 42 U.S.C. § 2000e-2(a)(1). . . . During the course of the proceedings in these long-running disputes, both Mr. Zarda and Ms. Stephens have passed away. But their estates continue to press their causes for the benefit of their heirs. . . .

II

This Court normally interprets a statute in accord with the ordinary public meaning of its terms at the time of its enactment. After all, only the words on the page constitute the law adopted by Congress and approved by the President. If judges could add to, remodel, update, or detract from old statutory terms inspired only by extratextual sources and our own imaginations, we would risk amending statutes outside the legislative process reserved for the people's representatives. And we would deny the people the right to continue relying on the original meaning of the law they have counted on to settle their rights and obligations. See *New Prime Inc. v. Oliveira*, 139 S.Ct. 532 (2019).

. . . .

A

The only statutorily protected characteristic at issue in today's cases is "sex"— and that is also the primary term in Title VII whose meaning the parties dispute. Appealing to roughly contemporaneous dictionaries, the employers say that, as used here, the term "sex" in 1964 referred to "status as either male or female [as] determined by reproductive biology." The employees counter by submitting that, even in 1964, the term bore a broader scope, capturing more than anatomy and reaching at least some norms concerning gender identity and sexual orientation. But because nothing in our approach to these cases turns on the outcome of the parties' debate, and because the employees concede the point for argument's sake, we proceed on the assumption that "sex" signified what the employers suggest, referring only to biological distinctions between male and female.

. . . . The question isn't just what "sex" meant, but what Title VII says about it. [T]he statute prohibits employers from taking certain actions "because of " sex. And, as this Court has previously explained, "the ordinary meaning of 'because of' is 'by reason of' or 'on account of.'" *University of Tex. Southwestern Medical Center v. Nassar*, 570 U.S. 338 (2013) (citing *Gross v. FBL Financial Services, Inc.*, 557 U.S. 167 (2009)). In the language of law, this means that Title VII's "because of" test incorporates the "'simple'" and "traditional" standard of but-for causation. *Nassar*. That form of causation is established whenever a particular outcome would not have happened "but for" the purported cause. *See Gross.* In other words, a but-for test directs us to change one thing at a time and see if the outcome changes. If it does, we have found a but-for cause.

This can be a sweeping standard. Often, events have multiple but-for causes. So, for example, if a car accident occurred both because the defendant ran a red light and because the plaintiff failed to signal his turn at the intersection, we might call each a but-for cause of the collision. When it comes to Title VII, the adoption of the traditional but-for causation standard means a defendant cannot avoid liability just by citing some other factor that contributed to its challenged employment decision. So long as the plaintiff's sex was one but-for cause of that decision, that is enough to trigger the law.

. . . Congress. . . . could have added "solely" to indicate that actions taken "because of" the confluence of multiple factors do not violate the law. . . . If anything, Congress has moved in the opposite direction, supplementing Title VII in 1991 to allow a plaintiff to prevail merely by showing that a protected trait like sex was a "motivating factor" in a defendant's challenged employment practice. Civil Rights Act of 1991, § 107, 105 Stat. 1075, codified at 42 U.S.C. § 2000e-2(m). Under this more forgiving standard, liability can sometimes follow even if sex wasn't a but-for cause of the employer's challenged decision. Still, because nothing in our analysis depends on the motivating factor test, we focus on the more traditional but-for causation standard that continues to afford a viable, if no longer exclusive, path to relief under Title VII. § 2000e–2(a)(1).

. . . Title VII does not concern itself with everything that happens "because of" sex. The statute imposes liability on employers only when they "fail or refuse to hire," "discharge," "or otherwise . . . discriminate against" someone because of a statutorily protected characteristic like sex. . . . By virtue of the word *otherwise*, the employers suggest, Title VII concerns itself not with every discharge, only with those discharges that involve discrimination.

Accepting this point, too, for argument's sake, the question becomes: What did "discriminate" mean in 1964? [I]t meant then roughly what it means today: "To make a difference in treatment or favor (of one as compared with others)." WEBSTER'S NEW INTERNATIONAL DICTIONARY (2d ed. 1954). To "discriminate against" a person, then, would seem to mean treating that individual worse than others who are similarly situated. See *Burlington N. & S.F.R. Co. v. White*, 548 U.S. 53 (2006). In so-called "disparate treatment" cases like today's, this Court has also held that the difference in treatment based on sex must be intentional. *See, e.g., Watson v. Fort Worth Bank & Trust*, 487 U.S. 977 (1988). So, taken together, an employer who intentionally treats a person worse because of sex—such as by firing the person for actions or attributes it would tolerate in an individual of another sex—discriminates against that person in violation of Title VII.

At first glance, another interpretation might seem possible. Discrimination sometimes involves "the act, practice, or an instance of discriminating categorically rather than individually." WEBSTER'S NEW COLLEGIATE DICTIONARY 326 (1975); *see also post*, at n. 22 (ALITO, J., dissenting). On that understanding, the statute would require us to consider the employer's treatment of groups rather than individuals, to see how a policy affects one sex as a whole versus the other as a whole. . . .

The statute. . . . tells us three times—including immediately after the words "discriminate against"—that our focus should be on individuals, not groups:

Employers may not "fail or refuse to hire or . . . discharge any *individual*, or otherwise . . . discriminate against any *individual* with respect to his compensation, terms, conditions, or privileges of employment, because of such *individual's* . . . sex." § 2000e–2(a)(1) (emphasis added). . . .

The consequences of the law's focus on individuals rather than groups are anything but academic. Suppose an employer fires a woman for refusing his sexual advances. It's no defense for the employer to note that, while he treated that individual woman worse than he would have treated a man, he gives preferential treatment to female employees overall. The employer is liable for treating *this* woman worse in part because of her sex. Nor is it a defense for an employer to say it discriminates against both men and women because of sex. This statute works to protect individuals of both sexes from discrimination, and does so equally. So an employer who fires a woman, Hannah, because she is insufficiently feminine and also fires a man, Bob, for being insufficiently masculine may treat men and women as groups more or less equally. But in both cases the employer fires an individual in part because of sex. Instead of avoiding Title VII exposure, this employer doubles it.

B

From the ordinary public meaning of the statute's language at the time of the law's adoption, a straightforward rule emerges: An employer violates Title VII when it intentionally fires an individual employee based in part on sex. . . . If the employer intentionally relies in part on an individual employee's sex when deciding to discharge the employee — put differently, if changing the employee's sex would have yielded a different choice by the employer — a statutory violation has occurred. Title VII's message is "simple but momentous": An individual employee's sex is "not relevant to the selection, evaluation, or compensation of employees." *Price Waterhouse v. Hopkins*, 490 U.S. 228 (1989) (plurality opinion).

The statute's message for our cases is equally simple and momentous: An individual's homosexuality or transgender status is not relevant to employment decisions. That's because it is impossible to discriminate against a person for being homosexual or transgender without discriminating against that individual based on sex. Consider, for example, an employer with two employees, both of whom are attracted to men. The two individuals are, to the employer's mind, materially identical in all respects, except that one is a man and the other a woman. If the employer fires the male employee for no reason other than the fact he is attracted to men, the employer discriminates against him for traits or actions it tolerates in his female colleague. Put differently, the employer intentionally singles out an employee to fire based in part on the employee's sex, and the affected employee's sex is a but-for cause of his discharge. Or take an employer who fires a transgender person who was identified as a male at birth but who now identifies as a female. If the employer retains an otherwise identical employee who was identified as female at birth, the employer intentionally penalizes a person identified as male at birth for traits or actions that it tolerates in an employee identified as female at birth. Again, the individual employee's sex plays an unmistakable and impermissible role in the discharge decision.

[H]omosexuality and transgender status are inextricably bound up with sex. . . . because to discriminate on these grounds requires an employer to intentionally treat individual employees differently because of their sex.

Nor does it matter that, when an employer treats one employee worse because of that individual's sex, other factors may contribute to the decision. Consider an employer with a policy of firing any woman he discovers to be a Yankees fan. Carrying out that rule because an employee is a woman and a fan of the Yankees is a firing "because of sex" if the employer would have tolerated the same allegiance in a male employee. Likewise here. When an employer fires an employee because she is homosexual or transgender, two causal factors may be in play — both the individual's sex and something else (the sex to which the individual is attracted or with which the individual identifies). But Title VII doesn't care. If an employer would not have discharged an employee but for that individual's sex, the statute's causation standard is met, and liability may attach.

Reframing the additional causes in today's cases as additional intentions can do no more to insulate the employers from liability. [I]ntentional discrimination based on sex violates Title VII, even if it is intended only as a means to achieving the employer's ultimate goal of discriminating against homosexual or transgender employees. There is simply no escaping the role intent plays here: Just as sex is necessarily a but-for cause when an employer discriminates against homosexual or transgender employees, an employer who discriminates on these grounds inescapably intends to rely on sex in its decisionmaking. Imagine an employer who has a policy of firing any employee known to be homosexual. The employer hosts an office holiday party and invites employees to bring their spouses. A model employee arrives and introduces a manager to Susan, the employee's wife. Will that employee be fired? If the policy works as the employer intends, the answer depends entirely on whether the model employee is a man or a woman. To be sure, that employer's ultimate goal might be to discriminate on the basis of sexual orientation. But to achieve that purpose the employer must, along the way, intentionally treat an employee worse based in part on that individual's sex.

An employer musters no better a defense by responding that it is equally happy to fire male and female employees who are homosexual or transgender. Title VII liability is not limited to employers who, through the sum of all of their employment actions, treat the class of men differently than the class of women. Instead, the law makes each instance of discriminating against an individual employee because of that individual's sex an independent violation of Title VII. So just as an employer who fires both Hannah and Bob for failing to fulfill traditional sex stereotypes doubles rather than eliminates Title VII liability, an employer who fires both Hannah and Bob for being gay or transgender does the same.

At bottom, these cases involve no more than the straightforward application of legal terms with plain and settled meanings. For an employer to discriminate against employees for being homosexual or transgender, the employer must intentionally discriminate against individual men and women in part because of sex.

That has always been prohibited by Title VII's plain terms—and that "should be the end of the analysis." [*Zarda v. Altitude Express, Inc.*, 883 F.3d 100, 135 (2d Cir. 2018)] (Cabranes, J., concurring in judgment).

[C]

In *Phillips v. Martin Marietta Corp.*, 400 U.S. 542 (1971) (per curiam), a company allegedly refused to hire women with young children, but did hire men with children the same age. Because its discrimination depended not only on the employee's sex as a female but also on the presence of another criterion—namely, being a parent of young children—the company contended it hadn't engaged in discrimination "because of" sex. The company maintained, too, that it hadn't violated the law because, as a whole, it tended to favor hiring women over men. Unsurprisingly by now, these submissions did not sway the Court. . . .

In *Los Angeles Dept. of Water and Power v. Manhart*, 435 U.S. 702 (1978), an employer required women to make larger pension fund contributions than men. The employer sought to justify its disparate treatment on the ground that women tend to live longer than men, and thus are likely to receive more from the pension fund over time. By everyone's admission, the employer was not guilty of animosity against women or a "purely habitual assumptio[n] about a woman's inability to perform certain kinds of work"; instead, it relied on what appeared to be a statistically accurate statement about life expectancy. . . . True, women as a class may live longer than men as a class. But "[t]he statute's focus on the individual is unambiguous," and any individual woman might make the larger pension contributions and still die as early as a man. . . .

In *Oncale v. Sundowner Offshore Services, Inc.*, 523 U.S. 75 (1998), a male plaintiff alleged that he was singled out by his male co-workers for sexual harassment. The Court held it was immaterial that members of the same sex as the victim committed the alleged discrimination. Nor did the Court concern itself with whether men as a group were subject to discrimination or whether something in addition to sex contributed to the discrimination, like the plaintiff 's conduct or personal attributes. "[A]ssuredly," the case didn't involve "the principal evil Congress was concerned with when it enacted Title VII." But, the Court unanimously explained, it is "the provisions of our laws rather than the principal concerns of our legislators by which we are governed." Because the plaintiff alleged that the harassment would not have taken place but for his sex—that is, the plaintiff would not have suffered similar treatment if he were female—a triable Title VII claim existed.

The lessons these cases hold for ours are by now familiar.

First, it's irrelevant what an employer might call its discriminatory practice, how others might label it, or what else might motivate it. In *Manhart*, the employer called its rule requiring women to pay more into the pension fund a "life expectancy" adjustment necessary to achieve sex equality. In *Phillips*, the employer could have accurately spoken of its policy as one based on "motherhood." In much the same way, today's employers might describe their actions as motivated by their employees' homosexuality or transgender status. But just as labels and additional intentions or motivations didn't make a difference in *Manhart* or *Phillips*, they cannot make a difference here. When an employer fires an employee for being homosexual or transgender, it necessarily and intentionally discriminates against that individual in part because of sex. And that is all Title VII has ever demanded to establish liability.

Second, the plaintiff's sex need not be the sole or primary cause of the employer's adverse action. In *Phillips*, *Manhart*, and *Oncale*, the defendant easily could have pointed to some other, nonprotected trait and insisted it was the more important factor in the adverse employment outcome. So, too, it has no significance here if another factor—such as the sex the plaintiff is attracted to or presents as—might also be at work, or even play a more important role in the employer's decision.

Finally, an employer cannot escape liability by demonstrating that it treats males and females comparably as groups. As *Manhart* teaches, an employer is liable for intentionally requiring an individual female employee to pay more into a pension plan than a male counterpart even if the scheme promotes equality at the group level. Likewise, an employer who intentionally fires an individual homosexual or transgender employee in part because of that individual's sex violates the law even if the employer is willing to subject all male and female homosexual or transgender employees to the same rule.

III

. . . . For present purposes, [the employers] do not dispute that they fired the plaintiffs for being homosexual or transgender. . . . Rather, the employers submit that even intentional discrimination against employees based on their homosexuality or transgender status supplies no basis for liability under Title VII.

[A]

Maybe most intuitively, the employers assert that discrimination on the basis of homosexuality and transgender status aren't referred to as sex discrimination in ordinary conversation. If asked by a friend (rather than a judge) why they were fired, even today's plaintiffs would likely respond that it was because they were gay or transgender, not because of sex. . . .

. . . . In conversation, a speaker is likely to focus on what seems most relevant or informative to the listener. So an employee who has just been fired is likely to identify the primary or most direct cause rather than list literally every but-for cause . . . But these conversational conventions do not control Title VII's legal analysis, which asks simply whether sex was a but-for cause. In *Phillips*, for example, a woman who was not hired under the employer's policy might have told her friends that her application was rejected because she was a mother, or because she had young children. . . . But the Court did not hesitate to recognize that the employer in *Phillips* discriminated against the plaintiff because of her sex. Sex wasn't the only factor, or maybe even the main factor, but it was one but-for cause—and that was enough. You can call the statute's but-for causation test what you will—expansive, legalistic, the dissents even dismiss it as wooden or literal. But it is the law.

Trying another angle, the defendants before us suggest that an employer who discriminates based on homosexuality or transgender status doesn't intentionally discriminate based on sex, as a disparate treatment claim requires. But, as we've seen, an employer who discriminates against homosexual or transgender employees necessarily and intentionally applies sex-based rules. An employer that announces it will not employ anyone who is homosexual, for example, intends to penalize male employees for being attracted to men and female employees for being attracted to women.

. . . . Maybe the employers mean they don't intend to harm one sex or the other as a class. But as should be clear by now, the statute focuses on discrimination against individuals, not groups. Alternatively, the employers may mean that they don't perceive themselves as motivated by a desire to discriminate based on sex. But nothing in Title VII turns on the employer's labels or any further intentions (or motivations) for its conduct beyond sex discrimination. In *Manhart*, the employer intentionally required women to make higher pension contributions only to fulfill the further purpose of making things more equitable between men and women as groups. In *Phillips*, the employer may have perceived itself as discriminating based on motherhood, not sex, given that its hiring policies as a whole favored women. But in both cases, the Court set all this aside as irrelevant. The employers' policies involved intentional discrimination because of sex, and Title VII liability necessarily followed.

Aren't these cases different, the employers ask, given that an employer could refuse to hire a gay or transgender individual without ever learning the applicant's sex? Suppose an employer asked homosexual or transgender applicants to tick a box on its application form. The employer then had someone else redact any information that could be used to discern sex. The resulting applications would disclose which individuals are homosexual or transgender without revealing whether they also happen to be men or women. Doesn't that possibility indicate that the employer's discrimination against homosexual or transgender persons cannot be sex discrimination?

No, it doesn't. Even in this example, the individual applicant's sex still weighs as a factor in the employer's decision. Change the hypothetical ever so slightly and its flaws become apparent. Suppose an employer's application form offered a single box to check if the applicant is either black or Catholic. If the employer refuses to hire anyone who checks that box, would we conclude the employer has complied with Title VII, so long as it studiously avoids learning any particular applicant's race or religion? Of course not: By intentionally setting out a rule that makes hiring turn on race or religion, the employer violates the law, whatever he might know or not know about individual applicants.

The same holds here. There is no way for an applicant to decide whether to check the homosexual or transgender box without considering sex. To see why, imagine an applicant doesn't know what the words homosexual or transgender mean. Then try writing out instructions for who should check the box without using the words man, woman, or sex (or some synonym). It can't be done. Likewise, there is no way an employer can discriminate against those who check the homosexual or transgender box without discriminating in part because of an applicant's sex. By discriminating against homosexuals, the employer intentionally penalizes men for being attracted to men and women for being attracted to women. By discriminating against transgender persons, the employer unavoidably discriminates against persons with one sex identified at birth and another today. Any way you slice it, the employer intentionally refuses to hire applicants in part because of the affected individuals' sex, even if it never learns any applicant's sex.

Next, the employers turn to Title VII's list of protected characteristics—race, color, religion, sex, and national origin. Because homosexuality and transgender status can't be found on that list and because they are conceptually distinct from sex, the employers reason, they are implicitly excluded from Title VII's reach. Put another way, if Congress had wanted to address these matters in Title VII, it would have referenced them specifically.

But that much does not follow. We agree that homosexuality and transgender status are distinct concepts from sex. But, as we've seen, discrimination based on homosexuality or transgender status necessarily entails discrimination based on sex; the first cannot happen without the second. Nor is there any such thing as a "canon of donut holes," in which Congress's failure to speak directly to a specific case that falls within a more general statutory rule creates a tacit exception. Instead, when Congress chooses not to include any exceptions to a broad rule, courts apply the broad rule. And that is exactly how this Court has always approached Title VII. "Sexual harassment" is conceptually distinct from sex discrimination, but it can fall within Title VII's sweep. *Oncale.* Same with "motherhood discrimination." *See Phillips.* Would the employers have us reverse those cases on the theory that Congress could have spoken to those problems more specifically? Of course not. As enacted, Title VII prohibits all forms of discrimination because of sex, however they may manifest themselves or whatever other labels might attach to them.

Since 1964, [the employers] observe, Congress has considered several proposals to add sexual orientation to Title VII's list of protected characteristics, but no such amendment has become law. Meanwhile, Congress has enacted other statutes addressing other topics that do discuss sexual orientation. This postenactment legislative history, they urge, should tell us something.

But what? There's no authoritative evidence explaining why later Congresses adopted other laws referencing sexual orientation but didn't amend this one. Maybe some in the later legislatures understood the impact Title VII's broad language already promised for cases like ours and didn't think a revision needed. Maybe others knew about its impact but hoped no one else would notice. Maybe still others, occupied by other concerns, didn't consider the issue at all. All we can know for certain is that speculation about why a later Congress declined to adopt new legislation offers a "particularly dangerous" basis on which to rest an interpretation of an existing law a different and earlier Congress did adopt. *Pension Benefit Guaranty Corporation v. LTV Corp.*, 496 U.S. 633 (1990).

That leaves the employers to seek a different sort of exception. Maybe the traditional and simple but-for causation test should apply in all other Title VII cases, but it just doesn't work when it comes to cases involving homosexual and transgender employees. The test is too blunt to capture the nuances here. The employers illustrate their concern with an example. When we apply the simple test to Mr. Bostock — asking whether Mr. Bostock, a man attracted to other men, would have been fired had he been a woman — we don't just change his sex. Along the way, we change his sexual orientation too (from homosexual to heterosexual). If the aim is to isolate whether a plaintiff's sex caused the dismissal, the employers stress, we must hold sexual orientation constant — meaning we need to change both his sex and the sex to which he is attracted. So for Mr. Bostock, the question should be whether he would've been fired if he were a woman attracted to women. And because his employer would have been as quick to fire a lesbian as it was a gay man, the employers conclude, no Title VII violation has occurred.

. . . . The employers might be onto something if Title VII only ensured equal treatment between groups of men and women or if the statute applied only when sex is the sole or primary reason for an employer's challenged adverse employment action. But both of these premises are mistaken. Title VII's plain terms and our precedents don't care if an employer treats men and women comparably as groups; an employer who fires both lesbians and gay men equally doesn't diminish but doubles its liability. . . . Nor does the statute care if other factors besides sex contribute to an employer's discharge decision. Mr. Bostock's employer might have decided to fire him only because of the confluence of two factors, his sex and the sex to which he is attracted. But exactly the same might have been said in *Phillips*, where motherhood was the added variable.

. . . . Consider an employer eager to revive the workplace gender roles of the 1950s. He enforces a policy that he will hire only men as mechanics and only women as secretaries. When a qualified woman applies for a mechanic position and is denied, the "simple test" immediately spots the discrimination: A qualified man would have been given the job, so sex was a but-for cause of the employer's refusal to hire. But like the employers before us today, this employer would say not so fast. By comparing the woman who applied to be a mechanic to a man who applied to be a mechanic, we've quietly changed two things: the applicant's sex and her trait of failing to conform to 1950s gender roles. The "simple test" thus overlooks that it is really the applicant's bucking of 1950s gender roles, not her sex, doing the work. So we need to hold that second trait constant: Instead of comparing the disappointed female applicant to a man who applied for the same position, the employer would say, we should compare her to a man who applied to be a secretary. And because that jobseeker would be refused too, this must not be sex discrimination.

No one thinks *that*, so the employers must scramble to justify deploying a stricter causation test for use only in cases involving discrimination based on sexual orientation or transgender status. Such a rule would create a curious discontinuity in our case law, to put it mildly. Employer hires based on sexual stereotypes? Simple test. Employer sets pension contributions based on sex? Simple test. Employer fires men who do not behave in a sufficiently masculine way around the office? Simple test. But when that same employer discriminates against women who are attracted to women, or persons identified at birth as women who later identify as men, we suddenly roll out a new and more rigorous standard? Why are *these* reasons for taking sex into account different from all the rest? Title VII's text can offer no answer.

B

Ultimately, the employers are forced to abandon the statutory text and precedent altogether and appeal to assumptions and policy. Most pointedly, they contend that few in 1964 would have expected Title VII to apply to discrimination against homosexual and transgender persons. . . .

. . . . This Court has explained many times over many years that, when the meaning of the statute's terms is plain, our job is at an end. . . . Of course, some Members of this Court have consulted legislative history when interpreting ambiguous statutory language. But that has no bearing here. "Legislative history, for those who take it into account, is meant to clear up ambiguity, not create it." *Milner v. Department of Navy*, 562 U.S. 562 (2011). And as we have seen, no ambiguity exists about how Title VII's terms apply to the facts before us. To be sure, the statute's application in these cases reaches "beyond the principal evil" legislators may have intended or expected to address. *Oncale*. But 'the fact that [a statute] has been applied in situations not expressly anticipated by Congress'" does not demonstrate ambiguity; instead, it simply "'demonstrates [the] breadth'" of a legislative command. *Sedima, S.P.R.L. v. Imrex Co.*, 473 U.S. 479 (1985). And "it is ultimately the provisions of" those legislative commands "rather than the principal concerns of our legislators by which we are governed." *Oncale*.

. . . . Because the law's ordinary meaning at the time of enactment usually governs, we must be sensitive to the possibility a statutory term that means one thing today or in one context might have meant something else at the time of its adoption or might mean something different in another context. And we must be attuned to the possibility that a statutory phrase ordinarily bears a different meaning than the terms do when viewed individually or literally. To ferret out such shifts in linguistic usage or subtle distinctions between literal and ordinary meaning, this Court has sometimes consulted the understandings of the law's drafters as some (not always conclusive) evidence. . . .

The employers, however, advocate nothing like that here. They do not seek to use historical sources to illustrate that the meaning of any of Title VII's language has changed since 1964 or that the statute's terms, whether viewed individually or as a whole, ordinarily carried some message we have missed. To the contrary, as we have seen, the employers agree with our understanding of all the statutory language— "discriminate against any individual . . . because of such individual's . . . sex." Nor do the competing dissents offer an alternative account about what these terms mean either when viewed individually or in the aggregate. Rather than suggesting that the statutory language bears some other meaning, the employers and dissents merely suggest that, because few in 1964 expected today's result, we should not dare to admit that it follows ineluctably from the statutory text. When a new application emerges that is both unexpected and important, they would seemingly have us merely point out the question, refer the subject back to Congress, and decline to enforce the plain terms of the law in the meantime.

That is exactly the sort of reasoning this Court has long rejected. Admittedly, the employers take pains to couch their argument in terms of seeking to honor the statute's "expected applications" rather than vindicate its "legislative intent." But the concepts are closely related. One could easily contend that legislators only intended expected applications or that a statute's purpose is limited to achieving applications foreseen at the time of enactment. However framed, the employer's logic impermissibly seeks to displace the plain meaning of the law in favor of something lying beyond it.

. . . .

One could also reasonably fear that objections about unexpected applications will not be deployed neutrally. Often lurking just behind such objections resides a cynicism that Congress could not possibly have meant to protect a disfavored group. Take this Court's encounter with the Americans with Disabilities Act's directive that no "'public entity'" can discriminate against any "'qualified individual with a disability.'" *Pennsylvania Dept. of Corrections v. Yeskey*, 524 U.S. 206 (1998). . . . Pennsylvania argued that "Congress did not 'envisio[n] that the ADA would be applied to state prisoners.'" This Court emphatically rejected that view, explaining that, "in the context of an unambiguous statutory text," whether a specific application was anticipated by Congress "is irrelevant." As *Yeskey* and today's cases exemplify, applying protective laws to groups that were politically unpopular at the time of the law's passage — whether prisoners in the 1990s or homosexual and transgender employees in the 1960s — often may be seen as unexpected. But to refuse enforcement just because of that, because the parties before us happened to be unpopular at the time of the law's passage, would not only require us to abandon our role as interpreters of statutes; it would tilt the scales of justice in favor of the strong or popular and neglect the promise that all persons are entitled to the benefit of the law's terms.

. . . . [T]he initial proponent of the sex discrimination rule in Title VII, Representative Howard Smith[, ...] may have wanted (or at least was indifferent to the possibility of) broad language with wide-ranging effect. Not necessarily because he was interested in rooting out sex discrimination in all its forms, but because he may have hoped to scuttle the whole Civil Rights Act and thought that adding language covering sex discrimination would serve as a poison pill. Certainly nothing in the meager legislative history of this provision suggests it was meant to be read narrowly.

Whatever his reasons, thanks to the broad language Representative Smith introduced, many, maybe most, applications of Title VII's sex provision were "unanticipated" at the time of the law's adoption. In fact, many now-obvious applications met with heated opposition early on, even among those tasked with enforcing the law . . .

Over time, though, the breadth of the statutory language proved too difficult to deny. By the end of the 1960s, the EEOC reversed its stance on sex-segregated job advertising. In 1971, this Court held that treating women with children differently from men with children violated Title VII. *Phillips*. And by the late 1970s, courts began to recognize that sexual harassment can sometimes amount to sex discrimination. While to the modern eye each of these examples may seem "plainly [to] constitut[e] discrimination because of biological sex," post (ALITO, J., dissenting), all were hotly contested for years following Title VII's enactment. And as with the discrimination we consider today, many federal judges long accepted interpretations of Title VII that excluded these situations. Cf. post (KAVANAUGH, J., dissenting) (highlighting that certain lower courts have rejected Title VII claims based on homosexuality and transgender status). . . .

The weighty implications of the employers' argument from expectations also reveal why they cannot hide behind the no-elephants-in-mouseholes canon. That canon recognizes that Congress "does not alter the fundamental details of a regulatory scheme in vague terms or ancillary provisions." *Whitman v. American Trucking Assns., Inc.*, 531 U.S. 457 (2001). But it has no relevance here. We can't deny that today's holding—that employers are prohibited from firing employees on the basis of homosexuality or transgender status—is an elephant. But where's the mousehole? Title VII's prohibition of sex discrimination in employment is a major piece of federal civil rights legislation. It is written in starkly broad terms. It has repeatedly produced unexpected applications, at least in the view of those on the receiving end of them. Congress's key drafting choices—to focus on discrimination against individuals and not merely between groups and to hold employers liable whenever sex is a but-for cause of the plaintiff's injuries—virtually guaranteed that unexpected applications would emerge over time. This elephant has never hidden in a mousehole; it has been standing before us all along.

With that, the employers are left to abandon their concern for expected applications and fall back to the last line of defense for all failing statutory interpretation arguments: naked policy appeals. If we were to apply the statute's plain language, they complain, any number of undesirable policy consequences would follow. *Cf.* post (ALITO, J., dissenting). Gone here is any pretense of statutory interpretation; all that's left is a suggestion we should proceed without the law's guidance to do as we think best. But that's an invitation no court should ever take up. . . . As judges we possess no special expertise or authority to declare for ourselves what a self-governing people should consider just or wise. And the same judicial humility that requires us to refrain from adding to statutes requires us to refrain from diminishing them.

What are these consequences anyway? The employers worry that our decision will sweep beyond Title VII to other federal or state laws that prohibit sex discrimination. And, under Title VII itself, they say sex-segregated bathrooms, locker rooms, and dress codes will prove unsustainable after our decision today. But none of these other laws are before us; we have not had the benefit of adversarial testing about the meaning of their terms, and we do not prejudge any such question today. Under Title VII, too, we do not purport to address bathrooms, locker rooms, or anything else of the kind. . . . As used in Title VII, the term "'discriminate against'" refers to "distinctions or differences in treatment that injure protected individuals." *Burlington N. & S.F.R.* Firing employees because of a statutorily protected trait surely counts. Whether other policies and practices might or might not qualify as unlawful discrimination or find justifications under other provisions of Title VII are questions for future cases, not these.

Separately, the employers fear that complying with Title VII's requirement in cases like ours may require some employers to violate their religious convictions. We are also deeply concerned with preserving the promise of the free exercise of religion enshrined in our Constitution; that guarantee lies at the heart of our pluralistic society. But worries about how Title VII may intersect with religious liberties are nothing new; they even predate the statute's passage. As a result of its deliberations in adopting the law, Congress included an express statutory exception for religious organizations. § 2000e-1(a). This Court has also recognized that the First Amendment can bar the application of employment discrimination laws "to claims concerning the employment relationship between a religious institution and its ministers." *Hosanna-Tabor Evangelical Lutheran Church and School v. EEOC*, 565 U.S. 171 (2012). And Congress has gone a step further yet in the Religious Freedom Restoration Act of 1993 (RFRA), 107 Stat. 1488, codified at 42 U.S.C. § 2000bb et seq. That statute prohibits the federal government from substantially burdening a person's exercise of religion unless it demonstrates that doing so both furthers a compelling governmental interest and represents the least restrictive means of furthering that interest. § 2000bb-1. Because RFRA operates as a kind of super statute, displacing the normal operation of other federal laws, it might supersede Title VII's commands in appropriate cases. See § 2000bb-3.

But how these doctrines protecting religious liberty interact with Title VII are questions for future cases too. Harris Funeral Homes did unsuccessfully pursue a RFRA-based defense in the proceedings below. In its certiorari petition, however, the company declined to seek review of that adverse decision, and no other religious liberty claim is now before us. So while other employers in other cases may raise free exercise arguments that merit careful consideration, none of the employers before us today represent in this Court that compliance with Title VII will infringe their own religious liberties in any way.

* * *

. . . . Ours is a society of written laws. Judges are not free to overlook plain statutory commands on the strength of nothing more than suppositions about intentions or guesswork about expectations. In Title VII, Congress adopted broad language making it illegal for an employer to rely on an employee's sex when deciding to fire that employee. We do not hesitate to recognize today a necessary consequence of that legislative choice: An employer who fires an individual merely for being gay or transgender defies the law.

The judgments of the Second and Sixth Circuits in Nos. 17-1623 and 18-107 are affirmed. The judgment of the Eleventh Circuit in No. 17-1618 is reversed, and the case is remanded for further proceedings consistent with this opinion.

It is so ordered.

Justice ALITO, with whom Justice THOMAS joins, dissenting.

There is only one word for what the Court has done today: legislation. The document that the Court releases is in the form of a judicial opinion interpreting a statute, but that is deceptive.

Title VII of the Civil Rights Act of 1964 prohibits employment discrimination on any of five specified grounds: "race, color, religion, sex, [and] national origin." Neither "sexual orientation" nor "gender identity" appears on that list. For the past 45 years, bills have been introduced in Congress to add "sexual orientation" to the list, and in recent years, bills have included "gender identity" as well. But to date, none has passed both Houses.

Last year, the House of Representatives passed a bill that would amend Title VII by defining sex discrimination to include both "sexual orientation" and "gender identity," H. R. 5, 116th Cong., 1st Sess. (2019), but the bill has stalled in the Senate. . . .

The Court tries to convince readers that it is merely enforcing the terms of the statute, but that is preposterous. Even as understood today, the concept of discrimination because of "sex" is different from discrimination because of "sexual orientation" or "gender identity." And in any event, our duty is to interpret statutory terms to "mean what they conveyed to reasonable people *at the time they were written.*" A. SCALIA & B. GARNER, READING LAW: THE INTERPRETATION OF LEGAL TEXTS (2012) (emphasis added). If every single living American had been surveyed in 1964, it would have been hard to find any who thought that discrimination because of sex meant discrimination because of sexual orientation—not to mention gender identity, a concept that was essentially unknown at the time.

The Court attempts to pass off its decision as the inevitable product of the textualist school of statutory interpretation championed by our late colleague Justice Scalia, but no one should be fooled. The Court's opinion is like a pirate ship. It sails under a textualist flag, but what it actually represents is a theory of statutory interpretation that Justice Scalia excoriated—the theory that courts should "update" old statutes so that they better reflect the current values of society. . . .

Many will applaud today's decision because they agree on policy grounds with the Court's updating of Title VII. But the question in these cases is not whether discrimination because of sexual orientation or gender identity should be outlawed. The question is whether Congress did that in 1964.

It indisputably did not.

I

A

[I]n 1964, it was as clear as clear could be that [discrimination because of sex] meant discrimination because of the genetic and anatomical characteristics that men and women have at the time of birth. Determined searching has not found a single dictionary from that time that defined "sex" to mean sexual orientation, gender identity, or "transgender status."

. . . [Therefore —Eds.] discrimination because of sex means discrimination because the person in question is biologically male or biologically female, not because that person is sexually attracted to members of the same sex or identifies as a member of a particular gender.

. . . . [T]he question we must decide comes down to this: . . . . if an employer takes an employment action solely because of the sexual orientation or gender identity of an employee or applicant, has that employer necessarily discriminated because of biological sex?

. . . . According to the Court, the text is unambiguous.

The arrogance of [its] argument is breathtaking. [T]here is not a shred of evidence that any Member of Congress interpreted the statutory text that way when Title VII was enacted. . . .

The Court's argument. . . . fails on its own terms. "Sex," "sexual orientation," and "gender identity" are different concepts, as the Court concedes. And neither "sexual orientation" nor "gender identity" is tied to either of the two biological sexes. *See ante* (recognizing that "discrimination on these bases" does not have "some disparate impact on one sex or another"). Both men and women may be attracted to members of the opposite sex, members of the same sex, or members of both sexes. And individuals who are born with the genes and organs of either biological sex may identify with a different gender.

. . . . [D]iscrimination because of sexual orientation or gender identity does not in and of itself entail discrimination because of sex. We can see this because it is quite possible for an employer to discriminate on those grounds without taking the sex of an individual applicant or employee into account. An employer can have a policy that says: "We do not hire gays, lesbians, or transgender individuals." And an employer can implement this policy without paying any attention to or even knowing the biological sex of gay, lesbian, and transgender applicants. In fact, at the time of the enactment of Title VII, the United States military had a blanket policy of refusing to enlist gays or lesbians, and under this policy for years thereafter, applicants for enlistment were required to complete a form that asked whether they were "homosexual."

At oral argument, the attorney representing the employees, a prominent professor of constitutional law, was asked if there would be discrimination because of sex if an employer with a blanket policy against hiring gays, lesbians, and transgender individuals implemented that policy without knowing the biological sex of any job applicants. Her candid answer was that this would "not" be sex discrimination. And she was right.

The attorney's concession was necessary, but it is fatal to the Court's interpretation, for if an employer discriminates against individual applicants or employees without even knowing whether they are male or female, it is impossible to argue that the employer intentionally discriminated because of sex. An employer cannot intentionally discriminate on the basis of a characteristic of which the employer has no knowledge. And if an employer does not violate Title VII by discriminating on the basis of sexual orientation or gender identity without knowing the sex of the affected individuals, there is no reason why the same employer could not lawfully implement the same policy even if it knows the sex of these individuals. . . . [A] disparate treatment case requires proof of intent—*i.e.*, that the employee's sex motivated the firing. . . .

[T]he Court offers its own hypothetical. . . . [Alito then quotes the "black or Catholic" application box hypo.]

How this hypothetical proves the Court's point is a mystery. A person who checked that box would presumably be black, Catholic, or both, and refusing to hire an applicant because of race or religion is prohibited by Title VII. Rejecting applicants who checked a box indicating that they are homosexual is entirely different because it is impossible to tell from that answer whether an applicant is male or female.

The Court follows this strange hypothetical with an even stranger argument. The Court argues that an applicant could not answer the question whether he or she is homosexual without knowing something about sex. If the applicant was unfamiliar with the term "homosexual," the applicant would have to look it up or ask what the term means. And because this applicant would have to take into account his or her sex and that of the persons to whom he or she is sexually attracted to answer the question, it follows, the Court reasons, that an employer could not reject this applicant without taking the applicant's sex into account.

This is illogical. Just because an applicant cannot say whether he or she is homosexual without knowing his or her own sex and that of the persons to whom the applicant is attracted, it does not follow that an employer cannot reject an applicant based on homosexuality without knowing the applicant's sex.

[A]nother hypothetical case offered by the Court is telling. But what it proves is not what the Court thinks. The Court posits:

> "Imagine an employer who has a policy of firing any employee known to be homosexual. The employer hosts an office holiday party and invites employees to bring their spouses. A model employee arrives and introduces a manager to Susan, the employee's wife. Will that employee be fired? If the policy works as the employer intends, the answer depends entirely on whether the model employee is a man or a woman."

This example disproves the Court's argument because it is perfectly clear that the employer's motivation in firing the female employee had nothing to do with that employee's sex. The employer presumably knew that this employee was a woman before she was invited to the fateful party. Yet the employer, far from holding her biological sex against her, rated her a "model employee." At the party, the employer learned something new, her sexual orientation, and it was this new information that motivated her discharge. So this is another example showing that discrimination because of sexual orientation does not inherently involve discrimination because of sex.

[T]he Court makes two other arguments. . . . The first [is] essentially that sexual orientation and gender identity are closely related to sex. The Court argues that sexual orientation and gender identity are "inextricably bound up with sex," and that discrimination on the basis of sexual orientation or gender identity involves the application of "sex-based rules." . . . .

. . . . Title VII prohibits discrimination because of sex itself, not everything that is related to, based on, or defined with reference to, "sex." Many things are related to sex. Think of all the nouns other than "orientation" that are commonly modified by the adjective "sexual." Some examples yielded by a quick computer search are "sexual harassment," "sexual assault," "sexual violence," "sexual intercourse," and "sexual content."

Does the Court really think that Title VII prohibits discrimination on all these grounds? Is it unlawful for an employer to refuse to hire an employee with a record of sexual harassment in prior jobs? Or a record of sexual assault or violence?

To be fair, the Court. . . . draws a distinction between things that are "inextricably" related [to sex] and those that are related in "some vague sense." Apparently the Court would graft onto Title VII some arbitrary line separating the things that are related closely enough and those that are not.[16] And it would do this in the name of high textualism.

. . . .

The Court's remaining argument is based on a hypothetical that the Court finds instructive. In this hypothetical, an employer has two employees who are "attracted to men," and *to the employer's mind* the two employees are "materially identical" except that one is a man and the other is a woman. (emphasis added). The Court reasons that if the employer fires the man but not the woman, the employer is necessarily motivated by the man's biological sex. After all, if two employees are identical

---

16. Notably, Title VII itself already suggests a line, which the Court ignores. The statute specifies that the terms "because of sex" and "on the basis of sex" cover certain conditions that are biologically tied to sex, namely, "pregnancy, childbirth, [and] related medical conditions." This definition should inform the meaning of "because of sex" in Title VII more generally. Unlike pregnancy, neither sexual orientation nor gender identity is biologically linked to women or men."

in every respect but sex, and the employer fires only one, what other reason could there be?

The . . . Court loads the dice. [I]n the mind of an employer who does not want to employ individuals who are attracted to members of the same sex, these two employees are not materially identical in every respect but sex. On the contrary, they differ in another way that the employer thinks is quite material. And until Title VII is amended to add sexual orientation as a prohibited ground, this is a view that an employer is permitted to implement. As noted, other than prohibiting discrimination on any of five specified grounds, "race, color, religion, sex, [and] national origin." Title VII allows employers to decide whether two employees are "materially identical." Even idiosyncratic criteria are permitted; if an employer thinks that Scorpios make bad employees, the employer can refuse to hire Scorpios. Such a policy would be unfair and foolish, but under Title VII, it is permitted. And until Title VII is amended, so is a policy against employing gays, lesbians, or transgender individuals.

Once this is recognized, what we have in the Court's hypothetical case are two employees who differ in two ways—sex and sexual orientation—and if the employer fires one and keeps the other, all that can be inferred is that the employer was motivated either entirely by sexual orientation, entirely by sex, or in part by both. We cannot infer with any certainty, as the hypothetical is apparently meant to suggest, that the employer was motivated even in part by sex. . . .

The Court tries to avoid this inescapable conclusion by arguing that sex is really the only difference between the two employees. This is so, the Court maintains, because both employees "are attracted to men." Of course, the employer would couch its objection to the man differently. It would say that its objection was his sexual orientation. So this may appear to leave us with a battle of labels. If the employer's objection to the male employee is characterized as attraction to men, it seems that he is just like the woman in all respects except sex and that the employer's disparate treatment must be based on that one difference. On the other hand, if the employer's objection is sexual orientation or homosexuality, the two employees differ in two respects, and it cannot be inferred that the disparate treatment was due even in part to sex.

The Court insists that its label is the right one, and that presumably is why it makes such a point of arguing that an employer cannot escape liability under Title VII by giving sex discrimination some other name. That is certainly true, but so is the opposite. Something that is not sex discrimination cannot be converted into sex discrimination by slapping on that label. So the Court cannot prove its point simply by labeling the employer's objection as "attract[ion] to men." Rather, the Court needs to show that its label is the correct one.

And a labeling standoff would not help the Court because that would mean that the bare text of Title VII does not unambiguously show that its interpretation is right. The Court would have no justification for its stubborn refusal to look any further.

As it turns out, however, [i]t can easily be shown that the employer's real objection is not "attract[ion] to men" but homosexual orientation.

In an effort to prove its point, the Court carefully includes in its example just two employees, a homosexual man and a heterosexual woman, but suppose we add two more individuals, a woman who is attracted to women and a man who is attracted to women. . . . We now have the four exemplars listed below, with the discharged employees crossed out:

~~Man attracted to men~~

Woman attracted to men

~~Woman attracted to women~~

Man attracted to women

The discharged employees have one thing in common. It is not biological sex, attraction to men, or attraction to women. It is attraction to members of their own sex — in a word, sexual orientation. And that, we can infer, is the employer's real motive.

. . . .

But even if the words of Title VII did not definitively refute the Court's interpretation, that would not justify the Court's refusal to consider alternative interpretations. [To say that the Court's interpretation is the only [textually — Eds.] possible reading is indefensible.

B

Although the Court relies solely on the arguments discussed above, several other arguments figure prominently in the decisions of the lower courts and in briefs submitted by or in support of the employees. The Court apparently finds these arguments unpersuasive, and so do I, but for the sake of completeness, I will address them briefly.

1

One argument, which relies on our decision in *Price Waterhouse v. Hopkins*, 490 U.S. 228 (1989) (plurality opinion), is that discrimination because of sexual orientation or gender identity violates Title VII because it constitutes prohibited discrimination on the basis of sex stereotypes. The argument goes like this. Title VII prohibits discrimination based on stereotypes about the way men and women should behave; the belief that a person should be attracted only to persons of the opposite sex and the belief that a person should identify with his or her biological sex are examples of such stereotypes; therefore, discrimination on either of these grounds is unlawful.

This argument fails because it is based on a faulty premise, namely, that Title VII forbids discrimination based on sex stereotypes. It does not. It prohibits discrimination because of "sex," and the two concepts are not the same. *See Price Waterhouse*. [Evidence] that a challenged decision was based on a sex stereotype[is] relevant to prove discrimination because of sex, and it may be convincing where the trait that is inconsistent with the stereotype is one that would be tolerated and perhaps even valued in a person of the opposite sex. *See ibid.*

Much of the plaintiff's evidence in *Price Waterhouse* was of this nature. The plaintiff was a woman who was passed over for partnership at an accounting firm, and some of the adverse comments about her work appeared to criticize her for being forceful and insufficiently "feminin[e]."

. . . .

Plaintiffs who allege that they were treated unfavorably because of their sexual orientation or gender identity are not in the same position as the plaintiff in *Price Waterhouse*. In cases involving discrimination based on sexual orientation or gender identity, the grounds for the employer's decision—that individuals should be sexually attracted only to persons of the opposite biological sex or should identify with their biological sex—apply equally to men and women. "[H]eterosexuality is not a *female* stereotype; it not a *male* stereotype; it is not a *sex-specific* stereotype at all." [*Hively v. Ivy Tech Community College of Ind.*, 853 F.3d 339 (7th Cir. 2017)] (Sykes, J., dissenting).

To be sure, there may be cases in which a gay, lesbian, or transgender individual can make a claim like the one in *Price Waterhouse*. That is, there may be cases where traits or behaviors that some people associate with gays, lesbians, or transgender individuals are tolerated or valued in persons of one biological sex but not the other. But that is a different matter.

2

A second prominent argument made in support of the result that the Court now reaches analogizes discrimination against gays and lesbians to discrimination against a person who is married to or has an intimate relationship with a person of a different race. Several lower court cases have held that discrimination on this ground violates Title VII. And the logic of these decisions, it is argued, applies equally where an employee or applicant is treated unfavorably because he or she is married to, or has an intimate relationship with, a person of the same sex.

This argument totally ignores the historically rooted reason why discrimination on the basis of an interracial relationship constitutes race discrimination. And without taking history into account, it is not easy to see how the decisions in question fit the terms of Title VII.

Recall that Title VII makes it unlawful for an employer to discriminate against an individual "because of *such individual's race*." 42 U.S.C. § 2000e-2(a) (emphasis added). So if an employer is happy to employ whites and blacks but will not employ any employee in an interracial relationship, how can it be said that the employer is discriminating against either whites or blacks "because of such individual's race"? This employer would be applying the same rule to all its employees regardless of their race.

The answer is that this employer is discriminating on a ground that history tells us is a core form of race discrimination.[18] "It would require absolute blindness to the history of racial discrimination in this country not to understand what is at stake in such cases. . . . A prohibition on 'race-mixing' was . . . grounded in bigotry against a particular race and was an integral part of preserving the rigid hierarchical distinction that denominated members of the black race as inferior to whites." [*Zarda v. Altitude Express, Inc.*, 883 F.3d 100 (2d Cir. 2018)] (Lynch, J., dissenting).

Discrimination because of sexual orientation is different. It cannot be regarded as a form of sex discrimination on the ground that applies in race cases since discrimination because of sexual orientation is not historically tied to a project that aims to subjugate either men or women. An employer who discriminates on this ground might be called "homophobic" or "transphobic," but not sexist. *See Wittmer v. Phillips 66 Co.*, 915 F.3d 328 (5th Cir. 2019) (Ho, J., concurring).

[II]

A

So far, I have not looked beyond dictionary definitions of "sex," but textualists like Justice Scalia do not confine their inquiry to the scrutiny of dictionaries. Dictionary definitions are valuable because they are evidence of what people at the time of a statute's enactment would have understood its words to mean. But they are not the only source of relevant evidence, and what matters in the end is the answer to the question that the evidence is gathered to resolve: How would the terms of a statute have been understood by ordinary people at the time of enactment?

. . . . Suppose that, while Title VII was under consideration in Congress, a group of average Americans decided to read the text of the bill with the aim of writing or calling their representatives in Congress and conveying their approval or disapproval. What would these ordinary citizens have taken "discrimination because of sex" to mean? Would they have thought that this language prohibited discrimination because of sexual orientation or gender identity?

B

The answer could not be clearer. In 1964, ordinary Americans reading the text of Title VII would not have dreamed that discrimination because of sex meant discrimination because of sexual orientation, much less gender identity. The ordinary meaning of discrimination because of "sex" was discrimination because of a person's biological sex, not sexual orientation or gender identity. The possibility that discrimination on either of these grounds might fit within some exotic understanding of sex discrimination would not have crossed their minds.

---

18. Notably, Title VII recognizes that in light of history distinctions on the basis of race are always disadvantageous, but it permits certain distinctions based on sex. Title 42 U.S.C. § 2000e-2(e)(1) allows for "instances where religion, sex, or national origin is a bona fide occupational qualification reasonably necessary to the normal operation of [a] particular business or enterprise." Race is wholly absent from this list.

1

In 1964, the concept of prohibiting discrimination "because of sex" was no novelty. It was a familiar and well-understood concept, and what it meant was equal treatment for men and women.

Long before Title VII was adopted, many pioneering state and federal laws had used language substantively indistinguishable from Title VII's critical phrase, "discrimination because of sex." [The opinion then canvasses numerous examples since the late 1800s.]

In short, the concept of discrimination "because of," "on account of," or "on the basis of" sex was well understood. It was part of the campaign for equality that had been waged by women's rights advocates for more than a century, and what it meant was equal treatment for men and women.

2

Discrimination "because of sex" was not understood as having anything to do with discrimination because of sexual orientation or transgender status. Any such notion would have clashed in spectacular fashion with the societal norms of the day.

For most 21st-century Americans, it is painful to be reminded of the way our society once treated gays and lesbians, but any honest effort to understand what the terms of Title VII were understood to mean when enacted must take into account the societal norms of that time. And the plain truth is that in 1964 homosexuality was thought to be a mental disorder, and homosexual conduct was regarded as morally culpable and worthy of punishment.

In its then-most recent *Diagnostic and Statistical Manual of Mental Disorders* (1952) (DSM–I), the American Psychiatric [Association] classified same-sex attraction as a "sexual deviation," a particular type of "sociopathic personality disturbance," . . . .

Society's treatment of homosexuality and homosexual conduct was consistent with this understanding. Sodomy was a crime in every State but Illinois, and in the District of Columbia, a law enacted by Congress made sodomy a felony punishable by imprisonment for up to 10 years and permitted the indefinite civil commitment of "sexual psychopath[s]."

This view of homosexuality was reflected in the rules governing the federal work force. In 1964, federal "[a]gencies could deny homosexual men and women employment because of their sexual orientation," and this practice continued until 1975. . . .

In 1964, individuals who were known to be homosexual could not obtain security clearances, and any who possessed clearances were likely to lose them if their orientation was discovered. A 1953 Executive Order provided that background investigations should look for evidence of "sexual perversion," as well as "[a]ny criminal, infamous, dishonest, immoral, or notoriously disgraceful conduct." . . . .

The picture in state employment was similar. In 1964, it was common for States to bar homosexuals from serving as teachers. . . .

Individuals who engaged in homosexual acts also faced the loss of other occupational licenses, such as those needed to work as a "lawyer, doctor, mortician, [or] beautician."

In 1964 and for many years thereafter, homosexuals were barred from the military. . . .

Homosexuals were also excluded from entry into the United States. The Immigration and Nationality Act of 1952 (INA) excluded aliens "afflicted with psychopathic personality." 8 U.S.C. § 1182(a)(4) (1964 ed.). In *Boutilier v. INS*, 387 U.S. 118 (1967), this Court, relying on the INA's legislative history, interpreted that term to encompass homosexuals and upheld an alien's deportation on that ground. Three Justices disagreed with the majority's interpretation of the phrase "psychopathic personality."[27] But it apparently did not occur to anyone to argue that the Court's interpretation was inconsistent with the INA's express prohibition of discrimination "because of sex." That was how our society—and this Court—saw things a half century ago. Discrimination because of sex and discrimination because of sexual orientation were viewed as two entirely different concepts.

To its credit, our society has now come to recognize the injustice of past practices, and this recognition provides the impetus to "update" Title VII. But that is not our job. Our duty is to understand what the terms of Title VII were understood to mean when enacted, and in doing so, we must take into account the societal norms of that time. . . .

C

While Americans in 1964 would have been shocked to learn that Congress had enacted a law prohibiting sexual orientation discrimination, they would have been bewildered to hear that this law also forbids discrimination on the basis of "transgender status" or "gender identity," terms that would have left people at the time scratching their heads. The term "transgender" is said to have been coined "'in the early 1970s,'" and the term "gender identity," now understood to mean "[a]n internal sense of being male, female or something else," apparently first appeared in an academic article in 1964. Certainly, neither term was in common parlance; indeed, dictionaries of the time still primarily defined the word "gender" by reference to grammatical classifications.

. . . .

The first widely publicized sex reassignment surgeries in the United States were not performed until 1966, and the great majority of physicians surveyed in 1969 thought that an individual who sought sex reassignment surgery was either "'severely neurotic'" or "'psychotic.'"

---

27. Justices Douglas and Fortas thought that a homosexual is merely "one, who by some freak, is the product of an arrested development."

It defies belief to suggest that the public meaning of discrimination because of sex in 1964 encompassed discrimination on the basis of a concept that was essentially unknown to the public at that time.

D

1

The Court's main excuse for entirely ignoring the social context in which Title VII was enacted is that the meaning of Title VII's prohibition of discrimination because of sex is clear. . . .

In arguing that we must put out of our minds what we know about the time when Title VII was enacted, the Court relies on Justice Scalia's opinion for the Court in *Oncale v. Sundowner Offshore Services, Inc.*, 523 U.S. 75 (1998). . . .

Properly understood, *Oncale* does not provide the slightest support for what the Court has done today. For one thing, it would be a wild understatement to say that discrimination because of sexual orientation and transgender status was not the "principal evil" on Congress's mind in 1964. Whether we like to admit it now or not, in the thinking of Congress and the public at that time, such discrimination would not have been evil at all.

But the more important difference between these cases and *Oncale* is that here the interpretation that the Court adopts does not fall within the ordinary meaning of the statutory text as it would have been understood in 1964 . . . And the reasoning of *Oncale* does not preclude or counsel against our taking those norms into account. They are relevant, not for the purpose of creating an exception to the terms of the statute, but for the purpose of better appreciating how those terms would have been understood at the time.

[2]

The Court extracts three "lessons" from *Phillips*, *Manhart*, and *Oncale*, but none sheds any light on the question before us. The first lesson is that "it's irrelevant what an employer might call its discriminatory practice, how others might label it, or what else might motivate it." This lesson is obviously true but. . . . simply takes us back to the question whether discrimination because of sexual orientation or gender identity is a form of discrimination because of biological sex. [It] is not.

It likewise proves nothing of relevance here to note that an employer cannot escape liability by showing that discrimination on a prohibited ground was not its sole motivation. . . .

The Court makes much of the argument that "[i]n *Phillips*, the employer could have accurately spoken of its policy as one based on 'motherhood.'" But motherhood, by definition, is a condition that can be experienced only by women, so a policy that distinguishes between motherhood and parenthood is necessarily a policy that draws a sex-based distinction. . . .

Lesson number two—"the plaintiff's sex need not be the sole or primary cause of the employer's adverse action"—is similarly unhelpful. The standard of causation in these cases is whether sex is necessarily a "motivating factor" when an employer discriminates on the basis of sexual orientation or gender identity. 42 U.S.C. § 2000e-2(m). But the essential question—whether discrimination because of sexual orientation or gender identity constitutes sex discrimination—would be the same no matter what causation standard applied. The Court's extensive discussion of causation standards is so much smoke.

Lesson number three—"an employer cannot escape liability by demonstrating that it treats males and females comparably as groups"—is also irrelevant. There is no dispute that discrimination against an individual employee based on that person's sex cannot be justified on the ground that the employer's treatment of the average employee of that sex is at least as favorable as its treatment of the average employee of the opposite sex. Nor does it matter if an employer discriminates against only a subset of men or women, where the same subset of the opposite sex is treated differently, as in *Phillips*. That is not the issue here. An employer who discriminates equally on the basis of sexual orientation or gender identity applies the same criterion to every affected individual regardless of sex. *See* Part I–A, *supra*.

III

A

. . . . Many Justices of this Court, both past and present, ... when there is ambiguity in the terms of a statute, . . . have found it appropriate to look to other evidence of "congressional intent," including legislative history.

So, why in these cases are congressional intent and the legislative history of Title VII totally ignored? Any assessment of congressional intent or legislative history seriously undermines the Court's interpretation.

B

[T]he legislative history of Title VII's prohibition of sex discrimination is brief, but it is nevertheless revealing. The prohibition of sex discrimination was "added to Title VII at the last minute on the floor of the House of Representatives," by Representative Howard Smith, the Chairman of the Rules Committee. Representative Smith had been an ardent opponent of the civil rights bill, and it has been suggested that he added the prohibition against discrimination on the basis of "sex" as a poison pill. On this theory, Representative Smith thought that prohibiting employment discrimination against women would be unacceptable to Members who might have otherwise voted in favor of the bill and that the addition of this prohibition might bring about the bill's defeat. But if Representative Smith had been looking for a poison pill, prohibiting discrimination on the basis of sexual orientation or gender identity would have been far more potent. However, neither Representative Smith nor any other Member said one word about the possibility that the prohibition of sex discrimination might have that meaning. Instead, all the debate concerned discrimination on the basis of biological sex.

Representative Smith's motivations are contested, but whatever they were, the meaning of the adoption of the prohibition of sex discrimination is clear. . . . It grew out of "a long history of women's rights advocacy that had increasingly been gaining mainstream recognition and acceptance," and it marked a landmark achievement in the path toward fully equal rights for women. "Discrimination against gay women and men, by contrast, was not on the table for public debate . . . [i]n those dark, pre-Stonewall days." *Hively* (Lynch, J., dissenting).

[C]

Post-enactment events only clarify what was apparent when Title VII was enacted. As noted, bills to add "sexual orientation" to Title VII's list of prohibited grounds were introduced in every Congress beginning in 1975, and two such bills were before Congress in 1991 when it made major changes in Title VII. At that time, the three Courts of Appeals to reach the issue had held that Title VII does not prohibit discrimination because of sexual orientation, two other Circuits had endorsed that interpretation in dicta, and no Court of Appeals had held otherwise. Similarly, the three Circuits to address the application of Title VII to transgender persons had all rejected the argument that it covered discrimination on this basis. These were also the positions of the EEOC. In enacting substantial changes to Title VII, the 1991 Congress abrogated numerous judicial decisions with which it disagreed. If it also disagreed with the decisions regarding sexual orientation and transgender discrimination, it could have easily overruled those as well, but it did not do so.[42]

After 1991, six other Courts of Appeals reached the issue of sexual orientation discrimination, and until 2017, every single Court of Appeals decision understood Title VII's prohibition of "discrimination because of sex" to mean discrimination because of biological sex. Similarly, the other Circuit to formally address whether Title VII applies to claims of discrimination based on transgender status had also rejected the argument, creating unanimous consensus prior to the Sixth Circuit's decision below.

The Court observes that "[t]he people are entitled to rely on the law as written, without fearing that courts might disregard its plain terms," but it has no qualms about disregarding over 50 years of uniform judicial interpretation of Title VII's plain text. . . .

IV

What the Court has done today . . . is virtually certain to have far-reaching consequences. Over 100 federal statutes prohibit discrimination because of sex. See Appendix C, *infra*; *e.g.*, 20 U.S.C. § 1681(a) (Title IX); 42 U.S.C. § 3631 (Fair Housing Act); 15 U.S.C. 1691(a)(1) (Equal Credit Opportunity Act). The . . . Court waves those considerations aside. As to Title VII itself, the Court dismisses questions

---

42. In more recent legislation, when Congress has wanted to reach acts committed because of sexual orientation or gender identity, it has referred to those grounds by name. *See, e.g.,* 18 U.S.C. § 249(a)(2)(A) (hate crimes) (enacted 2009); 34 U.S.C. § 12291(b)(13)(A) (certain federally funded programs) (enacted 2013).

about "bathrooms, locker rooms, or anything else of the kind." And it declines to say anything about other statutes whose terms mirror Title VII's.

[This] is irresponsible. If the Court had allowed the legislative process to take its course, Congress would have had the opportunity to consider competing interests and might have found a way of accommodating at least some of them. In addition, Congress might have crafted special rules for some of the relevant statutes. But . . . the Court has greatly impeded—and perhaps effectively ended—any chance of a bargained legislative resolution. . . .

[The] Court may wish to avoid [the] subject, but it is a matter of concern to many people who are reticent about disrobing or using toilet facilities in the presence of individuals whom they regard as members of the opposite sex. For some, this may simply be a question of modesty, but for others, there is more at stake. For women who have been victimized by sexual assault or abuse, the experience of seeing an unclothed person with the anatomy of a male in a confined and sensitive location such as a bathroom or locker room can cause serious psychological harm.

Under the Court's decision, however, transgender persons will be able to argue that they are entitled to use a bathroom or locker room that is reserved for persons of the sex with which they identify. . . . Thus, a person who has not undertaken any physical transitioning may claim the right to use the bathroom or locker room assigned to the sex with which the individual identifies at that particular time. The Court provides no clue why a transgender person's claim to such bathroom or locker room access might not succeed.

A similar issue has arisen under Title IX, which prohibits sex discrimination by any elementary or secondary school and any college or university that receives federal financial assistance. In 2016, a Department of Justice advisory warned that barring a student from a bathroom assigned to individuals of the gender with which the student identifies constitutes unlawful sex discrimination, and some lower court decisions have agreed.

[Another] issue that may come up under both Title VII and Title IX is the right of a transgender individual to participate on a sports team or in an athletic competition previously reserved for members of one biological sex. This issue has already arisen under Title IX, where it threatens to undermine one of that law's major achievements, giving young women an equal opportunity to participate in sports. The effect of the Court's reasoning may be to force young women to compete against students who have a very significant biological advantage, including students who have the size and strength of a male but identify as female and students who are taking male hormones in order to transition from female to male. . . .

[The] Court's decision may lead to Title IX cases against any college that resists assigning students of the opposite biological sex as roommates. . . . Similar claims may be brought under the Fair Housing Act. *See* 42 U.S.C. § 3604.

Briefs filed by a wide range of religious groups—Christian, Jewish, and Muslim—express deep concern that the position now adopted by the Court "will trigger open conflict with faith-based employment practices of numerous churches, synagogues, mosques, and other religious institutions." They argue that "[r]eligious organizations need employees who actually live the faith," and that compelling a religious organization to employ individuals whose conduct flouts the tenets of the organization's faith forces the group to communicate an objectionable message.

This problem is perhaps most acute when it comes to the employment of teachers. A school's standards for its faculty "communicate a particular way of life to its students," and a "violation by the faculty of those precepts" may undermine the school's "moral teaching." . . . .

[Healthcare] benefits may emerge as an intense battleground under the Court's holding. Transgender employees have brought suit under Title VII to challenge employer-provided health insurance plans that do not cover costly sex reassignment surgery. Similar claims have been brought under the Affordable Care Act (ACA), which broadly prohibits sex discrimination in the provision of healthcare.

Such claims present difficult religious liberty issues because some employers and healthcare providers have strong religious objections to sex reassignment procedures, and therefore requiring them to pay for or to perform these procedures will have a severe impact on their ability to honor their deeply held religious beliefs.

[The] Court's decision may even affect the way employers address their employees and the way teachers and school officials address students. . . . Some jurisdictions, such as New York City, have ordinances making the failure to use an individual's preferred pronoun a punishable offense, and some colleges have similar rules. After today's decision, plaintiffs may claim that the failure to use their preferred pronoun violates one of the federal laws prohibiting sex discrimination.

The Court's decision may also pressure employers to suppress any statements by employees expressing disapproval of same-sex relationships and sex reassignment procedures. Employers are already imposing such restrictions voluntarily, and after today's decisions employers will fear that allowing employees to express their religious views on these subjects may give rise to Title VII harassment claims.

[Finally], despite the important differences between the Fourteenth Amendment and Title VII, the Court's decision may exert a gravitational pull in constitutional cases. Under our precedents, the Equal Protection Clause prohibits sex-based discrimination unless a "heightened" standard of review is met. *Sessions v. Morales-Santana*, 137 S.Ct. 1678 (2017); *United States v. Virginia*, 518 U.S. 515 (1996). By equating discrimination because of sexual orientation or gender identity with discrimination because of sex, the Court's decision will be cited as a ground for subjecting all three forms of discrimination to the same exacting standard of review.

Under this logic, today's decision may have effects that extend well beyond the domain of federal antidiscrimination statutes. This potential is illustrated by pending and recent lower court cases in which transgender individuals have challenged a variety of federal, state, and local laws and policies on constitutional grounds. [Alito cites constitutional challenges to a "state law prohibiting transgender students from competing in school sports in accordance with their gender identity," to the "military's ban on transgender members," to a "state health plan's exclusion of coverage for sex reassignment procedures," to rules regarding "change of gender on birth certificates," by a "transgender student forced to use gender neutral bathrooms at school," to a "school policy requiring students to use the bathroom that corresponds to the sex on birth certificate," by a "transgender prisoner denied hormone therapy and ability to dress and groom as a female," by a "transgender prisoner [denied] sex reassignment surgery," and by a "transgender individual fired for gender non-conformity."]

. . . . The entire Federal Judiciary will be mired for years in disputes about the reach of the Court's reasoning.

* * *

The updating desire to which the Court succumbs no doubt arises from humane and generous impulses. Today, many Americans know individuals who are gay, lesbian, or transgender and want them to be treated with the dignity, consideration, and fairness that everyone deserves. But the authority of this Court is limited to saying what the law is.

. . . .

I respectfully dissent.

Justice KAVANAUGH, dissenting.

Like many cases in this Court, this case boils down to one fundamental question: Who decides? . . . . The question here is whether Title VII should be expanded to prohibit employment discrimination because of sexual orientation. . . .

The policy arguments for amending Title VII are very weighty. The Court has previously stated, and I fully agree, that gay and lesbian Americans "cannot be treated as social outcasts or as inferior in dignity and worth." *Masterpiece Cakeshop, Ltd. v. Colorado Civil Rights Comm'n*, 138 S.Ct. 1719 (2018).

But we are judges, not Members of Congress. And in Alexander Hamilton's words, federal judges exercise "neither Force nor Will, but merely judgment." *The Federalist No. 78.* Under the Constitution's separation of powers, our role as judges is to interpret and follow the law as written, regardless of whether we like the result. Our role is not to make or amend the law. As written, Title VII does not prohibit employment discrimination because of sexual orientation.[1]

---

1. Although this opinion does not separately analyze discrimination on the basis of gender identity, this opinion's legal analysis of discrimination on the basis of sexual orientation would apply in much the same way to discrimination on the basis of gender identity.

[I]

. . . .

For the sake of argument, I will assume that firing someone because of their sexual orientation may, as a very literal matter, entail making a distinction based on sex. But to prevail in this case with their literalist approach, the plaintiffs must also establish one of two other points. The plaintiffs must establish that courts, when interpreting a statute, adhere to literal meaning rather than ordinary meaning. Or alternatively, the plaintiffs must establish that the ordinary meaning of "discriminate because of sex"—not just the literal meaning—encompasses sexual orientation discrimination. The plaintiffs fall short on both counts.

First, courts must follow ordinary meaning, not literal meaning. And courts must adhere to the ordinary meaning of phrases, not just the meaning of the words in a phrase.

. . . . As Justice Scalia explained, "the good textualist is not a literalist." A. SCALIA, A MATTER OF INTERPRETATION 24 (1997). Or as Professor Eskridge stated: The "prime directive in statutory interpretation is to apply the meaning that a reasonable reader would derive from the text of the law," so that "for hard cases as well as easy ones, the ordinary meaning (or the 'everyday meaning' or the 'commonsense' reading) of the relevant statutory text is the anchor for statutory interpretation." W. ESKRIDGE, INTERPRETING LAW 33, 34–35 (2016). . . . The ordinary meaning that counts is the ordinary public meaning at the time of enactment—although in this case, that temporal principle matters little because the ordinary meaning of "discriminate because of sex" was the same in 1964 as it is now.

Judges adhere to ordinary meaning for two main reasons: rule of law and democratic accountability. A society governed by the rule of law must have laws that are known and understandable to the citizenry. And judicial adherence to ordinary meaning facilitates the democratic accountability of America's elected representatives for the laws they enact. Citizens and legislators must be able to ascertain the law by reading the words of the statute. Both the rule of law and democratic accountability badly suffer when a court adopts a hidden or obscure interpretation of the law, and not its ordinary meaning.

. . . . The difference between literal and ordinary meaning becomes especially important when—as in this case—judges consider phrases in statutes. (Recall that the shorthand version of the phrase at issue here is "discriminate because of sex.")[3] Courts must heed the ordinary meaning of the phrase as a whole, not just the meaning of the words in the phrase. That is because a phrase may have a more precise or confined meaning than the literal meaning of the individual words in

---

3. . . . . This opinion uses "discriminate because of sex" as shorthand for "discriminate . . . because of . . . sex." Also, the plaintiffs do not dispute that the ordinary meaning of the statutory phrase "discriminate" because of sex is the same as the statutory phrase "to fail or refuse to hire or to discharge any individual" because of sex.

the phrase. Examples abound. An "American flag" could literally encompass a flag made in America, but in common parlance it denotes the Stars and Stripes. . . .

If the usual evidence indicates that a statutory phrase bears an ordinary meaning different from the literal strung-together definitions of the individual words in the phrase, we may not ignore or gloss over that discrepancy. . . .

[T]his Court's precedents and longstanding principles of statutory interpretation teach a clear lesson: Do not simply split statutory phrases into their component words, look up each in a dictionary, and then mechanically put them together again, as the majority opinion today mistakenly does. To reiterate Justice Scalia's caution, that approach misses the forest for the trees.

. . . .

Second, in light of the bedrock principle that we must adhere to the ordinary meaning of a phrase, the question in this case boils down to the ordinary meaning of the phrase "discriminate because of sex." Does the ordinary meaning of that phrase encompass discrimination because of sexual orientation? The answer is plainly no.

. . . . Both common parlance and common legal usage treat sex discrimination and sexual orientation discrimination as two distinct categories of discrimination — back in 1964 and still today.

As to common parlance, few in 1964 (or today) would describe a firing because of sexual orientation as a firing because of sex. As commonly understood, sexual orientation discrimination is distinct from, and not a form of, sex discrimination. . . . In common parlance, Bostock and Zarda were fired because they were gay, not because they were men.

. . . .

Consider the employer who has four employees but must fire two of them for financial reasons. Suppose the four employees are a straight man, a straight woman, a gay man, and a lesbian. The employer with animosity against women (animosity based on sex) will fire the two women. The employer with animosity against gays (animosity based on sexual orientation) will fire the gay man and the lesbian. Those are two distinct harms caused by two distinct biases that have two different outcomes. To treat one as a form of the other — as the majority opinion does — misapprehends common language, human psychology, and real life. *See Hively v. Ivy Tech Community College of Ind.*, 853 F.3d 339, 363 (7th Cir. 2017) (Sykes, J., dissenting).

It also rewrites history. Seneca Falls was not Stonewall. The women's rights movement was not (and is not) the gay rights movement. . . . So to think that sexual orientation discrimination is just a form of sex discrimination is not just a mistake of language and psychology, but also a mistake of history and sociology.

. . . .

Many federal statutes prohibit sex discrimination, and many federal statutes also prohibit sexual orientation discrimination. But those sexual orientation statutes expressly prohibit sexual orientation discrimination in addition to expressly prohibiting sex discrimination. Every single one. To this day, Congress has never defined sex discrimination to encompass sexual orientation discrimination. Instead, when Congress wants to prohibit sexual orientation discrimination in addition to sex discrimination, Congress explicitly refers to sexual orientation discrimination. [Footnote citing statutes from 2009 and later omitted.]

. . . . When Congress chooses distinct phrases to accomplish distinct purposes, and does so over and over again for decades, we may not lightly toss aside all of Congress's careful handiwork. . . .

. . . . Congress knows how to prohibit sexual orientation discrimination. So courts should not read that specific concept into the general words "discriminate because of sex." We cannot close our eyes to the indisputable fact that Congress — for several decades in a large number of statutes — has identified sex discrimination and sexual orientation discrimination as two distinct categories.

. . . .

The story is the same with bills proposed in Congress. Since the 1970s, Members of Congress have introduced many bills to prohibit sexual orientation discrimination in the workplace. Until very recently, all of those bills would have expressly established sexual orientation as a separately proscribed category of discrimination. The bills did not define sex discrimination to encompass sexual orientation discrimination.

The proposed bills are telling not because they are relevant to congressional intent regarding Title VII. Rather, the proposed bills are telling because they, like the enacted laws, further demonstrate the widespread usage of the English language in the United States: Sexual orientation discrimination is distinct from, and not a form of, sex discrimination.

Presidential Executive Orders reflect that same common understanding. . . . In 1998, President Clinton charted a new path and signed an Executive Order prohibiting sexual orientation discrimination in federal employment. . . .

Like the relevant federal statutes, the 1998 Clinton Executive Order expressly added sexual orientation as a new, separately prohibited form of discrimination. . . . President Clinton's 1998 Executive Order indicates that the Executive Branch, like Congress, has long understood sexual orientation discrimination to be distinct from, and not a form of, sex discrimination.

Federal regulations likewise reflect that same understanding. . . .

The States have proceeded in the same fashion. A majority of States prohibit sexual orientation discrimination in employment, either by legislation applying to most workers, an executive order applying to public employees, or both. Almost every state statute or executive order proscribing sexual orientation discrimination expressly prohibits sexual orientation discrimination separately from the State's ban on sex discrimination.

That common usage in the States underscores that sexual orientation discrimination is commonly understood as a legal concept distinct from sex discrimination.

And it is the common understanding in this Court as well. Since 1971, the Court has employed rigorous or heightened constitutional scrutiny of laws that classify on the basis of sex. *See United States v. Virginia*, 518 U.S. 515 (1996); . . . *Reed v. Reed*, 404 U.S. 71 (1971). Over the last several decades, the Court has also decided many cases involving sexual orientation. But in those cases, the Court never suggested that sexual orientation discrimination is just a form of sex discrimination. . . .

Did the Court in all of those sexual orientation cases just miss that obvious answer—and overlook the fact that sexual orientation discrimination is actually a form of sex discrimination? That seems implausible. . . . [P]resumably . . . everyone on this Court, too, has long understood that sexual orientation discrimination is distinct from, and not a form of, sex discrimination.

In sum, all of the usual indicators of ordinary meaning—common parlance, common usage by Congress, the practice in the Executive Branch, the laws in the States, and the decisions of this Court—overwhelmingly establish that sexual orientation discrimination is distinct from, and not a form of, sex discrimination. The usage has been consistent across decades, in both the federal and state contexts.

Judge Sykes summarized the law and language this way: "[. . . .] Classifying people by sexual orientation is different than classifying them by sex. The two traits are categorically distinct and widely recognized as such.[. . .]" *Hively* (dissenting opinion).

. . . .

II

Until the last few years, every U.S. Court of Appeals to address this question concluded that Title VII does not prohibit discrimination because of sexual orientation. . . .

The unanimity of those 30 federal judges shows that the question as a matter of law, as compared to as a matter of policy, was not deemed close. . . .

To be sure, the majority opinion today does not openly profess that it is judicially updating or amending Title VII. *Cf. Hively* (Posner, J., concurring). But the majority opinion achieves the same outcome by seizing on literal meaning and overlooking the ordinary meaning of the phrase "discriminate because of sex." . . . .

The majority opinion deflects that critique by saying that courts should base their interpretation of statutes on the text as written, not on the legislators' subjective intentions. . . .

But in my respectful view, the majority opinion makes a fundamental mistake by confusing ordinary meaning with subjective intentions. To briefly explain: In the early years after Title VII was enacted, some may have wondered whether Title VII's prohibition on sex discrimination protected male employees. After all, covering male employees may not have been the intent of some who voted for the statute. Nonetheless, discrimination on the basis of sex against women and discrimination on the basis of sex against men are both understood as discrimination because of sex (back in 1964 and now) and are therefore encompassed within Title VII. So too, regardless of what the intentions of the drafters might have been, the ordinary meaning of the law demonstrates that harassing an employee because of her sex is discriminating against the employee because of her sex with respect to the "terms, conditions, or privileges of employment," as this Court rightly concluded. . . .

By contrast, this case involves sexual orientation discrimination, which has long and widely been understood as distinct from, and not a form of, sex discrimination. . . . To fire one employee because she is a woman and another employee because he is gay implicates two distinct societal concerns, reveals two distinct biases, imposes two distinct harms, and falls within two distinct statutory prohibitions.

. . . . [M]any Americans will not buy the novel interpretation unearthed and advanced by the Court today. Many will no doubt believe that the Court has unilaterally rewritten American vocabulary and American law—a "statutory amendment courtesy of unelected judges." *Hively* (Sykes, J., dissenting). Some will surmise that the Court succumbed to "the natural desire that beguiles judges along with other human beings into imposing their own views of goodness, truth, and justice upon others." *Furman v. Georgia*, 408 U.S. 238 (1972) (Rehnquist, J., dissenting).

I have the greatest, and unyielding, respect for my colleagues and for their good faith. But when this Court usurps the role of Congress, as it does today, the public understandably becomes confused about who the policymakers really are in our system of separated powers, and inevitably becomes cynical about the oft-repeated aspiration that judges base their decisions on law rather than on personal preference. The best way for judges to demonstrate that we are deciding cases based on the ordinary meaning of the law is to walk the walk, even in the hard cases when we might prefer a different policy outcome.

* * *

In judicially rewriting Title VII, the Court today cashiers an ongoing legislative process, at a time when a new law to prohibit sexual orientation discrimination was probably close at hand. After all, even back in 2007—a veritable lifetime ago in American attitudes about sexual orientation—the House voted 235 to 184 to prohibit sexual orientation discrimination in employment. In 2013, the Senate overwhelmingly approved a similar bill, 64 to 32. In 2019, the House voted 236 to 173 to amend Title VII to prohibit employment discrimination on the basis of sexual orientation. H.R. 5, 116th Cong., 1st Sess. It was therefore easy to envision a day, likely just in the next few years, when the House and Senate took historic votes on a bill that would prohibit employment discrimination on the basis of sexual orientation.

It was easy to picture a massive and celebratory Presidential signing ceremony in the East Room or on the South Lawn.

It is true that meaningful legislative action takes time—often too much time, especially in the unwieldy morass on Capitol Hill. But the Constitution does not put the Legislative Branch in the "position of a television quiz show contestant so that when a given period of time has elapsed and a problem remains unsolved by them, the federal judiciary may press a buzzer and take its turn at fashioning a solution." Rehnquist, *The Notion of a Living Constitution*, 54 TEXAS L. REV. 693, 700 (1976). . . .

. . . . Under the Constitution and laws of the United States, this Court is the wrong body to change American law in that way. The Court's ruling "comes at a great cost to representative self-government." *Hively* (Sykes, J., dissenting). And the implications of this Court's usurpation of the legislative process will likely reverberate in unpredictable ways for years to come.

Notwithstanding my concern about the Court's transgression of the Constitution's separation of powers, it is appropriate to acknowledge the important victory achieved today by gay and lesbian Americans. Millions of gay and lesbian Americans have worked hard for many decades to achieve equal treatment in fact and in law. They have exhibited extraordinary vision, tenacity, and grit—battling often steep odds in the legislative and judicial arenas, not to mention in their daily lives. They have advanced powerful policy arguments and can take pride in today's result. Under the Constitution's separation of powers, however, I believe that it was Congress's role, not this Court's, to amend Title VII. I therefore must respectfully dissent from the Court's judgment.

Discussion

1. How, if at all, will this decision be likely to affect other state and federal constitutions, statutes, and cases addressing sex discrimination? What legal changes do you expect will occur in the second edition of this casebook?

2. By some estimates about 75% of employment discrimination cases are dismissed on summary judgment, Nancy Gertner, *The Judicial Repeal of the Johnson/ Kennedy Administration's "Signature" Achievement*, 5–6 & n. 25 (2014), available at http://ssrn.com/abstract=2406671. Many plaintiffs lose on summary judgment because their evidence is adjudged insufficient to allow a reasonable jury to find that discrimination was the but-for cause of an adverse employment action after defendants meets their burden of production of a legitimate, non-discriminatory reason for its action. How could the Supreme Court's *Bostock* opinion affect this?

3. Justice Alito accuses Justice Gorsuch of being a literalist, rather than a textualist. Does Justice Gorsuch seem to accept the label? What other legal issues outside of the sex discrimination context that have previously been analyzed by reference to legislative history might Justice Gorsuch's textualism affect? Justice Alito also criticizes the majority for having "no qualms about disregarding over 50 years of

uniform judicial interpretation of Title VII's plain text." For an argument that "the first forty years of circuit precedent got Title VII wrong" by "rel[ying] on their era's misunderstanding of LGBTQ identities as pathological, unnatural, and deviant" instead of "relying on the statutory text," see Jessica A. Clarke, *How the First Forty Years of Precedent Got Title VII's Sex Discrimination Provision Wrong*, 98 Tex. L. Rev. Online 83 (2019). For a critique of the oral argument presented to the Supreme Court in Aimee Stephens's case, see Ezra Ishmael Young, *What the Supreme Court Could Have Heard in* R.G. & G.R. Harris Funeral Homes v. EEOC and Aimee Stephens, 11 Cal. L. Rev. Online 9 (2020).

4. Why might the Court have opted not to rely upon *Price Waterhouse v. Hopkins*, 490 U.S. 228 (1989), in its reasoning when so many lower court judges have found it helpful? Is anything in the majority opinion in *Bostock* inconsistent with any of the reasoning of Justice Brennan's opinion in *Price Waterhouse*?

Note on Bostock's Treatment of But-For Causation

The Court's decision in *Bostock* may affect not only LGBTQ employees, but all discrimination cases. Prior to *Bostock*, the court sometimes discussed "because of" in discrimination statutes as requiring that the plaintiff show that discrimination is "*the* but-for cause" of an adverse employment action. *See, e.g., Gross v. FBL Fin. Servs., Inc.*, 557 U.S. 167, 176, 177, 178, 180 (2009) (emphasis added) (interpreting Age Discrimination in Employment Act of 1967 (ADEA), 29 U.S.C. §623(a)); *University of Tex. Southwestern Medical Center v. Nassar*, 570 U.S. 338, 343, 348, 352 (2013) (interpreting anti-retaliation provision of Civil Rights Act of 1964, 42 U.S.C. §2000e-3(a)); *but see Burrage v. United States*, 571 U.S. 204, 211, 213–16 (2014) (writing of "a but-for cause" in interpreting penalty enhancement provision of Controlled Substance Act, 21 U.S.C. §841(b)(1)(C)). But-for causation is generally understood to mean that the plaintiff must show that had the bias not been taken into account, the employer would not have taken the adverse employment action.[b] Does "*the* but-for cause" mean something is the sole factor in a decision, the primary factor, or something else? Lower courts used various formulations to implement the requirement that an employer's biased motive be "the but-for cause" of, for example, a firing.

---

b. 42 U.S.C. §2000e-2(m) allows an alternate causation standard in Title VII discrimination cases. The plaintiff may establish liability by showing only that bias was a "motivating" factor; employers may as an affirmative defense limit the relief available if they show that they would have taken the same action in the absence of that impermissible motivating factor, *see* 42 U.S.C. §2000e-5(g)(2)(B). These provisions, adopted in 1991, changed the law stated in *Price Waterhouse*, which only required the burden shift to the employer if a plaintiff proved that bias was a "substantial" factor. This did not affect 42 U.S.C. §2000e-2(a), which refers to adverse actions "because of" a protected category, referring to the but-for causation test. Thus, a plaintiff could prove either the but-for case or the motivating factor case.

In *Bostock*, the Court adopted the test of an employer's motive being "<u>a</u> but-for cause" under Title VII along the way to its conclusion that discrimination against gay and lesbian and trans employees is discrimination "because of" sex. In so doing, the Court changed the standard in a subtle but meaningful way. The Court made clear that even where an employer has a legitimate reason for terminating a gay or trans employee, if the decision would not have been reached absent the gay or trans status of an employee, then sex is "*a* but-for cause" of the termination. This distinction between "a" but-for cause and "the" but-for cause may prove significant. *See 'But-For' Causation Under Bostock*, 10:228 NATIONAL LAW REVIEW, Aug. 16, 2020, at https://www.natlawreview.com/article/causation-under-bostock (https://perma.cc/FYP9-64C4). This may mean that the federal courts will be less open to ruling in favor of an employer based on its recitation of a legitimate reason for an adverse employment action against a worker, and more open to plaintiffs who argue that the claimed reason is only one of a number of the employer's actual reasons, one of which was discriminatory and which, in combination with any other motivations, caused an adverse action that otherwise wouldn't have happened to the employee. Whether this proves true will be a function of future court rulings.

Examining how one litigates causation in practice is useful in understanding the shift in the but-for causation standard from how the Court used it outside discriminatory treatment Title VII cases. After a plaintiff worker shows that bias is involved in the employer's adverse action against the plaintiff, the burden then commonly shifts to the employer to produce a legitimate, *i.e.*, nondiscriminatory reason for its action, such as the plaintiff's violation of a work rule or poor performance. *McDonnell Douglas Corp. v. Green*, 411 U.S. 792, 802 (1973). If the employee can prove that the employer's proffered reason was not true and merely a pretext for discrimination, then defendant is liable. *Id at* 804–05. That is fairly simple, and is valid in cases in which there is only a single reason alleged by either side for the adverse action. However, this procedure does not work simply in the many cases involving mixed causation, where both a legitimate reason and an illegitimate (statutorily unlawful) one co-exist. The plaintiff cannot then show which was "the" "true" reason, because the plaintiff concedes that both were true reasons, but argues that, the because of presence of the illegal reason, the employer's action violates Title VII. For example, an employee could be refused promotion because supervisors conclude she is abrasive, but that conclusion is reached by some managers because they feel a woman should not be abrasive although they are fine with male managers who are abrasive. In such a situation, it makes little sense to require the plaintiff to prove that the employer's reason was untrue, because it is concededly true. The question instead is whether the plaintiff's sex was one of the employer's motives or reasons for its action against her. The parties in such circumstances will often spar over how much a part of the motivation must it be, and how a plaintiff can prove whether the illegal reason played enough of a role when a defendant can simply assert that it played little or no role.

The Supreme Court addressed this kind of "mixed motive" situation in *Price Waterhouse v. Hopkins*, 490 U.S. 228 (1989), concluding that where a plaintiff shows that an illegal reason was a substantial factor in addition to the employer's legitimate, non-discriminatory reason, the burden of proof shifts to the employer to show that it would have taken the same action in the absence of bias. *Price Waterhouse*, 490 U.S. at 244–45 (1989) (plurality opinion using "motivating factor" for plaintiff's burden); *id.* at 259–60 (1989) (White, J., concurring in the judgment) (using "substantial factor" in arguably narrower reasoning than plurality, since it allows liability in narrower circumstances than the plurality, in Ann Hopkins's case upholding a finding of liability, which could make it the holding of the *Price Waterhouse* Court under *Marks v. United States*, 430 U.S. 188 (1977)); and *id.* at 265–66 (O'Connor, J. concurring in the judgment) (same). Some lower courts interpreted this as requiring the employer's unlawful reason be the "primary" factor in its decision; others held that it need only be a "significant" factor. *See* Lawrence D. Rosenthal, *A Lack of "Motivation," or Sound Legal Reasoning? Why Most Courts Are Not Applying Either* Price Waterhouse*'s or the 1991 Civil Rights Act's Motivating-Factor Analysis to Title VII Retaliation Claims in A Post-*Gross *World (But Should)*, 64 ALA. L. REV. 1067, 1079 (2013). All agreed it did not need to be the "sole" factor. However, as a practical matter, courts granted summary judgment to employers in the large majority of cases on the grounds that no reasonable jury could find that bias caused the adverse action once the employer gave a legitimate reason, even if the reason was factually incorrect, totally subjective, or involved credibility determinations that would normally be within the province of a jury. *See* Nancy Gertner, *The Judicial Repeal of the Johnson/Kennedy Administration's "Signature" Achievement*, 5–6, 6 n.25 (2014), available at http://ssrn.com/abstract=2406671 (citing statistics for employment discrimination claims in the Northern District of Georgia of 95% partial summary judgment dismissal, and 81% in full, compared to 74–77% rate for the nation).

In *Bostock*, the Court ruled that discrimination based on "homosexuality" or "transgender status" is "because of" sex. It did so because it understood but-for cause to be any bias that contributed enough, among any other factors, to push an employer over the edge to an adverse action decision. Because a gay or lesbian or trans employee would not have been subjected to the adverse action had they been of a different sex, the Court held that sex is "a" but-for cause of an adverse action based on gay or lesbian or trans status. In explaining its decision, the Court explicitly states that but-for cause does not mean sole cause, primary cause, or even just the most significant cause. *Bostock* states of but-for causation:

> This can be a sweeping standard. Often, events have multiple but-for causes. So, for example, if a car accident occurred both because the defendant ran a red light and because the plaintiff failed to signal his turn at the intersection, we might call each a but-for cause of the collision. *Cf. Burrage v. United States*, 571 U. S. 204, 211–212 (2014). When it comes to Title VII, the adoption of the traditional but-for causation standard means a defendant cannot avoid liability just by citing some other factor that contributed to its challenged employment decision. So long as the plaintiff's sex was one

but-for cause of that decision, that is enough to trigger the law. *See ibid.*; *University of Tex. Southwestern Medical Center v. Nassar*, 570 U.S. 338, 350 (2013).

As Congress did not write "primarily because of" into the law, the prohibited factor need not be the main cause of the defendant's challenged employment decision. *Bostock.* The *Bostock* holding teaches that but-for cause is "a sweeping standard." *Bostock.* It need not be a primary factor, but may be one element in a chain of causation, *id.*, "the straw that broke the camel's back," as stated in *Burrage v. United States*, 571 U. S. 204, 211 (2014), cited by the Court in *Bostock.* Thus, it could be a minor cause, so long as without that "last straw" the adverse action would not have happened.

This means where there is more than one cause, the defendant will be liable if the nondiscriminatory causes are not sufficient for termination. For example, if the employer shows that there is an objective rule requiring termination, and that plaintiff violated the rule in failing to wear a safety vest, the employer will have demonstrated as a matter of law that the alleged bias was not a but-for cause of termination, and judgment may be given under Fed. R. Civ. P. 50 or 56. By contrast, where the lawful causes are not sufficient to cause termination, or it is unclear whether they were sufficient to cause termination, then it is a factual question as to whether bias could have been one of a number of but-for causes for termination. For example, if the employer shows a rule that that could result in a range of penalties, and the employer also alleges some subjectively-determined poor performance, it is a question of fact as to whether the bias was a but-for cause of the termination.

By changing "the" but-for cause to "a" but-for cause, *Bostock* could be thought to have changed the causation standard in discrimination cases to make it easier for plaintiffs to show that discriminatory bias is a but-for cause of the adverse action. How this will play out in the courts will remain to be seen.

E. Workplace Restroom Access

As transgender advocate and Judge Phyllis Frye has observed (albeit in somewhat dated terminology), "If a company wants to fire a trangendered [*sic*] employee, the restroom issue is often the chosen way to do so. When co-workers or the employer oppose a transitioning transgendered employee, objections at the workplace frequently center around the transgender's [*sic*] change in restroom use from the women's to the men's room or from the men's to the women's room." Phyllis Randolph Frye, *The International Bill of Gender Rights vs. The Cider House Rules: Transgenders Struggle with the Courts over What Clothing They Are Allowed to Wear on the Job, Which Restroom They Are Allowed to Use on the Job, Their Right to Marry, and the Very Definition of Their Sex*, 7 Wm. & Mary J. Women & L. 133, 182 (2000).

The Supreme Court did not expressly address such questions in *Boston v. Clayton County, Georgia*, 140 S. Ct. 1731 (2020), Section D, *supra.* "Under Title VII," the

Bostock majority wrote, "we do not purport to address bathrooms, locker rooms, or anything else of the kind." This section of the casebook examines some of the law grappling with whether such firings or restrictions on restroom use unlawfully discriminate against transgender employees on the basis of sex or instead are required to protect other employees from discrimination.

Reading Guide for Cruzan v. Special School District No. 1

1. Although most of the case law in this area concerns challenges to employer's restrictions on their restroom use brought by workers who are transgender, this decision presents the opposite situation of a suit by cisgender worker objecting to an employer letting a transgender co-worker use restrooms consistent with her gender identity. Ruling per curiam (*i.e.*, with an opinion "by the court," rather than one whose authorship is attributed to a specific judge or judges), the court of appeals in *Cruzan* rejects a cisgender teacher's claims that the school's allowing a transgender woman to use the women's faculty restroom discriminated against the plaintiff on the basis of religion and discriminated against her on the basis of sex (gender) by creating a hostile environment. What is the essentially procedural ground on which the court affirms dismissal of the religious discrimination claim? Even without that procedural obstacle, does the opinion describe facts sufficient to support the plaintiff's claim that she was discriminated against on the basis of religion?

2. The court of appeals also holds that the school's alleged actions did not create a working environment that was hostile on the basis of sex. Why didn't they?

Cruzan v. Special School District, # 1 et al.

294 F.3d 981 (8th Cir. 2002)

[The defendant school district was supported on appeal by amici curiae American Civil Liberties Union; Outfront Minnesota; Gay, Lesbian and Straight Education Network of Minnesota; Harry Benjamin International Gender Dysphoria Association; and the National Center for Lesbian Rights.]

Before: HANSEN, Chief Judge, FAGG and BOWMAN, Circuit Judges.

PER CURIAM.

Carla Cruzan, a female teacher at Minneapolis Special School District, # 1, brought this action [against the district and principal Dr. Robert McAuley in his official and individual capacities] alleging the school district discriminated against her on the basis of her sex and her religion by allowing a transgendered [*sic*] coworker to use the women's faculty restroom. The district court granted summary judgment to the school district. *Cruzan v. Minneapolis Pub. Sch. Sys.*, 165 F. Supp. 2d 964 (D. Minn. 2001). Cruzan appeals, and we affirm.

David Nielsen began working for the school district in 1969. Nearly thirty years later, in early 1998, Nielsen informed school administration that he was transgendered, that is, a person who identifies with and adopts [*sic*] the gender identity of a member of the other biological sex. Nielsen informed administration he would "transition from male to female" and be known as Debra Davis in the workplace. To plan for the transition, the school district collaborated with Davis, legal counsel, the parent teacher association, students' parents, and psychologists. Cruzan asked whether Davis would be allowed to use the school's women's restrooms, and administration informed her other arrangements would be made. Later, legal counsel informed the school that under the Minnesota Human Rights Act (MHRA), which prohibits discrimination on the basis of a person's "self-image or identity not traditionally associated with one's biological maleness or femaleness," MINN. STAT. § 363.01 subd. 45 (1998), Davis had the right to use the women's restroom. Thus, after Davis's transition in the spring of 1998, the school district permitted Davis to use the women's faculty restroom.

A few months later, in October 1998, Cruzan entered the women's faculty restroom and saw Davis exiting a privacy stall. Cruzan immediately left, found the principal in the hallway among students, and complained about encountering Davis in the restroom. The principal asked Cruzan to either wait in his office or to make an appointment to discuss the matter. Cruzan did not do so, and never approached the principal about her concerns again.

Instead, Cruzan filed a complaint with the Minnesota Department of Human Rights, which dismissed Cruzan's charge, concluding there was no probable cause to believe an unfair discriminatory practice had occurred. The Department stated the MHRA neither requires nor prohibits restroom designation according to self-image of gender or according to biological sex. *See Goins v. West Group*, 635 N.W.2d 717, 723 (Minn. 2001) (stating same). After exhausting administrative remedies, Cruzan filed this action under Title VII and the MHRA asserting claims of religious discrimination and hostile work environment sex discrimination. Davis retired in 2001.

[To] establish a prima facie case of religious discrimination, Cruzan had to show she had a bona fide religious belief that conflicted with an employment requirement, she informed the school district of her belief, and she suffered an adverse employment action. *Seaworth v. Pearson*, 203 F.3d 1056, 1057 (8th Cir. 2000) (per curiam). The district court concluded that assuming without deciding Cruzan had a bona fide religious belief that conflicted with the restroom policy, she failed to inform the school district of her belief and did not suffer an adverse employment action because of it.

Although Cruzan expressed general disapproval of Davis's transition and the school district's decision to allow Davis to use the women's faculty restroom, Cruzan did not disclose or discuss the reason for her disapproval with her employer beyond asserting her personal privacy. Cruzan argues that she met the notice requirement by completing paperwork for her MDHR charge. We disagree. Even assuming such paperwork could satisfy the notice requirement, the school district did not receive the MDHR intake questionnaire until the discovery phase of this litigation, and

Cruzan's MDHR charge of discrimination alleges sex discrimination, not religious discrimination.

To show she suffered an adverse employment action, Cruzan had to establish a "'tangible change in duties or working conditions that constitute a material employment disadvantage.'" *Cossette v. Minnesota Power & Light,* 188 F.3d 964, 972 (8th Cir. 1999). Mere inconvenience without any decrease in title, salary, or benefits is insufficient to show an adverse employment action. *Harlston v. McDonnell Douglas Corp.,* 37 F.3d 379, 382 (8th Cir. 1994). Here, it is undisputed that Davis's use of the female staff restroom had no effect on Cruzan's title, salary, or benefits. Cruzan concedes that to avoid sharing a restroom with Davis, she used the female students' restroom, which is closer to her classroom and was never used by Davis. Single-stall, unisex bathrooms are also available. We thus agree with the district court that the school district's decision to allow Davis to use the women's faculty restroom does not rise to the level of an actionable adverse employment action. Because Cruzan failed to establish a prima facie case of religious discrimination, the district court properly granted summary judgment to the school district on this claim.

To establish a sexual harassment claim based on hostile work environment, Cruzan had to show, among other things, that the harassment affected a term, condition, or privilege of her employment. *Rheineck v. Hutchinson Tech, Inc.,* 261 F.3d 751 (8th Cir. 2001). The harassment must be so severe or pervasive that it alters the conditions of employment and creates an abusive working environment. *Id.* To make this showing, Cruzan had to establish the school was "permeated with discriminatory intimidation, ridicule, and insult." *Id.* Courts examine the totality of the circumstances, and consider whether a reasonable person would have found the environment hostile or abusive. *Id.* We agree with the district court that Cruzan failed to show the school district's policy allowing Davis to use the women's faculty restroom created a working environment that rose to this level. The school district's policy was not directed at Cruzan and Cruzan had convenient access to numerous restrooms other than the one Davis used. Cruzan does not assert Davis engaged in any inappropriate conduct other than merely being present in the women's faculty restroom. Given the totality of the circumstances, we conclude a reasonable person would not have found the work environment hostile or abusive.

Cruzan argues it is an abuse of the summary judgment procedure for a male judge to decide that reasonable women could not find their working environment is abusive or hostile when they must share bathroom facilities with a coworker who self-identifies as female, but who may be biologically male. No case law supports Cruzan's assertion, however. Judges routinely decide hostile environment sexual harassment cases involving plaintiffs of the opposite sex.

We thus affirm the district court.

Discussion

1. Federal employment discrimination law requires that employers "reasonably" "accommodate" employees' religious beliefs in some contexts. *See* Chapter 10, *infra*. Cruzan apparently did not bring a religious accommodation claim in this suit. If she had, and had persuaded a judge or jury that it conflicted with her sincere religious beliefs to use a multi-user restroom with a transgender woman, are there any different arrangements the school might reasonably have made to accommodate those beliefs?

2. In rejecting Cruzan's hostile environment claim, the court noted that Cruzan "had convenient access to numerous restrooms other than the one" her transgender coworker used. In part the court believed this showed that the school did not effectively alter a term or condition of Cruzan's work environment. Should we think that by allowing its employees to use restrooms consistent with their gender identity, the school takes an adverse action against or alters the terms or conditions of an employee who objects to sharing a restroom with a transgender coworker? What if the common (shared) women's faculty restroom were the only convenient one open to Cruzan — would that make the school's restroom policy amount to an objectively hostile one on the basis of sex?

3. There was at the time of Cruzan's suit some precedent about presumably cisgender men — rather than transgender women — using common women's restrooms. In *State v. Williams*, 279 N.W.2d 847 (Neb. 1979), the state supreme court upheld a man's conviction under a loitering statute for entering a women's restroom, possibly because the men's room was fully occupied and the defendant had diarrhea, though his explanations for his conduct were contradictory. The court explained that "[t]here is no requirement in the ordinance that any person be actually alarmed by the conduct, only that the circumstances, to wit, time, place, or manner of the loitering or prowling, are not usual for law-abiding individuals and warrants alarm for safety. The presence of a male in the public female restroom where women are likely to enter at any time is, in the absence of a credible explanation, sufficient to warrant alarm." And it concluded that the judge who conducted the bench trial clearly did not believe the defendant's explanation.

In *Commonwealth v. Young*, 370 Pa. Super. 42 (1988), a divided panel of the Superior Court of Pennsylvania affirmed the conviction of a man for disorderly conduct for his actions entering a common women's restroom in a women's floor of a college dorm. After the defendant and another man were let into the women's dorm by a resident and visited a student they knew there,

> on their way out of the dormitory, the two men walked into the women's restroom. A woman student was sitting on the toilet in one of the stalls. Appellant walked over to the stall, which did not lock, opened the door and said: "Hey baby, what you doing." The woman screamed, pulled up her pants and chased the men out of the dormitory. She testified that she was extremely frightened by the incident as she was not sure of the men's intentions when they opened the stall door.

The statute at issue provided in relevant part: "A person is guilty of disorderly conduct if, with intent to cause public inconvenience, annoyance or alarm, or recklessly creating a risk thereof, he: . . . creates a hazardous or physically offensive condition by any act which serves no legitimate purpose of the actor." The court found the risk-of-public-alarm element satisfied because "[a]ny number of women, in various states of undress, could have been using the showers, sinks and toilets in the area." It found the hazardous-or-physically-offensive-condition element satisfied because "the evidence establishes that appellant's conduct created a physically offensive condition to the victim. She was performing a private bodily function. She feared that appellant and his companion were going to assault her. Any reasonable woman in her situation would have been offended by appellant's actions."

The dissenting judge would have ruled that the restroom was not "public" due to the restrictions on access to the dormitory floor in which it was located. Interestingly, he would also have ruled that the defendant's conduct did not satisfy the hazardous-or-physically-offensive condition element:

> I do not agree with the majority that the complainant's embarrassment while performing a private bodily function and her fear of further assault amounted to a physically offensive condition. The statute specifically provides an *objective* standard requiring the creation of a *hazardous* or *physically* offensive condition. The majority's focus on the subjective feelings of one individual is misplaced. Appellant's conduct was morally offensive and embarrassing to the victim, but that conduct was in no way hazardous or physically offensive. The actions did not affect the women's physical being, but rather her sense of decency. I do not here make light of the woman's fright and distress nor condone appellant's reprehensible behavior. However, although appellant committed a wrongdoing, he did not commit the crime of disorderly conduct. "The crime of disorderly conduct is not intended as a catchall for every act which annoys or disturbs people . . . it is intended to preserve the public peace; it thus has a limited periphery beyond which the prosecuting authorities have no right to transgress. . . ." *Commonwealth v. Greene*, 189 A.2d 141 (Pa. 1963). That periphery has been transgressed here.

Is there anything in the facts of *Cruzan* that indicate that Ms. Davis did anything that would violate this other state's disorderly conduct law? Should privacy rights extend beyond the hazardous or physically offensive conditions reached by this law to include objectively objectionable offense and embarrassment? Even if they should, did Ms. Davis do anything that would rise to that level?

Note on Kastl v. Maricopa County Community College School District

In *Kastl v. Maricopa County Community College District*, 2004 WL 2008954, 2004 U.S. Dist. LEXIS 29825 (D. Ariz. June 3, 2004), transgender woman Rebecca Kastl sued her employer for unlawful discrimination after she refused its demand that she use the men's restroom pursuant to its policy. The complaint, filed by transgender attorney and activist Randi Barnabee, alleged that Ms. Kastl's personal physician determined her to be biologically female. Kastl brought claims for sex and disability discrimination in violation of Title VII of the Civil Rights Act of 1964, Title IX of the Education Amendments of 1972, and the ADA, and 42 U.S.C. § 1983. The defendant sought to dismiss, arguing that its policy, contrary to plaintiff's allegations, segregated restroom use by genitalia, not by sex. Because the court must generally accept the facts as pleaded by the plaintiff on a motion to dismiss for failure to state a claim, the court denied the motion as to Ms. Kastl's sex discrimination claims under Title VII and Title IX. It also allowed the § 1983 claims to proceed, for which a plaintiff must allege that a right secured by the Constitution or laws of the United States was violated. The court agreed that Kastl pled viable claims based on three sets of constitutional rights: 1) substantive due process and right to privacy, 2) equal protection, and 3) First Amendment freedom of speech. Regarding Kastl's right to privacy claim, the court ruled that the defendant's demand for information regarding Kastl's genitalia before it would let her use women's restrooms did not pass the "fit" prong of strict scrutiny required to justify infringing her right to privacy. On her equal protection claim the court reasoned that "singl[ing] out nonconforming individuals . . . for a greater intrusion upon their privacy" did not appear rationally related to the defendant's legitimate interest in protecting privacy and safety of its patrons, absent "baseless assumptions" that transsexual people pose a greater risk to the safety of minors and woman than other groups, and that the presence of a woman with male genitalia invades the privacy and threatens the safety of other women. The court also ruled that Kastl adequately pled a First Amendment claim that the defendant was violating her right to express her gender. Because she was suing as a public employee, to be protected her expression had to relate to a matter of public concern, rather than a purely private concern about her job. Following Ninth Circuit precedent, the court noted that speech on a matter of public concern includes "'almost *any* matter other than speech that relates to internal power struggles within the workplace.'" The Court distinguished this from (possibly?) unprotected disputes such as "employee complaints about dress codes, scheduling, or other personnel issues" on the ground that Kastl's expression had "its genesis not in the minutiae of workplace life, but in her everyday existence."

Subsequently, the district court granted the defendant's motion for summary judgment. *Kastl v. Maricopa County Community College District*, 2006 WL 2460636 (D. Ariz. Aug. 22, 2006), aff'd, 325 Fed. Appx. 492 (9th Cir. 2009)). The court ruled that Kastl failed to establish her claim that she was discriminated against as a biological woman in violation of her Title VII, Title IX, privacy, and equal protection rights. The court concluded that Ms. Kastl did not properly present supporting evidence of her theory that there are determinants of biological sex other than genitalia, which applied to her, or that she was diagnosed a biological female in 2001. Interestingly, this suggests that, had Kastl presented proper non-hearsay and expert evidence of her theory, and her physician's diagnosis, she might have prevailed on the motion for summary judgment. The court rebuffed her right of privacy claim. The court also rejected her First Amendment claim because she did not show evidence of the necessary elements of the claim: 1) that she engaged in protected speech; (2) that the employer took adverse employment action; and (3) that his or her speech was a substantial or motivating factor for the adverse employment action.

On appeal, a panel of the Ninth Circuit Court of Appeals comprising Judges Betty Fletcher and Margaret McKeown along with then-Tenth Circuit Judge Neil M. Gorsuch sitting by designation affirmed in an unsigned memorandum opinion. *Kastl v. Maricopa Cnty. Comm. Coll. Dist.*, 325 Fed. Appx. 492 (9th Cir. 2009). Although the panel agreed that Ms. Kastl presented a prima facie case of gender discrimination based on gender stereotyping, it held that she did not provide sufficient evidence that the defendant was motivated by her gender to rebut the defendant's proffered safety justification for forbidding her to use women's restrooms. The court also stated without further explanation that the defendant "was entitled to summary judgment on Kastl's constitutional privacy and expression claims also due to insufficient evidence[]" and that "Kastl's other challenges to the district court's decision also fail." In so doing, the Ninth Circuit panel sidestepped the necessity of deciding the issue of whether anti-transgender discrimination is sex discrimination under Title VII. While it is widely assumed that the Ninth Circuit Court of Appeals would so rule, there is no case from that court squarely on point. The Supreme Court addressed that question in *Bostock v. Clayton County, Georgia*, 140 S. Ct. 1731 (2020), holding that discrimination based on a person's "transgender status" is sex discrimination within the meaning of Title VII. The Court stated that it was not deciding restroom usage issues.

Reading Guide for Etsitty v. Utah Transit Authority *(appellate opinion)*

1. Unlike the district court opinion in this case, *Etsity v. Utah Transit Authority*, 2005 WL 1505610 (June 24, 2005), the opinion of the Tenth Circuit Court of Appeals acknowledges that *Oncale v. Sundowner Offshore Services, Inc.*, 523 U.S. 75 (1998), *supra* Section B, elevates statutory text above legislative expectations in statutory interpretation. Why does the court nonetheless conclude that Title VII does not forbid anti-transgender discrimination as necessarily a form of sex discrimination (that is, does not make transgender persons a "protected class") but only offers them more limited protection against discrimination based on sex stereotyping in particular circumstances?

2. The court of appeals assumes without holding that Krystal Etsitty established a prima facie case that the transit authority's firing of her was because of her sex. Because that was merely a probabilistic inference, based on what many courts would consider "indirect evidence," the Supreme Court's decision in *McDonnell Douglas Corp. v. Green*, 411 U.S. 792 (1973), allows a defendant to rebut it by articulating a "legitimate, nondiscriminatory reason" for the discrimination, which if not shown to be pretextual will shield the defendant from Title VII liability. What was the transit authority's reason that the court of appeals accepts? Should it be seen as truly not discriminatory on the basis of sex?

3. The court of appeals considers the possibility that the transit authority's stated reason was pretextual. Even though it is to draw all factual inferences in favor of Ms. Etsitty when assessing the authority's motion to dismiss, the court concludes that she did not show pretext. Why not? Is the court correct to dismiss her comparative evidence as insufficient?

Etsitty v. Utah Transit Authority et al.

502 F.3d 1215 (10th Cir. 2007)

Before HENRY and MURPHY, Circuit Judges, and FIGA,* District Judge.

MURPHY, Circuit Judge.

. . . .

II. Background

[Krystal] Etsitty is a transsexual [*sic*] who has been diagnosed with Adult Gender Identity Disorder. Although Etsitty was born as a biological male and given the name "Michael," she identifies herself as a woman and has always believed she was born with the wrong anatomical sex organs. Even before she was diagnosed with a gender identity disorder, Etsitty lived and dressed as a woman outside of work and used the female name of "Krystal." Eventually, Etsitty began to see an endocrinologist who prescribed her female hormones to prepare for a sex reassignment surgery in the future. Etsitty made the decision at that time to live full time as a woman. While she has begun the transition from male to female by taking female hormones, she has not yet completed the sex reassignment surgery. Thus, Etsitty describes herself as a "pre-operative transgendered individual." Nearly four years after Etsitty had begun taking female hormones, she applied for a position as a bus operator with [Utah Transit Authority ("UTA")]. She was hired and, after successfully completing a six-week training course, was assigned to a position as an extra-board operator. As an operator on the extra board, Etsitty was not assigned to a permanent route or shift. Instead, she would fill in for regular operators who were on vacation or called in sick. As a result, Etsitty drove many of UTA's 115 to 130 routes in the Salt Lake City area over approximately ten weeks as an extra-board operator. While on their routes, UTA employees use public restrooms.

Throughout her training period at UTA, Etsitty presented herself as a man and used male restrooms. Soon after being hired, however, she met with her supervisor, Pat Chatterton, and informed him that she was a transsexual. She explained that she would begin to appear more as a female at work and that she would eventually change her sex. Chatterton expressed support for Etsitty and stated he did not see any problem with her being a transsexual. After this meeting, Etsitty began wearing

---

* The Honorable Phillip S. Figa, District Judge, United States District Court for the District of Colorado, sitting by designation.

makeup, jewelry, and acrylic nails to work. She also began using female restrooms while on her route.

Shirley, the operations manager of the UTA division where Etsitty worked, heard a rumor that there was a male operator who was wearing makeup. She spoke with Chatterton and he informed her Etsitty was a transsexual and would be going through a sex change. When Chatterton told her this, Shirley expressed concern about whether Etsitty would be using a male or female restroom. Shirley told Chatterton she would speak with Human Resources about whether Etsitty's restroom usage would raise any concerns for UTA.

Shirley then called Bruce Cardon, the human resources generalist for Shirley's division, and they decided to set up a meeting with Etsitty. At the meeting, Shirley and Cardon asked Etsitty where she was in the sex change process and whether she still had male genitalia. Etsitty explained she still had male genitalia because she did not have the money to complete the sex change operation. Shirley expressed concern about the possibility of liability for UTA if a UTA employee with male genitalia was observed using the female restroom. Shirley and Cardon also expressed concern that Etsitty would switch back and forth between using male and female restrooms.

Following their meeting with Etsitty, Shirley and Cardon placed Etsitty on administrative leave and ultimately terminated her employment. Shirley explained the reason Etsitty was terminated was the possibility of liability for UTA arising from Etsitty's restroom usage. Cardon similarly explained to Etsitty that the reason for her termination was UTA's inability to accommodate her restroom needs. Shirley felt it was not possible to accommodate Etsitty's restroom usage because she typically used public restrooms along her routes rather than restrooms at the UTA facility. Shirley also testified she did not believe it was appropriate to inquire into whether people along UTA routes would be offended if a transsexual with male genitalia were to use the female restrooms. On the record of termination, Shirley indicated Etsitty would be eligible for rehire after completing sex reassignment surgery. At the time of the termination, UTA had received no complaints about Etsitty's performance, appearance, or restroom usage.

Etsitty filed suit against UTA and Shirley, alleging they had engaged in unlawful gender discrimination, in violation of Title VII and the Equal Protection Clause of the Fourteenth Amendment. She claimed she was terminated because she was a transsexual and because she failed to conform to UTA's expectations of stereotypical male behavior. The defendants filed a motion for summary judgment, arguing transsexuals are not a protected class under Title VII or the Equal Protection Clause and that Etsitty was not terminated for failing to conform to male stereotypes. The district court granted the motion. In doing so, it agreed transsexuals are not a protected class and concluded there was no evidence that Etsitty was terminated for any reason other than Shirley's stated concern about Etsitty's restroom usage.

III. Analysis

This court reviews a district court's decision to grant summary judgment de novo. Summary judgment is appropriate "if the pleadings, depositions, answers to interrogatories, and admissions on file, together with the affidavits, if any, show that there is no genuine issue as to any material fact and that the moving party is entitled to a judgment as a matter of law." FED. R. CIV. P. 56(c). In making the determination of whether summary judgment was appropriate, this court views all the evidence and draws all reasonable inferences in favor of the nonmoving party.

A. Title VII

In the Title VII context, this court applies the three-part burden-shifting framework established in *McDonnell Douglas Corp. v. Green*, 411 U.S. 792 (1973).[1] *Plotke v. White*, 405 F.3d 1092 (10th Cir. 2005). Under this framework, the plaintiff must first establish a prima facie case of prohibited employment action. If the plaintiff does so, the burden shifts to the employer to articulate a "legitimate, nondiscriminatory reason for its adverse employment action." If the employer satisfies this burden, "summary judgment is warranted unless the employee can show there is a genuine issue of material fact as to whether the proffered reasons are pretextual." Because this court concludes transsexuals are not a protected class under Title VII and because Etsitty has failed to raise a genuine issue of material fact as to whether UTA's asserted non-discriminatory reason for her termination is pretextual, this court concludes the district court properly granted summary judgment on Etsitty's Title VII claims.

1. Prima Facie Claim

Title VII provides that "[i]t shall be an unlawful employment practice for an employer . . . to discharge any individual, or otherwise to discriminate against any individual . . . because of such individual's . . . sex." While Title VII is a remedial statute which should be liberally construed, it should not be treated as a "general civility code" and should be "directed only at discrimination because of sex." *Oncale v. Sundowner Offshore Servs., Inc.*, 523 U.S. 75 (1998). . . . The question of whether, and to what extent, a transsexual may claim protection from discrimination under Title VII is a question this court has not previously addressed. On appeal, Etsitty presents two separate legal theories in support of her contention that she was discriminated against because of sex in violation of Title VII. First, she argues discrimination based on an individual's identity as a transsexual is literally discrimination

---

1. Etsitty contends it is unnecessary for this court to engage in the *McDonnell Douglas* analysis because it is "undisputed" that UTA had a discriminatory motive. *See Heim v. Utah*, 8 F.3d 1541 (10th Cir. 1993) (noting *McDonnell Douglas* burden-shifting analysis is inapplicable where there is direct evidence of discrimination). When viewed in context, however, the evidence directly supports only the conclusion that Etsitty was terminated because of UTA's concerns regarding her restroom usage, a motive which is not discriminatory for reasons further discussed below. Because Etsitty cannot establish an "existing policy which itself constitutes discrimination," her claim of unlawful discrimination rests on indirect evidence and the *McDonnell Douglas* analysis applies. *See Jones v. Denver Post Corp.*, 203 F.3d 748 (10th Cir. 2000).

because of sex and that transsexuals are therefore a protected class under Title VII *as transsexuals*. Alternatively, she argues that even if Title VII does not prohibit discrimination on the basis of a person's transsexuality, she is nevertheless entitled to protection under Title VII because she was discriminated against for failing to conform to sex stereotypes. *See Price Waterhouse v. Hopkins*, 490 U.S. 228 (1989) . . . .

a. Transsexuals as a Protected Class

Etsitty. . . . argues that because a person's identity as a transsexual is directly connected to the sex organs she possesses, discrimination on this basis must constitute discrimination because of sex. Although this court has not previously considered whether transsexuals are a protected class under Title VII, other circuits to specifically address the issue have consistently held they are not. *See Ulane v. E. Airlines, Inc.*, 742 F.2d 1081 (7th Cir. 1984); *Sommers v. Budget Mktg., Inc.*, 667 F.2d 748 (8th Cir. 1982); *Holloway v. Arthur Andersen & Co.*, 566 F.2d 659 (9th Cir.1977). . . .

This court agrees with *Ulane* and the vast majority of federal courts to have addressed this issue and concludes discrimination against a transsexual based on the person's status as a transsexual is not discrimination because of sex under Title VII. In reaching this conclusion, this court recognizes it is the plain language of the statute and not the primary intent of Congress that guides our interpretation of Title VII. See *Oncale* ("[S]tatutory prohibitions often go beyond the principal evil to cover reasonably comparable evils, and it is ultimately the provisions of our laws rather than the principal concerns of our legislators by which we are governed."). Nevertheless, there is nothing in the record to support the conclusion that the plain meaning of "sex" encompasses anything more than male and female. In light of the traditional binary conception of sex, transsexuals may not claim protection under Title VII from discrimination based solely on their status as a transsexual. Rather, like all other employees, such protection extends to transsexual employees only if they are discriminated against because they are male or because they are female.

While Etsitty argues for a more expansive interpretation of sex that would include transsexuals as a protected class, she acknowledges that few courts have been willing to adopt such an interpretation. Even the Sixth Circuit, which extended protection to transsexuals under the *Price Waterhouse* theory discussed below, explained that an individual's status as a transsexual should be irrelevant to the availability of Title VII protection. *Smith v. City of Salem*, 378 F.3d 566 (6th Cir. 2004). . . .

Scientific research may someday cause a shift in the plain meaning of the term "sex" so that it extends beyond the two starkly defined categories of male and female. *See Schroer v. Billington*, 424 F. Supp. 2d 203 (D.D.C. 2006) (noting "complexities stem[ming] from real variations in how the different components of biological sexuality . . . interact with each other, and in turn, with social psychological, and legal conceptions of gender"); *cf. Brown v. Zavaras*, 63 F.3d 967, 971 (10th Cir. 1995) (stating that the possibility that sexual identity may be biological suggests reevaluating whether transsexuals are a protected class for purposes of the Equal Protection Clause). At this point in time and with the record and arguments before this court, however, we conclude discrimination against a transsexual because she is a transsexual is not "discrimination because of sex." Therefore, transsexuals are not a protected class under Title VII and Etsitty cannot satisfy her prima facie burden on the basis of her status as a transsexual.[2]

b. *Price Waterhouse* Theory

Etsitty next argues that even if transsexuals are not entitled to protection under Title VII as transsexuals, she is nevertheless entitled to protection as a biological male who was discriminated against for failing to conform to social stereotypes about how a man should act and appear.[3] She argues that although courts have previously declined to extend Title VII protection to transsexuals based on a narrow interpretation of "sex," this approach has been supplanted by the more recent rationale of *Price Waterhouse*. Etsitty contends that after *Price Waterhouse*, an employer's discrimination against an employee based on the employee's failure to conform to stereotypical gender norms is discrimination "because of sex" and may provide a basis for an actionable Title VII claim.

. . . .

A number of courts have relied on *Price Waterhouse* to expressly recognize a Title VII cause of action for discrimination based on an employee's failure to conform to stereotypical gender norms. . . .

This court need not decide whether discrimination based on an employee's failure to conform to sex stereotypes always constitutes discrimination "because of sex" and we need not decide whether such a claim may extend Title VII protection to transsexuals who act and appear as a member of the opposite sex. Instead, because we conclude Etsitty has not presented a genuine issue of material fact as to whether UTA's stated motivation for her termination is pretextual, we assume, without deciding, that such a claim is available and that Etsitty has satisfied her prima facie burden.

2. Legitimate Nondiscriminatory Reason

Assuming Etsitty has established a prima facie case under the *Price Waterhouse* theory of gender stereotyping, the burden then shifts to UTA to articulate a legitimate, nondiscriminatory reason for Etsitty's termination. *Plotke*. At this stage of the

---

2. This court is aware of the difficulties and marginalization transsexuals may be subject to in the workplace. The conclusion that transsexuals are not protected under Title VII *as transsexuals* should not be read to allow employers to deny transsexual employees the legal protection other employees enjoy merely by labeling them as transsexuals. *See Smith* ("Sex stereotyping based on a person's gender non-conforming behavior is impermissible discrimination, irrespective of the cause of that behavior; a label, such as 'transsexual,' is not fatal to a sex discrimination claim where the victim has suffered discrimination because of his or her gender nonconformity."). If transsexuals are to receive legal protection apart from their status as male or female, however, such protection must come from Congress and not the courts. *See Ulane* ("[I]f the term 'sex' as it is used in Title VII is to mean more than biological male or biological female, the new definition must come from Congress").

3. Although Etsitty identifies herself as a woman, her *Price Waterhouse* claim is based solely on her status as a biological male. Etsitty does not claim protection under Title VII as a woman who fails to conform to social stereotypes about how a woman should act and appear.

McDonnell Douglas framework, UTA does not "need to litigate the merits of the reasoning, nor does it need to prove that the reason relied upon was bona fide, nor does it need to prove that the reasoning was applied in a nondiscriminatory fashion." *EEOC v. Flasher Co.*, 986 F.2d 1312 (10th Cir. 1992). Rather, UTA need only "explain its actions against the plaintiff in terms that are not facially prohibited by Title VII." *Jones v. Denver Post Corp.*, 203 F.3d 748 (10th Cir. 2000).

UTA has explained its decision to discharge Etsitty was based solely on her intent to use women's public restrooms while wearing a UTA uniform, despite the fact she still had male genitalia. The record also reveals UTA believed, and Etsitty has not demonstrated otherwise, that it was not possible to accommodate her bathroom usage because UTA drivers typically use public restrooms along their routes rather than restrooms at the UTA facility. UTA states it was concerned the use of women's public restrooms by a biological male could result in liability for UTA. This court agrees with the district court that such a motivation constitutes a legitimate, non-discriminatory reason for Etsitty's termination under Title VII.

Etsitty argues UTA's concern regarding which restroom she would use cannot qualify as a facially non-discriminatory reason because the use of women's restrooms is an inherent part of Etsitty's status as a transsexual and, thus, an inherent part of her non-conforming gender behavior. Therefore, she argues, terminating her because she intended to use women's restrooms is essentially another way of stating that she was terminated for failing to conform to sex stereotypes.

Title VII's prohibition on sex discrimination, however, does not extend so far. It may be that use of the women's restroom is an inherent part of one's identity as a male-to-female transsexual and that a prohibition on such use discriminates on the basis of one's status as a transsexual. As discussed above, however, Etsitty may not claim protection under Title VII based upon her transsexuality *per se*. Rather, Etsitty's claim must rest entirely on the *Price Waterhouse* theory of protection as a man who fails to conform to sex stereotypes. However far *Price Waterhouse* reaches, this court cannot conclude it requires employers to allow biological males to use women's restrooms. Use of a restroom designated for the opposite sex does not constitute a mere failure to conform to sex stereotypes. *Cf. Nichols* (explaining that not all gender-based distinctions are actionable under Title VII and that "there is [no] violation of Title VII occasioned by reasonable regulations that require male and female employees to conform to different dress and grooming standards").

The critical issue under Title VII "is whether members of one sex are exposed to disadvantageous terms or conditions of employment to which members of the other sex are not exposed." *Oncale*. Because an employer's requirement that employees use restrooms matching their biological sex does not expose biological males to disadvantageous terms and does not discriminate against employees who fail to conform to gender stereotypes, UTA's proffered reason of concern over restroom usage is not discriminatory on the basis of sex. Thus, it is not "facially prohibited by Title VII" and may satisfy UTA's burden on the second part of the *McDonnell Douglas* framework.

3. Pretext

Once UTA has advanced a legitimate, nondiscriminatory reason for Etsitty's termination, the burden shifts back to Etsitty to "show there is a genuine issue of material fact as to whether the proffered reason [][is] pretextual." *Plotke*. "A plaintiff demonstrates pretext by showing either that a discriminatory reason more likely motivated the employer or that the employer's proffered explanation is unworthy of credence." *Stinnett v. Safeway, Inc.,* 337 F.3d 1213 (10th Cir. 2003). Such a showing may be made by revealing "such weaknesses, implausibilities, inconsistencies, incoherence, or contradictions, in the employer's proffered legitimate reasons for its action that a reasonable factfinder could . . . infer that the employer did not act for the asserted non-discriminatory reasons." *Jencks v. Modern Woodmen of Am.,* 479 F.3d 1261 (10th Cir. 2007). Although this court must resolve all doubts in Etsitty's favor, "[m]ere conjecture that the employer's explanation is pretext is insufficient to defeat summary judgment." *Anderson v. Coors Brewing Co.,* 181 F.3d 1171 (10th Cir. 1999).

In support of Etsitty's contention that she was terminated for failing to conform to gender stereotypes and not because of UTA's concern regarding her restroom usage, she relies primarily on the testimony of Shirley and Cardon. Specifically, she points to Shirley's deposition testimony in which she stated, "We both felt that there was an image issue out there for us, that we could have a problem with having someone who, even though his appearance may look female, he's still a male because he still had a penis." Additionally, Cardon testified, "We have expectations of operators and how they appear to the public. . . . [I]f we see something that is considered radical or could be interpreted by the public as being inappropriate, we talk to the operators about that and expect them to have a professional appearance." Etsitty argues these statements provide sufficient evidence to allow a rational jury to conclude she was terminated because she was a biological male who did not act and appear as UTA believed a man should.

If these statements stood alone, they may constitute sufficient evidence of pretext to preclude summary judgment. A complete review of the deposition testimony, however, indicates otherwise. Although the specific statements cited by Etsitty address Etsitty's appearance, they fall within the larger context of an explanation of UTA's concerns regarding Etsitty's restroom usage. Immediately after Shirley mentions Etsitty's appearance, she explains the problem with this appearance is that she may not be able to find a unisex bathroom on the route and that liability may arise if Etsitty was using female restrooms. When Cardon was asked what he found unprofessional about Etsitty's appearance, he similarly responded with concerns about her restroom usage. Thus, the isolated and tangential comments about Etsitty's appearance are insufficient to alone permit an inference of pretext. Instead, the testimony of Shirley and Cardon, viewed in its entirety and in context, provides further support for UTA's assertion that Etsitty was terminated not because she failed to conform to stereotypes about how a man should act and appear, but because she was a biological male who intended to use women's public restrooms.

In addition to the statements made by Shirley and Cardon, Etsitty argues UTA's asserted reason for her termination must be pretextual because UTA had no reason to be concerned regarding her use of women's restrooms. In support of this claim, Etsitty makes the following arguments: (1) UTA could not be subject to liability, as a matter of law, for allowing a male-to-female transsexual employee to use women's restrooms; (2) UTA had received no complaints regarding Etsitty's restroom usage; (3) UTA made no attempt to investigate whether there were unisex restrooms available; and (4) because Etsitty looked and acted like a woman, no one would know she was not biologically female and therefore could not take offense to her use of women's restrooms.

None of the arguments raised by Etsitty is sufficient to raise a genuine issue as to whether UTA's asserted concern regarding her use of the women's restrooms is pretext. Although Etsitty states in her brief that there is no evidence she intended to use female restrooms, she admitted at oral argument that she was required to use female restrooms and that she informed Shirley of this at their meeting prior to her termination. Thus, UTA's belief that Etsitty intended to use female restrooms was well-grounded. While Etsitty contends this fact should not have given rise to her termination, her argument is more akin to a challenge to UTA's business judgment than a challenge to its actual motivation. Nevertheless, "[t]he relevant inquiry is not whether [the defendant's] proffered reasons were wise, fair or correct, but whether [it] honestly believed those reasons and acted in good faith upon those beliefs." *Exum v. United States Olympic Comm.*, 389 F.3d 1130 (10th Cir. 2004).

While this court may disagree with UTA that a male-to-female transsexual's intent to use women's restrooms should be grounds for termination before complaints have arisen, there is insufficient evidence to permit an inference that UTA did not actually terminate Etsitty for this reason. To the contrary, all of the evidence suggests UTA did in fact terminate Etsitty because of its concerns about her restroom usage. Both at the time of Etsitty's termination and in subsequent deposition testimony, Shirley consistently explained the termination decision in terms of her concerns regarding liability for UTA and the inability of UTA to accommodate Etsitty's restroom needs. Although Shirley and Cardon specifically asked Etsitty whether she possessed male genitalia, such an inquiry is not the "smoking gun" Etsitty suggests. Rather, the record is clear that this inquiry was only relevant to UTA's evaluation of whether Etsitty's restroom usage could become a problem.

UTA's legitimate explanation is not made implausible by any of the circumstantial evidence relied on by Etsitty in her brief. The fact UTA had not yet received complaints about Etsitty's restroom usage at the time of the termination does not mean UTA could not have been concerned about such complaints arising in the future, especially where Etsitty had only recently begun using the women's restroom. Similarly, Etsitty has pointed to nothing in the record to indicate the feasibility of an investigation into the availability of unisex restrooms along each of UTA's routes or the likelihood complaints would arise. Therefore, in this case, Shirley's failure to conduct such an investigation has little, if any, bearing on the veracity of her stated concern.

Etsitty's reliance on *Cruzan v. Special School District # 1* to call into question UTA's asserted motivation is also misplaced. 294 F.3d 981 (8th Cir. 2002). In *Cruzan*, the Eighth Circuit held that a male-to-female transsexual's use of the women's employee restroom does not create a hostile work environment for purposes of a Title VII sexual harassment claim. Even if such a rule were to be adopted in this circuit and applied to actions arising outside the employment context, however, it would say nothing about whether UTA was nevertheless genuinely concerned about the possibility of liability and public complaints. The question of whether UTA was legally correct about the merits of such potential lawsuits is irrelevant. *See Exum* ("To show pretext, the plaintiff must call into question the honesty or good faith of the [employer].")

Finally, Etsitty argues that because UTA typically resolves complaints about its employees' restroom usage simply by requiring the employees to stop using the restroom for which the complaint was received, Etsitty was treated differently than similarly situated employees. *See Kendrick v. Penske Transp. Servs., Inc.,* 220 F.3d 1220 (10th Cir. 2000) (noting plaintiff may show pretext "by providing evidence that he was treated differently from other similarly-situated, nonprotected employees"). The prior complaints received by UTA, however, involved problems with the cleanliness of the restrooms and with UTA employees congregating around a hotel swimming pool. An employee's use of bathrooms designated for the opposite sex is sufficiently different from these prior problems as to make UTA's treatment of restroom complaints in the past of little significance to the question of pretext in the case at bar.

Thus, there is no evidence in the record of any "weaknesses, implausibilities, inconsistencies, incoherence, or contradictions" in UTA's asserted legitimate, nondiscriminatory reason for Etsitty's termination. *Jencks.* Etsitty has therefore failed to raise a genuine issue as to whether UTA's proffered reason is pretextual and the district court properly granted summary judgment on Etsitty's Title VII claim.

B. Equal Protection

With respect to Etsitty's Equal Protection claims brought pursuant to § 1983, she makes no arguments aside from her Title VII claim that she was discriminated against because of sex. [Because] Etsitty does not argue there was a violation of the Equal Protection Clause separate from her Title VII sex discrimination claim, her Equal Protection claim fails for the same reasons discussed above. *Cf. Smith v. City of Salem,* 378 F.3d 566 (6th Cir. 2004) (holding transsexual plaintiff was not a member of a protected class for purposes of the Equal Protection Clause).

IV. Conclusion

For the foregoing reasons, this court AFFIRMS the district court's grant of summary judgment to the defendants.

Discussion

1. Even if sincere, would a concern about potential liability from Krystal Etsitty's use of women's restrooms be a non-discriminatory (not sex-based) reason? If Etsitty were to have used men's restrooms though presenting as a woman, would that have been better? For whom?

2. As the trial and appellate opinions may illustrate, assessing sex-discrimination arguments in this area may be challenging in part because of the broadly accepted sex-segregation of restrooms. Is there a way for transgender plaintiffs to challenge exclusion from restrooms consistent with their gender identity without calling into question the legality of separate men's and women's rooms? If there is not, should that consequence be fatal to their Title VII or other statutory or constitutional sex discrimination claims?

3. Compare *Etsitty* with *Goins v. West Group*, 635 N.W.2d 717 (Minn. 2001), an early case considering the question of how anti-discrimination protections affect restroom access for transgender people. Julienne Goins, a transgender woman, brought claims of "sexual orientation" discrimination under the Minnesota Human Rights Act, enacted in 1993, which defined that term to include "having or being perceived as having a self-image or identity not traditionally associated with one's biological maleness or femaleness." It is important to note that the Court adopted an earlier meaning of the word *transgender*, stating that "[t]ransgender people seek to live as a gender other than that attributed to them at birth but without surgery." The term is now generally considered to refer to both those who obtain or desire surgery and those who do not. West Group maintained that it designated restrooms and restroom use on the basis of "biological gender." The phrase "biological gender" may seem odd to those who understand gender to refer to non-biological traits, but the courts have often used *sex* and *gender* interchangeably and without distinction. The trial court granted summary judgment to West, but the intermediate appeals court reversed that decision and remanded the case for trial. The Minnesota Supreme Court in turn reversed again, holding in favor of the employer. The court noted that Goins was not arguing the statute prohibited employers from sex-segregating restrooms, but rather that it prohibited restroom designation by "biological gender" rather than "self-image of gender." Her argument tracks the words of the statute, but the court rejected her argument because "the traditional and accepted practice in the employment setting is to provide restroom facilities that reflect the cultural preference for restroom designation based on biological gender," and a contrary result was "a result not likely intended by the legislature." Note, though, that the subsequent jurisprudential trend, certainly with respect to federal

statutory interpretation, has been to subordinate or eliminate analysis based on legislative intent in favor of a focus on the meaning of the words in the statutory text.

Goins may be seen as one end of the rhetorical antipodes of denial of relief to transgender plaintiffs. The Tenth Circuit decision in *Etsitty*, by contrast, is the other. *Etsitty* specifically disavowed the use of legislative intent, the mainstay of the *Goins* opinion. Instead, it relied on precedent, the "plain language" of the statute, and the "traditional meaning" and apparently the meaning "[a]t this point in time" of "sex." This rhetorical shift essentially unmoored the meaning of sex in Title VII from legislative intent. On this view, the issue in a Title VII case brought by a transgender plaintiff is not what the term "sex" meant in 1964; the issue is what it means now. This may seem surprising given that the meaning of sex has arguably changed so radically since 1964, including Supreme Court rulings broadening the meaning of Title VII's ban on sex discrimination to include discrimination against males as well as females, "verbal or physical conduct of a sexual nature," predictive and prescriptive use of stereotypes regarding male or female behavior, and same-sex sexual harassment. If the meaning of sex has changed broadly, that would call into question the *Goins* result.

The Tenth Circuit opinion in *Etsitty* tried to address this conceptual problem by suggesting that the shift from legislative intent (relied on in earlier precedents that it "agree[d] with") to plain language made no difference in the case. According to the Tenth Circuit, "sex" means now, as it meant in 1964, only the traditional binary conception of male and female anatomy. The court claimed that the meaning of sex has not changed since the law was written more than forty years ago.

This is a somewhat unconvincing argument, which may help explain why it has been supplemented by some by use of an "original public meaning" argument in more recent litigation. That argument refers to the suggestion that, while putting aside the specific intent of the legislature, we should look at the meaning of the statutory text to members of the public at the time that the statute was enacted. This is similar to arguments of constitutional originalism, in which the meaning of the words of the US Constitution are understood from the point of view of their "public meaning" at the time of their adoption. Deemphasizing statements from legislators, original public meaning originalists consult dictionaries, newspapers, and other publications of the time. (This may seem very similar to legislative intent.) As explained by Judge James Ho of the U.S. Court of Appeals for the Fifth Circuit in *Wittmer v. Phillips 66 Co.*, 915 F.3d 328, 335 (5th Cir. 2019), a case addressing in dicta whether Title VII's ban on sex discrimination forbids anti-trans discrimination: "the point is not whether members of Congress subjectively intended that result—rather, the point is whether they should have expected it, in light of the words of the statute as they were generally understood at the time." In other words, we must hypothesize what legislators at the time would have predicted about how courts would interpret their words decades later, and which meanings they would consider legitimate. For a discussion of the issues of the meaning of "sex" in Title VII, at different moment's in the statute's history, see Jillian Todd Weiss, *Transgender Identity,*

Textualism, and the Supreme Court: What Is the "Plain Meaning" of "Sex" in Title VII of the Civil Rights Act of 1964?, 18 TEMPLE POL. & C.R. L. REV. 574 (2009). For the Supreme Court's understanding of the meaning of the words of Title VII's sex discrimination ban in sexual orientation and gender identity contexts, an understanding purportedly fixed in 1964, see *Bostock v. Clayton County, Georgia*, 140 S. Ct. 1731 (2020), Section D, *supra* at p. 244.

Reading Guide for Lusardi v. McHugh

1. Upon what statute does transgender woman Tamara Lusardi rely in her complaint of unlawful discrimination before the Equal Employment Opportunity Commission ("EEOC")? What relevant kind of discrimination does that statute forbid? What reasons does the EEOC give for concluding that the federal agency that employed Ms. Lusardi discriminated against her on that basis? Note that the aspects of her claims based on the names and pronouns by which she was addressed at work are treated primarily in Chapter 15, *infra* at p. 1081.

2. What arguments did the agency make for why its treatment of Lusardi's restroom access should be judged lawful? What reasons does the EEOC give for rejecting those arguments?

Lusardi v. John J. McHugh, Secretary, Department of the Army

No. 0120133395, 2015 WL 1607756 (E.E.O.C. Apr. 1, 2015)

. . . .

Issue Presented

The issue presented is whether Complainant proved that she was subjected to disparate treatment and harassment based on sex when the Agency restricted her from using the common female restroom, and a team leader ([supervisor 3, hereinafter] S3) intentionally and repeatedly referred to her by male pronouns and made hostile remarks.

Background[3]

This case concerns allegations of disparate treatment on the basis of sex in the terms and conditions of Complainant's employment and allegations that harassment based on sex subjected Complainant to a hostile work environment. . . . Complainant was employed at the [Army Aviation and Missile Research Development and Engineering Center ("AMRDEC")] Software Engineering Directorate ("SED") under the supervision of [supervisor 1, hereinafter] S1, the Quality Division Chief.

---

3. The factual background as laid out here is not exhaustive. Two comprehensive reports of the facts relevant to this case have already been compiled: the EEO Report of Investigation and the Agency's Final Agency Decision. We have considered those documents as well as the Complainant's Brief in Support of Appeal and the extensive transcript from the Fact-Finding Conference conducted [by the EEOC]. The facts pertinent to the legal analysis necessary are largely not in dispute.

During the relevant time period, . . . Complainant . . . worked as a Software Quality Assurance Lead under the direction of [supervisor 3, hereinafter] S3, the Software Engineering Lead, who was in turn supervised by [supervisor 2, hereinafter] S2, the Technical Chief. In August 2011, Complainant returned to her primary job at SED.

Complainant's Transition and Bathroom Access

[Transgender woman Tamara Lusardi discussed her gender identity with S1 as early as 2007 and began transitioning her gender presentation/expression in 2010. In April 2010, she secured an Alabama court order changing her name to a conventionally feminine one and requested that the government change her name and sex on all personnel records. The Office of Personnel Management ("OPM") did so on October 13, causing her work e-mail address to change to reflect her new name.]

On October 26, . . . at the request of S2, Complainant met with S2 and S1 to discuss the process of transitioning from presenting herself as a man to living and working, in conformance with her gender identity, as a woman. At that meeting, Complainant and her supervisors discussed how Complainant would explain her transition to colleagues and the estimated timeline for any medical procedures.

As part of that meeting, they also discussed which bathrooms Complainant would use when she began presenting as a woman. The plan, written in the form of a memorandum from Complainant to management, indicated that Complainant would use a single-user restroom referred to as the "executive restroom" or the "single shot rest room" rather than the multi-user "common women's restroom" until Complainant had undergone an undefined surgery.

S2 testified that in his recollection no one "insisted" that Complainant utilize only the executive restroom but that the plan was mutually crafted by himself, S1, and Complainant. According to Complainant, "We agreed up front in order to allow people to become accustomed to me and not feel uncomfortable that I would use the front bathroom for a period of time." She testified that she agreed to use the executive bathroom for the initial period "[b]ecause I have a good heart and I did believe there were people who might have issues with it and the ability for them to grow comfortable with who I was . . . would have provided it." S1 expressed at the time that it was her belief, after consulting with Human Resources, that because Complainant was a woman, she was free to use whichever women's restroom she wanted.

Regardless of the motivations behind the creation of the transition plan, it apparently had to be "approved" by higher level management. The Deputy Program Manager of the Program Executive Office testified that he made the final decision as to which bathroom Complainant would use. He stated:

> I made the decision based on the fact that I have a significant number of women in my building who would probably be extremely uncomfortable having an individual, despite the fact that she is conducting herself as a female, is still basically a male, physically.
>
> And that would cause as many problems if more problems [*sic*] than having the individuals use a private bathroom. I also thought that under the

circumstances, a male restroom would be inappropriate. So, that was left [*sic*] to use the single use bathrooms.

Additionally, a Lieutenant who supervised S2 testified that Complainant's bathroom access was conditioned on a medical procedure:

> [W]e all agreed back then that there was a procedure, operation that was to take place that would essentially signify a complete transformation to a female . . . And that procedure would be the point of where all the bathrooms would be on limits for or within limits for [the Complainant] to use for that point.

The transition plan was given final approval by the Deputy Program Manager in early November 2010. Complainant e-mailed the entire staff on November 22, 2010, explaining her situation and indicating that for an initial period, she would use the executive restroom. She began presenting as a woman at work following the Thanksgiving holiday. Complainant regularly used the executive restroom except on three occasions in early 2011. On one occasion, the executive restroom was out of order for several days. On another occasion, the executive restroom was being cleaned. In these incidents, Complainant felt that her only options were to leave the facility to locate a restroom off-site, use the common women's restroom, or use the common men's restroom. She chose to use the restroom associated with her gender. After each incident, Complainant was confronted by S2 who told her she'd been observed using the common women's restroom, that she was making people uncomfortable, and that she had to use the executive restroom until she could show proof of having undergone the "final surgery."

Complainant testified that in January 2011 when S2 confronted her about using the common women's restroom, she responded, "I am legally female. I used it."

Harassment

During the relevant time period, S3 repeatedly referred to Complainant by her former male name, by male pronouns, and as "sir." . . . .

After Complainant's e-mail address changed to reflect her name, but before she began presenting as female, curious coworkers questioned Complainant about the situation. As a result of the questions S2 asked Complainant to "hold down the chatter with people that were inquiring" about her transition.

Complainant testified that, although she did not inform management that she felt she was being subjected to a hostile work environment, she did tell Colonel 2 that there were "some issues."

EEO Investigation and Final Agency Decision

Complainant initiated EEO counselor contact on September 6, 2011, and filed a formal complaint on March 14, 2012 . . . . The Agency accepted the complaint and conducted an investigation, including a fact-finding conference. The Agency issued Complainant a copy of the investigative file and a notice of right to request a hearing before an EEOC Administrative Judge (AJ) or an immediate final agency decision

(FAD). Complainant elected an immediate FAD, which the Agency issued on September 5, 2013.

In its final decision, the Agency concluded that Complainant failed to prove that the Agency subjected her to discrimination or harassment as alleged. Specifically, the Agency concluded that it had provided legitimate, non-discriminatory reasons for its requirement that she use the executive restroom, and that Complainant failed to show that the explanations were pretext for unlawful discrimination. The Agency determined that, during a meeting with management, Complainant agreed to use the "single shot" executive restroom until she "had surgery," and that testimony and e-mails between Complainant and management reflected that management was supportive of Complainant and "committed to ensuring [Complainant] would be treated with dignity and respect." Additionally, the Agency concluded that Complainant had not shown that she was subjected to disparate treatment based on sex because Complainant did not tell management that the amenities in the executive restroom were inadequate compared to the common female restroom facility and, therefore, management did not deny her access to equal facilities.

The Agency further determined that, although S2 reminded Complainant about the bathroom access plan she had with management, the comments were not sufficiently severe or pervasive to constitute harassment.

With respect to Complainant's claim that S3 referred to her by male pronouns, names, and titles, the Agency concluded that these were isolated incidents that were not sufficiently severe or pervasive to constitute a hostile work environment.

On September 23, 2013, Complainant filed this appeal of the agency's final decision.

Contentions on Appeal

Complainant contends that the Agency erred when it found that she failed to show that she was subjected to sex discrimination and harassment. Complainant contends that, by restricting her to the single stall restroom because she is transgender, the Agency changed the terms and conditions of her employment solely based on her sex, in violation of Title VII. Complainant also reiterates her claim that the Agency subjected her to a hostile work environment by allowing S3 to refer to her by a male name and pronouns. . . . Complainant maintains that "these daily humiliations and reminders that the Agency did not accept her gender identity created a hostile work environment."

[The] Agency maintains that, taking into account the concerns of Complainant's female co-workers who had known her as male for years, management asked Complainant to use the single-stall restroom in the executive suite, and she agreed to do so until her surgery was "complete." The Agency maintains that there is no law that mandates that agencies allow transgender individuals to use restrooms that are consistent with their gender identity. The Agency further maintains that, if it had been aware of Complainant's concerns about the restroom facilities, arrangements could have been made to accommodate her needs, but it is unclear whether her inability to use a restroom with equivalent amenities constitutes an adverse action. The Agency contends that the record reflects that it was "very supportive of the complainant's transition from male to female," and that Complainant was grateful for her managers' and co-workers' support. The Agency concludes that, in the absence of legal precedent, management worked out a "fair solution" that took into account the concerns of all employees.

. . . .

Analysis and Findings
Disparate Treatment: Restroom Facilities

Title VII states that "[a]ll personnel actions affecting [federal] employees or applicants for employment . . . shall be made free from any discrimination based on . . . sex." 42 U.S.C. § 2000e-16(a). This provision is analogous to the section of Title VII governing employment discrimination in the private sector at 42 U.S.C. § 2000e-2(a)(1), (2) (making it unlawful for a covered employer to "fail or refuse to hire or to discharge any individual, or otherwise to discriminate with respect to his compensation, terms, conditions, or privileges of employment," or to "limit, segregate, or classify his employees or applicants for employment in any way which would deprive or tend to deprive any individual of employment opportunities or otherwise adversely affect his status as an employee" because of sex).

To establish a claim of disparate treatment on the basis of sex, a complainant must show the agency took an adverse employment action against the complainant because of the complainant's sex. This can be shown through either direct or indirect evidence.

"Direct evidence" is either written or verbal evidence that, on its face, demonstrates bias and is linked to an adverse action. *Pomerantz v. Dep't of Veterans Affairs*, EEOC Appeal No. 01990534 (Sept. 13, 2002). Where there is direct evidence of discrimination, there is no need to prove a prima facie case or facts from which an inference of discrimination can be drawn. *Trans World Airlines, Inc. v. Thurston*, 469 U.S. 111 (1985). Moreover, where the trier of fact finds that there is direct evidence of discrimination, liability is established. GUIDANCE ON RECENT DEVELOPMENTS IN DISPARATE TREATMENT THEORY, No. 915.002, July 14, 1992, Section III; EEOC COMPLIANCE MANUAL § 604.3, "Proof of Disparate Treatment" (June 1, 2006).

Complainant is a transgender individual. . . . In this case, Complainant identified as female and has consistently presented herself as female since at least November 2010.

Complainant alleges that the Agency subjected her to sex discrimination when it treated her differently than other employees because she is transgender. In *Macy v. Department of Justice*, EEOC Appeal No. 0120120821 (April 20, 2012), [presented in Section D, *supra* at p. 228,] the Commission held that discrimination against a transgender individual because that person is transgender is, by definition, discrimination "based on ... sex," and such discrimination violates Title VII, absent a valid defense. We stated:

> When an employer discriminates against someone because the person is transgender, the employer has engaged in disparate treatment "related to the sex of the victim." This is true regardless of whether an employer discriminates against an employee because the individual has expressed his or her gender in a non-stereotypical fashion, because the employer is uncomfortable with the fact that the person has transitioned or is in the process of transitioning from one gender to another, or because the employer simply does not like that the person is identifying as a transgender person. In each of these circumstances, the employer is making a gender-based evaluation, thus violating the Supreme Court's admonition that "an employer may not take gender into account in making an employment decision."

Here, the Agency acknowledges that Complainant's transgender status was *the* motivation for its decision to prevent Complainant from using the common women's restroom. The Deputy Program Manager testified that the restriction was imposed due to the Agency's belief that a significant number of women in the building would be "extremely uncomfortable having an individual [use the common female restroom because], despite the fact that she is conducting herself as a female, [the individual] is still basically a male, physically." Likewise, the Agency acknowledges that it restricted Complainant from the common women's restroom because of concerns about employee reaction to Complainant as a transgender individual. S1, for example, testified that management limited Complainant to the front executive restroom because it otherwise would have been a "real shocker for everyone in the workplace." This constitutes direct evidence of discrimination on the basis of sex.

The Agency defends its actions in part by pointing out that the Complainant agreed to use the "single shot" restroom while other employees adjusted to her transition. In this case, the "agreement" in question was a one-page memorandum from the Complainant to the management team. It outlined the reasons for Complainant's transition and a tentative list of next steps under the heading "Path Forward." The first step, starting in mid-November, was for Complainant to start dressing consistent with her gender identity. During this time, her plan said she would "use [the] single shot restroom." The next step, set to occur about a month later, was for Complainant to undergo an undefined "Surgical Procedure" and then put in a request to use the common facility. In accordance with her plan, Complainant used the single-shot restroom in the period following her change in dress. She apparently did not undergo a surgical procedure in December and did not submit a formal request to use the common facility exclusively. On two occasions, however, she found that the single-shot restroom was out-of-order or closed and decided to use the common facility. She was confronted by S2 after each time she used the common facility. He told her that she could not use those facilities until she had undergone "final surgery." Complainant asserted in response that she was "legally female" and entitled to use the women's restroom if needed.

This case represents well the peril of conditioning access to facilities on any medical procedure. Nothing in Title VII makes any medical procedure a prerequisite for equal opportunity (for transgender individuals, or anyone else). An agency may not condition access to facilities — or to other terms, conditions, or privileges of employment — on the completion of certain medical steps that the agency itself has unilaterally determined will somehow prove the bona fides of the individual's gender identity.[4]

On this record, there is no cause to question that Complainant — who was assigned the sex of male at birth but identifies as female — *is* female. And certainly where, as here, a transgender female has notified her employer that she has begun living and working full-time as a woman, the agency must allow her access to the women's restrooms. This "real life experience" often is crucial to a transgender employee's transition. As OPM points out:

> [C]ommencement of the real life experience [i]s often the most important stage of transition, and, for a significant number of people, the last step necessary for them to complete a healthy gender transition. As the name suggests, the real life experience is designed to allow the transgender individual to experience living full-time in the gender role to which he or she is transitioning.... [O]nce [a transitioning employee] has begun living and working full-time in the gender that reflects his or her gender identity, agencies should allow access to restrooms and (if provided to other employees) locker room facilities consistent with his or her gender identity.... [T]ransitioning employees should not be required to have undergone or to provide proof of any particular medical procedure (including gender reassignment surgery) in order to have access to facilities designated for use by a particular gender.

OPM Transgender Guidance

Agencies are certainly encouraged to work with transgender employees to develop plans for individual workplace transitions. For a variety of reasons, including the personal comfort of the transitioning employee, a transition plan might include a

---

4. Gender reassignment surgery is in no way a fundamental element of a transition. Transitions vary according to individual needs and many do not involve surgery at all. As the Office of Personnel Management has explained:

> Some individuals will find it necessary to transition from living and working as one gender to another. These individuals often seek some form of medical treatment such as counseling, hormone therapy, electrolysis, and reassignment surgery. Some individuals, however, will not pursue some (or any) forms of medical treatment because of their age, medical condition, lack of funds, or other personal circumstances. Managers and supervisors should be aware that not all transgender individuals will follow the same pattern, but they all are entitled to the same consideration as they undertake the transition steps deemed appropriate for them, and should all be treated with dignity and respect.

Office of Personnel Management (OPM), *Guidance Regarding the Employment of Transgender Individuals in the Federal Workplace* ("*OPM Transgender Guidance*"), available online at http://www.opm.gov/policy-data-oversight/diversity-and-inclusion/reference-materials/gender-identity-guidance/.

limited period of time where the employee opts to use a private facility instead of a common one. *See id.*

Circumstances can change, however and an employee is never in a position to prospectively waive Title VII rights. *See Alexander v. Gardner-Denver Co.*, 415 U.S. 36 (1974) ("[W]e think it clear that there can be no prospective waiver of an employee's rights under Title VII."); *see also Vigil v. Dep't of the Army*, EEOC Request No. 05960521 (June 22, 1998) ("... [an] agreement that waives prospective Title VII rights is invalid as violative of public policy"). Agencies should, as the OPM Guidance suggests, view any plan with a transitioning employee related to facility access as a "temporary compromise" and understand that the employee retains the right under Title VII to use the facility consistent with his or her gender. *OPM Transgender Guidance.*[5]

The Agency states that it would not allow Complainant to use the common female restroom because co-workers would feel uncomfortable with this approach. We recognize that certain employees may object — some vigorously — to allowing a transgender individual to use the restroom consistent with his or her gender identity. Some, like the Agency decision makers in this case, may not believe a transgender woman is truly female, and thus entitled or eligible to use a female bathroom, unless she has had gender reassignment surgery. Some co-workers may be confused or uncertain about what it means to be transgender, and/or embarrassed or even afraid to share a restroom with a transgender co-worker.

But supervisory or co-worker confusion or anxiety cannot justify discriminatory terms and conditions of employment. Title VII prohibits discrimination based on sex whether motivated by hostility, by a desire to protect people of a certain gender, by gender stereotypes, or by the desire to accommodate other people's prejudices or discomfort. *See Macy*; *see also Fernandez v. Wynn Oil Co.*, 653 F.2d 1273 (9th Cir. 1981) (female employee could not lawfully be fired because employer's foreign clients would only work with males); *Diaz v. Pan American World Airways, Inc.*, 442 F.2d 385 (5th Cir. 1971) (rejecting customer preference for female flight attendants as justification for discrimination against male applicants). Allowing the preferences of co-workers to determine whether sex discrimination is valid reinforces the very stereotypes and prejudices that Title VII is intended to overcome.[6] *See Diaz* ("While

---

5. This is not to say that plans have no place in the transition process. Properly developed, transition plans ensure that a transitioning employee is treated with dignity and respect. The process of developing a plan also opens important channels of communication between the transitioning employee and management. The plans should not, however, be used as a means for restricting a transitioning employee. Rather, they should serve as tools for enabling the employee to complete his or her transition in an open and welcoming way.

6. Thus, for instance, employers may not prohibit a transgender female worker from using the female bathroom based on speculation or stereotypes that such workers are somehow inherently dangerous or prone to violence, any more than a sheriff's office can exclude men from supervisory positions in female inmate housing based on unsubstantiated concerns that substantially all male deputies are likely to engage in sexual misconduct. *See Ambat v. City & County of San Francisco,*

we recognize that the public's expectation of finding one sex in a particular role may cause some initial difficulty, it would be totally anomalous if we were to allow the preferences and prejudices of the customers to determine whether the sex discrimination was valid. Indeed, it was, to a large, extent, these very prejudices the Act was meant to overcome"); . . . *cf. Cruzan v. Special Sch. Dist., No. 1*, 294 F.3d 981 (8th Cir. 2002) (school's policy of allowing transgender women to use women's faculty restroom did not create a hostile work environment for other employees).[7]

Finally, the Agency maintains that it is unclear whether restricting Complainant from using the common restrooms is even an adverse employment action. The Commission has long held that an employee is aggrieved for purposes of Title VII if she has suffered a harm or loss with respect to a term, condition, or privilege of employment. *Diaz v. Dep't of Air Force*, EEOC Request No. 05931049 (Apr. 21, 1994). Equal access to restrooms is a significant, basic condition of employment. *See, e.g.,* OSHA, Interpretation of 20 C.F.R. 1910.141 § (c)(1)(i): Toilet Facilities (Apr. 4, 1998) (requiring that employers provide access to toilet facilities so that all employees can use them when they need to do so). Here the Agency refused to allow the

---

757 F.3d 1017 (9th Cir. July 14, 2014) (concluding the assumption that "'all or substantially all' male deputies are likely to perpetrate sexual misconduct [against female inmates]" without evidence to support it "amount[s] to 'the kind of unproven and invidious stereotype that Congress sought to eliminate from employment decisions when it enacted Title VII'"). Of course, if a transgender woman using a common female restroom were to assault a co-worker using the same restroom, then the matter could and should be dealt with like any other workplace conduct violation — just as it would be if any other woman using a common female restroom assaulted a co-worker.

7. For this reason, the Commission disagrees with the holdings of cases like *Kastl v. Maricopa County Cmty. College Dist.*, 325 Fed. Appx. 492 (9th Cir. 2009), and *Etsitty v. Utah Transit Auth.*, 502 F.3d 1215 (10th Cir. 2007). . . . The Commission finds the rationale of these cases unpersuasive. First, an employee need not use the *McDonnell Douglas* framework when there is direct evidence that an adverse employment action has been taken on the basis of a sex-based consideration such as an employee's transgender status. Second, where an employer proffers an explanation inextricably linked to the protected trait — such as admitting that it refused to allow a transgender worker to use a restroom consistent with the worker's gender identity because of a belief that the worker's transgender status might raise safety or liability issues — that rationale is not non-discriminatory. Instead, that proffered justification is indistinguishable from the protected trait at issue and thus cannot serve as a "legitimate" explanation. *Cf. Johnson v. State of NY*, 49 F. 3d 75 (2d Cir. 1995) (holding that a policy requiring active membership in an organization where membership was automatically rescinded at age 60 was not neutral; it was, instead, "inextricably linked" with age). Indeed, the *Etsitty* Court itself acknowledged that: "It may be that use of the women's restroom is an inherent part of one's identity as a male-to-female transsexual and that a prohibition on such use discriminates on the basis of one's status as a transsexual." However, as the *Etsitty* court went on to explain, it had already concluded that "Etsitty may not claim protection under Title VII based upon her transexuality [*sic* — Eds.] per se" and thus Etsitty's claim had to "rest entirely on the *Price Waterhouse* theory of protection as a man who fails to conform to sex stereotypes." In light of that fact, the *Etsitty* court concluded that "[h]owever far *Price Waterhouse* reaches, this court cannot conclude it requires employers to allow biological males to use women's restrooms." Of course, as noted previously, the Commission in *Macy* has held that discrimination on the basis of transgender status is per se sex discrimination, finding that a plaintiff need not have specific evidence of gender stereotyping by the employer because "consideration of gender stereotypes will inherently be part of what drives discrimination against a transgendered individual."

Complainant to use a restroom that other persons of her gender were freely permitted to use. That constitutes a harm or loss with respect to the terms and conditions of Complainant's employment.[8]

But the harm to the Complainant goes beyond simply denying her access to a resource open to others. The decision to restrict Complainant to a "single shot" restroom isolated and segregated her from other persons of her gender. It perpetuated the sense that she was not worthy of equal treatment and respect. *Cf.* 42 U.S.C. §2000e-2(a)(2) (making it unlawful to "segregate" employees in any way that deprives or tends to deprive them of equal employment opportunities); [EEOC,] *Religious Garb and Grooming in the Workplace: Rights and Responsibilities*, Q. 8 and Ex. 8 (limiting employees who wear religious attire that might make customers uncomfortable to "back room" positions constitutes religious segregation and violates Title VII). The Agency's actions deprived Complainant of equal status, respect, and dignity in the workplace, and, as a result, deprived her of equal employment opportunities. In restricting her access to the restroom consistent with her gender identity, the Agency refused to recognize Complainant's very identity. Treatment of this kind by one's employer is most certainly adverse.[9]

In sum, we find that the Agency's decision to restrict Complainant's access to the common women's restroom on account of her gender identity violated Title VII. We further find that the record contains direct evidence that the decision was based on the gender identity of the Complainant. The Agency, therefore, erred when it found that Complainant was not subjected to sex-based disparate treatment.

Harassment: Gender Pronouns, Titles, and Access to Facilities

. . . .

In this case, Complainant contends that she was subjected to a hostile work environment because management restricted her from using the common women's restroom even after Complainant made clear that she no longer agreed with the initial plan restricting her to the executive bathroom facility, and S3 engaged in demeaning behavior toward her by refusing to refer to her correct name and gender.

---

8. In this case, the Agency's restroom policy also deprived Complainant of the use of common locker and shower facilities that non-transgender employees could use, which also constituted a material employment disadvantage for Complainant.

9. *Cf. John Doe, et al. v. Regional School Unit*, 86 A.3d 600 (Maine 2014) (where it has been clearly established that a student's psychological well-being and educational success depend upon being permitted to use the communal bathroom consistent with her gender identity, denying access to the appropriate bathroom constitutes sexual orientation discrimination in violation of the Maine Human Rights Act); *Mathis v. Fountain-Fort Carson School District 8*, Colo. Dep't of Regulatory Agencies, Div. of Civil Rights, Charge No. P20130034X, Determination available at http:// www .transgenderlegal.org/media/uploads/doc529.pdf (June 18, 2013) (restroom restriction placed on female transgender student created "an exclusionary environment which tended to ostracize the [student]"); Statement of Interest of the United States in *Tooley v. Van Buren Public Schools*, No. 2:14-cv-13466 (E.D. Mich. Feb. 20, 2015) (citing *Doe* and *Mathis*).

[In this section of its opinion, the EEOC concludes that "[p]ersistent failure to use the employee's correct name and pronoun may constitute unlawful, sex-based harassment if such conduct is either severe or pervasive enough to create a hostile work environment when 'judged from the perspective of a reasonable person in the employee's position." The Commission concluded that "S3's actions and demeanor made clear that S3's use of a male name and male pronouns in referring to Complainant was not accidental, but instead was intended to humiliate and ridicule Complainant. As such, S3's repeated and intentional conduct was offensive and demeaning to Complainant and would have been so to a reasonable person in Complainant's position." Moreover, because "S3's actions must be considered in the context of the Agency's actions related to Complainant's restroom access[,]" the Commission ruled that "Complainant established that she was subjected to a level of severe or pervasive sex-based harassment that meets the Title VII standard for liability." This aspect of the Commission's analysis is primarily addressed in Chapter 14, *infra* at p. 1081.]

Conclusion

Consequently, based on a thorough review of the record and the contentions on appeal, including those not specifically addressed herein, the Commission REVERSES the Agency's final decision. We REMAND this matter to the Agency to take remedial actions in accordance with this decision and the ORDER below.

. . . .

FOR THE COMMISSION:

Bernadette B. Wilson

Acting Executive Officer

Executive Secretariat

April 1, 2015

Discussion

1. Note that the EEOC concludes that Tamara Lusardi "is" a woman and so must have the same access to work facilities as other women employees. Presumably the EEOC is asserting that Ms. Lusardi is a woman within the meaning of Title VII sex discrimination doctrine. What basis might there be for concluding that under this particular statute transgender women are (legally) "women"? Those opposed to allowing transgender women access to women-only spaces such as communal ("common") restrooms strongly contest this conclusion and insist that people simply *are* (with the possible exception of certain people with intersex conditions, *see* Chapter 2, *supra*) members of the sex they were assigned at birth; many of them hold this view regardless of any transition-related surgeries a person may have had.

2. Why do you suppose that the supervisors and co-workers to whose conduct Ms. Lusardi objected treated her that way? Why should we understand sex

discrimination laws either to insist that transgender employees be treated as members of the sex consistent with their gender identity or not to require that?

3. Suppose the agency had defended its policy excluding trans women from common women's restrooms on the ground that it was not discriminating on the basis of gender identity, but simply using genitalia as the basis for allocating access to mens' and women's restrooms. Would that be sex discrimination under the reasoning of *Bostock v. Clayton County, Georgia*, 140 S. Ct. 1731 (2020), Section D, *supra*? Would having any separate restrooms limited to women or to me be sex discrimination on *Bostock*'s reasoning?

Chapter 6

Military Service

Although it is common to speak of "military service," one should not overlook that U.S. servicemembers are in fact employees of the federal government. The United States Department of Defense is often said to be the largest employer in the world, with *Forbes* reporting it having some 3.2 million employees in 2015. This includes civilian employees as well as members of the armed forces, but active duty servicemembers together with reservists account for more than 2.1 million of the DOD workforce as of 2019. But the armed forces are not just massive employers. As Kenneth Karst has argued,

> [w]hat is special about the [U.S. armed] forces is their position in American life. When they deny or seriously restrict the eligibility of a group of Americans for service, they do not merely impair opportunities for training or leadership. Much more is at stake, both for the people excluded and for the nation. The individual is denied equal citizenship, and the nation is denied a vital support for democracy.

Kenneth L. Karst, *The Pursuit of Manhood and the Desegregation of the Armed Forces*, 38 UCLA L. REV. 499, 501 (1991).

And make no mistake about it. The armed forces have a long history of discrimination. Writing in the early 1990s, Professor Karst recounted some of that history:

> Not until the Korean War did black Americans begin to take their rightful place in the services. Even today, women are excluded from combat positions, and thus denied the opportunities that are most valuable as they seek promotion to leadership. The services also purport to exclude gay men and lesbians altogether. Both the segregation of women into non-combat positions and the exclusion of gay and lesbian servicemembers are under challenge in the halls of Congress and in federal courts across the land. . . . [T]hese exclusions are inconsistent with the fourteenth amendment's principle of equal national citizenship.

Id. at 500. Even at that time, though unremarked upon by Karst, the U.S. armed forces also excluded service by people known or discovered to be transgender. It did so through multiple regulations regulating physical and psychological fitness for service. Like other exclusions of socially disfavored groups, trans people were denied the opportunities afforded by military service despite their ability to achieve at high levels.

Although this exclusion started to phase out in the last days of the Obama administration, Donald J. Trump rather unilaterally dictated a reversal of the Obama era reforms, starting with a startling announcement via tweet approximately six months into his term as President. This section details some of the history of the exclusion of trans people from U.S. military service and the challenges to the attempted restoration of that ban under the Trump administration, challenges that were ongoing as of the writing of this casebook. It starts with background on the pre-Obama-administration regulation and a critique thereof.

The Invisible Army: Why the Military Needs to Rescind Its Ban on Transgender Service Members[*]
Allison Ross

I. Introduction

. . . Although the military now allows gay, lesbian, and bisexual persons to serve openly, members of the transgender community are still categorically barred from service because of medical and psychological regulations. The military must rescind its ban on transgender persons from serving and recognize that there is nothing that makes this group inherently or uniformly unfit for the military.

Part II of this Note gives necessary background information to support the main argument. It explains the gender binary and what it means to be a transgender person, and then details the current military policies that exclude transgender persons from serving.

Part III argues that the military should rescind its categorical ban because transgender persons are not per se incapable of serving in the military. Section A argues that the current medical regulations are unwarranted because transgender persons are not uniformly incapable of or unfit for military service, and thus the regulations' blanket exclusions are arbitrary. Further undermining the regulations, the type of medical care that transgender service members would require is analogous to the kind of medical care that the military already provides for its female, pregnant, and diabetic service members. Section B argues that the military should remove Gender Identity Disorder ("GID") as a disqualifying condition because of the controversies over whether it is an actual mental illness and because the American Psychiatric Association changed the name of the diagnosis from GID to gender dysphoria to reflect a less pathologized and less "mentally disordered" medical condition.

Part IV presents and counters objections to allowing transgender persons to serve in the military. First, it attacks the unit cohesion argument by looking at the U.S. military's history with racial integration and the repeal of Don't Ask, Don't Tell; it

---

[*] Excerpted from Allison Ross, *The Invisible Army: Why the Military Needs to Rescind Its Ban on Transgender Service Members*, 23 S. Cal. Interdisc. L.J. 185 (2014). Reprinted with permission of the Southern California Interdisciplinary Law Journal.

describes other nations' experiences with transgender service members to illustrate that unit cohesion will not suffer; and it suggests that disclosure of gender identity might actually improve unit cohesion. Part IV further argues that transgender service will not be costly to the military. Finally, it argues that any "implementation problems" that might arise if transgender service members are allowed to serve are not overly problematic and could be easily solved by relying on the policies toward and regulations of transgender service members in other countries. Finally, the Conclusion briefly addresses how repeal might occur in practice.

II. Background

. . . .

C. Current Military Policy

Issues for transgender persons may arise at enlistment, during service, and in the inactive reserve. This Section addresses each in turn.

1. Enlistment

In order to join the military, potential service members must go through both a physical and a psychological examination, either of which may disqualify a transgender prospective service member. Each branch of the military has its own medical disqualifications. The Army's Standards of Medical Fitness, which is representative of the other branches' standards, lists numerous ways in which a current or prospective service member may be medically disqualified, including sex-reassignment surgery and identification as a transgender person. Although some medical conditions may be waived, scholars have been unable to find a circumstance in which a transgender service member received a waiver.

Transgender persons who have undergone sex-reassignment surgery are disqualified under a medical regulation during the physical exam. Transmen who have had sex-reassignment surgery may be excluded for "major abnormalities or defects of the genitalia" and change of sex. Transwomen who have had sex-reassignment surgery may be excluded for penis amputation, "major abnormalities or defects of the genitalia," and change of sex.

Transgender persons who have not had sex-reassignment surgery but who identify as transgender are disqualified under the psychological examination. Specifically, transgender persons may be disqualified for a long list of disorders, including transvestism, transsexualism, psychosexual conditions, and GID.

Pursuant to the Standards of Medical Fitness, after each evaluation, the service member is either marked "medically acceptable" or "medically unacceptable." Being "medically unacceptable" is a cause for rejection from service.

2. During Service

Transgender service members who wish to remain in the military must "pass" as their biological sex, which means they cannot take hormones or pursue sex-reassignment surgeries, and they must conceal their gender identities and transgenderism. Service members who wish to transition during service may be discharged for an enlistment violation. Transgender service members could also be discharged for cross-dressing even though dressing consistently with their gender identities is pivotal to their gender expressions and transition processes.

The military does not currently provide any support for transitioning service members. Because the military will not provide health care for transitioning and because there is limited doctor-patient confidentiality within the military, some transgender service members try to receive medical assistance with their transition from civilian medical practitioners. The military regularly schedules physical exams, so if a transitioning service member has sex-reassignment surgery or starts taking hormones secretly, the changes will likely become known during the exam. Moreover, some branches of the military require service members to report any medical care obtained from civilian providers, so failure to disclose could lead to disciplinary action as well as potential discharge. Transgender service members who wish to transition during service could therefore face disciplinary penalties as well as a potential discharge, which may or may not be honorable.

3. Members of Inactive Reserve

Recalled members of the inactive reserve are subject to the same medical examinations that active service members undergo at enlistment and on a yearly basis. Being recalled to active duty poses at least three potential problems for transgender service members. First, service members may have to halt the transition process. Ceasing hormone therapy could lead to discomfort and an increased risk for certain diseases or conditions. Second, because returning service members must take a physical exam, transitioning or post-transitioned service members could be medically disqualified upon their examination. Third, service members who identify as transgender but who have not begun hormone therapy or sex-reassignment surgery could be disqualified under the psychological regulation as administratively unfit. Essentially, recalled transgender service members must choose between seeking discharge from the military in order to continue their transitions and hiding a central part of their identities in order to go back into service.

III. The Case for Rescinding the Ban on Transgender Military Service

This Part argues that transgender service members should not be categorically barred from serving in the military. Section A exposes the flaws in the medical regulations that bar transgender service members by looking at examples of successful, high-achieving, transgender military service members and demonstrating that current military medical provisions for cisgender service members could be easily adapted to deal with transgender service members' medical needs. Section B argues that the military should rescind its ban on persons diagnosed with GID. Subsection 1 explores the controversy over this ostensible disorder to contend that a diagnosis should not uniformly disqualify every transgender person who exhibits its symptoms. Subsection 2 examines the American Psychiatric Association's decision to change the diagnosis from GID to gender dysphoria and suggests that this diagnostic change should prompt a reevaluation of the transgender exclusion in favor of removing the service bar.

A. Medical Regulations

1. Being Transgender Does Not Per Se Affect Service Capability

The following case study of S.C., a transgender pilot, illustrates several key points that should prompt the military to rescind its ban on transgender persons. First, despite the fact that she was a transgender person, S.C. had a successful military career, logging thousands of practice and combat hours. S.C. was capable of doing her job, regardless of her gender identity. Second, after her surgery, S.C. was able to return to work as a pilot without any limiting medical complications. This example suggests that transgenderism does not make a person per se unfit for the military and that post-transition soldiers can successfully reintegrate into the military. Transgender persons who have had sex-reassignment surgery should not be disqualified solely on that basis. Third, S.C. experienced distress with her GID until she was able to disclose her gender identity and undergo surgery to realign her body with that identity. After this disclosure and her sex-reassignment surgery, she resumed her military position with no complications. Hence, disclosure of one's identity as a transgender person might lead to better, more capable military service. . . . .

The military's ban on transgender service members is counterproductive; in many cases, the transgender service member is academically more qualified than a non-transgender service member, and these case studies vividly illustrate that transgender service members can have successful and high-achieving careers. It is detrimental to military strength to turn away qualified, willing, and educated service members because of their gender identities or because they have had sex-reassignment surgeries.

2. Utilizing Current Military Medical Policies for Transgender Medical Needs

Disqualifying transgender service members because of medical concerns is inconsistent with how the military generally addresses other medical conditions and diagnoses. As an initial matter, many transgender persons do not need constant treatment, nor do all transgender persons want sex-reassignment surgery. However, if transgender persons do wish to receive surgery or treatment, their medical needs could be addressed consistently with existing military medical policies. The military's policies toward oral contraceptives, pregnant servicewomen, and diabetics represent three ways that the military could address transgender service members' medical needs without having to entirely ban their service.

First, the military currently allows women to regularly take hormones, in the form of oral contraceptives, during military service. According to one study, roughly thirty-four percent of women in the military used contraceptives. . . . Of the approximately 214,000 women in the military, that means about 72,000 women take contraceptives.

Because the military allows women to take hormones, it should also allow transgender service members, many of whom take hormones as part of their transitions or in lieu of sex-reassignment surgeries, to do the same. Although there is no official data on the number of transgender persons who are currently in the military, it is certainly a significantly smaller number than the number of women in the military taking oral contraceptives. It would not be overly burdensome or costly for the military to allow transgender persons to take hormones. Furthermore, because women are allowed to take hormones and this has not affected their ability to serve, there is no reason to assume that allowing transgender service members to take hormones will impact their abilities to serve. Finally, the military would not have to change its policy drastically for transgender service members. Both transmen and transwomen can take their transition hormones by pill. Indeed, most transwomen take their hormones by pill. Because the military allows cisgender women to take hormones orally, the military should also allow transmen and transwomen to take hormones orally.

The military's provisions for diabetics offer another alternative as to how the military could treat transgender service members who take hormones. In addition to its provisions on birth control, the military also makes provisions for diabetic service members who require insulin injections. In the Army, for example, diabetic service members who take insulin cannot be deployed to areas where insulin cannot be stored or where "appropriate medical support cannot be reasonably assured." . . . .

As with diabetics who require insulin, the military could require that transgender persons who take hormones only be deployed to areas where the hormones could be properly stored or where appropriate medical care can be assured. If the military allows diabetics to receive insulin injections several times a day, the military could also allow transgender persons to receive their hormones by injection.

Finally, the military's provisions on leaves of absence for pregnant women could address the needs of transgender service members who require time off for sex-reassignment surgery. Although the military formerly considered pregnancy and motherhood incompatible with military service, there are now regulations in place that allow pregnant women to continue serving during and after their pregnancy. Approximately fifty-eight percent of hospitalizations among active-duty women are for pregnancy. Current policies stress that pregnancy by itself should not restrict tasks normally assigned to servicewomen. It is the service woman's responsibility to try and plan pregnancies to fit in with her military duties. Studies have shown that pregnant military women lose no more time from work than military men, who might lose time from service because of injuries or for disciplinary reasons.

These provisions demonstrate ways in which the military could make similar accommodations for transgender service members who require surgeries. First, like pregnancy, transgenderism by itself should not disqualify a person from service, nor should it restrict service members to certain types of tasks. . . . Second, transgender service members who wish to transition mid-service could be required to plan their transition so as not to conflict with important military duties, just as pregnant servicewomen must try and plan pregnancies responsibly. Finally, recovery from sex-reassignment surgery takes about six weeks, which is the same amount of time given to women in the military for postpartum care. Admittedly, transgender persons often undergo more than one surgery in order to complete their transition. However, if women are allowed to have multiple pregnancies and take time off for each recovery, transgender persons should similarly be allowed to undergo surgeries and take the required time off to recover for each one.

Because the military already makes provisions for service members who take hormones, take insulin, or become pregnant, the military could clearly make similar provisions for transgender service members who take hormones or who require surgery to complete their transitions. Being diabetic, taking birth control, and becoming pregnant do not bar one from service because none of those conditions are per se incapacitating. Nor should being transgender bar one from service. As one author aptly summarizes, "[g]iven the commonality of medical issues throughout a career, and the rarity of [transgender persons], [a transgender service member wishing to transition] is unlikely to place a significant burden on the force, especially since the timing of sex-reassignment surgery can be scheduled to have minimal impact on readiness." Instead of banning an entire group of service members because of potentially non-existing complications from hormone treatment or sex-reassignment surgery, the military should recognize that transgender persons are generally as fit for service as any other service members and rescind the medical bans. In the place of the medical bans, the military can adopt medical provisions—similar to those for diabetics, pregnant women, and women who take contraceptive hormones—that would ensure transgender service members receive adequate medical support.

B. Psychological Regulations

Transgender service members who are not disqualified by the medical regulations discussed in Part A can also be disqualified if they are diagnosed with GID, which the military considers a mental disorder.

The *Diagnostic and Statistical Manual* . . . , published by the American Psychiatric Association, defines the criteria for diagnosing and classifying mental disorders. GID is the psychiatric diagnosis for transgender persons in the DSM-IV. The military, though not bound to the DSM, relies on it and currently lists GID as a disqualifying psychiatric condition. In May 2013, the newest edition of the DSM, DSM-V, changed the diagnosis from GID to gender dysphoria. The change is meant to depathologize the diagnosis. It remains unclear whether or how the military will respond to the new DSM. However, this diagnostic change provides the military with an impetus to modify its policies on transgender service members. Rather than simply update the psychological regulations to reflect the new diagnosis, the military could remove the diagnosis as a disqualifying condition. Although this change would not completely rescind the transgender ban, it would be an important step to fully integrated military service.

Like transgender persons who seek sex-reassignment surgery or hormone therapy, persons who are diagnosed with GID are not inherently unfit for military service. In light of the debate over whether GID is properly considered a mental illness and the changes to the DSM — which make the diagnosis of gender dysphoria less of a mental disorder and more of a "temporary mental state" — the military should recognize that transgender persons are capable of successful military service and rescind the categorical ban on persons diagnosed with GID.

. . . .

IV. Other Objections to Transgender Service

This Part addresses other arguments in opposition to transgender military service. First, Section A responds to the position that unit cohesion will suffer if transgender persons are allowed to openly serve. Section B refutes the idea that transgender inclusion poses significant financial costs for the military. Finally, Section C addresses post-integration implementation concerns that some opponents have about transgender military service.

A. Unit Cohesion

One objection to transgender military service is that unit cohesion will suffer. This objection is analyzed under three subsections. Subsection 1 summarizes the unit cohesion argument, then investigates the repeal of Don't Ask, Don't Tell and the racial integration of the military, and concludes that this unit cohesion argument is implausible. Subsection 2 evaluates a number of countries with openly transgender service members to reject unit cohesion as an adequate basis for categorical transgender exclusion. Subsection 3 establishes that open transgender service members might improve, rather than harm, unit cohesion.

1. Inclusion of Openly Transgender Service Members Will Not Harm Unit Cohesion

One prominent argument against transgender inclusion in the military is that unit cohesion, defined as "the bonds of trust among individual service members," will suffer if transgender people are allowed to serve. . . . This argument was first advanced to support the Army's racial segregation; it was then resurrected to prevent women, and later, openly lesbian, gay, and bisexual people from serving. For each of these restrictions, this argument was undermined and the military ultimately reversed its initial position.

. . . . It will likely prove similarly false for gender identity and transgender service members.

2. Other Countries Allow Open Service for Transgender Persons

The experiences of other countries that accept transgender service members further suggests that unit cohesion offers an inadequate basis for the U.S. military's categorical exclusion. Currently, at least thirteen countries allow transgender persons to serve openly in the military including the United Kingdom, Canada, Israel, Thailand, the Czech Republic, Spain, Australia, Norway, Uruguay, and New Zealand. Additionally, Belgium, the Netherlands, and Brazil allow service under certain restrictions. In comparison, at the time Don't Ask, Don't Tell was repealed, approximately twenty-five countries allowed gays and lesbians to serve openly in the military. Their experiences supported the repeal of Don't Ask, Don't Tell. Likewise, other countries' recent experiences in successfully integrating their militaries to include transgender persons obligates the U.S. military to reconsider, and repeal, its ban on transgender service members.

Of the countries that allow transgender service members, none have reversed that decision. Although few reports discuss the impact of transgender service members on the military as a whole, either positive or negative, at least one study found that military performance has not been negatively affected by their inclusion. This Canadian study found that Canada's "decision to lift its [ban on gay, lesbian, and transgender service members] had no impact on military performance, readiness, cohesion, or morale." This study is supported by a 1995 announcement from the Human Rights Policy Bureau of the Canadian Department of National Defense, which reported that despite the anxiety about lifting the gay ban, the military had not been negatively affected. Although the authors refer to the exclusion as the "gay ban," the ban prohibited gay, lesbian, and transgender service members. Once this ban was lifted, the Canadian military enacted policies and practices "that were meant to preserve military effectiveness and simultaneously decrease the fear and anxiety of soldiers who self-identify as sexual minorities." The Canadian military "places paramount importance on getting the job done and respecting the chain of command, regardless of one's attitude concerning homosexuality." In addition, the Canadian military emphasized the distinction between beliefs and behavior: personal feelings were respected, but soldiers were expected to "put personal feelings aside to accomplish military objectives and to uphold the law." Therefore, instead of discriminating against capable service members because of their gender identities, the U.S. military should show the same support for transgender persons as the Canadian military does.

. . . .

C. Post-Integration Implementation

This Section will briefly consider some of the "implementation problems" that might arise if transgender persons were allowed to openly serve in the military. Implementation problems raised by opponents of transgendered military service include the assignment of jobs that the transgender service member can occupy while transitioning and what uniforms the transitioning or transitioned service member should wear.

The U.S. military could look to other countries' militaries to address these implementation concerns. For example, the U.S. military should not be concerned that transitioning service members will be unable to hold a service-related job during the [entirety] of their transition processes. In the United Kingdom, a transgender service member was given a desk job during his transition so that he could continue serving. The United Kingdom Army treats transgenderism as a long-term medical condition and makes allowances for service during a service member's transition. The United States could mirror this policy and permit transitioning service members to occupy temporary, low-risk jobs that allow them to take time off for the required surgeries.

Once they are fully recovered, they could switch from their interim jobs to their usual positions in the military. Allowing service members time to transition and undergo sex-reassignment surgeries affects military readiness no differently than allowing non-transgender service members to receive medical care for injuries sustained in battle, pregnancy-related interruptions of service, or corrective surgeries like laser eye-surgery, which the military regularly provides free of charge.

The assignment of uniforms to transgendered service members might pose a challenge because Articles 133 and 134 in the Uniform Code of Military Justice ("UCMJ") have been interpreted to restrict things like cross-dressing and other gender non-conforming behaviors. To provide uniforms to transgendered service members, the UCMJ must be interpreted to hold that transgender persons who wear the uniforms of their lived genders are not cross-dressing. The U.S. military can base its uniform policy on Canada's, in which transgender service members wear the uniforms of their lived genders. The United States should also treat transgender service members according to their lived genders and allow them to wear gender-appropriate uniforms.

. . . .

Discussion

1. Is Ms. Ross's analogy between oral hormone treatments for transgender persons and oral contraceptives for women persuasive? Is there anything more you would want to know about either before reaching a conclusion?

2. Is her analogy between injected hormones for transgender persons and insulin for people with diabetes persuasive?

3. Is the analogy between pregnancies and genital reconstruction surgeries persuasive?

4. Ought assessments of the U.S. military's policy toward transgender service members take account of the experiences of other nations' armed forces?

Elimination of the Transgender Military Servicemember Ban Under the Obama Administration and Reinstatement by Donald Trump

The path toward eliminating the exclusion of people from military service because they are transgender differs from how the exclusion of people from military service because they are lesbigay was repealed. Like the transgender ban, the LGB ban had been embodied in military regulations. However, following Bill Clinton's 1992 campaign promise to eliminate the LGB ban, Congress reacted by enshrining that ban in federal legislation, which Clinton acquiesced to and signed in 1993. Accordingly, administrative reform was not an option with respect to the sexual orientation ban.

After much (mostly unsuccessful) litigation in the lower federal courts seeking to overturn the ban on constitutional grounds, it was eventually eliminated by federal legislation—the Don't Ask Don't Tell Repeal Act of 2010, which President Obama signed into law in December 2010. P.L. 111-321, 124 Stat. 3515–3517 (2010). The Act specified a process for effectuating repeal, which involved a determination by the President, the Secretary of Defense, and the Chairman of the Joint Chiefs of Staff after completion of a comprehensive review (already underway) by the Department of Defense that implementing the repeal would be "consistent with the standards of military readiness, military effectiveness, unit cohesion, and recruiting and retention of the Armed Forces." The certification was transmitted to Congress in July 2011, and the statutory ban was terminated in September 2011.

The ban on transgender service was never codified in statute, so the Obama administration was able to address it regulatorily without need of congressional action. Under that administration, the armed forces eliminated the categorical regulatory ban on service by transgender persons, convened a working group to consider further change, and commissioned a study by an independent nonprofit research institution. After receiving the study and the working group's unanimous conclusion in support of allowing transgender persons to serve in the armed forces, the Department moved toward allowing open service by transgender people, with full reform of the relevant regulations to be adopted by July 1, 2017.

On June 30, 2017, Donald Trump's then-Secretary of Defense James Mattis announced that the military was conducting further study of service by transgender persons and that accession would be deferred to January 1, 2018.

Less than a month later, Trump announced by tweet that transgender people would *not* be allowed to serve in the armed forces "in any capacity." Lawsuits challenging this apparently unilateral conclusion of the country's Commander-in-Chief quickly followed, and the policy itself underwent some refinement as the administration toiled to defend the legality of this latest military discrimination. These cases quickly granted preliminary injunctions to the plaintiffs, and the initial opinion of the first court to do so appears next.

Reading Guide for Doe 1 v. Trump *(preliminary injunction)*

1. For a federal court to have subject matter jurisdiction over a plaintiff's suit, the suit must constitute a "case" or "controversy" within the meaning of Article III of the Constitution. That requires that plaintiffs have suffered or imminently will suffer an "injury in fact" fairly traceable to the defendants' challenged conduct that would likely be redressable by a favorable court ruling. *See, e.g., Lujan v. Defenders of Wildlife*, 504 U.S. 555 (1992).

The plaintiffs in this case challenged three aspects of the ban on military service by transgender people first announced by Donald Trump via tweet. What are they? Which two does the court hold they have standing to challenge? What two injuries does the court accept as sufficient for standing? For what reasons did the defendants argue the plaintiffs lacked standing? What reasons does the court give for rejecting the defense position? Why does the court hold that the plaintiffs lack standing to challenge the third aspect of the Trump ban?

2. In analyzing whether the plaintiffs are likely to succeed on the merits of their claim that the ban unconstitutionally discriminates against them, how does the court first frame the kind of discrimination at issue? What level of judicial scrutiny of the plaintiffs' discrimination claim does the court accordingly adopt, and based on what factors? How does the court also frame the discrimination in the alternative, why does it conclude that the policy includes that kind of discrimination, and what level of scrutiny does the court hold applies on that basis?

3. In setting the level of scrutiny, and again in applying it to the challenged policy, the court addresses whether, how much, and what kind of deference to extend to the to the defendants in reviewing the policy. What deference does it conclude is or is not appropriate?

4. The court concludes that the Trump policy cannot survive constitutional scrutiny. It basically reasons that the policy does not sufficiently closely fit its ostensible justifications to pass the fit prong of the relevant equal protection scrutiny—why not? The court also may suggest that the alleged governmental interests might not be sufficient to pass the purpose prong. In ruling that the policy likely fails constitutional scrutiny, what "circumstances" does the court think are relevant?

5. To secure a preliminary injunction based on a likely constitutional violation, plaintiffs must establish that they would face irreparable injury. What injury or injuries does the court conclude these plaintiffs have adequately alleged? In addition, plaintiffs must show that the balance of hardships (to the plaintiffs of denying relief versus to the defendants of granting relief) favors them. Why does the court conclude the plaintiffs have shown that as well?

Doe 1 v. Trump

275 F. Supp. 3d 167 (2017) [*vacated*, Doe 2 v. Shanahan,
755 Fed. Appx. 19 (D.C. Cir. 2019)]

[The plaintiffs here were represented by private counsel, the National Center for Lesbian Rights, and GLBTQ Legal Advocates & Defenders (GLAD).]

Memorandum Opinion

COLLEEN KOLLAR-KOTELLY, United States District Judge

On July 26, 2017, President Donald J. Trump issued a statement via Twitter announcing that "the United States Government will not accept or allow transgender individuals to serve in any capacity in the U.S. Military." A formal Presidential Memorandum followed on August 25, 2017. Before the Presidential Memorandum, the Department of Defense had announced that openly transgender individuals would be allowed to enlist in the military, effective January 1, 2018, and had prohibited the discharge of service members based solely on their gender identities. The Presidential Memorandum reversed these policies. First, the Memorandum indefinitely extends a prohibition against transgender individuals entering the military, a process formally referred to as "accession" (the "Accession Directive"). Second, the Memorandum requires the military to authorize, by no later than March 23, 2018, the discharge of transgender service members (the "Retention Directive").

The Department of Defense is required to submit a plan implementing the directives of the Presidential Memorandum by February 21, 2018. On September 14, 2017, Secretary of Defense James Mattis promulgated Interim Guidance establishing Department of Defense policy toward transgender service members until the directives of the Presidential Memorandum take effect. Pursuant to the Presidential Memorandum and the Interim Guidance, the protections afforded to transgender service members against discharge lapse early next year.

. . . .

[The defendants' standing] arguments, while perhaps compelling in the abstract, wither away under scrutiny. The Memorandum unequivocally directs the military to prohibit indefinitely the accession of transgender individuals and to authorize their discharge. This decision has already been made. These directives must be executed by a date certain, and there is no reason to believe that they will not be executed. Plaintiffs have established that they will be injured by these directives, due both to the inherent inequality they impose, and the risk of discharge and denial of accession that they engender. Further delay would only serve to harm the Plaintiffs. Given these circumstances, the Court is in a position to preliminarily adjudicate the propriety of these directives, and it does so here.

The Court holds that Plaintiffs are likely to succeed on their Fifth Amendment claim. As a form of government action that classifies people based on their gender identity, and disfavors a class of historically persecuted and politically powerless individuals, the President's directives are subject to a fairly searching form of scrutiny. Plaintiffs claim that the President's directives cannot survive such scrutiny because they are not genuinely based on legitimate concerns regarding military effectiveness or budget constraints, but are instead driven by a desire to express disapproval of transgender people generally. The Court finds that a number of factors—including the sheer breadth of the exclusion ordered by the directives, the unusual circumstances surrounding the President's announcement of them, the fact that the reasons given for them do not appear to be supported by any facts, and the recent rejection of those reasons by the military itself—strongly suggest that Plaintiffs' Fifth Amendment claim is meritorious.

. . .

I. Background
A. The Military's Policy Toward Transgender Service
1. Military Policy Prior to 2014

[The court here recounts how military regulations prior to 2014 categorically forbade transgender persons from joining the military (accession regulations) and authorized the termination of military service by transgender persons (retention regulations) on the basis of "Sexual Gender and Identity Disorders, including Sexual Dysfunctions and Paraphilias."]

2. August 2014 Regulation and July 28, 2015 Memorandum

[The court here recounts how the DoD under the Obama administration issued a new regulation, DODI 1332.18, Disability Evaluation System (DES), in August 2014 eliminating the armed forces-wide ban on retention of openly transgender persons and directing each branch to determine whether that and other medical condition-based retention bans were justified. Then, on July 28, 2015, Secretary of Defense Ash Carter issued a memorandum to the secretaries of the military departments directing that as of July 13, 2015, no servicemember would be "separated or denied reenlistment or continuation of active or reserve service on the basis of their gender identity, without the personal approval of the Under Secretary of Defense for Personnel and Readiness." The memo also ordered the Undersecretary of Defense for Personnel and Readiness to "chair a working group composed of senior representatives from each of the Military Departments, Joint Staff, and relevant components from the Office of the Secretary of Defense to formulate policy options for the DoD regarding the military service of transgender Service members."]

3. The Working Group and the RAND Report

The working group convened by the Undersecretary consisted of senior uniformed officers and senior civilian officers from each department of the military. The Working Group sought to identify any possible issues related to open military service of transgender individuals. It considered a broad range of information provided by senior military personnel, various types of experts, health insurance companies, civilian employers, transgender service members themselves, and representatives from the militaries of other nations who allow open service by transgender people. Finally, the Working Group commissioned the RAND Corporation's National Defense Research Institute to conduct a study on the impact of permitting transgender service members to serve openly. RAND is a nonprofit research institution that provides research and analysis to the Armed Services.

The RAND Corporation subsequently issued a 91-page report entitled "Assessing the Implications of Allowing Transgender Personnel to Serve Openly." The RAND Report found no evidence that allowing transgender individuals to serve would have any effect on "unit cohesion," and concluded that any related costs or impacts on readiness would be "exceedingly small," "marginal" or "negligible." The RAND Report also found that "[i]n no case" where foreign militaries have allowed transgender individuals to serve "was there any evidence of an effect on the operational effectiveness, operational readiness, or cohesion of the force."

Based on all of the information it collected, the Working Group unanimously concluded that transgender people should be allowed to serve openly in the military. Not only did the group conclude that allowing transgender people to serve would not significantly affect military readiness or costs, it found that prohibiting transgender people from serving undermines military effectiveness and readiness because it excludes qualified individuals on a basis that has no relevance to one's fitness to serve, and creates unexpected vacancies requiring expensive and time-consuming recruitment and training of replacements.[2]

The Working Group communicated its conclusion to the Secretary of Defense, along with detailed recommendations for policies and procedures for open transgender service.

4. June 30, 2016 Directive-Type Memorandum 16-005

On June 30, 2016, the Secretary of Defense Ash Carter issued a Directive-type Memorandum ("DTM") establishing a policy, assigning responsibilities, and prescribing procedures for "the retention, accession, separation, in-service transition and medical coverage for transgender personnel serving in the Military Services." The DTM took effect immediately. In the DTM, the Secretary of Defense stated his conclusion that open service by transgender Americans was "consistent with military readiness and with strength through diversity." Accordingly, the DTM stated that it was the policy of the Department of Defense that "service in the United States military should be open to all who can meet the rigorous standards for military service and readiness" and that, "consistent with the policies and procedures set forth in [the DTM], transgender individuals shall be allowed to serve in the military."

Retention

The DTM. . . . stated that "[e]ffective immediately, no otherwise qualified Service member may be involuntarily separated, discharged or denied reenlistment or continuation of service, solely on the basis of their gender identity," or on their "expressed intent to transition genders." The DTM stated that "Transgender Service members will be subject to the same standards as any other Service member of the

---

2. *See generally* . . . Fanning Decl. ¶¶ 25–26 ("At the conclusion of its discussion and analysis, the members of the Working Group did not identify any basis for a blanket prohibition on open military service of transgender people. . . . The Working Group communicated its conclusions to the Secretary of Defense, including that permitting transgender people to serve openly in the United States military would not pose any significant costs or risks to readiness, unit cohesion, morale, or good order and discipline."); Mabus Decl. ¶ 21 (stating that "all members of the Working Group . . . expressed their agreement that transgender people should be permitted to serve openly in the United States Armed Forces" and that "President Trump's stated rationales for reversing the policy and banning military service by transgender people make no sense," "have no basis in fact and are refuted by the comprehensive analysis of relevant data and information that was carefully, thoroughly, and deliberately conducted by the Working Group") . . . .

same gender; they may be separated, discharged, or denied reenlistment or continuation of service under existing processes and basis, but not due solely to their gender identity or an expressed intent to transition genders."

Accession

With respect to accession procedures, the DTM stated that by no later than July 1, 2017, DODI 6130.03 would be updated to allow for the accession of (i) individuals with gender dysphoria, (ii) individuals that have received medical treatment for gender transition, and (iii) individuals that have undergone sex reassignment surgeries. The policies and procedures generally provided that these conditions would be disqualifying unless the acceding service member was medically stable in their chosen gender for at least 18 months. The DTM also provided that, effective October 1, 2016, the Department of Defense would "implement a construct by which transgender Service members may transition gender while serving."

Equal Opportunity

Finally, the DTM stated that it is "the Department's position, consistent with the U.S. Attorney General's opinion, that discrimination based on gender identity is a form of sex discrimination."

5. June 30, 2016 Remarks by Secretary of Defense Ash Carter

On June 30, 2016, then-Secretary of Defense Ash Carter announced from the Pentagon briefing room that "we are ending the ban on transgender Americans in the United States military." . . .

Secretary Carter gave three reasons for the Department's decision. First, he stated that "the Defense Department and the military need to avail ourselves of all talent possible in order to remain what we are now—the finest fighting force the world has ever known." He added that "[w]e invest hundreds of thousands of dollars to train and develop each individual, and we want to take the opportunity to retain people whose talent we've invested in and who have proven themselves." Second, he stated that "the reality is that we have transgender service members serving in uniform today," and they and their commanders need "clearer and more consistent guidance than is provided by current policies." And third, he stated that, as a matter of principle, "Americans who want to serve and can meet our standards should be afforded the opportunity to come to do so."

. . . .

8. July 26, 2017 Statement by President Donald J. Trump

On July 26, 2017, President Donald J. Trump issued a statement via Twitter, in which he announced that[3]

---

3. The full text reads: "After consultation with my Generals and military experts, please be advised that the United States Government will not accept or allow Transgender individuals to serve in any capacity in the U.S. Military. Our military must be focused on decisive and overwhelming victory and cannot be burdened with the tremendous medical costs and dis-

9. August 25, 2017 Presidential Memorandum

On August 25, 2017, President Trump issued a memorandum entitled "Presidential Memorandum for the Secretary of Defense and the Secretary of Homeland Security." The memorandum. . . . stated that "the previous Administration failed to identify a sufficient basis to conclude that terminating the Departments' longstanding policy and practice would not hinder military effectiveness and lethality, disrupt unit cohesion, or tax military resources, and there remain meaningful concerns that further study is needed to ensure that continued implementation of last year's policy change would not have those negative effects."

The memorandum has two operative sections, one general, and the other more specific. Section 1(b) directs "the Secretary of Defense, and the Secretary of Homeland Security with respect to the U.S. Coast Guard, to return to the longstanding policy and practice on military service by transgender individuals that was in place prior to June 2016 until such time as a sufficient basis exists upon which to conclude that terminating that policy and practice would not have the negative effects discussed above." [The] memorandum defines the pre-June 2016 policy as one under which the military "generally prohibited openly transgender individuals from accession into the United States military and authorized the discharge of such individuals." The directive set forth in section 1(b) takes effect on March 23, 2018. The memorandum provides that the "Secretary of Defense, after consulting with the Secretary of Homeland Security, may advise [the President] at any time, in writing, that a change to this policy is warranted."

---

ruption that transgender [*sic*] in the military would entail. Thank you." Donald J. Trump (@real DonaldTrump), Twitter (July 26, 2017, 5:55 AM), https://twitter.com/realDonaldTrump/status /890193981585444864; Donald J. Trump (@realDonaldTrump), Twitter (July 26, 2017, 6:04 AM), https://twitter.com/realDonaldTrump/status/890196164313833472; Donald J. Trump (@realDonald Trump), Twitter (July 26, 2017, 6:08 AM), https://twitter.com/realDonaldTrump/status/890197 095151546369.

Section 2 contains two specific directives to the Secretary of Defense and the Secretary of Homeland Security. First, section 2(a) directs the Secretaries to "maintain the currently effective policy regarding accession of transgender individuals into military service beyond January 1, 2018, until such time as the Secretary of Defense, after consulting with the Secretary of Homeland Security, provides a recommendation to the contrary that [the President finds] convincing. . . ." This section takes effect on January 1, 2018.

Second, section 2(b) directs the Secretaries to "halt all use of DoD or DHS resources to fund sex reassignment surgical procedures for military personnel, except to the extent necessary to protect the health of an individual who has already begun a course of treatment to reassign his or her sex." This section, like section 1(b), takes effect on March 23, 2018.

By February 21, 2018, the Secretaries must submit a plan to the President "for implementing both the general policy set forth in section 1(b) of this memorandum and the specific directives set forth in section 2 of this memorandum." *Id.* § 3. This implementation plan must "determine how to address transgender individuals currently serving in the United States military." Until that determination is made — and it must be made as part of the implementation plan, which must be submitted by February 21, 2018 — "no action may be taken against such individuals under the policy set forth in section 1(b) of this memorandum." That is, only after February 21, 2018, may the Secretaries take actions toward reverting to the pre-June 2016 policy, which by the terms of the memorandum is a policy under which the military "generally prohibited openly transgender individuals from accession into the United States military and authorized the discharge of such individuals." *Id.* § 1(a).

Retention Directive

In sum, by March 23, 2018, the Secretaries are required by the plain text of the President's directive to revert to a policy under which the military "authorized the discharge of [transgender] individuals." *Id.* §§ 1(a), 1(b), 3. The protections of the memorandum with respect to discharge and other adverse action expire on February 21, 2018. *Id.* § 3.

Accession Directive

With respect to accession, the memorandum indefinitely delays the implementation of the accession policy of the June 2016 DTM, which was previously set for implementation on January 1, 2018, and by March 23, 2018, requires the Secretaries to revert to a policy by which the military "generally prohibit[s] openly transgender individuals from accession. . . ." *Id.* §§ 1(a), 1(b), 2(a), 3.

. . . .

11. September 14, 2017 Interim Guidance

On September 14, 2017, Secretary Mattis issued interim guidance that took "effect immediately and will remain in effect until [he] promulgate[s] DoD's final policy in this matter." The Interim Guidance states that "[n]ot later than February 21, 2018,

[Secretary Mattis] will present the President with a plan to implement the policy and directives in the Presidential Memorandum." The "implementation plan will establish the policy, standards and procedures for transgender individuals serving in the military."

Accession

With respect to accession, the Interim Guidance provides that the procedures previously set forth in a 2010 policy instruction, "which generally prohibit the accession of transgender individuals into the Military Services, remain in effect. . . ."

Medical Care and Treatment

With respect to medical care and treatment, the Interim Guidance provides that "[s]ervice members who receive a gender dysphoria diagnosis from a military medical provider will be provided treatment for the diagnosed medical condition," but that "no new sex reassignment surgical procedures for military personnel will be permitted after March 22, 2018, except to the extent necessary to protect the health of an individual who has already begun a course of treatment to reassign his or her sex."

Retention

With respect to the separation or retention of transgender service members, the Interim Guidance provides that "[a]n otherwise qualified transgender Service member whose term of service expires while this Interim Guidance remains in effect, *may*, at the Service member's request, be re-enlisted in service under existing procedures." (emphasis in original).

Finally, the Interim Guidance states that "[a]s directed by the [Presidential] Memorandum, no action may be taken to involuntarily separate or discharge an otherwise qualified Service member solely on the basis of a gender dysphoria diagnosis or transgender status."

. . . .

III. Discussion

. . . .

A. Subject Matter Jurisdiction

. . . .

For the reasons stated below, the Court concludes that it has jurisdiction to adjudicate the propriety of the directives of the Presidential Memorandum with respect to the accession and retention of transgender individuals for military service, which corresponds with sections 1(b) and 2(a) of the Presidential Memorandum (*i.e.*, the Accession and Retention Directives). The Court does not have jurisdiction over section 2(b), which prohibits the use of military resources to fund sex reassignment surgical procedures, because no Plaintiff has demonstrated that they are substantially likely to be impacted by this directive (the "Sex Reassignment Surgery Directive").

1. Standing

. . . .

The familiar requirements of Article III standing are:

> (1) that the plaintiff have suffered an "injury in fact"—an invasion of a judicially cognizable interest which is (a) concrete and particularized and (b) actual or imminent, not conjectural or hypothetical; (2) that there be a causal connection between the injury and the conduct complained of—the injury must be fairly traceable to the challenged action of the defendant, and not the result of the independent action of some third party not before the court; and (3) that it be likely, as opposed to merely speculative, that the injury will be redressed by a favorable decision.

Bennett v. Spear, 520 U.S. 154 (1997).

. . . . Plaintiffs have carried their burden of demonstrating a substantial likelihood of standing on the basis of at least two distinct injuries. First, Plaintiffs are subject to a competitive barrier that violates equal protection. Second, they are subject to a substantial risk of being denied accession, or being discharged from the military, due to their transgender status. Furthermore, Plaintiffs have demonstrated satisfactorily that both of these injuries are caused by the directives of the Presidential Memorandum, and that they are redressable by this Court.

a. The Import of the Presidential Memorandum

. . . .

According to Defendants, the Court lacks subject-matter jurisdiction with respect to the directives of the Presidential Memorandum because . . . the Presidential Memorandum merely commissioned an additional policy review; that review is underway; nothing is set in stone, and what policy may come about is unknown; and regardless, Plaintiffs are protected by the Interim Guidance. And while accession by transgender individuals is not permitted, they may obtain waivers. [These] arguments are a red herring.

The President controls the United States military. The directives of the Presidential Memorandum, to the extent they are definitive, are the operative policy toward military service by transgender service members. The Court must and shall assume that the directives of the Presidential Memorandum will be faithfully executed. Consequently, the Interim Guidance must be read as implementing the directives of the Presidential Memorandum, and any protections afforded by the Interim Guidance are necessarily limited to the extent they conflict with the express directives of the memorandum. Finally, to the extent there is ambiguity about the meaning of the Presidential Memorandum, the best guidance is the President's own statements regarding his intentions with respect to service by transgender individuals. . . . On August 25, 2017, the President issued the Presidential Memorandum. There, ... in section 1(b), the President directs the military "to return to the longstanding policy and practice on military service by transgender individuals that was in place prior to June 2016 . . . ." Accordingly, the military has been directed by section 1(b) to return to a policy under which: (i) transgender individuals are generally prohibited from accession; and (ii) the military is authorized to discharge individuals who are transgender.

This change in policy must occur by March 23, 2018, except that the prohibition on accession is extended indefinitely as of January 1, 2018. Likewise, as of March 23, 2018, the military is expressly prohibited from funding sex reassignment surgeries, except as necessary to protect the health of an already transitioning individual. . . .

. . . . Consequently, while the Court cannot presently adjudicate the merits of the yet-undecided details of how the directives will be carried out, it can adjudicate the constitutionality of the directives themselves, which are definite, and must be implemented by the military.

. . . . Accordingly, for purposes of its standing analysis, the Court concludes that there is a substantial likelihood that transgender individuals will be indefinitely prevented from acceding to the military as of January 1, 2018, and that the military shall authorize the discharge of current service members who are transgender as of March 23, 2018.

b. Equal Protection Injury

i. Relevant Case Law

The primary injury alleged by Plaintiffs, and which forms the basis of the Court's decision on the merits, is that the directives of the Presidential Memorandum violate the guarantee of equal protection afforded by the Due Process Clause of the Fifth Amendment. . . .

The Supreme Court and this Circuit have made clear that the "injury in fact element of standing in an equal protection case is the denial of equal treatment resulting from the imposition of the barrier." *Am. Freedom Law Ctr. v. Obama*, 821 F.3d 44 (D.C. Cir. 2016) (citing *Ne. Florida Chapter of Associated Gen. Contractors of Am. v. City of Jacksonville, Fla.*, 508 U.S. 656 (1993) (Thomas, J.)). In *City of Jacksonville*, the Supreme Court. . . . held that:

> When the government erects a barrier that makes it more difficult for members of one group to obtain a benefit than it is for members of another group, a member of the former group seeking to challenge the barrier need not allege that he would have obtained the benefit but for the barrier in order to establish standing. The "injury in fact" in an equal protection case of this variety is the denial of equal treatment resulting from the imposition of the barrier, not the ultimate inability to obtain the benefit. . . .

ii. Application to Plaintiffs

. . . Plaintiffs fall into two groups: Named Plaintiffs—who have yet to accede—and the Pseudonym Plaintiffs [such as lead plaintiff Jane Doe 1—Eds.]—who are currently in the military and fear that they will be discharged. [They] challenge the two fundamental directives of the Presidential Memorandum as unconstitutional:

a reversion of accession and retention policy with respect to transgender individuals (*i.e.*, the Accession and Retention Directives). For the following reasons, the Court concludes that: (i) the Accession and Retention Directives of the Presidential Memorandum impose a competitive barrier that the Named and Pseudonym Plaintiffs are substantially likely to encounter, and (ii) that this barrier constitutes an injury in fact sufficient to imbue the Named and Pseudonym Plaintiffs with standing to challenge the propriety of the Accession and Retention Directives of the Presidential Memorandum.

The Accession Directive

Plaintiff [Regan] Kibby—one of the Named Plaintiffs [and a transgender man]—has demonstrated a substantial likelihood that he is able and ready to accede to the military in the relatively near future, and consequently, that he is in a position to challenge the Accession Directive to the extent it imposes a barrier on him from acceding based on his transgender status.

. . . . Defendants represent that "Plaintiff Kibby currently is on medical leave and faces no impediment to returning to the Naval Academy when that leave ends in May 2018." The Commandant of Midshipmen at the Naval Academy, Robert B. Chadwick, has represented that Plaintiff Kibby "was afforded much support from the Brigade Medical Unit, his chain of command, and [the Commandant's] legal advisors in developing his [transition] plan and submitting his request [for medical leave]." According to the Commandant, the "purpose of the [medical] leave is to allow MIDN Kibby to undergo hormone treatment, and to [obtain] a period of gender stability of sufficient length under current policy and guidance to ensure his eligibility to accept a commission in May 2020 if he successfully completes the course of instruction upon return to [the Naval Academy]."

Upon his return, Plaintiff Kibby will be required to meet the male fitness requirements, which are more difficult than their female counterpart, as well as the Academy's academic standards. Plaintiff Kibby has represented that during the medical year of absence, he is "completing a rigorous exercise and training regimen so that [he] will be able to meet the male fitness standards upon [his] return[.]" Given his prior academic success at the Naval Academy, the support afforded to his transition plan by senior officials, and his representations regarding his fitness training, the Court finds that Plaintiff Kibby has demonstrated a substantial likelihood that he will be able to meet the graduation requirements of the Naval Academy. Following graduation, he will be in a position to accede to the Navy or Marine Corps. Defendants have not argued or presented any evidence that Plaintiff Kibby will be unable to graduate from the Naval Academy—an unsurprising position, given that dismissal stemming from the inability of transgender individuals to accede would itself likely be an injury sufficient to confer standing to challenge the constitutionality of the Presidential Memorandum.

Consequently, Plaintiff Kibby has demonstrated that he is "able and ready" to apply for accession. . . . Indeed, Plaintiff Kibby has demonstrated a greater likelihood of his being subject to the competitive barrier than many of the plaintiffs in the equal protection cases discussed above. . . . Plaintiff Kibby is on a defined track toward graduation from the Naval Academy and accession to the military. . . .

The remaining question is whether Plaintiff Kibby is substantially likely to "hit" a barrier when he applies for accession to the military. As of January 2018, transgender individuals shall be prohibited entry to the military, until such time that the President receives a recommendation to the contrary that he finds convincing. Given the President's pronouncement that "the United States government will not accept or allow transgender individuals to serve in any capacity in the U.S. military," there is no reason to believe that this directive will change by the time Plaintiff Kibby is ready to apply for accession in May 2020. . . . Nor does the potential availability of a waiver change this conclusion. First, Defendants have presented no evidence that waivers are actually made available to transgender individuals, or that they will be; and the only record evidence on this point suggests that transgender individuals are not entitled to waivers for accession purposes. Second, even if a bona fide waiver process were made available, Plaintiff Kibby would still be subject to a competitive barrier due to his transgender status. For accession purposes, he would be presumptively disqualified because of his transgender status, unless he obtains a waiver. Those who are not transgender are not subject to the same blanket proscription. . . . Accordingly, Plaintiff Kibby has demonstrated that he is substantially likely to attempt to accede, and to encounter a competitive barrier at the time of his accession due to his status as a transgender individual, which he claims is violative of equal protection. This is sufficient to confer standing to challenge the Accession Directive at this preliminary stage.

With respect to the Pseudonym Plaintiffs, there is no real doubt that they will remain in the military for long enough to hit the "barrier" that they claim is violative of equal protection. Each has submitted a declaration stating, and/or alleged, their intention to remain in military service, and Defendants have submitted declarations for each Pseudonym Plaintiff stating that they shall not be discharged until the military's new policy regarding transgender service members takes effect. There is also no real doubt that they will face a competitive barrier to their continued retention by the military. As of March 23, 2018, the military is required to effect a policy by which these service members can be discharged solely due to their transgender status. This barrier to their continued retention is imposed upon them, but not other service members. And Plaintiffs claim that this competitive barrier is violative of equal protection. Accordingly, at this preliminary stage, the Pseudonym Plaintiffs have demonstrated a substantial likelihood of standing to challenge the Presidential Memorandum's Retention Directive. . . .

iii. Substantial Risk of Injury

Plaintiffs have also established a substantial risk of two future injuries: denial of accession and discharge from military service. The substantial risk of these two future injuries is sufficient to constitute an injury in fact. As explained by the Supreme Court, "[a]n allegation of future injury may suffice if the threatened injury is certainly impending, or there is a substantial risk that the harm will occur." *Susan B. Anthony List v. Driehaus*, 134 S. Ct. 2334 (2014). Here, even assuming that the future injuries are not "certainly impending," there is a "substantial risk" of their occurrence.

. . . . In some circumstances, the chain of events that is necessary for the putative future harm to occur is too attenuated to constitute a substantial risk of that harm and to render that harm imminent. Consequently, in *Clapper*, the Supreme Court declined to find standing because the plaintiffs' "theory of standing [relied] on a highly attenuated chain of possibilities. . . ." *Clapper v. Amnesty Int'l USA*, 568 U.S. 398 (2013). . . . Here, there is no doubt that the denial of accession and discharge from the military constitute concrete and particularized injuries. Whether these are also imminent, based on the reasoning of *Clapper* and *Attias*, requires an analysis of the degree to which these future harms are separated from the present by a "series of contingent events. . . ." *Attias v. Carefirst, Inc.*, 865 F.3d 620 (D.C. Cir. 2017).

. . . .

Plaintiffs have demonstrated a chain of causation leading to concrete and particularized injuries in which there are few links and each link is substantially likely to occur. With respect to the Accession Directive, Plaintiff Kibby will suffer an injury in fact if he: (i) graduates from the Naval Academy; (ii) applies for accession; and (iii) is denied accession due to his transgender status. The first two links in this chain are substantially likely to occur for the reasons already stated. The third is likely to occur because the Presidential Memorandum indefinitely delays the accession of transgender individuals, and the President has unequivocally stated that transgender individuals shall not be permitted to serve in the military. Given this actuality, it is speculative to assume that transgender individuals will be permitted to accede by May 2020. At present, there is a substantial risk that accession will remain forbidden, and Plaintiff Kibby will be precluded from military service.

For the Pseudonym Plaintiffs, the chain of causation is even shorter. They will suffer an injury in fact if: (i) they remain in the military; and (ii) are discharged based on their transgender status after March 23, 2018 due to the Retention Directive. On the first point, there is no disagreement that the Pseudonym Plaintiffs are qualified service members who desire to remain in military service. On the second point, the available evidence is that the President—who ultimately controls the military—issued a statement that "the United States government will not . . . allow transgender individuals to serve in any capacity in the U.S. military," and shortly thereafter, issued a Presidential Memorandum that requires the military to authorize the discharge of transgender service members by March 23, 2018. True, it is conceivable that the Pseudonym Plaintiffs will not be discharged from the military, despite the head of the military stating that they will be. But in the absence of a crystal ball, and in light of these unequivocal factual circumstances, at the present time, the Pseudonym Plaintiffs face a substantial risk of discharge. This confers upon them an injury in fact.

. . . .

v. Plaintiffs Do Not Have Standing to Challenge the Sex Reassignment Surgery Directive

[None] of the Plaintiffs have demonstrated an injury in fact with respect to the Sex Reassignment Surgery Directive. First, only some Plaintiffs are implicated by the provision at all. For those that are, the risk of being impacted by the Sex Reassignment Surgery Directive is not sufficiently great to confer standing.

Jane Doe 1 alleges that "a transition-related procedure Jane Doe 1 was scheduled for was summarily canceled by the Defense Health Agency." However, Defendants have submitted a declaration representing that "Jane Doe 1's application for the supplemental health care waiver necessary to receive a transition-related surgery is currently being processed by the Defense Health Agency. Accordingly, Jane Doe 1 has not demonstrated that she will not receive the surgery prior to the effective date of the Sex Reassignment Surgery Directive.

Jane Doe 3 has developed a transition treatment plan, but will not begin her treatment until after she returns from active deployment in Iraq. Given the possibility of discharge, the uncertainties attended by the fact that she has yet to begin any transition treatment, and the lack of certainty on when such treatment will begin, the prospective harm engendered by the Sex Reassignment Surgery Directive is too speculative to constitute an injury in fact with respect to Jane Doe 3. Furthermore, John Doe 1 is scheduled for transition related-surgery on January 4, 2018, and Defendants have represented that this date remains unaffected by the Presidential Memorandum. Finally, the Named Plaintiffs are not currently in the military and it is speculative whether they will need surgery while in military service. Plaintiff Kibby, in particular, has stated that he will transition prior to applying for accession. Accordingly, no Plaintiffs have demonstrated that they are substantially likely to be impacted by the Sex Reassignment Surgery Directive, and none have standing to challenge that directive.

. . . .

C. Plaintiffs' Motion for Preliminary Injunction

Having determined that Plaintiffs have standing to challenge the Accession and Retention Directives . . . , the Court moves on to consider Plaintiffs' motion for preliminary injunction. Plaintiffs ask the Court to enjoin the enforcement of the Accession and Retention Directives pending the final resolution of this lawsuit. The Court will grant Plaintiffs' motion. The Court finds (1) that Plaintiffs have a likelihood of succeeding on their claim that the Accession and Retention Directives violate the Fifth Amendment, (2) that Plaintiffs would suffer irreparable injury in the absence of an injunction, and (3) that the balance of equities and the public interest favor granting injunctive relief.

1. Likelihood of Success on the Merits

. . . . The Due Process Clause of the Fifth Amendment provides that "No person shall be . . . deprived of life, liberty, or property, without due process of law." . . . . "In numerous decisions, [the Supreme Court] 'has held that the Due Process Clause of the Fifth Amendment forbids the Federal Government to deny equal protection of the laws.'" *Davis v. Passman*, 442 U.S. 228 (1979). To determine whether the Accession and Retention Directives violate the Due Process Clause's guarantee because they deny the equal protection of the laws to transgender Americans, the Court must decide (a) the level of scrutiny applicable, and (b) whether the Accession and Retention Directives are likely to survive that level of scrutiny.

a. Level of Scrutiny

. . . .

At this preliminary stage of the case, the Court is persuaded that it must apply a heightened degree of scrutiny to the Accession and Retention Directives. . . . First, on the current record, transgender individuals—who are alone targeted for exclusion by the Accession and Retention Directives—appear to satisfy the criteria of at least a quasi-suspect classification. "The Supreme Court has used several explicit criteria to identify suspect and quasi-suspect classifications." *Padula v. Webster*, 822 F.2d 97 (D.C. Cir. 1987). The Court has observed that a suspect class is one that has "experienced a 'history of purposeful unequal treatment' or been subjected to unique disabilities on the basis of stereotyped characteristics not truly indicative of their abilities." *Massachusetts Bd. of Ret. v. Murgia*, 427 U.S. 307 (1976). Also relevant is whether the group has been "relegated to such a position of political powerlessness as to command extraordinary protection from the majoritarian political process." *Id.* Finally, the Supreme Court has also considered whether the group "exhibit[s] obvious, immutable, or distinguishing characteristics that define them as a discrete group." *Lyng v. Castillo*, 477 U.S. 635 (1986).

The transgender community satisfies these criteria. Transgender individuals have immutable and distinguishing characteristics that make them a discernable class. *See, e.g.*, Medical Amici Brief (describing what it means to be transgender). As a class, transgender individuals have suffered, and continue to suffer, severe persecution and discrimination. *See, e.g.*, State Amici Brief (describing the discrimination the transgender community suffers); Trevor Project Amici Brief (discussing the harmful effects of discrimination against transgender youth). Despite this discrimination, the Court is aware of no argument or evidence suggesting that being transgender in any way limits one's ability to contribute to society. The exemplary military service of Plaintiffs in this case certainly suggests that it does not. Finally, transgender people as a group represent a very small subset of society lacking the sort of political power other groups might harness to protect themselves from discrimination. *See Adkins v. City of New York*, 143 F. Supp. 3d 134, 140 (S.D.N.Y. 2015) (noting that there is "no indication that there have ever been any transgender members of the United States Congress or the federal judiciary").

[This] Court . . . has taken note of the findings and conclusions of a number of other courts from across the country that have also found that discrimination on the basis of someone's transgender identity is a quasi-suspect form of classification that triggers heightened scrutiny. *See Evancho v. Pine-Richland Sch. Dist.*, 237 F. Supp. 3d 267 (W.D. Pa. 2017) (holding that "all of the indicia for the application of the heightened intermediate scrutiny standard are present" for transgender individuals); *Bd. of Educ. of the Highland Local Sch. Dist. v. United States Dep't of Educ.*, 208 F. Supp. 3d 850 (S.D. Ohio 2016) (finding that "transgender status is a quasi-suspect class under the Equal Protection Clause"); *Adkins*.

Second, the Court is also persuaded that the Accession and Retention Directives are a form of discrimination on the basis of gender, which is itself subject to intermediate scrutiny. It is well-established that gender-based discrimination includes discrimination based on non-conformity with gender stereotypes. *See Price Waterhouse v. Hopkins*, 490 U.S. 228 (1989) ("[W]e are beyond the day when an employer could evaluate employees by assuming or insisting that they matched the stereotype associated with their group"). The Accession and Retention Directives' exclusion of transgender individuals inherently discriminates against current and aspiring service members on the basis of their failure to conform to gender stereotypes. The defining characteristic of a transgender individual is that their inward identity, behavior, and possibly their physical characteristics, do not conform to stereotypes of how an individual of their assigned sex should feel, act and look. By excluding an entire category of people from military service on this characteristic alone, the Accession and Retention Directives punish individuals for failing to adhere to gender stereotypes. *See . . . Glenn v. Brumby*, 663 F.3d 1312 (11th Cir. 2011) (holding that "discrimination against a transgender individual because of her gender-nonconformity is sex discrimination"). A service member who was born a male is punished by the Accession and Retention Directives if he identifies as a woman, whereas that same service member would be free to join and remain in the military if he was born a female, or if he agreed to act in the way society expects males to act. The Accession and Retention Directives are accordingly inextricably intertwined with gender classifications.

For these two reasons, the Court will apply an intermediate level of scrutiny to Defendants' exclusion of transgender individuals from the military, akin to the level of scrutiny applicable in gender discrimination cases. [Meaningful] scrutiny of the constitutionality of the Accession and Retention Directives is appropriate despite the fact that they pertain to decisions about military personnel. Although the Court recognizes that deference to the Executive and Congress is warranted in the military context, the Court is not powerless to assess whether the constitutional rights of America's service members have been violated. The D.C. Circuit has explained that although "the operation of the military is vested in Congress and the Executive, and . . . it is not for the courts to establish the composition of the armed forces[,] . . . constitutional questions that arise out of military decisions regarding the composition of the armed forces are not committed to the other coordinate branches of government." *Emory v. Sec'y of Navy*, 819 F.2d 291 (D.C. Cir. 1987). "Where it is alleged, as it is here, that the armed forces have trenched upon constitutionally guaranteed rights through the promotion and selection process, the courts are not powerless to act." "The military has not been exempted from constitutional provisions that protect the rights of individuals" and, indeed, "[i]t is precisely the role of the courts to determine whether those rights have been violated."

b. Application of Intermediate Scrutiny

. . . . Under intermediate scrutiny, the government must demonstrate an "exceedingly persuasive justification" for its actions. *United States v. Virginia*, 518 U.S. 515 (1996). "The burden of justification is demanding and it rests entirely on" the government. The government "must show 'at least that the [challenged] classification serves important governmental objectives and that the discriminatory means employed are substantially related to the achievement of those objectives.'" "The justification must be genuine, not hypothesized or invented post hoc in response to litigation." "And it must not rely on overbroad generalizations about the different talents, capacities, or preferences of males and females." Finally, it is well established that "[t]he Constitution's guarantee of equality 'must at the very least mean that a bare . . . desire to harm a politically unpopular group cannot' justify disparate treatment of that group." *United States v. Windsor*, 133 S. Ct. 2675 (2013).

. . . Plaintiffs are likely to succeed in demonstrating that the Accession and Retention Directives' exclusion of transgender individuals from the military is unconstitutional. [The] Court reiterates precisely what is at issue in this case: a policy banning the accession, and allowing the discharge, of an entire category of individuals from the military solely because they are transgender, despite their ability to meet all of the physical, psychological, and other standards for military service. Defendants argue that this policy is necessary for three reasons. First, Defendants argue that "at least some transgender individuals suffer from medical conditions that could impede the performance of their duties." Second, Defendants argue that "there is room for the military to think" that certain medical conditions "may limit the deployability of transgender individuals as well as impose additional costs on the armed forces." Third, Defendants argue that "the President could reasonably conclude" that the presence of transgender individuals in the military would harm "unit cohesion."[9]

Plaintiffs do not dispute that maximizing military effectiveness, lethality and unit cohesion, and even budgetary considerations, are all important or at least legitimate government interests. They do challenge, however, whether Defendants can satisfy their burden of demonstrating that the discriminatory means that have been employed in the Presidential Memorandum . . . are "substantially related" to

---

9. Plaintiffs note that similar arguments were proffered in support of prior policies precluding service members from being openly gay, maintaining racially segregated ranks and excluding women from military colleges.

the achievement of these objectives. Based on the combined effect of a number of unusual factors, the Court finds it likely that Plaintiffs will succeed on this claim.

First, the reasons given for the decision to exclude transgender service members appear to be hypothetical and extremely overbroad. For instance, Defendants cite concerns that "some" transgender individuals "could" suffer from medical conditions that impede their duties. . . . As an initial matter, these hypothetical concerns could be raised about any service members. Moreover, these concerns do not explain the need to discharge and deny accession to all transgender people who meet the relevant physical, mental and medical standards for service. The Accession and Retention Directives are accordingly extremely overbroad when considered in the light of their proffered justifications. *See Romer v. Evans*, 517 U.S. 620 (1996) (holding that law's "sheer breadth is so discontinuous with the reasons offered for it that [it] seems inexplicable by anything but animus toward the class it affects"). The breadth of the Accession and Retention Directives is also discontinuous with the purported concern about costs, which, in addition to having been found to be minimal or negligible, apparently are primarily related to a surgical procedure that only a subset of transgender individuals will even need. Similarly, Defendants provide practically no explanation at all, let alone support, for their suggestion that the presence of transgender individuals may be harmful to "unit cohesion."[10] Indeed, Defendants themselves highlight the absence of any prior studies or evaluations supporting the proffered justifications by arguing that they must now conduct studies regarding transgender military service before they can adequately defend the President's decision. At most, Defendants' reasons appear therefore to be based on unsupported, "overbroad generalizations about the different talents, capacities, or preferences," of transgender people. *Virginia*.

Nonetheless, given the deference owed to military personnel decisions, the Court has not based its conclusion solely on the speculative and overbroad nature of the President's reasons. A second point is also crucial. As far as the Court is aware at this preliminary stage, all of the reasons proffered by the President for excluding transgender individuals from the military in this case were not merely unsupported, but were actually contradicted by the studies, conclusions and judgment of the military itself. As described above, the effect of transgender individuals serving in the military had been studied by the military immediately prior to the issuance of the Presidential Memorandum. [The] RAND National Defense Research Institute conducted a study and issued a report largely debunking any potential concerns about unit cohesion, military readiness, deployability or health care costs related to transgender military service. The Department of Defense Working Group, made up of senior uniformed officers and senior civilian officers from

---

10. To the extent this is a thinly-veiled reference to an assumption that other service members are biased against transgender people, this would not be a legitimate rationale for the challenged policy. "Private biases may be outside the reach of the law, but the law cannot, directly or indirectly, give them effect." *See Palmore v. Sidoti*, 466 U.S. 429 (1984).

each military department, unanimously concluded that there were no barriers that should prevent transgender individuals from serving in the military, rejecting the very concerns supposedly underlying the Accession and Retention Directives. In fact, the Working Group concluded that prohibiting transgender service members would undermine military effectiveness and readiness. Next, the Army, Air Force and Navy each concluded that transgender individuals should be allowed to serve. Finally, the Secretary of Defense concluded that the needs of the military were best served by allowing transgender individuals to openly serve. In short, the military concerns purportedly underlying the President's decision had been studied and rejected by the military itself.[11] This highly unusual situation is further evidence that the reasons offered for the Accession and Retention Directives were not substantially related to the military interests the Presidential Memorandum cited.

Third, the Court has also considered the circumstances surrounding the announcement of the President's policy. "In determining whether a law is motived by an improper animus or purpose, '[d]iscriminations of an unusual character' especially require careful consideration." *Windsor* (quoting *Romer*). The discrimination in this case was certainly of an unusual character. As explained above, after a lengthy review process by senior military personnel, the military had recently determined that permitting transgender individuals to serve would not have adverse effects on the military and had announced that such individuals were free to serve openly. Many transgender service members identified themselves to their commanding officers in reliance on that pronouncement. Then, the President abruptly announced, via Twitter—without any of the formality or deliberative processes that generally accompany the development and announcement of major policy changes that will gravely affect the lives of many Americans—that all transgender individuals would be precluded from participating in the military in any capacity. These circumstances provide additional support for Plaintiffs' claim that the decision to exclude transgender individuals was not driven by genuine concerns regarding military efficacy. *See Vill. of Arlington Heights v. Metro. Hous. Dev. Corp.*, 429 U.S. 252 (1977) (holding that "[t]he specific sequence of events leading up the challenged decision . . . may shed some light on the decisionmaker's purposes" and "[d]epartures from the normal procedural sequence also might afford evidence that improper purposes are playing a role").

In sum, even if none of the reasons discussed above alone would be sufficient for the Court to conclude that Plaintiffs were likely to succeed on their Fifth Amendment claim, taken together they are highly suggestive of a constitutional violation. The likelihood of success factor accordingly weighs in favor of granting preliminary injunctive relief. For the same reasons, the Court will deny Defendants' motion to dismiss Plaintiffs' claims under the Due Process Clause.

---

11. This differentiates this case from *Goldman v. Weinberger*, 475 U.S. 503 (1986), a case cited by Defendants, in which the court deferred to a decision that was based on the "considered professional judgment of the Air Force."

Defendants . . . argue that Plaintiffs cannot demonstrate a likelihood of success on the merits regarding the Presidential Memorandum's policy for enlisted service members in particular because Secretary Mattis' Interim Guidance is the "operative policy," and that guidance "does not impermissibly classify service members based on transgender status, but rather prohibits disparate treatment of existing service members based on transgender status." This may be true, but the focus of Plaintiffs' Amended Complaint is not the Interim Guidance, but the Presidential Memorandum. The Accession and Retention Directives of the Presidential Memorandum require the return to a policy that "generally prohibit[s] openly transgender individuals from accession into the United States military and authorize[s] the discharge of such individuals." Presidential Memorandum § 1(a). This overt disparate treatment, which will become effective when Secretary Mattis' Interim Guidance elapses early next year, is the subject of Plaintiffs' lawsuit.

Second, Defendants cite a number of cases for the proposition that the Presidential Memorandum "is subject to a highly deferential form of review." The Court has reviewed those cases and determined that none of them require the Court to apply a different level of scrutiny than has been applied here. Of primary importance is the Supreme Court's opinion in *Rostker v. Goldberg*, 453 U.S. 57 (1981). The Supreme Court in *Rostker* expressly declined to hold that the intermediate scrutiny applicable to gender discrimination did not apply in the military personnel context. Instead, the Court reviewed the particular facts before it and found that the district court in that case had not sufficiently deferred to the reasoned decision of Congress in the context of a particular military personnel-related decision.

The facts of that case are strikingly different than those presented here. In *Rostker*, the Court noted that "Congress did not act unthinkingly or reflexively and not for any considered reason," when it passed the challenged policy. To the contrary, the Court noted Congress' "studied choice of one alternative in preference to another," and relied on the fact that the policy at issue in that case had been "extensively considered by Congress in hearings, floor debate, and in committee." In other words, Congress had received extensive evidence on the issue, and simply chose one of two competing alternatives. The Supreme Court found that "[t]he District Court was quite wrong in undertaking an independent evaluation of this evidence, rather than adopting an appropriately deferential examination of Congress' evaluation of that evidence."

The study and evaluation of evidence that the *Rostker* Court found warranted judicial deference is completely absent from the current record. . . . [The] record at this stage of the case shows that the reasons offered for categorically excluding transgender individuals were not supported and were in fact contradicted by the only military judgment available at the time. Accordingly, unlike the district court in *Rostker*, the Court's analysis in this Opinion has not been based on an independent evaluation of evidence or faulting of the President for choosing between two alternatives based on competing evidence.

Third, Defendants seem to argue that they are free of the obligation of ratio-nalizing the Accession and Retention Directives because the directives are a mere continuation of a longstanding policy. This is false. The Accession and Retention Directives constituted a revocation from transgender people of rights they were pre-viously given. Before the Accession and Retention Directives, transgender people had already been given the right to serve openly and the right to accede by a date certain in early 2018. The Accession and Retention Directives took those rights away from transgender people and transgender people only. The targeted revocation of rights from a particular class of people which they had previously enjoyed — for however short a period of time — is a fundamentally different act than not giving those rights in the first place, and it will be the government's burden in this case to show that this act was substantially related to important government objectives. *See Perry v. Brown*, 671 F.3d 1052 (9th Cir. 2012), vacated and remanded *sub nom. Hollingsworth v. Perry*, 570 U.S. 693 (2013) ("Withdrawing from a disfavored group the right to obtain a designation with significant societal consequences is different from declining to extend that designation in the first place, regardless of whether the right was withdrawn after a week, a year, or a decade."). Targeted revocations of rights are a factor that has been present in a number of cases finding equal protec-tion violations. *See Romer* (holding that law that "withdr[ew] from homosexuals, but no others, specific legal protection . . . and . . . forb[ade] reinstatement of these laws and policies" was unconstitutional); *Windsor* (holding that the purpose of a law that "impose[d] a disability on [a] class by refusing to acknowledge a status" previously granted was to "disparage and to injure those" in that class).

Finally, Defendants argue that the military's previous study of transgender ser-vice cannot forever bind future administrations from looking into the issue them-selves. The Court fully agrees with this point. The Court by no means suggests that it was not within the President's authority to order that additional studies be under-taken and that this policy be reevaluated. If the President had done so and then decided that banning all transgender individuals from serving in the military was beneficial to the various military objectives cited, this would be a different case. But as discussed above, that is not the case before the Court. The Court can only assess Plaintiffs' equal protection claim based on the facts before it. At this time, it appears that the rights of a class of individuals were summarily and abruptly revoked for reasons contrary to the only then-available studies. As explained above, based on the cumulative effect of various unusual facts, the Court is convinced that Plaintiffs are likely to succeed on the merits of their Fifth Amendment claim. This finding in no way should be interpreted to prevent Defendants from continuing to study issues surrounding the service of transgender individuals in the military, as they have asserted that they intend to do.

The Court concludes this portion of its Memorandum Opinion with a caveat. This case comes before the Court on Plaintiffs' motion for a preliminary injunction and Defendants' motion to dismiss. It is accordingly still at its very earliest stages, and the record is necessarily limited. The Court's task at this time is to determine whether Plaintiffs have stated plausible claims and demonstrated a likelihood—not a certainty—of success based on the present record. The Court is persuaded that Plaintiffs have made these fairly modest showings, but this is not a final adjudication of the merits of Plaintiffs' claims.

2. Irreparable Injury

Next, the Court finds that Plaintiffs have demonstrated that they would suffer irreparable injury in the absence of preliminary injunctive relief. In order to satisfy the irreparable injury requirement, "[f]irst, the injury 'must be both certain and great; it must be actual and not theoretical.'" *Chaplaincy of Full Gospel Churches v. England*, 454 F.3d 290 (D.C. Cir. 2006). "Second, the injury must be beyond remediation." *Id.*

. . . . Absent an injunction, Plaintiffs will suffer a number of harms that cannot be remediated after that fact even if Plaintiffs were to eventually succeed in this lawsuit. The impending ban brands and stigmatizes Plaintiffs as less capable of serving in the military, reduces their stature among their peers and officers, stunts the growth of their careers, and threatens to derail their chosen calling or access to unique educational opportunities. *See Elzie v. Aspin*, 841 F. Supp. 439 (D.D.C. 1993) (holding that plaintiff would suffer irreparable injury in the absence of preliminary injunctive relief because "plaintiff faces the stigma of being removed from active duty as a sergeant in the Marine Corps [. . .] and labeled as unfit for service solely on the basis of his sexual orientation, a criterion which has no bearing on his ability to perform his job"). Money damages or other corrective forms of relief will not be able to fully remediate these injuries once they occur. Moreover, these injuries are also imminent, in that they are either ongoing or, at the latest, will begin when the Accession and Retention Directives take effect early next year.

These injuries are irreparable for the additional reason that they are the result of alleged violations of Plaintiffs' rights to equal protection of the laws under the Fifth Amendment. "It has long been established that the loss of constitutional freedoms, 'for even minimal periods of time, unquestionably constitutes irreparable injury.'" *Mills v. District of Columbia*, 571 F.3d 1304 (D.C. Cir. 2009) (quoting *Elrod v. Burns*, 427 U.S. 347 (1976)). Under this line of authority, Plaintiffs' allegation of constitutional injury is sufficient to satisfy the irreparable injury requirement for issuance of a preliminary injunction.

3. Balance of Equities and Public Interest

Finally, the Court finds that Plaintiffs have shown that the public interest and the balance of hardships weigh in favor of granting injunctive relief. "A party seeking a preliminary injunction must demonstrate both 'that the balance of equities tips in [its] favor, and that an injunction is in the public interest.'" *FBME Bank Ltd. v. Lew*, 125 F. Supp. 3d 109 (D.D.C. 2015). "These factors merge when the Government is the opposing party." *Id.*

As already established, the Presidential Memorandum is causing Plaintiffs serious ongoing harms and will cause them further harms in the near future absent

an injunction. On this record, there are no countervailing equities or public interest in precluding transgender service members from the military that outweigh
those harms. Defendants argue that "[t]he public has a strong interest in national
defense." They also argue that the military "is in the process of gathering a panel of
experts" to provide advice and recommendations regarding "the development and
implementation of the policy on military service by transgender individuals," and
that "[g]ranting Plaintiffs their requested relief would directly interfere with the
panel's work and the military's ability to thoroughly study a complex and important
issue regarding the composition of the armed forces."

Neither point passes muster. A bare invocation of "national defense" simply cannot defeat every motion for preliminary injunction that touches on the military.
On the record before the Court, there is absolutely no support for the claim that
the ongoing service of transgender people would have any negative effective on the
military at all. In fact, there is considerable evidence that it is the discharge and
banning of such individuals that would have such effects. The Court also notes that
fifteen States have filed an amici brief indicating that they and their residents will
be harmed by the Presidential Memorandum if it is not enjoined. Moreover, the
injunction that will be issued will in no way prevent the government from conducting studies or gathering advice or recommendations on transgender service. The
balance of equities and public interest accordingly weigh in favor of granting Plaintiffs' motion.

IV. Conclusion

For the reasons set out above, the Court will GRANT-IN-PART and DENY-IN-PART
Defendants' Motion to Dismiss and GRANT-IN-PART and DENY-IN-PART Plaintiffs'
Motion for Preliminary Injunction. The Court will grant Defendants' motion to
dismiss Plaintiffs' claims to the extent they are based on the Sex Reassignment Sur-
gery Directive. . . . Defendants' motion to dismiss is DENIED in all other respects.
Plaintiffs' motion for preliminary injunction is DENIED with respect to the Sex
Reassignment Surgery Directive. Plaintiffs' motion for preliminary injunction is
GRANTED, however, in that the Court will preliminarily enjoin enforcement of the
Accession and Retention Directives. The effect of the Court's Order is to revert to
the status quo with regard to accession and retention that existed before the issuance of the Presidential Memorandum—that is, the retention and accession poli-
cies established in the June 30, 2016 Directive-type Memorandum as modified by
Secretary of Defense James Mattis on June 30, 2017. An appropriate Order accompanies this Memorandum Opinion.

———————

Discussion

1. Is the court sufficiently deferential in reviewing this military service policy
declared by the President, who is the Commander in Chief of the armed forces?
Does the court adopt the right constitutional standard (level of scrutiny) for

assessing anti-transgender discrimination, or should the appropriate test be stronger or weaker than the court's?

2. If the justifications for the policy are as speculative and ill-fitting as the district court considers them, does that raise the question whether (as the plaintiffs suggested) something else—presumably something more constitutionally suspect or forbidden—was the real reason for the policy? How reluctant to declare a military policy pretextual should courts be? Compare *Trump v. Hawai'i*, 138 S. Ct. 2392 (2018), where a 5–4 majority of the Supreme Court insisted on treating as nondiscriminatory Donald Trump's "Muslim ban," which was facially neutral as to the religions of the people excluded from the United States but was limited primarily to majority-Muslim countries and was adopted by a President who as a candidate had publicly declaimed that he wanted to stop all immigration of Muslims.

Footnote 10 of the court's opinion relies on *Palmore v. Sidoti*, 466 U.S. 429 (1984), to reject unit cohesion as a justification for the ban "[t]o the extent that" it is predicated upon servicemembers' (and/or the public's?) "bias against transgender people." Eric Merriam has argued that the court should have gone further in following *Palmore* and held that, because the unit cohesion rationale is indeed "animus"-based, the trans ban "give[s] ... effect" to "[p]rivate biases" and hence is unconstitutional regardless of what other governmental purposes the law might also be argued to serve. *Fire, Aim, Ready! Militarizing Animus: "Unit Cohesion" and the Transgender Ban*, 123 Dick. L. Rev. 57 (2018). *Palmore* is presented in Chapter 7, *infra*, at p. 472.

3. The court suggests that had Trump ordered further studies, whose results warranted a reevaluation of the Obama administration military policy allowing service by openly transgender persons and a conclusion that a ban remained appropriate, that "would be a different case." (The court also emphasizes that it is ruling preliminarily, not on a full evidentiary record. Donald Trump sought to salvage his policy by taking advantage of this observation. *See Doe 2 v. Shanahan*, 755 Fed. Appx. 19 (D.C. Cir. 2019), *infra* at p. 359.)

4. Why might Donald Trump have instated this ban on transgender servicemembers? Professor Dara Purvis has argued that masculinities theory helps us understand "that a major reason for the [Trump Administration's] absolute hostility to transgender Americans is rooted in hegemonic masculinity," that recognizing "that transgender people face similar issues of gender discrimination as Ann Hopkins did at Price Waterhouse is to acknowledge that any deviation from the extreme norms of hegemonic masculinity is merely one step down a path that challenges the very concept of gender as binary," and therefore that it is "easy to understand ... why an administration captured by the values of hegemonic masculinity would perceive transgender servicemembers as such a threat and take such sudden and public actions ejecting transgender soldiers from the military and preventing any more from enlisting." Dara E. Purvis, *Trump, Gender Rebels, and Masculinities*, 54 WAKE FOREST L. REV. 423, 448–49 (2019).

Note on Stone v. Trump *(trial court opinion granting preliminary injunction)*

About three weeks after the federal judge in the District of Columbia granted a preliminary injunction against enforcement of the accession and retention directives — but not the surgery directive — of Trump's transgender military service policy in *Doe 1 v. Trump*, a U.S. District Judge in the District of Maryland enjoined the surgery directive in *Brock Stone et al. v. Donald J. Trump*, 280 F. Supp. 3d 747 (D. Md. 2017). The *Stone* plaintiffs, represented by the ACLU of Maryland and the national ACLU, argued that the Surgery Directive violated the equal protection component of the Fifth Amendment Due Process Clause, substantive due process, and 10 U.S.C. § 1074, pursuant to which active duty and reserve members of the armed services are entitled to medical and dental care in military treatment facilities.

The district court in *Stone* dismissed the statutory claim but allowed the possibility that the plaintiffs might seek further amendment of their complaint to press that claim with less conclusory factual allegations. The court did not reach the substantive due process claim, for it stopped its merits analysis after agreeing that the plaintiffs were likely to prevail on their equal protection claim. It ruled that, unlike the *Doe 1* plaintiffs, two of the named service member plaintiffs had standing to challenge the Surgery Directive. The court described their circumstances as alleged in the complaint:

1. Petty Officer First Class Brock Stone

Brock Stone is 34 years old and has served 11 years in the United States Navy, including a 9-month deployment to Afghanistan. Stone is currently assigned, until August 2020, to a unit at Fort Meade in Maryland, where he works as a computer analyst. Stone was awarded an achievement medal in connection with his deployment, and he has received multiple other commendations, including the Joint Commendation Medal, the Navy Commendation Medal, the Afghan Campaign Medal, a flag letter of commendation, and multiple recommendations for early promotion. He is currently eligible for promotion to Chief Petty Officer. Stone's goal is to serve for at least 20 years and qualify for retirement benefits. His current contract runs until 2023, which would end three years short of his achieving enough years in service to meet his retirement goal.

Stone has been undergoing hormone therapy as a medically-necessary part of his gender transition. Since arriving at Fort Meade in July 2017, he has received medically-necessary treatment related to his gender transition at Walter Reed National Military Medical Center in Bethesda, Maryland. Prior to his transfer to Fort Meade, Stone was close to finalizing a medical treatment plan that included surgery. After the transfer in July 2017, he had to restart the treatment plan, but it is now in the final approval stage. The treatment plan will be sent to the medical review board at Walter Reed in November 2017 and thereafter will be submitted to Navy Medical East for final medical approval. Plaintiffs assert that it is "highly likely that Petty Officer Stone will not receive one or both of his medically-necessary surgeries before March 23[, 2018]."

2. Staff Sergeant Kate Cole

Kate Cole is 27 years old and has served in the United States Army for almost ten years, including a one-year deployment to Afghanistan where she served as a team leader and designated marksman. Cole is currently stationed at Fort Polk, Louisiana, working as a Cavalry Scout, where she operates with a tank unit. Since enlisting at age 17, Cole has received seven achievement medals and two Army commendation medals. She recently received orders to enroll in Drill Sergeant School starting on January 3, 2018, with an anticipated graduation date of March 7, 2018. Following her return from Drill Sergeant School, she is scheduled to change station from Fort Polk, Louisiana, to Fort Benning, Georgia.

Cole has been undergoing hormone therapy and was scheduled to receive medically-necessary surgery related to her gender transition in or around September 2017. On September 8, 2017, she was informed that her surgical treatment was denied and her pre-surgical consultation was cancelled. Cancellation has been remedied, but "Cole's treatment plan calls for two additional surgeries, neither of which she will be able to undergo before March 23[, 2018], and one of which she is not even eligible for until after that date."

The court noted that there was "no dispute that the Plaintiffs have satisfied the causation and redressability elements of standing." The issue was whether the plaintiffs sufficiently alleged that they had suffered or imminently would suffer an injury-in-fact sufficient to support Article III standing to sue in federal court.

As the court worded it, the defendants argued "that no Plaintiff can demonstrate injury-in-fact because the military is continuing to provide transition-related medical care under the Interim Guidance. Any cancellations that occurred after the President's Memorandum have subsequently been remedied, so no one has been denied transition-related medical care." The court disagreed, concluding, rather, that plaintiffs Cole and Stone had standing to challenge the Surgery Directive:

> Plaintiff Cole has a final, approved medical plan that calls for two additional surgeries. Because Cole will be attending Drill Sergeant School from January 3, 2018, until March 7, 2018, it is impossible for her to have both surgeries before the March 23rd deadline.

> Plaintiff Stone has a near-final treatment plan that calls for two surgeries, needing only a final stamp of approval, which is not in doubt. The plan calls for the first of the surgeries in April 2018. Although Stone is trying to move the first surgery up to February in an attempt to meet the deadline, it seems unlikely, and the second surgery still needs to be scheduled.

Unlike the first plaintiff in *Doe 1*, Stone and Cole are highly unlikely to complete their medically-necessary surgeries before the effective date of the Directive. Unlike the second plaintiff in *Doe 1*, there is no lack of certainty regarding when transition treatment will begin for Stone and Cole since treatment has already begun, and Stone and Cole's surgeries are endangered by the Directive's deadline.

The court rejected the defendants' argument that the "exception in the Directive will 'cover' the plaintiffs who will not have completed all of their approved and medically-required sex-reassignment surgeries by the effective date." According to Section 2(b) of the President's Memorandum, the Secretaries are to "halt all use of DoD or DHS resources to fund sex reassignment surgical procedures for military personnel, *except to the extent necessary to protect the health of an individual who has already begun a course of treatment to reassign his or her sex*" (emphasis added). The defendants had argued that since "Plaintiffs have in fact started a course of treatment to reassign their sex, and have transition plans either submitted or already in place, the exception *may* in fact apply to them" (emphasis added).

"At the hearing, however," the court noted, "Defendants' counsel could not commit that the exception would apply to Plaintiffs." This was not enough to satisfy the court that the Surgery Directive was not threatening the plaintiffs with imminent harm:

Plaintiffs contend that the exception seems to refer to "situations in which complications arise from surgery performed before March 23." Plaintiffs add that it is not clear that "any service member with a medical need for surgery will receive that surgery—even if he or she received no surgical treatment before March 23." Plaintiffs argue that if the exception were to be interpreted under the broad terms proposed by Defendants, the "exception" would essentially nullify the Directive and contravene President Trump's premise about the cost of surgical care, adding that Defendants "may not evade judicial review by advancing (or, in this case, weakly suggesting) an interpretation of the challenged action that both is implausible and would fatally undercut the President's announced policy." At the hearing, Plaintiffs added that "the Government, as far as we're aware, is not scheduling anything for after March 22nd."

The Court finds that it is at the very least plausible that the exception would not apply to Stone and Cole's scheduled post-March-23rd surgeries. That conclusion is sufficient at this juncture to raise Plaintiffs' right to relief above the speculative and to the plausible level.

Accordingly, the Court finds that Plaintiffs have met their burden to demonstrate standing to challenge the . . . Surgery Directive.

Similarly, the court ruled that the plaintiffs' challenge to the Surgery Directive was not uncertain in a way that should preclude judicial review at that time. "The President directed that the military stop using military resources to fund sex-reassignment surgical procedures for military personnel. The President ordered an implementation plan and set definite implementation dates. The only uncertainties are how, not if, the policy will be implemented and whether, in some future context, the President might be persuaded to change his mind and terminate the policies he is now putting into effect. The validity of the Directives in the President's Memorandum is fit for review." Moreover, denying review now "would impose hardship on the Plaintiffs," the other major ripeness factor in addition to the fitness of the issues for review. The plaintiffs "demonstrated that they are already suffering harmful consequences such as the cancellation and postponements of surgeries, the stigma of being set apart as inherently unfit, facing the prospect of discharge and inability to commission as an officer, the inability to move forward with long-term medical plans, and the threat to their prospects of obtaining long-term assignments." Consequently, the court held that the plaintiffs' challenge to the Surgery Directive was ripe.

The court's analysis of the plaintiffs' likelihood of success on the equal protection challenge to the Surgery Directive was somewhat cursory. The court accepted the *Doe 1* court's analysis and conclusion that the directives should be subjected to intermediate scrutiny. But the *Stone* court offered little specific analysis about *the Surgery* Directive (rather than the Accession and Retention Directives). The court stated that it "agrees with the D.C. Court [in *Doe 1*] that there is sufficient support for Plaintiffs' claims that 'the decision to exclude transgender individuals was not driven by genuine concerns regarding military efficacy.'" But it said not one word of Trump's professed cost justifications. And in "adopt[ing] the D.C. Court's reasoning in the application of intermediate scrutiny to the Directives and find[ing] that the Plaintiffs herein are likely to succeed on their Equal Protection claim[,]" the *Stone* court failed to note that the *Doe* court provided *no* analysis of the equal protection challenge to the Surgery Directive because it had concluded the plaintiffs lacked standing to challenge it.

Note on Karnoski v. Trump *(district court decision granting preliminary injunction)*

Just under three weeks after a U.S. District Judge in Maryland entered the second injunction against Trump's ban on transgender service members (specifically, against the Accession, Retention, and Surgery Directives), a U.S. District Judge in Washington entered a third preliminary injunction against the ban in *Karnoski v. Trump*, C17-1297-MJP, 2017 WL 6311305 (W.D. Wash. Dec. 11, 2017). This suit, initially brought by Lambda Legal, OutServe-SLDN, and private counsel, challenged the policy on behalf of Ryan Karnoski and eight other individuals currently serving in or seeking to enlist in the military. The Human Rights Campaign, the Gender Justice League, the American Military Partner Association, and the State of Washington intervened as plaintiffs as well.

The court dismissed a claim that the policy violated the plaintiffs' procedural due process rights, ruling that they failed to state a valid claim. Citing a Ninth Circuit

Court of Appeals precedent without further explanation, the court conclusorily asserted that the complaint "allege[d] neither a 'protectible liberty or property interest' nor a 'denial of adequate procedural protections' as required for a procedural due process claim." The court did, however, rule that the plaintiffs alleged equal protection, substantive due process, and First Amendment claims that were likely to succeed.

On the equal protection claim, the court, with one sentence of analysis (citing statutory sex-stereotyping cases), concluded that transgender status is a quasi-suspect classification and hence subject to intermediate scrutiny. Stressing the early rejection of the very rationales for the Trump policy by the Department of Defense under the Obama administration, the court then found the policy not to be substantially related to important governmental interests. The court included a bit more detail of its analysis of the financial justification for the Surgery Directive than the opinion in *Stone v. Trump* provided:

> While Defendants raise concerns about transition-related medical conditions and costs, their concerns "appear to be hypothetical and extremely overbroad." *Doe 1.* For instance, Defendants claim that "at least some transgender individuals suffer from medical conditions that could impede the performance of their duties," including gender dysphoria, and complications from hormone therapy and sex reassignment surgery. But *all* service members might suffer from medical conditions that could impede performance, and indeed the working group [under the Obama administration] found that it is common for service members to be non-deployable for periods of time due to an array of such conditions. Defendants claim that accommodating transgender service members would "impose costs on the military." But the study preceding the June 2016 Policy indicates that these costs are exceedingly minimal. ("[E]ven in the most extreme scenario . . . we expect only a 0.13-percent ($8.4 million out of $6.2 billion) increase in [active component] health care spending."); ("[T]he maximum financial impact . . . is an amount so small it was considered to be 'budget dust,' hardly even a rounding error, by military leadership.'"). Indeed, the cost to discharge transgender service members is estimated to be *more than 100 times greater* than the cost to provide transition-related healthcare.

Karnoski added to the types of legal claims the judiciary was recognizing against the Trump ban, holding that the plaintiffs had likely stated that the policy violated their substantive due process rights. The court correctly observed that substantive due process doctrine "protects fundamental liberty interests in individual dignity, autonomy, and privacy from unwarranted government intrusion." But its analysis was not especially deep. It very broadly read the Supreme Court's marriage equality decision, *Obergefell v. Hodges*, 135 S. Ct. 2584 (2015), to hold that "[t]hese fundamental interests include the right to make decisions concerning bodily integrity and self-definition central to an individual's identity." That may be true, but the district court crucially should have specified that those fundamental interests include the right to make "some" such decisions, as the Supreme Court has held that not all such interests are in fact "fundamental" rights under the Due Process Clause. *Washington v. Glucksberg*, 521 U.S. 702 (1997). The court ruled that the policy did intrude on a fundamental liberty interest in "defin[ing] and express[ing] their gender identity," but it provided no reasoning to support that conclusion—it cited no precedent about how to identify fundamental rights and quoted no passages characterizing such rights, *e.g.*, "deeply rooted in this nation's history and tradition," *Glucksberg*.

In another new development, the *Karnoski* court also ruled that the plaintiffs were likely to prevail on their First Amendment argument. The court reasoned that the policy penalizes transgender service members—but not others—for disclosing their gender identity and is therefore a content-based restriction on speech. As such, it needed to survive strict scrutiny under the First Amendment, which the court held it was unlikely to do because the defendants had "not demonstrated that the intrusion upon protected expression furthers an important government interest," let alone that it was narrowly tailored to a compelling interest.

The court ruled that the plaintiffs satisfied the other prerequisites for injunctive relief. The plaintiffs faced irreparable injury because "[b]ack pay and other monetary damages proposed by Defendants will not remedy the stigmatic injury caused by the policy, reverse the disruption of trust between service members, nor cure the medical harms caused by the denial of timely health care." (The court also found that the state of Washington "demonstrated a likelihood of irreparable harm to its sovereign and quasi-sovereign interests if it is 'forced to continue to expend its scarce resources to support a discriminatory policy when it provides funding or deploys its National Guard.' Washington State has also demonstrated that its ability to recruit and retain service personnel for the Washington National Guard may be irreparably harmed.") Unconvinced "that reverting to the June 2016 Policy, which was voluntarily adopted by DoD after extensive study and review, and which has been in place for over a year without documented negative effects, will harm Defendants," and stressing that vindicating constitutional rights is in the public interest, the court concluded that the remaining injunctive relief factors favored the plaintiffs and so enjoined enforcement of the Trump policy.

Although the defendants appealed this decision, they subsequently voluntarily sought and obtained dismissal of their appeal, 2017 WL 8229552 (9th Cir. Dec. 30, 2017), possibly to avoid having the still somewhat liberal-leaning U.S. Court of Appeals for the Ninth Circuit render an adverse decision on the constitutionality of the policy as it was initially announced, when the Trump administration convened a panel to provide greater support for a perhaps cosmetically different version of the ban on military service by openly transgender persons.

Note on Stockman v. Trump *(district court decision granting preliminary injunction)*

Just 11 days after a U.S. District Judge in Washington entered the third injunction against Trump's transgender military ban (specifically, against the Accession, Retention, and Surgery Directives), a U.S. District Judge in California entered a fourth preliminary injunction against the ban on transgender service members in *Stockman v. Trump*, 2017 WL 9732572 (C.D. Cal. Dec. 22, 2017). This suit was brought by seven named or anonymous transgender men and women serving in or planning to serve in the armed forces along with Equality California ("EQCA"), "an organization dedicated to LGBTQ civil rights" whose "membership includes transgender individuals in active service, transgender military veterans, and transgender individuals who have intend to pursue long-term military careers."[a] District Judge Jesus G. Bernal denied the defendants' motion to dismiss for lack of standing and lack of a ripe dispute, ruling that the plaintiffs had standing to challenge the Access, Retention, and Surgery Directives.

As for the likelihood of the plaintiffs prevailing on the merits of their constitutional claims, the district court concluded that "discrimination on the basis of one's transgender status is equivalent to sex-based discrimination." Rejecting at that stage of the litigation the defendants' cost and unit cohesion arguments, the district court ruled that these justifications were not "exceedingly persuasive" as required by the intermediate equal protection scrutiny applicable to sex discrimination, and thus that the plaintiffs were likely to succeed on their equal protection claim. Since that was enough to support the grant of preliminary injunctive relief, the court expressed no views about the plaintiffs' due process, right to privacy, and First Amendment challenges to Trump's ban on military service by transgender persons.

Trump Trans Ban Version 2.0

In revisiting the exhaustive study of military service by transgender personnel conducted by the Obama administration, the Defense Department under Trump convened an ostensible panel of experts to study the issue more; the administration has been fighting litigation discovery efforts to identify the members of the panel. Citing multiple sources, *Slate* reported that "Vice President Mike Pence played a leading role in the creation of this report, along with Ryan Anderson, an anti-trans activist, and Tony Perkins, head of the Family Research Council, an anti-LGBTQ lobbying group." Mark Joseph Stern, *Trump's Trans Troop Ban Will Never Take Effect*, Slate, Mar. 24, 2018, available at https://slate.com/news-and-politics/2018/03/trumps-new-trans-troops-ban-is-still-unconstitutional.html. (The prediction in the title of this story proved inaccurate, primarily as a result of the Supreme

---

a One of this casebook's co-authors at the time served and continues to serve on the board of the Equality California Institute but was not involved in this case including the initial decision to bring it.

Court's eventually staying injunctions against the policy that lower courts had issued.) In February 2018, the panel completed a report recommending an implementation that would grandfather in certain transgender people already serving in the armed forces and some apparently small number of transgender people who meet several highly restrictive criteria. Also in February 2018, pursuant to the presidential memorandum Donald Trump issued the month after his July 2017 tweets announced his ban on military service by transgender people, Defense Secretary Mattis provided Trump with a memorandum containing a plan for implementing Trump's transgender service ban. The federal government sought to have litigation against its transgender military service ban dismissed as moot in light of its supposedly "new" policy, a position that met with a frosty reception among the district courts that had enjoined Trump's ban.

Note on Stockman v. Trump *(decision refusing to dissolve preliminary injunction)*

In *Stockman v. Trump*, 331 F. Supp. 3d 990 (C.D. Cal. 2018), vacated and remanded, 2019 WL 6125075 (9th Cir. Aug. 26, 2019), the district court denied the government's motion to dissolve its preliminary injunction in light of the Mattis implementation plan and subsequent 2018 presidential memorandum issued by Donald Trump. The district court concluded that "the new policy is essentially the same as the first policy."

Applying intermediate scrutiny, the court rejected the defendants' argument that the Trump ban was justified by an interest in "promoting military readiness based on deployability." Although the defendants claimed they were worried that people with gender dysphoria have greater mental instability, the court observed that

> a diagnosis of gender dysphoria is neither necessary nor sufficient to be excluded from the military under this policy. . . . People with gender dysphoria are explicitly exempted from this new policy as long as they do not present as transgender. Likewise, Defendants' concern that those who undergo gender transition surgery could negatively affect deployability is not substantially related to the actual effect of this policy. Defendants state the majority of current transgender service member treatment plans include a request for gender transition surgery. However, the Mattis Memorandum bans all individuals who present as transgender from the military, not only those who have undergone gender transition surgery.

The court consequently found the policy not substantially related to the defendant's proffered concerns as required under intermediate scrutiny.

The court also rejected the defendants' attempt to invoke unit cohesion to defend the policy. They appeared to argue that transgender people should not be allowed to serve unless they had genital reconstruction surgery, that if they did have such surgery they could not shower or be housed with either men or women without invading the reasonable "expectations of privacy of the non-transgender service members who share those quarters," and that it would not be practicable to provide separate facilities for transgender servicemembers. The court mentioned, in passing, precedents cited by the plaintiffs where courts "have held that allowing transgender individuals to live in accord with their identity does not threaten the privacy or safety interests of others." But it spent more time discussing the eventual rejection of the unit cohesion justification for the ban on lesbigay servicemembers. With a slight lacuna in its written argument, the court concluded:

> In the history of military service in this country, "the loss of unit cohesion" has been consistently weaponized against open service by a new minority group. Yet, at every turn, this assertion has been overcome by the military's steadfast ability to integrate these individuals into effective members of our armed forces. As with blacks, women, and gays, so now with transgender persons. The military has repeatedly proven its capacity to adapt and grow stronger specifically by the inclusion of these individuals. Therefore, the government cannot use "the loss of unit cohesion" as an excuse to prevent an otherwise qualified class of discrete and insular minorities from joining the armed forces. The Court finds this justification of the transgender ban is not exceedingly persuasive and cannot survive intermediate scrutiny.

On appeal, the U.S. Court of Appeals for the Ninth Circuit vacated the district court's order denying dissolution of the preliminary injunction and stayed that injunction pending that court's reconsideration of the motion to dissolve in light of the court of appeals decision in *Karnoski v. Trump*, 926 F.3d 1180 (9th Cir. 2019), and any appeal therefrom.

Stockman was not the only case where a district court rejected the Trump administration's attempt to wipe out preliminary injunctions against its trans ban. *Cf.* Jennifer L. Levi & Kevin M. Barry, *Transgender Tropes & Constitutional Review*, 37 Yale L. & Pol'y Rev. 589, 633, 640–46 (2019) (arguing that continued lower court rejection of "the familiar tropes used to justify laws that criminalized gender-nonconformity, den[ied] access to appropriate single-sex services, and deprive[d] transgender people of the protection of various anti-discrimination laws" has broad legal, doctrinal, theoretical, and symbolic implications). Another illustrative opinion is presented next in more detail.

Reading Guide for Doe 2 v. Trump

1. What does Secretary of Defense Mattis's implementation plan for Trump's transgender military service ban provide? (Whom does or doesn't it exclude?) To people with what sorts of conditions does the "Panel Report" compare transgender persons? Would these policies or recommendations exclude all transgender people from military service? Almost all? Would they exclude any people who are not transgender? Many such people?

2. In its analysis of the "injury-in-fact" prong of the constitutional "standing" doctrine, which must be satisfied for a person to be able to press a claim in federal court, in what ways does the court conclude Trump's ban as specified in the Mattis

implementation plan harms servicemembers despite the "grandfather" provision allowing a specific class of trans people to continue serving, and how does the policy harm them? What harms from the policy does the court identify for people who have already undergone gender transition but are not yet in the armed forces? What harms for people serving who have not yet received a gender dysphoria diagnosis, and what harms for Dylan Kohere?

3. What is the relationship the court articulates between Trump's initially announced policy and the Mattis plan? For what reasons does the court conclude that adoption of the Mattis plan does not render the plaintiffs' suit moot?

4. What reasons does the court give for concluding that the Mattis plan does not demonstrate the kind of changed circumstances that might justify the court in vacating the preliminary injunction the court had previously entered in favor of the plaintiffs?

Doe 2, et al. v. Trump, et al.

315 F. Supp. 3d 474 (D.D.C. 2018) [*rev'd*, Doe 2 v. Shanahan,
755 Fed. Appx. 19 (D.C. Cir. 2019)]

Memorandum Opinion

Colleen Kollar-Kotelly, United States District Judge.

On July 26, 2017, President Donald J. Trump issued a statement via Twitter announcing that "the United States Government will not accept or allow transgender individuals to serve in any capacity in the U.S. Military." A formal Presidential Memorandum followed on August 25, 2017. Before the 2017 Presidential Memorandum, the Department of Defense had announced that openly transgender individuals would be allowed to enlist in the military, effective January 1, 2018, and had prohibited the discharge of service members based solely on their gender identities. The 2017 Presidential Memorandum reversed these policies. It indefinitely extended the prohibition against transgender individuals entering the military (a process formally referred to as "accession"), and required the military to authorize the discharge of transgender service members. The President ordered Secretary of Defense James N. Mattis to submit a plan for implementing the policy directives of the 2017 Presidential Memorandum by February 2018. Plaintiffs filed suit and sought preliminary injunctive relief, which the Court granted.

Currently pending before the Court are Defendants' Motion to Dismiss Plaintiffs' Second Amended Complaint, or, in the Alternative, Defendants' Motion for Summary Judgment, and Defendants' Motion to Dissolve the Preliminary Injunction. . . . [T]he Court denies Defendants' Motion to Dismiss Plaintiffs' Second Amended Complaint, and denies Defendants' Motion to Dissolve the Preliminary Injunction. Both of these motions are based on the same fundamental premise: that Defendants have recently proposed a "new policy" that will now allow transgender individuals to serve in the military. Based on this premise, Defendants argue in these motions that Plaintiffs no longer have standing, that their claims are moot, and that there is no longer any need for this Court's preliminary injunction. For reasons discussed in more detail below, the Court is not persuaded by these arguments. This case shall proceed, and the Court's preliminary injunction shall continue to maintain the status quo ante.

I. Background

Plaintiffs are current and aspiring transgender service members. Many have years of experience in the military. Some have decades. They have been deployed on active duty in Iraq and Afghanistan. They have and continue to serve with distinction. All fear that the directives of the 2017 Presidential Memorandum will have devastating impacts on their careers and their families. Accordingly, they filed this lawsuit challenging those directives and moved this Court to enjoin the implementation of the 2017 Presidential Memorandum. They claimed that the President's directives violate the fundamental guarantees of due process afforded by the Fifth Amendment to the United States Constitution.

On October 30, 2017, the Court issued a preliminary injunction in this case. As particularly relevant here, the Court found that Plaintiffs had standing and were likely to succeed on their Fifth Amendment claim. . . . Accordingly, the Court enjoined Defendants from enforcing the President's directives. The effect of the Court's preliminary injunction was to revert to the status quo ante with regard to accession and retention that existed before the issuance of the 2017 Presidential Memorandum.

Defendants appealed, and moved this Court to stay the portion of its preliminary injunction that required Defendants to begin accepting transgender individuals into the military on January 1, 2018. On December 11, 2017, the Court denied Defendants' motion to stay.

Defendants then sought the same relief from the United States Court of Appeals for the District of Columbia Circuit. On December 22, 2017, the D.C. Circuit denied Defendants' motion to stay this Court's preliminary injunction. . . . After the D.C. Circuit's opinion was issued, Defendants voluntarily dismissed their appeal of this Court's preliminary injunction. The military began permitting openly transgender individuals to accede on January 1, 2018.

This case then moved forward into the discovery stage. Defendants strenuously resisted engaging in discovery. As noted above, the 2017 Presidential Memorandum had called for the Secretary of Defense to submit a plan to implement the President's policy directives by February 2018. Defendants repeatedly argued that discovery should be halted until that plan was submitted. Defendants even argued at one point that Plaintiffs were not entitled to discovery in this case at all. The Court repeatedly rejected Defendants' arguments and ordered Defendants to cooperate with discovery so that this case could move forward efficiently toward an ultimate resolution on the merits. Despite the Court's orders, discovery remains unfinished because Defendants have asserted that a substantial portion of the documents and information sought by Plaintiffs are privileged (pursuant to the deliberative process privilege and the presidential communications privilege), and the parties' disputes about these assertions of privilege remain outstanding.

In February 2018, as ordered by the 2017 Presidential Memorandum, Secretary of Defense Mattis presented a memorandum to the President that proposed a policy to effectively prevent transgender military service[] (hereinafter, the "Mattis Implementation Plan"). The Mattis Implementation Plan, unlike the President's 2017 tweet and memorandum, purports not to be a blanket ban on all "transgender individuals." However, the plan effectively implements such a ban by targeting proxies of transgender status, such as "gender dysphoria" and "gender transition," and by requiring all service members to serve "in their biological sex." Based on the conclusion "that there are substantial risks associated with allowing the accession and retention of individuals with a history or diagnosis of gender dysphoria and require, or have already undertaken, a course of treatment to change their gender," Mattis Implementation Plan at 2, the Mattis Implementation Plan proposes the following policies:

- Transgender persons with a history or diagnosis of gender dysphoria are disqualified from military service, except under the following limited circumstances: (1) if they have been stable for 36 consecutive months in their biological sex prior to accession; (2) Service members diagnosed with gender dysphoria after entering into service may be retained if they do not require a change of gender and remain deployable within applicable retention standards; and (3) currently serving Service members who have been diagnosed with gender dysphoria since the previous administration's policy took effect and prior to the effective date of this new policy, may continue to serve in their preferred gender and receive medically necessary treatment for gender dysphoria.

- Transgender persons who require or have undergone gender transition are disqualified from military service.

- Transgender persons without a history or diagnosis of gender dysphoria, who are otherwise qualified for service, may serve, like all other Service members, in their biological sex.

To summarize: under the Mattis Implementation Plan, individuals who require or have undergone gender transition are absolutely disqualified from military service; individuals with a history or diagnosis of gender dysphoria are largely disqualified from military service; and, to the extent that there are any individuals who identify as "transgender" but do not fall under the first two categories, they may serve, but only "in their biological sex." By definition, transgender persons do not identify or live in accord with their biological sex, which means that the result of the Mattis Implementation Plan is that transgender individuals are generally not allowed to serve openly in the military. There is only one narrow class of transgender individuals who are allowed to serve as openly transgender under the Mattis Implementation Plan. Pursuant to a "grandfather provision," those "currently serving Service members who have been diagnosed with gender dysphoria since the previous administration's policy took effect and prior to the effective date of" the policy set forth in the Mattis Implementation Plan, may continue to serve in their preferred gender.

The reasoning underlying the Mattis Implementation Plan is spelled out in a second memorandum that was sent from the Department of Defense to the President in February 2018[] (hereinafter, the "Panel Report"). Like the Mattis Implementation Plan, the Panel Report carefully avoids categorical language banning all transgender individuals. Instead, the document speaks in terms of individuals with "gender dysphoria" and those who have undergone or will require "gender transition" (both of which, again, are proxies for transgender status). Generally speaking, the Panel Report concludes that individuals with gender dysphoria or who have undergone or will require gender transition undermine the military. According to the report, these service members are fundamentally incompatible with the military's mental health standards, physical health standards, and sex-based standards. The report suggests that they are a detriment to military readiness and unit cohesion. It likens gender dysphoria to conditions such as "bipolar disorder, personality disorder, obsessive-compulsive disorder, suicidal behavior, and even body dysmorphic disorder." It concludes that individuals with gender dysphoria or who have undergone or will require gender transition are more likely to have other mental health conditions and substance abuse problems, and to commit suicide. The Panel Report also states that these individuals impose "disproportionate costs" on the military. For the most part, in lieu of affirmative evidence, the Panel Report repeatedly cites "uncertainty" in the medical field about these individuals as a reason to urge that the military "proceed with caution." Although not necessary to the outcome of this particular Memorandum Opinion, it is worth noting that these conclusions were immediately denounced by the American Psychological Association and the American Medical Association.

On March 23, 2018, Defendants filed a Notice informing the Court that President Trump had issued a second memorandum on military service by transgender individuals. In the 2018 Presidential Memorandum, the President stated that he "revokes" his 2017 Presidential Memorandum, "and any other directive [he] may have made with respect to military service by transgender individuals." The President ordered that "[t]he Secretary of Defense, and the Secretary of Homeland Security, with respect to the U.S. Coast Guard, may exercise their authority to implement any appropriate policies concerning military service by transgender individuals." To be clear, as has just been laid out, the "appropriate policies" that the Secretaries intended to implement had already been developed and proposed to the President at the time he issued this memorandum.

. . . . Defendants argue that the Mattis Implementation Plan represents a "new policy" divorced and distinct from the President's 2017 policy directives that were previously enjoined by this Court. They also contend that the Mattis Implementation Plan does not harm the Plaintiffs in this case. Accordingly, Defendants seek the dismissal of Plaintiffs' recently filed Second Amended Complaint for lack of jurisdiction because Plaintiffs lack standing and because their claims are now moot. For largely the same reasons, Defendants also argue that the Court's preliminary injunction should be dissolved. In sum, it is Defendants' view that they have pre-empted this lawsuit by drafting and issuing the Panel Report, the Mattis Implemen-tation Plan, and the 2018 Presidential Memorandum. The Court disagrees.

Summary: . . . . The Court first concludes that Plaintiffs have standing because they would all be harmed if the Mattis Implementation Plan were allowed to take effect. The Court next concludes that the Mattis Implementation Plan has not mooted Plaintiffs' claims because that plan is not a "new policy" that is meaning-fully distinct from the President's 2017 directives that were originally challenged in this case. Instead, at a fundamental level, the Mattis Implementation Plan is just that—a plan that implements the President's directive that transgender people be excluded from the military. For largely the same reasons, the rationale for the Court's preliminary injunction maintaining the status quo ante until the final reso-lution of this case remains intact. Nothing in this Memorandum Opinion repre-sents a final adjudication of whether Defendants' actions were constitutional. The Court merely holds that whatever legal relevance the Mattis Implementation Plan might have, it has not fundamentally changed the circumstances of this lawsuit such that Plaintiffs' claims should be dismissed for lack of jurisdiction, or that the need for the Court's preliminary injunction has dissipated.

. . . .

III. Discussion

. . . . Article III of the Constitution limits the jurisdiction of this Court to the adjudication of "Cases" and "Controversies." . . . . Defendants argue that the issu-ance of the 2018 Presidential Memorandum, the Mattis Implementation Plan, and the Panel Report have rendered this case moot and have deprived all Plaintiffs of standing. They contend that the Court must therefore dismiss the case for lack of jurisdiction. Defendants are wrong. In addition, for largely the same reasons that the Court continues to have jurisdiction over Plaintiffs' claims, Defendants have not satisfied their burden of demonstrating that the Court's preliminary injunction should be dissolved.

1. Standing

Standing is an element of the Court's subject-matter jurisdiction. . . . [S]tanding analysis is "especially rigorous when reaching the merits of the dispute would force [the court] to decide whether an action taken by one of the other two branches of the Federal Government was unconstitutional." *Clapper v. Amnesty Int'l USA*, 568 U.S. 398 (2013). "[A] plaintiff must demonstrate standing for each claim he seeks to press" and for each form of relief sought, *DaimlerChrysler Corp. v. Cuno*, 547 U.S. 332 (2006), but "the presence of one party with standing is sufficient to satisfy Article III's case-or-controversy requirement," *Rumsfeld v. Forum for Acad. & Insti-tutional Rights, Inc.*, 547 U.S. 47 (2006).

The familiar requirements of Article III standing are:

> (1) that the plaintiff have suffered an "injury in fact"—an invasion of a judicially cognizable interest which is (a) concrete and particularized and (b) actual or imminent, not conjectural or hypothetical; (2) that there be a causal connection between the injury and the conduct complained of—the injury must be fairly traceable to the challenged action of the defendant, and not the result of the independent action of some third party not before the court; and (3) that it be likely, as opposed to merely speculative, that the injury will be redressed by a favorable decision.

Bennett v. Spear, 520 U.S. 154, 167 (1997). With respect to the "injury in fact" requirement, which is predominantly at issue in this case, "future injury may suffice if the threatened injury is 'certainly impending,' or there is a 'substantial risk that the harm will occur.'" *Susan B. Anthony List v. Driehaus*, 134 S. Ct. 2334 (2014).

. . . . In its October 30, 2017 Memorandum Opinion, the Court explained in detail why the Plaintiffs in this case had standing. *See Doe 1 v. Trump*, 275 F. Supp. 3d 167 (D.D.C. 2017). The Court will assume familiarity with that discussion and will not repeat it here (although it does expressly incorporate that discussion into this Memorandum Opinion as though stated in full). . . . [I]n this Opinion the Court focuses more narrowly on Defendants' arguments about why the Mattis Implementation Plan has nullified Plaintiffs' standing. As explained above, the effect of that plan would be that individuals who require or have undergone gender transition would be absolutely disqualified from military service, individuals with a history or diagnosis of gender dysphoria would be largely disqualified from military service, and, to the extent that there are any individuals who identify as "transgender" but do not fall under the first two categories, they would be allowed serve, but only "in their biological sex" (which means that openly transgender persons would generally not be allowed to serve in conformance with their identity).

i. Current Service Members With Diagnoses of Gender Dysphoria Who Either Have Transitioned or Have Begun to Transition

Plaintiffs Regan Kibby, Jane Does 2 through 5, and John Doe 1 are current service members who have been diagnosed with gender dysphoria. The Mattis Implementation Plan generally bans individuals who have been diagnosed with gender dysphoria from military service on the grounds that they are mentally unstable and that their presence in the military disrupts unit cohesion, prevents good order and discipline, and is generally incompatible with military readiness and lethality. However, the Mattis Implementation Plan contains a limited exception from this ban for current service members who, like Plaintiffs Regan Kibby, Jane Does 2 through 5, and John Doe 1, were "diagnosed with gender dysphoria since the previous administration's policy took effect and prior to the effective date of this new policy." This "grandfather provision" purports to be based on the military's prior "commitment to these Service members" and "the substantial investment it has made in them." Panel Report. Defendants argue that the existence of this grandfather provision means that the Mattis Implementation Plan does not harm these Plaintiffs.

Defendants are wrong. The Mattis Implementation Plan clearly harms all current service members with gender dysphoria—even those who are allowed to remain in the military as a result of a narrow grandfather provision. It singles them out from all other service members and marks them as categorically unfit for military service. *See generally* Panel Report. It sends the message to their fellow service members and superiors that they cannot function in their respective positions. That they are mentally unstable. That their presence in the military is incompatible with military readiness, unit cohesion, good order, and discipline. In sum, it is an express statement that these individuals' very presence makes the military weaker and less combat-ready.

By singling these Plaintiffs out and stigmatizing them as members of an inherently inferior class of service members, the Mattis Implementation Plan causes Plaintiffs grave non-economic injuries that are alone sufficient to confer standing. *See Heckler v. Mathews*, 465 U.S. 728 (1984) ("[D]iscrimination itself, by perpetuating 'archaic and stereotypic notions' or by stigmatizing members of the disfavored group as 'innately inferior' and therefore as less worthy participants in the political community, can cause serious non-economic injuries to those persons who are personally denied equal treatment solely because of their membership in a disfavored group.") (internal citation omitted).

Defendants disagree that this "stigmatic" injury alone is sufficient to confer standing. They claim that "an alleged injury arising from discrimination 'accords a basis for standing only to those persons who are personally denied equal treatment by the challenged discriminatory conduct.'" But the principal case Defendants cite in support of this argument, *Allen v. Wright*, 468 U.S. 737 (1984), is readily distinguishable. The plaintiffs in *Allen* were the parents of African American public school children. They challenged the Internal Revenue Service's grant of tax-exempt status to racially segregated private schools. The Allen Court rejected the plaintiffs' claim of standing based on the "stigmatic injury, or denigration" that is "suffered by all members of a racial group when the Government discriminates on the basis of race." The Supreme Court held that "[t]here can be no doubt that this sort of non-economic injury is one of the most serious consequences of discriminatory government action and is sufficient in some circumstances to support standing." However, it concluded that such stigmatic injury did not support standing for the particular plaintiffs in *Allen* because their children had never applied to any of the private schools at issue, and therefore they had not been "personally denied equal treatment." Instead, they had merely alleged an "abstract stigmatic injury" that would be equally applicable to "all members" of an entire racial group, nationwide.

 The situation here is fundamentally different. Plaintiffs are not merely concerned members of the public or bystanders presenting a generalized grievance. They are members of the precisely defined group that the Mattis Implementation Plan discriminates against by labelling as unsuited for military service. The Mattis Implementation Plan sends a blatantly stigmatizing message to all members of the military hierarchy that has a unique and damaging effect on a narrow and identifiable set of individuals, of which Plaintiffs are members. Moreover, unlike the alleged injury in *Allen*, the stigmatic injury alleged by Plaintiffs is caused by their receiving unequal treatment under the Mattis Implementation Plan. Under that plan, Plaintiffs would be allowed to remain in the military but, unlike any other service members, only pursuant to an exception to a policy that explicitly marks them as unfit for service. No other service members are so afflicted. These Plaintiffs are denied equal treatment because they will be the only service members who are allowed to serve only based on a technicality; as an exception to a policy that generally paints them as unfit. In their words, "[w]hile other service members will enjoy the security and status of serving as honored, respected, and equal members of the Armed Forces," Plaintiffs "will serve only on conditional sufferance and therefore on objectively unequal terms."[5] Because their stigmatic injury derives from this unequal treatment, it is sufficient to confer standing.

Regardless, even assuming that the "stigmatic" aspects of Plaintiffs' injuries were not alone sufficient to confer standing, the Mattis Implementation Plan does more than just stigmatize Plaintiffs. It creates a substantial risk that Plaintiffs will suffer concrete harms to their careers in the near future. There is a substantial risk that the plan will harm Plaintiffs' career development in the form of reduced opportunities for assignments, promotion, training, and deployment. These harms are an additional basis for Plaintiffs' standing.

Defendants argue that these alleged harms are too "speculative," but the Court disagrees. The Secretary of Defense has personally issued a policy, with a lengthy supporting memorandum, that, in effect, instructs the entire armed forces that Plaintiffs' service is harmful to the military. There is nothing speculative about the proposition that, having been so instructed by the very top of the military hierarchy, Plaintiffs' supervisors will place less trust in Plaintiffs and be less likely to give Plaintiffs quality assignments and opportunities. The very nature of such a pronouncement from the Secretary of Defense creates a non-speculative and substantial risk that Plaintiffs' experience, career development, and growth in the military will be hampered. To pretend otherwise is fanciful. This fairly obvious conclusion is buttressed by evidence of the effects of prior negative proclamations about transgender service. For instance, Jane Doe 2 declares that she received an unfavorable work detail to keep her "separated from the rest of [her] unit because [she is] transgender and because of the President's ban, as [she] never had any problems with this kind of treatment in [her] old unit and [does] not know of any other reason [why] she would be treated this way." The detail requires Jane Doe 2 to "driv[e] far away from my base all day every day" and despite the fact that she is "supposed to be in charge of four or five other soldiers, [she has] yet to meet them." The conclusion is also

---

5. *In re Navy Chaplaincy*, 534 F.3d 756 (D.C. Cir. 2008) is also distinguishable. Unlike in that case, Plaintiffs here do not merely take offense to a message that can be interpreted from government action. Plaintiffs assert that they are directly injured by an explicit government message about their suitability as service members.

supported by the declarations of the former United States Secretaries of the Army and Navy. . . . *See, e.g.*, Supp. Decl. of Raymond E. Mabus, Jr. ("transgender service members are losing opportunities for assignments that they are capable of doing"); Supp. Decl. of Eric K. Fanning (transgender service members' "advancement and promotion opportunities in the military" are being substantially limited).

The grandfather provision of the Mattis Implementation Plan does not alleviate these harms. That provision does not state, nor does it appear to be based on, a conclusion that those who will be allowed to remain in the military like Regan Kibby, Jane Does 2 through 5, and John Doe 1 are somehow more fit to serve than those who will be banned. Instead, the provision is based—purportedly—on a conclusion that discharging these particular individuals would be unfair because they relied on the military's prior policy pronouncements, and also inefficient because the military has already invested time and money into their training. Accordingly, the message of the policy—that, under general circumstances, these Plaintiffs should not be in the military—remains intact. That message is substantially likely to harm Plaintiffs' careers in very real ways. Accordingly, the Court finds that Plaintiffs Regan Kibby, Jane Does 2 through 5, and John Doe 1 have standing.

ii. Prospective Service Members Who Have Undergone Gender Transition

Jane Doe 7 and John Doe 2 are prospective service members who have already undergone, or are currently undergoing, gender transition, and are also actively taking steps toward enlistment. If the Mattis Implementation Plan takes effect, these individuals will be barred from military service because they have undergone gender transition. Being barred from service is clearly an "injury in fact" sufficient to give these Plaintiffs standing.

Defendants argue that the Mattis Implementation Plan deprives these Plaintiffs of standing because (if they rush to enlist) they can still join the military while this Court's preliminary injunction is in effect and the Mattis Implementation Plan is not allowed to be implemented. . . . If Plaintiffs do not enlist right now while the preliminary injunction is in effect and take advantage of the grandfather provision, their harm is self-inflicted. Defendants argue that Plaintiffs cannot manufacture standing based on "self-inflicted" harm.

. . . . Plaintiffs challenge the constitutionality of the policies realized in the Mattis Implementation Plan, which Defendants are prepared to implement. Those policies, and that plan in particular, are not yet in effect, but only because the Court granted Plaintiffs' Motion for a Preliminary Injunction in this case, not because Defendants have decided to allow Plaintiffs to enlist as transgender military personnel during this period. All indications suggest that the Defendants have every intention of enforcing the plan as soon as they are no longer enjoined from doing so and, in fact, Defendants have moved this Court and other courts to dissolve injunctions so that they can accomplish that goal. That the plan does not harm Plaintiffs so long as the preliminary injunction is in force, of course, does not mean that Plaintiffs lack standing. To assess whether Plaintiffs have standing, the Court must determine whether that plan would harm them if the Court lifted its injunction and allowed the plan to go into effect. There is no dispute that if the Court did so, Jane Doe 7 and John Doe 2 would be barred from military service by the Mattis Implementation Plan. Accordingly, they have standing.

    . . . .

Finally, Defendants argue that, even assuming that the Mattis Implementation Plan has taken effect, and thus Jane Doe 7 and John Doe 2 are barred from military service, there would still be no injury because these Plaintiffs "would not be personally denied equal treatment[]" . . . . because Plaintiffs "have not shown that they would be treated differently than any other individual who seeks to join the military with a preexisting medical condition." This argument "concerns the merits. . . ." It has no relevance to the Court's assessment of standing. . . .

iii. Current Service Member Without a Diagnosis of Gender Dysphoria

Jane Doe 6 is a current service member who does not yet have a diagnosis of gender dysphoria. Jane Doe 6 had made a behavioral health appointment to obtain a transition plan and begin her gender transition, but—for obvious reasons—aborted that effort when President Trump tweeted that transgender individuals would not be permitted to serve. After that, Jane Doe 6 has not disclosed her transgender identity and has not received a military diagnosis of gender dysphoria because she is afraid that she will be discharged. Because she has not yet received a diagnosis of gender dysphoria, Jane Doe 6 would face discharge under the Mattis Implementation Plan if she sought such a diagnosis after the plan took effect.

    . . . . Defendants claim that if Jane Doe 6 seeks a diagnosis of gender dysphoria from a military doctor while this Court's preliminary injunction is still in place and the Mattis Implementation Plan has not yet gone into effect, she will be able to continue to serve under the plan's grandfather provision. Again, the Court rejects the logic of this argument. The Court asks whether the Mattis Implementation Plan, if allowed to go into effect, would harm Jane Doe 6. The answer is clear: it would. It would subject her to discharge if she sought a diagnosis of gender dysphoria and gender transition therapy.

    . . . . Jane Doe 6 does not lack standing simply because she has the option of either remaining in the military and disavowing her identity as a transgender person, or coming out and serving as a member of an officially branded inferior class of service members.

iv. Dylan Kohere

    . . . .

Finally, Defendants also argue that "[f]ar from being 'categorically barred because he is transgender' . . . under the new policy, Mr. Kohere would be allowed to serve in his biological sex." This argument misses the point. Mr. Kohere is transgender. That means that he does not identify with his biological sex. To serve in his biological sex would be to suppress his identity. To do so would be a harm in and of itself, sufficient to confer standing. The fact that a plaintiff can avoid the effect of a discriminatory policy by renouncing the characteristic that leads to the discrimination in the first place does not mean that the plaintiff lacks standing. . . .

2. Mootness

Defendants also argue that Plaintiffs' claims should be dismissed as moot. Defendants' mootness argument reduces to the following points: Plaintiffs' lawsuit challenges President Trump's 2017 policy of banning transgender military service. The Mattis Implementation Plan does not completely ban transgender military service. It is instead a "new policy" that is distinct from the policy directives announced by President Trump in 2017. Because Defendants are no longer attempting to implement the challenged policy, Plaintiffs' suit is now moot.

The Supreme Court has commanded that a party asserting mootness through cessation of challenged conduct carries a "heavy burden." *Hardaway v. D.C. Hous. Auth.*, 843 F.3d 973 (D.C. Cir. 2016) (citing *Friends of the Earth, Inc. v. Laidlaw Envtl. Servs. (TOC), Inc.*, 528 U.S. 167 (2000)). Defendants have not satisfied their burden here.

. . . . Plaintiffs have recently amended their complaint to challenge the Mattis Implementation Plan, and that challenge is clearly still live. . . . Accordingly, even if the Court were to accept Defendants' arguments regarding claims focused on the President's 2017 directives, Plaintiffs' lawsuit would not be moot to the extent that it challenges the Mattis Implementation Plan.

Regardless, the Court does not accept Defendants' argument that Plaintiffs' challenge to the President's 2017 directives is moot. This argument attempts to draw artificial and unwarranted boundaries between the various policy pronouncements in this case. As explained above, Defendants' mootness argument is based upon the premise that the Mattis Implementation Plan is a new and different policy than the one announced by President Trump in 2017. But Defendants have not demonstrated that this is the case in any meaningful way. To the contrary, the Mattis Implementation Plan appears to be just that — an implementation plan. The plan *implements* the President's 2017 directives that the military not allow transgender individuals to serve in the military.

. . . .

First, the 2017 Presidential Memorandum directed the Department of Defense to submit, by February 2018, a plan to *implement* the President's directives that transgender service be prohibited. It did not ask for the submission of a "new policy" on transgender service. In the 2017 Presidential Memorandum, the President directed the military to return to a policy under which: (i) transgender individuals are generally prohibited from accession and (ii) the military is authorized to discharge individuals who are transgender. The 2017 Presidential Memorandum ordered the Secretary of Defense to prepare an "implementation plan" that was circumscribed to suggestions about how to "implement a policy under which transgender accession is *prohibited*, and discharge of transgender service members is *authorized*." *Doe 1*. It is clear from the 2017 Presidential Memorandum that the "implementation plan" requested by the President was required to "prohibit transgender accession and authorize the discharge of transgender service members." *Id.* The plan was not intended to be a proposal for a "new policy" that *allowed* transgender service. *See Karnoski v. Trump*, 2018 WL 1784464 (W.D. Wash. Apr. 13, 2018) ("The 2017 Memorandum did not direct Secretary Mattis to determine *whether* or not the directives should be implemented, but instead ordered the directives to be implemented by specific dates and requested a plan for *how* to do so.") (emphasis in original).

Second, the actions and statements of Secretary Mattis, and the Department of Defense generally, during the time between the issuance of the 2017 Presidential Memorandum and the Mattis Implementation Plan indicate that the plan being developed was not a "new one" to propose to President Trump, but instead simply one to implement President Trump's 2017 policy directives. In an August 29, 2017 Statement, Secretary Mattis stated that the Department of Defense had "received the [2017] Presidential Memorandum" and would "carry out the president's policy direction." He further stated that he would establish a panel of experts not to consider "new policies," but instead simply "to provide advice and recommendations on the *implementation of the president's direction*." *Id.* (emphasis added). After the "panel reports its recommendations and following . . . consultation with the secretary of Homeland Security," Secretary Mattis stated that he would "provide [his] advice to the president concerning *implementation of his policy direction*." *Id.* (emphasis added).

In a September 14, 2017 document entitled "Military Service by Transgender Individuals—Interim Guidance," Secretary Mattis again stated that he would present the President with a "plan *to implement the policy and directives* in the [2017] Presidential Memorandum." (emphasis added). The Interim Guidance further stated that the Department of Defense would "*carry out the President's policy and directives*" and would "*comply with the [2017] Presidential Memorandum*." *Id.* (emphasis added). A separate document issued to direct the implementation process stated that Secretary Mattis had convened a panel to "develop[ ] an Implementation Plan on military service by transgender individuals, *to effect the policy and directives of the Presidential Memorandum*." (emphasis added). That document further acknowledges that the Department was required to "return to the longstanding policy and practice on military service by transgender individuals that was in place prior to June 2016," that is, the general prohibition on transgender service. It stated that the Department had been "direct[ed]" to prohibit accession by transgender individuals and asked the panel of experts merely how the "guidelines" for such a policy should be updated "to reflect currently accepted medical terminology." Acting Under Secretary of Defense for Personnel and Readiness, Anthony M. Kurta, also issued a memorandum in September 2017 that stated that the Department had convened a panel of experts "to support the . . . development of an Implementation Plan on military service by transgender individuals." Milgroom Decl., Ex. Y.[10]

Third, and most importantly, the Mattis Implementation Plan *in fact prohibits transgender military service*—just as President Trump's 2017 directives ordered. It is true that the plan takes a slightly less direct approach to accomplishing this goal than the President's 2017 tweet and memorandum. Instead of expressly banning all "transgender individuals" from military service, the Mattis Implementation Plan works by absolutely disqualifying individuals who require or have undergone gender transition, generally disqualifying individuals with a history or diagnosis of gender dysphoria, and, to the extent that there are any individuals who identify as "transgender" but do not fall under the first two categories, only allowing them to serve "in their biological sex" (which means that openly transgender persons are generally not allowed to serve in conformance with their identity).

But it is not at all surprising that an implementation plan, crafted over the course of months (clearly with assistance from lawyers and an eye to pending litigation) is a longer, more nuanced expression of the President's policy direction than the brief, blanket assertions made by the President himself in 2017. To determine whether Plaintiffs' claims are moot, the Court must look past these surface-level differences and ask whether, in effect, the Mattis Implementation Plan accomplishes the President's policy that is challenged in this case.

The Court concludes that the Mattis Implementation Plan does just that: it prevents service by transgender individuals. The plan succeeds at doing so in part by prohibiting individuals with traits associated with being transgender: those with "gender dysphoria" and who have undergone or require "gender transition." In addition, although the plan purports to allow some transgender individuals (those without a diagnosis of gender dysphoria or who have not undergone or require gender transition) to serve in the military under certain narrow circumstances, even this purported allowance is illusory. Under the Mattis Implementation Plan, those transgender persons who are not summarily banned are only allowed in the military if they serve *in their biological sex*. But by definition—at least the definition relevant to Plaintiffs' claims in this lawsuit—transgender persons *do not identify or live in accord with their biological sex*. Accordingly, the Mattis Implementation Plan effectively translates into a ban on transgender persons in the military. Tolerating a person with a certain characteristic only on the condition that they renounce that characteristic is the same as not tolerating them at all.[11] As Plaintiffs

---

10. Defendants cite statements from Secretary Mattis about the "independence" of the process that led to the creation of the Mattis Implementation Plan, but the context suggests that such "independence" related to how, not whether, to implement the President's policy directives.

11. Defendants argue that forcing all transgender service members to live in accordance with their biological sex is not the same as a ban on transgender service members because not all transgender individuals choose to come out as such and "live and work in accordance with [their] identity." That this would be the case is not at all surprising, and certainly does not demonstrate that Defendants' policy is not a ban on transgender service members. Decisions about whether and

correctly argue, "[j]ust as a policy allowing Muslims to serve in the military if they renounce their Muslim faith would be a ban of military service by Muslims, a policy requiring transgender individuals to serve in their birth sex *is* a ban on transgender service." Pls.' Opp'n at 10 (emphasis in original); *see also Karnoski* ("Requiring transgender people to serve in their 'biological sex' does not constitute 'open' service in any meaningful way, and cannot reasonably be considered an 'exception' to the Ban. Rather, it would force transgender service members to suppress the very characteristic that defines them as transgender in the first place."). Accordingly, despite superficial differences between it and the President's 2017 directives, the Mattis Implementation Plan essentially effectuates the policy announced by President Trump in 2017: the banning of military service by transgender individuals. It accordingly does not moot Plaintiffs' claims. *See Glob. Tel*Link v. Fed. Commc'ns Comm'n*, 866 F.3d 397 (D.C. Cir. 2017) ("replacing the challenged law 'with one that differs only in some insignificant respect' and 'disadvantages [petitioners] in the same fundamental way' does not moot the underlying challenge") (quoting *Ne. Fla. Chapter of Associated Gen. Contractors of Am. v. City of Jacksonville*, 508 U.S. 656 (1993)).[12]

Finally, Defendants repeatedly argue that the 2017 Presidential Memorandum has been "revoked." Even if the Court were to favor form over substance and accept this as an accurate description of what has genuinely occurred, it would not alone be enough to warrant a finding of mootness. As Defendants argue, "[w]hen a law is repealed and replaced, the relevant question is 'whether the new [policy] is sufficiently similar to the repealed [one] that it is permissible to say that the challenged conduct continues,' or, put differently, whether the policy 'has been sufficiently altered so as to present a substantially different controversy from the one . . . originally decided.'" Defs.' Mot. at 4 (quoting *Ne. Fla. Chapter of Associated Gen. Contractors of Am.*). Even assuming that the 2017 Presidential Memorandum has been "revoked," and the Mattis Implementation Plan could be viewed as a "new policy," at the very least, the new plan is sufficiently "similar" to the President's 2017 directives that Plaintiffs' claims are not moot. As already discussed, like the 2017 Presidential

---

when to admit one's transgender identity and initiate the process of gender transition are presumably affected by many factors, including career considerations, medical considerations, and fear of discrimination. Service members in particular might reasonably choose to delay due to upcoming deployments or other opportunities. That not all transgender service members have openly admitted to their status as such and sought to live in accordance with their gender identities by personal choice does not mean that an official policy forbidding them from doing so is not discriminatory.

12. Defendants argue that the Mattis Implementation Plan is similar to the currently operative policy on transgender service. *See, e.g.*, Defs.' Reply at 1. The Court disagrees. Any similarities Defendants are able to find between the policies are red herrings. The policies are fundamentally different because one allows transgender individuals to serve in accordance with their gender identity, and the other does not (with the exception of a small group of individuals who will be allowed to remain in the armed forces under a grandfather provision).

Memorandum, the Mattis Implementation Plan generally bars service by transgender individuals.[13]

* * *

In sum, whatever legal relevance the Mattis Implementation Plan and associated documents might have, they are not sufficiently divorced from, or different than, the President's 2017 directives such that Plaintiffs' claims are now moot.[14]

3. Motion to Dissolve the Preliminary Injunction

Finally, as the discussion above has likely already made clear, the Court will not dissolve its preliminary injunction. It is true that a preliminary injunction "may be dissolved where, for instance, changed circumstances eviscerate the justification therefor." However, the party seeking relief from an injunction bears the burden of establishing that changed circumstances warrant relief. The Court is not persuaded that the circumstances of this case have in fact genuinely changed in such a way that the Court's preliminary injunction is no longer warranted.

Like Defendants' mootness argument, the basic premise of Defendants' argument in support of dissolving the preliminary injunction is that the Mattis Implementation Plan is a "new policy" that does not implement the 2017 directives that were preliminarily enjoined by this Court. For the reasons already set forth above, Defendants have not persuaded the Court that this is the case. Instead, the Court finds that the Mattis Implementation Plan effectively implements the policy directives that were already at issue when the Court's preliminary injunction was ordered. Accordingly, Plaintiffs' challenge to those directives is not moot, and the need remains intact for the Court's preliminary injunction maintaining the *status quo ante* until the final resolution of this case on the merits.

The only material development that has occurred since the Court's preliminary injunction was issued is that the Defendants have prepared a plan to implement the

---

13. Defendants argue that the voluntary cessation doctrine does not apply to them. This argument does not survive scrutiny for two reasons. First, because the Court finds that the Mattis Implementation Plan is simply a plan that implements the Presidential directives that were already at issue in this case, the challenged conduct simply has not ceased, and the Court need not rely on the voluntary cessation doctrine. Second, the Court is not persuaded that the Defendants in this case—various Executive Branch departments and officials—are all immune from the doctrine. In a separate Memorandum Opinion and Order issued today, the Court has dismissed the President as a party from this case. Accordingly, at most, the Court would be applying the voluntarily cessation doctrine to lower Executive Branch officials. Defendants have not brought to the Court's attention any cases that hold that the voluntary cessation doctrine does not apply to such defendants. As indicated by the facts of this very case, the Executive Branch is able to change military policies back and forth with relative ease and speed, giving rise to the concerns that animate the voluntary cessation doctrine.

14. To the extent Defendants revive their motion to dismiss for failure to state a claim in this case, that motion is DENIED. . . . For the same reasons that the Mattis Implementation Plan does not moot Plaintiffs' claims, it also does not mean that their allegations now fail to state a claim.

enjoined directives, and a report that purportedly provides support for that plan. These developments do not change the Court's conclusion on any of the preliminary injunction factors.

On the merits, the Mattis Implementation Plan still accomplishes an extremely broad prohibition on military service by transgender individuals that appears to be divorced from any transgender individual's actual ability to serve. In the absence of the challenged policy, transgender individuals are subject to all of the same standards and requirements for accession and retention as any other service member. The Mattis Implementation Plan establishes a special *additional* exclusionary rule that precludes individuals who would otherwise satisfy the demanding standards applicable to all service members simply because they have certain traits that are associated with being transgender. Moreover, because the plan fundamentally implements the policy directives set forth by the President in 2017, the unusual factors associated with the issuance of the 2017 directives are still relevant. For example, the Court is still concerned that, immediately prior to the announcement of the 2017 Presidential directives, the military had studied the issue and found no reason to exclude transgender service members. The Court is likewise still concerned that the President's 2017 directives constituted an abrupt reversal in policy, and a *revocation* of rights, announced without any of the formality, deliberative process, or factual support usually associated with such a significant action. Although it makes no final ruling on the merits in this Memorandum Opinion, the Court is not convinced at this stage that the processes implemented by Defendants *after* President Trump's 2017 Presidential Memorandum, and the memoranda that they have issued since that time, resolve the constitutional issues that persuaded the Court that a preliminary injunction was warranted in the first place. Based on the record before the Court, these post hoc processes and rationales appear to have been constrained by, and not truly independent from, the President's initial policy decisions.

With regard to irreparable injury, Defendants argue again that the Mattis Implementation Plan protects Plaintiffs from any injury. The Court has already rejected those arguments. If the Court were to dissolve its injunction and allow the Mattis Implementation Plan to go into effect, Plaintiffs would suffer very real harms. Defendants also argue that Plaintiffs will not be irreparably injured if the Court dissolves its preliminary injunction because other courts have since issued injunctions that are still in place. The Court rejects this argument as well. The fact that other courts have similarly concluded that Defendants' policy is likely unconstitutional and warrants being preliminarily enjoined is no reason for this Court to lift its own injunction. This is especially so given that Defendants have moved to dissolve those preliminary injunctions, and have appealed the decision of the first court to deny such a motion. Finally, the Court's assessment of the balance of equities and public interest in its preliminary injunction Opinion still stands. It should not be forgotten that the United States military remains engaged in numerous armed conflicts throughout the world, and service members are still being injured and killed in those conflicts. The public interest and equities lie with allowing young men and women who are qualified and willing to serve our Nation to do so.

In short, because the Mattis Implementation Plan would effectively implement the very policies preliminarily enjoined by the Court, the development of that plan is not a reason to dissolve that injunction. To avoid any possible need for clarification, the Court states expressly: enforcing the Mattis Implementation Plan would violate the Court's October 30, 2017 preliminary injunction. All of the directives of that injunction remain in effect until further order of the Court.

IV. Conclusion

For the foregoing reasons, Defendants' Motion to Dismiss for lack of jurisdiction on standing and mootness grounds is DENIED. Defendants' Motion to Dissolve the Preliminary Injunction is also DENIED. The Court has made no final ruling on the merits of Plaintiffs' claims. It has simply held that all Plaintiffs still have standing to pursue their claims, this case is not moot, and there are no changed circumstances that justify dissolving the preliminary injunction. An appropriate Order accompanies this Memorandum Opinion.

Discussion

1. Note that under conventional constitutional equal protection doctrine, disability discrimination by government actors is subject to rational basis review when challenged in court, which is very deferential to the government. *See Board of Trustees of the University of Alabama v. Garrett*, 531 U.S. 356 (2001). There could be an exception to such deference if the discrimination is based on "a bare desire to harm a politically unpopular group." *See City of Cleburne, Texas v. Cleburne Living Center*, 473 U.S. 432, 446–47 (1985); *cf. Department of Agriculture v. Moreno*, 413 U.S. 528, 535 (1973); *Romer v. Evans*, 517 U.S. 620, 634–35 (1996); *Lawrence v. Texas*, 539 U.S. 558, 579–80 (O'Connor, J., concurring in the judgment). *But cf. Trump v. Hawai'i*, 138 S. Ct. 2392, 2420 (2018) (characterizing "common thread" among the cases using this language in majority opinions invalidating challenged laws as "lack [of] *any* purpose other than a 'bare . . . desire to harm a politically unpopular group.'") (emphasis added). What arguments might be made that the Trump administration's trans ban is motivated by a bare desire to harm a politically unpopular group? Can one reasonably argue that that is its *only* motivation?

2. Should the Mattis Implementation Plan's ostensibly more limited sweep than the ban as originally announced in Trump's tweets and August 2017 memorandum be sufficient to preclude the plaintiffs from challenging it in court? Should the court have concluded, as the government argued, that the plaintiffs are insufficiently harmed or threatened with harm to allow federal courts to adjudicate the plaintiffs' contentions, or is this instead a constitutional case that falls within the role of the federal judiciary?

3. Apropos various plaintiffs' attempts to secure discovery regarding the Trump trans ban, see, for example, *Karnoski v. Trump*, 2019 WL 6894510 (W.D. Wash.

Dec. 18, 2019); *Doe 2 v. Esper*, No. CV 17-1597 (CKK), 2019 WL 4394842 (D.D.C. Sept. 13, 2019); *Karnoski v. Trump*, 2019 WL 6894510 (W.D. Wash. Dec. 18, 2019); *Karnoski v. Trump*, 926 F.3d 1180 (9th Cir. 2019). *See also In re Center for Military Readiness*, 2019 WL 4733602 (E.D. Mich. Sept. 28, 2019) (discovery dispute from *Karnoski* litigation seeking to compel document production by nonprofit organization opposed to military service by LGBT people or combat service by women regarding its communications with government officials in connection with Trump's trans ban); *Stone v. Trump*, 402 F. Supp. 3d 153 (D. Md. 2019).

4. The district court's refusal to lift its preliminary injunction once the Mattis plan was promulgated was reversed less than five months later in *Doe 2 v. Shanahan*.

Reading Guide for Doe 2 v. Shanahan

1. What is the legal standard the court of appeals says governs a motion to dissolve an injunction? What is the applicable standard of appellate review that the court of appeals invokes?

2. What legal conclusions by the district court does the court of appeals argue are clearly erroneous? What reasons does the court of appeals give for concluding that the government meets the standard to dissolve the district court's injunction? Its logic on this point is not fully spelled out. What might the court of appeals think is the legal relevance of the district court's (supposed) errors to the merits of the plaintiffs' challenge to Trump's trans ban?

Doe 2, et al. v. Shanahan, et al.

755 Fed. Appx. 19 (D.C. Cir. 2019)

Before: GRIFFITH and WILKINS, Circuit Judges, and WILLIAMS,* Senior Circuit Judge.

Judgment

PER CURIAM

. . . . For the reasons stated below, it is

ORDERED and ADJUDGED that the District Court's denial of the government's motion to dissolve the preliminary injunction is REVERSED, the preliminary injunction is VACATED without prejudice, and the government's motion to stay is DENIED as moot.

I

We reverse the District Court's denial of the government's motion to dissolve the preliminary injunction and vacate the preliminary injunction without prejudice.

. . . . A party seeking to dissolve an injunction has the burden of showing "a significant change either in factual conditions or in law" such that continued enforcement

---

* Senior Circuit Judge Williams concurs in the result. Separate opinions will be filed at a later date.

of the injunction would be "detrimental to the public interest." *Horne v. Flores*, 557 U.S. 433 (2009). We review the denial of such a motion under an abuse of discretion standard. The District Court's factual findings are subject to clear error review and its legal conclusions are reviewed de novo. The merits of the preliminary injunction entered in October 2017 are not properly before us.

II

It was clear error to say there was no significant change with respect to at least two aspects of the policy recommended by Secretary of Defense James Mattis in February 2018 and approved by the President in March 2018 ("the Mattis Plan"). First, the District Court made an erroneous finding that the Mattis Plan was not a new policy but rather an implementation of the policy directives enjoined in October 2017. The government took substantial steps to cure the procedural deficiencies the court identified in the enjoined 2017 Presidential Memorandum. These included the creation of a panel of military and medical experts, the consideration of new evidence gleaned from the implementation of the policy on the service of transgender individuals instituted by then-Secretary of Defense Ash Carter ("the Carter Policy"), and a reassessment of the priorities of the group that produced the Carter Policy. Although the parties dispute whether these efforts were independent of the policy announced in the 2017 Presidential Memorandum, the record indicates that it was error for the district court to conclude that the Mattis Plan was foreordained.

Second, the District Court made an erroneous finding that the Mattis Plan was the equivalent of a blanket ban on transgender service. *Doe 2 v. Trump*, 315 F. Supp. 3d 474 (D.D.C. 2018). Although the Mattis Plan continues to bar many transgender persons from joining or serving in the military, the record indicates that the Plan allows some transgender persons barred under the military's standards prior to the Carter Policy to join and serve in the military. The Mattis Plan, for example, contains a reliance exemption that will allow at least some transgender service members to continue to serve and receive gender transition-related medical care. Also, Plaintiffs contended that the Mattis Plan's exclusion of transgender persons who have gender dysphoria or who are unwilling to serve in their biological sex constitutes a blanket ban, arguing this case as if all transgender individuals either (1) have gender dysphoria or (2) transition to their preferred gender. They characterized these as "essential" and "defining" aspects of being transgender, and the District Court agreed. Other than perhaps one passing statement by one of Plaintiffs' experts, we can find nothing in the record to support this definition of being transgender, as all of the reports supporting both the Carter Policy and the Mattis Plan defined transgender persons as "identifying" with a gender other than their biological sex. Indeed, those reports repeatedly state that not all transgender persons seek to transition to their preferred gender or have gender dysphoria, and the panel of experts convened by Secretary Mattis observed that there are transgender persons who "have served, and are serving, with distinction under the standards for their biological sex." Thus, the District Court erred in finding that the Mattis Plan was a blanket transgender ban.

III

"[M]ilitary interests do not always trump other considerations, and [the Supreme Court has] not held that they do." *Winter v. Nat. Res. Def. Council, Inc.*, 555 U.S. 7 (2008). Nonetheless, the "Constitution vests '[t]he complex, subtle, and professional decisions as to the composition, training, equipping, and control of a military force' exclusively in the legislative and executive branches," *Kreis v. Sec'y of Air Force*, 866 F.2d 1508 (D.C. Cir. 1989) (quoting *Gilligan v. Morgan*, 413 U.S. 1 (1973)), and it is "difficult to think of a clearer example of the type of governmental action that was intended by the Constitution to be left to the political branches directly responsible—as the Judicial Branch is not—to the electoral process," *Gilligan*. In *Rostker v. Goldberg*, 453 U.S. 57 (1981), and *Goldman v. Weinberger*, 475 U.S. 503 (1986), when addressing constitutional challenges to decisions by the executive and legislative branches regarding the composition and internal administration of combat-ready military forces, the Court explained that while the executive and legislative branches remain "subject to the limitations" of the Constitution, "the tests and limitations to be applied may differ because of the military context," *Rostker*, and "courts must give great deference to the professional judgment of military authorities concerning the relative importance of a particular military interest," *Goldman*. Courts "must be particularly careful not to substitute our judgment of what is desirable for that of [the executive and legislative branches], or our own evaluation of evidence for [their] reasonable evaluation" because "[i]t is difficult to conceive of an area of governmental activity in which the courts have less competence." *Rostker*.

Applying this standard in *Rostker*, the Supreme Court concluded that a facially discriminatory, sex-based draft-registration statute was "not invidious, but rather realistically reflect[ed] the fact that the sexes [were] not similarly situated." The Court explained that the sex-based classification was within constitutional bounds because Congress determined that the statute minimized "added burdens" and "administrative problems" and promoted "the important goal of military flexibility," and "[i]t is not for this Court to dismiss such problems as insignificant in the context of military preparedness and the exigencies of a future mobilization." Instead of an "independent evaluation" of the evidence, the Court adopted "an appropriately deferential examination of Congress' evaluation of that evidence." . . . . "None of this is to say that" the executive or legislative branch "is free to disregard the Constitution when it acts in the area of military affairs." But, as in *Rostker* and *Goldman*, any review must be "appropriately deferential" in recognition of the fact that the Mattis Plan concerned the composition and internal administration of the military.

We acknowledge that the military has substantial arguments for why the Mattis Plan complies with the equal protection principles of the Fifth Amendment. Although today's decision is not a final determination on the merits, we must recognize that the Mattis Plan plausibly relies upon the "considered professional judgment" of "appropriate military officials," *Goldman*, and appears to permit some transgender individuals to serve in the military consistent with established military mental health, physical health, and sex-based standards. In light of the substantial constitutional arguments and the apparent showing that the policy accommodates at least some of Plaintiffs' interests, we think that the public interest weighs in favor of dissolving the injunction.

————————

Discussion

1. The court of appeals appears impressed with the prospects of version 2.0 of Trump's transgender ban's surviving constitutional review. Besides judicial deference to the military, what might give the court such confidence? Why might it matter to the merits of the constitutional equal protection challenge to the policy if it is not viewed as "a blanket ban on transgender service"? Even if the policy does not exclude 100% of transgender people, might it not facially discriminate against transgender persons and therefore potentially be subject to a level of equal protection scrutiny greater than rational basis review (whether because the policy discriminates on the basis of sex, which precedent establishes is subject to intermediate scrutiny, or because anti-transgender discrimination should be viewed as suspect or quasi-suspect on its own terms and so subjected to some form of heightened scrutiny)? *Cf. Stone v. Trump*, 402 F. Supp. 3d 153 (D. Md. 2019) ("As the Court stated in its August 20, 2019 Memorandum Opinion, 'the Implementation Plan discriminates on the basis of transgender status, not a medical condition.' . . . . While the Implementation Plan may not ban all transgender persons from military service, it does ban individuals based on their transgender status. Thus, the Implementation Plan does indeed ban transgender persons from military service.").

2. *Rostker* did not involve any question of the eligibility of a group of people to serve in the military, but rather whether Congress could limit registration for potential mandatory service in the military to males. *Goldman* might seem a more on-point precedent as it upheld the constitutionality under the First Amendment of a military uniform (*i.e.*, attire) regulation with the effect of prohibiting anyone, even an Orthodox Jewish serviceman, from wearing a yarmulke. Some might argue this in effect amounts to a ban on service by Orthodox Jewish men. Is that uniform regulation distinguishable from Trump's trans ban, or is the *Goldman* precedent otherwise distinguishable from *Doe 2*?

3. Less than three weeks after the U.S. Court of Appeals dissolved the preliminary injunction in *Doe 2 v. Shanahan*, the Supreme Court of the United States issued orders — over the objections of Justices Ginsburg, Breyer, Sotomayor, and Kagan — granting the defendants' request to stay the injunctions in *Karnoski v. Trump* and *Stockman v. Trump* while the litigation proceeds. *Trump v. Karnoski*, 139 S. Ct. 950 (2019); *Trump v. Stockman*, 139 S. Ct. 950 (2019). Slightly more than six weeks after the Supreme Court acted, the U.S. District Court for the District of Maryland granted the defendants' motion to stay the last remaining preliminary injunction against Trump's trans ban. *Stone v. Trump*, 2019 WL 5697228 (D. Md. Mar. 7, 2019). As of the time of the writing of this book, there were no injunctions against the ban, and pursuant to Directive-type Memorandum-19-004 (Mar. 12, 2019), which

implemented the Mattis plan but by its terms expired March 12, 2020, most transgender people have been excluded from service since April 12, 2019. On May 14, 2020, the Navy announced that one servicemember, lead plaintiff Jane Doe in the *Doe v. Trump* litigation, was granted a waiver allowing her to serve despite the retention ban. Doe was the first such servicemember in over a year of the Trump policy. J.D. Simkins, *Navy Grants First Waiver Allowing Transgender Officer to Remain in Uniform*, NAVY TIMES, May 15, 2020, https://www.navytimes.com/news/your-navy/2020/05/15/navy-grants-first-waiver-allowing-transgender-officer-to-remain-in-uniform. Consider the extent if any to which this helps the administration in its defense of the claimed constitutionality of the policy.

None of the four suits discussed above has at this time advanced to a final judgment.

4. Michele Goodwin and Erwin Chemerinsky have argued that, although in their view the government's ostensible justifications cannot justify the revised transgender ban, "the Supreme Court's intervention to lift the preliminary injunctions bodes poorly for how the Court will address this issue and other LGBTQ rights issues to come." Michele Goodwin & Erwin Chemerinsky, *The Transgender Military Ban: Preservation of Discrimination Through Transformation*, 114 Nw. U. L. REV. 751 (2019). Notably, though, Professor Goodwin and Dean Chemerinsky were writing before the Supreme Court's historic decision in *Bostock v. Clayton County, Georgia*, 140 S. Ct. 1731 (2020), Chapter 5, Section D, *supra*, which held that discrimination against employees because of their transgender status is categorically sex discrimination within the meaning of Title VII of the Civil Rights Act of 1964. While the equal protection issue in challenges to the ban relies on a different source of law from the suits resolved in *Bostock*, the conceptual reasoning in *Bostock* lends significant support to the argument that Trump's transgender service ban should receive equal protection heightened scrutiny as a form of sex discrimination. The administration, if it does not change after the 2020 presidential election, can be expected to insist that, at least as revised, its policy should be seen not as discriminating on the basis of transgender status but as properly taking account of a mental disorder (gender dysphoria) that some servicemembers or aspiring servicemembers have. Is that a persuasive characterization of the policy for constitutional purposes? Is it relevant here that *Bostock* said that it doesn't matter if discrimination is motivated by additional reasons beyond an employee's transgender status because if it based on the latter, it is still sex discrimination under Title VII?

Transgender Veterans' Healthcare

Pursuant to statutory direction, the U.S. Department of Veterans Affairs ("VA") provides a wide range of healthcare to veterans as part of their benefits package, generally covering treatments and procedures that are considered medically necessary. This includes a variety of care related to transgender identities and transition.

[The] VA provides mental health counseling and hormone therapy for transgender veterans experiencing gender dysphoria. The VA also provides preoperative evaluation for transgender veterans, as well as continuing hormone replacement therapy and postoperative care to veterans who have received sex reassignment surgery outside the VA health care system. Indeed, reflecting its commitment to provide medically needed care to transgender veterans, the VA has recently opened clinics in Cleveland and Tucson that specialize in providing medical care to those veterans. In addition, the VA Boston Healthcare System has formed the Interdisciplinary Transgender Treatment Team, which provides medical care tailored to the needs of transgender veterans. As the VA also has acknowledged, the agency actually provides "the majority" of the care needed for transgender veterans. . . .

Brief for Petitioners, *Fulcher v. Secretary of Veterans Affairs*, No. 17-460, 2017 WL 2799671 (Fed. Cir. June 21, 2017). Indeed, "In 2011, the VA implemented a Transgender Healthcare Directive, which instruct[ed] all VA staff to provide care to transgender patients 'without discrimination in a manner consistent with care and management of all Veteran patients.'" Sally Fisher Curran & Adam Martin, *Serving Transgender Veterans*, 91 N.Y. St. B.J. 37, 38–39 (2019). The notable exception is gender-affirming surgery.

Separate from the surgery directive of Trump's transgender servicemember ban, which as described above forbids the use of military resources to fund "sex reassignment surgeries" for military personnel, another VA regulation specifically excludes "gender alterations" from the medical benefits package available to veterans. 38 C.F.R. § 17.38(c)(4). Veterans Health Administration "Directive 2013-003 (the 'Directive') clarifies that this exclusion constitutes an absolute bar to coverage for 'sex reassignment surgery,' which the Directive defines to encompass 'any of a variety of surgical procedures . . . done simultaneously or sequentially with the explicit goal of transitioning from one sex to another.'" (This included, for example, breast augmentation for transgender women and mastectomies for transgender men.) Brief for Petitioners, *Fulcher*. This exclusion was predicated upon the notion that sexual confirmation surgeries were not medically necessary.

This exclusion was challenged by Dee Fulcher, a Marine Corps vet who is a transgender woman, Giuliano Silva, an Army vet who is a transgender man, and a group to which Mr. Silva belongs, the Transgender American Veterans Association ("TAVA"). TAVA is a non-profit organization that works with Congress, the VA, and other interested individuals and organizations to improve the psychological and medical care of transgender veterans. Fulcher and Silva have been unable to secure medically recommended transition surgeries through the VA. In May of 2016 Fulcher, Silva, and TAVA submitted a petition to the VA requesting that it engage in rulemaking to eliminate the exclusion of "gender alterations" from VA medical benefits. Roughly contemporaneously, sometime in spring 2016 (under the Obama administration), the VA drafted a Notice of Proposed Rulemaking ("NPRM") suggesting elimination of that surgical exclusion in light of the by-then predominant medical understanding that gender-affirming surgeries including phalloplasty and vaginoplasty are indeed medically necessary treatment for some, though not all, transgender people. In response to a number of congressional inquiries about the NPRM, the Under Secretary for Health at the time (subsequently, the Secretary of Veterans Affairs from February 2017 through March 2018) wrote in reply, two days after Trump was elected to the presidency, that the VA was withdrawing the NPRM from the federal government's "Fall 2016 Unified Agenda for Federal Regulatory and Deregulatory Actions" and that any potential change to the gender surgery exclusion was "not imminent."

Fulcher, Silva, and TAVA ("the petitioners") filed suit in the U.S. Court of Appeals for the Federal Circuit, seeking review of the VA's denial of their petition for rulemaking. "On January 19, 2017, after the petition for review was filed . . . , the VA reissued VHA Directive 2013-003, reiterating the Department's categorical position that '[s]ex reassignment surgery cannot be performed or funded by VA.'" The petitioners argued that the exclusion and failure to repeal it were arbitrary and capricious within the meaning of U.S. administrative law, and that the exclusion violates petitioners' equal protection rights guaranteed from federal interference by the Due Process Clause of the Fifth Amendment.

Thereafter, "[a]fter Lambda Legal and [the Transgender Law Center] sought review from the U.S. Court of Appeals for the Federal Circuit, the [VA] announced on July 8, 2018, that it would seek comments 'as part of its ongoing consideration of the petition.'" Lambda Legal & Transgender Law Center, *Comments in response to "Notice of Petition for Rulemaking and request for comments—Exclusion of Gender Alterations from the Medical Benefits Package*," Sept. 7, 2018, https://www.lambdalegal.org/sites/default/files/legal-docs/downloads/us_fulcher_20180907_comments-by-lambda-legal-transgender-law-center.pdf. The same month, the petitioners voluntarily dismissed their federal circuit case against the VA, *see* Lambda Legal, *Fulcher v. Secretary of Veterans Affairs, History*, https://www.lambdalegal.org/in-court/cases/fulcher-v-secretary-of-va (last visited Jan. 5, 2020). They then submitted detailed comments, underscoring the arbitrariness of the exclusion in light of contemporary medical knowledge, contesting factually unfounded cost-based defenses of the exclusion (important in light of Trump's invocation of supposedly "tremendous" costs and "disruption" as justification for his surgery directive), and devastatingly critiquing on numerous grounds, including factual inaccuracy, the Defense Department's February 22, 2018, panel report prepared to support Trump's reversal of the Obama administration's lifting of the ban on military service by transgender persons.

Chapter 7

Public Accommodations and Housing

Humans are social creatures, and most of us interact with others in numerous settings, from the corner store where we buy a pack of gum to the property holder to whom we pay rent. Anti-discrimination laws in such settings provide "protections against exclusion from an almost limitless number of transactions and endeavors that constitute ordinary civic life in a free society." *Romer v. Evans*, 517 U.S. 620, 631 (1996). As of the writing of this book, no federal statute regarding housing or public accommodations expressly prohibits gender identity discrimination in its terms. Some laws, such as the federal Fair Housing Act (FHA), 42 U.S.C. § 3601 *et seq.*, forbid *sex* discrimination in housing; under the reasoning of *Bostock v. Clayton Country, Georgia*, 140 S. Ct. 1731 (2020), Chapter 5, Section D, *supra*, which held that discrimination because someone is transgender is sex discrimination under Title VII of the Civil Rights Act of 1964, courts may begin to interpret the FHA as forbidding anti-transgender discrimination. In addition, a number of states and local governments have adopted laws that specifically ban gender identity discrimination in public accommodations and housing. Section A of this chapter addresses public accommodations, and Section B turns to housing discrimination.

A. Public Accommodations

Public accommodations are businesses, facilities, or programs that serve the public. Numerous states have laws prohibiting some range of public accommodations from various forms of discrimination, often on specified grounds. Even while ruling that the First Amendment protected a parade organizer from being legally required to include groups it chose to exclude, Justice David Souter, writing for a unanimous U.S. Supreme Court in *Hurley v. Irish-American Gay, Lesbian and Bisexual Group of Boston*, 515 U.S. 557 (1995), emphasized the general propriety of public accommodations laws:

> At common law, innkeepers, smiths, and others who "made profession of a public employment," were prohibited from refusing, without good reason, to serve a customer. As one of the 19th-century English judges put it,

the rule was that "[t]he innkeeper is not to select his guests[;] [h]e has no right to say to one, you shall come into my inn, and to another you shall not, as every one coming and conducting himself in a proper manner has a right to be received; and for this purpose innkeepers are a sort of public servants."

After the Civil War, the Commonwealth of Massachusetts was the first State to codify this principle to ensure access to public accommodations regardless of race. *See* Act Forbidding Unjust Discrimination on Account of Color or Race, 1865 Mass. Acts, ch. 277 (May 16, 1865). In prohibiting discrimination "in any licensed inn, in any public place of amusement, public conveyance or public meeting," the original statute already expanded upon the common law, which had not conferred any right of access to places of public amusement As with many public accommodations statutes across the Nation, the legislature continued to broaden the scope of legislation, to the point that the law today prohibits discrimination on the basis of "race, color, religious creed, national origin, sex, sexual orientation . . . , deafness, blindness or any physical or mental disability or ancestry" in "the admission of any person to, or treatment in any place of public accommodation, resort or amusement." Provisions like these are well within the State's usual power to enact when a legislature has reason to believe that a given group is the target of discrimination, and they do not, as a general matter, violate the First or Fourteenth Amendments.

As the Court explained in *Romer v. Evans*, 517 U.S. 620 (1996), "contemporary statutes and ordinances prohibiting discrimination by providers of public accommodations" commonly enumerate grounds on which discrimination in covered establishments is forbidden because the "general" duty of the common law "proved insufficient in many instances." After an eighteenth-century Supreme Court ruling invalidated an early federal public accommodations non-discrimination law, *see The Civil Rights Cases*, 109 U.S. 3 (1883), "most States have chosen to counter discrimination by enacting detailed statutory schemes," *Romer*. And, rejecting the state of Colorado's argument that its ban on laws or policies forbidding discrimination against lesbian, gay, and bisexual people only took "special rights" off the table, *Romer* concluded:

> We find nothing special in the protections Amendment 2 withholds. These are protections taken for granted by most people either because they already have them or do not need them; these are protections against exclusion from an almost limitless number of transactions and endeavors that constitute ordinary civic life in a free society.

To this date, there is no general federal public accommodations law expressly protecting people from gender identity discrimination. Only the District of Columbia and 21 states have statewide laws expressly prohibiting gender identity discrimination in public accommodations: California, Colorado, Connecticut, Delaware, Hawai'i, Illinois, Iowa, Maine, Maryland, Massachusetts, Minnesota, Nevada, New

Hampshire, New Jersey, New Mexico, New York, Oregon, Rhode Island, Vermont, Virginia, and Washington.[a]

The lack of protection for trans people in public accommodations matters in daily life, or "ordinary civic life" to quote *Romer*. As Williams Institute scholar Jody Herman summarized pertinent findings from the U.S. Transgender Survey in her testimony to Congress on the proposed Equality Act:

> Nearly one-third (31%) of USTS respondents who utilized places of public accommodation, including restaurants, hotels, retail establishments, and

---

a. *See* Cal. Civ. Code §51.5 (West 2019) (discrimination in business establishments based on sex, defined to include gender identity); Colo. Rev. Stat. §24-34-601 (2014) (discrimination in public accommodations based on sexual orientation, defined to include transgender status, Colo. Rev. Stat. §24-34-301 (2014)); Conn. Gen. Stat. §46a-64 (2017) (discrimination in public accommodations based on gender identity or expression); Del. Code Ann., tit. 6, §4504 (2019) (discrimination in public accommodations based on gender identity); D.C Code §2-1402.31(a) (1) (2006) (discrimination in public accommodations based on gender identity or expression); Haw. Rev. Stat. Ann. §489-3 (2019) (discriminatory practices in public accommodations based on gender identity or expression); 775 Ill. Comp. Stat. 5/5-102 (2007) (discrimination in public accommodations based on sexual orientation, defined to include "gender-related identity, whether or not traditionally associated with the person's designated sex at birth," 775 Ill. Comp. Stat. 5/1-103 (O-1) (2019)); Iowa Code §216.7 (2019) (discrimination in public accommodations based on gender identity); Me. Stat. tit. 5, §4592 (1) (2019) (discrimination in public accommodations based on sexual orientation, defined to include "gender identity or expression," Me. Stat. Ann. tit. 5, §4553(9-C) (2019)); Md. Code Ann., State Gov't §20-304 (West 2014) (discrimination in public accommodations based on gender identity); Mass. Gen. Laws ch. 272, §98 (2016) (discrimination in public accommodations based on gender identity); Minn. Stat. §363A.11 (2001) (discrimination in public accommodations based on sexual orientation, defined to include "having or being perceived as having an emotional, physical, or sexual attachment to another person without regard to the sex of that person or having or being perceived as having an orientation for such attachment, or having or being perceived as having a self-image or identity not traditionally associated with one's biological maleness or femaleness," Minn. Stat. §363A.03(44) (2018)); Nev. Rev. Stat. §651.070 (2011) (discrimination in public accommodations based on gender identity or expression, excepting differential pricing based on sex to promote or market the place of public accommodation, which may implicate gender identity, *see* Nev. Rev. Stat. §651.065 (2011)); N.H. Rev. Stat. Ann. §354-A:17 (2018) (discrimination in public accommodations based on gender identity); N.J. Stat. Ann. §10:5-12 (f)(1) (West 2019) (discrimination in public accommodations based on gender identity or expression); N.M. Stat. Ann. §28-1-7(F) (2019) (discrimination in public accommodations based on gender identity); N.Y. Exec. Law §296(2)(a) (McKinney 2019) (discrimination in public accommodations based on gender identity or expression); Or. Rev. Stat. §659A.403 (2015) (discrimination in public accommodations based on sexual orientation, defined to include gender identity for all Oregon state statutes, Or. Rev. Stat. §174.100 (2015)); 11 R.I. Gen. Laws §11-24-2 (2001) (discrimination in public accommodations based on gender identity or expression); Vt. Stat. Ann. tit. 9, §4502(a) (2015) (discrimination in public accommodations based on gender identity); Va. Code Ann. §2.2-3904 (2020) (discrimination in public accommodations based on gender identity); Wash. Rev. Code §49.60.215 (2018) (discrimination in public accommodations based on sexual orientation, defined to include "gender expression or identity," defined as "having or being perceived as having a gender identity, self-image, appearance, behavior, or expression, whether or not that gender identity, self-image, appearance, behavior, or expression is different from that traditionally associated with the sex assigned to that person at birth," Wash. Rev. Code §49.60.040(26) (2018)).

other places, experienced being denied equal treatment, verbal harassment, and/or physical assault because they are transgender. USTS respondents also reported having one or more of these experiences in the past year when using public transportation (34%), when visiting public assistance offices or other government benefits offices (17%), Departments of Motor Vehicles (DMV) (14%), a courtroom or court house (13%), and a Social Security office (11%).

Jody L. Herman, *Written testimony in support of H.R. 5, The Equality Act, to Subcommittee on Civil Rights and Human Services, Committee on Education and Labor, U.S. House of Representatives* (Apr. 19, 2019), https://williamsinstitute.law.ucla.edu/wp -content/uploads/Herman-Equality-Act-Testimony.pdf.

Incidents of discrimination in public accommodations are all too common among trans people. One transgender male military vet reported that a barber shop proprietor refused him service citing the proprietor's religious belief that he could not cut women's hair. Tim Murphy, *This Calif. barbershop turned away a transgender male military vet*, LGBTQ NATION (Mar. 20, 2016), at http://www.lgbtqnation .com/2016/03/this-calif-barbershop-turned-away-a-transgender-male-military -vet/. An employee of a Macy's department store in Texas reportedly refused to let a trans woman—whom the employee "described as a man in makeup and woman's clothes"—use the women's changing room, also citing religious beliefs. *See* Kate Shellnut, *Macy's worker reportedly fired for not allowing transgender shopper into dressing room*, HOUSTON CHRONICLE (Dec. 6, 2011), https://blog.chron .com/believeitornot/2011/12/macy's-worker-reportedly-fired-for-not-allowing -transgender-shopper-into-dressing-room/; *Macy's Fires Employee for Refusing to Let Transgender Customer Use the Women's Dressing Room*, HUFFPOST (Dec. 7, 2011), https://www.huffpost.com/entry/macys-employee-fired-transgender_n_1133831. "[T]rans women of color receive more and worse harassment, discrimination, and violence than other groups," reported Jillian Weiss, the Executive Director of the Transgender Legal Defense and Education Fund. Dawn Ennis, *Dining While Trans: One Woman Describes Humiliating Experience*, NBC OUT (Apr. 24, 2017), http:// www.nbcnews.com/feature/nbc-out/dining-while-trans-one-woman-describes -humiliating-experience-n750301. Isabella Red Cloud, for example, reported being turned away from a soup kitchen in South Dakota for "dress[ing] inappropriately" and told not to return until she was "dressed like a man." Dawn Ennis, *Transgender woman denied food at soup kitchen because she was wearing a dress*, LGBTQ NATION (Apr. 24, 2017), https://www.lgbtqnation.com/2017/04/transgender-woman-ejected -church-soup-kitchen-wearing-dress/.

Consider whether courts have interpreted public accommodations laws and lawsuits to enforce them in ways adequately protective of trans people.

Reading Guide for McGrath v. Toys "R" Us

1. Courts can award "nominal damages"—generally, one dollar—to plaintiffs who establish that the defendants violated their right or rights but either were not injured by that violation or suffered damages that could not be quantified or failed adequately to establish the extent of any injury. In the following case, a retail store open to the public was found to have discriminated against customers who were transgender in violation of a New York City public accommodations law. The chief issue here is whether the plaintiffs, who received only nominal damages, would nonetheless be eligible for an award of attorney's fees.

2. Federal law greatly limits the availability of attorney's fee awards in nominal damages cases, and New York's highest state court, the "Court of Appeals," rules here that the same general standards apply under New York law. Why does it so hold?

3. The original fee award was approved by the U.S. District Court, which is a federal trial court. On appeal, the U.S. Court of Appeals certified the question of attorney's fees under New York law to the New York Court of Appeals, that state's highest court. What standard of review does the Court of Appeals apply in assessing the propriety of the district court's fee award?

4. What exception to the general rule against attorney's fee awards in cases with only nominal damages does the Court of Appeals hold applies here—on what factors does it rely? Why do the defendant and the dissent argue the exception was not satisfied here, and why does the majority reject their position?

McGrath v. Toys "R" Us, Inc.

821 N.E.2d 519 (N.Y. 2004)

Opinion of the Court

Graffeo, J.

. . . .

I

The three plaintiffs in this action, who identify themselves as preoperative trans-sexuals [*sic*—Eds.], commenced a federal action against defendant Toys "R" Us alleging that they were harassed by store employees while shopping in a Toys "R" Us store in December 2000. Plaintiffs contended that defendant's employees violated the New York City Human Rights Law, a civil rights statute that prohibits discrimination in public accommodation. . . .

. . . . At trial, plaintiffs' attorney requested substantial compensatory and punitive damages, but did not seek injunctive relief. The jury rendered a verdict in favor of plaintiffs, finding that the conduct of defendant's employees violated plaintiffs' rights under the New York City Human Rights Law, but awarded damages of only $1 for each plaintiff.

Following the trial, plaintiffs applied for attorney's fees in the amount of approximately $206,000. Defendant opposed the request, arguing that a fee award was not warranted because plaintiffs had received only nominal damages. Noting that the attorney's fee provision in the New York City Human Rights Law is similar to the fee provisions in the federal civil rights statutes, the court applied the rule articulated by the United States Supreme Court in *Farrar v. Hobby,* 506 U.S. 103 (1992). In *Farrar,* the Supreme Court held that it will rarely be appropriate to grant attorney's fees in a case where plaintiff obtained only nominal damages unless the case served a significant public purpose. [The] District Court in this case concluded that "[t]his case is one of those unusual and infrequent instances in which attorneys fees should be awarded." The court observed that this was the first public accommodation discrimination case to proceed to trial under the New York City Human Rights Law and the first case in which the rights of transsexuals were asserted and vindicated. In addition, at the time this action was commenced, it was unclear whether the New York City Human Rights Law covered transsexuals as the law was not amended to specifically include that class of individuals until just prior to trial. Ultimately, the District Court awarded attorney's fees in the amount of $193,551, the "lodestar" figure calculated by multiplying the number of hours reasonably expended on the litigation by a reasonable hourly rate.

Defendant appealed the attorney's fee determination to the Second Circuit, which noted that there are virtually no New York cases interpreting or applying the fee provision in the New York City Human Rights Law. Accordingly, the Second Circuit certified the following questions to this Court:

> 1. In determining whether an award of attorney's fees is reasonable under New York City Administrative Code § 8-502(f), does New York apply the standards set forth in *Farrar v. Hobby, i.e.,* (a) that "the most critical factor . . . is the degree of success," and (b) that when a party is awarded nominal damages, "the only reasonable fee is usually no fee at all"?

> 2. If the *Farrar* standard does not apply, what standard should a court use to determine what constitutes a reasonable fee award for a prevailing party who has received only nominal damages?

> 3. If the *Farrar* standard applies, does Administrative Code § 8-502(f) authorize a fee award to a prevailing plaintiff who receives only nominal damages but whose lawsuit served a significant public purpose?

> 4. If New York recognizes "service of a significant public purpose" as a factor warranting an attorney's fee award to a plaintiff recovering only nominal damages, would a plaintiff who is the first to secure a favorable jury verdict on a claim of unlawful discrimination against transsexuals in public accommodation, *see* N.Y. City Admin. Code § 8-107.4(a), be entitled to a fee award even though the law's prohibition of discrimination against transsexuals in employment, *see id.* § 8-107.1(a), has previously been recognized?

We accepted the certified questions and now answer questions 1, 3 and 4 in the affirmative, rendering question 2 academic.

II

. . . .

In New York, civil rights are cherished and highly protected. Legislation at the state and local levels prohibits discrimination in many spheres, including housing, employment, and public accommodation. The litigation in this case was brought under the public accommodation provision of the New York City Human Rights Law, which protects against discrimination based on "actual or perceived race, creed, color, national origin, age, gender, disability, marital status, sexual orientation or alienage or citizenship status." Admin. Code of City of N.Y. § 8-107[4][a].

A private action under the New York City Human Rights Law has been authorized since 1991 when the City Council amended the Code to grant the right to sue to any individual in a protected class who is subjected to discriminatory treatment. The legislation also gave a private party who prevailed in the lawsuit the right to seek attorney's fees. The fee provision states: "[i]n any civil action commenced pursuant to this section, the court, in its discretion, may award the prevailing party costs and reasonable attorney's fees." Admin. Code § 8-502[f].

The attorney's fee provision is indistinguishable from provisions in comparable federal civil rights statutes. For example, title VII of the Civil Rights Act of 1964's attorney's fee statute authorizes a court, in its discretion, to "allow the prevailing party . . . a reasonable attorney's fee . . . as part of the costs." 42 U.S.C. § 2000e-5[k]. Similarly, 42 U.S.C. § 1988(b), applicable to a myriad of civil rights claims, provides that "the court, in its discretion, may allow the prevailing party, other than the United States, a reasonable attorney's fee as part of the costs."

Where our state and local civil rights statutes are substantively and textually similar to their federal counterparts, our Court has generally interpreted them consistently with federal precedent. . . . Where state and local provisions overlap with federal statutes, our approach to resolution of civil rights claims has been consistent with the federal courts in recognition of the fact that, whether enacted by Congress, the State Legislature or a local body, these statutes serve the same remedial purpose — they are all designed to combat discrimination.

. . . .

In its 1992 decision in *Farrar v. Hobby*, the Supreme Court addressed a particular type of partial success case — the circumstance where a plaintiff obtains a favorable civil rights judgment on the merits but the only relief granted is nominal damages. . . .

All nine members of the Supreme Court concluded that plaintiffs were prevailing parties under the federal statutes, clarifying that "the prevailing party inquiry does not turn on the magnitude of the relief obtained." The Court explained that "a plaintiff 'prevails' when actual relief on the merits of his claim materially alters the legal relationship between the parties by modifying the defendant's behavior in a way that directly benefits the plaintiff." . . . [The] Court held that the fact that plaintiff obtained only nominal damages went to the second part of the attorney's fee inquiry—the reasonableness of the award.

. . . .

Justice O'Connor concurred, but wrote separately to clarify that the difference between the amount of damages recovered and the amount sought is not the only factor to be considered in determining the degree of a plaintiff's success in a nominal damages case. In appropriate cases, the court can consider the significance of the legal issue on which plaintiff prevailed and whether the litigation "accomplished some public goal other than occupying the time and energy of counsel, court, and client." This analysis has been referred to as the "significant public purpose" exception to the *Farrar* rule.

Federal courts have interpreted *Farrar* as holding that "while there is no *per se* rule that a plaintiff recovering nominal damages can never get a fee award . . . the award of fees in such a case will be rare," *Pino v. Locascio,* 101 F.3d 235 (2d Cir. 1996), and is appropriate only when plaintiff's success can be viewed as significant despite the failure to obtain more meaningful relief. . . .

Primarily relying on the legislative history of the 1991 amendment to the New York City Human Rights Law, plaintiffs in this case argue that the *Farrar* standard should not be applied to attorney's fee claims under the local law. . . . We are unpersuaded. There are many general statements in the legislative history indicating that the private right of action provision, adopted to keep the City at the forefront of human rights protection, should be liberally construed. . . . But, in this instance, such broad expressions of overriding policy offer no basis to overlook the textual similarities between the local law fee provision and the federal statutes or to abandon our general practice of interpreting comparable civil rights statutes consistently, particularly since these broad policies are identical to those underlying the federal statutes.

. . . .

III

The Second Circuit has not asked us to apply the *Farrar* standard to the facts and circumstances of this case, or to review whether it was appropriate for the District Court to grant attorney's fees in the full lodestar figure given the extent of relief plaintiffs obtained. These tasks it has reserved to itself. As we understand question 4, we are to determine whether this claim could have fallen within the "significant public purpose" exception addressed in the *Farrar* concurrence even though, prior to this litigation, some courts had held that transsexuals were protected from employment discrimination under the New York City Human Rights Law. We answer the fourth question in the affirmative because we cannot say, as a matter of law, that a court that reached that conclusion would have abused its discretion.

New York City Administrative Code §8-107(4)(a) prohibits discrimination in public accommodation on the following grounds: "actual or perceived race, creed, color, national origin, age, gender, disability, marital status, sexual orientation or alienage or citizenship status." Administrative Code §8-107(1)—which covers discrimination in employment—protects the same classes of individuals. At the time this litigation was commenced, the term gender was not defined in the Administrative Code and the term "sexual orientation" was defined as "heterosexuality, homosexuality, or bisexuality." Thus, the former provision did not explicitly encompass discrimination based on transsexualism.

There were lower court decisions concluding that employment discrimination based on transsexualism fell under the anti-discrimination umbrella of the Code. For example, in *Maffei v. Kolaeton Indus.*, 164 Misc. 2d 547, 626 N.Y.S.2d 391 (Sup. Ct., N.Y. County 1995), the trial court ruled that a person who identified herself as a transsexual had stated a claim under the New York City Human Rights Law's prohibition of gender discrimination in employment, despite the failure of the Code to expressly cover transsexuals. The New York City Commission on Human Rights had reached the same conclusion in administrative decisions. *See e.g. Matter of Arroyo v. New York City Health & Hosp. Corp.*, No. EM01120-04-12-89-DE, 1994 WL 932424 (N.Y. City Comm'n on Human Rights Mar. 11, 1994).

About two months before this case went to trial, the City Council passed legislation that added a new definition of "gender" to the New York City Human Rights Law, erasing any doubt about whether transsexuals were protected under the Code. *See* ADMIN. CODE §8-102[23]; Local Law No. 3 of City of New York (2002).[4] The legislative history of the local law indicates that the City Council believed that the scope of the existing gender-based discrimination provision required clarification. In other words, the City Council determined that, in its view, the Code already protected transsexuals but was concerned that, without the amendment, the law could be misinterpreted as excluding this class of individuals from coverage.

In the District Court and again in this Court, defendant has emphasized that at the time this action was commenced, there were lower court decisions interpreting the Code as protecting transsexuals from discrimination in employment. As such, defendant argues that this litigation was not significant. We do not believe that the latter necessarily follows from the former. As was apparent to the City Council, the fact that a handful of lower courts had interpreted the statute broadly did not put to rest the scope of coverage issue.

In this case, the District Court reasoned that the verdict was significant and performed a public purpose because it involved a series of "firsts"—*e.g.*, it was the first

---

4. The law now provides: "The term 'gender' shall include actual or perceived sex and shall also include a person's gender identity, self-image, appearance, behavior or expression, whether or not that gender identity, self-image, appearance, behavior or expression is different from that traditionally associated with the legal sex assigned to that person at birth." ADMIN. CODE §8-102[23].

public accommodation case that went to verdict under the New York City Human Rights Law, and was the first judgment in favor of transsexuals. We cannot conclude that a judgment in favor of a historically unrecognized group can never serve an important public purpose; a groundbreaking verdict can educate the public concerning substantive rights and increase awareness as to the plight of a disadvantaged class. Particularly in the civil rights arena, a jury verdict can communicate community condemnation of unlawful discrimination. It is therefore reasonable for a court to consider whether the verdict served this function in determining the significance of the relief obtained, although this is neither the only factor that may be considered nor will it necessarily be determinative.

Given the uncertain state of the law at the time this action was commenced and the fact that the breadth of the Code was not clarified until shortly before trial, many city residents might have been unaware at the time of verdict that discrimination against transsexuals was prohibited. We are therefore unpersuaded that the fact that a few lower courts had interpreted the Code as covering transsexuals rendered plaintiffs' verdict—the first of its kind—insignificant as a matter of law. In light of the procedural posture of this case, the fact-dependent nature of the "significant public purpose" inquiry and the limits of certified question 4, we have no occasion to further address the District Court determination in this regard.

Accordingly, certified questions 1, 3, and 4 should be answered in the affirmative and certified question 2 not answered upon the ground that it has been rendered academic.

Chief Judge KAYE and Judges G.B. SMITH, CIPARICK, and ROSENBLATT concur with Judge GRAFFEO.

READ, J. (dissenting).

I dissent with respect to certified question 4 only, which I would answer in the negative.

. . . .

. . . [Here], the purportedly groundbreaking legal principle—the recognition of transsexuals as members of a protected class safeguarded against discrimination by the New York City Human Rights Law—had already been supported by the only courts to have considered the question. *See Maffei; Rentos v. Oce-Office Sys.*, No. 95 Civ. 7908 (LAP), 1996 WL 737215, 1996 U.S. Dist. LEXIS 19060 (S.D.N.Y., Dec. 24, 1996). [The] New York City Commission on Human Rights, the administrative agency responsible for interpreting and enforcing the New York City Human Rights Law, had endorsed the same reading of the Human Rights Law in its administrative decisions.

. . . . Once the [New York City Human Rights Law] amendment was enacted on April 30, 2002, . . . plaintiffs' trial, which did not begin until about two months later, was rendered even more obviously irrelevant to establishing the protection of transsexuals under the New York City Human Rights Law.

In fact, the law was so certain that defendant Toys "R" Us never challenged plaintiffs' assertion that, as pre-operative transsexuals, they were members of a protected class under Administrative Code §8-107(4). . . .

Judge READ dissents in part and votes to answer certified question 4 in the negative in [the preceding] separate opinion in which Judge R.S. SMITH concurs.

Discussion

1. The standard practice in the United States is known as the "American rule," that is, parties to a lawsuit pay their own attorney's fees. What is the point of deviating from that rule and allowing prevailing parties to recover their attorney's fees from their opponents in certain classes of cases? What is the point with respect to the New York City Human Rights Law ("NYCHRL")? Was that purpose advanced by the award of fees in *McGrath*?

2. The dissent observes that Toys "R" Us did not contest the applicability, even before it was amended, of the NYCHRL to forbid anti-trans discrimination. The dissent says this shows that the NYCHRL was so clear before the plaintiffs' case that the litigation could not be deemed to serve a significant public purpose. Is there any other reason the defendant might not have contested the statute's coverage of gender identity discrimination?

Reading Guide for Hispanic AIDS Forum v. Estate of Bruno

1. In this real estate rental discrimination case, the trial court had rejected the defendants' motion to dismiss the plaintiff's complaint. The defendants appealed that decision. The appellate court here effectively assumes for the sake of argument that the statutes on which the plaintiff relies do forbid anti-transgender discrimination. It nonetheless concludes that the trial court should have dismissed the plaintiff's complaint for failing to make the allegations necessary to show a violation of those statutes.

2. According to the *Hispanic AIDS Forum* majority, what specific conduct by the defendants does the plaintiff contend was unlawfully discriminatory? How does the majority interpret the complaint's allegations to reach that conclusion? Why does it believe such conduct was not discrimination?

3. In dissent, Justice Saxe reads the plaintiff's complaint as alleging more discriminatory conduct than the majority sees. On what in the complaint does he rely? Why does he object to the majority's interpretation of the complaint's allegations?

4. The dissent reaches the statutory interpretation question of whether the laws on which the plaintiffs rely prohibit anti-transgender discrimination, answering "yes." How does it interpret discrimination "because of . . . sex"? Why does it conclude that the state's law banning sex discrimination with respect to real estate

reaches the conduct they see alleged here despite the state legislature's failure at that time to have amended the law expressly to protect transgender persons? How is the federal Rehabilitation Act relevant for the dissent? (How do the majority and the dissent disagree about the significance of *McGrath v. Toys "R" Us, supra*?) Why does the dissent conclude that New York City's law reaches the conduct challenged in the complaint despite the city's subsequent action to amend it expressly to protect transgender persons?

Hispanic AIDS Forum v. Estate of Bruno, et al.

16 A.D.3d 294 (N.Y. App. Div. 2005)

[Both sides were represented by private counsel. Amici supporting the plaintiff/appellant included the Harry Benjamin International Gender Dysphoria Association, the Transgender Law and Policy Institute, the Sylvia Rivera Law Project, and, with Roberta A. Kaplan as counsel, Legal Momentum.]

Saxe, J.P., Marlow, Sullivan, Nardelli, Catterson, JJ.

[Per curiam. — Eds.]

Opinion

. . . .

While it is true that in considering a motion to dismiss brought pursuant to [New York's Civil Practice Laws & Rules] CPLR 3211(a)(7), the court must presume the facts pleaded to be true and must accord them every favorable inference, it is also axiomatic that factual allegations that consist of bare legal conclusions are not entitled to such consideration.

Plaintiff Hispanic AIDS Forum is, according to the complaint, an organization that offers prevention and education programs that foster an increased awareness and knowledge of HIV/AIDS in Latino communities and addresses attitudes, beliefs and behaviors that place Latinos at risk. Defendant Estate of Joseph Bruno, and defendant Trustees of the Estate, own and operate the building designated as 74-09 37th Avenue, Jackson Heights, Queens. Plaintiff, beginning in 1991, maintained its offices in the building pursuant to various lease agreements. By 1995, plaintiff needed additional space, which resulted in the execution of two separate lease agreements, effective through April 2000, for two suites on the third floor of the building. Plaintiff was required to share the common areas, such as the restrooms, with the other commercial tenants on the third floor.

Plaintiff alleged that in April 2000, the parties successfully negotiated a five-year renewal lease, which was to take effect on May 1, 2000. In the interim, during the first few months of 2000, plaintiff noted that its transgender population increased because it had formed a support group for the transgender [*sic* — Eds.]. Plaintiff claimed that it executed the renewal lease, but was subsequently informed by defendants' office manager that the lease would not be renewed due to various complaints regarding the use of the bathrooms by its transgender clientele.

Plaintiff's remaining two causes of action[5] seek redress under the New York State and New York City Human Rights Law. The New York State Human Rights Law, in effect at the relevant time, provided, in pertinent part, that:

It shall be an unlawful discriminatory practice . . . [t]o refuse to sell, rent, lease or otherwise deny to or withhold from any person . . . land or commercial space because of the race, creed, color, national origin, sex, age, disability, marital status, or familial status of such person or persons . . .

EXECUTIVE LAW § 296[5][b] former [1].

The New York City Human Rights Law, in force at the time of the allegations set forth herein, provided, inter alia, that:

It shall be an unlawful discriminatory practice . . . [t]o refuse to sell, rent, lease . . . or otherwise deny or to withhold from any person or group of persons land or commercial space . . . because of the actual or perceived race, creed, color, national origin, gender, age, disability, sexual orientation, marital status or alienage or citizenship status . . .

NEW YORK CITY ADMIN. CODE § 8-107[5][b][1].

The New York City Human Rights Law was subsequently amended in 2002 to provide specifically that the term "gender" includes "a person's gender identity, self-image, appearance, behavior or expression, whether or not that gender identity, self-image, appearance, behavior or expression is different from that traditionally associated with the legal sex assigned to that person at birth." ADMIN. CODE § 8-102[23]. The State Legislature declined to adopt a similar amendment which would have specifically included transgender individuals under the State Human Rights Law's protective umbrella.

The parties herein . . . extensively address the issues of whether the City and State Human Rights Laws in effect at the time were applicable to transgender individuals. . . .[6] We, however, at this juncture, decline to address those issues, for the complaint, as it stands, fails to state a cause of action regardless of the applicability of the statutes to transgender individuals.

The allegations set forth in the complaint assert, despite plaintiff's attempt to paint them with a broader brush, that defendants refused to execute the lease

---

5. Plaintiff's third and fourth causes of action, asserting discrimination based on disability under the New York State Human Rights Law, and the New York City Administrative Code, respectively, were dismissed without prejudice.

6. We note that the dissent, in discussing pre-amendment discrimination decisions applying anti-discrimination protection to transsexuals, states that these decisions were not called into question, "but in fact are accepted as prevailing law by the Court of Appeals in *McGrath v. Toys 'R' Us*," adding that we cannot now ignore them. While we are aware that it would be unwise to ignore any precedent, those cases are certainly not controlling. Moreover, the Court in *McGrath*, in addressing the significance of those cases, opined that "the fact a handful of lower courts had interpreted the statute broadly did not put to rest the scope of coverage issue."

renewal because plaintiff's transgender clients were using the common area rest-rooms that did not coincide with their biological sex and that the other tenants in the building were complaining. Specifically, the complaint attributes the following statements to specific individuals: Lucy Delgado, an employee of a travel agent that shared space on the third floor of the building with plaintiff, explained that two of the travel agent's employees did not like "'those men that look like women using the [women's] bathroom'"; Dorothy Novotny, the landlord's office manager, purport-edly told plaintiff's representative that "other tenants were complaining because 'men who think they're women are using the women's bathroom'"; Novotny later explained to a different representative of plaintiff that the landlord had received complaints from other tenants, and had issues with "'men who think they are women using the women's bathrooms'"; and Jeff Henry, the landlord's property manager, who "complained" to Leon Quintero, plaintiff's attorney, that "'men dressed as women [were] coming into the building and using the bathrooms,'" after which Henry stated "'[t]hey can't use the wrong restrooms.'"

The complaint, in one sentence of its three-paragraph "Introduction," makes the claim that plaintiff was "told ... the lease would not be renewed unless [plaintiff] prevented its transgender clients from using common areas in the building, includ-ing the main entrance and bathrooms." The ultimatum is attributed to "they," or further back in the sentence to defendants, but nowhere in the complaint is a spe-cific individual, *i.e.*, any of the Trustees, or their agents, credited with making that particular threat. Indeed, at one point, Quintero is alleged to have informed Henry that plaintiff "could not legally restrict its transgender clients' use of the building entrance, hallways or bathrooms," yet the complaint is devoid of any allegation that Henry, or anyone else other than "they," made such a threat.

[The] dissent ... endeavors to expand the scope of the complaint well beyond the allegations set forth therein. The dissent emphasizes that the defendants would only renew the lease "if plaintiff agreed, *in writing*, to preclude *all* of its transgender cli-ents from using *any* of the building's public restrooms, and even the building's main entrance" (emphasis supplied in original). Yet, a careful review of the complaint reveals no such allegation; in fact, the only instance in which a written agreement is mentioned, and which is apparently the springboard for the dissent's conclusions, purportedly occurred in the following conversation between Quintero and Henry as conveyed in paragraph 23 of the complaint:

> Quintero and Henry had several conversations in which Henry insisted that [plaintiff] *agree in writing that its clients would no longer use the public bathrooms in the building.* Henry told Quintero that the Landlord needed such an agreement because other tenants were complaining about "the type of clientele" coming in and out of the building and using the bathrooms. *Specifically*, Henry complained about "men dressed as women coming into the building and using the bathrooms." *When Quintero asked whether Henry was referring to transgendered clients, Henry responded "I don't care what they are. They can't use the wrong restrooms"* (emphasis added).

No reference in the complaint regarding the use of the building's entrances is attributed to any identified individual, and it certainly was never associated with a request for a written agreement.

In sum, the complaint, as it stands, alleges not that the transgender individuals were selectively excluded from the bathrooms, which might trigger one or both of the Human Rights Laws, but that they were excluded on the same basis as all biological males and/or females are excluded from certain bathrooms—their biological sexual assignment. In this vein, we find the Minnesota Supreme Court's decision in *Goins v. West Group*, 635 N.W.2d 717 (Minn. 2001), to be instructive. In *Goins*, plaintiff claimed that defendant discriminated against her[7] based upon her sexual orientation by designating restrooms and restroom use on the basis of biological gender, in violation of the Minnesota Human Rights Act (MHRA), Minn. Stat. § 363.03(1)(2) (2000). The MHRA was clearly written to encompass transgender individuals, and provides that the definition of "sexual orientation" includes "having or being perceived as having a self-image or identity not traditionally associated with one's biological maleness or femaleness." Nevertheless, the court concluded that the defendants' designation of restroom use, applied uniformly, on the basis of "biological gender," rather than biological self-image, was not discrimination. We agree with this rationale and . . . we reverse and dismiss the complaint, on the merits, as, at this juncture, the only discernible claim set forth in the complaint is that plaintiff's transgender clients were prohibited from using the restrooms not in conformance with their biological sex, as were all tenants. Inasmuch as plaintiff makes vague allusions to a connection between defendants' refusal to renew the lease and plaintiff's refusal to prohibit its transgender clients from using the building's common areas, including the main entrance, we grant leave to replead if plaintiff chooses to pursue those assertions with an adequate degree of specificity.

All concur except SAXE, J.P. who dissents in a memorandum as follows:

SAXE, J.P. (dissenting).

A very simple and direct pleading issue is presented on this appeal: Does it constitute sex discrimination under the New York State Human Rights Law, Executive Law § 296(5)(b)(1), or gender discrimination under the New York City Human Rights Law, New York City Admin. Code § 8-107(5)(b)(1), when a landlord refuses to renew the lease of a tenant who provides services for transgender clients, unless the tenant prevents those transgender clients from using the building's restrooms and common areas?

While acknowledging that such an allegation "might trigger one or both of the Human Rights Laws," the majority nevertheless dismisses plaintiff's causes of action for sex and gender discrimination. This puzzling ruling, in effect, amounts to the preemptive issuance of an advisory opinion on a question not yet before the court, a question which might not necessarily be presented at all in this litigation.

---

7. Biologically, Goins was a male.

To accomplish this, the majority artfully eliminates the complaint's central allegation, and instead focuses solely on those factual allegations that provide background information. Having misstated what the complaint alleges, the majority then concludes, as a matter of law, that the allegations (as misstated) do not demonstrate discrimination. Finally, it issues an invitation to replead, which would presumably permit plaintiff to allege again that which it has already alleged: that defendants violated the Human Rights Laws by denying plaintiff a renewal lease unless it agreed to prevent its transgender clients from using the building's restrooms and common areas. This elaborate procedure allows the majority to issue a premature ruling on an issue not presented for decision at this time: whether it constitutes discrimination when a transgender individual is prevented from using the restroom corresponding with his or her adopted gender.

Background

. . . . It is alleged that following successful negotiations for a five-year renewal lease to take effect May 1, 2000, and after plaintiff executed the lease, defendants' office manager, Dorothy Novotny, informed plaintiff that defendants would not renew the lease, due to complaints from the other building tenants regarding the use of the building's restrooms by plaintiff's transgender clients, referred to by other tenants as "men who think they're women."

The complaint further alleges that Jeff Henry, defendants' property manager, thereafter advised Leon Quintero, plaintiff's attorney, that defendants would not renew the lease unless plaintiff agreed that its transgender clients would not use the building's public restrooms. Moreover, during subsequent negotiations, Henry allegedly insisted, on account of the complaints from the other tenants, that plaintiff agree in writing that its transgender clients would no longer use the public restrooms in the building. Furthermore, the introductory section of the complaint also alleges that defendants would not renew the lease unless plaintiff also prevented its transgender clients from using the building's main entrance. In addition, it is alleged, Henry informed Quintero that he just needed to get rid of "all these queens."

Plaintiff received an eviction notice on June 30, 2000. Defendants then commenced an eviction proceeding in housing court, and plaintiff stipulated to vacate the premises without prejudice to these claims. Plaintiff then commenced this action, asserting that defendants unlawfully discriminated by refusing to lease the space to plaintiff because of its transgender clients. The first cause of action alleges sex discrimination under the New York State Human Rights Law, and the second alleges gender discrimination under the New York City Administrative Code.

. . . .

Discussion

The basis for the claims of discrimination here is not merely that defendants sought to prevent people from using any bathroom other than that corresponding with their biological gender; it is that defendants discriminated by refusing to renew the lease unless plaintiff would exclude its transgender clients from the building's public restrooms and main entrance.

While the complaint sets forth that the difficulties initially arose when others in the building complained about biological males using the women's bathroom, it goes on to assert that when the time came to renew the lease, defendants would only do so if plaintiff agreed, in writing, to preclude all of its transgender clients from using any of the building's public restrooms; elsewhere it alleges, without attribution to a particular individual, that defendants also asked that plaintiff's clients even be precluded from using the building's main entrance.

On a motion to dismiss pursuant to CPLR 3211, the only issue is whether the allegations manifest any cause of action, giving the plaintiff the benefit of every possible favorable inference, and we must accept the allegations as true. There is no basis in the CPLR to exclude from consideration factual allegations contained in the complaint's introductory paragraphs, or alleged statements not attributed to a particular individual, whose source may be clarified in the context of a bill of particulars or during discovery. Nor may the court eliminate from consideration alleged statements that it deems to have been "clarified" or in effect retracted by an alleged subsequent statement. The only question here is whether the allegations, including the assertion that the landlord refused to renew plaintiff's lease unless it prevented its clients from using building restrooms and main entrance, may be said to constitute a violation of the New York State Human Rights Law and the New York City Human Rights Law.

The majority recognizes that the complaint includes an allegation that Jeff Henry, defendant's property manager, sought a written agreement that plaintiff would prohibit its clients from using all the restrooms; however, it then proceeds with its analysis as if another alleged statement by Mr. Henry ("I don't care what they are. They can't use the wrong restrooms.") completely nullifies his other statement. This amounts to an act of factual interpretation inappropriate in the context of a CPLR 3211 motion. Moreover, as to the majority's suggestion that the complaint is insufficient in not attributing alleged statements to a particular individual, any such lack is not fatal, but may be clarified in the context of a bill of particulars.

In holding that its allegations fail to set forth a cause of action, the majority quotes from the portion of the complaint that sets forth these allegations, including the assertion that "[Jeff] Henry insisted that [plaintiff] agree in writing that its clients would no longer use the public bathrooms in the building." Yet, it remarks that "a careful review of the complaint reveals no such allegation." Clearly, the quoted portion of the complaint includes a factual assertion that suffices to assert a cause of action for discrimination.

Executive Law § 296(5)(b)(1), New York State's Human Rights Law, as effective at the time of the alleged discrimination, provided:

> It shall be an unlawful discriminatory practice . . . to refuse to sell, rent, lease or otherwise deny to or withhold from any person or group of persons

land or commercial space because of the race, creed, color, national origin, sex, age, [or] disability . . . of such person or persons. . . .

New York City Administrative Code § 8-107(5)(b)(1) contained parallel language, except for the inclusion of the phrase "actual or perceived" and the use of the term "gender" instead of the word "sex."

Because these anti-discrimination statutes are remedial, they must be interpreted liberally to achieve their intended purpose. *See Matter of N.Y. County DES Litig.* [*Wetherill v. Eli Lilly & Co.*], 678 N.E.2d 474 (N.Y. 1997). Indeed, a broad interpretation is particularly appropriate since "the very purpose of the Human Rights Law was . . . to eliminate all forms of discrimination, those then existing as well as any later devised." *Brooklyn Union Gas Co. v. New York State Human Rights Appeal Bd.*, 359 N.E.2d 393 (N.Y. 1976).

Protected Class

In any discrimination claim, the first thing the plaintiff must establish is that the plaintiff is a member of a group that the statute intends to protect. . . .

New York State Executive Law

As to the New York State Human Rights Law, "[t]he standards for establishing unlawful discrimination under section 296 of the Human Rights Law are the same as those governing title VII cases under the Federal Civil Rights Act of 1964." *Mittl v. New York State Div. of Human Rights*, 794 N.E.2d 660 (N.Y. 2003). Because Title VII and the New York State Human Rights Law have many similarities, federal case law has been looked to in analyzing questions under state law.

Defendant takes the position that the term sex discrimination only applies to actions or decisions taken because of the victim's gender, or what the perpetrator perceived the victim's gender to be, and not actions taken based upon the victim's adoption of the other gender's trappings. However, *Price Waterhouse v. Hopkins*, 490 U.S. 228 (1989), established that sex discrimination may occur based upon actions taken because of the victim's failure to conform with sex stereotypes, rather than because of his or her gender *per se.* . . . As the [*Price Waterhouse*] Court explained, "[i]n the specific context of sex stereotyping, an employer who acts on the basis of a belief that a woman cannot be aggressive, or that she must not be, *has acted on the basis of gender.*" (emphasis added).

By the same token, an anatomical male who puts on what he believes to be the trappings of femininity, and is treated differently for doing so, is experiencing sex discrimination, under Title VII and no less under New York Executive Law. Even though the treatment is not because of his gender *per se*, it is sex discrimination when it occurs because the victim is behaving in a manner contrary to defendants' sex-stereotyped expectations of how a man ought to behave.

That the Legislature declined to amend the Executive Law so as to specifically include transgender people in its list of protected classes cannot be taken to necessarily mean that the Legislature intended that they be excluded from its coverage. Given the existence of prior case law under the statutes applicable here, applying anti-discrimination protections to transsexuals (*see Richards v. United States Tennis Assn.*, 93 Misc. 2d 713, 400 N.Y.S.2d 267 (1977); *Maffei v. Kolaeton Industry*, 164 Misc. 2d 547, 626 N.Y.S.2d 391 (1995); *Rentos v. Oce-Office Sys.*, 95 Civ. 7908 (LAP), 1996 U.S. Dist. LEXIS 19060, 1996 WL 737215 (S.D.N.Y. Dec. 24, 1996)), the decision not to include "transgender" in the statute's list is not dispositive. Indeed, it is arguably more meaningful that the Legislature did not specifically exclude the transgendered [*sic*—Eds.] from the statute's application, as Congress did in the Americans with Disabilities Act, *see* 42 USC §12211(b)(1), and the Rehabilitation Act, *see* 29 USC §705(20)(F)(i). The decision not to affirmatively add transgender individuals to the list of those covered by the statute's protection is quite different from affirmatively repealing or revising the protection already indicated by prior cases.

Furthermore, since those earlier discrimination decisions were not called into question, but in fact were accepted as prevailing law by the Court of Appeals in *McGrath v. Toys "R" Us*, *supra*, we cannot now ignore them.

Nor does the analysis change because in those earlier cases the plaintiffs may have physically altered their secondary sex characteristics to some extent.[3] The concept of discrimination does not apply in different ways to those who have completed the gender reassignment process and those who have not begun it, and there is no case holding otherwise. The prohibition against sex discrimination applies to transgender individuals regardless of where the particular victim falls on the gender-reassignment spectrum.

New York City Administrative Code

Similarly, plaintiff's transgender clients are covered under the New York City Human Rights Law even as it existed at the relevant time. It is true that the subsequent 2002 amendment clarified the intended scope of the term "gender" in the City's anti-discrimination law so as to leave no doubt that transgender people are covered. But this modification was specifically referred to by the City Council as a clarification rather than an expansion. Indeed, the Court of Appeals, in *McGrath v. Toys "R" Us*, remarked in regard to the adoption of the 2002 amendment that "the City Council determined that, in its view, the code already protected transsexuals but was concerned that, without the amendment, the law could be misinterpreted as excluding this class of individuals from coverage."

. . . .

---

3. In *Richards*, the plaintiff tennis player had undergone gender reassignment surgery. In *Rentos*, the plaintiff had "started, but had not completed, the process of changing her sex from male to female at the time of her hiring." In *Maffei*, the record was said to be unclear as to "what extent the plaintiff completed his metamorphosis from a female to a male."

Discriminatory Conduct

Once it is established that a plaintiff is a member of the class protected by the anti-discrimination statute at issue, there remains the matter of whether the complained-of conduct may be found to constitute discrimination on that basis. Here, the question is whether it is discrimination on the basis of gender or sex to deny a tenant a renewal lease unless the tenant prevents its transgender clients from using any of the restrooms. While defendant repeatedly contends that it is not discriminatory to prevent individuals who are anatomically male from using the women's restroom (and vice versa), that is not the issue presented here.

For purposes of this CPLR 3211 motion, the claim that issuance of a renewal lease was conditioned on the exclusion of plaintiff's transgender clients from public portions of the building, and in particular the bathrooms—all the bathrooms—asserts enough to state a claim under the City and State Human Rights Laws. The question of what actually occurred and whether it amounted to discrimination must await the development of a factual record.

Similarly, because this CPLR 3211 motion does not involve any factual determination, it would be premature to adopt the reasoning suggested by defendants, that they had a proper, non-discriminatory business purpose in denying plaintiff a renewal lease, because plaintiff's clients persisted in flouting clear, reasonable building rules about using the bathrooms.

I recognize that plaintiff and its clients, as well as the organizations submitting amicus curiae briefs, seek to press the point that anti-discrimination laws require that sex-segregated restrooms permit access to not only those of that biological gender, but to those who psychologically identify as belonging to that gender. On the other side of that coin, defendants raise the spectre of female-identified biological males insisting on using the women's locker rooms at sports clubs and gyms.

These issues of gender identity and its ramifications in the context of the Human Rights Law must and will be addressed by the courts. However, as tempting as it may be to weigh in on that issue now, it is, if not entirely irrelevant to the issues before us, certainly premature. Should it be established that defendants were merely seeking to limit people to the restroom matching their anatomical or biological gender, it would then be appropriate to address the issue of what restrictions or limitations, if any, may properly be imposed on transgender individuals. But, if it is demonstrated that defendants proposed as a condition of renewing the lease that these transgender individuals be prohibited from using any building restrooms, there may be no basis to consider whether reasonable restrictions are proper.

In view of the foregoing, defendants' application to dismiss the first and second causes of action was properly denied.

Discussion

1. Both the majority and the dissent in *Hispanic AIDS Forum* purport to exercise judicial restraint: the majority declines to decide whether specific state and city laws banning sex discrimination cover anti-transgender discrimination, and the dissent declines to decide whether requiring everyone to use restrooms based on their sex assigned at birth discriminates against transgender persons on the basis of sex. Whose posture regarding their judicial restraint is more persuasive, if either?

2. Is the view of equality presupposed by the majority in its reasoning (*i.e.*, that there was no discrimination alleged in the transgender plaintiffs' complaint) one of formal equality or substantive equality? Which kind of equality should courts seek to advance when interpreting and applying public accommodations statutes or other anti-discrimination laws?

Reading Guide for Department of Fair Employment and Housing v. Marion's Place

1. In *Department of Fair Employment and Housing v. Marion's Place*, what kinds of policies with respect to transgender persons does the Fair Employment and Housing Commission of California specify are or are not at issue? The Commission, consistent with precedent, takes the state's public accommodations statute (the Unruh Civil Rights Act or Unruh Act) to reach only intentional discrimination; what evidence supports the conclusion that Marion's Place intentionally discriminated?

2. In deciding whether the defendant violated the Unruh Act, the Commission follows a three-step analysis set forth by the California Supreme Court in *Harris v. Capital Growth Investors XIV*, 805 P.2d 873 (Cal. 1991). First, the Commission considers the language of the statute. What is the kind of discrimination that it sees at issue in the case and why? Second, the Commission considers whether the defendant's challenged policy was reasonably related to legitimate business reasons that might justify access to public accommodations. What does the Commission conclude on this point and why? Third, the Commission looks to the consequences of holding the challenged policy unlawful, which in some cases might support the conclusion that the legislature would have intended to reach the conduct at issue but in others might give courts a reason to refrain from interpreting the Unruh Act to hold a practice unlawful. Here, how did the Commission assess such concerns?

3. Were the award of damages to Ms. Arreola and its magnitude appropriate?

Department of Fair Employment and Housing v. Marion's Place

No. U-200203 C-0008-00-s, 2006 WL 1130912
(Cal. Fair Emp't & Housing Comm'n Feb. 1, 2006)

Decision

The Fair Employment and Housing Commission hereby adopts the attached Proposed Decision as the Commission's final decision in this matter and designates it precedential. . . .

. . . .

HUNT, Administrative Law Judge

Proposed Decision

Administrative Law Judge Caroline L. Hunt heard this matter on behalf of the Fair Employment and Housing Commission on February 22 and 23, 2005, in Salinas, California. . . . Christopher Daley, Esq., of the Transgender Law Center, participated in after-hearing briefing as amicus curiae. . . .

After consideration of the entire record, the administrative law judge makes the following findings of fact, determination of issues, and order.

Findings of Fact

Procedural Setting

On May 5, 2003, Francis Arreola (Arreola or complainant) filed written, verified complaints with the Department of Fair Employment and Housing (Department) against Muriano's [*sic*] Club, Marion's Place, [Mary] Ann Lopez Dewitt dba Marion's Place, and Marion Lopez dba Marion's Place. The complaints alleged that, within the preceding year, Marion Lopez (Lopez), owner of Muriano's [*sic*] Club and Marion's Place, located at 494 and 487 E. Market Street, Salinas, California, denied complainant full and equal privileges because of complainant's sex (male) and gender identity (transgender). The complaints alleged that Marion's Place denied entry to Arreola, who was wearing a dress, based on a "trousers only" dress code, and told Arreola to use only the men's restroom, and that this conduct constituted unlawful practices in violation of the Fair Employment and Housing Act (FEHA or Act), incorporating Civil Code section 51. (Gov. Code, § 12900 et seq., Civ. Code § 51.)

The Department is an administrative agency empowered to issue accusations under Government Code section 12930, subdivision (h). On May 4, 2004, Jill Peterson, in her then official capacity as Interim Director of the Department, issued an accusation. . . . The accusation alleged that respondents denied complainant full and equal accommodations, advantages, facilities, privileges, and services based on complainant's actual or perceived sex, gender identity, and sexual orientation, in violation of Civil Code section 51, as incorporated into the FEHA by Government Code section 12948. The accusation alleged that respondents denied complainant entry into their business establishment, Marion's Place, unless complainant adhered to the men's dress code by wearing pants, rather than a dress. . . .

Factual Setting

Complainant Arreola identifies herself as a male-to-female transgender [*sic*—Eds.]. She was born Francisco Arreola, a biological and anatomical male, on February 11, 1973, in Michoacán, Mexico. From an early age, Arreola considered herself female. In Mexico, she faced harassment and ostracism as a result of her sexual identity. On her arrival in the United States in about 1998, Arreola began publicly identifying herself as female in her daily life, by wearing women's clothes, jewelry, make-up, and hair styles.

Arreola underwent hormone therapy, taking female hormones prescribed by her doctor. Arreola considered but, primarily for financial reasons, had not undergone sex reassignment surgery.

At the time of the acts alleged in this case, Marion's Place was a nightclub owned and run, for about 38 years, by Respondent Marion J. Lopez (respondent Lopez). Marion's Place catered to a predominantly Hispanic, seasonal farm worker clientele. It offered a venue for drinking and dancing, with live music and cover charge on Friday, Saturday, and Sunday nights. . . . It held about 250 customers and was popular and crowded, especially on weekends.

Both prior to and after incorporation of the business, respondent Lopez managed the nightclub, supervising all employees. . . .

Transgender Customers at Marion's Place

Starting in about 2000, Marion's Place began to attract a transgender clientele, in addition to its existing customers and clients. By mid-to late 2002, the number of transgender customers at Marion's Place averaged around 25 on a Saturday night. Some of the male-to-female transgender customers wore dresses or skirts, clothing associated as traditionally "feminine" clothing, at the nightclub. Some women and transgender customers wore skirts or dresses that were very closely tailored and revealing, referred to as "mini skirts."

On occasion, fights or arguments took place at Marion's Place, at times involving verbal threats or physical altercations. The nightclub's security staff was headed by Alejandro (Alex) Gomez. Members of the security staff, including Gomez, were responsible for checking customers' identification documents (IDs) at the front entrance, checking for concealed weapons or alcohol, and intervening in the event of arguments and fights among clientele.

In both 2001 and 2002, several altercations at Marion's Place involving heterosexual and transgender patrons required intervention by . . . Gomez. In one such incident, a male customer became angry and physically violent on realizing that his dance partner was transgender. Gomez intervened to prevent a fistfight. In other incidents, transgender customers were assaulted or yelled at. From time to time, certain male customers became irate when they put their hands up the skirt of the person they were with, to discover that person was transgender. Each time, Gomez responded quickly to prevent an escalation to any further physical violence.

Marion's Place management and security personnel also dealt with a number of non-transgender females' soliciting sex acts both inside the club and outside in the parking lot.

Sometime in about 2002 at Marion's Place, a transgender [*sic*—Eds.], not identified in the record, came to the nightclub wearing a skirt without underwear. Several non-transgender customers complained and left, threatening never to return, when the transgender individual danced in a provocative manner, showing male genitalia. Gomez discussed this incident with respondent Lopez, who responded, "No more guys with skirts."

In late 2002, respondents instituted a dress code for its clientele. The dress code provided that:

> Women can wear a dress or pants. Men can wear pants but not dresses or skirts. Tank tops on men are prohibited. Shoes are required.

On adoption of the dress code at Marion's Place, transgender individuals who were perceived by the security staff at the door of the club to be males were not permitted entry to the club if they were wearing dresses or skirts. Male-to-female transgender individuals were still welcomed as customers at Marion's Place, as long as they abided by the male dress code, and wore pants.

One evening in November 2002, complainant Arreola went to Marion's Place for the first time. She was accompanied by a friend, Jesus Morales. Arreola wore a skirt, blouse, scarf, and nylons. At the entrance of the nightclub, Arreola was stopped by security and told that she needed to wear pants, not a skirt, because of the rules of the club. Arreola and Morales then left the nightclub.

Arreola was upset that respondents would not allow her into the nightclub wearing a skirt. She felt humiliated. This humiliation was particularly acute because she had been identified by respondents as a man, rather than as a woman, in front of her friend.

The next day, Arreola returned to the club with . . . Morales to speak to the owner, respondent Lopez. Lopez told Arreola that at Marion's Place, under the club's rules, men had to wear pants, not dresses.

Arreola's treatment at Marion's Place led to her experiencing simultaneous feelings of impotence and anger. She cried when she reflected on how she had been humiliated. She had been trying to live her life as a woman, had even applied for political asylum, and now the rejection and humiliation by Marion's Place rendered her both powerless and angry. She felt that respondents' security personnel had ridiculed her because of her gender identity. Previously, she had enjoyed dressing up to look her best, to go out with friends. She no longer enjoyed confidence in her appearance because of her treatment at the nightclub.

After six to seven months, Arreola reluctantly returned to Marion's Place, at the urging of her friends. When she went back, however, in about May 2003, she did not feel confident enough to dress in a skirt. Instead, she wore pants, because she feared being embarrassed once more at the club if she wore a skirt or dress. That evening, she was admitted to the club.

Arreola visited the nightclub two additional times later in 2003. She remained fearful of being embarrassed, so wore pants, not a skirt, and each time was admitted to the nightclub.

Some time prior to the events alleged in the accusation, Arreola applied for political asylum with the then United States Immigration and Naturalization Service, based on the persecution she faced in Mexico as a transgender. On about June 4, 2003, the I.N.S. issued Arreola an Employment Authorization Card. The I.N.S. designated complainant's sex as "female." On August 15, 2003, Arreola was issued a California Department of Motor Vehicles ID card. That ID also designated Arreola as "female."

At the time of hearing, respondents continued to maintain their dress code policy at Marion's Place, prohibiting prospective customers respondents considered to be men from entering the club wearing skirts or dresses. There were still fights and verbal disputes at the nightclub from time to time. Of approximately 25 fights at Marion's Place in the past five years, about two or three involved transgenders in skirts or dresses. In at least two incidents after adoption of the dress code, transgenders wearing pants were subjected to physical attacks.

Determination of Issues

Liability

Complainant Arreola, as a male-to-female transgender individual, asserts her right to wear traditionally feminine clothing, *i.e.*, a skirt or a dress, as a customer in Marion's Place.

The Department alleges that respondents' refusal to allow complainant Arreola to enter Marion's Place when dressed in a skirt constituted arbitrary discrimination under the Unruh Civil Rights Act, as incorporated into the FEHA by Government Code section 12948. (Civ. Code, §51, Gov. Code, §12948.) Both the Department and amicus curiae [Transgender Law Center] argue that complainant is protected under the Unruh Civil Rights Act based on her sex and gender identity, and that respondents' dress code barring men from wearing a dress or skirt violates the Act's prohibition against arbitrary, discriminatory conduct by a business establishment.

Respondents deny any violation of the Unruh Civil Rights Act or the FEHA, asserting that they have never discriminated against transgender individuals, and that respondents' dress code prohibiting men from wearing skirts or dresses is reasonable and justified for legitimate business reasons.

The Unruh Civil Rights Act

At the time of the acts alleged in the second amended accusation, Civil Code section 51, subdivision (b), stated: "All persons within the jurisdiction of this state are free and equal, and no matter what their sex, race, color, religion, ancestry, national origin, disability, or medical condition are entitled to the full and equal accommodations, advantages, facilities, privileges, or services in all business establishments of every kind whatsoever."

. . . .

It is well settled that a bar or nightclub, such as the one at issue in this case, qualifies as a "business establishment." *Stoumen v. Reilly*, 37 Cal. 2d 713 (1951). Thus, Marion's Place is a business establishment within the meaning of the Unruh Civil Rights Act.

It is important to recognize that the issue of barring all transgenders from the nightclub is not presented in this case. It is the mode of attire of customers, specifically transgender customers, that is being regulated. On its face, respondents' dress code delineates permissible attire for customers expressly and unambiguously based on their sex — whether they are men or women. Respondents' intent in adopting the policy, however, and the effect of the dress code as applied at Marion's Place, were to regulate the dress of transgender customers. See *Harris v. Capital Growth Investors XIV*, 52 Cal. 3d 1142 (1991) (the Unruh Civil Rights Act requires a showing of intentional discrimination, and the Title VII or FEHA's disparate impact analysis does not apply; however, relevant evidence of disparate impact may be probative of intentional discrimination in the appropriate case."). Respondents' dress code, in effect, precludes male-to-female transgender customers from patronizing Marion's Club if they choose to dress in the clothing most traditionally associated in this culture with exclusively female attire — a dress or skirt.

The Unruh Civil Rights Act is to be liberally construed to effectuate the purposes for which it was enacted and to promote justice. *Rotary Club of Duarte v. Bd. of Directors of Rotary Internat., et al.*, 178 Cal. App. 3d 1035 (1986), *aff'd*, 481 U.S. 537 (1987). One of the policies underlying the enactment of the Unruh Civil Rights Act is the eradication of sex discrimination by business establishments in the furnishing of "accommodations, advantages, facilities, privileges, or services." Civ. Code, § 51; *Rotary Club of Duarte*. The Unruh Civil Rights Act is "clearly a declaration of California's public policy mandate and objective that men and women be treated equally." *Koire v. Metro Car Wash*, 40 Cal. 3d 24, 28 (1985).

California courts have held that, in addition to the particular forms of discrimination specifically enumerated in the statute, the Unruh Civil Rights Act also protects judicially recognized classifications: unconventional dress or appearance, *In re Cox*, 3 Cal. 3d 205 (1970); family status, *Marina Point, Ltd. v. Wolfson*, 30 Cal. 3d 721 (1982); sexual orientation, *Rolon v. Kulwitzky*, 153 Cal. App. 3d 289 (1984); and persons under the age of 18, *O'Connor v. Village Green Owners Assn.*, 33 Cal. 3d 790 (1983).

Thus, in addition to making arbitrary sex discrimination by a business unlawful, the Unruh Civil Rights Act also prohibits a business establishment's barring a prospective customer solely on that individual's manner or mode of dress or unorthodox appearance. *Cox*. In *Cox*, the California Supreme Court held that the Unruh Civil Rights Act protected prospective customers with long hair and unconventional dress from arbitrary exclusion from a shopping center.

This is not to suggest that dress codes *per se* are unlawful. As the *Cox* Court notes, "[a] business establishment may, of course, promulgate reasonable deportment regulations that are rationally related to the services performed and the facilities provided." *Cox; see Orloff v. Los Angeles Turf Club*, 36 Cal. 2d 734 (1951).

In *Harris*, the Supreme Court adopted a three-part analysis, subsequently consistently followed by the courts, to determine the future reach of the Unruh Civil Rights Act consistent with legislative intent. In determining whether the dress code in issue in this case violates the Unruh Civil Rights Act, this decision follows the *Harris* three-part analysis by examining first, the language of the statute, second, the legitimate business interests asserted by the defendants, and finally, the consequences of allowing the discrimination claim.

Application of Harris' Three-Part Analysis
1. Sex as a Protected Basis Under the Language of the Statute

By its clear and unambiguous wording, respondents' dress code expressly bars "men" from wearing dresses or skirts. "Women" are permitted to wear either pants or dresses. Thus, the dress code, on its face, treats prospective customers differently based on their sex.

Such a sex-based dress code in a business establishment may violate the Unruh Civil Rights Act. In *Hales v. Ojai Valley Inn and Country Club*, 73 Cal. App. 3d 25 (1977), the court held that a male patron in a "leisure suit" who was refused service at the country club because he was not wearing a tie, while female patrons in leisure suits were served food and drink, stated a cause of action for sex discrimination under the Unruh Civil Rights Act.

The Department and amicus curiae assert that respondents' dress code, as applied specifically and intentionally against transgenders, is a form of sex stereotyping. They argue that such sex stereotyping constitutes unlawful discrimination based on sex, as recognized by the United States Supreme Court in the Title VII employment case *Price Waterhouse v. Hopkins*, 490 U.S. 228 (1989). In *Price Waterhouse*, the Supreme Court held that being treated differently by one's employer for not conforming to sex stereotypes of "femininity" is cognizable as sex discrimination under Title VII, 42 U.S.C. § 2000e et seq.

The Unruh Civil Rights Act prohibits "all forms of stereotypical discrimination. . . ." *Koire*. In *Koire*, the California Supreme Court held that a business establishment's policy of charging men and women different prices constituted "sex-based discounts [which] impermissibly perpetuate sexual stereotypes," in violation of the Unruh Civil Rights Act.

Here, respondents' policy is both based on and promulgates the sex stereotype that men should not wear clothing traditionally associated with exclusively "feminine" attire. As such, the policy is a form of discrimination on sex-based stereotypes. And as the Department and amicus persuasively argue, under the Unruh Civil Rights Act, the exclusion of a prospective customer for failing to conform to such sex stereotypes is unlawful, under *Koire*, unless it can be justified by a legitimate business reason.

Moreover, to the extent that dresses or skirts are not conventionally, in this culture, worn by men, respondent's dress code on its face also regulates "unconventional" dress or appearance, a protected category first recognized by the California Supreme Court in *Cox*.

Whether respondents' dress code is arbitrary discrimination that violates the Unruh Civil Rights Act, however, requires analysis of the legitimacy of respondents' business interests underlying the dress code and whether there is a rational relationship between the dress code and respondents' club and facilities. *Harris*; *Cox*.

2. Legitimate Business Reasons

Respondents assert that their dress code is justified for legitimate business reasons relating to the safety and security of the nightclub. Specifically, respondents assert that prior to institution of the dress code, customers mistook "men wearing dresses" for anatomical females, and fights resulted. Respondents also assert that some transgenders [*sic*— Eds.] wearing skirts danced provocatively and offended other customers. Respondents next assert that some of the transgender individuals at the club were involved in acts of solicitation. Finally, respondents assert that it is more difficult to check for a weapon at the door if a "man is dressed in a skirt."

. . . .

While a business must take reasonable steps to preserve the safety and security of their place of business, *Cox*, the security issues identified by respondents here relate to customers' conduct, not their attire. The offending individuals, none of whom was identified in the record, were all customers at the club whose behavior deviated from socially acceptable norms— dancing lewdly or provocatively, fighting, carrying weapons or soliciting sex acts. Respondents' dress code is misguided, because it focuses on attire, not the underlying problem behavior. And notably, the record showed that it was non-transgender customers who instituted most of the objectionable conduct at the nightclub.

It is significant that there was never a suggestion or even a hint of evidence in the record that complainant Arreola ever participated in any improper conduct, whether at Marion's Place or elsewhere.

As the Court noted in *Cox*, "Clearly, an entrepreneur need not tolerate customers who damage property, injure others, or otherwise disrupt his business." However, an individual who has committed no misconduct cannot be excluded solely because he or she falls within a class of persons whom the owner believes is more likely to engage in misconduct than other classes. *Marina Point, Ltd.*; *Orloff*; *Stoumen*; *Rolon*. Thus, under established Unruh case law, complainant may not be excluded simply because other customers, even transgender customers in skirts, engaged in misconduct.

Furthermore, the evidence in this case does not support respondents' assertion that the dress code bears a rational relationship to the safety and security of the business. The record showed, for example, that non-transgender female pros-titutes came to respondents' club and solicited sex acts on the premises. Respon-dents, however, did not impose a dress code to regulate female prostitutes' clothing. Respondents further assert that the dress code prevented fights. The record showed, however, that most fights at the club did not involve transgenders in skirts. Respon-dents next assert that it is men who carry weapons, and that if men are allowed to wear skirts, security can not perform weapons searches. This argument is unper-suasive. Respondents, of course, have a legitimate interest in preventing customers' from bringing weapons into their club, but how a skirt thwarts an effective search was not made clear.

Respondents also objected to lewd and provocative dancing by certain transgen-der individuals wearing short skirts. Respondent Lopez testified that these individ-uals would "wiggle their butts and it didn't look right," indicating that respondents' objection had more to do with subjective opinion on what was "appropriate," rather than issues of safety or security. One particular incident shortly preceded respondents' adoption of the dress code. [Gomez] testified that one night a trans-gender dancing in a very short skirt bared male genitalia, and that when Gomez informed respondent Lopez of the incident, Lopez announced, "No more guys in skirts." Respondents' decision at that time was to bar all "men in skirts," rather than address the conduct of that particular individual to prohibit nude displays of genitalia.

As applied, respondents' dress code requires that respondents' security personnel at the club entrance exercise the power to ascertain a prospective customer's sex. As amicus persuasively argues, "Short of performing genital checks on all patrons . . . wearing a dress or a skirt, . . . security staff is forced to rely on unlawful sex stereo-types in order to enforce this dress code." Such reliance on subjective perceptions of who appears "sufficiently feminine" or "too masculine" runs the inherent danger of arbitrarily imposing unlawful sex stereotypes to bar or permit a prospective cus-tomer into the club if wearing a skirt.

In sum, respondents' articulated business reasons of safety and security are not shown in this case to be rationally related to respondents' adoption of the dress code.

3. Consequences of Recognizing This Claim

The Department asserts that recognizing this claim furthers the purpose of the Unruh Civil Rights Act to guarantee access to public accommodations by all per-sons, regardless of their sex or other protected characteristic that has "no bearing on a person's status as a responsible consumer." *Harris.* Respondents argue that if their dress code is found to violate the Unruh Civil Rights Act "no business owner may impose any dress code."

The Department's argument is persuasive. Recognizing complainant's right not to be excluded from respondents' club based on her apparel upholds the intent and underlying purposes of the Unruh Civil Rights Act. The evidence did not establish that complainant's wearing a dress or skirt had any bearing on her being a responsible customer in the nightclub.

Moreover, contrary to respondents' dire predictions, the right of a business to regulate the conduct of its business by reasonable deportment regulations is preserved. This decision is a narrow one, finding that dress codes *per se* are not unlawful; however, where a dress code impermissibly and arbitrarily discriminates on the basis of sex, as occurred here, and is not justified by legitimate business reasons, it is in violation of the Unruh Civil Rights Act.

Thus, based on the foregoing, the Department established that respondents' dress code violates the Unruh Civil Rights Act, as incorporated in the FEHA. . . .

. . . .

Remedy

Having established that respondents violated the Act, the Department is entitled to whatever forms of relief are necessary to make complainant whole for any loss or injury she suffered as a result. The Department must demonstrate, where necessary, the nature and extent of the resultant injury, and respondent must demonstrate any bar or excuse it asserts to any part of these remedies. Gov. Code, § 12970, subd. (a); Cal. Code Regs., tit. 2, § 7286.9; *Donald Schriver, Inc. v. Fair Empl. & Hous. Com.*, 220 Cal. App. 3d 396 (1986).

The Department's second amended accusation seeks compensatory damages for emotional distress, out-of-pocket losses, attorney's fees, an administrative fine, and affirmative relief.

A. Make-Whole Relief

1. Compensatory Damages for Emotional Distress

The Department seeks an award of compensatory damages as a result of emotional injury complainant suffered as a result of respondents' unlawful conduct. . . .

Government Code section 12970, subdivision (a)(3), authorizes the Commission to award damages to compensate for emotional pain, suffering, inconvenience, mental anguish, loss of enjoyment of life, and other nonpecuniary losses in an amount not to exceed, in combination with any administrative fines imposed, $150,000 per aggrieved person per respondent. In determining whether to award damages for emotional injuries, and the amount of any award for these damages, the Commission considers relevant evidence of the effects of discrimination on the aggrieved person with respect to: physical and mental well-being; personal integrity, dignity, and privacy; ability to work, earn a living, and advance in his or her career; personal and professional reputation; family relationships; and, access to the job and ability to associate with peers and coworkers. The duration of the injury and the egregiousness of the discriminatory practice are also factors to be considered. Gov. Code, § 12970, subd. (b).

The evidence at hearing established that Arreola was humiliated and angry by being denied admission into Marion's Place because she was dressed in a skirt. She felt embarrassed and humiliated to be judged a man, and felt ridiculed by the security staff. These feelings were particularly acute because it had happened in front of her friend, Jesus Morales. Up to that point, Arreola had very much enjoyed dressing her best to go out with her friends at a club. She no longer enjoyed confidence in her appearance because of her treatment at respondents' nightclub. The rejection by Marion's Place also made Arreola cry with feelings of powerlessness and anger, as for so many years she had been trying to live her life as a woman and had applied for political asylum, based on her transgender identity.

It was more than six or seven months before Arreola, with some reluctance, and only after being urged by friends, went back to Marion's Place. Too afraid to wear a skirt, she instead wore tailored pants, and was admitted to the nightclub. Arreola visited Marion's Place twice more in 2003. She remained fearful of being rejected at the door and embarrassed, so wore pants, not a skirt, and was admitted to the nightclub.

Considering the facts of this case in light of the factors set forth in Government Code section 12970, subdivision (a)(3), respondents will be ordered to pay complainant $2,500 in actual damages for her emotional distress. Interest will accrue on this amount, at the rate of ten percent per year, compounded annually, from the effective date of this decision until the date of payment.

2. Out of Pocket Losses

. . . .

Complainant credibly testified that she missed two days of work in order to attend the hearings, and that she normally worked an eight-hour shift and was paid at the hourly rate of $7.25. To compensate complainant's out of pocket losses, she will be awarded $116 in lost wages. Interest shall accrue on this amount, at the rate of ten percent per year, compounded annually, from the effective date of this decision until the date of payment.

B. Administrative Fine

The Department seeks an order of an administrative fine for respondents' "willful, intentional and purposeful discrimination." The Commission has the authority to order administrative fines where it finds, by clear and convincing evidence, a respondent guilty of oppression, fraud, or malice, express or implied, as required by Civil Code section 3294. Gov. Code, § 12970, subd. (d). The amount of an administrative fine, in combination with any amount awarded to compensate for emotional distress, can not exceed $150,000 per respondent. Gov. Code, § 12970, subd. (a)(3). . . .

In determining the appropriate amount of an administrative fine, the Commission shall consider relevant evidence of, including but not limited to, the following: willful, intentional, or purposeful conduct; refusal to prevent or eliminate discrimination; conscious disregard for the rights of the complainant; commission of unlawful conduct; intimidation or harassment; conduct without just cause or excuse, or multiple violations of the Act. Gov. Code, § 12970, subd. (d).

Here, respondents' imposition of a dress code in an attempt to address issues between some of its transgender and heterosexual customers, while misconceived and arbitrary, and found in this decision to be in violation of the Unruh Civil Rights Act, does not rise to the level of willful, malicious, oppressive or fraudulent conduct envisaged under Government Code section 12970 or Civil Code section 3294. Thus, this proposed decision will not order an administrative fine.

C. Affirmative Relief

The Department asks that respondents be ordered to: cease and desist from discriminating against complainant and all other of their customers on the bases of actual or perceived sex, sexual orientation or gender identity; develop and implement a written policy prohibiting discrimination; conduct training for all owners, managers, supervisors and employees regarding that policy; develop and implement a formal complaint process for customers; and the posting of notices, as forms of affirmative relief, under the Act.

The Act authorizes the Commission to order affirmative relief, including an order to cease and desist from any unlawful practice, and an order to take whatever other actions are necessary, in the Commission's judgment, to effectuate the purposes of the Act. Gov. Code, § 12970, subd. (a)(5).

Respondents will be ordered to cease and desist from imposing its dress code to the extent that it discriminates against individuals based on sex. Respondent will also be ordered to post a notice acknowledging its unlawful conduct toward complainant . . . along with a notice of customers' rights and obligations regarding unlawful discrimination under the Act. . . . Finally, respondents will be ordered to provide training on discrimination under the Unruh Civil Rights Act to its corporate president, directors and officers, current managers and supervisors, and all employees currently working at Marion's Place.

. . . .

Discussion

1. Although the Commission notes more than once that it believes it is not addressing the question whether a public accommodation such as the defendant nightclub could have a dress code for customers *per se*, is there anything in its reasoning that would *not* lead to the conclusion that any *sex-discriminatory* (or *sex-specific*, as some would have it) dress code would be unlawful under the Unruh Act?

2. Should bans on sex discrimination be understood to prevent covered businesses from forbidding (or requiring) some people to wear specific attire that it allows (or does not require) other people to wear? For what reason or reasons might a nightclub, say, specify different acceptable clothing for people it considers women and people it considers men? Are those reasons ones the law should respect where privately owned (*i.e.*, non-governmental) businesses are concerned? What might

the reasoning of *Bostock v. Clayton Country, Georgia*, 140 S. Ct. 1731 (2020), Chapter 5, Section D, *supra*, suggest?

B. Housing

Housing constitutes one key area in which trans people face discrimination. The U.S. Transgender Survey contains numerous findings regarding the vulnerability of trans people in this domain:

* Nearly one-quarter (23%) of respondents experienced some form of housing discrimination in the past year, such as being evicted from their home or denied a home or apartment because of being transgender.

* Nearly one-third (30%) of respondents have experienced homelessness at some point in their lives.

* In the past year, one in eight (12%) respondents experienced homelessness because of being transgender.

* More than one-quarter (26%) of those who experienced homelessness in the past year avoided staying in a shelter because they feared being mistreated as a transgender person. Those who did stay in a shelter reported high levels of mistreatment: seven out of ten (70%) respondents who stayed in a shelter in the past year reported some form of mistreatment, including being harassed, sexually or physically assaulted, or kicked out because of being transgender.

Sandy E. James et al., National Center for Transgender Equality, The Report of the 2015 U.S. Transgender Survey 13 (2016).

These survey results may understate the housing discrimination trans people face. Using funding from the federal Department of Housing and Urban Development (HUD), the Suffolk University Law School Housing Discrimination Testing Program conducted a study in 2015 and 2016. It sent matched pairs of testers, one transgender or gender non-conforming, to randomly selected housing renters in the metropolitan Boston area. "This study found that transgender and gender-nonconforming people received *discriminatory differential treatment 61% of the time*. In addition, they were 27% less likely to be shown additional areas of the apartment complex, 21% less likely to be offered a financial incentive to rent, 12% more likely to be told negative comments about the apartment and the neighborhood, and 9% more likely to be quoted a higher rental price than people who were not transgender and conformed to gender stereotypes. The study also analyzed data separately for transgender and gender-nonconforming people, with similar findings." Jamie Langowski et al., *Transcending Prejudice: Gender Identity and Expression-Based Discrimination in the Metro Boston Rental Housing Market*, 29 Yale J.L. & Feminism 321, 322 (2018) (emphasis added). Do these findings, in light of the fact that discrimination in rental housing on the basis of gender identity has been expressly unlawful in

Massachusetts since 2012, *see* Mass. Gen. Laws ch. 151B, §4(7) (2012), raise concerns about the efficacy of anti-discrimination rules to protect trans people, generally or in this particular setting?

The federal Fair Housing Act, Title VIII of the Civil Rights Act of 1968, Pub. L. No. 90-284, 82 Stat. 73, 81–89 (1968), codified as amended at 42 U.S.C. §§ 3601–19 (2000), forbids discrimination on the basis of sex by specified covered entities, *see* § 3604, but whether that proscription reaches gender identity discrimination has been contested. Under the presidential administration of Barack Obama, HUD adopted three final rules "focusing on ensuring fair and equal access to housing for all Americans, regardless of their sexual orientation, gender identity, nonconformance with gender stereotypes, or marital status." *HUD LGBTQ Resources*, HUD .gov/U.S. Department of Housing and Urban Development, https://www .hud.gov/LGBT_resources (last visited June 28, 2019). These rules "require[] that a determination of eligibility for housing that is assisted by HUD or subject to a mortgage insured by the Federal Housing Administration" be made without regard to actual or perceived sexual orientation or gender identity, prohibit such discrimination in HUD core shelter projects, and generally require such non-discrimination in HUD's Native American and Native Hawai'ian programs.

Since Donald Trump took office in early 2017, however, HUD has signaled retreat from at least some of these positions. Rapidly following Trump's inauguration, HUD "removed a half-dozen resource documents from its website that were aimed at helping emergency homeless shelters and other housing providers comply with HUD nondiscrimination rules and keep transgender people safe." *HUD Purges Publications That Helped Shelters Keep Transgender People Safe* (Apr. 27, 2017), National Center for Transgender Equality, https://transequality.org /press/releases/hud-purges-publications-that-helped-shelters-keep-transgender -people-safe. Subsequently, in the spring of 2019, HUD publicly disclosed that it was working on a proposed rulemaking that would seemingly remove the requirement that core shelter program providers offering single-sex accommodations do so on the basis of residents' gender identity. Instead, under the proposed rule, shelter providers could "consider a range of factors in making such determinations, including privacy, safety, practical concerns, religious beliefs, any relevant considerations under civil rights and nondiscrimination authorities, the individual's sex as reflected in official government documents, as well as the gender which a person identifies with." HUD, *Revised Requirements Under Community Planning and Development Housing Programs* (FR-6152) (Spring 2019), www.reginfo.gov, https://www.reginfo.gov/public/do/eAgendaViewRule?pubId=201904&RIN=2506 -AC53. It was reported in June of 2020 that HUD would indeed soon be proposing such a regulatory rollback. *See, e.g.*, Paige Winfield Cunningham, *HUD to Change Transgender Rules for Single-sex Homeless Shelters* (June 13, 2020), Wash. Post, https://www.washingtonpost.com/politics/hud-to-change-transgender-rules-for -single-sex-homeless-shelters/2020/06/12/d47a5744-ad03-11ea-9063-e69bd6520940 _story.html (last visited June 28, 2020).

Scant case law addresses the FHA's applicability to anti-trans housing discrimination. In *Kaeo-Tomaselli v. Piʻikoi Recovery House for Women*, No. 11-00670 LEK-RLP, 2011 WL 5572603 (D. Haw. Nov. 16, 2011), a federal district court concluded that an incarcerated transgender woman's pro se complaint against a group home for formerly incarcerated women stated a claim for sex discrimination under the FHA. The court seemingly accepted that this conclusion might be reached either through a sex stereotyping theory or "on the theory that the perpetrator was motivated by the victim's real or perceived failure to conform to socially-constructed gender norms." Subsequently, however, the court dismissed the suit, ruling that the still-incarcerated plaintiff had not shown that she was rejected from the group home for being transgender. *Kaeo-Tomaselli v. Butts*, No. 11-00670 LEK/BMK, 2013 WL 5295710 (D. Haw. Sept. 17, 2013).

A federal district court in Colorado considered the extent to which the FHA's ban on sex discrimination reaches anti-transgender discrimination in the next case.

Reading Guide for Smith v. Avanti

1. The plaintiff, Tonya Smith, and her wife, Rachel Smith, a transgender woman, relied on several statutes to sue the landlord who would not rent to them. In part they argued that anti-transgender discrimination is necessarily sex discrimination within the meaning of the federal Fair Housing Act ("FHA"). Why does the court not rule in their favor on this basis?

2. For what reasons does the court rule in the plaintiffs' favor on their FHA sex discrimination claim?

3. For what reason does the court rule in the plaintiffs' favor on their sex discrimination claim under the Colorado Anti-Discrimination Act ("CADA")? For what reasons does the court rule in the plaintiffs' favor on their "sexual orientation" discrimination claim under CADA?

Tonya Smith, Individually and as Next Friend and Parent of K.S. and I.S., Minor Children; Joseph Smith, a/k/a Rachel Smith, Individually and as Next Friend and Parent of K.S. and I.S., Minor Children; K.S., A Minor Child; and, I.S., A Minor Child v. Deepika Avanti

249 F. Supp. 3d 1194 (D. Colo. 2017)

[The plaintiffs were represented by Lambda Legal and local private counsel.]

Order

RAYMOND P. MOORE, United States District Judge

This matter is before the Court on Plaintiffs' Unopposed Motion for Partial Summary Judgment . . . on the issue of liability as to all claims for relief. . . . Defendant does not oppose the motion; she did not file a response. The Court has considered the Motion; applicable statutes, rules, and case law; and relevant portions of the court file. Upon such consideration, and being otherwise fully advised, the Court grants the Motion for the reasons stated herein.

I. Factual and Procedural Background

This case arises from Defendant Deepika Avanti's refusal to rent properties she owns in Gold Hill, Colorado to Plaintiffs. Defendant refused because of Plaintiff Tonya and Rachel Smith's[1] "kids and the noise" and their "unique relationship."

. . . . As of April 24, 2015, Defendant had rented one of the townhouses [she owns] to a couple (Matthew and Chiara) and was advertising on Craigslist the other townhouse ("Townhouse") as available for rent.

Rachel Smith is a transgender woman. She and Tonya Smith (the "Smiths") have been married for more than five years. They are the parents of Plaintiff K.S. and I.S., minor children (the Smiths and their children, collectively, the "Smith Family" or "Plaintiffs"). In April 2015, Plaintiffs, residents of Colorado, began looking for a new home as the place they were living in was being sold. On April 24, 2015, the Smiths found Defendant's rental advertisement on Craigslist for the Townhouse; Tonya Smith responded to the advertisement and emailed Defendant. In the email, among other things, Tonya discussed her family, including mentioning that Rachel is transgender. Defendant responded by email that the Townhouse and the three-bedroom living space [also owned by Defendant] were available for rent, and asked Tonya to send photos of all of them. Tonya replied via email; she agreed to meet with Defendant that evening, and sent a photo of the Smith Family as requested.

The parties met that evening at the Properties. The Smith Family viewed the Townhouse and the three-room housing unit. They also met the family that lived in

---

1. Plaintiff Rachel Smith's legal name is Joseph Smith, but she is known by and uses the name Rachel Smith in accordance with her female gender identity. The Motion refers to Joseph Smith as Rachel Smith, and the Court does so as well.

the other townhouse. After returning home, Defendant emailed Tonya Smith twice that night. In the first email, Defendant told Tonya they were not welcome to rent the Townhouse because of Matt and Chiara's concerns regarding their children and "noise." In the second email, Defendant said she talked to her husband and they have "kept a low profile" and "want to continue it" that way. Essentially, Defendant conveyed she would not rent either residence to the Smith Family.

The next morning, April 25, Tonya responded to Defendant's email, asking her what she meant by "low profile." Defendant replied that the Smiths' "unique relationship" and "uniqueness" would become the town focus and would jeopardize Defendant's "low profile" in the community; and that Defendant talked to a "psychic friend" who "has a transvestite friend herself." Defendant refused to rent either of the properties to the Smith Family. But, Defendant continued to attempt to rent housing on her property at Gold Hill.

Plaintiffs searched for several months thereafter for another place to live, but were unable to find a rental before they had to move out of their apartment. Thus, they had to move into Rachel's mother's house for a week; in doing so, they had to get rid of many of their possessions as the house was too small for them to keep all of their belongings. They finally were able to move into another apartment on July 1, 2015, but it does not meet their family's needs as well. Defendant's Properties were of higher quality, were located in a better school district, and had nicer surroundings. The move also required an hour's commute for Rachel, whereas Defendant's Properties would have only required a 20 minutes' commute for work. Rachel has since changed jobs, which is closer to the parties' new apartment.

As of result of Defendant's actions, Plaintiffs filed this lawsuit asserting the following claims: (1) Count I (the Smiths)—Sex Discrimination in violation of the Fair Housing Act, 42 U.S.C. § 3604(a) & (c); (2) Count II (Smith Family)—Discrimination based on Familial Status in violation of the Fair Housing Act, 42 U.S.C. § 3604(a) & (c); (3) Count III (the Smiths)—Sex Discrimination in violation of the Colorado Anti-Discrimination Act, C.R.S. § 24-34-502; (4) Count IV (the Smiths)—Sexual Orientation Discrimination in violation of the Colorado Anti-Discrimination Act, C.R.S. § 24-34-502; and (5) Count V (Smith Family)—Discrimination based on Familial Status, in violation of the Colorado Anti-Discrimination Act, C.R.S. § 24-34-502. As stated, Plaintiffs move for summary judgment on the issue of liability as to all claims.

II. Legal Standard

. . . . [The] Court may not grant an unopposed motion for summary judgment unless the moving parties have met their burden of production and demonstrate they are legally entitled to judgment under Rule 56. . . .

[The] moving party must demonstrate there are no genuine issues of material fact and that the moving party is entitled to judgment as a matter of law. *E.g., Reed v. Bennett*, 312 F.3d at 1195. . . . "The court should accept as true all material facts asserted and properly supported in the summary judgment motion." *Id.* . . .

III. Analysis

A. Counts I & II — Discrimination in violation of the Fair Housing Act, 42 U.S.C. § 3604(a) & (c)

1. The Fair Housing Act and Defendant's Properties and Emails

Plaintiffs contend Defendant violated two provisions of the Fair Housing Act ("FHA"), 42 U.S.C. § 3604(a) & (c). Under § 3604(a), it is unlawful "[to] refuse to sell or rent after the making of a bona fide offer, or to refuse to negotiate for the sale or rental of, or otherwise make unavailable or deny, a dwelling to any person because of . . . sex, familial status, or national origin." And, under § 3604(c), it unlawful "[t]o make, print, or publish, or cause to be made, printed, or published any notice, statement, or advertisement, with respect to the sale or rental of a dwelling that indicates any preference, limitation, or discrimination based on . . . sex, . . . familial status, or national origin, or an intention to make any such preference, limitation, or discrimination." In other words, the FHA prohibits refusals to rent or negotiate for the rental of a dwelling space on the basis of sex and/or familial status, as well as statements indicating such discrimination. *Morgan v. Sec'y of Hous. & Urban Dev.*, 985 F.2d 1451 (10th Cir. 1993). . . .

Starting with § 3604(a), the undisputed material facts show that Defendant refused to rent and negotiate for the rental of the Townhouse and the three-bedroom housing unit. Plaintiffs have also shown that such properties constitute a "dwelling" within the meaning of the FHA. . . .[2] As for the last requirement, that Defendant refused to rent to Plaintiffs "because of sex" and/or "because of familial status," the Court addresses this requirement below.

Next, as to § 3604(c), Defendant's emails to Plaintiffs certainly were made "with respect to the sale or rental of a dwelling." . . . . [T]he Tenth Circuit has stated the FHA prohibits statements indicating prohibited discrimination, *Morgan*, and Defendant's emails certainly were "statements" concerning reasons why she would not rent to Plaintiffs. Accordingly, the Court finds them to be "statements." As with Plaintiffs' claim based on § 3604(a), the Court addresses below § 3604(c)'s last inquiry of whether Defendant's statements were discriminations "based on sex" and/or "based on familial status."

2. Count I — Discrimination Based on Sex Stereotypes

Plaintiffs argue that discrimination based on sex stereotypes is "discrimination based on sex" under the FHA. The Tenth Circuit looks to Title VII discrimination cases for guidance in addressing discrimination issues under the FHA. *Mtn. Side*

---

2. . . . . Under 42 U.S.C. § 3603(b), . . . § 3604(a) does not apply to "any single-family house sold or rented by an owner: *Provided*, That such private individual owner does not own more than three such single-family houses at any one time. . . ." (Emphasis in original.) Here, even assuming the "dwellings" Defendant owns constitute "single-family houses," Defendant owned more than three at the time of the alleged discriminatory acts. Accordingly, Defendant's Properties are not exempt dwellings.

Mobile Estates Partnership v. Sec'y of Hous. & Urban Dev., 56 F.3d 1243 (10th Cir. 1995). And, as the law currently stands, the Tenth Circuit "has explicitly declined to extend Title VII protections to discrimination based on a person's sexual orientation." *Etsitty v. Utah Transit Auth.*, 502 F.3d 1215 (10th Cir. 2007). In addition, "discrimination against a transsexual based on the person's status as a transsexual is not discrimination because of sex under Title VII." *Etsitty*. However, the Smiths' sex discrimination claim at issue is brought on the basis of gender stereotyping under *Price Waterhouse v. Hopkins*, 490 U.S. 228 (1989), and its progeny, and recognized as a possibility by the Tenth Circuit in *Etsitty*.

In *Etsitty*, the transgender plaintiff argued, among other things, that she was entitled to protection as a biological male for failing to conform to social stereotypes about how a man should act and appear. The Tenth Circuit recognized that a number of courts have relied on *Price Waterhouse* to expressly recognize a Title VII cause of action based on an employee's failure to conform to stereotypical gender norms. The Tenth Circuit, however, did not reach the issue of "whether discrimination based on an employee's failure to conform to sex stereotypes always constitutes discrimination 'because of sex'" and "whether such a claim may extend Title VII protection to transsexuals who act and appear as a member of the opposite sex," but assumed, without deciding, that such a claim is available. *Etsitty*. And, in a footnote, the Tenth Circuit cited with approval to *Smith v. City of Salem*, 378 F.3d 566 (6th Cir. 2004), quoting the Sixth Circuit's statement that "[s]ex stereotyping based on a person's gender non-conforming behavior is impermissible discrimination, irrespective of the cause of that behavior; a label, such as 'transsexual,' is not fatal to a sex discrimination claim where the victim has suffered discrimination because of his or her gender nonconformity." Further, subsequently, the Tenth Circuit has implicitly recognized that claims based on failure to conform to stereotypical gender norms may be viable. *See McBride v. Peak Wellness Ctr., Inc.*, 688 F.3d 698 (10th Cir. 2012); *Potter v. Synerlink Corp.*, 562 Fed. Appx. 665, 674 (10th Cir. 2014).

In this case, the Smiths contend that discrimination against women (like them) for failure to conform to stereotype norms concerning to or with whom a woman should be attracted, should marry, and/or should have children is discrimination on the basis of sex under the FHA. The Court agrees. Such stereotypical norms are no different from other stereotypes associated with women, such as the way she should dress or act (*e.g.*, that a woman should not be overly aggressive, or should not act macho), and are products of sex stereotyping. *See Price Waterhouse* ("an employer who acts on the basis of a belief that a woman cannot be aggressive, or that she must not be, has acted on the basis of gender"); *id.* ("we are beyond the day when an employer could evaluate employees by assuming or insisting that they matched the stereotype associated with their group").

The Smiths also contend that discrimination against a transgender [*sic*—Eds.] (here, Rachel) because of her gender-nonconformity is sex discrimination. In other words, that discrimination based on applying gender stereotypes to someone who was assigned a certain sex (here, male) at birth, constitutes discrimination based on sex. To the extent the Smiths contend that discrimination against Rachel because she does not conform to gender norms of a male, *e.g.*, does not act or dress like the stereotypical notions of a male, the Court agrees. *See, e.g., Smith.* To the extent the Smiths argue something more — that the FHA has been violated based on sex stereotyping as they have been discriminated against solely because of Rachel's status as a transgender, and that the Smiths were discriminated against because of their sexual orientation or identity — the Court declines to do so.

The Court declines to do so for two reasons. First, the Motion as to Count I is based on sex stereotyping, and Count I's reliance on sex stereotype as "discrimination based on sex" did not include such allegations. Second, Count I also relies on discrimination based on sexual orientation and gender identity/expression, but the Motion was not based on such theories. To the extent Plaintiffs are attempting to bootstrap such other theories onto their sex stereotype theory, the Court declines to consider something not pled.

Applying the principles stated above, the undisputed material facts show Defendant violated the FHA by discriminating against the Smiths based on their sex. For example, in referring to the Smiths' "unique relationship" and their family's "uniqueness," Defendant relies on stereotypes of, to, or with whom a woman (or man) should be attracted, should marry, or should have a family. Accordingly, the Motion is granted in favor of the Smiths as to Count I based on sex stereotypes of men and/or women.

3. Count II — Discrimination based on Familial Status

. . . . Defendant clearly stated, in writing, that she preferred to have a couple without children living in the Townhouse. As such, Defendant violated §§ 3604(a) and 3604(c) of the FHA in preferring to rent the Townhouse to someone without children and in refusing, in the emails, to rent the Townhouse to the Smith Family. Summary judgment is therefore granted to the Smith Family as to Count II.

B. Counts III, IV, & V — Discrimination Under the Colorado Anti-Discrimination Act

1. The Colorado Anti-Discrimination Act applies to Defendant and her Properties

Under the Colorado Anti-Discrimination Act ("CADA"), Colo. Rev. Stat. § 24-34-502(1)(a), "[i]t shall be an unfair housing practice and unlawful and hereby prohibited: (a) For any person to refuse to . . . rent, or lease, . . . or otherwise make unavailable or deny or withhold from any person such housing because of . . . sex, sexual orientation, . . . [or] familial status. . . ." It is also unlawful for any person "to cause to be made any written or oral inquiry or record concerning the . . . sex, sexual orientation, . . . [or] familial status . . . of a person seeking to purchase, rent, or lease any housing. . . ." Colo. Rev. Stat. § 24-34-502(1)(a). . . . Defendant was a "person" whose Properties are subject to the CADA. The question is whether Defendant's actions violated the CADA, as Plaintiffs have alleged.

2. Count III — Discrimination Based on Sex

The CADA contains several definitions, but "sex" is not one of them. But, "federal cases interpreting the Federal Fair Housing Act are persuasive in interpreting provisions of the CFHA."[4] *May v. Colo. Civil Rights Comm'n*, 43 P.3d 750 (Colo. App. 2002). As discussed above, discrimination based on sex stereotypes, as alleged, are protected under the FHA. The Court finds no reason why the analysis under the FHA should not be equally applicable under the CADA. Accordingly, in refusing to rent or make unavailable the properties Plaintiffs' viewed, Defendant engaged in unlawful conduct and discriminated against the Smiths "because of sex" in violation of the CADA. In addition, through her email setting forth the reasons ("uniqueness") for her refusal to rent to the Smiths, Defendant unlawfully "cause[d] to be made" a "written record" "concerning the sex" of the Smiths. Summary judgment is therefore granted in favor of the Smiths as to Count III.

3. Count IV — Discrimination Based on Sexual Orientation

The Smiths assert Defendant violated the CADA by discriminating against them on the basis of their sexual orientation and Rachel's transgender status. Under the CADA, "sexual orientation" "means an individual's orientation toward . . . homosexuality . . . or transgender status. . . ." Colo. Rev. Stat. § 24-34-301(7). Thus, the CADA expressly prohibits discrimination based on a person's sexual orientation, including transgender status. And, based on the undisputed material facts, reasonable minds could not differ that Defendant's conduct and statements (via email) also encompasses unlawful discrimination against the Smiths due to their relationship and Rachel's transgender status. Defendant's written statements (record) concerning the Smiths' "uniqueness" and that she also has a "transvestite" friend demonstrate her refusal to rent to the Smiths was also because of their sexual orientation. As such, Defendant violated the CADA based on sexual orientation, which includes Rachel's transgender status. Summary judgment in favor of the Smiths is also appropriate as to Count IV.

4. Count V — Discrimination Based on Familial Status

As stated, CADA prohibits discrimination based on "familial status.". . . . For the same reasons the Court found Defendant liable under the FHA for discrimination based on familial status, Defendant is liable under this provision of the CADA. . . . Accordingly, summary judgment in favor of Plaintiffs is appropriate as to Count V.

IV. Conclusion

Based on the foregoing, the Court ORDERS that Plaintiffs' Unopposed Motion for Partial Summary Judgment is GRANTED.

---

4. The Colorado Fair Housing Act is a part of the Colorado Anti-Discrimination Act.

Discussion

1. Why might the defendant have mentioned her "transvestite friend" to the Smiths when refusing to rent to them?

2. Why might the defendant, who owned several rental properties in Colorado, not have opposed the plaintiffs' motion seeking summary judgment on her liability?

3. The plaintiffs' summary judgment motion ruled on above did not seek to establish the amount of damages they suffered. What harms to them from the defendant's refusal to rent to them can you identify?

4. Should we conclude that the Fair Housing Act's ban on sex discrimination makes discrimination based on someone's "transgender status" unlawful without the need to show anything else (such as the degree or nature of a transgender person's gender nonconformity)? For one source arguing the answer should be "yes," see Joseph J. Railey, *Married on Sunday, Evicted on Monday: Interpreting the Fair Housing Act's Prohibition of Discrimination "Because of Sex" to Include Sexual Orientation and Gender Identity*, 36–37 Buff. Pub. Int. L.J. 99 (2019). How helpful is *Bostock v. Clayton Country, Georgia*, 140 S. Ct. 1731 (2020), Chapter 5, Section D, *supra* in answering that question?

———————

In addition to the federal Fair Housing Act, some state laws also forbid housing discrimination on the basis of sex or even expressly on the basis of gender identity. The District of Columbia and 22 states have such gender-identity-specific state-wide laws: California, Colorado, Connecticut, Delaware, Hawai'i, Illinois, Iowa, Maine, Maryland, Massachusetts, Minnesota, Nevada, New Hampshire, New Jersey, New Mexico, New York, Oregon, Rhode Island, Utah, Vermont, Virginia, and Washington.[b]

———————

b. *See* Cal. Gov't Code § 12955(a) (West 2019) (housing discrimination based on gender identity or gender expression); Colo. Rev. Stat. § 24-34-502(1) (2014) (housing discrimination based on sexual orientation, defined to include transgender status, Colo. Rev. Stat. § 24-34-301 (2014)); Conn. Gen. Stat. § 46a-64c (2017) (housing discrimination based on gender identity or expression); Del. Code Ann. tit. 6, § 4603 (2019) (housing discrimination based on gender identity); D.C. Code § 2-1402.21(a)-(b) (2006) (housing discrimination based on gender identity or expression); Haw. Rev. Stat. Ann. § 515-3 (2011) (housing discrimination based on gender identity or expression); 775 Ill. Comp. Stat. 5/3-102 (2019) (housing discrimination based on sexual orientation, defined to include "gender-related identity, whether or not traditionally associated with the person's designated sex at birth," 775 Ill. Comp. Stat. 5/1-103 (O-1) (2019)); Iowa Code § 216.8 (2009) (housing discrimination based on gender identity); Me. Stat. tit. 5, § 4581-A (2011) (housing discrimination based on sexual orientation, defined to include "gender identity or expression," Me. Stat. Ann. tit. 5, § 4553(9-C) (2019)); Md. Code Ann., State Gov't § 20-705 (2014) (housing discrimination based on gender identity); Mass. Gen. Laws ch. 151B, § 4(6)-4(8) (2018) (housing discrimination based on gender identity); Minn. Stat. § 363A.09 (2001) (housing discrimination based on sexual orientation, defined to include "having or being perceived as having a self-image or identity not traditionally associated with one's biological maleness or femaleness," Minn. Stat. § 363A.03(44) (2018)); Nev. Rev. Stat. § 118.100 (2011) (housing discrimination based on gender identity or expression); N.H. Rev. Stat. Ann. § 354-A:10 (2018) (housing discrimination based

In addition to states, some localities forbid gender identity discrimination in housing. New York City is the largest to do so, and it has administratively adopted guidance concerning what nondiscrimination requires in this context, and how it will enforce its ban on gender identity discrimination.

Legal Enforcement Guidance on Discrimination on the Basis of Gender Identity or Expression: Local Law No. 3 (2002); N.Y.C. Admin. Code § 8-102(23)

N.Y.C. COMMISSION ON HUMAN RIGHTS (Dec. 21, 2015)

The New York City Human Rights Law ("NYCHRL") prohibits discrimination in employment, public accommodations, and housing. It also prohibits discriminatory harassment and bias-based profiling by law enforcement. . . .

The New York City Commission on Human Rights (the "Commission") is the City agency charged with enforcing the NYCHRL. Individuals interested in vindicating their rights under the NYCHRL can choose to file a complaint with the Commission's Law Enforcement Bureau within one (1) year of the discriminatory act or file a complaint in New York State Supreme Court within three (3) years of the discriminatory act.

The NYCHRL prohibits unlawful discrimination in public accommodations, housing and employment on the basis of gender. Gender is defined as one's "actual or perceived sex and shall also include a person's gender identity, self-image, appearance, behavior or expression, whether or not that gender identity, self-image, appearance, behavior or expression is different from that traditionally associated with the legal sex assigned to that person at birth."[3] This document serves as the Commission's legal enforcement guidance of the NYCHRL's protections as they apply to discrimination based on gender, and gender identity and gender expression, which constitute gender discrimination under the NYCHRL. This document

---

on gender identity); N.J. STAT. ANN. § 10:5–12(g) (West 2019) (housing discrimination based on gender identity or expression); N.M. STAT. ANN. § 28-1-7(G) (2019) (housing discrimination based on gender identity); N.Y. EXEC. LAW § 296(2-a)(a)-(2-a)(c-1) (McKinney 2019) (housing discrimination based on gender identity or expression); OR. REV. STAT. § 659A.421(2)(a) (2014) (housing discrimination based on sexual orientation, defined to include gender identity for all Oregon state statutes, OR. REV. STAT. § 174.100 (2015)); 34 R.I. GEN. LAWS § 34-37-4 (a) (2015) (housing discrimination based on gender identity or expression); UTAH CODE ANN. § 57-21-5 (LexisNexis 2015) (housing discrimination based on gender identity); VT. STAT. ANN. tit. 9, § 4503(a)(1)-(8), (12) (2019) (housing discrimination based on gender identity); VA. CODE ANN. § 39-96.3 (2020) (housing discrimination based on gender identity); WASH. REV. CODE § 49.60.222-.224 (2007) (housing discrimination based on sexual orientation, defined to include "gender expression or identity," defined as "having or being perceived as having a gender identity, self-image, appearance, behavior, or expression, whether or not that gender identity, self-image, appearance, behavior, or expression is different from that traditionally associated with the sex assigned to that person at birth," WASH. REV. CODE § 49.60.040(26) (2018)).

3. Local Law No. 3 (2002); N.Y.C. ADMIN. CODE § 8-102(23).

is not intended to serve as an exhaustive list of all forms of gender-based discrimination claims under the NYCHRL.

I. Legislative Intent

In 2002, the New York City Council passed the Transgender Rights Bill to expand the scope of the gender-based protections guaranteed under the NYCHRL, and ensure protection for people whose "gender and self-image do not fully accord with the legal sex assigned to them at birth."[4] The City's intent in amending the law was to make explicit that the law prohibits discrimination against transgender people.[5]

The legislative history reflects that transgender people face frequent and severe discrimination such that protection from discrimination is "very often a matter of life and death." Recognizing the profoundly debilitating impact of gender-based discrimination on transgender and other gender non-conforming individuals, the amendment makes clear that "gender-based discrimination—including, but not limited to, discrimination based on an individual's actual or perceived sex, and discrimination based on an individual's gender identity, self-image, appearance, behavior, or expression—constitutes a violation of the City's Human Rights Law."

. . . .

II. Definitions

These definitions are intended to help people understand the following guidance as well as their rights and responsibilities under the NYCHRL.

. . . .

Gender Identity:

one's internal deeply-held sense of one's gender which may be the same or different from one's sex assigned at birth. One's gender identity may be male, female, neither or both, *e.g.*, non-binary. Everyone has a gender identity. Gender identity is distinct from sexual orientation.

Gender Expression:

the representation of gender as expressed through, for example, one's name, choice of pronouns, clothing, haircut, behavior, voice, or body characteristics. Gender expression may not be distinctively male or female and may not conform to traditional gender-based stereotypes assigned to specific gender identities.

Gender:

an individual's actual or perceived sex, gender identity, self-image, appearance, behavior, or expression, whether or not that gender identity,

---

4. *Id.*

5. *Report of the Governmental Affairs Division, Committee on General Welfare, Intro. No. 24, to amend the administrative code of the city of New York in relation to gender-based discrimination* (April 24, 2002), *accessible through* http://legistar.council.nyc.gov/Legislation.aspx.

self-image, appearance, behavior or expression is different from that traditionally associated with the sex assigned at birth.

. . . .

III. Violations of the New York City Human Rights Law's Prohibitions on Gender Discrimination

Gender discrimination under the NYCHRL includes discrimination on the basis of gender identity, gender expression, and transgender status.[6] The definition of gender also encompasses discrimination against someone for being intersex. Under the NYCHRL, gender discrimination can be based on one's perceived or actual gender identity, which may or may not conform to one's sex assigned at birth, or on the ways in which one expresses gender, such as through appearance or communication style. Gender discrimination is prohibited in employment, housing, public accommodations, discriminatory harassment, and bias-based profiling by police and exists whenever there is disparate treatment of an individual on account of gender. When an individual is treated "less well than others on account of their gender,"[7] that is gender discrimination under the NYCHRL.

Harassment motivated by gender is a form of discrimination. Gender-based harassment can be a single or isolated incident of disparate treatment or repeated acts or behavior. Disparate treatment can manifest in harassment when the incident or behavior creates an environment or reflects or fosters a culture or atmosphere of sex stereotyping, degradation, humiliation, bias, or objectification. Under the NYCHRL, gender-based harassment covers a broad range of conduct and occurs generally when an individual is treated less well on account of their gender. While the severity or pervasiveness of the harassment is relevant to damages, the existence of differential treatment based on gender is sufficient under the NYCHRL to constitute a claim of harassment. Gender-based harassment can include unwanted sexual advances or requests for sexual favors; however, the harassment does not have to be sexual in nature. For example, refusal to use a transgender employee's preferred name, pronoun, or title may constitute unlawful gender-based harassment. Comments, unwanted touching, gestures, jokes, or pictures that target an individual based on gender constitute gender-based harassment.

Unlawful gender-based discrimination is prohibited in the following areas:

. . . .

Public Accommodations:

It is unlawful for providers of public accommodations, their employees, or their agents to deny any person, or communicate intent to deny, the services, advantages, facilities or privileges of a public accommodation directly or indirectly because of their actual or perceived gender, including actual or

---

6. N.Y.C. ADMIN. CODE § 8-102(23).

7. *Williams v. N.Y.C. Hous. Auth.*, 872 N.Y.S.2d 27, 39 (App. Div. 2009).

perceived status as a transgender person. Simply put, it is unlawful to deny any person full and equal enjoyment of a public accommodation because of gender.

Housing:

It is unlawful to refuse to sell, rent, or lease housing to someone because of their actual or perceived gender, including actual or perceived status as a transgender person. It is unlawful to withhold from any person full and equal enjoyment of a housing accommodation because of their gender.[8]

1. Failing to Use an Individual's Preferred Name or Pronoun

The NYCHRL requires . . . covered entities to use an individual's preferred name, pronoun and title (*e.g.*, Ms./Mrs.) regardless of the individual's sex assigned at birth, anatomy, gender, medical history, appearance, or the sex indicated on the individual's identification. . . . [The name and pronoun provisions of the NYC guidance are addressed in Chapter 15, *infra* at pp. 1094–95.— Eds.]

2. Refusing to Allow Individuals To Utilize Single-Sex Facilities and Programs Consistent with Their Gender

The NYCHRL requires that individuals be permitted to use single-sex facilities, such as bathrooms or locker rooms, and participate in single-sex programs, consistent with their gender, regardless of their sex assigned at birth, anatomy, medical history, appearance, or the sex indicated on their identification. The law does not require entities to make existing bathrooms all-gender or construct additional restrooms. Covered entities that have single-occupancy restrooms should make clear that they can be used by people of all genders.[9]

Some people, including, for example, customers, other program participants, tenants, or employees, may object to sharing a facility or participating in a program with a transgender or gender non-conforming person. Such objections are not a lawful reason to deny access to that transgender or gender non-conforming individual.

Examples of Violations

a. Prohibiting an individual from using a particular program or facility because they do not conform to sex stereotypes. For example, a women's shelter may not turn away a woman because she looks too masculine nor may a men's shelter deny service to a man because he does not look masculine enough.

b. Prohibiting a transgender or gender non-conforming person from using the single-sex program or facility consistent with their gender identity or

---

8. Protections on the basis of gender under the NYCHRL are subject to the same limitations as all other protected categories. *See* N.Y.C. Admin. Code §§ 8-102(5); 8-107(5)(a)(4)(1),(2); 8-107(4)(b).

9. A single-occupancy restroom is a room with a single toilet, walls, a sink, and a door.

expression. For example, it is an unlawful discriminatory practice to prohibit a transgender woman from using the women's bathroom.

c. Requiring a transgender or gender non-conforming individual to provide proof of their gender in order to access the appropriate single-sex program or facility.

d. Requiring an individual to provide identification with a particular sex or gender marker in order to access the single-sex program or facility corresponding to their gender.

e. Barring someone from a program or facility out of concern that a transgender or gender non-conforming person will make others uncomfortable.

f. Forcing a transgender or gender non-conforming person to use the single-occupancy restroom.

Covered entities may avoid violations of the NYCHRL, by, wherever possible, providing single-occupancy restrooms and providing private space within multi-user facilities for anyone who has privacy concerns. Covered entities may accommodate an individual's request to use a single-occupancy restroom because of their gender. For example, an individual who is non-binary or who is in the process of transitioning may wish to use a single-occupancy restroom. As noted above, however, it is unlawful to *require* an individual to use a single-occupancy restroom because they are transgender or gender non-conforming. Covered entities should create policies to ensure that all individuals are allowed to access the single-sex facility consistent with their gender identity or expression and train all employees, but particularly all managers and employees who have contact with members of the public, on compliance with the policy, and their obligation under the NYCHRL to provide nondiscriminatory access to single-sex facilities including for transgender and gender non-conforming people. Covered entities should post a sign in all single-sex facilities that states, "Under New York City Law, all individuals have the right to use the single-sex facility consistent with their gender identity or expression." Covered entities may adopt policies or codes of conduct for single-sex facilities delineating acceptable behavior for the use of the facilities that are not themselves discriminatory and do not single out transgender or gender non-conforming people.

An individual's assessment of their own safety should be a primary consideration. Covered entities should offer opportunities for people to come to them if they have safety concerns and should establish a corresponding safety plan if needed. For example, if a transgender resident requests assignment to a facility corresponding to their sex assigned at birth instead of a placement corresponding to their gender identity, that request should be honored.

3. Sex Stereotyping

Discrimination based on an individual's failure to conform to sex stereotypes is a form of gender discrimination under the NYCHRL. Sex stereotypes are widely-held over-simplified expectations about how people of a particular sex or gender should be or how they should act. They include expectations of how an individual represents or communicates gender to others, such as behavior, clothing, hairstyle, activities, voice, mannerisms, or body characteristics. Sex stereotypes also relate to the roles or behaviors assigned to those who identify as male or female. Covered entities may not require individuals to conform to stereotypical norms of masculinity or femininity. The law also recognizes that unlawful sex stereotyping often manifests itself as antigay epithets, or attributing a particular sexual orientation to individuals who do not conform to sex stereotypes.

Examples of Violations

a. Using anti-gay epithets when speaking to or about an individual based on their non-conformity with gender norms. . . .

Covered entities may avoid violations of the NYCHRL by training all staff on creating and maintaining an environment free from sex stereotyping.

4. Imposing Different Uniforms or Grooming Standards Based on Sex or Gender

Under the NYCHRL, employers and covered entities may not require dress codes or uniforms, or apply grooming or appearance standards, that impose different requirements for individuals based on sex or gender. Under federal law, differing standards based on sex or gender are permitted so long as they do not impose an undue burden, an evidentiary standard that the plaintiff must prove. Differences that have been perceived by courts to be slight or that do not impose significantly greater burdens based on gender have generally been permitted; for example, courts have upheld requirements that female bartenders wear makeup, or that male servers wear ties. While some courts have found uniforms and grooming standards that perpetuate sex stereotypes impermissible in extreme cases—for example, where an employer required only female employers to wear an overtly sexualized uniform— courts have generally upheld such standards when courts deem them innocuous or based in long-held, traditional gender norms.

In keeping with the requirements of the Restoration Act of 2005, the NYCHRL looks to these cases as a floor rather than a ceiling, and to that end, does not require a showing that different uniform or grooming standards create an unequal burden or disparate effect to qualify as gender discrimination. Under the NYCHRL, the fact that the grooming standard or dress code differentiates based on gender is sufficient for it to be considered discriminatory, even if perceived by some as harmless. Holding individuals to different grooming or uniform standards based on gender serves no legitimate non-discriminatory purpose and reinforces a culture of sex stereotypes and accepted cultural norms based on gender expression and identity.

The variability of expressions associated with gender and gender norms contrast vastly across culture, age, community, personality, style, and sense of self. Placing the burden on individuals to justify their gender identity or expression and demonstrate why a particular distinction makes them uncomfortable or does not conform to their gender expression would serve to reinforce the traditional notion of gender that our law has disavowed. Differing standards based on gender will always be rooted in gender norms and stereotypes, even when they may be perceived by some as innocuous. When an individual is treated differently because of their gender and required to conform to a specific standard assigned to their gender, that is gender discrimination regardless of intent, and that is not permissible under the NYCHRL.

Employers and covered entities are entitled to enforce a dress code, or require specific grooming or appearance standards; however it must be done without imposing restrictions or requirements specific to gender or sex. It will not be a defense that an employer or covered entity is catering to the preferences of their customers or clients.

Examples of Violations

a. Maintaining grooming and appearance standards that apply differently to individuals who identify as men or women or which have gender-based distinctions. For example, requiring different uniforms for men and women, or requiring that female bartenders wear makeup. . . .

c. Permitting only individuals who identify as women to wear jewelry or requiring only individuals who identify as male to have short hair. . . .

d. Permitting female but not male residents at a drug treatment facility to wear wigs and high heels.

e. Requiring all men to wear ties in order to dine at a restaurant.

Covered entities may avoid violations of the NYCHRL by creating gender-neutral dress codes and grooming standards. For example, a covered entity may require individuals to either wear their hair short or pulled back from the face or require that workers must wear either a pantsuit or a skirt suit. . . .

7. Engaging in Discriminatory Harassment

The NYCHRL prohibits discriminatory harassment or violence motivated by a person's actual or perceived gender identity or expression that attempts to interfere with, or actually interferes with, the free exercise of a legal right. Discriminatory harassment includes violence, the threat of violence, a pattern of threatening verbal harassment, the use of force, intimidation or coercion, defacing or damaging real property and cyberbullying. For example, a tenant assaulting or threatening to assault a neighbor because of her gender expression, in addition to committing a crime, is also violating the NYCHRL.

8. Engaging in Retaliation

The NYCHRL prohibits retaliation against an individual for opposing discrimination or requesting a reasonable accommodation for a disability based on gender identity or expression. Opposing discrimination includes, but is not limited to, making an internal complaint about discrimination, making an external complaint of discrimination to the Commission or another government agency, or participating in an investigation of discrimination. An action taken against an individual that is reasonably likely to deter them from engaging in such activities is considered unlawful retaliation. The action need not rise to the level of a final action or a materially adverse change to the terms and conditions of employment, housing, or participation in a program to be retaliatory under the NYCHRL. When an individual opposes what they believe in good faith to be unlawful discrimination, it is unlawful to retaliate against the individual even if the conduct they opposed is not ultimately determined to violate the NYCHRL.

Examples of Violations

. . . .

d. Refusing to advance a program participant to the next stage of the program despite their successful completion of the previous stage because the participant raised concerns about unequal treatment.

Covered entities may avoid violations of the NYCHRL by implementing internal antidiscrimination policies to educate employees, tenants, and program participants of their rights and obligations under the NYCHRL with respect to gender identity and expression and regularly train staff on these issues. Covered entities should create procedures for employees, tenants, and program participants to internally report violations of the law without fear of adverse action and train those in supervisory capacities on how to handle those claims when they witness discrimination or instances are reported to them by subordinates. Covered entities that engage with the public should implement a policy for interacting with the public in a respectful, non-discriminatory manner consistent with the NYCHRL, respecting gender diversity, and ensuring that members of the public do not face discrimination, including with respect to single-sex programs and facilities.

IV. Penalties in Administrative Actions

The Commission can impose civil penalties up to $125,000 for violations, and up to $250,000 for violations that are the result of willful, wanton, or malicious conduct. The amount of a civil penalty will be guided by the following factors, among others:

- The severity of the particular violation;
- The existence of previous or subsequent violations;
- The employer's size, considering both the total number of employees and its revenue; and
- The employer's actual or constructive knowledge of the NYCHRL.

These penalties are in addition to the other remedies available to people who successfully resolve or prevail on claims under the NYCHRL, including, but not limited to, back and front pay, along with other compensatory and punitive damages. The Commission may consider the lack of an adequate anti-discrimination policy as a factor in determining liability, assessing damages, and mandating certain affirmative remedies.

Discussion

1. As interpreted by the Commission in its Guidance, one aspect of the NYCHRL is that it, in effect, forbids covered entities such as providers of housing and public accommodations, including shelters, from defining eligibility to use single-sex facilities on the basis of gendered anatomy and instead requiring eligibility for such facilities to be accorded on the basis of gender identity. In what sense can this be understood as necessary for gender identity equality? (Does this reflect a formal or substantive understanding of gender identity equality?)

2. Would *Hispanic AIDS Forum v. Estate of Bruno*, 16 A.D.3d 294 (N.Y. App. Div. 2005), Section A, *supra* at p. 394, come out the same if a court applied the Commission's Guidance to the dispute (a) on the majority's understanding of what the complaint alleged, or (b) on the dissent's understanding of what the facts alleged?

3. To what extent are legal prohibitions on discrimination in housing responsive to the needs of transgender people? *See, e.g.*, Patrick Saunders, *Jamie Roberts: Affordable Housing Crisis Hits Transgender Community Hard*, The Georgia Voice (Aug. 21, 2017), https://thegavoice.com/outspoken/jamie-roberts-affordable-housing-crisis -hits-transgender-community-hard/ (identifying "barriers to affordable housing" as particularly burdensome for transgender people); Kate Abbey-Lambertz, *The Subtle Ways Landlords Keep Out Transgender Renters*, HuffPost (Mar. 31, 2017), https://www.huffpost.com/entry/transgender-housing-discrimination_n_58dd 5898e4b08194e3b86483 ("Transgender and gender-nonconforming individuals face pervasive housing discrimination, ... and the people being discriminated against may not even know it."); Diane K. Levy et al., *A Paired-Testing Pilot Study of Housing Discrimination against Same-Sex Couples and Transgender Individuals*, Urban Institute (June 30, 2017), https://www.urban.org/research/publication /paired-testing-pilot-study-housing-discrimination-against-same-sex-couples-and -transgender-individuals (finding that "in the early stages of the rental search process, housing providers discriminate against . . . transgender people on some treatment measures" but noting limits of study including "only capture the early stage of the housing search process and not all differential treatment that a renter might face, such as during the application stage, when negotiating and signing the lease, and during occupancy" and that "testers posed as well-qualified renters rather than average or marginally qualified homeseekers, which might have influenced how providers treated them").

Chapter 8

Parenting

Many transgender people are parents. The single best source of available data is the U.S. Transgender Survey (USTS) (commonly pronounced "Eustace")—not a "representative" sample in the statistical sense, but the most comprehensive data on the lives of transgender and gender non-conforming people in the United States, collected from over 27,000 "respondents from all fifty states, the District of Columbia, American Samoa, Guam, Puerto Rico, and U.S. military bases overseas." Sandy E. James et al., National Center for Transgender Equality, The Report of the 2015 U.S. Transgender Survey 64 (2016). Almost one in five (18%) of the respondents were parents. *Id.* at 64. Of those, "more than two-thirds (69%) reported that they were out as transgender to at least one of their children." *Id.* at 68.

Other studies show similar substantial rates of parenting by transgender persons (although not as high as in the entire adult U.S. population). A late 2014 report reviewing the extant literature, conducted by scholars associated with the Williams Institute, found most surveys to show between one-fourth and one-half of transgender people reporting being parents. Rebecca L. Stotzer et al., The Williams Institute, Transgender Parenting: A Review of Existing Research 2 (Oct. 2014).

More than one in four (27% of) USTS respondents who were out as trans to a spouse or partner "reported that a spouse or partner ended their relationship solely or partly because they were transgender. . . ." James et al., *supra*, at 67. Thus, a person's gender identity or status can become a flashpoint in disputes attending the dissolution of a relationship. And this is true even though "[s]tudies on the outcomes for children with transgender parents have found no evidence that having a transgender parent affects a child's gender identity or sexual orientation development, nor has an impact on other developmental milestones." Stotzer et al., *supra*, at 2. Indeed, trans parents "have reported discrimination—either formally through the courts or informally by the child(ren)'s other parent—in child custody and visitation arrangements." *Id.*

Reading Guide for Christian v. Randall

1. What standard of review does the Colorado Court of Appeals apply in *Christian*? Why does it conclude that the decision below does not pass that standard?

2. How did the court of appeals treat the financial circumstances of the transgender parent Mark Randall? How did it treat the trial court's finding of mental disturbance on the part of Randall's daughters?

Duane E. Christian v. Mark Avle Randall

516 P.2d 132 (Colo. App. 1973)

Silverstein, Chief Judge.

Duane Christian filed a petition in the District Court of Delta County seeking custody of his four daughters who were then in the custody of respondent [Mark Avle Randall], his former wife, pursuant to a 1964 Nevada divorce decree. The trial court granted the petition, and the respondent appeals from that judgment. We reverse.

The parties to this action were married in 1953, and four daughters were born of the marriage. The children lived with the respondent continuously following the divorce, having resided in Colorado for six years at the time this action was brought. On September 27, 1972, after a hearing upon the petition, the trial court awarded custody of the girls to the petitioner, a Nevada resident.

The issues in this appeal are whether there was sufficient evidence before the trial court to support its conclusion that it would be in the best interests of the children to transfer custody from the respondent to the petitioner and whether in so doing the trial court abused its discretion.

In reviewing an order affecting the custody of a child, appellate courts will make every reasonable presumption in favor of the action of the trial court. We are always reluctant to disturb rulings of the trial court in custody matters, absent circumstances clearly disclosing an abuse of discretion. In the present case, however, our review of the record persuades us that, there being no evidence to support its conclusion, the trial court clearly abused its discretion. Under such circumstances the order cannot be allowed to stand.

The applicable statute, 1971 Perm. Supp., C.R.S. 1963, 46-1-31(2)(a), provides, "The court shall not modify a prior custody decree unless it finds . . . that a change has occurred in the circumstances of the child or his custodian and that the modification is necessary to serve the best interests of the child." Thus, a mere change of circumstances alone is insufficient to justify a change of custody.

Section 46-1-31(2)(a) further dictates that, in applying the above standards:

(T)he court *shall retain* the custodian established by the prior decree *unless:* . . . (d) The child's present environment endangers his physical health or significantly impairs his emotional development and the harm likely to be caused by a change of environment is outweighed by the advantage of a change to the child. (emphasis supplied)

Further, 1971 Perm. Supp., C.R.S. 1963, 46-1-24(1), provides:

(a) . . . In determining the best interests of the child, the court shall consider all relevant factors including:

(b) The wishes of the child's parent or parents as to his custody;

(c) The wishes of the child as to his custodian;

(d) The interaction and interrelationship of the child with his parent or parents, his siblings, and any other person who may significantly affect the child's best interests;

(e) The child's adjustment to his home, school, and community; and

(f) The mental and physical health of all individuals involved.

The record contains no evidence that the environment of respondent's home in Colorado endangered the children's physical health or impaired their emotional development. On the contrary, the evidence shows that the children were happy, healthy, well-adjusted children who were doing well in school and who were active in community activities.

The evidence included a letter from the school principal to the petitioner stating that he was well acquainted with the children and that he thought they were "wonderful" and that the older three girls (ages 11, 13 and 16) who were in his school ranked "very high on our Iowa Tests of Basic Skills."

The investigative report prepared for the court by the Delta County Family and Children's Services stated:

> All of the girls have good report cards. Also each one has various special achievement awards such as art, music, etc. The oldest girl, Lou Ann, was elected Cherry Queen. All of the girls have many friends and enjoy school immensely.

. . . .

Conclusions

> From my interview with this family it would appear that all of the girls are being well cared for and provided with the necessities of life. Also there are no indications of any emotional or social retardation as a result of their home life for any of the children in this family. There appears to be a close and warm relationship between all of the children and between the children and the adults.

1971 PERM. SUPP., C.R.S. 1963, 46-1-31(2)(d) recognizes that a modification of custody is likely to result in some harm to the child involved. At the hearing two experts testified that it would be traumatic for the children to leave a happy home where they were well adjusted. The evidence failed to show that the anxiety and confusion created by a change of custody would be outweighed by any advantages to the children resulting from such a change.

In its order at the close of the hearing the court found that respondent was "going through a transsexual change" and based its conclusion that a change of custody would be to the best interest of the children solely on that ground. The evidence shows that, subsequent to the 1964 divorce, the respondent has been going through a transsexual change from female to male, that the respondent's name was legally changed from Gay Christensen Christian to Mark Avle Randall, and that subsequent to the filing of the petition respondent married a woman. 1971 PERM. SUPP., C.R.S. 1963, 46-1-24(2), specifically directs that, in determining best interests, "The court *shall not* consider conduct of a proposed custodian that does not affect his relationship with the child." (emphasis supplied) The record discloses that the above circumstances did not adversely affect respondent's relationship with the children nor impair their emotional development.

In expanded findings made after a hearing on respondent's motion for new trial the court found that respondent had suffered financial reverses. There was no showing, however, that respondent's income from earnings and support was inadequate to provide for the children.

The earlier financial reverses and the status of the respondent are not sufficient grounds for changing custody in view of the uncontradicted evidence of the high quality of the environment and home life of respondent and the children. . . .

The court further stated that, from testimony of the children in the courtroom and separate interviews in chambers, it was concerned because there was an indication that the older two girls were mentally disturbed. This concern of the court is not justified by the record. First, the record does not disclose that any testimony by the children was taken in the courtroom. Second, the interviews with the four girls indicate no abnormality whatsoever, but only a sincere desire to remain with respondent, on lucid, logical bases.

We recognize that a trial court need not accept at face value all of the evidence introduced in a proceeding; however, when there is no evidence to support a finding or conclusion and such finding or conclusion is manifestly against the weight of the evidence, it cannot be permitted to stand.

In *Anderson v. Cold Spring Tungsten, Inc.*, 458 P.2d 756 (Colo. 1969), the [Colorado] Supreme Court said,

> In reviewing such issues of fact, this Court has taken the position that it will not set aside the findings of the trial judge where they are sustained by competent and adequate evidence, *amply appearing from the record. . . .* But such restraint in no way limits the power of this Court to reject the findings and conclusions of the trial judge where they are not supported by any evidence in the record or where the law has not been applied correctly.

The judgment of the trial court is reversed, and the cause is remanded with directions to enter an order denying the petition for modification of custody.

COYTE AND RULAND, JJ., concur.

Discussion

Christian v. Randall stands out among other reported U.S. cases over custody, visitation, or parental rights by transgender or gender nonconforming parents, which have often ruled against the trans parent. *See, e.g., Cisek v. Cisek*, No. 80 C.A. 113, 1982 WL 6161 (Ohio Ct. App. July 20, 1982); *In re Marriage of B.*, 184 A.D.2d 609 (N.Y. App. Div. 1992); *Daly v. Daly*, 715 P.2d 56 (Nev. 1986); *In re Marriage of Simmons*, 825 N.E.2d 303 (Ill. Ct. App. 2005); and *M.B. v. D.W.*, 236 S.W.3d 31 (Ky. Ct. App. 2007), all *infra* this chapter.

Reading Guide for Cisek v. Cisek

1. What standard of review does the Ohio Court of Appeals apparently use in evaluating the trial court's refusal to terminate Joni Christian's visitation with her daughters? On what grounds does the appeals court conclude that the trial judge's ruling failed that standard?

2. How does the appeals court discuss Joni Christian's transition? On what does it base its discussion thereof?

Rosemarie P. Cisek, nka Rosemarie P. Cool v. John Cisek, nka Joni Christian

No. 80 C.A. 113, 1982 WL 6161 (Ohio Ct. App. July 20, 1982)

Before Hon. JOHN J. LYNCH, Hon. JOSEPH E. O'NEILL, Hon. JOSEPH DONOFRIO, JJ.

O'NEILL, J.

The parties were married on June 3, 1972. Shortly thereafter, appellee-husband adopted Dawn, the daughter of appellant who was born prior to the marriage. During the marriage the couple also had a child of their own, Kimberly. On February 23, 1976, the Mahoning County Common Pleas Court decreed a Dissolution of their Marriage, at which time appellant was awarded custody of the two minor children with ordinary visitation privileges granted to appellee.

Shortly thereafter, appellee underwent a complete change of sex and now presents himself as a woman. Appellee had his name legally changed to Joni Christian. Appellee conducts himself as a woman at all times and circumstances, dresses and presents as a woman, and dates men. Appellee has become a public figure in the local community, and has appeared on several local television interview programs in connection with the promotion of his career as a vocalist.

Throughout and following these events appellee continued his visitation with the children until appellant refused to allow further visitation. Following institution of contempt proceedings by appellee, visitation was resumed under Court order.

On March 12, 1979, appellant filed a motion to terminate the previously ordered visitation. Following a number of hearings on this motion, the Common Pleas Court entered Judgment . . . denying appellant's motion. Appellant then filed her Notice of Appeal to this Court. . . .

Counsel and this court agree that this is a case of first impression. Our approach must be guarded and basic.

When a trial court comes on to consider a modification of a prior decree, his discretion is called into play. "(B) The court may make any just and reasonable order or decree permitting any parent who is deprived of the care, custody, and control of the children to visit them at the time and under the conditions that the court directs." Section 3109.05 O.R.C.

The exercise of this discretion has the goal of the "best interest of the child." It would be sufficient to conclude that if there was presented to a court evidence that visitations with a parent would be contrary to the best interest of the child, the court must deny such visitations. To rule otherwise would amount to an unreasonable, arbitrary, and unconscionable act by the court, an abuse of discretion.

In the case at hand, the appellant testified and related some of the confusion which the children had experienced and related to her.

Dr. James Giannini, a medical doctor with a specialty in psychiatry, was called by appellant. Dr. Giannini had examined both children. It was his opinion that the transsexualism of the appellee would have a sociopathic affect [*sic*—Eds.] on the child, Dawn, without appropriate intervention. Dr. Giannini also expressed the opinion that Kimberly would have difficulties in adjusting to her relationship with an individual, who though her father, is physically a woman. He felt that physical contact should be stopped.

We are bothered by these negative medical opinions. We are further bothered by any substantial basis [*sic*—perhaps "lack of any substantial basis"?—Eds.] explaining the motivations of the father. He presented no evidence that he was compelled by some mental imbalance to opt for a change in his sex. Was his sex change simply an indulgence of some fantasy? Whatever the nature, the change certainly worked a burden upon the two minors. The duty of all the courts is to protect these two girls from whatever physical, mental, or social impact might occur. There is evidence that there might be mental harm. Common sense dictates that there can be social harm.

It is our opinion that since the trial court had originally ordered visitation, there has been a substantial change in circumstances. This substantial change was justification for a reconsideration of the original order. In light of the evidence presented, there is a strong conclusion that absent adequate therapy, the two minor children are in harm's way.

We, therefore, vacate the judgment of the trial court and reverse the judgment for the reason that the appellant mother has produced sufficient evidence of substantial change in circumstances and, by medical testimony, mental and emotional trauma.

By this ruling, we do not permanently preclude visitation by the appellee. If and when by growth and maturity of the children and proper evidence presented by the appellee, and with a thorough investigation by the trial court with expert investigation and advice there may be a time when the trial court can order visitation by appellee, with a continuing plan protecting the best interests of the two children.

Judgment reversed.

———————

Discussion

1. How does the appellate court characterize the "duty" of the trial court? (Note that the full opinion cites no authority for this proposition.) If one took the appellate court literally, what kinds of interventions into family life could be warranted?

2. What might Joni Christian's lawyer have sought to do to try to produce a better outcome for her?

3. With what degree of confidence (or based on what quality of evidence) should a court determine that visitation with a child's parent would cause harm, and how much harm, before the law should deem it appropriate to deny the parent contact with the child? For an argument that even if children exposed to transgender parents were more likely to be trans than children not so "exposed" (though they are not), that should not be counted as a "harm" for family law purposes, see Shannon Shafron Perez, *Is It a Boy or a Girl? Not the Baby, the Parent: Transgender Parties in Custody Battles and the Benefit of Promoting a Truer Understanding of Gender*, 9 Whittier J. Child & Fam. Advoc. 367 (2010).

Note on the Varying Relevance of Marital Status to Trans Parenthood Determinations

Not all courts appear equally concerned with the technical legal validity of a trans person's marriage even when children are involved. Consider the contrasting rulings, for example, in *Karin T. v. Michael T.*, 127 Misc. 2d 14, 484 N.Y.S.2d 780 (Fam. Ct. 1985), and *In re Marriage of Simmons*, 825 N.E.2d 303 (Ill. App. 2005).

Michael T. and Robert Sterling Simmons were both transgender men, and each identified as female at birth. Each began presenting as male at some point, and each civilly married a woman (Karin T. and Jennifer Simmons, respectively). Michael had legally changed his name before marrying and never changed the gender marker on his birth certificate. Robert, subsequent to marrying, changed his name legally and had his birth certificate changed to indicate he was male. After marrying, each couple entered into an agreement regarding so-called artificial insemination, and each couple had one or more children by that method. Both couples' relationships soured.

Either Michael T. or Karin T. sought in superior court to have the marriage declared null and void, and Robert sued for divorce and sole custody of his and Jennifer's child. It was unclear whether or what gender confirmation surgeries Michael ever had, though the family court in the eventual child support case against him ruled that he was female. Robert had surgeries removing his uterus, ovaries, and Fallopian tubes after he was married and before Jennifer gave birth. A county social services department sued Michael seeking child support on his children's behalf, with Karin arguing that Michael was their father; Michael countered that he was female, neither a biological nor adoptive parent, and thus not the children's father nor eligible to bear child support obligations under New York law. In Robert's divorce and custody suit, Jennifer argued that Robert was female, that their purported marriage was therefore void, and that Robert accordingly was not a legal, equitable, or de facto parent under any of the potentially relevant Illinois laws.

In *Michael T.*, the family court rejected Michael's efforts to avoid child support obligations. Although its analysis was not the most precise, the family court appeared to hold the children to be third-party beneficiaries of the insemination agreement and Michael equitably estopped from denying his parentage of the children and hence his support obligations, though the court also may in the alternative have held that Michael was "a parent" within the meaning of a state domestic relations law provision specifying that only a parent—undefined in the statute—could be held to owe child support.

In *In re Marriage of Simmons*, in contrast, the trial court agreed with Jennifer that Robert was female and their marriage void, granted Jennifer sole custody, and denied Robert parental rights and standing to seek custody but granted Robert visitation with the child. The Illinois appeals court unanimously affirmed the judgment below. It concluded that Robert was not male, was never lawfully married to Jennifer, was therefore not a parent under any potentially applicable Illinois law, and was not entitled to seek custody of his 12-year-old child. Jennifer made no claim of fraud or deception by Robert, and she had acknowledged his paternity in their artificial insemination agreement. Yet the court held that Jennifer could not be estopped from challenging Robert's paternity because the agreement was invalid, reasoning that Robert was never a "husband" within the meaning of the statute governing such agreements. And the court reached these conclusions despite reading binding state case law "to stand for the proposition that . . . matters of financial support and parental responsibility may be brought under common law theories of breach of an oral contract and promissory estoppel."

What might account for the differing approaches and outcomes of these courts? Consider the following possibilities:

(A) *Michael T.*, decided 20 years before *In re Marriage of Simmons*, held the transgender man to be a parent without concern for the validity of the underlying marriage; *In re Marriage of Simmons*, the more recent case, rejected the validity of the transgender man's claimed marriage and his claim to parental rights. Evolving social mores therefore do not seem to account for the differences between the case outcomes.

(B) Gender identity/transgender persons are often conflated with sexual orientation/LGB persons. In 2004, 17 states had considered (and most enacted) state constitutional amendments designed to prevent their having to allow same-sex couples to marry civilly. In January 2005, George W. Bush endorsed a similar federal constitutional amendment in his State of the Union address. Thus, the relevant social context for questions of LGBT identity had changed from 1985 to 2005, but at the latter time, recent social progress had been set back by dramatic developments in the campaign to deny same-sex couples the right to marry.

(C) Technical differences between New York law and Illinois law and/or the differing political complexions of the states and/or their judiciaries may account for the differences between these two opinions.

(D) In *Michael T.*, the court rejected the transgender man's arguments against his marriage's validity because they were designed to avoid child support obligations that the government was trying to enforce for the children's benefit, while in *In re Marriage of Simmons*, the court rejected the transgender man's arguments for his marriage's validity because no question of support for the minor child was on the table in the litigation to that point.

Reading Guide for In re Marriage of B.

In the following case, a decision from the New York Supreme Court, which you'll recall is the name for the trial court in that state, denied a divorced (and remarried) father's motion to expand his minor son's visitation to include overnight stays with him. For what reasons does the Appellate Division affirm?

In re Marriage of B., aka B. (Anonymous) v. B. (Anonymous)
184 A.D.2d 609 (N.Y. App. Div. 1992)

Before Harwood, J.P., and Balleta, O'Brien and Ritter, JJ.

Memorandum by the Court.

In a matrimonial action in which the parties were divorced by judgment dated April 15, 1987, the defendant father appeals from an order . . . entered January 29, 1991 which denied his application to expand his visitation rights with the parties' son.

Ordered that the order is affirmed, with costs.

The parties were married on December 4, 1977, and divorced pursuant to a judgment dated April 15, 1987. They have one child, born August 9, 1984, who is the subject of this proceeding. The judgment of divorce awarded custody of the child to the mother and established a visitation schedule for the father. That schedule was subsequently modified and the father is presently entitled to visitation (a) every Saturday from 9:00 A.M. until 8:30 P.M., (b) from the eve of religious holidays until 8:30 P.M. (when there is no school for the child the following day), (c) various religious holidays, (d) alternate legal holidays, (e) the child's birthday in alternate years, (f) Father's Day, and (g) the father's birthday. The father moved for an order expanding this visitation schedule to provide for overnight visitation. The mother opposed any modification based upon, inter alia, her belief that the father was not an appropriate role model for the young child as evidenced by the father's history of cross-dressing. After a full and complete hearing where both parents, the father's present wife, an Orthodox Rabbi, two psychologists, and a psychiatrist testified, the hearing court denied the father's application. We affirm.

Any custody or visitation determination depends heavily upon the court's assessment of the credibility of the witnesses and of the character and temperament of the parents, and, therefore, the findings of the trial court are generally accorded the greatest respect. Moreover, where there is a conflict in the evidence, this court accords deference to the hearing court which has seen and evaluated the evidence firsthand. The record here contains contradictory testimony from the parties and their witnesses regarding the duration and extent of the father's cross-dressing activities. Although the Supreme Court improperly relied on hearsay evidence concerning the then five-year-old child's preferences in making its determination, we conclude that the decision not to expand visitation so as to include overnight stays with the father by this impressionable child has a sound and substantial basis in the record and that, at this point, the visitation schedule should not be changed.

Discussion

1. Note that only some but not all men who "cross-dress," that is, wear clothing conventionally judged appropriate for women but not men, have a female gender identity and would thus be considered "transgender" in narrower senses of the term. See discussion of forms of gender nonconformity and associated terminology in Chapter 1, *supra*.

2. On what basis or bases might a parent or judge believe that a father who sometimes cross-dresses is thereby an inappropriate role model for his five-year-old son? Is judicial reliance on such reasons consistent with the U.S. constitutional guarantee of equal protection of the laws, which has been held to forbid government action that classifies based on sex if it is based on gender stereotypes or otherwise lacks "an exceedingly persuasive justification"? Consider whether this, or other negative treatment of "cross-dressing" (*see, e.g.*, Chapter 3, *supra*), should be analyzed as sex discrimination, particularly given the reasoning in *Bostock v. Clayton County, Georgia*, 140 S. Ct. 1731 (2020), Chapter 5, Section D, *supra*, which held that discrimination because of an employee's "transgender status" is necessarily discrimination because of sex, for purposes of Title VII of the Civil Rights Act of 1964.

3. Shannon Minter, legal director of the National Center for Lesbian Rights, has argued that recent cases involving transgender parents tend to involve more subtle forms of discrimination than earlier cases, reflecting a "tendency to subject a parent's transition process to extremely close scrutiny and to penalize the parent for any possible missteps or failures of judgment." Shannon Price Minter, *Transgender Family Law*, 56 Fam. Ct. Rev. 410 (2018).

Reading Guide for J.L.S. v. D.K.S.

1. In *J.L.S.*, the majority and the dissent disagree about how to characterize the trial court's order authorizing visitation with the transgender parent to commence after one year and whether that provision was lawful under the circumstances. Whose position is better supported? (Was the majority right to treat the trial court as having implicitly found that immediate contact between the parent and children would have emotionally harmed the children?)

2. Was the appellate court right to hold that the parties could not be afforded joint legal custody? Does that holding reward the mother for violating the trial court's earlier orders regarding contact between the transgender parent and the children?

3. What rationale does the court give for preventing the transgender parent from "cohabit[ing] with other transsexuals or sleep[ing] with another female" while the children were visiting? On what assumptions about transgender persons and/or their children do such restrictions rest?

J.L.S. v. D.K.S.

943 S.W.2d 766 (Mo. Ct. App. 1997)

Simon, Judge.

. . . .

The decree must be affirmed if it is supported by substantial evidence, it is not against the weight of the evidence, and it neither erroneously declares nor applies the law. We must accept as true the evidence and permissible inferences therefrom in the light most favorable to the decree and disregard all contrary evidence and inferences. Where there is a conflict in testimony, we defer to the trial court's determination of the credibility of the witnesses.

[Mother] and father were married on March 19, 1983 and two sons were born. . . . The oldest child was eight at the time of trial and the youngest was five.

Circumstances, occurring before and during the marriage, culminated in father having male to female "sex-reassignment" surgery. Father told mother of a few instances of cross-dressing he had prior to the marriage, but assured her that they were resolved. However, throughout the marriage, father secretly struggled with urges to cross-dress.

In June 1991, the parties were living in Clinton, Maryland. The marriage was strained at this time. Mother brought the two children to Missouri to visit her family. When she returned to Maryland, father told her he had seen a social worker about his problems. The parties saw a series of counselors and psychologists. Father requested a separation for one year while he participated in a "Real Life Test," during which he would live as a woman "24 hours a day." Prior to the separation, mother and father had a talk with the boys about the pending separation, but nothing was mentioned about the "Real Life Test" or father's struggle with his gender.

On August 1, 1992, the parties separated. They signed a separation agreement which father drafted. They agreed mother would have sole, permanent care and custody of the children, and father would refrain from visiting them for at least one year while he participated in his "Real Life Test." . . . . Father told a court-appointed psychologist that he did not intend to end the marriage. . . . Instead, he planned to have sex-reassignment surgery and remain married. Father proposed that the parties continue to live together and that his sons call him "Aunt Sharon." . . . .

Mother moved to Missouri with her sons and father has had no face-to-face contact with the boys since the . . . separation. He tried to contact the boys by telephone and letter but mother refused to allow any contact. Both boys have experienced emotional difficulties since the parties' separation and have been under the care of a psychologist. The oldest boy expressed "suicidal ideations" and had been unhappy because he and mother had to move away from father. He was prescribed antidepressant medication. The youngest boy was diagnosed with attention deficit disorder.

In 1993, . . . Mother filed a petition for dissolution in Missouri which alleged in pertinent part:

15. That [father] has behaved in such a manner that [mother] cannot reasonably be expected to live with him.

16. That [father] has adopted a lifestyle such that it would be extremely harmful to the minor children for them to be placed even in the temporary custody of or visitation with [father]. That denying visitation and temporary custody to [father] is clearly in the best interests of the minor children.

Father filed a response to the petition alleging that he had been diagnosed "gender dysphoric" and had pursued treatment and rehabilitation medically indicated by this condition. Father denied that he "adopted a lifestyle," but rather that the change in his lifestyle was medically necessary for his health. He also denied that the change in his lifestyle would be "injurious per se" to the children. Further, father alleged that mother had failed to inform him about the children's development and health and denied him any contact with the children.

. . . .

About two months before trial, father underwent "sex-reassignment" surgery. At trial mother and father testified and each presented the testimony of two experts. Mother testified that the boys had adjustment problems as to the move and the separation of the parents and were under the care of a psychologist. . . . Mother asked the trial court for full physical and legal custody and that "under these circumstances that there be no face-to-face visitation between father and the boys."

Father testified that he wanted to be part of the boys' lives and that he loved them but agreed that they would need counseling in order to understand what was going on and to help with their adjustment.

Three experts testified in court and a fourth's testimony was presented by deposition. The trial court found father's experts to be credible. Both had significant experience with gender identity disorders and relationships of transsexuals to their children. The court found that father's expert, Dr. Brown, was an "expert's expert." Further, it found that mother's experts lacked credibility because neither had any experience in gender identity disorders or transsexualism. Although the trial court found that one of mother's experts "formed his opinions after one or two sessions with [mother] without ever seeing the children," the testimony of the experts as set forth in the record on appeal clearly indicates that each of mother's experts, including Mr. Wilkinson, interviewed the children, while father's experts did not interview the children.

 . . . .

On June 1, 1995, the trial court entered its Decree and Judgment of Dissolution of Marriage. The court amended the decree on June 20, 1995, and mother filed a motion for new trial on June 28, 1995, contending that the amended decree was not in accord with the credible evidence and that father's temporary custody is against the best interest of the minor children.

On July 19, 1995, the trial court entered its Findings of Fact and Second Amended Decree and Judgment. The trial court found, while "there was no request for findings, the court finds and believes from the evidence that it would be in the best interest and welfare of the minor children, that they be reunited with [father]." It noted that the evidence clearly established that father was a loving and caring father and that mother would not have a problem with his contact with the children if he was not acting like a woman. Further, it found that mother had interfered with the relationship of the minor children and their father. Additionally, the court found mother evasive in her answers regarding whether she would comply with the court's order of visitation and temporary custody. The Second Amended Decree reads in pertinent part:

IT IS FURTHER ORDERED, ADJUDGED AND DECREED AS FOLLOWS:

1. *Family Counseling:*

(a) That [mother], [father] and the minor children engage in family counseling not less often than once each month for a period of twelve months, in order to effectuate the reunification of the family and contact with [father] . . .

2. *Child Custody:*

(a) That [mother] is awarded the primary care, custody and control of the parties' minor children, . . . subject to reasonable rights of visitation and temporary custody in [father], provided during those periods in which the minor children are in the temporary custody of [father], [father] shall not cohabit with other transsexuals or sleep with another female. Said visitation and temporary custody shall commence on the third full weekend of the month on the twelfth month after the Entry of the Decree of Dissolution as follows:

i) The third full weekend of each month . . .

ii) Two weeks during the summer . . .

iii) Alternating major holidays . . .

(b) That [father] shall immediately be allowed telephone contact with the minor children at all times, . . . [and] [f]or the first sixty (60) days following the entry of the Decree, [father] shall not discuss with the minor children gender related issues.

(c) That [father] shall immediately be allowed to send letters, gifts, and other correspondence to the minor children, and [mother] is ordered to deliver those items to the children. For the first sixty (60) days following the entry of the Decree, [father] shall not discuss with the children gender related issues.

(d) That the parties shall confer with one another in the exercise of the decision-making rights, responsibilities and authority and have an equal voice on issues regarding the children's training, education and rearing,. . . .

Since mother's appeal is directed to the visitation and legal custody provisions of the decree and father's cross-appeal is directed to a restriction on his association and cohabitation during the exercise of his visitation rights, the remainder of the decree is affirmed.

In her first point on appeal, mother . . . essentially contends that the trial court erred in removing restrictions on father's visitation on a specified date in the future without requiring, as a precondition to the removal of the restrictions, a hearing or an affirmative showing by father of rehabilitation and treatment.

[Here,] we are addressing the original grant of visitation rights to father which is covered by [§ 452.400.2 RSMo 1994] subsection 1 which provides in pertinent part:

1. A parent not granted custody of the child is entitled to reasonable visitation rights unless the court finds, after a hearing, that visitation would endanger the child's physical health or impair his emotional development.

. . . .

The trial court's order provided that father's visitation rights would not begin until twelve months after the entry of the decree. Thus, the trial court placed a restriction on father's visitation. When the trial court places a restriction on father's visitation rights it ordinarily should make a finding of impairment of emotional development. Here, although the trial court did not make an express finding of impairment, it is implicit from its finding of no immediate contact, that immediate contact between the children and father would impair the boys' emotional development.

Further, the implicit finding is clearly supported by the evidence. All the experts agreed that father's immediate contact with the children would cause harm to them. When father's expert, Dr. Brown, was asked how long the reunification process should take, he responded, "I wouldn't be able to predict that for you." He also stated that it would be "emotionally confusing" for the boys to see their father as a woman immediately, and that the adjustment process could take a year. Moreover, father testified that the boys would need counseling to understand what has occurred and to help them adjust. . . .

The record on appeal indicates that the twelve-month period restricting father's visitation has expired. However, the record is absent of any showing that counseling has occurred or the present mental and emotional state of the children and parents. During oral argument, it was indicated that the boys have been told nothing of father's status. Clearly, in the best interest of the children, a reevaluation of all parties must occur before the boys are exposed to a situation that father's experts deemed as harmful to them if they have not been correctly prepared. . . .

This is a unique situation and it is imperative that evaluations of the parents and children are made prior to the children's face-to-face reunification with father. [As] of the date of this opinion, approximately twenty months have passed since the entry of the decree. Thus, on remand the trial court should determine the mental and emotional status of the parents and children to determine what is in the best interest of the children. Based upon those findings the trial court should decide what remedial measures, if any, should be taken to insure the best interests of the children are served while working toward their reunification with father. Likewise, the trial court should structure a visitation schedule appropriate to the children's best interest.

In her second point on appeal, mother contends that the trial court erred in that there is no substantial evidence to support the visitation provisions of the decree in that . . . the counseling provisions of the decree are unduly vague and grossly inadequate to serve the purposes of preparing the minor children for visitation with father at some time in the future. . . .

[Under] the terms of the decree, mother and the children were to engage in counseling at least once a month for a period of twelve months and father was to engage in counseling with his own counselor.

Mother argues that the counseling provisions are vague and inadequate because the provisions do not require: 1) communication between or among the counselors; 2) the issuance of formal or informal reports; and, 3) the presence or participation of the counselors during the unsupervised visitation father is to have in the future. In light of the unusual issues involved in this case, and the delicate age of the children, mother argues that the counseling provisions fail to serve the best interest of the children.

In light of the fact that we are requiring the trial court to conduct a hearing to evaluate the children's progress toward physical reunification with their father, we also believe that the court should require evidence of successful counseling before implementing reunification. Given the dramatic change in father's new identity, it is impossible to predict what effect his sex reassignment will have upon the children.

We believe that the children's best interest require [*sic*] that the counseling provisions insure that reunification proceeds with as little emotional trauma or psychological damage to the children as possible. If the trial court finds, after the hearing, that the children are not emotionally and mentally suited for physical contact with their father, then the trial court should not order visitation until such time as the parties demonstrate it is in the children's best interest to do so.

In her final point, mother contends the trial court erred in that the award of joint legal custody is not in the best interest of the children, it is unsupported by substantial evidence, and the overwhelming evidence indicates that the parties now do not share any commonality of beliefs regarding the raising of the minor children. We agree.

Joint legal custody means that the parents share in the decision-making regarding the important events in the child's life. A commonality of beliefs concerning parental decisions and the parties' ability to cooperate and function as a parental unit are important considerations when determining whether joint legal custody is in the best interest of the child.

The statutory preference for joint custody "is not that of a forced joint custody in order to induce the parents to find a common ground," but it is a preference in favor of parents who demonstrate "the willingness and ability to share the rights and responsibilities of child-rearing even after they have dissolved the marriage." *In re Marriage of Johnson*, 865 S.W.2d 412 (Mo. Ct. App. 1993) . . . .

In order to support an award of joint legal custody, there must be substantial evidence that the parties have a commonality of beliefs regarding the parental decisions and the willingness and ability to function as a parental unit in making decisions. It is error for the trial court to award joint legal custody if no substantial evidence exists. The lack of evidence of conflict between the parents over raising the child does not meet the affirmative proof required to demonstrate that the parents are equipped to function as a unit to make parental decisions. *Johnson.* The record here is void of substantial evidence that these parents have a commonality of beliefs concerning parental decisions or are capable of functioning as a parental unit in making those decisions.

Father argues that. . . . the record demonstrates that it was necessary for the trial court to award joint legal custody because otherwise mother would continue to interfere with his relationship with his children. . . . We find that father's argument is without merit. Joint legal custody was not designed to insure that a parent maintains his or her relationship with the child, but was designed to facilitate the best interest of the child by allowing both parents to share in the decision-making of raising the child.

Additionally, the evidence adduced at trial does not support the award of joint legal custody. First, mother and father have not functioned as a parental unit for at least four years. In that period of time, father has not actively engaged in the decision-making of raising his two children. Second, the ability of mother and father to make decisions regarding the children is further frustrated by the fact that mother and children live in Missouri while father lives elsewhere. Finally, there was no substantial evidence adduced at trial regarding how father's sex reassignment surgery and new identity will affect the manner in which mother and father function as a parental unit when making important decisions regarding the children.

There was no basis for concluding that the parents are willing to share the rights and responsibilities of raising their children. We find the order granting joint legal custody is unsupported by substantial evidence. . . . [We] reverse the trial court's finding of joint legal custody and award mother sole legal custody.

In his cross-appeal, father contends the trial court erred in ordering that during father's temporary custody "[he] shall not cohabit with other transsexuals or sleep with another female. . . ." Father contends that the trial court's order places an undue hardship on him, is in violation of his constitutional rights and bears no relationship to the best interest and welfare of the minor children. However, father cites no authority for his position.

The trial court is vested with broad discretion in determining child custody and our principal concern is, as is the trial court's in awarding custody, the best interest of the children. In determining the best interest of the children, the court may consider the conduct of the parents. There must be consideration of what conduct a parent may inspire by example, or what conduct of a child a parent may foster by condonation. Past and present activities may be a reliable guide to the priorities of a parent. Consideration of conduct is not limited to that which has in fact detrimentally affected the children.

Here, father testified that he is living as a woman with two other women, one of whom is a transsexual. He admitted that he has, on at least one occasion, had a female stay at his home and sleep in his bed, but denied having any sexual relations since the surgery.

Father argues that the "restriction on [his] cohabitation and private life is beyond the purview of the trial court and an abuse of discretion." However, the court cannot ignore the effect which the conduct of a parent may have on a child's moral development. There is substantial evidence to support the judgment of the trial court. We do not find an abuse of discretion. Point denied.

. . . .

Rhodes Russell, P.J., concurs.

Karohl, Judge, dissenting in part.

Except for an award of joint legal custody the trial court entered a remarkable decree in a difficult and unique case. It ruled without the benefit of factual precedent on the only source of dispute, father is a gender dysphoric [*sic* — Eds.]. Mother did not allege or offer evidence to support a finding D.K.S. was not a loving father in all respects, at all times, except for his condition. She alleged his "adopted . . . lifestyle [would be] extremely harmful to the children." For that reason *alone* she would have the court deny the children any contact with their father, even visitation.

The trial court expressly found "[t]he evidence clearly established that Respondent was a loving and caring father; that the children had a significant bond with their father." The key to a review of the decree is the court's recollection of mother's testimony, "she would not have a problem with his contact with [the boys] on an overnight basis . . . if he acted in no way like a woman." Another insight into the wisdom of the trial court are the provisions employed to reintroduce the children where the court found "Petitioner had interfered with the relationship of the minor children with their father, refusing to allow even telephone contact or letters to be received by the children, even though the children asked to see their father and had told Petitioner they missed him."

The decree was supported by findings of the court that mother's two experts had no experience in "gender identity disorders or transsexualism." One of mother's witnesses never saw the children. Mother's other expert acknowledged the expertise of father's expert and the court found his opinion did "not appear . . . to be supported by medical authority as competent as that of [father's] authority." Mother's witnesses would not support a finding, expressed or implied, of endangerment. The trial court found their testimony unconvincing and we are bound by that finding.

Father's expert, Dr. Brown, ... recommended "that it was imperative that the children be reunited with their father . . . [denial] . . . would be the worst thing the court could do." We must defer to the trial court where its findings and conclusions are supported by the evidence on all issues, including temporary custody, except the award of joint legal custody. Dr. Brown did not testify immediate visitation would cause the children harm because of his condition. He supported a gradual re-introduction to avoid harm. The court made no express finding of endangerment because of father's condition. Considering the careful, lengthy and detailed decree, it is very unlikely it reached any implied finding of endangerment. The delay of temporary custody was supported as a matter of kindness and good judgment without evidence father was dangerous. He was not. The decree awarded delayed, unrestricted temporary custody to permit a gradual adjustment, not to change father or his new persona. The trial judge is no longer in office. The only certain result of a reconsideration of the temporary custody is hardship and continued estrangement. My analysis of this appeal follows.

J.L.S. (Mother) appeals from a decree of dissolution of marriage. D.K.S. n/k/a S.D.S. (Father[1]) cross-appeals from the same decree. . . .

. . . .

---

1. D.K.S. n/k/a S.D.S. has undergone male to female "sex-reassignment" surgery. We [*sic*] will use the term "Father" to refer to D.K.S. n/k/a S.D.S. throughout the opinion. Father objected during the trial to any usage of male pronouns to describe Father. To avoid confusion and not out of any disrespect for Father's wishes, we will use pronouns applicable to the parties when their children were born.

[At] trial, four health care experts testified about visitation issues. On July 19, 1995, the trial court entered its "SECOND AMENDED *DECREE AND JUDG-MENT OF DISSOLUTION OF MARRIAGE.*" The trial court. . . . noted:

> [t]he recommendations of both Dr. Brown and Ms. Marcus were that it was imperative that the children be reunited with their father. Both suggested that there be a period of counseling, in order for the children to adapt to the situation and to learn to deal with it.

. . . .

Subsection 1 [of § 452.400 RSMo Cum. Supp. 1993] addresses the court's power to grant visitation rights in the first instance. The relevant portion of subsection 1 states, "1. A parent not granted custody of the child is entitled to reasonable visitation rights unless the court finds, after a hearing, that visitation would endanger the child's physical health or impair his emotional development." The trial court must determine what "reasonable visitation rights" are under the circumstances of each case. In this case, the trial court honored the statute. It did not "restrict" visitation rights, rather it granted what it found to be reasonable visitation rights without finding endangerment. It made no finding of endangerment. We have no authority to impose an implied finding where it is not possible for an appellate court to determine, with certainty, the motive for the delay. The long separation alone, the separation and Father's condition, or only Father's condition may be the basis for the trial court's decision. In the absence of evidence to support a finding where there is the possibility of various findings, there is no basis to reject the allowed visitation. In *VanPelt v. VanPelt,* 824 S.W.2d 135 (Mo. Ct. App. 1992) the court considered a very different issue with reference to an implied finding of endangerment. There was only one possible basis for *denying mother any visitation.* The statute is unambiguous in assigning that responsibility to the trial court. The one-year delay is not a "restriction" for purposes of the statute, therefore no finding of endangerment to the boys' physical health or impairment of their emotional development is necessary. There is no evidence to support the conclusion the implicit reason for the delay is impairment of the boys' emotional development. It is an accommodation to the years of absence of contact caused by both parents. The relevant inquiry in this case is whether the trial court abused its discretion in awarding visitation to Father with no restrictions beginning on a certain date in the future, together with provisions designed to effectuate the reintroduction of Father with the children and children with Father. In *Roberts v. Roberts,* 810 S.W.2d 65 (Mo. Ct. App. 1990), we affirmed the requirement of temporary arrangements guiding father's visitation rights without a showing that this visitation would endanger the children's physical health or impair their emotional development. In *Roberts* we found:

> [a] review of the evidence in the case discloses a lack of emotional control on the part of appellant and respondent incident to the breakup of their marriage and an inevitable effect upon the children. The trial court, within the authority granted pursuant to § 452.400, RSMo 1986, concluded

that temporary restrictions on appellant's rights of visitation would aid the healing process.

The court did not abuse its discretion in imposing a temporary arrangement delaying father's visitation rights. Under the circumstances of that case such an arrangement was reasonable.

In this case, Father's own evidence supported the temporary delay of face-to-face contact for one year, to give all parties, especially the children, time to adapt to the dissolution and Father's new identity. Responding to a question about what would be the appropriate process for reuniting Father with his children, Father's expert testified, "It would start with telephone contact, conference call situations and then move on to personal contact down the road, depending on how things progressed." Father's expert also agreed with the statement that he was "not recommending to the Court . . . that tomorrow or next Monday, whenever his order come [*sic*] down, that there be immediate contact [between Father and the children], . . ." He suggested that the parties and the children would need counseling before personal contact to deal with the confusion which would naturally be felt by the children. Father's expert invited the court to order a delay before Father see the children face-to-face. Under these circumstances, the temporary delay of face-to-face contact for a year while get-acquainted activities were in process was reasonable. Here, the parent not granted custody of the children was granted reasonable visitation rights in accord with his own evidence.

Furthermore, the provision in the judgment for the parties and the children to seek counseling "to effectuate the reunification of the family and contact with [Father]" is not a statutory restriction on Father's visitation rights. The success or completion of counseling was not ordered as a pre-condition or limitation on the starting date of Father's temporary custody and visitation rights. . . . The parties' failure to benefit from the court's request for counseling may be relevant to future proceedings. However, the counseling provision constitutes a request, rather than a restriction on Father's visitation rights.

. . . .

The one-year delay. . . . applies an accepted and kindly approach to allow parent and child to be reacquainted after a pre-dissolution estrangement. . . .

Mother also argues the psychological counseling provisions of the decree are unduly vague and grossly inadequate to serve the purpose of preparing the minor children for visitation with Father at some time in the future. . . . The success or completion of counseling was not a pre-condition or limitation on the starting date of Father's temporary custody and visitation rights. Accordingly, the counseling provisions constitute a request which both parties ignore at their peril. It is clear from the evidence and the decree that the trial court wanted the parties and the children to seek counseling for the sole purpose of helping the children to adapt to Father's absence for four years and his new identity. Consultation among counselors, or the issuance of reports may benefit the parties and the children and may occur but were reasonably thought to be unnecessary to the decree.

In her final point, Mother argues the trial court's award of joint legal custody is unsupported by substantial evidence, an abuse of discretion and a misapplication of the law. . . .

There was evidence to support a finding Mother and Father are not willing and able to function as a parental unit in making decisions involving child rearing. . . . Furthermore, Mother and Father have not acted as a parental unit for at least four years. This occurred originally by Father's choice and subsequently by Mother's restrictions on the children's contact with Father.

[The] record is devoid of any substantial evidence of Mother and Fathers' [*sic*] beliefs concerning parental decisions on education and health issues. The parties simply did not try the issue of joint legal custody to assist the trial court in following the relevant statute. The order granting joint legal custody is not supported by substantial evidence. I would remand to permit trial on that issue. The best interests of the children and the necessity for informed appellate review require the parties to present evidence to the fact-finder concerning their ability and willingness to function as a parental unit.

Father argues in his cross-appeal, the trial court erred in ordering "[Father] shall not cohabit with other transsexuals or sleep with another female" during those periods in which the minor children are in his temporary custody. He argues this prohibition bears no relationship to the best interest and welfare of the minor children, is an undue hardship on him, and violates his constitutional rights. Father cites no cases to support his argument. His point violates Rule 84.04(d). If, as is the case here, the point is "one for which precedent is appropriate and available, it is the obligation of [Father] to cite such authority." *Thummel v. King,* 570 S.W.2d 679 (Mo. banc 1978). A point of error unsupported by a citation of relevant, available authority is deemed abandoned. *Earl v. St. Louis University,* 875 S.W.2d 234 (Mo. Ct. App. E.D. 1994).

Even if Father had not abandoned his point, because of the nature of the issue, we could hold the trial court did not err in prohibiting Father from cohabiting with other transsexuals or sleeping with other women during the times when the children are in his custody. In *J.P. v. P.W.,* 772 S.W.2d 786 (Mo. Ct. App. 1989) we discussed several Missouri cases involving the custodial and visitation rights of homosexual parents. We held that even when a two-year old child showed no ill effects from being exposed to homosexual behavior, "[t]he court does not need to wait . . . till the damage is done." In *P.L.W. v. T.R.W.,* 890 S.W.2d 688 (Mo. Ct. App. S.D. 1994), we affirmed the trial court's order denying the mother's motion to modify the father's visitation rights because father had engaged in unusual sexual activities during the marriage. In the opinion, we noted that the father's actions had never occurred in the physical presence of the children. I would adopt the analysis in *J.P.*

v. P.W. In this case, the decree prohibits Father from cohabiting with a transsexual or sleeping with a female while the children are in his temporary custody. The prohibition is directed to behavior which would occur in the children's presence.

The decree should be affirmed in all respects except the award of joint legal custody.

Discussion

1. If J.L.S. and D.K.S. had remained married throughout J.L.S.'s transition, and J.L.S. did not move away for it, the children would have been "exposed" to that transition. Should the state be able to intervene in such an "intact" family out of concerns about the emotional effects of a parent's gender transition? If not, should the state be allowed to preclude contact between divorced transgender parents such as J.L.S. and their children? What freedoms are at stake in either situation?

2. The courts in this case also restricted J.L.S.'s choice of living or sleeping partners. Such restrictions used to be not uncommon with respect to lesbigay parents. *See, e.g.,* Courtney G. Joslin, Shannon P. Minter & Catherine Sakimura, Lesbian, Gay, Bisexual and Transgender Family Law § 1:21 *Restrictions preventing parent from living with nonmarital same-sex partner or prohibiting nonmarital same-sex partner from being present during residential time upheld* (Aug. 2018 Update) ("Two restrictions . . . on both custody and visitation that continue to be imposed with some regularity are restrictions prohibiting a parent from living with a nonmarital same-sex partner and restrictions preventing a nonmarital same-sex partner from being present during residential time."); *but see id.* ("While general anti-paramour provisions may be more difficult to challenge than restrictions limited to same-sex partners, courts increasingly have struck down such provisions."). "Today, most courts will only forbid overnight visitation with a parent who is cohabiting if there is a showing of adverse impact on the child." Linda D. Elrod, Child Custody Prac. & Proc. § 6:16 *Sexual conduct of parent* (Feb. 2019 Update). What liberties are curtailed by such restrictions, and what government interests might — or might not — justify such deprivations?

Reading Guide for In re Marriage of Magnuson

1. Do the majority and dissent disagree about the standard a reviewing court is to use to assess a trial court's grant of primary residential custody? Do they disagree about whether a trial court may lawfully restrict a parent's rights based on the parent's transgender status?

2. On what facts does the majority base its decision? On what facts does the dissent rely? Do the two opinions fully engage with their colleagues' analyses?

In re the Marriage of Tracy A. Magnuson

170 P.3d 65 (Wash. Ct. App. 2007)

BROWN, J.

In this parenting plan dispute, Robert S. Magnuson contends the trial court erred by improperly considering transgender status when it granted primary residential placement of the parties' children to Dr. Tracy A. Magnuson. But the court properly focused on the children's needs in making the residential placement decision, not transgender status, conforming to principles established in sexual preference cases. We agree with this extension of principle. Accordingly, we affirm.

Facts

In 1985, "Robbie" Magnuson and Tracy A. Magnuson (now Berg) were married. They had two children, Brian (born [1991]) and Meridith (born [1998]). Tracy is a surgeon and Robbie is an attorney. Robbie eventually "announced that [s]he needed to, and would be transitioning from male to female." She took a leave of absence from work and ultimately resigned. Robbie and Tracy separated in October 2004, and Tracy filed to dissolve their marriage.

After an eight-day trial, the court entered numerous findings, including: "Both parents are good and loving parents. . . . The children's relationship with each parent is approximately equal. Each has performed equal but very different roles with the children. . . . Historically, the parties were a dual professional family, relying on the assistance of nannies[,] and [i]t is somewhat disingenuous for either parent to claim the historical role of primary parent in this case."

The court found both parents acted in ways adversely affecting the children's stability. For example, Tracy denigrated Robbie in front of the children; Robbie's conduct had an "unimaginable impact on Meridith" when she showed up at Meridith's school, pushed Meridith's maternal grandmother out of the way, and "grabbed Meridith, such that observers actually thought a kidnapping was going on." Further, "[Robbie] has indicated she will be undergoing sexual reassignment surgery sometime in the very near future. . . . [Robbie's] surgery may be everything [she] has hoped for, or it may be disastrous. No one knows what is ahead[,] and [t]he impact of gender reassignment surgery on the children is unknown."

The court found while Robbie left her job, Tracy "maintained her professional career, has provided for the children in the 'former' family home, and provides an oasis of stability in all of this ongoing change." A previous shared co-equal residential placement did not work, and "[t]hese children, in particular, need environmental and parental stability." Finally, "[w]hile the margin is somewhat slim in this particular case, [Tracy] is in a more stable and predictable place in her life right now to act as the children's primary care giver." Robbie appealed.

Analysis

The issue is whether the trial court abused its discretion by impermissibly considering Robbie's transgender status in granting residential placement of the parties' two minor children to Tracy. Robbie contends the court erred in rejecting the guardian ad litem's (GAL) recommendation, in finding "[t]he impact of gender reassignment surgery on the children is unknown," in failing to properly address the factors in RCW 26.09.187(3)(a), and in restricting Robbie's parental rights.

We review a trial court's child placement decision for abuse of discretion. . . . A court abuses its discretion only if its decision is manifestly unreasonable or based on untenable grounds or reasons. . . .

Certain factors must be considered when establishing the residential provisions in a permanent parenting plan. These include: the parent/child relationship, the parents' responsibilities in performing parenting functions, parent agreements, "[e]ach parent's past and potential for future performance of parenting functions," the child's "emotional needs and developmental level," the child's relationships and activities, including schooling, the parent's wishes, the wishes of a mature child, and the parents' employment schedules. RCW 26.09.187 (3)(a)(iii)(iv).

First, the trial court carefully considered each child's relationship with each parent. . . . The court did not interview the children, but relied upon specific evidence given by the parties and the GAL when finding the impact of Robbie's surgery on the children was unknown. The court acted within its fact-finding discretion when drawing inferences from the given evidence of the children's present uncomfortable and nervous behavior to make the future impact finding. While Robbie points to evidence of the children's adjustment, we are in no position to find facts, reweigh the evidence, or decide witness credibility.

Second, the court was not bound by the GAL's recommendation. *In re Marriage of Swanson*, 944 P.2d 6 (Wash. Ct. App. 1997). The court's oral ruling and its extensive findings of fact show the factors in RCW 26.09.187(3)(a) that were considered; the court is not required to enter written findings on each factor. The record does not support Robbie's assertion that by rejecting the GAL's recommendation, the court impermissibly based its placement decision on transgender status.

Indeed, the court found Robbie was "undergoing an authentic gender transformation," and "has a right to be happy in her chosen life ahead." And, Robbie received substantial residential time with the children without limitation or restriction. *See In re Marriage of Cabalquinto*, 669 P.2d 886 (Wash. 1983) ("Visitation rights must be determined with reference to the needs of the child rather than the sexual preferences of the parent."). The *Cabalquinto* court's reasoning in a sexual preference visitation context is equally applicable in this transgender residential placement context.

In sum, the need of each child, not Robbie's transgender status, was the court's focus in determining residential placement. The court focused on the children's need for "environmental and parental stability" in granting the majority of residential time to Tracy, a permissible statutory factor addressing the children's emotional needs. RCW 26.09.187(3)(a). The trial court did not err in entering the final parenting plan. . . .

Affirmed.

I concur: Sweeney, C.J.

Kulik, J. (dissenting).

I agree with the majority's conclusion that the Supreme Court's reasoning in *In re Marriage of Cabalquinto* is equally applicable to transgender persons. *Cabalquinto* held that a trial court cannot restrict a parent's rights based on sexual orientation, and the majority here extends that holding to transgender persons. However, the trial court erred by doing exactly what the majority here prohibits—the court awarded primary residential placement to Tracy based on Robbie's transgender status. This is a manifest abuse of discretion and, therefore, I respectfully dissent.

As the majority states, we review challenged findings of fact for substantial evidence. And we do not engage in fact finding, or determine witness credibility. However, an abuse of discretion is found if the trial court applies the wrong legal standard or bases its ruling on an erroneous view of the law.

The trial court's Findings of Fact (FF) 2.21 X provides: "The impact of gender reassignment surgery on the children is unknown." But the trial court's other findings refute the assertion that substantial evidence supports FF 2.21 X. Contrary to the unrebutted expert opinion of Dr. Walter [Bockting, rendered by the dissent as Bochting—Eds.], the court found that the impact of the gender reassignment surgery on the children was unknown. Dr. [Bockting] is a national expert in transgender parenting. He presented uncontradicted testimony that transgender status does not ultimately have an impact on the parent's ability to parent.

The court found that the children had approximately equal relationships with each parent. Significantly, the court made no finding that Robbie's transgender status endangered the physical, mental, or emotional health of the children. And, the trial court found that Robbie was the more nurturing parent.

The guardian ad litem (GAL) conducted an exhaustive investigation. He interviewed 23 lay witnesses and 15 professional and expert witnesses, and prepared a 214-page report. The court found that the GAL had done a thorough job and had performed his role in an exemplary way.

The GAL testified that Robbie was the primary parent based on sabbaticals and involvement with the children on a day-to-day basis. The GAL concluded that Robbie was the more nurturing and engaged parent, and he recommended that the court designate Robbie as the primary residential parent. The GAL also concluded that Tracy had always been the secondary parent. Another expert, Dr. Paul Wert, the court-appointed psychologist, stated that psychologically and emotionally, Robbie was capable of continuing to extensively parent.

The trial court also erroneously based its decision to place the children with Tracy on a misreading of RCW 26.09.187(3)(a)(i). Under this statute, the greatest weight shall be given to the "relative strength, nature, and stability of the child's relationship with each parent." Here, the trial court found a lack of stability based on Robbie's transgender status. "The respondent has indicated she will be undergoing sexual reassignment surgery sometime in the very near future. Said surgery may be everything respondent has hoped for, or it may be disastrous. No one knows what is ahead."

However, the statute requires a review of the stability of the child's relationship with the parent—not a review of whether the parent may have a surgery that impacts the parent. The trial court's conclusion that Robbie's life was not stable because of her planned surgery was directly and impermissibly related to Robbie's transgender status. And again, there was no evidence and no finding that Robbie's transgender status would cause any harm or detriment to the children.

Moreover, the proper test of parental fitness is the present condition of the parent. The court's speculation about the future is not an appropriate basis for awarding custody. *See In re Marriage of Nordby*, 705 P.2d 277 (Wash. Ct. App. 1985); *In re Custody of Stell*, 783 P.2d 615 (Wash. Ct. App. 1989).

Finally, the trial court itself recognized that Robbie's transgender status caused no harm to the children when it placed no restrictions on Robbie's visitation with the children. The court agreed that the children's relationships with each parent were approximately equal. Apparently, the only difference between the parents was that Robbie, the primary parent, planned to have gender reassignment surgery.

"A trial court abuses its discretion when its decision is manifestly unreasonable or based on untenable grounds." *In re Parentage of J.H.*, 49 P.3d 154 (Wash. Ct. App. 2002). One parent's transgender status is not a tenable ground upon which to decide residential placement.

Accordingly, I respectfully dissent.

Discussion

1. In earlier times, courts would commonly deny custody or visitation by lesbigay parents based solely upon the fact of their sexual orientation. *See, e.g., Roe v. Roe*, 324 S.E.2d 691 (Va. 1985). Scholars sometimes describe this as a "per se" approach. *See, e.g.,* Julie Shapiro, *Custody and Conduct: How the Law Fails Lesbian and Gay Parents and their Children*, 71 Ind. L.J. 623, 626, 633 (1996). Over time, this approach was largely superseded by a rule that minority sexual orientation in and of itself was irrelevant to such family law decisions but could be considered only insofar as that orientation in a particular case affected the children in a pertinent way, that is, bore a "nexus" to the children's wellbeing. *Id. See, e.g., Damron v. Damron*, 670 N.W.2d 871 (N.D. 2003); *Van Driel v. Van Driel*, 525 N.W.2d 37 (S.D. 1994). Some scholarship has advocated that courts deciding transgender parents' rights should adopt a version of the "nexus" text developed in family law cases involving lesbigay persons. *See, e.g.,* Helen Y. Chang, *My Father Is a Woman, Oh No!: The Failure of the Courts to Uphold Individual Substantive Due Process Rights for Transgender Parents Under the Guise of the Best Interest of the Child*, 43 Santa Clara L. Rev. 649 (2003).

In building upon *In re Marriage of Cabalquinto*, 669 P.2d 886 (Wash. 1983), the *Magnuson* court does appear to haved adopt such a "nexus" test. *But see* Carlos A. Ball, The Right to Be Parents: LGBT Families and the Transformation of Parenthood 197 (2012) (arguing that court "essentially" applied a per se test by treating Tracy's decision to transition as evidence of parental instability); Sonia Katyal & Ilona Turner, *Transparenthood*, 117 Mich. L. Rev. 1593, 1657 (2019) (making that point about actual use of nexus test in trans parent cases generally). Katyal and Turner have concluded that more recent cases involving disputes over transgender parents' rights have eschewed applying *per se* tests, but that judicial opinions nonetheless still reflect anti-trans bias. *Id.* at 1600. As a result, they argue that "the only way to guarantee fair consideration that takes into account both the rights of transgender parents and the actual needs of their children is to completely prohibit consideration of a parent's transgender identity or expression, as well as consideration of any factors that may be used as proxies for such status, such as concerns about stigma or a child's anxiety about transition." *Id.* at 1600–01; *see also id.* at 1663–64 (enumerated more factors to be deemed inadmissible). Do you agree?

2. What might advocates for transgender parents or their ex-spouses do, consistent with professional ethics for lawyers, to increase or to reduce the chance of a transgender parent gaining primary custody of a child?

Reading Guide for Daly v. Daly

1. The following opinion concerns a termination of the parental rights of a transgender person. As the Nevada Supreme Court had interpreted the relevant state statutes (following a general approach some other states had adopted), "there are two kinds of grounds necessary to be considered in termination proceedings. One relates to parental conduct or incapacity and the parent's suitability as a parent; the other relates to the best interest of the child." *Champagne v. Welfare Div. of Nevada State Dep't of Human Res.*, 691 P.2d 849, 854 (Nev. 1984). That is, "there must be jurisdictional grounds for termination—to be found in some specific fault or condition directly related to the parents—and dispositional grounds—to be found by a general evaluation of the child's best interest." *Id.* As the court elaborated:

> "The jurisdictional question is whether the biological parent, by behavior [or incapacity not the fault of the parent—Eds.], has forfeited all rights in the child. The dispositional question is whether terminating parental rights would be in the best interest of the child. The first question focuses on the action, or inaction, of the natural parent. The second focuses on the placement which will be most beneficial to the child. If it is first decided that the parent has forfeited his rights in the children, then the court moves on to the second question. On the other hand, if it is decided that the biological parent's behavior does not violate minimum standards of parental conduct so as to render the parent unfit, then the analysis ends and termination is denied. In these latter instances, the court never reaches the question of

whether the child's future well-being would be better served by placement with the substitute or psychological parent."

Id. (quoting Orman W. Ketcham & Richard F. Babcock, Jr., *Statutory Grounds for the Involuntary Termination of Parental Rights*, 29 RUTGERS L. REV. 530 (1976)).

This doctrinal framework was later overruled in *In re Termination of Parental Rights as to N.J.*, 8 P.3d 126 (Nev. 2000).)

2. What is the basis for the majority's holding that it had "jurisdictional grounds" (a prerequisite for the Colorado judiciary's considering terminating parental rights) in this case? Upon what statutory element did the trial court rely and the state supreme court affirm? What was the "clear and convincing" evidentiary basis that the circumstances satisfied that element? For what various reasons do the dissenters reject each of the jurisdictional grounds upon which the trial court relied?

3. What is the ("clear and convincing") evidentiary basis for the majority's holding that "dispositional grounds" warrant the termination of Suzanne Daly's parental rights? For what reasons does the dissent reject each of those grounds?

Suzanne Lindley Daly, Formerly Known as Tim Daly v. Nan Toews Daly

715 P.2d 56 (1986)

STEFFEN, Justice:

Appellant . . . contends that there is no legal basis for the order terminating her parental rights and that the lower court is merely and improperly enforcing the private prejudices of the respondent. *Palmore v. Sidoti,* 466 U.S. 429 (1984). . . .

Respondent Nan Daly is the natural mother of the child. Appellant Suzanne Daly is the natural father of the child. Appellant's name was changed from Tim Daly [in] 1982. Appellant underwent sex-reassignment surgery, changing her sexual anatomy from male to female, [in] 1983, after a trial period of living as a female for approximately one year.

The parties were married [in] 1969 . . . . The minor child at issue in this action, Mary Toews Daly, was born [in] 1973 . . . . A final decree of divorce was entered February 17, 1981, at Reno, Nevada. . . . Respondent was awarded custody and control of Mary, subject to the visitation rights of appellant. Initially, appellant regularly exercised visitation rights under the decree, seeing the child approximately one weekend per month, alternate holidays and one month in the summer of 1981.

While Mary was with appellant in August, 1981, appellant revealed that she was a transsexual and would be undergoing hormonal and surgical reassignment as a female under the care of medical professionals.[11] Appellant told Mary that neither

---

11. Soon thereafter, Suzanne introduced Mary to the community of alternate lifestyles by taking her to a session at the Pacific Center where other transsexuals gather for support and counseling and discuss their experiences with one another.

respondent nor her grandmother, who lives with respondent, should know of appellant's plans. Mary did not reveal appellant's intentions for six months.

When Mary returned from her visit to Oakland in August of 1981, respondent noticed she was withdrawn and afraid to tell her something. On February 14, 1982, Mary revealed her father's plans to her mother. Mary was taken to a psychologist and evaluated by Dr. Towle, who advised respondent that it was very dangerous to allow Mary to be in the company of her father again.

Respondent testified that when Mary returned from the August visitation with her father, she would vacillate from being wide awake to being very sluggish. A certified academically talented child since seven years of age, she would sit at the kitchen table for hours cutting a large piece of paper into small pieces. She would take a pencil and trace the grain of the oak floor for hours. She wet the bed and, in fact, was incontinent in class a week prior to trial. Mary had not wet the bed since she was two years old. She had a short attention span and could not follow instructions, nor perform simple tasks. She also became inattentive and her handwriting degenerated into a scrawl. In addition, Mary became quiet and withdrawn.

In May of 1982, the respondent mother petitioned the lower court to terminate appellant's parental rights. On April 11, 1983, the court rendered its decision terminating appellant's parental rights. Appellant thereafter appealed.

[This] Court in *Cloninger v. Russell,* 655 P.2d 528 (Nev. 1982), adopted the clear and convincing evidence standard of proof in parental rights termination proceedings as set forth in *Santosky v. Kramer,* 455 U.S. 745 (1982). NRS 128.110 authorizes the termination of parental rights upon finding grounds pursuant to NRS 128.105. In the recent decision of *Champagne v. Welfare Division of the Nevada State Department of Human Resources,* 691 P.2d 849 (Nev. 1984), we elaborated on the grounds set forth in NRS 128.105 and held that there must be a finding of both jurisdictional and dispositional grounds in order to justify issuance of a termination order. [This particular framework was overruled in *In re Termination of Parental Rights as to N.J.,* 8 P.3d 126 (Nev. 2000) — Eds.] [In] the instant case . . . both grounds were satisfied.

Jurisdictional Grounds

NRS 128.105[12] specifies the jurisdictional grounds for termination. The district court primarily focused upon the risk of serious physical, mental, or emotional

---

12. NRS 128.105 recognizes the following jurisdictional grounds:
    1. Abandonment of the child;
    2. Neglect of the child;
    3. Unfitness of the parent;
    4. Risk of serious physical, mental or emotional injury to the child if he were returned
    to, or remains in, the home of his parent or parents;
    5. Only token efforts by the parent or parents:
      (a) To support or communicate with the child;
      (b) To prevent neglect of the child;
      (c) To avoid being an unfit parent;

injury to the child if visitation were resumed and the child were forced to maintain contact with appellant.

At trial Dr. Weiheir, respondent's expert witness who examined Mary, testified that there is a serious risk of emotional or mental injury to the child if she were allowed to be in her father's presence. In addition, the doctor testified that Mary would not be injured if she did not see her father again. The doctor also considered alternatives, such as consultation with psychologists and psychiatrists and testified there was no guarantee it would work and that there would be a serious risk of emotional injury.[13] It is precisely this risk that the lower court was asked to eliminate. [In] termination proceedings, the interests of the child are paramount and a child should not be forced to undergo psychological adjustments, especially in view of the risk involved, solely to avoid termination of a parent's rights. Certainly a parent's rights should be preserved if at all possible, but not at the expense of the child.

Appellant's expert witness also provided support for respondent's position by testifying that there are children who are not able to accept a parent as a transsexual. This witness also stated this was a new area and concluded there is a risk that there would be harm done in either direction. Dr. Weiheir, however, had the opportunity to observe and interview Mary and determined the risk to Mary would exist only if visitation were forced upon Mary.

Notwithstanding the possible harm that would befall Mary if visitation were resumed, NRS 128.107 provides that the child's desires regarding the termination should be a specific consideration, if the child has sufficient capacity to express his or her desires. Considering Mary's age and intelligence, the lower court found her to have the requisite capacity. We agree with the court's finding. In the present case, Mary told Dr. Weiheir and the trial judge that she did not want to see her father. Mary also said it would be disturbing to visit with her father and made it graphically clear that she didn't want to see him again.

The evidence presented in this case decisively establishes the jurisdictional grounds necessary to terminate parental rights. Therefore, our attention will now focus upon the dispositional grounds.

(d) To eliminate the risk of serious physical, mental or emotional injury to the child, or

6. With respect to termination of parental rights of one parent, the abandonment by that parent.

13. While other courts have imposed certain restrictions upon visitation with the child, such as the length of visitation, the location, or type of permissible activity, in this case such restrictions would accomplish nothing. The court recognized the effect appellant's transsexualism had upon Mary; any modification in visitation would not change that fact. To reiterate, the court did not conclude that appellant was an unfit parent merely because she is a transsexual. Rather, the court recognized the effect the situation had upon Mary in this time of her life and the serious risk of emotional or mental injury if visitation were allowed. Mary is very uncomfortable about the possibility of resuming visitation and is presently unprepared to cope with such a prospect.

Dispositional Grounds

Dispositional grounds are satisfied when it is found that the termination is in the child's best interests. At trial, it was undisputed that Mary's mother, Nan, is a very loving and conscientious mother who provides a desirable environment for her daughter. Nan always keeps Mary well fed and clothed and is absolutely dedicated to her child. At the present time, Mary is happy and well adjusted. Nevertheless, if visitation were permitted, there would be a risk of serious maladjustment, mental or emotional injury. Hence, recognizing Mary's present situation, her attitude and feelings, and the substantial risk of emotional or mental injury were she forced to visit with her father, it appears clear that termination of appellant's parental rights is in Mary's best interest.[14]

The trial court was fully aware of the seriousness and finality of a decree terminating parental rights, noting that such a remedy should be applied with caution. The court carefully considered the record and found abandonment and risk of serious mental and emotional harm. The court also found Suzanne to be a selfish person whose own needs, desires, and wishes were paramount and were indulged without regard to their impact on the life and psyche of the daughter, Mary.

Our review of the record indicates that the district court's findings are fully supported therein. Suzanne's efforts to regain visitation rights are shown to be a continuing source of apprehension to the child. Suzanne's solution is to subject the child to psychiatric counseling in order to change her mental attitude concerning her father's condition. Inferentially, the child will be more likely to succumb to a process of mental conditioning if she realizes that she will be forced to endure periods of visitation with Suzanne. However, expert testimony at trial reflects substantial doubt as to the success of such counseling at best, and a serious risk of further emotional injury to the child at worst. Such considerations are further complicated by the apparent degree of Mary's revulsion over Suzanne and the irretrievable loss of Suzanne's former relationship with Mary as a parent-father. The future prospects for emotional family stability are also dimmed by Suzanne's indication that Mary should know lesbians, homosexuals, and transsexuals and "be a part of their lives" if "they are my [Suzanne's] friends." Suzanne, who admitted that many of her friends are to be found among the aforementioned groups, has thus postured herself in a position of recurring conflict with the child's mother and the "traditional" upbringing enjoyed by Mary during her formative years. The resulting equation does not bode well for the emotional health and well-being of the child. This Court

---

14. It was shown that Mary is at the tender age when she is very much concerned about the impression of her peers and doesn't want to have any sort of uncomfortable fears. Mary would prefer to have her personal life remain a private event. By terminating Suzanne's parental rights, Mary will finally have the assurance and comfort of knowing the visitation matter is settled. Also, Mary's emotional state is preserved, thereby providing her the forum to mature and resolve the situation in her own way. There is nothing to prevent Mary from rekindling the relationship with her father in later years if she so desires, but that choice should be hers, made at a time when the risk of emotional or mental injury is eliminated.

can perceive no basis for such disruption of Mary's life. Nor do we see the necessity for inflicting a continuing sense of instability and uneasiness on this child. As noted previously, when Mary reaches the age of majority she can decide whether to reinstate a relationship with Suzanne. In the meantime, given the circumstances concerning Mary's view of Suzanne and the extent of her opposition to further ties with a vestigial parent, it can be said that Suzanne, in a very real sense, has terminated her own parental rights as a father. It was strictly Tim Daly's choice to discard his fatherhood and assume the role of a female who could never be either mother or sister to his daughter.

In sum, the record discloses the fact that appellant has paid no support for over a year, and what little communication there was during this time may be appropriately described as "token." Moreover, the court concluded that termination of appellant's parental rights would be in Mary's best interest. We have determined that the trial court's findings and decision are clearly and convincingly supported by the evidence. Both the jurisdictional and dispositional requisites for the termination of appellant's rights as a parent have been satisfied.

The trial court had all the parties before it, observed their demeanor and weighed their credibility. In this area of such sensitivity, we must accord the lower court due deference. We have considered appellant's remaining contentions and conclude they either lack merit or do not require a reversal. Accordingly, we affirm the lower court's decision.

Mowbray, C.J., and Young, J., concur.

Gunderson, Justice, with whom Springer, Justice, concurs, dissenting:

The natural mother of Mary Toews Daly (Mary), Nan Toews Daly (Nan), filed a petition to terminate the parental rights of the natural father of Mary, who is now legally known as Suzanne Lindley Daly.[1] After a hearing, the district court ter-

---

1. The father's name formerly was Tim Daly. He [*sic*] changed his legal name to Suzanne Lindley Daly in December, 1982. In this opinion, to avoid confusion I shall refer to the parties as the "mother" and the "father."

The father was a transsexual. A transsexual, or a person with sexual dysphoria, is biologically the member of one gender while considering himself as a member of the other gender. Green, *Sexual Identity of 37 Children Raised by Homosexual or Transsexual Parents*, 135 Am. J. Psych. 692, 692 (1978). The medical profession does not know the etiology of transsexuality; however, a person's self-identification as a transsexual appears to occur early in life, probably by the age of four, but might even occur prenatally. *See* Doe v. McConn, 489 F. Supp. 76, 78 (S.D. Tex. 1980); M.T. v. J.T., 355 A.2d 204, 205 (N.J. Super. Ct. 1976). Currently, psychotherapy appears to be an ineffective treatment for transsexuality. *See* Doe v. Department of Pub. Welfare, 257 N.W.2d 816, 819 (Minn. 1977). According to Ira Pauly, M.D., a psychiatrist and expert in transsexuality, who testified at trial, the medical profession believes that sex reassignment surgery is the best treatment available for a transsexual. For further information on transsexuality, see Comment, M.T. v. J.T.: *An Enlightened Perspective on Transsexualism*, 6 Cap. L. Rev. 403, 403–10 (1976–1977); Comment, *The Law and Transsexualism: A Faltering Response to a Conceptual Dilemma*, 7 Conn. L. Rev. 288, 288–94 (1974–1975); Comment, *Transsexualism, Sex Reassignment Surgery, and the Law*, 56 Cornell L. Rev. 963, 965–72 (1970–1971).

minated the father's parental rights over Mary. He then filed the instant appeal. We should reverse, because the district court lacked clear and convincing evidence which demonstrated the need to terminate parental rights over Mary. *At the outset, it should be emphasized that the father does not seek visitation rights at the present time. Hence, with all respect to my brethren in the majority, it seems inappropriate to bottom a ruling against him on the supposition that visitation with him could injure Mary.*

I

[The dissent starts with a lengthy counter-narrative of the case; this structure could suggest that it was originally drafted as a potential majority opinion. Because it provides a dramatically different picture of the situation, much of its detail is presented here.] After the separation, the mother worked and resided with Mary in Reno. The father lived in Oakland, California, where he worked at the Lawrence Berkeley Laboratory, a part of the University of California. . . .

In 1983, the mother petitioned the court to terminate her former husband's parental rights. The key issue underlying her petition appears to be his transsexuality. Prior to the 1981 medical diagnosis that the father was a transsexual, he had led a seemingly normal life. After high school, he received an appointment to the United States Naval Academy; however, he was unable to attend Annapolis because of poor eyesight. Instead, he enlisted in the United States Army and served honorably. Upon discharge, he attended the University of California at Berkeley. While at Berkeley, he worked at the Lawrence Berkeley Laboratory and double majored in Anthropology and in Slavic Language and Literature. After graduation, he continued to work for the Lawrence Berkeley Laboratory. His job, as a scientific research specialist, requires him to design and build complex research equipment and experimental devices. The parties also started to raise a family.

After their separation, the father had doubts about his gender identity. He consulted with Lynn Frazier, Ph.D., a psychotherapist specializing in the treatment of transsexuals. Dr. Frazier evaluated him for a potential gender identity problem and, using medical guidelines for the diagnosis of transsexuals, Dr. Frazier diagnosed him as a transsexual. Following Dr. Frazier's advice, the father then entered into the preoperative treatment regimen prescribed for transsexuals.

At the termination hearing, Ira Pauly, M.D., a psychiatrist and recognized expert in the field of transsexualism testified about the standards employed to screen candidates for sex reassignment surgery. Those standards require the candidate to undergo at least six months of psychological evaluation, to undergo a full year of hormonal therapy which allows the candidate to develop the secondary sexual characteristics of the opposite gender, and to undergo the "real life test" which requires the candidate to dress and act as a member of the opposite gender. According to Dr. Pauly, the length and depth of these tests permit the medical professionals evaluating the candidate to determine if he is psychologically prepared to live the remainder of his life as a member of the other gender. The testing also permits the candidate to decide whether he wants to go through the sex reassignment surgery. When the father completed the evaluation phase, Dr. Frazier decided that he was a proper candidate for the surgical phase of the treatment. The surgery was then performed.

In 1981, after having been evaluated as a legitimate candidate[2] for sex reassignment surgery, the father revealed to his daughter that he had been diagnosed as a transsexual, and that his doctors had advised him to undergo sex reassignment therapy. Seeking to prepare her, he discussed with Mary what transsexuality is and what was going to happen to him. Mary, a bright child, apparently developed a reasonable understanding of what he explained to her. Before Mary returned to her mother, the father asked her to keep information secret from her mother; for he believed, correctly as matters turned out, that the mother would seek to use the information against him.

In February of 1982, Mary informed her mother that her father was a transsexual. Upon hearing this disclosure, the mother claimed to be worried about Mary's condition. After Mary had returned from her visit to Tim during the summer of 1981, the mother, in hindsight, thought that Mary had been quieter than normal. However, prior to the disclosure, it appears the mother had no special concerns over Mary's behavior. In addition, a neighbor and school teacher, both of whom knew Mary, did not notice any particular problems with Mary during this period either.

To resolve her concerns, the mother consulted a lawyer and had Mary visit a psychologist. As a result of these discussions, the mother unilaterally decided to deny the father visitation privileges, in violation of the divorce decree. Soon after the mother had made that decision, the father attempted to visit Mary in Reno. However, the mother, using the pretext of a nonexistent court order, had two sheriff's deputies intercept and deter the father before he was able to visit with Mary. Then, in August of 1982, the mother refused to pick up the father's birthday present for Mary at the post office. She also requested him to not telephone their residence.

Once again, in January of 1983, the father was barred from contacting Mary based upon the mother's assertion of another nonexistent court order. Later that day, he attempted to visit Mary at home; however, he was deterred by Mary's gun-wielding grandmother, who would not permit him to enter the premises.

After this incident, the mother sought and received a restraining order prohibiting the father from contacting Mary. She then initiated the instant proceedings to terminate his parental rights. At the termination hearing, both parties testified. Expert testimony was also provided on transsexuality, on the father's medical treatment for transsexuality, and on Mary's psychological condition.

---

2. Dr. Pauly stated, for example, that homosexuals are not appropriate candidates for sex reassignment surgery because, unlike a transsexual who does not accept his biological gender, a homosexual accepts his biological gender and thus does not require this surgery.

The district court then terminated the father's parental rights. In reaching its decision, the district court basically concluded that Mary would be better off if she did not visit him. The court reached this conclusion based upon its evaluation of the father's emotional stability and upon the potential influence of his friends on Mary. The district court also noted that his "selfishness" did not serve Mary's interests. In addition, the district court found that he had failed to support Mary.

II

[I] turn . . . to consider application of the *Champagne* test to the district court's order.

A

The district court identified several jurisdictional grounds. First, the district court noted that the father had abandoned Mary because of a lack of support and communication over a period of six months or longer. The mother, however, played an instrumental role in inhibiting contacts with Mary, and manipulated sheriff's deputies and school officials to obstruct attempted visits. Considering these facts and others, we cannot properly ignore the obstacles the mother placed in the father's way.[4] *See In re Adoption of Doe,* 677 P.2d 1070, 1074, *cert. denied,* 677 P.2d 624 (N.M. 1984). Despite such barriers, the father continued to maintain medical insurance for Mary. Unlike the case of *Pyborn v. Quathamer,* where no "real attempt" to communicate or to support the child occurred, 605 P.2d 1147 (Nev. 1980), he attempted to visit Mary, attempted to communicate with Mary, and did help support Mary. There is thus no clear and convincing showing of a conscious abandonment of Mary. Therefore, this jurisdictional ground fails.

The district court also found that Mary faced a risk of serious physical, emotional or mental injury *if the father exercises any parental rights*. However, without the exercise of visitation rights, which he is voluntarily foregoing, such injury admittedly cannot occur. Thus, this jurisdictional ground fails also.

Finally, the district court found that the father's selfishness, his unrealistic thinking about Mary, and his lifestyle adversely affect his ability to be a parent. Because he does not ask to exercise visitation rights, however, these considerations do not currently affect Mary's life. Therefore, the jurisdictional grounds invoked by the district court fail to provide an adequate basis to terminate the father's parental rights.

B

The district court also found several categories of dispositional grounds. The district court noted that Mary should not be around someone with a gender identity

---

4. We further note that the father was attempting to regain visitation rights during this same period; he was hindered by counsel who evidently did not expeditiously aid his cause. Where a parent attempts through an attorney to regain his rights, we obviously should not hold that he has abandoned his child merely because of the seemingly ineffective assistance of counsel.

problem, should not be in an environment where she might confront sexual minorities, and does not presently wish to be with her father. Again, without visitation, none of these concerns have substance. Therefore, this first category of dispositional grounds fails to justify a termination of the father's parental rights.

The second category of dispositional grounds raised by the district court concerned Mary's anxieties over the dispute between her parents. Yet, no judicial resolution of the instant appeal can stop any hostilities that exist between the parties. With the father foregoing any contact with Mary, little else can be done to resolve Mary's anxieties. Thus, this dispositional ground fails to justify a termination of all parental rights.

Finally, the district court noted that Mary does not now desire to be with appellant and believes he is no longer her father. I recognize the importance of considering a child's views of her parents where the child can sufficiently articulate her desires. NRS 128.107(2). Still, we also should recognize the importance of not severing a parent's rights where a less restrictive alternative exists to permit preservation of a family tie. *E.g., In re Brooks,* 618 P.2d 814, 822 (Kan. 1980). While Mary may no longer have a father figure, she still has a second parent who desires to contribute to her financial support, and who might someday in the future provide her with needed comfort, affection, and help.

III

In conclusion, I reiterate that Mary and her father currently are totally separated, for he is willing to forego visitation rights at present, in order to maintain his legal status as Mary's parent. This separation protects Mary from all of the concerns, imagined or real, which underlay the district court's termination of parental rights.

A close reading of the majority opinion simply underscores this fundamental point. In attempting to justify the district court's ruling, the majority recite, *inter alia:* "The district court primarily focused upon the risk of serious physical, mental, or emotional injury to the child *if visitation were resumed and the child were forced to maintain contact with appellant.*" (Emphasis added.) The majority also state: "At trial Dr. Weiheir, respondent's expert witness who examined Mary, testified that there is a serious risk of emotional or mental injury to the child *if she were allowed to be in her father's presence.*" (Emphasis added.) Again, the majority point out: "Dr. Weiheir, however, had the opportunity to observe and interview Mary and determined the risk to Mary would exist *only if visitation were forced upon Mary.*" (Emphasis added.) The majority go on to assert: "Nevertheless, *if visitation were permitted,* there would be a risk of serious maladjustment, mental or emotional injury." (Emphasis added.) Hence, . . . the majority opinion is premised, not upon fact, but upon suppositions which are contrary to the facts and which ignore the appellant father's basic legal position.

As previously noted, the appellant father in this matter is a well educated person, long employed by one of this nation's eminent academic institutions. He served this country honorably in its armed forces, and, the record indicates, has never been known to violate any of our country's laws. Appellant fathered Mary Daly in wedlock, and, since divorce, has maintained an interest in her and has continued attempts to provide for her, even though the respondent has improperly impeded those legitimate efforts.

In psychological distress, the father has consulted legitimate and respected medical authorities. The advice given by those medical authorities may offend the religious precepts of many. In the ultimate judgment of history, such advice may well yet be condemned as quackery. Still, I respectfully submit that a court of law should not stigmatize an emotionally distressed person for following the advice of highly trained and licensed physicians, who are practicing medicine under government authority, and who possess the most exalted credentials their profession can bestow. Nor should any parent be stigmatized for attempting to forewarn a child concerning medical procedures the parent is about to undergo pursuant to such advice.

Recognizing that the medical procedures he has undergone currently occasion distress to her child, the father does not contend he should now be allowed visitation rights. Rather, he contends merely that he has done nothing to warrant severing his formal legal parental tie to Mary Daly, apparently hoping that the passage of time will restore in Mary a desire to know him. In the meantime, the father recognizes, he would have to accept the duty of contributing to Mary's support, while foregoing visitation with the child.

As I assess the record, the fact that the appellant father has suffered emotional problems which are foreign to the experience of this court's members, and has followed the possibly poor advice of eminent medical authorities in his attempt to relieve them, does not justify a total and irrevocable severance of appellant's formal legal tie to a child he obviously cares about and desires to help nurture. By holding that such a severance is justified in these facts, it seems to me, we are being unnecessarily and impermissibly punitive to the exercise of a medical option we personally find offensive, thereby depriving a child of a legal relationship which might well be to the child's advantage in the future.

SPRINGER, J., concurs.

Discussion

1. What language or assertions in the majority opinion might reflect bias against trans people? Does the majority opinion contain arguments that respond effectively to the dissent's contentions?

2. For a contrasting treatment of a question of the termination of a transgender person's parental rights, see *Pierre v. Pierre*, 898 So. 2d 419 (La. Ct. App. 2004). There, Lauraleigh Cefalu Pierre and transgender man Andrew R. Pierre divorced after Lauraleigh bore two children via assisted reproduction during their marriage. At their divorce Lauraleigh and Andrew stipulated to joint legal custody of their children, with Andrew having visitation rights with them. Subsequently,

after Lauraleigh's new boyfriend and eventual husband moved in with her and the children, Lauraleigh sought to have the divorce decree modified to grant her sole custody and terminate Andrew's visitation on the grounds that Andrew should be adjudged legally female and therefore unable to have married Lauraleigh. The district court found not credible Lauraleigh's conflicting testimony regarding her claim of ignorance of Andrew's reproductive history (he had had hormone therapy and surgery). Despite that and despite Andrew's legally changed birth certificate indicating his sex as male, the district judge nevertheless purported to terminate his parental rights but granted Andrew visitation rights as in the children's best interests, in accord with the recommendations of the court-appointed family therapist. Andrew's attorney failed timely to appeal the custody and parental rights rulings, but Lauraleigh appealed the visitation order. The court of appeal held that the district court had lacked jurisdiction over the parental rights termination and ruled, over one judge's dissent, that the trial judge had not abused his discretion in allowing Andrew continued visitation. (Along the way, the majority stated that "the court, legal counsel, and parties became "distracted by the issues surrounding sexual organs," rather than focusing on the best interests of the children as the appointed therapist's report had urged.)

3. Note that neither the majority nor the dissenting justices in *Daly v. Daly* address Suzanne Daly's argument that the trial court judge's termination of her parental rights violated *Palmore v. Sidoti*, 466 U.S. 429 (1984), rendered after the trial court ruled but before the state supreme court's decision. Since the dissent would have reversed the termination judgment on other grounds, its omission is not particularly significant. The majority, however, must reject all of Suzanne's arguments supporting reversal in order to uphold the trial court, yet substantively the majority simply ignores the argument after they note it in their opening paragraph. (The end of their opinion contains a conclusory labeling of Suzanne Daly's "remaining contentions" as "either lack[ing] merit or . . . not requir[ing] dismissal.") Consider the potential relevance of *Palmore*, next, in parenting disputes involving trans parents (and especially footnote 5 of the majority opinion).

Palmore v. Sidoti

466 U.S. 429 (1984)

Chief Justice BURGER delivered the opinion of the Court.

We granted certiorari to review a judgment of a state court divesting a natural mother of the custody of her infant child because of her remarriage to a person of a different race.

I

When petitioner Linda Sidoti Palmore and respondent Anthony J. Sidoti, both Caucasians, were divorced in May 1980 in Florida, the mother was awarded custody of their 3-year-old daughter.

In September 1981 the father sought custody of the child by filing a petition to modify the prior judgment because of changed conditions. The change was that the child's mother was then cohabiting with a Negro, Clarence Palmore, Jr., whom she married two months later. Additionally, the father made several allegations of instances in which the mother had not properly cared for the child.

After hearing testimony from both parties and considering a court counselor's investigative report, the court noted that the father had made allegations about the child's care, but the court made no findings with respect to these allegations. On the contrary, the court made a finding that "there is no issue as to either party's devotion to the child, adequacy of housing facilities, or respectability of the new spouse of either parent."

The court then addressed the recommendations of the court counselor, who had made an earlier report "in [another] case coming out of this circuit also involving the social consequences of an interracial marriage. *Niles v. Niles*, 299 So. 2d 162 (Fla. 1974)." From this vague reference to that earlier case, the court turned to the present case and noted the counselor's recommendation for a change in custody because "[t]he wife [petitioner] has chosen for herself and for her child, a life-style unacceptable to the father *and to society*. . . . The child . . . is, or at school age will be, subject to environmental pressures not of choice." (emphasis added).

The court then concluded that the best interests of the child would be served by awarding custody to the father. The court's rationale is contained in the following:

> "The father's evident resentment of the mother's choice of a black partner is not sufficient to wrest custody from the mother. It is of some significance, however, that the mother did see fit to bring a man into her home and carry on a sexual relationship with him without being married to him. Such action tended to place gratification of her own desires ahead of her concern for the child's future welfare. *This Court feels that despite the strides that have been made in bettering relations between the races in this country, it is inevitable that Melanie will, if allowed to remain in her present situation and attains school age and thus more vulnerable to peer pressures, suffer from the social stigmatization that is sure to come.*" (emphasis added).

The Second District Court of Appeal affirmed without opinion, thus denying the Florida Supreme Court jurisdiction to review the case. We granted certiorari, and we reverse.

II

[The state] court's opinion, after stating that the "father's evident resentment of the mother's choice of a black partner is not sufficient" to deprive her of custody, then turns to what it regarded as the damaging impact on the child from remaining in a racially mixed household. This raises important federal concerns arising from the Constitution's commitment to eradicating discrimination based on race.

The Florida court did not focus directly on the parental qualifications of the natural mother or her present husband, or indeed on the father's qualifications to have custody of the child. The court found that "there is no issue as to either party's devotion to the child, adequacy of housing facilities, or respectability of the new spouse of either parent." This, taken with the absence of any negative finding as to the quality of the care provided by the mother, constitutes a rejection of any claim of petitioner's unfitness to continue the custody of her child.

The court correctly stated that the child's welfare was the controlling factor. But that court was entirely candid and made no effort to place its holding on any ground other than race. Taking the court's findings and rationale at face value, it is clear that the outcome would have been different had petitioner married a Caucasian male of similar respectability.

A core purpose of the Fourteenth Amendment was to do away with all governmentally imposed discrimination based on race. *See Strauder v. West Virginia*, 100 U.S. 303 (1880). Classifying persons according to their race is more likely to reflect racial prejudice than legitimate public concerns; the race, not the person, dictates the category. See *Personnel Administrator of Mass. v. Feeney*, 442 U.S. 256 (1979). Such classifications are subject to the most exacting scrutiny; to pass constitutional muster, they must be justified by a compelling governmental interest and must be "necessary . . . to the accomplishment" of their legitimate purpose, *McLaughlin v. Florida*, 379 U.S. 184 (1964). See *Loving v. Virginia*, 388 U.S. 1 (1967).

The State, of course, has a duty of the highest order to protect the interests of minor children, particularly those of tender years. In common with most states, Florida law mandates that custody determinations be made in the best interests of the children involved. The goal of granting custody based on the best interests of the child is indisputably a substantial governmental interest for purposes of the Equal Protection Clause.

It would ignore reality to suggest that racial and ethnic prejudices do not exist or that all manifestations of those prejudices have been eliminated. There is a risk that a child living with a stepparent of a different race may be subject to a variety of pressures and stresses not present if the child were living with parents of the same racial or ethnic origin.

The question, however, is whether the reality of private biases and the possible injury they might inflict are permissible considerations for removal of an infant child from the custody of its natural mother. We have little difficulty concluding that they are not. The Constitution cannot control such prejudices but neither can it tolerate them. Private biases may be outside the reach of the law, but the law cannot, directly or indirectly, give them effect. "Public officials sworn to uphold the Constitution may not avoid a constitutional duty by bowing to the hypothetical effects of private racial prejudice that they assume to be both widely and deeply held." *Palmer v. Thompson*, 403 U.S. 217 (1971) (White, J., dissenting).

This is by no means the first time that acknowledged racial prejudice has been invoked to justify racial classifications. In *Buchanan v. Warley*, 245 U.S. 60 (1917), for example, this Court invalidated a Kentucky law forbidding Negroes to buy homes in white neighborhoods. "It is urged that this proposed segregation will promote the public peace by preventing race conflicts. Desirable as this is, and important as is the preservation of the public peace, this aim cannot be accomplished by laws or ordinances which deny rights created or protected by the Federal Constitution." *Id.* Whatever problems racially mixed households may pose for children in 1984 can no more support a denial of constitutional rights than could the stresses that residential integration was thought to entail in 1917. The effects of racial prejudice, however real, cannot justify a racial classification removing an infant child from the custody of its natural mother found to be an appropriate person to have such custody.

The judgment of the District Court of Appeal is reversed.

It is so ordered.

Discussion

1. Note that *Palmore* recites but does not simply apply the standard analysis of strict scrutiny. The Court does not hold that protecting children's best interests fails to count as a compelling governmental interest; it does not hold that there were less discriminatory means to protect the child Melanie from the harms flowing from social disapproval of her mother's interracial relationship. *Palmore* instead announces what philosophers might term a side constraint, a separate restriction on race-based governmental action: namely, regardless of the importance of the government's purpose or the narrowness of its use of race, governments may not respond to racial prejudices in ways that give them effect: "Private biases may be outside the reach of the law, but the law cannot, directly or indirectly, give them effect." *Accord* David B. Cruz, *The Sexual Freedom Cases: Contraception, Abortion, Abstinece, and the Constitution*, 35 Harv. C.R.-C.L. L. Rev. 299, 379–80 (2000); Richard D. Mohr, Gays/Justice 207–08 (1988).

2. This "*Palmore* principle" is not limited to types of discrimination or classification subject to strict scrutiny or even intermediate scrutiny under the constitutional guarantee of equal protection of the laws. The year after *Palmore*, a majority of the Supreme Court held in *Cleburne v. Cleburne Living Center, Inc.*, 473 U.S. 432 (1985), that discrimination on the basis of intellectual and developmental disability (which it then called "mental retardation") was subject only to rational basis review. Nevertheless, the *Cleburne* Court rejected the city's attempt to justify the special procedural burdens it placed on the proposed group home by reference to the negative attitudes of nearby property owners or school children toward people with such disabilities, quoting *Palmore*'s command that "[p]rivate biases may be outside the reach of the law, but the law cannot, directly or indirectly, give them effect." *Id.* at 448 (quoting *Palmore* at 433).

3. LGBT litigants have relied on *Palmore*, with mixed success. *Compare In re Marriage of Tipsword*, No. 1 CA-CV 12-0066, 2013 WL 1320444 (Ariz. Ct. App. Apr. 2, 2013) (citing *Palmore* to support irrelevance of societal prejudice against parent who was transgender woman in custody and visitation determinations); *Maxwell v. Maxwell*, 382 S.W.3d 892, 898–99 (Ky. Ct. App. 2012) (applying *Palmore* principle in custody proceedings to preclude use of prospect of private sexual orientation discrimination against mother with lesbian partner); *In re Marriage of Black*, 392 P.3d 1041 (Wash. 2017) (invoking *Palmore* to reject fear of bullying of children of lesbian mother divorcing her husband as basis for treating mother's sexual orientation as a negative factor in determining parenting plan), *with Lofton v. Secretary of Dept. of Children & Fam. Servs.*, 358 F.3d 804 (11th Cir. 2004) (ignoring plaintiffs' *Palmore* argument and upholding ban on same-sex couples adopting); *S.E.G. v. R.A.G.*, 735 S.W.2d 164 (Mo. Ct. App. 1987) (expressly relying on possibility of private anti-lesbigay prejudice in custody and visitation dispute involving lesbian mother and distinguishing *Palmore* as a strict scrutiny case albeit without so much as citing *Cleburne*). Should judicial reliance on a child's embarrassment, discomfiture, or fear about her friend's reactions to her transgender parent count as "giving effect to private prejudice" and hence be judged unconstitutional? *Cf. Daly v. Daly*, *supra* at p. 462 (sustaining termination of parental rights in part on such grounds without engaging with transgender parent's *Palmore* argument).

Reading Guide for M.B. v. D.W.

1. On what ground did the trial court decision reviewed here in *M.B. v. D.W.* base its termination of the transgender appellant's parental rights?

2. How does the appellate court deal with the appellant's objection that the trial court did not consider whether the best interests of appellant's daughter might be served by means less drastic than termination of parental rights?

M.B. Formerly M.B. v. D.W, B.W., and M.B., A Minor

236 S.W.3d 31 (Ky. Ct. App. 2007)

Before ACREE, HOWARD, and LAMBERT, Judges.

HOWARD, Judge.

This appeal is from a judgment of the Hardin Circuit Court granting the petition for adoption of the minor appellee, M.B., by her stepfather, D.W., without the consent of her biological father, the appellant, M.B (hereinafter the appellant). The appellant has undergone gender reassignment surgery and now lives as a woman. . . .

The appellant and the appellee, B.W., were married in June 1974 and three children were born of the marriage. The appellant and B.W. separated in 1997 and their marriage was dissolved [in] 1998. [They] agreed to joint custody of the two children who were not emancipated. B.W. was to provide the children's primary residence and the appellant received liberal visitation. The appellant was to pay $600 monthly for child support until certain specified real estate was sold. The agreement stated that the appellant's responsibility for "child support shall cease in lieu of the mortgage on the marital residence being paid off with proceeds from the sale of the acreage." The appellant was to provide health insurance for the two minor children until B.W. was eligible for insurance, at which time the appellant was to reimburse B.W. monthly for the insurance. Responsibility for uninsured medical expenses was to be divided equally between the appellant and B.W.

The appellees have not alleged that the appellant failed to satisfy any of the child support obligations. However, the record reflects that the appellant did fail to reimburse B.W. for any health insurance premiums or to pay his half of the medical expenses which were not covered by insurance. . . .

During the marriage the appellant cross-dressed with B.W.'s knowledge, but described this as merely a "fetish" and concealed the behavior from the children. After the divorce the appellant moved to Florida and ultimately began a medical gender reassignment procedure. The children visited with the appellant during the holidays in December 1998 and January 1999, and they noticed at that time that the appellant exhibited various feminine features. The appellant testified that all three of the children called after this visitation and said that they did not want to see the appellant again. M.B., who was nine years old at the time, did not see the appellant again until she testified in the present proceeding, at age fifteen.[1] The appellant underwent gender reassignment surgery in December of 1999.

In 2001 the appellant filed a motion . . . to enforce visitation rights with M.B., the only child not by then emancipated. However, M.B. still did not want to see the appellant, and was by this time in psychological counseling. In October 2001, the Jefferson Family Court entered an order restricting the appellant's contact with M.B. unless approved by M.B.'s guardian ad litem. By order entered on August 7, 2002, the Jefferson Family Court directed that the appellant have no contact with M.B. pending further orders of that court.

On December 15, 2003, B.W., her husband, D.W., and M.B. jointly filed in the Hardin Circuit Court a petition for adoption, without the consent of the appellant. Following an extensive hearing, the circuit court . . . granted the petition. . . .

An adoption without the consent of a living biological parent is, in effect, a proceeding to terminate that parent's parental rights. KRS 625.090 provides that parental rights may be involuntarily terminated only if, based on clear and convincing evidence, a circuit court finds: (1) that the child is abused or neglected as defined in KRS 600.020(1); (2) that termination is in the child's best interests; and (3) the

---

1. It has been pointed out to us that M.B. is now 18 and emancipated. We have been urged to hold that this matter is therefore moot. We do not believe it is moot because of the potential inheritance ramifications. However, we do note that any contact between M.B. and the appellant will now be an entirely voluntary matter between the two of them as adults, and neither the termination of the appellant's parental rights nor the refusal of the court to terminate those rights would have any effect on whether or not they choose to reestablish or maintain an ongoing relationship.

existence of one or more of ten specific grounds set out in KRS 625.090(2). These grounds include the following:

> (c) That the parent has continuously or repeatedly inflicted or allowed to be inflicted upon the child, by other than accidental means, physical injury or emotional harm. . . .
>
> . . . .
>
> (g) That the parent, for reasons other than poverty alone, has continuously or repeatedly failed to provide or is incapable of providing essential food, clothing, shelter, medical care, or education reasonably necessary and available for the child's well-being and that there is no reasonable expectation of significant improvement in the parent's conduct in the immediately foreseeable future, considering the age of the child. . . .

We begin our analysis of this case with the proposition that parental rights are "essential" and "basic" civil rights, "far more precious . . . than property rights." *Stanley v. Illinois*, 405 U.S. 645, 651 (1972). Parental rights cannot be terminated easily—"clear and convincing" evidence is required—and we believe the requirements of KRS 625.090 should be vigorously enforced.

However, this Court has also stated,

> The trial court has a great deal of discretion in determining whether the child fits within the abused or neglected category and whether the abuse or neglect warrants termination. . . . This Court's standard of review in a termination of parental rights action is confined to the clearly erroneous standard in CR 52.01 based upon clear and convincing evidence, and the findings of the trial court will not be disturbed unless there exists no substantial evidence in the record to support its findings. . . .
>
> . . . .
>
> [Substantial] evidence supports the circuit court's decision and it must therefore be affirmed.
>
> . . . .

The circuit court found that M.B. suffered emotional harm, that she "suffered an injury to her mental or psychological capacity or emotional stability as demonstrated by her ability to function within a normal range of performance and behavior." See KRS 600.020(24). Specifically, the court found that M.B. "suffered major depression, suicidal ideation, decline in school performance, physical symptoms of stomach pain and headaches and withdrawn behavior." The trial court further found that the appellant's behavior caused this injury. The appellant's actions, as found by the court, included exhibiting "physical changes in [the appellant's] appearance" when the children visited in Florida, such as long finger nails, "wearing tight shirts and short shorts (with shaved legs and arms) and breast augmentation," without any warning to prepare M.B. or the others for those changes; sending a letter to M.B.'s sister with a photograph of the appellant as a female and traveling to

Kentucky from Florida dressed as a woman and demanding visitation with M.B., knowing that M.B. did not want to see the appellant.

[Dr.] Charles K. Embry, a psychiatrist who treated M.B. after she discovered that her biological father underwent a gender reassignment, testified that M.B. became depressed over the appellant's sex change and that M.B.'s suicide ideation, decline in school performance and associated physical symptoms were related to the emotional injury occasioned by the appellant's actions.

M.B. herself testified poignantly and persuasively concerning the emotional distress the appellant's behavior caused her. She stated that she felt "abandoned," and that the worst part was "knowing that I did not have a father, where you go to school and say, 'I don't have a father, he's a woman.'" M.B.'s brother and mother also testified at length about the detrimental effects on M.B. brought about by the appellant's actions.

[The] circuit court did not find that the appellant's undergoing gender reassignment, by itself, inflicted M.B.'s emotional injury and justified termination of the appellant's parental rights. Rather, the court found that the entire series of events, including the appellant's behavior surrounding the sex change, caused the emotional injury. It is clear that M.B., as well as her two siblings, were not adequately prepared for the appellant's gender reassignment. Although one professional opined that the entire family mishandled informing and supporting M.B., we cannot say that the circuit court erred in holding the appellant primarily responsible for M.B.'s emotional injury. As the trial court accurately summarized the testimony,

> [The appellant] had no conversations with [B.W., the mother] to prepare the children for changes they observed during the Christmas, 1998 visit, and when [the appellant] telephoned [B.W.] in the summer of 2000, [the appellant] did not inform [B.W.] even then that [the appellant] had undergone a sex change, an omission manifesting at best an unconscionable indifference to the emotional welfare of other persons in [the appellant's] family in general and [M.B.] (then approximately eleven [11] years of age) in particular.

The circuit court's finding that the appellant continuously or repeatedly inflicted emotional harm on M.B. is supported by substantial evidence and therefore is not clearly erroneous.

The circuit court also found that the appellant failed to financially support M.B. [The] appellant did not reimburse B.W. for [the cost of M.B.'s health insurance and for half of her uninsured medical expenses], and that on only one occasion, in 1999, did the appellant even ask B.W. about the health insurance and medical expenses. [The] circuit court's finding that the appellant continuously or repeatedly failed to financially support M.B., as to her medical needs, is supported by substantial evidence and is not clearly erroneous.

The same evidence cited above regarding emotional harm supports the circuit court's finding that M.B. was neglected. KRS 600.020(1) defines an "[a]bused or neglected child" as, a child whose health or welfare is harmed or threatened with harm when his parent . . .

> (a) Inflicts or allows to be inflicted upon the child physical or emotional injury as defined in this section by other than accidental means. . . .

KRS 600.020(24) defines "emotional injury" as follows:

> "Emotional injury" means an injury to the mental or psychological capacity or emotional stability of a child as evidenced by a substantial and observable impairment in the child's ability to function within a normal range of performance and behavior with due regard to his age, development, culture, and environment as testified to by a qualified mental health professional[.]

[The] trial court expressly found that such an emotional injury occurred, closely echoing the statutory language. The circuit court's finding that M.B. was neglected by being inflicted with emotional injury is supported by substantial evidence and is not clearly erroneous.

The appellant argues that terminating the appellant's parental rights and allowing M.B. to be adopted by D.W. was not in M.B.'s best interests. The trial court found in this regard as follows:

> [The appellant] further acknowledges that her life and friends are different now from when she was [the appellant's former name], and, of even greater significance, [the appellant] acknowledges that the voluntary decision to undergo the sex change surgery was about doing what was good for [the appellant] in [the appellant's] own self-centered interest and not about what was good for, or otherwise in the best interest of, the parties' children, including [M.B.].

The appellant acknowledged knowing in advance that having a sex change would not be good for the children. Furthermore, the appellant's expert witness, Dr. Marilyn Volker, acknowledged that some children can accept transgendered parents and some cannot. She conceded that some children want their parent's parental rights terminated in this situation and that it is important for the transgendered parent to respect and honor the child's clear decision, or they will do more harm to the relationship. She felt that the ultimate decision to terminate parental rights or not should be made in the child's best interests.

M.B. testified at length and was very clear about her desire to be adopted by her stepfather. She stated that it was her decision to seek this adoption, and that, "I want to be able to have a father in my life, a legal father. I don't have that with my biological father and I don't want it with my biological father." As to D.W., her stepfather, she stated that if the adoption was granted, "I will be able to call him my real father. . . ." Likewise, M.B.'s mother, stepfather, brother and Dr. Embry all testified to the extent of her emotional injury occasioned by the appellant's actions and the benefits to M.B. of the adoption.[2] The circuit court's finding, that the termination of the appellant's parental rights and the granting of the adoption is in M.B.'s best interests, is clearly supported by substantial evidence and therefore is not clearly erroneous.

The appellant has also argued that there were other measures, less drastic than termination, which might have been effective in protecting the best interests of M.B. This court has held that a trial court should consider any such less drastic measures. However, it does not appear from the record that the appellant ever raised this issue in the trial court. [Pursuant] to CR 52.04,

> A final judgment shall not be reversed or remanded because of the failure of the trial court to make a finding of fact on an issue essential to the judgment unless such failure is brought to the attention of the trial court by a written request for a finding on that issue or by a motion pursuant to Rule 52.02.

Furthermore, we believe that the circuit court did make an implied finding in its discussion of M.B.'s best interests, that no remedy less drastic than termination would be sufficient to protect those interests. In this situation, where the emotional harm to M.B. was closely related to her feeling that she was abandoned by her father and her need to have a father figure in her life, we could not say that such a finding would be unsupported by the record.

[We] have been cited, and have been able to find, only one . . . case [dealing with termination of parental rights in a situation involving gender reassignment] from any . . . jurisdiction. In *Daly v. Daly*, 715 P.2d 56 (Nev. 1986) [*supra* at p. 462 — Eds.], the Nevada Supreme Court affirmed the termination of the parental rights of a biological father who had undergone gender reassignment surgery [and] affirmed the trial court's finding that the termination was in the child's best interests.

Although it did not involve termination, in *J.L.S. v. D.K.S.*, 943 S.W.2d 766 (Mo. Ct. App. E.D. 1997), the Missouri Court of Appeals affirmed an order temporarily prohibiting visitation and reversed an award of joint custody, based on the best interests of the children, where the biological father had undergone gender reassignment and there was substantial evidence that such had caused emotional harm to the children.

We do not . . . hold that a parent's undergoing gender reassignment is, in itself, grounds for [parental rights] termination. [However,] when the trial court has otherwise determined that the requirements of KRS 625.090 have been satisfied and that termination is in the child's best interests, we do not believe that a parent is exempt from having his rights terminated, or that his neglect or abuse of the child, leading to the termination, should be excused because that neglect or abuse

---

2. [The] Kentucky Cabinet for Health and Family Services filed a confidential report in this case, as they are required to do by KRS 199.510, and that report also recommended that the court approve the adoption, as being in M.B.'s best interests.

occurred in the process of his obtaining a gender reassignment. [The] circuit court's findings, which the court expressly stated were based on clear and convincing evidence . . . are supported by substantial evidence, and are not clearly erroneous.

. . . .

The judgment of the Hardin Circuit Court is affirmed.

ALL CONCUR.

Discussion

1. Although nominally adhering to the clear and convincing evidence standard for trial court terminations of parental rights, the court in *M. B.* insists that appellate review is limited to whether there was some (versus no) substantial evidence supporting the trial court determination. Is that constrained appellate review consistent with the heightened evidentiary standard, *i.e.*, clear and convincing evidence, that the Supreme Court requires for such decisions?

2. When parents transition and their children object to that transition (and/or views her father, for example, as no longer her father following a gender transition), should a judicial decision terminating parental rights be understood as giving effect to private prejudice and hence impermissible under *Palmore v. Sidoti* (*supra* at p. 472)?

Reading Guide for Note on In the Matter of M (Children)

The following note addresses a decision from the Court of Appeal of England and Wales that rejects a trial judge order denying any in-person visitation ("direct contact," as distinguished from, for example, telephone calls) of a transgender woman and her children. Does it better advance the *Palmore* principle (*see Palmore v. Sidoti*, *supra* at p. 472) than one or more of the U.S. decisions presented above? Does it adequately protect the children from harms that ought to be regarded seriously?

Note on In the Matter of M (Children)

The Court of Appeal of England and Wales considered a dispute between two parents, one of whom was transgender, in *In the Matter of M (Children)*, [2017] EWCA Civ 2164 (Dec. 20, 2017). J and B were a married couple who had five children together while J was presenting as a man. After the couple separated and J transitioned to live consistently with her gender identity as a woman, the children lived with their birth mother B. Subsequently, in a dispute over J's visitation rights, a family court judge denied direct contact between J and her children. On J's appeal, the Court of Appeal vacated the lower court's judgment and indicated that under English family law personal prejudices are an inappropriate basis for family law determinations even if the basis for such beliefs or attitudes was shared religion.

With the parents' agreement, the family lived in what was described as an ultra-Orthodox Jewish community in North Manchester, England, where the children grew up and reached ages 3 to 13 at the time of the Court of Appeal decision. The trial judge, Peter Jackson, had rejected the contention that J should have to live with the consequences of her transition because she had made "a lifestyle choice." Rather, he insisted, "[the] law . . . recognises the reality that one's true sexuality and gender are no more matters of choice than the colour of one's eyes or skin." He also rejected any significance of the notion "that transgenderism is a sin" because "[s]in is not valid legal currency. The currency of the law is the recognition, protection and balancing out of legal rights and obligations."

However, as Judge Jackson found and the Court of Appeal characterized it, "[b]ecause she is transgender — and for that reason alone — the father [J] is shunned by the North Manchester Charedi Jewish community (the community), and because she is transgender — and for that reason alone — the children face ostracism by the community if they have direct contact with her." Even though the trial judge found that "[t]he children will suffer serious harm if they are deprived of a relationship with [J]," Judge Jackson "reached the unwelcome conclusion that *the likelihood of the children and their mother being marginalised or excluded by the ultra-Orthodox community is so real, and the consequences so great, that this one factor, despite its many disadvantages, must prevail over the many advantages of [face-to-face] contact [with their transgender parent]* (emphasis added [by the Court of Appeal])."

The Court of Appeal accepted, despite recognizing conflicting testimony of differing rabbis, that the community's reaction was based on its members' religious beliefs. Nevertheless, the Court of Appeal recognized an obligation to decide this dispute between J and B "according to law, in this instance the law as laid down by Parliament in section 1(1)(a) of the Children Act 1989 . . . ." In pertinent part, that section articulates a paramountcy principle, namely, that "[w]hen a court determines any question with respect to . . . the upbringing of a child . . . the child's welfare shall be the court's paramount consideration."

The Court of Appeal reaffirmed that

> welfare is to be judged by reference to "the changing views, as the years go by, of reasonable men and women, the parents of children, on the proper treatment and methods of bringing up children"; and the task of the judge is to "act as the judicial reasonable parent." Section 1 of the 1989 Act is an "always speaking" statute. . . . What this means is that a child's welfare is to be judged today by the standards of reasonable men and women in 2017, not by the standards of their parents, grandparents or great-grand parents in 1989, 1971, 1925 or 1902. And fundamental to this is the need to have regard to the ever changing nature of our world: changes in our understanding of the natural world, technological changes, changes in social standards and, crucially for present purposes, *changes in social attitudes. . . .*

And, the Court continued, "[t]he fact is, as the daily business of the Family Division so vividly demonstrates, that we live today in a world where the family takes many forms and where surrogacy, IVF, same-sex relationships, same-sex marriage and transgenderism, for example, are no longer treated as they were in even the quite recent past." The court concluded that J was correct that Judge Jackson "ultimately lost sight of the paramountcy principle."

The Court of Appeal also reaffirmed that

> [if] the reasonable man or woman is receptive to change he or she is also broadminded, tolerant, easy-going and slow to condemn. We live, or strive to live, in a tolerant society increasingly alive to the need to guard against the tyranny which majority opinion may impose on those who, for whatever reason, comprise a small, weak, unpopular or voiceless minority. Equality under the law, human rights and the protection of minorities, particularly small minorities, have to be more than . . . "the incantations of legal rhetoric."

After reiterating that the ultra-Orthodox community's social shunning of the transgender parent's children would be harmful to those children, the Court of Appeal observed that:

> It will come as no surprise that there is a limit to freedom of religion where it involves significant physical harm to any person. In the light of our increased understanding in the twenty-first century about the psychological effects of others' behaviour, it ought equally to come as no surprise that there may equally be limits where that behaviour results in psychological harm to children.

The Court of Appeal faulted Judge Jackson for not acting cautiously enough after concluding that barring contact between J and her children would harm the children. The Court believed the judge should have asked himself, among other questions:

> Should I not directly and explicitly challenge the parents and the community with the possibility that, absent a real change of attitude on their part, the court may have to consider drastic steps such as removing the children from the mother's care, making the children wards of court, or even removing the children into public care? . . . . [How] can [the ban on direct contact] meet even the medium let alone the long-term needs and interests of the children? How can this order give proper effect to the reality, whether the community likes it or not, that the father, whether transgender or not, is and always will be the children's father and, as such, inescapably part of their lives, now, tomorrow and as long as they live? . . . .

The Court of Appeal remanded the case for reconsideration by a different family court judge for a hearing, consistent with the court's opinion but whose precise scope would be determined by that judge. But to assist the judge on remand, the Court of Appeal also addressed what it took to be relevant equality and European Convention of Human Rights ("Convention") law.

Article 14 of the Convention forbids discrimination with respect to Convention rights on various grounds, and the European Court of Human Rights has interpreted those to include sexual orientation discrimination and discrimination on the ground of transgender status. The Court of Appeal here pointedly remarked that "[w]hen the present case returns to the family court we anticipate that the court will wish to scrutinise with care the suggested justification for the apparent discrimination which the father faces on the ground of her transgender status, not least to ensure that the court itself does not breach its duty under section 6 of the [Human Rights Act,]" which requires the judiciary to comply with the Convention. Part of the expected analysis, it appeared from the court's discussion, would be to ensure that the family court judge on remand did not justify discrimination against the transgender parent based "not on objective factors . . . but on the subjective, negative attitudes of other[s]." The Court of Appeal observed that, on remand, "[in] directing contact with children, it would be open to a court to make an order, even if its implementation does not fully respect the religious beliefs, practices, and observances of the community of which the children are members, if those beliefs, practices, and observance were found not to be consistent with the values of the democratic society in this jurisdiction."

Chapter 9

Immigration by and Asylum for Transgender Persons

As difficult as life is for too many trans people in the United States, in part due to violence up to and including murder, *see, e.g.,* Human Rights Campaign, *Violence Against the Transgender Community in 2019*, https://www.hrc.org/resources /violence-against-the-transgender-community-in-2019, the rest of the globe is no haven. Even Europe, exemplar of the global/developed North/West, often noted for its respect for human rights, is blighted by the treatment of trans people there. A 2009 issue paper of the Commissioner for Human Rights of the Council of Europe detailed extensive rights violations, concluding that "[t]ransgender people experience a high degree of discrimination, intolerance, and outright violence. Their basic human rights are violated, including the right to life, the right to physical integrity, and the right to health." Thomas Hammarberg, *Human Rights and Gender Identity*, CommDH/Issue Paper (2009), https://rm.coe.int/16806da753. Circumstances in other parts of the world can be even more dire, leading one pair of scholars to conclude that "[anti-transgender] violence is not just an epidemic confined to the United States. It is, in fact, a *pandemic* which spans the globe, cutting across continents, cultures, and languages." Jeremy D. Kidd & Tarynn M. Witten, *Transgender and Transsexual Identities: The Next Strange Fruit—Hate Crimes, Violence and Genocide Against the Global Trans-Communities*, 6 J. HATE STUDIES 31, 44 (2007).

Thus, the United States can be a preferable location for some trans people in the world. As is the norm for nations, however, the United States does not simply allow within its borders anyone who wishes to come, nor simply allow everyone it admits to stay as long as they wish. U.S. immigration law requires visas for some people to enter the country, excludes some people entirely, limits durations of visits, and limits who may become "lawful permanent residents" with the possibility of naturalizing to become U.S. citizens. Exceptions to the usual statutory immigration limits, however, apply for non-citizens entitled to asylum under U.S. law implementing treaty obligations.

The 1967 Protocol Relating to the Status of Refugees expands upon the 1951 United Nations Convention Relating to the Status of Refugees. They (somewhat vaguely) define who counts as a refugee and ensure a right of non-refoulement, which bars signatory nations like the United States from returning refugees to their home countries under certain conditions. The United States has implemented the non-refoulement obligation at 8 U.S.C. § 1231(b)(3), labeling relief under this obligation as "withholding of removal." Refugees apply for entry into the United States through overseas applications made via the U.S. refugee resettlement program. Refugee applicants may be entitled to withholding if they are more likely than not to face persecution in their home country due to race, religion, nationality, membership in a particular social group, or political opinion.

The United States makes a distinction between applying for withholding of removal and applying for asylum. Asylum applications are generally made at the U.S. border or within the United States. Asylum applicants may be entitled to protection if they face "persecution or a well-founded fear of persecution on account of race, religion, nationality, membership in a particular social group, or political opinion." 8 U.S.C. § 1101(a)(42)(A). (Note the absence of "sex" from this list, an omission which limits the utility here of the Supreme Court's recent ruling that discrimination because a person is transgender is, at least for Title VII of the Civil Rights Act of 1964, a form of discrimination based on sex, *Bostock v. Clayton County, Georgia*, 140 S. Ct. 1731 (2020), Chapter 5, Section D, *supra*.) This legal test has an appreciably lower standard of proof than the test for withholding of removal; the Supreme Court has interpreted it to require something less than a preponderance of the evidence, *see I.N.S. v. Cardozo-Fonseca*, 480 U.S. 421 (1987), and lower courts have interpreted it to mean whether a reasonable person would be in fear of persecution, *see, e.g., Mamouzian v. Ashcroft*, 390 F.3d 1129 (9th Cir. 2004). Granting asylum to an applicant who meets this test is discretionary, while granting withholding of removal to an eligible applicant is mandatory. For examination of how federal regulations allow asylum applicants to prove a well-founded fear of persecution by showing a "pattern or practice" of persecution in their home country against groups of people to which the applicants belong, see Aaron Sussman, *Expanding Asylum Law's Pattern-or-Practice-of-Persecution Framework to Better Protect LGBT Refugees*, 16 U. Pa. J.L. & Soc. Change 111 (2013).

In addition, asylum and withholding both have mandatory bars to eligibility, but they are defined somewhat differently depending on the context; the mandatory bars can be found at 8 U.S.C. § 1158(b)(2)(A)-(B) for asylum and at 8 U.S.C. § 1231(b)(3)(B) for withholding. Both the asylum and withholding procedures have mandatory bars for applicants who have been convicted of a "particularly serious crime." Even then, though, the Convention Against Torture ("CAT"), to which the United States is a party, as implemented by statute and regulation, prohibits the United States from deporting unauthorized non-citizens who more likely than not would be tortured by, at the instigation of, or with the consent or acquiescence of public officials. 8 C.F.R. § 1208.16-.18. The bars to withholding of removal, however, still apply to CAT applications; if a bar is triggered and CAT eligibility is found, then regulations authorize continued detention of the individual if the individual is determined to be a risk to national security or a danger to the public.

Trans people fleeing to the United States to escape oppression in their home countries thus may seek to show that they would face persecution on grounds of their membership in a particular social group or would face torture if returned to their home countries. Virtually all asylum applications, withholding applications, and CAT applications are made as defensive applications in front of immigration judges during removal proceedings. If the government denies them protection and they are determined not to be CAT-eligible, they may be deported.

Reading Guide for Miranda v. INS

1. Suspensions or cancellations of deportations are discretionary forms of relief allowing a deportation-eligible non-citizen (*i.e.*, someone who is not a U.S. citizen) to remain in the United States if certain conditions are met/disqualifying conditions are not met. Similarly, under the law as it stood at the time of this case, reopening of deportation proceedings to allow a non-citizen to apply for suspension of deportation was only granted if the non-citizen established that she would face extreme hardship if deported. Such provisions are at issue in the next case. (This form of relief was eliminated by statute the following year.)

2. What did appellant Gina Miranda argue the INS improperly did in considering her evidence that she would face medical hardship if deported back to Honduras? Why does the court conclude the INS's treatment of the evidence did not violate the relevant standard of review the court applies?

3. What did appellant Gina Miranda argue the INS improperly did in considering her evidence that she would face social hardship if deported? Why does the court conclude the INS's treatment of the evidence did not violate the relevant standard of review the court applies?

4. Note that it was the immigration judge, not the INS, who made the fact findings and denied relief in the proceeding being reviewed—the court's reference to the INS being the factfinder/adjudicator is inaccurate.

Gina Ricarda Miranda, Also Known as Ricardo Pabel Miranda v. Immigration and Naturalization Service, et al.

51 F.3d 767 (8th Cir. 1995)

Before Fagg, Magill, and Loken, Circuit Judges.

Per curiam.

Gina Ricarda Miranda, a Honduran citizen, entered the United States illegally and has resided in this country for the past eleven years. Miranda is a transsexual who was born male, but has always believed she is female. The Immigration and Naturalization Service (INS) found Miranda to be deportable, denied her request for asylum, and granted her voluntary departure. Miranda appealed the INS decision to the Board of Immigration Appeals (BIA). While her BIA appeal was pending, Miranda had sexual reassignment surgery to become a woman. The BIA dismissed Miranda's appeal and ordered her to depart the country. Arguing her sexual reassignment surgery would cause her to face medical and social hardship if she returned to Honduras, Miranda moved to reopen the deportation proceedings to allow her to apply for a suspension of deportation under 8 U.S.C. § 1254(a)(1)

(1988 & Supp. V 1993). The BIA denied the motion because Miranda failed to make a prima facie showing of extreme hardship, which is necessary for reopening. *INS v. Jong Ha Wang*, 450 U.S. 139 (1981). Miranda appeals, and we affirm.

Miranda first contends the BIA abused its discretion in denying her motion to reopen, because the BIA distorted or failed to consider Miranda's evidence about the medical hardship Miranda would face in Honduras as a result of her sexual reassignment surgery. Specifically, Miranda argues the BIA mischaracterized the evidence by stating, "[T]here is no clear medical evidence, only [Miranda's] own unsupported assertions, that she could not obtain any needed follow-up medical care in Honduras." It is an abuse of discretion for the BIA to fail to consider all the relevant factors raised in support of a hardship claim, or to distort or disregard important aspects of the claim. *Barragan-Verduzco v. INS*, 777 F.2d 424 (8th Cir. 1985). The BIA's statement about Miranda's medical evidence, however, is a fair reading of the record rather than a distortion. Miranda submitted letters from two American and two Honduran doctors in addition to her affidavit, but these letters do not show Miranda would face medical hardship in Honduras. According to the American doctors, Miranda is a transsexual requiring treatment, but now that she has had surgery, the only medical care Miranda needs is hormone treatments and biannual checkups. The American doctors do not indicate appropriate checkups and hormone treatments are unavailable in Honduras. The letters from the Honduran doctors state, without explanation, that an "integral" or "integrated" treatment for transsexualism is not available in Honduras. The Honduran doctors wrote these letters before Miranda had her sexual reassignment surgery, and it is reasonable to assume surgery is a major part of an "integrated" treatment. Miranda no longer needs surgery, and the Honduran doctors do not state Miranda could not receive hormone treatments or checkups in Honduras. In fact, the Honduran doctors indicate Miranda was at least receiving psychiatric counseling for transsexualism before Miranda left Honduras. Thus, the BIA's statement about the lack of clear medical hardship evidence is not a distortion of the record.

Miranda also contends the BIA distorted and failed to consider fully her evidence about the social hardship she would experience if deported. According to Miranda, the BIA did not consider evidence that Miranda will face discrimination and governmental persecution in Honduras and cannot legally change her name and gender in Honduras. The BIA decision, however, specifically notes Miranda presented evidence about all these concerns, and the BIA acknowledged Miranda will face some social difficulties in Honduras as a result of her sexual reassignment surgery. The BIA did not consider the potential social hardship to be extreme because Miranda "lived as a woman in Honduras before she left . . . and was able to be employed there [as a woman]." Miranda contends this statement is a distortion of the evidence, because she lived as a man most of the time she was in Honduras and was never employed there as a woman. Contrary to Miranda's contention, the BIA's statement is a reasonable interpretation of the record. Miranda's own affidavit states that while she still resided in Honduras, Miranda "decided not to hide [her transsexualism] any longer" and began dressing as a woman. Although a supervisor at work threatened to fire her, another supervisor defended her and Miranda did not lose her job. Based on the record and the BIA's decision, we conclude the BIA did not ignore or distort Miranda's evidence about social hardship.

Miranda next contends the BIA abused its discretion by not adequately explaining the BIA's reasons for denying Miranda's motion to reopen. *See Carrete-Michel v. INS*, 749 F.2d 490, 494 (8th Cir. 1984). We disagree. The BIA does not need to discuss each of Miranda's contentions at length. *El-Gharabli v. INS*, 796 F.2d 935, 938 (7th Cir. 1986). Instead, the BIA is only required to "'announce its decision in terms sufficient to enable a reviewing court to perceive that [the BIA] has heard and thought and not merely reacted.'" *Hsi Sheng Liu v. United States Dep't of Justice*, 13 F.3d 1175 (8th Cir. 1994). In explaining its decision not to reopen, the BIA rejected Miranda's assertions about medical hardship because they were not supported by clear medical evidence. The BIA also stated that although Miranda would face some social difficulties in Honduras, she had lived and worked in Honduras as a woman. Having carefully reviewed the BIA's decision, we are satisfied the BIA thoughtfully considered the facts and arguments Miranda presented.

Finally, Miranda contends the BIA abused its discretion in concluding Miranda failed to present a prima facie case of extreme hardship. She argues the BIA interpreted the phrase "extreme hardship" more narrowly than Congress intended. Again, we disagree. The BIA has authority to interpret "extreme hardship" narrowly and to be restrictive in deciding when to reopen cases. *Jong Ha Wang*. The BIA's denial of Miranda's motion, on the grounds that Miranda's potential difficulty in readjusting to life in Honduras was insufficient to establish extreme hardship, was not an abuse of discretion. *See Sullivan v. INS*, 772 F.2d 609 (9th Cir. 1985) (no abuse of discretion in finding no extreme hardship to homosexual alien who claimed his friends and family at home had disowned him and he would not be able to find work there because of discrimination and poor economy).

We affirm the BIA's denial of Miranda's motion to reopen her deportation proceedings.

Discussion

1. The court of appeals asserts that "it is reasonable to assume surgery is a major part of an 'integrated' treatment [for transsexualism]." What reasoning or basis might underlie this pronouncement? Since the unavailability of "integrated" treatment was noted by the Honduran doctors before Miranda's "sex reassignment" surgery, could it instead be assumed to refer to a treatment that integrates psychotherapy with hormonal treatment, two of the common forms of "treatment" for people with gender dysphoria that often precede surgery? Even on such an interpretation, would that have supported Miranda's claim of medical hardship if she returned to Honduras?

2. As noted in the introduction to this chapter, asylum is a specific legal source of relief for non-citizens who would face a well-founded fear of "persecution" in their home country. At the time this case was decided, non-citizens not lawfully present in the United States who were deemed ineligible for asylum could try to seek suspension of deportation on grounds of "extreme hardship." This form of relief was replaced in 1996 by a more limited form of relief known as "cancellation of removal." 8 U.S.C. § 1225(b)(1). Under cancellation, "hardship" is no longer relevant, and applicants must instead show "that removal would result in exceptional and extremely unusual hardship to the alien's spouse, parent, or child, who is a citizen of the United States or an alien lawfully admitted for permanent residence." Thus, if a non-citizen does not have a qualifying spouse, parent, or child, they are barred from seeking cancellation.

3. Prior to its repeal, should the "hardship" standard have been understood as less extreme than "persecution"? How much disadvantage from being a member of a particular disfavored social group in one's home country, such as homosexual men or transgender women, would an applicant have had to endure to meet the standard for reopening deportation proceedings?

Reading Guide for Hernandez-Montiel v. INS

1. Note that although the court of appeals in the next case follows the testimony of the asylum applicant Geovanni Hernandez-Montiel's academic expert in referring to "gay men with female sexual identities," the applicant also self-described as a "transsexual" person. Although the expert's characterization may have captured social dynamics in Mexico, such persons today in the United States would most commonly be described by sympathetic persons as (heterosexual) transgender women.

2. What factors might account for the harassment, rape, and, generally, persecution to which Geovanni Hernandez-Montiel was subjected in Mexico?

3. How does the court define the social group to which Geovanni belonged in Mexico? For what reason does it adopt that definition? On what ground(s) does the court conclude that it counts as a "particular social group" within the meaning of the asylum statute, reversing the Board of Immigration Appeals? What role do notions of "immutability" play in the court's analysis? How does the court define "immutable" here?

4. Given the parts of the majority opinion's reasoning with which Judge Brunetti expressly agrees, what aspects of its "reasoning and rationale" might he consider unnecessarily "broad"?

Geovanni Hernandez-Montiel v. Immigration and Naturalization Service

225 F.3d 1084 (9th Cir. 2000)

[Hernandez-Montiel was represented by private counsel. Taylor Flynn, Suzanne Goldberg, Jon W. Davidson, and Shannon Minter represented her amici curiae American Civil Liberties Union of Southern California, Lambda Legal Defense & Education Fund, Inc., National Center for Lesbian Rights, and International Gay and Lesbian Human Rights Commission (now Outright Action International).]

Before: BRUNETTI and TASHIMA, Circuit Judges, and SCHWARZER, District Judge.

Opinion

TASHIMA, Circuit Judge:

Geovanni Hernandez-Montiel ("Geovanni"),[3] a native and citizen of Mexico, seeks review of a decision of the Board of Immigration Appeals ("BIA"), denying his application for both asylum and withholding of deportation. The BIA dismissed Geovanni's appeal because it agreed with the immigration judge ("IJ") that Geovanni failed to show that he was persecuted, or that he had a well-founded fear of future persecution, on account of his membership in a particular social group.

. . . We conclude as a matter of law that gay men with female sexual identities in Mexico constitute a "particular social group" [under the asylum statute] and that Geovanni is a member of that group. His female sexual identity is immutable because it is inherent in his identity; in any event, he should not be required to change it. Because the evidence compels the conclusion that Geovanni suffered past persecution and has a well-founded fear of future persecution if he were forced to return to Mexico, we conclude that the record compels a finding that he is entitled to asylum and withholding of deportation.

I. Factual Background

Geovanni testified that, at the age of eight, he "realized that [he] was attracted to people of [his] same sex." At the age of 12, Geovanni began dressing and behaving as a woman.

He faced numerous reprimands from family and school officials because of his sexual orientation. His mother registered him in a state-run Mexican school and informed the school authorities about what she deemed to be his "problem," referring to his sexual orientation. School authorities directed Geovanni to stop socializing with two gay friends. The father of a schoolmate grabbed Geovanni by the arm and threatened to kill him for "perverting" his son. He was even prevented from attending a school dance because of the way he was dressed. Shortly after the dance, the school asked Geovanni's mother to consent to his expulsion because he was

---

3. As does petitioner in his own briefs, we refer to Petitioner as "Geovanni," because he was a minor during the relevant events at issue.

not acting appropriately. He could not enroll in another school because the school refused to transfer his paperwork until he agreed to change his sexual orientation. Geovanni's parents threw him out of their home the day after his expulsion.

Beyond his school and family, Geovanni also suffered harassment and persecution at the hands of Mexican police officers. On numerous occasions, the Mexican police detained and even strip-searched Geovanni because he was walking down the street or socializing with other boys also perceived to be gay. In 1992, the Mexican police twice arrested Geovanni and a friend. The police told them that it was illegal for homosexuals to walk down the street and for men to dress like women. The police, however, never charged Geovanni with any crime.

Police officers sexually assaulted Geovanni on two separate occasions. In November 1992, when Geovanni was 14 years old, a police officer grabbed him as he was walking down the street, threw him into the police car, and drove to an uninhabited area. The officer demanded that Geovanni take off his clothes. Threatening him with imprisonment if he did not comply, the officer forced Geovanni to perform oral sex on him. The officer also threatened to beat and imprison Geovanni if he ever told anyone about the incident.

Approximately two weeks later, when Geovanni was at a bus stop with a gay friend one evening, the same officer pulled up in a car, accompanied by a second officer. The officers forced both boys into their car and drove them to a remote area, where they forced the boys to strip naked and then separated them. One of the officers grabbed Geovanni by the hair and threatened to kill him. Holding a gun to his temple, the officer anally raped Geovanni. Geovanni believes that his friend was also raped, although his friend refused to talk about the incident. Even before the boys could get dressed, the police officers threatened to shoot if they did not start running. The boys were left stranded in an abandoned area.

A few months after the second assault, in February 1993, Geovanni was attacked with a knife by a group of young men who called him names relating to his sexual orientation. He was hospitalized for a week while recovering from the attack.

Geovanni fled to the United States in October 1993, when he was 15 years old. He was arrested within a few days of his October 1993 entry.[4] When Geovanni returned to Mexico to live with his sister, she enrolled him in a counseling program, which ostensibly attempted to "cure" his sexual orientation by altering his female appearance. The program staff cut his hair and nails, and forced him to stop taking female hormones. Geovanni remained in the program from late January to late March 1994. Because his sister saw no changes in him, she brought Geovanni

---

4. Geovanni testified that while he was walking down the street in San Diego dressed in women's clothing, a man in a car pulled up and offered money in exchange for sex. Geovanni said he would not have sex, but asked the man for a ride. When the car turned the corner, police officers were waiting to arrest him. Geovanni was held in jail in San Diego for a week. There is no documentary evidence concerning the arrest in the record.

home to live with her. Soon thereafter, however, she forced Geovanni out of her house because he was not "cured" of his gay sexual orientation, despite his change in appearance. He again sought refuge in the United States.

II. Procedural Background

After a number of attempts to re-enter the United States, Geovanni last entered on or around October 12, 1994[;] . . . . [he] filed an application for asylum and withholding of deportation on February 22, 1995.

At his asylum hearing, Geovanni presented the testimony of Thomas M. Davies, Jr., a professor at San Diego State University and an expert in Latin American history and culture. Professor Davies, who has lived for extended periods of time in Mexico and elsewhere in Latin America, testified that certain homosexuals in Latin America are subjected to greater abuse than others. Professor Davies testified that it is "accepted" that "in most of Latin America a male before he marries may engage in homosexual acts as long as he performs the role of the male." A male, however, who is perceived to assume the stereotypical "female," *i.e.*, passive, role in these sexual relationships is "ostracized from the very beginning and is subject to persecution, gay bashing as we would call it, and certainly police abuse." Professor Davies testified that these gay men with "female" sexual identities in Mexico are "heavily persecuted by the police and other groups within the society. . . . [They are] a separate social entity within Latin American society and in this case within the nation of Mexico." According to Professor Davies, it is commonplace for police to "hit the gay street . . . and not only brutalize but actually rape with batons . . . homosexual males that are dressed or acting out the feminine role."

Professor Davies testified that gay men with female sexual identities are likely to become scapegoats for Mexico's present economic and political problems, especially since the recent collapse of the Mexican economy. Professor Davies specifically noted that Geovanni is "a homosexual who has taken on a primarily 'female' sexual role." Based on his expert knowledge, review of Geovanni's case, and interaction with Geovanni, Professor Davies opined that Geovanni would face persecution if he were forced to return to Mexico.

The IJ [*i.e.*, immigration judge] denied Geovanni asylum on both statutory and discretionary grounds. The IJ determined that Geovanni's testimony was "credible," "sincere," "forthright," "rational," and "coherent." The IJ found, however, that Geovanni had failed to demonstrate persecution "on account of a particular social group," classifying his social group as "homosexual males who wish to dress as a woman [*sic*]." The IJ noted that Geovannni "has altered certain outward physical attributes and his manner of dress to resemble a woman." The IJ found Geovanni's female gender identity not to be immutable, explaining:

> If he wears typical female clothing sometimes, and typical male clothing other times, he cannot characterize his assumed female persona as immutable or fundamental to his identity. The record reflects that respondent's

decision to dress as a women [*sic*] is volitional, not immutable, and the fact that he sometimes dresses like a typical man reflects that respondent himself may not view his dress as being so fundamental to his identity that he should not have to change it.

The IJ further found that Geovanni was not entitled to discretionary eligibility and denied voluntary departure in the exercise of discretion.

The BIA dismissed Geovanni's appeal from the IJ's decision. The BIA agreed that Geovanni gave credible testimony, but found that he failed to establish his statutory eligibility for asylum. The BIA found that Geovanni did not meet his burden of "establishing that the abuse he suffered was because of his membership in a particular social group," which the BIA classified as "homosexual males who dress as females." Concluding that the "tenor of the respondent's claim is that he was mistreated because of the way he dressed (as a male prostitute) and not because he is a homosexual," the BIA found that Geovanni failed to show that "his decision to dress as a female was an immutable characteristic." The BIA did not reach the alternative decision of whether Geovanni established his eligibility for asylum in the exercise of discretion, and it denied Geovanni's request for voluntary departure in the exercise of discretion.

. . . .

IV. Discussion

A. Standard of Review

Because the BIA conducted an independent review of the record, our review is limited to the BIA's decision. *See Gonzalez v. INS*, 82 F.3d 903 (9th Cir. 1996).

We review de novo determinations by the BIA of purely legal questions concerning requirements of the INA. *See Vang v. INS*, 146 F.3d 1114 (9th Cir. 1998). We examine the BIA's factual findings under the substantial evidence standard. *See Marcu v. INS*, 147 F.3d 1078, 1082 (9th Cir. 1998) ("Our task is to determine whether there is substantial evidence to support the BIA's finding, not to substitute an analysis of which side in the factual dispute we find more persuasive."). Under the substantial evidence standard, "[w]e will uphold the BIA's determination unless the evidence compels a contrary conclusion." *Prasad v. INS*, 101 F.3d 614 (9th Cir. 1996).

B. General Framework

The Attorney General may, in her discretion, grant asylum to an applicant determined to be a refugee, within the meaning of § 101(a)(42)(A) of the INA, 8 U.S.C. § 1101(a)(42)(A). An alien establishes refugee status if he is unable or unwilling to return to his country of nationality either because: (1) he was persecuted in the past; or (2) he has a well-founded fear of future persecution "on account of race, religion, nationality, membership in a *particular social group*, or political opinion." INA § 101(a)(42)(A), 8 U.S.C. § 1101(a)(42)(A) (emphasis added); *see also INS v. Cardoza-Fonseca*, 480 U.S. 421 (1987). The Attorney General must withhold deportation of any asylum applicant who establishes a "clear probability of persecution," which is a stricter standard than the "well-founded fear" standard for asylum. *INS v. Stevic*, 467 U.S. 407 (1984).

The applicant has the burden of proving his eligibility with "credible, direct, and specific evidence." *Prasad v. INS*, 47 F.3d 336 (9th Cir. 1995). We have held that where "the IJ expressly finds certain testimony to be credible, and where the BIA makes no contrary finding, we accept as indisputed the testimony given at the hearing before the IJ." *Velarde v. INS*, 140 F.3d 1305 (9th Cir. 1998). Here, the IJ found Geovanni's testimony to be "credible," "sincere," "forthright," "rational," and "coherent." The BIA agreed that "the respondent testified credibly regarding the events that occurred in his life." Thus, we also accept Geovanni's testimony.

C. Membership in a "Particular Social Group"

This case turns on the legal question of whether Geovanni was persecuted on account of his membership in a "particular social group." *See Fatin v. INS*, 12 F.3d 1233 (3d Cir. 1993) (reviewing de novo legal question of what constitutes a "particular social group"). Whether Geovanni is a member of a particular group is a question of fact, to which we apply the substantial evidence test. *See Prasad*. We first conclude that, as a matter of law, the appropriate "particular social group" is that group in Mexico made up of gay men with female sexual identities. Second, we conclude that the evidence compels the conclusion that Geovanni is a member of that group and was persecuted on account of his membership in that "particular social group."

1. Defining "Particular Social Group"

There is no definition of "particular social group" in the INA. The BIA, however, has recognized that the language comes directly from the United Nations Protocol Relating to the Status of Refugees ("Protocol"). *See Matter of Acosta*, 19 I. & N. Dec. 211 (BIA 1985). When Congress ratified the Protocol on October 4, 1968, it did not shed any further light on the definition of "particular social group." *See Sanchez-Trujillo v. INS*, 801 F.2d 1571 (9th Cir. 1986).

The case law regarding the definition of "particular social group" is not wholly consistent. In *Acosta*, the BIA interpreted "persecution on account of membership in a particular social group" to mean "persecution that is directed toward an individual who is a member of a group of persons all of whom share a common, immutable characteristic." The BIA explained that:

> The shared characteristic might be an innate one such as sex, color, or kinship ties, or in some circumstances it might be a shared past experience such as former military leadership or land ownership. The particular kind of group characteristic that will qualify under this construction remains to be determined on a case-by-case basis. However, whatever the common characteristic that defines the group, it must be one that the members of the group either cannot change, or should not be required to change because it is fundamental to their individual identities or consciences.

The BIA held that a group of taxi drivers did not meet the immutable characteristic requirement because an occupation can change; thus, driving a taxi is not fundamental to a person's identity. The BIA's interpretation is entitled to some deference. *See Arrieta v. INS*, 117 F.3d 429 (9th Cir. 1997) (citing *Chevron, U.S.A., Inc. v. Natural Resources Defense Council, Inc.*, 467 U.S. 837 (1984)).

The First, Third, and Seventh Circuits have adopted *Acosta*'s immutability analysis. *See Ananeh-Firempong v. INS*, 766 F.2d 621 (1st Cir. 1985) (recognizing *Acosta* in determining that family relations can be the basis of a "particular social group"); *Fatin* (noting that the subgroup of Iranian feminists who refuse to conform to the government's gender-specific laws and social norms could satisfy the statutory concept of "particular social group") (internal quotation marks omitted); *Lwin v. INS*, 144 F.3d 505 (7th Cir. 1998) (recognizing parents of Burmese student dissidents as part of a social group because they share a "common, immutable characteristic").

In *Sanchez-Trujillo*, we acknowledged that the social group category "is a flexible one which extends broadly to encompass many groups who do not otherwise fall within the other categories of race, nationality, religion, or political opinion." We stated that: "particular social group" implies a collection of people closely affiliated with each other, who are actuated by some common impulse or interest. Of central concern is the existence of a voluntary associational relationship among the purported members, which imparts some common characteristic that is fundamental to their identity as a member of that discrete social group.

The *Sanchez-Trujillo* court held that the class of working class, urban males of military age who maintained political neutrality in El Salvador did not constitute a "particular social group" for which the immigration laws provide protection from persecution. *See id.* (indicating that cognizable groups cannot "encompass every broadly defined segment of a population" but should be a "small, readily identifiable group").

We are the only circuit to suggest a "voluntary associational relationship" requirement. The Seventh Circuit has noted that this requirement "read literally, conflicts with *Acosta*'s immutability requirement." *Lwin*. Moreover, in *Sanchez-Trujillo*, we recognized a group of family members as a "prototypical example" of a "particular social group."[5] Yet, biological family relationships are far from "voluntary." We cannot, therefore, interpret *Sanchez-Trujillo*'s "central concern" of a voluntary associational relationship strictly as applying to every qualifying "particular social group." For, as *Sanchez-Trujillo* itself recognizes, in some particular social groups, members of the group are not voluntarily associated by choice.[6]

---

5. We have since held that a family cannot constitute a particular social group under 8 U.S.C. § 1101(a)(42)(A). *See Estrada-Posadas v. United States INS*, 924 F.2d 916 (9th Cir. 1991). [*But see* Discussion, note 1, *infra*.—Eds.]

6. Further, the statement in *Sanchez-Trujillo* that "[o]f central concern is the existence of a voluntary associational relationship among the purported members," is not essential to the holding of the case that the group—non-political, young, urban males—was simply too "all-encompassing"

We thus hold that a "particular social group" is one united by a voluntary association, including a former association, or by an innate characteristic that is so fundamental to the identities or consciences of its members that members either cannot or should not be required to change it.[7]

2. Sexual Identity as Basis for "Particular Social Group"

Sexual orientation and sexual identity are immutable; they are so fundamental to one's identity that a person should not be required to abandon them. Many social and behavioral scientists "generally believe that sexual orientation is set in place at an early age." Suzanne B. Goldberg, *Give Me Liberty or Give Me Death: Political Asylum and the Global Persecution of Lesbians and Gay Men*, 26 CORNELL INT'L L.J. 605 (1993). The American Psychological Association has condemned as unethical the attempted "conversion" of gays and lesbians. *See id.* Further, the American Psychiatric Association and the American Psychological Association have removed "homosexuality" from their lists of mental disorders. *See Boy Scouts of America v. Dale*, 530 U.S. 640 (2000) (Stevens, J. dissenting).

Sexual identity is inherent to one's very identity as a person. *See* Alfred Kinsey, et al., *"Sexual Behavior in the Human Male," in* CASES AND MATERIALS ON SEXUAL ORIENTATION AND THE LAW 1 (William B. Rubenstein ed., 2d ed., 1997) ("Even psychiatrists discuss 'the homosexual personality' and many of them believe that preferences for sexual partners of a particular sex are merely secondary manifestations of something that lies much deeper in the totality of that intangible which they call the personality."); cf. *Gay Rights Coalition of Georgetown Univ. Law Ctr. v. Georgetown Univ.*, 536 A.2d 1 (D.C. 1987) (observing that "homosexuality encompasses far more than people's sexual proclivities. Too often homosexuals have been viewed simply with reference to their sexual interests and activity. Usually the social context and psychological correlates of homosexual experience are largely ignored . . ."). Sexual identity goes beyond sexual conduct and manifests itself outwardly, often through dress and appearance. *See* Kenji Yoshino, *Suspect Symbols: The Literary Argument for Heightened Scrutiny for Gays*, 96 COLUM. L. REV. 1753 n.3 (1996) (defining gay identity as "the shared experience of having a sexual attachment to persons of the same sex and the oppression experienced because of that attachment"); Naomi Mezey, *Dismantling the Wall: Bisexuality and the Possibilities*

---

to be "the type of cohesive, homogeneous group to which . . . the term 'particular social group' was intended to apply." A group, such as a family, can be cohesive and homogeneous, without the existence of a voluntary associational relationship.

7. This formulation recognizes the holding of *Sanchez-Trujillo* and harmonizes it with *Acosta*'s immutability requirement. It is similar to the Supreme Court of Canada's definition of the term:

> A "particular social group" includes (1) groups defined by an innate or unchangeable characteristic; (2) groups whose members voluntarily associate for reasons so fundamental to their human dignity that they should not be forced to forsake that association; and (3) groups associated by a former voluntary status, unalterable due to its historical importance.

Canada (Attorney General) v. Ward [1993] S.C.R. 689.

of Sexual Identity Classification Based on Acts, 10 Berkeley Women's L.J. 98 (1995) (discussing the relationship of identity and conduct in arguing that "[s]eparating the way we speak of sexual acts and sexual identities is crucial" and arguing that the traditional binary system of heterosexuals and homosexuals is too restrictive); *see also* Gilbert Herdt, Same Sex, Different Cultures: Exploring Gay and Lesbian Lives 20 (1997).

In *Gay Rights Coalition of Georgetown Univ. Law Ctr.*, the District of Columbia Court of Appeals noted that:

> [H]omosexuality is as deeply ingrained as heterosexuality. . . . [E]xclusive homosexuality probably is so deeply ingrained that one should not attempt or expect to change it. Rather, it would probably make far more sense simply to recognize it as a basic component of a person's core identity.

Gay Rights Coalition of Georgetown Univ. Law Ctr. (quoting A. Bell, M. Weinberg & S. Hammersmith, Sexual Preference — Its Development in Men and Women (1981)).

Under the BIA's decision in *In the Matter of Toboso-Alfonso*, 20 I. & N. Dec. 819 (BIA 1990), sexual orientation can be the basis for establishing a "particular social group" for asylum purposes. In *Toboso-Alfonso*, the Cuban government had registered and tracked homosexual men for investigation over many years. The INS did not contest that homosexuality is an immutable characteristic, and the BIA held that sexual orientation establishes membership in a "particular social group." The Attorney General has designated the decision in *Toboso-Alfonso* to be "precedent in all proceedings involving the same issue or issues." Attorney General Order No. 1895 (June 19, 1994).

In determining that sexual orientation and sexual identity can be the basis for establishing a "particular social group," we also find persuasive the reasoning in *Matter of Tenorio*, No. A72-093-558 (IJ July 26, 1993). In *Tenorio*, the IJ granted asylum to a Brazilian gay man who had been beaten and stabbed by a group of people in Rio de Janeiro, who repeatedly used anti-gay epithets. The IJ found that Tenorio had a well-founded fear of future persecution due to his membership in a "particular social group" based on his sexual orientation. The BIA adopted the IJ's reasoning and dismissed the INS' appeal. *See Matter of Tenorio*, No. A72-093-558 (BIA 1999) (per curiam). The BIA held that the IJ's decision "correctly concludes that the respondent has established persecution or a well-founded fear of future persecution on account of one of the five grounds enumerated" in the INA.

3. Particular Social Group of Gay Men with Female Sexual Identities in Mexico

Based on the reasoning of the authorities discussed above, we conclude that the appropriate "particular social group" in this case is composed of gay men with female sexual identities in Mexico. Although not necessary to establish the "particular social group," the testimony of Professor Davies is helpful to our analysis. Professor Davies testified that gay men with female sexual identities in Mexico are "heavily persecuted by the police and other groups within the society. . . . [T]hey are a separate social entity within Latin American society and in this case within the nation of Mexico." Professor Davies expressly noted that as a subset of the gay male population, men with female sexual identities, are "ostracized from the beginning and [] subject to persecution, gay bashing as we would call it, and certainly police abuse."

We thus conclude that the BIA erred in defining the "particular social group" as "homosexual males who dress as females." Professor Davies did not testify that homosexual males are persecuted simply because they may dress as females or because they engage in homosexual acts. Rather, gay men with female sexual identities are singled out for persecution because they are perceived to assume the stereotypical "female," *i.e.*, passive, role in gay relationships. Gay men with female sexual identities outwardly manifest their identities through characteristics traditionally associated with women, such as feminine dress, long hair, and fingernails.

Gay men with female sexual identities in Mexico are a "small, readily identifiable group." *Sanchez-Trujillo.* Their female sexual identities unite this group of gay men, and their sexual identities are so fundamental to their human identities that they should not be required to change them. We therefore conclude as a matter of law that the "particular social group" in this case is comprised of gay men with female sexual identities in Mexico.

4. Geovanni's Membership

We find that the evidence compels the conclusion that Geovanni is a member of the "particular social group" of gay men in Mexico with female sexual identities. Professor Davies specifically classified Geovanni as "a homosexual who has taken on a primarily 'female' sexual role."[8] Geovanni has known that he was gay from the age of eight and began dressing as a woman when he was 12. He socialized with other gay boys in school, which led to his eventual expulsion. The BIA found that the police "temporarily detained [him] for walking the street and socializing with other young homosexual men." He was sexually assaulted twice by the police. After placing him in a therapy program to "convert" his sexuality, his sister eventually "realized that I was the same and the only thing that had changed was the fact that they had cut my hair and cut my nails." Geovanni's female sexual identity must be fundamental, or he would not have suffered this persecution and would have

---

8. In addition to being a gay man with a female sexual identity, Geovanni's brief states that he "may be considered a transsexual." A transsexual is "a person who is genetically and physically a member of one sex but has a deep-seated psychological conviction that he or she belongs, or ought to belong, to the opposite sex, a conviction which may in some cases result in the individual's decision to undergo surgery in order to physically modify his or her sex organs to resemble those of the opposite sex." Deborah Tussey, *Transvestism or Transsexualism of Spouse as Justifying Divorce*, 82 A.L.R.3d n.2 (2000); *see Farmer v. Haas*, 990 F.2d 319 (7th Cir. 1993) (Posner, J.) ("The disjunction between sexual identity and sexual organs is a source of acute psychological suffering that can, in some cases anyway, be cured or at least alleviated by sex reassignment—the complex of procedures loosely referred to as 'a sex-change operation.'"). We need not consider in this case whether transsexuals constitute a particular social group.

changed years ago. *See Fatin* (noting that "if a woman's opposition to the Iranian laws in question is so profound that she would choose to suffer the severe consequences of noncompliance, her beliefs may well be characterized as 'so fundamental to [her] identity or conscience that [they] ought not be required to change it'") (quoting *Acosta*).

Geovanni should not be required to change his sexual orientation or identity. *See Acosta*; *Tenorio*, No. A72-093-558 (IJ ("Sexual orientation is arguably an immutable characteristic, and one which an asylum applicant should not be compelled to change."). Because we conclude that Geovanni should not be required to change his sexual orientation or identity, we need not address whether Geovanni could change them. Geovanni's credible and uncontradicted testimony about the inherent and immutable nature of his sexual identity compels the conclusion that Geovanni was a member of the particular social group of gay men in Mexico with female sexual identities.

The BIA erroneously concluded that "tenor of [Geovanni's] claim is that he was mistreated because of the way he dressed (as a male prostitute) and not because he is a homosexual." This statement is not supported by substantial evidence; in fact, it is wholly unsupported by any evidence in the record. There is no evidence that Geovanni was a male prostitute, and we do not venture to guess the non-record basis of the BIA's assumption of how a male prostitute dresses.[9]

The BIA stressed that Geovanni could not remember how he was dressed on one occasion when he was arrested crossing the border between the United States and Mexico. The BIA, therefore, agreed with the IJ that "the decision to dress as a female was a volitional act, not an immutable trait." Geovanni did testify that he dresses as a man when he is going to a place where an effeminate style of dress would not be appropriate. That Geovanni could not remember how he was dressed on one occasion several years before does not support the BIA's conclusion that, because Geovanni can change his clothes, he can change his identity as quickly as the taxi drivers in *Acosta* can change jobs.

This case is about sexual identity, not fashion. Geovanni is not simply a transvestite "who dresses in clothing of the opposite sex for psychological reasons." AMERICAN HERITAGE DICTIONARY 1289 (2d Coll. Ed.) (1985). Rather, Geovanni manifests his sexual orientation by adopting gendered traits characteristically associated with women.

D. "On Account Of"

Geovanni must show that he was persecuted "on account of" his "membership in the particular social group." INA § 101(a)(42)(A); 8 U.S.C. § 1101(a)(42)(A). In satisfying the "on account of" requirement, the evidence compels a finding that

---

9. The only explicit reference to prostitution in the record is the INS attorney's question to Geovanni about whether he had ever worked as "a homosexual prostitute in the United States." Geovanni answered that he had not.

Geovanni's sexual identity was a significant motivation for the violence and abuse he endured. *See Lopez-Galarza v. INS*, 99 F.3d 954 (9th Cir. 1996) (holding that the petitioner must present "some evidence, direct or circumstantial, of the persecutor's motive, since 8 U.S.C. § 1101 requires 'persecution on account of' various characteristics"). The BIA explicitly noted that Geovanni was "stopped on numerous occasions . . . and temporarily detained for walking the street and socializing with other young homosexual men." The police were not going after people with long hair and nails, or everyone dressed in female clothing. Geovanni was sexually assaulted because of his outward manifestations of his sexual orientation.

The government's legal reasoning is unpersuasive when it argues that "the evidence does not compel the conclusion that the mistreatment [Geovanni] suffered by Mexican authorities was solely on account of his homosexual status." Geovanni is not required to prove that his persecutors were motivated by his sexual orientation to the exclusion of all other possible motivations. We have recognized that "persecutory conduct may have more than one motive, and so long as one motive is of one of the statutorily enumerated grounds, the requirements [for asylum] have been satisfied."

Professor Davies' testimony and the accompanying evidence highlight that the persecution Geovanni suffered was "on account of" his membership in the "particular social group" of men with female sexual identities in Mexico. Professor Davies testified that gay men with female sexual identities are recognized in Mexico as a distinct and readily identifiable group and are persecuted for their membership in that group. He testified that the police attack and even rape men with female sexual identities.

Attached to Professor Davies's declaration are numerous articles and reports documenting the violence against gay men in Mexico and throughout Latin America. A co-founder and general coordinator of a Mexican human rights organization stated: "The government has said it will not protect transvestites unless they are dressed like men, insinuating that it is okay to kill homosexuals if they are visible." *Anti-Queer Violence Continues in Mexico*, S.F. Bay Times, Feb. 25, 1993. There was also a New York Times article, documenting the granting of asylum to a gay man from Mexico. *See Gay Man Who Cited Abuse in Mexico is Granted Asylum*, N.Y. Times, March 26, 1994 at A5. The man had been arrested in Mexico for going to certain neighborhoods, attending certain parties and patronizing certain bars. The police falsely accused him of crimes, extorted him, and on one occasion, raped him. *See id.*

Also in evidence was an advisory opinion about Geovanni's case by the Office of Asylum Affairs of the United States Department of State, claiming that: "[o]ur Embassy in Mexico advises us that it has no evidence of the systematic persecution of homosexuals there although *random violence against homosexuals has occurred.*" (emphasis added). This evidence along with Geovanni's testimony compels the conclusion that Geovanni was persecuted "on account of" his membership in the "particular social group." The evidence is susceptible of no other conclusion.

E. Persecution

The BIA legally erred in finding that Geovanni failed to establish both past persecution and a well-founded fear of future persecution upon return to Mexico. *See* INA § 101(a)(42)(A), 8 U.S.C. § 1101(a)(42)(A); *see also Pitcherskaia v. INS*, 118 F.3d 641 (9th Cir. 1997) (reviewing de novo the legal question of the meaning of persecution). We have held that persecution involves "the infliction of suffering or harm upon those who differ . . . in a way regarded as offensive." *Desir v. Ilchert*, 840 F.2d 723 (9th Cir. 1988); *see Hernandez-Ortiz v. INS*, 777 F.2d 509 (9th Cir. 1985) (stating that persecution is "oppression . . . inflicted on groups or individuals because of a difference that the persecutor will not tolerate").

Geovanni must show that the persecution he suffered was "inflicted either by the government or by persons or organizations which the government is unable or unwilling to control." *Sangha v. INS*, 103 F.3d 1482 (9th Cir. 1997). The BIA was misguided when it concluded that Geovanni was not persecuted "even if the Mexican authorities give low priority to protection of gays." In this case, it was the police who actually perpetrated the violence. During the first sexual attack, Geovanni was abducted, ordered to remove his clothes, and forced to perform oral sex on the officer. The officer then told Geovanni that he would go to jail if he told anyone about the rape. During the second assault, Geovanni and a friend were abducted by two officers, driven to a secluded area, and ordered to remove their clothing. One officer sodomized Geovanni as he held a gun to his temple. Given these past assaults, Geovanni "is at risk of persecution at the hand of the very agency which purports to protect him by law. . . ." *In re Inaudi*, No. T91-04459 (Immigration and Refugee Board of Canada Apr. 9, 1992).

The sexual assaults Geovanni suffered at the hands of police officers undoubtedly constitute persecution. We have held that "rape or sexual assault . . . may constitute persecution." *Lopez-Galarza*; *see Lazo-Majano v. INS*, 813 F.2d 1432 (9th Cir. 1987) (finding persecution of a woman who was raped by a military sergeant whose clothing she was paid to wash), overruled on other grounds, *Fisher v. INS*, 79 F.3d 955 (9th Cir. 1996) (en banc). In *Lopez-Galarza*, we took note of:

> the numerous studies revealing the physical and psychological harms rape causes. A recent article in the *Journal of the American Medical Association* summarized several studies of the effects of rape, and concluded:
>
>> Rape commonly results in severe and long-lasting psychological sequelae that are complex and shaped by the particular social and cultural context in which the rape occurs. . . . Commonly reported feelings at the time of the rape include shock, a fear of injury or death that can be paralyzing, and a sense of profound loss of control over one's life. Longer-term effects can include persistent fears, avoidance of situations that trigger memories of the violation, profound feelings of shame, difficulty remembering events, intrusive thoughts of the abuse, decreased ability to respond to life generally, and difficulty reestablishing intimate relationships.

Lopez-Galarza. There is no reason to believe that the trauma for male victims of rape is any less severe than for female victims.[10]

The BIA gave the convoluted, inapposite, and irrelevant reasoning that "[w]hile *Toboso-Alfonso, supra,* provides a basis for finding that homosexuality is a basis for asylum, anti-sodomy laws are not persecution. *Bowers v. Hardwick*, 478 U.S. 186 (1986)." Geovanni did not argue, however, that he was being persecuted because of the prohibition of any anti-sodomy laws. Instead, he was raped twice by police officers who forced him to engage in sodomy. *Bowers* has no relevance to this case, and the BIA's reliance on that case is completely misplaced.

Further, the BIA erroneously reasoned that "the respondent's mistreatment arose from his conduct . . . thus the rape by the policemen, and the attack by a mob of gay bashers are not necessarily persecution. . . ." We are uncertain whether by "conduct" the BIA was referring to some alleged criminal conduct or to Geovanni's appearance and style of dress. Either way, substantial evidence compels a contrary result.

There is absolutely no evidence in the record that Geovanni's "mistreatment arose from his conduct," if conduct refers to criminal activity. There is no evidence in the record of any past convictions. In fact, the IJ explicitly noted that, despite police harassment in Mexico, Geovanni had "never been formally charged or convicted of any offense."

Perhaps, then, by "conduct," the BIA was referring to Geovanni's effeminate dress or his sexual orientation as a gay man, as a justification for the police officers' raping him. The "you asked for it" excuse for rape is offensive to this court and has been discounted by courts and commentators alike. *See e.g., Timm v. Delong*, 59 F. Supp. 2d 944 (D. Neb. 1998) (stating that Congress found that almost one quarter of state judges erroneously believe that rape victims precipitate their sexual assaults because of what they wear or their actions preceding the incidents); . . . Judith M. Billing & Brenda Murray, *Introduction to the Ninth Circuit Gender Bias Task Force Report: The Effects of Gender*, 67 S. Cal. L. Rev. 739 (1994) (stating that blaming women for bringing domestic violence on themselves is a common example of gender bias in the courts).

Further, the BIA had no basis for concluding that Geovanni's failure to respond to questions regarding his arrests in the United States "casts further doubt on his claim of persecution." It is true that "[t]here is no rule of law which prohibits officers charged with the administration of the immigration law from drawing an inference from the silence of one who is called upon to speak." *INS v. Lopez-Mendoza*, 468 U.S. 1032 (1984). Any inference to be drawn, however, must be reasonable. There simply is no logical connection between Geovanni's failure to answer questions regarding arrests in the United States and the rapes by police officers in Mexico.

---

10. Because we find that the two sexual assaults and accompanying police harassment constitute persecution, we need not examine Geovanni's additional claims that his expulsion from school, random stops by the police, and the knife assault by the group constitute persecution, individually and cumulatively.

Because Geovanni has established past persecution, there is a presumption that he has a well-founded fear of future persecution, which the INS must overcome by a preponderance of the evidence that country conditions have changed. See 8 C.F.R. § 208.13(b)(1)(I); *Singh v. Ilchert*, 63 F.3d (9th Cir. 1995). The INS presented no evidence that Mexico has taken effective steps to curb sexual orientation-based violence, including that perpetrated by the police. To the contrary, Professor Davies testified that the situation for gay men in Mexico has worsened because of the decline of the economy. Thus, the presumption must be given its full force.

F. Withholding of Deportation

Our analysis of past persecution also triggers a presumption that Geovanni has shown a "clear probability" of future persecution with respect to his withholding claim—a presumption that the INS may also rebut by an individualized showing of changed country conditions. See 8 C.F.R. § 208.16(b)(1); *Vallecillo-Castillo v. INS*, 121 F.3d 1237 (9th Cir. 1996). Again, there is nothing in the record to rebut that presumption. Accordingly, we conclude that Geovanni is also entitled to withholding of deportation.

V. Conclusion

We hold that the BIA's decision denying Geovanni asylum on statutory grounds is fatally flawed as a matter of law and is not supported by substantial evidence. Through police harassment and rape, Geovanni suffered past persecution in Mexico on account of his sexual orientation for being a gay man with a female sexual identity. Because that showing is unrebutted, we must presume that he has a well-founded fear of persecution if he returns. He is entitled to asylum and withholding of deportation. We therefore grant the petition for review and remand the case to the BIA with instructions to grant his application for withholding of deportation and to present this case to the Attorney General for the exercise of her discretion to grant asylum.

PETITION FOR REVIEW GRANTED and REMANDED with instructions.

Brunetti, Circuit Judge, specially concurring:

The majority's conclusion that Geovanni Hernandez-Montiel is entitled to asylum and withholding of deportation is correct. I do not agree, however, with the broad reasoning and rationale used by the majority in reaching its conclusion. I therefore must concur only in the result reached by the majority.

The evidence presented by Professor Davies supports the legal conclusion that in Mexico, gay men who have female sexual identities constitute a particular social group for asylum purposes. Hernandez-Montiel's uncontradicted testimony regarding his physical and mental state is sufficient to establish that he is a member of this particular social group. Professor Davies testified that gay men with female sexual identities are persecuted in Mexico. Hernandez-Montiel's testimony before the Immigration Judge that he suffered persecution on account of his membership in this social group was found credible by both the Immigration Judge and the Board of Immigration Appeals. Hernandez-Montiel is therefore entitled to asylum and withholding of deportation based on his well-founded fear of persecution should he be returned to Mexico.

Discussion

1. Note that insofar as *Hernandez-Montiel* or other decisions from the Ninth Circuit Court of Appeals may hold that families cannot constitute particular social groups under the asylum statute, *see* footnote 3 of the opinion, *supra*, they were overruled unanimously by an en banc panel in *Thomas v. Gonzales*, 409 F.3d 1177 (9th Cir. 2005). The judgment in *Thomas*, in turn, was vacated by the Supreme Court sub nomine *Gonzales v. Thomas*, 547 U.S. 183 (2006). The Supreme Court did not expressly call into question the conclusion by the en banc court of appeals panel that family members could constitute a particular social group; instead, it held that the lower court legally erred by failing to remand to the Board of Immigration Appeals for it to decide whether the specific family at issue qualified as "a particular social group."

2. In *Reyes-Reyes v. Ashcroft*, 384 F.3d 782, 785 (9th Cir. 2004), the Court of Appeals followed *Hernandez-Montiel* in accepting the characterization of an asylum applicant from El Salvador as "a homosexual male with a female sexual identity." Consider the following, basically contemporaneous assessment of this aspect of the *Hernandez-Montiel* opinion by Professor Sonia Katyal:

> The [analysis] highlights the possibility of redefining transgenderism to fall along a continuum of sexual orientation, without conflating the two, and without excluding one in favor of the other. Citing to various cases and texts that noted how fundamental sexual orientation is to a person's sexual identity, the court observed that sexual identity goes beyond sexual conduct and manifests itself outwardly, often through dress and appearance. Given the trauma which Geovanni faced throughout his life, the court concluded that his "female sexual identity must be fundamental, or he would not have suffered this persecution and would have changed years ago."
>
> Here, by focusing equally on the interior and exterior aspects of Geovanni's personality (his "homosexual" sexual orientation and "female" sexual identity, respectively), the Ninth Circuit's formulation ably transcended the overly rigid equation between identity and conduct favored by the substitutive model [of gay civil rights, which assumes that one's public sexual identity and private sexual conduct are interchangeable]. It accomplished this by protecting both Geovanni's gay subjectivity as well as his outward female appearance by concluding that Geovanni manifested his sexual orientation by adopting gendered traits characteristically associated with women. By rejecting the lower court's finding that he was not persecuted on account of his sexuality, the court observed that Geovanni's effeminate

dress and sexual orientation could not be classified as volitional behavior, observing, "[t]his case is about sexual identity, not fashion."

In this manner, the court broadly construed sexual orientation to include transgendered identification, drawing a key linkage between harassment based on transgender appearance and harassment based on sexual orientation. The opinion's conflation of the two is actually a protective move that captures protections for both sexual orientation and transgender identity through a single theory. It represents a milestone in ensuring protections for transgendered individuals and other sexual minorities because it unquestionably broadens the category of sexual orientation to include transgenderism. This linkage represents a complete break with many other cases in the United States which have refrained from protecting transsexuals on the basis of their sexual orientation or on the basis of gender. In sum, by observing that one's gender characteristics can comprise an outward manifestation of one's sexual orientation, the court ensures protection for both transgendered and gay-identified sexual minorities.

Sonia Katyal, *Exporting Identity*, 14 Yale J.L. & Feminism 97, 146–47 (2002). Are you persuaded? Should we think Geovanni's "female sexual identity" was an "exterior" aspect of his personality, rather than being a synonym for "gender identity," which is generally conceived of as an intrinsic (interior?) core aspect of one's psyche?

3. Note how asylum cases are intensely fact-specific, both as to an asylum applicant's membership in a particular social group and as to the past persecution or the well-foundedness or probability of the applicant's fear of future persecution on the basis of such membership. This is why asylum applicants who can connect to the necessary support resources generally seek to present expert testimony as to "country conditions," that is, how members of the social group at issue are commonly treated in the applicant's home country. Lack of such evidence can make it challenging for asylum applicants to satisfy an immigration judge or the Board of Immigration Appeals that they meet the statutory requirements to receive asylum. This can lead to their being deported to their home countries, where they may well face violence or violent death. *See, e.g.*, Nelson Renteria, *Trans asylum-seeker killed after U.S. deportation back to El Salvador*, Reuters (Feb. 22, 2019), https://www.reuters.com/article/us-usa-immigration-violence/trans-asylum-seeker-killed-after-u-s-deportation-back-to-el-salvador-idUSKCN1QC03L (reporting murder of Salvadoran transgender woman within approximately three months after deportation).

Reading Guide for Avendano-Hernandez v. Lynch

1. To be eligible for protection under the Convention Against Torture, precluding deportation and allowing a deportable non-U.S.-citizen to remain in the United States, the non-citizen must establish a future likelihood of what? What past conduct does the court here conclude amounted to torture of the petitioner non-citizen Avendano-Hernandez, and why? What kinds of governmental involvement in that

conduct does Avendano-Hernandez need to establish for deferral of removal, and what kind(s) of involvement does the court find on the record?

2. What kinds of evidence did the BIA maintain showed Avendano-Hernandez had not met her future likelihood showing? Why does the court conclude that substantial evidence did not support the BIA's conclusion?

Edin Carey Avendano-Hernandez v. Loretta E. Lynch, Attorney General

800 F.3d 1072 (9th Cir. 2015)

[Petitioner was represented by private counsel and the Public Law Center, Santa Ana, California. Supporting her as amici were the National Immigrant Justice Center, East Bay Community Law Center, The Florence Project, Immigration Equality, Lawyers' Committee for Civil Rights, and The National Center for Lesbian Rights.]

Before: Harry Pregerson, Barrington D. Parker, Jr., and Jacqueline H. Nguyen, Circuit Judges.

Opinion

Nguyen, Circuit Judge:

Edin Avendano-Hernandez is a transgender woman who grew up in a rural town in Oaxaca, Mexico. . . . Because of her gender identity and perceived sexual orientation, as a child she suffered years of relentless abuse that included beatings, sexual assaults, and rape. The harassment and abuse continued into adulthood, and, eventually, she was raped and sexually assaulted by members of the Mexican police and military. She ultimately sought refuge in the United States, applying for withholding of removal and relief under Article 3 of the Convention Against Torture ("CAT").

Avendano-Hernandez has a prior 2006 felony conviction for driving while having a .08 percent or higher blood alcohol level and causing bodily injury to another person, a violation of California Vehicle Code § 23153(b). The Board of Immigration Appeals ("BIA") concluded that this conviction constitutes a particularly serious crime, rendering Avendano-Hernandez ineligible for withholding of removal. We find that the BIA's decision was within its discretion. The immigration judge ("IJ") and the BIA erred, however, in denying her application for CAT relief, ironically exhibiting some of the same misconceptions about the transgender community that Avendano-Hernandez faced in her home country. The IJ failed to recognize the difference between gender identity and sexual orientation, refusing to allow the use of female pronouns because she considered Avendano-Hernandez to be "still male," even though Avendano-Hernandez dresses as a woman, takes female hormones, and has identified as a woman for over a decade. Although the BIA correctly used female pronouns for Avendano-Hernandez, it wrongly adopted the IJ's analysis, which conflated transgender identity and sexual orientation. The BIA also erred in assuming that recent anti-discrimination laws in Mexico have made life safer for transgender individuals while ignoring significant record evidence of violence targeting them. We grant the petition in part and remand for a grant of relief under CAT.

Background

Avendano-Hernandez, a native and citizen of Mexico, is a transgender woman. She knew from as young as five or six that she was different—she was feminine and loved to wear makeup and dress in her sister's clothes, and preferred the company of girls rather than boys of her age.[1] As a result, she was frequently targeted for harassment and abuse. Her father brutally beat her and called her "faggot" and "queer," and her schoolmates tormented her in class and physically assaulted her for being "gay." Soon, Avendano-Hernandez's older brothers and cousins began sexually abusing her. They forced her to perform oral sex, raped her, and beat her when she tried to resist their attacks. Her parents had reason to suspect this abuse was occurring, but did not intervene. When Avendano-Hernandez told her mother that her stomach hurt and she bled when using the restroom, her mother merely gave her herbal remedies to help alleviate her pain. Similarly, her father beat her for being a "faggot" after he saw a hickey left on her chest by her brother while he raped her. She was also harassed by a male teacher, who told her he knew she was gay, touched her inappropriately, and attempted to force her to perform oral sex.

The abuse continued as Avendano-Hernandez got older. In junior high school, her classmates would write "Edin is gay and likes men" on the blackboard or on notes they would stick to her back. People in her town, including members of the police and the military, would also call her "gay" when seeing her in public. At the age of 16, Avendano-Hernandez dropped out of high school and moved to Mexico City, where she worked at a nightclub. The club's customers also harassed her because of her feminine appearance and behavior, called her derogatory names, and, on one occasion, physically attacked her. She lived in constant fear.

A year later, Avendano-Hernandez returned to her hometown to care for her mother, who was battling cancer. One of her older brothers, who had raped her when she was a child, was also living in their parents' home and threatened to kill her if she did not leave the community. Shortly after her mother's death, in July 2000, Avendano-Hernandez unlawfully entered the United States and settled in Fresno, California. She began taking female hormones in 2005, and lived openly as a woman for the first time.

In the United States, Avendano-Hernandez struggled with alcohol abuse, and was twice convicted of driving under the influence of alcohol.... Her second offense... involved a head-on collision with another vehicle, causing injuries to

---

1. The IJ found Avendano-Hernandez to be credible, and the BIA affirmed this finding. Thus, "we accept the facts given by [the petitioner] and all reasonable inferences to be drawn from them as true." *Ornelas-Chavez v. Gonzales*, 458 F.3d 1052 (9th Cir. 2006).

both Avendano-Hernandez and the driver of the other car. This second offense led to a felony conviction on September 27, 2006 for driving while having a .08 percent or higher blood alcohol level and causing injury to another, a violation of California Vehicle Code § 23153(b). She was sentenced to 364 days incarceration and three years of probation. After her release from custody, she was removed to Mexico in March 2007 under a stipulated order of removal.

Back in Mexico, Avendano-Hernandez again faced harassment from her family and members of the local community because of her gender identity and perceived sexual orientation. One evening, when Avendano-Hernandez was on her way to visit family in Oaxaca's capital city, armed uniformed police officers stationed at a roadside checkpoint hurled insults at her as she walked past them. Four officers then followed her down a dirt road, grabbed her, forced her into the bed of their truck, and drove her to an unknown location. Shouting homophobic slurs, they beat her, forced her to perform oral sex, and raped her. One officer hit her in the mouth with the butt of his rifle, and another held a knife to her chin, cutting her hand when she tried to push it away. After the assault, the officers told her that they knew where she lived and would hurt her family if she told anyone about the attack.

This assault prompted Avendano-Hernandez to flee Mexico almost immediately. While attempting to cross the border with a group of migrants a few days later, Avendano-Hernandez encountered a group of uniformed Mexican military officers. Though the leaders of the migrant group had asked Avendano-Hernandez to dress differently to avoid attracting attention at the border, she was still visibly transgender, as she wore her hair in a ponytail and had been taking female hormones for several years. Calling her a "faggot," the officers separated Avendano-Hernandez from the rest of her group. One of the officers forced her to perform oral sex on him, while the rest of the group watched and laughed. The officer then told her to "get out of his sight." She successfully reentered the United States in May 2008 and returned to Fresno. Three years later, she was arrested for violating the terms of probation imposed in her 2006 felony offense for failing to report to her probation officer.

Placed in removal proceedings and fearful of returning to Mexico, Avendano-Hernandez applied for withholding of removal and CAT relief. The IJ denied her application for withholding of removal on the ground that Avendano-Hernandez's 2006 felony conviction constitutes a "particularly serious crime," barring her eligibility. *See* 8 U.S.C. § 1231(b)(3)(B)(ii). The BIA, conducting de novo review, reached the same conclusion. As to Avendano-Hernandez's CAT claim, the BIA denied relief on the ground that she failed to "demonstrate[] that a member of the Mexican government acting in an official capacity will more likely than not 'consent' to or 'acquiesce' in her torture; that is, come to have advance knowledge of any plan to torture or kill her and thereafter breach her legal responsibility to intervene to prevent such activity." This timely petition for review followed.

Discussion

I. Withholding of Removal

[Noncitizens are ineligible for withholding of removal, a form of relief entitling a deportable noncitizen to remain in the United States, if they] "having been convicted by a final judgment of a particularly serious crime [are] a danger to the community of the United States." 8 U.S.C. § 1231(b)(3)(B)(ii). An aggravated felony resulting in an aggregate sentence of five years imprisonment is a per se particularly serious crime. *Id.* § 1231(b)(3)(B). However, because the term "particularly serious crime" is not otherwise defined by statute, the Attorney General may also "designate offenses as particularly serious crimes through case-by-case adjudication as well as regulation." . . . .

[The court reviews the BIA's conclusions that an offense constitutes a particularly serious crime for an abuse of discretion. In this part, the court concludes that] [b]ecause the BIA properly found that Avendano-Hernandez's prior felony conviction constitutes a particularly serious crime, she is ineligible for withholding of removal.

II. Convention Against Torture

We now turn to Avendano-Hernandez's claim for relief under CAT. "We have jurisdiction pursuant to § 1252(a) to review the BIA's denial of [petitioner]'s claim for CAT deferral," *Delgado v. Holder,* 648 F.3d 1095 (9th Cir. 2011) (en banc), and review the factual findings behind the agency's conclusion for substantial evidence, *Zheng v. Ashcroft*, 332 F.3d 1186 (9th Cir. 2003). The BIA concluded that Avendano-Hernandez failed to show that the Mexican government will more likely than not consent to or acquiesce in her torture. This conclusion is not supported by the record.

A. Avendano-Hernandez's Rape and Sexual Assault by Mexican Officials Constitute Past Torture

To receive deferral of removal under CAT, Avendano-Hernandez must show that upon her return to Mexico "she is more likely than not to be tortured," 8 C.F.R. § 1208.17(a), either "by or at the instigation of or with the consent or acquiescence of a public official or other person acting in an official capacity," *id.* § 1208.18(a)(1). Torture is defined, in part, as "any act by which severe pain or suffering, whether physical or mental, is intentionally inflicted on a person . . . for any reason based on discrimination of any kind." *Id.* When evaluating an application for CAT relief, the IJ and the BIA should consider "all evidence relevant to the possibility of future torture, including . . . [e]vidence of past torture inflicted upon the applicant." *Id.* § 1208.16(c)(3).

. . . . Avendano-Hernandez was raped, forced to perform oral sex, beaten severely, and threatened. "Rape can constitute torture . . . [as it] is a form of aggression constituting an egregious violation of humanity." *Zubeda v. Ashcroft*, 333 F.3d 463 (3d Cir. 2003). Moreover, Avendano-Hernandez was singled out because of her transgender identity and her presumed sexual orientation. *See* 8 C.F.R. § 1208.18(a)

(1) (defining torture, in part, as "any act by which severe pain or suffering . . . is intentionally inflicted on a person . . . for any reason based on discrimination of any kind"). "[T]he officer[s]' words during the assaults make clear that [they were] motivated by [petitioner]'s sexuality." *Boer-Sedano v. Gonzales*, 418 F.3d 1082 (9th Cir. 2005). Rape and sexual abuse due to a person's gender identity or sexual orientation, whether perceived or actual, certainly rises to the level of torture for CAT purposes. *Cf. Hernandez-Montiel v. INS*, 225 F.3d 1084 (9th Cir. 2000) (finding that sexual assaults perpetrated against a transgender woman "undoubtedly constitute persecution"), *overruled on other grounds by Thomas v. Gonzales*, 409 F.3d 1177 (9th Cir. 2005).

The agency, however, wrongly concluded that no evidence showed "that any Mexican public official has consented to or acquiesced in prior acts of torture committed against homosexuals or members of the transgender community." In fact, Avendano-Hernandez was tortured "by . . . public official[s]"—an alternative way of showing government involvement in a CAT applicant's torture. 8 C.F.R. § 1208.18(a)(1). Avendano-Hernandez provided credible testimony that she was severely assaulted by Mexican officials on two separate occasions: first, by uniformed, on-duty police officers, who are the "prototypical state actor[s] for asylum purposes," *Boer-Sedano*, and second, by uniformed, on-duty members of the military. Such police and military officers are "public officials" for the purposes of CAT. *See also Muradin v. Gonzales*, 494 F.3d 1208 (9th Cir. 2007) (recognizing that abuse by military officers can constitute government torture in the CAT context). The BIA erred by requiring Avendano-Hernandez to also show the "acquiescence" of the government when her torture was inflicted *by* public officials themselves, as a plain reading of the regulation demonstrates.[2] 8 C.F.R. § 1208.18(a)(1) (specifying that the act must be inflicted "by *or* at the instigation of *or* with the consent or acquiescence of a public official") (emphasis added). *See also Baballah v. Ashcroft*, 367 F.3d 1067 (9th Cir. 2003) (finding "governmental involvement" to be "conclusively establish[ed]" where "there is no question that the perpetrators of the persecution were themselves government actors").

We reject the government's attempts to characterize these police and military officers as merely rogue or corrupt officials. The record makes clear that both groups of officers encountered, and then assaulted, Avendano-Hernandez while on the job and in uniform. Avendano-Hernandez was not required to show acquiescence by a higher level member of the Mexican government because "an applicant for CAT relief need not show that the entire foreign government would consent to or acquiesce in [her] torture." *Madrigal v. Holder*, 716 F.3d 499 (9th Cir. 2013). It is enough for her to show that she was subject to torture at the hands of local officials.

---

2. Alternatively, Avendano-Hernandez proved government acquiescence because several police and military officers stood by and watched their colleagues assault her. This assuredly constitutes "awareness of" her torture and "breach [of their] legal responsibility to intervene to prevent such activity." 8 C.F.R. § 1208.18(a)(7).

Thus, the BIA erred by finding that Avendano-Hernandez was not subject to past torture by public officials in Mexico.

B. The Record Evidence Compels a Finding of Likely Future Torture

"[P]ast torture is ordinarily the principal factor on which we rely when an applicant who has been previously tortured seeks relief under the Convention" because, absent changed circumstances, "if an individual has been tortured and has escaped to another country, it is likely that he will be tortured again if returned to the site of his prior suffering." *See Nuru v. Gonzales*, 404 F.3d 1207 (9th Cir. 2005). In addition, the agency must evaluate all other evidence relevant to the claim, including proof of "gross, flagrant, or mass violations of human rights" in the home country and other country conditions evidence. *Id.*

The BIA's conclusion that Avendano-Hernandez failed to show a likelihood of future torture is not supported by substantial evidence. The BIA primarily relied on Mexico's passage of laws purporting to protect the gay and lesbian community. The agency's analysis, however, is fundamentally flawed because it mistakenly assumed that these laws would also benefit Avendano-Hernandez, who faces unique challenges as a transgender woman.[3] There is no dispute that Mexico has extended some legal protections to gay and lesbian persons; for example, Mexico City legalized gay marriage and adoption in December 2009, and the Mexican Supreme Court has held that such marriages must be recognized by other Mexican states. U.S. Dep't of State, *Country Reports on Human Rights Practices for 2011*, ECF No. 6-1 at 530. But laws recognizing same-sex marriage may do little to protect a transgender woman like Avendano-Hernandez from discrimination, police harassment, and violent attacks in daily life.

While the relationship between gender identity and sexual orientation is complex, and sometimes overlapping, the two identities are distinct. Avendano-Hernandez attempted to explain this to the IJ herself, clarifying that she used to think she was a "gay boy" but now considers herself to be a woman. Of course, transgender women and men may be subject to harassment precisely because of their association with homosexuality. *See, e.g., Hernandez-Montiel* (surmising that "gay men with female sexual identities" may be singled out for persecution because of their presumed role in gay relationships); *cf. Latta v. Otter*, 771 F.3d 456 (9th Cir. 2014) (Berzon, J., concurring) ("[T]he social exclusion and state discrimination against lesbian, gay, bisexual, and transgender people reflects, in large part, disapproval of their nonconformity with gender-based expectations.") (footnote omitted). Avendano-Hernandez's own experiences in Mexico reflect this reality, as her persecutors have

---

3. While the record does mention two laws meant to protect the transgender community—a 2004 amendment to the Mexico City Civil Code allowing transgender people to change their registered name and sex on their birth certificates, and a national anti-discrimination law that includes protections for gender expression—neither the IJ nor the BIA appear to have specifically considered these protections or their effectiveness.

often labeled her as "gay" and called her a number of homophobic slurs that are also used against gay men.

Yet significant evidence suggests that transgender persons are often especially visible, and vulnerable, to harassment and persecution due to their often public nonconformance with normative gender roles.[4] Country conditions evidence shows that police specifically target the transgender community for extortion and sexual favors, and that Mexico suffers from an epidemic of unsolved violent crimes against transgender persons. Indeed, Mexico has one of the highest documented number of transgender murders in the world. Avendano-Hernandez, who takes female hormones and dresses as a woman, is therefore a conspicuous target for harassment and abuse. She was immediately singled out for rape and sexual assault by police and military officers upon first sight, and despite taking pains to avoid attracting violence when she attempted to cross the border, she was still targeted. Avendano-Hernandez's experiences reflect how transgender persons are caught in the cross-hairs of both generalized homophobia and transgender-specific violence and discrimination.

The BIA acknowledged record evidence regarding corruption among the Mexican police and military, but concluded that such evidence was unrelated to Avendano-Hernandez's fears of torture as a transgender woman because the corruption only occurred in the context of drug trafficking and accepting bribes. Again, this conclusion misreads the record. The evidence before the agency does not focus on drug trafficking-related police corruption, but instead shows an *increase* in violence against gay, lesbian, and transgender individuals during the years in which greater legal protections have been extended to these communities. *See Vitug v. Holder*, 723 F.3d 1056 (9th Cir. 2013) (noting that the emergence of gay rights activism in the Philippines and an ordinance protecting gays and lesbians from employment discrimination "do[] not indicate that there is any less violence against gay men or that police have become more responsive to reports of antigay hate crimes"). Avendano-Hernandez's expert explained that the passage of these laws has made the "situation . . . paradoxically become increasingly more perilous [for the gay, lesbian, and transgender community], as the public and authorities react to their expressions of a form of sexuality that the culture does not embrace and, in fact, fears." Indeed, the country's highest number of hate crimes in 2010 took place in Mexico City—where arguably the *most* efforts have been made to protect the rights of sexual minorities—and there is a continued failure to prosecute the perpetrators of homophobic hate crimes throughout Mexico. The agency's focus on drug-related

---

4. The Department of Homeland Security recently acknowledged the vulnerabilities of transgender persons, as Immigration and Customs Enforcement issued detailed guidance to its officers and employees regarding steps to assure the safety and proper care of transgender individuals held in immigration detention. Thomas Homan, Executive Associate Director, U.S. Immigration and Customs Enforcement, *Further Guidance Regarding the Care of Transgender Detainees*, June 19, 2015, *available at* https://www.ice.gov/sites/default/files/documents/Document/2015/ TransgenderCareMemorandum.pdf.

police corruption is inexplicable in light of the overwhelming record evidence of ineffective police protection of transgender persons.[5]

On this record, we find that Avendano-Hernandez is entitled to a grant of CAT relief on remand. . . . The agency's conflation of transgender and gay identity does not constitute the application of "an erroneous legal standard" that would normally require us to remand the case for further consideration. *Lopez v. Ashcroft*, 366 F.3d 799 (9th Cir. 2004). Instead, the agency's denial is based on its factual confusion as to what constitutes transgender identity and its erroneous conclusion that "[t]here is no substantial evidence in the record . . . to show that any Mexican public official has consented to or acquiesced in prior acts of torture committed against . . . members of the transgender community." In light of Avendano-Hernandez's past torture, and unrebutted country conditions evidence showing that such violence continues to plague transgender women in Mexico, "no questions remain — she was tortured and there is a substantial danger that she will be, if returned." *Edu v. Holder*, 624 F.3d 1137 (9th Cir. 2010). We grant Avendano-Hernandez's petition in part and remand her case for a grant of CAT relief.

Conclusion

The unique identities and vulnerabilities of transgender individuals must be considered in evaluating a transgender applicant's asylum, withholding of removal, or CAT claim. Here, the BIA properly found Avendano-Hernandez ineligible for withholding of removal because of her conviction for a particularly serious crime. We thus deny the petition in part as to her withholding of removal claim. We grant the petition in part and remand for the agency to grant CAT deferral relief because the record compels the conclusion that she will likely face torture if removed to Mexico.

PETITION DENIED IN PART, GRANTED IN PART, AND REMANDED.

Discussion

1. Note how the court's discussion here does not treat LGBT people or LGBT rights as monolithic; neither does it equate antidiscimination laws on the books to people's daily experiences of discrimination. *Hernandez-Montiel v. INS, supra* at p. 493, and *Avendano-Hernandez* differ in their approaches regarding the importance of judges' not conflating sexual orientation and gender identity, or gay men and (heterosexual) trans women. What advantages or disadvantages do you see to the approach of each? Does the *Avendano-Hernandez* court's approach reject the

---

5. Thus, this case is distinguishable from *Madrigal v. Holder*, where the agency's failure to consider the effectiveness of the Mexican government's "willingness to control Los Zetas" required remand for consideration of the question in the first instance. Here, in contrast, the agency appears to have considered the question of whether police protections are effective, but its conclusion that they are only ineffective in the context of collaboration with drug traffickers is not supported by substantial evidence.

counsel of the passages from Prof. Sonia Katyal excerpted in the Discussion following *Hernandez-Montiel*?

2. If government actors and others in Mexican society in fact conflate sexual orientation and gender identity, is the court right here to reject the argument that legal advances such as the increasing opening of marriage rights to same-sex couples make it unlikely that Avendano-Hernandez would face persecution were she to return again to Mexico? For an argument emphasizing differences between anti-LGB discrimination and anti-trans discrimination, as well as an argument that recognition of transgender women as particular social group in asylum law could lead to protection of cisgender women through treatment of "women" themselves as a particular social group, see Adena L. Wayne, *"Unique Identities and Vulnerabilities": The Case for Transgender Identity as a Basis for Asylum*, 102 Cornell L. Rev. 241 (2016).

Reading Guide for Matter of Christian J.C.U. a/k/a Monica C.U. (Jorge R.C.)

1. On what basis does the New York Family Court exercise jurisdiction over the guardianship petition of Monica C.U., given that she was being held in a detention unit for transgender persons outside the state? Why might New York law give its family court such jurisdiction?

2. "Lawful permanent residents (LPRs), also known as 'green card' holders, are non-citizens who are lawfully authorized to live permanently within the United States. LPRs may accept an offer of employment without special restrictions, own property, receive financial assistance at public colleges and universities, and join the Armed Forces. They also may apply to become U.S. citizens if they meet certain eligibility requirements." Department of Homeland Security, *Lawful Permanent Residents*, https://www.dhs.gov/immigration-statistics/lawful-permanent-residents (last visited Oct. 13, 2019). "If an SIJ is given lawful permanent resident status, she may eventually apply for United States citizenship." *Reyes v. Cissna*, 737 Fed. App'x 140 (4th Cir. 2018). What does the family court here have to conclude in order for federal law to allow it to proceed to make findings as to whether Monica was eligible for Special Immigrant Juvenile Status ("SJIS"), which might allow her LPR status? To be eligible for SIJS status under federal law, what does the court have to find? On what grounds does the court make such findings?

In re a Proceeding for the Appointment of a Guardian Pursuant to Family Court Act of the Person of Christian J.C.U. a/k/a Monica C.U., v. Jorge R.C. and Maria N.U.

60 Misc. 3d 706, 77 N.Y.S. 3d 834 (Fam. Ct. 2018)

[Monica C.U. was represented by counsel from Catholic Migration Services, Brooklyn, NY; her desired guardian Ms. W. appeared pro se; and Monica's parents did not appear.]

Opinion

Javier E. Vargas, J.

The Motion by Petitioner Christian J. C.U. a/k/a Monica C.U. . . . , for the appointment of a guardian and the issuance of an Order making Special Immigrant Juvenile Status ["SIJS"] findings, is granted and SIJS findings made in accordance with the following decision.

The following facts are undisputed. Monica was born biologically as male in Honduras to Respondents Maria N. U.P. ("Mother") and Jorge A. C.M. ("Father") on April 26, 1997. From an early age, however, Monica's gender identity has been female. Because of a family tragedy blamed on her, the Parents disliked and abandoned Monica in a Honduran orphanage when she was three years old, but she was rescued by her paternal grandmother, who took her in, nurtured and provided for her schooling throughout her childhood. Despite this, the parents continued to abuse and mistreat Monica with brutal beatings, which once resulted in broken ribs requiring medical attention, as well as by inflicting cigarette burns and scars. She was also victimized at the hands of one of her older brothers, Jorge C., who repeatedly raped and sexually abused her during her infancy. Although Monica told the grandmother about the rapes, her brother continued the sexual abuse after only a short reprieve.

On one occasion, Monica's father saw her dressed in a manner consistent with her gender identity, and he beat her up to the point that she was taken to the hospital and the Honduran child protective authorities were called and investigated, yet nothing was done civilly or criminally against the father to subvert the abuse. To the contrary, the father resumed his physical abuse against Monica, threatening that if she continued to dress as a woman or be a "fa***t" that he was going to beat her until she became a man, make her disappear or institutionalize her. Everything came to a head upon the passing of her grandmother in 2013, when Monica was 16 years of age and left all her little property to her. In 2014, Monica fled her native Honduras escaping her nightmarish parents and brother's abuse, threats, and harassment because of her gender identity, and searched for a new life and peace in the United States. She crossed the U.S. border illegally and was returned to Honduras.

Upon re-entering in 2017, Monica was captured by the U.S. Immigration & Customs Enforcement and detained at the transgendered [*sic*—Eds.] section of the Cibola County Detention Center located in Milan, New Mexico, where she is currently detained. Catholic Migration Services took over Monica's defense and the totality of her personal property in Brooklyn, consisting of her backpack with clothing, a purse, a wallet, medication and other items. By petition dated April 17, 2018, just days before her 21st birthday, Monica commenced the instant Family Court Act article 6 proceeding against her parents in the Kings County Family Court, seeking the appointment of her friend and mentor, respondent Alisha W., as her guardian for the purpose of obtaining SIJS findings in order to petition to the United States Citizenship and Immigrations Services ("USCIS") for [SIJS] pursuant to 8 U.S.C. § 1101(a)(27)(J). Thereafter, by order to show cause dated April 18, 2018, Monica moved for an order making the requisite declaration and specific findings so as to enable her to petition for SIJS, alleging that she is unmarried, under 21 years of age, that reunification with one or both of her parents is not viable due to abuse, neglect and abandonment, and that it would not be in her best interests to be returned to Honduras.

Given her dire circumstances and the proximity of Monica's 21st birthday, this court expedited the guardianship petition and afforded counsel time to locate and serve the parents with the petition by order to show cause. Following counsel's unsuccessful search for their whereabouts, the court waived service upon the parents on the return date pursuant to Surrogate's Court Procedure Act ("SCPA") § 1705(2) based on their abandonment of Monica. On April 20, 2018, the Family Court (Vargas, J.) conducted a hearing on the guardianship petition finding that the court has jurisdiction over the person of Monica based on the location of her property in Brooklyn, New York, pursuant to SCPA 1702(1)(b), and crediting Ms. W.'s hopeful testimony and plans she has in assuming the guardianship and care of Monica once she is released from the USCIS detention in New Mexico and travels to Brooklyn. A final order of guardianship was issued appointing Ms. W. as Monica's guardian until she turned 21. The court heard additional testimony and accepted into evidence Monica's affidavit retelling her harrowing life story in Honduras, thereby granting Monica's SIJS Motion and issuing an SIJS order (Vargas, J.) dated April 20, 2018, finding that she is eligible to petition for SIJS status, that reunification with both of her parents is not viable due to their neglect and abandonment, and that it would not be in her best interests to be returned to Honduras. However, the Court reserved the opportunity to write an opinion on the novel jurisdictional issues presented and expound on the rulings made.

Preliminarily, the novel, threshold jurisdictional issue presented is whether SCPA 1702 confers the Family Court with jurisdiction over Monica's guardianship petition based not on her physical presence in New York, but on the location of her "property" here. The Family Court "is a court of limited jurisdiction, constrained to exercise only those powers granted to it by the State Constitution or by statute." *Matter of H.M. v. E.T.*, 930 N.E.2d 206 (N.Y. 2010). However, pursuant to Family Court Act § 661 and SCPA 103(27), the Family Court, concurrently with the Surrogate's Court, has jurisdiction to make judicial determinations regarding the care, control, guardianship and custody of minors, which include within its definition juveniles up to the age of 21 years old. SCPA 1706; *see Matter of Marisol N.H.*, 115 A.D.3d 185 (N.Y. App. Div. 2d Dept. 2014). Where a minor has no guardian, the Family Court

> "may appoint a guardian of his person or property, or of both, in the following cases:
>
> (a) Where the infant is domiciled in that county or has sojourned therein immediately preceding the application, or
>
> (b) *Where the infant is a non-domiciliary of the state but has property situated in that county*" (SCPA 1702 (emphasis supplied)).

Courts have long recognized a Surrogate's jurisdiction to appoint a guardian of a minor who resides outside the state, but has property in the county in question. *See Matter of Thorne*, 148 N.E. 630 (N.Y. 1925); *Matter of Klineman*, 105 Misc. 2d 896, 898 (Sur. Ct., N.Y. County 1980) (infant's "property" consisted of securities and cash, valued at approximately $120,000, on bank deposit)).

Applying these legal principles to the matter at bar, the Court finds that the Family Court has the same jurisdiction over Monica's guardianship proceeding as the Surrogate's Court would. It is undisputed that Monica is currently detained by USCIS in New Mexico and, as such, is a "non-domiciliary of the state." But, as the statute provides, Monica "has property situated in [the] county," consisting of her personal property located in Kings County. It does not consist of real estate property, substantial assets or any significant monetary property, but merely Monica's own personal property items, including her backpack, clothing, purse, wallet and medicines. Nevertheless, those items are Monica's only "property" in the world! Unlike the Civil and Supreme Court which have monetary minimums for their jurisdiction, the Family Court is the real "People's Court" which welcomes all parties with open arms regardless of their gender, sexual orientation, gender identity, race, national origin, financial or citizenship status. That Monica's property is de minimis should not stymie her jurisdictional right to pursue her Guardianship proceeding here. "When considering guardianship appointments, the infant's best interests are paramount." *Matter of Axel S.D.C. v. Elena A.C.*, 139 A.D.3d 1050 (N.Y. App. Div. 2d Dept. 2016); *see Matter of Alamgir A.*, 81 A.D.3d 937 (N.Y. App. Div. 2d Dept. 2011); SCPA 1707(1). As such, this court rules that it has subject matter jurisdiction over the person of Monica to rule on her Guardianship Petition and hereby appoints Ms. W. as Monica's guardian until she turns 21.

Once subject matter jurisdiction has been established, the Court may proceed with its SIJS findings. Pursuant to the Immigration and Nationality Act, 8 U.S.C. § 1101(a)(27)(J) (as amended by the William Wilberforce Trafficking Victims Protection Reauthorization Act of 2008, Pub. L. 110-457, 122 U.S. Stat 5044); 8 C.F.R. 204.11 (2009), Congress provided a pathway for abused, neglected or abandoned non-citizen children to obtain lawful permanent residence in the U.S. through SIJS, if they are, inter alia, under 21 years of age, unmarried, and dependent upon a juvenile court or legally committed to an individual appointed by a state or juvenile court. It must also be established that reunification with one or both parents is not viable due to their prior misconduct, *see* 8 U.S.C. § 1101(a)(27)(J)(i); *Matter of Trudy-Ann W. v. Joan W.*, 73 A.D.3d 793 (N.Y. App. Div. 2nd Dept. 2010), and that it would not be in the child's best interests to be returned to his or her previous country of nationality or country of last habitual residence, *see* 8 U.S.C. § 1101(a)(27)(J)(ii); 8 CFR 204.11(c)(6); *Matter of Trudy-Ann W.* "Ultimately, the determination of whether to grant SIJS to a particular juvenile rests with USCIS and its parent agency, the U.S. Department of Homeland Security. Thus, when making the requisite SIJS findings, the state or juvenile court is not actually 'rendering an immigration determination.'" *Matter of Enis A.C.M. [Blanca E.M.-Carlos V.C.P.]*, 152 A.D.3d 690 (N.Y. App. Div. 2nd Dept. 2017).

Here, this Court found that Monica is fully entitled to SIJS findings. The record establishes that Monica meets the age and marital status requirements for special immigrant status, and the dependency requirement has been satisfied by the Family Court granting her guardianship to Ms. W.

Moreover, Monica's parents have violently rejected her, physically abused and refused to accept her gender identity issues since very early in her short life. Her father neglected her by burning her with cigarettes and using excessive corporal punishment, as defined by Family Court Act § 1012(f)(i)(B), that impaired Monica's emotional and physical condition, *see Matter of Padmine M.*, 84 A.D.3d 806 (N.Y. App. Div. 2nd Dept. 2011); *Matter of Justyce M.*, 77 A.D.3d 1407, 908 N.Y.S.2d 783 (4th Dept. 2010). Nor have they shown any inclination to support her financially, emotionally, educationally or medically in any way since 2014. Therefore, reunification with either of her parents is not viable, even impossible, *see Matter of Luis R. v. Maria Elena G.*, 120 A.D.3d 581 (N.Y App. Div. 2nd Dept. 2014); *Matter of Cristal M.R.M.*, 118 A.D.3d 889, 891 (N.Y. App. Div. 2nd Dept. 2014). This court further finds that it would certainly not be in Monica's best interests to be returned to Honduras — her previous country of nationality and last habitual residence — given the evidence establishing that there is no one there who loves or is able to care for her, and that she was threatened with violence or worse if she were to return, *see Matter of Keilyn GG.*, 159 A.D.3d 1295 (N.Y. App. Div. 3d Dept. 2018).

Monica's harrowing life cries for her to be permitted to remain, restart and enjoy her new life on these shores of New York City. As the words of Emma Lazarus's famous 1883 sonnet "The New Colossus," emblazoned on our Statue of Liberty, exhorts:

> Give me your tired, your poor,
> Your huddled masses yearning to breathe free,
> The wretched refuse of your teeming shore.
> Send these, the homeless, tempest-tost to me,
> I lift my lamp beside the golden door!

In accordance with the foregoing, the court grants Monica's guardianship petition, and her motion for SIJS findings in her favor, as per the Order (Vargas, J.) dated April 20, 2018. The foregoing constitutes the Decision and Order of this Court.

Discussion

1. Note the confluence of circumstances that resulted in the (partial) relief that Monica obtained here: She obtained partial protection from her grandparents after her parents initially rejected her. She managed to travel from Honduras to the United States twice, the first time entering as a minor. She obtained legal representation through Catholic Migration Services. She connected with a responsible adult willing to mentor her and serve as her guardian. And her case came before a judge presumably not hostile toward LGBT persons, *see* Arthur S. Leonard, *New York Family Court Appoints Guardian and Renders Special Immigrant Juvenile Status Findings for Transgender Honduran Girl*, 2018 LGBT Law Notes 301 (June 2018) ("Judge Vargas is an esteemed judicial member of LeGaL [the LGBT Bar of New York]."), who broadly interpreted the relevant jurisdictional statutes. Far from all trans noncitizen youth who make it to the United States seem likely to be so fortunate.

2. Note also that while the order in this case may well have been necessary to enable Monica to remain in the United States, it is not sufficient. The USCIS presented with an application for SJIS must conclude that the juvenile court that made the SJIS findings had sufficient factual predicates for its findings to be considered reasonable. *Reyes v. Cissna*, 737 F. Appx. 140 (4th Cir. 2018). Moreover, USCIS will not give the consent to SJIS required by statute if its review of the juvenile court's order does not lead it to conclude "that the juvenile court order was sought to obtain relief from abuse, neglect, abandonment, or a similar basis under state law, and not primarily or solely to obtain an immigration benefit." *Id.*

Reading Guide for In re Lovo-Lara

1. Federal law specifies that certain "immediate relatives" receive special, preferential treatment for purposes of immigrating to the United States under the Immigration and Nationality Act ("INA"). In the following case, a trans woman petitioned for a visa for her husband, but the petition was denied. On what ground?

2. On appeal, the Board of Immigration Appeals ("BIA") affirms that petitioner's marriage is valid under North Carolina law. For what reasons does it reach this conclusion?

3. The BIA next concludes that the federal so-called Defense of Marriage Act ("DOMA") excludes petitioner's marriage from qualifying as a "marriage" under the INA. How does the Department of Homeland Security, which defended the denial of the petition before the BIA, argue that DOMA should be interpreted? Why does the BIA reject that position? How does the BIA conclude "man" and "woman" should be interpreted for purposes of DOMA and the INA?

In re Jose Mauricio Lovo-Lara, Beneficiary of a Visa Petition Filed by Gia Teresa Lovo-Ciccone, Petitioner

23 I. & N. Dec. 746 (B.I.A. May 18, 2005)

[Petitioner was represented by Sharon McGowan. Over her legal career, McGowan was, inter alia, a Staff Attorney with the ACLU's Lesbian Gay Bisexual Transgender & AIDS Project, Acting General Counsel and Deputy General Counsel for Policy at the U.S. Office of Personnel Management (OPM), the Principal Deputy Chief of the Appellate Section of the Civil Rights Division in the Department of Justice, and the Chief Strategy Officer and Legal Director of Lambda Legal.]

BEFORE: Board Panel: GRANT, HESS and PAULEY, Board Members.

GRANT, Board Member:

In a decision dated August 3, 2004, the Nebraska Service Center ("NSC") director denied the visa petition filed by the petitioner to accord the beneficiary immediate relative status as her husband pursuant to section 201(b)(2)(A)(i) of the Immigration and Nationality Act ["INA"], 8 U.S.C. § 1151(b)(2)(A)(i) (2000). The petitioner has appealed from that decision. The appeal will be sustained.

I. Factual and Procedural History

The petitioner [Gia Teresa Lovo-Ciccone], a United States citizen, married the beneficiary [Jose Mauricio Lovo-Lara], a native and citizen of El Salvador, in North Carolina on September 1, 2002. On November 20, 2002, the petitioner filed the instant visa petition on behalf of the beneficiary based on their marriage. The record reflects that when the petitioner was born in North Carolina on April 16, 1973, she was of the male sex. However, an affidavit from a physician reflects that on September 14, 2001, the petitioner had surgery that changed her sex designation completely from male to female.

In support of the visa petition, the petitioner submitted, among other documents, her North Carolina birth certificate, which lists her current name and indicates that her sex is female; the affidavit from the physician verifying the surgery that changed the petitioner's sex designation; a North Carolina court order changing the petitioner's name to her current name; the North Carolina Register of Deeds marriage record reflecting the marriage of the petitioner and the beneficiary; and a North Carolina driver's license listing the petitioner's current name and indicating that her sex is female.

On August 3, 2004, the NSC director issued his decision denying the instant visa petition. In support of his denial, the NSC director stated that defining marriage under the immigration laws is a question of Federal law, which Congress clarified in 1996 by enacting the Defense of Marriage Act, Pub. L. No. 104-199, 110 Stat. 2419 (1996) ("DOMA"). Pursuant to the DOMA, in order to qualify as a marriage for purposes of Federal law, one partner to the marriage must be a man and the other partner must be a woman. In his decision the NSC director stated as follows:

While some states and countries have enacted laws that permit a person who has undergone sex change surgery to legally change the person's sex from one to the other, Congress has not addressed the issue. Consequently, without legislation from Congress officially recognizing a marriage where one of the parties has undergone sex change surgery . . . , this Service has no legal basis on which to recognize a change of sex so that a marriage between two persons born of the same sex can be recognized.

The NSC director concluded that "since the petitioner and beneficiary were born of the same sex, their marriage is not considered valid for immigration purposes and the beneficiary is not eligible to be classified as the spouse of the petitioner under section 201(b) of the Act."

The petitioner filed a timely Notice of Appeal (Form EOIR-29) and subsequently filed a brief in support of her appeal. The Department of Homeland Security ("DHS") Service Center Counsel also filed a brief in support of the NSC director's decision.

II. Issue

The issue presented by this case is whether a marriage between a postoperative male-to-female transsexual and a male can be the basis for benefits under section 201(b)(2)(A)(i) of the Act, where the State in which the marriage occurred recognizes the change in sex of the postoperative transsexual and considers the marriage valid.

III. Analysis

In order to determine whether a marriage is valid for immigration purposes, the relevant analysis involves determining first whether the marriage is valid under State law and then whether the marriage qualifies under the [INA]. *See Adams v. Howerton*, 673 F.2d 1036 (9th Cir. 1982). The issue of the validity of a marriage under State law is generally governed by the law of the place of celebration of the marriage. *Id*

. . . . Section 51-1 of the General Statutes of North Carolina provides that "[a] valid and sufficient marriage is created by the consent of a male and female person who may lawfully marry, presently to take each other as husband and wife, freely, seriously and plainly expressed by each in the presence of the other." The terms "male" and "female" are not defined in the statute, but section 51-1 makes it clear by its terms that the State of North Carolina does not permit individuals of the same sex to marry each other. *See also* N.C. Gen. Stat. § 51-1.2 (2004).

Section 130A-118 of the General Statutes of North Carolina governs the amendment of birth certificates. That statute provides, in relevant part, as follows:

A new certificate of birth shall be made by the State Registrar when:

. . .

(4) A written request from an individual is received by the State Registrar to change the sex on that individual's birth record because of sex reassignment

surgery, if the request is accompanied by a notarized statement from the physician who performed the sex reassignment surgery or from a physician licensed to practice medicine who has examined the individual and can certify that the person has undergone sex reassignment surgery.

N.C. Gen. Stat. § 130A-118(b)(4) (2004).

As noted above, the documents submitted by the petitioner reflect that she underwent sex reassignment surgery. Consequently, the State of North Carolina issued her a new birth certificate that lists her sex as female and registered her marriage to the beneficiary, listing her as the bride. In light of the above, we find that the petitioner's marriage to the beneficiary is considered valid under the laws of the State of North Carolina. [Neither] the NSC director nor the DHS counsel has asserted anything to the contrary on this point.

The dispositive issue in this case, therefore, is whether the marriage of the petitioner and the beneficiary qualifies as a valid marriage under the [INA]. Section 201(b)(2)(A)(i) of the [INA] provides for immediate relative classification for the "children, spouses, and parents of a citizen of the United States." The Act does not define the word "spouse" in terms of the sex of the parties. However, the DOMA did provide a Federal definition of the terms "marriage" and "spouse" as follows:

> In determining the meaning of any Act of Congress, or of any ruling, regulation, or interpretation of the various administrative bureaus and agencies of the United States, the word "marriage" means only a legal union between one man and one woman as husband and wife, and the word "spouse" refers only to a person of the opposite sex who is a husband or a wife.

DOMA § 3(a) (codified at 1 U.S.C. § 7 (2000)).

Neither the DOMA nor any other Federal law addresses the issue of how to define the sex of a postoperative transsexual or such designation's effect on a subsequent marriage of that individual. The failure of Federal law to address this issue formed the main basis for the NSC director's conclusion that this marriage cannot be found valid for immigration purposes. . . .

In determining the effect of the DOMA on this case, we look to the rules of statutory construction. The starting point in statutory construction is the language of the statute. *See INS v. Cardoza-Fonseca*, 480 U.S. 421 (1987). If the language of the statute is clear and unambiguous, judicial inquiry is complete, as we clearly "must give effect to the unambiguously expressed intent of Congress." *Chevron, U.S.A., Inc. v. Natural Resources Defense Council, Inc.*, 467 U.S. 837 (1984). We find that the language of section 3(a) of the DOMA . . . is clear on its face. There is no question that a valid marriage can only be one between a man and a woman. Marriages between same-sex couples are clearly excluded.

This interpretation is further supported by the legislative history of the DOMA. The House Report specifically states that the DOMA was introduced in response to a 1993 decision of the Hawai'i Supreme Court that raised the issue of the potential legality of same-sex marriages in Hawai'i. *See* H.R. Rep. No. 104-664, at 2–6 (1996) (citing *Baehr v. Lewin*, 852 P.2d 44 (Haw. 1993) (remanding for application of strict scrutiny under the Hawai'i equal protection clause to the question of the denial of marriage licenses to same-sex couples)). Throughout the House Report, the terms "same sex" and "homosexual" are used interchangeably. The House Report also repeatedly refers to the consequences of permitting *homosexual couples* to marry.

However, with regard to one of the specific issues we are facing in this case, *i.e.*, whether the DOMA applies to invalidate, for Federal purposes, a marriage involving a postoperative transsexual, it is notable that Congress did not mention the case of *M.T. v. J.T.*, 355 A.2d 204 (N.J. Super. Ct. App. Div. 1976) [Chapter 17, *infra* at p. 1190, which recognized a transsexual marriage.[6] Nor did it mention the various State statutes that at the time of consideration of the DOMA provided for the legal recognition of a change of sex designation by postoperative transsexuals. Rather, Congress's focus, as indicated by its consistent reference to homosexuals in the floor discussions and in the House Report, was fixed on, and limited to, the issue of homosexual marriage.

Furthermore, a specific statement in the House Report's section-by-section analysis provides support for the conclusion that Congress did not consider transsexual marriages to be per se violative of the DOMA. According to that statement, "*Prior to the Hawai'i lawsuit*, no State has ever permitted homosexual couples to marry. Accordingly, federal law could rely on state determinations of who was married without risk of inconsistency or endorsing same-sex 'marriage.'" H.R. Rep. No. 104-664, at 30 (emphasis added). As noted above, *M.T. v. J.T.* and the statutory provisions in several States recognizing a legal change of sex after surgery were in existence at the time the House Report was issued.

We therefore conclude that the legislative history of the DOMA indicates that in enacting that statute, Congress *only* intended to restrict marriages between persons of the same sex. There is no indication that the DOMA was meant to apply to

---

6. . . . . The court . . . directly confronted the issue "whether the marriage between a male and a postoperative transsexual, who has surgically changed her external sexual anatomy from male to female, is to be regarded as a lawful marriage between a man and a woman." The court concluded that "for marital purposes if the anatomical or genital features of a genuine transsexual are made to conform to the person's gender, psyche or psychological sex, then identity by sex must be governed by the congruence of these standards." *Id.* at 209. On this basis, the court affirmed the finding of the trial court that the postoperative male-to-female transsexual was a female at the time of her marriage and entered into a valid marriage.

In 1977, the Department of Health, Education, and Welfare prepared a Model State Vital Statistics Act that specifically provided for the amendment of a birth certificate upon proof of a change of sex by surgical procedure in section 21(e). By 1996, at the time of consideration of the DOMA, several States had enacted legislation patterned after section 21(e) to provide a mechanism for amending a person's birth certificate to reflect a change of sex upon submission of a court order recognizing a sex change by surgical procedure. A recent review of State legislation indicates that 22 States and the District of Columbia have now enacted provisions specifically permitting legal recognition of changes of sex by postoperative transsexuals.

a marriage involving a postoperative transsexual where the marriage is considered by the State in which it was performed as one between two individuals of the opposite sex.[7]

There is also nothing in the legislative history to indicate that, other than in the limited area of same-sex marriages, Congress sought to overrule our long-standing case law holding that there is no Federal definition of marriage and that the validity of a particular marriage is determined by the law of the State where the marriage was celebrated. *See Matter of Hosseinian*, 19 I. & N. Dec. 453 (B.I.A. 1987). While we recognize, of course, that the ultimate issue of the validity of a marriage for immigration purposes is one of Federal law, that law has, from the inception of our nation, recognized that the regulation of marriage is almost exclusively a State matter. *See, e.g., Boddie v. Connecticut*, 401 U.S. 371 (1971); *Sherrer v. Sherrer*, 334 U.S. 343 (1948).[8] Interestingly, with regard to this point, the House Report stated the following:

> If Hawai'i or some other State eventually recognizes homosexual "marriage," Section 3 will mean simply that that "marriage" will not be recognized as a "marriage" for purposes of federal law. *Other than this narrow federal requirement*, the federal government will continue to determine marital status in the same manner it does under current law.

H.R. Rep. No. 104-664, at 31 (emphasis added). Therefore, we also conclude that Congress need not act affirmatively to authorize recognition of even an atypical marriage before such a marriage may be regarded as valid for immigration purposes, assuming that the marriage is not deemed invalid under applicable State law.[9]

---

7. Our conclusion in this regard is consistent with an April 16, 2004, Interoffice Memorandum from William R. Yates, Associate Director for Operations of the United States Citizenship and Immigration Services ("CIS"), respecting the "Adjudication of Petitions and Applications Filed by or on Behalf of, or Document Requests by, Transsexual Individuals." That memorandum acknowledges that "neither the DOMA nor any other Federal statute addresses whether a marriage between (for example) a man and a person born a man who has undergone surgery to become a woman should be recognized for immigration purposes or considered invalid as a same-sex marriage."

8. In deference to this fundamental aspect of our system of government, Federal statutes purporting to outlaw certain types of marriage are few and far between, and no Federal statute affirmatively authorizing a type of marriage appears to exist. Apart from the DOMA, the only other Federal statutory provisions purporting to outlaw certain types of marriage that our research has discovered are found at section 101(a)(35) of the [INA], 8 U.S.C. § 1101(a)(35) (2000), which, in defining the terms "spouse," "husband," and "wife" for purposes of the Act, specifically excludes recognition of so-called proxy marriages "where the contracting parties thereto are not physically in the presence of each other, unless the marriage shall have been consummated," and in the Mann Act, which was construed by the Supreme Court to prohibit the interstate transportation of women for purposes of engaging in polygamy. *See Cleveland v. United States*, 329 U.S. 14 (1946); *see also* section 212(a)(10)(A) of the [INA], 8 U.S.C. § 1182(a)(10)(A) (2000) (rendering inadmissible any immigrant coming to the United States to practice polygamy). Section 3(a) of the DOMA would also appear to have as an incidental effect the declaration of invalidity of polygamy, as it provides that "the word 'marriage' means only a legal union between *one man and one woman* as husband and wife." (Emphasis added.)

9. This conclusion is entirely consistent with *Adams v. Howerton*, relied on by the DHS. In that case, the court held that even if a homosexual marriage between an American citizen and

The DHS counsel appears to argue that in determining whether a particular marriage is valid under the DOMA, we must look to the common meanings of the terms "man" and "woman," as they are used in the DOMA. Counsel asserts that these terms can be conclusively defined by an individual's chromosomal pattern, *i.e.*, XX for female and XY for male, because such chromosomal patterns are immutable. However, this claim is subject to much debate within the medical community. According to medical experts, there are actually eight criteria that are typically used to determine an individual's sex. They are [genetic or chromosomal sex—XX or XY; gonadal sex—testes or ovaries; internal morphologic sex—seminal vesicles/prostate or vagina/uterus/fallopian tubes; external morphologic sex—penis/scrotum or clitoris/labia; hormonal sex—androgens or estrogens; phenotypic sex (secondary sexual features)—facial and chest hair or breasts; assigned sex and gender of rearing; and sexual identity [more commonly known as gender identity—Eds.].] *See* Julie A. Greenberg, *Defining Male and Female: Intersexuality and the Collision Between Law and Biology*, 41 Ariz. L. Rev. 265, 278 (1999).

While most individuals are born with 46 XX or XY chromosomes and all of the other factors listed above are congruent with their chromosomal pattern, there are certain individuals who have what is termed an "intersexual condition," where some of the above factors may be incongruent, or where an ambiguity within a factor may exist. For example, there are individuals with a chromosomal ambiguity who do not have the typical 46 XX or XY chromosomal pattern but instead have the chromosomal patterns of XXX, XXY, XXXY, XYY, XYYY, XYYYY, or XO. Therefore, because a chromosomal pattern is not always the most accurate determination of an individual's gender, the DHS counsel's reliance on chromosomal patterns as the ultimate determinative factor is questionable.

Moreover, contrary to the suggestion of the DHS counsel, reliance on the sex designation provided on an individual's original birth certificate is not an accurate way to determine a person's gender.[10] Typically, such a determination is made by the birth attendant based on the appearance of the external genitalia. However, intersexed individuals may have the normal-appearing external genitalia of one sex, but have the chromosomal sex of the opposite gender. Moreover, many incongruities between the above-noted factors for determining a person's sex, and even

---

an alien was valid under Colorado law, the parties were not "spouses" under section 201(b) of the [INA]. The court reached its result through an interpretation of section 201(b) itself and the term "spouse" as used therein, not by finding a general Federal public policy against the recognition of such marriages.

10. We note that there could be anomalous results if we refuse to recognize a postoperative transsexual's change of sex and instead consider the person to be of the sex determined at birth in accordance with the DHS's suggestion. For example, the marriage of a postoperative male-to-female transsexual to a female in a State that recognizes marriages between both opposite-sex and same-sex couples would be considered valid, not only under State law, but also under Federal law, because, under the DHS's interpretation, the postoperative transsexual would still be considered a male, despite having the external genitalia of a female.

some ambiguities within a factor, are not discovered until the affected individuals reach the age of puberty and their bodies develop differently from what would be expected from their assigned gender.

We are not persuaded by the assertions of the DHS counsel that we should rely on a person's chromosomal pattern or the original birth record's gender designation in determining whether a marriage is between persons of the opposite sex. Consequently, for immigration purposes, we find it appropriate to determine an individual's gender based on the designation appearing on the current birth certificate issued to that person by the State in which he or she was born.

IV. Conclusion

We have long held that the validity of a marriage is determined by the law of the State where the marriage was celebrated. The State of North Carolina considers the petitioner to be a female under the law and deems her marriage to the beneficiary to be a valid opposite-sex marriage. We find that the DOMA does not preclude our recognition of this marriage for purposes of Federal law. As the NSC director did not raise any other issues regarding the validity of the marriage, we conclude that the marriage between the petitioner and the beneficiary may be the basis for benefits under section 201(b)(2)(A)(i) of the Act. Accordingly, the petitioner's appeal will be sustained, and the visa petition will be approved.

ORDER: The petitioner's appeal is sustained, and the visa petition is approved.

Discussion

1. What do you think the physician's affidavit means when it avers that Gia Teresa Lovo-Ciccone had "*surgery* that changed her sex *designation* completely from male to female" (emphases added)?

2. The BIA concludes that "reliance on the sex designation provided on an individual's original birth certificate is not an accurate way to determine a person's gender." What might the notion of "accuracy" mean as the BIA uses it here? In what sense is the hypothetical in footnote 5 "anomalous"?

3. The BIA concludes that federal immigration law should use state birth certificate sex designations to determine whether a couple is a validly married, different-sex couple for immigration purposes. Whether someone's current birth certificate reflects their current sex is a function of state law, so this might seem to accord with the principle from precedent that federal law generally accepts state law definitions of valid marriages. But (at least at a time when marriage was restricted to different-sex couples) state law might not necessarily treat current birth certificate sex designations as determining people's sexes for state marriage law. Why shouldn't federal immigration law use whatever sex designation state law treats as relevant for state marriage law purposes? Does the BIA take federalism into account properly?

4. For various scholarly treatments of immigration and asylum issues regarding transgender persons in addition to the sources cited above, see, for example, Luis Medina, *Immigrating While Trans: The Disproportionate Impact of the Prostitution Ground of Inadmissibility and Other Provisions of the Immigration and Nationality Act on Transgender Women*, 19 SCHOLAR 253 (2017).; Owen Cahill Bement, Note, *A Diplomatic Solution: The Continued Failure of Gender Classification in Immigration and Customs Enforcement's Transgender Care Memorandum*, 30 GEO. IMMIGR. L.J. 489 (2016); Benjamin Rumph, Avendano-Hernandez v. Lynch: *Twenty-First-Century Values and Transgender Communities' Impact on Immigration Policy and Foreign Relations*, 24 TUL. J. INT'L & COMP. L. 391 (2016); Adena L. Wayne, Note, *"Unique Identities and Vulnerabilities": The Case for Transgender Identity as a Basis for Asylum*, 102 CORNELL L. REV. 241 (2016); Munmeeth Soni, *A Call to Service: Ensuring Every Gay, Bisexual, Transgender Asylum Seeker Detained at the Santa Ana City Jail Has Access to Justice*, 57-OCT ORANGE COUNTY LAW. 32 (2015); Angela Devolld, *Refugee Roulette: Wagering on Morality, Sexuality, and Normalcy in U.S. Asylum Law*, 92 NEB. L. REV. 627 (2014); Shana Tabak & Rachel Levitan, *LGBTI Migrants in Immigration Detention: a Global Perspective*, 37 HARV. J.L. & GENDER 1 (2014); The National Lawyers Guild, San Francisco Bay Area Chapter, *A Know-Your-Rights Manual for the Transgender Community: Immigration Law*, 70 NAT'L LAW. GUILD REV. 145 (2013); Bijal Shah, *LGBT Identity in Immigration*, 45 COLUM. HUM. RTS. L. REV. 100 (2013); Olga Tomchin, Comment, *Bodies and Bureaucracy: Legal Sex Classification and Marriage-Based Immigration for Trans People*, 101 CALIF. L. REV. 813 (2013); Pooja Gehi, *Gendered (In)Security: Migration and Criminalization in the Security State*, 35 HARV. J.L. & GENDER 357 (2012); Christi Jo Benson, *Crossing Borders: A Focus on Treatment of Transgender Individuals in U.S. Asylum Law and Society*, 30 WHITTIER L. REV. 41 (2008). For a manual aimed at lawyers on U.S. asylum law in LGBT/HIV cases (with sources dating through 2016), see IMMIGRATION EQUALITY, ASYLUM MANUAL (2006), available at https://immigrationequality .org/asylum/asylum-manual/ (last visited July 27, 2020); for a "close reading" of this manual critical of "the limits of neo-liberal rights frameworks that produce gender-variant people as subjects who must pefectly perform regulatory procedures to gain access to rights," see Aren Z. Aizura, *Transnational and Transgender Rights and Immigration Law, in* TRANSFEMINIST PERSPECTIVES IN AND BEYOND TRANSGENDER AND GENDER STUDIES 133-150 (Anne Enke ed., 2012).

Chapter 10

Religious Exemptions from Anti-Discrimination Protections

As legal protections against discrimination on the basis of gender identity and expression have emerged in the contemporary United States of America, so, too, have claims to be exempt from such laws on the ground that complying would violate the regulated individuals' or entities' rights to exercise their religion. This chapter takes up this latest area of conflict between civil rights laws and religiously justified resistance to such laws. Section A presents a general overview of free exercise of religion law and doctrine. Section B provides a brief historical and contemporary examination of these sorts of clashes between equality and liberty in a variety of civil rights movements in the United States. Section C then examines particular instances where individuals and organizations have claimed a right to disregard laws forbidding discrimination against transgender and gender-nonconforming persons because, they claim, to do otherwise would require them to take action violative of their religious beliefs.

A. Foundations and Evolution of Free Exercise Law

The First Amendment to the Constitution provides that "Congress shall make no law respecting an establishment of religion, nor prohibiting the free exercise thereof. . . ." Although only expressly naming Congress and the laws that it makes, the Religion Clauses have long been interpreted to apply to all federal governmental actors and actions and not merely to legislation. The guarantees of these Clauses also have been interpreted to apply to state and local governmental actors through the Fourteenth Amendment via the "incorporation doctrine," by which almost all rights in the Bill of Rights have been held to apply to state and local government even though the Supreme Court has long ruled that the Bill of Rights directly restricts only the federal government, *see, e.g., Barron v. Baltimore*, 32 U.S. (7 Pet.) 243 (1833) (ruling Fifth Amendment's just compensation requirement for land taken for public use inapplicable to municipal taking).

With the exception of 27 years in U.S. constitutional history, the Supreme Court's treatment of the general rule of the Free Exercise Clause (the second of the Religion Clauses that open the First Amendment) has been that it forbids government action targeting people or actions *because* they are religious but that it does not privilege conduct by providing people exemptions from laws simply because of their religious motivations. *See, e.g., Church of Lukumi Babalu Aye, Inc. v. Hialeah*, 508 U.S. 520 (1993) (using strict scrutiny to invalidate under incorporated Free Exercise Clause a set of municipal ordinances targeted at religious animal sacrifice by practitioners of the religion Santeria). Thus, for example, in the late nineteenth century the Supreme Court rejected the position that the Free Exercise Clause should grant members of the Church of Jesus Christ of Latter-Day Saints (casually, the Mormon church) an exemption from criminal bans on polygamy on the ground that their polygamous practice was motivated by their religious beliefs. *Reynolds v. United States*, 98 U.S. 145 (1878). More than half a century later, the Supreme Court similarly rejected the claim that it violated the Free Exercise Clause to penalize Jehovah's Witnesses who due to their religious beliefs refused to salute the flag and recite the Pledge of Allegiance. *Minersville School District v. Gobitis*, 310 U.S. 586 (1940). When the Court reversed course and overruled *Gobitis* just three years later in the landmark case *West Virginia State Board of Education v. Barnette*, 319 U.S. 624 (1943), it did *not* hold that the Free Exercise Clause required an exemption for *religious* objectors. Rather, *Barnette* held that general freedom of speech and conscience principles of the First Amendment barred the government from requiring *any* person who objected to recite the Pledge.

It was not until 1963 that the Supreme Court used the Free Exercise Clause to require an exemption of sorts for someone because of the religious nature of their motivation. In *Sherbert v. Verner*, 374 U.S. 398 (1963), the state of South Carolina refused to grant unemployment compensation benefits to a member of the Seventh-Day Adventist Church who was fired from her job after she refused to work on the day she observed as the Sabbath. The state did not consider her refusal to work to be justified by "good cause," which disqualified her from benefits under its statutory scheme. The U.S. Supreme Court, however, held that this in effect penalized her for her Sabbatarian beliefs. Because the state's action substantially burdened her exercise of religion, the Court subjected its action to strict scrutiny, which the Court held the state failed and thereby violated the Free Exercise Clause. In subsequent years, the Court followed the approach of *Sherbert* and reversed state refusals to grant unemployment compensation benefits to people with religious reasons for refusing particular work in three more cases. *See Thomas v. Review Board*, 450 U.S. 707 (1981); *Hobbie v. Unemployment Appeals Commission*, 480 U.S. 136 (1987); *Frazee v. Illinois Department of Employment Security*, 489 U.S. 829 (1989). In addition to those four rulings, the Court held in favor of a religious claimant in one additional case, deciding that the Free Exercise Clause barred Wisconsin from applying its truancy laws to compel members of an Old Order Amish sect to send their children to organized schooling generally for ninth and tenth grades. *See Wisconsin v. Yoder*, 406 U.S. 205 (1972).

In all other free exercise cases the Court decided on the merits from 1963 to 1990, it either ruled that the challenged state action survived strict scrutiny or held that strict scrutiny was not required for some reason or other. Then, in 1990, the Court decided one more unemployment compensation case, where it largely repudiated its doctrine of strict scrutiny whenever laws imposed a substantial burden on someone's religious exercise. *See Employment Division, Department of Human Resources v. Smith*, 494 U.S. 872 (1990). In *Smith*, two drug counselors lost their jobs after they used peyote sacramentally in a ritual of the Native American Church. The state denied them unemployment compensation on grounds of "misconduct"; Oregon law criminalized the use of peyote, with (it turned out) no exemption for religious use. In the claimants' suit against the state, the U.S. Supreme Court ultimately held that, as a general matter, neutral, generally applicable laws — such as a criminal peyote ban that applied generally — did not violate the Free Exercise Clause, and hence Oregon did not have to provide unemployment compensation benefits here. It distinguished the *Sherbert* line of cases and *Yoder* as involving either laws that had systems of individual exemptions or "a hybrid situation" involving "the Free Exercise Clause in conjunction with other constitutional protections, such as freedom of speech and of the press."

Unhappy with the Court's repudiation of the compelled-exemptions view of the Free Exercise Clause, Congress enacted the Religious Freedom Restoration Act of 1993, 42 U.S.C. § 2000bb-1. As its title suggests, the widespread belief in Congress was that it was restoring judicial doctrine from the pre-*Smith* era, forbidding government from substantially burdening a person's exercise of religion unless the government shows that application of the burden to the person furthers a compelling governmental interest and is the least restrictive means of furthering that interest.

Seemingly unhappy with Congress's attempt to overrule one of its constitutional decisions with a mere statute, four years later the Supreme Court held that RFRA was not a permissible exercise of congressional power to enforce constitutional rights and thus that it could not be applied to state or local governmental action. RFRA remains applicable to the federal government on the theory that whatever grant of power lets the federal government take a particular action suffices, at least in conjunction with the Necessary and Proper Clause of the Constitution, Art. I § 8 cl. 18, for the government to bind itself not to burden substantially people's exercise of religion unless it can pass strict scrutiny. Pursuant to this remainder of RFRA, the Supreme Court has held that the federal government was properly subject to a preliminary injunction barring it from applying the Controlled Substances Act's ban on a particular hallucinogen used in a sacramental tea by a Christian Spiritist sect. *Gonzales v. O Centro Espírita Beneficente Uniã do Vegetal*, 126 S. Ct. 1211 (2006). *Accord Holt v. Hobbs*, 135 S. Ct. 853 (2015) (applying federal Religious Land Use and Institutionalized Persons Act, subjecting both federal and state or local governments to the same standard as RFRA in narrower domain, to require exemption for Muslim prisoner asking to wear ½" long beard from federal Bureau of Prisons rule barring beards on inmates).

RFRA was most notoriously interpreted and applied by the Supreme Court in *Burwell v. Hobby Lobby Stores, Inc.*, 573 U.S. 682 (2014). There, three closely-held for-profit corporations and the individuals who owned or controlled them challenged regulations that the Department of Health and Human Services promulgated under the Patient Protection and Affordable Care Act of 2010 ("ACA" or "Affordable Care Act") that generally require employers with 50 or more employees to include coverage for specified forms of contraception with no additional costs to the covered workers. The corporations sued, arguing that the requirement would coerce them to act contrary to their religious beliefs in violation of RFRA. By a 5–4 vote, the more conservative Justices of the Supreme Court agreed.

Hobby Lobby held that by protecting "persons," RFRA extended at least to closely held corporations whether they were religious or secular, non-profit or for-profit. It ruled that the challenged regulation imposed a substantial burden on the plaintiffs' exercise of religion by forcing them either to engage in acts they believe violate their religious beliefs or to face very large monetary penalties for not complying with the regulation. The government had argued that the connection between providing health insurance that includes contraceptive coverage for the companies' workers and destruction of a fertilized human egg was too attenuated because that destruction would only occur depending on the independent choices of workers. Thus, the government maintained that this connection was insufficient for the employers to be morally complicit in a way that should count as a substantial burden on the exercise of their religion within the meaning of the statute. The Supreme Court rejected that contention; all that mattered for RFRA, the Court held, was that the plaintiff individuals had a "sincere belief" or "honest conviction" that the provision of such insurance went against their religious beliefs and that adhering to their convictions would cost them "an enormous sum." Having found a substantial burden on the plaintiffs' exercise of religion, the majority applied strict scrutiny under the statute. Because RFRA requires that the application of the challenged law to the challenger be in furtherance of a compelling governmental interest, the Court, following precedent (*O Centro Espírita*), insisted that "broadly formulated interests" such as "public health" or "gender equality" writ large were inadequate. Rather, the government must consider the claimed harm of granting "specific exemptions to particular religious claimants." The majority accepted for sake of argument "that the interest in guaranteeing cost-free access to the four challenged contraceptive methods is compelling within the meaning of RFRA"—although it expressed skepticism of that position in light of various exemptions to the requirement that employers provide insurance including the regulatorily specified forms of contraception.

The majority did not need to rule that out because it held that even were that interest compelling, the regulation was not the least restrictive means of furthering that interest. It floated the idea that a less restrictive way for the government to assure such access "would be for the Government to assume the cost of providing the four contraceptives at issue to any women who are unable to obtain them under their health-insurance policies due to their employers' religious objections." But "[in] the end" the majority did not rely on the possibility of such a new governmental program, instead emphasizing the fact that the government had worked out a way to accommodate the religious objections of non-profit organizations while still ensuring that their female employees had coverage for all the specified forms of contraception; the organizations simply had to complete a form specifying their religious objection to coverage, and the insurers would ensure the workers received coverage nonetheless at no extra cost to the organizations or their employees. This accommodation, the court said, could be provided to closely-held for-profit corporations with religious objections with "precisely zero" effect on their women employees.

In a paragraph potentially significant for later clashes between anti-discrimination laws and religiously motivated discrimination, the majority wrote:

> The principal dissent raises the possibility that discrimination in hiring, for example on the basis of race, might be cloaked as religious practice to escape legal sanction. Our decision today provides no such shield. The Government has a compelling interest in providing an equal opportunity to participate in the workforce without regard to race, and prohibitions on racial discrimination are precisely tailored to achieve that critical goal.

The narrow tailoring logic seems applicable to laws forbidding disparate treatment on any ground—color, religion, national origin, sex, disability, transgender status, and more. A question could perhaps arise if a law were understood to require accommodations rather than merely formally equal treatment.

In addition, the *Hobby Lobby* majority only asserted here that government has a compelling interest (itself carefully worded) *with respect to race*. Whether a majority of the Court will be willing to recognize other antidiscrimination interests as compelling remains to be seen. With regard to the last point, it may be worth noting that during the drafting of RFRA, the House of Representatives rejected an amendment that would have defined "compelling state interest" to include only antidiscrimination laws *based on race or national origin. See* David B. Cruz, *Piety and Prejudice: Free Exercise Exemption from Laws Prohibiting Sexual Orientation Discrimination*, 69 N.Y.U. L. Rev. 1176, 1232 n.325 (1994) (citing H.R. Rep. No. 88, 103d Cong., 1st Sess. 16–17 n.6 (1993)).

Hobby Lobby thus reads RFRA expansively to require a regime of religious exemptions likely broader than pre-*Smith* case law demanded. *See, e.g., City of Boerne v. Flores*, 521 U.S. 507, 535 (1997) (contending that RFRA "imposes in every case a least restrictive means requirement—a requirement that was not used in the pre-*Smith* jurisprudence RFRA purported to codify"). But the field of such exemptions is narrower than before *Smith*: RFRA applies only to federal governmental action after *Boerne*, and the Religious Land Use and Institutionalized Persons Act of 2000 ("RLUIPA") applies the same test to federal, state, and local *land use* regulations and to governmentally imposed burdens on "a person residing in or confined to an institution" including jails, residential facilities for people with mental illnesses or disabilities, juvenile group homes, and more.

Additionally, there is a notable exception to *Smith*'s rule that neutral, generally applicable laws do not violate the Free Exercise Clause: the "ministerial exception" to anti-discrimination laws' applicability to employment of people considered "ministers." As the Supreme Court noted in *Hosanna-Tabor Evangelical Lutheran Church and School v. E.E.O.C.*, 565 U.S. 171 (2012):

> Since the passage of Title VII of the Civil Rights Act of 1964, 42 U.S.C. § 2000e et seq., and other employment discrimination laws, the Courts of Appeals have uniformly recognized the existence of a "ministerial exception," grounded in the First Amendment, that precludes application of such legislation to claims concerning the employment relationship between a religious institution and its ministers.

In *Hosanna-Tabor*, the Court embraced this doctrine under the Free Exercise Clause and the Establishment Clause of the First Amendment:

> Requiring a church to accept or retain an unwanted minister, or punishing a church for failing to do so, intrudes upon more than a mere employment decision. Such action interferes with the internal governance of the church, depriving the church of control over the selection of those who will personify its beliefs. By imposing an unwanted minister, the state infringes the Free Exercise Clause, which protects a religious group's right to shape its own faith and mission through its appointments. According the state the power to determine which individuals will minister to the faithful also violates the Establishment Clause, which prohibits government involvement in such ecclesiastical decisions.

On the facts of *Hosanna-Tabor*, the Court held that Cheryl Perich, a "called teacher" of kindergarten and fourth grade students at a Christian school, counted as a "minister" and so could not sue her former employer for disability discrimination in violation of the Americans with Disabilities Act. And this was true even though she abandoned her claim for reinstatement and was seeking only damages and attorney's fees:

> An award of such relief would operate as a penalty on the Church for terminating an unwanted minister, and would be no less prohibited by the First Amendment than an order overturning the termination. Such relief would depend on a determination that Hosanna-Tabor was wrong to have relieved Perich of her position, and it is precisely such a ruling that is barred by the ministerial exception.

Whether the "ministerial" employee's claim was based on federal law or state law was immaterial—all such actions were barred by the First Amendment.

The Court did not offer a definition of "minister" for purposes of the ministerial exception, declining to adopt "a rigid formula" and instead reaching its judgment that Perich was a minister based on "all the circumstances of her employment." These circumstances included "the formal title given Perich by the Church, the substance reflected in that title, her own use of that title, and the important religious functions she performed for the Church."

Most employers in the U.S. are not churches or "religious groups," and certainly most employees are not "ministers." The ministerial exception is thus unlikely to directly affect most transgender workers. Where it applies, however, it is potent.

Note also that, as this book is going to press, the Supreme Court has granted review in *Fulton v. City of Philadelphia*, 922 F.3d 140 (3d Cir. 2019), *cert. granted*, 140 S. Ct. 1104 (2020). Philadelphia requires the social services agencies with which it contracts not to discriminate on the basis of, inter alia, sexual orientation. One such agency, Catholic Social Services, refused to work with same-sex couples as potential foster parents; it would only place foster children with single or married people but not cohabiting couples, and its position is that only different-sex couples are married (in their religious view of marriage). Philadelphia refused to renew its contract with CSS, which responded by suing, alleging violations of its rights under the free speech, free exercise, and establishment clauses of the U.S. Constitution and Pennsylvania's Religious Freedom Protection Act (RFPA). The lower courts denied CSS a preliminary injunction, ruling that they were not likely to prevail on the merits of any of their claims. They reasoned in part that the non-discrimination requirement was a neutral law of general applicability, that the city's decision was apparently based on CSS's discriminatory conduct and not the religious character of the beliefs that motivated that conduct, that the city was not compelling agencies to adopt particular religious views about marriage nor to endorse the city's views on marriage, and that the city did not substantially burden CSS's exercise of religion within the meaning of RFPA.

CSS's cert petition granted by the Supreme Court included three questions it maintained were presented by the case. One was whether the U.S. Court of Appeals for the Third Circuit wrongly insisted that the only way to establish that a law was not neutral or generally applicable is to show that a governmental actor would have treated differently someone with different religious views who engaged in the same conduct. This question arguably seeks to adhere to *Smith* and *Church of the Lukumi Babalu Aye*, if perhaps to underscore *Smith*'s distinguishing of prior precedent that involved "individualized exemptions." Another "question presented" is whether conditioning agencies' participation in the foster care system on "taking actions and making statements" that contradict an agency's religious beliefs violates the First Amendment. Yet CSS does not appear to deny that same-sex couples can be civilly married, nor has it shown that Philadelphia is claiming that same-sex couples who civilly marry are married in a religious sense. (CSS alleges a couple statements in the record that might bear some resemblance to the comments of some Colorado Civil Rights Commission members that grounded the Court's finding of a free exercise violation in *Masterpiece Cakeshop, Ltd. v. Colorado Civil Rights Commission*, 138 S. Ct. 1719 (2018).) Most sweepingly, the third question presented is whether *Employment Division v. Smith* should be revisited. While it is troubling to imagine that the Supreme Court could hold that the Constitution requires the government to include groups that will discriminate against some of the citizenry when it hires private organizations to assist its exercise of governmental functions, the order granting certiorari, as always, does not explain why at least four members of the Court chose to take up this case.

B. Religiously Justified Resistance to Civil Equality

Laws expressly forbidding discrimination on the basis of gender identity or expression are fairly new, and so therefore are objections to them from certain religious individuals and organizations. Yet religiously based justifications for resistance to civil equality are not new. In the nineteenth century, defenders of race-based chattel slavery in the United States at times invoked the Bible as supporting enslavement or, later, racial segregation and bans on interracial marriages. During the twentieth century, individuals argued that the federal government could not enforce laws forbidding race or sex discrimination against them because of their freedom of religion. For example, in *Brown v. Dade Christian Schools, Inc.*, 556 F.2d 310, 312 (5th Cir. 1977) (en banc), the full U.S. Court of Appeals for the Fifth Circuit rejected the effort of a Christian school to interpose a free exercise of religion defense to a suit brought against it under a federal law prohibiting racial discrimination in contracting by the parents of children denied admission solely because they were African American. The plurality deferred to the trial court and affirmed the rejection of the religious exemption on the ground that the trial court was not clearly erroneous in finding the school's racially discriminatory admissions to be the result of a policy choice and not of religious belief. The concurring and dissenting judges disagreed, finding ample evidence of a religious foundation for the admissions policy; the concurrence rejected the free exercise claim on the merits, finding the governmental nondiscrimination interests to outweigh the religious exemption claim. *See also, e.g., Newman v. Piggie Park Enterprises, Inc.*, 256 F. Supp. 941, 945 (D.S.C. 1966), *aff'd in relevant part and rev'd in part on other grounds*, 377 F.2d 433 (4th Cir. 1967), *aff'd and modified on other grounds*, 390 U.S. 400 (1968) (rejecting free exercise argument that restaurant owner's religious beliefs against racial integration exempted him from law forbidding race discrimination by public accommodations).

Similarly, defendants have attempted to deploy the Free Exercise Clause as a defense to laws forbidding sex discrimination. In *EEOC v. Pacific Press Publishing Association*, 676 F.2d 1272 (9th Cir. 1982), for example, a nonprofit publishing house affiliated with the Seventh-Day Adventist Church that printed religiously oriented material claimed that the sex discrimination and retaliation provisions of Title VII of the Civil Rights Act of 1964 could not be applied to it consistently with the First Amendment. The Court of Appeals disagreed, holding that "the government's compelling interest in assuring equal employment opportunities" justified any burden on the publishing house's exercise of religion. In *EEOC v. Fremont Christian School*, 781 F.2d 1362 (9th Cir. 1986), the court rejected the free exercise defense of a Christian school that paid for health insurance for married employees only if they were male, based on its religious views about who is a "head of household." And in *Ohio*

Civil Rights Commission v. Dayton Christian Schools, 477 U.S. 619 (1986), a Christian school refused to renew the contracts of women with young children but not men, but the Supreme Court did not reach the merits of whether Ohio's nondiscrimination laws violated the Free Exercise Clause as applied here.

Sexual orientation civil rights laws are no exception to this pattern. For example, when Hawai'i amended its employment discrimination statute to forbid sexual orientation discrimination, a potpourri of plaintiffs including various churches, religious leaders, and a Christian pre-school filed suit contending that the new prohibition violated their First Amendment rights to speech and religion. *Voluntary Association of Religious Leaders, Churches, and Organizations v. Waihee*, 800 F. Supp. 882, 883 (D. Haw. 1992). Similarly, when New Jersey added sexual orientation to its Law Against Discrimination (reaching discrimination in employment, labor organization membership, public accommodations, and real estate, financial, and business transactions), the Orthodox Presbyterian Church—a small splinter denomination from the Presbyterian Church (U.S.A.)—filed suit within three months of the law's effective date, arguing that the law violated its, its pastors', and its members' free exercise of religion as well as their freedom of association and freedom of speech. *See Presbytery of New Jersey of Orthodox Presbyterian Church v. Florio*, 830 F. Supp. 241, 245 (D.N.J. 1993), *aff'd in part & rev'd in part*, 40 F.3d 1454, 1458 (3d Cir. 1994). Both of those suits failed essentially because the plaintiffs failed to show that the challenged laws would restrict their freedom in any unconstitutional way.

By and large, claims for religious exemptions from laws against sexual orientation discrimination were rejected by the courts when statutes or constitutional clauses did not categorically exempt some field of endeavor from general laws. Such claims nevertheless seemed to pick up as sexual orientation equality picked up momentum in legislatures and courts. Indeed, writing the year before the Supreme Court held exclusion of same-sex couples from civil marriage unconstitutional in *Obergefell v. Hodges*, 135 S. Ct. 2584 (2015), an opinion piece in the conservative *Washington Examiner* claimed that "conservatives see religious liberty arguments as the last redoubt in the culture war: *you guys won your gay marriages*, permissive abortion laws, taxpayer-subsidized birth control, and divorce-on-demand; *let us just live our lives according to our own consciences.*" Timothy P. Carney, *Peace in the culture wars — if the Left wants it*, Washington Examiner (Mar. 25, 2014), https://www.washingtonexaminer.com/peace-in-the-culture-wars-if-the-left-wants-it. As U.S. law evolves away from its overwhelmingly anti-lesbigay normative position, favored in some conservative quarters, sweeping understandings of religious exemptions broadly asserted may give an opportunity to preserve as much of the former normative order as possible. Law professors Doug NeJaime and Reva Siegel have argued that

> [m]any who join in cross-denominational coalitions to assert complicity-based conscience claims endorse laws concerning abortion or same-sex marriage that would preserve traditional morality for the society as a

whole. Some invoke complicity-based conscience claims when they cannot entrench traditional morality through laws of general application. As the conditions of conflict change and arguments rooted in traditional morality lose their ability to persuade, movement leaders have advocated shifting to religious liberty arguments for exemption as part of a long-term effort to shape community-wide norms.

Douglas NeJaime & Reva Siegel, *Conscience Wars: Complicity-Based Conscience Claims in Religion and Politics*, 124 Yale L.J. 2516, 2543 (2015). Frederick Clarkson argues that this increasing turn to religious exemptions strives to "shrink the public sphere and the arenas within which the government has legitimacy to defend people's rights, including . . . LGBTQ rights." Frederick Clarkson, When Exemption Is the Rule: The Religious Freedom Strategy of the Christian Right vi (2016).

Law professor Kyle Velte has suggested that when it comes to the rights of transgender persons, "the Religious Right still takes an outwardly attacking stance" rather than one which depicts religiously motivated discriminators as persecuted minorities. *See* Kyle C. Velte, *All Fall Down: A Comprehensive Approach to Defeating the Religious Right's Challenges to Antidiscrimination Statutes*, 49 Conn. L. Rev. 1, 9 & n.23 (2016). Laws requiring transgender persons to use restrooms reserved for people of the sex to which they were assigned at birth might be seen as one illustration of her point. Laws facilitating the exercise of anti-trans discrimination might be understood as another. One of the broadest anti-LGBT exemption laws is Mississippi's H.B. 1523, adopted out of displeasure with the U.S. Supreme Court's marriage equality decision *Obergefell v. Hodges*, 135 S. Ct. 2584 (2015). For an account of the genesis of the bill, see *Barber v. Bryant*, 193 F. Supp. 3d 677, 691–93 (S.D. Miss. 2016), *rev'd*, 860 F.3d 345 (5th Cir. 2017).

Mississippi's H.B. 1523

(As Sent to Governor)

AN ACT TO CREATE THE "PROTECTING FREEDOM OF CONSCIENCE FROM GOVERNMENT DISCRIMINATION ACT"; TO PROVIDE CERTAIN PROTECTIONS REGARDING A SINCERELY HELD RELIGIOUS BELIEF OR MORAL CONVICTION FOR PERSONS, RELIGIOUS ORGANIZATIONS AND PRIVATE ASSOCIATIONS; TO DEFINE A DISCRIMINATORY ACTION FOR PURPOSES OF THIS ACT; TO PROVIDE THAT A PERSON MAY ASSERT A VIOLATION OF THIS ACT AS A CLAIM AGAINST THE GOVERNMENT; TO PROVIDE CERTAIN REMEDIES; TO REQUIRE A PERSON BRINGING A CLAIM UNDER THIS ACT TO DO SO NOT LATER THAN TWO YEARS AFTER THE DISCRIMINATORY ACTION WAS TAKEN; TO PROVIDE CERTAIN DEFINITIONS; AND FOR RELATED PURPOSES.

BE IT ENACTED BY THE LEGISLATURE OF THE STATE OF MISSISSIPPI:

SECTION 1. This act shall be known and may be cited as the "Protecting Freedom of Conscience from Government Discrimination Act."

SECTION 2. The sincerely held religious beliefs or moral convictions protected by this act are the belief or conviction that:

(a) Marriage is or should be recognized as the union of one man and one woman;

(b) Sexual relations are properly reserved to such a marriage; and

(c) Male (man) or female (woman) refer to an individual's immutable biological sex as objectively determined by anatomy and genetics at time of birth.

SECTION 3. (1) The state government shall not take any discriminatory action against a religious organization wholly or partially on the basis that such organization:

(a) Solemnizes or declines to solemnize any marriage, or provides or declines to provide services, accommodations, facilities, goods or privileges for a purpose related to the solemnization, formation, celebration or recognition of any marriage, based upon or in a manner consistent with a sincerely held religious belief or moral conviction described in Section 2 of this act;

(b) Makes any employment-related decision including, but not limited to, the decision whether or not to hire, terminate or discipline an individual whose conduct or religious beliefs are inconsistent with those of the religious organization, based upon or in a manner consistent with a sincerely held religious belief or moral conviction described in Section 2 of this act; or

(c) Makes any decision concerning the sale, rental, occupancy of, or terms and conditions of occupying a dwelling or other housing under its control, based upon or in a manner consistent with a sincerely held religious belief or moral conviction described in Section 2 of this act.

(2) The state government shall not take any discriminatory action against a religious organization that advertises, provides or facilitates adoption or foster care, wholly or partially on the basis that such organization has provided or declined to provide any adoption or foster care service, or related service, based upon or in a manner consistent with a sincerely held religious belief or moral conviction described in Section 2 of this act.

(3) The state government shall not take any discriminatory action against a person who the state grants custody of a foster or adoptive child, or who seeks from the state custody of a foster or adoptive child, wholly or partially on the basis that the person guides, instructs or raises a child, or intends to guide, instruct, or raise a child based upon or in a manner consistent with a sincerely held religious belief or moral conviction described in Section 2 of this act.

(4) The state government shall not take any discriminatory action against a person wholly or partially on the basis that the person declines to participate in the provision of treatments, counseling, or surgeries related to sex reassignment or gender identity transitioning or declines to participate in the provision of psychological, counseling, or fertility services based upon a sincerely held religious belief or moral conviction described in Section 2 of this act. This subsection (4) shall not be

construed to allow any person to deny visitation, recognition of a designated representative for health care decision-making, or emergency medical treatment necessary to cure an illness or injury as required by law.

(5) The state government shall not take any discriminatory action against a person wholly or partially on the basis that the person has provided or declined to provide the following services, accommodations, facilities, goods, or privileges for a purpose related to the solemnization, formation, celebration, or recognition of any marriage, based upon or in a manner consistent with a sincerely held religious belief or moral conviction described in Section 2 of this act:

(a) Photography, poetry, videography, disc-jockey services, wedding planning, printing, publishing or similar marriage-related goods or services; or

(b) Floral arrangements, dress making, cake or pastry artistry, assembly-hall or other wedding-venue rentals, limousine or other car-service rentals, jewelry sales and services, or similar marriage-related services, accommodations, facilities or goods.

(6) The state government shall not take any discriminatory action against a person wholly or partially on the basis that the person establishes sex-specific standards or policies concerning employee or student dress or grooming, or concerning access to restrooms, spas, baths, showers, dressing rooms, locker rooms, or other intimate facilities or settings, based upon or in a manner consistent with a sincerely held religious belief or moral conviction described in Section 2 of this act.

(7) The state government shall not take any discriminatory action against a state employee wholly or partially on the basis that such employee lawfully speaks or engages in expressive conduct based upon or in a manner consistent with a sincerely held religious belief or moral conviction described in Section 2 of this act, so long as:

(a) If the employee's speech or expressive conduct occurs in the workplace, that speech or expressive conduct is consistent with the time, place, manner and frequency of any other expression of a religious, political, or moral belief or conviction allowed; or

(b) If the employee's speech or expressive conduct occurs outside the workplace, that speech or expressive conduct is in the employee's personal capacity and outside the course of performing work duties.

(8) (a) Any person employed or acting on behalf of the state government who has authority to authorize or license marriages, including, but not limited to, clerks, registers of deeds or their deputies, may seek recusal from authorizing or licensing lawful marriages based upon or in a manner consistent with a sincerely held religious belief or moral conviction described in Section 2 of this act. Any person making such recusal shall provide prior written notice to the State Registrar of Vital Records who shall keep a record of such recusal, and the state government shall not take any discriminatory action against that person wholly or partially on the basis

of such recusal. The person who is recusing himself or herself shall take all necessary steps to ensure that the authorization and licensing of any legally valid marriage is not impeded or delayed as a result of any recusal.

(b) Any person employed or acting on behalf of the state government who has authority to perform or solemnize marriages, including, but not limited to, judges, magistrates, justices of the peace or their deputies, may seek recusal from performing or solemnizing lawful marriages based upon or in a manner consistent with a sincerely held religious belief or moral conviction described in Section 2 of this act. Any person making such recusal shall provide prior written notice to the Administrative Office of Courts, and the state government shall not take any discriminatory action against that person wholly or partially on the basis of such recusal. The Administrative Office of Courts shall take all necessary steps to ensure that the performance or solemnization of any legally valid marriage is not impeded or delayed as a result of any recusal.

SECTION 4. (1) As used in this act, discriminatory action includes any action taken by the state government to:

(a) Alter in any way the tax treatment of, or cause any tax, penalty, or payment to be assessed against, or deny, delay, revoke, or otherwise make unavailable an exemption from taxation of any person referred to in Section 3 of this act;

(b) Disallow, deny or otherwise make unavailable a deduction for state tax purposes of any charitable contribution made to or by such person;

(c) Withhold, reduce, exclude, terminate, materially alter the terms or conditions of, or otherwise make unavailable or deny any state grant, contract, subcontract, cooperative agreement, guarantee, loan, scholarship, or other similar benefit from or to such person;

(d) Withhold, reduce, exclude, terminate, materially alter the terms or conditions of, or otherwise make unavailable or deny any entitlement or benefit under a state benefit program from or to such person;

(e) Impose, levy or assess a monetary fine, fee, penalty or injunction;

(f) Withhold, reduce, exclude, terminate, materially alter the terms or conditions of, or otherwise make unavailable or deny any license, certification, accreditation, custody award or agreement, diploma, grade, recognition, or other similar benefit, position, or status from or to any person; or

(g) Refuse to hire or promote, force to resign, fire, demote, sanction, discipline, materially alter the terms or conditions of employment, or retaliate or take other adverse employment action against a person employed or commissioned by the state government.

(2) The state government shall consider accredited, licensed or certified any person that would otherwise be accredited, licensed or certified, respectively, for any purposes under state law but for a determination against such person wholly or

partially on the basis that the person believes, speaks or acts in accordance with a sincerely held religious belief or moral conviction described in Section 2 of this act.

SECTION 5. (1) A person may assert a violation of this act as a claim against the state government in any judicial or administrative proceeding or as defense in any judicial or administrative proceeding without regard to whether the proceeding is brought by or in the name of the state government, any private person or any other party.

(2) An action under this act may be commenced, and relief may be granted, in a court of the state without regard to whether the person commencing the action has sought or exhausted available administrative remedies.

(3) Violations of this act which are properly governed by Chapter 46, Title 11, Mississippi Code of 1972 [regarding state and local immunity for torts—Eds.], shall be brought in accordance with that chapter.

SECTION 6. An aggrieved person must first seek injunctive relief to prevent or remedy a violation of this act or the effects of a violation of this act. If injunctive relief is granted by the court and the injunction is thereafter violated, then and only then may the aggrieved party, subject to the limitations of liability set forth in Section 11-46-15, seek the following:

(a) Compensatory damages for pecuniary and nonpecuniary losses;

(b) Reasonable attorneys' fees and costs; and

(c) Any other appropriate relief, except that only declaratory relief and injunctive relief shall be available against a private person not acting under color of state law upon a successful assertion of a claim or defense under this act.

SECTION 7. A person must bring an action to assert a claim under this act not later than two (2) years after the date that the person knew or should have known that a discriminatory action was taken against that person.

SECTION 8. (1) This act shall be construed in favor of a broad protection of free exercise of religious beliefs and moral convictions, to the maximum extent permitted by the state and federal constitutions.

(2) The protection of free exercise of religious beliefs and moral convictions afforded by this act are in addition to the protections provided under federal law, state law, and the state and federal constitutions. Nothing in this act shall be construed to preempt or repeal any state or local law that is equally or more protective of free exercise of religious beliefs or moral convictions. Nothing in this act shall be construed to narrow the meaning or application of any state or local law protecting free exercise of religious beliefs or moral convictions. Nothing in this act shall be construed to prevent the state government from providing, either directly or through an individual or entity not seeking protection under this act, any benefit or service authorized under state law.

(3) This act applies to, and in cases of conflict supersedes, each statute of the state that impinges upon the free exercise of religious beliefs and moral convictions

protected by this act, unless a conflicting statute is expressly made exempt from the application of this act. This act also applies to, and in cases of conflict supersedes, any ordinance, rule, regulation, order, opinion, decision, practice or other exercise of the state government's authority that impinges upon the free exercise of religious beliefs or moral convictions protected by this act.

SECTION 9. As used in Sections 1 through 9 of this act, the following words and phrases shall have the meanings ascribed in this section unless the context clearly indicates otherwise:

(1) "State benefit program" means any program administered or funded by the state, or by any agent on behalf of the state, providing cash, payments, grants, contracts, loans or in-kind assistance.

(2) "State government" means:

(a) The State of Mississippi or a political subdivision of the state;

(b) Any agency of the state or of a political subdivision of the state, including a department, bureau, board, commission, council, court or public institution of higher education;

(c) Any person acting under color of state law; and

(d) Any private party or third party suing under or enforcing a law, ordinance, rule or regulation of the state or political subdivision of the state.

(3) "Person" means:

(a) A natural person, in his or her individual capacity, regardless of religious affiliation or lack thereof, or in his or her capacity as a member, officer, owner, volunteer, employee, manager, religious leader, clergy or minister of any entity described in this section;

(b) A religious organization;

(c) A sole proprietorship, or closely held company, partnership, association, organization, firm, corporation, cooperative, trust, society or other closely held entity operating with a sincerely held religious belief or moral conviction described in this act; or

(d) Cooperatives, ventures or enterprises comprised of two (2) or more individuals or entities described in this subsection.

(4) "Religious organization" means:

(a) A house of worship, including, but not limited to, churches, synagogues, shrines, mosques and temples;

(b) A religious group, corporation, association, school or educational institution, ministry, order, society or similar entity, regardless of whether it is integrated or affiliated with a church or other house of worship; and

(c) An officer, owner, employee, manager, religious leader, clergy or minister of an entity or organization described in this subsection (4).

(5) "Adoption or foster care" or "adoption or foster care service" means social services provided to or on behalf of children, including:

(a) Assisting abused or neglected children;

(b) Teaching children and parents occupational, homemaking and other domestic skills;

(c) Promoting foster parenting;

(d) Providing foster homes, residential care, group homes or temporary group shelters for children;

(e) Recruiting foster parents;

(f) Placing children in foster homes;

(g) Licensing foster homes;

(h) Promoting adoption or recruiting adoptive parents;

(i) Assisting adoptions or supporting adoptive families;

(j) Performing or assisting home studies;

(k) Assisting kinship guardianships or kinship caregivers;

(l) Providing family preservation services;

(m) Providing family support services; and

(n) Providing temporary family reunification services.

SECTION 10. The provisions of Sections 1 through 9 of this act shall be excluded from the application of Section 11-61-1 [the Mississippi Religious Freedom Restoration Act—Eds.].

SECTION 11. This act shall take effect and be in force from and after July 1, 2016.

—————

Discussion

1. Note that Section 2(c) of H.B. 1523 seems to be protecting a belief that "sex change" or "sex reassignment" is impossible and that most, if not all, transgender people are really members of the sex they were assigned at birth rather than the sex consistent with their gender identity, regardless of what medical procedures or legal documentation changes a person may have undergone—at least on a casual reading of the text. Note that Section 3(4) and 3(6) specifically protect forms of anti-trans conduct.

2. Note the tremendously broad coverage of the statute, particularly as evidenced by the litanies of circumstances in Sections 3, 4, 8, and 9. In this respect, H.B. 1523 is reminiscent of Colorado's anti-gay state constitutional Amendment 2, which featured many strings of multiple disjunctions in an apparent effort to ensure that lesbigay people would not be protected from sexual orientation discrimination in any circumstance. Amendment 2 was held unconstitutional by the Supreme Court in

the landmark case *Romer v. Evans*, 517 U.S. 620 (1996). *Cf.* Klint W. Alexander, *The Masterpiece Cakeshop Decision and the Clash Between Nondiscrimination and Religious Freedom*, 71 Okla. L. Rev. 1069, 1075 (2019) ("Some of these [religious exemption] laws, like Mississippi's House Bill 1523, are simply licenses to discriminate and strongly favor those companies or individuals who do not wish to provide services to LGBT people."); Ronald J. Krotoszynski, Jr., *Agora, Dignity, and Discrimination: On the Constitutional Shortcomings of "Conscience" Laws That Promote Inequality in the Public Marketplace*, 20 Lewis & Clark L. Rev. 1221 (2017) (arguing that H.B. 1523 violates Equal Protection Clause).

3. A group of individuals and organizations filed suit in federal court to try to prevent H.B. 1523 from taking effect, and the district court held that it violated religious neutrality and hence violated the Establishment Clause, and that it denied LGBT and unmarried persons equal protection of the law in violation of the Equal Protection Clause. *Barber v. Bryant*, 193 F. Supp. 3d 677 (S.D. Miss. 2016). (*Cf.* Wyatt Fore, *Trans/forming Healthcare Law: Litigating Antidiscrimination Under the Affordable Care Act*, 28 Yale J.L. & Feminism 243 (2017) (arguing that healthcare providers' "categorical exclusion" of all transition-care from the medical services they will provide a patient "based on non-medical factors" such as their religious or other personal beliefs about transition "raises a significant and dangerous . . . problem of secondary discrimination" under *Palmore v. Sidoti*, 466 U.S. 429 (1984), *supra* Chapter 8). On the state's appeal, however, the U.S. Court of Appeals for the Fifth Circuit ruled that all the plaintiffs lacked standing, reversed the district court's injunction, and dismissed the case. *Barber v. Bryant*, 860 F.3d 345 (5th Cir. 2017), *cert. denied*, 138 S. Ct. 652 (2018), and *Campaign for Southern Equality v. Bryant*, 138 S. Ct. 671 (2018).

4. Jordan Woods has criticized H.B. 1523 in the course of a broader examination of "conflicts between religious liberty and child welfare issues pertaining to LGBTQ youth." Jordan Blair Woods, *Religious Exemptions and LGBTQ Child Welfare*, 103 Minn. L. Rev. 2343, 2349 (2019). Professor Woods argues that "current religious exemptions involving LGBTQ child welfare . . . harm[] LGBTQ youth and undermin[e] LGBTQ equality inside of the child welfare system, [and] have short-term and long-term spillover effects that undermine LGBTQ equality in society at large." *Id.* at 2350–51. Are such exemptions defensible as promoting parental rights, family autonomy, and/or moral diversity across the United States?

C. Contemporary Gender Identity Non-Discrimination Exemption Claims

Contemporarily, religious exemptions have become one of the key ways in which opponents of LGBTQ rights seek to undermine legal protections. States are passing broad religious exemption laws, sometimes targeted at sexual orientation and gender identity protections, as in Mississippi's H.B. 1523, *supra* at p. 540. The federal government under the administration of Donald Trump has attempted dramatically to broaden the circumstances under which exemptions might be claimed. Less than four months after taking office, Trump signed an executive order "Promoting Free Speech and Religious Liberty" that proclaims federal policy "to vigorously enforce Federal law's robust protections for religious freedom." Exec. Order No. 13798 (May 4, 2017). More recently, the administration proposed a new rule to guarantee faith-based groups with federal government contracts broader authority to hire and fire based on their religious beliefs, which organizations advancing the rights of LGBTQ people worry will be used to allow more discrimination against LGBTQ people and unmarried pregnant people. *See* Implementing Legal Requirements Regarding the Equal Opportunity Clause's Religious Exemption, 41 C.F.R. pt. 60-1 (Aug. 15, 2019). Litigation is yet another vehicle by which people are seeking to use religion to gain exemption from laws protecting LGBTQ persons.

Reading Guide for Franciscan Alliance v. Burwell

1. What canon of statutory interpretation does the court invoke to hold that the failure of the regulation implementing Section 1557 of the Affordable Care Act to include the religion- and abortion-related exceptions found in Title IX of the Education Amendments of 1972 renders the regulation contrary to Section 1557? To what part of the statute does the court apply this interpretive canon? What meaning is the court apparently giving to the statutory term "ground" in Section 1557?

2. For what reasons does the court conclude that the regulation at issue imposes a substantial burden on the exercise of the non-governmental plaintiffs' religion within the meaning of the Religious Freedom Restoration Act ("RFRA")? For what reasons does the court doubt that the regulation advances one or more compelling governmental interests that might justify applying the regulation to the plaintiffs despite such burden?

3. Why does the court conclude that the regulation fails RFRA's least restrictive means requirement?

4. Why does the court conclude that the balance of hardships as well as the interest of the public support enjoining the challenged rule? Why does the court conclude that the rule should be enjoined nationally, forbidding the defendant federal agency from enforcing it against anyone regardless of whether they're a plaintiff or a member of a plaintiff organization?

Franciscan Alliance, Inc., et al. v. Sylvia Burwell, Secretary of the United States Department of Health and Human Services, and United States Department of Health and Human Services

227 F. Supp. 3d 660 (N.D. Tex. 2016)

[The plaintiffs were represented by The Becket Fund for Religious Liberty and by Austin Nimocks, who was then in the Texas Attorney General's Office, but who earlier served as Senior Counsel for the Christian Right legal advocacy organization Alliance Defending Freedom.]

Opinion
Order

Reed O'Connor, United States District Judge

. . . .

The Plaintiffs challenge a regulation enacted pursuant to the Patient Protection and Affordable Care Act ("ACA") that covers nearly every healthcare provider in the country and reaches into one of the most intimate relationships: that between a physician and her patient. . . . While this lawsuit involves many issues of great importance — state sovereignty, expanded healthcare coverage, anti-discrimination protections, and medical judgment — ultimately, the question before the Court is whether Defendants exceeded their authority under the ACA in the challenged regulations' interpretation of sex discrimination and whether the regulation violates the Religious Freedom Restoration Act as applied to Private Plaintiffs. . . .

I. Background

The following factual recitation is taken from Plaintiffs' First Amended Complaint unless stated otherwise. Plaintiffs are composed of eight states (collectively "State Plaintiffs") and three private healthcare providers, Franciscan Alliance, Inc. ("Franciscan") [now, "Franciscan Health"—Eds.], its wholly owned entity Specialty Physicians of Illinois, LLC ("Specialty Physicians"), and the Christian Medical & Dental Society ("CMDA"), doing business as the Christian Medical & Dental Associations (collectively "Private Plaintiffs"). They have sued the U.S. Department of Health and Human Services ("HHS"), and HHS Secretary Sylvia Burwell ("Burwell") (collectively "Defendants"), challenging a new rule issued by HHS entitled Nondiscrimination in Health Programs & Activities (the "Rule"). 81 Fed. Reg. 31376–31473, (May 18, 2016) (codified at 45 C.F.R. § 92).

. . . .

On October 21, 2016, Plaintiffs moved for partial summary judgment, or in the alternative, a preliminary injunction. To resolve the matter before the Rule's insurance provision goes into effect on January 1, 2017, at which time Plaintiffs would be forced to "make significant, expensive changes to their insurance plans," the Court set an expedited briefing schedule and held a hearing on the preliminary injunction motions on December 20, 2016. Plaintiffs' motions for preliminary injunction are now ripe for review.

A. The Rule

. . . . After notice and comment, the final Rule was published on May 18, 2016. The Rule took partial effect on July 18, 2016, and the insurance provisions will be effective on January 1, 2017. The Rule purports to implement Section 1557 [of the ACA] which provides:

> [A]n individual shall not, *on the ground prohibited under* title VI of the Civil Rights Act of 1964 (42 U.S.C. 2000d et seq.) ["Title VI"], title IX of the Education Amendments of 1972 (20 U.S.C. 1681 et seq.) ["Title IX"], the Age Discrimination Act of 1975 (42 U.S.C. 6101 et seq.) ["ADA"], or section 504 of the Rehabilitation Act of 1973 (29 U.S.C. 794) ["Section 504"], be excluded from participation in, be denied the benefits of, or be subjected to discrimination under, any health program or activity, any part of which is receiving Federal financial assistance. . . .

42 U.S.C. § 18116(a) (emphasis added). Section 1557 does not create new bases of prohibited discrimination, but rather incorporates the grounds of four longstanding federal nondiscrimination statutes: Title VI, Title IX, the ADA, and Section 504. The implementing Rule claims to merely "clarif[y] and codif[y] *existing* nondiscrimination requirements," incorporated in Section 1557. 81 Fed. Reg. at 31376 (emphasis added). . . .

When implementing the Title IX portion of Section 1557, HHS defined discrimination "on the basis of sex" to include "termination of pregnancy" and "gender identity." 45 C.F.R. § 92.4. The Rule does not define termination of pregnancy but defines gender identity as "an individual's internal sense of gender, which may be male, female, neither, or a combination of male and female, and which may be different from an individual's sex assigned at birth." *Id.* The Rule explains that the "gender identity spectrum includes an array of possible gender identities beyond male and female." 81 Fed. Reg. at 31392.

. . . .

1. Health Coverage

One of the "discriminatory actions prohibited" under the Rule is "hav[ing] or implement[ing] a categorical [insurance] coverage exclusion or limitation for all health services related to gender transition." 45 C.F.R. § 92.207(b). The Rule declares that categorizations of all transition-related treatment as cosmetic or experimental are now "outdated and not based on current standards of care." 81 Fed. Reg. at 31429. The "range of transition-related services" contemplated by the Rule includes treatment for gender dysphoria[4] and is "not limited to surgical treatments and may include, but is not limited to, services such as hormone therapy and psychotherapy, which may occur over the lifetime of the individual." 81 Fed. Reg. at 31435–36.

Because the Rule contains no age limitation, Plaintiffs are concerned it may require health insurance coverage of transitions for children and they note that

---

4. Gender dysphoria is defined as "a distressed state arising from conflict between a person's gender identity and the sex the person has or was identified as having at birth." Merriam-Webster Medical Dictionary (2016) https://www.merriam-webster.com/medical/genderdysphoria.

transition-related procedures are viewed by many in the medical community as harmful, including HHS's own medical experts.[5] ....

2. Health Services

Plaintiffs also allege the Rule requires doctors or healthcare providers to perform (or refer patients for) transition-related procedures if the entity provides an analogous service in a different context. For example, the Rule's preamble explains that "[a] provider specializing in gynecological services that previously declined to provide a medically necessary hysterectomy [removal of the uterus] for a transgender man would have to revise its policy to provide the procedure for transgender individuals in the same manner it provides the procedure for other individuals." 81 Fed. Reg. at 31455.

.... Plaintiffs interpret this to mean that if a doctor performs mastectomies as part of a medically necessary treatment for breast cancer, he would be forced to perform the same procedure for a gender transition, even if the doctor believed removing healthy breast tissue was contrary to the patient's medical interest. Private Plaintiffs also perform certain procedures for a miscarriage (such as dilation and curettage) and they fear the Rule will require them to perform those procedures for abortions to avoid discrimination on the basis of "termination of pregnancy."

. . . .

3. Enforcement

Although Title IX provides the grounds of prohibited sex discrimination, covered entities who violate the Rule's prohibition of sex discrimination are subject to the penalties associated with a violation of Title VI of the Civil Rights Act of 1964. Those in violation of the Rule face the loss of federal funding, debarment from doing business with the government, and false claims liability.[6] Covered entities are required to record and submit compliance reports upon request to HHS's Office of Civil Rights ("OCR") and post public notices of compliance. The Rule also provides for enforcement proceedings by the Department of Justice and private lawsuits for damages and attorney's fees.

---

5. *See* . . . Centers for Medicare & Medicaid Services, *Proposed Decision Memo for Gender Dysphoria and Gender Reassignment Surgery* (June 2, 2016) ("Based on a thorough review of the clinical evidence available at this time, there is not enough evidence to determine whether gender reassignment surgery improves health outcomes for Medicare beneficiaries with gender dysphoria. There were conflicting (inconsistent) study results—of the best designed studies, some reported benefits while others reported harms.").

6. Franciscan would risk losing $900 million in federal funds; Texas would risk losing more than $42.4 billion in federal funds; and CMDA members would risk losing a significant amount of federal funds.

4. Plaintiffs

Franciscan and CMDA's members are covered entities under the Rule because they both receive federal financial assistance and provide employee health insurance.[7] Franciscan is a Roman Catholic faith-based hospital system founded by a Roman Catholic order, the Sisters of St. Francis of Perpetual Adoration. Healthcare and religion have been inextricably intertwined in the delivery of their services since their first hospital building opened, serving as both a convent and a hospital. Since opening their doors in 1875, they have been focused on serving the most vulnerable of society with the values of the Sisters of St. Francis, including: respect for life, fidelity to Franciscan's mission, compassionate concern, and Christian stewardship. Franciscan's hospitals provide many resources to accommodate the spiritual needs of their employees, patients, and their families — including daily Mass and 24-hour access to a chapel for individuals of all faiths to pray and meditate. Franciscan now provides $900 million in Medicare and Medicaid services annually to the poor, disabled, and elderly; and stands to lose that funding and significantly more if federal funding is withdrawn.

Franciscan provides all of its standard medical services to every individual, including those who identify as transgender. But Franciscan's religious beliefs do not allow them to perform or cover transition-related procedures.

> Franciscan holds religious beliefs that sexual identity is an objective fact rooted in nature as male or female persons. Like the Catholic Church it serves, Franciscan believes that a person's sex is ascertained biologically, and not by one's beliefs, desires, or feelings. Franciscan believes that part of the image of God is an organic part of every man and woman, and that women and men reflect God's image in unique, and uniquely dignified, ways.

Am. Compl. 37. . . . Franciscan does not believe transition-related procedures are ever in the best interests of its patients and providing or covering any transition-related service would violate their deeply held religious beliefs.

CMDA is the nation's largest faith-based organization of doctors, including nearly 18,000 members who sign a statement of faith to join and rely on CMDA to advocate on behalf of their religious beliefs and medical judgments in the public square. CMDA members hold values similar to Franciscan and CMDA's approved Ethics Statement affirms the "obligation of Christian healthcare professionals to care for patients struggling with gender identity with sensitivity and compassion" but states clear opposition to medical assistance with gender transition and

---

7. The Rule applies to "every health program or activity, any part of which receives Federal financial assistance provided or made available by the Department; every health program or activity administered by the Department; and every health program or activity administered by a Title I entity." 45 C.F.R. § 92.2(a). HHS estimated the Rule would "likely cover almost all licensed physicians because they accept Federal financial assistance. . . ." 81 Fed. Reg. at 31445.

abortion. CMDA members treat transgender individuals for health issues ranging from the common cold to cancer, and several members have already received requests for transition-related procedures that they cannot provide without violating their religious beliefs. . . .

Private Plaintiffs' religious beliefs also prevent them from being able to participate in, refer for, or cover elective sterilizations or abortion-related procedures. . . .

Franciscan and CMDA's members also provide health insurance coverage for their employees in accordance with their religious beliefs. . . . Private Plaintiffs sincerely believe that participating in, referring for, or providing insurance coverage of gender transitions, sterilizations, or abortions would constitute "impermissible material cooperation with evil."

The State Plaintiffs receive billions in federal financial assistance each year, and are subject to the Rule as providers of both health care and health insurance. State Plaintiffs prohibit insurance coverage for abortions and gender transition procedures, but to comply with the Rule, State Plaintiffs must rescind these categorical exclusions. Texas, one of the named State Plaintiffs, is already being forced to comply with an investigation by [OCR] and stands to lose more than $42.4 billion in federal healthcare funding . . . if it does not change its policies. State Plaintiffs claim the Rule "undermines the longstanding sovereign power of the States to regulate healthcare, ensure appropriate standards of medical judgment, and protect its citizens' constitutional and civil rights." State Plaintiffs also argue the Rule forces them to incur significant costs to post required notices of compliance, train personnel, adjust insurance coverage, and increase service offerings to include transition-related procedures. HHS estimates that states will need to contribute $17.8 million to train 7,637,306 state workers under the new Rule.

Together, Plaintiffs claim the Rule violates the Administrative Procedure Act ("APA") because its definition of prohibited sex discrimination is contrary to law and arbitrary and capricious. Accordingly, the Court begins with the law governing APA claims and the relevant standards in considering a preliminary injunction.

. . . .

III. Analysis

Plaintiffs argue the Rule should be enjoined because it violates: (1) the [APA]; (2) the Religious Freedom Restoration Act; (3) the First Amendment's Free Speech Clause; and (4) the Spending Clause of Article I.

. . . .

B. Preliminary Injunction
1. Likelihood of Success on the Merits

The first consideration in determining whether to grant Plaintiffs' motions for preliminary injunction is whether Plaintiffs have shown a likelihood of success on the merits for their claims . . .

a. Administrative Procedure Act

. . . .

Because the authority to issue the Rule was given in Section 1557 of the ACA, the Court begins with the language of Section 1557. Section 1557 clearly incorporates Title IX's prohibition of sex discrimination. [With] no ambiguity in the statute as to what is prohibited sex discrimination, the Court next analyzes the incorporated text to determine whether HHS's interpretation of the incorporated statute was in line with the text of Title IX. Title IX provides that "[n]o person in the United States shall, *on the basis of sex*, be excluded from participation in, be denied the benefits of, or be subjected to discrimination under any education program or activity receiving Federal financial assistance. . . ." 20 U.S.C. § 1681(a) (emphasis added).

[The court goes on to conclude that Section 1557, like Title IX itself as this district judge has previously interpreted it, "is clear and unambiguously prohibits discrimination" only on the basis of "the biological and anatomical differences between male and female" persons "as determined at their birth."] In promulgating the Rule, HHS revised the core of Title IX sex discrimination under the guise of simply incorporating it. . . .

[Having so concluded, the court for essentially the same reason concludes that the regulation does not lawfully implement Section 1557 but instead violates it and thus violates the Administrative Procedure Act. This analysis is presented in more detail in Chapter 11 Section A, *infra* at p. 595.]

iii. Title IX Unincorporated Religious Exemptions

Plaintiffs also claim the Rule's failure to incorporate Title IX's religious exemptions renders the Rule arbitrary, capricious, and contrary to law under the APA. Title IX does not apply to covered entities controlled by a religious organization if its application would be inconsistent with the religious tenets of such organization. 20 U.S.C. § 1681(a)(3) (the "religious exemption"). Title IX also states that it cannot be "construed to require or prohibit any person, or public or private entity, to provide or pay for any benefit or service, including the use of facilities, related to an abortion." 20 U.S.C. § 1688 (the "abortion exemption"). The Rule did not incorporate Title IX's religious or abortion exemption even though it incorporated the exemptions of the other three federal nondiscrimination statutes.[29]

[When] determining whether the failure to incorporate the exemptions is contrary to law, the Court must examine the text of Section 1557. This examination requires the Court to again apply well settled rules of construction which include giving the statutory text its plain and ordinary meaning, construing the statute as a whole, and giving effect to every word of the statute. The canon disfavoring surplusage is "one

---

29. "The exceptions applicable to Title VI apply to discrimination on the basis of race, color, or national origin under this part. The exceptions applicable to Section 504 apply to discrimination on the basis of disability under this part. The exceptions applicable to the Age Act apply to discrimination on the basis of age under this part." 45 C.F.R. § 92.101(c).

of the most basic interpretive canons." *Corley v. United States*, 556 U.S. 303 (2009). In construing a statute, courts are obligated to give effect to all its provisions "so that no part will be inoperative or superfluous, void, or insignificant." *Id.*

The text of Section 1557 prohibits discrimination "on the ground prohibited under . . . [T]itle IX of the Education Amendments of 1972 (20 U.S.C. 1681 et seq.) . . . ." Congress specifically included in the text of Section 1557 "20 U.S.C. 1681 et seq." That Congress included the signal "et seq.," which means "and the following," after the citation to Title IX can only mean Congress intended to incorporate the entire statutory structure, including the abortion and religious exemptions. Title IX prohibits discrimination on the basis of sex, but exempts from this prohibition entities controlled by a religious organization when the proscription would be inconsistent with its religious tenets. 20 U.S.C. § 1681(a)(3). Title IX also categorically exempts any application that would require a covered entity to provide abortion or abortion-related services. 20 U.S.C. § 1688. Therefore, a religious organization refusing to act inconsistent with its religious tenets on the basis of sex does not discriminate on the ground prohibited by Title IX. Failure to incorporate Title IX's religious and abortion exemptions nullifies Congress's specific direction to prohibit only the ground proscribed by Title IX. That is not permitted. By not including these exemptions, HHS expanded the "ground prohibited under" Title IX that Section 1557 explicitly incorporated. The Rule's failure to include Title IX's religious exemptions renders the Rule contrary to law.

. . . .

b. Religious Freedom Restoration Act

The Court next evaluates in the alternative whether Plaintiffs have established a substantial likelihood of success on their RFRA claim. Private Plaintiffs allege the Rule violates RFRA because it substantially burdens their exercise of religion. . . .

RFRA provides that the "[g]overnment may substantially burden a person's exercise of religion only if it demonstrates that application of the burden to the person . . . is the least restrictive means of furthering [a] compelling government interest." 42 U.S.C. § 2000bb-1(b). . . . Courts evaluating a claim under RFRA must first determine if the challenged rule imposes a "substantial burden" on plaintiffs' religious exercise and if so, then whether the rule satisfies strict scrutiny.

As to the first prong, the Court must (a) identify a sincere religious exercise, and (b) determine whether the government has placed substantial pressure on Plaintiffs to abstain from that religious exercise. *Burwell v. Hobby Lobby Stores, Inc.*, 134 S. Ct. 2751 (2014). Defendants do not question or contest the sincerity of Private Plaintiffs' religious beliefs or exercise, and the Court is careful not to weigh or evaluate the relevant doctrines of faith.[31] As discussed above, the Court finds that Private

---

31. *See Hernandez v. Comm'r*, 490 U.S. 680 (1989) ("It is not within the judicial ken to question the centrality of particular beliefs or practices to a faith, or the validity of particular litigants' interpretations of those creeds.").

Plaintiffs' refusal to perform, refer for, or cover transitions or abortions is a sincere religious exercise. Private Plaintiffs have demonstrated they sincerely believe such procedures would harm their patients and force their employees to "engage in material cooperation with evil." The Supreme Court has explained that the exercise of religion includes "business practices that are compelled or limited by the tenets of a religious doctrine." *Hobby Lobby.*

In regards to whether the Rule places substantial pressure on Plaintiffs to abstain from religious exercise, the Court finds—and the parties agree—that the Rule's prohibition of categorical exclusions of transitions and abortions forces Plaintiffs to make an individualized assessment of every request for performance of such procedures or coverage of the same. The Rule therefore places substantial pressure on Plaintiffs to perform and cover transition and abortion procedures. The Rule's prohibition of categorical exclusions also forces Plaintiffs to provide the federal government a nondiscriminatory and "exceedingly persuasive justification" for their refusal to perform or cover such procedures. 45 C.F.R. § 92.101. Private Plaintiffs' long-held view that such procedures are immoral and inappropriate in every circumstance is now at odds with the Rule's interpretation of sex discrimination because it requires them to remove the categorical exclusion of transitions and abortions (a condition they assert is a reflection of their religious beliefs and an exercise of their religion) and conduct an individualized assessment of every request for those procedures. "A law that 'operates so as to make the practice of . . . religious beliefs more expensive' in the context of business activities imposes a burden on the exercise of religion." *Hobby Lobby* (quoting *Braunfeld v. Brown*, 366 U.S. 599 (1961)). Accordingly, the Rule imposes a substantial burden on Private Plaintiffs' religious exercise.

As to the second prong, the government bears the burden to show the Rule satisfies strict scrutiny—*i.e.*, "demonstrate[] that the application of the burden to the person represents the least restrictive means of advancing a compelling interest." *Gonzales v. O Centro Espírita Beneficente Uniã do Vegetal*, 546 U.S. 418 (2006). The Fifth Circuit has held that to satisfy strict scrutiny under RFRA, the government "must show by specific evidence that [Private Plaintiffs'] religious practices jeopardize its stated interests." *Merced v. Kasson*, 577 F.3d 578 (5th Cir. 2009). Defendants do not provide a compelling interest in their briefing and Private Plaintiffs dispute that one exists. Although the preamble to the Rule claims broadly that the government has "a compelling interest in ensuring that individuals have nondiscriminatory access to health care and health coverage," Defendants have failed to brief the basis of its compelling interest, leaving the Court unable to determine whether Private Plaintiffs' religious practices jeopardize its purpose. A compelling interest is one the government would be willing to pursue itself. Yet, the government's own health insurance programs, Medicare and Medicaid, do not mandate coverage for transition surgeries; the military's health insurance program, TRICARE, specifically excludes coverage for transition surgeries; and the government's own medical experts reported "conflicting" study results of transition procedures—"some reported benefits while others reported harms." Centers for Medicare & Medicaid Services, *Proposed Decision Memo for Gender Dysphoria and Gender Reassignment Surgery* (June 2, 2016); see *Hobby Lobby* (significant carve outs and exceptions may indicate the government lacks a compelling interest). Therefore, it appears the government has failed to adequately carry its burden and show the Rule advances a compelling interest.[32]

Nevertheless, the Court assumes the Rule pursues a compelling interest, because even if it does, the government has failed to prove the Rule employs the least restrictive means. The least-restrictive-means standard requires the government to "sho[w] that it lacks other means of achieving its desired goal without imposing a substantial burden on the exercise of religion by the objecting part[y]." *Hobby Lobby.* If the government wishes to expand access to transition and abortion procedures, "[t]he most straightforward way of doing this would be for the government to assume the cost of providing the [procedures] at issue to any [individuals] who are unable to obtain them under their health-insurance policies due to their employers' religious objections." *Id.* The government could also assist transgender individuals in finding and paying for transition procedures available from the growing number of health-care providers who offer and specialize in those services. The government has failed to demonstrate how exempting Private Plaintiffs pursuant to their religious beliefs would frustrate the goal of ensuring "nondiscriminatory access to health care and health coverage," and the government has numerous less restrictive means available to provide access and coverage for transition and abortion procedures. Accordingly, Private Plaintiffs have demonstrated a substantial likelihood of success on their claim that the challenged Rule violates RFRA.

2. Threat of Irreparable Harm

Next, Plaintiffs must demonstrate they are "likely to suffer irreparable harm in the absence of preliminary relief." *Winter v. Nat. Res. Def. Council*, 555 U.S. 7 (2008). "[H]arm is irreparable where there is no adequate remedy at law, such as monetary damages." *Janvey v. Alguire*, 647 F.3d at 600 (5th Cir. 2011). An injunction is appropriate only if the anticipated injury is imminent and not speculative. *Winter.*

. . . . The State Plaintiffs claim they are currently suffering injury under the ongoing HHS investigation into their insurance plans and all Plaintiffs will suffer irreparable harm on January 1, 2017, when they are forced to alter their insurance coverage plans. Plaintiffs also point out several entities with similar insurance

---

32. While Putative Intervenors [the American Civil Liberties Union of Texas and River City Gender Alliance—Eds.] proposed several compelling interests in their briefing (including "eradicating all forms of invidious discrimination," "making sure that federal funds are not used to subsidize discrimination," "making sure people are able to access healthcare coverage and services on a nondiscriminatory basis," and "safeguarding the public health") it is the government's view that controls. *Hobby Lobby*, 134 S. Ct. at 2776.

policies that have already been sued under the Rule since it was issued on May 18, 2016. State Plaintiffs allege the Rule is in direct conflict with state law that mandates a physician's independent medical judgment be given paramount consideration when providing treatment because the Rule makes a physician's independent medical judgment one of many factors in evaluating compliance.

A state suffers irreparable harm anytime it is prevented from enforcing a statute enacted by representatives of its people. *Planned Parenthood of Greater Texas Surgical Health Servs. v. Abbott*, 734 F.3d 406 (5th Cir. 2013) ("When a statute is enjoined, the State necessarily suffers the irreparable harm of denying the public interest in the enforcement of its laws."); *Maryland v. King*, 567 U.S. 1301 (2012) ("[A]ny time a State is enjoined by a court from effectuating statutes enacted by representatives of its people, it suffers a form of irreparable injury.").

Because the Rule is in conflict with state law, one of the State Plaintiffs is already undergoing investigation by the HHS's OCR, and entities similarly situated to Private Plaintiffs have already been sued under the Rule since it took partial effect on May 18, 2016, the Court finds Plaintiffs have demonstrated that they face a substantial threat of irreparable harm in the absence of an injunction.

3. Balance of Hardships and Public Interest

The Court next considers whether the threatened injury to Plaintiffs outweighs any damage the proposed injunction may cause Defendants and its impact on the public interest. The threatened injury to Plaintiffs outweighs any potential harm to Defendants. Without an injunction, Plaintiffs will be threatened with substantial harm, including the risk of federal funding withdrawal and civil liability.

On the other hand, HHS will suffer no harm from delaying implementation of the challenged portion of the Rule. The agency's six-year delay in issuing the Rule strengthens the Court's conclusion that the delay imposed by the injunction would work no significant harm on Defendants. The injunction would merely maintain the status quo—allowing HHS to prohibit sex discrimination in healthcare services as defined by Title IX and incorporated by Section 1557. If the Rule is invalid, it will be set aside in its entirety and the public interest will be served by the injunction. But even if the Rule is valid, the injunction will merely delay its implementation, pending final review on the merits.

Defendants allege that Plaintiffs' delay in seeking relief should weigh in favor of denying the injunction. But the Court finds that filing suit one month after the first parts of the Rule became effective constitutes prompt action, notwithstanding the inadvertent mistake that led to a delay in serving the U.S. Attorney for the Northern District of Texas. Further, Defendants' six-year delay in promulgating the Rule since the ACA's enactment demonstrates that Defendants and the public interest would suffer no irreparable injury in the face of an injunction to maintain the status quo.

For the foregoing reasons, the Court finds that Plaintiffs have satisfied all prerequisites for a preliminary injunction.

C. Scope of Injunction

Finally, the Court must determine the scope of the injunction. Plaintiffs seek a nationwide injunction as to the challenged portions of the Rule—prohibiting discrimination on the basis of "gender identity" and "termination of pregnancy." Defendants argue the injunction should be limited to Plaintiffs.

"[D]istrict courts enjoy broad discretion in awarding injunctive relief." *Nat'l Min. Ass'n v. U.S. Army Corps of Eng'rs*, 145 F.3d 1399 (D.C. Cir. 1998). "[T]he Constitution vests the District Court with 'the judicial power of the United States.' That power is not limited to the district wherein the court sits but extends across the country. It is not beyond the power of a court, in appropriate circumstances, to issue a nationwide injunction." *Texas v. United States*, 809 F.3d 134, 188 (5th Cir. 2015). "[T]he scope of injunctive relief is dictated by the extent of the violation established, not by the geographical extent of the plaintiff class." *Califano v. Yamasaki*, 442 U.S. 682, 702 (1979). A nationwide injunction is appropriate when a party brings a facial challenge to agency action under the APA. *See, e.g., Nat'l Mining* (invalidating an agency rule and affirming the nationwide injunction); *Harmon v. Thornburgh*, 878 F.2d 484 (D.C. Cir. 1989) ("When a reviewing court determines that agency regulations are unlawful, the ordinary result is that the rules are vacated—not that their application to the individual petitioners is proscribed.").

CMDA's membership extends across the country and the Rule applies broadly to "almost all licensed physicians." Accordingly, the Rule's harm is felt by healthcare providers and states across the country, including all of CMDA's members, and the Court finds a nationwide injunction appropriate. Because the Rule includes a severability provision, none of the unchallenged provisions are enjoined. 45 C.F.R. §92.2(c). Only the Rule's command this Court finds is contrary to law and exceeds statutory authority—the prohibition of discrimination on the basis of "gender identity" and "termination of pregnancy"—is hereby enjoined.

. . . .

IV. Conclusion

For the foregoing reasons, the Court finds that Plaintiffs' motions for preliminary injunction should be and are hereby GRANTED. Defendants are hereby ENJOINED from enforcing the Rule's prohibition against discrimination on the basis of gender identity or termination of pregnancy.

So ORDERED on this 31st day of December, 2016.

Discussion

1. The court draws a key inference: "[t]hat Congress included the signal *'et seq.'* . . . after the citation to Title IX can only mean Congress intended to incorporate the entire statutory structure, including the abortion and religious exemptions." Is there any other possible explanation for Congress's referring in the ACA

to discrimination on "the ground prohibited under . . . [T]itle IX of the Education Amendments of 1972 (20 U.S.C. 1681 *et seq.*)"? Note also that the court cites no authority for applying the canon against surplusage to statutory citation signals such as "*et seq.*" Why should we treat part of a signal pointing to "Title IX," which is, after all, a federal act encompassing more than one subsection, as "part of" the ACA such that failure to attribute specific effect to "*et seq.*" would make "part" of the statute "inoperative or superfluous, void, or insignificant," in the language of the surplusage canon?

2. Is the court right that because Title IX contains exemptions from its coverage, an entity falling within the terms of those exemptions is in fact not discriminating on the ground prohibited in Title IX? Isn't "the *ground* prohibited under" Title IX simply "sex," and the exemptions merely specifying *when/in what areas* sex discrimination is prohibited?

3. *Hobby Lobby* held that RFRA applied not just to natural persons (*i.e.*, real human individuals) but also to closely held for-profit corporations (there, family-owned corporations). The Court has also applied RFRA to religious institutions such as churches or orders of nuns. *See Gonzales v. O Centro Espírita Beneficente Uniã do Vegetal*, 126 S. Ct. 1211 (2006); *Little Sisters of the Poor Home for the Aged v. Sebelius*, 571 U.S. 1171 (2014). Here, the court applies it to a large hospital system. Whether or not that was the intent of the Congress that enacted RFRA in 1993, is that an otherwise appropriate construction of the term "person" in a statute that protects the free exercise of religion by "any person"? Why or why not?

4. What kinds of governmental interests should suffice to override the statutory protection for religious exercise provided by RFRA? Note that the court provides no citation for its assertion that "[a] compelling interest is one the government would be willing to pursue itself."

5. The district court cites *Hobby Lobby* for the proposition that "if the government wishes to expand access to transition and abortion procedures, the most straightforward way of doing this would be for the government to assume the cost of providing the procedures at issue to any individuals who are unable to obtain them under their health-insurance policies due to their employers' religious objections." (Internal quotation marks and alterations omitted.) Note that the *Hobby Lobby* majority continued its analysis and concluded "[i]n the end, however, we need not rely on the option of a new, government-funded program in order to conclude that the HHS regulations fail the least-restrictive-means test." Rather, the fact that HHS had made an accommodation for nonprofit organizations convinced the court that it could do the same for for-profit close corporations whose small group of owners had similar religious objections. Should we think that the government taking on the costs that other entities in a given field have to bear should be a requirement of RFRA?

Even if this argument addressed the insurance coverage question of who pays for services, it doesn't address the challenge to regulations guaranteeing nondiscriminatory access to medical procedures. The court's answer seems to be that the government could set up a web site or app to provide information to transgender persons on where to find medical care providers who would not discriminate against them. Should we think RFRA would require government to publish a "greenbook" listing businesses that would not discriminate against African Americans if people were to assert—as people in fact have—religious reasons for their racial discrimination? Would such an approach satisfy the equality aims of antidiscrimination laws?

Note also that the court cites *Hobby Lobby* for the proposition that only the government's view of the compelling interests served by a challenged law matters ("controls"). The cited page of the *Hobby Lobby* opinion, however, makes an argument that the Supreme Court would not reach a least restrictive means argument made by amici that was not presented in the lower courts and with which the opponents had had no opportunity to engage.

6. The challenged nondiscrimination regulation covers both health insurance and access to healthcare. Do all aspects of the court's preliminary injunction analysis fully cover both sorts of obligations?

Is the court acting consistently in treating any injunction against the state enforcing its laws as "irreparable injury" to the state but insisting that "HHS will suffer *no* harm from delaying implementation of the challenged portion of the Rule" (emphasis added)?

7. The plaintiff's suit also argued that the challenged regulation barring discrimination on the basis of gender identity or termination of pregnancy was not authorized by the statutory ban on sex discrimination in Section 1557 of the Affordable Care Act and therefore was in violation of the Administrative Procedure Act. This aspect of the suit is presented in Chapter 11, *infra* at p. 595. (As to that issue, consider the possible significance of the reasoning of *Bostock v. Clayton County, Georgia*, 140 S. Ct. 1731 (2020), presented in detail in Chapter 5 Section D, *supra*, which held that the ban on sex discrimination in Title VII of the Civil Rights Act of 1964 forbids discrimination based on someone's "transgender status.") The Discussion following the opinion in Chapter 11 recounts the subsequent history of this case, culminating in the court "setting aside" the challenged aspects of the regulation as unlawful and remanding the matter for the Department of Health and Human Services to act consistently with the court's ruling.

Reading Guide for EEOC v. Harris Funeral Homes

1. In the following case, the defendant Harris Funeral Homes was sued for firing funeral director Aimee Stephens after she informed it that she would be transitioning and no longer presenting as male on the job (or elsewhere). The defendant argued that it did not violate Title VII of the federal Civil Rights Act of 1964 to insist its employees comply with sex-differentiated dress codes according to their ("God-given") sex. The defendant also argued that even if its conduct were to violate Title VII, that statute could not be applied to it because doing so would substantially

burden its exercise of religion in a way that would not survive the strict scrutiny required by the federal Religious Freedom Restoration Act ("RFRA"). The court of appeals concludes that the firing of Ms. Stephens violated Title VII and that applying the law there did not violate RFRA. The defendants appealed the Title VII issue to the Supreme Court, which affirmed in *Bostock v. Clayton County, Georgia*, 140 S. Ct. 1731 (2020), presented in detail in Chapter 5 Section D, *supra*. The *Harris Funeral Home* defendants did not appeal their loss on the RFRA issue, leaving the court of appeals ruling on that point in place. The court of appeals' analysis presented below focuses on the defendants' RFRA religious exemption claim.

2. Even though the funeral home did not rely on the "ministerial exception" to Title VII (see discussion of *Hosanna-Tabor Evangelical Lutheran Church & Sch. v. EEOC*, 565 U.S. 171 (2012), *supra* at p. 536), the court nevertheless considers whether Aimee Stephens falls within its scope. Why does it address the issue? The court concludes that Stephens's firing is not protected by the doctrine for two independent reasons. What is the court's reasoning regarding each? Is the court right on each?

3. RFRA protects against governmental imposition of burdens on the exercise of religion. Why does the court apply it to this dispute arising from the firing of an individual employee by a private corporation? And on the merits, what is the relevant "exercise of religion" by the corporation's owner Thomas Rost? Note that as in *Hobby Lobby*, discussed *supra* at pp. 534–35, the corporation's exercise of religion is equated to that of its owner or owners. (Is that proper?)

4. The defendant alleges two burdens on its exercise of religion. The court rejects the first one on both factual and legal grounds. What is the court's factual argument? What is its doctrinal argument? The court also rejects the defendant's claimed second burden, again on two grounds. What is the first, arguably factually-driven argument that the court gives for rejecting the second claimed burden? What is its second, legally based ruling for rejecting the legal sufficiency of the alleged second burden for the defendant's RFRA claim?

5. In the alternative, the court of appeals rules that the plaintiff has satisfied strict scrutiny and therefore has not violated RFRA. How does the defendant characterize the governmental interest supporting application of Title VII to it? For what reasons does the court reject that characterization? How does the court articulate the governmental interest, and for what reasons does it judge that interest "compelling"? (Note that some of the court's reasoning on this point, dealing with the harm to Stephens or other employees, may sound like it goes to the next element of the RFRA analysis—whether applying the law to the RFRA claimant is the least restrictive means of advancing a compelling governmental interest.)

6. The court concludes that enforcing Title VII's sex discrimination ban against the defendant is the least restrictive means of furthering the government's compelling interest. Why does it reject the sufficiency of the defendant's suggested less restrictive alternatives? On what precedents does the court rely, and for what points?

Equal Employment Opportunity Commission, Plaintiff-Appellant, Aimee Stephens, Intervenor v. R.G. & G.R. Harris Funeral Homes, Inc., Defendant-Appellee

884 F.3d 560 (6th Cir. 2018), *cert. granted in part*, 139 S. Ct. 1599 (2019)

[In the Court of Appeals, the intervenor Aimee Stephens was represented by the national ACLU and the ACLU of Michigan; the defendant Harris Funeral Homes was represented by the Alliance Defending Freedom; participating as amici supporting Harris Funeral Homes were organizations including Public Advocate of the United States (a private organization advocating conservative religious policies in the political sphere) and the Conservative Legal Defense and Education Fund; and participating as amici supporting the EEOC and Stephens were many organizations including Lambda Legal, the Human Rights Campaign, the Unitarian Universalist Association, Americans United for Separation of Church and State, Muslim Advocates, the Union for Reform Judaism, the United Synagogue of Conservative Judaism, and The Private Rights/Public Conscience Project at Columbia Law School (now the Law, Rights, and Religion Project).]

Before: MOORE, WHITE, and DONALD, Circuit Judges.

Opinion

KAREN NELSON MOORE, Circuit Judge.

Aimee Stephens . . . was born biologically male.[1] While living and presenting as a man, she worked as a funeral director at R.G. & G.R. Harris Funeral Homes, Inc. ("the Funeral Home"), a closely held for-profit corporation that operates three funeral homes in Michigan. Stephens was terminated from the Funeral Home by its owner and operator, Thomas Rost, shortly after Stephens informed Rost that she intended to transition from male to female and would represent herself and dress as a woman while at work. Stephens filed a complaint with the Equal Employment Opportunity Commission ("EEOC"), which investigated Stephens's allegations that she had been terminated as a result of unlawful sex discrimination. During the course of its investigation, the EEOC learned that the Funeral Home provided its male public-facing employees with clothing that complied with the company's dress code while female public-facing employees received no such allowance. The EEOC subsequently brought suit against the Funeral Home in which the EEOC charged the Funeral Home with violating Title VII of the Civil Rights Act of 1964 ("Title VII") by (1) terminating Stephens's employment on the basis of her transgender or transitioning status and her refusal to conform to sex-based stereotypes; and (2) administering a discriminatory-clothing-allowance policy.

The parties submitted dueling motions for summary judgment. . . .

---

1. We refer to Stephens using female pronouns, in accordance with the preference she has expressed through her briefing to this court.

The district court granted summary judgment in favor of the Funeral Home on both claims. For the reasons set forth below, we hold that (1) the Funeral Home engaged in unlawful discrimination against Stephens on the basis of her sex; (2) the Funeral Home has not established that applying Title VII's proscriptions against sex discrimination to the Funeral Home would substantially burden Rost's religious exercise, and therefore the Funeral Home is not entitled to a defense under [the Religious Freedom Restoration Act ("RFRA")]; (3) even if Rost's religious exercise were substantially burdened, the EEOC has established that enforcing Title VII is the least restrictive means of furthering the government's compelling interest in eradicating workplace discrimination against Stephens; and (4) the EEOC may bring a discriminatory-clothing-allowance claim in this case because such an investigation into the Funeral Home's clothing-allowance policy was reasonably expected to grow out of the original charge of sex discrimination that Stephens submitted to the EEOC. Accordingly, we REVERSE the district court's grant of summary judgment on both the unlawful-termination and discriminatory-clothing-allowance claims, GRANT summary judgment to the EEOC on its unlawful-termination claim, and REMAND the case to the district court for further proceedings consistent with this opinion.

I. Background

. . . .

Stephens moved to intervene in this appeal on January 26, 2017, after expressing concern that changes in policy priorities within the U.S. government might prevent the EEOC from fully representing Stephens's interests in this case. We . . . granted Stephens's motion to intervene on March 27, 2017. . . .

II. Discussion

. . . .

B. Unlawful Termination Claim

Title VII prohibits employers from "discriminat[ing] against any individual with respect to his compensation, terms, conditions, or privileges of employment, because of such individual's race, color, religion, sex, or national origin." . . .

Here, the district court correctly determined that Stephens was fired because of her failure to conform to sex stereotypes, in violation of Title VII. The district court erred, however, in finding that Stephens could not alternatively pursue a claim that she was discriminated against on the basis of her transgender and transitioning status. Discrimination on the basis of transgender and transitioning status is necessarily discrimination on the basis of sex. . . .

. . . . [We] hold that the EEOC could pursue a claim under Title VII on the ground that the Funeral Home discriminated against Stephens on the basis of her transgender status and transitioning identity. The EEOC should have had the opportunity, either through a motion for summary judgment or at trial, to establish that the Funeral Home violated Title VII's prohibition on discrimination on the basis of sex by firing Stephens because she was transgender and transitioning from male to female.

3. Defenses to Title VII Liability

Having determined that the Funeral Home violated Title VII's prohibition on sex discrimination, we must now consider whether any defenses preclude enforcement of Title VII in this case. [The] district court held that the EEOC's enforcement efforts must give way to the Religious Freedom Restoration Act ("RFRA"), which prohibits the government from enforcing a religiously neutral law against an individual if that law substantially burdens the individual's religious exercise and is not the least restrictive way to further a compelling government interest. [In] addition, certain amici ask us to affirm the district court's grant of summary judgment on different grounds—namely that Stephens falls within the "ministerial exception" to Title VII and is therefore not protected under the Act.

We hold that the Funeral Home does not qualify for the ministerial exception to Title VII; the Funeral Home's religious exercise would not be substantially burdened by continuing to employ Stephens without discriminating against her on the basis of sex stereotypes; the EEOC has established that it has a compelling interest in ensuring the Funeral Home complies with Title VII; and enforcement of Title VII is necessarily the least restrictive way to achieve that compelling interest. We therefore REVERSE the district court's grant of summary judgment in the Funeral Home's favor and GRANT summary judgment to the EEOC on the unlawful-termination claim.

a. Ministerial Exception

We turn first to the "ministerial exception" to Title VII, which is rooted in the First Amendment's religious protections, and which "preclude[s] application of [employment discrimination laws such as Title VII] to claims concerning the employment relationship between a religious institution and its ministers." *Hosanna-Tabor Evangelical Lutheran Church & Sch. v. EEOC*, 565 U.S. 171 (2012). "[I]n order for the ministerial exception to bar an employment discrimination claim, the employer must be a religious institution and the employee must have been a ministerial employee." *Conlon v. InterVarsity Christian Fellowship/USA*, 777 F.3d 829 (6th Cir. 2015). "The ministerial exception is a highly circumscribed doctrine. It grew out of the special considerations raised by the employment claims of clergy, which 'concern[] internal church discipline, faith, and organization, all of which are governed by ecclesiastical rule, custom, and law.'" *Gen. Conf. Corp. of Seventh-Day Adventists v. McGill*, 617 F.3d 402 (6th Cir. 2010).

Public Advocate of the United States and its fellow amici argue that the ministerial exception applies in this case because (1) the exception applies both to religious and non-religious entities, and (2) Stephens is a ministerial employee. Tellingly, however, the Funeral Home contends that the Funeral Home "is not a religious organization" and therefore, "the ministerial exception has no application" to this case. Although the Funeral Home has not waived the ministerial-exception defense by failing to raise it, *see Conlon* (holding that private parties may not "waive the First Amendment's ministerial exception" because "[t]his constitutional protection is . . . structural"), we agree with the Funeral Home that the exception is inapplicable here.

[The] ministerial exception applies only to "religious institutions." *Id*. While an institution need not be "a church, diocese, or synagogue, or an entity operated by a traditional religious organization," *id*., to qualify for the exception, the institution must be "marked by clear or obvious religious characteristics," *id*. . . .

The Funeral Home . . . has virtually no "religious characteristics." Unlike the campus mission in *Conlon*, the Funeral Home does not purport or seek to "establish and advance" Christian values. As the EEOC notes, the Funeral Home "is not affiliated with any church; its articles of incorporation do not avow any religious purpose; its employees are not required to hold any particular religious views; and it employs and serves individuals of all religions." . . . [The] Funeral Home's sole public displays of faith, according to Rost, amount to placing "Daily Bread" devotionals and "Jesus Cards" with scriptural references in public places in the funeral homes, which clients may pick up if they wish. The Funeral Home does not decorate its rooms with "religious figures" because it does not want to "offend[] people of different religions." . . .

Nor is Stephens a "ministerial employee" under *Hosanna-Tabor*. [We] have identified four factors to assist courts in assessing whether an employee is a minister covered by the exception: (1) whether the employee's title "conveys a religious—as opposed to secular—meaning"; (2) whether the title reflects "a significant degree of religious training" that sets the employee "apart from laypersons"; (3) whether the employee serves "as an ambassador of the faith" and serves a "leadership role within [the] church, school, and community"; and (4) whether the employee performs "important religious functions . . . for the religious organization." *Conlon*. Stephens's title—"Funeral Director"—conveys a purely secular function. The record does not reflect that Stephens has any religious training. Though Stephens has a public-facing role within the funeral home, she was not an "ambassador of [any] faith," and she did not perform "important religious functions," *see id*.; rather, Rost's description of funeral directors' work identifies mostly secular tasks—making initial contact with the deceased's families, handling the removal of the remains to the funeral home, introducing other staff to the families, coaching the families through the first viewing, greeting the guests, and coordinating the families' "final farewell." The only responsibilities assigned to Stephens that could be construed as religious in nature were, "on limited occasions," to "facilitate" a family's clergy selection, "facilitate the first meeting of clergy and family members," and "play a role in building the family's confidence around the role the clergy will play, clarifying what type of religious message is desired, and integrating the clergy into the experience." Such responsibilities are a far cry from the duties ascribed to the employee in *Conlon*, which "included assisting others to cultivate 'intimacy with

God and growth in Christ-like character through personal and corporate spiritual disciplines.'" In short, Stephens was not a ministerial employee and the Funeral Home is not a religious institution, and therefore the ministerial exception plays no role in this case.

b. Religious Freedom Restoration Act

.... RFRA precludes the government from "substantially burden[ing] a person's exercise of religion even if the burden results from a rule of general applicability," unless the government "demonstrates that application of the burden to the person—(1) is in furtherance of a compelling governmental interest; and (2) is the least restrictive means of furthering that compelling governmental interest." 42 U.S.C. § 2000bb-1. ...

i. Applicability of the Religious Freedom Restoration Act

We have previously made clear that "Congress intended RFRA to apply only to suits in which the government is a party." *Seventh-Day Adventists.* Thus, if Stephens had initiated a private lawsuit against the Funeral Home to vindicate her rights under Title VII, the Funeral Home would be unable to invoke RFRA as a defense because the government would not have been party to the suit. Now that Stephens has intervened in this suit, she argues that the case should be remanded to the district court with instructions barring the Funeral Home from asserting a RFRA defense to her individual claims. The EEOC supports Stephens's argument.

The Funeral Home, in turn, argues that the question of RFRA's applicability to Title VII suits between private parties "is a new and complicated issue that has never been a part of this case and has never been briefed by the parties." Because Stephens's intervention on appeal was granted, in part, on her assurances that she "seeks only to raise arguments already within the scope of this appeal," the Funeral Home insists that permitting Stephens to argue now in favor of remand "would immensely prejudice the Funeral Home and undermine the Court's reasons for allowing Stephens's intervention in the first place."

The Funeral Home is correct. ...

.... The merits of a remand have been addressed only in passing by the parties, and thus have not been discussed with "sufficient clarity and completeness" to enable us to entertain Stephens's claim.[8]

---

8. For a similar reason, we decline to consider the argument raised by several amici that reading RFRA to "permit a religious accommodation that imposes material costs on third parties or interferes with the exercise of rights held by others" would violate the Establishment Clause of the First Amendment. *See* Private Rights/Public Conscience Br. at 15; Americans United Br. at 6-15. Amici may not raise "issues or arguments [that] . . . 'exceed those properly raised by the parties.'" *Shoemaker v. City of Howell*, 795 F.3d 553 (6th Cir. 2015). Although Stephens notes that the Establishment Clause "requires the government and courts to account for the harms a religious exemption to Title VII would impose on employees," no party to this action presses the broad constitutional argument that amici seek to present. We therefore will not address the merits of amici's position.

ii. Prima Facie Case Under RFRA

To assert a viable defense under RFRA, a religious claimant must demonstrate that the government action at issue "would (1) substantially burden (2) a sincere (3) religious exercise." *Gonzales v. O Centro Espírita Beneficente Uniã do Vegetal*, 546 U.S. 418 (2006). In reviewing such a claim, courts must not evaluate whether asserted "religious beliefs are mistaken or insubstantial." *Burwell v. Hobby Lobby Stores, Inc.*, 134 S. Ct. 2751 (2014). Rather, courts must assess "whether the line drawn reflects 'an honest conviction.'" *Id.* In addition, RFRA, as amended by the Religious Land Use and Institutionalized Persons Act of 2000 ("RLUIPA"), protects "any exercise of religion, whether or not compelled by, or central to, a system of religious belief." 42 U.S.C. § 2000cc-5(7)(A).

. . . . The Funeral Home . . . contends that the "very operation of [the Funeral Home] constitutes protected religious exercise" because Rost feels compelled by his faith to "serve grieving people" through the funeral home, and thus "[r]equiring [the Funeral Home] to authorize a male funeral director to wear the uniform for female funeral directors would directly interfere with — and thus impose a substantial burden on — [the Funeral Home's] ability to carry out Rost's religious exercise of caring for the grieving."

If we take Rost's assertions regarding his religious beliefs as sincere, which all parties urge us to do, then we must treat Rost's running of the funeral home as a religious exercise — even though Rost does not suggest that ministering to grieving mourners by operating a funeral home is a tenet of his religion, more broadly. The question then becomes whether the Funeral Home has identified any way in which continuing to employ Stephens would substantially burden Rost's ability to serve mourners. The Funeral Home purports to identify two burdens. "First, allowing a funeral director to wear the uniform for members of the opposite sex would often create distractions for the deceased's loved ones and thereby hinder their healing process (and [the Funeral Home's] ministry)," and second, "forcing [the Funeral Home] to violate Rost's faith . . . would significantly pressure Rost to leave the funeral industry and end his ministry to grieving people." Neither alleged burden is "substantial" within the meaning of RFRA.

The Funeral Home's first alleged burden — that Stephens will present a distraction that will obstruct Rost's ability to serve grieving families — is premised on presumed biases. As the EEOC observes, the Funeral Home's argument is based on "a view that Stephens is a 'man' and would be perceived as such even after her gender transition," as well as on the "assumption that a transgender funeral director would so disturb clients as to 'hinder healing.'" The factual premises underlying this purported burden are wholly unsupported in the record. Rost testified that he has never seen Stephens in anything other than a suit and tie and does not know how Stephens would have looked when presenting as a woman. Rost's assertion that he believes his clients would be disturbed by Stephens's appearance during and after her transition to the point that their healing from their loved ones' deaths would be hindered, at the very least raises a material question of fact as to whether his clients would actually be distracted, which cannot be resolved in the Funeral Home's favor at the summary-judgment stage. Thus, even if we were to find the Funeral Home's argument legally cognizable, we would not affirm a finding of substantial burden based on a contested and unsupported assertion of fact.

But more to the point, we hold as a matter of law that a religious claimant cannot rely on customers' presumed biases to establish a substantial burden under RFRA. Though we have seemingly not had occasion to address the issue, other circuits have considered whether and when to account for customer biases in justifying discriminatory employment practices. In particular, courts asked to determine whether customers' biases may render sex a "bona fide occupational qualification" under Title VII have held that "it would be totally anomalous . . . to allow the preferences and prejudices of the customers to determine whether the sex discrimination was valid." *Diaz v. Pan Am. World Airways, Inc.*, 442 F.2d 385 (5th Cir. 1971); *see also Bradley v. Pizzaco of Nebraska, Inc.*, 7 F.3d 795 (8th Cir. 1993) (holding grooming policy for pizza deliverymen that had disparate impact on African-American employees was not justified by customer preferences for clean-shaven deliverymen because "[t]he existence of a beard on the face of a delivery man does not affect in any manner Domino's ability to make or deliver pizzas to their customers"); *Fernandez v. Wynn Oil Co.*, 653 F.2d 1273 (9th Cir. 1981) (rejecting claim that promoting a female employee would "'destroy the essence' of [the defendant's] business"—a theory based on the premise that South American clients would not want to work with a female vice-president—because biased customer preferences did not make being a man a "bona fide occupational qualification" for the position at issue). . . .

Of course, cases like *Diaz*, *Fernandez*, and *Bradley* concern a different situation than the one at hand. We could agree that courts should not credit customers' prejudicial notions of what men and women can do when considering whether sex constitutes a "bona fide occupational qualification" for a given position while nonetheless recognizing that those same prejudices have practical effects that would substantially burden Rost's religious practice (*i.e.*, the operation of his business) in this case. But the Ninth Circuit rejected similar reasoning in *Fernandez*, and we reject it here. In *Fernandez*, the Ninth Circuit held that customer preferences could not transform a person's gender into a relevant consideration for a particular position even if the record supported the idea that the employer's business would suffer from promoting a woman because a large swath of clients would refuse to work with a female vice-president. Just as the *Fernandez* court refused to treat discriminatory promotion practices as critical to an employer's business, notwithstanding any evidence to that effect in the record, so too we refuse to treat discriminatory policies as essential to Rost's business—or, by association, his religious exercise.

The Funeral Home's second alleged burden also fails. Under *Holt v. Hobbs*, 135 S. Ct. 853 (2015), a government action that "puts [a religious practitioner] to th[e] choice" of "'engag[ing] in conduct that seriously violates [his] religious beliefs' [or] . . . fac[ing] serious" consequences constitutes a substantial burden for the purposes of RFRA. *See id.* (quoting *Hobby Lobby*). Here, Rost contends that he is being put to such a choice, as he either must "purchase female attire" for Stephens or authorize her "to dress in female attire *while representing* [the Funeral Home] and serving the bereaved," which purportedly violates Rost's religious beliefs, or else face "significant[] pressure . . . to leave the funeral industry and end his ministry to grieving people." Appellee Br. (emphasis in original). Neither of these purported choices can be considered a "substantial burden" under RFRA.

First, though Rost currently provides his male employees with suits and his female employees with stipends to pay for clothing, this benefit is not legally required and Rost does not suggest that the benefit is religiously compelled. In this regard, Rost is unlike the employers in *Hobby Lobby*, who rejected the idea that they could simply refuse to provide health care altogether and pay the associated penalty (which would allow them to avoid providing access to contraceptives in violation of their beliefs) because they felt religiously compelled to provide their employees with health insurance. And while "it is predictable that the companies [in *Hobby Lobby*] would face a competitive disadvantage in retaining and attracting skilled workers" if they failed to provide health insurance, the record here does not indicate that the Funeral Home's clothing benefit is necessary to attract workers; in fact, until the EEOC commenced the present action, the Funeral Home did not provide any sort of clothing benefit to its female employees. Thus, Rost is not being forced to choose between providing Stephens with clothing or else leaving the business; this is a predicament of Rost's own making.

Second, simply permitting Stephens to wear attire that reflects a conception of gender that is at odds with Rost's religious beliefs is not a substantial burden under RFRA. . . . [We] hold that, as a matter of law, tolerating Stephens's understanding of her sex and gender identity is not tantamount to supporting it.

Most circuits, including this one, have recognized that a party can sincerely believe that he is being coerced into engaging in conduct that violates his religious convictions without actually, as a matter of law, being so engaged. Courts have recently confronted this issue when non-profit organizations whose religious beliefs prohibit them "from paying for, providing, or facilitating the distribution of contraceptives," or in any way "be[ing] complicit in the provision of contraception" argued that the Affordable Care Act's opt-out procedure—which enables organizations with religious objections to the contraceptive mandate to avoid providing such coverage by either filling out a form certifying that they have a religious objection to providing contraceptive coverage or directly notifying the Department of Health and Human Services of the religious objection—substantially burdens their religious practice. *See Eternal Word Television Network, Inc. v. Sec'y of U.S. Dep't of Health & Human Servs.*, 818 F.3d 1122 (11th Cir. 2016).

Eight of the nine circuits to review the issue, including this court, have determined that the opt-out process does not constitute a substantial burden. The courts reached this conclusion by examining the Affordable Care Act's provisions and determining that it was the statute—and not the employer's act of opting out—that "entitle[d] plan participants and beneficiaries to contraceptive coverage." *See, e.g., Eternal Word.* As a result, the employers' engagement with the opt-out process, though legally significant in that it leads the government to provide the organizations' employees with access to contraceptive coverage through an alternative route, does not mean the employers are facilitating the provision of contraceptives in a way that violates their religious practice.

We view the Funeral Home's compliance with antidiscrimination laws in much the same light. Rost may sincerely believe that, by retaining Stephens as an employee, he is supporting and endorsing Stephens's views regarding the mutability of sex. But as a matter of law, bare compliance with Title VII—without actually assisting or facilitating Stephens's transition efforts—does not amount to an endorsement of Stephens's views. As much is clear from the Supreme Court's Free Speech jurisprudence, in which the Court has held that a statute requiring law schools to provide military and nonmilitary recruiters an equal opportunity to recruit students on campus was not improperly compelling schools to endorse the military's policies because "[n]othing about recruiting suggests that law schools agree with any speech by recruiters," and "students can appreciate the difference between speech a school sponsors and speech the school permits because legally required to do so, pursuant to an equal access policy." *Rumsfeld v. Forum for Acad. & Institutional Rights, Inc.,* 547 U.S. 47 (2006); *see also Rosenberger v. Rector & Visitors of the Univ. of Va.,* 515 U.S. 819 (1995) (being required to provide funds on an equal basis to religious as well as secular student publications does not constitute state university's support for students' religious messages). Similarly, here, requiring the Funeral Home to refrain from firing an employee with different religious views from Rost does not, as a matter of law, mean that Rost is endorsing or supporting those views. Indeed, Rost's own behavior suggests that he sees the difference between employment and endorsement, as he employs individuals of any or no faith, "permits employees to wear Jewish head coverings for Jewish services," and "even testified that he is not endorsing his employee's religious beliefs by employing them."[10]

At bottom, the fact that Rost sincerely believes that he is being compelled to make such an endorsement does not make it so. *Cf. Eternal Word* ("We reject a framework that takes away from courts the responsibility to decide what action the government requires and leaves that answer entirely to the religious adherent. Such a framework improperly substitutes religious belief for legal analysis regarding the operation of federal law."). Accordingly, requiring Rost to comply with Title VII's proscriptions on discrimination does not substantially burden his religious practice. The district

---

10. Even ignoring any adverse inferences that might be drawn from the incongruity between Rost's earlier deposition testimony and the Funeral Home's current litigation position, as we must do when considering whether summary judgment is appropriate in the EEOC's favor, we conclude as a matter of law that Rost does not express "support[] [for] the idea that sex is a changeable social construct rather than an immutable God-given gift" by continuing to hire Stephens, *see* Rost Aff. ¶¶ 43, 45—even if Rost sincerely believes otherwise.

court therefore erred in granting summary judgment to the Funeral Home on the basis of its RFRA defense, and we REVERSE the district court's decision on this ground. As Rost's purported burdens are insufficient as a matter of law, we GRANT summary judgment to the EEOC with respect to the Funeral Home's RFRA defense.

iii. Strict Scrutiny Test

Because the Funeral Home has not established that Rost's religious exercise would be substantially burdened by requiring the Funeral Home to comply with Title VII, we do not need to consider whether the EEOC has adequately demonstrated that enforcing Title VII in this case is the least restrictive means of furthering a compelling government interest. However, in the interest of completeness, we reach this issue and conclude that the EEOC has satisfied its burden. We therefore GRANT summary judgment to the EEOC with regard to the Funeral Home's RFRA defense on the alternative grounds that the EEOC's enforcement action in this case survives strict scrutiny.

(a) Compelling Government Interest

Under the "to the person" test, the EEOC must demonstrate that its compelling interest "is satisfied through application of the challenged law [to] . . . the particular claimant whose sincere exercise of religion is being substantially burdened." *Gonzales*. This requires "look[ing] beyond broadly formulated interests justifying the general applicability of government mandates and scrutiniz[ing] the asserted harm of granting specific exemptions to particular religious claimants." *Id.*

As an initial matter, the Funeral Home does not seem to dispute that the EEOC "has a compelling interest in the 'elimination of workplace discrimination, including sex discrimination.'" Appellee Br. at 41 (quoting Appellant Br. at 51). However, the Funeral Home criticizes the EEOC for "cit[ing] a general, broadly formulated interest" to support enforcing Title VII in this case. According to the Funeral Home, the relevant inquiry is whether the EEOC has a "specific interest in forcing [the Funeral Home] to allow its male funeral directors to wear the uniform for female funeral directors while on the job." The EEOC instead asks whether its interest in "eradicating employment discrimination" is furthered by ensuring that Stephens does not suffer discrimination (either on the basis of sex-stereotyping or her transgender status), lose her livelihood, or face the emotional pain and suffering of being effectively told "that as a transgender woman she is not valued or able to make workplace contributions." *See, e.g.,* Appellant Br. Stephens similarly argues that "Title VII serves a compelling interest in eradicating all the forms of invidious employment discrimination proscribed by the statute," and points to studies demonstrating that transgender people have experienced particularly high rates of "bodily harm, violence, and discrimination because of their transgender status."

The Funeral Home's construction of the compelling-interest test is off-base. Rather than focusing on the EEOC's claim—that the Funeral Home terminated Stephens because of her proposed gender nonconforming behavior—the Funeral Home's test focuses instead on its defense (discussed above) that the Funeral Home merely wishes to enforce an appropriate workplace uniform. But the Funeral Home has not identified any cases where the government's compelling interest was framed as its interest in disturbing a company's workplace policies. For instance, in *Hobby Lobby*, the issue, which the Court ultimately declined to adjudicate, was whether the government's "interest in guaranteeing cost-free access to the four challenged contraceptive methods" was compelling—not whether the government had a compelling interest in requiring closely held organizations to act in a way that conflicted with their religious practice.

The Supreme Court's analysis in cases like *Wisconsin v. Yoder*, 406 U.S. 205 (1972), and *Holt* guides our approach. In those cases, the Court ultimately determined that the interests generally served by a given government policy or statute would not be "compromised" by granting an exemption to a particular individual or group. Thus, in *Yoder*, the Court held that the interests furthered by the government's requirement of compulsory education for children through the age of sixteen (*i.e.*, "to prepare citizens to participate effectively and intelligently in our open political system" and to "prepare[] individuals to be self-reliant and self-sufficient participants in society") were not harmed by granting an exemption to the Amish, who do not need to be prepared "for life in modern society" and whose own traditions adequately ensure self-sufficiency. Similarly, in *Holt*, the Court recognized that the Department of Corrections has a compelling interest in preventing prisoners from hiding contraband on their persons, which is generally effectuated by requiring prisoners to adhere to a strict grooming policy, but the Court failed to see how the Department's "compelling interest in staunching the flow of contraband into and within its facilities . . . would be seriously compromised by allowing an inmate to grow a 1/2-inch beard."

Here, the same framework leads to the opposite conclusion. Failing to enforce Title VII against the Funeral Home means the EEOC would be allowing a particular person—Stephens—to suffer discrimination, and such an outcome is directly contrary to the EEOC's compelling interest in combating discrimination in the workforce. *See, e.g., United States v. Burke*, 504 U.S. 229 (1992) ("[I]t is beyond question that discrimination in employment on the basis of sex . . . is, as . . . this Court consistently has held, an invidious practice that causes grave harm to its victims.").[12] In this regard, this case is analogous to *Eternal Word*, in which the Eleventh Circuit determined that the government had a compelling interest in requiring a particular

---

12. Courts have repeatedly acknowledged that Title VII serves a compelling interest in eradicating all forms of invidious employment discrimination proscribed by the statute. As the Supreme Court stated, the "stigmatizing injury" of discrimination, "and the denial of equal opportunities that accompanies it, is surely felt as strongly by persons suffering discrimination on the basis of their sex as by those treated differently because of their race." *Roberts v. U.S. Jaycees*, 468 U.S. 609 (1984); *see also EEOC v. Pac. Press Publ'g Ass'n*, 676 F.2d 1272 (9th Cir. 1982) ("By enacting Title VII, Congress clearly targeted the elimination of all forms of discrimination as a 'highest priority.' Congress' purpose to end discrimination is equally if not more compelling than other interests that have been held to justify legislation that burdened the exercise of religious convictions.").

nonprofit organization with religious objections to the Affordable Care Act's contraceptive mandate to follow the procedures associated with obtaining an accommodation to the Act because

> applying the accommodation procedure *to the plaintiffs in these cases* furthers [the government's] interests because the accommodation ensures that the plaintiffs' female plan participants and beneficiaries — who may or may not share the same religious beliefs as their employer — have access to contraception without cost sharing or additional administrative burdens as the ACA requires.

(emphasis added). The *Eternal Word* court reasoned that "[u]nlike the exception made in *Yoder* for Amish children," who would be adequately prepared for adulthood even without compulsory education, the "poor health outcomes related to unintended or poorly timed pregnancies apply to the plaintiffs' female plan participants or beneficiaries and their children just as they do to the general population." Similarly, here, the EEOC's compelling interest in eradicating discrimination applies with as much force to Stephens as to any other employee discriminated against based on sex.

It is true, of course, that the specific harms the EEOC identifies in this case, such as depriving Stephens of her livelihood and harming her sense of self-worth, are simply permutations of the generic harm that is always suffered in employment discrimination cases. But *O Centro*'s "to the person" test does not mean that the government has a compelling interest in enforcing the laws only when the failure to enforce would lead to uniquely harmful consequences. Rather, the question is whether "the asserted harm of granting specific exemptions to particular religious claimants" is sufficiently great to require compliance with the law. *O Centro*. Here, for the reasons stated above, the EEOC has adequately demonstrated that Stephens has and would suffer substantial harm if we exempted the Funeral Home from Title VII's requirements.

Finally, we reject the Funeral Home's claim that it should receive an exemption, notwithstanding any harm to Stephens or the EEOC's interest in eradicating discrimination, because "the constitutional guarantee of free exercise[,] effectuated here via RFRA . . . [,] is a higher-order right that necessarily supersedes a conflicting statutory right." This point warrants little discussion. The Supreme Court has already determined that RFRA does not, in fact, "effectuate . . . the First Amendment's guarantee of free exercise," because it sweeps more broadly than the Constitution demands. *See City of Boerne v. Flores*, 521 U.S. 507 (1997). And in any event, the Supreme Court has expressly recognized that compelling interests can, at times, override religious beliefs — even those that are squarely protected by the Free Exercise Clause. *See Cutter v. Wilkinson*, 544 U.S. 709 (2005) ("We do not read RLUIPA to elevate accommodation of religious observances over an institution's need to maintain order and safety. Our decisions indicate that an accommodation must be measured so that it does not override other significant interests."). We therefore decline to hoist automatically Rost's religious interests above other compelling governmental concerns. The undisputed record demonstrates that Stephens has been and would be harmed by the Funeral Home's discriminatory practices in this case, and the EEOC has a compelling interest in eradicating and remedying such discrimination.

(b) Least Restrictive Means

The final inquiry under RFRA is whether there exist "other means of achieving [the government's] desired goal without imposing a substantial burden on the exercise of religion by the objecting part[y]." *Hobby Lobby*. "The least-restrictive-means standard is exceptionally demanding," and the EEOC bears the burden of showing that burdening the Funeral Home's religious exercise constitutes the least restrictive means of furthering its compelling interests. Where an alternative option exists that furthers the government's interest "equally well," *Hobby Lobby*, the government "must use it," *Holt*. In conducting the least-restrictive-alternative analysis, "courts must take adequate account of the burdens a requested accommodation may impose on nonbeneficiaries." *Hobby Lobby*. Cost to the government may also be "an important factor in the least-restrictive-means analysis." *Id*.

The district court found that requiring the Funeral Home to adopt a gender-neutral dress code would constitute a less restrictive alternative to enforcing Title VII in this case, and granted the Funeral Home summary judgment on this ground. According to the district court, the Funeral Home engaged in illegal sex stereotyping only with respect to "the clothing Stephens [c]ould wear at work," and therefore a gender-neutral dress code would resolve the case because Stephens would not be forced to dress in a way that conforms to Rost's conception of Stephens's sex and Rost would not be compelled to authorize Stephens to dress in a way that violates Rost's religious beliefs.

Neither party endorses the district court's proposed alternative, and for good reason. The district court's suggestion, although appealing in its tidiness, is tenable only if we excise from the case evidence of sex stereotyping in areas other than attire. Though Rost does repeatedly say that he terminated Stephens because she "wanted to *dress* as a woman" and "would no longer *dress* as a man" (emphasis added), the record also contains uncontroverted evidence that Rost's reasons for terminating Stephens extended to other aspects of Stephens's intended presentation. For instance, Rost stated that he fired Stephens because Stephens "was no longer going to *represent himself* as a man,"(emphasis added), and Rost insisted that Stephens presenting as a female would disrupt clients' healing process because female clients would have to "share a bathroom with a man dressed up as a woman." The record thus compels the finding that Rost's concerns extended beyond Stephens's attire and reached Stephens's appearance and behavior more generally.

At the summary-judgment stage, where a court may not "make credibility determinations, weigh the evidence, or draw [adverse] inferences from the facts," the district court was required to account for the evidence of Rost's non-clothing-based sex stereotyping in determining whether a proposed less restrictive alternative furthered the government's "stated interests equally [as] well," *Hobby Lobby.* Here, as the evidence above shows, merely altering the Funeral Home's dress code would not address the discrimination Stephens faced because of her broader desire "to represent [her]self as a [wo]man." Indeed, the Funeral Home's counsel conceded at oral argument that Rost would have objected to Stephens's coming "to work presenting clearly as a woman and acting as a woman," regardless of whether Stephens wore a man's suit, because that "would contradict [Rost's] sincerely held religious beliefs."

The Funeral Home's proposed alternative—to "permit businesses to allow the enforcement of sex-specific dress codes for employees who are public-facing representatives of their employer, so long as the dress code imposes equal burdens on the sexes and does not affect employee dress outside of work"—is equally flawed. The Funeral Home's suggestion would do nothing to advance the government's compelling interest in preventing and remedying discrimination against Stephens based on her refusal to conform at work to stereotypical notions of how biologically male persons should dress, appear, behave, and identify. Regardless of whether the EEOC has a compelling interest in combating sex-specific dress codes—a point that is not at issue in this case—the EEOC does have a compelling interest in ensuring that the Funeral Home does not discriminate against its employees on the basis of their sex. The Funeral Home's proposed alternative sidelines this interest entirely.[13]

The EEOC, Stephens, and several amici argue that searching for an alternative to Title VII is futile because enforcing Title VII is itself the least restrictive way to further EEOC's interest in eradicating discrimination based on sex stereotypes from the workplace. We agree.

To start, the Supreme Court has previously acknowledged that "there may be instances in which a need for uniformity precludes the recognition of exceptions to generally applicable laws under RFRA." *O Centro.* The Court highlighted *Braunfeld v. Brown*, 366 U.S. 599 (1961), as an example of a case where the "need for uniformity" trumped "claims for religious exemptions." *O Centro.* In *Braunfeld*, the plurality "denied a claimed exception to Sunday closing laws, in part because . . . [t]he whole point of a 'uniform day of rest for all workers' would have been defeated by exceptions." *O Centro. Braunfeld* thus serves as a particularly apt case to consider here, as it too concerned an attempt by an employer to seek an exemption that would elevate its religious practices above a government policy designed to benefit

---

13. In its district court briefing, the Funeral Home proposed three additional purportedly less restrictive alternatives: the government could hire Stephens; the government could pay Stephens a full salary and benefits until she secures comparable employment; or the government could provide incentives to other employers to hire Stephens and allow her to dress as she pleases. Not only do these proposals fail to further the EEOC's interest enabling Stephens to work for the Funeral Home without facing discrimination, but they also fail to consider the cost to the government, which is "an important factor in the least-restrictive-means analysis." *Hobby Lobby.* We agree with the EEOC that the Funeral Home's suggestions—which it no longer pushes on appeal—are not viable alternatives to enforcing Title VII in this case, as they do not serve the EEOC's interest in eradicating discrimination "equally well." *See id.*

employees. If the government's interest in a "uniform day of rest for all workers" is sufficiently weighty to preclude exemptions, *see O Centro*, then surely the government's interest in uniformly eradicating discrimination against employees exerts just as much force.

The Court seemingly recognized Title VII's ability to override RFRA in *Hobby Lobby*, as the majority opinion stated that its decision should not be read as providing a "shield" to those who seek to "cloak[] as religious practice" their efforts to engage in "discrimination in hiring, for example on the basis of race." As the *Hobby Lobby* Court explained, "[t]he Government has a compelling interest in providing an equal opportunity to participate in the workforce without regard to race, and prohibitions on racial discrimination are precisely tailored to achieve that critical goal." We understand this to mean that enforcement actions brought under Title VII, which aims to "provid[e] an equal opportunity to participate in the workforce without regard to race" and an array of other protected traits, *see id.*, will necessarily defeat RFRA defenses to discrimination made illegal by Title VII. The district court reached the opposite conclusion, reasoning that *Hobby Lobby* did not suggest that "a RFRA defense can never prevail as a defense to Title VII" because "[i]f that were the case, the majority would presumably have said so." But the majority did say that anti-discrimination laws are "precisely tailored" to achieving the government's "compelling interest in providing an equal opportunity to participate in the workforce" without facing discrimination. *Hobby Lobby*.

As Stephens notes, at least two district-level federal courts have also concluded that Title VII constitutes the least restrictive means for eradicating discrimination in the workforce. *See Redhead v. Conf. of Seventh-Day Adventists*, 440 F. Supp. 2d 211 (E.D.N.Y. 2006) (holding that "the Title VII framework is the least restrictive means of furthering" the government's interest in avoiding discrimination against non-ministerial employees of religious organization), *adhered to on reconsideration*, 566 F. Supp. 2d 125 (E.D.N.Y. 2008); *EEOC v. Preferred Mgmt. Corp.*, 216 F. Supp. 2d 763 (S.D. Ind. 2002) ("[I]n addition to finding that the EEOC's intrusion into [the defendant's] religious practices is pursuant to a compelling government interest," — *i.e.*, "the eradication of employment discrimination based on the criteria identified in Title VII" — "we also find that the intrusion is the least restrictive means that Congress could have used to effectuate its purpose.").

We also find meaningful Congress's decision not to include exemptions within Title VII to the prohibition on sex-based discrimination. As both the Supreme Court and other circuits have recognized, "[t]he very existence of a government-sanctioned exception to a regulatory scheme that is purported to be the least restrictive means can, in fact, demonstrate that other, less-restrictive alternatives could exist." *McAllen Grace Brethren Church v. Salazar*, 764 F.3d 465 (5th Cir. 2014) (citing *Hobby Lobby*); *see also Church of the Lukumi Babalu Aye, Inc. v. City of Hialeah*, 508 U.S. 520 (1993) ("It is established in our strict scrutiny jurisprudence that 'a law cannot be regarded as protecting an interest of the highest order . . . when it leaves appreciable damage to that supposedly vital interest unprohibited.'" (omission in original)). Indeed, a driving force in the *Hobby Lobby* Court's determination that the government had failed the least-restrictive-means test was the fact that the Affordable Care Act, which the government sought to enforce in that case against a closely held organization, "already established an accommodation for nonprofit organizations with religious objections." Title VII, by contrast, does not contemplate any exemptions for discrimination on the basis of sex. Sex may be taken into account only if a person's sex "is a bona fide occupational qualification reasonably necessary to the normal operation of [a] particular business or enterprise," 42 U.S.C. § 2000e-2(e)(1)—and in that case, the preference is no longer discriminatory in a malicious sense. Where the government has developed a comprehensive scheme to effectuate its goal of eradicating discrimination based on sex, including sex stereotypes, it makes sense that the only way to achieve the scheme's objectives is through its enforcement.

State courts' treatment of RFRA-like challenges to their own antidiscrimination laws is also telling. In several instances, state courts have concluded that their respective antidiscrimination laws survive strict scrutiny, such that religious claimants are not entitled to exemptions to enforcement of the state prohibitions on discrimination with regard to housing, employment, medical care, and education. These holdings support the notion that antidiscrimination laws allow for fewer exceptions than other generally applicable laws.

As a final point, we reject the Funeral Home's suggestion that enforcing Title VII in this case would undermine, rather than advance, the EEOC's interest in combating sex stereotypes. According to the Funeral Home, the EEOC's requested relief reinforces sex stereotypes because the agency essentially asks that Stephens "be able to dress in a stereotypical feminine manner." This argument misses the mark. Nothing in Title VII or this court's jurisprudence requires employees to reject their employer's stereotypical notions of masculinity or femininity; rather, employees simply may not be discriminated against for a failure to conform. *See Smith v. City of Salem*, 378 F.3d 566 (6th Cir. 2004) (holding that a plaintiff makes out a prima facie case for discrimination under Title VII when he pleads that "his *failure to conform* to sex stereotypes concerning how a man should look and behave was the driving force behind" an adverse employment action (emphasis added)). Title VII protects both the right of male employees "to c[o]me to work with makeup or lipstick on [their] face[s]," *Barnes v. City of Cincinnati*, 401 F.3d 729 (6th Cir. 2005), and the right of female employees to refuse to "wear dresses or makeup," *Smith*, without any internal contradiction.

. . . .

[The court's analysis of the discriminatory clothing-allowance claim is omitted.]

III. Conclusion

Discrimination against employees, either because of their failure to conform to sex stereotypes or their transgender and transitioning status, is illegal under Title VII. The unrefuted facts show that the Funeral Home fired Stephens because she refused to abide by her employer's stereotypical conception of her sex, and therefore the EEOC is entitled to summary judgment as to its unlawful-termination claim. RFRA provides the Funeral Home with no relief because continuing to employ Stephens would not, as a matter of law, substantially burden Rost's religious exercise, and even if it did, the EEOC has shown that enforcing Title VII here is the least restrictive means of furthering its compelling interest in combating and eradicating sex discrimination. We therefore REVERSE the district court's grant of summary judgment in favor of the Funeral Home and GRANT summary judgment to the EEOC on its unlawful-termination claim. We also REVERSE the district court's grant of summary judgment on the EEOC's discriminatory-clothing-allowance claim, as the district court erred in failing to consider the EEOC's claim on the merits. We REMAND this case to the district court for further proceedings consistent with this opinion.

Discussion

1. After losing in the court of appeals, the funeral home sought certiorari from the Supreme Court. The Alliance Defending Freedom ("ADF") abandoned its RFRA claim in its July 2018 cert petition, contesting only the applicability of Title VII's sex discrimination ban to anti-trans discrimination. Why might ADF, a religious liberty advocacy organization, have elected not to pursue its religious exemption claim under RFRA?

After almost nine months and listing the petition for consideration at conference multiple times, the Supreme Court granted review on April 19, 2019. The Court limited its grant "to the following question: Whether Title VII prohibits discrimination against transgender people based on (1) their status as transgender (2) sex stereotyping under *Price Waterhouse v. Hopkins*, 490 U.S. 228, 109 S. Ct. 1775, 104 L. Ed. 2d 268 (1989)." The Supreme Court heard oral arguments in *Harris Funeral Homes* and two cases raising claims of sexual orientation discrimination under Title VII (with the Trump administration contending that Title VII's ban on sex discrimination did not prohibit gender identity or sexual orientation discrimination) on October 8, 2019. On June 15, 2020, the Court held that discriminating against someone because of their status as transgender was sex discrimination under Title VII. *Bostock v. Clayton County, Georgia*, 140 S. Ct. 1731 (2020), Chapter 5, Section D, *supra*.

2. Should the "ministerial exception" to Title VII and similar statutes, shielding employers from liability for discriminating against employees who count as "ministers," be available only to religious institutions, as the U.S. Court of Appeals for the Sixth Circuit has held, or available to all entities without respect to whether they are religious or non-religious as some amici urged here?

3. The court of appeals relied on cases about the BFOQ exception to Title VII's ban on sex discrimination—which refuse to treat customer's gender-based prejudices,

even if real and material, as a basis for treating gender as legally relevant—to rule that likewise customer prejudices cannot provide the basis for a substantial burden on religious exercise under RFRA. Is that proper? One might think that law, and in particular Title VII, properly treats notions of business necessity as objective and for principled and/or strategic reasons not countenancing sex-based prejudice. But does that mean that a burden on a person's exercise of religion under RFRA should likewise be treated as objective rather than subjective to the particular religious adherent? Wouldn't doing that be in tension with the majority's approach to burdens in *Hobby Lobby*, which seemed to focus on the claimants' personal religious beliefs about various contraception methods? It might also be in tension with the Supreme Court's granting of injunctions against the federal government's requiring religious nonprofit entities with religious objections to covering contraceptives in their employee insurance plans to file a specified form to be exempt from providing that coverage. *See Wheaton College v. Burwell*, 134 S. Ct. 2806 (2014). The objectors had argued that in their religious view, they would still be complicit in religiously objectionable practices if they had to file such a form, regardless of whether anyone else thought their belief in their own complicity reasonable; the courts of appeals had disagreed about whether RFRA exempted such objectors from the obligation to file the form. The appeals court here recognized the existence of such claims. Note also that the court relies on free speech jurisprudence about (objective) expressions of agreement or endorsement to justify rejecting as a matter of law the contention that continuing to employ Stephens after her transition would burden Rost's (subjective) exercise of religion.

4. ADF's proffered characterization of the government's allegedly compelling interest in the case is framed in terms of Rost's religious reasons for wishing to terminate Stephens. The court rejects it as an inapt, odd framing, but this is not the only case where one sees religious objectors to civil laws attempting to recast the governmental interest into something facially objectionable. In *Fulton v. City of Philadelphia*, 922 F.3d 140 (3d Cir. 2019), *cert. granted*, 140 S. Ct. 1104 (2020), Catholic Social Services ("CSS"), a Catholic foster care agency, objected to the city's insisting that it not discriminate against same-sex couples who wished to foster children. It argued that the city was singling it out for disfavor because of its religious beliefs, but the court of appeals dismissed that contention:

> CSS's theme devolves to this: the City is targeting CSS because it discriminates against same-sex couples; CSS is discriminating against same-sex couples because of its religious beliefs; therefore the City is targeting CSS for its religious beliefs. But this syllogism is as flawed as it is dangerous. It runs directly counter to the premise of *Smith* that, while religious belief is always protected, religiously motivated conduct enjoys no special protections or exemption from general, neutrally applied legal requirements. That CSS's conduct springs from sincerely held and strongly felt religious beliefs does not imply that the City's desire to regulate that conduct springs from antipathy to those beliefs. If all comment on religiously motivated conduct

by those enforcing neutral, generally applicable laws against discrimination is construed as ill will against the religious belief itself, then *Smith* is a dead letter, and the nation's civil rights laws might be as well. As the Intervenors rightly state, the "fact that CSS's non-compliance with the City's non-discrimination requirements is based on its religious beliefs does not mean that the City's enforcement of its requirements constitutes anti-religious hostility."

CSS was represented by the conservative Becket Fund for Religious Liberty in that case, and the Alliance Defending Freedom was an amicus supporting CSS. For a brief explanation of the issue that the Supreme Court will be deciding as it reviews this case, see *supra* at p. 537.

5. In arguing that enforcement of Title VII against the defendant was the least restrictive means of advancing the government's compelling interests, the court of appeals treats as relevant the lack of exemptions from Title VII's sex discrimination prohibition. But why isn't the BFOQ provision of Title VII, which allows otherwise unlawful discrimination on the basis of sex, for example, when sex is a bona fide occupational qualification for a particular position, properly characterized as an "exemption"? (For that matter, why doesn't the limitation of Title VII to employers of 15 or more employees, 42 U.S.C. §2000e(b), undermine arguments that Title VII's bans on discrimination on grounds of race, color, religion, national origin, and sex serve compelling interests by the least restrictive means?)

Chapter 11

Health Insurance Exclusion and Discrimination

Unlike the vast majority of developed nations, the U.S. government does not provide health care for all its citizenry. It does provide health care to poor Americans through the Medicaid program, and to senior citizens through Medicare. Otherwise, people largely are on their own to secure health care through insurance they purchase individually or through an employer's plan, through paying directly for services they receive, or through visiting a hospital emergency room. Access to health insurance is thus important for many people in the United States. One-fourth of respondents to the U.S. Transgender Survey, the largest study of the experiences of transgender people in the United States, with over 27,000 respondents from every state, D.C., three federal territories, and overseas military bases, reported experiencing "a problem in the past year with their insurance related to being transgender, such as being denied coverage for care related to gender transition or being denied coverage for routine care because they were transgender." SANDY E. JAMES ET AL., NATIONAL CENTER FOR TRANSGENDER EQUALITY, THE REPORT OF THE 2015 U.S. TRANSGENDER SURVEY 10 (2016). "More than half (55%) of those who sought coverage for transition-related surgery in the" year prior to the survey reported being denied coverage, as did one fourth "of those who sought coverage for hormones."

These statistics by themselves could paint a rosier picture than warranted, for 33% of survey respondents reported that in the year preceding the survey they "did not go to a health care provider when needed because they could not afford it." This makes health insurance vitally important for transgender people in particular. Section A of this chapter focuses on individual insurance, and Section B focuses on Medicaid and other government insurance programs.

A. Individual Insurance

Litigation is not an ideal way for someone to secure payment from their insurance company for medical procedures. It can be expensive, time-consuming, and itself a source of stress, which can exacerbate health problems. If one is transgender, it can also lead to unwanted publicity of one's transgender status or health history. Thus, this section starts with a case where the transgender plaintiff sought to proceed anonymously, using a pseudonym.

Reading Guide for Doe v. Blue Cross & Blue Shield

1. What does the underlying litigation in this case concern? According to the court, what is the general rule that applies to the question whether the plaintiff may sue about that using a pseudonym? What does the court say is the right analysis to use to determine whether the plaintiff is entitled to an exception from that general rule?

2. Upon what factors does the court rely in reaching its decision on whether to allow the plaintiff to proceed as "John Doe"? Do the precedents upon which it relies furnish apt analogies? How does it distinguish *John Doe and Jane Doe v. Prudential Insurance Co.*?

John Doe v. Blue Cross & Blue Shield of Rhode Island

794 F. Supp. 72 (D.R.I. 1992)

Memorandum and Order

Pettine, Senior District Judge.

Defendant . . . has filed a Motion to Strike Plaintiff's Amended Complaint. In essence, defendant objects to plaintiff's use of a fictitious name. . . .

I

Plaintiff, a transsexual, has filed suit against Blue Cross & Blue Shield of Rhode Island in an attempt to recoup medical expenses he incurred in connection with his sex change. Blue Cross contends that sex changes are expressly excluded from the insurance coverage afforded plaintiff through his group employee benefits plan.

Plaintiff wishes to pursue this litigation under a fictitious name

> in order to avoid public identification as a transsexual. Plaintiff seeks to avoid the social stigmatization which would flow from his identity as a transsexual. Plaintiff also seeks, through the use of a fictitious name, to protect his privacy, as well as to insulate himself from harassment that could result from his public identification as a transsexual. And plaintiff seeks to avoid the destruction of his ability to earn a living. Indeed Plaintiff, an insurance agent, lost the endorsement of two insurance carriers after they had learned that he was a transsexual. As a result, Plaintiff fears that other carriers would refuse to conduct business with him, and that his ability to pursue his chosen occupation, or any other, would be jeopardized by public revelation of his transsexuality.

Defendant counters that neither "social embarrassment [nor] potential economic loss . . . is sufficient to overcome the presumption that one who seeks the assistance of the courts should conduct that litigation under his/her own name."

II

Few courts have been faced with the precise question of whether transsexuals are entitled to sue under pseudonymous names.[14] However, in at least three such cases, transsexual litigants were permitted to proceed under fictitious names. In *McClure v. Harris*, 503 F. Supp. 409 (N.D. Cal. 1980), *rev'd on other grounds*, *Schweiker v. McClure*, 456 U.S. 188 (1982), the Court granted plaintiff Ann Doe's motion to proceed by a fictitious name. Ms. Doe's lawsuit was premised on a denial of Medicare reimbursement for her sex-change operation. The Court in *Doe v. McConn*, 489 F. Supp. 76 (S.D. Tex. 1980), explained that "The Jane Doe Plaintiffs and Plaintiff M.B., in various stages of sexual transition, are suing under fictitious names to insulate themselves from possible harassment, to protect their privacy, and to protect themselves from prosecution resulting from this action."[15] Finally, in *Doe v. Alexander*, 510 F. Supp. 900 (D. Minn. 1981), the Court, without comment, permitted the transsexual plaintiff to litigate pseudonymously.

. . . . In balancing plaintiff's right to privacy and security against the dual concerns of (1) public interest in identification of the litigants; and (2) harm to the defendant stemming from falsification of plaintiff's name,[16] this Court is cognizant of the highly sensitive and personal nature of each person's sexuality. Particularly in this era of seemingly increased societal intolerance toward "unconventional" sexual behavior, I will not strip plaintiff of the cloak of privacy which shields him from the stigmatization he might otherwise endure.

In assessing the potential harm to plaintiff if he is forced to reveal his identity, a useful analogy may be drawn to homosexuals and others whose sexuality also expose them to public derision and discrimination. This analogy was acknowledged in Steinman, *Public Trial, Pseudonymous Parties: When Should Litigants be Permitted to Keep Their Identities Confidential?*, 37 HASTINGS L.J. 1, 51 (1985), a scholarly article on the subject of pseudonymous litigants:

> [P]eople may have a right not to disclose their sexual histories and preferences, and a strong interest in nondisclosure. Matters of sexual identity and sexual preference are exceedingly personal. . . . [W]hile sex-change

---

14. Under most circumstances, parties to a lawsuit are required to proceed under their real names. See, *e.g.*, Fed. R. Civ. P. 10(a); *Southern Methodist Univ. Ass'n v. Wynne & Jaffe*, 599 F.2d 707 (5th Cir. 1979). This general rule has been broken on occasion, however. See *Roe v. Wade*, 410 U.S. 113 (1973). . . .

15. Blue Cross correctly points out *McConn* is distinguishable from the instant case in that the plaintiff transsexuals in *McConn* were in danger of prosecution for violating a city ordinance making it unlawful for persons to cross-dress in public. Here, the plaintiff faces no such threat of criminal sanctions; nonetheless, the *McConn* plaintiffs and the present plaintiff share other, equally valid, concerns regarding divulgence of their true identities.

16. "The decision [as to whether a party may sue anonymously] requires a balancing of considerations calling for maintenance of a party's privacy against the customary and constitutionally-embedded presumption of openness in judicial proceedings." *Doe v. Stegall*, 653 F.2d 180 (5th Cir. 1981).

operations are too new to carry a long history of condemnation and stigma, the experience of homosexuals and transvestites strongly indicates a similar public response.

I need cite no authority for the proposition that homosexuals in the United States today are frequently met with scorn or hatred. While transsexuality and homosexuality are not the same or even related phenomena, bigoted persons are no more likely to tolerate one than the other of these sexual practices.

Homosexual plaintiffs have been permitted to litigate their cases pseudonymously to protect their privacy and to shield them from social stigmatization. In *Doe v. United Services Life Ins. Co.*, 123 F.R.D. 437 (S.D.N.Y. 1988), a heterosexual male sued a life insurance carrier which erroneously classified him as homosexual based on certain aspects of his lifestyle, and then attempted to add a surcharge to his premium on the basis of its inaccurate categorization. In permitting plaintiff to litigate under a fictitious name, the Court reasoned that "[c]ases where a party risks identification as a homosexual . . . raise privacy concerns that have supported an exception to the general rule of disclosure [of the litigant's name]." Cautioning that "[c]ourts should not permit parties to proceed pseudonymously just to protect the parties' professional or economic life," the Court granted plaintiff's motion to litigate pseudonymously.

I find persuasive the analysis of litigants' requests for pseudonymity set forth in *Doe v. Rostker*, 89 F.R.D. 158 (N.D. Cal. 1981). The Court explained that the general rule requiring plaintiffs to include the names of all parties in their complaints is not set in stone:

> Courts have carved out limited exceptions to [this rule] where the parties have strong interests in proceeding anonymously. Although no express standard exists setting forth these exceptions, this court's review of numerous cases has uncovered some classifiable characteristics. The most common instances are cases involving abortion, mental illness, personal safety, homosexuality, transsexuality and illegitimate or abandoned children in welfare cases. The common thread running through these cases is the presence of some social stigma or the threat of physical harm to the plaintiffs attaching to disclosure of their identities to the public record.

The Court continued:

> A plaintiff should be permitted to proceed anonymously in cases where a substantial privacy interest is involved. The most compelling situations involve matters which are highly sensitive, such as social stigmatization, real danger of physical harm, or where the injury litigated against would occur as a result of the disclosure of the plaintiff's identity. That the plaintiff may suffer some embarrassment or economic harm is not enough. There must be a strong social interest in concealing the identity of the plaintiff.

The plaintiff in this case does have a substantial privacy interest at stake. Unquestionably, one's sexual practices are among the most intimate parts of one's life. When those sexual practices fall outside the realm of "conventional" practices which are generally accepted without controversy, ridicule or derision, that interest is enhanced exponentially. As a transsexual, plaintiff's privacy interest is both precious and fragile, and this Court will not cavalierly permit its invasion.

III

Defendant contends that other factors outweigh plaintiff's privacy interest in keeping his identity from the public at large. First, defendant attempts to analogize between the instant case and *John Doe and Jane Doe v. Prudential Insurance Co.*, 744 F. Supp. 40 (D.R.I. 1990). The underlying dispute in Prudential involved a claim by the parents of a deceased homosexual for the proceeds of the decedent's life insurance policy. The parents filed a motion to proceed under fictitious names, presumably because they did not wish to publicize their son's homosexuality or the fact that he died from AIDS. The Court denied plaintiffs' motion, explaining that:

> [P]laintiffs . . . rely on an understandable desire to prevent what they consider to be "personal, private, and family matters" from becoming public information. . . . However, it is inappropriate for the Court to bar access to otherwise public records solely on the basis of subjective feelings of confidentiality or embarrassment of the type asserted here.

Prudential is easily and appropriately distinguished from the case at bar. In *Prudential*, the individual whose sexual preferences and practices were to be exposed in the course of litigation was dead. He would, therefore, suffer no stigmatization following disclosure of his identity. While the individual's parents did have a privacy interest at stake, due to its largely vicarious nature, their interest was insufficient to outweigh public interest in disclosure. In the instant case, the plaintiff seeks to mask his identity; it is his sexuality which will become public knowledge unless he proceeds under a fictitious name. He may suffer stigmatization for the duration of his life if his identity is disclosed. Thus, the privacy interest he asserts is vastly greater than that of the plaintiffs in *Prudential*. Moreover, as detailed in the previous Section, this Court finds that plaintiff's interests in nondisclosure are more than "mere embarrassment or threat of economic harm,"[17] as described by defendant.

Defendant also argues that it

> seriously doubts that this case will need to reach the issue of the "medical necessity" of plaintiff's surgery, which, according to plaintiff, purportedly would bring into minute scrutiny the details of his treatment. Blue Cross' primary defense in this case is that the treatment for which reimbursement is sought is unambiguously and categorically excluded from coverage under plaintiff's subscriber agreement. . . . In view of this clear and unambiguous

---

17. Plaintiff argues that he has already, and will likely continue to, lose professional clients once his status as a transsexual is no longer confidential. The Court need not address this, since I find that the probability of social stigmatization is sufficient to override any public interest in identity disclosure in this case.

contract exclusion, Blue Cross submits that it is likely to prevail on a motion for summary judgment. Medical testimony may never be required in this case.

This argument essentially asks this Court to engage in unwarranted speculation. Defendant has thus far not filed a summary judgment motion, and I will not join with defendant in hypothesizing that it would indeed prevail on a summary judgment motion which does not now even exist. Plaintiff presently has a substantial privacy interest at stake, which must be protected from the start of litigation if it is to be worth anything at all. Defendant's prediction that it will prevail at the summary judgment phase has no bearing on this Court's balancing of plaintiff's interests against those of the public.

. . . . I find that plaintiff has a substantial privacy interest in maintaining confidentiality as to his identity; I further find little if any evidence that the public interest in disclosure is sufficient to override plaintiff's security interest. Nor do I find that any significant harm will befall defendant if plaintiff proceeds under a fictitious name. Accordingly, I authorize the plaintiff to pursue this litigation using a pseudonym, and I deny defendant's motion to strike the amended complaint.

So ordered.

Discussion

1. The closet has been a mixed blessing for LGB persons, at times offering a measure of protection from anti-LGB prejudice and hostility, but also taking a tremendous toll both personally and in terms of the social and political influence that LGB people might have if they come out. Similar concerns have been voiced with respect to transsexual persons in conjunction with the possibility of their "disappearing" or "passing" after completing medical transitions. *See* Sandy Stone, *The Empire Strikes Back: A Posttranssexual Manifesto, in* Susan Stryker & Stephen Whittle, Eds., The Transgender Studies Reader 221 (2006). One should be cognizant that "the term 'passing' . . . is quite contested among transgender people. . . ." Leigh Goodmark, *Transgender People, Intimate Partner Abuse, and the Legal System*, 48 Harv. C.R.-C.L. L. Rev. 51, 59 (2013). For discussions of some of the complexities of notions of passing in this context, see, for example, Kate Bornstein, Gender Outlaw: On Men, Women, and the Rest of Us 125–128 (1995); Pat Califia, Sex Changes: The Politics of Transgenderism 210, 225 (1997); A. Finn Enke, *The Education of Little Cis: Cisgender and the Discipline of Opposing Bodies, in* Transfeminist Perspectives in and Beyond Transgender and Gender Studies 60, 64–66, 74–77 (Anne Enke ed., 2012); Jamison Green, *Look! No, Don't! The Visibility Dilemma for Transsexual Men, in* The Transgender Studies Reader 499 (Susan Stryker & Stephen Whittle eds., 2006); Alecia D. Anderson et al., *"Your Picture Looks the Same as My Picture": An Examination of Passing in Transgender Communities*, 37 Gender Issues 44 (2020). And notions of passing can be closely related to

notions of deception. *See, e.g.*, Talia Mae Bettcher, *Evil Deceivers and Make-Believers: On Transphobic Violence and the Politics of Illusion, in* The Transgender Studies Reader 2 278 (Susan Stryker & Aren Z. Aizura eds., 2013).

2. If the court is correct that pseudonymous plaintiffs cannot withhold evidence necessary to defend a lawsuit, for what reason might the insurer here have contested the permissibility of John Doe's proceeding via a pseudonym?

Note on Radtke v. Miscellaneous Drivers & Helpers Union Local #638

In *Christine Alisen Radtke v. Miscellaneous Drivers & Helpers Union Local #638 Health, Welfare, Eye & Dental Fund*, 867 F. Supp. 2d 1023 (D. Minn. 2012), the court ruled that an insurance plan had unlawfully terminated coverage of Christine Radtke, a transgender woman, on the professed ground that she was not a covered dependent of the primarily insured worker.

Christine had undergone treatment for gender dysphoria including "sex reassignment surgery" and had her Wisconsin birth certificate amended pursuant to court order to change her name and designate her sex as female. She subsequently married undisputed male Calvin Radtke in Minnesota and enrolled in his union's health plan as Calvin's dependent, defined by the plan to include his "legal spouse." After the plan learned that Christine was transgender (after she needed medical care to deal with a burst breast implant), counsel for the union's plan decided that the Radtkes were not legally married because Minnesota limited civil marriage to different-sex couples and directed the termination of Christine's coverage.

Christine sued the plan under the Employment Retirement Income Security Act ("ERISA"), by which it was governed. "Under ERISA, a plan beneficiary has the right to judicial review of a benefits determination. *See* 29 U.S.C. § 1132(a)(1)(B)." Judge Michael J. Davis summarized his opinion as follows:

> . . . . The Fund breached the terms of the Plan when it terminated Plaintiff's enrollment based on its erroneous and unreasonable interpretation of Minnesota law. The State of Minnesota law recognizes the Radtkes' marriage as a marriage between a man and a woman because Minnesota law recognizes Plaintiff's sex as female. Ms. Radtke is Mr. Radtke's legal spouse under Minnesota law and an eligible dependent under the Plan.
>
> The Plan was unambiguously written to allow all persons who are legal spouses under Minnesota law to be eligible family dependents. The Fund's role was to ascertain Minnesota law. It was not the Fund's role to impose its own definitions of gender and marriage upon its participants. In this case, the Fund ignored all evidence of the State of Minnesota's view of Plaintiff's sex and marital status. The Fund's decision was not only wrong, under a de novo review, it was a flagrant violation of its duty under any standard of review. In sum, the Fund erred when it terminated Plaintiff's participation

as an eligible family dependent. The Fund's termination of Ms. Radtke is reversed and she is reinstated as a participant as of April 19, 2010.

The court applied "a de novo standard of review because the Fund's denial is based upon its interpretation of Minnesota law, not on its interpretation of the Plan terms." On the merits, the court deemed irrelevant "decades-old Title VII cases" such as *Ulane v. Eastern Airlines, Inc.*, 742 F.2d 1081 (7th Cir. 1984), Chapter 5, Section A, *supra* at p. 146, and *Sommers v. Budget Marketing., Inc.*, 667 F.2d 748 (8th Cir. 1982), Chapter 5, Section A, *supra* at p. 138, because those precedents "analyz[ed] the meaning of 'sex' in Title VII, not under Minnesota law, and the opinions specifically base[d] their conclusion on a close analysis of Title VII and its particular legislative history." (The court also judged that "the 'narrow view' of the term 'sex' in Title VII in *Ulane* and *Sommers* 'has been eviscerated by *Price Waterhouse.*' *Smith v. City of Salem*, 378 F.3d 566, 573 (6th Cir. 2004) (citing *Price Waterhouse v. Hopkins*, 490 U.S. 228 (1989))".)

The court rejected the Fund's contention that Minnesota marriage law relied upon a person's sex assigned at birth. Rather, following *In re Lovo-Lara*, 23 I. & N. Dec. 746 (B.I.A. 2005), Chapter 9, *supra* at p. 523, the court reasoned that "it is logical to look to 'the designation appearing on the current birth certificate issued to that person by the State in which he or she was born,' *id.* at 753, and to the official government documents issued by the State of Minnesota, including court orders and marriage certificates and licenses." The court saw nothing in Minnesota's marriage statute suggesting the parties' sex should be treated differently from their age or lack of marriage to anyone else, which clearly must be assessed at the time of marriage (not birth or another time).

And the court believed Minnesota would accept the sex designation on Christine's amended birth certificate. "The only logical reason to allow the sex identified on a person's original birth certificate to be amended is to permit that person to actually use the amended certificate to establish his or her legal sex for other purposes, such as obtaining a driver's license, passport, or marriage license." The court noted numerous federal and state agencies that recognize Christine as female and/or as Calvin's spouse. Rejecting the notion of variable sex floated in marriage non-recognition cases such as *Corbett v. Corbett*, 2 All E.R. 33 (1970) (Eng.), Chapter 17, *infra* at p. 1178, the court concluded that "[t]here is no basis to conclude that Minnesota recognizes Plaintiff as female for some purposes—birth records and driver's licenses, but not for others—marriage certificates." The court bolstered its conclusion by noting that judicial decisions had recognized such marriages involving a transgender person for decades, yet Minnesota never amended its marriage laws to bar them expressly. Lacking any indication that Minnesota courts would follow some of the few reported non-recognition decisions denying transgender people the right to marry as a member of the sex consistent with their gender identity, the federal court refused to adopt such a rule here.

The court concluded by addressing a 2011 plan amendment limiting marriage to couples who were designated members of different sexes at their birth, which the

Fund adopted during the litigation. Because the 2010 termination was unlawful, the court reversed that action, leaving it to the Fund going forward to determine whether the 2011 amendment would apply to Christine even though it had always treated her coverage as governed by the plan terms in place when she became covered in 2005 rather than by other subsequent amendments.

If, following this litigation, the plan determined to apply its 2011 amendment to Ms. Radtke, what might she argue based on the Affordable Care Act and Title VII of the Civil Rights Act of 1964? What circumstances or factors might affect her likelihood of prevailing on either or both of those claims?

Consider the numerous medical and legal steps Christine Radtke took to effectuate her transition and live consistently with her gender identity. There was no problem with her husband's insurance covering her until after an accident occurred with one of her breast implants, which led to a doctor revealing her transgender status to the insurance plan. The advent of nationwide marriage equality in the United States, making one's sex irrelevant to the lawfulness of one's marriage as far as the federal and state governments are concerned, reduces one source of precarity in the lives of transgender people. What else might law, perhaps even insurance law, do to make transgender people more secure?

Note on Davidson v. Aetna Life & Casualty Insurance *and* Mario v. P & C Food Markets

Consider the following two cases from New York decided almost a quarter century apart. Each was reviewing an insurance plan administrator's decision to deny coverage for medical gender confirmation procedures, with the earlier decision ruling in favor of coverage for a transgender woman's "sex-reassignment surgery" or, more technically, genitoplasty; the later decision denied coverage for a transgender man's hormone therapy and mastectomy as well as any future services related to his gender transition. The courts took dramatically differing views about what treatments for gender dysphoria had or had not been shown to be "medically necessary."

In *Davidson v. Aetna Life & Casual Insurance Co.*, 101 Misc. 2d 1, 420 N.Y.S.2d 450 (Sup. Ct. 1979), the chemical company that employed transgender woman Victoria Lee Davidson had an employee benefits plan underwritten and administered by defendant Aetna Life & Casualty Insurance Co.; the plan's medical insurance coverage excluded "cosmetic surgery" unless it was "necessary for the repair of a non-occupational injury which occurs" during the coverage period. An Aetna employee rejected coverage of Ms. Davidson's genitoplasty pursuant to the cosmetic surgery exclusion, insisting that such surgeries are "cosmetic in nature" and citing Aetna's medical director, a physician who "lack[ed] expertise on the subject of gender dysphoria and transsexualism," and who insisted that "surgical intervention is not necessary and is unreasonable" apparently because in his view "there is nothing physically wrong with a transsexual's [*sic*] body, the problem, rather, being purely mental."

Judge Louis Grossman engaged in "an extensive reading of applicable literature," including the standards of care for patients with gender dysphoria then recently published by the Harry Benjamin International Gender Dysphoria Association (now named the World Professional Association for Transgender Health (WPATH)). He emphasized that "[t]he over-all process of sex-reassignment surgery is both long and arduous" and irreversible. He rejected the plan administrator's conclusion that Ms. Davidson's planned genitoplasty was cosmetic, optional, or elective, concluding instead from her evidence that "in order for the plaintiff to live a normal life, sex-reassignment surgery is imperative and necessary." Having recounted much of the technical details of gonadectomy and vaginoplasty, the judge observed that "[w]hile many seem appalled at such surgery, it nevertheless has demonstrated proven benefits for its recipients, although psychological in nature." Accordingly, he "conclude[d] that the treatment and surgery involved in the sex change operation of the plaintiff is of a medical nature and is feasible and required for the health and well-being of the plaintiff," and therefore not "cosmetic surgery" within the meaning of the policy. Hence, "the court [found] that the defendant Aetna Life & Casualty Insurance Co. is responsible for all medical expenses incurred by plaintiff herein as a result of her undergoing sex reassignment."

Although the court ruled that the health insurance plan Victoria Davidson enjoyed through her work was obliged to cover her gender confirmation surgery, one commentator has asserted that "many insurance companies avoided covering future sex-reassignment surgeries by creating policies with an explicit clause denying coverage to all conditions related to SRS. No longer a matter of contract interpretation, the narrowed clause became a bargained-for contractual term, precluding further private actions against an insurer." Kari E. Hong, *Categorical Exclusions: Exploring Legal Responses to Health Care Discrimination Against Transsexuals*, 11 COLUM. J. GENDER & L. 88, 100 (2002). The author cites no supporting evidence for that claim, although one could envision sophisticated attorneys for employers or insurance plans reacting to *Davidson* in this fashion.

Twenty-three years later, the U.S. Court of Appeals for the Second Circuit took a different view of medical necessity as shown by the evidence in *Marc Andrew Mario v. P & C Food Markets, Inc.*, 313 F.3d 758 (2d Cir. 2002). Former Yale Law School Dean and Circuit Judge Guido Calabresi, joined by Judges McLaughlin and B.D. Parker, Jr., sustained the denial of coverage by Mario's employer's self-funded plan for medical services related to Mr. Mario's "gender reassignment."

The court of appeals rejected Mario's claim that the plan improperly denied him coverage in violation of §§ 502 and 510 of the Employee Retirement Income and Security Act of 1974 ("ERISA"), 29 U.S.C. §§ 1132, 1140. The plan at issue excluded coverage for treatments that were not "medically necessary," which the court interpreted as "refer[ring] to what is medically necessary for a particular patient, and hence entails an individual assessment rather than a general determination of what works in the ordinary case." After research into "the issue of transsexualism, inquiry into the policies of other employers and insurance carriers concerning coverage of gender reassignment procedures, consultation with medical centers having special-ized knowledge of transsexualism and sexual reassignment surgeries, and consulta-tion with medical personnel employed by [the third-party plan administrator North American Administrators ("NAA")], including a psychiatrist retained by NAA," the plan administrator "concluded that there was substantial disagreement in the medi-cal community about whether gender dysphoria was a legitimate illness and uncer-tainty as to the efficacy of reassignment surgery." (The administrator relied in part on the retained psychiatrist's affidavit attesting that "the surgical removal of healthy organs, for no purpose other than gender dysphoria, would fall into the category of cosmetic surgery, and would therefore not be 'medically necessary.'") And the court of appeals did not believe the plaintiff had presented evidence that he was "different from the usual in ways that make the treatment medically necessary for him. . . ."

The court also affirmed the district court's dismissal of Mario's claim that he was discriminated against for failing to conform to sex stereotypes, in violation of Title VII of the Civil Rights Act of 1964. The court reasoned that "[s]pecifically, Mario claim[ed] that his employer, having accepted him as a male, denied coverage for medical procedures that are closely identified with being female, and that his claims would have been approved had they been made by female employees. . . ." With-out explanation, the court ruled that Mario failed "to make out a prima facie case because he presented no evidence to support his contention that P & C's denial of benefits occurred under circumstances giving rise to an inference of discrimination based on . . . his failure to conform to gender stereotypes." Ruling in the alternative, the court also affirmed dismissal of the Title VII claim because it believed that the lack of medical necessity for the surgeries was a legitimate, nondiscriminatory rea-son for the plan administrator to deny coverage.

Mario was decided almost a quarter century after *Davidson*. Should courts today agree with *Mario* about the lack of medical necessity for surgical gender transition procedures? Kathryn Kennedy has suggested that the answer should be "no":

> The controversy regarding treatment for gender dysphoria that the Second Circuit was referring to arguably has been rebutted since 2002. The Ameri-can Medical Association . . . issued a resolution in 2008, declaring its sup-port for public and private health insurance coverage for the treatment of GID as there was sufficient medical research that proved the medical neces-sity of mental health therapy, hormone therapy and sex reassignment sur-gery. In its resolution, it states "GID, if left untreated, can result in clinically significant psychological distress, dysfunction, debilitation, depression and, for some people without access to appropriate medical care and treatment, suicidality and death." Likewise, the American Psychiatric Association (APA) regards the treatment of gender transition surgeries as . . . medically necessary and therefore recommends their coverage by public and private insurers. The APA also opposes categorical exclusions of coverage for such medically necessary treatment when prescribed by a physician. [WPATH] affirms that medical procedures to confirm the gender that the individual

identifies with are not "cosmetic" or "elective" or "for the mere convenience of the patient.

Kathryn J. Kennedy, *Coverage in Transition: Considerations When Expanding Employer-Provided Health Coverage to LGBTI Employees and Beneficiaries*, 24 CARDOZO J. EQUAL RTS. & SOC. JUST. 1, 22–23 (2017) (footnotes omitted).

The Affordable Care Act

After Democratic candidate Barack Obama was elected President of the United States in November 2008, the next Congress began working on health care reform. Controlled by Democrats, the Senate and the House of Representatives were in 2010 able to pass, and President Obama signed, the Patient Protection and Affordable Care Act, Pub. L. 111-148, 124 Stat. 119-1025. The Affordable Care Act, or "Obamacare," was widely known for its so-called "individual mandate," the requirement that people maintain health insurance with specified minimum coverage. The Supreme Court upheld that provision in its high-profile decision in *National Federation of Independent Business v. Sebelius*, 567 U.S. 519 (2012), as an exercise of Congress's power to tax. But among the other provisions of this 900-plus page law was Section 1557, which by reference to other federal statutes prohibits discrimination in health programs or activities that receive some federal funding on the basis of, among other forbidden grounds, "sex." The U.S. Department of Health and Human Services subsequently engaged in formal "notice and comment" rulemaking and promulgated a rule that the ban on discrimination because of sex included discrimination because of gender identity and discrimination because of termination of pregnancy. 45 C.F.R. §92.4. While seemingly promising important protections to people from sex discrimination understood broadly, the regulation was fairly quickly challenged in federal court in *Franciscan Alliance v. Burwell*, 227 F. Supp. 3d 660 (N.D. Tex. 2016), presented next.

Reading Guide for Franciscan Alliance v. Burwell

1. Chapter 10, *supra* at p. 548, provides a fuller presentation of the background to and contentions of this litigation, brought by eight states and three private health care providers including Franciscan Alliance, Inc., now known as "Franciscan Health." It focuses on the religious exemptions claim pressed by the plaintiffs in this case.

2. Section 1557 of the Affordable Care Act prohibits discrimination in, inter alia, health insurance, by reference to forms of discrimination banned by other statutes; as relevant here, the ACA incorporates a ban on discrimination on the "the ground prohibited under" Title IX—which prohibits sex discrimination. The government, defending the statute, argues that the statutory texts of the ACA and Title IX do not clearly dictate those laws' application to anti-transgender discrimination; the plaintiffs argue that the laws clearly do not reach such discrimination (and thus that the court owes no deference to the non-discrimination regulation the Department of Health and Human Services adopted to implement Section 1557). How does the

district court resolve this disagreement about what the statutory text unambiguously forbids, and for what reasons does it reach its conclusion?

3. How broad is the injunctive relief that the court grants in this case? How does it justify this relief?

Franciscan Alliance, Inc., et al. v. Sylvia Burwell, Secretary of the United States Department of Health and Human Services, and United States Department of Health and Human Services

227 F. Supp. 3d 660 (N.D. Tex. 2016)

[The plaintiffs were represented by The Becket Fund for Religious Liberty and by Austin Nimocks who was then in the Texas Attorney General's Office, but who earlier served as Senior Counsel for the Alliance Defending Freedom.]

Opinion
Order

REED O'CONNOR, United States District Judge

. . . .

The Plaintiffs challenge a regulation enacted pursuant to the Patient Protection and Affordable Care Act ("ACA") that covers nearly every healthcare provider in the country and reaches into one of the most intimate relationships: that between a physician and her patient . . . While this lawsuit involves many issues of great importance—state sovereignty, expanded healthcare coverage, anti-discrimination protections, and medical judgment—ultimately, the question before the Court is whether Defendants exceeded their authority under the ACA in the challenged regulations' interpretation of sex discrimination and whether the regulation violates the Religious Freedom Restoration Act as applied to Private Plaintiffs. . . .

For the following reasons, the Court concludes that . . . the regulation violates the Administrative Procedure Act ("APA") by contradicting existing law and exceeding statutory authority. . . . Accordingly, Plaintiffs' Motions for Preliminary Injunction should be and are hereby GRANTED.

I. Background

. . . . [Plaintiffs] challeng[e] a new rule issued by HHS entitled Nondiscrimination in Health Programs & Activities (the "Rule"). 81 Fed. Reg. 31376-31473, (May 18, 2016) (codified at 45 C.F.R. §92).

The Rule implements Section 1557 of the ACA ("Section 1557"), which prohibits discrimination by any health program or activity receiving federal financial assistance on the grounds prohibited under four federal nondiscrimination statutes incorporated by Section 1557. 45 C.F.R. §92.1. The ground at issue in this case is Section 1557's incorporation of the prohibited sex discrimination under Title IX of the Education Amendments of 1972 ("Title IX"). Plaintiffs challenge the Rule's interpretation of discrimination "on the basis of sex" under Title IX as encompassing "gender identity" and "termination of pregnancy." 45 C.F.R. § 92.4. Plaintiffs argue that because Section 1557 incorporates the statutory prohibition of sex discrimination in Title IX, its scope should be limited by Title IX's unambiguous definition of "sex" as the immutable, biological differences between males and females "as acknowledged at or before birth." State Pls.' Br. at 13, 27. The Plaintiffs also assert that the Rule's definition of sex does not apply to them because the text of Section 1557 incorporates the religious and abortion exemptions of Title IX, and the Rule's failure to incorporate those exemptions renders it contrary to law.

. . . .

A. The Rule

. . . . After notice and comment, the final Rule was published on May 18, 2016. The Rule took partial effect on July 18, 2016, and the insurance provisions will be effective on January 1, 2017. The Rule purports to implement Section 1557 [of the ACA] which provides:

> [A]n individual shall not, *on the ground prohibited under* title VI of the Civil Rights Act of 1964 (42 U.S.C. 2000d et seq.) ["Title VI"], title IX of the Education Amendments of 1972 (20 U.S.C. 1681 et seq.) ["Title IX"], the Age Discrimination Act of 1975 (42 U.S.C. 6101 et seq.) ["ADA"], or section 504 of the Rehabilitation Act of 1973 (29 U.S.C. 794) ["Section 504"], be excluded from participation in, be denied the benefits of, or be subjected to discrimination under, any health program or activity, any part of which is receiving Federal financial assistance. . . .

42 U.S.C. § 18116(a) (emphasis added). Section 1557 does not create new bases of prohibited discrimination, but rather incorporates the grounds of four longstanding federal nondiscrimination statutes: Title VI, Title IX, the ADA, and Section 504. The implementing Rule claims to merely "clarif[y] and codif[y] *existing* nondiscrimination requirements," incorporated in Section 1557. 81 Fed. Reg. at 31376 (emphasis added). . . .

When implementing the Title IX portion of Section 1557, HHS defined discrimination "on the basis of sex" to include "termination of pregnancy" and "gender identity." 45 C.F.R. § 92.4. The Rule does not define termination of pregnancy but defines gender identity as "an individual's internal sense of gender, which may be male, female, neither, or a combination of male and female, and which may be different from an individual's sex assigned at birth." *Id.* The Rule explains that the "gender identity spectrum includes an array of possible gender identities beyond male and female." 81 Fed. Reg. at 31392.

. . . .

1. Health Coverage

One of the "discriminatory actions prohibited" under the Rule is "hav[ing] or implement[ing] a categorical [insurance] coverage exclusion or limitation for all health services related to gender transition." 45 C.F.R. § 92.207(b). The Rule declares that categorizations of all transition-related treatment as cosmetic or experimental are now "outdated and not based on current standards of care." 81 Fed. Reg. at 31429. The "range of transition-related services" contemplated by the Rule includes treatment for gender dysphoria[4] and is "not limited to surgical treatments and may include, but is not limited to, services such as hormone therapy and psychotherapy, which may occur over the lifetime of the individual." 81 Fed. Reg. at 31435–36.

Because the Rule contains no age limitation, Plaintiffs are concerned it may require health insurance coverage of transitions for children and they note that transition-related procedures are viewed by many in the medical community as harmful, including HHS's own medical experts.[5] . . . .

. . . .

Plaintiffs claim the Rule pressures covered entities to perform and provide insurance coverage for abortion- and transition-related procedures. But Defendants argue the Rule does not require the performance or insurance coverage of any procedure, but merely prohibits policies from "operating in a discriminatory manner, both in design and implementation." Defendants claim that "neutral nondiscriminatory application of evidence-based criteria" can be used to "make medical necessity or coverage determinations" and that "a legitimate nondiscriminatory reason" can justify a limitation of services. At the hearing on this matter however, Defendants' Counsel argued it would be "very difficult to imag[in]e" any medical justification for a categorical exclusion of health services or coverage of all transition-related procedures.

. . . .

4. Plaintiffs

Franciscan and CMDA's members are covered entities under the Rule because they both receive federal financial assistance and provide employee health insurance. . . .

CMDA is the nation's largest faith-based organization of doctors, including nearly 18,000 members who sign a statement of faith to join and rely on CMDA to advocate on behalf of their religious beliefs and medical judgments in the public square. Accordingly, CMDA is bringing suit on behalf of its members. CMDA members hold values similar to Franciscan and CMDA's approved Ethics Statement affirms the "obligation of Christian healthcare professionals to care for patients struggling with gender identity with sensitivity and compassion" but states clear opposition to medical assistance with gender transition and abortion. . . .

---

4. Gender dysphoria is defined as "a distressed state arising from conflict between a person's gender identity and the sex the person has or was identified as having at birth." Merriam-Webster Medical Dictionary (2016) https://www.merriam-webster.com/medical/genderdysphoria.

5. *See* . . . Centers for Medicare & Medicaid Services, *Proposed Decision Memo for Gender Dysphoria and Gender Reassignment Surgery* (June 2, 2016) ("Based on a thorough review of the clinical evidence available at this time, there is not enough evidence to determine whether gender reassignment surgery improves health outcomes for Medicare beneficiaries with gender dysphoria. There were conflicting (inconsistent) study results — of the best designed studies, some reported benefits while others reported harms.").

. . . .

Franciscan and CMDA's members also provide health insurance coverage for their employees in accordance with their religious beliefs. For example, both groups exclude coverage for services related to gender transition, sterilizations, and abortions. Franciscan's employee health benefit plan specifically excludes coverage for any "[t]reatment, drugs, medicines, services, and supplies related to gender transition; sterilizations; abortions." Private Plaintiffs sincerely believe that participating in, referring for, or providing insurance coverage of gender transitions, sterilizations, or abortions would constitute "impermissible material cooperation with evil."

The State Plaintiffs receive billions in federal financial assistance each year, and are subject to the Rule as providers of both health care and health insurance. State Plaintiffs prohibit insurance coverage for abortions and gender transition procedures, but to comply with the Rule, State Plaintiffs must rescind these categorical exclusions. Texas, one of the named State Plaintiffs, is already being forced to comply with an investigation by HHS's Office of Civil Rights and stands to lose more than $42.4 billion in federal healthcare funding—jeopardizing the availability of healthcare for the nation's most vulnerable citizens if it does not change its policies. State Plaintiffs claim the Rule "undermines the longstanding sovereign power of the States to regulate healthcare, ensure appropriate standards of medical judgment, and protect its citizens' constitutional and civil rights." State Plaintiffs also argue the Rule forces them to incur significant costs to post required notices of compliance, train personnel, adjust insurance coverage, and increase service offerings to include transition-related procedures. HHS estimates that states will need to contribute $17.8 million to train 7,637,306 state workers under the new Rule.

Together, Plaintiffs claim the Rule violates the Administrative Procedure Act ("APA") because its definition of prohibited sex discrimination is contrary to law and arbitrary and capricious. *See* Am. Compl., ECF No. 21. Accordingly, the Court begins with the law governing APA claims and the relevant standards in considering a preliminary injunction.

. . . .

III. Analysis

Plaintiffs argue the Rule should be enjoined because it violates: (1) the [APA]; (2) the Religious Freedom Restoration Act; (3) the First Amendment's Free Speech Clause; and (4) the Spending Clause of Article I.

. . . .

B. Preliminary Injunction
1. Likelihood of Success on the Merits

The first consideration in determining whether to grant Plaintiffs' motions for preliminary injunction is whether Plaintiffs have shown a likelihood of success on the merits for their claims . . .

a. Administrative Procedure Act

Plaintiffs claim the Rule violates the APA because it is contrary to law and exceeds statutory authority by (1) interpreting Title IX's prohibition of sex discrimination to include gender identity; (2) failing to include the religious and abortion exemptions of Title IX; (3) contradicting the commands of Title VII; and (4) attempting to commandeer the states in violation of the Tenth Amendment. In response, Defendants argue the Rule is lawful and argue the Rule's interpretation of sex discrimination is entitled to *Chevron* deference.[20]

In evaluating agency action under the APA, courts must "hold unlawful and set aside" agency actions that are "not in accordance with the law" or "in excess of statutory jurisdiction, authority, or limitations, or short of statutory right." 5 U.S.C. § 706(2). . . .

i. *Chevron* Deference

In reviewing an agency's construction of a statute it administers, courts follow the familiar two-step framework articulated in *Chevron* and ask first whether Congress has directly spoken to the precise question at issue. *Chevron, U.S.A., Inc. v. Nat. Res. Def. Council, Inc.*, 467 U.S. 837 (1984). If so, this is the end of the matter as the court and agency must give effect to Congress's unambiguously expressed intent. If not, the court must defer to the agency's construction of the statute so long as it is permissible. *Food and Drug Admin. v. Brown & Williamson Tobacco Corp.*, 529 U.S. 120, 121 (2000).

For *Chevron* deference to apply, an agency must have received congressional authority to determine the particular matter at issue in the particular manner adopted. *City of Arlington, Tex. v. F.C.C.*, 569 U.S. 290 (2013)). When a statute is silent or ambiguous with respect to a specific issue, courts assume the implementing agency has been granted an implicit delegation from Congress to fill in the statutory gaps, and proceed to ask whether the agency's construction is permissible. *Brown & Williamson*. . . .

. . . .

Because the authority to issue the Rule was given in Section 1557 of the ACA, the Court begins with the language of Section 1557. Section 1557 clearly incorporates Title IX's prohibition of sex discrimination.[23] Therefore, with no ambiguity in the statute as to what is prohibited sex discrimination, the Court next analyzes the incorporated text to determine whether HHS's interpretation of the incorporated

---

20. Defendants also argue Plaintiffs are unlikely to succeed on their First or Fifth Amendment claims, but because the Court is working on an expedited briefing schedule it does not reach Plaintiffs' constitutional arguments or Defendants' constitutional defenses.

23. "[A]n individual shall not, on the ground prohibited under . . . [T]itle IX of the Education Amendments of 1972 . . . be excluded from participation in, be denied the benefits of, or be subjected to discrimination under, any health program or activity, any part of which is receiving Federal financial assistance. . . ." 42 U.S.C. § 18116(a).

statute was in line with the text of Title IX. 42 U.S.C. § 18116(a), (c). Title IX provides that "[n]o person in the United States shall, *on the basis of sex*, be excluded from participation in, be denied the benefits of, or be subjected to discrimination under any education program or activity receiving Federal financial assistance. . . ." 20 U.S.C. § 1681(a) (emphasis added).

Plaintiffs assert that the plain language of Title IX (incorporated by Section 1557) is clear and unambiguously prohibits biological sex discrimination. They argue Congress spoke directly to the contested issue—the meaning and scope of prohibited sex discrimination. . . . Defendants assert that Section 1557's definition of sex discrimination is ambiguous because it fails to explicitly address transgender individuals and the Rule simply fills the statutory gap, implementing Section 1557.

The precise question at issue in this case is: What constitutes Title IX sex discrimination? The text of Section 1557 is neither silent nor ambiguous as to its interpretation of sex discrimination. Section 1557 clearly adopted Title IX's existing legal structure for prohibited sex discrimination. For the reasons set out more fully below, this Court has previously concluded: the meaning of sex in Title IX unambiguously refers to "the biological and anatomical differences between male and female students as determined at their birth." *Texas v. United States*, 201 F. Supp. 3d 810 (N.D. Tex. Aug. 21, 2016). In promulgating the Rule, HHS revised the core of Title IX sex discrimination under the guise of simply incorporating it.

In addition to the statutory text, the Supreme Court has emphasized a common-sense approach when determining whether Congress was likely to delegate a "policy decision of such economic and political magnitude to an administrative agency." *Brown & Williamson*. The challenged Rule undoubtedly implicates significant policy questions—namely, the scope and meaning of sex discrimination prohibited by Title IX and incorporated by Section 1557. If Congress wished to assign that decision to HHS, it surely would have done so expressly. *King v. Burwell*, 135 S. Ct. 2480 (2015).

. . . . Because Congress clearly addressed the question at issue by incorporating Title IX's existing legal structure, and HHS had no authority to interpret such a significant policy decision—the scope of sex discrimination under Title IX—*Chevron* deference does not apply and the Court need not reach step two of the analysis.

ii. Title IX Sex Discrimination

Because HHS is not entitled to *Chevron* deference, the Court now considers whether Plaintiffs have demonstrated a likelihood of success on their claim that the Rule violates the APA. Plaintiffs claim the Rule is contrary to law under the APA because its definition of prohibited sex discrimination conflicts with that incorporated by Section 1557. Congress's intent in enacting Section 1557 is clear because the statute explicitly incorporates Title IX's prohibition of sex discrimination. *See* 42 U.S.C. § 18116(a). It is also clear from Title IX's text, structure, and purpose that Congress intended to prohibit sex discrimination on the basis of the biological differences between males and females. *See* 20 U.S.C. § 1681.

The text of Title IX indicates Congress's binary definition of "sex." *See* 20 U.S.C. §1681 (referring to "students of one sex," "both sexes," "students of the other sex"). When interpreting a statute, courts look to its ordinary meaning at the time it was enacted. *See, e.g., Carcieri v. Salazar*, 555 U.S. 379 (2009) ("We begin with the ordinary meaning of the word 'now,' as understood when the [statute] was enacted.") .... When Title IX was enacted in 1972, the term "sex" was commonly understood to refer to the biological differences between males and females.[24] Even the early users of the term "gender identity" recognized the distinction between "sex" and "gender identity."[25] If Congress had intended to enact a new, different, or expansive definition of prohibited sex discrimination in Section 1557, it knew how to do so and would not have chosen to explicitly incorporate its meaning from Title IX. The structure of 20 U.S.C. §1681 *et seq.* (Title IX) supports this conclusion. For example, in §1686 Congress authorized covered institutions to provide different arrangements for each of the sexes. 20 U.S.C. §1686. These authorized distinctions based on sex can only reasonably be interpreted to be necessary for the protection of personal privacy, and confirm Congress's biological view of the term "sex." *See G.G. ex rel. Grimm v. Gloucester Cty. Sch. Bd.*, 822 F.3d 709 (4th Cir. 2016), *recalling mandate & issuing stay*, 136 S. Ct. 2442 (2016). Accordingly, the text, structure, and purpose reveal that the definition of sex in Title IX's prohibition of sex discrimination unambiguously prevented discrimination on the basis of the biological differences between males and females.

But even if, as Defendants argue, the definition of sex discrimination was determined in 2010 when the ACA incorporated Title IX's prohibition of sex discrimination, the Court is not persuaded it was passed with the Rule's expansive scope in mind because: (1) Congress knew how but did not use language indicating as much, and (2) in 2010 no federal court or agency had interpreted Title IX sex discrimination to include gender identity.[26] That Congress did not understand "sex"

---

24. *See, e.g.,* American Heritage Dictionary 1187 (1976) ("The property or quality by which organisms are classified according to their reproductive functions."); Webster's Third New International Dictionary 2081 (1971) ("The sum of the morphological, physiological, and behavioral peculiarities of living beings that subserves biparental reproduction with its concomitant genetic segregation and recombination which underlie most evolutionary change . . ."); 9 Oxford English Dictionary 578 (1961) ("The sum of those differences in the structure and function of the reproductive organs on the ground of which beings are distinguished as male and female, and of the other physiological differences consequent on these.").

25. *See, e.g.,* Robert [Stoller, mis-rendered by the court as] Stroller (UCLA psychoanalyst who coined the term "gender identity") believed "sex was biological but gender was social." David Haig, *The Inexorable Rise of Gender and the Decline of Sex: Social Change in Academic Titles*, 1945–2001, 33 Archives of Sexual Behavior 93 (Apr. 2004); Virginia Prince (Transgender activist who coined the term "transgender") stated that "I, at least, know the difference between sex and gender." Virginia Prince, *Change of Sex or Gender*, 10 Transvestia 53, 60 (1969).

26. Defendants argued at the hearing that Section 1557's definition of prohibited sex discrimination [was] determined in 2010 when the ACA was passed.

But even if the definition of sex discrimination was determined in 2010, promulgation of the proposed Rule five years later included a new and expanded definition, as evidenced by commentators' to include "gender identity" when it passed the ACA is evidenced by the employment of the phrase "gender identity" by the same Congress to include protections against crimes motivated by gender identity. *See* 18 U.S.C. § 249(a)(2)(A) (hate crimes legislation passed by Congress in 2010 protecting "gender identity" and "sexual orientation"); *see also Brown & Williamson* (subsequent analogous statutes more specifically addressing a topic in an earlier statute shape the focus of the earlier statute's meaning). In addition, the 2013 amendments to the Violence Against Women Act, legislation designed to protect women, added protections for "gender identity" and simultaneously reinforced the longstanding, binary definition of "sex" by employing both terms as separate and distinct bases of discrimination prohibited by the statute. *See* 42 U.S.C. § 13925(b)(13)(A) (specifically addressing both sex and gender identity, declaring: "No person . . . shall, on the basis of . . . race, color, religion, national origin, sex, gender identity . . . be subjected to discrimination. . . ."). These subsequent enactments confirm that Title IX and Congress's incorporation of it in the ACA unambiguously adopted the binary definition of sex. *See Brown & Williamson.*

Finally, the government's usage of the term sex in the years since Title IX's enactment bolsters the conclusion that its common meaning in 1972 and 2010 referred to the binary, biological differences between males and females. Prior to the passage of the ACA in 2010 and for more than forty years after the passage of Title IX in 1972, no federal court or agency had concluded sex should be defined to include gender identity.[28] Accordingly, HHS's expanded definition of sex discrimination exceeds the grounds incorporated by Section 1557.

iii. Title IX Unincorporated Religious Exemptions

[Here, the court accepted the plaintiffs' argument that the Rule's failure to incorporate Title IX's religious exemptions renders the Rule arbitrary, capricious, and

---

depictions of the Rule as "groundbreaking." Lena H. Sun & Lenny Bernstein, *U.S. Moves to Protect Women, Transgender People in Health Care*, Washington Post, Sept. 3, 2015 (The new Rule "for the first time includes bans on gender identity discrimination as a form of sexual discrimination, language that advocacy groups have pushed for and immediately hailed as groundbreaking.").

28. Defendants' briefing and the Rule's preamble relied on *Price Waterhouse* to show that "sex" discrimination encompasses "gender identity." *See* 81 Fed. Reg. at 31387-90; *Price Waterhouse v. Hopkins*, 490 U.S. 228 (1989) (holding that Title VII's prohibition of sex discrimination includes discrimination based on stereotypical notions of appropriate behavior, appearance, or mannerisms for males and females). But *Price Waterhouse* dealt with the definition of "sex" in the Title VII context, not the incorporated statute at issue here: Title IX. *Price Waterhouse* was decided in 1989, twenty years before the ACA was enacted. If Congress intended to prohibit the newly-expanded version of sex discrimination that Defendants claim includes "gender identity" it could have incorporated Title VII's prohibition of sex discrimination instead of Title IX. But even in *Price Waterhouse*, the Supreme Court seems to acknowledge the binary nature of sex and focuses mainly on sex stereotypes. 490 U.S. at 251 ("[i]n forbidding employers to discriminate against individuals because of their sex, Congress intended to strike at the entire spectrum of disparate treatment of men and women resulting from sex stereotypes").

contrary to law under the APA. This analysis is presented in the treatment of this case in chapter 10, *supra* at p. 548.]

b. Religious Freedom Restoration Act

[Here the court concludes that the non-state plaintiffs demonstrated a substantial likelihood of success on their claim that the challenged Rule violates RFRA. This analysis is presented in the treatment of this case in Chapter 10, *supra* at p. 548.

[The analysis of other prerequisites for a preliminary injunction, including that the plaintiffs face a threat of irreparable harm if denied an injunction and that the threatened harm to the plaintiffs outweighs any harm the injunction would have upon the defendants or the public interest, is presented in Chapter 10, *supra* at p. 548.]

C. Scope of Injunction

Finally, the Court must determine the scope of the injunction. Plaintiffs seek a nationwide injunction as to the challenged portions of the Rule—prohibiting discrimination on the basis of "gender identity" and "termination of pregnancy." Defendants argue the injunction should be limited to Plaintiffs.

"[D]istrict courts enjoy broad discretion in awarding injunctive relief." *Nat'l Min. Ass'n v. U.S. Army Corps of Eng'rs*, 145 F.3d 1399 (D.C. Cir. 1998). "[T]he Constitution vests the District Court with 'the judicial power of the United States.' That power is not limited to the district wherein the court sits but extends across the country. It is not beyond the power of a court, in appropriate circumstances, to issue a nationwide injunction." *Texas v. United States*, 809 F.3d 134 (5th Cir. 2015). "[T]he scope of injunctive relief is dictated by the extent of the violation established, not by the geographical extent of the plaintiff class." *Califano v. Yamasaki*, 442 U.S. 682 (1979). A nationwide injunction is appropriate when a party brings a facial challenge to agency action under the APA. *See, e.g., National Min. Ass'n v. U.S. Army Corps of Engineers*, 145 F.3d 1399 (D.C. Cir. 1998) (invalidating an agency rule and affirming the nationwide injunction); *Harmon v. Thornburgh*, 878 F.2d 484 (D.C. Cir. 1989) ("When a reviewing court determines that agency regulations are unlawful, the ordinary result is that the rules are vacated—not that their application to the individual petitioners is proscribed.").

CMDA's membership extends across the country and the Rule applies broadly to "almost all licensed physicians."[37] Accordingly, the Rule's harm is felt by healthcare providers and states across the country, including all of CMDA's members, and the Court finds a nationwide injunction appropriate. Because the Rule includes a severability provision, none of the unchallenged provisions are enjoined. 45 C.F.R. §92.2(c). Only the Rule's command this Court finds is contrary to law and exceeds statutory authority—the prohibition of discrimination on the basis of "gender identity" and "termination of pregnancy"—is hereby enjoined.

---

37. CMDA has members "in all [the] states." Hr'g Tr. 93:5.

IV. Conclusion

For the foregoing reasons, the Court finds that Plaintiffs' motions for preliminary injunction should be and are hereby GRANTED. *See* FED. R. CIV. P. 65. Defendants are hereby ENJOINED from enforcing the Rule's prohibition against discrimination on the basis of gender identity or termination of pregnancy.

So ORDERED on this 31st day of December, 2016.

———————

Discussion

1. In footnote 28, the court tries to diminish the significance of *Price Waterhouse v. Hopkins*, whose 1989 reasoning has been read by many courts and commentators to entail that discrimination on the basis of sex forbidden by Title VII of the Civil Rights Act of 1964 includes discrimination on the basis of gender identity. The court here apparently suggests that if Congress wanted to incorporate that understanding in Section 1557 of the Affordable Care Act, it would, could, and should have referred expressly to Title VII rather than Title IX. This is a somewhat curious dodge, for the same judge in an earlier case ruled that the Department of Justice–Department of Education guidance interpreting Title IX to reach gender identity discrimination was an incorrect interpretation of Title IX; in its opinion there, the court stated that it was using Title VII "to help explain the legislative intent and purpose of Title IX because the two statutes are commonly linked." *Texas v. United States*, 201 F. Supp. 3d 810, 819 n.7 (N.D. Tex. 2016).

2. Even if "sex" only means what the plaintiffs here term "biological sex," "discrimination" "on the ground" of sex still conceptually reaches anti-transgender discrimination. *See, e.g.*, Brief of Statutory Interpretation and Equality Law Scholars as Amici Curiae in Support of the Employees, *Bostock v. Clayton County, Georgia*, Nos. 17-1618, 17-1623, 18-107, 2019 WL 2915037, at 3 (U.S. July 3, 2019) (arguing that "Title VII does not prohibit discrimination based on sexual orientation and gender identity because 'sex' *means* 'sexual orientation' or 'gender identity.' Rather, it does so because discrimination based on an employee's sexual orientation or gender identity is also necessarily 'because of such individual's . . . sex.'"). Now that the Supreme Court embraced precisely this conclusion in *Bostock v. Clayton County, Georgia*, 140 S. Ct. 1731 (2020), Chapter 5, Section D, *supra*, this leaves the reasoning in *Franciscan Alliance* on shaky ground at best.

3. In a case not involving health insurance but actual provision of medical care, *Prescott v. Rady Children's Hospital-San Diego*, 265 F. Supp. 3d 1090 (S.D. Cal. 2017), a district court concluded that the *Franciscan Alliance* decision above did not affect the plaintiff's lawsuit because the *Prescott* court was relying only on the text of Section 1557 of the ACA, not the regulation at issue in *Franciscan Alliance*, to rule that the ACA forbade anti-transgender discrimination. For an argument that this is the correct interpretation of Section 1557 and criticism of *Franciscan Alliance*, see, for

example, Derek Waller, *Recognizing Transgender, Intersex, and Nonbinary People in Healthcare Antidiscrimination Law*, 103 Minn. L. Rev. 467 (2018).

4. The government never appealed the nationwide preliminary injunction granted in this case. Instead, they sought first delays and then a remand to the Department of Health and Human Services to let the agency reconsider the Obama-era regulation implementing Section 1557. Rather than remand, the district court stayed the case to allow such reconsideration. *Franciscan Alliance, Inc. v. Price*, No. 7:16-CV-00108-O, 2017 U.S. Dist. LEXIS 145416 (N.D. Tex. July 10, 2017).

Seemingly tired of waiting, the plaintiffs filed briefs in support of renewed motions for summary judgment on February 4, 2019. Two months later the Department of Justice filed its response, stating the Trump administration's position that "the term 'sex' in Title VII does not refer to gender identity, and there is no reason why Section 1557 . . . should be treated differently." The defendants requested that the court defer ruling on the plaintiffs' summary judgment motions in light of the administration's "ongoing efforts to amend the Rule"; they represented they expected to "publish a proposed rule soon, which, if finalized, may moot this case."

HHS posted its proposed rule online on May 24, 2019, which, as expected, adopted the position that the term "sex" in Section 1557 does not include gender identity. *See* Dep't of Health & Human Services, HHS Proposes to Revise Section 1557 Rule to Enforce Civil Rights in Healthcare, Conform to Law, and Eliminate Billions in Unnecessary Costs (May 24, 2019), https://www.hhs .gov/about/news/2019/05/24/hhs-proposes-to-revise-aca-section-1557-rule.html; *see also Nondiscrimination in Health and Health Education Programs or Activities*, 84 Fed. Reg. 115 (proposed May 23, 2019) (to be codified at 42 C.F.R. pts. 438, 440, and 460 & 45 C.F.R. pts. 86, 92, 147, 155, and 156).

Just over two months after the period for public comments on the proposed rule closed on August 13, with no final rule having been issued, Judge O'Connor vacated and remanded the "unlawful portions" of the regulation implementing Section 1557 of the Affordable Care Act for the defendants' "further consideration in light of this opinion." *Franciscan Alliance v. Azar*, 414 F. Supp. 3d 928 (N.D. Tex. 2019). Specifically, the court held, consistent with its preliminary injunction ruling above, that the regulation's prohibitions on discrimination on the basis of gender identity and termination of pregnancy are unlawful under the Administrative Procedure Act and the Religious Freedom Restoration Act. O'Connor stayed the plaintiffs' claims regarding whether the regulation violated Title VII (perhaps in light of the Title VII cases argued before the Supreme Court the week before this ruling), the Spending Clause of the Constitution, and the First, Tenth, and Eleventh Amendments.

5. Even if Section 1557 were interpreted to prohibit discrimination on the basis of gender identity, it may well not suffice to assure transgender people health care, as lack of insurance is one major barrier facing trans people. For a discussion of some of the promise and limits of Section 1557, see, for example, Rachel C. Kurzweil, *"Justice*

Is What Love Looks Like in Public": How the Affordable Care Act Falls Short on Transgender Health Care Access, 21 Wash. & Lee J. Civil Rts. & Soc. Just. 199 (2014).

Note on Medical Cost Tax Deductions as Quasi-Insurance

The U.S. tax code provides for the taxation of people's income at specified rates. It also contains deductions, which are certain sorts of expenditures by which people may reduce their income before calculating the tax that they owe. At least some of these deductions can be conceived of as forms of insurance. For decades, for example, taxpayers could use a casualty loss deduction to reduce their taxable income (subject to some limitations) by the (uninsured) amount of certain fairly sudden damage to property, for example, things resulting from earthquakes, fires, floods, or hurricanes. (This changed in 2018 when Congress enacted and Donald Trump signed the Tax Cuts and Jobs Act of 2017, Pub L. 115-97, 131 Stat. 2054, which dramatically curtailed the availability of such deductions for individuals, as opposed to businesses, from 2018 through 2025.) Instead of paying for insurance to cover the cost of such losses, persons for free could use the deduction to reduce their taxable income, and thus the amount of tax they had to spend, thereby receiving partial coverage of their losses.

Another such deduction is the one for (uninsured) medical expenses. And indeed, according to noted law and economics scholar Louis Kaplow, "the most convincing rationales offered for the casualty loss and medical expense deductions implicitly appeal to notions relating to insurance." Louis Kaplow, *The Income Tax as Insurance: The Casualty Loss and Medical Expense Deductions and the Exclusion of Medical Insurance Premiums*, 79 Calif. L. Rev. 1485, 1487 (1991). Thus, Professor Kaplow refers to "the free partial insurance provided through the tax rules." *Id.*

Because the medical expense deduction acts as a form of insurance to help some individuals to defray the costs of maintaining their health, and because health insurance plans have so broadly excluded transition-related care from their coverage, *see, e.g.*, David B. Cruz, O'Donnabhain v. Commissioner of Internal Revenue, *in* Feminist Judgments: Rewritten Tax Opinions 274, 283–84 (Bridget J. Crawford & Anthony C. Infanti, eds. 2017),[a] the following case about the tax deductibility of expenses for transition-related care is included in this section on private health insurance.

Reading Guide for O'Donnabhain v. Commissioner of Internal Revenue

1. As Tax Court Judge Holmes stated in his concurring opinion in this case, "the medical-expense provisions in the Code [can be viewed] as creating a series of rules and exceptions. Section 262(a) creates a general rule that personal expenses are not deductible. Section 213(a) and (d)(1) then creates an exception to the general rule

---

a. Prof. Cruz thanks Prof. Anthony Infanti for raising the quasi-insurance point in commenting on a draft of the rewritten *O'Donnabhain* opinion.

for the expenses of medical care if they exceed a particular percentage of adjusted gross income. Section 213(d)(9) then creates an exception to the exception for cosmetic surgery. And Section 213(d)(9)(A) then creates a third-order exception restoring deductibility for certain types of cosmetic surgery." 134 T.C. 34, 90 (2010). In more detail, as one of this casebook's authors reads the statute,

> Rhiannon O'Donnabhain's medical expenses are deductible if (1) either (A) they are "for the diagnosis, cure, mitigation, treatment, or prevention of disease" or (B) they are "for the purpose of affecting any structure or function of the body"; and (2) (A) either they are not "directed at improving the patient's appearance" or they do "meaningfully promote the proper function of the body or prevent or treat illness or disease" or (B) they are "necessary to ameliorate a deformity arising from, or directly related to, a congenital abnormality, a personal injury resulting from an accident or trauma, or disfiguring disease." Condition (1) brings a procedure within the general definition of "medical care." One of its subconditions must be satisfied for deductibility. In addition, either a procedure must not be cosmetic surgery, or if it is, it must satisfy one of the saving conditions in §213(d)(9)(A). Condition (2) (A) is the negation of the definition "cosmetic surgery," and condition (2) (B) restates the saving conditions.

Cruz, O'Donnabhain v. Commissioner of Internal Revenue, *supra*, at 276.

2. What reasons does Judge Gale's majority opinion give for concluding that gender identity disorder ("GID") is a "disease" within the meaning of the relevant tax code provisions? For what reasons does the majority opinion reject the narrow definition of disease espoused by the Commissioner's expert Dr. Dietz regarding Section 213 of the code? For what reasons does the majority opinion reject the Commissioner's argument that Ms. O'Donnabhain was not properly diagnosed as having GID?

3. For what reasons does the majority conclude that hormone therapy and genitoplasty "treat" GID within the meaning of the tax code? For what reasons does it conclude that O'Donnabhain's breast augmentation surgery was not deductible medical care?

4. Although not resolving the question whether the tax code limits medical care deductions to care that is "medically necessary," the majority opinion concludes that O'Donnabhain's hormone therapy and genitoplasty were medically necessary. For what reasons does it so conclude?

5. Why does Judge Halpern argue, contrary to largely dissenting Judge Gustafson, that O'Donnabhain's transition procedures "treated" her GID even though they did not and were not designed to change her belief that she was female (*i.e.*, her gender identity)?

6. For what reasons does Judge Holmes object to the majority's discussion of medical necessity and its reliance on the Benjamin standards for transition care? For what reasons does Holmes distinguish O'Donnabhain's hormones and genitoplasty from her breast augmentation?

7. Why does Judge Gustafson's largely dissenting opinion reject (in footnote 4) the argument that the genitoplasty was "functional" and thus not cosmetic surgery? For what reasons does the dissent reject the conclusion that the medical care expenses Ms. O'Donnabhain sought to deduct "treated" her GID?

Rhiannon G. O'Donnabhain v. Commissioner of Internal Revenue

134 T.C. 34 (2010)

[Rhiannon O'Donnabhain was represented by counsel including then-LGBT movement attorneys Karen L. Loewy, Bennett H. Klein, and Jennifer L. Levi.]

GALE, Judge.[2]

. . . .

Findings of Fact

. . . .

I. Petitioner's Background

Rhiannon G. O'Donnabhain (petitioner) was born a genetic male with unambiguous male genitalia. However, she[3] was uncomfortable in the male gender role from childhood and first wore women's clothing secretly around age 10. Her discomfort regarding her gender intensified in adolescence, and she continued to dress in women's clothing secretly.

As an adult, petitioner earned a degree in civil engineering, served on active duty with the U.S. Coast Guard, found employment at an engineering firm, married, and fathered three children. However, her discomfort with her gender persisted. She felt that she was a female trapped in a male body, and she continued to secretly wear women's clothing.

Petitioner's marriage ended after more than 20 years. After separating from her spouse in 1992, petitioner's feelings that she wanted to be female intensified and grew more persistent.

II. Petitioner's Psychotherapy and Diagnosis

By mid-1996 petitioner's discomfort with her male gender role and desire to be female intensified to the point that she sought out a psychotherapist to address them. After investigating referrals, petitioner contacted Diane Ellaborn, a licensed independent clinical social worker (LICSW) and psychotherapist, and commenced psychotherapy sessions in August 1996.

. . . .

---

2. Unless otherwise indicated, all section references are to the Internal Revenue Code of 1986, as amended and in effect in the year in issue, and all Rule references are to the Tax Court Rules of Practice and Procedure. [Relocated footnote. — Eds.]

3. Reflecting petitioner's preference, we use the feminine pronoun to refer to her throughout this Opinion.

In early 1997, after approximately 20 weekly individual therapy sessions, Ms. Ellaborn's diagnosis was that petitioner was a transsexual suffering from severe gender identity disorder (GID), a condition listed in the *Diagnostic and Statistical Manual of Mental Disorders* (4th ed. 2000 text revision) (DSM-IV-TR), published by the American Psychiatric Association. The DSM-IV-TR states that a diagnosis of GID is indicated where an individual exhibits (1) a strong and persistent desire to be, or belief that he or she is, the other sex; (2) persistent discomfort with his or her anatomical sex, including a preoccupation with getting rid of primary or secondary sex characteristics; (3) an absence of any physical intersex (hermaphroditic) condition; and (4) clinically significant distress or impairment in social, occupational, or other important areas of functioning as a result of the discomfort arising from the perceived incongruence between anatomical sex and perceived gender identity. Under the classification system of the DSM-IV-TR, a severity modifier — mild, moderate, or severe — may be added to any diagnosis. The term "Transsexualism" is currently used in the DSM-IV-TR to describe GID symptoms that are severe or profound.

Both the DSM-IV-TR and its predecessor the DSM-IV contain the following "Cautionary Statement":

> The purpose of DSM-IV is to provide clear descriptions of diagnostic categories in order to enable clinicians and investigators to diagnose, communicate about, study, and treat people with various mental disorders. It is to be understood that inclusion here, for clinical and research purposes, of a diagnostic category * * * does not imply that the condition meets legal or other non-medical criteria for what constitutes mental disease, mental disorder, or mental disability. * * *

III. Treatment of GID

The World Professional Association for Transgender Health (WPATH), formerly known as the Harry Benjamin International Gender Dysphoria Association, Inc., is an association of medical, surgical, and mental health professionals specializing in the understanding and treatment of GID.[8] WPATH publishes "Standards of Care" for the treatment of GID (hereinafter Benjamin standards of care or Benjamin standards). . . .

Summarized, the Benjamin standards of care prescribe a "triadic" treatment sequence for individuals diagnosed with GID consisting of (1) hormonal sex reassignment; *i.e.*, the administration of cross-gender hormones to effect changes in physical appearance to more closely resemble the opposite sex; (2) the "real-life" experience (wherein the individual undertakes a trial period of living full time in

---

8. Harry Benjamin, M.D. (1885–1986), was an endocrinologist who in conjunction with mental health professionals in New York did pioneering work in the study of transsexualism. The parties have stipulated that the term "gender dysphoria" was coined by Dr. Norman Fisk (Dr. Fisk) in 1973 to describe patients presenting with dissatisfaction and unhappiness with their anatomic and genetic sex and their assigned gender. The parties have further stipulated that, according to a 1974 article by Dr. Fisk, transsexualism represents the most extreme form of gender dysphoria.

society as a member of the opposite sex); and (3) sex reassignment surgery, consisting of genital sex reassignment and/or nongenital sex reassignment. . . .

Under the Benjamin standards, an individual must have the recommendation of a licensed psychotherapist to obtain hormonal or surgical sex reassignment. Hormonal sex reassignment requires the recommendation of one psychotherapist and surgical sex reassignment requires the recommendations of two. The recommending psychotherapist should have diagnostic evidence for transsexualism for a period of at least 2 years, independent of the patient's claims.

The Benjamin standards state that hormonal sex reassignment should precede surgical sex reassignment because the patient's degree of satisfaction with hormone therapy "may indicate or contraindicate later surgical sex reassignment." The Benjamin standards further state that "Genital sex reassignment shall be preceded by a period of at least 12 months during which time the patient lives full-time in the social role of the genetically other sex." The standards provide that breast augmentation surgery may be performed as part of sex reassignment surgery for a male-to-female patient "if the physician prescribing hormones and the surgeon have documented that breast enlargement after undergoing hormone treatment for 18 months is not sufficient for comfort in the social gender role."

IV. Ms. Ellaborn's Treatment Plan for Petitioner

. . . .

A. Petitioner's Hormone Treatments

[Petitioner] commenced taking hormones in September 1997. She remained on feminizing hormones continuously through the taxable year in issue (2001).

After beginning hormone therapy petitioner told Ms. Ellaborn that she felt calmer and better emotionally and that she felt positive about her physical changes. Ms. Ellaborn viewed petitioner's positive reactions to hormone therapy as validation of the GID diagnosis.

. . . .

B. Petitioner's "Real-Life" Experience

In consultation with Ms. Ellaborn, petitioner decided to undertake the Benjamin standards' "real-life" experience; *i.e.*, to present in public as female on a full-time basis in March 2000. Petitioner legally changed her name from Robert Donovan to Rhiannon G. O'Donnabhain and arranged to have the gender designation on her driver's license changed, on the basis of her GID diagnosis. She underwent surgery to feminize her facial features,[16] and with the cooperation of her employer commenced

---

16. Ms. Ellaborn had observed that, notwithstanding 18 months of hormone therapy, petitioner had distinctly male facial features which interfered with her "passing" as female. Ms. Ellaborn referred petitioner to a plastic surgeon who in March 2000 performed procedures designed to feminize petitioner's facial features, including a rhinoplasty (nose reshaping), a facelift, and a tracheal shave (reducing cartilage of the "Adam's apple"). Petitioner was dissatisfied with the initial results,

presenting as a female at work around April of that year. Petitioner informed Ms. Ellaborn that her transition at work went smoothly and that the "real-life" experience had been "incredibly easy." Ms. Ellaborn viewed petitioner's positive response to her "real-life" experience as further validation of the GID diagnosis.

C. Petitioner's Sex Reassignment Surgery

Petitioner's anxiety as a result of having male genitalia persisted,[17] however, and Ms. Ellaborn concluded that her prognosis without genital surgical sex reassignment (sex reassignment surgery) was poor, in that petitioner's anxiety over the lack of congruence between her perceived gender and her anatomical sex would continue in the absence of surgery and would impair her ability to function normally in society. In November 2000 Ms. Ellaborn wrote a referral letter to Dr. Toby Meltzer (Dr. Meltzer), a board-certified plastic and reconstructive surgeon, with over 10 years' experience specializing in sex reassignment surgery, to secure a place for petitioner on his waiting list.

After three additional therapy sessions with petitioner in mid-2001, Ms. Ellaborn concluded that petitioner had satisfied or exceeded all of the Benjamin standards' criteria for sex reassignment surgery, including time spent satisfactorily on feminizing hormones and in the "real-life" experience. In July 2001 Ms. Ellaborn wrote a second letter to Dr. Meltzer certifying petitioner's GID diagnosis and satisfaction of the Benjamin standards' criteria for sex reassignment surgery, and formally recommending petitioner for the surgery. Another licensed psychotherapist with a doctoral degree in clinical psychology, Dr. Alex Coleman (Dr. Coleman), examined petitioner and provided a second recommendation for her sex reassignment surgery, as required by the Benjamin standards. Dr. Coleman's letter to Dr. Meltzer observed that petitioner "appears to have significant breast development secondary to hormone therapy."

Petitioner . . . went for a consultation and examination by Dr. Meltzer in June 2001 at his offices in Portland, Oregon. Dr. Meltzer concluded that petitioner was a good candidate for sex reassignment surgery. Dr. Meltzer's notes of his physical examination of petitioner state: "Examination of her breasts reveal [*sic*] approximately B cup breasts with a very nice shape."

In mid-October 2001 petitioner returned to Portland, and she underwent sex reassignment surgery. . . .

Dr. Meltzer also performed breast augmentation surgery designed to make petitioner's breasts, which had experienced some development as a result of feminizing hormones, more closely resemble the breasts of a genetic female.

---

and in December 2000 the surgeon performed further surgery to revise the effects of the earlier procedures. The surgeon also gave petitioner a Botox treatment at that time. The deductibility of the foregoing procedures is not at issue.

17. In one instance, petitioner held a knife and had an urge to cut off her penis.

In May 2002 Dr. Meltzer performed followup surgery on petitioner to refine the appearance of her genitals and remove scar tissue. In February 2005 Dr. Meltzer performed further surgery on petitioner's face, designed to feminize her facial features.

V. Petitioner's Claim for a Medical Expense Deduction

During 2001 petitioner incurred and paid the following expenses (totaling $21,741) in connection with her hormone therapy, sex reassignment surgery, and breast augmentation surgery: (1) $19,195 to Dr. Meltzer for surgical procedures, including $14,495 for vaginoplasty and other procedures, $4,500 for breast augmentation, and $200 towards a portion of petitioner's postsurgical stay at Dr. Meltzer's facility; (2) $60 for medical equipment; (3) $1,544 in travel and lodging costs away from home for presurgical consultation and surgery; (4) $300 to Ms. Ellaborn for therapy; (5) $260 for the consultation for a second referral letter for surgery; and (6) $382 for hormone therapy. These payments were not compensated for by insurance or otherwise.

On her Federal income tax return for 2001, petitioner claimed an itemized deduction for the foregoing expenditures as medical expenses, which respondent subsequently disallowed in a notice of deficiency.

. . . .

Opinion
I. Medical Expense Deductions Under Section 213
A. In General

Section 213(a) allows a deduction for expenses paid during the taxable year for medical care that are not compensated for by insurance or otherwise and to the extent that such expenses exceed 7.5 percent of adjusted gross income. In addition, section 213(d)(1)(B) and (2) provides that certain amounts paid for transportation and lodging, respectively, may qualify as amounts paid for medical care under section 213(a) if a taxpayer's travel away from home is primarily for and essential to receiving medical care.[25]

B. Definition of Medical Care

Congress first provided an income tax deduction for medical expenses in 1942. The original provision was codified as section 23(x) of the 1939 Internal Revenue Code and read as follows:

SEC. 23. DEDUCTIONS FROM GROSS INCOME.

In computing net income there shall be allowed as deductions:

* * * * * * *

---

25. The parties have stipulated that if any part of petitioner's sex reassignment surgery is determined by the Court to be deductible under sec. 213, then petitioner's travel and lodging costs incurred in connection with her consultation and surgery by Dr. Meltzer are also deductible.

(x) Medical, Dental, Etc., Expenses.—Except as limited under paragraph (1) or (2), expenses paid during the taxable year * * * for medical care of the taxpayer * * *. The term "medical care," as used in this subsection, shall include amounts paid for the diagnosis, cure, mitigation, treatment, or prevention of disease, or for the purpose of affecting any structure or function of the body * * *.

. . . .

The core definition of "medical care" originally set forth in section 23(x) of the 1939 Code has endured over time and is currently found in section 213(d)(1)(A), which provides as follows:

SEC. 213 (d). Definitions.—For purposes of this section—

(1) The term "medical care" means amounts paid—

(A) for the diagnosis, cure, mitigation, treatment, or prevention of disease, or for the purpose of affecting any structure or function of the body * * *

Thus, since the inception of the medical expense deduction, the definition of deductible "medical care" has had two prongs. The first prong covers amounts paid for the "diagnosis, cure, mitigation, treatment, or prevention of disease" and the second prong covers amounts paid "for the purpose of affecting any structure or function of the body."

The regulations interpreting the statutory definition of medical care. . . . state in relevant part:

(e) Definitions—(1) General. (i) The term "medical care" includes the diagnosis, cure, mitigation, treatment, or prevention of disease. Expenses paid for "medical care" shall include those paid for the purpose of affecting any structure or function of the body or for transportation primarily for and essential to medical care. * * *

(ii) * * * Deductions for expenditures for medical care allowable under section 213 will be confined strictly to expenses incurred primarily for the prevention or alleviation of *a physical or mental defect or illness.* * * * [Sec. 1.213-1(e)(1), Income Tax Regs.; emphasis added.]

Notably, the regulations . . . treat "disease" as used in the statute as synonymous with "a physical or mental defect or illness." The language equating "mental defect" with "disease" was in the first version of the regulations promulgated in 1943 and has stood unchanged since. In addition, to qualify as "medical care" under the regulations, an expense must be incurred "primarily" for alleviation of a physical or mental defect, and the defect must be specific. "[A]n expenditure which is merely beneficial to the general health of an individual, such as an expenditure for a vacation, is not an expenditure for medical care." Sec. 1.213-1(e)(1)(ii), Income Tax Regs.

Given the reference to "mental defect" in the legislative history and the regulations, it has also long been settled that "disease" as used in section 213 can extend to mental disorders. *See, e.g., Fischer v. Commissioner*, 50 T.C. 164, 173 n.4 (1968).

[A] taxpayer seeking a deduction under section 213 must show: (1) "the present existence or imminent probability of a disease, defect or illness—mental or physical" and (2) a payment "for goods or services directly or proximately related to the diagnosis, cure, mitigation, treatment, or prevention of the disease or illness." *Jacobs v. Commissioner*, 62 T.C. 813 (1974). Moreover, where the expenditures are arguably not "wholly medical in nature" and may serve a personal as well as medical purpose, they must also pass a "but for" test: the taxpayer must "prove both that the expenditures were an essential element of the treatment and that they would not have otherwise been incurred for nonmedical reasons." *Id.*

C. Definition of Cosmetic Surgery

. . . . The Internal Revenue Service, relying on the second prong [of the statutory definition of "medical care," concerning amounts paid "for the purpose of affecting any structure or function of the body"], had determined in two revenue rulings that deductions were allowed for amounts expended for cosmetic procedures (such as facelifts, hair transplants, and hair removal through electrolysis) because the procedures were found to affect a structure or function of the body within the meaning of section 213(d)(1)(A).

In 1990 Congress responded to these rulings by amending section 213 to include new subsection (d)(9) which, generally speaking, excludes cosmetic surgery from the definition of deductible medical care. . . . Congress deemed the amendment necessary to clarify that deductions for medical care do not include amounts paid for "an elective, purely cosmetic treatment."[27]

Section 213(d)(9) defines "cosmetic surgery" as follows:

SEC. 213(d). Definitions.—For purposes of this section—

---

27. . . . . The report of the Senate Finance Committee . . . contrasted "cosmetic" procedures with "medically necessary procedures" as follows:

For purposes of the medical expense deduction, the IRS generally does not distinguish between procedures which are medically necessary and those which are purely cosmetic.
* * * * * * *

* * * Expenses for purely cosmetic procedures that are not medically necessary are, in essence, voluntary personal expenses, which like other personal expenditures (*e.g.*, food and clothing) generally should not be deductible in computing taxable income.
* * * * * * *

* * * [U]nder the provision, procedures such as hair removal electrolysis, hair transplants, lyposuction [*sic*], and facelift operations generally are not deductible. In contrast, expenses for procedures that are medically necessary to promote the proper function of the body and only incidentally affect the patient's appearance or expenses for the treatment of a disfiguring condition arising from a congenital abnormality, personal injury or trauma, or disease (such as reconstructive surgery following removal of a malignancy) continue to be deductible * * *.

(9) Cosmetic surgery. —

(A) In general. — The term "medical care" does not include cosmetic surgery or other similar procedures, unless the surgery or procedure is necessary to ameliorate a deformity arising from, or directly related to, a congenital abnormality, a personal injury resulting from an accident or trauma, or disfiguring disease.

(B) Cosmetic surgery defined. — For purposes of this paragraph, the term "cosmetic surgery" means any procedure which is directed at improving the patient's appearance and does not meaningfully promote the proper function of the body or prevent or treat illness or disease.

. . . .

III. Analysis

. . . .

A. Statutory Definitions

. . . . Both the statutory definition of "medical care" and the statute's exclusion of "cosmetic surgery" from that definition depend in part upon whether an expenditure or procedure is for "treatment" of "disease." Under section 213(d)(1)(A), if an expenditure is "for the * * * treatment * * * of disease," it is deductible "medical care"; under section 213(d)(9)(B), if a procedure "[treats] * * * disease," it is not "cosmetic surgery" that is excluded from the definition of "medical care."

. . . .

B. Is GID a "Disease"?

Petitioner argues that she is entitled to deduct her expenditures for the procedures at issue because they were treatments for GID, a condition that she contends is a "disease" for purposes of section 213. Respondent maintains that petitioner's expenditures did not treat "disease" because GID is not a "disease" within the meaning of section 213. Central to his argument is respondent's contention that "disease" as used in section 213 has the meaning postulated by respondent's expert, Dr. [Park] Dietz; namely, "a condition * * * [arising] as a result of a pathological process * * * [occurring] within the individual and [reflecting] abnormal structure or function of the body at the gross, microscopic, molecular, biochemical, or neurochemical levels."

[Respondent] . . . urges . . . that a "disease" for this purpose must have a demonstrated organic or physiological origin in the individual. . . .[33]

. . . . The meaning of "disease" as used in section 213 must be resolved by the Court, using settled principles of statutory construction, including reference to

---

33. The experts all agree and the Court accepts, for purposes of deciding this case, that no organic or biological cause of GID has been demonstrated.

the Commissioner's interpretive regulations, the legislative history, and caselaw precedent.

. . . . Numerous cases have treated mental disorders as "diseases" for purposes of section 213 without regard to any demonstrated organic or physiological origin or cause. These cases found mental conditions to be "diseases" where there was evidence that mental health professionals regarded the condition as creating a significant impairment to normal functioning and warranting treatment. . . . . We have also considered a condition's listing in a diagnostic reference text as grounds for treating the condition as a "disease," without inquiry into the condition's etiology.

[We] reject respondent's interpretation of "disease" because it is incompatible with the stated intent of the regulations and legislative history to cover "mental defects" generally and is contradicted by a consistent line of cases finding "disease" in the case of mental disorders without regard to any demonstrated etiology.

. . . . [Respondent] . . . argues that GID is "not a significant psychiatric disorder" but instead is a "social construction"—a "social phenomenon" that has been "medicalized." . . . .

[We] conclude that GID is a "disease" within the meaning of section 213. [Two] caselaw factors influenc[e] a finding of "disease" in the context of mental conditions: (1) A determination by a mental health professional that the condition created a significant impairment to normal functioning, warranting treatment, *see Fay v. Commissioner*, 76 T.C. 408 (1981), or (2) a listing of the condition in a medical reference text, *see Starrett v. Commissioner*, 41 T.C. 877 (1964). Both factors involve deference by a court to the judgment of medical professionals.

. . . GID is listed as a mental disorder in the DSM-IV-TR, which all three experts agree is the primary diagnostic tool of American psychiatry. GID or transsexualism is also listed in numerous medical reference texts, with descriptions of their characteristics that are similar to those in the DSM-IV-TR.

Even if one accepts respondent's expert Dr. [Chester W. Schmidt, Jr.'s] assertion that the validity of the GID diagnosis is subject to some debate in the psychiatric profession, the widespread recognition of the condition in medical literature persuades the Court that acceptance of the GID diagnosis is the prevailing view. . . .

Second, GID is a serious, psychologically debilitating condition. Respondent's characterization of the condition on brief as a "social construction" and "not a significant psychiatric disorder" is undermined by both of his own expert witnesses and the medical literature in evidence. All three expert witnesses agreed that, absent treatment, GID in genetic males is sometimes associated with autocastration, autopenectomy, and suicide. Respondent's expert Dr. Schmidt asserts that remaining ambiguous about gender identity "will tear you apart psychologically." Petitioner's expert Dr. [George R.] Brown likewise testified that GID produces significant distress and maladaption.

. . . .

Third, respondent's position that GID is not a significant psychiatric disorder is at odds with the position of every U.S. Court of Appeals that has ruled on the question of whether GID poses a serious medical need for purposes of the Eighth Amendment, which has been interpreted to require that prisoners receive adequate medical care. . . . No U.S. Court of Appeals has held otherwise.

In view of (1) GID's widely recognized status in diagnostic and psychiatric reference texts as a legitimate diagnosis, (2) the seriousness of the condition as described in learned treatises in evidence and as acknowledged by all three experts in this case; (3) the severity of petitioner's impairment as found by the mental health professionals who examined her; (4) the consensus in the U.S. Courts of Appeal that GID constitutes a serious medical need for purposes of the Eighth Amendment, we conclude and hold that GID is a "disease" for purposes of section 213.

C. Did Petitioner Have GID?

Respondent also contends that petitioner was not correctly diagnosed with GID, citing his expert Dr. Schmidt's contentions that certain comorbid conditions such as depression or transvestic fetishism had not been adequately ruled out as explanations of petitioner's condition.

We find that petitioner's GID diagnosis is substantially supported by the record. Ms. Ellaborn was licensed under State law to make such a diagnosis. A second licensed professional concurred, as did petitioner's expert, a recognized authority in the field. Ms. Ellaborn's testimony concerning her diagnosis was persuasive. She considered and ruled out comorbid conditions, including depression and transvestic fetishism, and she believed her initial diagnosis was confirmed by petitioner's experience with the steps in the triadic therapy sequence.

Absent evidence of a patent lack of qualifications, *see, e. g., Flemming v. Commissioner*, T.C. Memo. 1980-583 (rejecting diagnosis of cancer and kidney disease by dentist), this Court has generally deferred, in section 213 disputes, to the judgment of the medical professionals who treated the patient. All three witnesses who supported petitioner's GID diagnosis interviewed petitioner. Since Dr. Schmidt did not, his analysis is entitled to considerably less weight, and we conclude that there is no persuasive basis to doubt the diagnosis.

D. Whether Cross-Gender Hormones, Sex Reassignment Surgery and Breast Augmentation Surgery "Treat" GID

1. Cross-Gender Hormones and Sex Reassignment Surgery

Our conclusions that GID is a "disease" for purposes of section 213, and that petitioner suffered from it, leave the question of whether petitioner's hormone therapy, sex reassignment surgery, and breast augmentation surgery "[treated]" GID within the meaning of section 213(d)(1)(A) and (9)(B).

In contrast to their dispute over the meaning of "disease," the parties have not disputed the meaning of "treatment" or "treat" as used in section 213(d)(1)(A) and

(9)(B), respectively. We accordingly interpret the words in their ordinary, everyday sense. *See Crane v. Commissioner*, 331 U.S. 1 (1947).

"Treat" is defined in standard dictionaries as: "to deal with (a disease, patient, etc.) in order to relieve or cure," Webster's New Universal Unabridged Dictionary 2015 (2003); "to care for or deal with medically or surgically," Merriam Webster's Collegiate Dictionary 1333 (11th ed. 2008); . . . .

The regulations provide that medical care is confined to expenses "incurred primarily for the prevention or *alleviation* of a physical or mental defect or illness." Sec. 1.213-1(e)(1)(ii), Income Tax Regs. (emphasis added). A treatment should bear a "direct or proximate therapeutic relation to the * * * condition" sufficient "to justify a reasonable belief the * * * [treatment] would be efficacious." *Havey v. Commissioner*, 12 T.C. 409, 412 (1949). In *Starrett v. Commissioner, supra*, this Court concluded that the taxpayer's psychoanalysis was a treatment of disease because the taxpayer was "thereby relieved of the physical and emotional suffering attendant upon" the condition known as anxiety reaction.

Hormone therapy, sex reassignment surgery and, under certain conditions, breast augmentation surgery are prescribed therapeutic interventions, or treatments, for GID outlined in the Benjamin standards of care. . . . Several courts have accepted the Benjamin standards as representing the consensus of the medical profession regarding the appropriate treatment for GID or transsexualism.

. . . . [Even] assuming some debate remains in the medical profession regarding acceptance of the Benjamin standards or the scientific proof of the therapeutic efficacy of sex reassignment surgery, a complete consensus on the advisability or efficacy of a procedure is not necessary for a deduction under section 213. *See, e.g., Dickie v. Commissioner*, T.C. Memo. 1999-138 (naturopathic cancer treatments deductible); *Crain v. Commissioner*, T.C. Memo. 1986-138 (holistic cancer treatments deductible but for failure of substantiation); *Tso v. Commissioner*, T.C. Memo. 1980-399 (Navajo "sings" (healing ceremonies) deductible); Rev. Rul. 72-593, 1972-2 C.B. 180 (acupuncture deductible); Rev. Rul. 55-261, 1955-1 C.B. 307 (services of Christian Science practitioners deductible). It is sufficient if the circumstances "justify a reasonable belief the * * * [treatment] would be efficacious." *Havey v. Commissioner*. That standard has been fully satisfied here. The evidence is clear that a substantial segment of the psychiatric profession has been persuaded of the advisability and efficacy of hormone therapy and sex reassignment surgery as treatment for GID, as have many courts.

Finally, the Court does not doubt that . . . some medical professionals shun transsexual patients and consider cross-gender hormone therapy and sex reassignment surgery unethical because they disrupt what is considered to be a "normally functioning hormonal status or destroy healthy, normal tissue." However, the Internal Revenue Service has not heretofore sought to deny the deduction for a medical procedure because it was considered unethical by some. *See, e.g.*, Rev. Rul. 73-201, 1973-1 C.B. 140 (cost of abortion legal under State law is deductible medical care under section 213); Rev. Rul. 55-261, *supra* (services of Christian Science practitioners deductible). Absent a showing of illegality, any such ground for denying a medical expense deduction finds no support in section 213.

. . . . We therefore conclude and hold that petitioner's hormone therapy and sex reassignment surgery "[treated] * * * disease" within the meaning of section 213(d)(9)(B) and accordingly are not "cosmetic surgery" as defined in that section.

. . . .

2. Breast Augmentation Surgery

We consider separately the qualification of petitioner's breast augmentation surgery as deductible medical care. . . . Because petitioner had normal breasts before her surgery, respondent argues, her breast augmentation surgery was "directed at improving * * * [her] appearance and [did] not meaningfully promote the proper function of the body or prevent or treat illness or disease," placing the surgery squarely within the section 213(d)(9)(B) definition of "cosmetic surgery."

. . . . [We] find that petitioner has failed to show that her breast augmentation surgery "[treated]" GID. The Benjamin standards provide that breast augmentation surgery for a male-to-female patient "may be performed if the physician prescribing hormones and the surgeon have documented that breast enlargement after undergoing hormone treatment for 18 months is not sufficient for comfort in the social gender role." The record contains no documentation from the endocrinologist prescribing petitioner's hormones at the time of her surgery. To the extent Ms. Ellaborn's or Dr. Coleman's recommendation letters to Dr. Meltzer might be considered substitute documentation for that of the hormone-prescribing physician, Ms. Ellaborn's two letters are silent concerning the condition of petitioner's presurgical breasts, while Dr. Coleman's letter states that petitioner "appears to have significant breast development secondary to hormone therapy." The surgeon here, Dr. Meltzer, recorded in his presurgical notes that petitioner had "approximately B cup breasts with a very nice shape." Thus, all of the contemporaneous documentation of the condition of petitioner's breasts before the surgery suggests that they were within a normal range of appearance, and there is no documentation concerning petitioner's comfort level with her breasts "in the social gender role."

Dr. Meltzer testified with respect to his notes that his reference to the "very nice shape" of petitioner's breasts was in comparison to the breasts of other transsexual males on feminizing hormones and that petitioner's breasts exhibited characteristics of gynecomastia, a condition where breast mass is concentrated closer to the nipple as compared to the breasts of a genetic female. Nonetheless, given the contemporaneous documentation of the breasts' apparent normalcy and the failure to adhere to the Benjamin standards' requirement to document breast-engendered anxiety to justify the surgery, we find that petitioner's breast augmentation surgery did not fall within the treatment protocols of the Benjamin standards and therefore did not "treat" GID within the meaning of section 213(d)(9)(B). Instead, the surgery merely improved her appearance.

The breast augmentation surgery is therefore "cosmetic surgery" under the section 213(d)(9)(B) definition unless it "meaningfully [promoted] the proper function of the body." The parties have stipulated that petitioner's breast augmentation "did not promote the proper function of her breasts." Although petitioner expressly declined to stipulate that the breast augmentation "did not meaningfully promote the proper functioning of her body within the meaning of I.R.C. §213," we conclude that the stipulation to which she did agree precludes a finding on this record, given the failure to adhere to the Benjamin standards, that the breast augmentation surgery "meaningfully [promoted] the proper function of the body" within the meaning of section 213(d)(9)(B). Consequently, the breast augmentation surgery is "cosmetic surgery" that is excluded from deductible "medical care."[52]

E. Medical Necessity

. . . . We find it unnecessary to resolve respondent's claim that section 213(d)(9) should be interpreted to require a showing of "medical necessity" notwithstanding the absence of that phrase in the statute. [Respondent's] contention would not bar the deductions at issue, inasmuch as we are persuaded . . . that petitioner has shown that her sex reassignment surgery was medically necessary.

. . . . Dr. Schmidt conceded in his report that a significant segment of those physicians who are knowledgeable concerning GID believes that sex reassignment surgery is medically necessary. . . . [Petitioner's] expert Dr. Brown believes that sex reassignment surgery is often the only effective treatment for severe GID, and a number of courts have concurred. . . .

The mental health professional who treated petitioner concluded that petitioner's GID was severe, that sex reassignment surgery was medically necessary, and that petitioner's prognosis without it was poor. Given Dr. Brown's expert testimony,[56] the judgment of the professional treating petitioner, the agreement of all three experts

---

52. Respondent also argues that the various surgical procedures petitioner underwent to feminize her facial features in 2000 and 2005 demonstrate a propensity for cosmetic surgery that is relevant in assessing whether petitioner's hormone therapy and sex reassignment surgery were undertaken for the purpose of improving petitioner's appearance rather than treating a disease.

We disagree. The deductibility of petitioner's facial surgery, undertaken in years other than the year in issue, is not at issue in this case. However, there is substantial evidence that such surgery may have served the same therapeutic purposes as (genital) sex reassignment surgery and hormone therapy; namely, effecting a female appearance in a genetic male. Both Ms. Ellaborn and Dr. Meltzer testified that petitioner had masculine facial features which interfered with her passing as female. The expert testimony confirmed that passing as female is important to the mental health of a male GID sufferer, and the Benjamin standards contemplate surgery to feminize facial features as part of sex reassignment for a male GID sufferer. Thus, we conclude that the facial surgery does not suggest, as respondent contends, that petitioner had a propensity for conventional cosmetic surgery.

56. When weighing Dr. Brown's and Dr. Schmidt's opposing views on whether sex reassignment surgery is medically necessary, we consider that Dr. Brown is widely published in peer-reviewed medical journals and academic texts on the subject of GID, whereas Dr. Schmidt is not. Accordingly, there is a reasonable basis to conclude that Dr. Brown's views are more widely recognized and accepted in the psychiatric profession.

that untreated GID can result in self-mutilation and suicide, and, as conceded by Dr. Schmidt, the views of a significant segment of knowledgeable professionals that sex reassignment surgery is medically necessary for severe GID, the Court is persuaded that petitioner's sex reassignment surgery was medically necessary.

IV. Conclusion

. . . . Given our holdings that GID is a "disease" and that petitioner's hormone therapy and sex reassignment surgery "[treated]" it, petitioner has shown the "existence * * * of a disease" and a payment for goods or services "directly or proximately related" to its treatment. *See Jacobs v. Commissioner*, 62 T.C. at 818. She likewise satisfies the "but for" test of *Jacobs*, which requires a showing that the procedures were an essential element of the treatment and that they would not have otherwise been undertaken for nonmedical reasons. Petitioner's hormone therapy and sex reassignment surgery were essential elements of a widely accepted treatment protocol for severe GID. The expert testimony also establishes that . . . petitioner would not have undergone hormone therapy and sex reassignment surgery except in an effort to alleviate the distress and suffering attendant to GID. Respondent's contention that petitioner undertook the surgery and hormone treatments to improve appearance is at best a superficial characterization of the circumstances that is thoroughly rebutted by the medical evidence.

Petitioner has shown that her hormone therapy and sex reassignment surgery treated disease within the meaning of section 213 and were therefore not cosmetic surgery. Thus petitioner's expenditures for these procedures were for "medical care" as defined in section 213(d)(1)(A), for which a deduction is allowed under section 213(a).

To reflect the foregoing and concessions by the parties,

Decision will be entered under Rule 155.

Reviewed by the Court.

Colvin, Cohen, Thornton, Marvel, Wherry, Paris, and Morrison, JJ., agree with this majority opinion.

Halpern, J., concurring:

I substantially agree with the majority. I write separately to offer one comment on the majority's rationale for disallowing petitioner's deduction for her breast augmentation surgery and to offer additional comments on positions taken in other side opinions.

I. Breast Augmentation Surgery

. . . . For me, that petitioner failed to prove her doctors adhered to the Benjamin standards requirement that they document her breast-engendered anxiety is sufficient to find that the surgery did not fall within those standards. The majority's added reason, "the breasts' apparent normalcy," I find superfluous and potentially misleading. . . . Dr. Meltzer testified that the surgery was different from the surgery he would perform on a biological female: "[I]t was to give her a female looking breast, which is quite different from a male breast." In response to a question from the Court, he testified that the primary purpose of the breast surgery was not to improve petitioner's appearance but "to assign her to the appropriate gender." His medical notes should not be taken out of context.

II. Statutory Interpretation

. . . . My colleagues raise arguments in support of respondent that he did not make. Because they are not addressed by the majority, I use this opportunity to address some of them.

. . . .

For Judge Gustafson, petitioner's disease was the "delusion" that she was a female. Judge Gustafson cannot fathom that someone with a healthy male body who believes he is female is not sick of mind. Yet the record suggests that the disease is more than that. . . . [The] "delusion" itself is not the disease. Instead, for someone suffering from severe GID (like petitioner) the medical problem — the disease — is the symptoms. For a significant part of the medical community, sex reassignment surgery is an accepted approach to eliminating a sufficient number of those symptoms so that a diagnosis of GID will no longer hold. And if the diagnosis will no longer hold, then the patient is cured.

. . . . If petitioner could be cured, then she could be treated, and, as the majority makes clear, we do not ground decisions as to medical care on the efficacy of the treatment. . . .

HOLMES, J., concurring:

On this record, for this taxpayer, and on the facts found by the Judge who heard this case, I agree with the majority's conclusion — that O'Donnabhain can deduct the cost of her hormone therapy and sex-reassignment surgery, but not her breast-augmentation surgery. I also agree with the majority that GID is a mental disorder, and therefore a disease under section 213. But I disagree with the majority's extensive analysis concluding that sex reassignment is the proper treatment — indeed, medically necessary at least in "severe" cases — for GID. It is not essential to the holding and drafts our Court into culture wars in which tax lawyers have heretofore claimed noncombatant status.

I

A

What does it mean for a person born male to testify, as did O'Donnabhain, that "I was a female. The only way for me to — the only way for me to be the real person that I was in my mind was to have this surgery"?

. . . .

In the crash course on transsexualism that this case has forced on us, there are at least four approaches that those who've studied the phenomenon of such feelings have had. One response, curtly dismissed by the majority, is that this is a form of delusion:

> It is not obvious how this patient's feeling that he is a woman trapped in a man's body differs from the feeling of a patient with anorexia nervosa that she is obese despite her emaciated, cachectic state. We don't do liposuction on anorexics. Why amputate the genitals of these poor men? Surely, the fault is in the mind and not the member.

McHugh, *Psychiatric Misadventures*, Am. Scholar 497, 503 (1992). For such psychiatrists, gender follows sex, is a fundamental part of human nature, and is not easily amenable to change. Those who take this view look at transsexual persons to uncover what they suspect are comorbidities—other things wrong with their patients that might explain the undoubtedly powerful feeling that they are wrongly sexed and whose treatment might alleviate the stress that it causes them.

A second approach focuses on the notion of "feeling female." What does this mean? The answer adopted by the majority and urged by O'Donnabhain is that this is a shorthand way of saying that a transsexual person's gender (*i.e.*, characteristic way of feeling or behaving, and conventionally labeled either masculine or feminine) is strongly perceived by her as mismatched to her sex (*i.e.*, biological characteristics). This, too, is highly contested territory—gender being thought by many, particularly feminists, to be entirely something society imposes on individuals. To such theorists, transsexualism is likewise a social construct:

> The medical profession need not direct the gender dissatisfied to surgery. Counselling is possible to encourage clients to take a more political approach to their situation and to realize that they can rebel against the constraints of a prescribed gender role, and relate to their own sex in their native bodies.

Jeffreys, *Transgender Activism: A Lesbian Feminist Perspective*, 1 J. Lesbian Stud. 55, 70 (1997) (suggesting SRS be proscribed as "crime against humanity"); *see also id.* at 56 (citing Raymond, The Transsexual Empire (Teachers College Press 1994)).

Yet a third school of thought is that the origins of at least many (but not all) transsexual feelings—particularly those with extensive histories of secret transvestism—is that it's not about gender, but about a particular kind of erotic attachment. *See, e.g.*, Blanchard, *Typology of Male-to-Female Transsexualism*, 14 Archives Sexual Behav. 247 (1985). Scholars of this school regard SRS as justified—not so much to cure a disease, but because SRS relieves suffering from an intense, innate, fixed, but otherwise unobtainable desire. *See, e.g.*, Dreger, *The Controversy Surrounding The Man Who Would Be Queen: A Case History of the Politics of Science, Identity, and Sex in the Internet Age*, 37 Archives Sexual Behav. 366, 383–84 (2008).

. . . . The fourth and currently predominant view among those professionally involved in the field is the one urged by O'Donnabhain, and not effectively contested by the Commissioner: that the reason a transsexual person seeks SRS is to correct a particular type of birth defect—a mismatch between the person's body and her gender identity. That mismatch has a name—GID—if not yet any clinically verifiable origin, and SRS (plus hormone therapy) is simply the correct treatment of the disorder.

I profess no expertise in weighing the merits of biodeterminism, feminism, or any of the competing theories on this question. But the majority's decision to devote significant analysis to the importance of characterizing GID as a disease, and SRS as its medically necessary treatment, pulls me into such matters to give context to the majority's analysis.

B

The. . . . consensus of WPATH is not necessarily the consensus of the entire medical community. The membership of WPATH is limited, consisting of professionals that work with transsexual patients, including social workers, psychiatrists, and surgeons that perform SRS.

The Commissioner's expert, Dr. Schmidt, testified that the Benjamin standards are merely guidelines rather than true standards of care and that they enjoy only limited acceptance in American medicine generally. The majority cites several psychiatric textbooks that mention the Benjamin standards to refute Dr. Schmidt's claim and as evidence of their general acceptance in the psychiatric profession. But the textbooks treat the Benjamin standards as mere guidelines—which may or may not be followed—rather than clearly endorsing SRS. . . .

WPATH is also quite candid that it is an advocate for transsexual persons, and not just interested in studying or treating them. . . .

And even WPATH's method of identifying candidates for SRS—the method we describe and effectively endorse today—is very much contestable. A leading article (admittedly ten years old at this point, but still oft cited), concluded on this topic that "[u]nfortunately, studies evaluating the indispensability of components of the currently employed procedures are nonexistent." Cohen-Kettenis & Gooren, *Transsexualism: A Review of Etiology, Diagnosis and Treatment*, 46 J. Psychosomatic Res. 315 (1999).

II

The majority reasons that O'Donnabhain's hormone therapy and SRS treat a disease, and so their costs are deductible expenses of medical care. It then adds a coda to the opinion holding that these treatments are "medically necessary."[3]

---

3. . . . .

I must, however, note the Commissioner's alternative argument [to his narrow definition of disease,] that "negative myths and ignorance that permeate social thinking in the United States regarding transgendered persons" and the "many laws and legal situations [that] are highly discriminatory for persons with GID" mean that the "suffering experienced by GID patients is primarily inflicted by an intolerant society." . . . . It is not effective advocacy to denigrate the people whose government one is representing. [relocated footnote—Eds.]

. . . . If [the majority] had reasoned simply that to "treat" illness in section 213(d)(9)(B) meant the same low standard that it does in section 213(d)(1) — a subjective good-faith therapeutic intent on the part of the patient — and stopped, we wouldn't be doing anything controversial. . . .

. . . . But the majority tacks on an extra section onto its opinion concluding that SRS and hormone therapy for transsexual persons are "medically necessary." Avoidance would have been the sounder course, because "medically necessary" is a loaded phrase. Construing it puts us squarely, and unnecessarily, in the middle of a serious fight within the relevant scientific community, and the larger battle among those who are deeply concerned with the proper response to transsexual persons' desires for extensive and expensive surgeries.

. . . .

Our discussion of the science is, though, weak even by the low standards expected of lawyers. Tucked into a footnote is our opinion on the relative merits of the scientific conclusions of Dr. Brown (O'Donnabhain's witness in favor of the medical necessity of SRS) and Dr. Schmidt (the Commissioner's witness who was opposed). Majority op. note 56. The reasoning in that footnote in favor of Dr. Brown's opinion is that he is more widely published than Dr. Schmidt. But Dr. Schmidt was Chair of the Sexual Disorders Work Group that drafted part of the DSM-IV on which the majority relies, and is a longtime psychiatry professor at Johns Hopkins and a founder of its Sexual Behavior Consultation Unit. . . .

The majority also criticizes Dr. Schmidt for citing a religious publication. It's true that one of the sources Dr. Schmidt cited was an article by the former chairman of Johns Hopkins's Psychiatry Department in *First Things*. But it is inadequate, if we're going to weigh in on this debate, to imply that Johns Hopkins's conclusion was based merely on an essay in "a religious publication."

First Things, like *Commentary* and a host of other general-interest but serious periodicals, seeks out the small subset of specialists who can write well. Essays by such people don't aspire to be original research, but they are often based on original research. And so was the *First Things* article by Dr. McHugh, which summarized the research of a third member of the Hopkins Psychiatry Department, Dr. Jon Meyer. Meyer & Reter, *Sex Reassignment*, 36 ARCHIVES GEN. PSYCHIATRY 1010 (1979). . . . Unlike authors of previous studies, Meyer included both unoperated GID patients and post-SRS patients in his study. . . . Using patient interviews, he issued initial and followup adjustment scores. . . . Both the operated and unoperated subjects' mean scores improved after the followup period, but there was no significant difference between the improvement of each group. The operated group failed to demonstrate clear objective superiority over the unoperated group — in other words, SRS didn't provide any objective improvement to the GID patients. [For more on the essay by McHugh, see Discussion note, *infra* at p. 1120. — Eds.]

There are numerous other clues that the picture of scientific consensus that the majority presents is not quite right. Consider where the surgeries are currently performed. SRS was for many years primarily undertaken in research hospitals that had "gender identity clinics." These clinics would conduct research on SRS and evaluate its effectiveness. Johns Hopkins, under the leadership of Dr. John Money, opened the first U.S. gender identity clinic in 1965. Money & Schwartz, *Public Opinion and Social Issues in Transsexualism: A Case Study in Medical Sociology, in* Transsexualism and Sex Reassignment 253 (Green & Money, eds., 1969). After Johns Hopkins took the lead, other university-based clinics jumped at the opportunity to research transsexualism and perform SRS. But the first research clinic to perform and study SRS was also the first to cut it off. The Meyer study had found no significant difference in adjustment between those who had SRS and those who didn't, and in light of that study Johns Hopkins announced in 1979 that it would no longer perform SRS. *No Surgery for Transsexuals*, Newsweek, Aug. 27, 1979, at 72. After the Hopkins clinic closed, the other university-based clinics either closed or ended their university affiliations. Denny, *The University-Affiliated Gender Clinics, and How They Failed to Meet the Needs of Transsexual People*, Transgender Tapestry #098, Summer 2002, available at http://www.ifge .org/ Article59.phtml (last visited Jan. 7, 2010). Stanford, for example, in 1980 spun off its university-affiliated clinic to a private center that performed SRS but didn't conduct research.

Eventually, all university-based research clinics stopped the practice of SRS.[8] Today, SRS in the United States is primarily the purview of a few boutique surgery practices. While such surgeons—including O'Donnabhain's—are undoubtedly skilled in their art, they do not have the capacity to conduct research on the medical necessity of SRS like the research hospitals. Their practices use the Benjamin standards, but do not seem to conduct peer-reviewed studies of their efficacy.

It is true that the Meyer piece has been the subject of lively controversy[9] . . . . If we needed to opine on the medical necessity of SRS, some sensitivity to that academic controversy, particularly the problem of how to set up a proxy control group for those undergoing sex reassignment, as well as some sensitivity to defining and

---

8. Some research hospitals, Stanford among them, will perform SRS on a referral basis—but the clinical research on SRS at these hospitals has been shut down. Levy, *Two Transsexuals Reflect on University's Pioneering Gender Dysphoria Program*, Stanford Rep., May 3, 2000.

9. There has been at least one study that reached a different conclusion using a somewhat similar methodology. *See* Mate-Kole et al., *A Controlled Study of Psychological and Social Change After Surgical Gender Reassignment in Selected Male Transsexuals*, 157 Brit. J. Psychiatr. 261 (1990). There have also been numerous studies without controls (or the sort of quasi-controls that Meyer used) that report transsexual persons generally satisfied with the results of SRS. Such studies are as problematic as would be drug studies without double-blind control groups. The question is further complicated by the possibility that different types of transsexuals, *see* Blanchard, *Typology of Male-to-Female Transsexualism*, 14 Archives Sexual Behav. 247 (1985), will experience different outcomes; as might female-to-male transsexuals compared to male-to-female transsexuals. *See generally* Cohen-Kettenis & Gooren, *supra*.

My point is not to pick Meyer over Mate-Kole, but only to suggest the problem is much more complicated than the majority lets on. It is certainly beyond the competence of tax judges.

measuring the effectiveness of surgery, would have to be shown. I do not believe we should have addressed the issue.

. . . .

III

. . . . Hormones and SRS are . . . directed at treating GID in this sense and do not so much improve appearance as create a new one.

But the breast-augmentation surgery is different. O'Donnabhain's new baseline having been established through hormones, I would hold that that surgery was directed at improving—in the sense of focused on changing what she already had—her already radically altered appearance. Denying the deduction for this procedure while allowing it for the hormones and SRS also seems a reasonable distinction—breast surgery is likely one of the commonest types of cosmetic surgery and (if not undergone after cancer surgery or trauma or the like) highly likely to be within the common public meaning of that phrase.

That leaves only the question of whether O'Donnabhain's breast-augmentation surgery meets one of the exceptions to the nondeductibility of cosmetic surgery listed in subsection (d)(9)(A). This is easy—O'Donnabhain never argued her breasts were deformed by "a congenital abnormality, a personal injury resulting from an accident or trauma, or disfiguring disease."

I therefore respectfully concur with majority's result, if not its reasoning.

GOEKE, J., agrees with this concurring opinion.

[Judge Goeke's opinion concurring in the result only, joined by Judge Holmes is omitted, as is Judge Foley's opinion concurring in part and dissenting in part, joined by Judges Wells, Vasquez, Kroupa, and Gustafson.]

GUSTAFSON, J., concurring in part and dissenting in part:

I concur with the result of the majority opinion to the extent that it disallows a medical care deduction under section 213 for breast enhancement surgery, but I dissent to the extent that the majority allows a deduction for genital sex reassignment surgery.

Petitioner is the father of three children from a marriage that lasted 20 years. Although physically healthy, he was unhappy with his male anatomy and became profoundly so, to the point of contemplating self-mutilation. Mental health professionals diagnosed him as suffering from Gender Identity Disorder (GID). With their encouragement, he received medical procedures: In years before the year at issue here, he received injections of female hormones and underwent facial surgery and other plastic surgery; and then in the year at issue he paid a surgeon about $20,000 to remove his genitals, fashion simulated female genitals, and insert breast implants. After these procedures, petitioner "passed" as female and became happier. She claimed an income tax deduction for the cost of this "sex reassignment surgery" (SRS). The question in this case is whether section 213 allows this deduction.

. . . . We decide today whether SRS is deductible "medical care" or instead is non-deductible "cosmetic surgery or other similar procedures." "Whether and to what extent deductions shall be allowed depends upon legislative grace; and only as there is *clear provision* therefor can any particular deduction be allowed." *New Colonial Ice Co. v. Helvering*, 292 U.S. 435 (1934) (emphasis added). This case therefore requires us to determine whether there is "clear provision" for the deduction of SRS expenses. I conclude that section 213 is anything but clear in allowing such a deduction.

. . . .

The definition of deductible "medical care" in section 213(d)(1)(A) and the definition of non-deductible "cosmetic surgery" in the exception in subsection (d)(9) (B) must be construed in tandem. . . .[4]

. . . . "[M]edical care" is defined in subsection (d)(1)(A) by five terms — *i.e.*, "diagnosis, cure, mitigation, treatment, or prevention." . . . [I]t seems likely that when this "medical care" deduction was first enacted in 1942, Congress simply intended to enact a broad definition of medical care and therefore chose terms to convey that breadth, without particular intention about the potential distinctive meanings of those terms. . . .

However, we consider here the very different and specific congressional intent 48 years later in 1990, when Congress enacted subsection (d)(9) to disallow deductions for cosmetic surgery. Congress provided an exception to this new disallowance, and allowed a deduction in the case of an otherwise cosmetic procedure, if

---

4. . . . Judge Goeke's concurrence would allow a deduction for the genital SRS because it "was not directed at improving petitioner's appearance but rather was functional." His concurrence thus rightly discerns that section 213(d)(9)(B) distinguishes "improving * * * *appearance*" from "promot[ing] * * * proper *function*" (emphasis added); but there is no basis for the conclusion that SRS is "functional." Petitioner's SRS did not involve any attempt to confer female reproductive function. No one undertaking to "promote" sexual "function" would perform a penectomy and a castration on a healthy male body. On the contrary, SRS drastically terminates a male patient's functioning sexuality. SRS did not change petitioner into a "function[ing]" female, but removed his salient male characteristics and attempted to make him resemble a woman — *i.e.*, by petitioner's lights, to "improve[] the patient's appearance." The majority shows that the SRS surgeon does try to salvage, as much as possible, some possibility for subsequent sexual response, and observes that SRS "alter[s] appearance (and, *to some degree*, function)" (emphasis added); but the majority makes no finding that petitioner proved that any identifiable portion of the SRS expense can be allocated to restoration of "function." On our record, petitioner's SRS must be said to have been directed at improving appearance rather than promoting function, and it is therefore within the definition of "cosmetic surgery." Judge Holmes's concurrence, on the other hand, attempts no analysis of function versus appearance, but rather proposes a different distinction not explicit in the statute: He would hold that SRS did not "so much *improve* [petitioner's male] appearance as *create* a new [female] one." (emphasis added). This ingenious distinction, if accepted, might well undo the disallowance of deductions for cosmetic surgery, since plastic surgery is often marketed and purchased on the grounds that it supposedly creates a "new appearance." But in fact, any surgery that gives the patient a "new appearance" has thereby "improved" the patient's former appearance and is "cosmetic surgery" under section 213(d)(9)(B). [Relocated footnote.—Eds.]

it "*prevent[s] or treat[s]* illness or disease." Sec. 213(d)(9)(B) (emphasis added). . . . Missing from this short list of deductible modes of care in subsection (d)(9)(B) . . . are three of the five terms in subsection (d)(1)(A), including "mitigation." . . . . Under the wording Congress adopted, if an otherwise cosmetic procedure "mitigates" a disease but cannot be said to "treat" or "prevent" it, then under the plain terms of the statute, one would have to conclude that the expense of that procedure is non-deductible.

. . . . The majority implicitly holds that "prevent or treat" in section 213(d)(9) (A) is equivalent to, or is shorthand for, "diagnos[e], cure, mitigat[e], treat[], or prevent[]" in subsection (d)(1)(A) and that no narrow meaning should be ascribed to "treat." . . . . [Ascribing] this broad or loose meaning to "treat * * * disease" is untenable under section 213, where "treat" must be distinguished from "mitigate," and where the direct object is "disease" (not "patient" or "symptom") . . . .

. . . . When "treat" and "mitigate" are distinguished, rather than being blended, "treatment" addresses underlying causes and "mitigation" lessens effects. . . .

. . . [In] section 213(d)(9)(B), the object of the verb "treat" is "disease." The breadth of the dictionary definitions cited by the majority is attributable in part to the fact that one may "treat" a disease, *or* a patient, *or* a symptom. Consequently, a general definition of "treat" that is not confined—as section 213 is confined— to treatment *of a disease* should and will reflect shades of meaning appropriate for treatment of symptoms, which shades of meaning overlap more with "mitigate." For that reason these general dictionary definitions are not very illuminating in this instance, where the question is whether to "treat" *disease* is or is not the same as to "mitigate" *disease.*

As a part of "medical care," one could "treat" a *patient* with palliative care or could "treat" his painful *symptoms* with morphine (both of which could also be said to "mitigate," and the expenses of which would be deductible under section 213(a))—all the while leaving his disease un-"treated," strictly speaking. When Congress intends to enact a provision that turns on "treatment of *patients*"[8] or on "treatment of *symptoms*,"[9] it knows how to do so; but it did not do so in section 213(d)(9)(B), which allows deductions for procedures that "treat * * * *disease.*" (Emphasis added.) . . . .

---

8. *See* sec. 168(i)(2)(C) (emphasis added).

9. *See* 8 U.S.C. sec. 1611(b)(1)(C) (2006) (emphasis added). Focusing on treatment of symptoms, Judge Halpern emphasizes (emphasis added) that petitioner's expert pronounced petitioner "cured" (even though petitioner's belief about her sex was unchanged) in the sense that "the *symptoms* of the disorder were no longer present", *e.g.,* "she had been free for a long time of clinically significant distress or impairment"; and Judge Halpern equates a removal of symptoms with a "cure" of the disease (and therefore a "treatment" of the disease). However, when treatment of symptoms makes a psychiatric patient content with his delusion, he has not been cured, and his "disease" has not been "treat[ed]" for purposes of section 213(d)(9)(B).

. . . . The majority's loose interpretation of subsection (d)(9)(B) . . . invites arguments for the deduction not only of GID patients' SRS expenses but also of the cosmetic surgery expenses of any psychiatric patient who is (or claims to be) pathologically unhappy with his body. . . .

. . . . Where Congress was explicitly setting out to shut down deductions for cosmetic surgery, the restricting language it employed can hardly be taken as careless or unintentional.

. . . .

Because the particular question in this case is whether SRS falls within the definition of cosmetic surgery for which expenses are *disallowed* in subsection (d)(9)(B), the majority gives short shrift to subsection (d)(9)(A). Subsection (d)(9)(A) shows the sorts of exceptional procedures for which Congress meant to *preserve* deductions — *i.e.*, procedures that are "necessary to ameliorate a deformity arising from, or directly related to, a congenital abnormality, a personal injury resulting from an accident or trauma, or disfiguring disease" — and thus illuminates the congressional purpose. Someone like petitioner who suffers from GID has no deformities that are addressed by SRS; he has no "congenital abnormality"; he has suffered no "accident or trauma, or disfiguring disease." There is thus no indication that Congress explicitly intended to carve out, from its new disallowance, an exception that would reach SRS expenses. The wording choices in the statute that limit deductibility must be taken at face value in order to vindicate the undisputed congressional purpose.

. . . .

It appears that doctors sometimes use the word "treat" in [a] loose sense, so that they discuss SRS as a "treatment" for GID. . . . In testimony in this case, doctors manifestly used the terms "care" and "treatment" almost interchangeably, without particular attention to whether it is the patient, the symptoms, or the disease that is being addressed; in section 213(d), however, "care" is a general term of which "treatment" is a mode distinct from "mitigation", and deductible care is directed to "disease" (or "illness"), not to the patient or her symptoms. There is thus no indication that doctors' usage of these words respects the distinctions that are important in section 213.

. . . .

IV. SRS does not "treat" GID for purposes of section 213(d)(9)(B).

For the GID patient there is a dissonance between, on the one hand, his male body . . . and, on the other hand, his perception of himself as female. The male body conflicts with the female self-perception and produces extreme stress, anxiety, and unhappiness.

One could analyze the GID patient's problem in one of two ways: (1) His anatomical maleness is normative, and his perceived femaleness is the problem. Or (2) his perceived femaleness is normative, and his anatomical maleness is the problem.

If one assumes option 2, then one could say that SRS *does* "treat" his GID by bringing his problematic male body into simulated conformity (as much as is possible) with his authentic female mind.

However, the medical consensus as described in the record of this case is in stark opposition to the latter characterization and can be reconciled only with option 1: Petitioner's male body was healthy, and his mind was disordered in its female self-perception. GID is in the jurisdiction of the psychiatric profession — the doctors of the mind — and is listed in that profession's definitive catalog of "*Mental* Disorders." *See* DSM-IV-TR at 576-582. When a patient presents with a healthy male body and a professed subjective sense of being female, the medical profession does not treat his body as an anomaly, as if it were infected by the disease of an alien maleness. Rather, his male body is taken as a given, and the patient becomes a *psychiatric* patient because of his disordered feeling that he is female. The majority concludes (emphasis added), that GID is a "serious *mental* disorder" — *i.e.*, a disease in petitioner's mind — and I accept that conclusion.

A procedure that changes the patient's healthy male body (in fact, that disables his healthy male body) and leaves his mind unchanged (*i.e.*, with the continuing misperception that he is female) has not treated his mental disease. On the contrary, that procedure has given up on the mental disease, has capitulated to the mental disease, has arguably even changed sides and joined forces with the mental disease. In any event, the procedure did not (in the words of *Havey v. Commissioner*, 12 T.C. at 412) "bear directly on the * * * condition in question", did not "deal with" the disease (per *Webster's*), did not "treat" the mental disease that the therapist diagnosed. Rather, the procedure changed only petitioner's healthy body and undertook to "mitigat[e]" the effects of the mental disease.

Even if SRS is medically indicated for the GID patient — even if SRS is the best that medicine can do for him — it is an otherwise cosmetic procedure that does not "treat" the mental disease. Sex reassignment surgery is therefore within "cosmetic surgery or other similar procedures" under section 213(d)(9)(A), and the expense that petitioner incurred for that surgery is not deductible under section 213(a).

WELLS, FOLEY, VASQUEZ, and KROUPA, JJ., agree with this concurring in part and dissenting in part opinion.

———————

Discussion

1. Note that the current version of the WPATH Standards of Care makes clear that transgender persons who wish to transition need not undergo psychotherapy, hormones, and surgery in that fixed order, and indeed that not all of these interventions are appropriate for all trans persons. WORLD PROFESSIONAL ASSOCIATION FOR TRANSGENDER HEALTH, STANDARDS OF CARE FOR THE HEALTH OF TRANSSEXUAL, TRANSGENDER, AND GENDER NONCONFORMING PEOPLE, Version 7, at 9 (2011) ("For individuals seeking care for gender dysphoria, a variety of therapeutic options

can be considered. The number and type of interventions applied and the order in which these take place may differ from person to person.").

2. Should it matter to deductibility under the tax code whether or not Rhiannon O'Donnabhain was correctly diagnosed with GID given that qualified medical personnel rendered that diagnosis and she thereupon underwent medical treatments for that condition? Consider also that Julie Youngman and Courtney Hauck have argued that *O'Donnabhain* wrongly examined whether particular transition-related medical treatments were "'medically necessary' and 'widely accepted' in the medical community," requirements that the federal tax code does not impose." Julie Furr Youngman & Courtney D. Hauck, *Medical Necessity: A Higher Hurdle for Marginalized Taxpayers?*, 51 Loy. L.A. L. Rev. 1, 6 (2018).

3. Does Justice Holmes's discussion of "alternative" views of "transsexualism" give credence to those in a way that embroils him in the so-called "culture wars" in which he accuses the majority of wrongly intervening, or is he just correcting an imbalance the majority created?

4. For further discussion of *O'Donnabhain*, see, for example, David B. Cruz, O'Donnabhain v. Commissioner of Internal Revenue, *in* Feminist Judgments: Rewritten Tax Opinions 274 (Bridget J. Crawford & Anthony C. Infanti, eds. 2017); Nancy J. Knauer, *Commentary on* O'Donnabhain v. Commissioner, *in* Feminist Judgments: Rewritten Tax Opinions 266; Lindsey Dennis, *"I Do Not Suffer from Gender Dysphoria. I Suffer from Bureaucratic Dysphoria": An Analysis of the Tax Treatment of Gender Affirmation Procedures Under the Medical Expense Deduction*, 34 Berkeley J. Gender L. & Just. 215 (2019); Ann Mumford, *"Rhiannon O'Donnabhain Is a Taxpayer": Tax and the Social Contract in* O'Donnabhain v. Commissioner, 16 Pitt. Tax Rev. 145 (2019); Julie Furr Youngman & Courtney D. Hauck, *Medical Necessity: A Higher Hurdle for Marginalized Taxpayers?*, 51 Loy. L.A. L. Rev. 1 (2018); Katherine Pratt, *The Tax Definition of "Medical Care": A Critique of the Startling IRS Arguments in* O'Donnabhain v. Commissioner, 23 Mich. J. Gender & L. 313 (2016); Stephanie Chen, *Examining* O'Donnabhain v. Commissioner, *134 T.C. No. 4 (2010): Sex Reassignment Surgery as a Tax Deductible Medical Expense*, 21 S. Cal. Interdisc. L.J. 603 (2012); Lauren Herman, *A Non-Medicalized Medical Deduction?* O'Donnabhain v. Commissioner *& the IRS's Understanding of Transgender Medical Care*, 35 Harv. J. L. & Gender 487 (2012); Alesdair H. Ittelson, *Trapped in the Wrong Phraseology:* O'Donnabhain v. Commissioner — *Consequences for Federal Tax Policy and the Transgender Community*, 26 Berkeley J. Gender L. & Just. 356, 356 (2011); Susan L. Megaard, *Scope of the Medical Expense Deduction Clarified and Broadened by New Tax Court Decision*, 112 J. Tax'n 353 (110).

B. Medicare, Medicaid, and Other Government Health Insurance

Note on G.B. v. Lackner

In *G.B. v. Jerome Lackner*, 80 Cal. App. 3d 64, 145 Cal. Rptr. 555 (1978), the court considered whether Medi-Cal, the state's Medicaid program that financially assists low-income persons with medical care, had to cover genitoplasty for G.B., a transgender woman. Her surgeon John Brown had concluded that the surgery was medically necessary to treat G.B.'s gender dysphoria and applied for authorization through Medi-Cal. "Dr. Wayne Erdbrink, a Medi-Cal consultant who [was] an ophthalmologist," denied the claim, a position sustained by the Director of the California Department of Health. The director concluded that "[t]he proposed operation . . . is . . . a cosmetic operation that would change the appearance of the claimant's external genitalia. Inasmuch as the proposed operation is to be performed solely for that purpose, it must be considered a cosmetic operation that is not covered under the Medi-Cal Program." The court reversed.

In the majority's view, "[t]he Director's conclusion that castration and penectomy changes the appearance of male genitalia seems strained." The court recounted testimony of numerous doctors who provided testimony in support of G.B.; noted the Minnesota Supreme Court's conclusion that "[t]he only medical procedure known to be successful in treating the problem of transsexualism is the radical sex conversion surgical procedure," *Doe v. State, Dept. of Public Welfare*, 257 N.W.2d 816 (Minn. 1977); and quoted the conclusion of *Richards v. United States Tennis Ass'n*, 93 Misc. 2d 713 (Sup. Ct. 1977), that "Medical Science has not found any organic cause or cure (other than sex reassignment surgery and hormone therapy) for transsexualism, nor has psychotherapy been successful in altering the transsexual's identification with the other sex or his desire for surgical change."

The director had relied on regulations denying Medi-Cal coverage for cosmetic surgery, defined as:

> Surgery to alter the texture or configuration of the skin and its relationship with contiguous structures of any feature of the human body. [¶] This alteration would be considered by the average prudent observer to be within the range of normal and acceptable appearance for the patient's age and ethnic background and by competent medical opinion to be without risk to the patient's physical or mental health. [¶] It means only surgery which is sought by the patient for personal reasons and is not used to denote surgery which is needed to correct or improve physical features which may be functionally normal but which attracts undue attention or even ridicule by his peers, or which an average person would consider to be conspicuous, objectionable, abnormal or displeasing to others. [¶] Operations performed to correct congenital anomalies, to remove tumors, or restore parts which were removed in treatment of a tumor or repair a deformity or scar

resulting from injury, infection, or other disease process is obviously not cosmetic even though the appearance may be improved by the procedure.

"Surely," the majority here reasoned, "castration and penectomy cannot be considered surgical procedures to alter the texture and configuration of the skin and the skin's relationship with contiguous structures of the body. Male genitals have to be considered more than just skin, one would think." (What might the court mean by that last sentence?)

The court thought that to fit within this definition, genitoplasty as treatment for gender dysphoria would have to be "considered by the average prudent observer to be within the range of normal and acceptable appearance for the patient's age and ethnic background." Yet, the majority believed, "[t]he average prudent observer probably has no desire and will not observe what is under the skirts or trousers of either a pre-or postoperative transsexual. It is not a generally recognized characteristic of transsexuals to move about in public in the nude." In sum, and based on the evidence presented, the court adjudged that it would be "clearly impossible to conclude that transsexual surgery is cosmetic surgery, even using the definition relied on by the Director." It ruled that the director's contrary characterization of the prescribed surgery for G.B. as cosmetic was arbitrary, set aside his decision, and remanded the case to the trial court to order the director to cover G.B.'s surgery.

Acting Presiding Justice Scott wrote a lengthy dissent, more than four times as long as the majority opinion. He would have extended deference to the director's regulation barring coverage of cosmetic surgery and held that the director acted within his statutory discretion in denying Medi-Cal payment for G.B.'s surgery. In his view, "[a]lthough transsexual surgery is more drastic than most other cosmetic procedures, the procedure bears some resemblance to an operation to reduce the size of a nose, or to reduce the size of female breasts. In all of these operations an incision is made, parts of the organs are removed, and a new body part is fashioned by plastic surgery." Discounting the gravity of G.B.'s gender dysphoria as insufficient to overcome the evidentiary deference due the director, Scott contended that "[i]n transsexual surgery, as in other kinds of cosmetic surgery, nothing is physically amiss with the function of the portion of the body which is altered. The surgery is performed in an effort to alleviate the patient's emotional distress which is caused by his subjective perception of his body." And, although his logic was not pellucid, Scott's conclusion that G.B.'s surgery (which she had and was seeking reimbursement for) "alter[ed] a normal, healthy part of the body to conform the appearance of that part, as nearly as is medically possible, to the patient's misperception of himself [*sic*]" made it in his view reasonable for the director to "conclude that this operation [was] not 'reasonable and necessary for the prevention, diagnosis, or treatment of disease, illness, or injury,' as those terms are used in the regulations of the Department of Health."

Justice Scott also rejected G.B.'s constitutional challenges to the exclusion of her surgery from Medi-Cal. Following cases such as *Holloway v. Arthur Andersen & Co.*, 566 F.2d 659 (9th Cir. 1977), Scott applied rational basis review to G.B.'s equal protection claim and argued that California's "legitimate interest in using limited funding in the most efficient way" reasonably justified the state's consistent exclusion in all circumstances of "the surgical removal and reconstruction by plastic surgery of organs not diseased, damaged, or deformed." Justice Scott also rejected G.B.'s argument that the state violated her rights under the Due Process Clause of the Fourteenth Amendment, relying in part on the Supreme Court's decision in *Maher v. Roe*, 432 U.S. 464 (1977), denying a constitutional obligation for government to fund women's exercise of their fundamental constitutional right to choose to terminate their pregnancies.

How should one assess whether the dissent or the majority better characterizes genitoplasty-as-treatment-for-gender-dysphoria as "cosmetic" or not? What significance should one attribute to disagreement of medical doctors about the medical necessity of surgery as treatment for a particular person's gender dysphoria? Or for all people with gender dysphoria, in the case of doctors—an apparent minority among those who treat transgender patients—who believe surgery never to be appropriate?

Note on Rush v. Parham

In *Carolyn Rush (Pseudonym) v. T.M. "Jim" Parham*, 625 F.2d 1150 (5th Cir. 1980), the U.S. Court of Appeals considered a transgender woman's suit against various state and federal officials seeking coverage by Georgia's Medicaid program for what the judicial opinions called "transsexual surgery" or "sex reassignment surgery." By the time of the district court's decision, Ms. Rush had been seeking surgery for eight years. Georgia invoked the state's Medicaid plan and policies that denied coverage for "experimental surgery[,] *e.g.*, . . . transsexual operations." "The district court, on Rush's motion for summary judgment, ordered state defendants to pay for the surgery, holding that a state Medicaid program cannot, consistent with [the federal Medicaid act], categorically deny funding for necessary medical services. The district court also ordered federal defendants to disapprove that portion of Georgia's Medicaid plan that 'irrebuttably den[ies] Medicaid coverage for transsexual surgery [*sic*—Eds.].'" The court of appeals concluded that the grant of summary judgment to Rush was erroneous, reversed, and remanded for the state to attempt to defend its action here on either of two approaches.

First, the court of appeals disapproved the district court's conclusion that under the federal Medicaid statute, a state must pay for whatever treatments the doctors of people enrolled in the state's Medicaid program determine in their individual discretion are medically necessary for their patients. Rather, as a matter of statutory interpretation the court of appeals ruled "instead that a state may adopt a definition of medical necessity that places reasonable limits on a physician's discretion. One such limitation is the one Georgia contends it used in denying the surgery: a ban against reimbursement for experimental forms of treatment, *i.e.*, treatment not generally recognized as effective by the medical profession." Accordingly, if on remand Georgia showed that it, "in fact, had a policy prohibiting payment for experimental services when it first rejected plaintiff's application; and, if it did, [if] its determination that transsexual surgery is experimental [was] reasonable[,]" then the state would not have to pay for Rush's surgery.

Second, the court of appeals held that even if Georgia were unable to avail itself of that first path to denying coverage, the district court on remand should rule in the state's favor if it could establish a second legal justification for its denial. Specifically, "[i]f on remand, the district court finds that the state defendants' decision to deny payment for Rush's surgery was not based on a prohibition against reimbursement for experimental treatment,[b] or if it finds that transsexual surgery was not experimental, it must consider defendants' second contention: that they reached a proper administrative determination that transsexual surgery was inappropriate treatment for Rush." The court of appeals then specified a two-track standard for the state to review Rush's doctor's recommendation. On one hand, if "transsexual surgery was experimental" and Georgia allowed experimental surgeries only in exceptional cases, then its denial of coverage "should be sustained unless Rush was able to show compelling reasons why an exception should be made for her. To show such reasons, we think Rush was required to present convincing evidence that no other form of treatment would improve her condition, and that transsexual surgery was unlikely to worsen it." On the other hand, "[i]f the district court finds that Georgia did not have a policy limiting payment for experimental surgery to exceptional cases (or that transsexual surgery was not experimental)," then the denial of coverage should be upheld by the district court only if "the physician's diagnosis, or his opinion that the prescribed treatment was appropriate to the diagnosis, was without any basis in fact."

It is unclear that *Rush* has much precedential value today. Adult gender confirmation surgery is no longer considered experimental by experts in transition care (such as the World Professional Association for Transgender Health) and mainstream medical organizations (such as the American Medical Association). Are there types of trans medical treatments that might still be considered "experimental" today? *But cf.*, *e.g.*, Brief of Amicus Curiae Dr. Paul R. McHugh, M.D., Professor of Psychiatry in Support of Petitioner, *R.G. & G.R. Harris Funeral Homes, Inc. v. Equal Employment Opportunity Commission, et al.*, No. 18-107 (filed Aug. 22, 2019) (arguing that "[t]here is no good evidence that this dramatic surgery produces the benefits espoused by the [American Medical Association].").

Reading Guide for Pinneke v. Preisser

1. What was Iowa's justification for categorically excluding surgery to treat gender dysphoria from its Medicaid program? How did Iowa characterize such surgeries?

---

b. The court seems to be alluding to the fact that, at the time of the initial denial, there was no exclusion for experimental treatments, something that seems to have been added in response to the plaintiff's request for medical treatment. [— Eds.]

What provision of the Medicaid statute does the court of appeals hold this exclusion violates?

2. According to the court, where does the Medicaid statute place the authority to make determinations of medical necessity?

3. Under what exclusion from the requirements of the Medicaid statute does Iowa try to fit its refusal to reimburse for gender confirmation surgery? What does the court hold regarding that claim?

Verna Pinneke v. Victor Preisser, Commissioner of Iowa Department of Social Services, and Monica Murray, Director of the Cerro Gordo County Department of Social Services, Individually and in Their Official Capacities

623 F.2d 546 (8th Cir. 1980)

Before Heaney, Circuit Judge, Gibson, Senior Circuit Judge, and Stephenson, Circuit Judge.

Opinion

Floyd R. Gibson, Senior Circuit Judge.

Appellants are state and local officials in charge of administering the State of Iowa's Medicaid program. They appeal from the District Court's order requiring them to reimburse Appellee-Plaintiff Pinneke $3,024.52 for her expenses incurred for sex reassignment surgery and awarding her $500 as compensation for mental anguish and suffering resulting from the wrongful denial of benefits, together with attorney fees. . . .

Pinneke began life as a male, but quickly became uncomfortable with the male gender identity. After extensive testing, doctors concluded that she had a transsexual personality, and required sex reassignment surgery. She underwent sex reassignment surgery on April 20, 1976. As a Supplemental Security Income recipient, Pinneke was eligible for benefits under the Medicaid program, 42 U.S.C. § 1396 (1976). She applied for funding of her sex reassignment surgery under the Medicaid program, but the Cerro Gordo County office of the Iowa Department of Social Services refused funding. The Commissioner of the Iowa Department of Social Services affirmed this decision on the basis that the State of Iowa's Medicaid plan specifically excludes coverage for sex reassignment surgery. Pinneke then filed this suit seeking remedial injunctive and declaratory relief from the denial of her constitutional rights to equal protection and due process and her statutory right to Medicaid benefits.

On May 11, 1979, the District Court declared that the policy of denying Medicaid benefits for sex reassignment surgery where it is a medical necessity for treatment of transsexualism is contrary to the provisions of Title XIX of the Social Security Act, 42 U.S.C. § 1396 (1976) . . . . It declared the relevant parts of the Iowa State Plan void, and permanently enjoined the administration and enforcement of the Iowa Medicaid program in a manner to deny benefits for medically necessary care and treatment incident to sex reassignment surgery or subsequent corrective surgery.

. . . .

[Appellants] assert that Congress conferred upon the states considerable latitude and discretion in shaping their medical assistance programs under Title XIX, and that the State of Iowa has properly exercised this discretion to formulate an irrebuttable presumption that treatment of transsexualism by alteration of healthy tissue cannot be considered "medically necessary."[1] Appellants apparently concede that Pinneke suffers from transsexualism, but contend that the state may make an irrebuttable presumption prohibiting a certain manner of treatment, even though medical testimony establishes that this treatment, sex reassignment surgery, is the only procedure available for treatment of the condition from which Pinneke suffers, transsexualism, and was medically necessary for her, based upon an individualized medical evaluation.

From this record, it appears that radical sex conversion surgery is the only medical treatment available to relieve or solve the problems of a true transsexual. As noted by the Minnesota Supreme Court in *Doe v. Minnesota Department of Public Welfare and Hennepin County Welfare Board*, 257 N.W.2d 816 (Minn.1977):

> Given the fact that the roots of transsexualism are generally implanted early in life, the consensus of medical literature is that psychoanalysis is not a successful mode of treatment for the adult transsexual. * * * The only medical procedure known to be successful in treating the problem of transsexualism is the radical sex conversion surgical procedure requested by Doe in the present case:
>
> > "It is the alternative that is sobering. In the light of present knowledge, there is no known approach to treatment of transsexualism other than the surgical route. Nothing else holds promise. Granted that the surgical route is difficult and clearly second-best to a method of preventing these tragic reversals of gender identity and role, yet it seems to be all that there is to offer at present." Hastings, *Postsurgical Adjustment of Male Transsexual Patients*, 1 CLINICS IN PLASTIC SURGERY 335, 344.
>
> Thus, it is not unreasonable to conclude that transsexualism is a very complex medical and psychological problem which is generally developed by individuals early in life. By the time an individual reaches adulthood, the problem of gender role disorientation and the transsexual condition

---

1. The State of Iowa does not appear to challenge the use of "medically necessary" as the standard for determining when it must provide coverage, but rather argues that sex reassignment surgery simply is considered not "medically necessary," but more in the nature of cosmetic surgery. This standard of medical necessity is not explicit in the statute, but has become judicially accepted as implicit to the legislative scheme and is apparently endorsed by the Supreme Court. *Beal v. Doe*, 432 U.S. 438 (1977).

resulting therefrom are so severe that the only successful treatment known to medical science is sex conversion surgery.

The State of Iowa, in choosing to participate in Title XIX, the Medicaid program, by establishing a Medical Assistance Program, has bound itself to abide by certain provisions of the federal legislation. Title XIX, 42 U.S.C. § 1396a(13)(B), mandates that five basic categories of medical assistance be provided to all categorically needy persons when the assistance is medically necessary. These five categories, listed in section 1396d(a) include "inpatient hospital services (other than services in an institution for tuberculosis or mental diseases)" and "physicians' services furnished by a physician (as defined in section 1395x(r)(1) of this title), whether furnished in the office, the patient's home, a hospital, or a skilled nursing facility, or elsewhere."

The state's plan is subject further to regulations promulgated by the federal Department of Health, Education, and Welfare. In particular, 42 C.F.R. 449.10(a)(5)(i) (1977), now codified at 42 C.F.R. § 440.230(c) (1979), provides in pertinent part:

> [T]he State may not arbitrarily deny or reduce the amount, duration or scope of, such services to an otherwise eligible individual solely because of the diagnosis, type of illness, or condition. Appropriate limits may be placed on services based on such criteria as medical necessity or those contained in utilization or medical review procedures.

We find that a state plan absolutely excluding the only available treatment known at this stage of the art for a particular condition must be considered an arbitrary denial of benefits based solely on the "diagnosis, type of illness, or condition." *Doe v. Minnesota Department of Public Welfare*, 257 N.W.2d 816 (Minn. 1977); *see White v. Beal*, 555 F.2d 1146 (3d Cir. 1977). *Cf. G.B. v. Lackner*, 145 Cal. Rptr. 555 (1978) (classification of sex reassignment surgery as cosmetic is arbitrary).

Furthermore, Iowa's policy is not consistent with the objectives of the Medicaid statute. Without any formal rulemaking proceedings or hearings, the Iowa Department of Social Services established an irrebuttable presumption that the procedure of sex reassignment surgery can never be medically necessary when the surgery is a treatment for transsexualism and removes healthy, undamaged organs and tissue. This approach reflects inadequate solicitude for the applicant's diagnosed condition, the treatment prescribed by the applicant's physicians, and the accumulated knowledge of the medical community. The Supreme Court has emphasized the importance of a professional medical judgment in this context. *See Beal v. Doe*, 432 U.S. 438 (1977). The legislative history also supports the conclusion that Congress intended medical judgments to play a primary role in the determination of medical necessity.[2] S. Rep. No. 404, 89th Cong., 1st Sess., reprinted in (1965) U.S. Code Cong. & Admin. News, p. 1943, 1986–89. . . . .

---

2. Senate Report No. 404, 89th Congress, 1st session, U.S. Code Cong. & Admin. News 1965, p. 1986, states in part:

The decision of whether or not certain treatment or a particular type of surgery is "medically necessary" rests with the individual recipient's physician and not with clerical personnel or government officials. And, as stated in *White v. Beal*, "The regulations permit discrimination in benefits based upon the degree of medical necessity but not upon the medical disorders from which the person suffers." Here Pinneke proved a real need for the only medical service available to alleviate her condition, and the record indicates her condition has improved since the surgery.

Appellants lastly argue that transsexual surgery is excluded by the language of 42 U.S.C. § 1396d(a), providing two exclusions for mental diseases. The clear language of these exclusions, however, strictly limits them to situations involving payment for "services in an institution for tuberculosis or mental disease." Appellants' only attempt to fit within these exclusions is the suggestion that Pinneke's medical condition requiring surgery was a mental disease. The statutory limitations, however, do not apply to mental health problems in general. Pinneke's transsexual surgery thus comes within the medical assistance categories of "inpatient hospital services" and "physicians' services furnished by a physician," and must be covered under the state's Medicaid plan unless not medically necessary.

The decision of the District Court is affirmed.

————————

Discussion

1. *Pinneke v. Preisser* was decided the same year as *Rush v. Parham*, 625 F.2d 1150 (5th Cir. 1980), *supra* at p. 635. What factors might account for the Fifth Circuit and Eighth Circuit Court of Appeals panels' seemingly different attitudes concerning whether or not gender confirmation surgeries are medically necessary?

2. As noted in the Discussion after *Rush*, the American Medical Association and the World Professional Association for Transgender Health both recognize that transition-related surgeries are not "experimental" but are indeed medically necessary as part of the treatment for gender dysphoria of those trans persons for whom it is prescribed. One might have expected after *Pinneke* that transgender people under the care of competent medical professionals should not have experienced difficulties securing Medicaid coverage of their surgeries at least within the Eighth Circuit. But consider the following decision two decades later.

————————

3(a) Conditions and limitations on payment for services.

(1) Physicians' role

The committee's bill provides that the physician is to be the key figure in determining utilization of health services and provides that it is a physician who is to decide upon admission to a hospital, order tests, drugs and treatments, and determine the length of stay. For this reason the bill would require that payment could be made only if a physician certifies to the medical necessity of the services furnished. * * *

Reading Guide for Smith v. Rasmussen

1. Why did Iowa deny Medicaid coverage to transgender man John Smith for phalloplasty? What kind of input went into Iowa's mid-1990s rulemaking that ended in a revision to its rule regarding the kinds of gender dysphoria treatments that were covered by its Medicaid program? How does the regulation characterize gender confirmation surgeries?

2. What considerations lead the court to conclude that Iowa's new regulation was reasonable and consistent with the federal Medicaid statute? Why does the court reject Smith's argument that the regulation violates a provision in the Medicaid act banning arbitrary denials of coverage based on diagnosis, type of illness, or condition?

John Smith v. Jessie K. Rasmussen, in her Official Capacity as Director of the Iowa Department of Human Services

249 F.3d 755 (8th Cir. 2001)

BEFORE: WOLLMAN, Chief Judge, BEAM, Circuit Judge, and PANNER,[1] District Judge.

Opinion

WOLLMAN, Chief Judge.

The Iowa Department of Human Services (the Department or State) appeals from the district court's judgment that the Department violated the mandates of Title XIX of the Social Security Act, 42 U.S.C. § 1396 et seq. (1992 & Supp. 2000) (Medicaid Act or Act), when it refused to fund surgery for the plaintiff, John Smith (pseudonym). We reverse.

I

Smith, now 41 years old, was born with the physiology of a female. He[2] suffers from the psychiatric condition "gender identity disorder," which, when severe, equates with what is popularly known as transsexualism. Dr. Sharon Satterfield, Smith's primary treating psychiatrist and a specialist in gender identity disorder, has determined that sex reassignment surgery (essentially a transition from female to male physical features) is the necessary treatment for Smith. This transformation involves several different surgical procedures, hormonal treatment, and psychological counseling. Smith has already undergone the surgery for breast reduction and contouring. At this stage, Smith seeks payment from the Department for the final surgical procedure, which is a phalloplasty, the creation of a body part that simulates a penis. The Department's administrator of the division of medical services, Donald Herman, testified at trial that the State's Medicaid program covers

---

1. The Honorable Owen M. Panner, United States District Judge for the District of Oregon, sitting by designation.

2. As did the parties during the proceedings in the district court, we will refer to Smith, in accordance with his preference, by using masculine pronouns.

psychotherapy and medication prescribed for psychiatric conditions such as gender identity disorder, but that surgical procedures are not covered. The Department has funded procedures for Smith, such as a hysterectomy, that were medically necessary for diagnosed conditions other than his gender identity disorder.

Medicaid is a federal-state program through which the federal government provides funds for the provision of health care services to needy individuals through the participation of the states, which act as administrators of the funds. 42 U.S.C. § 1396; *Arkansas Med. Soc'y, Inc. v. Reynolds*, 6 F.3d 519 (8th Cir. 1993). States are not required to participate in the Medicaid program, but if they do they must comply with the requirements of the Medicaid Act and its regulations. *Reynolds*. . . .

The Medicaid Act defines "medical assistance" as "payment of part or all of the cost of [enumerated] care and services. . . ." 42 U.S.C. § 1396d(a). As a general matter, a state may choose which enumerated services to provide, but some services are mandated for most categories of needy persons who receive services under the plan. 42 U.S.C. §§ 1396a(a)(10)(A), 1396d(a); 42 C.F.R. § 440.220. As the Seventh Circuit has stated, under the Medicaid Act "[there are essentially] three categories of potential recipients — the 'categorically needy,' the 'medically needy,' and those whose need is determined in relation to the poverty level." *Addis v. Whitburn*, 153 F.3d 836 (7th Cir. 1998). A state plan must provide for medical assistance to the categorically needy, but the state may choose whether to provide services to those persons within the classification of medically needy, who "do not qualify for some forms of federal assistance but who nonetheless lack the resources to obtain adequate medical care." *Hodgson v. Board of County Comm'rs, County of Hennepin*, 614 F.2d 601 (8th Cir. 1980). . . . .

Smith is within a covered "medically needy" classification of Medicaid recipients, but the Department refused payment for a phalloplasty because the procedure is excluded by a state regulation that prohibits funding for plastic surgery for certain purposes and which specifically excludes sex reassignment surgery. On May 19, 1997, Smith brought suit under 42 U.S.C. § 1983, alleging that the Medicaid Act provides an enforceable federal right to "reasonable standards" for the determination of the extent and scope of services that a state will provide and contending that the regulation that excludes funding for surgery for gender identity disorder is unreasonable and thus violates his right under the Act.

The Department does not dispute that Smith is eligible for coverage under the medically needy classification of Medicaid or that he is ready for the phalloplasty. The Department contends that Smith does not have an enforceable right under section 1983, that the district court erred in an evidentiary ruling that limited the testimony of its expert witness, and that the district court erred when it concluded that the application of the regulation violated Smith's right. Assuming for the purposes of this case that Smith has an enforceable federal right, we reverse the district court's judgment because the Department's regulation does not violate that right.

. . . .

III

Turning to the merits, we have held that "[t]he Medicaid statute and regulatory scheme create a presumption in favor of the medical judgment of the attending physician in determining the medical necessity of treatment." *Weaver v. Reagen*, 886 F.2d 194 (8th Cir. 1989); *see Pinneke v. Preisser*, 623 F.2d 546 (8th Cir. 1980). At the same time, "Medicaid was . . . designed . . . to provide the largest number of necessary medical services to the greatest number of needy people." *Ellis v. Patterson*, 859 F.2d 52 (8th Cir. 1988). The Act "confers broad discretion on the States to adopt standards for determining the extent of medical assistance, requiring only that such standards be 'reasonable' and 'consistent with the objectives' of the Act." *Beal v. Doe*, 432 U.S. 438 (1977). A state must "specify the amount, duration, and scope of each service" that it provides and "may place appropriate limits on a service based on such criteria as medical necessity or on utilization control procedures." 42 C.F.R. §440.230. A provided service, however, must "be sufficient in amount, duration, and scope to reasonably achieve its purpose." *Id.* The Act and its regulations both protect and limit the states' discretion. . . .

As a preliminary matter, the Department argues that an enforceable right to reasonable standards would not require the State to use a standard of medical necessity in making funding determinations, as Smith argues. At oral argument, however, the Department's counsel admitted that the State had not changed its service coverage determination standards since our *Pinneke* decision, in which we concluded that "medical necessity" was implicitly the State's determinative standard. The Department has articulated no other standard (such as utilization controls) for the determination of the scope and extent of medical services provided in the program. . . . .

The district court considered itself bound by *Pinneke* and determined that the Department's regulation failed to meet the mandates of Medicaid, finding both procedural and substantive fault in the regulation. The Department argues that the district court erred in invalidating the regulation because both the legal and medical landscapes have changed since *Pinneke*.

In *Pinneke*, the Department's predecessor had developed an exclusionary policy precluding funding for surgeries such as Smith's but had not followed a formal rule-making process, had not consulted medical professionals, and had disregarded the current accumulated knowledge of the medical community. *Pinneke*. We required the State to fund the surgery because the record showed that the procedure was the only medical treatment available to relieve or cure the plaintiff's condition, and thus the denial of funding based on a non-medical presumption, particularly one not promulgated through a proper rulemaking process, was arbitrary. In contrast, here the Department has followed a rulemaking process and has considered the knowledge of the medical community. We thus conclude that *Pinneke* is not outcome-determinative in this case.

The State's current regulation provides: "Cosmetic, reconstructive, or plastic surgery performed in connection with certain conditions is specifically excluded." 441

IOWA ADMIN. CODE r. 78.1(4)(b). Procedures related to gender identity disorder are specifically excluded. 441 IOWA ADMIN. CODE r. 78.1(4)(b)(2). We review the rule-promulgation actions of a state agency administering federal Medicaid funding as we would review non-adjudicatory federal agency action; that is, we decide whether the action is arbitrary, capricious, an abuse of discretion, or otherwise not in accordance with the law. *Weaver.* This is a question of law that we review de novo.

In 1993, the Department contracted with the Iowa Foundation for Medical Care (the Foundation) to provide a review and recommendation regarding the coverage of treatment for disorders like gender identity disorder. . . . Foundation personnel conducted a review of the medical literature and contacted various organizations, including the National Institute for Mental Health and the Harry Benjamin International Gender Dysphoria Association [now, the World Professional Association for Transgender Health—Eds.]. The Foundation reported a lack of consensus on definition, diagnosis, and treatment and referred to post-*Pinneke* research that indicated that hormone treatments, psychotherapy, and situational treatment may be more appropriate, and at times more effective, than sex reassignment surgery. The literature also revealed that the surgery can be appropriate and medically necessary for some people and that the procedure was not considered experimental. The final recommendation for the Department, prepared by a Foundation review committee consisting of physicians of various specialties, was that, given the lack of consensus in the medical community and the availability of other treatment options, the Department should not fund sex reassignment surgery.

Following the receipt of the Foundation's report, the Department commenced a rulemaking process by publishing a notice of intended action that included a mention of fiscal concerns and a lengthy discussion of the medical literature and which solicited public comment.[4] [Iowa surveyed state Medicaid agencies in 1994.] Of the forty-four state agencies that [responded], thirty-six stated that they did not fund [sex reassignment] surgery. . . .[5] The proposed regulation was thereafter considered at a public meeting of the Department's policy-making body and then reviewed by the administrative rules committee of the state legislature. The regulatory exclusion was then adopted. . . . Accordingly, we cannot say that these procedures were problematic, unreasonable, or inadequate.

In the light of the evidence before the Department questioning the efficacy of and the necessity for sex reassignment surgery, given other treatment options, we cannot conclude as a substantive matter that the Department's regulation is unreasonable, arbitrary, or inconsistent with the Act, which is designed to provide "necessary medical services to the greatest number of needy people," *Ellis*, in a reasonable

---

4. The only comment received in response to the notice was that from Smith's current counsel.

5. The Department performed a similar survey in 1998 during this litigation that showed that of the forty-seven states that responded, forty, including Minnesota, now do not provide coverage for sex reassignment surgery.

manner. See *Weaver*; *Beal*. "Medicaid programs do not guarantee that each recipient will receive that level of health care precisely tailored to his or her particular needs," as long as the care and services that the states provide "are provided in the best interests of the recipients." *Alexander v. Choate*, 469 U.S. 287 (1985). As described above, the Department's research demonstrated the evolving nature of the diagnosis and treatment of gender identity disorder and the disagreement regarding the efficacy of sex reassignment surgery. . . . Although Dr. Satterfield's testimony generally supports the conclusion that sex reassignment surgery may be medically necessary in some cases, it is not as unequivocal an endorsement of the surgery as Smith argues. Indeed, Dr. Satterfield's testimony noted that the efficacy of the surgery has been questioned within the medical community. Accordingly, we conclude that the State's prohibition on funding of sex reassignment surgery is both reasonable and consistent with the Medicaid Act.

Finally, we briefly consider 42 C.F.R. § 440.230(c), cited by the district court, which prohibits an arbitrary denial of coverage based on diagnosis, type of illness, or condition. Smith cites the regulation broadly, but we note that, by its own terms, it applies solely to 42 C.F.R. §§ 440.210 and 440.220, which list required services for the classifications of categorically needy and medically needy, respectively. The Department points out that the categories of required services for medically needy persons do not include those that would be required for sex reassignment surgery, *see* 42 C.F.R. § 440.220, and Smith has not attempted to persuade us otherwise. We conclude, therefore, that the State regulation does not conflict with the contours of section 440.230(c). . . .

The Department's rulemaking process has resulted in a reasonable regulation that overcomes the presumption in favor of the determination of Smith's treating psychiatrist. *See Weaver*. Accordingly, the judgment is reversed, and the case is remanded with directions to dismiss the complaint.

Discussion

1. If, as the court concedes, "sex reassignment surgery may be medically necessary in some cases," why is it reasonable to categorically deem such surgery cosmetic and deny coverage even for transgender people for whom it is medically necessary?

2. How much medical disagreement about the efficacy of any given treatment for gender dysphoria would suffice under the reasoning of *Smith v. Rasmussen* to justify a state's categorical exclusion of that treatment from its Medicaid program? *Cf. Gonzales v. Carhart*, 550 U.S. 124, 162 (2007) (upholding federal ban on certain abortion procedures even without a health exception, required of abortion regulations by prior Supreme Court precedent, because there was "documented medical disagreement whether the Act's prohibition would ever impose significant health risks on women").

Reading Guide for Good v. Iowa Department of Human Services

1. What reason did the managed care organizations give for dismissing the applications of transgender women EerieAnna Good and Carol Beal for Medicaid to pay for their gender-affirming surgeries?

2. What are the Iowa Department of Human Services' (DHS) statutory arguments for why it should not be considered a public accommodation covered by the Iowa Civil Rights Act (ICRA)? What are the several reasons given by the Iowa Supreme Court for rejecting DHS's contention?

3. What is DHS's argument that its regulation denying Medicaid coverage for gender-affirming surgical procedures, Iowa Admin. Code r. 441-78.1(4), does not discriminate on the basis of gender identity? What reasons does the court offer for rejecting DHS's argument?

4. How does the court explain its decision not to address whether the challenged regulation violates the equal protection clause of the Iowa state constitution?

Eerieanna Good and Carol Beal v. Iowa Department of Human Services

924 N.W.2d 853 (Iowa 2019)

[The challengers to Iowa's regulation were represented by the ACLU of Iowa, the national ACLU LGBT & HIV Project, and private counsel. They were supported by amici Iowa Scholars of Law, History, Bioethics, Gender, and Sexuality; medical associations including the American Medical Association; Iowan LGBT organizations; LGBT organizations including Lambda Legal, National Center for Transgender Equality, Transcend Legal, and the Transgender Legal Defense and Education Fund; health and civil rights organizations; and the left-leaning social justice organization the Impact Fund, National Women's Law Center, and 25 legal and advocacy organizations including GLBTQ Advocates and Defenders and the National Center for Lesbian Rights.]

Opinion

CHRISTENSEN, Justice.

In 2007, the Iowa legislature amended Iowa Code chapter 216—the Iowa Civil Rights Act (ICRA)—to add "gender identity" to the list of protected characteristics. *See* 2007 IOWA ACTS ch. 191, §§ 5, 6 (codified at IOWA CODE § 216.7(1)(a) (2009)). We must now determine whether the language of Iowa Administrative Code rule 441-78.1(4) pertaining to the prohibition of Iowa Medicaid coverage of surgical procedures related to "gender identity disorders" violates the ICRA or the Iowa Constitution. The appellees are transgender women and Iowa Medicaid recipients who sought Medicaid coverage for gender-affirming surgical procedures to treat their gender dysphoria. The appellees' managed care organizations (MCOs) denied coverage for their surgeries pursuant to rule 441-78.1(4). An administrative law judge

(ALJ) and the director of the Iowa Department of Human Services (DHS) affirmed the MCOs' decisions based on rule 441-78.1's exclusion of coverage for gender-affirming procedures.

After exhausting intra-agency appeals, the appellees sought judicial review. The district court consolidated their cases and concluded the challenged portions of rule 441-78.1(4) violate the ICRA and the equal protection clause of the Iowa Constitution. The district court also determined the DHS's denial of Medicaid coverage for gender-affirming surgeries was reversible because it would result in a disproportionate negative impact on private rights and the decision was unreasonable, arbitrary, and capricious. We retained the DHS's appeal. On our review, we affirm the judgment of the district court because the rule violates the ICRA's prohibition against gender-identity discrimination. Because of this, we adhere to the doctrine of constitutional avoidance and do not address the constitutional claim.

I. Background Facts and Proceedings.

EerieAnna Good and Carol Beal are transgender women who have gender dysphoria. . . . At their administrative hearings, Good and Beal each entered into the record an affidavit in support of their appeal from Dr. Randi Ettner, Ph.D., a specialist and international expert in the field of gender dysphoria. Dr. Ettner concluded that the findings of the Iowa Foundation Report, the DHS Rulemaking Notice, and the DHS Rule Adoption Notice used to justify rule 441-78.1(4) "are not reasonably supported by scientific or clinical evidence, or standards of professional practice, and fail to take into account the robust body of research that surgery relieves or eliminates Gender Dysphoria." She explained, "Without treatment, gender dysphoric individuals experience anxiety, depression, suicidality, and other attendant mental health issues." Dr. Ettner described the accepted standards of medical care to alleviate gender dysphoria, which involve the following options: socially transitioning to live consistently with one's gender identity, counseling, hormone therapy, and gender-affirming surgery to conform one's sex characteristics to one's gender identity. The State presented no evidence to the contrary.

According to Dr. Ettner, "[o]f those individuals who seek treatment for [g]ender [d]ysphoria, only a subset requires surgical intervention." Good and Beal are among the subset of individuals seeking treatment for gender dysphoria whose physicians have concluded that gender-affirming surgery is necessary to treat their gender dysphoria.

Good is a twenty-nine-year-old transgender woman and Medicaid recipient who was officially diagnosed with gender dysphoria in 2013, though she began presenting herself as a female fulltime in 2010. Good began hormone therapy in 2014 and legally changed her name, birth certificate, driver's license, and social security card to align with her gender identity in 2016. Good's gender dysphoria intensifies her depression and anxiety. After her healthcare providers determined that surgery was medically necessary to treat her gender dysphoria, Good initiated the process to seek Medicaid coverage of her gender-affirming orchiectomy procedure from her MCO, AmeriHealth Caritas Iowa (AmeriHealth), in January 2017.

Beal is a forty-three-year-old transgender woman and Medicaid recipient who was officially diagnosed with gender dysphoria in 1989. Beal began presenting herself as a female fulltime at the age of ten and began hormone therapy in 1989. She legally changed her name, birth certificate, driver's license, and Social Security card to align with her gender identity in 2014. Beal experiences depression and anxiety due to her gender dysphoria. Beal's healthcare providers have concluded gender-affirming surgery is medically necessary to treat her gender dysphoria. She began seeking Medicaid coverage for a gender-affirming vaginoplasty, penectomy, bilateral orchiectomy, clitoroplasty, urethroplasty, labiaplasty, and preineoplasty from her MCO, Amerigroup of Iowa Inc. (Amerigroup), in June 2017.

Medicaid is a joint federal-state program established under Title XIX of the Social Security Act that helps states provide medical assistance to eligible low-income individuals. The Iowa DHS manages Iowa's Medicaid program consistent with state and federal requirements through a managed care model that requires Medicaid recipients' enrollment in an MCO. The MCO is required to "provide, at a minimum, all benefits and services deemed *medically necessary* that are covered under the contract with the agency" in accordance with the DHS's standards. Iowa Admin. Code r. 441-73.6(1) (emphasis added).

Iowa Medicaid generally provides coverage for medically necessary services and supplies provided by physicians subject to a few exclusions and limitations.

> For the purposes of this program, cosmetic, reconstructive, or plastic surgery is surgery which can be expected primarily to improve physical appearance or which is performed primarily for psychological purposes or which restores form but which does not materially correct or materially improve the bodily functions. When a surgical procedure primarily restores bodily function, whether or not there is also a concomitant improvement in physical appearance, the surgical procedure does not fall within the provisions set forth in this subrule. Surgeries for the purpose of sex reassignment are not considered as restoring bodily function and are excluded from coverage.
>
> . . . .
>
> b. Cosmetic, reconstructive, or plastic surgery performed in connection with certain conditions is specifically excluded. These conditions are:
>
> . . . .
>
> (2) Procedures related to transsexualism, hermaphroditism, *gender identity disorders*, or body dysmorphic disorders.
>
> (3) Cosmetic, reconstructive, or plastic surgery procedures performed primarily for psychological reasons or as a result of the aging process.
>
> (4) Breast augmentation mammoplasty, surgical insertion of prosthetic testicles, penile implant procedures, and surgeries for the purpose of sex reassignment.
>
> . . . .

d. Following is a partial list of cosmetic, reconstructive, or plastic surgery procedures which are not covered under the program. This list is for example purposes only and is not considered all-inclusive.

. . . .

(2) Cosmetic, reconstructive, or plastic surgical procedures which are justified primarily on the basis of a psychological or psychiatric need.

. . . .

(15) Sex reassignment.

Iowa Admin. Code r. 441-78.1(4)(b)(2)-(4), (d)(2), (15) (emphasis added).

. . . . AmeriHealth denied Good's request based on the rule excluding any surgical procedure for the purpose of sex reassignment. . . .

Good filed a petition for judicial review in district court . . . , arguing Iowa Administrative Code rule 441-78.1(4) violates the ICRA's prohibitions against sex and gender identity discrimination and the equal protection clause of the Iowa Constitution. . . . The DHS filed a preanswer motion to dismiss for failure to state a claim upon which relief can be granted, which the district court denied. . . .

Beal filed her request for Medicaid preapproval from Amerigroup to cover the expenses of her gender-affirming surgical procedures. . . . Amerigroup denied Beal's request based on the rule excluding surgical procedures for the purpose of sex reassignment. Beal initiated an internal appeal, which Amerigroup also denied. . . .

Beal filed a petition for judicial review in district court . . . presenting the same arguments as Good. The DHS also filed a motion to dismiss on Beal's case. . . . The district court denied this motion and consolidated Good's case with Beal's. . . .

[The] district court reversed the DHS's decision to deny Good and Beal Medicaid coverage for their gender-affirming surgical procedures. The district court concluded the DHS is a public accommodation under the ICRA, and rule 441-78.1(4), which denies coverage for gender-affirming surgeries, violates the ICRA's prohibition on gender-identity discrimination. However, the district court rejected appellees' claim that the rule also violates the ICRA's prohibition on sex discrimination, relying on our holding in *Sommers v. Iowa Civil Rights Commission*, which held that sex discrimination under the ICRA does not include "transsexuals." 337 N.W.2d 470, 474 (Iowa 1983). [*See* Chapter 14, *infra*, at p. 963 for a note on Sommers's disability discrimination suit.—Eds.] The district court also concluded rule 441-78.1(4) violates the equal protection clause of the Iowa Constitution. . . . The DHS appealed the district court ruling, and we retained the appeal.

II. Standard of Review.

. . . . It is proper for a district court to grant relief "if the agency action prejudiced the substantial rights of the petitioner and if the agency action falls within one of the criteria listed in [Iowa Code] section 17A.19(10)(a) through (n)." *Brewer-Strong v. HNI Corp.*, 913 N.W.2d 235 (Iowa 2018). . . . "We affirm the district court decision when we reach the same conclusion." *Id.* [We] review the DHS's interpretation of the law de novo. *See Bearinger v. Iowa Dep't of Transp.*, 844 N.W.2d 104 (Iowa 2014).

III. Analysis.

The DHS raises several challenges to the district court's ruling on appeal. . . .

A. Public Accommodations Under the ICRA.

Iowa Code section 216.7 addresses "[u]nfair practices — accommodations or services." In relevant part, this section provides,

> It shall be an unfair or discriminatory practice for any . . . manager . . . of any public accommodation or any agent or employee thereof . . . [t]o refuse or deny any person because of . . . sex . . . [or] gender identity . . . in the furnishing of such accommodations, advantages, facilities, services, or privileges.

Iowa Code § 216.7(1)(a). Iowa Code section 216.2(13)(b) states that a public accommodation "includes each state and local government unit or tax-supported district of whatever kind, nature, or class that offers services, facilities, benefits, grants, or goods to the public, gratuitously or otherwise." *Id.* § 216.2(13)(b). The DHS challenges the district court's conclusion that it is a "public accommodation." It asserts that the term is limited to physical places, establishments, or facilities.

The ICRA does not define "government unit." . . . . Here, our prior decisions, dictionary definitions, and the title of the statute prohibiting public accommodations from certain types of discrimination under the ICRA all support our conclusion that the DHS is a "government unit" within the ICRA's definition of a "public accommodation."

Our prior cases discussing a "government unit" are limited, but our past use of the term supports our interpretation that public accommodations are not limited to a physical place, establishment, or facility. For example, in *Warford v. Des Moines Metropolitan Transit Authority*, we noted Iowa's statute governing tort liability of governmental subdivisions "anticipates that a 'municipality' will be some unit of local government." 381 N.W.2d 622 (Iowa 1986). Further, the dictionary definitions of "unit" reinforce our holding that the DHS is a "government unit" within the ICRA's definition of a "public accommodation" when it issues benefits determinations concerning Medicaid. Though the dictionary has multiple definitions for the word "unit," the most applicable definition of "unit" defines it as "a single thing or person or group that is a constituent and isolable member of some more inclusive whole." Unit, Webster's Third New International Dictionary (unabr. ed. 2002). This definition aligns with the Black's Law Dictionary definition of "governmental unit" as "[a] subdivision, *agency*, department . . . or other unity of government of a country or state" because the DHS is a government agency. Governmental Unit, Black's Law Dictionary (10th ed. 2014) (emphasis added).

Additionally, Iowa Code section 216.2(13)(b) makes clear that a "public accommodation" includes a unit of state government that offers "benefits [or] grants . . . to the public." Medicaid is such a benefit or grant. Government benefits and grants are not normally dispersed in person at physical locations. This further undermines the DHS's limited view of what constitutes a public accommodation under the ICRA.

The title of the statute Good and Beal rest their ICRA claims on—"Unfair practices—accommodations or services"—also informs our determination that the legislature intended to include the DHS as a "public accommodation" under the ICRA. *See* Iowa Code § 216.7. The title of this section and its definition of a "public accommodation" reveal the legislature intended to include government agencies in its prohibition on discriminatory practices based on gender identity "in the furnishing of [an agency's] accommodations, advantages, facilities, services, or privileges." *See id.* § 216.7(1)(a). The DHS is an agency that furnishes Medicaid services through its implementation and oversight of the Iowa Medicaid services that MCOs provide. Therefore, it is a public accommodation under the ICRA.

Finally, while the ICRA does define "covered multifamily" as "[a] building consisting of four or more dwelling *units* if the building has one or more elevators" or "the ground floor *units* of a building consisting of four or more dwelling *units*," this usage of "unit" does not conflict with our interpretation of it in section 216.7 as the DHS claims. Iowa Code § 216.2(4) (emphasis added). The use of the term "unit" to describe a "covered multifamily dwelling" is vastly different from the use of "government unit" within the definition of "public accommodation" given the context in which both terms are used. Thus, the legislature's references to the word "unit" to describe a structure does not inform or limit our definition of "government unit." For these reasons, we affirm the district court's ruling that he DHS is a public accommodation under the ICRA.

B. The ICRA's Prohibition on Gender Discrimination.

The DHS maintains rule 441-78.1(4) does not discriminate based on gender identity because transgender Medicaid beneficiaries and nontransgender Medicaid beneficiaries in Iowa alike are not entitled to gender-affirming surgical procedures. This position is based on the DHS's argument that the requested surgical procedures are performed primarily for psychological purposes. Further, the DHS claims the rule's explicit exclusion of gender-affirming surgeries and cosmetic surgery related to "transsexualism" is merely a specified example within the broader category of "cosmetic, reconstructive, and plastic surgeries" excluded from coverage under the rule.

In 2007, the Iowa legislature amended the ICRA to add "gender identity" to the list of protected groups. *See* 2007 Iowa Acts ch. 191, §§ 5, 6 (codified at Iowa Code § 216.7(1)(a) (2009)). Section 216.7(1)(a) provides that it is "unfair or discriminatory" for any "agent or employee" of a "public accommodation" to deny services based on "gender identity." Iowa Code § 216.7(1)(a). The ICRA's gender identity classification encompasses transgender individuals—especially those who have gender dysphoria—because discrimination against these individuals is based on the nonconformity between their gender identity and biological sex. This prohibition against denying coverage for Good's and Beal's gender-affirming surgical procedures extends to the director and staff of the DHS, as well as its agents, the MCOs.

The record does not support the DHS's position that rule 441-78.1(4) is nondiscriminatory because its exclusion of coverage for gender-affirming surgical procedures encompasses the broader category of "cosmetic, reconstructive, or plastic surgery" that is "performed primarily for psychological purposes." Iowa Admin. Code r. 441-78.1(4). The DHS expressly denied Good and Beal coverage for their surgical procedures because they were "related to transsexualism . . . [or] gender identity disorders" and "for the purpose of sex reassignment." Moreover, the rule authorizes payment for some cosmetic, reconstructive, and plastic surgeries that serve psychological purposes—*e.g.,* "[r]evision of disfiguring and extensive scars resulting from neoplastic surgery" and "[c]orrection of a congenital anomaly." *Id.* r. 441-78.1(4)(a). Yet, it prohibits coverage for this same procedure if [*sic*—if for?— Eds.] a transgender individual. *Id.* r. 441-78.1(4)(b).

Further, the history behind the rule supports our holding that the rule's express bar on Medicaid coverage for gender-affirming surgical procedures discriminates against transgender Medicaid recipients in Iowa under the ICRA. Nearly forty years ago, the United States Court of Appeals for the Eighth Circuit ruled in *Pinneke v. Preisser* that it was improper for the Iowa DHS to informally characterize sex reassignment surgery as "cosmetic surgery" in its denial of sex reassignment surgery. 623 F.2d 546, 548 n.2 (8th Cir. 1980). Prior to *Pinneke,* the DHS had an unwritten policy of excluding sex reassignment surgeries from Medicaid coverage based on Medicaid's coverage limitations on "cosmetic surgery" and "mental diseases." *Id.* at 548 n.2, 549–50. After the Eighth Circuit rejected this informal policy, the DHS amended the rule to clarify that the rule excluded Medicaid coverage for "sex reassignment procedures" and "gender identity disorders." 17 Iowa Admin. Bull. 730–34 (Nov. 9, 1994) (effective Feb. 1, 1995); *see also Smith v. Rasmussen,* 249 F.3d 755, 760 (8th Cir. 2001). Consequently, the rule expressly excludes Iowa Medicaid coverage for gender-affirming surgery specifically because this surgery treats gender dysphoria of transgender individuals. After the DHS amended the rule to bar Medicaid coverage for gender-affirming surgery, the legislature specifically made it clear that individuals cannot be discriminated against on the basis of gender identity under the ICRA. *See* 2007 Iowa Acts ch. 191, §§ 5, 6 (codified at Iowa Code § 216.7(1)(a) (2009)).

C. Doctrine of Constitutional Avoidance.

Given our holding that rule 441-78.1(4)'s exclusion of Medicaid coverage for gender-affirming surgery violates the ICRA as amended by the legislature in 2007, we need not address the other issues raised on appeal. In doing so, we adhere to the time-honored doctrine of constitutional avoidance. This doctrine "instructs us that we should 'steer clear of "constitutional shoals" when possible.'" *Nguyen v. State,* 878 N.W.2d 744 (Iowa 2016) (quoting *State v. Iowa Dist. Ct.,* 843 N.W.2d 76 at 85). "Such judicial restraint is an essential component of our system of federalism and separation of powers." *State v. Williams,* 695 N.W.2d 23 (Iowa 2005). The doctrine of constitutional avoidance recognizes the wisdom of this process, "and we continue to subscribe to it today." *Id.*

IV. Conclusion.

For the aforementioned reasons, we affirm the district court judgment.

AFFIRMED.

All justices concur except McDonald, J., who takes no part.

————

Discussion

1. Although the Midwest might not at first blush seem the most hospitable region in the country for LGBT people, the jurisprudence of the Iowa Supreme Court has nonetheless been progressive. Presumably in part for that reason, one of the earlier, successful marriage equality lawsuits was filed in Iowa state court, culminating in a unanimous win for the plaintiffs in *Varnum v. Brien*, 763 N.W.2d 862 (Iowa 2009). That said, following a campaign that targeted Iowa Supreme Court justices who ruled in favor of marriage equality, the Iowa electorate voted to remove all three (of the marriage equality majority of four) who faced their periodic judicial retention elections in November 2010. *See, e.g.,* Grant Schulte, *Iowans dismiss three justices,* DES MOINES REGISTER, Nov. 3, 2010.

2. With what sense or kind of equality might the *Good* court be operating in rejecting DHS's argument that rule 441-78.1(4) does not discriminate on the basis of gender identity because it denies gender-affirming surgical procedures to everyone, whether or not they are transgender (*i.e.,* whether or not a person's gender identity matches their natally assigned sex) and regardless of anyone's gender identity? If only transgender people (albeit only *some* transgender people) have gender dysphoria, is a ban on covering a specific treatment for gender dysphoria discriminating against transgender people? Consider in this regard the highly criticized U.S. Supreme Court decision in *Geduldig v. Aiello*, 417 U.S. 484 (1974), wherein a majority of the Court reasoned that a California law excluding coverage of certain disabilities resulting from pregnancy from the scope of the state's disability insurance system did not discriminate on the basis of sex in part because "[t]he program divides potential recipients into two groups — pregnant women and nonpregnant persons. While the first group is exclusively female, the second includes members of both sexes. The fiscal and actuarial benefits of the program thus accrue to members of both sexes." Should we similarly think that the benefits of Iowa's Medicaid program accrued to people of all gender identities, and in particular to both transgender and cisgender people, and should that suffice for constitutionality?

————

Although the cases in this section are primarily about Medicaid, the joint federal-state program to help ensure health care for low-income people, since 1989 Medicare, the national health insurance program primarily covering people at least 65 years of age, had categorically ruled gender confirmation surgery to be a non-covered practice, *i.e.*, one for which Medicare funds are unavailable, pursuant to National Coverage Determination 140.3 ("NCD 140.3"). NCD 140.3 was predicated upon the conclusions of a 1981 report from the National Center for Healthcare Technology. The NCD was challenged by a septuagenarian Army veteran, Denee Mallon, whose requested gender confirmation surgery coverage was denied by Medicare on the authority of NCD 140.3. She appealed and, under the Obama administration, prevailed before the Department of Health and Human Services Departmental Appeals Board in late 2014. *See* Jessica McLaughlin, *Sexual Reassignment Surgery: The Path to Medicare Coverage*, LawStreet (Apr. 18, 2015), https://www.lawstreetmedia.com /issues/health-science/sexual-reassignment-surgery-effects-medicares-lifted-ban/ (last visited Sept. 27, 2019).

Department of Health and Human Services, Departmental Appeals Board
NCD 140.3, Transsexual Surgery
Docket No. A-13-87, Decision No. 2576 (May 30, 2014)

Decision

The Board has determined that the National Coverage Determination (NCD) denying Medicare coverage of all transsexual surgery as a treatment for transsexualism is not valid under the "reasonableness standard" the Board applies. The NCD was based on information compiled in 1981. The record developed before the Board in response to a complaint filed by the aggrieved party (AP), a Medicare beneficiary denied coverage, shows that even assuming the NCD's exclusion of coverage at the time the NCD was adopted was reasonable, that coverage exclusion is no longer reasonable. This record includes expert medical testimony and studies published in the years after publication of the NCD. The Centers for Medicare & Medicaid Services (CMS), which is responsible for issuing and revising NCDs, did not defend the NCD or the NCD record in this proceeding and did not challenge any of the new evidence submitted to the Board.

Effect of this decision

Since the NCD is no longer valid, its provisions are no longer a valid basis for denying claims for Medicare coverage of transsexual surgery, and local coverage determinations (LCDs) used to adjudicate such claims may not rely on the provisions of the NCD. The decision does not bar CMS or its contractors from denying individual claims for payment for transsexual surgery for other reasons permitted by law. Nor does the decision address treatments for transsexualism other than transsexual surgery. The decision does not require CMS to revise the NCD or issue a new NCD, although CMS, of course, may choose to do so. CMS may not reinstate the invalidated NCD unless it has a different basis than that evaluated by the Board. 42 C.F.R. § 426.563.

CMS must implement this Board decision within 30 days and apply any resulting policy changes to claims or service requests made by Medicare beneficiaries other than the AP for any dates of service after that implementation. With respect to the AP's claim in particular, CMS and its contractors must "adjudicate the claim without using the provision(s) of the NCD that the Board found invalid." 42 C.F.R. § 426.560(b)(1).

Legal background

With exceptions not relevant here, section 1862(a)(l)(A) of the Social Security Act (Act) (42 U.S.C. § 1395y(a)(l)(A)) bars Medicare payment for items or services "not reasonable and necessary for the diagnosis or treatment of illness or injury[.]"[2] CMS refers to this requirement as the "medical necessity provision." 67 Fed. Reg. 54,534, 54,536 (Aug. 22, 2002). . . . When CMS issues NCDs, they apply nationally and are binding at all levels of administrative review of Medicare claims. CMS and its contractors use applicable NCDs in determining whether a beneficiary may receive Medicare reimbursement for a particular item or service.

. . . .

Prior to issuing a decision, the Board must review any "new evidence" admitted to the record before the Board and determine whether it "has the potential to significantly affect" the Board's evaluation. 42 C.F.R. §§ 426.340(a), (b), 426.505(d)(3). "New evidence" is defined as "clinical or scientific evidence that was not previously considered by . . . CMS before the . . . NCD was issued." 42 C.F.R. § 426.110. If the Board so concludes, the Board stays proceedings for CMS "to examine the new evidence, and to decide whether [to] initiate[] . . . a reconsideration" of the NCD. 42 C.F.R. § 426.340(d). If CMS does not reconsider the NCD, or reconsiders it but does not change the challenged provision, the Board lifts the stay and the NCD challenge process continues. 42 C.F.R. § 426.340(f). At the end of that process, the Board closes the record and issues a decision that the challenged "provision of the NCD is valid" or "is not valid under the reasonableness standard."[4] 42 C.F.R. § 426.550. The Board's decision "constitutes a final agency action and is subject to judicial review" on appeal by an aggrieved party. 42 C.F.R. § 426.566.

Case background
The NCD and the NCD record

The challenged NCD, titled "140.3, Transsexual Surgery," states:[5]

---

2. The table of contents to the current version of the Social Security Act, with references to the corresponding United States Code chapter and sections, can be found at http://www.socialsecurity .gov/OP_Home/ssact/ssact-toc.htm.

4. Section 426.547(b) states that the Board must make the decision available at the HHS Medicare Internet site and that "the posted decision does not include any information that identifies any individual, provider of service, or supplier." CMS has indicated in the preamble to the Part 426 regulations that this provision was meant to protect the privacy of Medicare beneficiaries such as the AP. *See, e.g.,* 68 Fed. Reg. 63,692, 63,708 (Nov. 7, 2003) ("Board decisions regarding NCDs will be made available on the Medicare Internet site, without beneficiary identifying information").

5. NCDs are available at http://www.cms.gov/medicare-coverage-database/overview-and -quick- search.aspx?list_type=ncd.

Item/Service Description

Transsexual surgery, also known as sex reassignment surgery or intersex surgery, is the culmination of a series of procedures designed to change the anatomy of transsexuals to conform to their gender identity. Transsexuals are persons with an overwhelming desire to change anatomic sex because of their fixed conviction that they are members of the opposite sex. For the male-to-female, transsexual surgery entails castration, penectomy and vulva-vaginal construction. Surgery for the female-to-male transsexual consists of bilateral mammectomy, hysterectomy and salpingo-oophorectomy, which may be followed by phalloplasty and the insertion of testicular prostheses.

Indications and Limitations of Coverage

Transsexual surgery for sex reassignment of transsexuals is controversial. Because of the lack of well controlled, long-term studies of the safety and effectiveness of the surgical procedures and attendant therapies for transsexualism, the treatment is considered experimental. Moreover, there is a high rate of serious complications for these surgical procedures. For these reasons, transsexual surgery is not covered.

. . . . The NCD quotes or paraphrases portions of an 11-page report that the former National Center for Health Care Technology (NCHCT) of the HHS Public Health Service (PHS) issued in 1981, titled "Evaluation of Transsexual Surgery" (1981 report).[7] The NCHCT forwarded the 1981 report to [CMS's predecessor, the Health Care Financing Administration (HCFA),] with a May 6, 1981 memorandum stating that the 1981 report "concludes that transsexual surgery should be considered experimental because of the lack of proven safety and efficacy of the procedures for the treatment of transsexualism" and recommending "that transsexual surgery not be covered by Medicare at this time."

The NCD record includes three April 1982 letters from the American Civil Liberties Union (ACLU) of Southern California disagreeing with HCFA's noncoverage determination. The ACLU submitted letters and affidavits from physicians and therapists supporting the medical necessity of transsexual surgery and taking issue with the non-coverage determination. On May 11, 1982, the HCFA physicians panel, by a vote of five to two, recommended against referring the ACLU's submissions to PHS, "on the basis that it does not contain information about new clinical studies or other medical and scientific evidence sufficiently substantive to justify reopening

---

7. The concluding summary of the 1981 NCHTC report stated in relevant part:
   Transsexual surgery for sex reassignment of transsexuals is controversial. There is a lack of well controlled, long-term studies of the safety and effectiveness of the surgical procedures and attendant therapies for transsexualism. There is evidence of a high rate of serious complications of these surgical procedures. The safety and effectiveness of transsexual surgery as a treatment of transsexualism is not proven and is questioned. Therefore, transsexual surgery must be considered still experimental.

the previous PHS assessment." Thus, although the NCD was issued in 1989, it was based on the analysis of medical and scientific publications in the 1981 report.

The NCD complaint

The AP in this case, a Medicare beneficiary whose insurer denied a physician's order for sex reassignment surgery (transsexual surgery), filed an acceptable NCD complaint and supporting materials. CMS submitted the NCD record on May 15, 2013, and the AP submitted a statement of why the NCD record is not complete or adequate to support the validity of the NCD under the reasonableness standard (AP Statement) on June 14, 2013. The Board granted unopposed requests by six advocacy organizations to participate as amici curiae in the NCD review by filing written briefs arguing that the NCD was invalid. . . .[8]

The record developed before the Board

The record before the Board consists of the NCD record, the briefs submitted by the AP and the amici and evidence submitted by the AP and [HRC]. Since neither party submitted argument or evidence (except for the [curricula vitae of the AP's witnesses]) after the Board's Ruling, the Board treats the AP statement as the AP's brief in this appeal. The AP submitted written declarations made under penalty of perjury from a clinical psychologist and a physician, and two notarized physician letters submitted to an Administrative Law Judge in the Department of Health and Human Services Office of Medicare Hearings and Appeals in another matter. The AP described the witnesses, who are active in the field of treating transgender persons, as experts and submitted their resumes or CVs.

. . . . In this decision we use the term "new evidence" to refer to the evidence submitted to us by the AP and amici to distinguish it from the evidence used to support the NCD which, as noted, consists principally of the 1981 report. . . .

Standard of review

The Board "evaluate[s] the reasonableness" of an NCD by determining whether it "is valid [or] is not valid under the reasonableness standard," which requires us to uphold the NCD "if the findings of fact, interpretations of law, and applications of fact to law by . . . CMS are reasonable" based on the NCD record and the relevant record developed before us. Act § 1869(f)(1)(A)(iii); 42 C.F.R. §§ 426.110, 426.531(a), 426.550(a). The Board "defer[s] only to the reasonable findings of fact, reasonable interpretations of law, and reasonable applications of fact to law by the Secretary." Act § 1869(f)(1)(A)(iii); 42 C.F.R. § 426.505(b).

. . . . CMS has explained that "[s]o long as the outcome [in the NCD] is one that could be reached by a rational person, based on the evidence in the record as a whole

---

8. The six amici are the Human Rights Campaign (HRC) and the World Professional Association for Transgender Health (WPATH), which each submitted briefs, and the FORGE Transgender Aging Network, the National Center for Transgender Equality, the Sylvia Rivera Law Project, and the Transgender Law Center, which submitted a joint brief.

(including logical inferences drawn from that evidence), the determination must be upheld," and that if CMS "has a logical reason as to why some evidence is given more weight than other evidence," the Board "may not overturn the determination simply because they would have accorded more weight to the evidence in support of coverage." 68 Fed. Reg. at 63,703.

Analysis

The NCD is invalid because a preponderance of the evidence in the record as a whole supports a conclusion that the NCD's stated bases for its blanket denial of coverage for transsexual surgery are not reasonable.

As previously stated, the NCD was based principally on the 1981 report findings that the safety and effectiveness of transsexual surgery had not been proven. The AP argues that these findings are not "supportable by the current state of medical science" and "not reasonable in light of the current state of scientific and clinical evidence and current medical standards of care" and are contradicted by studies conducted in the 32 years since the 1981 report.... [The] new evidence, which is unchallenged, indicates that the bases stated in the NCD and the NCD record for denying coverage, even assuming they were reasonable when the NCD was issued, are no longer reasonable.

A. The fact that the new evidence is unchallenged and the NCD record undefended is significant.

[The] AP has the burden of proof by a preponderance of the evidence that an NCD is invalid under a reasonableness standard. In deciding whether the AP has met this burden, we must weigh the evidence in the record before us.... [The] only evidence before us, other than the record for the NCD, which consists principally of the 1981 report, is the new evidence submitted by the AP and the amicus HRC. CMS submitted the NCD record, as it was required to do, but has not argued that that record or any other evidence supports the NCD.... The preamble to the regulations that implement the NCD statute states that the "reasonableness standard ... recognizes the *expertise of ... CMS in the Medicare program—specifically, in the area of coverage requiring the exercise of clinical or scientific judgment*." 68 Fed. Reg. at 63,703 (emphasis added). Accordingly, in determining whether the NCD is valid under the reasonableness standard, we must accord some deference to CMS's position, and its decision not to defend the NCD or challenge the new evidence in this case has some significance for our decision-making.

Apart from the absence of any challenge to the new evidence or defense of the NCD record, we find the new evidence credible and persuasive on its face. We have no difficulty concluding that the new evidence, which includes medical studies published in the more than 32 years since issuance of the 1981 report underlying the NCD, outweighs the NCD record and demonstrates that transsexual surgery is safe and effective and not experimental. Thus, as we discuss below, the grounds for the NCD's exclusion of coverage are not reasonable, and the NCD is invalid.

B. The new evidence indicates acceptance of criteria for diagnosing transsexualism.

Transsexual surgery is a treatment option for the medical condition of transsexualism. The NCD recognized that transsexualism is a diagnosed medical condition. The 1981 report stated that transsexualism "is defined as an overwhelming desire to change anatomic sex stemming from the fixed conviction that one is a member of the opposite sex." The 1981 report recognized that the American Psychiatric Association's *Diagnostic and Statistical Manual of Mental Disorders* issued in 1980 (DSM-III) had "included for the first time the diagnostic category of 'Transsexualism.'" Nonetheless, the 1981 report expressed concern that diagnosing transsexualism was "problematic" because, the report contended, the criteria for establishing the diagnosis "vary from center to center and have changed over time."

One of the AP's expert witnesses, Randi Ettner, Ph.D., a clinical psychologist, testified that the expressed basis for this concern is "completely untrue now." Dr. Ettner stated that "Gender Identity Disorder is a serious medical condition codified in the *International Classification of Diseases* (10th revision; World Health Organization) and the [DSM]."[13] She described the condition as follows:

> The disorder is characterized by intense and persistent discomfort with one's primary and secondary sex characteristics—one's birth sex. The suffering that arises is often described as "being trapped in the wrong body." The psychiatric term for this severe and unremitting emotional pain is "gender dysphoria."

Dr. Ettner's declaration and CV state that she has a doctorate in psychology, has evaluated or treated between 2,500 and 3,000 individuals with GID and mental health issues related to gender variance, has published three books, including Principles of Transgender Medicine and Surgery, has authored articles in peer-reviewed journals, and is a member of the board of directors of the World Professional Association for Transgender Health (WPATH) and an author of the *WPATH Standards of Care for the Health of Transsexual, Transgender, and Gender-Nonconforming People*.

We find nothing in the new evidence that would undercut Dr. Ettner's statement. The DSM-IV-TR (text revision), published in 2000, continues to recognize "transsexualism" as a diagnosed medical condition, although it refers to the same disorder as GID and identifies criteria for diagnosing GID in adolescents and adults that are consistent with Dr. Ettner's description, albeit more detailed. [Quotations from the criteria omitted.—Eds.] The WPATH brief indicates that transsexualism or GID remains a diagnostic category in the fifth edition of the DSM issued in 2013 (DSM-V), which uses the term "Gender Dysphoria."

---

13. The record indicates that the term "transsexualism" that was used in the NCD and the DSM-III was succeeded in the DSM-IV and DSM-V by the terms "Gender Identity Disorder" (GID) and "gender dysphoria." AP Statement at 1 n.1; Ettner Supp. Decl. at ¶ 6; Hsiao Decl. at ¶ 11; AP Ex. 7, at 208; WPATH Br. at 2 n.3. In this decision, we use the term "transsexualism" because it is used in the NCD, but our decision should be read as encompassing the successor terminology as well.

. . . .

We conclude that to the extent the NCD was based on concerns expressed in the NCD record about problems diagnosing transsexualism, that concern is unreasonable based on the new evidence.

C. The new evidence indicates that transsexual surgery is safe.

The 1981 report stated that transsexual surgery "cannot be considered safe because of the high complication rates." . . . . The AP argues that "advancements in surgical techniques have dramatically reduced the risk of complications from sex reassignment surgery and the rates of serious complications from such surgeries are low" and that the studies cited in the 1981 report "evaluated outdated surgical techniques that have been replaced with improved, safer procedures." The new evidence supports the AP.

Expert witness Katherine Hsiao, M.D., testified that hysterectomies and mastectomies are common procedures used to treat gender GID in transgender men (FM) and "are routinely performed in other contexts, such as in cases of breast cancer, ovarian cancer, uterine cancer and/or cervical cancer. . . ." These procedures, she stated, "have low rates of complications" and are "generally identical whether performed on transgender men to treat gender dysphoria or to treat women for these other conditions." . . . . Dr. Hsiao testified that based on her own practice of providing surgery to transgender men, "gender affirming surgeries for transgender men are extremely safe and have very low rates of serious complications" . . . .

Dr. Hsiao further stated, regarding MF transsexual surgery, that she has been part of a surgical team that performed surgery to create a neovagina in women born with a congenital "complete or partial absence of a vagina, cervix, and uterus," a condition called Mayer-Rokitansky-Kuster-Hauser syndrome, or MRKH. She stated that this procedure has "a low rate of complications" . . . .

Dr. Ettner stated that "[t]here is no scientific or medical basis" for the NCD's statement that sex reassignment surgery has not been proven safe and has a high rate of serious complications; that the "[r]ates of complications during and after sex reassignment surgery are relatively low, and most complications are minor;" and that the risk of complications "has, moreover, been dramatically reduced since 1985." . . . . She stated that [the Chicago Gender Clinic] "as a whole has a 12 percent complication rate for genital surgery" and that "the vast majority of those complications [were] minor, all were easily corrected, and none involved surgical site infection or readmission." Dr. Ettner stated the 1981 report's discussion of surgical complication rates was "outdated and irrelevant based on current medical practices and procedures." In particular, she stated that one of the studies cited in the 1981 report's discussion of complications (Laub & Fisk 1974) reflected the use of a MF surgical technique that "led to unacceptably high rates of fistulae and other complications" and was later abandoned by the study's authors.

Another of the AP's expert witnesses, Marci L. Bowers, M.D., stated in her notarized letter that in her experience of performing gender-related surgeries, transsexual surgery "does not have a higher rate of complication than any other surgery, and in fact has very few complications, which are mainly minor in nature." Dr. Bowers stated that she performs approximately 220 gender-related surgeries annually and has performed over 1000 "Male to Female Gender Corrective Surgeries."

. . . . Dr. Hsiao testified that she reviewed five studies in the AP exhibits "that include complication rate data and information for gender affirming surgeries performed in recent years" and that "[n]one of these five studies reported high rates of serious complications."

Dr. Hsiao further stated that Eldh et al. (1997) compared complication rates for surgeries performed before and after 1986 and showed that "[n]early all of the surgical complication rates decreased significantly over time." Dr. Hsiao stated, showed that "[t]here is not a high rate of serious complications in any of the surgeries performed after 1986" and she noted that "there have been nearly 20 years of additional surgical progress since the last surgery tracked."

. . . .

. . . . We have conducted our own review of the studies cited by Dr. Hsiao and Dr. Ettner and find them consistent with these opinions and representations. We note, for example, that [Jan Eldh, et al., *Long-Term Follow Up After Sex Reassignment Surgery*, 31 SCAND. J. PLAST. RECONSTR. SURG. HAND SURG. 39–45 (1997),] which divided the study group into those operated on before 1986 and those operated on from 1986–1995, made findings tending to support these expert opinions. The Eldh study states:

> After 1985 the outcome of surgery became much better not only because of changes in management but also because of improvements in surgical technique, preoperative planning, and postoperative treatment. Total time spent in hospital decreased dramatically after 1985 because the number of procedures was less and the rate of early and late postoperative complications dropped. Haemorrhage and haematoma were common in both groups, predominantly originating from the spongious tissue of the urethra. Infections occurred less often in the late group perhaps as a result of peroperative antibiotic prophylaxis. Serious complications like fistula formation and partial flap necrosis were rare after 1985, though they were common before then. The reason for the lower fistula rate in the later group may be ascribed to better anatomical knowledge of this region and a more precise surgical technique. There was only one rectovaginal fistula after 1985 and this fistula closed spontaneously.

. . . .

We conclude that the AP has shown that the NCD's statement that transsexual surgery is unsafe and has a high rate of complications is not reasonable in light of the evolution of surgical techniques and the studies of outcomes discussed in the unchallenged new evidence presented here.

D. The new evidence indicates that transsexual surgery is an effective treatment option in appropriate cases.

1. The expert testimony and studies on which the experts rely support the surgery's effectiveness.

The AP argues that studies conducted after the 1981 report was issued confirm that transsexual surgery is an effective treatment for persons with severe gender dysphoria, and the expert testimony and studies support that argument.

. . . . Dr. Ettner testified that "more than three decades of research confirms that sex reassignment surgery is therapeutic and therefore an effective treatment for Gender Identity Disorder" and that "for many patients with severe Gender Identity Disorder, sex reassignment surgery is the only effective treatment."[23] She concluded that "[t]he NCD's determination regarding efficacy is not reasonably supported by scientific or clinical evidence, or standards of professional practice, and fails to take into account the robust body of research establishing that surgery relieves, and very often completely eliminates, gender dysphoria."

Dr. Bowers stated that "[m]any patients report a dramatic improvement in mental health following surgery, and patients have been able to become productive members of society, no longer disabled with severe depression and gender dysphoria." She concluded that "Gender Corrective Surgery has been shown to be a life-saving procedure, and is unequivocally medically necessary." Dr. Leis stated that "[m]edical literature reports a dramatic drop in the incidence of depression and suicide attempt[s] by individuals who have undergone gender reassignment, indicating that many lives have been saved because of this surgery. . . ."

Dr. Ettner cited 20 studies published between 1987 and 2010 as showing the effectiveness of transsexual surgery. She emphasized three studies, two of which were published in 1998 and 2007 and analyze other studies of the treatment of transsexuals published during the years 1961 to 1991 and 1990 to 2007, respectively. . . . As "general results," the researchers in the 1998 study stated that the studies they reviewed concluded "that gender reassigning treatments are effective," that positive, desired results outweigh the negative or non-desired effects, and that "[p]robably the most important change that is found in most research is the increase of subjective satisfaction [which] contrasts markedly to the subjectively unsatisfactory start position of the patients."

. . . .

The 2007 study, [Luk Gijs & Anne Brewaeys, *Surgical Treatment of Gender Dysphoria in Adults and Adolescents: Recent Developments, Effectiveness, and Challenges*, 18 ANN. REV. SEX RES. 178-224 (2007)], which examined the results of 18 studies

---

23. Dr. Ettner in her declaration focuses on genital surgery for the male-to-female (MF) transsexual. Dr. Hsiao's testimony addressed procedures performed on FM patients. [Relocated footnote—Eds.]

published between 1990 and 2006, states that sex reassignment "is the most appropriate treatment to alleviate the suffering of extremely gender dysphoric individuals" and that "96% of the persons who underwent [surgery] were satisfied and regret was rare." Two of the reviewed studies showed that "[s]uicidality was significantly reduced postoperatively" and that in MF patients there were no suicide attempts after surgery as opposed to three attempts before surgery.

. . . .

Based on our own review of the cited studies, we find no reason to question the expert testimony about them. In general, the studies included interviewing postoperative patients with a variety of surveys or questionnaires to assess changes in different aspects of their lives and psychological symptoms following surgery. The studies also generally used statistical techniques to assess the results. The studies were conducted in countries including the United States, Canada, Sweden, the Czech Republic, Israel, Brazil, The Netherlands, and Belgium.

We note that these studies are scientific writings and do not make sweeping pronouncements or claim discoveries beyond possible doubt. Indeed, the authors sometimes qualify the results and caution against drawing overly broad and simplistic conclusions. This, in our view, enhances their facial credibility. Nonetheless, even keeping in mind the possible limitations of these studies, they support the AP's position that transsexual surgery has gained broad acceptance in the medical community.

2. The 1981 report's expressed concern about an alleged lack of controlled, long-term studies is not reasonable in light of the new evidence.

The 1981 report summarized the findings of nine studies on "[t]he result or outcome of" transsexual surgery. With respect to those studies, the report stated that "surgical complications are frequent, and a very small number of postsurgical suicides and psychotic breakdowns are reported." However, the report also acknowledged that eight of those nine studies "report that most transsexuals show improved adjustment on a variety of criteria after sex reassignment surgery, and that "[i]n all of these studies the large majority of those who received surgery report that they are personally satisfied with the change[.]" Notwithstanding its discussion of these studies, the 1981 report (and the NCD) cited an alleged "lack of well controlled, long term studies of the safety and effectiveness of the surgical procedures and attendant therapies for transsexualism" as a ground for finding the procedures "experimental." The 1981 report did not define "long term" for the purpose of assigning weight to study results and the NCD record provided no clarification of that phrase. The 1981 report noted "post-operative followup" and "followup" times for eight of the nine studies on the outcomes of surgery, with "average," "mean" or "median" periods ranging from 25 months to over eight years, and individual periods from three months to 13 years. If these studies do not qualify as acceptable long-term studies, the basis for such a conclusion is not adequately explained in the NCD record.

Even assuming the studies cited in the 1981 report could be viewed as not sufficiently "long-term," Dr. Ettner stated that "there are numerous long-term follow-up studies on surgical treatment demonstrating that surgeries are effective and have low complication rates. . . ." CMS does not challenge this statement, and we find no reason to question it. We note that the participants in one study Dr. Ettner cited had a mean interval since vaginoplasty of 75.46 months. We also note that the 18 studies published between 1990 and 2006 and encompassing 807 MF and FM patients analyzed in Gijs & Brewaeys (2007) had mean follow-up durations ranging from six months to as long as (in one study) 168 months. Additionally, two studies Dr. Ettner cited appear to be long term in that they studied patients who had undergone surgery during periods of 14 and 20 years, respectively. Those studies reported favorable overall results.

Dr. Ettner also testified that two studies from 1987 and 1990 used control groups and found improved psychosocial outcomes in surgery patients. . . . The study found that patients who underwent surgery "demonstrated dramatically improved psychosocial outcomes, compared to the still-waiting controls" and "were more active socially and had significantly fewer psychiatric symptoms." *See also* WPATH Br. at 8 (study found "comparative improvements in neurotic symptoms and social activity for the group receiving surgery"). Dr. Ettner described the 1990 study as the "best example of a well-controlled investigation." Dr. Ettner also described a 1987 study comparing transsexuals who had undergone surgery with "those who had not, but were otherwise matched (control group)" as finding that "the patients who underwent surgery were better adjusted psychosocially, had improved financial circumstances, and reported increased satisfaction with sexual experiences, as compared to the unoperated group."

Nothing in the record puts into question the authoritativeness of the studies cited in the new evidence based on methodology (or any other ground). Even if questions about methodology had been raised, we would be hard pressed to find that this alone would justify our not crediting the new evidence that transsexual surgery is effective and safe. This is particularly true since the 1981 report itself suggested it might be impossible to find the kind of adequate control groups needed to assuage this criticism. We note that in the local coverage determination (LCD) context, CMS guidance for contractors states that the determinations "shall be based on the strongest evidence available." CMS Medicare Program Integrity Manual (MPIM), CMS Pub. 100- 08, Ch. 13, §13.7.1.33 . . . . While the guidance applies to contractors, who develop LCDs but not NCDs, it is instructive here as representing CMS's determination of the type of evidence that may support Medicare coverage. Regardless of whether the new evidence here meets the first option for meeting the evidentiary standard set forth in the guidance (and CMS does not assert that it does not), it clearly meets the second option because it indicates a consensus among researchers and mainstream medical organizations that transsexual surgery is an effective, safe and medically necessary treatment for transsexualism.

Based on the record as a whole, including the new evidence discussed above, we conclude that the AP has shown that transsexual surgery is an effective treatment option for transsexualism in appropriate cases.

E. The new evidence indicates that the NCD's rationale for considering the surgery experimental is not valid.

The NCD asserted that transsexual surgery was considered experimental because it had not been shown to be safe and effective. The 1981 report stated that transsexual surgery "must be considered still experimental" because "[t]he safety and effectiveness of transsexual surgery as a treatment of transsexualism is not proven and is questioned." As discussed above, the unchallenged new evidence indicates that transsexual surgery is a safe and effective treatment option for transsexualism in appropriate cases. Accordingly, the NCD's reasons for asserting that transsexual surgery was experimental are no longer valid.

In addition, the new evidence independently indicates that transsexual surgery is not considered experimental in a broader sense relating to its acceptance as a treatment for transsexualism. . . . . Dr. Hsiao testified that there is "no scientific or medical basis for [the NCD's] description of gender affirming surgeries as 'experimental.'" Dr. Hsiao, as noted, stated that some of the procedures involved in transsexual surgery are routinely performed in other contexts, and that surgery to create a neovagina is performed on women born MRKH. *See* Ettner Supp. Decl. at ¶ 15 ("mastectomies, hysterectomies and salpingo-oophorectomies, which are . . . excluded from coverage under [the NCD] are performed frequently . . . when indicated for medical conditions other than gender dysphoria").

Dr. Hsiao cited the "increasing coverage of sex affirming surgeries by private and public medical plans" and the inclusion of those surgeries "in prominent surgical text books" as showing that "gender affirming surgeries . . . are the standard of care and are not experimental." Dr. Hsiao cited California managed care guidance "clarifying that any attempt 'to exclude insurance coverage of [] transsexual surgery'" would violate California law, and she stated that Vermont, Colorado, Oregon, and Washington, D.C. "have issued similar insurance directives prohibiting discrimination based on gender identity with respect to healthcare policies." . . . Letter No. 12-K: Gender Nondiscrimination Requirements, Calif. Dep't of Managed Health Care (Apr. 9, 2013).[36] "These events in the private and public sector," Dr. Hsiao stated, "solidify what the medical community has known for years—that gender affirming surgeries to treat gender dysphoria are evidence-based, medically necessary, and the standard of care for these patients."

. . . . Dr. Leis also stated that "[m]edical and mental health professionals who are knowledgeable and experienced in this field recognize that counseling or psychotherapy, hormone therapy and genital reassignment surgery are medically necessary

---

36. http://www.dmhc.ca.gov/library/reports/news/dl12k.pdf, accessed May 14, 2014.

treatment modalities for many individuals with [GID]" and that those therapies "are widely accepted treatments for individuals with significant [GID] in the United States and in many other countries." Dr. Leis also pointed to the acceptance of transsexual surgery procedures "as standard therapy by leading medical and mental health organizations" including the American Medical Association, the National Association of Social Workers, the American Psychological Association, the American Psychiatric Association, "and experts in the field belonging to" WPATH.

. . . .

Dr. Bowers, Dr. Hsiao and Dr. Ettner cited acceptance of the WPATH standards of care, which were first published in 1979 and last revised in 2011, as evidence that transsexual surgery is not experimental. *See also* AP Ex. 3 (AMA resolution stating that "[h]ealth experts in GID, including WPATH, have rejected the myth that such treatments are "cosmetic" or "experimental" and have recognized that these treatments can provide safe and effective treatment for a serious health condition"). The new evidence indicates that the WPATH standards of care have attained widespread acceptance.[38] *See* Hsiao Decl. ("the WPATH established standards of care for patients with gender dysphoria . . . have been endorsed by the American Medical Association, the Endocrine Society, the American Psychological Association, and the American College of Obstetricians and Gynecologists"); AP Ex. 3 (AMA resolution stating that WPATH is "the leading international, interdisciplinary professional organization devoted to the understanding and treatment of gender identity disorders" and that its "internationally accepted Standards of Care for providing medical treatment for people with GID . . . are recognized within the medical community to be the standard of care for treating people with GID"). Federal courts have recognized the acceptance of the WPATH standards of care. *See, e.g., De'lonta v. Johnson*, 708 F.3d 520 (4th Cir. 2013) (WPATH standards of care "are the generally accepted protocols for the treatment of GID"); *Glenn v. Brumby*, 724 F. Supp. 2d 1284 (N.D. Ga. 2010) ("there is sufficient evidence that statements of WPATH are accepted in the medical community").[39] The acceptance of the WPATH standards of care also suggests that transsexual surgery is no longer considered experimental.

. . . .

---

38. WPATH was "formerly the Harry Benjamin International Gender Dysphoria Association." Harry Benjamin, M.D. "was an endocrinologist who in conjunction with mental health professionals in New York did pioneering work in the study of transsexualism." *O'Donnabhain v. Comm'r of Internal Revenue*, 134 T.C. 34 (2010). The 1981 report cites a 1966 study by Dr. Benjamin finding a positive outcome from MF transsexual surgery as "perhaps the first report" on transsexual surgery "in the literature."

39. The general acceptance of a set of standards of care for the treatment of transsexuals appears to render invalid one of the 1981 report criticisms of the studies it discussed, that "therapeutic techniques are not standardized."

We note that in addition to stating that transsexual surgery was experimental, the NCD and the 1981 report stated that transsexual surgery was "controversial." NCD Record (1981 report stating that "[o]ver and above the medical and scientific issues, it would also appear that transsexual surgery is controversial in our society"). The AP and the new evidence dispute the relevance of this statement. The AP objected that this point relies on two "polemics" that are "are either completely unscientific or fall far outside the scientific mainstream," and Dr. Ettner stated that the views expressed therein "fall far outside the mainstream psychological, psychiatric, and medical professional consensus, and call into question the objective reasonableness of the NCD." CMS has not asserted that the Board's decision may be based on factors "over and above the medical and scientific issues" involved. Considerations of social acceptability (or nonacceptability) of medical procedures appear on their face to be antithetical to Medicare's "medical necessity" inquiry, which is based in science, and such considerations do not enter into our decision that the NCD is not valid.

For the reasons stated above, we conclude that citing the alleged "experimental" nature of transsexual surgery as a basis for noncoverage of all transsexual surgery is not reasonable in light of the unchallenged new evidence and contributes to our conclusion that the NCD is not valid.

Conclusion

For the reasons explained above, we conclude that the AP has shown that NCD 140.3 is not valid under the reasonableness standard.

/s/   Leslie A. Sussan

/s/   Constance B. Tobias

/s/   Sheila Ann Hegy

Presiding Board Member

Discussion

1. This decision by the Board of Departmental Appeals that National Coverage Determination 140.3 is invalid paves the way for more states' Medicare programs to cover transition-related care for transgender seniors. Nevertheless, the invalidation of NCD 140.3 does not, by itself, require states to include such care. That would take additional litigation challenging exclusions or such care and/or state legislative or administrative will to cover such care expressly.

2. The repeal of this across-the-board non-coverage determination is an important advance for transgender people's ability to secure adequate health care. But while such "[w]holesale categorical exclusions are increasingly viewed as invalid, whether under Affordable Care Act regulations or as a matter of Medicare coverage determinations or federal Medicaid law," Samuel Rosh has observed that even some

jurisdictions that repealed their blanket bans deem a range of transition-related care — including "electrolysis, facial reconstruction, voice therapy, and sexual reassignment surgery" — "cosmetic" and thus uncovered, despite the contrary view of modern medicine. Samuel Rosh, *Beyond Categorical Exclusions: Access to Transgender Healthcare in State Medicaid Programs*, 51 Colum. J.L. & Soc. Probs. 1, 2 (2017). Such rules, Rosh argues, violate the Affordable Care Act. *Id.*

Chapter 12

Incarcerated and Institutionalized Persons' Safety and Health Care

Jails and prisons in the United States are too often sites of grotesque violence against inmates, and transgender inmates are particularly vulnerable. The respondents to the U.S. Transgender Survey, or "USTS"—the largest survey of the life experiences of transgender and gender nonconforming people in the United States, with over 27,000 respondents including people from every state, D.C., three territories, and overseas military bases—who in the previous year were incarcerated in jails, prisons, or juvenile detention facilities, reported incidents that showed them to be "over five times more likely to be sexually assaulted by facility staff than the U.S. population in jails and prisons, and over nine times more likely to be sexually assaulted by other inmates." Sandy E. James et al., National Center for Transgender Equality, The Report of the 2015 U.S. Transgender Survey 15 (2016).

Transgender people also have difficulty receiving adequate medical care while incarcerated. Thirty-seven percent of USTS respondents who had been taking hormones prior to incarceration were forbidden to continue that form of therapy in jail, prison, or juvenile detention. *Id.* at 193. Sometimes, transgender inmates who were not on hormone therapy before incarceration are denied access to hormones due to "freeze-frame" policies that deny transgender inmates medical care that they were not receiving "outside"—even when such care may be medically necessary for treatment of gender dysphoria. And prisons across the country vigorously resist providing gender confirmation surgeries to inmates.

Many of the challenges faced by transgender persons during incarceration can be traced to the practice of segregating jails, prisons, and juvenile detention facilities on the basis of sex. That, combined with a binary notion of sex and a refusal to treat transgender people as members of the sex consistent with their gender identity, at least in the absence of genital reconstruction surgery, can result in a particularly dire living situation for transgender women, who are typically housed in (more violent) men's prisons.

A. Failures of Care

Because inmates are not free to ensure their own safety nor to provide their own health care, the government has duties of care toward those they incarcerate, detain, or otherwise institutionalize. Particularly with respect to transgender people, these duties have too often been observed in the breach. Subsection 1 here deals with jail officials' failures to protect transgender inmates from violence during incarceration. Subsection 2 then turns to jail officials' failure to provide legally required medical care to transgender inmates, including transition-related or gender-affirming care.

1. Failure to Protect

The Constitution of the United States is frequently said to be, in general, one that assures "negative liberties," freedom *from* the government's doing certain things to people (like abridging their freedom of speech), rather than "positive liberties," affirmative rights to government *provision of* certain things (like education or health care). Thus, the Supreme Court concluded in *DeShaney v. Winnebago County Department of Social Services*, 489 U.S. 189 (1989), "the Due Process Clauses generally confer no affirmative right to governmental aid, even where such aid may be necessary to secure life, liberty, or property interests of which the government itself may not deprive the individual." There are limited exceptions, notably, for example, where individuals are incarcerated and thus not free to care for themselves. *See, e.g., Estelle v. Gamble*, 429 U.S. 97 (1976). Accordingly, prison administrators "are under an obligation to take reasonable measures to guarantee the safety of the inmates themselves." *Hudson v. Palmer*, 468 U.S. 517, 526–27 (1984).

When prisons fail to keep inmates safe, what recourse might they have? This subsection presents efforts to use the Eighth Amendment (in conjunction with 42 U.S.C. § 1983, a federal statute generally authorizing suits against state and local officials for violating constitutional rights), the Gender Motivated Violence Act (a federal law later held unconstitutional by the Supreme Court), and state tort law to redress jailers' failures to protect transgender inmates.

Reading Guide for Farmer v. Brennan

1. The following judicial decision concerns the constitutional standards governing prisons' failures to protect inmates imposed by the Eight Amendment's ban on cruel and unusual punishment. The lawsuit was filed by Dee Farmer, a black transgender woman who alleged that she was repeatedly raped and attacked in prison. She sued pursuant to the Supreme Court's decision in *Bivens v. Six Unknown Fed. Narcotics Agents*, 403 U.S. 388 (1971), which authorized civil suits against federal government officials for money damages for violation of one's constitutional rights in certain circumstances.

2. The Court identifies two required elements of an Eighth Amendment violation when prisoners are harmed by fellow inmates according to its decision in

Wilson v. Seiter, 501 U.S. 294 (1991). What are they? This case focuses on the definition of the second requirement. How does the Court define that requirement, that is, what must a plaintiff satisfy to establish it? What reasons does the Court give for rejecting Ms. Farmer's argument for a wholly objective definition of the standard? What role does the text of the Eighth Amendment play in the Court's reasoning? The Court identifies specific times at which a plaintiff seeking injunctive relief must make the required showing—when must these showings occur? (Farmer also sought injunctive relief, although a plaintiff seeking an injunction need not rely on *Bivens*, which is needed solely for money damages.) How, according to the Court, must defendants respond to a risk of which they are aware to avoid Eighth Amendment liability?

3. How does the Court dispose of Farmer's appeal? For what reason does the Court choose that disposition?

4. Justice Blackmun joins the Court's opinion and files a concurring opinion. In what respect(s) does he disagree with the majority in Part I of his concurrence, and for what reasons? Whose position is more persuasive, his or the majority's? Given Blackmun's disagreements with the majority, why does he nonetheless join the opinion of the Court?

5. Justice Thomas does not join the majority opinion but instead concurs in the judgment. Why does he refuse to join the Court's opinion? With what aspect of the majority's reasoning does Thomas agree, and why?

Dee Farmer v. Edward Brennan, Warden, et al.

511 U.S. 825 (1994)

Souter, J., delivered the opinion of the Court, in which Rehnquist, C.J., and Blackmun, Stevens, O'Connor, Scalia, Kennedy, and Ginsburg, JJ., joined. Blackmun, J., and Stevens, J., filed concurring opinions. Thomas, J., filed an opinion concurring in the judgment.

A prison official's "deliberate indifference" to a substantial risk of serious harm to an inmate violates the Eighth Amendment. *See Helling v. McKinney*, 509 U.S. 25 (1993); *Wilson v. Seiter*, 501 U.S. 294 (1991); *Estelle v. Gamble*, 429 U.S. 97 (1976). This case requires us to define the term "deliberate indifference," [which] we do by requiring a showing that the official was subjectively aware of the risk.

I

The dispute before us stems from a civil suit brought by petitioner, Dee Farmer, alleging that respondents, federal prison officials, violated the Eighth Amendment by their deliberate indifference to petitioner's safety. Petitioner, who is serving a federal sentence for credit card fraud, has been diagnosed by medical personnel of the Bureau of Prisons as a transsexual, one who has "[a] rare psychiatric disorder in which a person feels persistently uncomfortable about his or her anatomical sex," and who typically seeks medical treatment, including hormonal therapy and surgery, to bring about a permanent sex change. For several years before being convicted and sentenced in 1986 at the age of 18, petitioner, who is biologically male, wore women's clothing (as petitioner did at the 1986 trial), underwent estrogen therapy, received silicone breast implants, and submitted to unsuccessful "black market" testicle-removal surgery. *See Farmer v. Haas*, 990 F.2d 319 (7th Cir. 1993). Petitioner's precise appearance in prison is unclear from the record before us, but petitioner claims to have continued hormonal treatment while incarcerated by using drugs smuggled into prison, and apparently wears clothing in a feminine manner, as by displaying a shirt "off one shoulder." The parties agree that petitioner "projects feminine characteristics." The practice of federal prison authorities is to incarcerate preoperative transsexuals with prisoners of like biological sex, . . . and over time authorities housed petitioner in several federal facilities, sometimes in the general male prison population but more often in segregation. While there is no dispute that petitioner was segregated at least several times because of violations of prison rules, neither is it disputed that in at least one penitentiary petitioner was segregated because of safety concerns.

On March 9, 1989, petitioner was transferred for disciplinary reasons from the Federal Correctional Institute in Oxford, Wisconsin (FCI-Oxford), to the United States Penitentiary in Terre Haute, Indiana (USP-Terre Haute). [Penitentiaries] are typically higher security facilities that house more troublesome prisoners than federal correctional institutes. After an initial stay in administrative segregation, petitioner was placed in the USP-Terre Haute general population. Petitioner voiced no objection to any prison official about the transfer to the penitentiary or to placement in its general population. Within two weeks, according to petitioner's allegations, petitioner was beaten and raped by another inmate in petitioner's cell. Several days later, after petitioner claims to have reported the incident, officials returned petitioner to segregation to await, according to respondents, a hearing about petitioner's HIV-positive status.

Acting without counsel, petitioner then filed a *Bivens* complaint, alleging a violation of the Eighth Amendment. *See Bivens v. Six Unknown Fed. Narcotics Agents*, 403 U.S. 388 (1971); *Carlson v. Green*, 446 U.S. 14 (1980). As defendants, petitioner named respondents: the warden of USP-Terre Haute and the Director of the Bureau of Prisons (sued only in their official capacities); the warden of FCI-Oxford and a case manager there; and the Director of the Bureau of Prisons North Central Region Office and an official in that office (sued in their official and personal capacities). As later amended, the complaint alleged that respondents either transferred petitioner to USP-Terre Haute or placed petitioner in its general population despite knowledge that the penitentiary had a violent environment and a history of inmate assaults, and despite knowledge that petitioner, as a transsexual who "projects feminine characteristics," would be particularly vulnerable to sexual attack by some USP-Terre Haute inmates. This allegedly amounted to a deliberately indifferent failure to protect petitioner's safety, and thus to a violation of petitioner's Eighth Amendment rights. Petitioner sought compensatory and punitive damages, and an injunction barring future confinement in any penitentiary, including USP-Terre Haute [as distinguished from a less secure federal correctional institute].[1]

[T]he District Court . . . granted summary judgment to respondents, concluding that there had been no deliberate indifference to petitioner's safety. The failure of prison officials to prevent inmate assaults violates the Eighth Amendment, the court stated, only if prison officials were "reckless in a criminal sense," meaning that they had "actual knowledge" of a potential danger. Respondents, however, lacked the requisite knowledge, the court found. "[Petitioner] never expressed any concern for his [*sic*—Eds.] safety to any of [respondents]. Since [respondents] had no knowledge of any potential danger to [petitioner], they were not deliberately indifferent to his safety."

The United States Court of Appeals for the Seventh Circuit summarily affirmed without opinion. We granted certiorari because Courts of Appeals had adopted inconsistent tests for "deliberate indifference." . . . .

II

A

The Constitution "does not mandate comfortable prisons," *Rhodes v. Chapman*, 452 U.S. 337 (1981), but neither does it permit inhumane ones, and it is now settled that "the treatment a prisoner receives in prison and the conditions under which he is confined are subject to scrutiny under the Eighth Amendment," *Helling*. In its prohibition of "cruel and unusual punishments," the Eighth Amendment places restraints on prison officials, who may not, for example, use excessive physical force against prisoners. *See Hudson v. McMillian*, 503 U.S. 1 (1992). The Amendment also imposes duties on these officials, who must provide humane conditions of confinement; prison officials must ensure that inmates receive adequate food, clothing, shelter, and medical care, and must "take reasonable measures to guarantee the safety of the inmates," *Hudson v. Palmer*, 468 U.S. 517 (1984). *See Helling*; *Washington v. Harper*, 494 U.S. 210 (1990); *Estelle*. *Cf. DeShaney v. Winnebago County Dept. of Social Servs.*, 489 U.S. 189 (1989).

In particular, as the lower courts have uniformly held, and as we have assumed, "prison officials have a duty . . . to protect prisoners from violence at the hands of other prisoners." *Cortes-Quinones v. Jimenez-Nettleship* (1st Cir.), *cert. denied*, 488 U.S. 823 (1988). Having incarcerated "persons [with] demonstrated proclivit[ies] for antisocial criminal, and often violent, conduct," *Hudson v. Palmer*, having stripped them of virtually every means of self-protection and foreclosed their access to outside aid, the government and its officials are not free to let the state of nature take its course. Prison conditions may be "restrictive and even harsh," *Rhodes*,

---

1. Petitioner also sought an order requiring the Bureau of Prisons to place petitioner in a "co-correctional facility" (*i.e.*, one separately housing male and female prisoners but allowing coeducational programming). Petitioner tells us, however, that the Bureau no longer operates such facilities, and petitioner apparently no longer seeks this relief.

but gratuitously allowing the beating or rape of one prisoner by another serves no "legitimate penological objectiv[e]," *Hudson v. Palmer* (STEVENS, J., concurring in part and dissenting in part), any more than it squares with "'evolving standards of decency,'" *Estelle* (quoting *Trop v. Dulles*, 356 U.S. 86 (1958) (plurality opinion)). Being violently assaulted in prison is simply not "part of the penalty that criminal offenders pay for their offenses against society." *Rhodes.*

It is not, however, every injury suffered by one prisoner at the hands of another that translates into constitutional liability for prison officials responsible for the victim's safety. Our cases have held that a prison official violates the Eighth Amendment only when two requirements are met. First, the deprivation alleged must be, objectively, "sufficiently serious," *Wilson*; a prison official's act or omission must result in the denial of "the minimal civilized measure of life's necessities," *Rhodes.* For a claim (like the one here) based on a failure to prevent harm, the inmate must show that he is incarcerated under conditions posing a substantial risk of serious harm. *See Helling.*

The second requirement follows from the principle that "only the unnecessary and wanton infliction of pain implicates the Eighth Amendment." *Wilson.* To violate the Cruel and Unusual Punishments Clause, a prison official must have a "sufficiently culpable state of mind." *Ibid.; see also Hudson v. McMillian.* In prison-conditions cases that state of mind is one of "deliberate indifference" to inmate health or safety, *Wilson.* . . . The parties disagree . . . on the proper test for deliberate indifference. . . .

B

1

. . . . The term ["deliberate indifference"] first appeared in the United States Reports in *Estelle v. Gamble*, and [it] describes a state of mind more blameworthy than negligence. In considering the inmate's claim in *Estelle* that inadequate prison medical care violated the Cruel and Unusual Punishments Clause, we distinguished "deliberate indifference to serious medical needs of prisoners," from "negligen[ce] in diagnosing or treating a medical condition," holding that only the former violates the Clause. . . . Eighth Amendment liability requires "more than ordinary lack of due care for the prisoner's interests or safety." *Whitley v. Albers*, 475 U.S. 312 (1986). [The deliberate indifference test] is satisfied by something less than acts or omissions for the very purpose of causing harm or with knowledge that harm will result. [T]he "deliberate indifference standard in inappropriate" . . . when "officials stand accused of using excessive physical force." *Hudson v. McMillian.* In such situations, where the decisions of prison officials are typically made "'in haste, under pressure, and frequently without the luxury of a second chance,'" *Hudson v. McMillian* (quoting *Whitley*), an Eighth Amendment claimant must show more than "indifference," deliberate or otherwise. The claimant must show that officials applied force "maliciously and sadistically for the very purpose of causing harm," *Hudson v. McMillian*, or, as the Court also put it, that officials used force with "a knowing willingness that

[harm] occur." This standard of purposeful or knowing conduct is not, however, necessary to satisfy the *mens rea* requirement of deliberate indifference for claims challenging conditions of confinement; "the very high state of mind prescribed by *Whitley* does not apply to prison conditions cases." *Wilson*. . . .

[The] Courts of Appeals have routinely equated deliberate indifference with recklessness. [A]cting or failing to act with deliberate indifference to a substantial risk of serious harm to a prisoner is the equivalent of recklessly disregarding that risk. That does not, however, fully answer the pending question about the level of culpability deliberate indifference entails, for the term recklessness is not self-defining. . . .

We reject petitioner's invitation to adopt an objective test for deliberate indifference. We hold instead that a prison official cannot be found liable under the Eighth Amendment for denying an inmate humane conditions of confinement unless the official knows of and disregards an excessive risk to inmate health or safety; the official must both be aware of facts from which the inference could be drawn that a substantial risk of serious harm exists, and he must also draw the inference. This approach comports best with the text of the Amendment as our cases have interpreted it. The Eighth Amendment does not outlaw cruel and unusual "conditions"; it outlaws cruel and unusual "punishments." [An] official's failure to alleviate a significant risk that he should have perceived but did not, while no cause for commendation, cannot under our cases be condemned as the infliction of punishment.

In *Wilson v. Seiter,* we rejected a reading of the Eighth Amendment that would allow liability to be imposed on prison officials solely because of the presence of objectively inhumane prison conditions. As we explained there, our "cases mandate inquiry into a prison official's state of mind when it is claimed that the official has inflicted cruel and unusual punishment." Although "state of mind," like "intent," is an ambiguous term that can encompass objectively defined levels of blameworthiness, it was no accident that we said in *Wilson* and repeated in later cases that Eighth Amendment suits against prison officials must satisfy a "subjective" requirement. . . .

To be sure, the reasons for focusing on what a defendant's mental attitude actually was (or is), rather than what it should have been (or should be), differ in the Eighth Amendment context from that of the criminal law. Here, a subjective approach isolates those who inflict punishment; there, it isolates those against whom punishment should be inflicted. But the result is the same: to act recklessly in either setting a person must "consciously disregar[d]" a substantial risk of serious harm. MODEL PENAL CODE § 2.02(2)(c).

. . . .

2

Our decision that Eighth Amendment liability requires consciousness of a risk is thus based on the Constitution and our cases, not merely on a parsing of the phrase "deliberate indifference." . . . . "[D]eliberate indifference" is a judicial gloss, appearing neither in the Constitution nor in a statute. . . . deliberate indifference serves under the Eighth Amendment to ensure that only inflictions of punishment carry liability, *see Wilson*. . . .

. . . . Needless to say, moreover, considerable conceptual difficulty would attend any search for the subjective state of mind of a governmental entity, as distinct from that of a governmental official. For these reasons, we cannot accept petitioner's argument . . . that a prison official who was unaware of a substantial risk of harm to an inmate may nevertheless be held liable under the Eighth Amendment if the risk was obvious and a reasonable prison official would have noticed it.

We are no more persuaded by petitioner's argument that, without an objective test for deliberate indifference, prison officials will be free to ignore obvious dangers to inmates. Under the test we adopt today, an Eighth Amendment claimant need not show that a prison official acted or failed to act believing that harm actually would befall an inmate; it is enough that the official acted or failed to act despite his knowledge of a substantial risk of serious harm. We doubt that a subjective approach will present prison officials with any serious motivation "to take refuge in the zone between 'ignorance of obvious risks' and 'actual knowledge of risks.'" Brief for Petitioner 27. Whether a prison official had the requisite knowledge of a substantial risk is a question of fact subject to demonstration in the usual ways, including inference from circumstantial evidence, and a factfinder may conclude that a prison official knew of a substantial risk from the very fact that the risk was obvious. *Cf.* [W. LaFave & A. Scott, Substantive Criminal Law § 3.7, p. 335 (1986)] ("[I]f the risk is obvious, so that a reasonable man would realize it, we might well infer that [the defendant] did in fact realize it; but the inference cannot be conclusive, for we know that people are not always conscious of what reasonable people would be conscious of"). For example, if an Eighth Amendment plaintiff presents evidence showing that a substantial risk of inmate attacks was "longstanding, pervasive, well-documented, or expressly noted by prison officials in the past, and the circumstances suggest that the defendant-official being sued had been exposed to information concerning the risk and thus 'must have known' about it, then such evidence could be sufficient to permit a trier of fact to find that the defendant-official had actual knowledge of the risk." Brief for Respondents 22.[8]

---

8. While the obviousness of a risk is not conclusive and a prison official may show that the obvious escaped him, he would not escape liability if the evidence showed that he merely refused to verify underlying facts that he strongly suspected to be true, or declined to confirm inferences of risk that he strongly suspected to exist (as when a prison official is aware of a high probability of facts indicating that one prisoner has planned an attack on another but resists opportunities to obtain final confirmation; or when a prison official knows that some diseases are communicable and that a single needle is being used to administer flu shots to prisoners but refuses to listen to a subordinate who he strongly suspects will attempt to explain the associated risk of transmitting disease). When instructing juries in deliberate indifference cases with such issues of proof, courts should be careful to ensure that the requirement of subjective culpability is not lost. It is not enough merely to find that a reasonable person would have known, or that the defendant should have known, and juries should be instructed accordingly.

Nor may a prison official escape liability for deliberate indifference by show-ing that, while he was aware of an obvious, substantial risk to inmate safety, he did not know that the complainant was especially likely to be assaulted by the specific prisoner who eventually committed the assault. The question under the Eighth Amendment is whether prison officials, acting with deliberate indifference, exposed a prisoner to a sufficiently substantial "risk of serious damage to his future health," *Helling*, and it does not matter whether the risk comes from a single source or multiple sources, any more than it matters whether a prisoner faces an excessive risk of attack for reasons personal to him or because all prisoners in his situation face such a risk. *See* Brief for Respondents 15 (stating that a prisoner can estab-lish exposure to a sufficiently serious risk of harm "by showing that he belongs to an identifiable group of prisoners who are frequently singled out for violent attack by other inmates"). If, for example, prison officials were aware that inmate "rape was so common and uncontrolled that some potential victims dared not sleep [but] instead . . . would leave their beds and spend the night clinging to the bars nearest the guards' station," *Hutto v. Finney*, 437 U.S. 678 (1978), it would obviously be irrel-evant to liability that the officials could not guess beforehand precisely who would attack whom.

Because, however, prison officials who lacked knowledge of a risk cannot be said to have inflicted punishment, it remains open to the officials to prove that they were unaware even of an obvious risk to inmate health or safety. That a trier of fact may infer knowledge from the obvious, in other words, does not mean that it must do so. Prison officials charged with deliberate indifference might show, for example, that they did not know of the underlying facts indicating a sufficiently substantial dan-ger and that they were therefore unaware of a danger, or that they knew the under-lying facts but believed (albeit unsoundly) that the risk to which the facts gave rise was insubstantial or nonexistent.

In addition, prison officials who actually knew of a substantial risk to inmate health or safety may be found free from liability if they responded reasonably to the risk, even if the harm ultimately was not averted. A prison official's duty under the Eighth Amendment is to ensure "'reasonable safety,'" *Helling*; *see also Washing-ton v. Harper*; *Hudson v. Palmer*, a standard that incorporates due regard for prison officials' "unenviable task of keeping dangerous men in safe custody under humane conditions," *Spain v. Procunier*, 600 F.2d 189 (9th Cir. 1979) (Kennedy, J.); *see also Bell v. Wolfish*, 441 U.S. 520 (1979). Whether one puts it in terms of duty or deliber-ate indifference, prison officials who act reasonably cannot be found liable under the Cruel and Unusual Punishments Clause.

We address, finally, petitioner's argument that a subjective deliberate indiffer-ence test will unjustly require prisoners to suffer physical injury before obtaining court-ordered correction of objectively inhumane prison conditions. "It would," indeed, "be odd to deny an injunction to inmates who plainly proved an unsafe, life-threatening condition in their prison on the ground that nothing yet had hap-pened to them." *Helling*. But nothing in the test we adopt today clashes with that common sense. Petitioner's argument is flawed for the simple reason that "[o]ne does not have to await the consummation of threatened injury to obtain preventive relief." *Pennsylvania v. West Virginia*, 262 U.S. 553 (1923). Consistently with this principle, a subjective approach to deliberate indifference does not require a prisoner seeking "a remedy for unsafe conditions [to] await a tragic event [such as an] actua[l] assaul[t] before obtaining relief." *Helling*.

In a suit such as petitioner's, insofar as it seeks injunctive relief to prevent a substantial risk of serious injury from ripening into actual harm, "the subjective factor, deliberate indifference, should be determined in light of the prison authorities' current attitudes and conduct," *Helling*: their attitudes and conduct at the time suit is brought and persisting thereafter. An inmate seeking an injunction on the ground that there is "a contemporary violation of a nature likely to continue," *United States v. Oregon State Medical Soc.*, 343 U.S. 326 (1952), must adequately plead such a violation; to survive summary judgment, he must come forward with evidence from which it can be inferred that the defendant-officials were at the time suit was filed, and are at the time of summary judgment, knowingly and unreasonably disregarding an objectively intolerable risk of harm, and that they will continue to do so; and finally to establish eligibility for an injunction, the inmate must demonstrate the continuance of that disregard during the remainder of the litigation and into the future. In so doing, the inmate may rely, in the district court's discretion, on developments that postdate the pleadings and pretrial motions, as the defendants may rely on such developments to establish that the inmate is not entitled to an injunction.[9] *See* Fed. Rule Civ. Proc. 15(d). If the court finds the Eighth Amendment's subjective and objective requirements satisfied, it may grant appropriate injunctive relief. *See Hutto v. Finney* (upholding order designed to halt "an ongoing violation" in prison conditions that included extreme overcrowding, rampant violence, insufficient food, and unsanitary conditions). Of course, a district court should approach issuance of injunctive orders with the usual caution, *see Bell v. Wolfish* (warning courts against becoming "enmeshed in the minutiae of prison operations"), and may, for example, exercise its discretion if appropriate by giving prison officials time to rectify the situation before issuing an injunction.

. . . . When a prison inmate seeks injunctive relief, a court need not ignore the inmate's failure to take advantage of adequate prison procedures, and an inmate

---

9. If, for example, the evidence before a district court establishes that an inmate faces an objectively intolerable risk of serious injury, the defendants could not plausibly persist in claiming lack of awareness, any more than prison officials who state during the litigation that they will not take reasonable measures to abate an intolerable risk of which they are aware could claim to be subjectively blameless for purposes of the Eighth Amendment, and in deciding whether an inmate has established a continuing constitutional violation a district court may take such developments into account. At the same time, even prison officials who had a subjectively culpable state of mind when the lawsuit was filed could prevent issuance of an injunction by proving, during the litigation, that they were no longer unreasonably disregarding an objectively intolerable risk of harm and that they would not revert to their obduracy upon cessation of the litigation.

who needlessly bypasses such procedures may properly be compelled to pursue them. *Cf.* 42 U.S.C. § 1997e (authorizing district courts in § 1983 actions to require inmates to exhaust "such plain, speedy, and effective administrative remedies as are available"). Even apart from the demands of equity, an inmate would be well advised to take advantage of internal prison procedures for resolving inmate grievances. When those procedures produce results, they will typically do so faster than judicial processes can. And even when they do not bring constitutionally required changes, the inmate's task in court will obviously be much easier.

Accordingly, we reject petitioner's arguments and hold that a prison official may be held liable under the Eighth Amendment for denying humane conditions of confinement only if he knows that inmates face a substantial risk of serious harm and disregards that risk by failing to take reasonable measures to abate it.

III

. . . .

In granting summary judgment to respondents on the ground that petitioner had failed to satisfy the Eighth Amendment's subjective requirement, the District Court[, which was summarily affirmed without briefing by the Court of Appeals for the Seventh Circuit,] may have placed decisive weight on petitioner's failure to notify respondents of a risk of harm. That petitioner "never expressed any concern for his safety to any of [respondents]" was the only evidence the District Court cited for its conclusion that there was no genuine dispute about respondents' assertion that they "had no knowledge of any potential danger to [petitioner]." But with respect to each of petitioner's claims, for damages and for injunctive relief, the failure to give advance notice is not dispositive. Petitioner may establish respondents' awareness by reliance on any relevant evidence. *See supra.*

The summary judgment record does not so clearly establish respondents' entitlement to judgment as a matter of law on the issue of subjective knowledge that we can simply assume the absence of error below. For example, in papers filed in opposition to respondents' summary-judgment motion, petitioner pointed to respondents' admission that petitioner is a "non-violent" transsexual who, because of petitioner's "youth and feminine appearance" is "likely to experience a great deal of sexual pressure" in prison. And petitioner recounted a statement by one of the respondents, then warden of the penitentiary in Lewisburg, Pennsylvania, who told petitioner that there was "a high probability that [petitioner] could not safely function at USP-Lewisburg," an incident confirmed in a published District Court opinion. *See Farmer v. Carlson*, 685 F. Supp. 1335 (M.D. Pa. 1988) ("Clearly, placing plaintiff, a twenty-one year old transsexual, into the general population at [USP-] Lewisburg, a [high-]security institution, could pose a significant threat to internal security in general and to plaintiff in particular").

We cannot, moreover, be certain that additional evidence is unavailable to petitioner because in denying petitioner's Rule 56(f) motion for additional discovery the District Court may have acted on a mistaken belief that petitioner's failure to notify was dispositive. Petitioner asserted in papers accompanying the Rule 56(f) motion that the requested documents would show that "each defendant had knowledge that USP-Terre Haute was and is, a violent institution with a history of sexual assault, stabbings, etc., [and that] each defendant showed reckless disregard for my safety by designating me to said institution knowing that I would be sexually assaulted." But in denying the Rule 56(f) motion, the District Court stated that the requested documents were "not shown by plaintiff to be necessary to oppose defendants' motion for summary judgment," a statement consistent with the erroneous view that failure to notify was fatal to petitioner's complaint.

Because the District Court may have mistakenly thought that advance notification was a necessary element of an Eighth Amendment failure-to-protect claim, we think it proper to remand for reconsideration of petitioner's Rule 56(f) motion and, whether additional discovery is permitted or not, for application of the Eighth Amendment principles explained above.[10]

. . . .

IV

The judgment of the Court of Appeals is vacated, and the case is remanded for further proceedings consistent with this opinion.

So ordered.

Justice BLACKMUN, concurring.

I agree with Justice STEVENS that inhumane prison conditions violate the Eighth Amendment even if no prison official has an improper, subjective state of mind. This Court's holding in *Wilson v. Seiter*, to the effect that barbaric prison conditions may be beyond the reach of the Eighth Amendment if no prison official can be deemed individually culpable, in my view is insupportable in principle and is inconsistent with our precedents interpreting the Cruel and Unusual Punishments Clause. Whether the Constitution has been violated "should turn on the character of the punishment rather than the motivation of the individual who inflicted it." *Estelle v. Gamble* (1976) (STEVENS, J., dissenting). *Wilson v. Seiter* should be overruled.

Although I do not go along with the Court's reliance on *Wilson* in defining the "deliberate indifference" standard, I join the Court's opinion, because it creates no new obstacles for prison inmates to overcome, and it sends a clear message to prison officials that their affirmative duty under the Constitution to provide for the safety of inmates is not to be taken lightly. Under the Court's decision today, prison officials may be held liable for failure to remedy a risk so obvious and substantial that

---

10. The District Court's opinion is open to the reading that it required not only advance notification of a substantial risk of assault, but also advance notification of a substantial risk of assault posed by a particular fellow prisoner. *See* App. 124 (referring to "a specific threat to [a prisoner's] safety"). The Eighth Amendment, however, imposes no such requirement. *See supra*, 511 U.S. at 842–844.

the officials must have known about it, see *ante*, and prisoners need not "'await a tragic event [such as an] actua[l] assaul[t] before obtaining relief,'" *ante*.

I

. . . . Homosexual rape or other violence among prison inmates serves absolutely no penological purpose. "Such brutality is the equivalent of torture, and is offensive to any modern standard of human dignity." *United States v. Bailey*, 444 U.S. 394 (1980) (Blackmun, J., dissenting). The horrors experienced by many young inmates, particularly those who, like petitioner, are convicted of nonviolent offenses, border on the unimaginable. Prison rape not only threatens the lives of those who fall prey to their aggressors, but is potentially devastating to the human spirit. Shame, depression, and a shattering loss of self-esteem accompany the perpetual terror the victim thereafter must endure. Unable to fend for himself without the protection of prison officials, the victim finds himself at the mercy of larger, stronger, and ruthless inmates. Although formally sentenced to a term of incarceration, many inmates discover that their punishment, even for nonviolent offenses like credit card fraud or tax evasion, degenerates into a reign of terror unmitigated by the protection supposedly afforded by prison officials.

The fact that our prisons are badly overcrowded and understaffed may well explain many of the shortcomings of our penal systems. But our Constitution sets minimal standards governing the administration of punishment in this country, see *Rhodes*, and thus it is no answer to the complaints of the brutalized inmate that the resources are unavailable to protect him from what, in reality, is nothing less than torture. I stated in dissent in *Bailey*:

> "It is society's responsibility to protect the life and health of its prisoners. '[W]hen a sheriff or a marshall [*sic*] [alteration in *Farmer*] takes a man from the courthouse in a prison van and transports him to confinement for two or three or ten years, *this is our act. We* have tolled the bell for him. And whether we like it or not, we have made him our collective responsibility. We are free to do something about him; he is not' (emphasis in original). Address by The Chief Justice, 25 Record of the Assn. of the Bar of the City of New York 14, 17 (Mar. 1970 Supp.)."

The Court in *Wilson v. Seiter* (1991), held that any pain and suffering endured by a prisoner that is not formally a part of his sentence — no matter how severe or unnecessary — will not be held violative of the Cruel and Unusual Punishments Clause unless the prisoner establishes that some prison official intended the harm. The Court justified this remarkable conclusion by asserting that only pain that is intended by a state actor to be punishment is punishment.

The Court's analysis is fundamentally misguided; indeed it defies common sense. "Punishment" does not necessarily imply a culpable state of mind on the part of an identifiable punisher. A prisoner may experience punishment when he suffers "severe, rough, or disastrous treatment," *see, e.g.,* Webster's Third New International Dictionary 1843 (1961), regardless of whether a state actor intended the cruel treatment to chastise or deter. *See also* Webster's New International Dictionary of the English Language 1736 (1923) (defining punishment as "[a]ny pain, suffering, or loss inflicted on *or suffered by* a person because of a crime or evil-doing") (emphasis added).

The Court's unduly narrow definition of punishment blinds it to the reality of prison life. Consider, for example, a situation in which one individual is sentenced to a period of confinement at a relatively safe, well-managed prison, complete with tennis courts and cable television, while another is sentenced to a prison characterized by rampant violence and terror. Under such circumstances, it is natural to say that the latter individual was subjected to a more extreme punishment. It matters little that the sentencing judge did not specify to which prison the individuals would be sent; nor is it relevant that the prison officials did not intend either individual to suffer any attack. The conditions of confinement, whatever the reason for them, resulted in differing punishment for the two convicts.

Wilson's myopic focus on the intentions of *prison officials* is also mistaken. Where a legislature refuses to fund a prison adequately, the resulting barbaric conditions should not be immune from constitutional scrutiny simply because no prison official acted culpably. . . . The responsibility for subminimal conditions in any prison inevitably is diffuse, and often borne, at least in part, by the legislature. Yet, regardless of what state actor or institution caused the harm and with what intent, the experience of the inmate is the same. . . . As Judge Noonan has observed:

> "The Framers were familiar from their wartime experience of British prisons with the kind of cruel punishment administered by a warden with the mentality of a Captain Bligh. *But they were also familiar with the cruelty that came from bureaucratic indifference to the conditions of confinement.* The Framers understood that cruel and unusual punishment can be administered by the failure of those in charge to give heed to the impact of their actions on those within their care."

Jordan v. Gardner, 986 F.2d 1521 (9th Cir. 1993) (emphasis added).

Before *Wilson,* it was assumed, if not established, that the conditions of confinement are themselves part of the punishment, even if not specifically "meted out" by a statute or judge. *See Wilson* (White, J., concurring in judgment), *citing Hutto v. Finney*; *Rhodes v. Chapman*. We examined only the objective severity of the conditions of confinement in the pre-*Wilson* cases, not the subjective intent of government officials, as we found that "[a]n express intent to inflict unnecessary pain is not required, . . . *and harsh 'conditions of confinement' may constitute cruel and unusual punishment* unless such conditions 'are part of the penalty that criminal offenders pay for their offenses against society.'" *Whitley v. Albers*, quoting *Rhodes* (emphasis added). This initial approach, which employed an objective standard to chart the boundaries of the Eighth Amendment, reflected the practical reality that "intent simply is not very meaningful when considering a challenge to an institution, such as a prison system," *Wilson* (White, J., concurring in judgment). It also, however, demonstrated a commitment to the principles underlying the Eighth Amendment. The Cruel and Unusual Punishments Clause was not adopted to protect prison officials with arguably benign intentions from lawsuits. The Eighth Amendment guarantees each prisoner that reasonable measures will be taken to ensure his safety. Where a prisoner can prove that no such reasonable steps were taken and, as a result, he experienced severe pain or suffering without any penological justification, the Eighth Amendment is violated regardless of whether there is an easily identifiable wrongdoer with poor intentions.

II

Though I believe *Wilson v. Seiter* should be overruled, and disagree with the Court's reliance upon that case in defining the "deliberate indifference" standard, I nonetheless join the Court's opinion. Petitioner never challenged this Court's holding in *Wilson* or sought reconsideration of the theory upon which that decision is based. More importantly, the Court's opinion does not extend *Wilson* beyond its ill-conceived boundaries or erect any new obstacles for prison inmates to overcome in seeking to remedy cruel and unusual conditions of confinement. . . . The opinion's clear message is that prison officials must fulfill their affirmative duty under the Constitution to prevent inmate assault, including prison rape, or otherwise face a serious risk of being held liable for damages or being required by a court to rectify the hazardous conditions. . . .

Justice STEVENS, concurring.

While I continue to believe that a state official may inflict cruel and unusual punishment without any improper subjective motivation, see *Estelle v. Gamble* (1976) (dissenting opinion); *Wilson v. Seiter* (1991) (White, J., concurring in judgment), I join Justice SOUTER's thoughtful opinion because it is faithful to our precedents.

Justice THOMAS, concurring in the judgment.

Prisons are necessarily dangerous places; they house society's most antisocial and violent people in close proximity with one another. Regrettably, "[s]ome level of brutality and sexual aggression among [prisoners] is inevitable no matter what the guards do . . . unless all prisoners are locked in their cells 24 hours a day and sedated." *McGill v. Duckworth*, 944 F.2d 344 (7th Cir. 1991). Today, in an attempt to rectify such unfortunate conditions, the Court further refines the "National Code of Prison Regulation," otherwise known as the Cruel and Unusual Punishments Clause. *Hudson v. McMillian* (THOMAS, J., dissenting).

I adhere to my belief, expressed in *Hudson* and *Helling v. McKinney* (THOMAS, J., dissenting), that "judges or juries—but not jailers—impose 'punishment.'" "[P]unishment," from the time of the Founding through the present day, "has always meant a 'fine, penalty, or confinement inflicted upon a person by the authority of the law and the judgment and sentence of a court, for some crime or offense committed by him.'" *Id.* (quoting BLACK'S LAW DICTIONARY 1234 (6th ed. 1990)). *See also* 2 T. SHERIDAN, A GENERAL DICTIONARY OF THE ENGLISH LANGUAGE (1780) (defining "punishment" as "[a]ny infliction imposed in vengeance of a crime"). Conditions of confinement are not punishment in any recognized sense of the term, unless imposed as part of a sentence. As an original matter, therefore, this case would be an easy one for me: Because the unfortunate attack that befell petitioner was not part of his sentence, it did not constitute "punishment" under the Eighth Amendment.

When approaching this case, however, we do not write on a clean slate. Beginning with *Estelle v. Gamble* (1976), the Court's prison condition jurisprudence has been guided, not by the text of the Constitution, but rather by "evolving standards of decency that mark the progress of a maturing society." *Id. See also ante*; *Helling; Hudson.* I continue to doubt the legitimacy of that mode of constitutional decision-making, the logical result of which, in this context, is to transform federal judges into superintendents of prison conditions nationwide. *See Helling* (THOMAS, J., dissenting). Although *Estelle* loosed the Eighth Amendment from its historical moorings, the Court is now unwilling to accept the full consequences of its decision and therefore resorts to the "subjective" (state of mind) component of post-*Estelle* Eighth Amendment analysis in an attempt to contain what might otherwise be unbounded liability for prison officials under the Cruel and Unusual Punishments Clause.

Although I disagree with the constitutional predicate of the Court's analysis, I share the Court's view that petitioner's theory of liability—that a prison official can be held liable for risks to prisoner safety of which he was ignorant but should have known—fails under even "a straightforward application of *Estelle.*" *Helling* (THOMAS, J., dissenting). In adopting the "deliberate indifference" standard for challenges to prison conditions, *Estelle* held that mere "inadverten[ce]" or "negligen[ce]" does not violate the Eighth Amendment.... Petitioner's suggested "should have known" standard is nothing but a negligence standard, as the Court's discussion implicitly assumes. Thus, even under *Estelle*, petitioner's theory of liability necessarily fails.

The question remains, however, what state of mind *is* sufficient to constitute deliberate indifference under *Estelle*. Given my serious doubts concerning the correctness of *Estelle* in extending the Eighth Amendment to cover challenges to conditions of confinement, I believe the scope of the *Estelle* "right" should be confined as narrowly as possible. In *Wilson,* the Court has already held that the highest subjective standard known to our Eighth Amendment jurisprudence—"maliciou[s] and sadisti[c]" action "for the very purpose of causing harm," *Whitley*—"does not apply to prison conditions cases." *Wilson.* The Court today adopts the next highest level of subjective intent, actual knowledge of the type sufficient to constitute recklessness in the criminal law, noting that "due regard" is appropriate "for prison officials' 'unenviable task of keeping dangerous men in safe custody under humane conditions.'"[1] *Ante* (quoting *Spain v. Procunier* (9th Cir. 1979) (Kennedy, J.)).

---

1. The facts of this case demonstrate how difficult that task can be. When petitioner was taken out of general prison population for security reasons at United States Penitentiary-Lewisburg, he [*sic*] asserted that he "d[id] not need extra security precautions" and filed suit alleging that placing

. . . I cannot join the Court's opinion. . . . Indeed, "[w]ere the issue squarely presented, . . . I might vote to overrule *Estelle.*" *Helling* (Thomas, J., dissenting). Nonetheless, the issue is not squarely presented in this case. Respondents have not asked us to revisit *Estelle,* and no one has briefed or argued the question. In addition to these prudential concerns, *stare decisis* counsels hesitation in overruling dubious precedents. For these reasons, I concur in the Court's judgment. . . .

Discussion

1. Should the *Farmer* standard apply to the denial of health care to a trans incarceree? (Why might it not?) And, if so, to what forms of trans health care should it be extended?

2. Would the *Farmer* standard apply to justify the placement of all trans incarcerees in solitary confinement on the grounds that they would otherwise be exposed to a known risk?

Note on Greene v. Bowles

In *Greene v. Bowles*, 361 F.3d 290 (6th Cir. 2004), the U.S. Court of Appeals 2–1 reversed a grant of summary judgment to Warden Anthony J. Brigano in a suit brought by Traci Greene, a transgender woman inmate housed in a men's prison, against Brigano and other corrections officials. She had sued under 42 U.S.C. § 1983 for violation of her Eighth Amendment rights, alleging that the defendants were deliberately indifferent to her safety. As recounted by the opinion of Judge Karen Moore, joined by Judge James Ryan,

> . . . . At the time of her incarceration at Warren Correctional Institution ("WCI"), [Greene] was preoperative [*sic*—Eds.], but still displayed female characteristics, including developed breasts and a feminine demeanor, and was undergoing hormone therapy. Because of her feminine appearance, Greene was placed in the Protective Custody Unit ("PCU") to guard against attacks from other inmates. In July 1996, a second inmate in the PCU, Hiawatha Frezzell ("Frezzell"), assaulted Greene on several occasions, culminating in a severe attack on July 12 in which Frezzell beat Greene with a mop handle and then struck her with a fifty-pound fire extinguisher. Frezzell had a long history of assaults on other inmates and was classified as a maximum-security prisoner; at the time of the attack, Greene was classified as medium-security. By Warden Brigano's own admission, Frezzell was a "predatory inmate." Frezzell had been placed in the PCU at WCI, however, in order to protect him from the repercussions of his testimony against

---

him in solitary confinement was unconstitutional. *See Farmer v. Carlson*, 685 F. Supp. 1335, 1342 (M.D. Pa. 1988). Petitioner's present claim, oddly enough, is essentially that *leaving him* in general prison population was unconstitutional because it subjected him to a risk of sexual assault.

his fellow prisoners in the Lucasville prison riot; Frezzell had been himself convicted of aggravated assault for beating two prisoners during that riot. Nonetheless, for Frezzell's protection from others, Frezzell was placed in PCU with Greene, a medium-security and vulnerable inmate.

After the attack, Frezzell was transferred from the PCU to the segregation unit, and criminally charged with attempted murder.

"Summary judgment was granted as to Warden Brigano and denied as to the other defendants; they earlier appealed that decision to" the court of appeals, "which affirmed the denial as to two defendants and reversed as to one." A jury trial ruled in favor of the defendants remaining in the suit, and Greene pursued her appeal of the grant of summary judgment to Brigano.

As the court of appeals explained, the trial court had granted Brigano summary judgment

on the narrow ground that Greene failed to introduce evidence from which a reasonable trier of fact could conclude that Warden Brigano knew of a substantial risk of serious harm to Greene. Specifically, the court held first that as Frezzell's attack on Greene wasn't sexual, Greene's status was irrelevant to the determination of a substantial risk, and second, that Greene had not offered "evidence from which a trier of fact could conclude that [Warden Brigano] knew of Mr. Frezzell's history of violence and, specifically, of attacks upon other inmates."

The court of appeals

reject[ed] the district court's ultimate conclusion for two reasons: first, evidence had been offered from which a trier of fact could conclude that Greene was vulnerable, not just to sexual assault, but also to physical assaults from her fellow inmates, such that her presence in the PCU with other inmates without segregation or protective measures presented a substantial risk to her safety of which Warden Brigano was aware; and second, Greene has presented evidence from which a trier of fact could conclude that Warden Brigano was in fact aware of the substantial risk Frezzell posed to any inmate with whom he was placed in the PCU.

Regarding the first ground, dealing with Greene's vulnerability, the court of appeals highlighted that Greene's evidence included

a Protective Control Screening form signed by [Brigano], noting that Greene was placed in the PCU for her personal safety; numerous Protective Control Review forms signed by . . . Brigano noting Greene's physical appearance as the reason for her placement in the PCU; [Brigano's] deposition testimony that transgendered [sic — Eds.] inmates are often placed in protective custody because of the greater likelihood of their being attacked by their fellow inmates; [his] admission that the universe of harm that can befall inmates like Greene includes attempted assault, assault, attempted murder, and murder; and [his] concessions that Greene was placed in the PCU to protect her from serious harm and that that serious harm could come from a fellow PCU inmate as well as an inmate in the general population.

Regarding the second ground, dealing with Frezzell's danger, the court of appeals pointed to evidence Greene presented to the trial court, including

> Frezzell's lengthy prison misconduct record, including . . . two convictions for felonious assault arising out of the Lucasville prison riot; [Brigano's] admission of Frezzell's status as a predatory inmate; [Brigano's] concessions that Frezzell had "a long institutional history of being a disruptive, violent inmate"; and the fact that Frezzell was a maximum-security inmate.

This, the court of appeals held, was enough to create a genuine issue of material fact about whether Brigano was deliberately indifferent to Greene's safety sufficient to preclude a grant of summary judgment to Brigano.

Circuit Judge John Marshall Rogers dissented. In his view,

> [t]he only evidence cited by Greene that suggests that Warden Brigano actually drew the inference that Greene faced a substantial risk of harm in the protective custody unit is [Brigano's] admission that harms may befall protective custody inmates. Such a statement can hardly be enough to create a triable issue of fact as to Warden Brigano's awareness of the risks facing Greene. At most, this admission is a concession that prison life is inherently dangerous, and particularly so for transgendered inmates. The fact that Warden Brigano recognized the existence of certain risks attendant with the placement of certain categories of inmates in protective custody, however, does not amount to an awareness of a significant risk of harm to Greene's health or safety. The Eighth Amendment requires, instead, that a warden actually recognize a significant risk of harm arising from particular facts. While the majority properly states that, in some contexts, a particular victim, or a particular perpetrator, need not be known, general recognition of some risks is not enough.

As he read the court's treatment of Greene's allegations, "[t]he effect of the majority's opinion in this case is to impose an objective standard of deliberate indifference—a position explicitly rejected by the Supreme Court [in *Farmer v. Brennan*, 511 U.S. 825 (1994)]."

Note on Schwenk v. Hartford

In 2000, the U.S. Court of Appeals for the Ninth Circuit upheld a transgender woman inmate's right to sue for sexual assault under the federal Gender Motivated Violence Act ("GMVA") in *Schwenk v. Hartford*, 204 F.3d 1187 (9th Cir. 2000). See Chapter 5, Section C, *supra*, for discussion of *Schwenk*'s sex discrimination/sex stereotyping reasoning. Two and a half months later, the Supreme Court held that the GMVA was not within Congress's commerce power or its power to enforce the Fourteenth Amendment. *United States v. Morrison*, 529 U.S. 528 (2000).

It remains to be seen whether the judiciary would uphold applications of the GMVA as applied to federal defendants on the theory that whatever power let Congress incarcerate them also suffices (in conjunction with Congress's power under the Necessary and Proper Clause of the Constitution) to let Congress ban sex discrimination against them and thus to sustain the GMVA as applied to them. This would be parallel to the theory by which courts are enforcing the Religious Freedom Restoration Act ("RFRA") against federal defendants even after the Supreme Court held that RFRA was not within Congress's Fourteenth Amendment enforcement powers in *City of Boerne v. Flores*, 521 U.S. 507 (1997). *See, e.g., Burwell v. Hobby Lobby Stores, Inc.* 573 U.S. 682, 695 (2014) ("As applied to a federal agency, RFRA is based on the enumerated power that supports the particular agency's work. . . .") (citing decisions from the Second and Ninth Circuit U.S. Courts of Appeals).

Reading Guide for Giraldo v. California Dep't of Corrections and Rehabilitation

1. The suit by plaintiff Alexis Giraldo, an incarcerated transgender woman, included three causes of action against the state for allegedly failing to protect her against repeated violence, including rapes, by other inmates. What happened in the trial court with each? What are the bottom-line conclusions of the California Court of Appeal on the first and third causes of action?

2. What is the reasoning of the court of appeal on the first cause of action? On what authorities does it rely in its analysis? What does it say is "the most important consideration"? What is the "caveat" the court provides to its holding on this cause of action? For what reasons does the court reject the defense arguments against the plaintiff's position that the court embraces?

3. On the third cause of action, what are the three factors from precedent that the court of appeal analyzes? How does the court reason that these factors lead to its conclusion on this cause of action?

4. What is the court's reasoning on the defendants' mootness argument?

Alexis Giraldo v. California Department of Corrections and Rehabilitation, et al.

85 Cal. Rptr. 3d 371 (Ct. App. 2008)

RICHMAN, J.

Plaintiff's appeal presents two questions never before decided in California: (1) whether the relationship between jailer and prisoner is a special relationship giving rise to a duty of care to the prisoner; and (2) whether there is a private right of action for damages for violation of the cruel or unusual punishment clause of the state Constitution, article I, section 17. We answer yes to the first question, no to the second.

Plaintiff Alexis Giraldo, describing herself as a male-to-female transgender person, was an inmate in the California prison system. Plaintiff filed an action against the California Department of Corrections and Rehabilitation (CDCR) and various

CDCR personnel (when referred to collectively, defendants) "challeng[ing] prison policies that place transgender inmates, such as [plaintiff], who have the physical appearance of women, in the male inmate population without any meaningful precaution to the obvious risk of sexual assault to them." The complaint made the specific claim that defendants failed to take action on plaintiff's repeated complaints that she was being beaten and raped by her cellmate at Folsom State Prison.

Plaintiff's complaint alleged three causes of action: (1) negligence; (2) intentional infliction of emotional distress; and (3) violation of the cruel or unusual punishment clause of the California Constitution. The law and motion judge sustained a demurrer to the first cause of action based on a failure to allege a cognizable duty. The second cause of action was rejected by a jury. And the trial judge dismissed the third cause of action on motion by defendants.

. . . .

I. Background
A. The Facts

[Plaintiff's] first claim for negligence was addressed via demurrer, which was sustained. . . . The relevant facts, therefore, are those contained in plaintiff's complaint. . . .

The operative complaint is the amended complaint. It is 34 pages long, with 175 paragraphs, and contains extensive details of horrific sexual abuse plaintiff allegedly suffered at the hands of her cellmate, abuse that, according to plaintiff, defendants were repeatedly told about and repeatedly disregarded. Those details are not necessary to our analysis here, and we set forth the essential facts alleged in the amended complaint, which are these:

On or about October 17, 2005, plaintiff was incarcerated at North Kern State Prison on a parole violation. Plaintiff was a male-to-female transgender inmate who "has the physical appearance of a woman, yet she [was] incarcerated with male inmates without any meaningful precaution to the obvious risk of sexual assault stemming from being unprotected from the countless male inmates she is housed with."

In December 2005, plaintiff was classified as a Level III Inmate with 36 points, which resulted in her having a primary placement recommendation for incarceration at either California Medical Facility (CMF) or California Men's Colony (CMC). CMF and CMC have higher concentrations of transgender inmates, and such inmates are relatively safer at both prisons than at other state prisons.

Contrary to that recommendation, however, plaintiff was in fact assigned to Folsom State Prison (FSP), to which she was transferred on January 4, 2006. Within a week of her assignment to FSP, an inmate employed as a lieutenant's clerk requested that plaintiff be assigned as his cellmate, which request was granted. Beginning almost immediately, and lasting through late January, the cellmate "sexually harassed, assaulted, raped and threatened" plaintiff on a daily basis.

During the time plaintiff was housed in this cell, her cellmate introduced her to his friend, another inmate, who in late January requested that plaintiff be transferred to his cell, which request was also granted. One to two weeks after plaintiff moved into this cell, her new cellmate began raping and beating her, again daily. Plaintiff reported the abuse to prison staff members, apparently on numerous occasions, repeatedly requesting transfer to a different cell. Her reports were ignored, and she was always returned to the same cell.[1] After one final incident on March 12, 2006, in which her cellmate raped her and attacked her with a box-cutter, plaintiff was finally placed in segregated housing.

As a result of these incidents, plaintiff suffered, and continued to suffer, "severe emotional distress that has caused severe depression and anxiety." Plaintiff was, at the time she filed her complaint, housed in a unit for psychologically troubled inmates at CMF and expressed her fear that she would "be released from the mental-health unit and into the general male-inmate population, which [would] significantly increase the risk that she [would] be sexually assaulted once again." Plaintiff also alleged that "[u]pon her release from custody, her transition to civilian life will be more difficult, which decreases her chances of successful rehabilitation. She will need to seek professional mental-health care for the rest of her life, and her ability to work and earn income will also be diminished for the rest of her life."

B. The Pretrial Proceedings

Plaintiff's first cause of action was for negligence, and alleged in fundamental part that "Defendants' custody of plaintiff created a situation of dependency, which resulted in detrimental reliance on them for protection. This, in turn, established a duty of care to protect [plaintiff] under *Williams v. State of California*, 34 Cal. 3d 18 (1983) and other applicable law discussing the doctrine of the 'special relationship.'" The second cause of action was for intentional infliction of emotional distress, and alleged that plaintiff had on multiple occasions informed various prison staff members that her cellmate was raping and beating her, yet they continued to place her

---

1. Our disclaimer about detail notwithstanding, two specific allegations about this timeframe are illustrative. First, plaintiff alleged that on March 8, 2006, she was able to get to the office of correctional counselor Jerry Ignasiak, and told him that "her cellmate had become violent, was forcing her to have unwanted sex with him on a daily basis, would beat her if she refused to have sex with him, and was physically abusing her." In fear for her life, plaintiff pleaded with Ignasiak to move her from the cell, showing him her CMF and CMC classification recommendations, and explaining that she was never supposed to be placed at FSP. Ignasiak told plaintiff to be "tough and strong," did nothing else, and "even discouraged [plaintiff] from taking any further action." He then returned her to her cell.

Second, on March 10, 2006, plaintiff sought protection by speaking to Amy Holliday, a FSP medical employee, telling her that her cellmate was raping and beating her daily. Holliday wrote the following entry in plaintiff's chronological interdisciplinary progress notes: "Inmate has been dealing with an abusive cellie [cellmate] who has become sexually demanding and overly possessive. I/M [inmate] would like transfer to transgendered [*sic*] unit but doesn't want to 'lock it up.' 'I don't want to get him into trouble.'"

back in the same cell with the knowledge that she would continue to be assaulted. The third cause of action was for violation of the California Constitution, article I, section 17, and alleged that defendants acted with "deliberate indifference" to plaintiff's safety needs, and that defendants' conduct was "shocking to the conscience" in violation of the cruel or unusual punishment clause of the California Constitution. Cal. Const., art. I, § 17.

. . . .

Plaintiff's prayer sought general and special damages, punitive damages, a permanent injunction prohibiting [CDCR Secretary James E. Tilton] and CDCR from violating the rights of transgender inmates, and a declaratory judgment that (1) the practice of housing transgender inmates with male inmates violates the prohibition against cruel or unusual punishment, and (2) prison officials owe a duty to protect inmates under the "special relationship" doctrine of tort law. Plaintiff also sought costs of suit and attorneys' fees.

. . . .

On July 13, 2007, plaintiff was released from prison on parole. That same day, defendants filed a motion to dismiss plaintiff's prayer for declaratory and injunctive relief, arguing that her claims for equitable relief were moot due to her release from CDCR custody and that her claims did not fall under the "general public interest" exception to the mootness doctrine. Additionally, defendants sought dismissal of plaintiff's claim for damages under the California Constitution, arguing that article I, section 17 does not support a private right of action for tort damages.

. . . .

II. Discussion

. . . .

B. The General Principles

In *Adams v. City of Fremont*, 80 Cal. Rptr. 2d 196 (Ct. App. 1998), we began our analysis with an exposition of the principles pertinent to the question of duty as it pertains to public employees, first setting forth the fundamental rule that the right to recover against public entities or their employees for injuries resulting from alleged negligent conduct has, since 1963, been defined by statute. We then went on: "Public employees are liable for injuries resulting from their acts or omissions to the same extent as private persons, except where otherwise exempted or immunized by law. [Govt. Code,] § 820. Public entities are correspondingly liable for the negligent acts or omissions of their employees acting within the scope of their employment except where either the employee or the public entity is immunized from liability by statute. [Govt. Code,] § 815.2. However, '[t]he exclusive sway of statutory rules does not foreclose the aid of common law tort doctrines and analogies in ascertaining and achieving imperfectly expressed statutory objectives.' Where a legal duty is not created by statute, the question of whether a legal duty exists is analyzed under general principles of tort law." . . . .

"The most important of [the] considerations in establishing duty is for[e]see-ability. As a general principle, a 'defendant owes a duty of care to all persons who are foreseeably endangered by his conduct, with respect to all risks which make the conduct unreasonably dangerous.'" *Tarasoff v. Regents of University of California*, 51 P.2d 334 (Cal. 1976).

Another general principle is "that, as a general matter, there is no duty to act to protect others from the conduct of third parties." *Delgado v. Trax Bar & Grill*, 113 P.3d 1159 (Cal. 2005); *Williams.* This general principle, however, is subject to a significant qualification, as *Delgado* also confirmed: "A defendant may owe an affirmative duty to protect another from the conduct of third parties if he or she has a 'special relationship' with the other person. Such can arise when the "defendant stands in some special relationship to either the person whose conduct needs to be controlled or in a relationship to the foreseeable victim of that conduct, *see* REST. 2D TORTS (1965) §§ 315–320.)" *Tarasoff.*

It has been observed that a typical setting for the recognition of a special rela-tionship is where "the plaintiff is particularly vulnerable and dependent upon the defendant who, correspondingly, has some control over the plaintiff's welfare." *Kockelman v. Segal*, 71 Cal. Rptr. 2d 552 (Ct. App. 1998), *citing* PROSSER & KEETON, TORTS (5th ed.1984) § 56, p. 374. Thus, and as our Supreme Court has noted, a spe-cial relationship has been found to exist between business proprietors such as shop-ping centers, restaurants, and bars, and their tenants, patrons, or invitees, and also between common carriers and passengers, innkeepers and their guests, and mental health professionals and their patients. *Delgado.*

C. There Exists a Special Relationship Between a Jailer and a Prisoner Giving Rise to a Duty of Care to Protect the Prisoner from Foreseeable Harm Inflicted by a Third Party

Plaintiff's negligence claim was . . . premised on the existence of a special rela-tionship between the prison employees and herself which, she claimed, gave rise to a duty to protect her from foreseeable harm—an issue that, surprisingly, no Cali-fornia court has apparently discussed, much less answered. But while California has not addressed the issue of whether the relationship of jailer and prisoner imposes a duty of care, recognition of such a duty finds support in numerous, if not all, perti-nent authorities.

The *Restatement Second of Torts*, cited with approval by the California Supreme Court in *Delgado*, says this in section 320: "Duty of Person Having Custody of Another to Control Conduct of Third Persons. [¶] One who is required by law to take or who voluntarily takes the custody of another under circumstances such as to deprive the other of his normal power of self-protection or to subject him to asso-ciation with persons likely to harm him, is under a duty to exercise reasonable care so to control the conduct of third persons as to prevent them from intentionally harming the other or so conducting themselves as to create an unreasonable risk of harm to him, if the actor [¶] (a) knows or has reason to know that he has the ability to control the conduct of the third persons, and [¶] (b) knows or should know of the necessity and opportunity for exercising such control."

The comment to section 320 begins as follows: "a. The rule stated in this Section is applicable to a sheriff or peace officer, a jailer or warden of a penal institution. . . ." The comments then go on, in comment c., with observations particularly apt here: "c. *Peculiar risks to which other exposed.* The custody of another may be taken under such circumstances as to associate the other with persons who are peculiarly likely to do him harm from which he cannot be expected to protect himself. If so, the actor who has taken custody of the other is required to exercise reasonable care to furnish the necessary protection. This is particularly true where the custody not only involves intimate association with persons of notoriously dangerous character, but also deprives the person in custody of his normal ability to protect himself, as where a prisoner is put in a cell with a man of known violent temper, or is required to work or take exercise with a group of notoriously desperate characters. In such a case, the fact that the person in custody is a prisoner precludes the possession of any self-defensive weapons, and thus makes him incapable of adequately protecting himself."

Professor Dobbs, likewise cited in *Delgado,* states the rule this way: "A person who has custody of another owes a duty of reasonable care to protect the other from foreseeable harm. A custodian may thus be held liable for failure to make reasonable efforts to protect a ward from a third person's attack or molestation and even to protect the ward from his own self-destructive inclinations. . . . [¶] *Jailers.* . . . Custodians include those who actually exercise control over their charges or who have legal authority to control them. One clear example is the jailer who holds prisoners in custody. By reason of his custody, the jailer owes the prisoner a duty of reasonable protection from attack. . . ." 2 Dobbs, The Law of Torts § 326 (2001).

The Prosser and Keeton hornbook is similar: "The general duty which arises in many relations to take reasonable precautions for the safety of others may include the obligation to exercise control over the conduct of third persons. Certain relationships are protective by nature, requiring the defendant to guard his charge against harm from others. Thus, the duty of a carrier toward its passengers may require it to maintain order in its trains and stations, and to use reasonable care to prevent not only conduct which is merely negligent, but also physical attacks or thefts of property on the part of other passengers or strangers. A similar obligation rests upon innkeepers towards their guests, landlords toward their tenants, employers toward their employees, *jailers toward their prisoners,* hospitals toward their patients, schools toward their pupils, business establishments toward their customers, and landlords toward their tenants." Prosser and Keeton, Torts, Acts and Omissions, § 56 (5th ed. 1984) (italics added).

Such relationship, and its concomitant duty, is also the rule set forth in legal encyclopedias. *E.g.,* 60 Am. Jur. 2d, Penal and Correctional Institutions § 181 (2007) ("A jailer, whether he is a sheriff or some other officer, owes a duty to the prisoner to keep him safe, to protect him from unnecessary harm, and to exercise reasonable and ordinary care for the prisoner's life and health.") And in law review articles. *E.g.*, 24 U. Tol. L. Rev. 807, 826 ("[T]ort law has long recognized that special relationships override the 'no duty to rescue' rule. Some special relationships, such as master and servant, arose from the benefit derived from another's services. Other special relationships were created by virtue of one party becoming the caretaker of another, as occurs between passenger and common carrier and jailer and inmate.").

That this is the rule is confirmed by the fact that apparently all cases that have considered the issue have recognized a duty owed by a jailer to a prisoner. Several cases hold that the duty arises because there is a special relationship, such as *Wilson v. City of Kotzebue*, 627 P.2d 623 (Alaska 1981) . . . .

Haworth v. State, 592 P.2d 820 (Haw. 1979), is similar: "It is well settled that a state, by reason of the special relationship created by its custody of a prisoner, is under a duty to the prisoner to take reasonable action to protect the prisoner against unreasonable risk of physical harm." Likewise *Thornton v. City of Flint*, 197 N.W.2d 485 (Mich. Ct. App. 1972), where the court held, "The duty which defendant owed to plaintiff arose out of this special relationship in which defendant was one 'required by law to take or who voluntarily takes the custody of another under circumstances such as to deprive the other of his normal opportunities for protection.'"

In addition, an unbroken string of cases starting in 1935 has recognized a duty of care, though not necessarily expressing it in terms of a special relationship. *See, e.g.*, *Sanchez v. State*, 36 A.D.3d 1065 (N.Y. App. Div. 2007) ("'Having assumed physical custody of inmates, who cannot protect and defend themselves in the same way as those at liberty can, [defendant] owes a duty of care to safeguard inmates, even from attacks by fellow inmates.'"); *Kemp v. Waldron*, 115 A.D.2d 869 (N.Y. App. Div. 1985) ("corrections officials have 'a duty to provide inmates with reasonable protection against foreseeable risks of attack by other prisoners'"); [rest of string cite omitted].

Federal law is in accord, as shown by *Farmer v. Brennan*, 511 U.S. 825 (1994), [*supra*, this text, at p. 671 — Eds.]. . . . [T]he United States Supreme Court . . . concluded that a subjective standard applies: "[A]s the lower courts have uniformly held, and as we have assumed, 'prison officials' have a duty . . . to protect prisoners from violence at the hands of other prisoners."

In addition to all the above, two recent statutes cited in the brief filed by amicus curiae Stop Prisoner Rape instruct us. The first is the Prison Rape Elimination Act (PREA), 42 U.S.C. § 15601 *et seq.*, enacted by the United States Congress in 2003, which expressly states its purposes are to: "establish a zero-tolerance standard for the incidence of prison rape in prisons in the United States," "increase the accountability of prison officials who fail to detect, prevent, reduce, and punish prison rape," and "protect the Eighth Amendment rights of Federal, State and local prisoners." The second statute is the Sexual Abuse in Detention Elimination Act (SADEA). SADEA was enacted by the California Legislature in 2005, and set forth practices to be instituted by CDCR concerning the prevention of, and response to, sexual abuse in California prisons. PEN. CODE, §§ 2635–2643. Indeed, CDCR acted to ensure compliance with PREA and SADEA, and in 2006 developed a Prison Rape Elimination Policy, memorialized in a manual detailing procedures for preventing, detecting, responding to, investigating, or tracking sexual abuse in CDCR facilities. CAL. DEPT. OF CORR. & REHAB., DEPT. OPERATIONS MANUAL (2006) Ch. 5, Art. 44 <http://www.cdcr.ca.gov/Regulations/ Adult_Operations/ docs/ DOM/ Ch_ 5_ Printed_ Final_DOM. pdf.>

That, therefore, is the background against which we reach the issue before us: whether there is a special relationship between jailer and prisoner, imposing on the former a duty of care to the latter. We hold that there is.

As quoted above, the most important consideration "in establishing duty is for[e]seeability." *Tarasoff.* It is manifestly foreseeable that an inmate may be at risk of harm, as the recently enacted PREA and SADEA show, recognizing the serious problem presented by sexual abuse in the prison environment. As also noted, important factors in determining whether a relationship is "special" include vulnerability and dependence. Prisoners are vulnerable. And dependent. Moreover, the relationship between them is protective by nature, such that the jailer has control over the prisoner, who is deprived of the normal opportunity to protect himself from harm inflicted by others. This, we conclude, is the epitome of a special relationship, imposing a duty of care on a jailer owed to a prisoner, and we today add California to the list of jurisdictions recognizing a special relationship between jailer and prisoner.

. . . .

Defendants . . . attempt to distinguish the four out-of-state authorities relied on by plaintiff. Defendants argue these cases are factually different from the situation here, and urge that "[n]one of these cases hold [*sic*] that a prison official is in a 'special relationship' with an inmate. . . ." While the cases may not use that term, such distinction does not undermine the point for which plaintiff cites them: court after court after court has recognized that jailers owe prisoners a duty of care to protect them from foreseeable harm, whether stated specifically in terms of a "special relationship" or otherwise.

We close our discussion with a caveat, necessary because of the manner in which the issue presents itself. Defendants' demurrer was, as noted, filed jointly on behalf of all defendants, and made the sweeping claim that no duty was owed by any defendant. Thus, no differentiation was made between or among defendants, no focus put on the position any particular defendant held at FSP or the role he or she was alleged to have played vis-à-vis plaintiff. It will also be recalled that the order sustaining the demurrer to the negligence claim was for "failure to plead cognizable duty," which order also did not differentiate between or among defendants.

Against that background, we issue this express caveat as to what it is we hold: there is a special relationship between jailer and prisoner which imposes a duty of care on the jailer to the prisoner. Who comes within the category of jailer is not before us, nor is the question of what law pertains to non-jailer defendants—questions that could not be decided on this record in any event. . . . Any such issues are left for another day.

D. There Is No Private Right of Action for Damages Arising out of an Alleged Violation of the Cruel or Unusual Punishment Clause of the California Constitution

[Following precedent, this court] turn[s] to the cruel or unusual punishment clause in the California Constitution and, as directed by *Katzberg*, "begin[s—Ed.] our inquiry by asking whether, when the constitutional provision at issue was adopted, the enactors intended that it include a damages remedy for its violation" . . . . [After a lengthy analysis—Eds.] we have found no indication—either on the face of the constitutional provision or in its history—that the enactors intended article I, section 17 of the state Constitution confer a private right of action for damages for a violation of the prohibition against the infliction of cruel or usual punishment.

Katzberg further instructs that we must now analyze "whether a constitutional tort action for damages to remedy the asserted constitutional violation should be recognized." Such question is to be considered in light of the three factors identified as relevant to this question, the first of which is "adequacy of existing remedies." . . . .

We conclude that there are adequate alternative remedies available for a claim such as that asserted by plaintiff here. First, we have concluded that California law imposes on at least some prison personnel a duty to protect prisoners from foreseeable harm caused by other inmates, breach of which could give rise to a claim for negligence. Additionally, and as defendants point out, plaintiff had available a claim pursuant to 42 U.S.C. § 1983 for violation of the Eighth Amendment to the federal Constitution. *Redman v. County of San Diego*, 942 F.2d 1435 (9th Cir. 1991) (directed verdict for defendants reversed; jury could find deliberate indifference in placement of pretrial detainee in cell with homosexual with history of trying to coerce others into sexual favors when detainee was later allegedly raped); *see also Farmer v. Brennan*. The "availability of the adequate alternative remedies militates against judicial creation of a tort cause of action for damages in the circumstances presented." *Katzberg*.

The second *Katzberg* factor is whether allowing private damages claims for violation of California Constitution article I, section 17 would change existing law. [D]efendants argue "this factor militates against inferring a claim for damages under the cruel-or-unusual punishment clause because this would change existing tort law [since] no court has recognized a claim for damages under this constitutional provision." We agree with defendants.

The final factor we consider is the nature of the cruel or unusual punishment clause and "the significance of the purpose that it seeks to effectuate." . . . . We agree that the due process right is fundamental. But absent the applicability of the other relevant factors discussed here, the relative importance of the constitutional right is of little help in determining the availability of a damages remedy for a violation of that right." *Carlsbad Aquafarm, Inc. v. State Dept. of Health Services*, 100 Cal. Rptr. 2d 87 (Ct. App. 2000); *see also Katzberg.*

Undoubtedly, the prohibition against the infliction of cruel or unusual punishment is a significant Constitutional right aimed at protecting, in plaintiff's words, "basic human dignity." However, when considered together with the other factors relevant to whether the claim for damages should be recognized—most significantly, the availability of adequate remedies—we conclude there is no basis to recognize a claim for damages under article I, section 17 of the California Constitution. Accordingly, we affirm the trial court's dismissal of plaintiff's claim for damages resulting from defendants' alleged violation of the cruel or unusual punishment clause.

E. The Trial Court's Dismissal of Plaintiff's Prayer for Injunctive and Declaratory Relief as Moot Was Supported by Substantial Evidence

[W]e review a trial court's determination of mootness for substantial evidence, and conclude that the determination here was supported by substantial evidence. It is clear that upon plaintiff's parole she was no longer under the physical control of CDCR, and the challenged conduct no longer applied to her. Thus, any injunction or declaratory judgment would not impact her. . . .

[P]laintiff argues that in the event that we affirm the trial court's mootness determination, her equitable claims fall under the "public importance" exception to the mootness doctrine such that either the trial court or this court should nevertheless consider them. [W]e will not exercise any such discretion here.

To begin with, the issues plaintiff presents are essentially factual, a recognized basis to refuse to decide a moot case. Beyond that, we lack an adequate record to address plaintiff's equitable claims. In short, nothing could come of our exercising our discretion to invoke the exception. . . .

III. Disposition

The trial court's order sustaining defendants' demurrer to plaintiff's claim for negligence on the ground that she failed to allege a cognizable duty is reversed. The order dismissing the claim for violation of the cruel or unusual punishment clause and the prayers for injunctive and declaratory relief is affirmed. The matter is remanded to the trial court for further proceedings consistent with the above.

We concur: KLINE, P.J., and HAERLE, J.

———————

Discussion

1. Does the court's analysis of the plaintiff's first cause of action impose too many burdens on correctional authorities, who must deal with the necessity of housing numerous dangerous inmates?

2. In analyzing the plaintiff's claimed third cause of action and the adequacy of alternative remedies, should the court have addressed the defense of qualified immunity available to individual state officers in suits brought to enforce plaintiffs' federal constitutional rights under 42 U.S.C. § 1983? *Cf.* David M. Shapiro & Charles Hogle, *The Horror Chamber: Unqualified Impunity in Prison*, 93 Notre Dame L. Rev. 2021 (2018) (discussing reasons why "the availability of federal litigation has not stopped prisoners from being tortured, maimed, killed, or otherwise made to suffer chilling abuse.").

———————

Consider the following excerpts from an "abolitionist"—meaning, advocating for the abolition of prisons—article arguing that "racialized gender violence" cannot be eliminated from prisons and thus for the government to preclude such violence from its penal facilities the government must eliminate those facilities.

The Only Way to End Racialized Gender Violence in Prisons Is to End Prisons2[*]
Dean Spade

. . . .

[An] analysis of the origins of imprisonment [as an adaptation of slavery] helps us understand imprisonment itself as racialized violence. Punishment and imprisonment were and are co-constitutive in the United States with processes of racialization. Today punishment systems are rationalized as race-neutral institutions for determining and punishing individual culpability, but such assertions are laughable in the face of the severe and obvious targeting of people of color in every aspect of policing, pre-trial imprisonment, prosecution, sentencing, imprisonment, probation, and parole. More than 60 percent of the people in prison are people of color, and one in every ten Black men age 30–39 is in prison or jail. Black youth are 16 percent of the youth population, but 28 percent of juvenile arrests, 37 percent of the youth in juvenile jails, and 58 percent of the youth sent to adult prisons. . . . The criminal punishment system in the United States . . . is justified by the idea that it contains and neutralizes dangerous law-breakers. In reality, race, not dangerousness or illegal action, determines who is imprisoned. US prisons are full of low-income people and people of color who were prosecuted for crimes of poverty and minor drug use. Racist tropes of Black dangerousness that have been a central part of US culture since slavery are invoked and mobilized in media to justify and normalize the continuing expansion of criminalization and imprisonment. . . .

Processes of racialization, like . . . slavery/criminalization processes . . . , are inherently gendered and gendering, and the construction and administration of

———————

[*] Excerpted from Dean Spade, *The Only Way to End Racialized Gender Violence in Prisons Is to End Prisons*, 3 Calif. L. Rev. Circuit 184 (2012). Reprinted with permission

gender categories is always racialized. . . . The specific vulnerabilities, responsibilities, and chances at life administered by US laws and institutions are racialized *and* gendered, not universal to all people assigned a particular gender or race category. . . .

Trans studies scholars have provided analysis of how racialized gender norms are administered in spaces of concentrated state violence in the contemporary United States. Across the country, the spaces where people of color and poor people are concentrated for surveillance, punishment, targeted abandonment, and premature death — shelters, foster care and juvenile punishment group homes, psychiatric facilities, immigration prisons, jails, and the like — are sex-segregated, rigidly enforcing notions of gender binarism. The enforcement of racialized gender norms in these spaces operates through coercion and violence overseen by state agents, including law enforcement and social service providers. The violence in these spaces includes identity documentation and surveillance, dress regulations, strip searches, sexual assault, forced prostitution, family dissolution, verbal harassment, medical neglect, murder, and other contributors to early death. . . .

. . . .

. . . . Prison reforms, abolitionists argue, tend to refine and reify the racialized-gendered control of prisons. In general, reforms that try to address the violence caused by state enforcement of racialized gender norms and categories by slightly altering the categories being enforced or by adding additional categories consistently fail to meaningfully alleviate that violence. A typical response to the assertion that trans people face significant violence in prisons and jails is the proposal to build trans prisons. . . . These kinds of proposals . . . will inevitably fail to address the harms identified. Instead, they will become new sites for racialized gender norms to be enforced as state agents take up their posts enforcing identity categories in ways that will inevitably operate to the detriment of people of color, poor people, people with disabilities, and immigrants. The fundamental projects of security that animate criminal punishment and identity surveillance are established in and exist to secure and protect white supremacy and patriarchy. It is not a design flaw that these systems and institutions are sites of transphobic and homophobic violence. . . .

. . . . What does it mean to assert individual privacy rights in a system where strip-searches and other forms of forced nudity are daily realities, where consensual sex is criminalized and rape is routine, where filing a grievance or lodging any kind of protest means risking severe violence or death? . . . . It is no secret that police, wardens, parole officers, corrections officers, and Immigration and Customs Enforcement do not follow the laws and policies that are supposed to prevent the outrageous violence and abuse they commit every day. Even when advocates win cases about the access to medical care or nutrition or protection from harm that law enforcement agents are supposed to provide, it is still inadequate, selective, or rarely provided, if at all. Selective enforcement, medical neglect, nutritional deprivation, harassment, and sexual violence are not anomalies in law enforcement systems: they are fundamental to them.

Because of the nature of our criminal systems and prisons, there is not a fair or safe way for queer, trans, and gender non-conforming people, or anyone, to be imprisoned. Starting from that premise, we can take different approaches to questions of reform, focusing more on decarcerating and dismantling systems of criminalization, and being extremely wary of reforms that purport to offer recognition and inclusion but actually expand and legitimize violent institutions. The best ways to protect queer, trans, and gender non-conforming people from police and prison violence is to keep them out of contact with police and prisons and to support them while they are locked up. . . . Some are working to oppose gang injunctions, "stop and frisk" practices, collaboration between immigration enforcement and criminal punishment systems, mandatory minimum sentences, prison building projects, and other expansions of criminalization. Some activists and advocates are focused on individual advocacy for current prisoners, knowing that broad-based policy reform often expands the system or provides an inappropriately "one size fits all" solution. Instead, they advocate on a case-by-case basis for the changes individual prisoners believe will make them safer in their current environment, recognizing that prisoners' situations and contexts differ and prisoners often have the best information about what might be safer in their particular circumstances. Others focus on establishing resources for people coming out of prison to prevent the poverty and housing insecurity that often results in further criminalization. Many are also working to establish community responses to violence that do not utilize police and courts, recognizing that calling the police often escalates violence for queer and trans people of color, immigrants, and people with disabilities. . . . This approach to addressing homophobia and transphobia in criminal punishment systems rejects the quest for inclusion and recognition in violent legal and administrative apparatuses and the fantasy that any constitutional claim before a court will bring relief, and instead seeks the abolition of criminal punishment and immigration enforcement. It properly identifies the fruitlessness of seeking safety at the hands of the most significant perpetrators of racialized gendered violence. . . .

Discussion

1. In the essay excerpted above, Dean Spade, who at the time of this textbook's writing was an Associate Professor at Seattle University School of Law, suggests that "racialized gender norms" are a fundamental aspect of imprisonment in the United States, an enterprise grounded in and serving "white supremacy and patriarchy." Due to the "fruitlessness" of trying to reform state institutions founded upon such forces so as to eliminate their patriarchal and white supremacist character, Prof. Spade favors solutions that strive toward "the abolition of criminal punishment and immigration enforcement." To what extent do you agree with Spade's description of the problem of state-inflicted gendered and racialized carceral violence and with his proposed aim? Given statistics demonstrating the vastly disproportionate effect of the U.S. criminal justice system on poor people and people of color, how if at all can

the U.S. justify a criminal justice system that seems to perpetuate and exacerbate poverty among and cruelty against racial, ethnic, and gender minorities? *Cf.* Daria Roithmayr, Reproducing Racism: How Everyday Choices Lock In White Advantage 4, 6 ("[W]e continue to see significant racial differences—in labor, housing, education, and wealth, in health care, political power and now incarceration—decade after decade. . . . [R]acial inequality reproduces itself automatically from generation to generation, in the everyday choices that people make about their lives. . . . [U]nfair advantage, acquired early in our nation's history, has now become self-reinforcing and cumulative.).

2. In his description of "violence" inflicted through racialized gender norms in government facilities, Prof. Spade includes "identity documentation and surveillance" and "dress regulations." In what ways are these practices harmful to trans and gender-nonconforming people? In what ways might it be accurate or helpful to characterize these practices as forms of "violence"?

3. To what extent should Spade's pessimistic outlook on "the quest for inclusion and recognition in violent legal and administrative apparatuses" be extended to society at large? Wouldn't his broad definition of "violence" indict many other forms of government administration, including, for example, government health care programs that may discriminate on the basis of gender identity (such as under regulations proposed by the Trump administration)? What roles should government play in addressing the harms that flow from gender and race ideologies? To what extent should we rely upon courts and legislatures to advance meaningful and necessary change for the lives of transgender and gender-nonconforming people?

4. Do you agree with Spade's contention that building separate prison facilities for TGNC people would be futile, since they would ultimately succumb to the same racialized gender norms enforced by state agents in general men's and women's prisons? What, if anything, would assigning trans inmates to sex-segregated prisons in accordance with their gender identity (as opposed to their sex assigned at birth) do to alleviate the various forms of violence and discrimination that they face?

Reading Guide for Transgender Offender Manual

1. As you read, consider the differences in tone and language between the Transgender Offender Manual (TOM) issued during the Obama administration and the revisions issued during the Trump administration. Aside from concrete policy differences, how might differences in the way regulations describe people and circumstances impact the manner in which government officials effectuate their obligations?

2. Bear in mind the evidence of the often-tragic experience of transgender individuals in prison, ranging from verbal harassment to denials of various necessary services to brutal violence and rape. As you weigh the differences between the two administrations' policies, consider whether either is well-suited to remedy the harms transgender inmates experience while incarcerated.

Note on U.S. Department of Justice, Federal Bureau of Prisons, Transgender Offender Manual

The Federal Bureau of Prisons ("BOP") is a subdivision of the U.S. Department of Justice. In the very last days of the administration of President Barack Obama, BOP issued a Transgender Offender Manual ("TOM"), Federal Bureau of Prisons, Program Statement 5200.04 CN-1: Transgender Offender Manual (Jan. 18, 2017). The purpose of the TOM was "[to] ensure the Bureau of Prisons (Bureau) properly identifies, tracks, and provides services to the transgender population." It called for creation of a "Transgender Executive Council" (TEC), which

> will consist of staff members from the Health Services Division, the Female Offender Branch, Psychology Services, the Correctional Programs Division, the Designation and Sentence Computation Center (DSCC), and the Office of General Counsel. The TEC will meet a minimum of quarterly to offer advice and guidance on unique measures related to treatment and management needs of transgender inmates and/or inmates with GD, including designation issues. Institution staff and DSCC staff may raise issues on specific inmates to the TEC through the Female Offender Branch. The National PREA Coordinator is consulted as needed.

Regulations adopted under the Obama Administration to implement the Prison Rape Elimination Act (PREA) provide:

> (c) In deciding whether to assign a transgender or intersex inmate to a facility for male or female inmates, and in making other housing and programming assignments, the agency shall consider on a case-by-case basis whether a placement would ensure the inmate's health and safety, and whether the placement would present management or security problems.

> (d) Placement and programming assignments for each transgender or intersex inmate shall be reassessed at least twice each year to review any threats to safety experienced by the inmate.

> (e) A transgender or intersex inmate's own views with respect to his or her own safety shall be given serious consideration.

> (f) Transgender and intersex inmates shall be given the opportunity to shower separately from other inmates.

> (g) The agency shall not place lesbian, gay, bisexual, transgender, or intersex inmates in dedicated facilities, units, or wings solely on the basis of such identification or status, unless such placement is in a dedicated facility, unit, or wing established in connection with a consent decree, legal settlement, or legal judgment for the purpose of protecting such inmates.

28 C.F.R. § 115.42(c)-(g) (2012). The original TOM further specified:

> The TEC will consider factors including, but not limited to, an inmate's security level, criminal and disciplinary history, current gender expression,

medical and mental health needs/information, vulnerability to sexual victimization, and likelihood of perpetrating abuse. The TEC may also consider facility-specific factors, including inmate populations, staffing patterns, and physical layouts (*e.g.*, types of showers available). *The TEC will recommend housing by gender identity when appropriate.*

TOM at 6 (emphasis added).

Less than a year and a half after Donald Trump succeeded Barack Obama, BOP released a revised TOM. Federal Bureau of Prisons, Program Statement 5200.04 CN-1: Transgender Offender Manual (May 11, 2018). The revision significantly qualified the purpose of the TOM, now providing: "To ensure the Bureau of Prisons (Bureau) properly identifies, tracks, and provides services to the transgender population, *consistent with maintaining security and good order in Federal prisons.*" *Id.* at 1 (emphasis added). The revision also eliminated the provision that "[t]he TEC will recommend housing by gender identity when appropriate." *Id.*at 6. Instead, it prioritizes (the undefined term) "biological sex":

> In deciding the facility assignment for a transgender or intersex inmate, the TEC should make the following assessments on a case-by-case basis:
>
> • The TEC will use biological sex as the initial determination for designation;
>
> • The TEC will consider the health and safety of the transgender inmate, exploring appropriate options available to assist with mitigating risk to the transgender offender, to include but not limited to cell and/or unit assignments, application of management variables, programming missions of the facility, etc.;
>
> • The TEC will consider factors specific to the transgender inmate, such as behavioral history, overall demeanor, and likely interactions with other inmates; and
>
> • The TEC will consider whether placement would threaten the management and security of the institution and/or pose a risk to other inmates in the institution (*e.g.*, considering inmates with histories of trauma, privacy concerns, etc.).
>
> The designation to a facility of the inmate's identified gender would be appropriate only in rare cases after consideration of all of the above factors and where there has been significant progress towards transition as demonstrated by medical and mental health history.

Id. at 6–7. The same considerations are to be used for transfers. *Id.* at 7–8.

The revision did leave intact some (somewhat) progressive Obama-era policies or procedures. Regarding pronouns and names: "Transgender inmates often prefer to be called by pronouns of their identified gender identity. Staff may choose to use these gender-specific pronouns or salutations per the inmate's request, and will not be disciplined for doing so." Regarding "pat searches": "For purposes of pat searching, inmates will be pat-searched in accordance with the gender of the institution, or housing assignment, in which they are assigned. Transgender inmates may request an exception. The exception must be pre-authorized by the Warden, after consultation with staff from Health Services, Psychology Services, Unit Management, and Correctional Services." Regarding clothing and commissary items: "Consistent with safety and security concerns, inmates with the CMA assignment of transgender will have the opportunity to have undergarments of their identified gender even if they are not housed with inmates of the identified gender. Institutional laundry will have available institutional undergarments that fulfill the needs of transgender inmates. Undergarments will not have metal components. . . . Additional items based on an individualized assessment of the transgender inmate may be approved by the Warden."

Discussion

1. The stated purpose of the TOM under the Obama administration was to ensure that the BOP "properly identifies, tracks, and provides services to the transgender population." The stated purpose of the TOM as revised under the Trump administration includes the same language but contains an additional clause: "consistent with maintaining security and good order in Federal prisons." This clause appears to qualify the original purpose; does it mean that any consideration of transgender inmates' experiences while incarcerated should be weighed against a general policy interest in prison security? Why would the Trump administration include that clause in its revised purpose? Should the revised purpose be interpreted to be less protective of transgender inmates than the original purpose? What, if any, concerns about housing inmates according to their gender identity are implied in the revised purpose?

2. Another significant difference between the original TOM and the revised TOM is the language about the likelihood of housing inmates according to their gender identity. The original TOM declares that inmates will be housed according to their gender identity "when appropriate." The revised TOM declares that doing so will only be appropriate in "rare cases" when an inmate has undergone "significant progress toward transition." What policy concerns might justify only housing inmates according to their gender identity when they have made "significant progress" toward their gender transition? How might this undefined "significant progress" standard be operationalized in practice? For example, could the TEC interpret this standard to require that transgender inmates have received hormone therapy at some point in their lives? (At some specified recent point? For a minimum duration?) Could the TEC interpret the standard to require that an inmate have had surgery (or some specific forms of surgery) to be housed consistent with their gender identity? Consider how various factors in an individual's life may impede their ability to meet various versions of a "significant progress" standard, in particular, how incarcerated individuals are often poor and/or people of color who may have lacked access to gender-affirming care prior to incarceration (and may not receive gender-affirming care while incarcerated).

3. The revised TOM states that "privacy concerns" are an example of how transgender inmates might threaten the "management and security" of an institution and/or "pose a risk to other inmates in the institution." How would housing an inmate according to their gender identity pose "privacy concerns" for others? More generally, how do concerns over the "privacy" of others underlie policymaking and political discourse regarding the treatment of transgender individuals? Are such concerns warranted in the prison context or elsewhere?

4. Although both the original TOM and revised TOM include various protections for transgender inmates, these protections may be ineffective or difficult to obtain. For example, the manual now provides only that prison staff "may choose" to refer to inmates by their preferred pronouns. Similarly, if transgender inmates want a pat-search conducted by someone of the sex consistent with their gender identity rather than by someone of the same sex as inmates generally housed in their facility, they need the backing of several different departments as well as the discretionary approval of the warden. Moreover, whether inmates may have access to gender-affirming clothing and commissary items (other than undergarments) is left to the discretion of the warden. Should pronoun usage, the sex of pat-searchers, and/or approval of most clothing and commissary items be at the discretion of prison officials? Might the discretion of prison officials lead to negative or dangerous consequences for transgender inmates? Does a discretionary approach in these contexts, as opposed to strict guarantees, better serve the interests of security and good order in federal prisons, and, if so, at what cost?

5. Even if anti-transgender discrimination were subject to intermediate equal protection scrutiny as a form of sex discrimination under the Title VII reasoning of *Bostock v. Clayton County, Georgia*, 140 S. Ct. 1731 (2020), Chapter 5, Section D, *supra*, as Justice Alito's dissent in that case speculated the opinion's logic might require, that would not necessarily doom any restrictions. Unlike Title VII of the Civil Rights Act of 1964, which flatly forbids sex discrimination that does not fit into exceptions for affirmative action or (narrow) bona fide occupational qualifications, intermediate scrutiny allows government to continue discriminating if it can establish that such discrimination is substantially related to an important governmental interest. Prison security and inmate safety would undoubtedly be considered important interests, so the question would be the fit of a discriminatory governmental policy to those interests—the more readily the government could use less discriminatory means, the less likely courts would be to uphold a challenged policy (though intermediate scrutiny does not require the government to use less restrictive means, as strict scrutiny would).

2. Failure to Treat

Inmates are dependent on prisons for all the necessities of life. This includes medical care. Too often those in charge of decisionmaking for a facility or system are either outright hostile to trans persons or do not understand transition-related care as medical care that can indeed be life-saving. Inmates are thus forced to use administrative grievance procedures to try to secure treatment, or to sue (often pro se) when that fails. Eventual victories with respect to gender presentation and hormone therapy are more common than successful suits for surgery—victories that have sometimes been mooted by release of a transgender inmate or reversed on appeal or rehearing. This subsection considers a variety of efforts by transgender prisoners to secure medically proper care.

Reading Guide for Brown v. Zavaras

1. What two constitutional rights does Josephine Brown, the pro se transgender inmate plaintiff in this case, allege the defendant correctional officials have violated by not providing her hormone treatments?

2. With respect to Ms. Brown's first claimed right, what does the court hold the governing rule is? How does the court dispose of the first claim, and for what reasons?

3. What does the court hold is the proper level of scrutiny for assessing Brown's second claimed constitutional violation? Why does the court raise questions about the propriety of that level of scrutiny? Why does it ultimately set aside those qualms? How does the court dispose of the second claim, and for what reasons?

Josephine Brown v. Aristedes Zavaras and Robert Furlong

63 F.3d 967 (10th Cir. 1995)

Before SEYMOUR, Chief Judge, McKAY and HENRY, Circuit Judges.

Opinion

HENRY, Circuit Judge.

Pro se plaintiff Josephine Brown appeals the summary judgment order of the district court dismissing his [*sic*—Eds.] 42 U.S.C. § 1983 civil rights action.[1] We . . . remand to the district court for further proceedings consistent with this opinion.

I. Background

Mr. Brown is an inmate at the Limon Correctional Facility, a Colorado state prison. In his complaint against two corrections officials, Mr. Brown states that he is a transsexual. The medical term for transsexuality is "gender dysphoria," and gender dysphoria is a medically recognized psychological disorder resulting from the "disjunction between sexual identity and sexual organs." *Farmer v. Haas*, 990 F.2d 319 (7th Cir. 1993) (collecting medical literature).

---

1. Although plaintiff identifies his true gender as female, plaintiff is biologically male and refers to himself with masculine pronouns throughout his pleadings. As is our practice, we refer to litigants as the record suggests they prefer to be addressed.

Mr. Brown alleged in his complaint that the defendants have violated his Eighth Amendment right to be free from cruel and unusual punishment and his Fourteenth Amendment equal protection rights. Specifically, he alleged that defendants have withheld medical care with deliberate indifference to his serious medical needs by not providing him with the female hormone estrogen and other medical treatment in contravention of the rule in *Estelle v. Gamble*, 429 U.S. 97 (1976).

The magistrate recommended that Mr. Brown's Eighth Amendment claim be dismissed because Mr. Brown had alleged only that Colorado had failed to provide estrogen treatment.

The district court accepted the magistrate's recommendation regarding the Eighth Amendment claim. The district court further noted that Mr. Brown was not a member of a "protected class" and dismissed the equal protection claim. On appeal, Mr. Brown argues that the district court erred in dismissing both his Eighth Amendment and Equal Protection claims.

II. Discussion

B. Eighth Amendment

Mr. Brown argues that the defendants have provided inadequate medical care under the Eighth Amendment. Deliberate indifference by prison officials to a prisoner's serious medical need constitutes cruel and unusual punishment in violation of the Eighth Amendment. *Estelle.*

This circuit was one of the first to consider whether transsexuals had an Eighth Amendment right to estrogen. *See Supre v. Ricketts*, 792 F.2d 958 (10th Cir. 1986). We held in the context of that case, where the provision of estrogen was medically controversial, that although prison officials must provide treatment to address the medical needs of transsexual prisoners, the law did not require prison officials to administer estrogen or provide any other particular treatment. Since *Supre*, most courts have reached the same conclusion. *Farmer v. Haas; White v. Farrier*, 849 F.2d 322 (8th Cir. 1988); *Meriwether v. Faulkner*, 821 F.2d 408 (7th Cir. 1987); *Long v. Nix*, 877 F. Supp. 1358 (S.D. Iowa 1995).[2]

The defendants' sole response to Mr. Brown's Eighth Amendment claim is that Mr. Brown failed to raise the issue in the district court. In light of our obligation to construe pro se pleadings liberally, *see Haines v. Kerner*, 404 U.S. 519 (1972), we

---

2. However, in addressing the Eighth Amendment claim of a preoperative transsexual who had taken estrogen before entering prison, the United States District Court for the Western District of Michigan has issued a preliminary injunction ordering prison officials to provide female hormones to the prisoner. *Phillips v. Michigan Dep't of Corrections*, 731 F. Supp. 792, 794 (W.D. Mich. 1990), *aff'd*, 932 F.2d 969 (6th Cir. 1991). The court reasoned that the plaintiff "suffer[ed] from a serious medical need," and that the denial of hormone treatment constituted cruel and unusual punishment.

Unlike the plaintiff in *Phillips*, however, Mr. Brown has not alleged that he received hormone treatment for gender dysphoria prior to his incarceration. *Phillips* is therefore inapplicable to this case.

cannot agree. In our view, Mr. Brown claimed a medical need and therefore a general right to medical treatment for gender dysphoria in his complaint. In addition, Mr. Brown clarified his pleadings, specifically alleging that he has not been offered any treatment at all, in his response to the magistrate's recommendation. *Cf. Green v. Johnson*, 977 F.2d 1383 (10th Cir. 1992) (remanding case to district court for factual development of issues raised in pro se supplemental brief).[3]

We therefore remand to the district court to properly determine whether Mr. Brown is being offered medical care consistent with *Supre*.

C. Equal Protection

Mr. Brown also asserts that he is being denied the equal protection of the laws because some prisoners receive estrogen treatment.[4] In this case, the district court observed that transsexuals are not a protected class and dismissed Mr. Brown's equal protection claim.

The Ninth Circuit has held that transsexuals are not a protected class. *Holloway v. Arthur Andersen & Co.*, 566 F.2d 659 (9th Cir. 1977). In *Holloway*, the court reasoned that transsexuality did not meet the traditional indicia of a suspect classification because transsexuals are not a discrete and insular minority, and because the plaintiff did not establish that "transsexuality is an 'immutable characteristic determined solely by the accident of birth' like race, or national origin." *Id.* (quoting *Frontiero v. Richardson*, 411 U.S. 677 (1973)).

Recent research concluding that sexual identity may be biological suggests reevaluating *Holloway*. *See Equality Found. v. City of Cincinnati*, 860 F. Supp. 417 (S.D. Ohio 1994) (concluding that sexual orientation is an issue beyond individual control), *aff'd in part and vacated in part*, 54 F.3d 261 (6th Cir. 1995); *Dahl v. Secretary of the United States Navy*, 830 F. Supp. 1319, 1324 n. 5 (E.D. Cal. 1993) (collecting research suggesting that sexual identity is biological). However, we decline to make such an evaluation in this case because Mr. Brown's allegations are too conclusory to allow proper analysis of this legal question. We therefore follow *Holloway* and hold that Mr. Brown is not a member of a protected class in this case. When the plaintiff is not a member of a protected class and does not assert a fundamental right, we determine only whether government classifications have a rational basis. *See Stephens v. Thomas*, 19 F.3d 498 (10th Cir. 1994).

Competing standards for resolving a plaintiff's equal protection claim under Rule 12 complicate our analysis when we review a plaintiff's claim under the rational

---

3. Although the documents defendants attached to their motion to dismiss suggest that it is the policy of the Colorado Department of Corrections to provide preoperative transsexual prisoners who have not taken hormones with counseling rather than hormones, we review Mr. Brown's claim under the Rule 12 standard, referring only to his complaint.

4. The documents that defendants attached to their motion to dismiss suggest that Colorado provides hormones to prisoners with low hormone levels and that the state will therefore give estrogen to postoperative transsexuals who suffer from a hormone imbalance. However, as we have noted, we review Mr. Brown's claim under the Rule 12 standard, referring only to his complaint.

basis standard. In *Wroblewski v. City of Washburn*, 965 F.2d 452 (7th Cir. 1992), the Seventh Circuit identified and considered this issue:

> A perplexing situation is presented when the rational basis standard meets the standard applied to a dismissal under Fed R. Civ. P. 12(b)(6). The rational basis standard requires the government to win if any set of facts reasonably may be conceived to justify its classification; the Rule 12(b)(6) standard requires the plaintiff to prevail if "relief could be granted under any set of facts that could be proved consistent with the allegations." *Hishon v. King & Spalding*, 467 U.S. 69 (1984). The rational basis standard, of course, cannot defeat the plaintiff's benefit of the broad Rule 12(b)(6) standard. . . .

The court then adopted a hybrid approach to reconcile the standards, holding that a plaintiff pursuing an equal protection claim must allege facts sufficient to overcome a presumption of government rationality. . . . Finally, the *Wroblewski* court reviewed possible government rationales for the actions at issue, noted that a court must presume that government actions are rational, and held that the plaintiff's "conclusionary assertions" were insufficient to state a claim under that standard. We find the Seventh Circuit's analysis sound and apply *Wroblewski* here.

It is a close question as to whether Mr. Brown's complaint raises an equal protection claim under the *Wroblewski* standard. However, Mr. Brown's allegations are merely conclusory in that they do not allege the factual basis for an equal protection claim, and even pro se litigants must do more than make mere conclusory statements regarding constitutional claims. *See United States v. Fisher*, 38 F.3d 1144 (10th Cir. 1994) (holding that conclusory allegations are insufficient to support a claim for relief); *Petrick v. Maynard*, 11 F.3d 991 (10th Cir. 1993) (holding that a pro se prisoner must do more than make conclusory allegations regarding access to a law library). Thus, even assuming the truth of Mr. Brown's allegation that some prisoners are given hormones and others are not, we hold that his conclusory allegations simply do not state a cause of action for which relief can be granted under an equal protection theory.

We REVERSE and REMAND this matter to the district court for proceedings consistent with this opinion regarding Mr. Brown's Eighth Amendment claim, but AFFIRM the decision of the district court regarding Mr. Brown's equal protection claim.

———

Discussion

1. What allegations by Brown would have made it appropriate for the court to address the question whether "sexual identity," as the court put it, is "biological"? Is it necessary that gender identity have a "biological" component in order to receive heightened scrutiny under the Equal Protection Clause?

2. What kind of facts would Brown have had to prove to prevail on the Equal Protection claim?

Reading Guide for Fields v. Smith

1. What constitutional guarantee do the plaintiffs contend the state's ban on hormonal and surgical treatments for inmates with gender identity disorder violates? What were the defendants' arguments for why the court should deem the ban constitutional?

2. What standard does the court say should be used to decide when denials of medical treatments violate inmates' rights? What element of such showing do the defendants concede? Why does the court hold that the plaintiffs succeeded in showing the other element? (What does the court reason about costs? What does it reason about alternative treatments? What does it say about the defendants' security rationale?)

Andrea Fields, et al. v. Judy P. Smith, et al.

653 F.3d 550 (7th Cir. 2011)

Before ROVNER and WOOD, Circuit Judges, and GOTTSCHALL, District Judge.

GOTTSCHALL, District Judge.

In this appeal, we are asked to review the decision of the district court invalidating a Wisconsin state statute which prohibits the Wisconsin Department of Corrections ("DOC") from providing transgender inmates with certain medical treatments. The Inmate Sex Change Prevention Act ("Act 105") provides in relevant part:

(a) In this subsection:

1. "Hormonal therapy" means the use of hormones to stimulate the development or alteration of a person's sexual characteristics in order to alter the person's physical appearance so that the person appears more like the opposite gender.

2. "Sexual reassignment surgery" means surgical procedures to alter a person's physical appearance so that the person appears more like the opposite gender.

(b) The [Wisconsin Department of Corrections] may not authorize the payment of any funds or the use of any resources of this state or the payment of any federal funds passing through the state treasury to provide or to facilitate the provision of hormonal therapy or sexual reassignment surgery. . . .

2005 WIS. ACT 105, codified at WIS. STAT. § 302.386(5m) (2010). The district court concluded that this provision violates the Eighth Amendment's ban on cruel and unusual punishment and the Fourteenth Amendment's Equal Protection Clause. Defendants, various DOC officials, now appeal.

I

A number of DOC inmates filed this lawsuit as a putative class action in the Eastern District of Wisconsin on behalf of all current and future DOC inmates with "strong, persistent cross-gender identification." The district court denied plaintiffs' motion for class certification, but permitted the case to proceed to trial on the individual claims of three plaintiffs.

The three plaintiffs—Andrea Fields, Matthew Davison (also known as Jessica Davison), and Vankemah Moaton—are male-to-female transsexuals. According to stipulated facts, each has been diagnosed with Gender Identity Disorder ("GID"). GID is classified as a psychiatric disorder in the DSM-IV-TR, the current edition of the American Psychiatric Association's *Diagnostic and Statistical Manual of Mental Disorders*. Individuals with GID identify strongly with a gender that does not match their physical sex characteristics. The condition is associated with severe psychological distress. Prior to the passage of Act 105, each of the plaintiffs had been diagnosed by DOC physicians with GID and had been prescribed hormones.

After a trial in which both sides presented expert testimony about GID, its treatment, and its potential effects on prison security, the district court ruled in favor of plaintiffs. The court ruled that Act 105 was unconstitutional, both as applied and on its face, under the Eighth and Fourteenth Amendments. The district court ultimately issued an injunction barring defendants from enforcing Act 105. We need not recount all the evidence presented at trial—the district court's 40-page opinion thoroughly describes the trial testimony, *see Fields v. Smith*, 712 F. Supp. 2d 830 (E.D. Wis. 2010)—but a brief review of the district court's critical factual findings is warranted.

The district court credited much of the testimony from plaintiffs' witnesses, including three experts in the treatment of GID. Plaintiffs' experts testified that, collectively, they had treated thousands of patients with GID and published numerous peer-reviewed articles and books on the subject. One expert had specifically studied transsexuals in the correctional setting. These experts explained that GID can cause an acute sense that a person's body does not match his or her gender identity. Even before seeking treatment and from an early age, patients will experience this dysphoria and may attempt to conform their appearance and behavior to the gender with which they identify.

The feelings of dysphoria can vary in intensity. Some patients are able to manage the discomfort, while others become unable to function without taking steps to correct the disorder. A person with GID often experiences severe anxiety, depression, and other psychological disorders. Those with GID may attempt to commit suicide or to mutilate their own genitals.

The accepted standards of care dictate a gradual approach to treatment beginning with psychotherapy and real life experience living as the opposite gender. For some number of patients, this treatment will be effective in controlling feelings of dysphoria. When the condition is more severe, a doctor can prescribe hormones, which have the effect of relieving the psychological distress. Hormones also have physical effects on the body. For example, males may experience breast development, relocation of body fat, and softening of the skin. In the most severe cases, sexual reassignment surgery may be appropriate. But often the use of hormones will be sufficient to control the disorder.

When hormones are withdrawn from a patient who has been receiving hormone treatment, severe complications may arise. The dysphoria and associated psychological symptoms may resurface in more acute form. In addition, there may be severe physical effects such as muscle wasting, high blood pressure, and neurological complications. All three plaintiffs in this case experienced some of these effects when DOC doctors discontinued their treatment following the passage of Act 105.[2]

Plaintiffs also called Dr. David Burnett, the DOC's Medical Director, and Dr. Kevin Kallas, the DOC Mental Health Director, to testify at trial. These officials explained that, prior to the enactment of Act 105, hormone therapy had been prescribed to some DOC inmates, including plaintiffs. DOC policies did not permit inmates to receive sex reassignment surgery. Drs. Kallas and Burnett served on a committee of DOC officials that evaluated whether hormone therapy was medically necessary for any particular inmate. Inmates are not permitted to seek any medical treatment outside the prison, regardless of their ability to pay. The doctors testified that they could think of no other state law or policy, besides Act 105, that prohibits prison doctors from providing inmates with medically necessary treatment.

II

We evaluate both the district court's grant of injunctive relief and the scope of that relief for abuse of discretion. *Knapp v. Nw. Univ.*, 101 F.3d 473 (7th Cir. 1996); *see Brown v. Plata*, 131 S. Ct. 1910 (2011) (Scalia, J., dissenting) (noting that under the Prison Litigation Reform Act ("PLRA"), "when a district court enters a new decree with new benchmarks, the selection of those benchmarks is . . . reviewed under a deferential, abuse-of-discretion standard of review"); *Russian Media Group, LLC v. Cable Am., Inc.*, 598 F.3d 302 (7th Cir. 2010) ("[T]he appropriate scope of the injunction is left to the district court's sound discretion."); *Thomas v. Bryant*, 614 F.3d 1288 (11th Cir. 2010) (applying abuse of discretion standard to evaluate scope of injunction in conformity with PLRA); *Crawford v. Clarke*, 578 F.3d 39 (1st Cir. 2009) (holding that district court did not abuse its discretion in awarding system-wide relief under the PLRA). The court's factual findings are reviewed for clear error, and any legal determinations are reviewed de novo. *Knapp*.

"Prison officials violate the Eighth Amendment's proscription against cruel and unusual punishment when they display 'deliberate indifference to serious medical needs of prisoners.'" *Greeno v. Daley*, 414 F.3d 645 (7th Cir. 2005) (quoting *Estelle v. Gamble*, 429 U.S. 97 (1976)). In this case, the district court held that plaintiffs suffered from a serious medical need, namely GID, and that defendants acted with deliberate indifference in that defendants knew of the serious medical need but refused to provide hormone therapy because of Act 105. Defendants do not challenge the district court's holding that GID is a serious medical condition. They

---

2. Defendants began reducing plaintiffs' hormone levels on January 12, 2006; on January 27, 2006, the district court granted a preliminary injunction barring defendants from continuing to withdraw plaintiffs' hormone therapy and ordering defendants to return plaintiffs to their previous hormone levels.

contend that Act 105 is constitutional because the state legislature has the power to prohibit certain medical treatments when other treatment options are available. And defendants argue that Act 105 is justified by a legitimate need to ensure security in state prisons.

Defendants rely primarily on two Seventh Circuit decisions which addressed constitutional challenges to refusals to provide treatment for gender dysphoria or transsexualism. Over twenty-four years ago, in *Meriwether v. Faulkner*, 821 F.2d 408 (7th Cir. 1987), this court reversed the dismissal of a complaint which alleged that the plaintiff, who had previously been taking hormones, was denied all treatment for her gender dysphoria upon entering prison. The court held that the plaintiff stated a claim that transsexualism was a serious medical need and that prison officials acted with deliberate indifference in refusing all treatment. The court noted in dicta that "[i]t is important to emphasize, however, that she does not have a right to any particular type of treatment, such as estrogen therapy which appears to be the focus of her complaint."

Ten years later, in *Maggert v. Hanks*, 131 F.3d 670 (7th Cir. 1997), this court, in two brief paragraphs, upheld a decision granting summary judgment [against— Eds.] a similar deliberate indifference claim where the plaintiff did not come forward with any evidence to rebut defendants' expert witness, who testified that plaintiff did not suffer from gender dysphoria. The court's opinion proceeded to address "a broader issue, having to do with the significance of gender dysphoria in prisoners' civil rights litigation." The court commented, again in dicta, that the Eighth Amendment does not require the provision of "esoteric" treatments like hormone therapy and sexual reassignment surgery which are "protracted and expensive" and not generally available to those who are not affluent. A prison would be required to provide some treatment for gender dysphoria, but not necessarily "curative" treatment because the Eighth Amendment requires only minimum health care for prison inmates.

The court's discussion of hormone therapy and sex reassignment surgery in these two cases was based on certain empirical assumptions—that the cost of these treatments is high and that adequate alternatives exist. More than a decade after this court's decision in *Maggert*, the district court in this case held a trial in which these empirical assumptions were put to the test. At trial, defendants stipulated that the cost of providing hormone therapy is between $300 and $1,000 per inmate per year. The district court compared this cost to the cost of a common antipsychotic drug used to treat many DOC inmates. In 2004, DOC paid a total of $2,300 for hormones for two inmates. That same year, DOC paid $2.5 million to provide inmates with quetiapine, an antipsychotic drug which costs more than $2,500 per inmate per year. Sex reassignment surgery is significantly more expensive, costing approximately $20,000. However, other significant surgeries may be more expensive. In 2005, DOC paid $37,244 for one coronary bypass surgery and $32,897 for one kidney transplant surgery. The district court concluded that DOC might actually incur greater costs by refusing to provide hormones, since inmates with GID might require other expensive treatments or enhanced monitoring by prison security.[3] In fact, at oral argument before this court, counsel for defendants disclaimed any argument that Act 105 is justified by cost savings. *See* Oral Argument at 15:18, *Fields v. Smith*, Nos. 10-2339 and 10-2466, available at http://www. ca7.uscourts.gov /fdocs/docs.fwx? dname=arg.

More importantly here, defendants did not produce any evidence that another treatment could be an adequate replacement for hormone therapy. Plaintiffs' witnesses repeatedly made the point that, for certain patients with GID, hormone therapy is the only treatment that reduces dysphoria and can prevent the severe emotional and physical harms associated with it. Although DOC can provide psychotherapy as well as antipsychotics and antidepressants, defendants failed to present evidence rebutting the testimony that these treatments do nothing to treat the underlying disorder. Defendants called their own expert to speak about GID: Dr. Daniel Claiborn, a Ph.D. in psychology who estimated he has treated only about fifty clients with GID over a period of twenty years in his private practice. Dr. Claiborn provided no testimony about the appropriate treatment for plaintiffs. He offered his opinion that GID is not properly characterized as a psychological disorder because a person with GID does not typically suffer from an impairment in psychological functions. However, defendants have now conceded that GID is a serious medical condition. Dr. Claiborn's testimony does not support the assertion that plaintiffs can be effectively treated without hormones.

It is well established that the Constitution's ban on cruel and unusual punishment does not permit a state to deny effective treatment for the serious medical needs of prisoners. The Supreme Court articulated this principle in *Estelle v. Gamble*:

> An inmate must rely on prison authorities to treat his medical needs; if the authorities fail to do so, those needs will not be met. In the worst cases, such a failure may actually produce physical "torture or a lingering death," the evils of most immediate concern to the drafters of the Amendment. In less serious cases, denial of medical care may result in pain and suffering which no one suggests would serve any penological purpose. . . . We therefore conclude that deliberate indifference to serious medical needs of prisoners constitutes the "unnecessary and wanton infliction of pain," proscribed by the Eighth Amendment.

Surely, had the Wisconsin legislature passed a law that DOC inmates with cancer must be treated only with therapy and pain killers, this court would have no trouble concluding that the law was unconstitutional. Refusing to provide effective treatment for a serious medical condition serves no valid penological purpose and amounts to torture. *Id.*; *see also Roe v. Elyea*, 631 F.3d 843 (7th Cir. 2011) (upholding verdict for plaintiff that prison policy on treatment of Hepatitis C was deliberately

---

3. Plaintiff Moaton, for example, experienced suicidal ideation after DOC officials began withdrawing hormone treatments.

indifferent); *Kelley v. McGinnis*, 899 F.2d 612, 616 (7th Cir. 1990) (reversing dismissal of complaint alleging that prison provided inadequate treatment for inmate's chronic foot problems). Although Act 105 permits DOC to provide plaintiffs with some treatment, the evidence at trial indicated that plaintiffs could not be effectively treated without hormones.

Defendants have also argued that Act 105 is justified by the state's interest in preserving prison security. Defendants' security expert, Eugene Atherton, testified that more feminine male inmates become targets for sexual assault in prisons. Because hormone therapy alters a person's secondary sex characteristics such as breast size and body hair, defendants argue that hormones feminize inmates and make them more susceptible to inciting prison violence. But the district court rejected this argument, noting that the evidence showed transgender inmates may be targets for violence even without hormones. Atherton himself, in his deposition, testified that it would be "an incredible stretch" to conclude that banning the use of hormones could prevent sexual assaults. In the Colorado Department of Corrections, where Atherton worked for many years, the state had a policy of providing necessary hormones to inmates with GID. Atherton testified that this policy was reasonable and had been implemented effectively in Colorado.

Defendants cite *Whitley v. Albers* for the proposition that "'[p]rison administrators . . . should be accorded wide-ranging deference in the adoption and execution of policies and practices that in their judgment are needed to preserve internal order and discipline and to maintain institutional security.'" 475 U.S. 312 (1986) (quoting *Bell v. Wolfish*, 441 U.S. 520 (1979)). But deference does not extend to "actions taken in bad faith and for no legitimate purpose." *Id.* The district court did not abuse its discretion in concluding that defendants' evidence failed to establish any security benefits associated with a ban on hormone therapy. The legislators who approved Act 105 may have honestly believed they were improving prison security, but courts "retain[] an independent constitutional duty to review factual findings where constitutional rights are at stake." *Gonzales v. Carhart*, 550 U.S. 124 (2007).

Finally, defendants contend that the district court's injunction violates the PLRA, 18 U.S.C. §3626(a), because it enjoins Act 105 in its entirety.[4] They argue that plaintiffs have never demonstrated a need for sex reassignment surgery, which the law also prohibits. For their part, plaintiffs argue that defendants waived this argument by failing to raise it before the district court. In fact, the record

---

4. The PLRA provides, in part:
   Prospective relief in any civil action with respect to prison conditions shall extend no further than necessary to correct the violation of the Federal right of a particular plaintiff or plaintiffs. The court shall not grant or approve any prospective relief unless the court finds that such relief is narrowly drawn, extends no further than necessary to correct the violation of the Federal right, and is the least intrusive means necessary to correct the violation of the Federal right. The court shall give substantial weight to any adverse impact on public safety or the operation of a criminal justice system caused by the relief.
18 U.S.C. §3626(a)(1)(A).

establishes an admission, not a waiver. On June 9, 2010 plaintiffs requested that the district court supplement its findings relating to the PLRA's so-called "need-narrowness-intrusiveness" standard. At a subsequent status conference, the court asked defendants' counsel not once, but twice, "whether or not the Defense believes the order as tendered . . . is as narrow as is required"; counsel replied that it was. As a practical matter, then, defendants are precluded from making this argument now.

Regardless, the district court's orders establish that the court evaluated the record as a whole and identified evidence that fully supports the scope of the injunctive relief granted. . . .

Having determined that the district court properly held that Act 105 violates the Eighth Amendment, both on its face and as applied to plaintiffs, we need not address the district court's alternate holding that the law violates the Equal Protection Clause. Plaintiffs have asserted a conditional cross-appeal of the district court's denial of class certification. But because we have upheld the district court's injunction, we also do not address the cross-appeal.

III

The judgment of the district court is affirmed.

Discussion

1. Why might the state of Wisconsin have enacted a categorical ban on state correctional facilities using any state or federal funds for hormone treatments, or what today would widely be called gender confirmation surgeries, for transgender inmates?

2. Is the court's limited-cancer-treatment analogy valid? Would it be more appropriate to compare conventional treatment of cancer with more costly genetic therapies?

3. The court relies on the Supreme Court majority's embrace in *Gonzalez v. Carhart*, 550 U.S. 124 (2007) (upholding the federal so-called Partial-Birth Abortion Ban Act), of an independent review of facts in constitutional cases. Is that reconcilable with rational basis review, where challenged government action is sustained "if there if there is any reasonably conceivable state of facts that could provide a rational basis for the classification," *F.C.C. v. Beach Commc'ns, Inc.*, 508 U.S. 307, 313 (1993)?

4. Note that the court's decision was rendered in reliance on the American Psychiatric Association's revised fourth edition of the *Diagnostic and Statistical Manual of Mental Disorders* ("DSM-IV-TR") and its diagnosis of "gender identity disorder" ("GID") (*see* discussion in Chapter 14, *infra* at pp. 941–42) when it wrote that "[i]ndividuals with GID identify strongly with a gender that does not match their physical

sex characteristics. The condition is associated with severe psychological distress." What that wording might not make clear is that identifying with a gender different from the one assigned at birth is not necessarily accompanied by severe psychological distress. The fifth edition of the DSM ("DSM-V") replaced the GID diagnosis with a new one termed "gender dysphoria" (see discussion in Chapter 14, *infra* at pp. 1017–22); DSM-V did so to clarify and emphasize that simply being transgender is not a mental illness, that cross-gender identification is not caused by the disorder gender dysphoria, and that it is the distress that need not but can be associated with living as a member of one's sex assigned at birth that is the mark of disorder. In addition, in contrast to the rigid presentation by the court, it is today recognized that the order in which a transgender person might receive counseling/therapy, hormones, and surgery can vary, and that not all trans people will want or need all or any of these interventions. *See, e.g.,* World Professional Association for Transgender Health (WPATH), Standard of Care for the Health of Transsexual, Transgender, and Gender-Nonconforming People 16 (7th ed. 2011).

Reading Guide for Kosilek v. Spencer

1. In the following case brought by an incarcerated transgender woman seeking surgery to treat her gender identity disorder, the district court ruled in the plaintiff's favor and a three-judge panel of the court of appeals initially affirmed, but a majority of the appeals court sitting en banc reversed.

2. What right does Michelle Kosilek argue that Massachusetts violated? What is the legal test for violations of that right (agreed to by the majority and dissenting justices)? What standard for appellate review does the en banc majority articulate?

3. What reasons does the majority give for rejecting the trial court's conclusion that Ms. Kosilek proved the treatment/treatment plans for her gender identity disorder was objectively inadequate? What is the majority's reasoning, about medicine and about security, for rejecting the district court's conclusion that Kosilek satisfied the subjective prong of the relevant constitutional doctrine?

4. The standard for Eighth Amendment violations contains an "objective" component. Why, in assessing it, does Judge Thompson's dissent disagree with the majority about the "prudence" of defense expert Dr. Schmidt? Why does it disagree about whether the care the prison gave and proposed to give to Ms. Kosilek was objectively adequate?

5. The standard for Eighth Amendment violations also contains a subjective component. In assessing it, why does Thompson's dissent disagree with the majority about the significance of any conflicting medical opinions about the medical necessity of gender confirmation surgery (here termed "sex reassignment surgery")? For what reasons does Thompson's dissent disagree about the import of the defendant's professed security concerns, including those dealing with housing and suicide risk?

6. What is the basic point Judge Kayatta emphasizes in his dissent?

Michelle Kosilek v. Luis S. Spencer, Commissioner of the Massachusetts Department of Correction

774 F.3d 63 (1st Cir. 2014) (en banc)

[The Massachusetts Family Institute filed an amicus curiae in support of the state. WPATH and a number of U.S. LGBT health and community organizations and institutions; the ACLU, ACLU of Massachusetts, and legal organizations serving prisoners; and LGBTQ legal and political organizations including transgender-specific ones all filed amicus briefs supporting plaintiff transgender inmate Michelle Kosilek.]

Before LYNCH, Chief Judge, TORRUELLA, HOWARD, THOMPSON, and KAYATTA, Circuit Judges.

Opinion En Banc

TORRUELLA, Circuit Judge.

. . . . We are asked to determine whether the district court erred in concluding that the Massachusetts Department of Correction ("DOC") has violated the Cruel and Unusual Punishment Clause of the Eighth Amendment by providing allegedly inadequate medical care to prisoner Michelle Kosilek ("Kosilek"). More precisely, we are faced with the question whether the DOC's choice of a particular medical treatment is constitutionally inadequate, such that the district court acts within its power to issue an injunction requiring provision of an alternative treatment — a treatment which would give rise to new concerns related to safety and prison security.

After carefully considering the community standard of medical care, the adequacy of the provided treatment, and the valid security concerns articulated by the DOC, we conclude that the district court erred and that the care provided to Kosilek by the DOC does not violate the Eighth Amendment. We therefore reverse the district court's grant of injunctive relief, and we remand with instructions to dismiss the case.

I. Background

This litigation has now spanned more than twenty years and produced several opinions of significant length. *See Kosilek v. Spencer,* 889 F. Supp. 2d 190 (D. Mass. 2012) ("*Kosilek II*"); *Kosilek v. Maloney,* 221 F. Supp. 2d 156 (D. Mass. 2002) ("*Kosilek I*"). In light of the expansive record, we recite here only the facts necessary to clarify the issues on appeal.

A. Michelle Kosilek

Michelle Kosilek . . . is an anatomically male prisoner in her mid-sixties who suffers from gender identity disorder ("GID")[1] and self-identifies as a female. In

---

1. The term "gender identity disorder" has recently been replaced with the term "gender dysphoria" in the medical community. *See* Am. Psychiatric Ass'n, *Gender Dysphoria*, http://www.

1992 Kosilek was convicted of first-degree murder and sentenced to a term of life imprisonment without parole for the 1990 strangulation of her then-wife, Cheryl McCaul. . . . While awaiting trial for McCaul's murder, Kosilek twice attempted to commit suicide. She also once tied a string around her testicles in an attempt at self-castration, but removed the string when it became painful. Since 1994, Kosilek has been housed at MCI-Norfolk, a medium security male prison in Massachusetts. Throughout the twenty-year duration of her incarceration at MCI-Norfolk, Kosilek has not attempted to harm herself.

B. *Kosilek I*

Kosilek first sued the DOC in 1992, alleging that its failure to provide direct treatment for her GID was a violation of the Eighth Amendment. At that time, Kosilek was receiving only "supportive therapy" to cope with the distress caused by her GID. . . .

The district court issued a decision in 2002, in which it concluded. . . . that the DOC was unaware that a failure to provide additional treatment to Kosilek might result in serious harm [and acted,] at least in part, [from] "sincere security concerns[]" and so . . . was not in violation of the Eighth Amendment.

Despite finding for the DOC, the district court's opinion made clear that Kosilek required additional treatment for her GID, and that the DOC would need to develop and implement an improved treatment plan. . . .

C. The DOC offers treatment

The DOC responded to *Kosilek I* by revamping its policy for GID treatment. [After] *Kosilek I* the DOC adopted a plan that allowed prisoners to receive additional treatment beyond the level of that received before entering prison, when such care was medically required. [Medical recommendations] would be made by the University of Massachusetts Correctional Health Program ("UMass"), a health-services provider contracted by the DOC. The DOC Commissioner and the DOC Director of Health Services were responsible for assessing whether any change in treatment would create increased security concerns.

Kosilek was evaluated by Dr. David Seil, a gender-identity specialist, who prescribed a course of treatment to alleviate the mental distress . . . associated with her GID. In line with Dr. Seil's recommendations, in 2003 the DOC began providing Kosilek with significant ameliorative treatment aimed at directly addressing the mental distress caused by GID. In addition to continued mental health treatment, she was provided female, gender-appropriate clothing and personal effects, and electrolysis was performed to permanently remove her facial hair. Kosilek also began a course of hormonal treatments recommended by an endocrinologist. These

---

dsm5.org/documents/gender%20dysphoria%20fact%20sheet.pdf (last visited June 3, 2014). To maintain consistency with prior related litigation and evidence in the record, we continue to use the term "GID" in this opinion.

treatments resulted in "breast development and shrinkage of her testicles." All of the treatments described continue to be offered to Kosilek to the present day.

D. Consideration of SRS

In line with the Harry Benjamin Standards of Care (the "Standards of Care" or "the Standards"),[3] Dr. Seil recommended that Kosilek be considered for SRS after one year of hormonal treatment. Accordingly, in 2004 the DOC began the process of finding an appropriate professional to evaluate Kosilek's eligibility for, and the necessity of, SRS. . . . The UMass Mental Health Program Director, Dr. Kenneth Appelbaum, suggested that the DOC consult with the Fenway Community Health Center [. . . .], a Boston-based facility focused on serving the lesbian, gay, bisexual, and transgender community. In contrast, the DOC's Director of Mental Health and Substance Abuse Services, Gregory Hughes . . . , suggested consulting with Cynthia Osborne . . . , a gender identity specialist employed at the Johns Hopkins School of Medicine who had experience working with other departments of correction regarding GID treatment.

Hughes expressed concern with using the Fenway Center because of "the perception that their approach was to come out with recommendations that globally endorsed a full panoply of treatments." It was thought that Osborne, in contrast, "may do more objective evaluations." Dr. Appelbaum noted, however, that the Fenway Center's approach was, to his knowledge, probably "more the norm than the exception." . . . .

The Fenway Center was retained by the DOC, and Kosilek was evaluated by Kevin Kapila, M.D., and Randi Kaufman, Psy.D., in a ninety-minute interview. Drs. Kapila and Kaufman also reviewed Kosilek's medical [records and] issued a report recommending that Kosilek receive SRS (the "Fenway Report"). The Fenway Report acknowledged Kosilek's positive response to the treatment provided by the DOC. . . .

Nonetheless, it also emphasized that Kosilek remained significantly distressed by "having male genitalia, as well as not having female genitalia." . . . .

The Fenway Report was received by the DOC and reviewed. . . . The UMass doctors informed the DOC that they found no clear contraindications to SRS. . . .

[The] DOC decided to have Osborne conduct a peer review of the Fenway Report. In a letter to Osborne, the DOC stated that it was requesting her services because

---

3. . . . . Relevant to *Kosilek II* is the sixth version of the Standards of Care. A seventh version of the Standards of Care was published in 2011, and adopts the Harry Benjamin Association's new name. *See* World Professional Ass'n for Transgender Health ("WPATH"), Standards of Care for the Health of Transsexual, Transgender, and Gender-Nonconforming People, Version 7 (2011). The Standards of Care "are intended to provide *flexible directions for the treatment* " of GID, and state that "[i]ndividual professionals and organized programs may modify" the Standards' requirements in response to "a patient's unique . . . situation" or "an experienced professional's evolving [treatment methodology]." Standards of Care at 1-2 (emphasis added).

"[t]he treatment of Gender Identity Disorder within a correctional environment is a complicated issue and one that the Department takes very seriously. . . ." . . . .

[The] DOC Director of Health Services, Susan Martin . . . , wrote UMass, stating her concern that UMass had not "address[ed] the lack of detail, clarity and specific recommendations in the evaluation done by the Fenway Clinic," and had failed to provide an independent recommendation as to the appropriateness of surgery. She also asked for specific logistical information, including a list of doctors who might provide the surgery, what procedures would be performed, and what recovery time could be expected.

[The UMass doctors] replied, indicating that they deferred to the Fenway Center's recommendation of surgery, as they were not experts in the area of SRS—a medical procedure specifically excluded from their contract to provide services to the DOC. They provided a preliminary list of surgeons to consider, none of whom were licensed to practice medicine in Massachusetts.

[Osborne] finished her peer review of the Fenway Report. [Her] review was limited to reading and evaluating the reports of others. [She] believed [there] to be a lack of comprehensiveness in the report and an inclination to minimize the possibility of comorbid conditions. . . . Osborne expressed belief that threats of self-harm or suicide should serve as a contraindication to surgery, and that such threats were not a valid or clinically acceptable justification for surgery. In consequence, she disagreed with the Fenway Center's statements that surgery was medically necessary as a means to diminish the likelihood that Kosilek would attempt suicide in the future.

Osborne's report also highlighted that the Standards of Care admit of flexible application, and noted that the Standards state that "the diagnosis of GID invites the consideration of a variety of therapeutic options, only one of which is the complete therapeutic triad." She emphasized that "[t]here is currently no universal professional consensus regarding what constitutes medical necessity in GID."

. . . Osborne noted that the Standards of Care include a criterion that candidates for SRS exhibit "satisfactory control of problems such as sociopathy, substance abuse, psychosis and suicidality." She believed that this requirement was inherently in conflict with the Standard's [sic] application to incarcerated persons, as she felt incarceration indicated a lack of mastery over such antisocial leanings. Moreover, Osborne noted that non-incarcerated individuals often face external constraints in their choice of treatments or determine, as a result of their "real life experience," that other, non-invasive treatments are personally preferable to SRS. In consequence, she felt that it was unrealistic for inmates to expect "that prison life [would] provide *no* constraints or obstacles to cross gender preferences" and that it was "outside[] the bounds of good clinical practice" for care providers to try to meet this expectation. . . .

After considering Osborne's peer review, Martin again reached out to the doctors at UMass[, expressing] continuing concern with the Fenway Report. . . .

. . . . The [UMass doctors' response] made clear that they were not experts in the treatment of GID, and that they deferred to the Fenway Center's treatment recommendation. Referring to the differences between the preferred treatment plans of the Fenway Center and Osborne, the doctors reminded Martin that Osborne's report had emphasized the "dearth of empirical research upon which to base treatment decisions" for GID and had highlighted the lack of "professional consensus" regarding the "medical necessity" of SRS.

The Fenway Center issued a follow-up report aimed at answering Osborne's critique of its initial recommendation. [This] report . . . noted that suicidal ideation was common among individuals suffering from GID, and that it often decreased with the provision of care. Therefore, the likelihood that Kosilek would become suicidal if denied surgery was, to the doctors, not a contraindication to her eligibility, but instead was a symptom that could be alleviated by provision of SRS. The doctors also disagreed with Osborne's belief that incarceration was a significant contraindication to surgery, noting that the Standards of Care specifically state that "[p]ersons who are receiving treatment for [GID] should continue to receive appropriate treatment . . . after incarceration [*i.e.*, after becoming incarcerated—Eds.]. For example, those who are receiving psychotherapy and/or cross-sex hormonal treatments should be allowed to continue this medically necessary treatment. . . ."

The Fenway Center doctors further discussed their belief that a key step of the triadic sequence, the "real-life experience," could occur in prison. . . . The purpose of this requirement is [to] ensure that GID patients have an opportunity to experience a full measure of life in a cross-gender role, including the social scrutiny that may arise among professional counterparts and peers. Prison, the Fenway Center's doctors surmised, might be considered a "more stringent" real-life experience, because a prisoner's gender presentation would be subject to full-time monitoring by prison personnel and other inmates. The report concluded by reiterating the Fenway Center's recommendation that Kosilek receive SRS. The doctors . . . emphasized that "hormone therapy and [SRS] are the only clinical treatments found to be effective for GID."

E. The DOC's Security Report

On April 25, 2005, the district court issued an order requiring that the DOC conduct a review of any potential safety and security concerns arising from the provision of SRS. In the next month, the DOC worked to formalize its security concerns into a report. . . .

On May 19, 2005, DOC Commissioner Kathleen Dennehy . . . convened a meeting with the Superintendent of MCI-Norfolk, Luis Spencer . . . , and the Superintendent of MCI-Framingham, Lynne Bissonnette . . . , as well as the DOC's legal counsel. . . . to formally discuss the security concerns previously expressed by both superintendents in phone conversations with Dennehy. . . .

The report focused mainly on issues of safety and security surrounding Kosilek's post-operative housing. Dennehy conveyed concern regarding housing Kosilek at MCI-Norfolk, noting that approximately twenty-five percent of male offenders in the Massachusetts prison system are classified as sex offenders and concluding that "Kosilek would clearly be a target for assault and victimization in a male prison." The report also expressed concerns with housing Kosilek at MCI-Framingham [Massachusetts's only female prison], including the absence of single-bed cells, such that all inmates had to share cells, and the possibility that Kosilek's presence might exacerbate mental distress among the significant portion of MCI-Framingham's population that had previously experienced domestic abuse and trauma at the hands of male partners.

Given the stated infeasibility of housing Kosilek in the general population of either MCI-Framingham or MCI-Norfolk, the report considered segregated housing in a protected ward. It expressed concern, however, about the possible deleterious impact on Kosilek's mental health caused by any housing solution that required long-term isolation. The report also noted that it was not within the DOC's ability to create a special ward for prisoners with GID, given that these prisoners present a significant range of criminal histories, security ratings, and treatment needs that are antithetical to co-housing.

On June 10, 2005, . . . the DOC informed the district court that it had chosen to continue Kosilek's current ameliorative treatment, but not to provide her with SRS.

F. *Kosilek II*

Trial commenced on May 30, 2006, with what would be the first of three rounds of testimony. . . . .

G. *Kosilek II* [*sic*]

The district court issued an extensive opinion on September 4, 2012. This opinion concluded that Kosilek had a serious medical need and that—based on the court's belief that [the defendant's expert Dr. Chester Schmidt, a licensed psychiatrist and Associate Director of the Johns Hopkins School of Medicine, who testified that he would not consider SRS medically necessary here] was not a prudent professional—the only adequate way to treat this need was through SRS. Moreover, the court determined that the DOC's stated security concerns were merely pretextual and concluded that the DOC had in fact made its decision based on public and political pressure [including angry letters from "outraged state politicians" to Harold Clarke, successor to Dennehy as DOC Commissioner]. This, the court concluded, amounted to deliberate indifference under the Eighth Amendment. Stating its belief that the DOC would continue to deny Kosilek adequate treatment in the future, the district court granted an injunction requiring that the DOC provide Kosilek with SRS. [The DOC appealed, and a panel of the First Circuit Court of Appeals affirmed 2–1. *Kosilek v. Spencer*, 740 F.3d 733 (1st Cir. 2014).]

II. Discussion

A. The Eighth Amendment and Medical Care in Prison

"Excessive bail shall not be required, nor excessive fines imposed, nor cruel and unusual punishments inflicted." U.S. Const. amend. VIII. From this brief amendment, courts have derived the principles that govern the permissible conditions under which prisoners are held and that establish the medical treatment those prisoners must be afforded. *See Farmer v. Brennan*, 511 U.S. 825 (1994). Where "society takes from prisoners the means to provide for their own needs," the failure to provide such care "may actually produce physical torture or a lingering death." *Brown v. Plata*, 563 U.S. 493 (2011). Undue suffering, unrelated to any legitimate penological purpose, is considered a form of punishment proscribed by the Eighth Amendment. *Estelle v. Gamble*, 429 U.S. 97 (1976). The Eighth Amendment is meant to prohibit "unnecessary and wanton infliction of pain," which is "repugnant to the conscience of mankind." *Id.*

The Amendment's focus on punishment means that not all shortages or failures in care exhibit the intent and harmfulness required to fall within its ambit. *See Farmer* (reasoning that the Eighth Amendment's prohibition of punishment implies an act done with intentionality). Therefore, to prove an Eighth Amendment violation, a prisoner must satisfy both of two prongs: (1) an objective prong that requires proof of a serious medical need, and (2) a subjective prong that mandates a showing of prison administrators' deliberate indifference to that need. *See Estelle.*

First, a medical need must be "serious." *Sires v. Berman*, 834 F.2d 9, 12 (1st Cir. 1987). This objective prong requires that the need be "one that has been diagnosed by a physician as mandating treatment, or one that is so obvious that even a lay person would easily recognize the necessity for a doctor's attention." *Gaudreault v. Municipality of Salem, Mass.*, 923 F.2d 203 (1st Cir. 1990). This prong does not impose upon prison administrators a duty to provide care that is ideal, or of the prisoner's choosing. *See United States v. Derbes*, 369 F.3d 579 (1st Cir. 2004) (stating that prison administrators are "by no means required to tailor a perfect plan for every inmate; while [they are] constitutionally obligated to provide medical services to inmates, these services need only be on a level reasonably commensurate with modern medical science and of a quality acceptable within prudent professional standards"); *Ferranti v. Moran*, 618 F.2d 888 (1st Cir. 1980) ("[A]llegations [that] simply reflect a disagreement on the appropriate course of treatment . . . fall[] short of alleging a constitutional violation."). Rather, the Constitution proscribes care that is "'so inadequate as to shock the conscience.'" *Torraco v. Maloney*, 923 F.2d 231 (1st Cir. 1991).[7]

---

7. Although these cases address the second, subjective prong of the Eighth Amendment analysis, we have recognized that "the subjective deliberate indifference inquiry may overlap with the objective serious medical need determination" and that "similar evidence . . . may be relevant to both components." *Leavitt v. Corr. Med. Servs., Inc.*, 645 F.3d 484 (1st Cir. 2011); *see also DesRosiers v. Moran*, 949 F.2d 15, 18–19 (1st Cir. 1991). As the adequacy of care is germane both to Kosilek's

Second, even if medical care is so inadequate as to satisfy the objective prong, the Eighth Amendment is not violated unless prison administrators also exhibit deliberate indifference to the prisoner's needs. *Estelle.* For purposes of this subjective prong, deliberate indifference "defines a narrow band of conduct," *Feeney v. Corr. Med. Servs. Inc.,* 464 F.3d 158 (1st Cir. 2006), and requires evidence that the failure in treatment was purposeful. *See Estelle* (holding that "an inadvertent failure to provide adequate medical care" is not a constitutional violation). "The obvious case would be a denial of needed medical treatment in order to punish the inmate." [*Watson v. Caton,* 984 F.2d 537 (1st Cir. 1993)]. While deliberate indifference may also be exhibited by a "wanton disregard" to a prisoner's needs, *Battista v. Clarke,* 645 F.3d 449 (1st Cir. 2011), such disregard must be akin to criminal recklessness, requiring consciousness of "'impending harm, easily preventable.'" *Watson.*

When evaluating medical care and deliberate indifference, security considerations inherent in the functioning of a penological institution must be given significant weight. *Battista* ("[S]ecurity considerations also matter at prisons . . . and administrators have to balance conflicting demands."). "[W]ide-ranging deference" is accorded to prison administrators "in the adoption and execution of policies and practices that in their judgement are needed to . . . maintain institutional security." *Whitley v. Albers,* 475 U.S. 312 (1986). In consequence, even a denial of care may not amount to an Eighth Amendment violation if that decision is based in legitimate concerns regarding prisoner safety and institutional security. *Cameron v. Tomes,* 990 F.2d 14 (1st Cir. 1993) (requiring courts to "embrace security and administration, . . . not merely medical judgments" in assessing claims of deliberate indifference); [*Sires v. Berman,* 834 F.2d 9 (1st Cir. 1987)] ("[S]afety factors are properly included in the evaluation of the medical needs of an inmate."). Importantly, prison administrators need only have "'responded reasonably to the risk.'" *Giroux v. Somerset Cnty.,* 178 F.3d 28 (1st Cir. 1999) (quoting *Farmer*).

B. Standard of Review

The test for establishing an Eighth Amendment claim of inadequate medical care encompasses a multitude of questions that present elements both factual and legal. Review of such "mixed questions" is of a variable exactitude; the more law-based a question, the less deferentially we assess the district court's conclusion. *In re Extradition of Howard,* 996 F.2d 1320 (1st Cir. 1993) ("The standard of review applicable to mixed questions usually depends upon where they fall along the degree-of-deference continuum. . . .").

The ultimate legal conclusion of whether prison administrators have violated the Eighth Amendment is reviewed *de novo.* Subsidiary legal questions, such as whether an actor's conduct amounted to deliberate indifference for purposes of the Eighth Amendment, are likewise reviewed *de novo. Cf. Ornelas v. United States,* 517 U.S.

---

objective need for surgery and to the DOC's alleged deliberate indifference to that need, the principles of these cases are relevant to both steps of our analysis.

690 (1996) (holding that, for Fourth Amendment purposes, reasonable suspicion and probable cause determinations should receive *de novo* appellate review); *United States v. Camacho*, 661 F.3d 718, 724 (1st Cir. 2011) (we review de novo a district court's subsidiary reasonable suspicion and probable cause determinations in evaluating a motion to suppress).

Our court awards deference to the district court's resolution of questions of pure fact and issues of credibility. *See, e.g., DesRosiers v. Moran*, 949 F.2d 15 (1st Cir. 1991) (reviewing factual findings regarding the adequacy of care deferentially); *Torraco* (finding that issues of culpability in a deliberate indifference inquiry are usually questions for a jury). We will reverse the district court's findings on such factual questions only for clear error. We find clear error when we are left with "'a strong, unyielding belief, based on the whole of the record,' that the judge made a mistake." *In re O'Donnell*, 728 F.3d 41 (1st Cir. 2013). We may also find clear error when the district court commits an error of law that affects its fact-finding analysis. *See Uno v. City of Holyoke*, 72 F.3d 973 (1st Cir. 1995).

. . . .

The considerations set forth in *Ornelas* . . . are equally relevant here. "Medical 'need' in real life is an elastic term," *Battista*, "that take[s its] substantive content from the particular context[] in which the standards are being assessed." *Ornelas*. Similarly, the "legal rules" for what constitutes care in violation of the Eighth Amendment "acquire content only through application"—a fact which favors *de novo* appellate review "to maintain control of, and to clarify, the legal principles." *See id.*

C. The Objective Prong: Serious Medical Need

To sustain a claim under the objective prong of the Eighth Amendment, Kosilek must show that she has a serious medical need for which she has received inadequate treatment. A significant risk of future harm that prison administrators fail to mitigate may suffice under the objective prong. *Helling v. McKinney,* 509 U.S. 25 (1993) . . . .

That GID is a serious medical need, and one which mandates treatment, is not in dispute in this case. . . . Rather, the parties disagree over whether SRS is a medically necessary component of Kosilek's care, such that any course of treatment not including surgery is constitutionally inadequate. . . .

Kosilek argues that the *only* constitutionally sufficient treatment regimen is to adhere to the Standards of Care's triadic sequence in full, including the provision of SRS. . . .

In contrast, the DOC argues that full progression through the Standards of Care's triadic sequence is not the only adequate treatment option, as Kosilek's GID may be appropriately managed with treatment short of SRS. The DOC maintains that the evidence does not meet the standards for negligent treatment of a medical condition, much less the higher Eighth Amendment standard. *See Estelle* ("Thus, a complaint that a physician has been negligent in diagnosing or treating a medical condition does not state a valid claim of medical mistreatment under the Eighth Amendment.").

Relying on the advice of accredited medical professionals, the DOC argues that its alternative course of treatment—which provides Kosilek such alleviative measures as psychotherapy, hormones, electrolysis, and the provision of female garb and accessories—is sufficient to treat Kosilek's GID and far exceeds a level of care that would be "so inadequate as to shock the conscience." *See Torraco.* Moreover, this course of treatment has, in practice, greatly diminished Kosilek's mental distress and allowed her a fair measure of contentment. Should suicidal ideation arise in the future, the DOC contends that—based on the advice of its medical experts and its own penological experience—it would be able to address that future risk appropriately through psychotherapy and antidepressants.

. . . .

1. The district court's medical prudence determination

The district court ruled that SRS was a medically necessary treatment, and that Dr. Schmidt's alternative belief was outside the bounds of medical prudence. However, the court's finding that Dr. Schmidt's views were medically imprudent was based on several erroneous determinations.

First, the court ruled that, unlike prudent medical professionals, Dr. Schmidt did not "follow" the Standards of Care in his treatment of GID. This finding ignored critical nuance in Dr. Schmidt's testimony and based its conclusion on a severely strained reading of Dr. Levine's expert testimony.

As an initial matter, the Standards of Care themselves admit of significant flexibility in their interpretation and application. They state, for example, that "[t]he Standards of Care [a]re Clinical *Guidelines*" and are "intended to provide *flexible directions*" to medical professionals in crafting treatment plans. Standards of Care (emphases added). The Standards of Care also specifically warn that "[a]ll readers should be aware of the limitations of knowledge in this area." "Individual professionals and organized programs," the Standards of Care continue on, "may modify [the standards]" as appropriate. Dr. Levine's testimony acknowledged this flexibility:

> [DR. LEVINE]: [T]he "Standards of Care" was a consensus document from people from seven different countries or something, you know, who come from different systems, and it was a political process that forged together a set of standards. . . . So "prudent" is a wonderful word, but it's not like it has one simple definition.
>
> . . .
>
> THE COURT: But is this an area in which you think prudent professionals can reasonably differ as to what is at least minimally adequate treatment for this condition?

[DR. LEVINE]: Yes, and do.

Moreover, the district court put great weight on the fact that the Standards of Care require that patients receive two letters of recommendation prior to SRS. The court concluded, therefore, that "prudent professionals who treat individuals suffering from severe gender identity disorders write such letters of recommendation," and it faulted Dr. Schmidt as imprudent for his failure to engage in this practice. In so doing, the court relied on Dr. Levine's testimony, which it believed stated that a prudent professional would not "[refuse] to write letters of recommendation."

Dr. Schmidt's testimony, however, makes clear that although he does not advocate or recommend surgery to his patients, if a patient chooses to seek SRS, he releases all of their medical files to a surgeon and writes that surgeon a letter confirming that the patient is eligible for surgery. Insofar as Dr. Schmidt had not advocated for the surgery, this neutrality aligns with what Dr. Levine describes as the accepted practice for doctors in the treatment of GID: "[i]f the patient meets eligibility requirements . . . we then write a letter of support . . . I understand how others may perceive this as a recommendation . . . [but] we tell ourselves we are opening a gate to their decision." Therefore, whatever the semantic force of the district court's distinction, we see no material difference between the letters written by Dr. Schmidt confirming a patient's readiness for surgery and what the Standards of Care refers to as a letter of recommendation.

The district court next concluded that Dr. Schmidt was imprudent because antidepressants and psychotherapy alone are inadequate to treat GID. Again, the court claimed that it relied on the testimony of Dr. Levine, but misconstrued his testimony in support of its conclusion. Dr. Levine did in fact state that "gender dysphoria is not significantly ameliorated . . . by treating [patients] with a prozac-like drug alone." He continued on, however, to explain that he did not believe this was the treatment plan advocated by Dr. Schmidt or the DOC. To the contrary, he understood that Kosilek would continue to receive ameliorative treatment for her GID and, if she entered a depressive or suicidal state based on her inability to receive SRS, antidepressants and psychotherapy would be used to help stabilize her mental state so as to alleviate the risk of suicide while working with her to craft new perspectives and life goals beyond surgery. He felt that the treatment might well be successful in this capacity, when combined with the direct alleviative treatments currently provided.

Finally, the district court found Dr. Schmidt imprudent because he did not believe that a real-life experience could occur in prison, given that it was an isolated, single-sex environment. The district court disagreed, stating that it had concluded a real-life experience could occur in prison, as Kosilek would remain incarcerated for her entire life. In reaching this determination, the court made a significantly flawed inferential leap: it relied on its own—non-medical—judgment about what constitutes a real-life experience to conclude that Dr. Schmidt's differing viewpoint was illegitimate or imprudent. Prudent medical professionals, however, do reasonably differ in their opinions regarding the requirements of a real-life experience—and this reasonable difference in medical opinions is sufficient to defeat Kosilek's argument.

In fact, Dr. Levine noted that an incarcerative environment might well be insufficient to expose Kosilek to the variety of societal, familial, and vocational pressures foreseen by a real-life experience. This viewpoint aligned with that of Dr. Schmidt and Osborne. And, although Dr. Forstein's written report appears to presume Kosilek had completed a real-life experience, it echoed this same point: "being in prison has helped [Kosilek] consolidate her desire . . . simplifying the issues, without the stressors and choices that she would have had to make out in the outside real world." We find no support for the district court's conclusion that no reasonable medical expert could opine that Kosilek lacked real-life experience, particularly in light of the contrary testimony from medical experts concerning the range of social, environmental, and professional considerations that are necessary to constitute a real-life experience under the Standards of Care. The district court thus erred by substituting its own beliefs for those of multiple medical experts.[10]

The district court's finding of medical imprudence relied heavily on inferences we do not believe can rightly be drawn from Dr. Levine's testimony; this finding also ignored significant contrary evidence regarding the breadth and variety of acceptable treatments for GID within the medical community. Its conclusion that the Fenway Center's recommendation constituted the sole acceptable treatment plan is, thus, contradicted by the record.

2. Adequacy of the DOC's treatment plan

Regarding the medical adequacy of Kosilek's treatment, the district court held that psychotherapy and antidepressants alone would not adequately treat Kosilek's GID. This finding mischaracterizes the issues on appeal and unduly minimizes the nature of the DOC's preferred treatment plan. The DOC does not claim that treating Kosilek's GID merely with therapy and antidepressants alone would constitute adequate care. *Cf. Fields v. Smith*, 653 F.3d 550 (7th Cir. 2011) (accepting, in the absence of contrary evidence, expert testimony that "psychotherapy as well as antipsychotics and antidepressants . . . do nothing to treat the underlying disorder [of GID]"). In fact, since *Kosilek I* the DOC has acknowledged the need to directly treat Kosilek's GID. Beginning in 2003, it has provided hormones, electrolysis, feminine clothing and accessories, and mental health services aimed at alleviating her distress. The

---

10. There are obvious reasons for the range of judgments in this area. Although the medical experts disagreed over whether experience in a prison setting could qualify as real-life experience, none of the experts who opined that it could do so appear to have considered the fact that after SRS, Kosilek would most likely be housed in the drastically different setting of a female facility. This distinction was reflected in Dr. Forstein's report, which stated that "[Kosilek's] 'real life experience' leads her to the conclusion that so long as she is in a male prison . . . she cannot perceive herself as a true woman." This statement acknowledges that any real-life experience available to Kosilek was shaped by her current, all-male prison environment. Kosilek introduced no evidence to show that her experience there would satisfy the requirement that she have real-life experience in her post-operative housing environment.

parties agree that this care has led to a real and marked improvement in Kosilek's mental state. [This] care would continue, whether or not SRS is provided.

The question before our court, therefore, ... is whether the decision not to provide SRS—in light of the continued provision of all ameliorative measures currently afforded Kosilek and in addition to antidepressants and psychotherapy—is sufficiently harmful to Kosilek so as to violate the Eighth Amendment. It is not. *See Smith v. Carpenter,* 316 F.3d 178 (2d Cir. 2003) ("[I]t's the particular risk of harm faced by a prisoner due to the challenged deprivation of care, rather than the severity of the prisoner's underlying medical condition, considered in the abstract, that is relevant for Eighth Amendment purposes."); *see also Estelle* (requiring proof of "acts or omissions sufficiently harmful" as to illustrate deliberate indifference to a serious medical need).

Kosilek admits that the DOC's current treatment regimen has led to a significant stabilization in her mental state. Kosilek's doctors testified to the same, highlighting her "joy around being feminized." This claim is also borne out by the passage of significant time since she exhibited symptoms of suicidal ideation or attempted to self-castrate. In addition to alleviating her depressive state, this treatment has also resulted in significant physical changes and an increasingly feminine appearance.

[The] risk of suicidal ideation is born from Kosilek's GID-related mental distress. Therefore an assessment of the gravity of that risk, and its appropriate treatment, must encompass the entirety of the DOC's treatment plan, not merely the potential addition of psychotherapy and antidepressants.

Kosilek is provided hormones, facial hair removal, feminine clothing and accessories, and access to regular mental health treatment. The DOC also stands ready to protect Kosilek from the potential for self-harm by employing its standard and accepted methods of treating any prisoner exhibiting suicidal ideation. Trial testimony established that this plan offers real and direct treatment for Kosilek's GID. It employs methods proven to alleviate Kosilek's mental distress while crafting a plan to minimize the risk of future harm. It does not wantonly disregard Kosilek's needs, but accounts for them.

The law is clear that where two alternative courses of medical treatment exist, and both alleviate negative effects within the boundaries of modern medicine, it is not the place of our court to "second guess medical judgments" or to require that the DOC adopt the more compassionate of two adequate options. *Layne v. Vinzant,* 657 F.2d 468 (1st Cir. 1981).

That the DOC has chosen one of two alternatives—both of which are reasonably commensurate with the medical standards of prudent professionals, and both of which provide Kosilek with a significant measure of relief—is a decision that does not violate the Eighth Amendment.[12]

---

12. This holding in no way suggests that correctional administrators wishing to avoid treatment need simply to find a single practitioner willing to attest that some well-accepted treatment is not

Kosilek warns, however, that upholding the adequacy of the DOC's course of treatment in this case—despite her medical history and record of good behavior—will create a de facto ban against SRS as a medical treatment for any incarcerated individual. We do not agree. For one, the DOC has specifically disclaimed any attempt to create a blanket policy regarding SRS. We are confident that the DOC will abide by this assurance, as any such policy would conflict with the requirement that medical care be individualized based on a particular prisoner's serious medical needs. *See, e.g., Roe v. Elyea*, 631 F.3d 843 (7th Cir. 2011) (holding that the failure to conduct an individualized assessment of a prisoner's needs may violate the Eighth Amendment).

For another, this case presents unique circumstances; we are simply unconvinced that our decision on the record before us today will foreclose all litigants from successfully seeking SRS in the future. Certain facts in this particular record—including the medical providers' non-uniform opinions regarding the necessity of SRS, Kosilek's criminal history, and the feasibility of postoperative housing—were important factors impacting the decision.

D. The Subjective Prong: Deliberate Indifference

1. The DOC's reliance on medical experts

The subjective element of an Eighth Amendment claim for injunctive relief requires not only that Kosilek show that the treatment she received was constitutionally inadequate, but also that the DOC was—and continues to be—deliberately indifferent to her serious risk of harm. *See Farmer.*[13] On the record presented, this is a burden Kosilek cannot meet. Even if the district court had been correct in its erroneous determination that SRS was the only medically adequate treatment for Kosilek's GID, the next relevant inquiry would be whether the DOC also knew or should have known this fact, but nonetheless failed to respond in an appropriate manner. *See Wilson v. Seiter*, 501 U.S. 294 (1991). In answering this question, it is not the district court's own belief about medical necessity that controls, but what was

---

necessary. We do not establish here a *per se* rule allowing a dissenting medical opinion to carry the day. Rather, our determination is limited to the particular record on appeal, which involves a medical condition that admits of a number of valid treatment options. This fact was testified to by Dr. Levine, recognized by the UMass doctors in their correspondence with the DOC, and corroborated by Dr. Forstein in his written report.

The DOC did not engage in a frenzy of serial consultations aimed at finding the one doctor out of a hundred willing to testify that SRS was not medically necessary. Rather, it made a considered decision to seek out a second opinion from an expert previously considered in its initial selection process....

13. Although the DOC has not specifically argued that the conflicting medical opinions preclude a finding of subjective deliberate indifference, we do not find this argument waived. As we have explained above, the subjective and objective analyses overlap. *See supra* note 7. The DOC's contention that the district court erred in deeming SRS medically necessary and in rejecting Dr. Schmidt's approach as imprudent necessarily entails the DOC's subjective belief that SRS was unnecessary....

known and understood by prison officials in crafting their policy. *Id.* (requiring a showing of purposefulness or intent on the part of prison administrators).

In this case, the DOC solicited the opinion of multiple medical professionals and was ultimately presented with two alternative treatment plans, which were each developed by different medical experts to mitigate the severity of Kosilek's mental distress. The choice of a medical option that, although disfavored by some in the field, is presented by competent professionals does not exhibit a level of inattention or callousness to a prisoner's needs rising to a constitutional violation.[14] *Cf. Torraco* ("[T]his court has hesitated to find deliberate indifference to a serious need '[w]here the dispute concerns not the absence of help, but the choice of a certain course of treatment,' [but] deliberate indifference may be found where the attention received is 'so clearly inadequate as to amount to a refusal to provide essential care.'" (internal citations omitted)). Moreover, a later court decision — ruling that the prison administrators were wrong in their estimation of the treatment's reasonableness does not somehow convert that choice into one exhibiting the sort of obstinacy and disregard required to find deliberate indifference.

2. The DOC's security concerns

The subjective prong also recognizes that, in issues of security, "[p]rison administrators . . . should be accorded wide-ranging deference in the adoption and execution of policies and practices that in their judgment are needed to preserve internal order and discipline and to maintain institutional security." [*Bell v. Wolfish*, 441 U.S. 520 (1979).] As long as prison administrators make judgments balancing security and health concerns that are "within the realm of reason and made in good faith," their decisions do not amount to a violation of the Eighth Amendment. *Battista.*

The DOC officials explained that they believed SRS would create new security issues, the most significant being the provision of safe housing options for Kosilek after her surgery. They further explained the importance of keeping other inmates from believing that they could use threats of suicide to extract concessions from the prison administration. Nonetheless, rather than deferring to the expertise of prison

---

14. If the prison itself should have been aware that some of the medical advice it was receiving was imprudent — that is, if any layperson could have realized that the advice was imprudent — then the decision to still follow that advice may qualify as deliberate indifference. *See Farmer*, 511 U.S. at 846 n.9 ("If, for example, the evidence before a district court establishes that an inmate faces an objectively intolerable risk of serious injury, the defendants could not plausibly persist in claiming lack of awareness. . . ."); *Hadix v. Johnson*, 367 F.3d 513 (6th Cir. 2004) ("If [the challenged prison conditions] are found to be objectively unconstitutional, then that finding would also satisfy the subjective prong because the same information that would lead to the court's conclusion was available to the prison officials."). The facts of this case, however, are highly distinct from such a scenario.

. . . . Moreover, even assuming arguendo that the DOC was on notice that its treatment was insufficient, the DOC's continued refusal also rested on valid security concerns, discussed below, such that its actions did not amount to deliberate indifference in any event.

administrators, the district court ignored the DOC's stated security concerns, reasoning both that Kosilek could be housed safely and that the DOC had not acted out of a legitimate concern for Kosilek's safety and the security of the DOC's facilities. As explained below, this was in error.

a. The DOC's concerns about safety and security were reasonable

Recognizing that reasonable concerns would arise regarding a post-operative, male-to-female transsexual being housed with male prisoners takes no great stretch of the imagination. *See Farmer* (summarizing evidence that a prison's refusal to provide segregated housing to a pre-operative male-to-female transsexual could pose significant security concerns). At the same time, as particularly relevant in Kosilek's case, the DOC's security report reflected that significant concerns would also arise from housing a formerly male inmate—with a criminal history of extreme violence against a female domestic partner—within a female prison population containing high numbers of domestic violence survivors. Nonetheless, in dismissing the DOC's concerns, the district court relied heavily on the fact that security issues have not yet arisen within MCI-Norfolk's general population. Rejecting the testimony of multiple individuals with decades of penological experience—all of whom acknowledged the risk of housing a female prisoner at MCI-Norfolk—the district court reasoned that Kosilek's *past* safety was indicative of a likelihood that she could reside safely at the prison after her operation.

This reasoning wrongly circumvents the deference owed to prison administrators: the appropriate inquiry was not whether the court believed that Kosilek could be housed safely, but whether the DOC has a reasoned basis for its stated concerns. Indeed, that Kosilek had so far been safe within MCI-Norfolk's prison population does not negate the DOC's well-reasoned belief that safety concerns would arise in the future after SRS. *Cf. Jones v. N.C. Prisoners' Labor Union,* 433 U.S. 119 (1977) (holding, in the First Amendment context, that the rights of prisoners may be abridged based on a reasonable belief that future harm or disruption may occur); *cf. Hudson v. Palmer,* 468 U.S. 517 (1984) (requiring prison administrators to implement prophylactic solutions to foreseeable security issues reasonably within the scope of their expertise). Moreover, the fact that, preoperatively, Kosilek has not been subject to assault or threats does not vitiate the concern that she would be victimized after receiving SRS.[15]

The district court also reasoned that "the DOC [could] reasonably assure the safety of Kosilek and others after sex reassignment surgery by housing Kosilek in a segregated protective custody unit." It then noted, however, that there existed a strong argument that such isolation would amount to "a form of extrajudicial punishment that is prohibited by the Eighth Amendment." This warning echoes the

---

15. These concerns were obvious to more than just those individuals within the DOC with significant penological experience. The likelihood that issues surrounding secure housing would arise after SRS was also acknowledged by Kosilek's treating psychologist, Mark Burrows, and by the Fenway Center doctors in their initial report.

very concerns highlighted by the DOC, which expressed disagreement with the use of long-term isolation as a housing solution for Kosilek, based on its potential negative effects on her mental health. The deference awarded to prison administrators cannot be defeated by such circular reasoning, which dismisses the DOC's concern in one breath only to recognize its validity in the next.

The prison administrators in this case have decades of combined experience in the management of penological institutions, and it is they, not the court, who are best situated to determine what security concerns will arise. The DOC's judgment regarding post-operative housing is without doubt "within the realm of reason," *Battista*, and the district court's alternative belief as to the possibility of safely housing Kosilek does not suffice to undermine this reasonableness.

The DOC officials also expressed concern that providing Kosilek SRS would incentivize the use of suicide threats by prisoners as a means of receiving desired benefits. Although the district court determined that, in this case, Kosilek's risk for suicidal ideation was very real, this finding does not invalidate the DOC's reasonable belief that providing SRS might lead to proliferation of false threats among other prisoners.

The DOC's concern—regarding the unacceptable precedent that would be established in dealing with future threats of suicide by inmates to force the prison authorities to comply with the prisoners' particular demands—cannot be discounted as a minor or invalid claim. Such threats are not uncommon in prison settings and require firm rejection by the authorities, who must be given ample discretion in dealing with such situations. Given the circumstances presented here, we cannot say that the DOC lacks reasonable security concerns.

b. Deference to the DOC's reasonable concerns about safety and security

The district court ultimately dismissed the DOC's concerns as pretextual, reasoning that DOC was in fact acting in response to "public and political criticism." The primary evidence on record tending to support this theory includes a press interview by Commissioner Dennehy, Dennehy's relationships with a state senator and the lieutenant governor, and the acknowledgment that the DOC was aware of negative news coverage regarding Kosilek's request for surgery.

In her testimony, Dennehy denied being influenced by such media and political pressures, and stated that the decision not to provide SRS was founded in bona fide security concerns alone. The district court, however, found this testimony non-credible, and this credibility finding is the sort of determination to which our court gives deference. Even accepting that Dennehy's motivations were colored by political and media pressure, however, does not take Kosilek's claim as far as it needs to go.

As an initial matter, the fact that Dennehy was motivated in part by concerns unrelated to prison security does not mean that the security concerns articulated by the DOC were irrelevant, wholly pretextual, or—most importantly—invalid on the merits. In *Battista*, our court held that deference to the decisions of prison administrators could be overcome where those administrators admittedly relied on inflated data, identified a security concern only several years after refusing to provide treatment for an acknowledged medical need, and engaged in a pattern of changing positions and arguments before the court. Such gross delays and misstatements were not present here.[16] Rather, the DOC testified consistently that it believed the postoperative security concerns surrounding Kosilek's treatment were significant and problematic.[17] Even if not entitled to deference, those concerns still matter insofar as they are reasonable and valid, and Kosilek did not put on any evidence showing that they wholly lacked merit.[18]

Second, when determining the appropriateness of injunctive relief, our focus must include "current attitudes and conduct." *Farmer* ("'[D]eliberate indifference[]' should be determined in light of the prison authorities' current attitudes and conduct': their attitudes and conduct at the time suit is brought and persisting thereafter."). Dennehy has not served as DOC Commissioner since 2007. Given the age of this litigation and the changes in DOC leadership that have occurred since the suit was filed, the district court's assumption that Dennehy's attitudes necessarily carried over to her successors and governed their actions is unsupported by the record. Although consideration of Dennehy's motivation is surely relevant, it is insufficient to show that the DOC continued to be motivated by public pressure even after her departure, or that this is what motivates the DOC presently.

Indeed, it was Commissioner Clarke—and not Dennehy—who made the decision here. And the only evidence tending to show that Commissioner Clarke may have considered public and political criticism were two letters *received* by

---

16. Great weight was placed on the fact that Dennehy told a reporter that there were significant security concerns about post-operative housing three days before she met with Superintendents Spencer and Bissonnette. The record reveals, however, that discussions about housing had previously occurred at Executive Staff Meetings, and Dennehy testified that she had conducted phone calls with both Superintendents prior to meeting to formalize their security report. This timeline, therefore, is far from sufficient to establish that the DOC's security assessments were unprincipled or invalid.

17. That the DOC may have, in the district court's assessment, engaged in a pattern of prevarication regarding whether they understood that SRS was being recommended by UMass as medically necessary, does not undercut the consistency with which they identified safety and security concerns—concerns which are within their expert province—that would arise from the surgery.

18. Kosilek did cross-examine Commissioner Clarke to show that a transgendered prisoner had safely been housed in a Washington State prison under his supervision. Left unexplored, however, were the numerous ways in which MCI-Norfolk's environment, facilities, or population might be distinct from this prison in Washington. Neither was there a comparison between that prisoner's criminal history and the criminal history of Kosilek. That an individual was housed safely by Commissioner Clarke while employed in another state does not rebut Superintendent Bissonnette's testimony that moving her to MCI-Framingham would cause climate problems in that particular prison. *See Feeley v. Sampson*, 570 F.2d 364 (1st Cir. 1978) (rejecting uniform housing conditions for detainees, without regard to their disparate criminal history, because "Constitutional rights cannot be defined in terms of literal comparisons of this nature").

Clarke—who did not respond—from Massachusetts legislators. These letters, however, relate almost in their entirety to concerns about the cost of SRS, and the district court soundly rejected any argument that the DOC, or Clarke specifically, had adopted its safety and security measures as a pretextual means of addressing the cost concerns raised by state legislators. Moreover, Clarke was never found by the court to be noncredible.[19]

The district court improperly imputed its belief that Commissioner Dennehy had acted out of concern for public and political pressure to its assessment of the motivations of future DOC Commissioners. This error ignores the requirement, in cases of injunctive relief, that a court consider the attitudes and beliefs of prison administrators at the time of its decision. *Farmer.* The effect of this error is particularly clear given that Clarke has now been replaced by Commissioner Spencer, so that Dennehy is now several administrations and more than seven years removed from the decisionmaking process. Without proof that the DOC remains motivated by pretextual or improper concerns with public pressure, even if it was assumed that Dennehy was improperly motivated, the district court's finding that injunctive relief was required is unsupportable.

III. Conclusion

We are not tasked today with deciding whether the refusal to provide SRS is uncompassionate or less than ideal. Neither finding would support Kosilek's claims of a constitutional violation. The Eighth Amendment, after all, proscribes only medical care so unconscionable as to fall below society's minimum standards of decency. *See Estelle.* In this case, the DOC has chosen to provide a form of care that offers direct treatment for Kosilek's GID. Moreover, it has done so in light of the fact that provision of SRS would create new and additional security concerns—concerns that do not presently arise from its current treatment regimen.

Given the positive effects of Kosilek's current regimen of care, and the DOC's plan to treat suicidal ideation should it arise, the DOC's decision not to provide SRS does not illustrate severe obstinacy or disregard of Kosilek's medical needs. *DesRosiers* ("[T]he complainant must prove that the defendants had a culpable state of mind and intended wantonly to inflict pain."). Rather, it is a measured response to the valid security concerns identified by the DOC. *Battista* ("Medical 'need' in real life is an elastic term: security considerations also matter at prisons. . . ."); *Cameron* ("Nothing in the Constitution mechanically gives controlling weight to one set of professional judgments."). Having reviewed the record before us, we conclude that Kosilek has failed, on these facts, to demonstrate an Eighth Amendment violation. Accordingly, we reverse the district court's order of injunctive relief and remand this case to the district court with instructions to dismiss the case.

---

19. We further note that the DOC has not defended this case based on cost considerations relating to the provision of SRS.

Reversed and Remanded.

Thompson, Circuit Judge, dissenting.

The majority turns a blind eye to binding precedent, opting instead to cobble together law from other circuits and non-Eighth Amendment jurisprudence to formulate a standard of review that, though articulated as one of variable exactitude, amounts to sweeping de novo review. Armed with the ability to take a fresh look at findings that clearly warranted deference, the majority easily steps into the trial judge's shoes—the inarguable superiority of the judge's ability to marshal facts, assess motive, and gauge credibility all but forgotten. The parameters set by the majority foretold the result. It concludes that the Massachusetts Department of Correction did not violate Michelle Kosilek's constitutional rights. That conclusion is erroneous, the majority's analytical path to it is misguided, and the fact that this case is even subject to en banc scrutiny in the first place is wrong. And so I dissent.

. . . .

II. Standard of Review

. . . . When deciding a post-bench-trial appeal, this court takes up questions of law de novo, but reviews findings of fact for clear error only. . . . With inquiries that are more of a mixed bag, there is a continuum. *Johnson v. Watts Regulator Co.*, 63 F.3d 1129 (1st Cir. 1995). The more fact-intensive the question, the more deferential our review. Conversely, the more law-dominated the query, the more likely our review is de novo.

. . . . The majority . . . utterly favors the de novo end of the spectrum. This approach does not accord with our case law. . . .

For one, the majority posits that the issue of deliberate indifference is a legal one to be reviewed de novo. It relies on Fourth Amendment jurisprudence, citing criminal cases that, in the context of deciding the validity of searches and seizures, hold that reasonable suspicion and probable cause determinations should receive de novo appellate review. I do not see how these cases are analogous to Kosilek's challenge, nor why we should look to Fourth Amendment cases rather than our Eighth Amendment jurisprudence.

In the context of the Eighth Amendment, we have explained that the existence of deliberate indifference is a "state-of-mind issue" that usually presents a jury question, *Torraco v. Maloney*, 923 F.2d 231 (1st Cir. 1991), or in other words, an issue for the finder of fact. This makes sense. Often intertwined in state-of-mind issues are determinations about credibility and motivation; those are classic examples of the judgment calls to which we give deference. . . .

The majority recognizes *Torraco*, citing it for the narrow proposition that "issues of culpability in a deliberate indifference inquiry are usually questions for a jury," in connection with its discussion about what standard of review findings of fact garner. But this is a mischaracterization of what *Torraco* held. Rather, the case states that "the *existence* of deliberate indifference," is a state-of-mind issue, which makes it a typical juror question. *Torraco* (emphasis added). The majority's slight spin on this holding allows it to ignore *Torraco,* and lean on Fourth Amendment jurisprudence instead to support the notion that deliberate indifference gets a fresh look from this court.

Similarly erroneous is the majority's position that we review de novo the district court's ultimate determination as to whether an Eighth Amendment violation occurred. For support it cites to a series of Eighth Amendment cases from other circuit courts. . . . The problem though is that the ultimate constitutional question is inextricably tied up with the factual details that emerged at trial, the credibility of the witnesses, and the questions of motivation. This counsels against pure de novo review and our own case law supports this notion.

As explained above, a state-of-mind issue such as the existence of deliberate indifference is typically left to the finder of fact. *Torraco.* And when reviewing a trial judge's determination on the adequacy of medical treatment following a bench trial, this court has applied the deferential clearly erroneous standard. *DesRosiers.* On top of this, it is well established that "elusive issues of motive and intent" (relevant here in connection with the Eighth Amendment's subjective prong) are typically fact-bound ones subject to the clearly erroneous rule. Thus the major pieces of the puzzle in an Eighth Amendment inquiry—adequacy of medical care, the existence of deliberate indifference, and the parties' motive and intent—are subject to the clearly erroneous standard, making unqualified de novo review a bad fit.

Policy concerns do not counsel otherwise, making the majority's reliance on *Ornelas,* a Fourth Amendment case, not particularly persuasive. *Ornelas,* which characterized the ultimate reasonable suspicion and probable cause determination as a mixed question of law and fact, decided that de novo review was the best fit for its resolution. The Supreme Court, as the majority points out, emphasized that "[i]ndependent review" by appellate courts can help "to maintain control of, and to clarify, the legal principles" in reasonable suspicion and probable cause cases. . . .

. . . . Cases dealing with the constitutional adequacy of medical care under the Eighth Amendment are incredibly fact-specific, resulting in distinctive issues. The trial judge must, among other things, have a handle on the prisoner's medical condition, the treatment sought, the treatment provided (if any), what treatment medical providers recommended, what the defendant knew and when, and what motivated its decisions. This court cannot hope to match the district judge's expertise in these areas, nor can I fathom why we would want to try. The "extremely fact-bound nature" of these cases means that "*de novo* review [will] have relatively little benefit," *id.* (Scalia, J., dissenting), leaving us unmoved by the uniformity-of-the-law considerations raised by the majority.

[T]he trial court heard testimony from no fewer than nineteen witnesses (*e.g.,* medical providers, medical experts, prison officials, and Kosilek) over the course of a trial that ultimately extended two years. The court scrutinized events that had transpired over a twenty-year period, including those relating to what treatment

Kosilek had requested, what treatment had been recommended, and what care was ultimately provided. The court considered evidence about the DOC's security review, how it was conducted, and the concerns it raised. It assessed the credibility of Kosilek, DOC officials, and the medical experts. The court reviewed a copious amount of exhibits, such as Kosilek's medical records, Kosilek's prison records, DOC policies, DOC contracts, DOC manuals, reports from Kosilek's medical providers, reports penned by each side's experts, DOC staff meeting notes, security reports, medical literature, correspondence, and deposition testimony. The end result was pages upon pages of factual findings made by the trial judge.

In other words, the district court "engaged in a careful and close analysis of the trial evidence," *Turner v. United States*, 699 F.3d 578 (1st Cir. 2012) to make its ultimate determination that the DOC, without any valid penological purpose, refused to provide medically necessary treatment for Kosilek's life-threatening condition. Given the clearly fact-intensive nature of the court's review, our own examination into whether the court was correct that the DOC violated the Eighth Amendment should be deferential, as opposed to the fresh look the majority proposes.[23] As ably said by the Supreme Court, "deferential review of mixed questions of law and fact is warranted when it appears that the district court is better positioned than the appellate court to decide the issue in question, or that probing appellate scrutiny will not contribute to the clarity of legal doctrine." *Salve Regina Coll. v. Russell*, 499 U.S. 225 (1991).

[In] actual application essentially no deference was paid. The only conclusion of the district court that the majority concedes warranted deference was the judge's determination that Commissioner Kathleen Dennehy's testimony was not credible. . . .

[The] district court drew inferences from the various medical providers' testimony to decide what constituted a prudent approach. It also considered what Commissioner [Clarke's] motivations were for denying sex reassignment surgery. It drew inferences from the DOC's conduct (*e.g.*, the timing of security reviews and the DOC's communications with Kosilek's medical providers) to determine that the DOC had engaged in prevarication and delay. The majority; however, does not appear to adjust its consideration of these issues to reflect any deference to the trial judge. Rather it decides anew what inferences should be drawn from the facts attested to at trial. Even under the majority's standard, this is not proper.

Without doubt, the level of scrutiny applied by a court permeates its analysis and guides the outcome. The impact here is clear. The Eighth Amendment is violated when prison officials fail to provide an inmate with adequate medical care, such

---

23. Plus, even assuming that the conclusion that the DOC's refusal to provide care constituted an Eighth Amendment violation lands closer to the law side of the mixed-question spectrum, a measure of deference is still appropriate. *See Battista* ("The legal labels applied to facts are reviewed on appeal more closely than a district court fact-finding, but often with some deference to the district judge.").

that "their 'acts or omissions [are] sufficiently harmful to evidence deliberate indifference to serious medical needs.'" *Leavitt v. Corr. Med. Servs., Inc.,* 645 F.3d 484 (1st Cir. 2011). The district court concluded that the evidence established the DOC had committed such a violation. The majority says otherwise but its analysis is plagued with flaws, starting with its determination as to the objective prong.

III. Eighth Amendment: Objective Prong

[A] prisoner with a "serious medical need," *Mahan v. Plymouth Cnty. House of Corr.,* 64 F.3d 14 (1st Cir. 1995), is entitled to adequate medical care, *i.e.,* "services at a level reasonably commensurate with modern medical science and of a quality acceptable within prudent professional standards." *United States v. DeCologero,* 821 F.2d 39 (1st Cir. 1987).

. . . . The disagreement—both between the parties and amongst this en banc court—centers around whether the district court correctly found that the DOC's proffered regimen of care was inadequate, and that sex reassignment surgery is the only appropriate treatment for Kosilek. Based on the record, and when one employs the proper standard of review, that conclusion was generously supported by the evidence.

A. Dr. Schmidt's Prudence

[The] district court's conclusion that the DOC's expert, Dr. Chester Schmidt, was not a prudent professional was not clearly erroneous. In his testimony, Dr. Schmidt expressed a good deal of disagreement with the Harry Benjamin Standards of Care, which were widely relied upon by the other medical providers who testified below and which have been generally accepted by courts. [numerous citations omitted—Eds.]

While . . . the Standards of Care have a built-in flexibility, that pliancy appears to stem from the uniqueness of patient needs and the evolution of the gender identity disorder field.[25] Dr. Schmidt's departure from the Standards appeared more fundamental. For instance, the [Standards] explained that sex reassignment surgery is not "experimental, investigational, elective, cosmetic, or optional in any meaningful sense." Dr. Schmidt disagreed. In his expert report, he wrote that sex reassignment surgery was a "voluntary, elective choice[ ] and procedure[ ]," calling the steps towards reassignment "equivalent to a variety of elective cosmetic nonsurgical procedures and elective cosmetic surgical procedures." Another example: the [Standards] provide that, for persons with severe gender identity disorder, sex reassignment surgery is effective, and when paired with hormone therapy and a real-life experience, "medically indicated and medically necessary." Dr. Schmidt again was not on board. He testified that generally he does not believe that sex reassignment surgery is medically necessary and his practice manifests this philosophy.

---

25. The Standards state: "Clinical departures from these guidelines may come about because of a patient's unique anatomic, social, or psychological situation, an experienced professional's evolving method of handling a common situation, or a research protocol."

In the approximately 300 patients he had evaluated, Dr. Schmidt never recalled seeing even one case of gender identity disorder serious enough to warrant surgery.[26]

. . . . In Dr. Schmidt's opinion, a real-life experience living as the opposite gender could not be effectively replicated in prison, and this counseled against surgery for Kosilek. The district court found that this viewpoint was not prudent. The majority claims that in doing so the court "relied on its own—non-medical—judgment about what constitutes a real-life experience." This is not accurate.

The court based its determination, back in *Kosilek I*, on the testimony of Dr. Marshall Forstein and Dr. George Brown, who "convincingly testified [that] Kosilek's 'real life' is prison." Then in *Kosilek II*, the court found the "credible evidence in the instant case confirmed the conclusion in *Kosilek I* that a person can have a 'real life experience' in prison." Evidence before the court in *Kosilek II* included an expert report from Dr. Forstein, and testimony from Dr. Randi Kaufman, both of whom indicated that Kosilek had undergone a real-life experience in prison. There was also the February 24, 2005 report from the Fenway doctors, . . . which explained that Kosilek had moved successfully through the steps outlined by the Standards of Care. Then, in their October 7, 2005 report, the Fenway doctors explained at length why Cynthia Osborne's review subtly distorted the concept of the real-life experience, and why Kosilek had completed the real-life test—a test made even more stringent by the fact that she was living as a female in an all-male prison. Dr. Brown. . . . testified that Kosilek had not only met the minimum real-life experience but had exceeded it. Dr. Brown focused on the significant amount of information that existed regarding Kosilek's time in prison, a record that his patients in the outside world would never have.[27]

The record is clear. The district court's determination that Dr. Schmidt's viewpoint about the feasibility of a real-life experience in prison was not based on the judge's own lay opinion. It was, as the district court alluded to, grounded in a significant amount of evidence offered by competent medical professionals, all of whom disagreed with Dr. Schmidt.[28]

---

26. The majority makes much of the district judge faulting Dr. Schmidt for not writing letters of recommendation for patients seeking sex reassignment surgery, suggesting that the judge did not appreciate the nuance between opening the door for surgery and advocating for it. I suspect the judge was more broadly concerned with the fact that Dr. Schmidt did not think sex reassignment was ever medically necessary, nor had he ever seen a case where it was warranted. And despite having this strident perspective, Dr. Schmidt nonetheless opened the door for patients to undergo this major medical procedure.

27. The majority mentions that none of the experts who opined that Kosilek completed a real-life experience considered that she might be housed in a female facility post-surgery. This is hardly surprising as this is a theory of my colleagues' own making. The DOC never made any argument that a potential post-surgery housing change rendered Kosilek unable to complete the real-life experience, nor did any provider opine that it was even a consideration.

28. The Seventh Version of the Standards of Care came out in 2011. Notably it contains a new section devoted to scenarios where persons with gender identity disorder are living in institutional environments such as prisons or long-term care facilities. It provides that those individuals' health

The same can be said about what course of treatment was appropriate for Kosilek. Dr. Schmidt testified that Kosilek had "made an excellent adaptation" on her current treatment regimen and that surgery would not "confer any additional functional capability." . . . . To minimize the risk of future harm to Kosilek, Dr. Schmidt thought employing psychotherapy and medication to reduce her dysphoria and, if needed, placing Kosilek in a medical facility would be effective. A majority of the testifying medical providers said otherwise though. When asked what they thought about Dr. Schmidt's suggested regimen, Drs. Kapila, Kaufman, Appelbaum, and Forstein all thought it unreasonable.[29] The common thinking was that Dr. Schmidt's approach was not likely to effectively reduce Kosilek's risk of self harm, given that the source of her dysphoria was her male genitalia.

In the Eighth Amendment context, the adequacy of medical care is "measured against 'prudent professional standards.'" *Nunes v. Mass. Dept. of Corr.*, 766 F.3d 136 (1st Cir. 2014). The district court here concluded that Dr. Schmidt was not a prudent professional. Given the above, I am not convinced that this determination was clearly erroneous. Dr. Schmidt's significant disagreement with widely accepted guidelines and the sharp contrast between his and the other well-credentialed providers' opinions, offer strong support for the court's finding.

B. Adequacy of the DOC's Treatment

[The] question remains whether the evidence supported its conclusion that the DOC's treatment was not medically adequate. . . .

The district court was of course well aware that the DOC was suggesting a more comprehensive treatment plan. . . . Nonetheless, as it repeatedly explained, it found that *all* treatment other than sex reassignment surgery was inadequate for Kosilek. [The] court did not minimize the DOC's regimen. Based on the testimony and evidence presented, it simply found the regimen did not, and would not going forward, adequately treat Kosilek's gender identity disorder. This finding was well within the court's purview to make. . . . In *De'lonta v. Johnson*, 708 F.3d 520 (4th Cir. 2013), the Fourth Circuit Court of Appeals found that an inmate, who sought sex reassignment surgery after her gender identity disorder failed to resolve despite receiving hormones, stated a plausible deliberate indifference claim. The court concluded that, though the Virginia Department of Corrections had provided the inmate with hormone therapy and psychological counseling consistent with the Standards of

---

care "should mirror that which would be available to them if they were living in a non-institutional setting" and that "[a]ll elements of assessment and treatment as described in the [Standards of Care] can be provided to people living in institutions."

29. Court-appointed expert, Dr. Stephen Levine, ultimately testified that from a purely medical perspective (absent considerations relative to the prison environment), a prudent professional would not deny Kosilek sex reassignment surgery. However, Dr. Levine initially opined that Dr. Schmidt's view was reasonable (if not popular), a discrepancy that apparently arose from Dr. Levine disregarding the district court's order to treat Kosilek as a patient in free society. Considering this incongruity, I do not list Dr. Levine as one of Dr. Schmidt's critics.

Care, "it does not follow that they have necessarily provided her with *constitutionally adequate* treatment."

The majority. . . . focus[es] heavily on the improvement Kosilek has made since being provided hormones, electrolysis, feminine garb and gear, and mental health treatment. [Despite] the short shrift the majority pays it, there was ample evidence supporting the district court's conclusion that this improvement was not sufficient to ease Kosilek's suffering to a point where she was no longer facing a life-threatening risk of harm.

. . . . The court chronicled the evidence: Kosilek's own testimony about her continued distress,[30] the Fenway Center report indicating Kosilek's ongoing angst over her male genitalia and the high likelihood of another suicide attempt, and the [similar] testimony of Kosilek's treating psychologist. . . . There was also Dr. Kaufman's testimony that, even with the treatment the DOC provided, Kosilek still suffered from clinically significant distress and severe dysphoria, a fact she found "quite notable." Dr. Brown testified similarly, explaining that Kosilek's treatment to date, including the hormones, had not obviated her need for surgery. Further, there was evidence that Kosilek's improvement was tangled up in her continuing hope that sex reassignment surgery would be provided. Dr. Brown testified: "And without that hope, the [DOC's] treatments are — I wouldn't say for naught, but they are not going to continue her level of improvement where she is now."

Thus, even with Kosilek's documented improvement, Drs. Brown, Kaufman, Forstein, Kapila, and Appelbaum all testified unequivocally that sex reassignment surgery was medically necessary and the only appropriate treatment for Kosilek. They further agreed that there was a serious risk of harm, most likely suicide, should Kosilek not receive the surgery, which was a concern the Fenway doctors voiced as early as 2005. . . .

The DOC's assertion that this future risk could be curbed with medication and psychotherapy cannot carry the day. As the district court found, treating the underlying disorder and its symptoms are two very different things, a distinction also drawn by the Seventh Circuit. *See Fields v. Smith,* 653 F.3d 550 (7th Cir. 2011). In *Fields,* the court found a Wisconsin statute that prohibited the state's correctional department from providing transgender inmates with hormones and sex reassignment surgery unconstitutional. The court, discussing how some patients require hormone therapy, found the department of corrections had not effectively rebutted the evidence that an offering of medication and psychotherapy would "do nothing to treat the underlying disorder." In the instant matter, Drs. Appelbaum and Kapila testified that the preferred approach is to treat the underlying problem — Kosilek's gender identity disorder — as opposed to the symptoms it might produce.

---

30. The court found Kosilek testified credibly that although hormone treatments had helped, she was distressed by her male genitalia and believed that she needed surgery. Antidepressants and psychotherapy, according to Kosilek, would not alter the fact that she did not want to continue living with her male genitalia.

As chronicled above, the consensus was that the only way to adequately treat that problem was with sex reassignment surgery.

. . . . The DOC is challenging the district court's grant of injunctive relief following a bench trial, meaning that due regard is paid to the judge's factual findings and credibility determinations. *See* [*Monahan v. Romney,* 625 F.3d 42, 46 (1st Cir. 2010)]. When the evidence yields competing inferences or two permissible views, we cannot second guess, "even if, had we been sitting as triers of the facts, we might have arrived at a different set of judgments." *N. Ins. Co. of N.Y. v. Point Judith Marina, LLC,* 579 F.3d 61 (1st Cir. 2009). . . . It is not for us to re-weigh the evidence and second-guess this determination, but that is exactly what the majority does.

What's more, by upholding the adequacy of the DOC's course of treatment, the majority in essence creates a de facto ban on sex reassignment surgery for inmates in this circuit. Its attempt to repudiate this notion is not compelling. [The] fact that the DOC has "disclaimed any attempt to create a blanket policy regarding SRS" is a non-starter. The issue is not whether correctional departments will voluntarily provide the surgery, it is whether the precedent set by this court today will preclude inmates from ever being able to mount a successful Eighth Amendment claim for sex reassignment surgery in the courts. Equally unconvincing is the majority's assertion that the "unique circumstances" presented by Kosilek's case will prevent any de facto ban. The first so-called anomaly cited by the majority—the divergence of opinion as to Kosilek's need for surgery—only resulted from the DOC disregarding the advice of Kosilek's treating doctors and bringing in a predictable opponent to sex reassignment surgery. It is no stretch to imagine another department of corrections stealing a page from this play book, *i.e.,* just bring in someone akin to Osborne. It is hardly a matchless scenario. The same goes for Kosilek's criminal history and post-surgical housing options, which the majority also points to. Rare will be the prisoner who does not pose some type of security concern, or harbor some potential for causing climate unrest. So the question remains, if Kosilek—who was time and again diagnosed as suffering from severe gender identity disorder, and who was uniformly thought by qualified medical professionals to require surgery—is not an appropriate candidate for surgery, what inmate is?

In sum, the majority's conclusion that the district court wrongly found that Kosilek satisfied the objective component of the Eighth Amendment inquiry is, in my opinion, flatly incorrect. I am no more convinced by the majority's examination of the subjective component.

IV. Eighth Amendment: Subjective Prong

. . . . The majority posits that the DOC, because it was faced with conflicting medical opinions about what treatment was appropriate for Kosilek, and because it proffered reasonable security concerns, was not deliberately indifferent to Kosilek's risk for serious harm. Both theories fail to convince.

A. Conflicting Medical Opinions

The idea that incompatible medical opinions serve to insulate the DOC from a deliberate indifference finding is a concept not advanced by the DOC, which rests on several faulty propositions and has very problematic implications.

The majority . . . claims [this argument] is not waived because "[t]he DOC's contention that the district court erred in deeming SRS medically necessary and in rejecting Dr. Schmidt's approach as imprudent necessarily entails the DOC's subjective belief that SRS was unnecessary."[31] This is a stretch. An argument advanced on appeal years after surgery was denied is not the equivalent of the DOC's subjective belief that sex reassignment surgery was unnecessary when it denied it. Moreover, the mere existence of contradictory medical opinions does not necessarily mean that the DOC did not deny Kosilek surgery for purely pretextual reasons. It is certainly conceivable that a correctional department could seize on an opinion from a medical provider, whether or not it found it compelling, as a means to justify denying treatment.

Another even more serious flaw in the majority's theory is that it is contradicted by the evidence. Commissioner Dennehy testified multiple times, and submitted a report to the same effect, that it was security concerns that motivated her decision to deny Kosilek surgery. During Dennehy's first round of testimony, when she was still claiming ignorance about whether UMass (the DOC's contracted health-services provider) was recommending surgery, she testified that based "strictly [on] safety and security concerns" she would still veto the surgery even if UMass told her that it was medically necessary. Then, once UMass's position that surgery was medically necessary became pellucid to Dennehy, she submitted a report to the court indicating that she was standing firm in her decision to deny surgery based on "alarming and substantial" safety and security concerns. Her final time on the stand, Dennehy testified that the only thing, in her view, preventing surgery for Kosilek was safety and security concerns; absent such concerns, Dennehy would have no reason to interfere with any medical order for treatment.

The evidence with regard to Commissioner Clarke's stance on the issue was similar. In his report to the court, Clarke disclaimed any ability to render an opinion on the validity of the medical opinions expressed at trial, and went on to explain his view that "the safety and security concerns presented by the prospect of undertaking sex reassignment surgery for Michelle Kosilek are insurmountable." Clarke then hammered home his security concerns on the stand. Therefore, even though there was contradictory opinions on whether surgery was medically necessary for

---

31. When the DOC first informed the district court that it would not be providing Kosilek with surgery (back in June 2005 under Dennehy's watch), Dr. Schmidt had not even evaluated Kosilek let alone communicated his findings. At the time, the DOC was only armed with the report of Cynthia Osborne who had not met with Kosilek but rather had simply peer reviewed the Fenway Report.

Kosilek, both Dennehy's and Clarke's decision to deny the procedure was, as they put it, based solely on security concerns.

The majority's presumption that the existence of varying medical opinions should insulate the DOC is not only an unpreserved, unsupported argument but it has very troubling implications. It gives correctional departments serious leeway with the Eighth Amendment. If they do not want to provide a prisoner with care recommended by one or more than one medical provider, they need only find a doctor with a differing mind set (typically not a difficult task). It is no stretch to think that might be what happened here. The DOC had the treatment recommendation of Drs. Kaufman and Kapila. . . . The doctors themselves were recommended by the DOC's own medical provider, UMass. Yet the DOC took the unusual step of having the Fenway doctors' recommendation peer reviewed by Cynthia Osborne, an out-of-state social worker with a known opinion about sex reassignment surgery. It seems highly unlikely that the DOC was simply looking for a more complete picture of Kosilek's treatment options, and that Osborne's predictable opposition to Kosilek being provided with surgery was a non-factor. The DOC knew that Osborne was working with the Virginia and Wisconsin departments of corrections to help defend lawsuits filed by transgender prisoners, and internal DOC meeting minutes noted that Osborne "may do more objective evaluations" and was "[m]ore sympathetic to DOC position." Predictably, Osborne was one-hundred percent sympathetic.

B. Security Concerns

There is no dispute that "security considerations . . . matter at prisons," leaving "ample room for professional judgment." *Battista*. . . . [At] some point a defendant forfeits the advantage of deference, for instance following a "pattern of delays, new objections substituted for old ones, misinformation and other negatives."[32] *Id.* The district court determined that the DOC had done just this, causing undue delay in Kosilek's treatment regimen, manufacturing security concerns, and orchestrating a half-hearted security review. . . .

Of course, it has been many years since medical providers began considering the propriety of surgery for Kosilek. . . . But right when she started as commissioner, Dennehy made a curious move. She reassessed the care being provided to all inmates suffering from gender identity disorder, despite the DOC's contract with UMass placing that medical care squarely in UMass's purview. [Once] the Fenway doctors opined in 2005 that Kosilek should be allowed to have surgery, the DOC frittered away time claiming not to understand that UMass recommended surgery for

---

32. The pattern in *Battista*—a case in which a transgender inmate sued the Massachusetts DOC for failing to provide doctor-recommended hormones—included an initial failure to take the inmate's diagnosis and hormone request seriously, the years it took for a solid security justification to be made, and the DOC's claim that withholding hormones or placing the inmate in severely constraining protective custody were the only two options. In other words, there are some marked similarities between that case and this one. That is, apart from their outcomes. In *Battista*, this court affirmed the district court's deliberate indifference determination.

Kosilek. The majority does not quibble with the court's finding that the DOC pre-varicated in this respect because it "does not undercut the consistency with which they identified safety and security concerns." This misses the point. To establish a subjective intent, "it is enough for the prisoner to show a wanton disregard sufficiently evidenced 'by denial, delay, or interference with prescribed health care.'" *Battista*; *see also Johnson v. Wright*, 412 F.3d 398 (2d Cir. 2005) (A "deliberate indifference claim can lie where prison officials deliberately ignore the medical recommendations of a prisoner's treating physicians."). That is precisely what the district court found happened here, and the evidentiary support for this determination is in the record.

The same goes for the court's conclusion that the DOC's security reviews were rushed and results-driven. Dennehy told a news outlet that the DOC would deny Kosilek's request for surgery despite only having "generalized discussions" and phone calls with the relevant players; she had not yet received written reports or convened a formal security meeting. When the DOC did meet, there was just a week left before its court-ordered security report was due—a report that was then penned predominantly by trial counsel and reviewed by Dennehy only a day or two before its filing. Once trial was underway, the hurriedness continued. A mere nine days before expert disclosures were due, Dennehy contacted the director of the Federal Bureau of Prisons looking for a security expert. And the experts the DOC ultimately did present at trial seemed ill prepared, failing to take into account important details about Kosilek's medical and disciplinary history.

For the district court, another reason not to esteem the DOC's proffered security concerns was the fact that they were "largely false" and "greatly exaggerated." This finding is not clearly erroneous. Yet the majority easily dismisses it, in part by limiting its focus to what it presumably perceives as the DOC's more valid security concerns—where to house Kosilek postoperatively and the deterrence of false suicide threats by inmates. The majority is conveniently forgetting the throw-it-up-and-see-what-sticks approach taken by the DOC below. It was this approach, in part, that led the court to question whether the DOC could be trusted to give an accurate picture of security concerns consequent to surgery.

For instance, the DOC repeatedly claimed that transporting Kosilek to surgery out of state would pose an insurmountable security risk. It is hardly surprising the district court thought this was an embellished concern. Kosilek had been transported to multiple doctor's appointments without issue, and it is illogical to think Kosilek would attempt to flee en route to the surgery she has dedicated decades of her life to obtaining. Also eminently unlikely is that during the transport home from highly invasive surgery, a sixty-five-year-old, recovering Kosilek would be able to escape the grasp of DOC personnel. Even Clarke thought it near certain that Kosilek could safely be transported to and from surgery.

[The] DOC painted Kosilek as a highly-polarizing escape risk who could not possibly safely reside in MCI-Framingham's general[, female] population. It pointed to the comparatively weaker perimeter of MCI-Framingham, alleging that

Kosilek's superior male strength and life sentence made her a flight risk. . . . Kosilek was advanced in age, physically slight, had taken female hormones for years, and had an excellent disciplinary record. And MCI-Framingham successfully housed approximately forty life offenders. The court also had reason to be skeptical of the DOC's adamant contention that Kosilek would cause inmate climate issues at MCI-Framingham due to the fact that she murdered her wife. Undoubtedly inmates find other inmates offensive for a plethora of reasons, such as, race, religion, gang affiliation, sexual orientation, or the crime committed. Prisons deal with these situations on a routine basis and the evidence established that MCI-Framingham had procedures in place to do just that.

The DOC even admitted at oral argument that had a postoperative, transgender person out in free society committed murder, the DOC would have to figure out where to house that person. The DOC, however, did not think this a particularly important point, protesting that Kosilek presents unique concerns. . . . I am unmoved. The fact that Kosilek's crime was one of violence against a woman could equally apply to another potential inmate. And the fact that Kosilek gained notoriety by litigating against the DOC all these years—in other words, successfully pursuing her constitutional right to adequate medical care—hardly seems a compelling consideration.

For the district court, also blunting the DOC's fervent cries of overwhelming security concerns were the alternatives to placing Kosilek in the general population of a Massachusetts prison. There was the option of transferring Kosilek to an out-of-state prison (though this scenario appears to have been left largely unexplored by the DOC). In fact, the evidence established that Clarke's former employer, the Washington Department of Corrections, housed a post-operative female transgender inmate, also serving a life sentence for murdering a female relative, without security or climate issues. The inmate's housing was so unremarkable that Clarke was not even aware of it during his tenure in Washington. Further, there was evidence that Kosilek's safety could be ensured by placing her in a segregated housing unit.

The DOC's past conduct was also relevant to the district court's credibility assessment. In connection with *Kosilek I*, then Commissioner Michael Maloney hammered the serious security concerns surrounding Kosilek remaining at MCI-Norfolk while receiving hormones, theorizing that an inmate living as a female (with female attributes) among sex offenders would create a risk of violence. However, once the DOC actually stopped to conduct a security review, it determined there were no current security concerns with Kosilek being provided estrogen therapy. Indeed no security issues ever arose. . . . The DOC's reversal on this issue calls into question its stance before this court about the non-feasibility of housing a post-surgical Kosilek at MCI-Norfolk.

The DOC also expressed concern that providing Kosilek with surgery would encourage inmates to utilize suicide threats to receive a desired benefit, and the majority deems this concern reasonable. I am not convinced, and neither was the district court. Not only is there absolutely no evidence that Kosilek is trying to game the system, but the DOC . . . employs mental health professionals and has policies in place to deal with suicidality. . . . That the DOC does not want to be inundated with a hypothetical influx of false suicide threats hardly seems a valid reason to deny a prisoner care deemed medically necessary.

For the district court, the public and political disapproval of Kosilek's surgical pursuit was another factor. It did not believe Dennehy's and Clarke's claims that the avoidance of controversy played no role in the DOC's decision to deny surgery. The majority concedes that it must give deference to the court's finding that Dennehy's motivations were colored by public pressure and so, instead, the majority hypes up the role of Commissioner Clarke by characterizing him as the ultimate decision maker. I see a few flaws with the majority's reasoning.

[The] majority says the district court improperly imputed Dennehy's motivations to Clarke, thus ignoring the injunctive-relief requirement that it take into account the DOC's then present-day stance.[33] *See Farmer* (The court considers deliberate indifference "'in light of the prison authorities' current attitudes and conduct,' . . . their attitudes and conduct at the time suit is brought and persisting thereafter."). The majority has it wrong. The court took testimony from Clarke, reviewed his written report, and spoke extensively in its decision about why it was not convinced that Clarke denied Kosilek surgery based on legitimate penological concerns. [Kosilek] sought to have Clarke inform the court of his position, and the DOC, which stipulated at trial that Dennehy was the operative decision maker, actually objected to Clarke even testifying as he was simply "maintain[ing] the position set forth by the DOC through former Commissioner Dennehy."

Furthermore, though the majority defers to the court's take on Dennehy, it refuses to do so for Clarke, claiming that "Clarke was never found by the court to be non-credible." This is not entirely accurate. Clearly the import of the court's conclusion that Clarke's articulated security concerns were either false or exaggerated as a pretext to deny surgery means that the court did not think Clarke a completely credible witness. *See* [*Kosilek II*] ("[T]he purported security considerations that Dennehy and Clarke claim motivated their decisions to deny Kosilek sex reassignment surgery are largely false and any possible genuine concerns have been greatly exaggerated to provide a pretext for denying the prescribed treatment.") In fact, the court specifically found certain claims made by Clarke not to be credible. *See id.* (finding that "neither Dennehy nor Clarke has provided a credible explanation

---

33. While a defendant's attitudes and conduct at the time a decision is rendered are relevant, what motivates the DOC today is not. This fact may be less than clear given the majority's reference to the DOC's present stance ("proof that the DOC remains motivated by pretextual or improper concerns") and the fact that Dennehy is now seven years removed from the decision-making process. To be clear, we are reviewing the district court's decision that the DOC, through Dennehy and Clarke, denied Kosilek surgery based on pretextual reasons. Indeed it would be an amazing feat of prescience for the district court to anticipate what the DOC's viewpoint would be two years after penning its decision.

for their purported belief that if Kosilek's genitalia are altered the risk to him and others at MCI Norfolk will be materially magnified" and "[t]he claims of Dennehy and Clarke that they have denied sex reassignment surgery for Kosilek in part because MCI Framingham is not sufficiently secure to prevent an escape by Kosilek, who has never attempted to flee, are not credible.") Therefore, as it did with Dennehy, the majority should be giving due regard to the court's conclusion that Clarke was not believable.

The majority also misses the mark with its contention that the "only evidence" tending to show Clarke may have considered public and political criticism were the two letters from the unhappy Massachusetts legislators. This is not the whole picture. In addition to the letters, what convinced the court that Clarke was improperly motivated was his advancing inflated security concerns following a hasty review, suggesting that he did not operate with an open mind. Having already detailed the evidence supporting the court's distrust of the DOC's proffered security concerns, I will not rehash.

As for the thoroughness of Clarke's review, the court criticized Clarke for not consulting with Luis Spencer, who was Superintendent of MCI-Norfolk at the time, and for not reviewing the DOC's security-expert trial testimony, prior to deciding whether to deny surgery. The DOC counters that Clarke, pursuant to the court's order, was not required to do either of those things. It is both conceivable that Clarke's review was too cursory, or that he felt constrained by the court's order, though the fact that Clarke did not know significant details such as Kosilek's age and excellent disciplinary record favors the former possibility. Either way, both views are permissible, which means that the district court's choice of one of them cannot be clearly erroneous. *See Monahan*. Nor is it appropriate for us to second-guess the court's tenable perception of Clarke's motivations, as deference extends to "inferences drawn from the underlying facts, and if the trial court's reading of the record [with respect to an actor's motivation] is plausible, appellate review is at an end." *Janeiro*. . . .

V. Conclusion

I am confident that I would not need to pen this dissent, over twenty years after Kosilek's quest for constitutionally adequate medical care began, were she not seeking a treatment that many see as strange or immoral. Prejudice and fear of the unfamiliar have undoubtedly played a role in this matter's protraction. Whether today's decision brings this case to a close, I cannot say. But I am confident that this decision will not stand the test of time, ultimately being shelved with the likes of *Plessy v. Ferguson*, 163 U.S. 537 (1896), deeming constitutional state laws requiring racial segregation, and *Korematsu v. United States*, 323 U.S. 214 (1944), finding constitutional the internment of Japanese-Americans in camps during World War II. I only hope that day is not far in the future, for the precedent the majority creates is damaging. It paves the way for unprincipled grants of en banc relief, decimates the deference paid to a trial judge following a bench trial, aggrieves an already marginalized community, and enables correctional systems to further postpone their adjustment to the crumbling gender binary.

I respectfully dissent.

KAYATTA, Circuit Judge, dissenting.

[There] is not a comma, much less a word, of the applicable law that the district court did not expressly and correctly explain and apply. . . .

Our decision in this case therefore necessarily turns on the facts themselves. And we begin our review knowing that Kosilek does indeed have a serious medical need, and the prison's own doctors, as well as the specialists retained by those doctors, informed DOC that treatment of Kosilek's medical condition in accordance with prudent professional standards requires sex reassignment surgery (SRS). That leaves only two factual questions: (1) Are the DOC's doctors correct that SRS is the only treatment for Kosilek's condition that is commensurate with modern medical science as practiced by prudent professionals;[35] and, if so, (2) Did prison officials nevertheless deny that treatment not because they disbelieved their own doctors, and not because of prison security considerations, but rather simply because they feared public ridicule. If the answer to each of these two questions is "yes," Kosilek should win. Otherwise, she loses.

. . . . Dr. Levine, who participated in drafting the Standards of Care, provided carefully nuanced and persuasive testimony that medical science has not reached a wide, scientifically driven consensus mandating SRS as the only acceptable treatment for an incarcerated individual with gender dysphoria. But I am not the trial judge in this case. Nor are my colleagues. And that is the rub.

The experienced jurist who was the trial judge in this case, and who actually sat and listened to the live testimony, found as a matter of fact that:

(1) Commensurate with modern medical science, no prudent professional would recommend any treatment for Kosilek other than SRS; and

(2) Prison officials nevertheless denied the treatment not because they rejected the accuracy of the medical advice tendered by their own doctors, and not because of security issues, but rather because they feared public ridicule. Their reasons for denying the necessary treatment were thus in bad faith.

The majority never explains why these two findings are not pure findings of fact, and are not therefore subject solely to review for clear error. . . .

. . . . Of course, deferring to the trial judge's fact-finding happens to produce a result in this case that some of us find surprising, and much of the public likely finds shocking. . . . The notion that hard-wired aspects of gender may not unerringly and inexorably correspond to physical anatomy is especially unnerving for many.

The solution, I think, is to trust our trial judges to resolve these factual issues when the evidence supports a finding either way. Some will get it wrong; most will

---

35. In the majority's words, "whether SRS is a medically necessary component of Kosilek's care, such that any course of treatment not including surgery is constitutionally inadequate."

get it right. The arc of decision-making, over time, will bend towards the latter. For each instance of error in fact-finding, such as possibly this case itself, $25,000 or so may be lost. But doctors and lawyers will refine their presentations and other trial judges will make their own findings, not bound in any way by the fact-finding in this case.

Instead, by deciding the facts in this case as an appellate court essentially finding law, the majority ends any search for the truth through continued examination of the medical evidence by the trial courts. It locks in an answer that binds all trial courts in the circuit: no prison may be required to provide SRS to a prisoner who suffers from gender dysphoria as long as a prison official calls up Ms. Osborne or Dr. Schmidt.[36] . . . I . . . decline the invitation to join the majority in embracing the authority to decide the facts. I suspect that our court will devote some effort in the coming years to distinguishing this case, and eventually reducing it to a one-off reserved only for transgender prisoners.

———————

Discussion

1. The majority holds that the plaintiff did not show that the defendant was failing to provide (objectively) adequate care for a serious medical need occasioned by her gender identity disorder. That alone would suffice to defeat the plaintiff's Eighth Amendment challenge to the defendant's denial of her surgery. Why then might the court have additionally held that the plaintiff did not show that the defendant was (subjectively) deliberately indifferent to any serious medical need, instead of exercising judicial restraint by not addressing issues not necessary to its judgment reversing the district court?

2. Why does the majority think that housing a transgender woman, who had murdered a female partner, in a women's prison would pose security concerns? Would not a cisgender woman who murdered a female partner also—and without question—be housed in a women's prison?

Note on Trump Administration BOP Regulations Regarding Medical Care for Trans Inmates

When the Trump administration Bureau of Prisons ("BOP") revised the Transgender Offender Manual ("TOM"), *see supra* at p. 703, it made some changes to the section concerning treatment of trans inmates. Whether these changes are consequential remains to be seen. In essence, they limit references to the care provided to medically "necessary" care. Section 10 of the Manual was renamed from "Hormone and Medical Treatment" to "Hormone and Necessary Medical Treatment." Its first sentence was changed to read "Hormone or other *necessary* medical treatment may be provided after an individualized assessment of the requested

———————

36. No prisoner is likely to have a more favorable record than Kosilek.

inmate by institution medical staff" (emphasis added). And it now provides that "Medical staff should request consultation from Psychology Services regarding the mental health benefits of hormone or other *necessary* medical treatment" (emphasis added). There is no indication that BOP previously provided any medical treatment that was *un*necessary or "elective," so these changes seem unlikely in and of themselves to effect any substantive policy change. They could, however, signify a newly skeptical approach to the provision of care to transgender inmates. It seems likely to be difficult to determine empirically whether that proves to have consequences for the actual care provided to federal inmates who are transgender.

Reading Guide for Keohane v. Jones

1. Based on the subset of the court's arguments in the edited opinion below, why does the court conclude that Reiyn Keohane's Eighth Amendment claim seeking access to hormones was not mooted when the defendant changed its policy regarding treatment for gender dysphoria?

2. Based on the edited reasoning, why does the court hold the denial of hormones to have violated the Eighth Amendment?

3. Why does the court order the defendants to allow Ms. Keohane to transition socially?

Reiyn Keohane v. Julie Jones, in her Official Capacity as Secretary of the Florida Department of Corrections

328 F. Supp. 3d 1288 (N.D. Fla. 2018)

Order on the Merits

Mark E. Walker, Chief United States District Judge.

"The basic concept underlying the Eighth Amendment is nothing less than the dignity of man." *Trop v. Dulles*, 356 U.S. 86 (1958).

This case involves an individual immersed in the process of transitioning gender roles when she[1] found herself in jail after a violent argument with her roommate. Reiyn Keohane was born anatomically male, but she began identifying as female around age eight. She says she's always had an "internal sense" of being female.[2] Since age fourteen, Ms. Keohane has worn women's clothing, makeup, and hair styles, adopted a feminine name, and used female pronouns at school and with family and friends. In short, she's lived as a woman in all aspects of her life since her early teens.

Ms. Keohane was formally diagnosed with gender dysphoria at age sixteen, and as soon as she was permitted—and it was safe to do so—she began a hormone

---

1. Out of respect for Ms. Keohane, this Court uses female pronouns when referring to her—a courtesy not all of Defendant's agents have extended, though Defendant is endeavoring to remedy this slight (among others).

2. "I know who I am, and have always felt this is who I am. I am a girl, female."

therapy regimen to ease her dysphoria and feminize her body. But shortly thereafter, she was arrested and cut off from the treatment she needed, including hormone therapy and the ability to dress and groom as a woman.

Ms. Keohane continuously grieved her denial of care during the first two years in Defendant's custody, but she faced roadblocks every step of the way.[3] At times, her untreated dysphoria caused such extreme anxiety that she says she's attempted to kill herself and to castrate herself to rid her body of its testosterone source.

Ms. Keohane's testimony at trial demonstrates the lengths to which she'll go to feel better in her own skin. On one occasion, she said she tied a rubber band around her scrotum to reduce circulation and cut down the center line in a place she estimated would lessen the chance of excessive blood loss. After breaking the skin, she said she tried to squeeze one of her testicles out of her body in what she perceived to be an attempt at self-castration, but her hands were shaking so badly from the pain that she couldn't finish the job.[4]

It wasn't until Ms. Keohane found a lawyer willing to take her case that things changed for the better. Defendant was staring down the barrel of a federal lawsuit when it suddenly changed course by securing hormone therapy and amending its policy formerly prohibiting new treatment for inmates with gender dysphoria—all within a matter of months after Ms. Keohane filed her complaint.

[The] essential issues before this Court can be distilled down to these; namely, was Defendant deliberately indifferent to Ms. Keohane's gender dysphoria—which both sides agree is a serious medical need—when it denied her hormone therapy for two years? Should this Court enter an injunction ordering Defendant to provide the requested treatment? Part and parcel to this second inquiry is whether Defendant's provision of hormone therapy and amendment to its policies has sufficiently remedied Ms. Keohane's injuries. And lastly, is the parallel treatment for gender dysphoria—namely, social transitioning through access to Defendant's female clothing and grooming standards—necessary to treat Ms. Keohane's gender dysphoria such that Defendant's refusal to provide treatment amounts to deliberate indifference?

When it comes to medical care in prison, reasonable minds may differ. One can be negligent, even grossly negligent, when treating an inmate without offending the United States Constitution. *Farrow v. West*, 320 F.3d 1235 (11th Cir. 2003). But while

---

3. The Defendant in this case is Julie Jones, sued in her official capacity as Secretary of the Florida Department of Corrections. "Since official-capacity suits generally represent another way of pleading an action against an entity of which an officer is an agent," this Court refers to Secretary Jones and the Florida Department of Corrections interchangeably as "Defendant" throughout this order.

4. Defendant disputes whether Ms. Keohane actually intended to remove her testicles. Instead, Defendant contends she made only a superficial cut to gain attention. But even so, this doesn't change the fact that Ms. Keohane took a razor to her scrotum because she was denied treatment for her gender dysphoria—some of which even Defendant now concedes is medically necessary.

the standard for establishing deliberate indifference is high, it is not impossible to meet. And if Ms. Keohane's treatment in Defendant's custody isn't deliberate indifference, then surely there is no such beast. Ultimately, this case is about whether the law, and this Court by extension, recognizes Ms. Keohane's humanity as a transgender woman. The answer is simple. It does, and I do.

I

Ms. Keohane is a transgender woman. Her assigned sex at birth was male—she was born with and still has male genitalia—but she identifies as a woman. When she was fourteen years old, Ms. Keohane told her parents about her gender identity. Thereafter until her incarceration at age nineteen, Ms. Keohane wore girls' or women's clothing and makeup, and grew her hair to a longer, traditionally feminine length. She adopted a feminine name—Jamie—and preferred using female pronouns. Later, Ms. Keohane legally changed her first name to Reiyn "to bring [it] into conformity with [her] gender identity." And at age sixteen, Ms. Keohane was formally diagnosed with gender identity disorder—now known as gender dysphoria.

A

Gender dysphoria generally "refers to discomfort or distress that is caused by a discrepancy between a person's gender identity and that person's sex assigned at birth." It is a psychiatric diagnosis in the *Diagnostic and Statistical Manual for Mental Disorders* published by the American Psychiatric Association, and manifests as "a set of symptoms that include anxiety, irritability, depression, and this sense of incongruence or mismatch between one's sex of assignment at birth and internally felt[] gender identity."

Ms. Keohane's expert at trial, Dr. George R. Brown, identified three criteria for a gender dysphoria diagnosis. First, a patient must have "experienced a significant incongruity between their sex of assignment at birth, their anatomy, and their internal sense of their gender for a minimum of six months." Second, a patient must meet a combination of several specific criteria such as "having a strong disgust or repulsion of one's own genitals, a desire to be rid of those genitals, [or] a desire to have treatment to approximate the other gender." The third requirement considers whether the first two criteria are "distressing enough or . . . cause enough dysfunction in your life and important areas of your functioning that they are clinically relevant." . . . .

In short, transgender people may feel some dysphoria, or anxiety, about their bodies and their gender identity. But not all transgender people are formally diagnosed with gender dysphoria—indeed, this Court recognizes that many transgender people may be perfectly at ease and even rejoice in their own skin. A formal diagnosis of gender dysphoria results only if a person's symptoms of dysphoria are severe enough and persist for so long that they become "clinically relevant." Pursuant to their pretrial stipulation, the parties agree and this Court finds that Ms. Keohane has been diagnosed, and is currently diagnosed, with gender dysphoria—a serious medical need.

B

. . . .

Dr. Brown explained at trial that several treatment options can alleviate a person's gender dysphoria. They primarily include psychotherapy, "hormonal management," and "surgical interventions . . . like genital confirmation surgery or sex reassignment surgery." And aside from these "three main domains," social transitioning is another option for treating gender dysphoria.

Social transitioning can include "changing identity documents, changing one's name, [and] changing one's gender role presentation."[5] For purposes of this order, "social transitioning" refers only to Ms. Keohane's request for access to Defendant's clothing and grooming standards for female inmates. . . . This includes the ability to possess and wear the same bras, panties, hairstyles, and makeup items permitted in Defendant's female facilities. All inmates, male and female, are severely limited when it comes to self-expression. For Ms. Keohane, aside from using the appropriate pronouns, the *only* way she can express her gender identity in prison is by wearing women's undergarments and grooming like a woman.

Hormone therapy involves taking prescribed male or female hormones consistent with one's gender identity. In male-to-female patients like Ms. Keohane, hormone therapy can cause physiological changes including the redistribution of body fat to create a more feminine physique, erectile dysfunction, and the development of breasts. In addition, hormone therapy may have beneficial psychological effects including a perceived reduction in the patient's anxiety or depression.

Treatment for gender dysphoria is multimodal. That is, the WPATH Standards recognize "[s]ome patients may need hormones, a possible change in gender role, but not surgery; others may need a change in gender role along with surgery but not hormones." But while some patients benefit from fewer than all primary treatment options, Dr. Brown opined that providing hormone therapy while denying the ability to socially transition is not only "medically and logically inconsistent," but also "potentially harmful." . . . .

C

Around September 22, 2013, Ms. Keohane was charged with attempted second-degree murder and was taken into custody at the Lee County Jail. Only about six weeks earlier, she had started hormone therapy under the care of her pediatric endocrinologist to treat her gender dysphoria. But when she was taken into custody in September, the jail refused her request to continue treatment. . . .

. . . .

---

5. The WPATH Standards also include "[c]hanges in gender expression and role (which may involve living part time or full time in another gender role, consistent with one's gender identity)," as an option for treating gender dysphoria.

This denial of care—premised on the notion that Ms. Keohane would not receive hormone therapy because she wasn't *already* receiving hormone therapy when she arrived in Defendant's custody—flows from the legally untenable "freeze-frame policy" in place at the time. The policy provided in part that "[i]nmates who have undergone treatment for [gender dysphoria] will be maintained only at the level of change that existed at the time they were received by the Department." Ultimately, Defendant did not permit Ms. Keohane to resume hormone therapy until September 2016, more than *two years* after she was committed to Defendant's custody and, notably, shortly after she filed her complaint and preliminary-injunction motion in this case.

D

For purposes of this litigation, Defendant's medical vendor, Wexford, arranged for an evaluation of Ms. Keohane's need for access to female clothing and grooming standards after she filed her complaint. Wexford's regional psychiatrist, Dr. Jose Santeiro, evaluated Ms. Keohane on September 27, 2016, specifically to determine whether she had a medical need to socially transition in prison. He concluded that Ms. Keohane had no medical need for access to female clothing and grooming standards. But this Court finds Dr. Santeiro's conclusions suspect for several reasons, including his admitted lack of experience treating gender dysphoria in prison, his lack of knowledge about the standards of care, and the limited information upon which he based his conclusion.

. . . . Moreover, like all of Defendant's witnesses, Dr. Santeiro's testimony focuses on the infeasibility of transitioning in prison based on security concerns instead of articulating any medical opinion as to whether social transitioning should be part of Ms. Keohane's treatment plan in addition to hormone therapy and counseling.

As far as this Court can discern from the record before it, nobody on Ms. Keohane's treatment team (composed of medical personnel employed through Wexford) has made a final treatment decision regarding access to female clothing and grooming standards. The primary rationale for not recommending such treatment or seeking an exception to Defendant's security policies is that those same policies—namely, Defendant's clothing and grooming standards—preclude social transitioning in prison. But Defendant's own expert witness, Dr. [Stephen] Levine, testified that *it is* appropriate or "psychologically helpful" to allow a transgender woman who is taking hormones—like Ms. Keohane—to outwardly express herself as a woman. . . .

. . . .

On several occasions, Defendant forcibly shaved Ms. Keohane's head after she protested Defendant's hair-length policy. And Defendant has confiscated Ms. Keohane's self-made bras and panties, labeling those items as contraband. These disciplinary actions have almost always contributed to the feelings of anxiety, disgust, and hopelessness accompanying Ms. Keohane's gender dysphoria, leading her to consider or attempt to harm herself.[6]

II

. . . Defendant asserts now that Ms. Keohane is receiving hormone therapy and Defendant has amended its policies to drop the "freeze-frame" language for the treatment of inmates with gender dysphoria, Ms. Keohane's claims for injunctive relief are moot to the extent they address both the old policy and the denial of hormone therapy. But in so doing, Defendant "bears the formidable burden of showing that it is absolutely clear the allegedly wrongful behavior could not reasonably be expected to recur." *Doe v. Wooten*, 747 F.3d 1317 (11th Cir. 2014). . . .

"Because of the unique characteristics of public defendants," courts "often give[] governmental actors 'more leeway than private parties in the presumption that they are unlikely to resume illegal activities.'" *Wooten*. The Eleventh Circuit has labeled "this leeway that we extend to government actors a 'rebuttable presumption,' or a 'lesser burden.'" *Id.* . . .

. . . . Defendant asserts Ms. Keohane must "overcome the rebuttable presumption necessary to establish the voluntary cessation doctrine." Not quite. Though courts have described Defendant's burden as a "rebuttable presumption," it's still Defendant's burden to show it's "absolutely clear the allegedly wrongful behavior could not reasonably be expected to recur." *Wooten*. Moreover, . . . Defendant, as a government actor, is only entitled to a "lesser burden" or "rebuttable presumption" once it's established an "unambiguous termination" of the challenged activity. This Defendant has not done.

In evaluating whether an unambiguous termination has occurred, this Court may consider several non-exhaustive factors, including "whether . . . the change in government policy or conduct appears to be the result of substantial deliberation, or is simply an attempt to manipulate jurisdiction," and "whether the government has 'consistently applied' a new policy or adhered to a new course of conduct." *Wooten*. In addition, "[t]he timing and content of the cessation decision are relevant in evaluating whether the defendant's stopping of the challenged conduct is sufficiently unambiguous." *Id.* This Court may be "'more likely to find a reasonable expectation of recurrence when the challenged behavior constituted a continuing practice or was otherwise deliberate.'" *Id.* . . .

The challenged practice in this case is Defendant's refusal to provide hormone therapy based on a "freeze-frame" policy stating that inmates who've been treated for gender dysphoria "will be maintained only at the level of change that existed at the time they were received by [Defendant]." When Ms. Keohane originally entered

---

6. For example, Ms. Keohane's self-described castration attempt promptly followed the confiscation of her female undergarments and a suicide attempt. ECF No. 145 . . . at 51 (describing feelings after forced haircuts as "[t]errible. Extremely depressed. Suicidal. Extremely . . . angry, upset that this could happen. I felt . . . disgusted with myself every time I would look at myself.").

Defendant's custody, Defendant denied her request for hormone therapy because she had "not received hormone treatment since 2013." Within a month of filing suit, Defendant finally arranged for Ms. Keohane to see an outside endocrinologist and began providing the long-sought-after hormone treatment. And within about two months, Defendant formally amended its policies to remove the "freeze-frame" provision.

. . . .

Defendant . . . fails to provide *any* explanation for the swift course correction regarding Ms. Keohane's visit to an outside endocrinologist and subsequent provision of hormone therapy soon after she filed her complaint. Though some witness testimony indicates a referral to an endocrinologist was in the works as early as February 2016, Defendant has not explained why it took more than *eighteen months* to reach this point. Nor does Defendant provide an explanation as to why it took Defendant at least *another five months* to show some urgency in finalizing the referral for Ms. Keohane to be evaluated for hormone therapy. . . .

. . . .

Given that Defendant's "freeze-frame" policy and denial of Ms. Keohane's hormone therapy constituted a deliberate practice during her first two years in Defendant's custody, the late-in-the-game timing and content of Defendant's decision to amend its policy and provide for hormone treatment, the lack of any evidence of "substantial deliberation" giving rise to the policy amendment, and at least one instance of inconsistent application of the new policy, this Court finds Defendant has failed to establish an "unambiguous termination" of the challenged "freeze-frame" policy and the denial of hormone treatment. As such, Defendant is *not* entitled to the rebuttable presumption that it's unlikely to resume its challenged conduct. And based on these same circumstances, it's plain to this Court that Defendant has failed to meet its "formidable burden" to show it's "absolutely clear the allegedly wrongful behavior could not reasonably be expected to recur." Accordingly, Ms. Keohane's claims for injunctive relief based on the denial of hormone therapy and Defendant's "freeze-frame" policy aren't mooted by Defendant's voluntary cessation of the challenged conduct.

. . . .

IV

. . . .

Despite Defendant's knowledge of Ms. Keohane's gender-dysphoria diagnosis, her continued requests for treatment, her self-harm, and her suicide attempts, Defendant initially denied, then delayed, treatment for two years—treatment which it now agrees is medically necessary. This Court finds this prolonged denial of hormone treatment under Defendant's "freeze-frame" policy constitutes deliberate indifference to Ms. Keohane's gender dysphoria. Defendant's decision to deny hormone therapy was based on an unconstitutional rule with no foundation in medical judgment. Moreover, the minimization of Ms. Keohane's condition and the slow-walking of her treatment by those in charge of her care only goes to show how inexperience and ignorance can needlessly prolong an inmate's suffering. Accordingly, so long as Ms. Keohane's hormone therapy is not medically contraindicated, Defendant is enjoined to continue providing her with hormone therapy as prescribed by her treating endocrinologist.

V

. . . .

This Court recognizes that no inmate is automatically entitled to the most state-of-the-art medical treatment while in the state's custody. But that's not what Ms. Keohane is seeking. Though she truly sees herself as a warrior queen[21] in this fight, Ms. Keohane is not demanding that Defendant bow down with offerings of frilly dresses, fancy shoes, or other frivolous badges of stereotypical femininity. Given the severe constraints placed on self-expression for male *and* female inmates, the *only* way it's even feasible for Ms. Keohane to express her gender identity is through pronouns, undergarments, and grooming. She's simply asking Defendant to see her and treat her as she is; namely, a woman stuck in a male body that's stuck in a cage for the foreseeable future. . . .

Now that Defendant is permitting hormone therapy, Ms. Keohane's body is changing, feminizing, and becoming more in tune with her internal sense of self. But still, Defendant is forcing Ms. Keohane to live outwardly as a man in ways that, though seemingly banal to some, strike at the heart of what it means to be perceived as a man or woman.[22] Ultimately, Defendant has chosen an easier course of treatment to maximize "uniformity," and ease "security concerns," by ignoring the substantial risk of harm to Ms. Keohane's mental health that results from denying such "minor accommodations" as panties and access to Defendant's female grooming standards. This ends now.

---

21. At trial, Ms. Keohane aptly compared herself to Daenerys Targeryen [*sic*] — "a queen and a warrior who has been through hardship and has learned how to survive it, who not only stands up for herself, but for other people and who values . . . human dignity and believes that all people should be able to have it." [The trial court's opinion was written many months before *Game of Thrones* Season 8, Episode 5 "The Bells" aired on May 12, 2019. — Eds.]

22. For example, former Maricopa County Sheriff Joe Arpaio didn't overlook the power of gendered undergarments when he forced male inmates housed in his jail to wear pink underwear. *See Arizona pink underwear inmate case to be settled: lawyer*, Reuters (Sept. 8, 2014, 7:47 PM), https://www.reuters.com/article/us-usa-arizona-underwear/arizona-pink-underwear-inmate -case-to-be-settled-lawyer-idUSKBN0H32GO20140908. "In 2012, the federal 9th U.S. Circuit Court of Appeals ruled that Arpaio's policy may be unconstitutional when applied to prisoners who had not been convicted of a crime." *Id.*; *see also* [Gabriel] Arkles, *Correcting Race and Gender: Prison Regulation of Social Hierarchy Through Dress*, 87 N.Y.U. L. Rev. 859, 904-05 (2012) (describing use of "non-dominant gendering" of prison clothing "as a form of punishment, humiliation, and control").

Defendant has stipulated "that if having longer hair or female undergarments or makeup were deemed to be medically necessary for an inmate with gender dysphoria, then the accommodation would be provided, with additional security measures taken if necessary." This Court finds such treatment is medically necessary to alleviate Ms. Keohane's gender dysphoria, and Defendant's denial of such treatment constitutes deliberate indifference. Defendant's deliberate denial of care—that is, the denial of access to female clothing and grooming standards despite its knowledge of her diagnosis and her history and risk of self-harm—has caused Ms. Keohane to continue to suffer unnecessarily and poses a substantial risk of harm to her health. Accordingly, Defendant is enjoined to permit Ms. Keohane access to the same undergarments, hair-length policy, and makeup items available for inmates housed in Defendant's female facilities so that she can socially transition to treat her gender dysphoria.

. . . .

VII

[The] fact remains that both Defendant's "freeze-frame" policy and its security policies governing clothing and grooming trumped the exercise of medical judgment when it came to treating Ms. Keohane's gender dysphoria.

While now recognizing Ms. Keohane's mental-health need for hormone therapy, Defendant persists in suggesting she is to blame for any victimization coming her way based on her gender role presentation. But after denying treatment based on its security policies—and offering expert witnesses to testify to myriad security concerns—Defendant abandoned this red herring on the eve of trial with its stipulation that if the requested treatments are medically necessary, they'll be provided with added security measures. Having so stipulated, Defendant is now put to that task. Ms. Keohane is not an animal. She is a transgender woman. Forthwith, Defendant shall treat her with the dignity the Eighth Amendment commands.

Discussion

1. Since the plaintiff was receiving hormone therapy prior to her arrest and was not taking hormones at the time she entered into DOC care only because of the Lee County Jail's denial policy, would the defendant have fared better had its policy looked to whether an inmate had a prior prescription by a doctor?

2. If the court's questioning of the defendant's doctor's expertise regarding gender dysphoria undermines the doctor's conclusions, what should correctional facilities do when prison doctors without experience in such issues are faced with decisions about transgender incarcerees?

3. If doctors should not use security concerns as criteria for their recommendations for care of inmates, are prisons handicapped in addressing legitimate security concerns?

4. On appeal, the defendants prevailed, procedurally or substantively, on each aspect of the district court's ruling. *See Keohane v. Florida Department of Corrections Secretary*, 952 F.3d 1257 (11th Cir. 2020), discussed in the next Note.

Note on Keohane v. Florida Department of Corrections Secretary *(appellate decision)*

Reiyn Keohane was a transgender woman incarcerated in a men's facility by the Florida Department of Corrections ("FDC"). She was denied hormone therapy pursuant to FDC's "freeze-frame" policy, which limited transgender inmates to the medical care for their gender dysphoria that they were receiving prior to being incarcerated, and denied access to female undergarments and cosmetics ("canteen items") necessary for social transition and subjected to forced haircuts pursuant to FDC's policy limiting attire and grooming of inmates in FDC's male facilities. She sued in federal district court, arguing that these denials of care amounted to deliberate indifference to a serious medical need in violation of the Eighth Amendment's ban on cruel and unusual punishment. She secured an injunction requiring FDC not to enforce its freeze-frame policy, to provide her hormone therapy, and to allow her to transition socially (to present as female). *Reiyn Keohane v. Julie Jones, in Her Official Capacity as Secretary of the Florida Department of Corrections*, 328 F. Supp. 3d 1288 (N.D. Fla. 2018), *supra*. On the FDC's appeal from that order, Ms. Keohane was represented by the ACLU of Florida, the ACLU, the Southern Poverty Law Center, and private counsel. She was supported by ten amici civil rights/LGBT advocacy and legal services organizations including Lambda Legal and the Center for Constitutional Rights, as well as by nine medical, mental health, and other health care associations including the World Professional Association for Transgender Health. The Court of Appeals vacated and reversed in part the district court's order, eliminating Keohane's legal victories. *Keohane v. Florida Department of Corrections Secretary*, 952 F.3d 1257 (11th Cir. 2020).

Writing for himself and U.S. District Judge for the Northern District of Alabama L. Scott Coogler, who was sitting by designation, Circuit Judge Kevin Newsom ruled in the majority opinion that Keohane's challenge to the freeze-frame policy was moot because FDC repealed it approximately two months after Keohane filed her lawsuit against the Department. Suggesting that the freeze-frame policy likely had been unconstitutional, the majority nonetheless judged this formal repeal and replacement with a new policy that required individualized consideration of an inmate's medical needs not to fall within the "voluntary cessation" exception to mootness doctrine. That exception allows courts to adjudicate otherwise moot cases if it is not unmistakably clear that the defendant will *not* resume the challenged conduct. Applying several factors relevant under circuit precedent, the majority emphasized both the "formal repeal of the freeze-frame policy" and the FDC's counsel's assurances to the court that it would not reinstate the policy. The majority also claimed that even the district court treated one post-repeal application of the freeze-frame policy to another transgender inmate as not "probative."

The majority similarly held that "Keohane's hormone-therapy-related challenge is moot" because the FDC started providing her hormones shortly after she filed suit and the majority saw no "reasonable basis" to conclude that the FDC would likely resume denying them so long as they were medically necessary for Keohane. Again, the FDC's practice combined with counsel's assurances to the court were weighty considerations for the majority.

Circuit Judge Charles R. Wilson dissented. He emphasized that while the district court's legal mootness/voluntary cessation analysis was reviewed de novo, the Court of Appeals was under circuit precedent to review the district court's factual findings relevant to its ruling on mootness under a deferential standard and reverse such findings only if they were "clearly erroneous." The dissent noted that the district judge had in fact treated the post-"repeal" application of the policy to another inmate as *relevant* to the mootness analysis, making the case that the majority selectively (mis)quoted the lower court opinion. At one point, Judge Wilson's dissent summarized its lengthy mootness reasoning, noting that the district court based its holding that Ms. Keohane's claims were not moot

> on a host of findings: that the timing of the FDC's concessions was suspect; that the FDC had no explanation for its delay; that the FDC's positions throughout the litigation were inconsistent; that the FDC's decision-making was a black box; that the FDC's prior practices were not accidental, but deliberate and historical; that the FDC refused to promise that it would not re-enact the freeze-frame policy; that the FDC still was adamant that its practices were valid, even after it claimed to change its ways; that the FDC delayed in providing Keohane's hormone therapy, even after it agreed that she needs it; and that, on at least one occasion, the FDC applied the repealed freeze-frame policy to bar hormone therapy for a patient with gender dysphoria.

> As the majority does not hold that any of these findings are clearly erroneous, they bind us. And these findings show that the FDC has not apologetically turned over a new leaf, but has acted to manipulate jurisdiction. . . .

For those reasons, the dissent would have affirmed "the district court's holding that these claims are not moot."

Because the FDC was still refusing to let Ms. Keohane socially transition ("[w]ith the lone exception of a sports bra to help with her hormone-related breast enlargement," the majority noted), the Court of Appeals agreed that that aspect of her suit was not moot. The majority, however, held that she failed to establish that the FDC was deliberately indifferent to a serious medical need of hers; rather it was at most negligent in denying her permission to engage in social transition measures, which is insufficient to violate the Eighth Amendment.

The majority said that it was using deferential clear error review for "subsidiary issues of fact" with de novo review for the district court's "ultimate determination 'that there was an Eighth Amendment violation warranting equitable relief.'" The majority and the dissent devoted pages to contesting the proper level of review and what review the majority was in practice applying. In many respects this discussion plays out the similar disputes between the en banc majority and the dissents in *Kosilek v. Spencer*, 774 F.3d 63, 84 (1st Cir. 2014) (en banc), *supra*. Ultimately, the majority added a defensive claim in a footnote—unpersuasive to the dissent—that it would reverse the district court's finding of an Eighth Amendment violation in the defendants' refusal to let Ms. Keohane transition socially even were the majority to apply deferential clear-error review.

The majority's primary reason for concluding that Ms. Keohane failed to show more than negligent disregard of a serious medical need of hers was that

> the testifying medical professionals were—and remain—divided over whether social transitioning is medically necessary to Keohane's gender-dysphoria treatment. Keohane's retained expert testified that it is. By contrast, the members of Keohane's medical-treatment team, Wexford's staff psychiatrist, the FDC's chief clinical officer, and the FDC's retained expert all testified that it isn't.

Such a "simple disagreement" about an inmate's proper medical treatment cannot violate the Eighth Amendment, the majority concluded. In addition, it reasoned, following *Kosilek*, that "the FDC denied Keohane's social-transitioning-related requests, at least in part, on the ground that they presented serious security concerns—including, most obviously, that an inmate dressed and groomed as a female would inevitably become a target for abuse in an all-male prison." The majority minimized the FDC's concession that were social transitioning judged (by *its* agents) medically necessary for Keohane, it would allow her to do so (and somehow deal with any security concerns). The majority also seemed to think it relevant that the "FDC has given Keohane some, but not all, of what she wants," as if treatment of a serious mental health condition were merely a matter of gratifying desires.

In dissent, following circuit precedent Judge Wilson emphasized at the outset of his analysis that satisfaction of the subjective, deliberate indifference element of an Eighth Amendment claim is a question of fact reviewed deferentially and reversed only if the district court's conclusion was clearly erroneous. He strenuously objected to the majority's limitation of that rule to what the majority deemed "historical facts" involved in the deliberate indifference determination, in effect replacing deferential review with de novo review of everything, in Wilson's eyes.

Judge Wilson explained that

> [t]he district court found that the FDC had [been subjectively deliberately indifferent] for two reasons. First, the FDC denied social transitioning because it blindly deferred to the FDC's clothing policy, effectively enacting a blanket ban on social transitioning without case-specific medical or security judgment. Second, the FDC denied Keohane access to medical

personnel competent enough to realize that she needs to transition to avoid severe self-harm.

He believed that the Court of Appeals was required to affirm because both of those findings had substantial record support and thus were not clearly erroneous.

One member of Keohane's prison medical treatment team never even assessed whether Ms. Keohane needed female underclothes or permission to grow her hair out because FDC policy forbade those; the FDC's regional medical director likewise testified that she "did not consider any medical exceptions to the FDC's clothing policy; and another treatment team member said they discussed whether Keohane needed access to female clothing 'but ultimately concluded that "it is out of our hands . . . there's nothing we can do."'" Indeed, "the FDC's final decisionmaker — its chief medical officer — would have refused an exception even if treatment team members had recommended it. . . . The district court also found that the officer made this decision without considering Keohane's specific circumstances. . . ." And, Judge Wilson observed, the district judge also found — with record support — that the chief medical officer's "prejudgment was also born of 'ignorance of gender dysphoria and bigotry toward transgender individuals in general[.]'"

The dissent objected to the majority's reversing the district court's ruling on deliberate indifference due to supposed security concerns. As Judge Williams read the decision below, "[t]he district court did not conclude that the FDC denied treatment because it considered Keohane's need for social transitioning and decided that the security risks outweighed her need. The court found that the FDC did not consider necessity or security at all when denying treatment, because prison officials blindly deferred to the FDC's clothing policy." This failure to consider Keohane's medical need, Williams argued, would amount to deliberate indifference "even under *Kosilek*," and the constitutional violation was exacerbated because prison officials didn't even "evaluate the security risks of social transitioning. . . ." Rather, they wrongly assumed that FDC policy would forbid social transitioning treatment so they didn't even investigate whether Keohane might be allowed to grow her hair out and wear women's undergarments. In sum, "[t]he record here shows . . . that Keohane's medical need and the security risks of her treatment played zero part in the FDC's decision to withhold social transitioning. That decision was driven by blind deference to FDC policy, without regard for medical need, no matter how dire the straits." This literally unreasoning deference amounted in Wilson's view to "a categorical, blanket ban on social transitioning and a level of disregard that rises above mere negligence."

In addition, Wilson argued that the prison's medical team was not competent to treat Keohane's gender dysphoria and, citing circuit precedent, that the FDC's provision of such unqualified physicians constituted deliberate indifference. "As the district court found, no member of Keohane's treatment team had ever treated a pre-transition patient with gender dysphoria. In fact, most of her team members had never treated a patient with gender dysphoria, period. Team members were not trained in the World Professional Association for Transgender Health (WPATH) standards—standards that the district court (and many others) have found authoritative for treating gender dysphoria in prison." Indeed, "Keohane's treatment team leader conceded that she was not qualified to decide whether Keohane needed social transitioning. And the FDC's chief medical officer admitted that he 'doesn't know one way or the other if social transitioning is helpful in treating gender dysphoria,' even though that treatment is standard for treating the illness." To make matters worse,

> the FDC's staff psychiatrist—a psychiatrist the FDC brought in post-litigation to say that Keohane doesn't need social transitioning—admitted that he lacked knowledge about the proper standard of care for gender dysphoria, that he had only read the parts of Keohane's record relevant to her psychiatric need (Keohane has never taken psychiatric medication while in FDC custody), and that he had never before "evaluated anyone in prison to determine a medical need for access to clothing or grooming standards to treat gender dysphoria." This led the district court to fairly conclude that his views deserved little, if any weight.

All this led the dissent to conclude that the district court's conclusion of deliberate indifference was not clearly erroneous and so should be affirmed. The majority's footnoted response was to assert that the medical team members were "minimally" competent, not so bad as to "shock the conscience," even though they lacked specialization or particular experience treating patients with Keohane's diagnosis. (Would the majority have thought that the failure to provide an oncologist for a patient with cancer was not conscience-shocking if the physician provided was in general "minimally competent"?)

The dissent rejected the majority's attempt to portray this as a mere case of reasonable medical disagreement. As the dissent reviewed the decision, both sides' "experts agreed that this treatment would be deeply helpful for Keohane's mental state (and that she would be at great risk of self-harm without it), [so] the [trial] court fairly found that '[e]xperts on both sides agreed at trial that [the FDC] should allow Ms. Keohane access to female clothing and grooming standards to treat her gender dysphoria.'" [First two alterations by Eds.] In sum, Wilson contended, "there is no genuine dispute or difference in medical opinion in this record. Both experts agreed at trial that Keohane should have this treatment. Team members recognized that Keohane remained in pain despite hormone therapy and knew that social conditioning could help her pain. And the district court found that the few officials who said social transitioning was unnecessary were incompetent and incredible."

Judge Wilson's dissent also found unpersuasive the majority's attempt "to distinguish several cases holding that the failure to provide social-transitioning treatment arises to deliberate indifference." Although the majority asserts "that, in those cases, medical providers all agreed that a certain medical treatment for gender dysphoria was medically necessary, while here they don't," the dissent points out with supporting citation that this was factually "wrong because medical providers in those cases did not all agree that a given type of treatment was necessary." (Wilson also found the incorrect claim "irrelevant because, again, the views of Keohane's treatment team had no role in its decision-making. Team members blindly deferred to prison policy, which caused them to deny care.")

Wilson also rejected the majority's assertion "that prison officials in those [other] cases denied care under a blanket ban, but here the FDC has rescinded the freeze-frame policy and has conceded that it will grant exceptions if social transitioning is medically necessary." Not only was the district court "right to treat Keohane's case as a blanket-ban case," in Wilson's view, but the "FDC's freeze-frame policy has nothing to do with its general security policy requiring all inmates to dress as their biological sex."

"Third, the majority says that it was clear in those cases that the patient's health was declining, but here the evidence shows that Keohane's symptoms improved after she received hormone therapy." But, the dissent objected, "it can be true that Keohane's treatment team knew that hormone therapy was helping and also knew that she still suffered from significant distress due to her lack of social transitioning. These facts are not mutually exclusive — although Tylenol dulls the pain of a gunshot wound, the patient still needs stitches." Even though hormones were helping Ms. Keohane's gender dysphoria, there was still "evidence showing that the FDC also knew that Keohane was still suffering from her inability to transition and yet did nothing more to treat her pain."

Accordingly, the dissent would have followed the approach of cases such as *Hicklin v. Precythe*, 2018 WL 806764 (E.D. Mo. Feb. 9, 2018), *supra*, *Soneeya v. Spencer*, 851 F. Supp. 2d 228 (D. Mass. 2012), and *Edmo v. Corizon, Inc.*, 2019 WL 3978329 (9th Cir. Aug. 23, 2019) (discussed in a Note, *infra*), where courts held "that the categorical refusal to adequately treat gender dysphoria amounts to deliberate indifference." "Because this record supports the district court's findings," Judge Wilson acidly closed his dissent, "we should affirm them, not shake the magic 8-ball until it gives us a different result. And on those findings, the FDC is liable for deliberate indifference to Keohane's gender dysphoria."

Reading Guide for Battista v. Clarke

1. Note that this next case involves a plaintiff, transgender woman Sandy Battista, who was civilly committed rather than criminally incarcerated. What potential significance does the court suggest this may have with regard to the governing doctrinal test for unconstitutional denial of treatment?

2. How does the court treat Ms. Battista's evidence of a defendant's suggestion that he considered punishment by withholding treatment for her gender identity disorder to be a factor in denying her hormone therapy?

3. Why does the court of appeals conclude that the defendants were not entitled to deference in this case? How does it address the defendants' argument that providing hormones would increase the risk of sexual assaults against Battista?

Sandy J. Battista v. Harold W. Clarke, Commissioner of the Massachusetts Department of Correction, et al.

645 F.3d 449 (1st Cir. 2011)

Before BOUDIN, Circuit Judge, SOUTER,* Associate Justice, and STAHL, Circuit Judge.

BOUDIN, Circuit Judge.

In 1983, in state court in Massachusetts, Sandy Battista . . . was convicted of the rape of a child, robbery, and kidnapping. After serving that sentence, Battista was involuntarily committed in 2003 in a civil proceeding, Mass. Gen. Laws ch. 123A, § 14 (2008), to the Massachusetts Treatment Center for Sexually Dangerous Persons ("Treatment Center") [an all-male facility]. . . .

. . . .

Battista is anatomically male but suffers from "gender identity disorder" ("GID"), a psychological condition involving a strong identification with the other gender. GID is a disorder recognized in the American Psychiatric Association's *Diagnostic and Statistical Manual of Mental Disorders* (4th ed. 1994). The diagnostic criteria include not only "cross-gender identification" but also "clinically significant distress or impairment in social, occupational, or other important areas of functioning."

In 1996, Battista changed her name to Sandy and began to seek treatment from the Department, including administration of female hormones and access to female garb. Her early demands were met with skepticism and resistance.[1] In 1997, a Department consultant diagnosed her GID, but the Department offered no further evaluation or treatment until 2004. . . .

Battista filed her complaint in the present suit in July 2005 and in October 2005 sought to castrate herself with a razor blade. The suit, against various officials of the Department, charged deliberate indifference to her medical needs in violation of the Eighth and Fourteenth Amendments and 42 U.S.C. § 1983 (2006), as well as state law, including Mass. Gen. Laws ch. 12, §§ 11H-11I. In particular, Battista sought an injunction requiring that hormone therapy and female garb and accessories be provided to her.

In and around 2005 and 2006, the Department fenced with its own healthcare provider, the University of Massachusetts Correctional Health Program, which offered strong support for the GID diagnosis, asserted that harm could easily occur without adequate treatment, and recommended hormone therapy as medically

---

* The Hon. David H. Souter, Associate Justice (Ret.) of the Supreme Court of the United States, sitting by designation.

1. In response to Battista's initial requests, a Department psychiatric consultant stated in 1997 that the name change and desired treatments were "bizarre at best, and psychotic at worst" and recommended various medical and psychological testing, as well as therapy. The consultant also considered Battista's requests to be "elective procedures" equivalent to "tummy tucks and liposuctions."

necessary. The Department instead hired another gender specialist, who then agreed that hormone treatment might be appropriate along with other therapy.

. . . .

In August 2008, the first security review by the Department concluded that a feminine appearance would endanger Battista. The core security concern throughout has been that sexual contacts or assaults by other detainees would be made more likely by female clothing and accessories and the enhancement of breasts due to hormone therapy. The report, however, was fairly cursory, comprising only a few paragraphs, and in December 2008 the district court entered a preliminary injunction requiring psychotherapy, access to women's attire and accessories, monthly reports on Battista's condition, and a recommendation on hormone therapy after a six-month review.

In the six-month report, the doctors again prescribed the hormones. A first dose was administered, but then the Department put another indefinite hold on treatment pending a second security review. The September 2009 review again found the safety risk too high. This new report was more substantial although it more or less duplicated an earlier report prepared for an inmate who also had requested and been denied hormone therapy. Its security evaluation is at the core of the Department's substantive objection to hormone therapy for Battista.

. . . .

. . . . In the course of the trial, Battista offered an evaluation from psychiatrist George Brown. He testified that Battista was eligible and ready for hormonal treatment, that the past treatment for her GID "falls below any reasonable standard of care," and that with a

> high degree of medical certainty . . . when this patient loses hope again regarding access to appropriate care, she will engage in surgical self-treatment by autocastration or will hire someone to do this for her. This could lead to an inadvertent death due to exsanguination.

On August 3, 2010, the court stated that it would enter a modified preliminary injunction order requiring hormone therapy to begin shortly. . . .

In its decision, the district court unqualifiedly required hormone therapy.[2] . . . . That directive was stayed by the district court pending appeal, as defendants requested, solely because the district court feared harm to Battista if hormone therapy were begun and later stopped again.

---

2. The modified preliminary injunction now on appeal was issued on August 23, 2010, and requires "[w]ithin seven (7) business days of the entry of this Order, the DOC shall provide hormone therapy to Battista in accordance with the recommendation of Dr. Levine, Dr. Zakai, and Ruth Khowais, Psy.D. on June 19, 2009, and the prescription by endocrinologist Dr. Mohammed Saad dated August 4, 2009 and August 14, 2009."

The district court's ultimate finding of "deliberate indifference" rests on several different subordinate findings, which can be recast and summarized under two headings: first, that Battista has an established medical need for hormone therapy, may suffer severe harm without it, and (implicitly) that such therapy is feasible despite safety concerns; and second, that the defendants' reliance on their administrative discretion in invoking and dealing with security concerns has been undercut by a collection of pretexts, delays, and misrepresentations.

. . . .

. . . . In the district court, the parties and the judge focused on the Eighth Amendment test used to assess medical care, or the lack of it, for criminal prisoners, namely, whether the defendants were "deliberately indifferent" to the needs of their charge. *Farmer v. Brennan*, 511 U.S. 825 (1994); *Estelle v. Gamble*, 429 U.S. 97 (1976). This choice of tests was hardly surprising: although protection of civilly committed persons rests on due process concepts rather than the Eighth Amendment, deliberate indifference is the familiar test for medical care.

The Eighth Amendment standard is in part one of subjective intent. *Farmer.* The phrasing itself implies at least a callous attitude, but subjective intent is often inferred from behavior and even in the Eighth Amendment context — contrary to the defendants' assertion — a deliberate intent to harm is not required. *Id.* Rather, it is enough for the prisoner to show a wanton disregard sufficiently evidenced "by denial, delay, or interference with prescribed health care." *DesRosiers v. Moran*, 949 F.2d 15 (1st Cir. 1991).

Because Battista is civilly committed, a different, more plaintiff-friendly standard arguably applies here: whether the defendant failed to exercise a reasonable professional judgment. *Youngberg v. Romeo*, 457 U.S. 307 (1982).[4] . . . . The two standards are not all that far apart and, to the extent that the *Youngberg* phrasing governs and is more helpful to Battista, that only reinforces the outcome reached by the district judge.

Both the *Farmer* and *Youngberg* tests leave ample room for professional judgment, constraints presented by the institutional setting, and the need to give latitude to administrators who have to make difficult trade-offs as to risks and resources. This is a regular theme in the Eighth Amendment cases, *Farmer*, and it is equally important under *Youngberg*. There, while stressing that civilly committed persons are entitled to an extra margin of protection, the Court also stated that there can

---

4. The decisions are not uniform. *Compare Ketchum v. Marshall*, No. 90-F-1627, 963 F.2d 382, 1992 WL 111209, at *2 (10th Cir. 1992) (unpublished table decision) (using deliberate indifference test for medical care for the civilly committed without mentioning *Youngberg*), *with Patten v. Nichols*, 274 F.3d 829 (4th Cir. 2001) (applying professional judgment test, not deliberate indifference), *with Sain v. Wood*, 512 F.3d 886 (7th Cir. 2008) (treating both standards as equivalent to deliberate indifference), and *Ambrose v. Puckett*, 198 Fed. Appx. 537 (7th Cir. 2006) (treating both standards as equivalent to professional judgment).

be more than one reasonable judgment, and that the choice in such cases is for the professional. *Youngberg.*

Finally, while an "intent to punish" is not required even under *Farmer,* it could certainly be highly significant under *Farmer* and, *a fortiori,* under *Youngberg.* So it is useful to dispose at the outset of plaintiff's claim that Robert Murphy — the superintendent of the Treatment Center — admitted that whether Battista should "be punished for her lack of good judgment by withholding medical care" was "a consideration" when Murphy wrote the security report rejecting hormone therapy.

This overreads Murphy's testimony. That Battista had regularly evaded Treatment Center restrictions and engaged in sexual contacts with other detainees was fully established, and it enhanced the danger to her in the future if her attractiveness to other detainees was increased. So that fact was legitimately a "consideration" that could affect whether hormone treatment could be safely allowed. . . .

However, even without an evil motive, the district court could reasonably find that there had been "denial," "delay" and "interference" under Eighth Amendment precedent and that a reasonable professional judgment had not been exercised under *Youngberg.* It has been fifteen years since Battista first asked for treatment, and for ten years, health professionals have been recommending hormone therapy as a necessary part of the treatment. When during the delay Battista sought to mutilate herself, the Department could be said to have known that Battista was in "substantial risk of serious harm." *Farmer.*

But the question remains whether the withholding of hormone therapy was "wanton" or outside the bounds of "reasonable professional judgement." Medical "need" in real life is an elastic term: security considerations also matter at prisons or civil counterparts, and administrators have to balance conflicting demands. The known risk of harm is not conclusive: so long as the balancing judgments are within the realm of reason and made in good faith, the officials' actions are not "deliberate indifference," *Farmer,* or beyond "reasonable professional" limits, *Youngberg.*

. . . .

The Treatment Center is the one facility where Battista can be housed as a civil inmate and, while the Department could establish a branch elsewhere, Mass. Gen. Laws ch. 123A, § 2, this would pose administrative difficulties and be isolating for Battista. The civil-side residents of the Treatment Center contain a disproportionate number of male sex offenders who might threaten one who presents herself as female. And Battista has a record of infractions and sexual contacts and risk-taking that colorably place her at greater risk from invited or uninvited sexual contact.

Nor is Battista's willingness to take risks for herself decisive. The defendants have an obligation to take reasonable measures to protect inmates, *Farmer,* and Battista is quite likely to sue if preventable harm occurs. Battista will bear some of the risk of the hormone therapy, but not all of it. And, while she could be kept in protective custody available at the Treatment Center, this custody — as currently structured—involves confinement for most of the day and other disadvantages that Battista is unwilling to tolerate.

. . . . [The] problem is not one of callous guards or inept medical care but of conflicting considerations. As we said in an earlier case involving the Treatment Center:

> Any professional judgment that *decides* an issue involving conditions of confinement must embrace security and administration, and not merely medical judgments. . . . The administrators are responsible to the state and to the public for making professional judgments of their own, encompassing institutional concerns as well as individual welfare. Nothing in the Constitution mechanically gives controlling weight to one set of professional judgments.

Cameron v. Tomes, 990 F.2d 14 (1st Cir. 1993).

Yet in this instance, as the record now stands, the defendants have forfeited the advantage of deference. Initially, the district judge was far from anxious to grant the relief sought. It was only after what the judge perceived to be a pattern of delays, new objections substituted for old ones, misinformation and other negatives that he finally concluded that he could not trust the defendants in this instance. The details are laid out in his oral opinion and the record contains support for his conclusion. Several examples stand out.

First, for some time, the Department refused to take the GID diagnosis and request for hormone therapy seriously. . . .

Second, once the medical prescription was clear, several years passed before the defendants produced a substantial security justification; and this, it turns out, depended in part on inaccurate data in paragraphs largely written by Department counsel and inserted at counsel's request *after* Murphy had made his decision and submitted his initial draft. . . .

Third, for some time, the defendants portrayed the choice facing the court as one between keeping Battista in a severely constraining protective custody unit and denying her hormone therapy. Defendants now show some signs of retreating from this all or nothing choice,[5] but not far: this is consistent with a pattern of slow retreats to the next redoubt. . . .

In the end, there is enough in this record to support the district court's conclusion that "deliberate indifference" has been established—or an unreasonable professional judgment exercised—even though it does not rest on any established sinister motive or "purpose" to do harm. Rather, the Department's action is undercut by a composite of delays, poor explanations, missteps, changes in position and rigidities—common

---

5. Finally faced with a decision by the district court to require therapy, defendants now say they have offered to create a modified protective custody arrangement that would provide Battista and others with both protection from other residents and "access to treatment, work, educational programs, and recreation." This may on investigation be less than the quotation suggests but that is another matter.

enough in bureaucratic regimes but here taken to an extreme. This, at least, is how the district court saw it, and it had a reasonable basis for that judgment.

There are a few loose ends to address. One is that the defendants say that the harm faced by Battista is neither immediate nor irreparable—common requisites for preliminary relief—but, as already noted, the injunction is not preliminary as to her entitlement to hormone therapy. And while the risk of self-mutilation is unpredictable, it grows as the litigation drags on. They also say that the risk of physical assault will be increased by therapy, which may be so but is not decisive: medical treatment often poses risks and invites trade-offs.

. . . .

Affirmed.

———————

Discussion

1. What is the distinction between professionally unreasonable judgment and indifference to medical need that the court draws here?

2. In *Fields v. Smith*, 653 F.3d 550, 557 (7th Cir. 2011), the U.S. Court of Appeals for the Seventh Circuit held that provision of hormones could not legitimately be withheld to prevent increased sexual assaults against transgender inmates. Which court is right?

3. What does *Battista*'s reasoning for sustaining the trial court's conclusion of deliberate indifference mean for future cases in which corrections officials and defense counsel may act with more care to seem reasonable? To what extent are the legal aspects of the case, in addition to the medical ones, part of the "reasonable judgment" or "deliberate indifference" standard?

4. Is the appellate court's reasoning about Murphy's testimony consistent with the full opinion's pronouncement on the applicable standards of review— "Legal issues are open to *de novo* review, factual findings are reviewed for clear error, and judgment calls by the district judge may get deference depending on the circumstances"?

Reading Guide for Hicklin v. Precythe

1. The next opinion consistently misspelled the name of lead defendant Missouri Department of Corrections Director Anne Precythe, including in the case caption (hence, some online resources have likewise misspelled it). The editors have corrected this in the version presented here.

2. What facts convince the district court that the plaintiff inmate, Jessica Hicklin, a transgender inmate denied hormone therapy and access to gender-appropriate "canteen items," was facing a threat of irreparable injury?

3. On what precedent do defendants rely to defend their denial of hormone therapy to Ms. Hicklin? How does the court deal with that precedent? Why does

the court conclude that "psychiatric care and counseling alone are constitutionally inadequate to address Ms. Hicklin's gender dysphoria"?

4. What is/are the basis/bases for the district court's conclusions regarding "'gender affirming' canteen items and permanent hair removal"?

5. In analyzing the balance of harms to determine whether to grant Hicklin a preliminary injunction, how does the court assess the defendants' professed penological concerns (safety and security) and cost concerns?

6. How does the court address the plaintiff's request to enjoin the freeze-frame policy of the Missouri Department of Corrections in general?

Jessica Hicklin v. Anne Precythe, et al.

No. 4:16-cv-01357-NCC, 2018 WL 806764, 2018 U.S. Dist. LEXIS 21516
(E.D. Mo. Feb. 9, 2018)

[Jessica Hicklin was represented by Lambda Legal attorneys Demoya Renee Gordon, Carl Solomon Charles, and Richard Saenz, and a number of private counsel.]

Memorandum and Order

Noelle C. Collins, United States Magistrate Judge

. . . . The parties have consented to the jurisdiction of the undersigned United States Magistrate Judge pursuant to 28 U.S.C. §636(c). . . .

I. Facts and Background

On August 22, 2016, Plaintiff Jessica Hicklin ("Ms. Hicklin")[3] filed this action for injunctive and declaratory relief pursuant to 42 U.S.C. §1983 against Defendant Corizon, LLC, the Individual Corizon Defendants,[6] and the MDOC Defendants (collectively "Defendants") for their alleged deliberate indifference to Ms. Hicklin's serious medical needs. Ms. Hicklin specifically alleges that despite knowing that she has gender dysphoria, a serious medical condition, Defendants have refused to provide Ms. Hicklin with medically necessary care including hormone therapy, permanent hair removal, and access to "gender-affirming" canteen items. Ms. Hicklin asserts that Defendants refuse to provide her with this hormone therapy, citing a policy or custom of providing hormone therapy only to those transgender inmates who were receiving it prior to incarceration (the so-called "freeze-frame" policy).

On April 4, 2017, Ms. Hicklin filed a Motion for Preliminary Injunction requesting a preliminary injunction order that (1) directs Defendants to provide Ms. Hicklin with care that her doctors deem to be medically necessary treatment for gender dysphoria, including but not limited to providing her hormone therapy, access to

---

3. In July 2015, Ms. Hicklin changed her name and has since updated her social security card and offender identification card as well as her prison-issued clothing. The parties have agreed to use female pronouns when addressing Plaintiff Jessica Hicklin.

6. Corizon and the Individual Corizon Defendants will be collectively referred to as the "Corizon Defendants."

permanent body hair removal, and access to "gender-affirming" canteen items; and (2) enjoins Defendants from enforcing the unconstitutional policies, customs, or practices that deny inmates with gender dysphoria individualized medically necessary treatment and care, which are contrary to widely accepted standards of care and the recommendations of Ms. Hicklin's treating mental health professionals. As to gender-affirming canteen items, Ms. Hicklin seeks to have access to, and purchase herself, the same items available to women in the MDOC.

. . . .

Ms. Hicklin is a thirty-eight year old pre-operative transgender woman in the custody of the Missouri Department of Corrections ("MDOC") and housed at Potosi Correctional Center ("PCC"), a facility for male inmates. . . . Ms. Hicklin has been in the custody of [MDOC] since the age of 16, serving a sentence of life without the possibility of parole and 100 years, to be served concurrently. Ms. Hicklin suffers from gender dysphoria (also known as gender identity disorder or transsexualism), a medical condition caused by the incongruence between a person's gender identify and the sex they were assigned at birth.

Gender Dysphoria Background

. . . .

According to the Declaration of Dr. Randi C. Ettner, a clinical and forensic psychologist retained by Ms. Hicklin as an expert, individuals with untreated gender dysphoria experience clinically significant depression, anxiety, and mental impairment, and, when left untreated, additional serious medical problems including suicidality and the compulsion to engage in self-castration and self-harm. Ms. Hicklin asserts that she should be provided treatment consistent with the World Professional Association for Transgender Health's ("WPATH") *Standards of Care for the Health of Transsexual, Transgender, and Gender-Nonconforming People* (the "Standards of Care"). Dr. Ettner notes that these Standards of Care are "the internationally recognized guidelines for the treatment of persons with gender dysphoria" and have been endorsed by numerous professional medical organizations including the American Medical Association, the American Psychological Association, the American Psychiatric Association, the World Health Organization, and the National Commission of Correctional Health Care. The Standards of Care explicitly state that they are equally applicable to patients in prison.

The Standards of Care

The following provisions of the Standards of Care are pertinent to this case. Once a diagnosis of gender dysphoria is established, individualized treatment should be initiated. Such treatment may include (1) living in the gender role that is consistent with one's gender identity, (2) hormone therapy to feminize or masculinize the body, (3) surgery to change primary and/or secondary sex characteristics and/or (4) psychotherapy. Changes in gender expression including clothing and grooming that affirm one's gender identity as well as permanent body hair removal are significant in alleviating gender dysphoria. "For individuals with persistent, well-documented gender dysphoria, hormone therapy is an effective, essential, medically indicated treatment to alleviate the distress of the condition." Dr. Ettner indicates that the therapeutic effects of hormone therapy are twofold: (1) the patient acquires congruent secondary sex characteristics (*i.e.*, breast development, retribution of body fat, cessation of male pattern baldness, and reduction of body hair) and (2) the hormones act directly on the brain lessening the gender dysphoria and associated psychiatric symptoms. In regards to psychotherapy:

> Merely providing counseling and/or psychotropic medication to a severely gender dysphoric patient is a gross departure from medically accepted practice. Inadequate treatment of this disorder puts an individual at serious risk of psychological and physical harm.

(quoting WPATH Medical Necessity Statement, 2016).

As Dr. Ettner explains,

> Psychotherapy can provide support for the many issues that arise in tandem with gender dysphoria. However, psychotherapy alone is not a substitute for medical intervention when medical intervention is required, nor is it a precondition for medically indicated treatment. By analogy, counseling can be useful for patients with diabetes by providing psychoeducation about living with chronic illness and nutritional information, but counseling doesn't obviate the need for insulin.

The Medical Record

Pursuant to PCC policy, on March 4, 2015, Ms. Hicklin requested an initial evaluation for gender dysphoria. As a result, Dr. Meredith Throop, a psychiatrist, evaluated Ms. Hicklin on March 23, 2015. Based on this assessment, Dr. Throop determined that Ms. Hicklin met the diagnostic criteria for gender dysphoria outlined in the DSM-V. Dr. Throop referred Ms. Hicklin to an endocrinologist "for evaluation of cross-sex hormone [treatment]. Currently, hormone therapy (estrogen, testosterone blockers) is the accepted treatment for individuals with [a] Gender Dysphoria diagnoses." [*sic*] In an addendum to Dr. Throop's notes from the evaluation, Dr. Throop notes, "after researching DOC protocols, it was found that endocrinology consult is NOT the appropriate next step for psychiatry in the [treatment] of Gender Dysphoria. Endocrinology consult was not requested." .... Dr. Throop continued to recommend hormone therapy, noting, "It is the opinion of this provider that neglecting to treat this [patient] with the currently accepted standards of care for gender dysphoria as per the APA and WPATH [Standards of Care] is detrimental to [her] mental/emotional/psychiatric well-being." ....

During the same time period, on June 19, 2015, Ms. Hicklin was evaluated for a TRIA hair removal device she requested or formal electrolysis.[9] Defendant Associ-

---

9. A laser hair-removal device for personal use at home. [footnote relocated to end of sentence — Eds.]

ate Regional Medical Director Dr. Glen Babich determined that neither treatment option was medically necessary.

Ms. Hicklin continued her treatment with a new psychiatrist, Dr. Evelynn Stephens. Dr. Stephens diagnosed Ms. Hicklin with "gender dysphoria with associated panic secondary to current body characteristics" on December 16, 2015. Dr. Stephens prescribed medication for panic and body anxiety symptoms. Dr. Stephens also recommended that Ms. Hicklin be treated with "hair removal device and hormone therapy as these are likely to greatly decrease patient's current level of discomfort and intrusive thoughts." After this initial evaluation, Dr. Stephens met with the gender dysphoria committee on January 13, 2016 to discuss next steps. Dr. Stephens noted that her "overall suggestion is to utilize the standard of care discussed by the 2012 APA task force on treatment of gender identity disorder (now gender dysphoria)" and specifies "the patient initially requires psychotherapy during a period that patient is presenting as desired gender, then I would suggest referral to medicine to initiate hormone therapy." Dr. Stephens added:

> [Ms. Hicklin's] symptoms are escalating with age given risk of male pattern baldness more likely at this time if hormone therapy not initiated. This should be taken into account when considering the time table for starting treatment. The patient does meet the requirements for diagnosis of gender dysphoria and has now been diagnosed by two psychiatrists.

. . . . [On] or about February 3, 2016, Dr. Stephens recommended "psychotherapy ongoing, 3–6 months living as a female with access to products that females in DOC have access to for self care [*sic*], then referral to medicine for hormone therapy. Suggest weekly psychotherapy if possible given the severity of illness." However, on March 14, 2016, Dr. Stephens suggests the use of medication to prevent hair loss as "this could be used while pending decision on DOC policy of use of hormone treatment of gender dysphoria diagnosed while incarcerated. Defer to medical." . . . . On June 6, 2016, . . . Dr. Stephens . . . states, "[f]ormal request for hormone therapy consideration was submitted again today as the patient has successfully lived as a female with ongoing therapy for over 6 months." On September 20, 2016, Dr. Stephens notes, "[g]iven this increased agitation, self harm [*sic*] thoughts and reported active symptoms of male pattern baldness will refer to gender dysphoria committee to consider dermatology referral and treatment for hair loss (head) and removal (body) as at this time symptoms [constitute] medical necessity."

[The] Gender Dysphoria Clinical Supervision Group ("GDCSG") . . . . members concurred with Dr. Stephens' diagnosis of gender dysphoria, and "[a] referral to the Gender Dysphoria Committee was agreed upon" and "[a]ppropriate hormone therapy was agreed upon." . . . .

On September 29, 2016, Dr. Stephens added an addendum to these notes indicating that. . . . Ms. Hicklin's agitation is at "higher levels than previously reported" as Ms. Hicklin describes an "'overwhelming feeling of dread,' in the context of thinning hair on head" and "increasing intrusive self harm thoughts to remove own testicles in order to remove offensive testosterone." . . . .

. . . .

During her treatment with Dr. Stephens, Ms. Hicklin reported "panic symptoms" with "active body anxiety, tachycardia, [shortness of breath], [with] diaphoresis noted almost daily." . . . . Ms. Hicklin also described "disgust surrounding [her] testicles for multiple reasons [including . . .] the fact that they produce testosterone which is causing [her] body to not look like [her] own." Indeed, Dr. Stephens diagnosed Ms. Hicklin with Anxiety [Not Otherwise Specified] occasionally as "acute exacerbation secondary to hair removal difficulty" . . . . Ms. Hicklin also reported experiencing intrusive thoughts of cutting off her testicles and counsel stated on the record that Ms. Hicklin has attempted to remove her testicles and has a past history of suicidal attempts.

As of today's date, Ms. Hicklin is not receiving hormone therapy and does not have access to "gender-affirming" canteen items or the means for permanent hair removal. The MDOC Defendants indicate that medical staff continues to provide Plaintiff with psychiatric care and counseling.

Expert Testimony — Dr. Ettner's Evaluation of Ms. Hicklin

On January 27, 2017, Plaintiff's expert, Dr. Ettner, met with and evaluated Ms. Hicklin. Dr. Ettner diagnosed Ms. Hicklin with "intractable, untreated gender dysphoria." Upon review of Ms. Hicklin's medical records, Dr. Ettner found that:

> [The] lack of appropriate treatment for gender dysphoria is causing Ms. Hicklin to experience serious psychological and physical symptoms including panic attacks, anxiety, racing heartbeat (tachycardia), shortness of breath, sleep disturbance, lack of appetite, headaches, and excessive sweating. She also experiences intrusive thoughts of cutting off her testicles, and has attempted to amputate them with a tourniquet[.]

Dr. Ettner further indicated that, "Ms. Hicklin has a history of suicide ideation and two suicide attempts." . . . . Dr. Ettner recommended the immediate initiation of feminizing hormone therapy. She further stated that, "[i]ntegral to successful treatment of gender dysphoria is the ability to present as a female" and,"[t]herefore, Ms. Hicklin should also be allowed access to items and clothing available to female inmates, and effective, permanent means of body hair removal."

Relevant Policy and Procedures

The MDOC Defendants have provided the Court with limited written policies and procedures relating to the care of transgender individuals within MDOC custody. First, the MDOC Defendants provide the Court with the Missouri Department of Corrections Institutional Services Procedure Manual Procedure IS5-3.1 titled "Offender Housing Assignments." The following are the relevant portions of this policy. . . . Each MDOC institution has a transgender committee comprised of the health service administrator, medical director, institutional chief of mental health services and the deputy warden or Prison Rape Elimination Act (PREA) site coordinator. "The transgender committee is responsible for determining a permanent housing assignment for each transgender . . . offender, and prior to this assignment shall meet with each offender to determine his vulnerability within the general population and length of time living as the acquired gender." Of note, the housing policy does not address any medical issues.

Second, during the Preliminary Injunction Hearing, the MDOC Defendants provided the Court and opposing counsel with a single paragraph on a sheet of paper without any identifying information and stated that it was the freeze-frame policy at issue (hereinafter "the Policy"). The Policy of unknown origin reads in its entirety as follows:

> [The Prison Rape Elimination Act (PREA)] is designed to keep all offenders safe from sexual assault and harassment, particularly those at greater risk of sexual victimization. The Department has adopted and is committed to enforce [*sic*] PREA zero tolerance of sexual abuse and harassment by complying with all PREA standards and making every effort to keep our offenders safe. The Department believes the initiation of Hormone Replacement Therapy (HRT) is not appropriate in a prison environment. An attempt at such transition in the prison venue severely compromises the safety of the offender and places them at substantial risk of sexual abuse and harassment. Therefore, after carefully balancing the potential benefit of HRT therapy [*sic*] to an offender, the increased risk to their personal safety as well as impact on the safety and security of other offenders and staff, we conclude such therapy is not appropriate in a prison setting and is not approved. Although HRT therapy is not approved, Mental Health is directed to and shall continue to provide all counseling and support deemed necessary.

Third, the MDOC Defendants also indicate that they, in conjunction with Corizon have developed explicit procedures to respond to inmates with gender dysphoria. In support of this assertion, the MDOC Defendants provide an August 2016 Corizon Memo regarding "Gender Dysphoria Patients." In the memo, Corizon outlines its "initial guidance into the treatment or continuation of treatment for patients with Gender Dysphoria." Corizon defines gender dysphoria using the DSM-V definition. . . . Relevant to the current case, the memo indicates that the following steps should be taken when a new diagnosis of Gender Dysphoria is under consideration or suspected, to be "ruled in or ruled out:"

> a. The patient will be scheduled with a Psychiatrist for an evaluation to include a thorough history and for a consideration of a provisional diagnosis of Gender Dysphoria.

> b. Before a diagnosis of Gender Dysphoria can be ruled in, the Gender Dysphoria Clinical Supervision Group must convene to review the case.

> c. During this meeting a review of all medical records, medication records, and independent reports detailing their findings, and evaluations by site staff must occur, and a diagnosis of Gender Dysphoria will be ruled in or ruled out.

d. Once the final diagnosis of Gender Dysphoria is ruled in, the individualized medical and mental health treatment plans will be developed by site health care staff and will then be forwarded to the Gender Dysphoria Clinical Supervision Group for their review and approval.

e. Once the treatment plans are approved by the Gender Dysphoria Clinical Supervision Group, they will forward such plans to the DOC Transgender Committee for their review and subsequent referral to the DOC Central Office.

f. At this time, the patient's diagnosis should be noted on the problem list and treatment documented and when implemented with the involvement of the offender within the electronic medical record.

g. On a case-by-case base, hormonal replacement therapy (HRT) may need to be considered. In such a situation, the Gender Dysphoria Clinical Supervision Group will be forward [*sic*] such decision on to the DOC Transgender Committee for their review and subsequent referral to DOC Central Office.

h. Upon review, DOC Central Office will provide direction to the DOC Transgender Committee, and copy the appropriate facility [Health Services Administrator (HSA)], facility medical director, and the [Intuitional Chief of Mental Health Services (ICMHS)].

i. With the approval of the DOC Central Office, the offender will be scheduled for a medical evaluation to include a thorough history, complete physical examination, and baseline laboratory studies and initiate HRT as clinically indicated.

j. Also, if the patient is transferred to another facility, it is expected the sending site HSA and ICMHS will notify the receiving site's HSA and ICMHS of this patient, treatment plan and expectations for fulfilling the requirements of this plan.

The Gender Dysphoria Clinical Supervision Group is comprised of the healthcare professionals who are assigned to work with a patient diagnosed with Gender Dysphoria, the contractual Regional Director of Psychiatry, the appropriate contractual Mental Health Director, the contractual Regional Medical Director, and a contractual Specialty Physician Consultant based upon identified need. This Group meets as needed to conduct an ongoing review of the management of patients diagnosed with Gender Dysphoria. Each Department of Corrections (DOC) institution will have a transgender committee comprised of the health services administrator (HSA), the medical director, institutional chief of mental health services (ICMHS) and the deputy warden or prison rape elimination act (PREA) site coordinator. Defendants also provided a copy of the Corizon Transgender MTF (Male to Female) Hormone Protocol and Patient Consent form.

. . . .

[When] Ms. Hicklin met with Defendant Nurse Diana Larkin to discuss whether [her] grievance could be resolved through discussion, Defendant Larkin informed Ms. Hicklin that she had received an email from Dwayne Kempker, previously named in this action as a defendant and the former Deputy Director, Division of Adult Institutions, MDOC, stating that Ms. Hicklin would not receive hormone therapy because MDOC policy prohibited an inmate who was not on such therapy upon entering MDOC from receiving it while in MDOC. . . .

II. Discussion

Federal Rule of Civil Procedure 65 gives courts the authority to grant preliminary injunctions. "A preliminary injunction is an extraordinary remedy never awarded as of right." *Winter v. Nat. Res. Def. Council, Inc.*, 555 U.S. 7 (2008). "Whether a preliminary injunction should issue involves consideration of (1) the threat of irreparable harm to the movant, (2) the state of the balance between this harm and the injury that granting the injunction will inflict on other parties litigant, (3) the probability that movant will succeed on the merits, and (4) the public interest." *Dataphase Sys., Inc. v. C.L. Sys., Inc.*, 640 F.2d 109 (8th Cir. 1981). Although "'no single factor is determinative,' the probability of success factor is the most significant." *Home Instead, Inc. v. Florance*, 721 F.3d 494 (8th Cir. 2013). . . .

A. Threat of Irreparable Harm

. . . .

The Court finds that Plaintiff has met her burden to show the threat of irreparable injury. . . . The medical records establish that Ms. Hicklin suffers and will continue to suffer from "panic symptoms" with "active body anxiety, tachycardia, sob, [with] diaphoresis noted almost daily." The record also reflects that these symptoms are as a result of Ms. Hicklin's gender dysphoria. Indeed, Plaintiff's expert, Dr. Ettner indicates, that:

> [The] lack of appropriate treatment for gender dysphoria is causing Ms. Hicklin to experience serious psychological and physical symptoms including panic attacks, anxiety, racing heartbeat (tachycardia), shortness of breath, sleep disturbance, lack of appetite, headaches, and excessive sweating.

The records further indicate that Ms. Hicklin's symptoms have been worsening and would continue to do so absent treatment for her gender dysphoria. For example, Dr. Stephens, upon receiving several letters from Ms. Hicklin and after an urgent follow-up appointment with her, found that Ms. Hicklin suffered from "some increased dysphoria symptoms with body/facial hair growth . . . and increase in intrusive thoughts to remove testicles with fear of active male pattern baldness symptoms".

The records also establish that Ms. Hicklin is at severe risk of self-harm. While Ms. Hicklin has consistently indicated that she does not have suicidal ideations or that she will commit self-harm, she has a history of suicide ideation and has indicated on more than one occasion the inclination to remove her own testicles. . . . Dr. Ettner notes that "Ms. Hicklin avoids contact with her genitals, and, typical of incarcerated gender dysphoric individuals without access to care, she has thoughts of removing them. On one occasion, Ms. Hicklin tried to amputate her testicles with a tourniquet . . ." "Emotional distress, anxiety, depression and other psychological problems can constitute irreparable injury." *Norsworthy v. Beard*, 87 F. Supp. 3d 1164 (N.D. Cal.) *See also cf.* [*sic*—Eds.] *Reid v. Kelly*, No. 5:13CV00249 JLH-JTK, 2013 WL 6231149 (E.D. Ark. Dec. 2, 2013) (suggesting self-harm may be sufficient to establish a threat of irreparable harm).

Finally, . . . the deprivation of Ms. Hicklin's constitutional rights under the Eighth Amendment is alone sufficient to establish irreparable harm. *See Elrod v. Burns*, 427 U.S. 347 (1976) (plurality opinion) ("The loss of First Amendment freedoms, for even minimal periods of time, unquestionably constitutes irreparable injury."); *Michigan State A. Philip Randolph Inst. v. Johnson*, 833 F.3d 656, 669 (6th Cir. 2016) ("When constitutional rights are threatened or impaired, irreparable injury is presumed."); *Mitchell v. Cuomo*, 748 F.2d 804 (2d Cir. 1984) ("When an alleged deprivation of a constitutional right is involved, most courts hold that no further showing of irreparable injury is necessary."). . . .

B. Likelihood of Success

The Court will next consider the likelihood that Plaintiff will succeed on the merits. . . . In considering this factor, the Court need not decide whether Ms. Hicklin . . . will ultimately succeed on her claims but, rather, whether Ms. Hicklin has a "fair chance of success on the merits." *Planned Parenthood Minn., N.D., S.D. v. Rounds*, 530 F.3d 724 (8th Cir. 2008). Here, Ms. Hicklin asserts that she suffers from an objectively serious medical condition that Defendants, acting with deliberate indifference, have failed to treat in violation of the Eighth Amendment.

"The Eighth Amendment forbids prison officials from 'unnecessarily and wantonly inflicting pain' on an inmate by acting with 'deliberate indifference' toward the inmate's serious medical needs." *Blackmore v. Kalamazoo Cnty.*, 390 F.3d 890 (6th Cir. 2004). The "deliberate indifference" standard applies to a prisoner's challenge to medical treatment. *Wilson v. Seiter*, 501 U.S. 294 (1991). Deliberate indifference has both subjective and objective components. A plaintiff must show (1) that she suffered from an objectively serious medical need and (2) that the prison officials actually knew of, but deliberately disregarded, that need. *Jolly v. Knudsen*, 205 F.3d 1094 (8th Cir. 2000).

1. Serious Medical Need

. . . . To be objectively serious, the medical need must be "one that has been diagnosed by a physician as requiring treatment, or one that is so obvious that even a layperson would easily recognize the necessity for a doctor's attention." *Johnson v. Busby*, 953 F.2d 349 (8th Cir. 1991). In this case, Ms. Hicklin asserts that both her diagnosis for gender dysphoria disorder and her risk of self-harm constitute serious medical needs. Defendants do not contest that Ms. Hicklin's gender dysphoria is a serious medical need. [The court's analysis is omitted.—Eds.]

2. Deliberate Indifference

"In order to demonstrate that a defendant actually knew of, but deliberately disregarded, a serious medical need, the plaintiff must establish a mental state akin to criminal recklessness: disregarding a known risk to the inmate's health." *Allard v. Baldwin*, No. 14-1087, 2015 WL 921006 (8th Cir. Mar. 5, 2015) (internal quotation omitted) Negligence or medical malpractice does not constitute a constitutional violation. *Estelle v. Gamble*, 429 U.S. 97 (1976).

The Court finds that Ms. Hicklin is likely to succeed in establishing that Defendants were deliberately indifferent to her serious medical need. Ms. Hicklin has presented compelling evidence that Defendants' refusal to provide her with hormone therapy after her diagnosis is based on the Policy rather than on a medical judgment concerning Ms. Hicklin's specific circumstances.

Medical professionals, including members of several reviewing committees, are generally in consensus that Ms. Hicklin requires hormone therapy to treat her gender dysphoria in accordance with the Standards of Care. Both of Ms. Hicklin's physiatrists, Dr. Throop and Dr. Stephens, recommended hormone therapy in accordance with the Standards of Care. The Gender Dysphoria Clinical Supervision Group also agreed on appropriate hormone therapy to treat Ms. Hicklin's gender dysphoria.

[The] decision to refuse Ms. Hicklin the hormone therapy rests solely on the Policy. The Policy is mentioned extensively throughout the medical record as the reason for the refusal to provide Ms. Hicklin with hormone therapy. . . . The MDOC Defendants also admit that when Ms. Hicklin met with Defendant Nurse Diana Larkin . . . , Defendant Larkin informed Ms. Hicklin that she had received an email from Dwayne Kempker, the former Deputy Director, Division of Adult Institutions, MDOC, stating that Ms. Hicklin would not receive hormone therapy because MDOC policy prohibited an inmate who was not on such therapy upon entering MDOC from receiving it while in MDOC. The denial of hormone therapy based on a blanket rule, rather than an individualized medical determination, constitutes deliberate indifference in violation of the Eighth Amendment. *See, e.g., Kosilek v. Spencer*, 774 F.3d 63 (1st Cir. 2014) (en banc); *Fields v. Smith*, 653 F.3d 550 (7th Cir. 2011); *De'lonta v. Angelone*, 330 F.3d 630 (4th Cir. 2003); *Allard v. Gomez*, 9 Fed. Appx. 793 (9th Cir. 2001) (unpublished).

The MDOC Defendants do not contest that the medical staff at PCC recommends hormone therapy for Ms. Hicklin nor do they appear to dispute that the treatment was denied based on the Policy[;] instead they argue, "there is an important distinction to be made between what medical professionals recommend and what the federal constitution requires." Citing *Smith v. Rasmussen*, 249 F.3d 755

(8th Cir. 2001), a case upholding a state Medicaid regulation prohibiting payment for sex reassignment surgery, the MDOC Defendants specifically assert that "[t]here is no constitutional right to sex-reassignment therapy." Reliance of [*sic*— Eds.] *Rasmussen* is misplaced here and Plaintiff has not asked for surgery. The MDOC Defendants also argue, citing portions of a report entitled, *Sexuality and Gender: Findings from the Biological, Psychological, and Social Services*, by Dr. Lawrence S. Mayer and Dr. Paul R. McHugh, that "there is a legitimate disagreement in the scientific community about what treatment is or is not appropriate for a patient with gender dysphoria." . . . . Defendants assert that Plaintiff is receiving extensive and continuing medical and psychological care for her gender dysphoria, "far more than that could possibly be required by the federal Constitution."

Defendants' decision to provide "*some* treatment" is inadequate and, therefore, not constitutional. *De'lonta v. Johnson (De'lonta II)*, 708 F.3d 520 (4th Cir. 2013) (emphasis in original). As aptly put by the District Court of Massachusetts, "if [Ms. Hicklin] had cancer, and was depressed and suicidal because of that disease, the DOC would discharge its duty to [her] under the Eighth Amendment by treating *both* [her] cancer and [her] depression." *Kosilek v. Maloney*, 221 F. Supp. 2d 156 (D. Mass. 2002) (emphasis added). *See also, e.g., Kothmann v. Rosario*, 558 Fed. Appx. 907 (11th Cir. 2014) (unpublished) (denying qualified immunity to prison official who denied transgender prisoner hormone therapy while providing anti-anxiety and anti-depression medications, mental health counseling, and psychotherapy treatments); *De'lonta II* (finding counseling and anti-depressants insufficient as defendants had not clearly demonstrated that this treatment was provided for the purpose of alleviating plaintiff's self-harm or that it was deemed to be a reasonable method of preventing further mutilation); *Fields* ("Although DOC can provide psychotherapy as well as antipsychotics and antidepressants, defendants failed to present evidence rebutting the testimony that these treatments do nothing to treat the underlying [gender dysphoria]."); *Soneeya v. Spencer*, 851 F. Supp. 2d 228 (D. Mass. 2012) (blanket ban on laser hair removal and surgery was deliberately indifferent even though transgender plaintiff was receiving some treatment, including psychotherapy and hormones). Accordingly, while Defendants are correct in their assertion that Ms. Hicklin is not constitutionally entitled to the treatment of her choice, the treatment must nevertheless be adequate to address the prisoner's serious medical need. In light of treating physicians' recommendations, psychiatric care and counseling alone are constitutionally inadequate to address Ms. Hicklin's gender dysphoria.

The Court further finds that Ms. Hicklin is likely to succeed on the merits as to her requests to have access to "gender-affirming" canteen items and permanent hair removal. Pursuant to the Standards of Care, individualized treatment for gender dysphoria may include living in the gender role that is consistent with one's gender identity. In line with and specifically noting the Standards of Care, Dr. Stephens suggested that Ms. Hicklin be given the opportunity to live as her desired gender.

In order to accomplish this, Dr. Stephens recommended "psychotherapy ongoing, 3–6 months living as a female with access to products that females in DOC have access to for self care." Dr. Stephens [notes], "[g]iven this increased agitation, self harm thoughts and reported active symptoms of male pattern baldness will refer to gender dysphoria committee to consider dermatology referral and treatment for hair loss (head) and removal (body) as at this time symptoms [constitute] medical necessity." The basis of the denial of these items is unclear from the record. At one point, in response to an internal grievance, Nurse Wade indicates Dr. Babich, Associate Regional Medical Director, stated that various forms of permanent hair removal were "not medically necessary." However, as discussed above, the medical evidence does not support this blanket assertion and the case law is clear — "gender-affirming" canteen items and permanent hair removal are not merely cosmetic treatments but, instead, medically necessary treatments to address a serious medical disease. *See Alexander v. Weiner*, 841 F. Supp. 2d 486 (D. Mass. 2012) (finding plaintiff sufficiently asserted factual allegations to support a claim of deliberate indifference to survive a motion to dismiss when she alleged that she was prescribed laser hair removal and/or electrolysis on at least three occasions but defendants "repeatedly ignored treatment prescriptions given to [p]laintiff by her doctors"). *See also Soneeya* (finding the department of corrections' blanket policy prohibiting, among other things, laser hair removal to be unconstitutional and, therefore, entering a permanent injunction enjoining the department of corrections from enforcing it); *Konitzer v. Frank*, 711 F. Supp. 2d 874 (E.D. Wis. 2010) (finding modest makeup, female undergarments, facial hair remover, and hair growth stimulators to be "part of the real-life experience" required under the applicable standards of care such that sufficient evidence supported the conclusion that these items may be medically necessary to survive summary judgment).

Accordingly, the Court finds that Ms. Hicklin is likely to succeed on the merits as to her Eighth Amendment claim that Defendants were deliberately indifferent by failing to provide her with hormone therapy, "gender-affirming" canteen items, and permanent hair removal to treat her serious medical of gender dysphoria.

C. Balance of Harms

[The court was unswayed by the defendants' claims that denial of the care sought served staff and inmate safety and security, observing that "other inmates within the MDOC system have received hormone therapy[,]" and it noted that the defendants had provided no information about costs.[13] Accordingly, the Court finds the balance of harms weighs heavily in favor of Ms. Hicklin.

---

13. By illustration, as noted by the Seventh Circuit, "[i]n 2004, [the Wisconsin Department of Corrections (DOC)] paid a total of $2,300 for hormones for two inmates. That same year, DOC paid $2.5 million to provide inmates with quetiapine, an antipsychotic drug which costs more than $2,500 per inmate." *Fields*. [Footnote by court.]

D. The Public Interest

Finally, the public interest weighs strongly in favor of issuing the preliminary injunction. . . . "[I]t is always in the public interest to prevent the violation of a party's constitutional rights." *Melendres v. Arpaio*, 695 F.3d 990 (9th Cir. 2012).

E. The Policy

Additionally, as relief in her Motion for Preliminary Injunction, Ms. Hicklin requests the Court enter an order "enjoining Defendants from enforcing the policies, customs, or practices that have served as a moving force behind their constitutional violations by denying inmates with gender dysphoria individualized medically necessary treatment and care, contrary to widely accepted standards of care and the recommendations of Ms. Hicklin's treating mental health professionals." Although unclear as to the precise meaning of this request, Ms. Hicklin appears to suggest that the Policy is itself unconstitutional and the MDOC Defendants should be enjoined from enforcing it. The Court notes that the Policy categorically restricts inmates who are diagnosed with gender dysphoria after entering the MDOC from receiving hormone treatment. There does not appear to be any rational relationship between the Policy and a legitimate governmental interest or penological purpose especially in light of the evidence indicating that other inmates in the MDOC system receive hormone therapy. *Turner v. Safley*, 482 U.S. 78 (1987) [(articulating legitimate penological interests test)—Eds.]. Further, failure to conduct an individualized review of a prisoner's needs may violate the Eighth Amendment. *Kosilek v. Spencer*, 774 F.3d 63 (1st Cir. 2014) (en banc) (citing *Roe v. Elyea*, 631 F.3d 843 (7th Cir. 2011)) (any blanket policy regarding sex reassignment surgery would conflict with the requirement that medical care be individualized based on a particular prisoner's serious medical needs and that such a failure may violate the Eighth Amendment). *See also Fields* (finding blanket law denying access to hormone treatment to be unconstitutional; "Refusing to provide effective treatment for a serious medical condition serves no valid penological purpose and amounts to torture."). However, Ms. Hicklin does not raise this issue in her Complaint nor did any of the Parties present argument on this claim either in their briefs or before the Court during the hearing.

The Court has considered the entire record and the arguments presented at the hearing on this matter. Based upon the foregoing consideration of all of the [preliminary injunction] factors, the Court finds that Ms. Hicklin is entitled to a preliminary injunction that Defendants' provide Ms. Hicklin with care that her doctors deem to be medically necessary treatment for her gender dysphoria, including hormone therapy, access to permanent body hair removal, and access to "gender-affirming" canteen items. However, Ms. Hicklin's has failed to meet her burden to warrant a preliminary injunction as to the Policy in general.

F. Bond

Federal Rule of Civil Procedure 65(c)'s instruction that "[n]o restraining order or preliminary injunction shall issue except upon the giving of security by the applicant, in such sum as the court deems proper" has long been interpreted to mean that a district court has discretion to grant injunctive relief without requiring bond or other security, especially when doing so would function to bar poor people from obtaining judicial redress. *See, e.g., Doctor's Assocs., Inc. v. Stuart*, 85 F.3d 975 (2d Cir. 1996). In this case, Ms. Hicklin is incarcerated and appears to lack sufficient resources from which to provide security. Requiring a bond in this case would effectively bar Ms. Hicklin from obtaining injunctive relief. Therefore, the Court will grant injunctive relief without requiring bond or other security. *See Johnson v. Bd. of Police Comm'rs*, 351 F. Supp. 2d 929 (E.D. Mo. 2004) ("[A] district court has discretion to grant injunctive relief without requiring bond or other security, especially when doing so would function to bar poor people from obtaining judicial redress.").

III. Conclusion

Accordingly,

It is hereby ordered that. . . . Plaintiff Jessica Hicklin's Motion for Preliminary Injunction is granted, in part and denied, in part.

The Court has carefully considered Plaintiff's specific requests for relief and finds the following injunctive relief to be appropriate:

> (1) Defendants are directed to provide Ms. Hicklin with care that her doctors deem to be medically necessary treatment for her gender dysphoria, including hormone therapy, access to permanent body hair removal, and access to "gender-affirming" canteen items.

————————

Discussion

1. Why might a prison adopt a "freeze-frame" policy limiting the transition-related medical treatment inmates receive to that which they were receiving when they became incarcerated? Why might such a policy disproportionately affect people who were incarcerated at relatively young ages?

2. Note that the defendants rely on a "report" co-authored by Paul R. McHugh and Lawrence S. Mayer. The court's opinion does not note that the piece, a review of scientific literature, was published in *The New Atlantis*, a non-peer reviewed journal founded by a social conservative advocacy group, the Ethics and Public Policy Center. In response to the McHugh and Mayer piece, over 500 "researchers and clinicians with expertise in gender and sexuality" published an open letter avowing that the *New Atlantis* report "misleads readers about the state of scientific research and evidence-based clinical practice guidelines addressing the health of people who are lesbian, gay, bisexual, transgender, and queer (LGBTQ)." These experts concluded that "the report's conclusions do not reflect current scientific or medical consensus about sexual orientation or gender identity research findings or clinical care recommendations." See discussion of another McHugh essay in *O'Donnabhain v. Commissioner of Internal Revenue*, Chapter 11, *supra* at p. 625.

McHugh was a key figure behind the closing of the Gender Program that had provided transition care, including surgeries, at Johns Hopkins University in 1979. More recently, McHugh "communicated with the [federal] Government regarding the implementation of an official federal policy of discrimination against transgender military service (the 'Ban')." Plaintiffs' Memorandum of Law in Support of Motion to Compel Discovery from Dr. Paul R. McHugh, MD, *Karnoski v. Trump*, case no. 2:17-CV-01297-MJP (W.D. Wash. Oct. 3, 2018).

Note on Edmo v. Idaho Department of Correction *and* Edmo v. Corizon, Inc.

In *Edmo v. Idaho Department of Correction*, 358 F. Supp. 3d 1103 (D. Idaho 2018), B. Lynn Winmill, Chief U.S. District Court Judge for the District of Idaho, granted the motion of inmate Adree Edmo, a Native American transgender woman, for an injunction ordering the Department to provide her "adequate medical care, including gender confirmation surgery." Ms. Edmo was represented by the National Center for Lesbian Rights and private counsel. The judge self-consciously sought to reassure readers (or reviewing judges): "the Court notes that its decision is based upon, and limited to, the unique facts and circumstances presented by Ms. Edmo's case. This decision is not intended, and should not be construed, as a general finding that all inmates suffering from gender dysphoria are entitled to gender confirmation surgery." The court's opinion, though, was both sympathetic to the plaintiff and respectful of precedent, as the opening paragraphs well convey:

> For more than forty years, the Supreme Court has consistently held that consciously ignoring a prisoner's serious medical needs amounts to cruel and unusual punishment in violation of the Eighth Amendment. *See Estelle v. Gamble*, 429 U.S. 97 (1976). After all, inmates have no choice but to rely on prison authorities to treat their medical needs, and "if the authorities fail to do so, those needs will not be met." *Id.* Prison authorities thus treat inmates with all manner of routine medical conditions — broken bones are set; diabetic inmates receive insulin; inmates with cancer receive chemotherapy; and so on. This constitutional duty also applies to far less routine, and even controversial, procedures — if necessary to address a serious medical need. And so it is here. Plaintiff Adree Edmo alleges that prison authorities violated her Eighth Amendment rights by refusing to provide her with gender confirmation surgery. [The] Court agrees and will order defendants to provide her with this procedure, a surgery which is considered medically necessary under generally accepted standards of care.

> The Court will explain its reasoning below but will first pause to place this decision in a broader context. The Rule of Law, which is the bedrock of our legal system, promises that all individuals will be afforded the full protection of our legal system and the rights guaranteed by our Constitution. This is so whether the individual seeking that protection is black,

white, male, female, gay, straight, or, as in this case, transgender. This decision requires the Court to confront the full breadth and meaning of that promise.

Adree Edmo is a male-to-female transgender prisoner in the custody of the Idaho Department of Correction ("IDOC"). She has been incarcerated since April 2012. In June 2012, soon after being incarcerated, an IDOC psychiatrist diagnosed Ms. Edmo with gender dysphoria. An IDOC psychologist confirmed that diagnosis a month later.

. . . . The treatment for gender dysphoria depends upon the severity of the condition. Many transgender individuals are comfortable living with their gender identity, role, and expression without surgery. For others, however, gender confirmation surgery, also known as gender or sex reassignment surgery ("SRS"), is the only effective treatment.

To treat Ms. Edmo's gender dysphoria, medical staff at the prison appropriately began by providing Ms. Edmo with hormone therapy. This continued until she was hormonally confirmed—meaning she had the same circulating sex hormones and secondary sex characteristics as a typical adult female. Ms. Edmo thus achieved the maximum physical changes associated with hormone treatment. But, Ms. Edmo continued to experience such extreme gender dysphoria that she twice attempted self-castration. . . .

. . . . [The] United States Supreme Court has held that deliberate indifference to a prisoner's serious medical needs constitutes cruel and unusual punishment in violation of the Eighth Amendment to the United States Constitution. To show such deliberate indifference, Ms. Edmo must establish two things. First, she must show a "serious medical need" by demonstrating that failure to treat a medical condition could result in significant further injury or the "unnecessary and wanton infliction of pain." Second, she must show that the prison officials were aware of and failed to respond to her pain and medical needs, and that she suffered some harm because of that failure.

Ms. Edmo's case satisfies both elements of the deliberate indifference test. She has presented extensive evidence that, despite years of hormone therapy, she continues to experience gender dysphoria so significant that she cuts herself to relieve emotional pain. She also continues to experience thoughts of self-castration and is at serious risk of acting on that impulse. With full awareness of Ms. Edmo's circumstances, IDOC and its medical provider Corizon refuse to provide Ms. Edmo with gender confirmation surgery. In refusing to provide that surgery, IDOC and Corizon have ignored generally accepted medical standards for the treatment of gender dysphoria. This constitutes deliberate indifference to Ms. Edmo's serious medical needs and violates her rights under the Eighth Amendment to the

United States Constitution. Accordingly, for the reasons explained in detail below, IDOC and Corizon will be ordered to provide Ms. Edmo with gender confirmation surgery.

In its findings of fact, the court pointedly noted that the defendants' experts had never recommended gender confirmation surgery as treatment for gender dysphoria (save one expert regarding two patients but with legally impossible preconditions), nor had the private corporate correctional health provider defendant Corizon ever had one of its providers recommend such surgery in any correctional facility where it provides services in the United States. The court also found that "Defendants' experts appear to misrepresent the WPATH Standards of Care by concluding that Ms. Edmo, despite presenting as female since her incarceration in 2012, cannot satisfy the WPATH criteria because she has not presented as female outside of the prison setting. But there is no requirement in the WPATH Standards of Care that a 'patient live for twelve months in his or her gender role outside of prison before becoming eligible for SRS.' *Norsworthy v. Beard*, 87 F. Supp. 3d 1164 (N.D. Cal. 2015)." And the court noted that the views of one of the defense experts were accorded scant weight by the *Norsworthy* court when he testified before it. That court did so because his "report [to the court] misrepresents the Standards of Care; overwhelmingly relies on generalizations about gender dysphoric prisoners, rather than an individualized assessment of Norsworthy; contains illogical inferences; and admittedly includes references to a fabricated anecdote."

On the defendants' appeal, Ms. Edmo was again represented by the National Center for Lesbian Rights and several private counsel and was supported by amici including former corrections officials, prison scholars, medical and mental health professional organizations, civil rights and nonprofit organizations, and others. In *Edmo v. Corizon, Inc.*, 935 F.3d 757 (9th Cir. 2019), a three-judge panel of the U.S. Court of Appeals for the Ninth Circuit removed some unnecessary defendants from the scope of the trial court's injunction but affirmed the substantive reach of that relief, primarily the requirement that Ms. Edmo be provided gender confirmation surgery. Like the trial court, the appeals court "emphasize[d] that the analysis here is individual to Edmo and rests on the record in this case. We do not endeavor to project whether individuals in other cases will meet the threshold to establish an Eighth Amendment violation[,]" it noted. On the merits, the court of appeals "rejected the State's portrait of a reasoned disagreement between qualified medical professionals." Rather, accepting what it characterized as "the district court's logical, well-supported factual findings," the court held

> that the responsible prison authorities have been deliberately indifferent to Edmo's gender dysphoria, in violation of the Eighth Amendment. The record before us, as construed by the district court, establishes that Edmo has a serious medical need, that the appropriate medical treatment is GCS, and that prison authorities have not provided that treatment despite full knowledge of Edmo's ongoing and extreme suffering and medical needs.

B. Sex-Segregated Prisons

Although the practice of segregating prisons and other correctional institutions by sex is widespread and has a long history, it has not been universal across all places and times. In the United States, as Barry Ruback notes, "women had occupied dungeons, almshouses, and jails with men and children since the mid-1600s in the American colonies." Barry Ruback, *The Sexually Integrated Prison: A Legal and Policy Evaluation, in* John Ortiz Smykla, Coed Prison 33, 33 (1990). Initially, jails were not sex-segregated. Dana M. Britton, At Work in the Iron Cage: The Prison as Gendered Organization 25 (2003). Facilities reserved for women appeared gradually, sometimes initially as a small building in an existing prison yard, and then, for greater numbers of women prisoners, across the street from a men's prison or somewhat farther away, with "nearly every state operat[ing] a custodial unit for women" by the late 1800s. Nicole Hahn Rafter, Partial Justice: Women, Prisons, and Social Control xvi-xvii (2d ed. 1990).

The practice of sex segregation, however, seems to presuppose agreement about the number of sexes — two, male and female — and about the sex to which any person sentenced to incarceration belongs. Presumably, such agreement is expected to be shared not only by governmental agents responsible for the imprisonment of convicts, but also by the convicts/inmates themselves. With transgender inmates, that is most often emphatically not the case. What ensues is all too frequently horrific:

> Upon incarceration, transgender individuals find themselves at the mercy of a hyper-gendered system: prisoners are sorted into sex-segregated facilities where traditional gender roles are strictly enforced. Transgender individuals are uniquely at odds with these gender stereotypes, and are singled out for assault because of their gender non-conformity. For most prisoners, incarceration is a violent coercive experience; transgender prisoners experience the violence and coercion to a heightened degree. In the absence of policies specifically addressing the needs of gender-transgressive individuals in such a gendered system, transgender prisoners are routinely forced into dangerous placements and denied gender-affirming medical care.

Sydney Tarzwell, *The Gender Lines Are Marked with Razor Wire: Addressing State Prison Policies and Practices for the Management of Transgender Prisoners*, 38 Colum. Hum. Rts. L. Rev. 167, 176–77 (2006).

Reading Guide for Rosenblum, "Trapped" in Sing Sing

1. What issues facing transgender inmates in the prison system does Darren Rosenblum identify? Which right(s) of these inmates are being violated due to the way the prison system treats and houses transgender inmates?

2. What are the methods Rosenblum, now Professor of Law at the Elisabeth Haub School of Law at Pace University, offers for eliminating or ameliorating the issues

faced by transgender inmates due to the sex-segregated prison system? What concerns does he discuss regarding these methods?

3. What biases regarding transgender people does the article mention in scholarship on and the legal treatment of transgender people?

"Trapped" in Sing Sing: Transgendered Prisoners Caught in the Gender Binarism[*]
Darren Rosenblum

A transgendered woman [today, the preferred term is "transgender woman" — Eds.], who has undergone extensive hormonal therapy and cosmetic surgery, is convicted and imprisoned. Because she still has a penis, albeit a nonfunctioning one, prison officials categorize her as a male, and place her in a men's prison. "You were born a boy, and you're going to stay a boy," the prison doctor says, rejecting continuation of her long-term estrogen treatment. Her body begins to regain the masculinity she had largely escaped. Bruised by the changes, her body no longer feels like her own, but one imposed on her by the criminal justice system. Her femininity stands out among the male prisoners who repeatedly rape and beat her. Trapped,[4] not only in her body, but in a prison that refuses to recognize and respect her gender identity, she castrates herself with glass and used razors. The prison hospital's hands forced, it finishes the job. Then, to compensate for the lost masculinity, the doctor orders testosterone replacement treatments. After this fails to restore her masculinity, the prison doctors return her to the estrogen treatments that preceded her incarceration. Shockingly, several transgendered women have experienced similar ordeals.[7] This Article will examine this human rights tragedy and explore its vital relevance. . . .

. . . . .

5. A Note Concerning Transgendered Men

Although transgendered men comprise about half of the transgender population, case law generally addresses the concerns of transgendered women. There is a concomitant skewing of scholarship toward this group. Reasons for the lack

---

* Excerpted from Darren Rosenblum, *"Trapped" in Sing Sing: Transgendered Prisoners Caught in the Gender Binarism*, 6 MICH. J. GENDER & L. 499 (1997), by permission of the author.

4. Transgendered people commonly speak of their situation as being "trapped in the wrong body," a prison metaphor that reflects the doubly incarcerated nature of transgendered prisoners' experiences. *See, e.g., Inmate's Transsexual Suit Tossed*, OMAHA WORLD HERALD, Mar. 8, 1994, at 18 (stating that Keith Smith, who prefers to be called Andrea Stevens, claims to be a "woman trapped in a man's body"). However transgendered writer and activist Kate Bornstein criticizes this hackneyed phrase as inaccurate: "I understand that many people may explain their pre-operative transgendered lives in this way, but I'll bet that it's more likely an unfortunate metaphor that conveniently conforms to cultural expectations, rather than an honest reflection of our transgendered feelings." KATE BORNSTEIN, GENDER OUTLAW 66 (1994).

7. *See Farmer v. Brennan*, 511 U.S. 825 (1994) [*supra* at p. 671 — Eds.]; *Supre v. Ricketts*, 792 F.2d 958 (10th Cir. 1986).

of emphasis on transgendered men include the fact that most gender clinics were directed at transgendered women rather than men; that phalloplasty is a relatively recent and expensive procedure compared with vaginoplasty; and perhaps most importantly, that there is male bias in the perspectives of researchers. Also, social pressures prevent women from self expression of gender and sexual identity.[63] The result is that many transgendered men choose to retain their female genitalia permanently. The gender binarism creates castes of transgendered people, in which the "post-operative" reap the approbation of the legal categorization of their acquired gender, including the right to marry someone of their former gender. Because of the relative difficulty of female-to-male surgery, trangendered men find themselves without the perks of full transformation.

. . . .

II. Doubly Imprisoned: Transgendered Prisoner Placement

"We're trying to not treat him differently than anyone else."
—Corrections officer about transgendered woman inmate.

A. The Cruel, the Unusual, and the Transgendered— Prison Law and Life

. . . . Once imprisoned, transgendered people find fighting for their gender identity a monumental task, as they confront the gender segregation, transphobia, and limited resources of the prison system.

. . . .

Courts view the principal issues facing transgendered prisoners through the lens of Eighth Amendment protections. When medical and living conditions fall below an allowable standard, they may constitute cruel and unusual punishment. . . .

Misplacement or mistreatment of transgendered people based on an erroneous understanding of sexual identity is cruel and unusual punishment. However, Eighth Amendment analysis prevents only the most egregious violations of prisoners' rights regarding living conditions and medical treatment, among other situations. Although transgendered prisoners' needs fall into these two areas, the greater issue of the right to gender self determination falls through the cracks of such analysis.

Transgendered prisoners' needs constitute one of many challenges facing correctional authorities who need to balance calls for humane treatment and Constitutional requirements with staffing and budget limitations. . . .

B. Categorizing Gender: Pre-Incarceration Processing

Whether in a holding cell or a maximum security institution, detainees and prisoners are segregated into men's and women's facilities or housing areas. The

---

63. *See* Leslie Martin Lothstein, Female-to-Male Transsexualism: Historical, Clinical and Theoretical Issues 6–7, 14 (1983), *cited in* Marjorie Garber, Vested Interests 101 (1992).

overwhelming majority of prisons segregate men and women, most often by maintaining separate prisons. The obvious conundrum of categorizing the transgendered for placement purposes arises directly from this policy of segregation. . . .

. . . . Pre-sentence reports provide sentencing judges with a portrait of the prisoner, and such reports should include a space for the presentencing officer to discuss gender issues more fully than currently permitted. Prisoners should be allowed to present medical, psychological, and even physical evidence to support their assertions of gender identity. This idea of demonstrating one's gender stems from the sexual declaratory hearing, in which a court determines the sex of the person.[104] If the pre-sentencing officer obviously misreports the gender identity of the prisoner, or if a prisoner requests reconsideration of the reporting, judges should intervene to insist that the prisoner is appropriately categorized and treated. Prison authorities should designate a sensitive, knowledgeable, and sympathetic person to deal with transgendered prisoner requests to prevent the arbitrary denial of appropriate treatment. Treatment of transgendered people should be standardized within prison systems to maximize the rationality of the practices assumed

Speedy and dignified treatment is essential for the sensitive handling of the pre-incarceration processing. In one case, an inmate was isolated for two weeks while prison authorities tried to determine whether she was a man or a woman. In that case, the Chief of Corrections of Chelan County Regional Jail in Washington stated "We isolated her, him. . . . We put her in an infirmary. Or him in an infirmary." The time that passed with the inmate in solitary was used to determine her sex and then to decide where to place her. Instituting policies regarding placement of transgendered prisoners would avert the delay and the indignity of having one's identity scrutinized.

Notably, the right to present such evidence has been denied in one case, albeit in a post-imprisonment setting. In 1986, Lavarita Meriwether sued primarily because prison authorities denied her medical treatment. She claimed that her equal protection rights were violated because, at an evidentiary hearing, she was not allowed to argue that she should be classified as a female and placed in a women's correctional institution. The district court's rejection of this claim was upheld by the Seventh Circuit, which decided that an administrative decision could not give rise to an equal protection claim without evidence of discriminatory intent.[107] The Seventh Circuit refused to deal with the fundamental challenge transgendered people pose to the sex-based system of incarceration.

The above-suggested reforms might prevent claims such as Ms. Meriwether's. In terms of the pre-incarceration period, no serious negative consequences to penal interests result from assigning a gender to a new prisoner and requiring

---

104. *See* Katherine M. Franke, *The Central Mistake of Sex Discrimination Law: The Disaggregation of Sex from Gender*, 144 U. Pa. L. Rev. 1, 41 n.157 (1995) (*citing Corbett v. Corbett*, 1971 P. 83 (1970), in which a court determined the meaning of the sex of one of the spouses).

107. *See Meriwether v. Faulkner*, 821 F.2d 408 (7th Cir. 1987).

the pre-sentencing officer and the sentencing judge to attend to the issue of gender with more care. Furthermore, the costs to the penal system of adopting such reforms are minimal. Altering forms to provide for more than just a check-box undoubtedly qualifies as a small expense. Instructing the relevant public officials on how to handle transgender issues appropriately in placement would require a more significant investment of resources, including training and the preparation and distribution of materials to ensure adequate compliance with the requirements. Nonetheless, this investment might be considered an "ounce of prevention" to preempt the need for a "pound of cure" later in the suffering and litigation that result from an erroneous placement.

C. Genitalia-Based Placement

However reasonable the aforementioned adjustments may be, such changes would require the prison system's acceptance that there are indeed more than two genders; this represents a monumental change in a system that still segregates on the basis of traditionally defined gender.

Prison authorities generally place transgendered prisoners, regardless of the extent of their nongenital transformation, based on their genitalia. "An inmate with a penis is considered male; one with a vagina is considered female. It doesn't matter whether nature or a surgeon provided the part." . . . .

Abuse often results from the placement of pre-operative transgendered people based on their genitalia. Dee Farmer was placed in the general population of a men's maximum security prison, even though she had already undergone several years of hormonal therapy with significant resulting feminization, including silicone breast implants and a failed surgical removal of her testicles. [*See Farmer v. Brennan, supra* at p. 671 — Eds.] Another case involved a transgendered woman who had already been castrated and was ordered to wear a brassiere despite her placement in a men's prison. The foolishness of always placing a transgendered woman with breasts and feminine features in a men's prison demonstrates the domination of the male/female binarism in prison organization. In one case, where a transgendered woman had undergone hormonal and surgical treatments including castration and her "penile tissue was atrophic" and nonfunctioning, she was denied a request for special treatment because "her presentence report identified her as a 32 year-old caucasian male." Unable and unwilling to allow for more complexity than the two categories of male and female, penal authorities rely on an anatomical aspect that to some people may be a very minor factor in their gender makeup.

The placement of transgendered people is determined by what is crude simplification of their gender identity. Because of such placement by genitalia, a transgendered prisoner who has not undergone genital transformation faces the profound stigma of being the only prisoner who identifies with the sex that the prison excludes. At best, this classification evokes her categorization according to a gender identity that less than fully captures her identity. At worst, it forces the assumption of a past gender identity.

1. The Mortal Dangers of Genitalia-Based Placement

Male prisons have an infamous history of creating and reinforcing barbarous hierarchies of economic, social, and sexual subjugation of the weak to the strong, hierarchies that affect and victimize all male prisoners. . . .

Dominant inmates seek to rape inmates who are young, less-streetwise, effeminate, or gay.[115] Transgendered prisoners often find themselves forced into the victim role in prison. Victims rarely report such rapes because other prisoners punish snitches, even with death. One study estimated that slightly less than a quarter of all inmates have been raped. Yet prison systems officially deny the existence of any sexual activity justifying their nonprovision of safe-sex instruction and resources. . . .

Unsurprisingly, the result of placing a transgendered woman in this environment is rape and abuse, endemic in an atmosphere of deliberate indifference. The illegality of rape apparently has not reduced the likelihood of its occurrence. Ms. Farmer's placement in the general population of a men's prison led to her violent rape. In another case, a sixty-one year old cross-dressed prisoner testified that she had been raped twice while imprisoned in the general men's population, both times while she was dressed as a woman.

Acts by the guards cross the line from deliberate indifference to acts of hostility and aggression. Not only do authorities turn a blind eye to abuse by prisoners of transgendered inmates, but they permit and occasionally encourage the mistreatment of transgendered inmates by prison employees. . . .

Another pre-operative transgendered woman who works as a street prostitute was harassed and arrested by the police, even though she was not working at that time, and the officers had not witnessed any work-related behavior. Without any evidence of criminal conduct, the policemen arrested her and took her to jail. They put her in the cell furthest from the guard station with forty-six men. She was finally released eight hours later, after being raped by nearly all of the men in the cell.

In another case, Rosio Melgoza, a transgendered woman, was arrested as a result of a wage dispute. The arresting officers reportedly touched her breasts and genitalia with their hands and a nightstick. Two days after the arrest, she was allegedly strip searched in front of sixty male inmates and then placed in a cell with them, where she was the victim of multiple sexual assaults. The charges against Ms. Melgoza were dropped. The offending police officers did not provide the prisoners with condoms, thereby elevating the foreseeable gang rape into a possible HIV infection or reinfection. This was likely the case in the other rapes discussed above, given the general absence of safe-sex practices in prisons. Finally, given the pattern of abuse in the reported cases, it is probable that most imprisoned transgendered women are raped or abused on a regular basis.

. . . .

---

115. *See* David M. Siegal, *Rape in Prison and AIDS: A Challenge for the Eighth Amendment Framework of* Wilson v. Seiter, 44 Stan. L. Rev. 1541, 1541–47 (1992) . . . .

2. The Failure to Eliminate Genitalia-Based Segregation:
The Co-Correctional Experiment

In theory, the most sweeping solution to gender segregation would be the establishment of co-correctional facilities. In the 1970s, prison reform groups saw segregation as the principal limitation for the development of equal treatment of women prisoners. Co-correctional institutions mix men and women prisoners by placing them in the same prison, separated by cell, hall, or cellblock.

Advocates argued that co-correctional prisons would afford prisoners many advantages over life in single-sex prisons. Geographical proximity to their families and access to the same recreational, vocational, and educational opportunities provided to men would improve life. Men would act differently in the context of a co-correctional institution, even with limited interaction with women. For example, scholars of women's prisons point to the construction of "play-families" among women prisoners that reveal "how the power structure within women's prisons may be very different from the power structure within men's prisons where gangs are the most common social grouping." A variant on co-correctional institutions is the "coordinate" model, which creates a women's institution next to a men's institution where resources are shared.

As promising as co-correctional prisons may seem in abolishing gender segregation, general consensus among prisoner's rights advocates is that the experiment was an utter failure. The overwhelmingly male population in co-correctional institutions led to security problems between men and women, which required placing women under higher levels of control and denying them resources. Mixed-sex facilities still exist, but the separation of the sexes within the facility hardly makes them co-correctional, since even recreational and educational programs are segregated.

One might argue that the abolition of gender segregation would benefit transgendered prisoners by lifting the iron curtain between the sexes. Placing a transgendered prisoner in a co-correctional facility would permit the transgendered person to live as she wished, with access to the resources of both men's and women's prisons.

This failure of the co-correctional remedy warns of the difficulty of abolishing the gender binarism's hold on contemporary society, and points to the challenge confronting prisons in placing individuals that do not easily fit into male or female categories.

3. Potential Reforms for Genitalia-Based Placement

Given the failure of attempts to end sex segregation, reform of the current system may be the best option for transgendered prisoners. Current placement methods put transgendered people into the general population of prisoners with like genitalia, which may be appropriate for some transgendered prisoners.[149] In cases where

---

149. *See* Jennifer Gonnerman, *Love Behind Bars: Lipstick, Love Letters and Laundry: Five Men Talk About Their Prison Romances*, Village Voice, May 13, 1997, at 46.

security issues arise, prison authorities often force transgendered people into segregation. These two placement options, as discussed above, do not provide sufficiently comfortable or safe environments for a transgendered inmate.

Certain practices could improve these situations. Prison authorities can break the cycle of deliberate indifference to prison rape, and protect transgendered inmates from such trauma. First, prison authorities should commit themselves to prosecuting inter-prisoner violence and rape. Second, they should identify potential or known attackers and put them on notice that violence will be severely punished. Third, prison officials can identify likely targets for aggression and assist them in dealing with sexual pressure, and to encourage them to report rape early to permit the identification and punishment of attackers. Fourth, prison authorities can strictly enforce the rules with regard to the treatment of transgendered prisoners by other inmates.

4. Centralization of Placement Resources

Another important reform is the centralization of resources among neighboring states. As one prison official commented, "[a]n inmate could go to California or New York, where the penal system has special units for transsexual offenders." Perhaps the most important argument in favor of centralization is that such a policy would foster a rationalization of prison procedures regarding transgendered inmates. Especially on the state and local levels, prison authorities appear to act in an ad hoc fashion by providing or denying special treatment to transgendered inmates as they see fit at the moment. Although one might ascribe such randomness to disrespect, the fact that there are so few transgendered inmates discourages the creation of set rules for treatment. By combining resources, different jurisdictions that take the lead on provision of appropriate placement and treatment might provide such services for inmates in other states. Differences in state policies, along with the privatization of some prison systems, might make such centralization difficult. Nonetheless such a policy, even if enacted in a limited fashion, might practically permit serious advances in the humane placement and treatment of transgendered prisoners.

D. Segregation

One common solution is to place the transgendered person in segregation, generally in a single cell. Segregation may provide greater security to the prisoner, as in Ms. Farmer's case, where she had requested segregation for security and was instead left in the general population. However, such segregation excludes the prisoner from equal participation in prison life. First, separating transgendered people might not make them safer because their segregation emphasizes their difference to the prison population, exposing them to ridicule. One transgendered woman was segregated in a men's prison to determine whether she would be released into the general population. After she was placed in the general population, she was attacked by another inmate. Prison officials returned her to a segregated cell as the investigation into the attack proceeded. Faced with the choice between segregation and genitalia-based placement, some transgendered people might choose to be placed in the general population, especially prisoners who no longer fear rape because of their age or appearance. For example, one [sexagenarian] transgendered woman did "not fear sexual attack by inmates as he [*sic*—Eds.] is 61 years old."

Automatic segregation may provide an improvement in safety, but at a high comfort cost to the transgendered prisoner. Other concerns arise. One pre-operative transgendered woman complained that segregation denied her adequate "recreation, living space, educational and occupational rehabilitation opportunities, and associational rights for nonpunitive reasons." Such differential treatment might leave the prisoner in a worse position than the other prisoners. Segregation should only be used as a protective measure. Rather than punish the transgendered inmate for the general population's intolerance, prison authorities should engage in the above-mentioned actions to improve life in the prison for the transgendered person. Only in two circumstances should a transgendered prisoner be placed in segregation: where she requests the segregation for her own safety or well-being, or where the danger to the prisoner is so patently clear that prison authorities would be exhibiting deliberate indifference to leave her in the general population.

E. Placement Based on the Gender Identity of the Prisoner

Placement based on self-defined gender identity would be ideal for transgendered people, given a sex-dichotomized prison system. One significant advantage to placing transgendered prisoners based on their gender identity is the avoidance of difficult situations with other prisoners.

The principal problem with this solution is the comfort and security of the traditionally-gendered prisoners in the prison in which the transgendered prisoner is placed. In one case, a transgendered man was placed among women, who complained, "there's a man in the tank." Likewise, one police officer, commenting on the incarceration of a transgendered woman "who looked more like a woman than the other women," would not fit in with male inmates. Potential intolerance toward a transgendered person, however, should not be the sole factor in determining the best placement: bigotry does not merit such accommodation. Because prisons principally concern themselves with order, prison officials would likely object to any reform that could cause disruption in the prison environment.

However, even if objections to housing transgendered women in a women's prison stem from homophobia, such objections require consideration. Legitimate objections to housing transgendered inmates according to their self-defined gender identity do exist. First, the prisoner who must share a cell with a transgendered person may object. One example is Juanita Crosby's claim in her case against a Maine county jail. [*See* Note on *Crosby v. Reynolds*, *infra* at p. 819—Eds.] In this case, the jail placed Ms. Cheyenne Lamson, a 6'1" pre-operative transsexual who had undergone estrogen treatments, developed breasts, and lost penile sexual function, in a women's prison. The doctor saw her placement with women as advantageous, especially when compared to living with male inmates, who would have caused Ms. Lamson "physical and psychological harm." Ms. Crosby, her cell-mate, sued because Ms. Lamson accidentally entered her part of the cell when she was on the toilet, a recurring discomfort. Ms. Crosby refrained from showering to avoid being nude in front of Ms. Lamson. The court determined that, given the lack of alternatives and the lack of established procedures, the authorities could not have understood their actions as violative of the plaintiff's Constitutional rights. In another case in which a transgendered woman was placed in a women's prison, prison authorities admitted that the other two female prisoners had difficulties coping with their new cellmate. Women have complained that their cellmate was growing a beard.

. . . .

Another legitimate challenge is that a transgendered woman might be violent against other women. However improbable this may seem, transgendered prisoners convicted of violent sex crimes, like all those convicted of such crimes, should be placed with the greatest care. Prison officials should not carelessly place those convicted of or known for sexual violence against a particular sex with members of that sex. Prison authorities have not shown the greatest sensitivity in dealing with sex offenders, placing them arbitrarily in the general prison population without regard to the dangers they might pose. As with any prison, prison authorities should be conscious of such dangers. In one case, Jean Marie Druley, an advanced pre-operative transgendered woman, was incarcerated for killing her girlfriend. Obviously, such an inmate would be an unsuitable candidate for placement among women.

Yet, placement according to the gender identity might be more [feasible] if the prison procedures were modified. First, concerns about the discomfort that may result from sharing a cell could be addressed by placing the transgendered inmate in a smaller, single bed cell. Second, to meet the needs of transgendered prisoners and avoid discomfort among the general prison population, prison officials could take a more active role in placement. For example, they could survey prisoners to determine the most tolerant cellmate before placement occurs. Surveying is easier in smaller prisons, where there is more personal contact between the guards and social service providers and the prisoners. In a prison where a transgendered prisoner would be housed, sensitivity training of prisoners and prison officials could ease the integration of the transgendered prisoner into the prison population.

The careful placement of transgendered people could cost the prisons far less than other remedies because it requires little change in prison organization. It also may be less disruptive to penal interests than placing the transgendered inmate among people of her initial sex, which might lead to more violence and disorder than would exist in a placement according to gender identity.

Finally, it must be noted that placing a transgendered woman in a women's prison will not necessarily improve her conditions, because women prisoners receive treatment inferior to that of male prisoners. Because women constitute a far smaller incarcerated population than men, many states incarcerate all women together, regardless of their crime, requiring many women's prisons to follow maximum security procedures, including body searches. Despite faster growth, resources in women's prisons rarely match those in men's prisons, which contain a population over eighteen times that of women's prisons. Vocational programs, for example, rarely equal those provided for men, often focusing on cosmetology and other "women's professions." The conditions of women's incarceration appropriately has given rise to many equal protection and Title IX suits.

F. Special Wards for Transgendered Prisoners

Another option for prison authorities charged with the safety and well-being of a transgendered inmate would be to create special wards for transgendered inmates, modeled on the gay wards that exist in some jurisdictions. In preparing this article, I interviewed the public relations officer of the New York City Department of Corrections. In response to my query about whether there was transsexual housing, I was asked, "what's the difference between transsexual and homosexual?" Indeed, upon further investigation, popular reports that a transgendered ward existed on Riker's Island turned out to be false: transgendered women are placed in the ward designed to house gay men. However, this 'gay' ward is thought by many to be a transgendered ward.

The fact that prison authorities conflate transgenderism with homosexuality requires closer attention. Given the high levels of male-to-male sexual contact in prison, what makes a man seek special housing based on sexual orientation? The answer, it would appear, is that some prisoners feel unsafe in the general population because their identity as gay men, as opposed to men who engage in same sex conduct, exposes them to violence. Indeed, it appears that those gay men who seek such protection do so because their femininity, interpreted as weakness in the prison context, places them at risk in the prison population. This prevalence of conflationist attitudes in prisons renders the line between gay men and transgendered women nearly indistinguishable.

. . . .

Specifically transgendered wards could look to gay housing that exists in the New York City jail system as a model. In that system, prisoners who request such housing, and prisoners deemed to require the protection afforded by such housing, are placed in the gay ward, which has a limited capacity of approximately fifty. Such housing for transgendered people would undoubtedly provide them with a space to express their gender identity freely. Rather than confront a dangerous, and humiliating environment, transgendered inmates would find a supportive, safe environment in which they would be able to freely express their gender and continue to develop healthy attitudes about their gender identity. This solution would cost little more than the dedication of a separate ward to this purpose, a cost that would obviously affect smaller prison systems more than those with numerous transgendered prisoners.

If the transgendered population in a particular jurisdiction were too small to constitute its own ward, states could pool resources with other jurisdictions to provide joint resources. In this manner, one jurisdiction's fair treatment of transgendered prisoners would permit other jurisdictions to do so as well. In addition, by establishing special wards, prisons could provide centralized services for transgendered prisoners. Finally, the costs of such a program would in some sense be lower than either placement of transgendered prisoners among their initial sex or their goal gender identity, because the prison would not have to manage the interaction between the transgendered and the traditionally gendered prisoners.

In summary, there are several possibilities for corrections authorities to improve placement options for transgendered prisoners. Transgendered wards and placement based on gender identity would improve upon the current system of genitalia-based placement. Each reform entails particular advantages and costs, but all provide a vast improvement over the dangerous and inhumane status quo placement policy.

. . . .

Discussion

1. Rosenblum offers a variety of solutions or methods to address the issues transgender inmates face due to the sex-segregated housing system within U.S. prisons, including both pre- and post-sentencing solutions. What advantages and disadvantages can you identify for the various methods of alleviating the issues faced by transgender inmates described in the article? How feasible are each of the proposed solutions, especially considering the reality of limited staffing and budgets available in the prison systems? Can combining two or more approaches make implementing a solution more feasible? What are the advantages and disadvantages of combining any of the methods addressed? Are there any other options that you can think of to address the pressing issues here?

2. Rosenblum suggests co-correctional facilities as a possible solution to the issues faced by transgender inmates in being forced into sex-segregated facilities based on the sex they were assigned but with which they do not identify, but also mentions the failure of this option in the past. How feasible is this solution currently? What changes would be needed for this option to be a feasible solution? Now-Professor Rosenblum suggests that abolishing the view of gender as binary would be necessary—do you agree? Are there changes beyond ceasing to house inmates based upon gender that would also need to be implemented to eliminate reliance on a binary view of gender in U.S. prison systems?

3. Is the proposed solution of including transgender inmates in "gay" prison wards appropriate? Are there any issues that may result from lumping these groups together? What issues might arise from housing these two (potentially overlapping, if one included trans men, though they are largely outside the scope of this article) groups together? Could the sorts of issues faced by transgender inmates held in prisons with inmates of their sex assigned at birth arise in a joint gay-trans ward? What issues could arise from assigning inmates to prisons based on their gender identity?

4. Rosenblum notes that the body of scholarship he relied on for this article focuses predominantly on transgender women. Could the literature's failure to examine in depth the circumstances of transgender men bear on the feasibility of

any of the proposed solutions to issues concerning prison housing for transgender inmates?

5. Rosenblum quotes a corrections officers who voices a goal of wanting to treat a transgender inmate the same as other inmates. Is the same treatment necessarily equal, or fair, treatment? Is it possible that treating a transgender inmate the same as other inmates could lead to an Eighth Amendment violation?

Note on Lamb v. Maschner

Lamb v. Maschner, 633 F. Supp. 351 (D. Kansas 1986), is one of few reported decisions addressing the constitutionality of housing a transgender woman in a men's prison. In *Lamb*, a federal court granted summary judgment to defendant prison officials in a suit brought (through counsel) by inmate Lamb, who professed being transsexual and sought relief that included being transferred from a men's prison to a women's prison. Despite settled case law requiring that factual inferences be drawn in favor of the party opposing summary judgment, a clearly skeptical judge appeared inclined to credit the defendant's evidence over the plaintiff's conflicting evidence, for example, on whether the plaintiff was indeed transsexual, rather than finding a genuine dispute of material fact. Regarding the plaintiff's claim for transfer to a women's prison, the court's reasoning was, at best, spare and conclusory:

> Plaintiff originally requested to be transferred to a women's prison because of his transsexualism. A male prisoner cannot be housed in a women's prison. Even though a transfer may relieve plaintiff's anxieties, clearly a violation of the women's rights would be at issue. Prison authorities must be given great deference to formulate rules and regulations that satisfy a rational purpose and segregation of the sexes is a rational purpose.

The court offered no definition of "male" and "female." It seemed in this reasoning to shift without explanation from the *rationality* of sex segregation to its *necessity* to protect the rights of women inmates. The court also treated sex segregation as an end in itself—"a . . . purpose"—rather than the means by which the Supreme Court's equal-protection sex-discrimination doctrine treated sex classifications even in 1986.

Reading Guide for Tates v. Blanas

1. In the following case, transgender woman inmate Jackie Tates was housed for a prolonged period in a form of administrative segregation in a county men's jail prior to trial. The defendants represented that

> [t]he general policy is to place such an individual in the general population of members of the same gender, unless there is reason to believe that doing so will jeopardize the safety of the inmate. Factors include whether the individual exhibits mannerisms and physical characteristics of the opposite sex.
>
> Plaintiff desired to be placed in the men's general population. Because of his female appearance and mannerisms, the Main Jail and classification

officers were concerned for his safety, as it is not unusual for such persons to be subject to physical assault and rape if housed in general population. Based on these and other factors, it was determined that Plaintiff should be classified as a total separation inmate and housed on the protective custody floor.

Tates v. Blanas, No. CIV. S-00-2539 OMP P, 2002 WL 32718055, 2002 U.S. Dist. LEXIS 27633 (E.D. Cal. Sept. 4, 2002). The court reads Tates's complaint to raise "an Equal Protection claim" as well as Eighth Amendment cruel and unusual punishment/due process claims. What constitutional right(s), if any, does the court specify the defendant correctional officials violated? What kind of scrutiny does the court, explicitly or implicitly, apply to judge the constitutionality of the jail's treatment of Ms. Tates?

2. The defendants in this case acknowledge classifying Tates as a "total separation" inmate for what reason? What kinds of discriminatory treatment of transgender inmates does the court find the jail engaged in? How does the court conclude those various forms of treatment do, or do not, relate to the justification for segregating Tates and other transgender inmates?

Jackie Tates v. Lou Blanas, Sheriff; Kevin Farrell, et al.

No. CIV S-00-2539 OMP P, 2003 U.S. Dist. LEXIS 26029, 2003 WL 23864868
(E.D. Cal. Mar. 11, 2003)

Owen M. Panner, J.

Opinion
Findings of Fact and Conclusions of Law

Plaintiff Jackie Tates is a pre-operative transgender, male to female, pretrial detainee at the Sacramento County Main Jail (the "Jail"). Tates contends his constitutional rights are violated by the conditions of his confinement. He brought this pro se civil rights action in November 2000 against Sacramento County Sheriff Lou Blanas and two Jail employees, Captain B. Kelly and Classification Deputy Kenneth Farrell. . . .

I previously determined that Tates is not entitled to recover damages from Defendant Farrell, citing qualified immunity. I denied defendants' motion for summary judgment regarding Tates' prayer for prospective injunctive relief.

. . . . All issues addressed in this opinion have been the subject of one or more grievances that were not satisfactorily resolved. Plaintiff has exhausted his administrative remedies as to those issues.

I conducted a court trial. . . . I now issue my findings of fact and conclusions of law. . . . Any finding of fact more properly characterized as a conclusion of law, and any conclusion of law more properly deemed a finding of fact, should be so construed.

Findings of Fact
Plaintiff Tates

Plaintiff Tates is a 36-year old biological male who has self-identified as female for at least the past 18 years. Tates is around 5'6" tall. He[2] weighed approximately 125 pounds when he arrived at the Jail, and about 154 pounds at the time of trial. He has not had sex change surgery yet, but is receiving female hormone treatment. He has described himself as "a very effeminate transgender." His voice, appearance, and demeanor are consistent with his self-identified gender. His breasts are sufficiently enlarged that the Jail medical staff authorized issuing him a bra. Tates wears women's clothing when not incarcerated, but—apart from requesting a bra for support—he wears men's clothing while in jail.

This action was commenced during Tates' confinement as a pretrial detainee at the Jail between October 20, 2000 and April 2001. Tates was next housed at Sacramento County's Rio Cosumnes Correctional Center in Elk Grove, California, from April 2001 until mid-August 2001. From there, he was transferred to Patton State Hospital and Atascadero State Hospital, for psychiatric evaluation in connection with his underlying criminal case. Tates was returned to the Sacramento Main Jail on or about February 20, 2002, where he remains to this day.

Tates has several prior felony convictions. . . . He is currently detained pending trial on charges of sending a threatening letter to the governor of California. Tates pled not guilty by reason of insanity, and has been undergoing psychiatric evaluations. On or about December 11, 2001, the Medical Director of Patton State Hospital certified that Tates "is now mentally competent" to stand trial.

Tates' written submissions to the court reflect a high degree of anxiety, obsession, and perhaps paranoia. However, during all court hearings, Tates behaved appropriately and appeared to have little difficulty comprehending the proceedings and rationally articulating his contentions. That Tates may have psychological issues does not, in itself, preclude the possibility that his allegations may have merit. In fact, a number of his factual assertions in this case ultimately have proven to be undisputed. Cognizant of the psychological concerns and his prior convictions, I have carefully scrutinized his allegations and sought independent corroboration when possible. In many instances, the court heard substantially similar testimony from inmate witnesses who had little opportunity or motive to coordinate their stories.

The Main Jail

The Main Jail opened in 1989. It presently houses approximately 2200 to 2300 inmates at any given time, more than double its original design capacity. Defendants describe the Jail as "extremely full." The floors the court viewed were divided

---

2. For purposes of this litigation, Tates chose to have the court refer to him using masculine pronouns, because he is in a men's jail.

into three "pods," each containing a "dayroom." Cell doors line the dayroom walls. A small window in each cell door lets guards peer inside the cell, and lets inmates view the dayroom. A typical pod has around 32 cells, arranged in two tiers. Most cells house two inmates, which equates to about 64 inmates per pod. The three pods on each floor are designed so a central control booth monitors all three pods, and remotely locks or unlocks individual cell doors.

The cells appeared to be roughly $6' \times 10'$ in dimension. Bunks, a toilet and sink, and two inmates, all must fit within that space, leaving little room for other in-cell activities. The shower and telephones are accessible only from the dayroom, as is the television. The Jail also has some fenced "outdoor recreation" facilities.

The T-Sep Classification

Upon arrival at the Jail, each inmate is "classified" by a Classification Officer. Most inmates are classified as "general population." Inmates believed to require special protection (*e.g.*, those particularly susceptible to victimization by other inmates, or likely to be the target of an attack) are housed in "protective custody" (aka "P.C."). Inmates who violate rules can be punished by placement in a special disciplinary category with very restricted privileges. The final classification mentioned in the record is "total separation," usually abbreviated as "T-sep." . . . .

Despite ample opportunity, defendants have provided the court with relatively little information concerning the T-sep classification. They have said it is not a disciplinary classification. In response to the court's questions at trial, defendants named only two groups of inmates who are placed in this category: certain gang members, and transgender inmates.

T-sep inmates are housed in the same pods as other inmates, but forbidden to have any contact with other inmates or even to be in the same room as them. As discussed below, T-sep inmates are subject to many burdens and restrictions not shared by other inmates.

Tates did not ask to be classified as T-sep. Rather, the Jail automatically classifies all biologically male transgender inmates as T-sep, regardless of their behavior, criminal history, whether they pose a danger to others, or any other characteristic. Although Jail policy requires that each inmate's classification be periodically re-examined, in practice an exception is made for transgender inmates, since there is no possibility that the Jail will change their classification.

Since his arrival at the Jail, Tates has repeatedly asked to be placed in the general population or, in the alternative, to be moved to the "P.C. Unit where I can get active program, recreational with other inmate's, rather than isolation program. . . ." His requests were all denied. In response to a grievance, Plaintiff was informed that, "You will remain a T-Sep for the duration of your stay. This topic has already been addressed and you were given your final answer dated 12-5-00." The latter document, which is signed by Defendant Farrell and Captain Kelly, states:

This will be the last time a grievance will be answered when it deals with your classification status. *Your status will never change as long as you are housed at this jail.* (emphasis added).

Defendants have repeatedly stated that Tates is classified as T-sep solely because he is transgender, and Defendants fear he might be harmed and they be held liable if he were given a less restrictive classification. Defendants have not asserted, nor is there any evidence to show, that he was classified as T-sep because he will likely try to harm a Jail employee or other inmate, or poses a particular risk of escaping, or for misconduct, or any reason unrelated to his transgender status.[5]

Other Transgender Inmates at the Sacramento Main Jail

The Jail does not house a large number of transgender inmates, but it is not a unique circumstance either. The Jail presently houses at least two transgender inmates, Plaintiff Tates and Luis(a) Espinoza,[6] and possibly more. There are references in the record to at least four other male to female transgenders [*sic*] who were inmates at the Jail at some point during this case. In addition, the court heard testimony regarding transgender inmates at other correctional institutions.

Given past patterns, it is likely that at any given time the Jail will house at least some transgender inmates. Issues such as the classification of transgenders, and their conditions of confinement, will continue to be a concern even after Tates moves onward. The record also reflects that the conditions Tates complains of are shared by other transgender inmates.

Housing Tates Separate from General Population

I initially thought that Defendants had acted properly in segregating transgenders from the general Jail population. Additional evidence received during the court trial, and an evaluation of all the testimony, makes clear that Defendants acted without due consideration of all factors and the rights of transgenders.

Shackling

The Jail treats transgender inmates in a manner ordinarily reserved for the most dangerous inmates. Unlike most other inmates, those classified as T-sep are heavily shackled and manacled while transported to court, or being moved inside the jail, and even while in a holding cell. This is done without regard to whether the particular individual poses a risk to the safety of other inmates or the staff, or is a threat to

---

5. Defendants' expert witness speculated that Tates must be a disciplinary problem because of the number of housing moves shown in his jail record. An examination of those documents reveals that the vast majority of "moves" were routine and lasted no more than a few hours, *e.g.*, attending court, or meeting with a nurse, social worker, or attorney. Several other "moves" were initiated by the Jail staff due to abuse directed against Tates. There were also inter-facility transfers. The court received no evidence that Tates had significant disciplinary problems at the Jail.

6. I have used feminine pronouns when referring to Espinoza, in accordance with her expressed preference. The court had an opportunity to observe her at trial. Her appearance, voice, and demeanor are consistent with her self-identified gender.

escape. During the trial in this case, Tates was brought into the courtroom wearing leg shackles and manacles chained to his waist. Despite the presence of numerous deputies in the room, Defendants proposed to keep Tates shackled in this fashion throughout the day-long trial.

Defendants insist such treatment is mandatory because Tates, and other transgender inmates, are classified as T-sep. However, the Jail ostensibly classifies transgenders as T-sep solely to protect them from being victimized. Defendants have failed to establish any legitimate reason for automatically treating transgender inmates as inherently more dangerous than most other inmates. The court had an opportunity to observe both Tates and Luis(a) Espinoza during the trial. Neither appears to pose a significant threat to Jail employees or other inmates, as compared to the risk posed by other inmates in general. There was testimony to the contrary, that while Tates occasionally is depressed, he is always compliant and cooperative with Jail employees and medical staff. Defendants offered no evidence to the contrary.

Religious Services

Transgender inmates are prohibited from attending religious services or bible study with other inmates, due to their T-sep classification. In theory, a Chaplain is available for one-on-one prayer sessions with transgender inmates, which Tates has requested. In practice this almost never occurs. Plaintiff attributes this to bias, but there are more plausible explanations. One is overcrowding. The Jail holds 2300 inmates, but has only one Chaplain and a couple of assistants.

Chaplain Ortiz also testified that, because Plaintiff is classified as T-sep, Jail rules require that a guard be present at all times when he meets with Tates. As guards are in short supply, Chaplain Ortiz is rarely able to meet with Tates or other transgender inmates. Chaplain Ortiz has not expressed any fear of Tates or requested that a guard be present. Rather, this appears to be an unintended and unnecessary consequence of classifying transgender inmates as T-sep. The floors viewed by the court had conference rooms, visible from the control room, that would allow the Chaplain to meet with Tates and other transgender inmates without compromising safety or security and without a guard being present in the room.

Tates and Espinoza both testified that their written requests for a Bible went unanswered for a long time.

Dayroom Access

The Sacramento County Main Jail Operations Order on Dayroom Use states that:

> Access to dayrooms shall be provided to inmates on a daily basis under normal circumstances. Use of the dayroom is intended to help maintain the inmates' social and emotional health by allowing them to participate in leisure activities. The dayrooms shall also be used for meal service and

for use of showers and telephones. . . . General population inmates shall be given as much access to the dayroom as possible.

As the Order recognizes, regular dayroom access is important. The cells are very small, and there is little in them to occupy an inmate's time. In addition, the shower and telephones are accessible only via the dayroom.

General population inmates are usually allowed out in large groups, either an entire pod or at least one tier. The Main Jail Operations Order makes special provision for T-sep inmates:

Each inmate on total separation status shall receive no less than one (1) hour of dayroom access daily. The dayroom shall not be used by more than one (1) Total Separation inmate at a time.

It is undisputed that Tates, and other transgender inmates, do not receive dayroom access for at least one hour daily as stated in the Jail policy. On many days, they never leave their cells. Nor do transgenders regularly receive an average of one hour of dayroom daily, *i.e.*, seven hours per week. Instead, Defendants have sought to reframe the issue in terms of whether Tates receives the minimum three hours per week required by state law, citing CAL. ADMIN. CODE title 15, § 1065(a).

Defendants produced in camera a logbook that records the amount of time that Tates and other inmates on his floor received dayroom during a period of several months. Tates disputes the accuracy of those records, insisting that guards sometimes falsely record an hour of dayroom time when he received just ten minutes, or write that he refused dayroom time or outdoor recreation when in fact it was never offered to him. Tates argues that, after being cooped in his cell for so long, he would not pass up the opportunity to use the dayroom or outdoor recreation areas, or take a shower. Defendants did not produce any witness who actually saw Tates using the dayroom or heard him refuse dayroom time. Instead, they rely entirely upon the business records hearsay exception.

It is not necessary to resolve this dispute. Even assuming the accuracy of the logbook, it is undisputed that Tates and other transgender inmates receive less dayroom and outdoor recreation than other inmates, both in terms of quantity and quality. This is largely a product of the Jail's decision to prohibit transgender inmates from having contact with other inmates, including each other.

When a T-sep inmate uses the dayroom, all other inmates must be excluded. Faced with the choice of letting thirty general population inmates use the dayroom for an hour, versus a single transgender inmate, the guards understandably try to accommodate the greater number. Indeed, requiring all other inmates to remain in their cells so a single inmate can use the dayroom may trigger resentment towards that one inmate, even though he is not at fault.

In addition, because the Jail prohibits T-sep inmates from using the dayroom together, the available T-sep time must be divided among the T-sep inmates. This significantly reduces the time allotted to each.

The dayroom time Tates does receive is often late at night while most other inmates are asleep, *i.e.*, between 11:00 p.m. and 4:00 a.m.[7] For example, during the week of June 23, 2002, Tates received only 13 minutes of dayroom time between the hours of 6:00 a.m. and 8:00 p.m. Two thirds of his total dayroom time that week was between the hours of midnight and 5:00 a.m. Tates has complained about this unusual schedule. Among other things, confining dayroom usage to late night hours limits his ability to make telephone calls to friends, family, or attorneys.

Lt. Powell explained that if the Jail doesn't provide transgenders enough dayroom time to satisfy state minimums during normal hours, the Jail makes it up during the night. This effort is admirable. Nevertheless, "dayroom" at two or three in the morning is not a comparable substitute for dayroom during normal hours, at least on a regular basis, unless the inmate prefers those hours for some reason.

Transgender inmates are forbidden to participate in recreational activities with other inmates, or to exercise or interact with them. Consequently, their activities in the dayroom, or outdoor recreation, are very limited. They can't play games, cards, sports, or even talk to another person. Tates claims he is now prohibited from even talking to any other inmate. He has suffered severe depression and emotional distress as a result of his isolation, which has lasted almost two years. Judging by the enormous volume of correspondence the court has received from Tates, he is extremely lonely and bored, with little to occupy his time each day. He has also gained 30 pounds since arriving at the Jail, which is consistent with inactivity.

Tates has repeatedly been denied permission to use the dayroom with other transgender inmates. This refusal is puzzling. Allowing two transgender inmates to use the dayroom together would effectively double the amount of time available for each, or reduce the total time that must be reserved for transgender inmates, freeing up more time for others. It also would enhance the quality of recreational activities available, while helping to alleviate the effects of long-term solitary confinement.

There is no evidence in the record that transgender inmates are more likely than other inmates to act inappropriately while in the dayroom together, and in any event they would be in full view of the guards. Defendants have suggested that there can be a "pecking order" even among transgenders, but point to no evidence that Tates and Espinoza are likely to harm each other. Nor have Defendants made

---

7. The unusual hours may explain some of the "refusals" recorded in the logbook. The logbook shows he was offered dayroom use at 2:11 a.m. on June 23, but declined. On the night of June 27–28, Tates was in the dayroom for an hour and 40 minutes, from 11:47 p.m. to 1:27 a.m. He was then offered dayroom at 1:33 a.m. on June 28 — six minutes after the end of the prior session — but "refused." The logbook also shows refusals at 11:50 p.m. on July 11; 12:05 a.m. on July 17; 2:25 a.m. on August 17; 2:15 a.m. on September 7; 1:10 a.m. on September 10; 11:50 p.m. on October 8; and 2:05 a.m. on October 18. It is not clear from the logbook whether Tates was even awake when he allegedly "refused" dayroom on these occasions.

Some other refusals recorded in the logbook, if accurate, seem less justified, *e.g.*, during normal hours. Tates insists he never refused dayroom. The record is insufficient to make a finding on that issue.

a case-by-case determination. Rather, Defendants' refusal to let transgenders share dayroom time is premised on a rigid classification-based argument: all transgenders are T-sep, and T-seps are forbidden to have contact with any other inmate.

Sanitation

Tates has repeatedly complained that his cell was filthy and asked that it be cleaned or that he be issued cleaning supplies. The court's examination of his cell during the tour was inconclusive. Tates was relocated days before the scheduled tour for reasons apparently unrelated to the court's visit, and his prior cells had been cleaned and repaired despite the court's order to the contrary. Tates testified that he had never seen those cells so clean during the entire time he was there. Tates also testified that a defective faucet that would spray water at him was repaired after he was transferred out of the cell.

Some conditions Tates complained of, such as plugged vents, are common to many cells.[8] . . . .

However, the court finds that the cells of Tates, Espinoza, and other transgenders are cleaned far less often than the cells of other inmates. Defendants essentially concede this point, but insist it is not the result of animosity. Most Jail inmates are issued cleaning supplies to maintain their own cells, or else inmate trustees perform the cleaning chores. However, T-sep inmates are never furnished cleaning supplies, apparently on the theory they might use those materials to harm someone. Nor could trustees enter and clean Tates' cell unless the dayroom was first emptied of all other inmates and a guard was present at all times, since his T-sep status precludes Tates from being around any other inmate, even a trustee. Consequently, Tates' cell was infrequently cleaned. A trustee described it as "pretty nasty," and testified that Espinoza's cell was rarely cleaned either. The latter testified that her cell was cleaned only once during a four month period.

Showers

Inmates ordinarily can shower only when permitted to use the dayroom. Since T-sep inmates are given limited access to the dayroom, Tates and other transgender inmates often must go two or more days without a shower, and sometimes up to a week. There was unrefuted testimony that Tates, Espinoza, and other transgender inmates are permitted to shower less often than other inmates. The record also contains grievances that Tates filed requesting a shower. They are corroborated by the logbook, which shows he had not been allowed out of his cell during the stated period. Defendants appear to have responded when prompted by a formal grievance, but it is impractical to require transgender inmates to file a grievance each time they need a shower.

---

8. The focus of this case is upon alleged disparities between the treatment received by Tates as compared to non-transgender inmates. I express no opinion regarding overall Jail conditions, as that issue is not before me.

Request for a Bra

After arriving at the Jail, Tates asked for a bra. In a grievance response dated December 3, 2000, and signed by Sgt. Brown and Captain Kelly, the Jail categorically refused to issue Tates a bra so long as he "still had a functioning penis and testicles." "You are a male inmate and therefore I am unable to allow you to have a womans [*sic*—Eds.] bra." The Jail attributed this decision to both the medical staff and classification officers; however, there is no evidence in the record that the medical staff has adopted such a policy.

On or about November 18, 2002, *i.e.*, between sessions of the court trial, the Jail medical staff authorized issuance of a bra to Tates for the duration of his stay. Once the trial was over, Sgt. Banning allegedly confiscated Tates' bra and refused to return it. Tates says he was told this action was due to a ruling by this court, though I am aware of no such ruling. Tates claims to be in "great pain" as a result of the lack of physical support. Tates has submitted post-trial documents showing that on January 24 and January 31, 2003, the medical staff again authorized issuance of a bra to him for the duration of his stay.

In deciding to issue a bra, the Jail medical staff presumably took into consideration the potential that a bra can be used as a weapon to strangle a person or as a noose in a suicide attempt. Tates has made suicidal statements during the course of this case, and his Jail admission records evidence past suicide attempts. Eight suicides reportedly took place at the Jail in a recent 12 month period.

Derision, Harassment, and Abuse

The court heard extensive testimony regarding ridicule and abuse allegedly directed at transgender inmates including Tates. Examples include the use of language such as "he/she," "it," "faggot," "bitch," "queer," and "homo;" serving transgenders' meals on the floor; grabbing their breasts or commenting on their physical attributes; threats of rape and other comments of a sexual nature; and unprovoked threats of violence.

Luisa Espinoza testified that she hears jokes about her daily; she was forced to dig in a trash can for items she needed; her food is served on the floor; she was asked to display her breasts; her cell was cleaned only once in four months; she often does not receive a response to her "kites" [inmates' written requests about something— Eds.]; her request for a Bible was ignored; and some guards simply ignore her when she speaks to them or makes requests.

Tates and Espinoza also complain that, to obtain clean clothes, they are forced to walk bare-breasted while the entire pod watches the show through the cell door windows. They find this humiliating.

Most of the alleged abuse originated with other inmates, including trustees. The Jail relies upon the latter, instead of regular employees, to reduce operating costs. I find that the trustees are not being adequately policed by Jail employees. There also is credible evidence that some guards have tolerated abusive conduct directed at transgenders, and that inmates believed they could harass transgenders without fear of punishment. Jail deputies receive some diversity training at the Academy, but apparently no training specifically concerning transgenders. I find that no reasonable attempts have been made to train trustees and guards to stop the harassment that transgenders are subjected to at the Jail.

Defendants' expert, William Naber, testified that many jails do not segregate transgender inmates in the manner practiced at the Sacramento County main Jail. He opined that this option was necessary at this Jail due to its particular design. Naber conceded that placing Tates in solitary confinement for several years, without any review of his classification, would be unconstitutional. Naber asserted that Plaintiff's status had been regularly reviewed, but his requests for reclassification had simply been denied. When confronted with the Jail's written response to Tates—"your status will never change as long as you are housed at this jail"— Naber suggested that Jail officials had probably "misspoken."

I find serious discrimination exists at this jail against transgenders. I find that this results from a failure of Defendants to promulgate rules and discipline to protect transgenders from discrimination.

Conclusions of Law

Pre-trial detainees, such as Tates, are entitled to the same constitutional protections as convicted criminal serving a sentence. *See Gibson v. County of Washoe, Nevada*, 290 F.3d 1175 (9th Cir. 2002). Courts must be careful not to usurp the legitimate role of prison officials. Nevertheless, there are occasions when the federal courts must intercede to ensure that basic rights are protected.

Transgender inmates pose unique concerns for prison officials. Prison officials cannot mistreat transgenders or deny them the benefits available to all other inmates, simply because of a bias against transgenders. When appropriate, though, prison officials can—and in some cases may even have a duty—to treat transgenders differently, *e.g.*, to protect them from violence at the hands of other prisoners. *Cf. Farmer v. Brennan*, 511 U.S. 825 (1994); *Redman v. County of San Diego*, 942 F.2d 1435 (9th Cir. 1991) (en banc).

Segregation of transgenders is not always required. Some correctional facilities choose to house transgenders with other inmates not perceived as posing an undue risk of violent or abusive behavior. Such determinations necessarily depend upon a variety of factors, including the design of the facility, whether it is adequately staffed and not overpopulated, the number of transgender inmates at the facility, and the characteristics of the general inmate population (*e.g*, whether the pod houses exclusively non-violent offenders).

The duty to protect Tates from harm may not be used to justify actions not reasonably related to accomplishing that purpose. Defendants erred by automatically classifying all transgender inmates as T-sep, as that classification is administered at this Jail. The necessary consequence of this classification scheme is to needlessly deprive transgender pretrial detainees of basic human needs and of privileges available to all other inmates, and to needlessly subject transgender inmates to harsh conditions, as discussed earlier in this opinion.

At the conclusion of the court trial, I pointed out various concerns, and asked Defendants "to file a post-trial brief discussing whether it is really necessary to classify all transgender inmates as T-Sep and whether a more suitable classification exists or could be established that would take into account their unique circumstances."

Defendants responded that "it is necessary to classify transgender inmates at the Sacramento County Main Jail as T-sep' and there is no other classification that exists or could *be established*. . . ." Defendant's Post-Trial Brief, p. 2 (emphasis added). The Jail's response is regrettable. I have no interest in micro-managing the Jail, and will extend considerable deference to reasonable decisions by Jail officials. Nevertheless, I have a duty to ensure that Plaintiff's constitutional rights are respected. Since Defendants have declined my invitation to remedy the problems voluntarily, I will order them to do make [*sic*] the necessary changes.

Defendants can, and must, adopt a classification scheme that more appropriately addresses the special circumstances of transgender inmates. Transgender inmates should not routinely be shackled and chained in circumstances where other inmates would not be subjected to such treatment. Transgender inmates should be permitted to socialize with each other unless there are particular safety concerns that would create an undue risk of harm. Such determinations must be based upon facts, not phobias.

Defendants need not treat every transgender inmate in the identical manner. If a particular transgender inmate is determined to be especially dangerous, Defendants could still classify that inmate as T-sep, or use shackles, so long as they would have made the same decision even if that inmate were not transgender. Likewise, transgender inmates are not immune from discipline for rules violations.

The determination of whether or not transgenders can attend group religious services must be made based on all factors and not simply because the person is a transgender. If a transgender is barred from group religious services, the transgender must be provided religious materials promptly and given prompt religious counseling. If Defendants believe a guard must be present, Defendants must make the necessary arrangements.

Transgender inmates must be allowed reasonable use of the dayroom, outdoor recreational facilities, and telephones during normal hours, not just very late at night. The Jail's Operations Order specifies that inmates will ordinarily receive a minimum of one hour of dayroom daily. Other inmates receive at least that much dayroom. Transgender inmates must be similarly treated.

Transgender inmates must have an adequate opportunity to shower, and to do so without being sexually assaulted or harassed. Their cells should be cleaned at least as often as those of other inmates in the same pod. If other inmates are provided cleaning supplies, transgender inmates should be similarly treated, absent reason to believe that a particular inmate will abuse that opportunity. If, for safety reasons, the cells of transgender inmates must be cleaned by a Jail employee or by a trustee with a guard present, then Defendants must see that it is done.

With regard to Tates' bra, the possibility that it could be misused as a weapon or noose must be balanced against any medical or psychological harm to him resulting from denial of a bra. Defendants presumably have existing policies in place for addressing these same concerns with regard to female Jail inmates, some of whom may be suicidal and whose needs for support vary. A similar analysis should apply here. I will leave the final determination to Jail officials, including the medical staff. Their decision must not be influenced by bias, nor may Defendants apply a categorical rule as they previously did that denies an inmate a bra simply because he is a transgender or is housed in a men's ward.

Transgender inmates are entitled to be treated with the same respect as other inmates. This attitude must be conveyed from the top on down. Sheriff Blanas, and senior Jail officials, must make it absolutely clear that abuse, ridicule, "faggot" jokes, and other inappropriate behavior will not be tolerated—whether by employees, trustees, or other inmates. Jail officials must take appropriate disciplinary measures if that policy is violated. An employee who witnesses such misconduct must report it to the appropriate supervisor. This topic shall be addressed when training new Jail employees, and in periodic refresher training of existing employees.

Defendants have until Tuesday, April 1, 2003, to furnish the court with a proposed plan for correcting the deficiencies noted herein.

DATED this 6 day of March, 2003.

Order

Defendants have until Tuesday, April 1, 2003, to furnish the court with a proposed plan for correcting the deficiencies identified in the findings of fact and conclusions of law.

DATED this 6 day of March, 2003.

OWEN M. PANNER

U.S. DISTRICT JUDGE

Discussion

1. Subsequently, the prison submitted a Proposed Plan re: Classification of Transgender Inmates on April 1, 2003, which the court adopted on May 12 in an opinion filed May 19. *Tates v. Blanas*, No. CIV S-00-2539 OMP P, 2003 U.S. Dist. LEXIS 26028 (E.D. Cal. May 19, 2003).

2. Why might the correctional defendants here have adopted and insisted on adhering to a policy of "total separation" of transgender inmates? How should jails

and prisons decide whether, when, and how to house transgender inmates with the general jail or prison population?

Note on Estate of DiMarco v. Wyoming Department of Corrections

In *Estate of Miki Ann DiMarco v. Wyoming Department of Corrections*, 473 F.3d 1334 (10th Cir. 2007), the court of appeals rejected claims that a prison had violated the due process rights of Ms. DiMarco, a woman inmate who was transgender or perhaps had an intersex condition, by imposing restrictive conditions on her confinement ("classifying her") and by not affording her an administrative hearing to contest her placement and living conditions.

According to the court, "Miki Ann DiMarco lived her life as a woman even though she was anatomically male." DiMarco was sentenced to incarceration in prison for a probation violation. "Not realizing DiMarco's medical condition and believing her to be a woman, the court placed her in Wyoming's women's correctional facility in Laramie." She was originally housed with the general female population in the county jail, but was then transferred to Wyoming's sole women-only prison. During the usual prison intake examination, "prison officials learned DiMarco was a hermaphrodite." The court explained in a footnote:

> According to the district court, DiMarco was a "hermaphrodite" or "intersexual." A hermaphrodite may have "both male and female characteristics, including in varying degrees reproductive organs, secondary sexual characteristics, and sexual behavior. This condition is the result of an abnormality of the sex chromosomes or a hormonal imbalance during the development of the embryo." DiMarco had a penis but apparently had her testicles removed as part of gender reassignment surgery; she had no female reproductive organs.

The general population was housed in the East wing of the prison, and higher risk prisoners were housed in the West wing. DiMarco was placed in the West wing, not in the "pod" where new prisoners were commonly housed for a month while the prison determined the appropriate assignment but in Pod 3, "the most restrictive and isolated housing pod used for inmates confined to administrative or protective custody." Its four cells were gray-painted cement blocks with sparse steel fixtures or furnishing, and the "day room" was comparably spartan. "Conditions in the West wing, by contrast, are more pleasant."

Although prison officials determined DiMarco to be a low security risk, they recommended she be housed "apart from the general population for three reasons: (1) DiMarco's safety and that of the general female inmate population, (2) her physical condition, and (3) the need to tailor programs for her condition." The warden said a "primary concern" was "that other inmates might try to harm DiMarco if they discovered her physical condition." Prison officials' reviews of her assignment each 90 days maintained her placement, for the same reasons. Each time, DiMarco had to sign a document avowing her understanding of the prison's decision; the "document explained, 'Inmate DiMarco based on medical testing has been determined to be a male and therefore requires housing from other inmates.'"

DiMarco's treatment in Pod 3 differed in numerous respects from that of the general inmate population there, beyond the physical aspects of her pod. Although her clothes were washed daily, she had two sets instead of five. With no table or chair in her cell, she had to sit on her bed or toilet to eat meals alone. She could only use the prison gym when it was unused by any other inmates. She "was not allowed day-to-day contact with the other inmates. Nor did she have access to some of the educational programs that would have put her in contact with other inmates." Indeed, she "was not allowed routine contact with other inmates. . . ."

After her release, DiMarco sued in federal court for money damages for alleged excessive punishment in violation of her Eighth Amendment right against cruel and unusual punishment, violation of her equal protection rights, and violations of her procedural and substantive due process rights. Following a bench trial the district court rejected the Eighth Amendment claim because she received "the basic necessities of food, shelter, clothing, and medical treatment" and because legitimate " institutional safety concerns created by '[p]lacing an inmate of the opposite gender in a facility like the WWC . . . mandated separate housing.'" It rejected DiMarco's equal protection claim under rational basis review because it believed both that "'individuals born with ambiguous gender' are not members of a quasi-suspect or constitutionally protected class" and that DiMarco's placement separate from the general inmate population "was rationally related to the legitimate purposes of ensuring the safety of Plaintiff and other inmates and security of the facility." The district court agreed with DiMarco that her confinement conditions departed sufficiently from the ordinary and that due process required she be provided with more procedure than she received. The defendants appealed the due process holding, but DiMarco did not appeal the Eighth Amendment and equal protection rulings, which therefore became final.

The Tenth Circuit Court of Appeals reversed in an opinion by Judge Timothy Tymkovich, who as Colorado's Solicitor General had previously, unsuccessfully defended the state's virulently anti-LGB state constitutional Amendment 2, which was held unconstitutional by the Supreme Court in *Romer v. Evans*, 517 U.S. 620 (1996); Tymkovich was appointed to the Court of Appeals by George W. Bush in 2001. In the view of the court of appeals, "[n]either the Due Process Clause itself nor the policies or regulations of the State of Wyoming allow DiMarco to challenge Wyoming's placement decision and conditions of confinement."

"[M]indful of the primary management role of prison officials who should be free from second-guessing or micro-management from the federal courts," the court thought the analysis should consider key factors without treating any as dispositive. "Relevant factors might include whether (1) the segregation relates to and furthers a legitimate penological interest, such as safety or rehabilitation; (2) the conditions of placement are extreme; (3) the placement increases the duration of confinement . . . ; and (4) the placement is indeterminate. . . ." In considering these factors, the court believed it helpful to keep in mind that DiMarco was an admittedly unique prisoner, with a physiological and psychological condition never before encountered by Wyoming prison officials. No one suggests the initial segregation for evaluative purposes was inappropriate or excessive. Prison officials consulted medical professionals in evaluating DiMarco's condition and relied, in part, on those opinions in their placement decision. DiMarco had access to prison staff and doctors throughout her confinement. Her placement was evaluated every ninety days, and she was given an opportunity to be heard at each evaluation. While her confinement was isolating, it provided the ordinary essentials of prison life. Finally, the prison had to consider the needs of the general prison population, including rehabilitative goals and programs designed for them. Perhaps most importantly, DiMarco does not contend that segregation itself was unreasonable.

The court then credited the security risks about which the prison asserted it was concerned. The court reasoned

> that DiMarco might be a risk if introduced to the general population of the prison. Many of the women confined in the prison were victims of sexual assault. Some might be fearful of DiMarco, even though she functioned as a woman; others might threaten DiMarco for different reasons.

It also thought the cost of transferring DiMarco to another state with adequate facilities for "transsexual inmates" was a legitimate concern, and that placing her in "Wyoming's men's prison was not a plausible alternative." It judged the conditions of her confinement "not atypical of protective custody," though the court acknowledged that "it is hard to believe the prison could not make better accommodations for her long-term placement. Many of her complaints about living conditions were commonplace and the petty denial of certain amenities borders on the absurd." Her segregated confinement did not extend her period of incarceration, and her placement was reviewed every 90 days.

The court therefore concluded that the prison did not "impose[] such an atypical and significant hardship on her" that it would give rise to a protected liberty interest necessary to trigger the protections of the Due Process Clause. And, reasoning in the alternative, the court ruled that it would reject DiMarco's due process claim even if it did find a protected liberty interest because "Wyoming provided adequate procedural protections to justify its placement decisions" under *Wilkinson v. Austin*, 545 U.S. 209 (2005), since it "allowed (1) a sufficient initial level of process, *i.e.*, a reasoned examination of the assignment; (2) [afforded] the opportunity for the inmate to receive notice and respond to the decision; and (3) safety and security concerns [were] weighed as part of the placement decision." Under the totality of the circumstances, it ruled, the defendants satisfied due process.

Note on Crosby v. Reynolds

In *Crosby v. Reynolds*, 763 F. Supp. 666 (D. Me. 1991), the district court addressed a damages suit by Juanita Crosby, a woman held before her federal trial at a county jail, who sued correctional officers for placing transgender woman Cheyenne Lamson in the same cell block as Crosby on two occasions in 1989, once for five days and once for 16 days. Crosby argued that this violated her constitutional right to privacy. (She also included a claim that a guard allegedly threatened to place her in solitary confinement if she continued to complain about Lamson. The district court held that Crosby failed to show how this violated her right to procedural due process.)

The court acknowledged that the U.S. Supreme Court and the First Circuit Court of Appeals recognized a constitutional right of privacy; it cited the reproductive autonomy cases *Roe v. Wade*, 410 U.S. 113 (1973) (invalidating criminal abortion ban), and *Griswold v. Connecticut*, 381 U.S. 479 (1965) (invalidating ban on use of contraception as applied to married couples), as well as a court of appeals decision rejecting a claim that a school board violated a principal's right to privacy by requiring him to submit to a psychiatric evaluation, *Daury v. Smith*, 842 F.3d 9 (1st Cir. 1988). And, in particular, it noted that "[o]ne Circuit has recognized that pretrial detainees have 'a general right, constitutionally protected, not to be subjected by state action to involuntary exposure in a state of nakedness to members of the opposite sex unless that exposure was reasonably necessary in maintaining her otherwise legal detention.'" (quoting *Fisher v. Washington Metropolitan Area Transit Authority*, 690 F.2d 1133 (4th Cir. 1982)). On the other hand, *Crosby* observed, "[a]nother Circuit [had] declared that such a right must give way to the needs of equal opportunity in hiring prison guards." (citing *Timm v. Gunter*, 917 F.2d 1093 (8th Cir. 1990)). Moreover, the *Crosby* court "found no decision setting forth the privacy rights of prisoners vis-a-vis other prisoners who are transsexual." As a result, and on the facts of this case—where "Lamson did not want to be segregated; it was physically and psychologically unsafe to place Lamson with males; and, as it turned out, some female inmates such as the plaintiff objected to Lamson being housed with them"—the district court "conclude[d] that the contours of that right [to privacy were] not clear when it comes to the determination of where to house transsexuals." Accordingly, the court granted the defendants qualified immunity, which shields individuals from money damages awards against them when the law they violated or were alleged to violate was not clearly established at the time, and hence the court granted the defendants' motion for summary judgment.

Chapter 13

Student Rights Under Title IX and Other Laws

LGBTQ students, particularly those who are transgender, often have negative experiences at school. These experiences are documented in the U.S. Transgender Survey (or "USTS") and indicate widespread problems. It found that more than three-quarters (77%) of the survey respondents "who were out or perceived as transgender while in school (K-12)" endured "some form of negative treatment," "including being verbally harassed (54%), physically attacked (24%), and sexually assaulted (13%) because they were transgender. Further, 17% experienced such severe mistreatment that they left a school as a result." Sandy E. James et al., National Center for Transgender Equality, The Report of the 2015 U.S. Transgender Survey 4, 131 (2016). As is often true, many transgender people of color were especially vulnerable; USTS found that American Indian, Middle Eastern, and multiracial respondents reported even higher rates of negative experiences at school. *Id.* at 132.

A number of school districts and some states around the country, including major school districts, have adopted policies to respect and protect trans students. *See, e.g.,* Cal. Ed. Code § 220 (barring discrimination based on gender, gender identity, and gender expression); Cal. Ed. Code § 221.5 (allowing students to participate in or use sex-segregated school programs, activities, and facilities in accordance with their gender identity); Los Angeles Unified School District Policy Bulletin, BUL 6224.2, Gender Identity and Students, Ensuring Equity and Nondiscrimination (May 17, 2019), https://achieve.lausd.net/cms/lib/CA01000043/Centricity/Domain /383/BUL-6224.2%20Transgender%20Policy%205%2013%2019.pdf ("best practices relating to recognition of each student's gender identity consistent with goals of reducing stigmatization and ensuring access for students"); Denver School District, Denver Public Schools Board of Education Policies, Section A: Foundations and Basic Commitments, Nondiscrimination/Equal Opportunity, http://go.boarddocs .com/co/dpsk12/Board.nsf/goto?open&id=AZRUZE72DEC0 (barring discrimination and setting goal of providing safe learning and working environment regardless of gender identity or transgender status); Conn. Gen. Stat. § 10-15c (barring discrimination based on gender identity in public schools); D.C. Code § 2.1402.21 (barring discrimination in educational institutions based on gender identity or expression); Iowa Code § 216.9 (barring discrimination based on gender identity in educational institutions); 5 Maine Rev. Stat. § 4601 (right to freedom from discrimination based on sexual orientation, defined as including actual or perceived gender identity or expression, in education and at educational institutions); Minn. Stat. § 363A.13 (barring discrimination in the full utilization of or benefit from any educational institution based on sexual orientation defined to include having or being perceived as having a self-image or identity not traditionally associated with one's biological maleness or femaleness);[a] N.J.A.C. § 6A:7-1.1 (declaring statutory purpose to ensure equal access to educational programs and services to students regardless of gender identity or expression); O.R.S. § 659.850 (prohibiting "any act that unreasonably differentiates treatment, intended or unintended, or any act that is fair in form but discriminatory in operation," on basis of sexual orientation defined to include "gender identity, regardless of whether the individual's gender identity, appearance, expression or behavior differs from that traditionally associated with the individual's sex at birth," but exempting enforcement of otherwise-valid dress codes provided that the school accommodates student health and safety on a case-by-case basis); Rev. Code Wash. § 28A.642.010 (barring discrimination based on sexual orientation, defined to include gender expression or identity, in public schools).

But even the presence of good laws on the books is not sufficient to ensure that the daily experience of trans youth in schools is positive. California had prohibitions on sexual orientation and gender identity discrimination in schools, *see* discussion of A.B. 1266, *infra* at p. 834, but LGBTQ students still experienced bullying and harassment. In 2019, the state passed A.B. 493, The Safe and Supportive Schools Act of 2019. Sponsored by Equality California, the law requires the state's education department to develop and/or update resources for public and charter schools teaching students grades 7–12 that can be used for training teachers and staff to "increase support for LGBTQ pupils and thereby improve overall school climate." Cal. Educ. Code tit. I, div. 1, pt. 1, ch. 2, art. 2.7, § 218. And to help encourage schools to adopt best practices under this act, the Equality California Institute has created the Safe and Supportive Schools Survey and, based on the survey results, the Safe and Supportive Schools Report Card to "shine[] a light on some of the successes and challenges that California unified school districts said they are experiencing when implementing LGBTQ-inclusive programs and policies." *See* Equality California Institute, *Safe and Supportive Schools Report Card*, https://safesupportiveschools .org (last visited Mar. 4, 2020). (One of this book's authors was on the Equality California Institute board when organizational decisions were made to pursue the Safe and Supportive Schools Act, Survey, and Report Card.)

The materials in this chapter mostly focus on primary and secondary schooling. For a brief treatment of issues regarding transgender and gender nonconforming

---

a. Note, though, that the Minnesota Supreme Court has interpreted that statutory language not to forbid excluding transgender workers from restrooms consistent with their gender identity if they have not had genital reconstruction surgery. *See Goins v. West Group*, 635 N.W.2d 717 (Minn. 2001).

people in higher education, where the authors argue that "the campus climates and institutional processes of colleges and universities must be radically changed if higher education is to be truly inclusive of gender-nonconforming students," see GENNY BEEMYN & SUSAN RANKIN, THE LIVES OF TRANSGENDER PEOPLE, chapter 5 (2011).

Reading Guide for Doe v. Yunits I

1. Note that the court refers to First Amendment "expressive speech" doctrine. That nomenclature is idiosyncratic. The predominant name is "expressive conduct" doctrine.

2. Why does the court conclude in Part II of its opinion that transgender girl Pat Doe's wearing certain specified conventionally feminine attire to school was expressive conduct potentially protected by (the Massachusetts state constitutional counterparts to) the First Amendment? Does that conclusion seem correct? Why does the court conclude that the school's policy forbidding Doe to wear such clothing was directed at her expression? Why does the court conclude that the school's policy is not a "content-neutral" regulation of conduct, which would be subject to a more deferential form of judicial review? Why does the court reject the defendants' argument that they were merely trying to prevent disruptive conduct by Doe?

3. In Part II.C of its opinion, the court addresses Doe's arguments that the state constitution's substantive protection of her liberty through the state's Due Process Clause is violated by the school's policy. What is the court's reasoning on that issue?

4. In Part II.D. of its opinion, the court addresses Doe's arguments that the school was unlawfully discriminating on the basis of sex. How had the school tried to defend its policy, and what does the court conclude is the proper question to answer in order to determine whether the school was discriminating on the basis of sex? Why does the court adopt that framing of the question? How does the court in a footnote distinguish the *Harper v. Edgewood Bd. of Education* decision (which, because it was issued by a federal trial court, would at most be persuasive precedent)? How, if at all, is that relevant to the sex discrimination claims the *Doe* court is analyzing at that point in the opinion? In a different footnote, the court distinguishes *LaFleur v. Bird-Johnson Co.* as involving discrimination against a "transvestite" as opposed to discrimination between biological males and females regarding what clothes they may wear; is this distinction coherent?

5. In Part II.E of its opinion, the court concludes that Doe is not likely to succeed on her state constitutional disability discrimination claim. Why does it so rule?

6. What irreparable harms does the court conclude Doe faces? Why does it conclude that the balance of the equities favors Doe and that the public interest would not be harmed by granting her relief?

Pat Doe v. John Yunits, et al. (Doe v. Yunits I)

No. 00-1060-A, 2000 WL 33162199 (Mass. Super. Ct. Oct. 11),
aff'd sub nom. Doe v. Brockton Sch. Comm., 2000 WL 33342399
(Mass. App. Ct. Nov. 30, 2000)

[Pat Doe was represented by GLAD, at the time acronymic for Gay & Lesbian Advocates & Defenders, now GLBTQ Legal Advocates & Defenders.]

Memorandum of Decision and Order on Plaintiff's Motion for Preliminary Injunction

Linda Giles, J.

Plaintiff Pat Doe ("plaintiff"), a fifteen-year-old student, has brought this action by her[4] next friend, Jane Doe, [plaintiff's grandmother and guardian,] requesting that this court prohibit defendants from excluding the plaintiff from South Junior High School, Brockton, Massachusetts, on the basis of the plaintiff's sex, disability, or gender identity and expression. . . . After a hearing, and for the reasons stated below, plaintiff's motion for preliminary injunction is ALLOWED.

Background

Plaintiff began attending South Junior High, a Brockton public school, in September 1998, as a 7th grader. In early 1999, plaintiff first began to express her female gender identity by wearing girls' make-up, shirts, and fashion accessories to school. South Junior High has a dress code which prohibits, among other things, "clothing which could be disruptive or distractive to the educational process or which could affect the safety of students." In early 1999, the principal, Kenneth Cardone, would often send the plaintiff home to change if she arrived at school wearing girls' apparel. On some occasions, plaintiff would change and return to school; other times, she would remain home, too upset to return. In June 1999, after being referred to a therapist by the South Junior High, plaintiff was diagnosed with gender identity disorder. Plaintiff's treating therapist . . . determined that it was medically and clinically necessary for plaintiff to wear clothing consistent with the female gender and that failure to do so could cause harm to plaintiff's mental health.

Plaintiff returned to school in September 1999, as an 8th grader, and was instructed by Cardone to come to his office every day so that he could approve the plaintiff's appearance. Some days the plaintiff would be sent home to change, sometimes returning to school dressed differently and sometimes remaining home. During the 1999–2000 school year, plaintiff stopped attending school, citing the hostile environment created by Cardone. Because of plaintiff's many absences during the 1999–2000 school year, plaintiff was required to repeat the 8th grade this year.

Over the course of the 1998–1999 and 1999–2000 school years, plaintiff sometimes arrived at school wearing such items as skirts and dresses, wigs, high-heeled

---

4. This court will use female pronouns to refer to plaintiff: a practice which is consistent with the plaintiff's gender identity and which is common among mental health and other professionals who work with transgender clients. [Relocated footnote. — Eds.]

shoes, and padded bras with tight shirts. The school faculty and administration became concerned because the plaintiff was experiencing trouble with some of her classmates. Defendants cite one occasion when the school adjustment counselor had to restrain a male student because he was threatening to punch the plaintiff for allegedly spreading rumors that the two had engaged in oral sex. Defendants also point to an instance when a school official had to break up a confrontation between the plaintiff and a male student to whom plaintiff persistently blew kisses. At another time, plaintiff grabbed the buttock of a male student in the school cafeteria. Plaintiff also has been known to primp, pose, apply make up, and flirt with other students in class. Defendants also advance that the plaintiff sometimes called attention to herself by yelling and dancing in the halls. Plaintiff has been suspended at least three times for using the ladies' restroom after being warned not to.

On Friday, September 1, 2000, Cardone and Dr. Kenneth Sennett, Senior Director for Pupil Personnel Services, met with the plaintiff relative to repeating the 8th grade. At that meeting, Cardone and Sennett informed the plaintiff that she would not be allowed to attend South Junior High if she were to wear any outfits disruptive to the educational process, specifically padded bras, skirts or dresses, or wigs. On September 21, 2000, plaintiff's grandmother tried to enroll plaintiff in school and was told by Cardone and Sennett that plaintiff would not be permitted to enroll if she wore any girls' clothing or accessories. . . . Plaintiff is not currently attending school, but the school has provided a home tutor for her to allow her to keep pace with her classmates.

On September 26, 2000, the plaintiff filed a complaint in this court claiming a denial of her right to freedom of expression in the public schools in violation of [Massachusetts General Laws] G.L.ch.71, § 82; a denial of her right to personal dress and appearance in violation of G.L. ch.76, § 83; a denial of her right to attend school in violation of G.L. ch.76, § 5; a denial of her right to be free from sex discrimination guaranteed by Articles I and XIV of the Declaration of Rights of the Massachusetts Constitution; a denial of her right to be free from disability discrimination guaranteed by Article CXIV of the said Declaration of Rights; a denial of her due process rights as guaranteed by G.L. ch.71, § 37 and G.L. ch.76, § 17; a denial of her liberty interest in her appearance as guaranteed by the Massachusetts Declaration of Rights, Art. I and X; and a violation of her right to free expression as guaranteed by the said Declaration of Rights, Art. I and X.

Discussion

I. Introduction

In evaluating a request for a preliminary injunction, the court must examine "in combination the moving party's claim of injury and chance of success on the merits." *Packing Industries Group, Inc. v. Cheney,* 380 Mass. 609 (1980). "If the judge is convinced that failure to issue the injunction would subject the moving party to a substantial risk of irreparable harm, the judge must then balance this risk against any similar risk of irreparable harm which granting the injunction would create for the opposing party . . . Only where the balance between these risks cuts in favor of the moving party may a preliminary injunction properly issue." *GTE Products Corp. v. Stewart,* 414 Mass. 721 (1993). In addition, where the injunction is sought against a public entity, as it is here, the court must consider the risk of injury to the public interest which would flow from the grant of the injunction. *Brookline v. Goldstein,* 388 Mass. 443 (1983).

II. The Likelihood of Plaintiff's Success on the Merits

Plaintiff's complaint asserts eight causes of action based on the Massachusetts Declaration of Rights and the General Laws. . . .

A. Freedom of Expression, Massachusetts Declaration of Rights, Art. II and X

The Massachusetts Declaration of Rights, Article XVI . . . provides, "[t]he right of free speech shall not be abridged." The analysis of this article is guided by federal free speech analysis. *See Hosford v. School Committee of Sandwich,* 421 Mass. 708 (1996). According to federal analysis, this court must first determine whether the plaintiff's symbolic acts constitute expressive speech which is protected, in this case, by Article VXI of the Massachusetts Declaration of Rights. *See Texas v. Johnson,* 491 U.S. 397 (1989), citing *Spence v. Washington,* 418 U.S. 405 (1974) (per curiam). If the speech is expressive, the court must next determine if the defendants' conduct was impermissible because it was meant to suppress that speech. *See Johnson,* citing *United States v. O'Brien,* 391 U.S. 367 (1968); *see also Spence.* If the defendants' conduct is not related to the suppression of speech, furthers an important or substantial governmental interest, and is within the constitutional powers of the government, and if the incidental restriction on speech is no greater than necessary, the government's conduct is permissible. *See O'Brien.* In addition, because this case involves public school students, suppression of speech that "materially and substantially interferes with the work of the school" is permissible. *See Tinker v. Des Moines Community School Dist.,* 393 U.S. 503 (1969).

1. The Plaintiff's Conduct is Expressive Speech Which is Understood by Those Perceiving it

Symbolic acts constitute expression if the actor's intent to convey a particularized message is likely to be understood by those perceiving the message. *See Spence* (finding that an upside-down flag with a peace symbol attached was protected speech because it was a purposeful message people could understand); *see also Chalifoux v. New Caney Independent School Dist.,* 976 F. Supp. 659 (S.D. Tex. 1997) (students wearing rosary beads as a sign of their religious belief was likely to be understood by others and therefore protected).

Plaintiff in this case is likely to establish that, by dressing in clothing and accessories traditionally associated with the female gender, she is expressing her identification with that gender. In addition, plaintiff's ability to express herself and her gender identity through dress is important to her health and well-being, as attested to by her treating therapist. Therefore, plaintiff's expression is not merely a personal preference but a necessary symbol of her very identity. Contrast *Olesen v. Board of*

Education of School District No. 228, 676 F. Supp. 820 (N.D. Ill. 1987) (school's anti-gang policy of prohibiting males from wearing earrings, passed for safety reasons, was upheld because plaintiff's desire to wear an earring as an expression of his individuality and attractiveness to girls was a message not within the scope of the First Amendment).

This court must next determine if the plaintiff's message was understood by those perceiving it, *i.e.,* the school faculty and plaintiff's fellow students. *See Bivens v. Albuquerque Public Schools,* 899 F. Supp. 556 (D.N.M. 1995) (student failed to provide evidence that his wearing of sagging pants to express his identity as a black youth was understood by others and, therefore, such attire was not speech). In the case at bar, defendants contend that junior high school students are too young to understand plaintiff's expression of her female gender identity through dress and that "not every defiant act by a high school student is constitutionally protected speech." *Id.* However, unlike *Bivens,* here there is strong evidence that plaintiff's message is well understood by faculty and students. The school's vehement response and some students' hostile reactions are proof of the fact that the plaintiff's message clearly has been received. Moreover, plaintiff is likely to establish, through testimony, that her fellow students are well aware of the fact that she is a biological male more comfortable wearing traditionally "female"-type clothing because of her identification with that gender.

2. The Defendants' Conduct was a Suppression of the Plaintiff's Speech

Plaintiff also will probably prevail on the merits of the second prong of the *Texas v. Johnson* test, that is, the defendants' conduct was meant to suppress plaintiff's speech. Defendants in this case have prohibited the plaintiff from wearing items of clothing that are traditionally labeled girls' clothing, such as dresses and skirts, padded bras, and wigs. This constitutes direct suppression of speech because biological females who wear items such as tight skirts to school are unlikely to be disciplined by school officials, as admitted by defendants' counsel at oral argument. Therefore, the test set out in [*O'Brien*], which permits restrictions on speech where the government motivation is not directly related to the content of the speech, cannot apply here. Further, defendants' argument that the school's policy is a content-neutral regulation of speech is without merit because, as has been discussed, the school is prohibiting the plaintiff from wearing clothes a biological female would be allowed to wear. Therefore, the plaintiff has a likelihood of fulfilling the *Texas v. Johnson* test that her speech conveyed a particularized message understood by others and that the defendants' conduct was meant to suppress that speech.

3. Plaintiff's Conduct is not Disruptive

This court also must consider if the plaintiff's speech "materially and substantially interferes with the work of the school." *Tinker.* Defendants argue that they are merely preventing disruptive conduct on the part of the plaintiff by restricting her attire at school. . . . Given the state of the record thus far, the plaintiff has demonstrated a likelihood of proving that defendants, rather than attempting to restrict plaintiff's wearing of distracting items of clothing, are seeking to ban her from donning apparel that can be labeled "girls' clothes" and to encourage more conventional, male-oriented attire. Defendants argue that any other student who came to school dressed in distracting clothing would be disciplined as the plaintiff was. However, defendants overlook the fact that, if a female student came to school in a frilly dress or blouse, make-up, or padded bra, she would go, and presumably has gone, unnoticed by school officials. Defendants do not find plaintiff's clothing distracting *per se*, but, essentially, distracting simply because plaintiff is a biological male.

In addition to the expression of her female gender identity through dress, however, plaintiff has engaged in behavior in class and towards other students that can be seen as detrimental to the learning process. This deportment, however, is separate from plaintiff's dress. Defendants vaguely cite instances when the principal became aware of threats by students to beat up the "boy who dressed like a girl" to support the notion that plaintiff's dress alone is disruptive. To rule in defendants' favor in this regard, however, would grant those contentious students a "heckler's veto." *See Fricke v. Lynch,* 491 F. Supp. 381, 387 (D.R.I. 1980). The majority of defendants' evidence of plaintiff's disruption is based on plaintiff's actions as distinct from her mode of dress. Some of these acts may be a further expression of gender identity, such as applying make-up in class; but many are instances of misconduct for which any student would be punished. Regardless of plaintiff's gender identity, any student should be punished for engaging in harassing behavior towards classmates. Plaintiff is not immune from such punishment but, by the same token, should not be punished on the basis of dress alone.

Plaintiff has framed this issue narrowly as a question of whether or not it is appropriate for defendants to restrict the manner in which she can dress. Defendants, on the other hand, appear unable to distinguish between instances of conduct connected to plaintiff's expression of her female gender identity, such as the wearing of a wig or padded bra, and separate from it, such as grabbing a male student's buttocks or blowing kisses to a male student. The line between expression and flagrant behavior can blur, thereby rendering this case difficult for the court. It seems, however, that expression of gender identity through dress can be divorced from conduct in school that warrants punishment, regardless of the gender or gender identity of the offender. Therefore, a school should not be allowed to bar or discipline a student because of gender-identified dress but should be permitted to ban clothing that would be inappropriate if worn by any student, such as a theatrical costume, and to punish conduct that would be deemed offensive if committed by any student, such as harassing, threatening, or obscene behavior. *See Bethel v. Fraser,* 478 U.S. 675 (1986).

B. G.L. ch. 71, §82

[The court concludes that the alleged limitation of this statute to secondary schools when South Junior High was a primary school is practically immaterial in light of its constitutional free expression analysis above.]

C. Liberty Interest in Appearance Massachusetts Declaration of Rights Article I and X

Plaintiff is also likely to prevail in this claim. A liberty interest under the First Amendment has been recognized to protect a male student's right to wear his hair as he wishes. *See Richards v. Thurston*, 424 F.2d 1281 (1st Cir. 1970), cited with approval *Bd. of Selectmen of Framingham v. Civil Service Commission*, 366 Mass. 547 (1974). The question in liberty interest cases is whether the government's interest in restricting liberty is strong enough to overcome that liberty interest. Given that plaintiff has a likelihood of success in proving that her attire is not distracting, as discussed above, she is likely to prove that defendants' interests do not overcome the recognized liberty interest in appearance.

D. Sex Discrimination G.L. ch.76, § 5 and Article I and XIV of the Massachusetts Declaration of Rights

G.L. ch.76, § 5 states that "Every person shall have the right to attend the public schools of the town where he actually resides . . . No person shall be excluded from or discriminated against in admission to a public school of any town, or in obtaining the advantages, privileges and course of study of such public school on account of race, color, sex, religion, national origin or sexual orientation." G.L. ch.76, § 5 (2000). Federal cases have recognized the impropriety of discriminating against a person for failure to conform with the norms of their biological gender. See *Price Waterhouse v. Hopkins*, 490 U.S. 228 (1989) (sex stereotyping occurred when members of an accounting firm denied female associate promotion because she failed to walk, talk, and dress femininely); *Rosa v. Park West Bank*, 214 F.3d 213 (1st Cir. 2000) (claim of sex discrimination may be sustained when cross-dressing man was denied a loan application until he went home to change clothes). This court finds plaintiff's reliance on such cases persuasive and the cases cited by defendants distinguishable, as discussed below.

Plaintiff contends that defendants' action[s] constitute sex discrimination because defendants prevented plaintiff from attending school in clothing associated with the female gender solely because plaintiff is male. Defendants counter that, since a female student would be disciplined for wearing distracting items of men's clothing, such as a fake beard, the dress code is gender-neutral. Defendants' argument does not frame the issue properly. Since plaintiff identifies with the female gender, the right question is whether a female student would be disciplined for wearing items of clothes plaintiff chooses to wear. If the answer to that question is no, plaintiff is being discriminated against on the basis of her sex, which is biologically male.[5] Therefore, defendants' reliance on cases holding that discrimination

---

5. This case is distinguishable from *Harper v. Edgewood Bd. of Education*, 655 F. Supp. 1353 (S.D. Ohio 1987). In *Harper*, the court granted summary judgment in favor of the defendants, who prevented two students dressed in clothing of the opposite gender from attending the prom against a claim that the plaintiffs' First Amendment rights were violated. The court found the school's action permissible because it fostered community values and maintained discipline. Plaintiff in

on the basis of sexual orientation, transsexualism, and transvestism are not controlling in this case because plaintiff is being discriminated against because of her gender. *See Ulane v. Eastern Airlines*, 742 F.2d 1081 (7th Cir. 1984). Furthermore, such cases have been criticized and distinguished under both Title VII and the First and Fourteenth Amendments.[6] *See Quinn v. Nassau County Police Dept.*, 53 F. Supp. 2d 347 (E.D.N.Y. 1999); *Blozis v. Mike Raisor Ford, Inc.*, 896 F. Supp. 805 (N.D. Ind. 1995); *Schwenk v. Hartford*, 204 F.3d 1187 (9th Cir. 2000).

In support of their argument, defendants cite cases in which gender-specific school dress codes have been upheld in the face of challenges based on gender discrimination and equal protection because the codes serve important governmental interests, such as fostering conformity with community standards. . . . Such cases are not binding on this court. This court cannot allow the stifling of plaintiff's selfhood merely because it causes some members of the community discomfort. "Our constitution . . . neither knows nor tolerates classes among citizens." *Plessy v. Ferguson,* 163 U.S. 537 (1896) (dissenting opinion of Harlan, J.). Thus, plaintiff in this case is likely to establish that the dress code of South Junior High, even though it is gender-neutral, is being applied to her in a gender discriminatory manner.

E. Disability Discrimination Article CXIV of the Massachusetts Declaration of Rights

Plaintiff does not have a likelihood of success in proving that the defendants' conduct constituted disability discrimination. Analysis of federal discrimination law is instructive in construing state disability discrimination law. *See Cox v. New England Tel. & Tel. Co.*, 414 Mass. 375 (1993). The federal Americans with Disabilities Act expressly excludes "transvestism, transsexualism . . . [and] gender identity disorders not resulting from physical impairments . . ." While noting that the courts of this state can, and often do, provide more protection than its federal counterpart, there is no authority to support the notion that Gender Identity Disorder is a protected disability under the Massachusetts Declaration of Rights of [*sic*] laws of this state.

---

this case, however, is not merely engaging in rebellious acts to demonstrate a willingness to violate community norms; plaintiff is expressing her personal identity, which cannot be suppressed by the school merely because it departs from community standards.

6. *LaFleur v. Bird-Johnson Co.,* 1994 W.L. 878831 (Mass. Super. Ct. Nov. 3, 1994), is also distinguishable. *LaFleur* was decided after *Price Waterhouse* but recognized the Supreme Judicial Court's holding in *Macauley v. MCAD,* 379 Mass. 279 (1979), that transsexual discrimination is not within the scope of this state's sexual discrimination law. However, the case at hand differs from *LaFleur,* where the plaintiff claimed she was discriminated against in the employment context because she was a transvestite, because the instant plaintiff is likely to establish that defendants have discriminated against her on the basis of sex by applying the dress code against her in a manner in which it would not be applied to female students.

F. Due Process G.L. ch.76, § 17

Plaintiff does not have a likelihood of success on the merits of this claim because, as defendants correctly point out, the plaintiff has not been expelled from school. Therefore, no process was due the plaintiff.

G. G.L. ch.71, § 83

Defendants again are correct in asserting that this section, which protects a student's right to personal dress, is a local option statute which applies only to jurisdictions that have chosen to adopt it. G.L. ch.71, § 86. Therefore, the plaintiff has not demonstrated a likelihood of success on the merits of this claim.

III. Irreparable Harm

The party seeking an injunction bears the burden of establishing irreparable harm, *i.e.*, that it may suffer a loss of rights that cannot be vindicated should it prevail after a full hearing on the merits. Plaintiff in this case has met the burden of establishing irreparable harm. The plaintiff is currently being home schooled because the defendants will not allow her to attend school in girls' attire. Therefore, plaintiff is being denied the benefits of attending school with her peers, learning in an interactive environment, and developing socially. Such harm is further exacerbated by the fact that the plaintiff has been the subject of much controversy over the past two years and now is noticeably absent from school. Defendants argue that any harm to the plaintiff is self-induced because plaintiff has chosen not to attend school under the conditions the defendants have put on her attire. This contention is without merit. Defendants are essentially prohibiting the plaintiff from expressing her gender identity and, thus, her quintessence, at school. Their actions have forced plaintiff to submit to home schooling. However, "in the field of public education the doctrine of 'separate but equal' has no place." *Brown v. Board of Education of Topeka*, 347 U.S. 483 (1954).

IV. The Balance of the Equities

The balance of the equities tips in favor of plaintiff in his case. The plaintiff attended South Junior High School for two academic years; and the school and its students, with the exception of new students entering this year, are accustomed to interacting with plaintiff and, thus, are capable of doing so again. Because the school is empowered to discipline plaintiff for conduct for which any other student would be disciplined, the harm to the school in readmitting plaintiff is minimal. On the other hand, if plaintiff is barred from school, the potential harm to plaintiff's sense of self-worth and social development is irreparable. Defendants cite cases that stand for the proposition that a school's interest in disciplining students by barring them from school outweigh the harm to the student. In this case, however, the school is not disciplining the plaintiff for certain conduct. The school is barring her from school on account of the expression of her very identity. Defendants maintain that plaintiff is free to enroll in school as long as she complies with the stated dress code. This is not entirely true because the defendants have placed specific restrictions on plaintiff's dress that may not be placed on other female students. This court does take note of the fact that defendants made efforts to accommodate the plaintiff's desire to dress in girl's clothes for over a year. However, their proscription of the items of clothing that can be worn by plaintiff is likely to be impermissible. Therefore, the harm to plaintiff by the actions of the defendants outweigh the harm to the defendants in granting this injunction.

V. The Harm to the Public Interest

Defendants have not made a showing that the granting of this injunction will harm the public interest. Although defendants contend that plaintiff's dress is disruptive to the learning process, the workings of the school will not be disrupted if they are permitted to discipline plaintiff according to normal procedures for truly disruptive attire and inappropriate behavior. Furthermore, this court trusts that exposing children to diversity at an early age serves the important social goals of increasing their ability to tolerate such differences and teaching them respect for everyone's unique personal experience in that "Brave New World" out there.

Order

For all the foregoing reasons, plaintiff's motion for preliminary injunction is ALLOWED; and it is hereby ORDERED THAT:

1. Defendants are preliminarily enjoined from preventing plaintiff from wearing any clothing or accessories that any other male or female student could wear to school without being disciplined.

2. Defendants are further preliminarily enjoined from disciplining plaintiff for any reason for which other students would not be disciplined.

3. If defendants do seek to discipline plaintiff in conformance with this order, they must do so according to the school's standing policies and procedures.

Discussion

1. In Part II.A.1 of its opinion, the court observes that "plaintiff's ability to express herself and her gender identity through dress is important to her health and well-being." Is this relevant to anything in First Amendment doctrine governing expressive conduct as detailed by the court? If not, why might the court have included this observation in its analysis?

2. In Part II.A.1, the court reasons that "[t]he school's vehement response and some students' hostile reactions are proof of the fact that the plaintiff's message clearly has been received." Might there be anything else that could account for the vehemence and hostility?

3. The court rejects the defendant's framing of the appropriate comparison for determining whether it was discriminating against Doe on the basis of sex. Is the court's framing of the issue the right way to analyze it? Does the logic of the court's

sex discrimination reasoning in Part II.D mean that a school must let boys wear anything it lets girls wear and let girls wear anything it lets boys wear, that is, that schools may not have sex-specific dress codes?

4. The court relies on *Plessy v. Ferguson*, 163 U.S. 537 (1896) (dissenting opinion of Harlan, J.), for the proposition that "[o]ur constitution . . . neither knows nor tolerates classes among citizens." How might late-nineteenth century Louisiana law requiring racial segregation in railroad service implicate "classes among citizens" in ways similar to or different from this early twenty-first century Massachusetts school's treatment of Pat Doe's permissible attire? The court also relies on *Brown v. Board of Education*, 347 U.S. 483 (1954), which repudiated *Plessy* at least in the context of public education. How much does *Brown* support the point that the trial court uses it to make?

5. What implications might reasonably be drawn from the fact that, unlike the federal Rehabilitation Act, Massachusetts disability law did not expressly exclude certain gender identity disorders from its ban on disability discrimination? Although Judge Giles found that Doe did not have a likelihood of success on her state constitutional disability discrimination claim, the case was subsequently reassigned to Judge Gants, who disagreed with Giles's analysis and rejected the defendants' motion to dismiss that claim. *See Doe v. Yunits II*, 2001 WL 664947 (Mass. Super. Ct. Feb. 26, 2001), Chapter 14, *infra* at p. 1011.

6. How might one argue that the court's reasoning about irreparable injury in Part III or about the balance of equities in Part IV means that only a transgender student wishing to challenge a sex-specific dress code or sex-specific dress code provision could secure injunctive relief? Or would a cisgender boy wishing to wear a skirt at Doe's school also be able to show irreparable injury?

7. Is the court substituting its policy judgment for the school's when it concludes that allowing Pat Doe to attend school wearing clothing other girls would wear would teach the students to respect diversity?

8. Mary Anne Case has noted that discussion of *Doe v. Yunits* is often paired with discussion of the case of Nikki Youngblood. Mary Anne Case, *Legal Protections for the "Personal Best" of Each Employee: Title VII's Prohibition on Sex Discrimination, the Legacy of* Price Waterhouse v. Hopkins, *and the Prospect of ENDA*, 66 Stan. L. Rev. 1333 (2014). As Professor Case explains:

> When having her yearbook photo taken, Youngblood objected to wearing the "velvet-like, ruffly, scoop neck drape" girls were required to wear and asked instead to pose in "a white shirt, tie, and dark jacket," as was required of boys. Her request was refused, her photo excluded from the yearbook, and she brought suit on the claim that her school had "created a discriminatory dress code policy . . . based on stereotypes of how they believe males and females should dress." Youngblood's complaint described her as someone who had long rejected "gender stereotypes," had not worn skirts since second grade, and would find it "emotionally damaging" to be forced to

wear "stereotypically feminine attire," but the only identity she claimed was "female." After briefing heavily featuring Title VII cases in which the school made an "equal burdens" defense, the district court dismissed Youngblood's complaint. In the course of an appeal to the Eleventh Circuit, the case settled, with an agreement providing that in the future "[s]tudents may request an exception to the dress code from the principal, who will grant the exception when good cause is shown." No specification, however, was made of what shall constitute "good cause." It is unsurprising, therefore, that a subsequent challenge to identical yearbook photo requirements in another Florida school noted the plaintiff was a lesbian and included a sexual orientation nondiscrimination provision in the resulting settlement.

For one pairing of *Yunits* and *Youngblood*, and an effort to provide litigation and non-litigation resouces for people seeking to help transgender students to express their gender identity, see Zenobia V. Harris, *Breaking the Dress Code: Protecting Transgender Students, Their Identities, and Their Rights*, 13 Scholar: St. Mary's Law Review on Minority Issues 149 (2010).

California Assembly Bill No. 1266

CHAPTER 85

An act to amend Section 221.5 of the Education Code, relating to pupil rights.

[Approved by Governor August 12, 2013. Filed with Secretary of State August 12, 2013.]

Legislative Counsel's Digest

AB 1266, Ammiano. Pupil rights: sex-segregated school programs and activities.

Existing law prohibits public schools from discriminating on the basis of specified characteristics, including gender, gender identity, and gender expression, and specifies various statements of legislative intent and the policies of the state in that regard. Existing law requires that participation in a particular physical education activity or sport, if required of pupils of one sex, be available to pupils of each sex.

This bill would require that a pupil be permitted to participate in sex-segregated school programs and activities, including athletic teams and competitions, and use facilities consistent with his or her gender identity, irrespective of the gender listed on the pupil's records.

The people of the State of California do enact as follows:

SECTION 1. Section 221.5 of the Education Code is amended to read:

221.5. (a) It is the policy of the state that elementary and secondary school classes and courses, including nonacademic and elective classes and courses, be conducted, without regard to the sex of the pupil enrolled in these classes and courses.

(b) A school district may not prohibit a pupil from enrolling in any class or course on the basis of the sex of the pupil, except a class subject to Chapter 5.6 (commencing with Section 51930) of Part 28 of Division 4 of Title 2.

(c) A school district may not require a pupil of one sex to enroll in a particular class or course, unless the same class or course is also required of a pupil of the opposite sex.

(d) A school counselor, teacher, instructor, administrator, or aide may not, on the basis of the sex of a pupil, offer vocational or school program guidance to a pupil of one sex that is different from that offered to a pupil of the opposite sex or, in counseling a pupil, differentiate career, vocational, or higher education opportunities on the basis of the sex of the pupil counseled. Any school personnel acting in a career counseling or course selection capacity to a pupil shall affirmatively explore with the pupil the possibility of careers, or courses leading to careers, that are nontraditional for that pupil's sex. The parents or legal guardian of the pupil shall be notified in a general manner at least once in the manner prescribed by Section 48980, in advance of career counseling and course selection commencing with course selection for grade 7 so that they may participate in the counseling sessions and decisions.

(e) Participation in a particular physical education activity or sport, if required of pupils of one sex, shall be available to pupils of each sex.

(f) A pupil shall be permitted to participate in sex-segregated school programs and activities, including athletic teams and competitions, and use facilities consistent with his or her gender identity, irrespective of the gender listed on the pupil's records.

———————

Discussion

Although the (quite large) Los Angeles Unified School District and others in the state already had similar policies, A.B. 1266 attracted more controversy, perhaps because it was adopted through legislation, rather than by administrative procedures, and applied statewide. Despite the controversy, it readily passed the legislature and was signed by the California governor. Opponents of A.B. 1266 sought to gather enough signatures for a referendum petition to ask the voters of California to repeal the law. Their initial effort failed to qualify for the ballot, but nothing in state law would procedurally bar a future effort to eliminate the protections afforded by A.B. 1266. Below are excerpts from a web page created by proponents of the proposed referendum.

Privacy for All Students, Frequently Asked Questions about the A.B. 1266 Referendum[*]

Wednesday, September 11th, 2013 @ 9:33AM

What is AB 1266?

. . . . The legislation creates the right of elementary and secondary school students to use sensitive sex-segregated school facilities such as showers, restrooms and locker rooms based on the student's perceived gender identity rather than their actual sex. . . .

What are the problems with AB 1266?

. . . . First, it's an invasion of student privacy to open sensitive school facilities such as showers, restrooms and locker rooms to students of the opposite sex. Further, the legislation is poorly drafted and flawed, a one-size-fits-all approach that contains no standards, guidelines or rules. The law does not require that a student have ever demonstrated any indication that he she or considers himself or herself as transgendered. A student can assert a gender identity at school at any time. Because gender identity is based on feelings and perceptions, he or she can be both transgender and heterosexual at the same time. Because of the lack of requirements, some teens and young adults will undoubtedly game the law. Additionally, the law contains no provisions to balance the interests of all students, including those who are transgender. Finally, it is so poorly conceived and drafted that it may result in harming those it intends to help. For example, it contains no provisions for parental involvement to help design an approach to accommodate the specific needs of a transgender student, and it may jeopardize existing local programs that provide less invasive approaches, such as access to single-stall gender-neutral restrooms, private changing areas, and use of faculty restroom facilities.

. . . .

Who is Privacy for All Students coalition? Do you have the expertise to successfully mount a referendum campaign?

The Privacy For All Students coalition is a group of advocacy, nonprofit and religious and civic groups, along with parents, students and educators who are concerned about the many problems . . . that will be created if AB 1266 is allowed to become law. . . .

The coalition is being advised by Frank Schubert who has twice been named the country's top political consultant. Mr. Schubert is a referendum and ballot initiative expert and has managed 14 California statewide referendum and ballot initiative campaigns, winning 13 of those contests.

. . . .

---

[*] On file with authors. Formerly available at http://privacyforallstudents.com/frequently-asked-questions-about-the-ab-1266-referendum. Copyright © 2013 Privacy for all Students.

Paid for by Privacy for all Students, [CA address omitted].

Discussion

1. Privacy for All Students (PFAS) contrasts a "student's perceived gender identity" with "their actual sex." They do not define either term in their FAQ. What might each mean here?

2. What does PFAS's privacy argument presuppose? What is their argument about what they take to be the nature of gender identity? (What in particular are they getting at when they seemingly lament that a student "can be both transgender and heterosexual at the same time"?)

3. Can you unpack PFAS's paternalistic argument speculating that A.B. 1266 could harm transgender students? How exactly would that happen?

4. Members of the PFAS coalition included the right-leaning legal advocacy organization Pacific Justice Institute; the self-professed "conservative political action" platform ActRight, founded and chaired by Brian Brown, co-founder, former Executive Director, and President of the anti-marriage equality group the National Organization for Marriage; and the California chapter of the right-wing, anti-feminist political organization Concerned Women for America. Their consultant, Frank Schubert, was described by liberal journalist and political commentator Michelangelo Signorile as follows:

> Schubert is the strategist who ran the campaign that convinced voters to pass Proposition 8 in California in 2008, using ads that, among other things, framed gay marriage as dangerous to children. He moved on from there to other states and helped in the campaign that got three judges who had ruled in favor of marriage equality removed from the Iowa Supreme court in retention elections in 2010. He successfully beat back marriage equality in Maine at the ballot box in 2009, and he got the marriage amendment passed in the brutal battle in North Carolina [in May 2011] . . . .

Michelangelo Signorile, *Anti-Gay Marriage Amendment Mastermind, Crumbles Under Questioning (AUDIO)*, The Blog, HuffPost (Oct. 19, 2012, updated Dec. 6, 2017), https://www.huffpost.com/entry/frank-schubert-anti-gay-marriage-amendment_b_1980260.

5. For two notes arguing against the propriety of A.B. 1266, see Tyler Brown, *The Dangers of Overbroad Transgender Legislation, Case Law, and Policy in Education: California's AB 1266 Dismisses Concerns About Student Safety and Privacy*, 2014 B.Y.U. Educ. & L.J. 287 (2014), and Emeline Garcia, *AB 1266: The School Success and Opportunity Act or a Violation of the Constitutional Right to Privacy*, 35 U. La Verne L. Rev. 243 (2014). For generally contrary assessments, see, for example, Lara Awad, *Chapter 85: Providing Greater Protections of Transgender Students*, 45 McGeorge L. Rev. 473 (2014), and the unfortunately titled Rachel E. Moffitt, *Keeping the John*

Open to Jane: How California's Bathroom Bill Brings Transgender Rights Out of the Water Closet, 16 Geo. J. Gender & L. 475 (2015).

6. Other efforts to try to deny transgender people use of common restrooms consistent with their gender identity have been more successful. *See, e.g., Carcaño v. Cooper*, No. 1:16-cv-236 2019 WL 3302208 (M.D.N.C. July 23, 2019) (resolving by consent decree claims against state executive branch officials in challenge to "North Carolina's Public Facilities Privacy & Security Act, 2016 N.C. Sess. Laws 3, known as House Bill 2 ('HB2'), which required, among other things, that public agencies ensure that multiple occupancy restrooms, showers, and other similar facilities be 'designated for and only used by' persons based on the 'biological sex' listed on their birth certificate"). A number of such efforts have taken the form of ballot measures put to the voters, sometimes to repeal anti-discrimination laws that would or might have assured transgender people's right to use facilities consistent with their gender identity. *See, e.g.*, Marie-Amélie George, *Framing Trans Rights*, 114 Nw. U. L. Rev. 555, 556 & nn.2–3 (2019). Professor George has critically examined the way that LGBT rights organizations have campaigned against such initiatives and referenda:

> Much as they once did for gay and lesbian rights, LGBT rights groups have tended to adopt the most assimilationist posture possible, in that the transgender individuals they feature in campaign materials are all-but-fully transitioned, conventionally attractive men and women. . . . The LGBT campaigns' imagery overtly reinforces a binary view of gender, despite the wide range of transgender people's presentations and experiences. . . . [The] campaigns' emphasis on binary trans individuals promotes a limited view of sex and gender that may undermine the movement's broader litigation goals. [It] ignores the many gender nonconforming individuals within the LGBT community[, risking] reinforcing social and legal impediments to the rights of the very individuals they are trying to serve." *Id.* at 559, 565.

Instead, George recommends options including "featuring nonbinary individuals, as well as their family members and elected representatives; highlighting how the laws force all citizens to conform to gender stereotypes; and emphasizing gender identity's immutability." *Id.* at 626. How likely is each of these approaches to prove successful? (How should success be identified in any given context of contest over an anti-trans ballot measure?)

Reading Guide for Doe v. Regional School Unit 26

1. The girl plaintiff in this case, who under the pseudonym Susan Doe sued to use school restrooms consistent with her gender identity, is Nicole Maines, today probably more well known for playing the first transgender superhero on U.S. network television, Nia Nal/Dreamer on the CW series *Supergirl*. For more detail on her life, see Amy Ellis Nutt, Becoming Nicole: The Transformation of an American Family (2015).

2. What is the unconventional definition of "sexual orientation" used by Maine's Human Rights Act (MHRA)? (*Cf.* the Minnesota Human Rights Act from *Goins v. West Group*, 635 N.W.2d 717 (Minn. 2001), discussed in Chapter 5, *supra* at p. 300.)

3. For what reason does the court conclude that the school's original policy toward Susan's restroom use did not violate the MHRA?

4. On what basis does the court conclude that the school's revised policy toward Susan's restroom use did violate the MHRA? To what factors does the majority point to delimit the scope of its holding?

5. Upon what canon of interpretation does the dissent rely to argue that Section 6501 trumps the MHRA?

John Doe et al. v. Regional School Unit 26

86 A.3d 600 (Me. 2014)

Silver, J.

[¶1] John and Jane Doe, parents of Susan Doe, and the Maine Human Rights Commission appeal from a summary judgment entered in the Superior Court in favor of Regional School Unit 26 ["RSU 26"] on the Does' complaint pursuant to the Maine Human Rights Act (MHRA), 5 M.R.S. §§ 4592(1), 4602(4) (2013). RSU 26 argues that the public accommodations section of the MHRA conflicts with a statutory provision regarding sanitary facilities in schools, 20-A M.R.S. § 6501 (2013). [We] vacate the Superior Court's judgment.

I. Background

A. Facts

[¶2] The following facts are supported by the summary judgment record, viewed in the light most favorable to the Does and the Commission as the nonprevailing parties.

[¶3] Susan Doe is a transgender girl. She was born male, but began to express a female gender identity as early as age two. Beginning in the first grade, she attended Asa Adams School in Orono. Susan generally wore gender-neutral clothing to school until her third-grade year, when her identity as a girl became manifest. At that time, the school principal first became aware that Susan was transgender.

[¶4] All third and fourth grade students at Asa Adams used single-stall bathrooms. Susan used the single-stall girls' bathroom with the support and encouragement of school staff. In third grade, teachers and students began referring to Susan as "she." By fourth grade, Susan was dressing and appearing exclusively as a girl.

[¶5] In early 2007, midway through Susan's fourth-grade year, school personnel implemented an educational plan, commonly referred to as a "504" plan, to address Susan's gender identity issues and her upcoming transition to the fifth grade, where students used communal bathrooms separated by sex. The 504 process is generally designed to identify impediments to learning for individual students and to implement steps to help those students succeed in school.

[¶6] By the time she was preparing to enter the fifth grade, Susan had received a diagnosis of gender dysphoria, which is the medical term for psychological distress resulting from having a gender identity different from the sex that one was assigned at birth. School officials recognized that it was important to Susan's psychological health that she live socially as a female. They did not interpret 20-A M.R.S. § 6501, or any other law, as prohibiting a person with Susan's diagnosis from using the girls' bathroom.

[¶7] A team consisting of Susan's mother, her teachers, the school guidance counselor, and the director of special services met in March 2007 to develop the 504 plan. The team agreed that school staff should refer to Susan, and encourage students to refer to Susan, by her female name. The school counselor expressed to the group that, for a transgender girl like Susan, using the communal girls' bathroom was the best practice. The team agreed that requiring Susan to use the boys' bathroom was not an acceptable option; the principal later testified that it would not have been safe for Susan to do so. The minutes of the 504 meeting reflected the team's recommendation that Susan use the girls' bathroom. The minutes also reflected the team's awareness that a unisex staff bathroom was available for Susan to use in the event that her use of the girls' bathroom became "an issue."

[¶8] Susan began the fifth grade in September 2007. Her use of the girls' bathroom went smoothly, with no complaints from other students' parents, until a male student followed her into the restroom on two separate occasions, claiming that he, too, was entitled to use the girls' bathroom. The student was acting on instructions from his grandfather, who was his guardian and was strongly opposed to the school's decision to allow Susan to use the girls' bathroom. The controversy generated significant media coverage. As a result of the two incidents, the school, over the Does' objections, terminated Susan's use of the girls' bathroom, requiring her instead to use the single-stall, unisex staff bathroom. That year, Susan was the only student instructed to use the staff bathroom.

[¶9] The 504 team met again in December 2007 to discuss Susan's upcoming transition to middle school. Over the Does' objections, school officials determined that Susan would not be permitted to use the girls' bathroom at the middle school. Again, Susan was required to use a separate, single-stall bathroom. As a result, at the end of Susan's sixth-grade year at Orono Middle School, the Doe family moved to another part of the state.

B. Procedural History

[¶10] On April 10, 2008, while Susan was still in elementary school, Jane Doe filed a complaint with the Commission alleging that the superintendent and other school district entities violated the MHRA by excluding Susan from the communal girls' bathroom at Asa Adams. The Commission unanimously found reasonable grounds to believe discrimination had occurred. The Does, as parents and next friends of Susan, and the Commission filed a complaint in the Superior Court on September 23, 2009, asserting claims for unlawful discrimination in education (Count I) and unlawful discrimination in a place of public accommodation (Count II) on the basis of sexual orientation.

[¶11] After the Superior Court denied the defendants' motion to dismiss all counts . . . , the Does and the Commission filed an amended complaint . . . , adding facts to Counts I and II based on Susan's exclusion from the girls' bathroom at Orono Middle School. The Superior Court granted RSU 26's motion for summary judgment on all counts. . . . The Does and the Commission appeal the Superior Court's entry of summary judgment on Counts I and II.

II. Discussion

[¶12] This is the first case that has required us to interpret the Legislature's 2005 amendments to the MHRA that prohibit discrimination based on sexual orientation in public accommodations, educational opportunities, employment, housing, and other areas. Particularly where young children are involved, it can be challenging for a school to strike the appropriate balance between maintaining order and ensuring that a transgender student's individual rights are respected and protected. Many of the school officials involved in Susan's education exhibited tremendous sensitivity and insight over several years. The record reveals that her counselors and teachers strove to provide her with a supportive environment and were largely successful. As a result of its efforts, the school came under intense public scrutiny, which caused it to reconsider the propriety of the steps it had taken up to that point and ultimately to reverse course. We appreciate the difficulty of the situation in which the school found itself; nevertheless, we must assess schools' obligations pursuant to the Legislature's amendments to the MHRA without regard to the public's potential discomfort with the result. It is for the Legislature, not this Court, to write laws establishing public policy, and we must respect that constitutional division of authority, absent the Legislature adopting a law violative of the Maine Constitution or the United States Constitution. . . .

[¶13] "We review a grant of summary judgment de novo." Summary judgment is properly granted "if the record reflects that there is no genuine issue of material fact and the movant is entitled to a judgment as a matter of law."

[¶14] This case requires us to examine the relationship between the public-accommodations provision of the MHRA and a provision of the Sanitary Facilities subchapter of title 20-A, which regulates education. "[O]ur first task when interpreting a statute is to ascertain the real purpose of the legislation." *State v. Niles*, 585 A.2d 181 (Me. 1990). Seemingly contradictory provisions should not be viewed as irreconcilable when they serve different purposes. *Trask v. Pub. Utils. Comm'n*, 731 A.2d 430 (Me. 1999). We give effect to the Legislature's intent, avoiding results that are inconsistent or illogical "if the language of the statute is fairly susceptible to such a construction." *Cote v. Georgia-Pacific Corp.*, 596 A.2d 1004 (Me. 1991). . . .

[¶15] In construing a statute, we may properly consider its "practical operation and potential consequences." *Clark v. State Emps. Appeals Bd.*, 363 A.2d 735 (Me. 1976). When one construction would lead to a result that is inimical to the public interest, and a different construction would avoid that result, the latter construction is to be favored unless the terms of the statute absolutely forbid it. Moreover, "[w]e have the power and duty . . . to interpret statutes so as to avoid absurd results." *State v. Hopkins*, 526 A.2d 945 (Me. 1987). "A court can even ignore the literal meaning of phrases if that meaning thwarts the clear legislative objective." *Niles.* Such an approach "is not judicial legislation; it is seeking and enforcing the true sense of the law notwithstanding its imperfection or generality of expression." *State v. Day*, 165 A. 163 (Me. 1933).

Section 4592(1) of the MHRA provides, in relevant part:

> It is unlawful public accommodations discrimination, in violation of this Act . . . [f]or any public accommodation or any person who is the . . . superintendent, agent, or employee of any place of public accommodation to directly or indirectly refuse, discriminate against or in any manner withhold from or deny the full and equal enjoyment to any person, on account of . . . sexual orientation . . . any of the accommodations . . . [or] facilities . . . of public accommodation. . . .

Section 4602(4) of the MHRA extends the same prohibition against discrimination based on sexual orientation to educational institutions and educational opportunities, subject only to an exception in section 4553(10)(G)(3) for religious institutions and programs that do not receive public funds.

[¶16] The MHRA defines a "public accommodation" to include a public entity that "operates a place of public accommodation." An elementary school is a place of public accommodation. The definition of "discriminate" "includes, without limitation, [to] segregate or separate." The definition of "sexual orientation" includes "a person's actual or perceived gender identity or expression." The MHRA provides no definition of "sex."

[¶17] On the other hand, 20-A M.R.S. § 6501 requires that sanitary facilities be provided as follows:

1. Toilets. A school administrative unit shall provide clean toilets in all school buildings, which shall be:

. . . .

B. Separated according to sex and accessible only by separate entrances and exits[.]

[¶18] Section 6501 is located in the "Sanitary Facilities" subchapter of the "Health, Nutrition, and Safety" chapter of title 20-A. It has not been amended since 1983. Its purpose is to establish cleanliness and maintenance requirements for school bathrooms, as well as requirements for the physical layout of toilet facilities.

It does not purport to establish guidelines for the use of school bathrooms. Nor does it address how schools should monitor which students use which bathroom, and it certainly offers no guidance concerning how gender identity relates to the use of sex-separated facilities. In contrast, the sole purpose of the public-accommodations and educational-opportunities provisions of the MHRA is to ensure equal enjoyment of and access to educational opportunities and public accommodations and facilities. The public-accommodations and educational-opportunities provisions were amended in 2005 to prohibit discrimination against transgender students in schools.

[¶19] Because these statutes serve different purposes, they are not irreconcilable; one makes it a violation of the Maine Human Rights Act to discriminate in providing access to school bathrooms based on sexual orientation and the other requires schools to provide children with "clean toilets" separated according to sex. Although school buildings must, pursuant to section 6501, contain separate bathrooms for each sex, section 6501 does not—and school officials cannot—dictate the use of the bathrooms in a way that discriminates against students in violation of the MHRA.

[¶20] RSU 26 argues that the sanitary-facilities provision preemptively created an exception to the MHRA's prohibition on sexual orientation discrimination twenty-two years in advance of the passage of the relevant sections of the MHRA. However, we must presume that the Legislature did not intend the MHRA to be construed as inconsistent with section 6501. In this case, a consistent reading of the two statutes avoids conflicting, illogical results and comports with the legislative intent by giving effect to both provisions. Therefore, we adopt a consistent reading of the two provisions.

[¶21] Because section 6501 does not mandate, or even suggest, the manner in which transgender students should be permitted to use sex-separated facilities, each school is left with the responsibility of creating its own policies concerning how these public accommodations are to be used. Those policies must comply with the MHRA. Here, RSU 26 agreed with Susan's family and counselors that, for this purpose (as for virtually all others), Susan is a girl. Based upon its determination that Susan is a girl, and in keeping with the information provided to the school by Susan's family, her therapists, and experts in the field of transgender children, the school determined that Susan should use the girls' bathroom. In so doing, the school provided her with the same access to public facilities that it provided other girls. In this regard, RSU 26 complied with both section 6501 and the MHRA.

[¶22] RSU 26's later decision to ban Susan from the girls' bathroom, based not on a determination that there had been some change in Susan's status but on others' complaints about the school's well-considered decision, constituted discrimination based on Susan's sexual orientation. She was treated differently from other students solely because of her status as a transgender girl. This type of discrimination is forbidden by the MHRA, and it is not excused by the school's compliance with section 6501. We vacate the Superior Court's entry of summary judgment and remand for entry of summary judgment in favor of the Does and the Commission.

[¶23] In vacating this judgment, we emphasize that in this case the school had a program carefully developed over several years and supported by an educational plan designed to sensitively address Susan's gender identity issues. The determination that discrimination is demonstrated in this case rests heavily on Susan's gender identity and gender dysphoria diagnosis, both of which were acknowledged and accepted by the school. The school, her parents, her counselors, and her friends all accepted that Susan is a girl.

[¶24] Thus, we do not suggest that any person could demand access to any school facility or program based solely on a self-declaration of gender identity or confusion without the plans developed in cooperation with the school and the accepted and respected diagnosis that are present in this case. Our opinion must not be read to require schools to permit students casual access to any bathroom of their choice. Decisions about how to address students' legitimate gender identity issues are not to be taken lightly. Where, as here, it has been clearly established that a student's psychological well-being and educational success depend upon being permitted to use the communal bathroom consistent with her gender identity, denying access to the appropriate bathroom constitutes sexual orientation discrimination in violation of the MHRA.

The entry is:

JUDGMENT VACATED.

Remanded for further proceedings consistent with this opinion.

SAUFLEY, C.J., concurring.

[¶25] I concur in the decision of the Court and write separately to highlight two aspects of the majority and dissent that may be lost amid the Court's necessarily detailed legislative analysis. First, as noted, the school system at issue in this case was working in uncharted territory and undertook a rational and compassionate approach to the challenges presented to it. The school's efforts should not be lost or minimized simply because, in the end, its actions, initially agreed to by the parents of the student, contravened the Legislature's statutory pronouncements. Second, the points made by the dissent regarding the ramifications of the Court's decision today, which as the dissent notes "inescapably lead to the conclusion that an individual may not be denied access to public bathrooms based upon sex," Dissenting Opinion ¶ 34 n.12, require legislative attention, and similarly should not be overlooked.

[¶26] With regard to the actions of the school, it bears repeating that the school system in this case accepted Susan as a girl, supported her parents' efforts to create a healthy school environment for Susan, and established a plan, memorialized in meeting minutes, by which all of the adults in Susan's life would work together in support of those goals. Critical to the issue before the Court today, the school actually anticipated the possibility that Susan could be required to use a single-user bathroom rather than the communal girls' bathroom, and the parents, at an earlier point in the planning, did not object to the school's anticipated action. Thus, although ultimately the parents, not unreasonably, sought to have their daughter treated identically to other girls at the school, and the law requires the school to do so, the school's actions in anticipating challenges and planning smooth transitions around those challenges were not unreasonable.

[¶27] Finally, I write to encourage, as has the dissent, legislative attention to the ramifications of the current language in the statutes that have been addressed by the Court today. Specifically, the Court has concluded, as it must based on the statutes, that discrimination in the public accommodation of communal bathrooms is prohibited based on sexual orientation. The statute requiring that result also prohibits discrimination based simply on "sex." Thus, the next logical step given the Court's inevitable interpretation of the existing statute is, as the dissent points out, the assertion that access to the public accommodation of designated communal bathrooms cannot be denied based on a person's sex. See Dissenting Opinion ¶ 34 n.12.

[¶28] Put simply, it could now be argued that it would be illegal discrimination for a restaurant, for example, to prohibit a man from using the women's communal bathroom, and vice versa. I agree with the dissent that it is highly unlikely that the Legislature actually intended that result. Accordingly, on this matter of public policy, it would benefit the public for the Legislature to act quickly to address the concern raised by the dissent in this matter.

Mead, J., dissenting.

[¶29] I agree with the broad principle confirmed in the Court's decision: the Maine Human Rights Act prohibits discrimination in access to public accommodations based upon sexual orientation. "Public accommodations" include multiple-user public bathrooms. "Sexual orientation" includes gender identity. Accordingly, a transgendered individual has the right to use a public bathroom that is designated for use by the gender with which he or she identifies. I depart and dissent, however, from the Court's final conclusion that RSU 26 has committed an act of illegal discrimination upon the facts of this case because well-established principles of statutory construction require a different result.

[¶30] A civilized society protects its citizens from discrimination that is based on petty prejudices and mean-spirited exclusionary practices. The MHRA identifies classes of persons who are entitled to specific protections from such discrimination. The Legislature has included sexual orientation as one of the categories entitled to protection, and rightfully so. Considering the issue presented here, transgendered persons who live their lives as a member of the sex with which they identify face unique challenges with regard to public multiple-user bathrooms. It is simply unreasonable to expect a transgendered person to enter a bathroom designated for use by the sex with which they do not identify. Doing so is likely to provoke confrontation, or even violence. If transgendered people are prohibited from using bathrooms designated for the sex with which they identify, they are left with no practical recourse in most public settings. This result is simply untenable.

[¶31] The Court's decision concludes, and I agree, that elementary schools are places of public accommodation. The MHRA provides that it is unlawful to withhold "facilities" in places of public accommodation, including bathrooms, from any person on account of "race or color, sex, sexual orientation, physical or mental disability, religion, ancestry or national origin."

[¶32] The broad principle established by the Court's interpretation of the MHRA is that access to multiple-user public bathrooms may not be denied based upon sexual orientation. That principle, by implication, applies equally to the other categories enumerated in the MHRA. Specifically, it means that no person may be denied access to a public bathroom in a school or other place of public accommodation on the basis of their race, color, physical or mental disability, religion, ancestry, national origin, or sex. Thus, the MHRA, as construed by the Court today, prevents the denial of access to any public bathroom on the basis of a person's sex. Obviously this result is an extraordinary departure from the well-established custom that public bathrooms are typically segregated by sex.

[¶33] The understandable response by those opposed to this inescapable result is: the Legislature would never have intended that! I do not disagree. But the plain language of the MHRA and the unavoidable implications of the Court's decision set a well-established societal custom (segregation of public bathrooms by sex) and the MHRA on a collision course.

[¶34] I repeat that the right of transgendered individuals to access public accommodations consistent with their gender identity must be protected. It falls to the Legislature to reconcile the plain language of the MHRA as it is currently written and interpreted by the Court with society's longstanding expectation of having multiple-user bathrooms segregated by sex.[12]

[¶35] I realize that this issue at its broadest is not specifically presented by the facts of this case. I address it to highlight the scope and potential ramifications of the Court's decision, to invite the Legislature to clarify its intent concerning this anomaly in the law, and to provide context for the statutory construction analysis required by this case that follows.

[¶36] RSU 26 is not guilty of unlawful public accommodations discrimination if the Legislature has approved segregating school bathrooms by sex in a way that supersedes the MHRA. Applying well-established rules of statutory construction, I conclude that it did so by purposely leaving 20-A M.R.S. § 6501 (2013) in its current

---

12. I can find no authority, statutory or otherwise, that allows public bathrooms, other than school bathrooms (discussed *infra*), to be segregated by sex. On the contrary, the plain language of the MHRA, read in conjunction with the principles announced by the Court today, inescapably lead to the conclusion that an individual may not be denied access to public bathrooms based upon sex.

form after amending the MHRA in 2005. At the very least, this circumstance raises enough of a question to require us to defer to the Legislature to resolve the uncertainty created by section 6501's apparent tension with the MHRA. Section 6501 provides:

1. Toilets. A school administrative unit shall provide clean toilets in all school buildings, which shall be:

. . . .

B. Separated according to sex and accessible only by separate entrances and exits[.]

[¶37] Section 6501, in the specific case of school bathrooms, thus establishes, and indeed mandates, an exception to the MHRA's general rule forbidding the segregation of facilities in schools by sex. We recently reaffirmed "the fundamental rule of statutory construction that we favor the application of a specific statutory provision over the application of a more general provision when there is any inconsistency." *Cent. Me. Power Co. v. Devereux Marine, Inc.*, 68 A.3d 1262, ¶ 22 (Me. 2013).

[¶38] Furthermore, the Legislature is "presumed to be aware of the state of the law . . . when it passes an act." *Stockly v. Doil*, 870 A.2d 1208, ¶ 14 (Me. 2005). Notwithstanding the Court's assertion that the purpose of section 6501 is merely "to establish . . . requirements for the physical layout of toilet facilities," and not to "address how schools should monitor which students use which bathroom," I presume as I must that the Legislature was aware of the interplay between section 6501 and the public accommodations discrimination provision of the MHRA. It would make little sense for the Legislature to require that school bathroom facilities be "[s]eparated according to sex and accessible only by separate entrances and exits," 20-A M.R.S. § 6501(1)(B), and at the same time mandate that schools allow the use of those sex-segregated facilities by students of either sex.

[¶39] The Court states: "[Section 6501] does not purport to establish guidelines for the use of school bathrooms." I vigorously disagree. The statutory directive to segregate bathrooms in schools by sex, and providing for separate entrances and exits for those bathrooms, clearly anticipates that the use of a bathroom would be restricted to the sex for which it has been designated. The statute is susceptible to no other reading. Thus I also disagree with the Court's announcement that Section 6501 somehow vests schools with the prerogative of "creating its own policies concerning how these public accommodations are to be used."

[¶40] Accordingly, I depart from the Court's casual dismissal of the fact that the plain language of a specific statute explicitly requires segregating school bathrooms by sex. The plain language of the provisions of section 6501 and the MHRA are in conflict, and I believe that principles of comity require us to defer to the representative branch of government to resolve the issue.

[¶41] I would therefore affirm the judgment of the Superior Court.

Discussion

1. The majority's reasoning about why banning "Susan" from common or communal girls' restrooms discriminates against her on the basis of her transgender status is not highly detailed. Can you elaborate upon what might be implicit in the majority's stated reasoning? Are the concurring and dissenting justices correct that, as a result of the state statutes at issue and the majority's interpretations thereof, individuals may not be denied access to any restroom on the basis of *sex*?

2. If the court were to rule, as the dissent urged, that the school did *not* violate the MHRA by excluding Susan Doe from common/communal girls' restrooms, in what sense would that be leaving it "to the Legislature to reconcile the plain language of the MHRA as it is currently written and interpreted by the Court with society's longstanding expectation of having multiple-user bathrooms segregated by sex" or "defer[ing] to the representative branch of government to resolve the issue"? Wouldn't it be the court adopting a resolution, and one inconsistent with what all the justices seem to accept, as the meaning of the plain words of the MHRA?

3. Is the upshot of the decision in *Doe* that covered entities may (and indeed must) label communal restrooms as male or female but cannot then exclude anyone from using such facilities on the basis of their sex?

––––––––––––

In 2011, Massachusetts enacted An Act Relative to Gender identity, Chapter 199 of the Acts of 2011, http://www.malegislature.gov/Laws/SessionLaws/Acts/2011 /Chapter199. The act added gender identity to several anti-discrimination statutes. In particular, the act amended the state law forbidding gender identity discrimination in education, effective 2012. Now, G.L. ch. 76, § 5 specifies: "No person shall be excluded from or discriminated against in admission to a public school of any town, or in obtaining the advantages, privileges and courses of study of such public school on account of race, color, sex, gender identity, religion, national origin or sexual orientation."

"In June 2012, the Massachusetts Board of Elementary and Secondary Education (Board) adopted revised Access to Equal Education Opportunity Regulations, 603 CMR 26.00, and Charter School Regulations, 603 CMR 1.00, to reflect the broadened student anti-discrimination provision in G.L. [ch]. 76, § 5. The Board also directed the Department of Elementary and Secondary Education (Department) to provide guidance to school districts to assist in implementing the gender identity provision." Massachusetts Department of Elementary and Secondary Education, Guidance for Massachusetts Public Schools: Creating a Safe and Supportive School Environment: Nondiscrimination on the Basis of Gender Identity (Feb. 15, 2015), http://www.doe.mass.edu/ssce/GenderIdentity .pdf. The following excerpt is from the relatively brief section (compared to the overall lengthy guidance) that provides advice to schools on naming and pronoun practices.

**Massachusetts Department of Elementary and
Secondary Education,** *Guidance for Massachusetts Public
Schools: Creating a Safe and Supportive School Environment:
Nondiscrimination on the Basis of Gender Identity*[*]
(Feb. 15, 2015)

. . . .

Names and Pronouns

The issue of the name and pronoun to use in referring to a transgender student is one of the first that schools must resolve to create an environment in which that student feels safe and supported. Transgender students often choose to change the name assigned to them at birth to a name that is associated with their gender identity. As with most other issues involved with creating a safe and supportive environment for transgender students, the best course is to engage the student, and[,] in the case of a younger student, the parent, with respect to name and pronoun use, and agree on a plan to initiate that name and pronoun use within the school. The plan also could include when and how this is communicated to students and their parents. In the case of a transgender student who is enrolling at a new school, it is important that the school respect the student's privacy (see the following section) and chosen name.

> In one situation where a transgender girl was entering high school, she and her parent asked the principal to inform her teachers that even though her school records indicate that her name is John, she goes by the name Jane and uses female pronouns. The school principal sent the following memorandum to the student's classroom teachers: "The student John Smith wishes to be referred to by the name Jane Smith, a name that is consistent with the student's female gender identity. Please be certain to use the student's preferred name in all contexts, as well as the corresponding pronouns. It is my expectation that students will similarly refer to the student by her chosen name and preferred pronouns. Your role modeling will help make a smooth transition for all concerned. If students do not act accordingly, you may speak to them privately after class to request that they do. Continued, repeated, and intentional misuse of names and pronouns may erode the educational environment for Jane. It should not be tolerated and can be grounds for student discipline. If you need any assistance to make sure that Jane Smith experiences a safe, nondiscriminatory classroom atmosphere, please contact me or Ms. O'Neill.—Mr. Jones, Principal."

Massachusetts' law recognizes common law name changes. An individual may adopt a name that is different from the name that appears on his or her birth certificate provided the change of name is done for an honest reason, with no fraudulent

---

[*] Available at http://www.doe.mass.edu/ssce/GenderIdentity.pdf

intent. Nothing more formal than usage is required.[13] Hence, when requested, schools should accurately record the student's chosen name on all records, whether or not the student, parent, or guardian provides the school with a court order formalizing a name change.

The Department has a procedure in place to update name changes and gender markers in the Student Information Management System (SIMS) upon request. The document Assigning State Assigned Student Identifiers (SASIDs) to Massachusetts' Public School Students, which may be found at http://www.doe.mass.edu /infoservices/data/sims/sasid/, guides schools through changing names and gender markers on school records.

In sum, school personnel should use the student's chosen name and pronouns appropriate to a student's gender identity, regardless of the student's assigned birth sex. For those students who have been attending a school and undergo gender transition while attending the same school, it is important to develop a plan for initiating use of the chosen name and pronouns consistent with the student's gender identity.

. . . .

———————

Numerous other government entities have issued similar guidance documents. *See, e.g.,* Chicago Public Schools, Guidelines Regarding the Support of Transgender and Gender Nonconforming Students (May 3, 2016), http://cps.edu /SiteCollectionDocuments/ TL_TransGenderNonconformingStudents_Guidelines. pdf; Oregon Department of Education, Guidance to School Districts: Creating a Safe and Supportive School Environment for Transgender Students (May 5, 2016),http:// media.oregonlive.com/education_impact/other/ Transgender%20Student%20Guidance%205-5-16.pdf; New York State Education Department, Guidance to School Districts for Creating a Safe and Supportive School Environment for Transgender and Gender Nonconforming Students (July 2015), http://www.p12.nysed.gov/dignityact /documents/Transg_GNCGuidanceFINAL.pdf.

The guidance for U.S. schools that received the highest level of visibility was issued during the Obama administration. In May of 2016, the U.S. Department of Justice and U.S. Department of Education issued joint guidance to schools (in the form of a "Dear Colleague Letter") on how to conform their treatment of transgender students with schools' obligations under Title IX of the Education Amendments of 1972, which prohibit sex discrimination in education programs by entities receiving federal funding.

———————

13. For certain transactions, such as banking and applying for governmental benefits or licenses, it may be necessary to have a formal legal document establishing one's change of name for identity and other purposes.

This Dear Colleague letter was presaged by a January 7, 2015 opinion letter to Emily T. Prince, Esq., from the United States Department of Education Office of Civil Rights. That opinion letter noted that "OCR enforces and interprets Title IX consistent with case law, and with the adjudications and guidance documents of other Federal agencies." (footnote omitted). Specifically, the letter observed that "The Department's Title IX regulations permit schools to provide sex-segregated restrooms, locker rooms, shower facilities, housing, athletic teams, and single-sex classes under certain circumstances. When a school elects to separate or treat students differently on the basis of sex in those situations, a school generally must treat transgender students consistent with their gender identity. OCR also encourages schools to offer the use of gender-neutral, individual-user facilities to any student who does not want to use shared sex-segregated facilities." (footnote omitted). It also observed that "In response to OCR's recent investigations of two complaints of gender identity discrimination, recipients [of federal education funds, specifically, Arcadia Unified School District and Downey Unified School District, both in California] have agreed to revise policies to make clear that transgender students should be treated consistent with their gender identity for purposes of restroom access."

Although subsequently repealed by Secretary of Education Elizabeth ("Betsy") DeVos and Attorney General Jefferson Beauregard ("Jeff") Sessions III under the Trump administration, the May 2016 Dear Colleague letter was for a short time a landmark achievement in the federal protection of transgender students.

U.S. Departments of Justice and Education, *Dear Colleague Letter*

U.S. Department of Justice	**U.S. Department of Education**
Civil Rights Division	**Office for Civil Rights**

May 13, 2016

Dear Colleague:

Schools across the country strive to create and sustain inclusive, supportive, safe, and nondiscriminatory communities for all students. In recent years, we have received an increasing number of questions from parents, teachers, principals, and school superintendents about civil rights protections for transgender students. Title IX of the Education Amendments of 1972 (Title IX) and its implementing regulations prohibit sex discrimination in educational programs and activities operated by recipients of Federal financial assistance.[1] This prohibition encompasses discrim-

---

1. 20 U.S.C. §§ 1681–1688; 34 C.F.R. Pt. 106; 28 C.F.R. Pt. 54. In this letter, the term schools refers to recipients of Federal financial assistance at all educational levels, including school districts, colleges, and universities. An educational institution that is controlled by a religious organization is exempt from Title IX to the extent that compliance would not be consistent with the religious tenets of such organization. 20 U.S.C. § 1681(a)(3); 34 C.F.R. § 106.12(a).

ination based on a student's gender identity, including discrimination based on a student's transgender status. This letter summarizes a school's Title IX obligations regarding transgender students and explains how the U.S. Department of Education (ED) and the U.S. Department of Justice (DOJ) evaluate a school's compliance with these obligations.

ED and DOJ (the Departments) have determined that this letter is *significant guidance*.[2] This guidance does not add requirements to applicable law, but provides information and examples to inform recipients about how the Departments evaluate whether covered entities are complying with their legal obligations. If you have questions or are interested in commenting on this guidance, please contact ED at ocr@ed.gov or 800-421-3481 (TDD 800-877-8339); or DOJ at education@usdoj.gov or 877-292-3804 (TTY: 800-514-0383).

Accompanying this letter is a separate document from ED's Office of Elementary and Secondary Education, *Examples of Policies and Emerging Practices for Supporting Transgender Students*. The examples in that document are taken from policies that school districts, state education agencies, and high school athletics associations around the country have adopted to help ensure that transgender students enjoy a supportive and nondiscriminatory school environment. Schools are encouraged to consult that document for practical ways to meet Title IX's requirements.[3]

. . . .

Compliance with Title IX

As a condition of receiving Federal funds, a school agrees that it will not exclude, separate, deny benefits to, or otherwise treat differently on the basis of sex any person in its educational programs or activities unless expressly authorized to do so under Title IX or its implementing regulations.[4] The Departments treat a student's gender identity as the student's sex for purposes of Title IX and its implementing regulations. This means that a school must not treat a transgender student differently from the way it treats other students of the same gender identity. The

---

2. Office of Management and Budget, Final Bulletin for Agency Good Guidance Practices, 72 Fed. Reg. 3432 (Jan. 25, 2007), www.whitehouse.gov/sites/default/files/omb/fedreg/2007/ 012507_good_guidance.pdf.

3. ED, *Examples of Policies and Emerging Practices for Supporting Transgender Students* (May 13, 2016), www.ed.gov/oese/oshs/emergingpractices.pdf. OCR also posts many of its resolution agreements in cases involving transgender students online at www.ed.gov/ocr/lgbt.html. While these agreements address fact-specific cases, and therefore do not state general policy, they identify examples of ways OCR and recipients have resolved some issues addressed in this guidance.

4. 34 C.F.R. §§ 106.4, 106.31(a). For simplicity, this letter cites only to ED's Title IX regulations. DOJ has also promulgated Title IX regulations. *See* 28 C.F.R. Pt. 54. For purposes of how the Title IX regulations at issue in this guidance apply to transgender individuals, DOJ interprets its regulations similarly to ED. State and local rules cannot limit or override the requirements of Federal laws. *See* 34 C.F.R. § 106.6(b).

Departments' interpretation is consistent with courts' and other agencies' interpretations of Federal laws prohibiting sex discrimination.[5]

The Departments interpret Title IX to require that when a student or the student's parent or guardian, as appropriate, notifies the school administration that the student will assert a gender identity that differs from previous representations or records, the school will begin treating the student consistent with the student's gender identity. Under Title IX, there is no medical diagnosis or treatment requirement that students must meet as a prerequisite to being treated consistent with their gender identity.[6] Because transgender students often are unable to obtain identification documents that reflect their gender identity (*e.g.*, due to restrictions imposed by state or local law in their place of birth or residence),[7] requiring students to produce such identification documents in order to treat them consistent with their gender identity may violate Title IX when doing so has the practical effect of limiting or denying students equal access to an educational program or activity.

A school's Title IX obligation to ensure nondiscrimination on the basis of sex requires schools to provide transgender students equal access to educational programs and activities even in circumstances in which other students, parents, or community members raise objections or concerns. As is consistently recognized in

---

5. *See, e.g., Price Waterhouse v. Hopkins*, 490 U.S. 228 (1989); *Oncale v. Sundowner Offshore Servs. Inc.*, 523 U.S. 75, 79 (1998); *G.G. v. Gloucester Cnty. Sch. Bd.*, No. 15-2056, 2016 WL 1567467, at *8 (4th Cir. Apr. 19, 2016); *Glenn v. Brumby*, 663 F.3d 1312, 1317 (11th Cir. 2011); *Smith v. City of Salem*, 378 F.3d 566, 572–75 (6th Cir. 2004); *Rosa v. Park W. Bank & Trust Co.*, 214 F.3d 213, 215–16 (1st Cir. 2000); *Schwenk v. Hartford*, 204 F.3d 1187, 1201–02 (9th Cir. 2000); *Schroer v. Billington*, 577 F. Supp. 2d 293, 306–08 (D.D.C. 2008); *Macy v. Dep't of Justice*, Appeal No. 012012082 (U.S. Equal Emp't Opportunity Comm'n Apr. 20, 2012). *See also* U.S. Dep't of Labor (USDOL), Training and Employment Guidance Letter No. 37-14, Update on Complying with Nondiscrimination Requirements: Discrimination Based on Gender Identity, Gender Expression and Sex Stereotyping are Prohibited Forms of Sex Discrimination in the Workforce Development System (2015), wdr.doleta.gov/directives/attach/TEGL/TEGL_37-14.pdf; USDOL, Job Corps, Directive: Job Corps Program Instruction Notice No. 14-31, Ensuring Equal Access for Transgender Applicants and Students to the Job Corps Program (May 1, 2015), https://supportservices.jobcorps.gov/Program%20Instruction%20Notices/pi_14_31.pdf DOJ, Memorandum from the Attorney General, Treatment of Transgender Employment Discrimination Claims Under Title VII of the Civil Rights Act of 1964 (2014), www.justice.gov/sites/default/files/opa/press-releases/attachments/2014/12/18/title_vii_memo.pdf; USDOL, Office of Federal Contract Compliance Programs, Directive 2014-02, Gender Identity and Sex Discrimination (2014), www.dol.gov/ofccp/regs/compliance/directives/dir2014_02.html.

6. *See Lusardi v. Dep't of the Army*, Appeal No. 0120133395 at 9 (U.S. Equal Emp't Opportunity Comm'n Apr. 1, 2015) ("An agency may not condition access to facilities—or to other terms, conditions, or privileges of employment—on the completion of certain medical steps that the agency itself has unilaterally determined will somehow prove the bona fides of the individual's gender identity.").

7. *See G.G.*, 2016 WL 1567467, at *1 n.1 (noting that medical authorities "do not permit sex reassignment surgery for persons who are under the legal age of majority").

civil rights cases, the desire to accommodate others' discomfort cannot justify a policy that singles out and disadvantages a particular class of students.[8]

1. Safe and Nondiscriminatory Environment

Schools have a responsibility to provide a safe and nondiscriminatory environment for all students, including transgender students. Harassment that targets a student based on gender identity, transgender status, or gender transition is harassment based on sex, and the Departments enforce Title IX accordingly.[9] If sex-based harassment creates a hostile environment, the school must take prompt and effective steps to end the harassment, prevent its recurrence, and, as appropriate, remedy its effects. A school's failure to treat students consistent with their gender identity may create or contribute to a hostile environment in violation of Title IX. For a more detailed discussion of Title IX requirements related to sex-based harassment, see guidance documents from ED's Office for Civil Rights (OCR) that are specific to this topic.[10]

2. Identification Documents, Names, and Pronouns

Under Title IX, a school must treat students consistent with their gender identity even if their education records or identification documents indicate a different sex.

---

8. 34 C.F.R. § 106.31(b)(4); *see G.G.*, 2016 WL 1567467, at *8 & n.10 (affirming that individuals have legitimate and important privacy interests and noting that these interests do not inherently conflict with nondiscrimination principles); *Cruzan v. Special Sch. Dist. No. 1*, 294 F.3d 981, 984 (8th Cir. 2002) (rejecting claim that allowing a transgender woman "merely [to be] present in the women's faculty restroom" created a hostile environment); *Glenn*, 663 F.3d at 1321 (defendant's proffered justification that "other women might object to [the plaintiff]'s restroom use" was "wholly irrelevant"). *See also Palmore v. Sidoti*, 466 U.S. 429, 433 (1984) ("Private biases may be outside the reach of the law, but the law cannot, directly or indirectly, give them effect."); *City of Cleburne v. Cleburne Living Ctr.*, 473 U.S. 432, 448 (1985) (recognizing that "mere negative attitudes, or fear . . . are not permissible bases for" government action).

9. *See, e.g.,* Resolution Agreement, *In re Downey Unified Sch. Dist., CA*, OCR Case No. 09-12-1095, (Oct. 8, 2014), www.ed.gov/documents/press-releases/downey-school-district-agreement.pdf (agreement to address harassment of transgender student, including allegations that peers continued to call her by her former name, shared pictures of her prior to her transition, and frequently asked questions about her anatomy and sexuality); Consent Decree, *Doe v. Anoka-Hennepin Sch. Dist. No. 11, MN* (D. Minn. Mar. 1, 2012), www.ed.gov/ocr/docs/investigations/05115901-d.pdf (consent decree to address sex-based harassment, including based on nonconformity with gender stereotypes); Resolution Agreement, *In re Tehachapi Unified Sch. Dist., CA*, OCR Case No. 09-11-1031 (June 30, 2011), www.ed.gov/ocr/docs/investigations/09111031-b.pdf (agreement to address sexual and gender-based harassment, including harassment based on nonconformity with gender stereotypes). *See also Lusardi*, Appeal No. 0120133395, at *15 ("Persistent failure to use the employee's correct name and pronoun may constitute unlawful, sex-based harassment if such conduct is either severe or pervasive enough to create a hostile work environment").

10. *See, e.g.,* OCR, Revised Sexual Harassment Guidance: Harassment of Students by School Employees, Other Students, or Third Parties (2001), www.ed.gov/ocr/docs/shguide.pdf; OCR, Dear Colleague Letter: Harassment and Bullying (Oct. 26, 2010), www.ed.gov/ocr/letters/colleague-201010.pdf; OCR, Dear Colleague Letter: Sexual Violence (Apr. 4, 2011), www.ed.gov/ocr/letters/colleague-201104.pdf; OCR, Questions and Answers on Title IX and Sexual Violence (Apr. 29, 2014), www.ed.gov/ocr/docs/qa-201404-title-ix.pdf.

The Departments have resolved Title IX investigations with agreements commit-ting that school staff and contractors will use pronouns and names consistent with a transgender student's gender identity.[11]

3. Sex-Segregated Activities and Facilities

Title IX's implementing regulations permit a school to provide sex-segregated restrooms, locker rooms, shower facilities, housing, and athletic teams, as well as single-sex classes under certain circumstances.[12] When a school provides sex-segregated activities and facilities, transgender students must be allowed to partici-pate in such activities and access such facilities consistent with their gender identity.[13]

> * **Restrooms and Locker Rooms**. A school may provide separate facilities on the basis of sex, but must allow transgender students access to such facilities consistent with their gender identity.[14] A school may not require transgender students to use facilities inconsistent with their gender identity or to use individual-user facilities when other students are not required to do so. A school may, however, make individual-user options available to all students who voluntarily seek additional privacy.[15]

> * **Athletics**. Title IX regulations permit a school to operate or sponsor sex-segregated athletics teams when selection for such teams is based upon competitive skill or when the activity involved is a contact sport.[16] A school may not, however, adopt or adhere to requirements that rely on overly broad generalizations or stereotypes about the differences between trans-gender students and other students of the same sex (*i.e.*, the same gender identity) or others' discomfort with transgender students.[17] Title IX does not prohibit age-appropriate, tailored requirements based on sound, current,

---

11. *See, e.g.*, Resolution Agreement, *In re Cent. Piedmont Cmty. Coll., NC*, OCR Case No. 11-14-2265 (Aug. 13, 2015), www.ed.gov/ocr/docs/investigations/more/11142265-b.pdf (agreement to use a transgender student's preferred name and gender and change the student's official record to reflect a name change).

12. 34 C.F.R. §§ 106.32, 106.33, 106.34, 106.41(b).

13. *See* 34 C.F.R. § 106.31.

14. 34 C.F.R. § 106.33.

15. *See, e.g.*, Resolution Agreement, *In re Township High Sch. Dist. 211, IL*, OCR Case No. 05-14-1055 (Dec. 2, 2015), www.ed.gov/ocr/docs/investigations/more/05141055-b.pdf (agreement to provide any student who requests additional privacy "access to a reasonable alternative, such as assignment of a student locker in near proximity to the office of a teacher or coach; use of another private area (such as a restroom stall) within the public area; use of a nearby private area (such as a single-use facility); or a separate schedule of use.").

16. 34 C.F.R. § 106.41(b). Nothing in Title IX prohibits schools from offering coeducational athletic opportunities.

17. 34 C.F.R. § 106.6(b), (c). An interscholastic athletic association is subject to Title IX if (1) the association receives Federal financial assistance or (2) its members are recipients of Federal finan-cial assistance and have ceded controlling authority over portions of their athletic program to the association. Where an athletic association is covered by Title IX, a school's obligations regarding transgender athletes apply with equal force to the association.

and research-based medical knowledge about the impact of the students' participation on the competitive fairness or physical safety of the sport.[18]

* **Single-Sex Classes.** Although separating students by sex in classes and activities is generally prohibited, nonvocational elementary and secondary schools may offer nonvocational single-sex classes and extracurricular activities under certain circumstances.[19] When offering such classes and activities, a school must allow transgender students to participate consistent with their gender identity.

* **Single-Sex Schools.** Title IX does not apply to the admissions policies of certain educational institutions, including nonvocational elementary and secondary schools, and private undergraduate colleges.[20] Those schools are therefore permitted under Title IX to set their own sex-based admissions policies. Nothing in Title IX prohibits a private undergraduate women's college from admitting transgender women if it so chooses.

* **Social Fraternities and Sororities.** Title IX does not apply to the membership practices of social fraternities and sororities.[21] Those organizations are therefore permitted under Title IX to set their own policies regarding the sex, including gender identity, of their members. Nothing in Title IX prohibits a fraternity from admitting transgender men or a sorority from admitting transgender women if it so chooses.

* **Housing and Overnight Accommodations.** Title IX allows a school to provide separate housing on the basis of sex.[22] But a school must allow transgender students to access housing consistent with their gender identity and may not require transgender students to stay in single-occupancy accommodations or to disclose personal information when not required of other

---

18. The National Collegiate Athletic Association (NCAA), for example, reported that in developing its policy for participation by transgender students in college athletics, it consulted with medical experts, athletics officials, affected students, and a consensus report entitled *On the Team: Equal Opportunity for Transgender Student Athletes* (2010) by Dr. Pat Griffin & Helen J. Carroll (On the Team), https://www.ncaa.org/sites/default/files/NCLR_TransStudentAthlete%2B(2).pdf. *See* NCAA Office of Inclusion, NCAA Inclusion of Transgender Student-Athletes 2, 30–31 (2011), https://www.ncaa.org/sites/default/files/Transgender_Handbook_2011_Final.pdf (citing *On the Team*). The *On the Team* report noted that policies that may be appropriate at the college level may "be unfair and too complicated for [the high school] level of competition." *On the Team* at 26. After engaging in similar processes, some state interscholastic athletics associations have adopted policies for participation by transgender students in high school athletics that they determined were age-appropriate.

19. 34 C.F.R. § 106.34(a), (b). Schools may also separate students by sex in physical education classes during participation in contact sports. *Id.* § 106.34(a)(1).

20. 20 U.S.C. § 1681(a)(1); 34 C.F.R. § 106.15(d); 34 C.F.R. § 106.34(c) (a recipient may offer a single-sex public nonvocational elementary and secondary school so long as it provides students of the excluded sex a "substantially equal single-sex school or coeducational school").

21. 20 U.S.C. § 1681(a)(6)(A); 34 C.F.R. § 106.14(a).

22. 20 U.S.C. § 1686; 34 C.F.R. § 106.32.

students. Nothing in Title IX prohibits a school from honoring a student's voluntary request for single-occupancy accommodations if it so chooses.[23]

* **Other Sex-Specific Activities and Rules**. Unless expressly authorized by Title IX or its implementing regulations, a school may not segregate or otherwise distinguish students on the basis of their sex, including gender identity, in any school activities or the application of any school rule. Likewise, a school may not discipline students or exclude them from participating in activities for appearing or behaving in a manner that is consistent with their gender identity or that does not conform to stereotypical notions of masculinity or femininity (*e.g.*, in yearbook photographs, at school dances, or at graduation ceremonies).[24]

4. Privacy and Education Records

Protecting transgender students' privacy is critical to ensuring they are treated consistent with their gender identity. The Departments may find a Title IX violation when a school limits students' educational rights or opportunities by failing to take reasonable steps to protect students' privacy related to their transgender status, including their birth name or sex assigned at birth.[25] Nonconsensual disclosure of personally identifiable information (PII), such as a student's birth name or sex assigned at birth, could be harmful to or invade the privacy of transgender students and may also violate the Family Educational Rights and Privacy Act (FERPA).[26] A school may maintain records with this information, but such records should be kept confidential.

* **Disclosure of Personally Identifiable Information from Education Records**. FERPA generally prevents the nonconsensual disclosure of PII from a student's education records; one exception is that records may be disclosed to individual school personnel who have been determined to have a legitimate educational interest in the information.[27] Even when a student has disclosed the student's transgender status to some members of the school community, schools may not rely on this FERPA exception to disclose PII from education records to other school personnel who do not have a legitimate educational interest in the information. Inappropriately disclosing (or requiring students or their parents to disclose) PII from education records

---

23. *See, e.g.*, Resolution Agreement, *In re Arcadia Unified. Sch. Dist., CA*, OCR Case No. 09-12-1020, DOJ Case No. 169-12C-70, (July 24, 2013), www.justice.gov/sites/default/files/crt/legacy/2013/07/26/arcadiaagree.pdf (agreement to provide access to single-sex overnight events consistent with students' gender identity, but allowing students to request access to private facilities).

24. *See* 34 C.F.R. §§ 106.31(a), 106.31(b)(4). *See also, In re Downey Unified Sch. Dist., CA, supra* n.9; *In re Cent. Piedmont Cmty. Coll., NC, supra* n.11.

25. 34 C.F.R. § 106.31(b)(7).

26. 20 U.S.C. § 1232g; 34 C.F.R. Part 99. FERPA is administered by ED's Family Policy Compliance Office (FPCO). Additional information about FERPA and FPCO is available at www.ed.gov/fpco.

27. 20 U.S.C. § 1232g(b)(1)(A); 34 C.F.R. § 99.31(a)(1).

to the school community may violate FERPA and interfere with transgender students' right under Title IX to be treated consistent with their gender identity.

* **Disclosure of Directory Information.** Under FERPA's implementing regulations, a school may disclose appropriately designated directory information from a student's education record if disclosure would not generally be considered harmful or an invasion of privacy.[28] Directory information may include a student's name, address, telephone number, date and place of birth, honors and awards, and dates of attendance.[29] School officials may not designate students' sex, including transgender status, as directory information because doing so could be harmful or an invasion of privacy.[30] A school also must allow eligible students (*i.e.*, students who have reached 18 years of age or are attending a postsecondary institution) or parents, as appropriate, a reasonable amount of time to request that the school not disclose a student's directory information.[31]

* **Amendment or Correction of Education Records.** A school may receive requests to correct a student's education records to make them consistent with the student's gender identity. Updating a transgender student's education records to reflect the student's gender identity and new name will help protect privacy and ensure personnel consistently use appropriate names and pronouns.

* Under FERPA, a school must consider the request of an eligible student or parent to amend information in the student's education records that is inaccurate, misleading, or in violation of the student's privacy rights.[32] If the school does not amend the record, it must inform the requestor of its decision and of the right to a hearing. If, after the hearing, the school does not amend the record, it must inform the requestor of the right to insert a statement in the record with the requestor's comments on the contested information, a statement that the requestor disagrees with the hearing decision, or both. That statement must be disclosed whenever the record to which the statement relates is disclosed.[33]

> * Under Title IX, a school must respond to a request to amend information related to a student's transgender status consistent with its general practices for amending other students' records.[34] If a student or parent

---

28. 34 C.F.R. §§ 99.3, 99.31(a)(11), 99.37.

29. 20 U.S.C. § 1232g(a)(5)(A); 34 C.F.R. § 99.3.

30. Letter from FPCO to Institutions of Postsecondary Education 3 (Sept. 2009), www.ed.gov /policy/gen/guid/fpco/doc/censuslettertohighered091609.pdf.

31. 20 U.S.C. § 1232g(a)(5)(B); 34 C.F.R. §§ 99.3. 99.37(a)(3).

32. 34 C.F.R. § 99.20.

33. 34 C.F.R. §§ 99.20–99.22.

34. *See* 34 C.F.R. § 106.31(b)(4).

complains about the school's handling of such a request, the school must promptly and equitably resolve the complaint under the school's Title IX grievance procedures.[35]

* * *

We appreciate the work that many schools, state agencies, and other organizations have undertaken to make educational programs and activities welcoming, safe, and inclusive for all students.

Sincerely,

/s/

Catherine E. Lhamon
Assistant Secretary for Civil Rights

U.S. Department of Education

/s/

Vanita Gupta
Principal Deputy Assistant Attorney General for Civil Rights

U.S. Department of Justice

Discussion

1. How does this Dear Colleague letter differ from the Enforcement Guidance on the NYCHRL, *see* Chapter 7, *supra* at p. 425? Note, for example, that this letter requires a student/parent to provide notice to the school that the student wants to assert a different gender identity than what is listed in school records, which will then trigger the various listed protections (*e.g.*, with respect to name/pronoun usage and the ability to use sex-segregated facilities in accordance with one's gender identity). Why might an anti-discrimination policy in schools require such notice? Should other anti-discrimination laws also be subject to similar notice requirements?

2. This letter cites the Supreme Court decision in *Price Waterhouse* as consistent with its reading of Title IX. *Price Waterhouse* established that discrimination on the basis of sex stereotypes may constitute sex discrimination under Title VII. In what way is *Price Waterhouse* consistent with this guidance? Could an opponent of this guidance argue that *Price Waterhouse* is inconsistent with or unrelated to matters of gender identity discrimination?

3. Perhaps the weakest protections afforded to transgender students in this guidance are contained in the "Athletics" section on sex-segregated facilities/activities. Although schools cannot rely on "overbroad generalizations" about students when segregating athletic activities, they may use "age-appropriate, tailored requirements based on sound, current, and research-based medical knowledge about the impact of the students' participation on the competitive fairness or physical safety of the sport." What types of segregation might be allowable under this guidance? For example, could schools segregate athletic activities based on students' testosterone levels? (Would schools have to test all student athlete's testosterone levels,

---

35. 34 C.F.R. § 106.8(b).

or would it be permissible, for example, to test only transgender female students' testosterone?)

———————

Donald J. Trump was inaugurated as the forty-fifth President of the United States on January 20, 2017. On February 22, 2017, the Justice Department and the Education Department withdrew this guidance (along with another pro-trans letter issued under the Obama administration). Josh Keefe, *Who Is Gavin Grimm? Trans Student's Lawyer Reacts to Trump Rescinding Rules on Transgender Guidance*, Int'l Business Times (Feb. 23, 2017), https://www.ibtimes.com/who-gavin-grimm-trans -students-lawyer-reacts-trump-rescinding-rules-transgender-2496021 (last visited Oct. 17, 2019); *see also* Allison Fetter-Harrott et al., *Sex Discrimination in Schools: Has Change in Administration Meant Change in Protections for Transgender Students and Educators?*, 44 U. Dayton L. Rev. 455 (2019) (summarizing judicial and administrative changes in recognition of rights of transgender students including restroom access rights). The Dear Colleague letter rescinding the guidance focused on doubts about whether Title IX and its implementing regulations "require access to sex-segregated facilities based on gender identity[,]" yet the Departments revoked the entirety of the guidance, even provisions dealing with harassment, names and pronouns, and educational records. U.S. Department of Justice Civil Rights Division & U.S. Department of Education Office of Civil Rights, Dear Colleague Letter, Feb. 22, 2017. Perhaps more weight should be attached to the revocation letter's federalism-related pronouncement, framed as an "addition[al]" consideration, that "there must be due regard for the primary role of the States and local school districts in establishing educational policy." The avowed purpose of the action to "withdraw and rescind" the guidance was "to further and more completely consider the legal issues involved." Although the new letter states that "The Departments [of Justice and Education] will not rely on the views expressed within" the revoked guidance, it does not affirmatively express the view that Title IX's ban on sex discrimination does *not* prohibit (to quote the Obama administration guidance) "discrimination based on a student's gender identity, including discrimination based on a student's transgender status." Whether it does or not is likely to be resolved in litigation.

In *Bostock v. Clayton County, Georgia*, 140 S. Ct. 1731 (2020), Chapter 5, Section D, *supra*, the Supreme Court held that discrimination against someone based on their "transgender status" or "for being . . . transgender" necessarily violates the ban on discrimination because of sex in Title VII of the Civil Rights Act of 1964. Since courts often draw on Title VII precedent in construing Title IX, and since *Bostock* was based on what the terms or concepts "sex," "discrimination," and "because of" mean, this decision will likely have significant ramifications regarding the extent to which Title IX protects transgender people in education. Consider the types of treatment that the now rescinded Obama administration guidance seeks to forestall. Regardless of the guidance, Title IX still governs. If the Court interprets sex discrimination under Title IX as it interpreted sex discrimination under Title VII, which of those forms of treatment would amount to discrimination based on "transgender status" or discrimination "for being transgender"? Would any other forms of treatment the guidance addresses count as "penaliz[ing] a person identified as male at birth for traits or actions that it tolerates in an employee identified as female at birth," *id.* at 1741, "intentionally appl[ying] sex-based rules," *id.* at 1745, or "weighing a student's sex] as a factor in the [school's] decision," *id* at 1746?

––––––––––

Much of the litigation over restroom access for transgender students has largely focused on Title IX issues. There are also serious *constitutional* equal protection questions that arise when students who are transgender are denied access to gender-appropriate common restrooms. Consider the differing approaches of the next two judicial opinions (one presented as a main case and one as a note case) to the analysis of such equal protection issues.

Reading Guide for Evancho v. Pine-Richland School District

1. The following suit was filed by three high school students who are transgender; one, Juliette Evancho, is the older sister of America's Got Talent finalist and classical/pop crossover singer Jackie Evancho, who performed the national anthem at Donald Trump's inauguration in January 2017.

2. What does the district court conclude was the nature or "basis" of the defendants' discriminatory treatment of the plaintiffs? Is the court's reasoning for that conclusion persuasive?

3. What factors does the court use to determine the appropriate level of scrutiny for the discrimination it identified? What level of scrutiny does the court adopt? What reasons does the court give for concluding that those factors support its chosen level of scrutiny?

4. For what reasons does the court conclude that the district did not satisfy that level of scrutiny? What reasons did the court give for rejecting the legal sufficiency of the district's "express rationales" for its Resolution 2 concerning restroom use by transgender students?

Juliet Evancho, et al. v. Pine-Richland School District, et al.

237 F. Supp. 3d 267 (W.D. Pa. 2017)

Opinion

Mark R. Hornak, United States District Judge

[Plaintiffs] are each transgender, and all are in their senior year at Pine-Richland High School. Two[,] Juliet Evancho and Elissa Ridenour, each over 18 years old, had "male" listed on their birth certificates when they were born.[1] That of the third

––––––––––

1. The Commonwealth of Pennsylvania has re-issued a birth certificate for Plaintiff Evancho that lists her sex as "female."

Plaintiff, A.S. (also a high school senior, but not yet 18 years old), said "female." For some time, Juliet Evancho and Elissa Ridenour have lived all facets of their lives as girls, and A.S. has done so as a boy.

The Defendant School District does not dispute that Plaintiffs identify as transgender, which means, among other things, that their gender identities are at odds with the sexes listed on their original birth certificates and with their external sex organs. It is undisputed that in all respects, the Plaintiffs have—at least for their high school years—lived every facet of their in-school and out-of-school lives consistently with their respective gender identities rather than their "assigned sexes."[3] Their teachers, school administrators, fellow students and others have treated the Plaintiffs consistently with their gender identities as they have lived and expressed them rather than according to their assigned sexes. According to the District, the Plaintiffs, except for purposes of excretory functions, are of the gender with which they identify, and the District treats the Plaintiffs' gender identities as their "sex" in all other interactions with the District.

The central issue now before the Court is whether the District acted in accord with federal law when it limited, by formal School Board Resolution 2,[4] the common school bathrooms that these Plaintiffs may use to either (a) single-user bathrooms or (b) the bathrooms labeled as matching their assigned sexes. The Plaintiffs argue that the District's application of Resolution 2 to prevent them from continuing to use common student restrooms that conform to their gender identities violates both Title IX of the Education Amendments of 1972, and the Equal Protection Clause . . . , in the former case by unlawfully discriminating against them based on their sexes, and in the latter case by impermissibly treating them differently than other District students based on their gender identities, and therefore their sexes. [Plaintiffs] seek an order . . . enjoining the District from enforcing Resolution 2 as to them and restoring the *status quo ante* as to how the District interacted with the Plaintiffs prior to the enactment of Resolution 2.

---

3. Solely for simplicity of reference, and because it is the focus of all of the arguments advanced by the Defendants, the Court will use the term "assigned sex" to refer to the physical characteristics of the external sex organs of a person being referenced. [T]his Court is reluctant to use any descriptive term that can have the unintended effect of reducing any person on any side of any case to a label, but it nonetheless uses this terminology because the District's asserted rationale for Resolution 2 turns on that single human characteristic. The Court will use the term "transgender" to refer to individuals who have expressed and live a gender identity that is different from their assigned sex at birth. The Court recognizes that each of the parties contends that such terms may have other meanings in a variety of contexts beyond the discrete issues now before the Court.

4. Resolution 2 provides:

This resolution agreed to by a majority of the Board of Directors of the Pine-Richland School District indicates our support to return to the long-standing practice of providing sex specific facility usage. All students will have the choice of using either the facilities that correspond to their biological sex or unisex facilities. This practice will remain in place until such time that a policy may be developed and approved..

The Court concludes that the Plaintiffs have a reasonable likelihood of success on the merits of their Equal Protection claim but not on the merits of their Title IX claim. The Court will therefore grant in part the Plaintiffs' Motion for a Preliminary Injunction. The Court will deny without prejudice the District's Motion to Dismiss both of the Plaintiffs' claims.

. . . .

III

[As] a preliminary matter, the Court concludes that on the record now before it, the Plaintiffs have shown that the District is treating them differently from other students who are similarly situated on the basis of their transgender status. The Plaintiffs are being distinguished by governmental action from those whose gender identities are congruent with their assigned sex. The Plaintiffs are the only students who are not allowed to use the common restrooms consistent with their gender identities.[28] [Evancho] and Ridenour fully identify as girls and are identified by others as girls. [A.S.] fully identifies as a boy and is identified by others as a boy. That is how they live, and have lived, their lives in all regards, and they are otherwise treated as such. . . . But unlike every other student, the Plaintiffs would have to use restrooms where they are wholly unlike everyone else in appearance, manner, mode of living, and treatment at school. Resolution 2 therefore discriminates based on transgender status. Just as other courts have recently concluded, for these analytical purposes, that discrimination based on transgender status in these circumstances is essentially the epitome of discrimination based on gender nonconformity, making differentiation based on transgender status akin to discrimination based on sex for these purposes.[30] *Glenn v. Brumby*, 663 F.3d 1312 (11th Cir. 2011); *Bd. of Educ. of Highland S.D. v. U.S. Dept. of Ed.*, 208 F. Supp. 3d 850 (S.D. Ohio 2016); *Carcaño v. McCrory*, 203 F. Supp. 3d 615 (M.D.N.C. 2016).

---

28. Equal Protection claims require proof of discriminatory purpose, which includes state action in which the decision maker selected or reaffirmed a course of action at least in part because of its effects on an identifiable group. Here, there is a clearly identifiable small group adversely impacted by the application of Resolution 2 to them, coupled with the District's stated intention to impact them, based at least in part on its stated desire to do so after a public insistence that it do just that. Given that the lead up to Resolution 2's passage and its explained rationales in this case were to expressly change the rules (or at least settled practices) as to Plaintiffs' restroom use, and to do so based on a criteria that knowingly and consciously related to *their* gender identities, the Court has no difficulty in concluding that the Plaintiffs have demonstrated a likelihood that they can establish the level of purposeful discrimination underlying a valid Equal Protection claim. *See Romer v. Evans*, 517 U.S. 620 (1996) (noting that separation based upon a specific characteristic raises an "inevitable inference" of animosity toward those affected by the classification).

30. Our Court of Appeals has recognized in cases arising under Title VII of the Civil Rights Act of 1964 that discrimination or differentiation based on gender, and gender nonconformity, is discrimination based on "sex." *Betz v. Temple Health Sys.*, 659 Fed. Appx. 137 (3d Cir. 2016); *Prowel v. Wise Bus. Forms, Inc.*, 579 F.3d 285 (3d Cir. 2009); *Bibby v. Phila. Coca Cola Bottling Co.*, 260 F.3d 257 (3d Cir. 2001).

Given that the classification at hand is the Plaintiffs' transgender status, the parties dispute which Equal Protection standard should apply. The District says [it's] the rational basis test. . . .

The District cites two reasons. . . . The first is that neither the Supreme Court nor our Court of Appeals has specifically weighed in as to the applicable Equal Protection standard as to classifications based on transgender status. . . . First, that means that applying an Equal Protection standard other than rational basis in such a setting is not contrary to settled law, and second, when an issue is fairly and squarely presented to a District Court, that Court must address it. Dodging the question is not an option.

The second reason . . . is that in *Johnston v. University of Pittsburgh*, 97 F. Supp. 3d 657 (W.D. Pa. 2015), another member of this Court ruled that the rational basis standard applies to distinctions based on transgender status. *Johnston* also acutely recognized that cases involving transgender status implicate a fast-changing and rapidly-evolving set of issues that must be considered in their own factual contexts. . . .

The Plaintiffs in turn approach this issue with a double-barreled argument. First, they say that in light of the factual record set out above, there simply is no rational basis for the enactment and enforcement of Resolution 2 — at least not as it relates to the use of the High School's restrooms by the Plaintiffs. They contend that there has been no rational basis that can be identified that would insulate Resolution 2 from an Equal Protection challenge, and that in any event the rational basis test, applied in its most accommodating iteration, still requires something, and what there is here is a desire to change the school restrooms that the Plaintiffs had been using without any factual basis to conclude that doing so is necessary or even advisable.

Beyond that, the Plaintiffs contend that the rational basis test is not the test to be applied to the classification enacted by Resolution 2. They say that . . . "intermediate scrutiny," which is applied to classifications based on sex, should apply here. . . .

The Supreme Court uses the following four factors to determine whether a "new" classification requires heightened scrutiny: (1) whether the class has been historically "subjected to discrimination," *Lyng v. Castillo*, 477 U.S. 635 (1986); (2) whether the class has a defining characteristic that "frequently bears no relation to ability to perform or contribute to society," *City of Cleburne v. Cleburne Living Ctr.*, 473 U.S. 432 (1985); (3) whether the class exhibits "obvious, immutable, or distinguishing characteristics that define them as a discrete group," *Lyng*; and (4) whether the class is "a minority or politically powerless." *Id.*

Against that backdrop, the Court concludes that an intermediate standard of Equal Protection review applies in this case. The record before the Court reflects that transgender people as a class have historically been subject to discrimination or differentiation; that they have a defining characteristic that frequently bears no relation to an ability to perform or contribute to society; that as a class they exhibit immutable or distinguishing characteristics that define them as a discrete group; and that as a class, they are a minority with relatively little political power. [*See*] *Adkins v. City of New York*, 143 F. Supp. 3d 134 (S.D.N.Y. 2015). Indeed, the documentary record advanced by the Plaintiffs, and not contested by the District, reveals that, as a class of people, transgender individuals make up a small (according to all parties, less than 1%) proportion of the American population. *Highland*. As to these Plaintiffs, their transgender characteristics are inherent in who they are as people. . . . As to these Plaintiffs, and more generally as to transgender individuals as a class, that characteristic bears no relationship to their ability to contribute to our society. [The] record reveals that the Plaintiffs are in all respects productive, engaged, contributing members of the student body at the High School. Thus, all of the indicia for the application of the heightened intermediate scrutiny standard are present here. *See Carcaño*; *Highland*.

Moreover, as to these Plaintiffs, gender identity is entirely akin to "sex" as that term has been customarily used in the Equal Protection analysis. It is deeply ingrained and inherent in their very beings. Like "sex," as to these Plaintiffs, gender identity is neither transitory nor temporary. Further, what buttresses that conclusion is the fact that the school community as a whole treats these Plaintiffs in all other regards consistently with their stated gender identities, along with the reality that these Plaintiffs live all facets of their lives in a fashion consistent with their stated and experienced gender identities. These are all factors that have informed the judgments of other courts in applying the intermediate scrutiny Equal Protection analysis in the case of classifications involving transgender status, and in this Court's estimation, they apply here. *See Glenn*; *Highland*; *Carcaño*; *Adkins*.

When measured against the legal standard for meeting the intermediate scrutiny test, the Court concludes that the Plaintiffs have a reasonable likelihood of success on the merits. [What] is missing from the record here are facts that demonstrate the "exceedingly persuasive justification" for the enforcement of Resolution 2 as to restroom use by these Plaintiffs . . .

First, such an application of Resolution 2 would not appear to be necessary to quell any actual or incipient threat, disturbance or other disruption of school activities by the Plaintiffs. There is no record of any such thing. . . . Nor would the application of Resolution 2 appear to be necessary to address any such threat or disturbance by anyone else in the High School restrooms, as there is no record evidence of that, either.

Second, Resolution 2 would appear to do little to address any actual privacy concern of any student that is not already well addressed by the physical layout of the bathrooms. . . . [According] to *Doe v. Luzerne Cty.*, 660 F.3d 169 (3d Cir. 2011), . . . that interest, like any stated governmental interest, must be considered in the context of the "facts on the ground," not only as a broadly stated goal, and *Doe* specifically rejected the application of any "bright line" test. Unlike the situation in *Doe*, the facts in this case do not establish any threatened or actually occurring violations of personal privacy.[36] Although the record reveals some specific concerns driven by the reputed presence (and presence alone) of a Plaintiff in a restroom matching her gender identity, there is no record evidence that this actually imperiled or risked imperiling any privacy interest of any person. And . . . given the actual physical layout of the student restrooms at the High School, it would appear to the Court that anyone using the toilets or urinals at the High School is afforded actual physical privacy from others viewing their external sex organs and excretory functions. Conversely, others in the restrooms are shielded from such views.[37]

Third, Resolution 2 would not appear to have been necessary in order to fill some gap in the District's code of student conduct or the positive law of Pennsylvania in order to proscribe unlawful malicious "peeping Tom" activity by anyone pretending to be transgender.[38] There is no evidence of such a gap. The existing disciplinary

_____

36. In *Doe*, the facts drove the rule our Court of Appeals applied. Here they are:

Two sheriff's deputies were swarmed by fleas while searching what appeared to be a crime scene. A decontamination unit was called. All did not go smoothly in setting it up, so the process was moved to a local hospital for decontamination efforts. An involved, flea-attacked female deputy was in the decontamination room there, and another female deputy was with her to examine her for fleas after the afflicted deputy had removed her clothes and taken a shower. The freshly-showered deputy could not find any towels, so she attempted to wrap herself in the thin paper that doctors use to cover their examination tables. Because it was really thin, when it stuck to her wet body it became either transparent or translucent.

Then two male deputies opened the unlocked wooden door to the decontamination area and not only covertly (at least at first) observed the deputy who was nude, but videotaped what was going on in the decontamination area under the rubric of making a "training tape" as to decontamination operations. There was record evidence that the deputy's breasts and buttocks were exposed and observed by the filmmaking deputies. It also appeared that the video captured a tattoo on the deputy's back that inferentially revealed that she was involved in a lesbian relationship. That video tape ended up back at the station house, with descriptive commentary about the female deputy's anatomy included in the "soundtrack" to that video.

After engaging in the requisite fact intensive and context specific analysis, our Court of Appeals had no trouble in concluding that there was at minimum a genuine issue of material fact as to whether the freshly-showered, tissue-paper wrapped, naked sheriff's deputy had a legitimate interest in her bodily privacy when she was both observed by male coworkers in that state, and then videotaped by them, with the video ending up on a public computer file in the sheriff's office (and labeled with the denominator "XXX's ass"). The *Doe* Court also focused on the real risk that the videotape could end up on the Internet.

Despite the reality that there are no similar facts present in this case, the District tells this Court that *Doe* means that in all cases, there is a constitutional "zone of privacy" that starts at the door to a restroom, and whether there is an actual or actually threatened exposure of intimate bodily parts is irrelevant. *Doe* held no such thing. What it does say is that there can be a constitutionally-protected privacy interest in not having parts of your body publicly exposed to others. . . .

37. Put directly, everyone using the toilets in the "girls room" is doing so in an enclosed stall with a locking door, and everyone using the toilets in the "boys room" is doing the same or is using a urinal with privacy screens.

38. In *Carcaño,* the Court noted that laws in North Carolina, similar to those existing in Pennsylvania, adequately dealt with potential "Peeping Tom" situations. Further, the record in that case revealed that there had never been any reported episodes of "imposter" transgender individuals entering a restroom anywhere in the entire University of North Carolina system, nor in any other educational institutions in that state.

rules of the District and the laws of Pennsylvania would address such matters. And as noted above, there is no record evidence of an actual or threatened outbreak of other students falsely or deceptively declaring themselves to be "transgender" for the purpose of engaging in untoward and maliciously improper activities in the High School restrooms.[39]

Fourth, such application of Resolution 2 also would not appear to be supported by any actual need for students to routinely use the corners of the restrooms for changing into athletic gear from street clothes. Even if pressed by such theoretical possibilities, it would appear to the Court that the dozen or so single-user rest-rooms sprinkled around the High School would easily fit the bill for private changing. There is also no record evidence that any student uses, has used, or will use any common restroom outside of its structurally privacy-protected areas in any state of undress or for "excretory functions," which the District advised was the focus of Resolution 2.

In light of where the factual record leads, the Court must next examine the express rationales set forth by the District for applying Resolution 2 to the Plaintiffs' restroom use.

[The] declarations of the Board members recite that some of them had received word that several parents had, and others would, move their children to other schools if the Board did not enact a policy akin to Resolution 2. Additionally, the record reflects that there were members of the community who attended one or more Board meetings and voiced support for Resolution 2. . . . [Like] the Court, [school board members] have sworn fealty to the Constitution and laws of the United States and the Commonwealth of Pennsylvania. If adopting and imple-menting a school policy or practice based on those individual determinations or preferences of parents—no matter how sincerely held—runs counter to the legal obligations of the District, then the District's and the Board's legal obligations must

---

39. To do so in a way that would place them on similar factual footing to the Plaintiffs would take quite a lot. It is undisputed that these Plaintiffs live their lives in all respects consistent only with their gender identities and not their assigned sexes. It is also undisputed that the District treats them that way, that their peers and instructors treat them that way, that their families treat them that way, and that they are in consultation with medical professionals as they undergo medi-cal interventions to fully transition in all physiological respects.

For an "imposter" to take such steps would be an extensive social and medical undertaking. That would appear to the Court to be a really big price to pay in order to engage in intentionally wrongful conduct that is unlawful under state law and contrary to the District's stated expecta-tions as to student conduct. The Court need not determine as a legal matter precisely where the line would fall between individuals who embody gender identities on the same terms as the Plain-tiffs and individuals who are *ad hoc* imposters, but it can observe with confidence that a one-off, episodic declaration of transgender status in an effort to escape the consequences of engaging in nefarious bathroom behavior would not support a factual finding of transgender "gender identity" as is present in this case.

prevail. Those obligations to the law take precedence over responding to constituent desires.[40] The Equal Protection Clause of the Fourteenth Amendment is neither applied nor construed by popular vote. *West Virginia State Bd. of Educ. v. Barnette*, 319 U.S. 624 (1943); *see Obergefell v. Hodges*, 135 S. Ct. 2584 (2015).

[The] District's counsel advised the Court that Resolution 2 was intended to place into concrete District policy certain societal norms and expectations about privacy as to bathroom use. In so doing, they say that the Board was responding to the desires of the public that elected them. Given the analytical construct directed by our Court of Appeals in *Doe*, however, the fact that such interests exist generally, or are longstanding, does not advance the analysis necessary here. There is insufficient record evidence that the steps already in place at the time of Resolution 2's adoption did not adequately and reasonably address them, or that there were any actual or actually threatened risks to any such privacy interests by the actions of these Plaintiffs.

[The] District asserts that there should not be an issue here because any student may use the single-user restrooms sprinkled around the High School. The District has proposed that those single-user bathrooms therefore provide a "safety valve" of sorts for the Plaintiffs if they do not feel comfortable using the common bathrooms matching their assigned sexes, but inconsistent with everything else about them. The Plaintiffs, on the other hand, contend that those single-user restrooms also provide a "safety valve" for any other students who may have especially heightened privacy concerns for whatever reason. Given that settled precedent provides that impermissible distinctions by official edict cause tangible Constitutional harm, *Hassan v. City of New York*, 804 F.3d 277 (3d Cir. 2015), the law does not impose on the Plaintiffs the obligation to use single-user facilities in order to "solve the problem." In these circumstances, that would compel them to use only restrooms inconsistent with their gender identities or to use the "special" restrooms. That is a choice directed by official edict, and it is not a choice compelled of other students. . . .

This all leads to the conclusion that under the intermediate scrutiny standard, the Plaintiffs have established a reasonable likelihood of success on their Equal Protection claim. That is because on the facts now present in the record, the District has not demonstrated that there is an exceedingly persuasive justification for applying Resolution 2 to common restroom use by the Plaintiffs that is substantially related to an important government interest, since there is insufficient record evidence of

---

40. The District also stated that the implementation of Resolution 2 as to the Plaintiffs furthered a "fundamental right" of parents to raise children. It did not explain how or why such rights of other District parents are to take precedence over the same rights of Plaintiffs' parents, who very much desire that Plaintiffs use restrooms conforming to their gender identities. In some ways, this and some other of the District's arguments boil down to contending that Resolution 2 is a legally-permissible restriction on Plaintiffs' use of school bathrooms because more residents who spoke at School Board meetings desired that outcome than not. Historically, that has not been the basis upon which the application of Constitutional rights is to be determined. *West Virginia State Bd. of Educ. v. Barnette*, 319 U.S. 624 (1943).

any actual threat to any legitimate privacy interests of any student by the Plaintiffs' use of such restrooms consistent with their gender identity, or that the set-up of the High School restrooms fails to fully protect the privacy interests of any and every student.[42]

Next, the Court must consider whether Plaintiffs have shown that they are likely to suffer irreparable harm absent injunctive relief and whether the balance of harms tips in their favor. As discussed at length above, the Plaintiffs have set forth — in considerable detail and without factual contradiction by the District — the actual, immediate and irreparable harm that they are experiencing. Courts have long recognized that disparate treatment itself stigmatizes members of a disfavored group as innately inferior, *Heckler v. Mathews*, 465 U.S. 728 (1984), and raises the "inevitable inference" of animosity toward those impacted by the involved classification. *Romer*. Given that the Plaintiffs had been using the restrooms consistent with their gender identities for several years without incident, and are now by formal District directive the discrete group barred from doing so, it is not a long leap, nor really a leap at all, to give credence to the Plaintiffs' assertions that they subjectively feel marginalized, and objectively are being marginalized, which is causing them genuine distress, anxiety, discomfort and humiliation. This Court is in no position to downplay or minimize the nature or consequence of such harm or the likelihood that Plaintiffs will prove it. Its relatively unquantifiable nature makes the Plaintiffs' harm no less real.[44] [That] Plaintiffs' harm is intangible and therefore cannot later be readily remedied by monetary relief is what makes it "irreparable" for these purposes, and is what makes a preliminary injunction appropriate in this case.

On the other hand, it would appear that the grant of relief ordered by the Court here would cause relatively little "harm" in the preliminary injunction sense — if any harm at all — to the District and the High School community. The record reveals that there were no problems with the Plaintiffs' restroom use prior to the Board actions that led to the passage of Resolution 2. Moreover, the record shows that the physical layout of the bathrooms at the High School appears to fully protect any legitimate privacy interests of both the Plaintiffs and all other bathroom users. And it would appear that the state of affairs advanced by applying Resolution 2 to

---

42. Even if the Court were to apply the District's preferred standard, rational basis review, it would likely come to the same conclusion as to Plaintiffs' likelihood of success on the merits. As discussed above, under rational basis review, the Court must "uphold the legislative classification so long as it bears a rational relation to some legitimate end." *Romer*. Here, measuring the factual record against the interests articulated by the District, it appears reasonably likely that Plaintiffs will demonstrate that Resolution 2 is not "narrow enough in scope and grounded in a sufficient factual context" to survive even that deferential standard.

44. Courts have long recognized, for example, that a bare equal protection violation is sufficient to constitute an injury in fact for the purposes of establishing Article III standing because unequal treatment under the law is harm unto itself. *See, e.g., Hassan*, 804 F.3d at 289, n.1 (explaining that the mere act of being singled out for unequal treatment by government edict is a judicially cognizable injury); *see also Northeastern Fla. Chap. Assoc. Gen. Contractors v. City of Jacksonville*, 508 U.S. 656, 666 (1993).

the Plaintiffs could actually risk further harm to their interests without benefitting the District or anyone else.

Finally, in light of the Constitutional import of the commands of the Equal Protection Clause, and in light of the minimal burdens that would flow from requiring the District to return to the mode of bathroom operations as to the Plaintiffs that existed prior to the passage of Resolution 2, which is the *status quo ante*, the public interest is furthered by the grant of a preliminary injunction in this case. Accordingly, the Plaintiffs' Motion for a Preliminary Injunction will be granted on the Plaintiffs' Equal Protection claim. *See Dodds v. U.S. Dept. of Educ.*, 845 F.3d 217 (6th Cir. 2016) (explaining that injunctive relief to protect constitutional rights is by definition in the public interest).

IV

[In this part, the court extensively reviews other litigation involving the rights of transgender students under Title IX to use common restrooms consistent with their gender identity; it gave great weight to the stay that the Supreme Court issued in the *Gavin Grimm* litigation. *See Gloucester County School Board v. G.G., by His Next Friend and Mother, Deirdre Grimm*, 136 S. Ct. 2442 (2016). At the time of the *Evancho* opinion, the Supreme Court had not yet vacated the decision and remanded to the Fourth Circuit Court of Appeals. *See Gloucester County School Bd. v. G.G. ex rel. Grimm*, 137 S. Ct. 1239 (2017).]

Put plainly, the law surrounding the Regulation and its interpretation and application to Title IX claims relative to the use of common restrooms by transgender students, including the impact of the 2017 Guidance [rescinding the Obama administration Guidance], is at this moment so clouded with uncertainty that this Court is not in a position to conclude which party in this case has the likelihood of success on the merits of that statutory claim.

The Court therefore concludes that the necessary showing of likely success on the merits on the Plaintiffs Title IX claim cannot be made at this juncture. Plaintiffs' request for preliminary injunctive relief on Title IX grounds will be denied.

V.

The Plaintiffs appear to the Court to be young people seeking to do what young people try to do every day—go to school, obtain an education, and interact as equals with their peers. The School Board's consideration of these matters appears to have been open, extended and highly engaged. From all accounts, the District's professional educators have worked hard to treat all students, including the Plaintiffs, with respect and to provide all students with an excellent education in an inclusive environment. In doing so, they have sought to comply with the law as their own oaths require while fulfilling the directives of the School Board as embodied in Resolution 2. Their effort to navigate the confluence of the competing demands present here was considerable, and it is likely not the easiest task they have ever confronted. All counsel have put their respective client's best foot forward in their written and oral presentations, and have in all respects brought their "A game" to the task with thoroughness and professionalism.

The Court's holding here need not and does not decide other questions that will arise over time in other school settings or in other situations. What it does do is apply established legal principles to fundamentally undisputed facts to conclude that the Plaintiffs have shown a reasonable likelihood of success on the merits of their claim that the District's enforcement of Resolution 2 as to their use of common school restrooms does not afford them equal protection of the law as guaranteed to them by the Fourteenth Amendment.

An appropriate Order will issue.

————————

Discussion

1. Should acceptance (or lack thereof) as a member of the sex corresponding to one's gender identity factor into a determination of an individual's right to use a particular gendered restroom? Who might be disadvantaged by weighing that factor? Is the district's stated concern about parents threatening to leave the district "giv[ing] effect to private prejudice," which the Supreme Court has said is not permissible under the Constitution? *See Palmore v. Sidoti*, 466 U.S. 429 (1984), Chapter 8, *supra* at p. 472.

2. To what extent, if any, would the court's analysis of restrooms apply to the exclusion of transgender students from *locker* rooms consistent with their gender identity?

3. Later in the summer following this decision, the Pine-Richland School District entered a settlement with Juliette Evancho and the other plaintiffs that "'enjoined [the District] from enforcing . . . any policy, practice, or custom . . . that denies transgender students the access and use of restrooms that match a student's consistently and uniformly expressed gender identity; and taking any formal or informal disciplinary action against transgender students for using the restrooms that match a student's consistently and uniformly asserted gender identity.'" The agreement "also requires the suburban Pittsburgh school district to include gender identity in its nondiscrimination policies and practices, and to adopt policies that respect transgender students' gender identity with respect to student records, names, pronouns, and restrooms, among other aspects." And it "includes new school district administrative regulations and an undisclosed monetary payment." Lambda Legal, *Lambda Legal Lawsuit Forces End to School District Anti-Transgender Bathroom Policy* (July 25, 2017), https://www.lambdalegal.org/news/pa_20170801_pine-richland -settlement.

Note on Whitaker v. Kenosha Unified Board of Education

In *Whitaker v. Kenosha Unified Board of Education*, 858 F.3d 1034 (7th Cir. 2017), the U.S. Court of Appeals for the Seventh Circuit reached a similar conclusion to that of the district court in *Evancho, supra* at p.861. This case was brought by Ashton "Ash" Whitaker, a transgender high school student at the time, who was represented by the Transgender Law Center. Ash sued the school district and its superintendent for excluding him from the boys' restroom based on an unwritten policy of uncertain content, ostensibly applied because, as described by the court of appeals, "it believed[] that his mere presence would invade the privacy rights of his male classmates." The first time Ash and his mother met with Ash's guidance counselor they were told that he could only use girls' restrooms or a gender-neutral restroom in the school's main office, far from his classes. Later, an assistant principal told them that Ash's exclusion was because "he was listed as a female in the school's official records and to change those records, the school needed unspecified 'legal or medical documentation.'" (The school subsequently offered Ash, and only Ash, the option to use two single-user gender-neutral restrooms also far from where he took classes.) Rejecting his pediatrician's letter attesting to Ash's gender identity and recommending he be allowed to use male-designated facilities, the school insisted—without explaining why—that he would have to "complete a surgical transition," which the court stated Ash could not lawfully do until he was 18. Ash did not use the office restroom because he was the only student allowed to and did not wish to further set himself apart from his classmates. He also tried to reduce his water consumption to avoid having to use the restroom during the school day, despite his doctor's recommendation that Ash drink six to seven bottles of water and a bottle of Gatorade daily to avoid fainting and/or seizures due to his vasovagal syncope, with the consequence that he suffered fainting and dizziness, which are symptoms of the condition.

The district court denied the defendants' motion to dismiss and granted Ash's motion for a preliminary injunction to assure him access to boys' restrooms at school and school-related functions, and the court of appeals affirmed in an opinion by Chief Judge Wood joined by Judges Rovner and Williams.[b] The court rejected the defendants' argument that Ash's injuries were "self-inflicted" since he chose not to avail himself of the options they offered; it upheld the district court's finding that Ash's use of boys' restrooms was key to success in his treatment for gender dysphoria, with which he had been diagnosed in accordance with the American Psychiatric Association's *Diagnostic and Statistical Manual of Mental Disorders* (5th ed. 2013) ("DSM-V"). [*See* Chapter 14, *infra*, at p. 1019 for pertinent excerpts from DSM-V.]

---

b. "Although not part of this appeal," the court noted, "Ash contends that he has also been subjected to other negative actions by the School District, including initially prohibiting him from running for prom king, referring to him with female pronouns, using his birth name, and requiring him to room with female students or alone on school-sponsored trips. Furthermore, Ash learned in May 2016 that school administrators had considered instructing its guidance counselors to distribute bright green wristbands to Ash and other transgender students so that their bathroom usage could be monitored more easily. Throughout this litigation, the School District has denied that it considered implementing the wristband plan."

The court of appeals affirmed the district court's conclusions that Ash suffi-ciently pled that he would suffer irreparable injury and that he lacked an adequate remedy at law; the court emphasized that the harms Ash pled the policy caused him led to a risk of his committing suicide, and it concluded that money damages would not adequately compensate him either for that risk or for "preventable 'life-long diminished well-being and life-functioning'" that Ash alleged. The court of appeals also concluded that the balance of harms favored Ash. In opposition to the harms he faced from the policy were it not enjoined, the court concluded, the school district did not show any harm to it or the public were it enjoined; Ash had used boys' restrooms at schools without incident or student complaint for six months, and amici school administrators from districts with a combined 1.4 million stu-dents represented that no harms materialized from their trans-inclusive restroom policies, in 21 states and the District of Columbia.

The court also concluded that Ash established a likelihood of success on the mer-its of his Title IX and equal protection claims. On the Title IX claim, the court rea-soned that Ash's allegation that he was denied access to the boys' restroom because he is transgender is sex discrimination under that statute, because in requiring him to use common restrooms that do not conform to his gender identity the school is punishing him for his gender non-conformity and because the "policy also subjects Ash, as a transgender student, to different rules, sanctions, and treatment than non-transgender students." (The court also rejected as factually inaccurate, given Ash's medical diagnosis and the fact that he had been living consistently with his gender identity, the defendants' refrain that Ash was improperly seeking to "unilaterally declare" his gender.)

On Ash's equal protection claim, the court of appeals wrote approvingly of Ash's argument that discrimination against transgender people should be protected by heightened scrutiny as a minority historically discriminated against based on gender identity, an immutable characteristic; it recounted "alarming" data about harassment and physical and sexual assault of transgender and gender non-conforming students in grades K-12 as reported in Jaime M. Grant et al., National Center for Transgender Equality, Injustice at Every Turn: A Report of the National Transgender Discrimination Survey 33 (2011) (available at http://www .transequality.org/sites/default/files/docs/resources/NTDS_Report.pdf). However, it did not rule on that contention because it concluded that the challenged policy classified on the basis of sex (and displayed sex stereotyping) and therefore was sub-ject to intermediate scrutiny under the Equal Protection Clause:

> Here, the School District's policy cannot be stated without referencing sex, as the School District decides which bathroom a student may use based upon the sex listed on the student's birth certificate. This policy is inher-ently based upon a sex-classification and heightened review applies. Fur-ther, the School District argues that since it treats all boys and girls the same, it does not violate the Equal Protection Clause. This is untrue. Rather, the School District treats transgender students like Ash, who fail to

conform to the sex-based stereotypes associated with their assigned sex at birth, differently. These students are disciplined under the School District's bathroom policy if they choose to use a bathroom that conforms to their gender identity. . . .

The court rejected the district's argument that, as the court put it, "[t]he mere presence of a transgender student in the bathroom . . . infringes upon the privacy rights of other students with whom he or she does not share biological anatomy." The court insisted that the defendants' interest in protecting privacy rights "must be weighed against the facts of the case and not just examined in the abstract, to determine whether this justification is genuine" as required under heightened scrutiny. But again, the court viewed the defendants' claim as "based upon sheer conjecture and abstraction" given the record of Ash's nearly half year of using boys' restrooms without incident (using stalls not urinals) and the policy's utter failure "to protect the privacy rights of each individual student vis-à-vis students who share similar anatomy." The court of appeals reasoned:

> A transgender student's presence in the restroom provides no more of a risk to other students' privacy rights than the presence of an overly curious student of the same biological sex who decides to sneak glances at his or her classmates performing their bodily functions. Or for that matter, any other student who uses the bathroom at the same time. Common sense tells us that the communal restroom is a place where individuals act in a discreet manner to protect their privacy and those who have true privacy concerns are able to utilize a stall. Nothing in the record suggests that the bathrooms at Tremper High School are particularly susceptible to an intrusion upon an individual's privacy. . . .

The court of appeals was suspicious of the bona fides of the district's policy and even its existence. The court noted that at oral argument the district insisted Ash would need to present a birth certificate designating his sex as male to use boys' restrooms, but this supposed requirement was never communicated to his mother before Ash's suit. Birth certificate sex designations are not based on chromosomes, and the court also noted that male or female designations thereon "would not adequately account for or reflect one's biological sex" in part due to the existence of people with various intersex conditions. In addition, states other than Wisconsin allow changes of birth certificate sex markers without requiring genitoplasty, so under the claimed policy a transgender male student "could move to Kenosha and be permitted to use the boys' restroom in one of the School District's schools even though he retains female anatomy." Moreover, the district accepts passports for new students in lieu of birth certificates, and the State Department does not require genitoplasty for changing a sex marker on a passport, which again underscored what the court considered "the arbitrary nature of the policy," which therefore lacked the "exceedingly persuasive justification" required at a minimum by heightened scrutiny. With Ash thus showing a likelihood of success on the merits, the court of appeals affirmed the grant of a preliminary injunction in his favor.

Discussion

1. Does the court's sex discrimination reasoning logically mean that excluding cisgender girls from boys' restrooms is sex discrimination that must survive intermediate scrutiny? Would the court's reasoning apply to the exclusion of a boy who is transgender from a boy's *locker room* at school? How *should* such an exclusion be analyzed under the Equal Protection Clause?

2. The defendants argued, as the court summarized it, that "implementing an inclusive policy will result in the demise of gender-segregated facilities in schools." If, in fact, as the full *Whitaker* opinion suggests (noting the experiences reported by amici school administrators with trans-inclusive restroom policies), "allowing transgender students to use facilities that align with their gender identity has actually reinforced the concept of separate facilities for boys and girls," should we regard that as positive or negative (a feature or a bug)? Mary Anne Case, for example, has expressed the view that sex-segregated restrooms come with more cost than benefit. Mary Anne Case, *Why Not Abolish Laws of Urinary Segregation*, in Toilet: Public Restrooms and the Politics of Sharing pp. 211–25 (Harvey Molotch & Laura Norén eds., 2010). For an account of a creative alliance among "genderqueer and disabled" people working, inter alia, "to push for more gender-neutral bathrooms and showers in the dormitories, and to investigate the feasibility of multi-stall gender-neutral bathrooms around campus as a whole" on one university campus, see Simone Chess et al., *Calling All Restroom Revolutionaries!, in* That's Revolting! Queer Strategies for Resisting Assimilation pp. 189–205 (Mattilda aka Matt Bernstein Sycamore ed., 2004).

3. Days after his victory in the Seventh Circuit Court of Appeals upholding the district court's preliminary injunction against the school board, Ash Whitaker graduated from George Nelson Tremper High School in June 2017. In January 2018, the Kenosha Unified Board of Education approved a settlement of Ash's case, withdrawing its Supreme Court cert petition, allowing Ash Whitaker to use men's restrooms should he visit campus as an alum or community member (though not assuring such access for other trans males), and paying $800,000 to Ash and his attorneys for the harms he endured and their reasonable attorney's fees and costs. Tasneem Nashrulla, *A School District Will Pay $800,000 to Settle a Transgender Student's Discrimination Lawsuit*, BuzzFeed News (Jan. 10, 2018), https://www.buzzfeednews.com/article/tasneemnashrulla/transgender-student-discrimination-settlement (last visited Oct. 19, 2019).

4. For an argument that gender confirmation surgery requirements for birth certificate sex marker amendment are unconstitutional, and therefore that such requirements cannot be used to forestall "Title IX relief for transgender students regarding the use of sex-segregated facilities," see Kyle C. Velte, *Mitigating the "LGBT Disconnect": Title IX's Protection of Transgender Students, Birth Certificate*

Correction Statutes, and the Transformative Potential of Connecting the Two, 27 Am. U. J. Gender Soc. Pol'y & L. 29, 35 (2019).

The Gavin Grimm Litigation

The highest profile litigation to date over appropriate access to restrooms for students (or any transgender persons, for that matter) has been that brought by Gavin Grimm seeking access to the boys' restrooms in his Virginia public high school. Although the suit was originally filed using his initials "G.G." because he was a minor, Gavin has been quite public throughout the legal dispute, which went up to the Supreme Court at least once. Although Gavin initially used boys' restrooms with the approval of his school's administration, the board of education for the county school district thereafter adopted a policy that excluded him from boys' rooms. Gavin sued in federal court, arguing that the board violated his equal protection rights and his rights against sex discrimination under Title IX of the Education Amendments of 1972. The district court dismissed his Title IX claim for failure to state a claim upon which relief could be granted, and without reaching the merits of his equal protection claim, denied his motion for a preliminary injunction on the ground that the balance of equities did not favor Gavin. Over one judge's dissent, the first decision by the court of appeals in the case granted deference to the January 2015 opinion letter of the Education Department and reversed the dismissal of the Title IX claim. It also vacated the denial of a preliminary injunction and remanded the case for the district court to apply the correct legal standard. The majority of the court of appeals did not reach the merits of Gavin's equal protection claim.

Reading Guide for Grimm v. Gloucester County School Board *(first appellate opinion)*

1. What is the court's reasoning for concluding that the Title IX regulation allowing schools to have sex-segregated restrooms was ambiguous? Having concluded that the regulation was ambiguous, what reasons did the majority offer for why the Department of Education's interpretation of that regulation (which was articulated in a January 7, 2015 opinion letter) was reasonable? What kind of weight did the court give to the Department's interpretation of the regulation?

2. Why did dissenting Judge Niemeyer maintain that the regulation was unambiguous? (Does he engage with the specific textual arguments the majority made to support its contrary view?)

3. What exactly is the dissenting judge's argument as to why assuring gendered restroom access according to gender identity would be "nonsensical"?

G.G., By His Next Friend and Mother, Deirdre Grimm
v. Gloucester County School Board

822 F.3d 709 (4th Cir. 2016)

[Gavin Grimm was represented by the ACLU and its Virginia affiliate. He was supported by amici including the United States; school administrators from ten states and the District of Columbia; nine "non-profit legal and advocacy groups with expertise in both Title IX and sex discrimination issues more broadly, and a non-profit professional organization for school and college Title IX Coordinators and other administrators charged with enforcing Title IX compliance"; WPATH and other organizations and professionals with expertise in transgender healthcare; "one transgender high school student and seven public interest organizations whose professional employees have served and supported transgender youth." The school board was supported by amici including four states and two governors; the conservative advocacy organization Eagle Forum Education and Legal Defense Fund; the conservative organization The Family Foundation of Virginia; students or parents of students attending school in Gloucester County, and other concerned residents of the county (represented by the anti-LGBT "family values" organization Alliance Defending Freedom); The Liberty Center for Child Protection a/k/a the Liberty Center for Child Protection Institute and its director Judith Reisman, a member of the faculty at Liberty University (represented by Christian Right advocacy organization Liberty Counsel).]

Before NIEMEYER and FLOYD, Circuit Judges, and DAVIS, Senior Circuit Judge.

FLOYD, Circuit Judge:

. . . .

I

. . . . Because this case comes to us after dismissal pursuant to Federal Rule of Civil Procedure 12(b)(6), the facts below are generally as stated in G.G.'s complaint.

A

G.G. is a transgender boy now in his junior year at Gloucester High School. G.G.'s birth-assigned sex, or so-called "biological sex," is female, but G.G.'s gender identity is male. G.G. has been diagnosed with gender dysphoria, a medical condition characterized by clinically significant distress caused by an incongruence between a person's gender identity and the person's birth-assigned sex. Since the end of his freshman year, G.G. has undergone hormone therapy and has legally changed his name to G., a traditionally male name. G.G. lives all aspects of his life as a boy. G.G. has not, however, had sex reassignment surgery.[1]

————————

1. The World Professional Association for Transgender Health (WPATH) has established Standards of Care for individuals with gender dysphoria. These Standards of Care are accepted as authoritative by organizations such as the American Medical Association and the American

Before beginning his sophomore year, G.G. and his mother told school officials that G.G. was a transgender boy. The officials were supportive and took steps to ensure that he would be treated as a boy by teachers and staff. Later, at G.G.'s request, school officials allowed G.G. to use the boys' restroom.[2] G.G. used this restroom without incident for about seven weeks. G.G.'s use of the boys' restroom, however, excited the interest of others in the community, some of whom contacted the Gloucester County School Board (the Board) seeking to bar G.G. from continuing to use the boys' restroom.

Board Member Carla B. Hook (Hook) added an item to the agenda for the November 11, 2014 board meeting titled "Discussion of Use of Restrooms/Locker Room Facilities." Hook proposed the following resolution (hereinafter the "transgender restroom policy" or "the policy"):

> Whereas the GCPS [*i.e.*, Gloucester County Public Schools] recognizes that some students question their gender identities, and
>
> Whereas the GCPS encourages such students to seek support, advice, and guidance from parents, professionals and other trusted adults, and
>
> Whereas the GCPS seeks to provide a safe learning environment for all students and to protect the privacy of all students, therefore
>
> It shall be the practice of the GCPS to provide male and female restroom and locker room facilities in its schools, and the use of said facilities shall be limited to the corresponding biological genders, and students with gender identity issues shall be provided an alternative appropriate private facility.

At the November 11, 2014 meeting twenty-seven people spoke during the Citizens' Comment Period, a majority of whom supported Hook's proposed resolution. Many of the speakers displayed hostility to G.G., including by referring pointedly to him as a "young lady." Others claimed that permitting G.G. to use the boys' restroom would violate the privacy of other students and would lead to sexual assault in restrooms. One commenter suggested that if the proposed policy were not adopted, non-transgender boys would come to school wearing dresses in order to gain access to the girls' restrooms. G.G. and his parents spoke against the proposed policy. Ultimately, the Board postponed a vote on the policy until its next meeting on December 9, 2014.

At the December 9 meeting, approximately thirty-seven people spoke during the Citizens' Comment Period. Again, most of those who spoke were in favor of the proposed resolution. Some speakers threatened to vote the Board members out of office if the Board members voted against the proposed policy. Speakers again referred to G.G. as a "girl" or "young lady." One speaker called G.G. a "freak" and

---

Psychological Association. The WPATH Standards of Care do not permit sex reassignment surgery for persons who are under the legal age of majority.

2. G.G. does not participate in the school's physical education programs. He does not seek here, and never has sought, use of the boys' locker room. Only restroom use is at issue in this case.

compared him to a person who thinks he is a "dog" and wants to urinate on fire hydrants. Following this second comment period, the Board voted 6–1 to adopt the proposed policy, thereby barring G.G. from using the boys' restroom at school.

G.G. alleges that he cannot use the girls' restroom because women and girls in those facilities "react[] negatively because they perceive[] G.G. to be a boy." Further, using the girls' restroom would "cause severe psychological distress" to G.G. and would be incompatible with his treatment for gender dysphoria. As a corollary to the policy, the Board announced a series of updates to the school's restrooms to improve general privacy for all students, including adding or expanding partitions between urinals in male restrooms, adding privacy strips to the doors of stalls in all restrooms, and constructing single-stall unisex restrooms available to all students. G.G. alleges that he cannot use these new unisex restrooms because they "make him feel even more stigmatized. . . . Being required to use the separate restrooms sets him apart from his peers, and serves as a daily reminder that the school views him as 'different.'" G.G. further alleges that, because of this stigma and exclusion, his social transition is undermined and he experiences "severe and persistent emotional and social harms." G.G. avoids using the restroom while at school and has, as a result of this avoidance, developed multiple urinary tract infections.

B

G.G. sued the Board on June 11, 2015. G.G. seeks an injunction allowing him to use the boys' restroom. . . . On July 27, 2015, the district court held a hearing on G.G.'s motion for a preliminary injunction and on the Board's motion to dismiss G.G.'s lawsuit. [The] district court orally dismissed G.G.'s Title IX claim and denied his request for a preliminary injunction, but withheld ruling on the motion to dismiss G.G.'s equal protection claim. . . .

[The] district court reasoned that Title IX prohibits discrimination on the basis of sex and not on the basis of other concepts such as gender, gender identity, or sexual orientation. The district court observed that the regulations implementing Title IX specifically allow schools to provide separate restrooms on the basis of sex. The district court concluded that G.G.'s sex was female and that requiring him to use the female restroom facilities did not impermissibly discriminate against him on the basis of sex in violation of Title IX. With respect to G.G.'s request for an injunction, the district court found that G.G. had not made the required showing that the balance of equities was in his favor. The district court found that requiring G.G. to use the unisex restrooms during the pendency of this lawsuit was not unduly burdensome and would result in less hardship than requiring other students made uncomfortable by G.G.'s presence in the boys' restroom to themselves use the unisex restrooms.

This appeal followed. . . . The United States, as it did below, has filed an amicus brief supporting G.G.'s Title IX claim in order to defend the government's interpretation of Title IX as requiring schools to provide transgender students access to restrooms congruent with their gender identity.

II

. . . . Title IX provides: "[n]o person . . . shall, on the basis of sex, be excluded from participation in, be denied the benefits of, or be subjected to discrimination under any education program or activity receiving Federal financial assistance." 20 U.S.C. § 1681(a). To allege a violation of Title IX, G.G. must allege (1) that he was excluded from participation in an education program because of his sex; (2) that the educational institution was receiving federal financial assistance at the time of his exclusion; and (3) that the improper discrimination caused G.G. harm. *See Preston v. Virginia ex rel. New River Cmty. Coll.*, 31 F.3d 203 (4th Cir. 1994) (citing *Cannon v. Univ. of Chi.*, 441 U.S. 677 (1979)). We look to case law interpreting Title VII of the Civil Rights Act of 1964 for guidance in evaluating a claim brought under Title IX. *Jennings v. Univ. of N.C.*, 482 F.3d 686 (4th Cir. 2007).

Not all distinctions on the basis of sex are impermissible under Title IX. For example, Title IX [provides]: "nothing contained [in Title IX] shall be construed to prohibit any educational institution receiving funds under this Act, from maintaining separate living facilities for the different sexes." 20 U.S.C. § 1686. The Department's regulations implementing Title IX permit the provision of "separate toilet, locker room, and shower facilities on the basis of sex, but such facilities provided for students of one sex shall be comparable to such facilities provided for students of the other sex." 34 C.F.R. § 106.33. The Department recently delineated how this regulation should be applied to transgender individuals. In an opinion letter dated January 7, 2015, the Department's Office for Civil Rights (OCR) wrote: "When a school elects to separate or treat students differently on the basis of sex . . . a school generally must treat transgender students consistent with their gender identity."[5]

A

G.G., and the United States as amicus curiae, ask us to give the Department's interpretation of its own regulation controlling weight pursuant to *Auer v. Robbins*, 519 U.S. 452 (1997). *Auer* requires that an agency's interpretation of its own

---

5. The opinion letter cites to OCR's December 2014 "Questions and Answers on Title IX and Single-Sex Elementary and Secondary Classes and Extracurricular Activities." This document, denoted a "significant guidance document" per Office of Management and Budget regulations, states: "All students, including transgender students and students who do not conform to sex stereotypes, are protected from sex-based discrimination under Title IX. Under Title IX, a recipient generally must treat transgender students consistent with their gender identity in all aspects of the planning, implementation, enrollment, operation, and evaluation of single-sex classes." Office of Civil Rights, Dept. of Educ., Questions and Answers on Title IX and Single-Sex Elementary and Secondary Classes and Extracurricular Activities 25 (2014) available at http://www2.ed.gov/about /offices/list/ocr/docs/faqs-title-ix-single-sex-201412.pdf.

The dissent suggests that we ignore the part of OCR's opinion letter in which the agency "also encourages schools to offer the use of gender-neutral, individual-user facilities to any student who does not want to use shared sex-segregated facilities," as the Board did here. However, because G.G. does want to use shared sex-segregated facilities, the agency's suggestion regarding students who do not want to use such shared sex-segregated facilities is immaterial to the resolution of G.G.'s claim. Nothing in today's opinion restricts any school's ability to provide individual-user facilities.

ambiguous regulation be given controlling weight unless the interpretation is plainly erroneous or inconsistent with the regulation or statute. . . .

. . . .

The United States contends that the regulation clarifies statutory ambiguity by making clear that schools may provide separate restrooms for boys and girls "without running afoul of Title IX." Br. for the United States as Amicus Curiae. However, the Department also considers § 106.33 itself to be ambiguous as to transgender students because "the regulation is silent on what the phrases 'students of one sex' and 'students of the other sex' mean in the context of transgender students." The United States contends that the interpretation contained in OCR's January 7, 2015 letter resolves the ambiguity in § 106.33 as that regulation applies to transgender individuals.

B

. . . . We determine ambiguity by analyzing the language under the three-part framework set forth in *Robinson v. Shell Oil Co.*, 519 U.S. 337 (1997). The plainness or ambiguity of language is determined by reference to (1) the language itself, (2) the specific context in which that language is used, and (3) the broader context of the statute or regulation as a whole.

[The] language itself—"of one sex" and "of the other sex"—refers to male and female students. Second, in the specific context of § 106.33, the plain meaning of the regulatory language is best stated by the United States: "the mere act of providing separate restroom facilities for males and females does not violate Title IX. . . ." Third, the language "of one sex" and "of the other sex" appears repeatedly in the broader context of 34 C.F.R. § 106 Subpart D, titled "Discrimination on the Basis of Sex in Education Programs or Activities Prohibited." This repeated formulation indicates two sexes ("one sex" and "the other sex"), and the only reasonable reading of the language used throughout the relevant regulatory section is that it references male and female. Read plainly then, § 106.33 permits schools to provide separate toilet, locker room, and shower facilities for its male and female students. By implication, the regulation also permits schools to exclude males from the female facilities and vice-versa.

. . . . Although the regulation may refer unambiguously to males and females, it is silent as to how a school should determine whether a transgender individual is a male or female for the purpose of access to sex-segregated restrooms. We conclude that the regulation is susceptible to more than one plausible reading because it permits both the Board's reading—determining maleness or femaleness with reference exclusively to genitalia—and the Department's interpretation—determining maleness or femaleness with reference to gender identity. It is not clear to us how the regulation would apply in a number of situations—even under the Board's own "biological gender" formulation. For example, which restroom would a transgender individual who had undergone sex-reassignment surgery use? What about an intersex individual? What about an individual born with X-X-Y sex chromosomes?

What about an individual who lost external genitalia in an accident? The Department's interpretation resolves ambiguity by providing that in the case of a transgender individual using a sex-segregated facility, the individual's sex as male or female is to be generally determined by reference to the student's gender identity.

C

Because we conclude that the regulation is ambiguous as applied to transgender individuals, the Department's interpretation is entitled to *Auer* deference unless the Board demonstrates that the interpretation is plainly erroneous or inconsistent with the regulation or statute. . . . An agency's view need only be reasonable to warrant deference. *Pauley v. BethEnergy Mines, Inc.*, 501 U.S. 680 (1991).

Title IX regulations were promulgated by the Department of Health, Education, and Welfare in 1975 and were adopted unchanged by the Department in 1980. Two dictionaries from the drafting era inform our analysis of how the term "sex" was understood at that time. The first defines "sex" as "the character of being either male or female" or "the sum of those anatomical and physiological differences with reference to which the male and female are distinguished. . . ." AMERICAN COLLEGE DICTIONARY (1970). The second defines "sex" as:

> the sum of the morphological, physiological, and behavioral peculiarities of living beings that subserves biparental reproduction with its concomitant genetic segregation and recombination which underlie most evolutionary change, that in its typical dichotomous occurrence is usu[ally] genetically controlled and associated with special sex chromosomes, and that is typically manifested as maleness and femaleness. . . .

WEBSTER'S THIRD NEW INTERNATIONAL DICTIONARY (1971).

Although these definitions suggest that the word "sex" was understood at the time the regulation was adopted to connote male and female and that maleness and femaleness were determined primarily by reference to the factors the district court termed "biological sex," namely reproductive organs, the definitions also suggest that a hard-and-fast binary division on the basis of reproductive organs — although useful in most cases — was not universally descriptive. The dictionaries, therefore, used qualifiers such as reference to the "sum of" various factors, "typical dichotomous occurrence," and "typically manifested as maleness and femaleness." Section 106.33 assumes a student population composed of individuals of what has traditionally been understood as the usual "dichotomous occurrence" of male and female where the various indicators of sex all point in the same direction. It sheds little light on how exactly to determine the "character of being either male or female" where those indicators diverge. We conclude that the Department's interpretation of how § 106.33 and its underlying assumptions should apply to transgender individuals is not plainly erroneous or inconsistent with the text of the regulation. The regulation is silent as to which restroom transgender individuals are to use when a school elects to provide sex-segregated restrooms, and the Department's interpretation, although perhaps not the intuitive one, is permitted by the varying physical, psychological, and social aspects—or, in the words of an older dictionary, "the morphological, physiological, and behavioral peculiarities"—included in the term "sex."

D

. . . .

Although the Department's interpretation is novel because there was no interpretation as to how § 106.33 applied to transgender individuals before January 2015, "novelty alone is no reason to refuse deference" and does not render the current interpretation inconsistent with prior agency practice. *See Talk Am., Inc. v. Mich. Bell Tel. Co.*, 564 U.S. 50 (2011). As the United States explains, the issue in this case "did not arise until recently," because schools have only recently begun citing § 106.33 as justification for enacting new policies restricting transgender students' access to restroom facilities. . . .

Nor is the interpretation merely a convenient litigating position. The Department has consistently enforced this position since 2014. *See J.A.* (providing examples of OCR enforcement actions to secure transgender students access to restrooms congruent with their gender identities). Finally, this interpretation cannot properly be considered a post hoc rationalization because it is in line with the existing guidances and regulations of a number of federal agencies—all of which provide that transgender individuals should be permitted access to the restroom that corresponds with their gender identities.[8] U.S. Br. 17 n. 5 & n. 6 (citing publications by the Occupational Safety and Health Administration, the Equal Employment Opportunity Commission, the Department of Housing and Urban Development, and the Office of Personnel Management). . . .

E

We conclude that the Department's interpretation of its own regulation, § 106.33, as it relates to restroom access by transgender individuals, is entitled to *Auer* deference and is to be accorded controlling weight in this case. We reverse the district court's contrary conclusion and its resultant dismissal of G.G.'s Title IX claim.

F

In many respects, we are in agreement with the dissent. We agree that "sex" should be construed uniformly throughout Title IX and its implementing regulations. We

---

8. We disagree with the dissent's suggestion that the result we reach today renders the enforcement of separate restroom facilities impossible because it "would require schools to assume gender identity based on appearances, social expectations, or explicit declarations of identity." Accepting the Board's position would equally require the school to assume "biological sex" based on "appearances, social expectations, or explicit declarations of [biological sex]." Certainly, no one is suggesting mandatory verification of the "correct" genitalia before admittance to a restroom. The Department's vision of sex-segregated restrooms which takes account of gender identity presents no greater "impossibility of enforcement" problem than does the Board's "biological gender" vision of sex-segregated restrooms.

agree that it has indeed been commonplace and widely accepted to separate public restrooms, locker rooms, and shower facilities on the basis of sex. We agree that "an individual has a legitimate and important interest in bodily privacy such that his or her nude or partially nude body, genitalia, and other private parts" are not involuntarily exposed.[10] It is not apparent to us, however, that the truth of these propositions undermines the conclusion we reach regarding the level of deference due to the Department's interpretation of its own regulations.

. . . . In a case such as this, where there is no constitutional challenge to the regulation or agency interpretation, the weighing of privacy interests or safety concerns[11]—fundamentally questions of policy—is a task committed to the agency, not to the courts.

. . . . Not only may a subsequent administration choose to implement a different policy, but Congress may also, of course, revise Title IX explicitly to prohibit or authorize the course charted here by the Department regarding the use of restrooms by transgender students. . . .

III

G.G. also asks us to reverse the district court's denial of the preliminary injunction he sought which would have allowed him to use the boys' restroom during the pendency of this lawsuit. . . .

The district court analyzed G.G.'s request only with reference to . . . the balance of hardships . . . and found that the balance of hardships did not weigh in G.G.'s favor. G.G. submitted two declarations in support of his complaint, one from G.G. himself and one from a medical expert, Dr. Randi Ettner, to explain what harms G.G. will suffer as a result of his exclusion from the boys' restroom. The district

---

10. We doubt that G.G.'s use of the communal restroom of his choice threatens the type of constitutional abuses present in the cases cited by the dissent. For example, G.G.'s use—or for that matter any individual's appropriate use—of a restroom will not involve the type of intrusion present in *Brannum v. Overton Cty. Sch. Bd.*, 516 F.3d 489 (6th Cir. 2008) (involving the videotaping of students dressing and undressing in school locker rooms), *Beard v. Whitmore Lake Sch. Dist.*, 402 F.3d 598 (6th Cir. 2005) (involving the indiscriminate strip searching of twenty male and five female students), or *Sepulveda v. Ramirez*, 967 F.2d 1413 (9th Cir. 1992) (involving a male parole officer forcibly entering a bathroom stall with a female parolee to supervise the provision of a urine sample).

11. The dissent accepts the Board's invocation of amorphous safety concerns as a reason for refusing deference to the Department's interpretation. We note that the record is devoid of any evidence tending to show that G.G.'s use of the boys' restroom creates a safety issue. We also note that the Board has been, perhaps deliberately, vague as to the nature of the safety concerns it has—whether it fears that it cannot ensure G.G.'s safety while in the restroom or whether it fears G.G. himself is a threat to the safety of others in the restroom. We are unconvinced of the existence of danger caused by "sexual responses prompted by students' exposure to the private body parts of students of the other biological sex." The same safety concern would seem to require segregated restrooms for gay boys and girls who would, under the dissent's formulation, present a safety risk because of the "sexual responses prompted" by their exposure to the private body parts of other students of the same sex in sex-segregated restrooms.

court refused to consider this evidence because it was "replete with inadmissible evidence including thoughts of others, hearsay, and suppositions."

[The Court of Appeals proceeds next to conclude that the district court erred in excluding evidence on Gavin's preliminary injunction motion using more stringent standards of admissibility at trial.]

. . . . We vacate the district court's denial of G.G.'s motion for a preliminary injunction and remand the case to the district court for consideration of G.G.'s evidence in light of the [proper] evidentiary standards. . . .

For the foregoing reasons, the judgment of the district court is

REVERSED IN PART, VACATED IN PART, AND REMANDED.

[Senior Circuit Judge Davis's concurring opinion is omitted. He argued that the evidence was such that the Court of Appeals could have properly granted the preliminary injunction Gavin sought. Judge Davis concluded the substance of his concurrence as follows: "It is to be hoped that the district court will turn its attention to this matter with the urgency the case poses. Under the circumstances here, the appropriateness and necessity of such prompt action is plain. By the time the district court issues its decision, G.G. will have suffered the psychological harm the injunction sought to prevent for an entire school year."]

NIEMEYER, Circuit Judge, concurring in part and dissenting in part:

. . . .

[The] majority's opinion, for the first time ever, holds that a public high school may not provide separate restrooms and locker rooms on the basis of biological sex. Rather, it must now allow a biological male student who identifies as female to use the girls' restrooms and locker rooms and, likewise, must allow a biological female student who identifies as male to use the boys' restrooms and locker rooms. This holding completely tramples on all universally accepted protections of privacy and safety that are based on the anatomical differences between the sexes. And, unwittingly, it also tramples on the very concerns expressed by G.G., who said that he should not be forced to go to the girls' restrooms because of the "severe psychological distress" it would inflict on him and because female students had "reacted negatively" to his presence in girls' restrooms. Surely biological males who identify as females would encounter similar reactions in the girls' restroom, just as students physically exposed to students of the opposite biological sex would be likely to experience psychological distress. As a result, schools would no longer be able to protect physiological privacy as between students of the opposite biological sex.

This unprecedented holding overrules custom, culture, and the very demands inherent in human nature for privacy and safety, which the separation of such facilities is designed to protect. More particularly, it also misconstrues the clear language of Title IX and its regulations. And finally, it reaches an unworkable and illogical result.

. . . .

Title IX and its implementing regulations are not ambiguous. . . . I would affirm the district court's dismissal of G.G.'s Title IX claim.

I

The relevant facts are not in dispute. . . .

. . . . The School Board . . . faced a dilemma. It recognized G.G.'s feelings, as he expressed them, that "[u]sing the girls' restroom[s][was] not possible" because of the "severe psychological distress" it would inflict on him and because female students had previously "reacted negatively" to his presence in the girls' restrooms. It now also had to recognize that boys had similar feelings caused by G.G.'s use of the boys' restrooms, although G.G. stated that he continued using the boys' restrooms for some seven weeks without personally receiving complaints from fellow students.

. . . .

II

G.G. . . . . argues, "discrimination against transgender people is necessarily discrimination based on sex because it is impossible to treat people differently based on their transgender status without taking their sex into account." He concludes that the School Board's policy addressing restrooms and locker rooms thus illegally fails to include transgender persons on the basis of their gender identity. In particular, he concludes that he is "prevent[ed] . . . from using the same restrooms as other students and relegat[ed] . . . to separate, single-stall facilities."

[The] School Board's policy designates the use of restrooms and locker rooms based on the student's biological sex; biological females are assigned to the girls' restrooms and unisex restrooms; biological males are assigned to the boys' restrooms and unisex restrooms. G.G. is thus assigned to the girls' restrooms and the unisex restrooms, but is denied the use of the boys' restrooms. He asserts, however, that because neither he nor the girls would accept his use of the girls' restroom, he is relegated to the unisex restrooms, which is stigmatizing.

The School Board contends that it is treating all students the same way, as it explains:

> The School Board's policy does not discriminate against any class of students. Instead, the policy was developed to treat all students and situations the same. To respect the safety and privacy of all students, the School Board has had a long-standing practice of limiting the use of restroom and locker room facilities to the corresponding biological sex of the students. The School Board also provides three single-stall bathrooms for any student to use regardless of his or her biological sex. Under the School Board's restroom policy, G.G. is being treated like every other student in the Gloucester Schools. All students have two choices. Every student can use a restroom associated with their anatomical sex, whether they are boys or girls. If students choose not to use the restroom associated with their anatomical sex, the students can use a private, single-stall restroom. No student is permitted

to use the restroom of the opposite sex. As a result, all students, including female to male transgender and male to female transgender students, are treated the same. . . .

. . . .

Title IX . . . provides, "Notwithstanding anything to the contrary contained in this chapter, nothing contained herein shall be construed to prohibit any educational institution receiving funds under this Act, from maintaining separate living facilities *for the different sexes.*" 20 U.S.C. § 1686 (emphasis added); *see also* 34 C.F.R. § 106.32(b) (permitting schools to provide "separate housing *on the basis of sex*" as long as the housing is "proportionate" and "comparable" (emphasis added)). Similarly, implementing Regulation 106.33 provides for particular separate facilities, as follows:

> A recipient may provide separate toilet, locker room, and shower facilities *on the basis of sex*, but such facilities provided for students of one sex shall be comparable to such facilities provided for students of the other sex.

34 C.F.R. § 106.33 (emphasis added). Thus, although Title IX and its regulations provide generally that a school receiving federal funds may not discriminate on the basis of sex, they also specify that a school does not violate the Act by providing, on the basis of sex, separate living facilities, restrooms, locker rooms, and shower facilities.

While G.G. only challenges the definition and application of the term "sex" with respect to separate restrooms, acceptance of his argument would necessarily change the definition of "sex" for purposes of assigning separate living facilities, locker rooms, and shower facilities as well. . . .

Across societies and throughout history, it has been commonplace and universally accepted to separate public restrooms, locker rooms, and shower facilities on the basis of biological sex in order to address privacy and safety concerns arising from the biological differences between males and females. An individual has a legitimate and important interest in bodily privacy such that his or her nude or partially nude body, genitalia, and other private parts are not exposed to persons of the opposite biological sex. Indeed, courts have consistently recognized that the need for such privacy is inherent in the nature and dignity of humankind. *See, e.g., Doe v. Luzerne Cnty.*, 660 F.3d 169 (3d Cir. 2011) (recognizing that an individual has "a constitutionally protected privacy interest in his or her partially clothed body" and that this "reasonable expectation of privacy" exists "particularly while in the presence of members of the opposite sex"); *Brannum v. Overton Cnty. Sch. Bd.*, 516 F.3d 489 (6th Cir. 2008) (explaining that "the constitutional right to privacy . . . includes the right to shield one's body from exposure to viewing by the opposite sex"); *Beard v. Whitmore Lake Sch. Dist.*, 402 F.3d 598 (6th Cir. 2005) ("Students of course have a significant privacy interest in their unclothed bodies"); *Sepulveda v. Ramirez*, 967 F.2d 1413 (9th Cir. 1992) (explaining that "[t]he right to bodily privacy is fundamental" and that "common sense, decency, and [state] regulations" require recognizing it in a parolee's right not to be observed by an officer of the opposite sex while producing a urine sample); *Lee v. Downs*, 641 F.2d 1117 (4th Cir. 1981) (recognizing that, even though inmates in prison "surrender many rights of privacy," their "special sense of privacy in their genitals" should not be violated through exposure unless "reasonably necessary" and explaining that the "involuntary exposure of [genitals] in the presence of people of the other sex may be especially demeaning and humiliating").

Moreover, we have explained that separating restrooms based on "acknowledged differences" between the biological sexes serves to protect this important privacy interest. *See Faulkner v. Jones*, 10 F.3d 226 (4th Cir. 1993) (noting "society's undisputed approval of separate public rest rooms for men and women based on privacy concerns"). Indeed, the Supreme Court recognized, when ordering an all-male Virginia college to admit female students, that such a remedy "would undoubtedly require alterations necessary to afford members of each sex privacy from the other sex." *United States v. Virginia*, 518 U.S. 515 (1996). Such privacy was and remains necessary because of the inherent "[p]hysical differences between men and women," which, as the Supreme Court explained, are "enduring" and render "the two sexes . . . not fungible," *id.* (distinguishing sex from race and national origin), not because of "one's sense of oneself as belonging to a particular gender," as G.G. and the government as amicus contend.

Thus, Title IX's allowance for the separation, based on sex, of living facilities, restrooms, locker rooms, and shower facilities rests on the universally accepted concern for bodily privacy that is founded on the biological differences between the sexes. This privacy concern is also linked to safety concerns that could arise from sexual responses prompted by students' exposure to the private body parts of students of the other biological sex. Indeed, the School Board cited these very reasons for its adoption of the policy, explaining that it separates restrooms and locker rooms to promote the privacy and safety of minor children, pursuant to its "responsibility to its students to ensure their privacy while engaging in personal bathroom functions, disrobing, dressing, and showering outside of the presence of members of the opposite sex. [That the school has this responsibility] is particularly true in an environment where children are still developing, both emotionally and physically."

The need to protect privacy and safety between the sexes based on physical exposure would not be present in the same quality and degree if the term "sex" were to encompass only a person's gender identity. Indeed, separation on this basis would function nonsensically. A biological male identifying as female could hardly live in a girls' dorm or shower in a girls' shower without invading physiological privacy needs, and the same would hold true for a biological female identifying as male in a boys' dorm or shower. G.G.'s answer, of course, is that he is not challenging the separation, on the basis of sex, of living facilities, locker rooms, and shower facilities, but only of restrooms, where the risks to privacy and safety are far reduced. . . . But this effort to restrict the effect of G.G.'s argument hardly matters when the term "sex" would have to be applied uniformly throughout the statute and regulations. . . .

The realities underpinning Title IX's recognition of separate living facilities, restrooms, locker rooms, and shower facilities are reflected in the plain language of the statute and regulations, which is not ambiguous. The text of Title IX and its regulations allowing for separation of each facility "on the basis of sex" employs the term "sex" as was generally understood at the time of enactment. . . . Title IX was enacted in 1972 and the regulations were promulgated in 1975 and readopted in 1980, and during that time period, virtually every dictionary definition of "sex" referred to the physiological distinctions between males and females, particularly with respect to their reproductive functions. . . .

   . . . .

[When] asserting that G.G. must be allowed to use the boys' restrooms and locker rooms as consistent with his gender identity, G.G., the government, and the majority must be arguing that "sex" as used in Title IX and its regulations means only gender identity. But this construction would, in the end, mean that a school could never meaningfully provide separate restrooms and locker rooms on the basis of sex. Biological males and females whose gender identity aligned would be required to use the same restrooms and locker rooms as persons of the opposite biological sex whose gender identity did not align. With such mixed use of separate facilities, no purpose would be gained by designating a separate use "on the basis of sex," and privacy concerns would be left unaddressed.

Moreover, enforcement of any separation would be virtually impossible. Basing restroom access on gender identity would require schools to assume gender identity based on appearances, social expectations, or explicit declarations of identity, which the government concedes would render Title IX and its regulations nonsensical:

> Certainly a school that has created separate restrooms for boys and girls could not decide that only students who dress, speak, and act sufficiently masculine count as boys entitled to use the boys' restroom, or that only students who wear dresses, have long hair, and act sufficiently feminine may use the girls' restroom. [Quoting Br. for the United States as Amicus Curiae.—Eds.]

Yet, by interpreting Title IX and the regulations as "requiring schools to treat students consistent with their gender identity," and by disallowing schools from treating students based on their biological sex, the government's position would have precisely the effect the government finds to be at odds with common sense.

Finally, in arguing that he should not be assigned to the girls' restrooms, G.G. states that "it makes no sense to place a transgender boy in the girls' restroom in the name of protecting student privacy" because "girls objected to his presence in the girls' restrooms because they perceived him as male." But the same argument applies to his use of the boys' restrooms, where boys felt uncomfortable because they perceived him as female. In any scenario based on gender identity, moreover, there would be no accommodation for the recognized need for physiological privacy.

. . . .

Because the Gloucester County School Board did not violate Title IX and Regulation 106.33 in adopting the policy for separate restrooms and locker rooms, I would affirm the district court's decision dismissing G.G.'s Title IX claim and therefore dissent.

I also dissent from the majority's decision to vacate the district court's denial of G.G.'s motion for a preliminary injunction. . . . Given the facts that the district court fully and fairly summarized in its opinion, including the hardships expressed both by G.G. and by other students, I cannot conclude that we can "form a definite and firm conviction that the court below committed a clear error of judgment," particularly when we are only now expressing as binding law an evidentiary standard that the majority asserts the district court violated.

As noted, however, I concur in Part IV of the court's opinion.

————————

Discussion

1. The opinion notes that Title IX allows sex-segregated "living facilities," but that the Department of Education's implementing regulation allows "separate toilet, locker room, and shower facilities on the basis of sex. . . . 34 C.F.R. § 106.33." (Note that dissenting Judge Niemeyer characterizes the regulations as allowing "separate living facilities, restrooms, locker rooms, and shower facilities"—in the conjunctive—rather than writing "separate living facilities *including* restrooms, locker rooms, and shower facilities.") Is that a permissible interpretation of the statute? Is "living facilities" ambiguous, or does it refer only to student housing (dorms, specific floors in dorms, apartments, etc.)? If there is ambiguity and the regulation permissibly extends it to, for example, sex-segregated toilets, would it be permissible for a covered educational institution to provide separate kitchens, lounges, and study rooms for males and females on the basis that, like toilets, changing rooms, and showers, such facilities are spaces in which one engages in the sorts of activities people conduct in the places in which they "liv[e]"? (And if that is not the principle that explains why toilet, locker room, and shower facilities count as "living facilities," what is?)

2. Note that Niemeyer's claim that "[a]cross societies and throughout history" sex-segregated "public restrooms, locker rooms, and shower facilities" have been "universally accepted" overlooks both the many societies that have provided or do provide public bathing and toileting facilities that are not sex-segregated as well as the development of such restrooms only centuries after the U.S. was first colonized. *Cf.* Terry Kogan, *Public Restrooms and the Distorting of Transgender Identity*, 95 N.C. L. Rev. 1205, 1212 (2017) (flagging that in the United States, "the multi-user public restroom . . . dates back only to the 1870s").

3. Some parties defending the exclusion of transgender school students from common restrooms consistent with their gender identity have tried to rely on

Faulkner v. Jones, 10 F.3d 226 (4th Cir. 1993). There, the court of appeals held that South Carolina violated the equal protection rights of Shannon Faulkner by revoking her admission to the Citadel, a state-run all-male military college, based on her sex. (Ms. Faulkner's application had made no mention of her sex). The court of appeals conditionally ordered her admitted, but in the course of its opinion referred to "society's undisputed approval of separate public rest rooms for men and women based on privacy concerns. The need for privacy justifies separation. . . ."

For example, plaintiffs challenging a school district policy allowing transgender students to use common restrooms consistent with their gender identity quoted this passage in support of their position. *Doe v. Boyertown Area School District*, 897 F.3d 518 (3d Cir. 2018), *infra* p.913. The *Boyertown* court, however distinguished *Faulkner*, noting that it neither held that "the Constitution *compels* separate bathroom facilities" for men and women nor "recognize[d] a constitutional mandate that bathrooms and locker rooms must be segregated by birth-determined sex." The Third Circuit Court of Appeals ultimately rejected the plaintiffs' challenge.

4. Can you precisely identify the "physiological privacy needs" Judge Niemeyer invokes? Is he saying our physiology somehow compels respect for certain privacy interests? Or that there are normative interests compelling us to keep aspects of our physiology private? If the latter, how are those not prescriptive gender norms, which are broadly condemned in U.S. constitutional and statutory sex discrimination law? He seems to be saying that people with penises and people with vaginas should not see each other nude, nor use restrooms together. But why, exactly? (Note that, while there may be relevant evidence in the record, Judge Niemeyer cites nothing to support his assertion that in fact "boys felt uncomfortable" with Gavin using boys' restrooms "because they perceived him as female"—and the district court opinion that the court of appeals reversed and vacated made no such assertion.)

————————

On remand, the district court entered an injunction requiring the school board to let Gavin use boys' restrooms, *G.G. v. Gloucester County School Board*, No. 4:15cv54, 2016 WL 3581852 (E.D. Va. June 23, 2016), and the district court and then the court of appeals denied the board's motion for a stay pending appeal, 654 Fed. Appx. 606 (4th Cir. 2016). With Justice Breyer's "courtesy" vote, the Supreme Court stayed the injunction on August 3, 2016, *Gloucester County School Board v. G.G.*,136 S. Ct. 2442 (2016), and then agreed to review the decision, granting certiorari on October 28, 2016, 137 S. Ct. 369 (2016).

Eighteen days after Donald Trump's inauguration, on February 7, 2017, the Senate (by a 51–50 vote with Vice President Pence breaking a tie) confirmed Betsy DeVos as Secretary of Education; on February 9, the Senate confirmed Jeff Sessions as Attorney General. Thirteen days later, on February 22, the Departments of Justice and Education jointly issued a Dear Colleague letter withdrawing the Obama administration guidance from the January 7, 2015, Department of Education opinion letter and the May 13, 2016, Dear Colleague letter that the Justice and Education

Departments had jointly issued. This February 22, 2017, guidance explicitly noted the Grimm litigation, and it purported to rescind the prior "guidance documents in order to further and more completely consider the legal issues involved." It also asserted, without elaboration, "that in this context, there must be due regard for the primary role of the States and local school districts in establishing educational policy."

Two weeks later, in March, the Supreme Court vacated the judgment of the court of appeals and remanded the case "for further consideration in light of the guidance document issued by the Department of Education and Department of Justice on February 22, 2017." 137 S. Ct. 1239 (2017). In April, the court of appeals vacated the preliminary injunction that had been entered by the district court and stayed by the Supreme Court, 853 F.3d 729 (4th Cir. 2017), with Judge Davis writing an extraordinary concurrence joined by Judge Floyd (the two members of the original panel majority). It is reprinted below in full.

G.G., By His Next Friend and Mother, Deirdre Grimm v. Gloucester County School Board

853 F.3d 729 (4th Cir. 2017)

Davis, Senior Circuit Judge, concurring:

I concur in the order granting the unopposed motion to vacate the district court's preliminary injunction and add these observations.

G.G., then a fifteen-year-old transgender boy, addressed the Gloucester County School Board on November 11, 2014, to explain why he was not a danger to other students. He explained that he had used the boys' bathroom in public places throughout Gloucester County and had never had a confrontation. He explained that he is a person worthy of dignity and privacy. He explained why it is humiliating to be segregated from the general population. He knew, intuitively, what the law has in recent decades acknowledged: the perpetuation of stereotypes is one of many forms of invidious discrimination. And so he hoped that his heartfelt explanation would help the powerful adults in his community come to understand what his adolescent peers already did. G.G. clearly and eloquently attested that he was not a predator, but a boy, despite the fact that he did not conform to some people's idea about who is a boy.[1]

Regrettably, a majority of the School Board was unpersuaded. And so we come to this moment. High school graduation looms and, by this court's order vacating the preliminary injunction, G.G.'s banishment from the boys' restroom becomes an enduring feature of his high school experience. Would that courtesies extended to others had been extended to G.G.

---

1. Footage of his compelling statement to the School Board is available at: https://www.youtube.com/watch?v=My0GYq_Wydw& feature=youtu.be.

Our country has a long and ignominious history of discriminating against our most vulnerable and powerless. We have an equally long history, however, of brave individuals—Dred Scott, Fred Korematsu, Linda Brown, Mildred and Richard Loving, Edie Windsor, and Jim Obergefell, to name just a few—who refused to accept quietly the injustices that were perpetuated against them. It is unsurprising, of course, that the burden of confronting and remedying injustice falls on the shoulders of the oppressed. These individuals looked to the federal courts to vindicate their claims to human dignity, but as the names listed above make clear, the judiciary's response has been decidedly mixed. Today, G.G. adds his name to the list of plaintiffs whose struggle for justice has been delayed and rebuffed; as Dr. King reminded us, however, "the arc of the moral universe is long, but it bends toward justice." G.G.'s journey is delayed but not finished.

G.G.'s case is about much more than bathrooms. It's about a boy asking his school to treat him just like any other boy. It's about protecting the rights of transgender people in public spaces and not forcing them to exist on the margins. It's about governmental validation of the existence and experiences of transgender people, as well as the simple recognition of their humanity. His case is part of a larger movement that is redefining and broadening the scope of civil and human rights so that they extend to a vulnerable group that has traditionally been unrecognized, unrepresented, and unprotected.

G.G.'s plight has shown us the inequities that arise when the government organizes society by outdated constructs like biological sex and gender. Fortunately, the law eventually catches up to the lived facts of people; indeed, the record shows that the Commonwealth of Virginia has now recorded a birth certificate for G.G. that designates his sex as male.

G.G.'s lawsuit also has demonstrated that some entities will not protect the rights of others unless compelled to do so. Today, hatred, intolerance, and discrimination persist—and are sometimes even promoted—but by challenging unjust policies rooted in invidious discrimination, G.G. takes his place among other modern-day human rights leaders who strive to ensure that, one day, equality will prevail, and that the core dignity of every one of our brothers and sisters is respected by lawmakers and others who wield power over their lives.

G.G. is and will be famous, and justifiably so. But he is not "famous" in the hollowed-out Hollywood sense of the term. He is famous for the reasons celebrated by the renowned Palestinian-American poet Naomi Shihab Nye, in her extraordinary poem, *Famous*. Despite his youth and the formidable power of those arrayed against him at every stage of these proceedings, "[he] never forgot what [he] could do."[2]

—————————

2. *See* N.S. Nye, *Famous*:
   The river is famous to the fish.
   The loud voice is famous to silence,
   which knew it would inherit the earth

Judge Floyd has authorized me to state that he joins in the views expressed herein.

———————

Discussion

Is this kind of statement appropriate for a judge (or a federal judge in particular) to make? To whom is it addressed? What might be the advantages or disadvantages of a court's publishing such a statement? Should courts issue *more* such statements?

———————

Following the vacatur of the district court's injunction, in August 2017 the same panel of the court of appeals, following supplemental briefing, remanded the case to the district court to determine whether it had become moot by virtue of Gavin's having graduated from high school. *Gavin Grimm v. Gloucester County School Board*, 869 F.3d 286 (4th Cir. 2017). Following further briefing, the new district court judge to whom the case was reassigned while the court of appeals and Supreme Court review process unfolded, the Hon. Arenda L. Wright Allen, dismissed Gavin's claims for an injunction or prospective declaratory relief with his consent. *Gavin Grimm v. Gloucester County School Board*, No. 4:15-cv-54, 2017 WL 9882602 (E.D. Va. Dec. 12, 2017) However, Judge Wright "conclude[d] that Plaintiff's graduation did not moot either his request for nominal damages for the School Board's alleged past violations of his rights under Title IX and the Equal Protection Clause or his request for a declaratory judgment regarding these alleged violations."

Five months later, Judge Wright Allen—who four years earlier had ruled Virginia's exclusion of same-sex couples from civil marriage unconstitutional in *Bostic v. Rainey*, 970 F. Supp. 2d 456 (E.D. Va.), *aff'd sub nom. Bostic v. Schaefer*, 760 F.3d 352 (4th Cir. 2014)—rejected the defendants' motion to dismiss the amended complaint Gavin had filed.

———————

before anybody said so.
The cat sleeping on the fence is famous to the birds
watching him from the birdhouse.
The tear is famous, briefly, to the cheek.
The idea you carry close to your bosom
is famous to your bosom.
The boot is famous to the earth,
more famous than the dress shoe,
which is famous only to floors.
The bent photograph is famous to the one who carries it
and not at all famous to the one who is pictured.
I want to be famous to shuffling men
who smile while crossing streets,
sticky children in grocery lines,
famous as the one who smiled back.
I want to be famous in the way a pulley is famous,
or a buttonhole, not because it did anything spectacular,
but because it never forgot what it could do.

Reading Guide for *Grimm v. Gloucester County School Board* (May 2018 district court opinion)

1. What different reasons does the court give for reconsidering Gavin Grimm's claim against the school board for its policy barring him from using boys' restrooms under Title IX of the Education Amendments of 1972?

2. It is not entirely clear, but with regard to Mr. Grimm's Title IX claim, what does the court reason about the difference between "physical characteristics" and "biological gender"?

3. For what reason does the court conclude that 34 C.F.R. § 106.33, one of the regulations purportedly implementing Title IX, is ambiguous? What does the court conclude the ban on sex discrimination in Title VII of the Civil Rights Act says about anti-transgender discrimination? What is the relevance of that interpretation of Title VII to Grimm's Title IX claim? What reasons does the court give for concluding that "that Mr. Grimm has sufficiently pled a Title IX claim of sex discrimination"?

4. The court concludes that heightened scrutiny of the school's restroom policy is required under Gavin Grimm's equal protection challenge for two distinct reasons. What are those, and what is the court's reasoning supporting each? What reasons does the court give for concluding that the policy fails intermediate scrutiny?

Gavin Grimm v. Gloucester County School Board

302 F. Supp. 3d 730 (E.D. Va. 2018)

Order

Pending before the Court is an Amended Motion to Dismiss pursuant to Federal Rule of Civil Procedure 12(b)(6) filed by Defendant Gloucester County School Board. For reasons set forth herein, the Motion is DENIED.

I. Factual and Procedural Background

When ruling on a motion to dismiss for failure to state a claim, courts accept a complaint's well-pled factual allegations as true, and draw any reasonable inferences in favor of the plaintiff. Accordingly, the Court reviews the facts as alleged by Plaintiff Gavin Grimm.

Mr. Grimm is an eighteen-year-old man who attended Gloucester High School, a public school in Gloucester County, Virginia, from September 2013 through his graduation in June 2017. When Mr. Grimm was born, hospital staff identified him as female. However, Mr. Grimm has known from a young age that he has a male gender identity—that is, he has a "deeply felt, inherent sense of being a boy, a man, or male," rather than a sense of being "a girl, a woman, or a female." Because his gender identity differs from the sex assigned to him at birth, he is transgender.

Like many of his transgender peers, after the onset of puberty, Mr. Grimm began suffering from "debilitating levels of distress" as the result of gender dysphoria, "a condition in which transgender individuals experience persistent and clinically significant distress caused by the incongruence between their gender identity and the sex assigned to them at birth." There is a medical and scientific consensus that treatment for gender dysphoria includes allowing transgender individuals to live in accordance with their gender identity, including "use of names and pronouns consistent with their identity, grooming and dressing in a manner typically associated with that gender, and using restrooms and other sex-separated facilities that match their gender identity."[1] Furthermore, when medically appropriate, treatment also includes hormone therapy and surgery so that transgender individuals "may develop physical sex characteristics typical of their gender identity." In addition, under widely accepted standards of care, "boys who are transgender may undergo medically necessary chest-reconstruction surgery after they turn [sixteen years old]."

In 2014, by the end of his freshman year of high school, Mr. Grimm experienced such distress from his untreated gender dysphoria that he was unable to attend class. At this time, he informed his parents of his male gender identity. He began treatment with a psychologist experienced in counseling transgender youth and, as part of the medically-necessary treatment for his gender dysphoria, commenced the process of transitioning to live in accordance with his male identity. By the time he began his sophomore year, Mr. Grimm had legally changed his first name to Gavin and had begun using male pronouns. He wore clothing and a hairstyle in a manner consistent with other males, and used men's restrooms in public venues without incident. He also obtained a treatment documentation letter from his medical providers confirming that he was receiving treatment for gender dysphoria and was to be treated as a male in all respects—including restroom use.

In August 2014, prior to the beginning of his sophomore year, Mr. Grimm and his mother met with the Gloucester High School Principal and the Guidance Counselor, explaining that Mr. Grimm is a transgender boy and would be attending school as a boy. Mr. Grimm and his mother also provided the Principal and Counselor with the treatment documentation letter. At the time of the meeting, the Board lacked a policy addressing the restrooms that transgender students would use. Mr. Grimm initially requested the use of the restroom in the nurse's office. However, that restroom was located remotely, and using it left Mr. Grimm feeling stigmatized and isolated. That restroom was also far from many of his classrooms, causing Mr. Grimm to be late for class when he used it. After a few weeks, Mr. Grimm sought permission to use the boys' restrooms. With the Principal's support, he began using the boys' restrooms on October 20, 2014, and did so without incident for approximately seven weeks.[3]

---

1. The consensus within medical and mental health communities is that excluding transgender individuals from using restrooms consistent with their gender identity "is harmful to their health and wellbeing. When excluded from the common restrooms, transgender [individuals] often avoid using the restroom entirely, either because the separate restrooms are too stigmatizing or too difficult to access." As a result, they suffer from physical consequences, and their risk of depression and self-harm is increased.

3. He also requested permission to complete his physical education requirements through a homebound program, bypassing any need to use the locker rooms at the school.

The Principal and Superintendent informed the Board that they had authorized Mr. Grimm to use the boys' restrooms, but otherwise kept the matter confidential. However, several adults in the community learned of a transgender student's use of the boys' restrooms. They contacted the Board, demanding that the transgender student be barred from the boys' restrooms. The Board considered the matter in a private meeting and took no action for several weeks. However, one Board member proposed a policy regarding the use of restrooms by transgender students and submitted the policy for public debate at a Board meeting scheduled for November 11, 2014. In pertinent part, the policy proposed that "[i]t shall be the practice of the [Gloucester County Public Schools ("GCPS")] to provide male and female restroom and locker room facilities in its schools, and the use of said facilities shall be limited to the corresponding biological genders, and students with gender identity issues shall be provided an alternative appropriate private facility."

At the meeting, Mr. Grimm decided to address the issue publicly, describing how he sought to use the restrooms "in peace" and had experienced "no problems from students" when using the boys' restrooms, "only from adults." The School Board deferred a vote on the proposed policy until its December 9, 2014 meeting. Before the next meeting, the Board announced plans to add or expand partitions between urinals in the male restrooms, add privacy strips to the doors of stalls in all restrooms, and to designate single-stall, unisex restrooms "to give all students the option for even greater privacy."

Despite the announced plans, speakers at the December 9, 2014 meeting continued to demand that Mr. Grimm be excluded from using the boys' restrooms immediately. The Board then passed the policy at the meeting by a six-to-one vote. The following day, Mr. Grimm was informed by the principal that he could no longer use the boys' restrooms. The Board then installed three single-user restrooms, none of which was located near Mr. Grimm's classes. Although any student was allowed to use them, no student besides Mr. Grimm did.

Because using the single-user restrooms underscored his exclusion and left him physically isolated, Mr. Grimm refrained from using any restroom at school. He developed a painful urinary tract infection and had difficulty concentrating in class because of his physical discomfort. When he attended school football games, no restroom was available for Mr. Grimm's use. As a result, Mr. Grimm was forced to have his mother pick him up from games early.

Throughout his sophomore, junior, and senior years of high school, Mr. Grimm continued the process of transitioning to live in accordance with his male identity. In December 2014, the middle of his sophomore year, he had begun hormone therapy, which altered his bone and muscle structure, deepened his voice, and caused him to grow facial hair. In June 2015, prior to the beginning of his junior year, the Virginia Department of Motor Vehicles issued Mr. Grimm a state identification card designating his gender as male. A year later, prior to the beginning of his senior year, Mr. Grimm underwent chest-reconstruction surgery, in accordance with the medical standards of care for treating gender dysphoria. Later that year, in September 2016, the Gloucester County Circuit Court issued an order changing his sex under Virginia state law and directing the Virginia Department of Health to issue Mr. Grimm a birth certificate listing his sex as male; this certificate was issued in October 2016. Throughout the process of these changes — up through Mr. Grimm's graduation in June 2017 — the School Board maintained that Mr. Grimm's "biological gender" was female and prohibited administrators from permitting Mr. Grimm to use the boys' restrooms.

Mr. Grimm commenced this action against the Gloucester County School Board in July 2015, alleging that the Board's policy of assigning students to restrooms based on their biological sex violated Title IX of the Education Amendments of 1972, 20 U.S.C. § 1681(a), as well as the Equal Protection Clause of the Fourteenth Amendment to the United States Constitution. [Eventually, the] case was remanded to this Court for consideration of the Title IX claim. The Equal Protection Claim also remains pending before this Court.

Following the filing of Mr. Grimm's Amended Complaint, the School Board filed the instant Motion to Dismiss. . . .

II. Legal Standard

"To survive a Rule 12(b)(6) motion to dismiss, a complaint must 'state a claim to relief that is plausible on its face.'" *United States ex rel. Nathan v. Takeda Pharm. N. Am., Inc.*, 707 F.3d 451 (4th Cir. 2013). . . . [The] "'[f]actual allegations must be enough to raise a right to relief above the speculative level,' thereby 'nudg[ing] [the plaintiff's] claims across the line from conceivable to plausible.'" *Vitol, S.A. v. Primerose Shipping Co.*, 708 F.3d 527 (4th Cir. 2013).

At this stage, "(1) the complaint is construed in the light most favorable to the plaintiff, (2) its allegations are taken as true, and (3) all reasonable inferences that can be drawn from the pleading are drawn in favor of the pleader." 5B Charles A. Wright et al., Federal Practice & Procedure § 1357 & n.11 (3d ed.) (collecting cases).

. . . .

III. Analysis

A. Reconsideration of the Interlocutory Order

As a preliminary matter, this Court must consider whether it is bound by the previous dismissal of the Title IX claim. . . .

The . . . Board contends that because Mr. Grimm's "current Title IX claim is virtually identical to the claim that [the previous judge] already dismissed, [Mr. Grimm] is essentially asking the Court to reconsider" the original decision. . . .

Such reconsiderations are governed by Federal Rule of Civil Procedure 54(b), which provides that:

> any order or other decision, however designated, that adjudicates fewer than all the claims or rights and liabilities of fewer than all the parties does

not end the action as to any of the claims or parties and may be revised at any time before the entry of a judgment adjudicating all the claims and all the parties' rights and liabilities.

Both parties acknowledge that district courts retain the discretion to revise an interlocutory order at any time before the entry of a judgment adjudicating all the claims. *Carlson v. Boston Scientific Corp.*, 856 F.3d 320 (4th Cir. 2017).

[A] "court may review an interlocutory order under the same circumstances in which it may depart from the law of the case: (1) a subsequent trial producing substantially different evidence; (2) a change in applicable law; or (3) clear error causing manifest injustice." *Id.*

. . . . First, there has been a significant change in the applicable law since the Motion to Dismiss the Title IX claim was initially considered in 2015. The Sixth and Seventh Circuits have since held that excluding boys and girls who are transgender from the restrooms that align with their gender identity may subject them to discrimination on the basis of sex under Title IX, the Equal Protection Clause, or both.

A number of district courts have also reached the same conclusion.

Recently, the District of Maryland denied a strikingly similar Motion to Dismiss a transgender student's Title IX and Equal Protection claims stemming from his school's policy of barring him from using the boys' locker room. *M.A.B. v. Bd. of Educ. of Talbot Cty.*, 286 F. Supp. 3d 704 (D. Md. 2018). Although these precedents are not binding upon this Court, the thorough analyses of analogous questions provided by the rulings proves persuasive. Moreover, to the extent that the Fourth Circuit's consideration of the Title IX claim provides meaningful guidance for this Court's analysis of the Title IX regulation, the earlier dismissal of the Title IX claim lacked such guidance.

Second, a number of factual developments warrant reconsideration of the original decision to dismiss the Title IX claim. When Mr. Grimm filed his initial complaint in 2015, he alleged that the Board's policy violated his rights under Title IX on the day the policy was first issued, which occurred in the middle of his sophomore year. The Amended Complaint alleges that the Board violated his rights under Title IX when the policy was issued, and also throughout the remainder of his time as a student at Gloucester High School. Since the previous dismissal of the Title IX claim, Mr. Grimm has received chest reconstruction surgery, obtained an order from Gloucester County Circuit Court legally changing his sex under Virginia law, and has received a new birth certificate from the Virginia Department of Health listing his sex as male. The previous decision was rendered without any opportunity to consider whether the Board's policy violated Title IX throughout the remainder of Mr. Grimm's time at Gloucester High School, and in light of these factual developments.

For these reasons, the Court concludes that revisiting the question of whether Mr. Grimm has stated a plausible Title IX claim is warranted. . . .

B. Title IX Claim

Title IX provides that no person "shall, on the basis of sex, be excluded from participation in, be denied the benefits of, or be subjected to discrimination under any educational program or activity receiving Federal financial assistance. . . ." 20 U.S.C. § 1681(a); see also 34 C.F.R. § 106.31. A covered institution may not, on the basis of sex, (1) provide different aid, benefits, or services; (2) deny aid, benefits, or service, or (3) subject any person to separate or different rules, sanctions, or treatment. 34 C.F.R. § 106.31(b)(2)-(4).

However, "[n]ot all distinctions on the basis of sex are impermissible under Title IX." The statute's regulations permit an institution to provide separate bathroom, shower, and locker facilities by sex, so long as the facilities are comparable. 34 C.F.R. § 106.33.

1. A Plaintiff's Claim of Discrimination on the Basis of Transgender Status Constitutes a Claim of Sex Discrimination Under Title IX

. . . . Neither Title IX nor its regulations defines the term "sex.". . . .

The Board notes that § 106.33 permits schools to establish separate facilities on the basis of sex. The Board also contends that the term "sex" "at a minimum includes the physiological distinction between men and women." Therefore, the Board argues, this Court must interpret Title IX as applying only to discrimination on the basis of physiological sex, rather than gender identity.

[The] Board argues that the Policy "distinguishes boys and girls based on physical sex characteristics alone," but fails to acknowledge that there are individuals who possess both male and female physical sex characteristics. As Mr. Grimm contends, attempting to draw lines based on physiological and anatomical characteristics proves unmanageable: how would the Board's policy apply to individuals who have had genital surgery, individuals whose genitals were injured in an accident, or those with intersex traits who have genital characteristics that are neither typically male nor female? In Mr. Grimm's situation, how would the Board have continued to implement the Policy after Mr. Grimm's medical procedures? Mr. Grimm had attained some secondary male physical sex characteristics after hormone therapy and chest reconstruction surgery. Accordingly, acts of discrimination on the basis of physiological sex certainly could have occurred.

The Policy in question assigned restrooms based on "biological gender," not physiological characteristics. This term has not been accepted by the medical community, because "sex"—the "attributes that characterize biological maleness or femaleness" (such as sex-determining genes, sex chromosomes, internal and external genitalia, and secondary sex characteristics)—is distinct from "gender," or the "internal, deeply held sense" of being a man or a woman. *See* Wylie C. Hembree et al., *Endocrine Treatment of Gender-dysphoric/Gender-Incongruent Persons: An Endocrine Society Clinical Practice Guideline*, 102(11) J. CLIN. ENDOCRINOLOGY & METABOLISM 3869, 3875 (2017) (noting that the terms "biological male or female" should be avoided because not all individuals have physical attributes that align perfectly with biological maleness or femaleness, such as individuals with XY chromosomes who may have female-appearing genitalia). Given the Policy's disregard for these distinctions, its use of the term "biological gender" functioned as a proxy for physiological characteristics that a student may or may not have had. The term allowed the Board to isolate, distinguish, and subject to differential treatment any student who deviated from what the Board viewed a male or female student should be, and from the physiological characteristics the Board believed that a male or female student should have.

The Court next turns to consideration of § 106.33. . . .

The Board asks this Court to resolve this issue by cabining the definition of sex to the "then-universal understanding of 'sex' as a binary term encompassing the physiological distinctions between men and women," as understood during the passage of Title IX and the promulgation of § 106.33. However, as noted above, this fails to address the question of how § 106.33 is to be interpreted regarding transgender students or other individuals with physiological characteristics associated with both sexes.

The Court has some guidance in resolving § 106.33's ambiguity. Courts may "look to case law interpreting Title VII of the Civil Rights Act of 1964," as amended, 42 U.S.C. §§ 2000e et seq. (2018)—which prohibits employment discrimination on the basis of, among other qualities, sex—"for guidance in evaluating a claim brought under Title IX."

In *Price Waterhouse v. Hopkins*, 490 U.S. 228 (1989), the Supreme Court considered whether the plaintiff, a woman who was denied partnership in an accounting firm, had an actionable Title VII claim against the firm because the firm had allegedly denied her a promotion because she failed to conform to certain gender stereotypes related to women. . . . Six Justices of the *Price Waterhouse* Court agreed that Title VII barred discrimination not only based on the plaintiff's gender, but based on "sex stereotyping" because the plaintiff had failed to act in accordance with gender stereotypes associated with women. In noting that "we are beyond the day when an employer could evaluate employees by assuming or insisting that they match[] the stereotype associated with their group," the *Price Waterhouse* Court recognized that Title VII's prohibition on sex discrimination necessarily includes a prohibition on gender stereotyping.

Price Waterhouse, by its own terms, took an expansive view as to the forms of sex discrimination that Title VII was meant to reach, expressly leaving open the possibility of other forms of gender stereotyping. "By focusing on [gender stereotypes associated with appearance and behavior], however, we do not suggest a limitation on the possible ways of proving that stereotyping played a motivating role in an employment decision. . . ."

The Supreme Court's expansion recognizes that the prohibition on sex discrimination pursuant to Title VII also includes same-sex harassment claims. *Oncale v. Sundowner Offshore Services, Inc.*, 523 U.S. 75 (1998)

The First, Second, Third, Seventh, and Ninth Circuits have all recognized that based on the logic of *Price Waterhouse*, a gender stereotyping allegation generally is actionable sex discrimination under Title VII. *Hively v. Ivy Tech Cmty. Coll.*, 853 F.3d 339 (7th Cir. 2017) (en banc) (holding that a lesbian plaintiff could state a Title VII claim under a sex stereotyping theory); *Christiansen v. Omnicom Grp., Inc.*, 852 F.3d 195, 200-01 (2d Cir. 2017) (per curiam) (holding that a plaintiff had stated a plausible Title VII claim based on a gender stereotyping theory); *Prowel v. Wise Bus. Forms, Inc.*, 579 F.3d 285 (3d Cir. 2009); *Nichols v. Azteca Rest. Enters., Inc.*, 256 F.3d 864 (9th Cir. 2001); *Higgins v. New Balance Athletic Shoe, Inc.*, 194 F.3d 252 (1st Cir. 1999).

[T]his Court joins the District of Maryland in concluding that "discrimination on the basis of transgender status constitutes gender stereotyping because 'by definition, transgender persons do not conform to gender stereotypes.'" *M.A.B.* The Court also concludes that, pursuant to the logic of *Price Waterhouse*, transgender discrimination is per se actionable sex discrimination under Title VII. *Id.*

This conclusion comports with decisions from the First, Sixth, Ninth, and Eleventh Circuits, all of which recognize that based on the gender-stereotyping theory from *Price Waterhouse*, claims of discrimination on the basis of transgender status are per se sex discrimination under Title VII or other federal civil rights laws. *See EEOC v. R.G. & G.R. Harris Funeral Homes, Inc.*, 884 F.3d 560 (6th Cir. 2018) (... Title VII); *Glenn v. Brumby*, 663 F.3d 1312 (11th Cir. 2011) (... Title VII and the Equal Protection Clause ...); *Smith v. City of Salem, Ohio*, 378 F.3d 566 (6th Cir. 2004) (... Title VII); *Rosa v. Park W. Bank & Trust Co.*, 214 F.3d 213 (1st Cir. 2000) (... Equal Credit Opportunity ...); *Schwenk v. Hartford*, 204 F.3d 1187 (9th Cir. 2000) (... Gender Motivated Violence Act ...).

Numerous district courts have also concluded that a transgender individual can state a claim under Title VII for sex discrimination on the basis of a sex or gender-stereotyping theory.

Accordingly, allegations of gender stereotyping are cognizable Title VII sex discrimination claims and, by extension, cognizable Title IX sex discrimination claims.[11] ... "[C]laims of discrimination on the basis of transgender status are per se actionable under a gender stereotyping theory" under Title IX. Mr. Grimm has properly brought a Title IX claim of discrimination "on the basis of sex" — that is, based on his transgender status.

---

11. The Board's argument that Title IX must explicitly refer to discrimination against transgender students to fulfill the notice requirements under *Pennhurst State School & Hospital v. Halderman*, 451 U.S. 1 (1981), is unavailing. Title IX funding recipients "have been on notice that they could be subjected to private suits for intentional sex discrimination under Title IX since 1979," when the Supreme Court decided *Cannon v. University of Chicago*, 441 U.S. 677 (1979), and "have been put on notice by the fact that ... cases since *Cannon* ... have consistently interpreted Title IX's private cause of action broadly to encompass diverse forms of intentional sex discrimination." *Jackson v. Birmingham Bd. of Educ.*, 544 U.S. 167 (2005); *see also West Virginia Dep't of Health & Human Resources v. Sebelius*, 649 F.3d 217, 223 (4th Cir. 2011).

2. Mr. Grimm Has Sufficiently Pled a Title IX Claim

. . . . To state a claim under Title IX, a plaintiff must allege: (1) that he or she was excluded from participation in an education program because of his or her sex; (2) that the educational institution was receiving federal financial assistance at the time of his or exclusion; and (3) that the improper discrimination caused the plaintiff harm. . . .

. . . . The Seventh Circuit concluded that a policy that requires transgender students to use bathrooms not in conformity with their gender identity subjects "a transgender student . . . to different rules, sanctions, and treatment than non-transgender students," and amounts to discrimination on the basis of transgender status in violation of Title IX. *Whitaker v. Kenosha Unified School Dist. No. 1 Board of Education*, 858 F.3d 1034 (7th Cir. 2017). This conclusion is sound. Furthermore, the provision of a gender-neutral alternative is insufficient to relieve a school board of liability, "as it is the policy itself which violates [Title IX]." *See id. at 1050.* Offering restroom alternatives that impose hardships like unreasonable distances to a student's classroom and increased stigma on a student is inadequate. *See id.*

In *M.A.B.*, the District of Maryland recognized that because the plaintiff had alleged that the school board had denied him access to the boys' locker rooms because of his transgender status, the policy subjected him to sex discrimination under a gender stereotyping theory. *M.A.B.* concluded that the plaintiff had sufficiently alleged discrimination under Title IX. Given the persuasive reasoning in *Whitaker* and *M.A.B.*, the Court concludes that Mr. Grimm has sufficiently pled that the Policy subjected him to sex discrimination under a gender stereotyping theory.

[Second,] GCPS and Gloucester High School "are education programs receiving Federal financial assistance[.]" [Third,] Mr. Grimm has sufficiently alleged that the discrimination harmed him. The location of the bathrooms, coupled with the stigmatization and physical and mental anguish inflicted upon Mr. Grimm, caused harm. . . . After full consideration of the facts presented and the compelling scope of relevant legal analyses, the Court concludes that Mr. Grimm has sufficiently pled a Title IX claim of sex discrimination under a gender stereotyping theory.

C. Equal Protection Claim

Mr. Grimm also brings a claim under the Equal Protection Clause of the Fourteenth Amendment to the United States Constitution, which provides that "[n]o State shall . . . deny to any person within its jurisdiction the equal protection of the laws." . . . .

Sex-based classifications are subject to heightened scrutiny. The state bears the burden of demonstrating that its proffered justification for the use of a sex-based classification is "exceedingly persuasive." *United States v. Virginia*, 518 U.S. 515 (1996). That is, the state is required to demonstrate that the classification "serves important governmental objectives and that the discriminatory means employed are substantially related to the achievement of those objectives." Hypothesized or post hoc justifications created in response to litigation are insufficient to meet this burden, as are justifications based on overbroad generalizations about sex. Furthermore, "[i]f a state actor cannot defend a sex-based classification by relying upon overbroad generalizations, it follows that sex-based stereotypes are also insufficient sustain a classification." *Whitaker*.

1. The Board's Policy Warrants Intermediate Scrutiny

. . . . The Board contends that rational basis review should apply because transgender individuals do not constitute a quasi-suspect class under the Equal Protection Clause. Mr. Grimm contends that classification based upon transgender status amounts to classification based on sex, and so warrants heightened scrutiny.

The Fourth Circuit has not considered the question of whether transgender classifications are sex-based. The Seventh and Eleventh Circuits have considered the issue and have concluded that heightened scrutiny applies. This Court agrees and concludes that intermediate scrutiny is warranted for at least two reasons.

First, transgender individuals constitute at least a quasi-suspect class, and the Policy classified Mr. Grimm on the basis of his transgender status. Four factors are used to determine whether a group of people who have been classified by a state amount to a suspect or quasi-suspect class: (1) whether the class has historically been subject to discrimination, *Bowen v. Gilliard*, 483 U.S. 587 (1987); (2) whether the class has a defining characteristic that bears a relation to ability to perform or contribute to society, *Cleburne*; (3) whether the class exhibits obvious, immutable, or distinguishing characteristics that define the class as a discrete group, *Bowen*; and (4) whether the class is a minority or politically powerless. *Id.* This Court joins the District of Maryland in concluding that transgender individuals meet all four factors and constitute at least a quasi-suspect class.

As to the first factor, there is no doubt that transgender individuals historically have been subjected to discrimination on the basis of their gender identity, including high rates of violence and discrimination in education, employment, housing, and healthcare access. *See Whitaker*; *M.A.B.*; *see also Evancho v. Pine-Richland Sch. Dist.*, 237 F. Supp. 3d 267 (W.D. Pa. 2017); *Bd. of Educ. of the Highland Local Sch. Dist. v. U.S. Dep't of Educ.*, 208 F. Supp. 3d 850 (S.D. Ohio 2016); *Adkins v. City of New York*, 143 F. Supp. 3d 134 (S.D.N.Y. 2015).

The second factor is also met because transgender status has no bearing on a transgender individual's ability to contribute to society. *See M.A.B.*

As to the third factor, "transgender status is immutable." *Id.* Furthermore, transgender individuals have distinguishing characteristics—the disparity between the gender they were assigned at birth and the gender they identify with—that define them as a discrete group. *Id.*

As to the fourth factor, there can be no doubt that transgender individuals are a minority and are politically powerless, comprising just a fraction of the population and frequently subjected to discriminatory federal policies and state laws. *Id.* This Court joins the District of Maryland, as well as a host of other district courts, in concluding that because transgender individuals are part of a quasi-suspect class, classifications based on transgender status are per se entitled to heightened scrutiny.

Second, intermediate scrutiny is also warranted because, as Mr. Grimm has pled the matter, the Board Policy at issue relies on sex stereotypes. Accordingly, Mr. Grimm's claims amount to an allegation of a sex-based classification and, therefore, an allegation of sex-based discrimination in violation of the Equal Protection Clause. *See M.A.B.*

. . . .

This Court joins other courts that have concluded that because the Policy relies on sex-based stereotypes, it is a sex-based classification. The Policy classified Mr. Grimm differently on the basis of his transgender status and, accordingly, subjected him to sex stereotyping. The Equal Protection Clause protects Mr. Grimm from impermissible sex stereotypes—just as Title IX does, for the reasons articulated previously— and the Court need only find that the Board's Policy demonstrated sex stereotyping under the Equal Protection Clause. Mr. Grimm was subjected to sex discrimination because he was viewed as failing to conform to the sex stereotype propagated by the Policy. Because the Policy relies on sex-based stereotypes, the Court finds that review of the Policy is subject to intermediate scrutiny.

2. As Pled by Mr. Grimm, the Policy was Not Substantially Related to Achieving an Important Governmental Objective

. . . .

The Board argues that the Policy is substantially related to an important governmental objective: protecting the privacy rights of its students. The Board expands this argument by contending that concerns over student privacy extend to protecting students like Mr. Grimm who, for whatever reason, may be uncomfortable using a restroom corresponding with their physiological sex. The Board argues that by permitting such students to use a single-user restroom, the Board is also protecting the privacy of students like Mr. Grimm.

The Board's argument rings hollow. In *Whitaker*, the Seventh Circuit concluded that although the school's privacy justification may be a legitimate and important interest, the policy was not genuine because it is "based upon sheer conjecture and abstraction."

Such conjecture is obvious. First, the plaintiff in *Whitaker*—like Mr. Grimm— used the boys' bathrooms for weeks without incident before other adults in the community—not students—complained of this use. Second, as the Seventh Circuit observed, a "transgender student's presence in a restroom provides no more of a risk to other students' privacy rights than the presence of an overly curious student of the same biological sex who decides to sneak glances at his or her classmates performing their bodily functions." *Whitaker*. Third, if school districts were genuinely concerned with protecting the privacy of students who have different-looking anatomies, "then it would seem that separate bathrooms also would be appropriate for pre-pubescent and post-pubescent children who do not look alike anatomically," which the school district had not provided. *Id*. This Court declines to further evaluate the legitimacy of the purported privacy concerns. The record here is less developed than it was in *Whitaker*. However, the Court underscores that, as pled by Mr. Grimm, Mr. Grimm used the boys' bathrooms for weeks without incident.

The Court concludes that, as pled by Mr. Grimm, the policy at issue was not substantially related to protecting other students' privacy rights. There were many other ways to protect privacy interests in a non-discriminatory and more effective manner than barring Mr. Grimm from using the boys' restrooms. For example, the Board had taken steps "to give all students the option for even greater privacy" by installing partitions between urinals and privacy strips for stall doors. Additionally, students who wanted greater privacy for any reason could have used one of the new single-stall restrooms made available upon implementation of the policy. Furthermore, as the *M.A.B.* court recognized, it is significant when a school board fails to provide "any explanation for why completely barring [the transgender student] from the boys' [segregated facility] protects the privacy of other boys," "while the availability of single-use restrooms or locker stalls does not." As in *Whitaker* and *M.A.B.*, preventing Mr. Grimm from using the boys' restrooms did nothing to protect the privacy rights of other students, but certainly singled out and stigmatized Mr. Grimm.

Similarly, the Board's argument that the policy should not be construed as violating the Equal Protection Clause because the policy treated all boys and girls the same is unavailing. The Policy singled out Mr. Grimm for differing treatment because it "treat[ed] transgender students . . . who fail to conform to the sex-based stereotypes associated with their assigned sex at birth[] differently," whereas a boy making the personal choice to change clothes in or use a single-stall restroom would not have been singled out by the school policy. *Whitaker*; *see also G.G. ex rel. Grimm v. Gloucester County Sch. Bd.*, 822 F.3d 709, 729 (4th Cir. 2016) (Davis, J., concurring) ("For other students, using the single-stall restrooms carries no stigma whatsoever, whereas for G.G., using those same restrooms is tantamount to humiliation and a continuing mark of difference among his fellow students."), *vacated and remanded*, 137 S. Ct. 1239 (2017).

For these reasons, the Court concludes that Mr. Grimm has sufficiently pled that the Policy was not substantially related to protecting other students' privacy rights, because there were many other ways to protect privacy interests in a non-discriminatory and more effective manner than barring Mr. Grimm from using the boys' restrooms. The Board's argument that the policy did not discriminate against any one class of students is resoundingly unpersuasive. Accordingly, the Court declines to dismiss his Equal Protection Claim.

IV. Conclusion

For the reasons set forth herein, the Amended Motion to Dismiss (ECF No. 135) is DENIED. . . .

It is so ordered.

Discussion

1. To justify reconsidering an earlier order in the case, the district court asserts that "there has been a significant change in the applicable law since the Motion to Dismiss the Title IX claim was initially considered. . . ." It states that the evidence about "the applicable law" is comprised of decisions from other circuit and district courts—none of which is binding on this court. Should that kind of change in law be sufficient to justify this kind of reconsideration? (Even if not, either the reasoning of the intervening Fourth Circuit Court of Appeals regarding Gavin Grimm's Title IX claim or factual developments might justify reconsideration, as the district court notes.)

2. If the school board eschewed the vague terms "biological gender" and "physiological characteristics" and instead based common restroom usage on genitalia, would there be a question about how it applied to Grimm? Would it be legally erroneous to interpret Title IX and its implementing regulations' usage of "sex" to mean "sex (male or female) as determined by genital inspection," perhaps with the qualifier "at birth"? If so, since minors are generally unable to have genital reconstruction surgery, would this give the school board the result it seemingly desired? Would such a policy be administrable?

Note on Grimm v. Gloucester County School Board

The district court permitted Gavin to file a second amended complaint on February 15, 2019, arguing that the school board continued to violate his rights under Title IX and the Equal Protection Clause by refusing to update his official school transcripts to reflect his sex as male. Subsequently, both sides filed summary judgment motions. In an August 9, 2019 order, Judge Wright Allen granted Gavin's motion and denied the school board's motion. *Grimm v. Gloucester County School Board*, 400 F. Supp. 3d 444 (E.D. Va. 2019).

Judge Wright Allen refused to revisit her earlier decision denying the board's motion to dismiss Gavin's suit (*see supra*), observing that no case law subsequent to her order undermined her conclusion there "that claims of discrimination on the basis of transgender status are per se actionable under a gender stereotyping theory." "To the contrary," she noted, "every court to consider the issue since May 22, 2018, has agreed with the analysis relied upon by this Court," citing *Doe v. Boyertown Area Sch. Dist.*, 897 F.3d 518 (3d Cir. 2018); *Adams v. Sch. Bd. of St. Johns Cty.*, 318 F. Supp. 3d 1293 (M.D. Fla. 2018), appeal docketed, No. 18-13592 (11th Cir. Aug. 24, 2018); and *Parents for Privacy v. Dallas Sch. Dist. No. 2*, 326 F. Supp. 3d

1075, 1106 (D. Or. 2018) [subsequently affirmed, *Parents for Privacy v. Barr*, 949 F.3d 1210 (9th Cir. 2020), *infra* at p. 936].

Judge Wright Allen also rejected the board's contention that its policy did not involve sex stereotypes under *Price Waterhouse*. Beyond the analysis of her previous order, she reasoned:

> Moreover, the Board has inadequately explained the physiological and anatomical characteristics it relies upon to enforce its policy. For example, Mr. Grimm has had chest reconstruction surgery. The Gloucester County Circuit Court referred to Mr. Grimm's chest reconstruction surgery as "gender reassignment surgery," relying on that surgery in part in determining that Mr. Grimm is a male. However, this surgery is insufficient under the Board's policy. At the summary judgment hearing, counsel for the Board argued that an individual must have "the primary genitals and sex characteristic of a particular gender." "Primary genitals" may be sufficiently clear, but "sex characteristic" is troublingly ambiguous. Many aspects of biology determine a person's sex, including genitalia, and also including hormones, genes, chromosomes, and other factors that comprise a person's biological makeup. The policy at issue uses some of these factors to define sex and ignores others. In determining the physical characteristics that define male and female and the characteristics that are disregarded, the Board has crafted a policy that is based on stereotypes about gender. *See Glenn v. Brumby*, 663 F.3d 1312 (11th Cir. 2011) ("A person is defined as transgender precisely because of the perception that his or her behavior transgresses gender stereotypes. . . . There is thus a congruence between discriminating against transgender and transsexual individuals and discrimination on the basis of gender-based behavioral norms."); *City of L.A., Dep't of Water & Power v. Manhart*, 435 U.S. 702 (1978) (stating that protections from sex discrimination are not limited to discrimination based on "myths and purely habitual assumptions," but also extend to discrimination based on generalizations that are "unquestionably true").

> Additionally, Mr. Grimm has both a valid court order and a state-issued birth certificate identifying him as male. All other students with male birth certificates at Gloucester High School are permitted to use male restrooms. Mr. Grimm was the only student with a male birth certificate excluded from the male restrooms. This constitutes discriminatory treatment by the Board.

> Furthermore, the Board has refused to update Mr. Grimm's transcripts and education documents, despite his amended birth certificate. The Board argues that his amended birth certificate does not comply with Virginia law and questions its authenticity. Such questions have been dispelled by the Declaration of Janet M. Rainey. Ms. Rainey is the State Registrar and Director of the Division of Vital Records and administers Virginia's system of vital records in accordance with Virginia law. She issued Gavin

Grimm an amended birth certificate on October 27, 2016 that identifies him as male. Regardless of prior concerns about the amended birth certificate's authenticity,[6] the Board's continued recalcitrance in the face of Ms. Rainey's Declaration and the court order from the Gloucester County Circuit Court is egregious. It is also discriminatory. Other students in the Gloucester County School system with male birth certificates also have male transcripts. Undeniably, the Board discriminates against Mr. Grimm in violation of Title IX in refusing to afford him the same dignity.

The Board also argues that Mr. Grimm has not proven that his use of male restrooms was medically necessary. However, the questions presented in this case do not require a finding that Mr. Grimm's use of a male restroom was medically necessary. The Board treated Mr. Grimm differently than other students on the basis of sex and, as established below, he suffered some measure of harm from that treatment. The existence of other methods of social transition for transgender individuals is, for the purposes of resolving the questions presented, irrelevant.

As a result, the court concluded that "the Board has discriminated against Gavin Grimm on the basis of his transgender status in violation of Title IX."

Judge Wright Allen also rejected the school district's arguments that various harms Gavin suffered were not sufficient to show Title IX liability because Gavin's testimony as to those harms was not supported by expert testimony. She noted that there is no such evidentiary requirement in the law, and that the board's counsel had conceded that Gavin's testimony could support a finding of harm supporting at least nominal damages. She likewise concluded that the refusal to update Gavin's records was causing him harm every time he had to present his transcript to others, such as new employers, and hence be marked as different from other (non-transgender) males.

As she did with Gavin's Title IX claim, the judge rejected the board's request that she revisit her holding that its discrimination against Gavin was subject to intermediate scrutiny, again noting that case law since her order denying the board's motion to dismiss agreed with that conclusion; she cited as illustrative *Karnoski v. Trump*, 926 F.3d 1180 (9th Cir. 2019), a case challenging Donald Trump's ban on military service by transgender persons, and *Adams*. On the merits, although she accepted that "students have a privacy right in avoiding exposure of their unclothed bodies," she found that the board's policy was not substantially related to such interest as required to satisfy intermediate scrutiny:

---

6. It is obvious from the face of the amended birth certificate that the photocopy presented to the Board was marked "void" because it was a copy of a document printed on security paper, not because it was fabricated. *See* ECF No. 184–6 (a copy of Mr. Grimm's birth certificate, stating that it the original is printed on security paper and is void without a watermark). In any event, given Ms. Rainey's Declaration, the Board rationalizes its continuing denial of Mr. Grimm's amended birth certificate on specious grounds: that a photocopy was marked void.

At the summary judgment hearing, defense counsel conceded that there is no privacy concern for other students when a transgender student walks into a stall and shuts the door. However, the Board's . . . witness, Troy Andersen, testified that privacy concerns are implicated when students use the urinal, use the toilet, or open their pants to tuck in their shirts. When asked why the expanded stalls and urinal dividers could not fully address those situations, Mr. Andersen responded that he "was sure" the policy also protected privacy interests in other ways, but that he "[couldn't] think of any other off the top of [his] head. This Court is compelled to conclude that the Board's privacy argument "is based upon sheer conjecture and abstraction."

Judge Wright Allen also rejected the board's attempts to rely on "[bathroom] use relying on the social norms of binary sexes." She quoted *City of Cleburne v. Cleburne Living Center*, 473 U.S. 432 (1985), for the proposition that "mere negative attitudes, or fear, unsubstantiated by factors which are properly cognizable . . . are not permissible bases" for discrimination. And she found concerns about the legality of Gavin's amended birth certificate eliminated by Janet Rainey's declaration in the case. Thus, she ruled that the board had not met its burden of showing an exceedingly persuasive justification for its discrimination. She also ruled that Gavin had satisfied the requirements for a permanent injunction regarding updating his school records. And for all the foregoing reasons, she rejected the board's motion for summary judgment in its favor.

Judge Wright Allen concluded her opinion with a coda of sorts, reminiscent of Judge Davis's opinion concurring in the vacatur of the preliminary injunction Gavin had obtained in the litigation:

> Nelson Mandela said that "[h]istory will judge us by the difference we make in the everyday lives of children." One need only trace the arduous journey that this litigation has followed since its inception over four years ago to understand that passion and conviction have infused the arguments and appeals along the way. The Board undertook the unenviable responsibility of trying to honor expressions of concern advanced by its constituency as it navigated the challenges presented by issues that barely could have been imagined or anticipated a generation ago. This Court acknowledges the many expressions of concern arising from genuine love for our children and the fierce instinct to protect and raise our children safely in a society that is growing ever more complex. There can be no doubt that all involved in this case have the best interests of the students at heart.
>
> At the same time, the Court acknowledges that for seven weeks, the student body at Gloucester High School accommodated Mr. Grimm without incident as he — assisted by compassionate school and medical representatives — took new paths in his everyday life. This Court is compelled to acknowledge too that some of the external challenges seeking to reroute these new paths inflicted grief, pain, and suicidal thoughts on a child.

> However well-intentioned some external challenges may have been and however sincere worries were about possible unknown consequences arising from a new school restroom protocol, the perpetuation of harm to a child stemming from unconstitutional conduct cannot be allowed to stand. These acknowledgements [*sic*] are made in the hopes of making a positive difference to Mr. Grimm and to the everyday lives of our children who rely upon us to protect them compassionately and in ways that more perfectly respect the dignity of every person.

She therefore declared "that the Board's policy violated Mr. Grimm's rights under the Fourteenth Amendment to the United States Constitution and Title IX . . . on the day the policy was first issued and throughout the remainder of his time as a student at Gloucester High School" and "that the Board's refusal to update Mr. Grimm's official school transcript to conform to the 'male' designation on his birth certificate violated and continues to violate his rights under" the Equal Protection Clause and Title IX. She awarded him nominal damages of $1 and reasonable attorney's fees, and enjoined the board to conform Gavin's school records to "the male designation on his updated birth certificate" and to make copies thereof available to Gavin within 10 days.

This did not end the saga, however, as the school board timely filed an appeal with the Fourth Circuit Court of Appeals on September 3, 2019.

Discussion

1. Judge Wright Allen argues that the school board treated Gavin Grimm discriminatorily because Gavin "was the only student with a male birth certificate excluded from the male restrooms." (She reasons similarly about the sex marker on Gavin's transcript.) Title IX, however, is not violated by most forms of "discriminatory treatment," but only by *sex* discrimination. If the relevant Title IX regulations allow schools to exclude from male restrooms students who were identified as female at birth on their birth certificate, what more might the judge have included in her reasoning to show that this discrimination was because of sex in a distinguishable way?

2. Compare and contrast Judge Wright Allen's closing passages to Judge Davis's earlier concurring opinion (*supra* at p. 892). Is one more justified than the other? More fair to all sides? More likely to be efficacious (toward what object)?

3. Chan Tov McNamarah has argued that "the Gavin Grimm case . . . is a model of formal equality." Chan Tov McNamarah, *On the Basis of Sex(ual Orientation or Gender Identity): Bringing Queer Equity to School with Title IX*, 104 Cornell L. Rev. 745, 749 (2019). But McNamarah has criticized this litigation strategy, contending that "[i]n the Gavin Grimm case and the larger Title IX sphere, formal equality arguments are shortsighted, ignore the statute's legislative history, and frustrate the purpose of the statute." *Id.* at 751. This note argues that "simply guaranteeing queer students equal access to existing educational services—the requirement of formal

equality—is insufficient to ensure that LGBT students *actually* receive equal access to the benefits of educational opportunities." *Id.* at 751–52. Why might one think that these critiques are or are not well taken?

—————

Not all litigation over transgender students' rights to use sex-segregated facilities consistent with their gender identity has been brought by trans students seeking access. Some litigation has been filed by the parents of cisgender students seeking to invalidate trans-inclusive school policies. Thus far, they have largely been met with defeat, as in the next case.

Reading Guide for Doe v. Boyertown Area School District

1. The following case differs from most suits regarding transgender students' access to gender appropriate restrooms, where students have sued over exclusionary policies; here, cisgender parents and students are suing to block a public school from maintaining its trans-inclusive policy. With some of their counsel from the Alliance Defending Freedom, a Christian Right legal advocacy organization, the plaintiffs sought a preliminary injunction requiring the exclusion of transgender students from restrooms consistent with their gender identity—which the court denies in the opinion below.

2. What constitutional privacy rights cases does the court examine, and what reasons does it give for concluding that the plaintiffs had not established a likelihood of prevailing on the claim that the defendants had violated their constitutional rights as protected by those precedents?

3. The court also analyzes the plaintiffs' apparent invocation of formulations of a constitutional privacy right broader than those precedents protected. What does the court say is the test for determining whether such a claimed substantive due process right amounts to a fundamental right that can only be overcome where the defendant's challenged policy survives strict scrutiny? Why does the court conclude the plaintiff's alleged right does not meet that test?

4. The court also rules that the plaintiffs have not established a likelihood of prevailing on their claim that the defendants discriminated against them on the basis of sex in violation of Title IX of the federal Education Amendments of 1972. The court gives multiple reasons for its conclusion—what are they? (Pay attention to the required elements of any Title IX claim and of a hostile environment sexual harassment claim in particular.)

5. What is the plaintiffs' state law tort claim, what are its elements, and what reasons does the court give for concluding the plaintiffs have not shown a likelihood of success on that claim?

6. What other requirements or factors for plaintiffs to receive a preliminary injunction does the court address, and for what reasons does it conclude those requirements/factors do not support granting such relief here?

Joel Doe, A Minor, by and Through his Guardians, John Doe and Jane Doe [et al.] v. Boyertown Area School District [et al.]

276 F. Supp. 3d 324 (E.D. Penn. 2017)

[The plaintiffs were represented by private counsel, the Alliance Defending Freedom, and the Independence Law Center.]

Memorandum Opinion

Edward G. Smith, J.

Here, the court is presented with four students, three who will be seniors for the upcoming 2017–18 school year and one student who recently graduated, claiming that the defendant school district's practice of allowing transgender students (who the plaintiffs choose to identify as "members of the opposite sex" rather than as transgender students) to access bathrooms and locker rooms consistent with their gender identity violates (1) their constitutional right to privacy under the Fourteenth Amendment, (2) their right of access to educational opportunities, programs, benefits, and activities under Title IX because they are subject to a hostile environment, and (3) their Pennsylvania common law right of privacy preventing intrusion upon their seclusion while using bathrooms and locker rooms. . . . At bottom, the plaintiffs are opposed to the mere presence of transgender students in locker rooms or bathrooms with them because they designate them as members of the opposite sex and note that, *inter alia*, society has historically separated bathrooms and locker rooms on the basis of biological sex to preserve the privacy of individuals from members of the opposite biological sex.

[The court] finds that the plaintiffs are not entitled to preliminary injunctive relief because they have not shown that they are likely to succeed on the merits on any of their causes of action and they have failed to show irreparable harm. Accordingly, the court will deny the plaintiffs' motion for a preliminary injunction.

[III. Procedural History]

. . . . On April 3, 2017, Aidan DeStefano, who was then a senior at the Boyertown Area Senior High School [("BASH")], and the Pennsylvania Youth Congress Foundation ("PYC"), a youth-led, statewide LGBTQ advocacy organization, filed a motion to intervene in this litigation.

[IV. Findings of Fact]

After . . . assigning such weight to the evidence as the court deemed proper and disregarding the testimony that the court found to lack credibility, the pertinent [417! — Eds.] facts are as follows:

[7.] There were 1659 students at BASH during the 2016–17 school year. . . .

[28.] Based on the May 2016 Dear Colleague Letter and consultation with the School District's solicitor, since the beginning of the 2016–17 school year, the School

District has, upon request, permitted transgender students to use restrooms and locker rooms aligned with their gender identity on a case-by-case basis.

[37.] During the 2016–17 school year, the School District . . . granted permission to another transgender male (Student A) [in addition to senior Aidan DeStefano] permission to use the boys' restrooms and locker rooms, and one transgender female (Student B) to use the girls' restrooms because those facilities were aligned with their gender identity. Cooper Dep. at 86-93.

[58.] BASH has undergone significant renovations over the past one to two years.

[61.] During the renovations, the showers in the locker rooms were changed from "gang showers" to single-user showers which have curtains for privacy. . . .

67. All of the multi-user bathrooms at BASH have individual toilet stalls, each with a locking door for privacy. . . . .

V. Discussion

A. Standard — Motion for a Preliminary Injunction

"A preliminary injunction is an extraordinary remedy never awarded as of right." *Winter v. Natural Res. Def. Council*, 555 U.S. 7 (2008). A district court should not grant a motion for preliminary injunctive relief unless the moving party shows "(1) a likelihood of success on the merits; (2) that [the moving party] will suffer irreparable harm if the injunction is denied; (3) that granting preliminary relief will not result in even greater harm to the nonmoving party; and (4) that the public interest favors such relief." . . . .

Generally, "[a] primary purpose of a preliminary injunction is maintenance of the status quo until a decision on the merits of a case is rendered." *Acierno v. New Castle Cty.*, 40 F.3d 645 (3d Cir. 1994). Thus, "[a] party seeking a mandatory preliminary injunction that will alter the status quo bears a particularly heavy burden in demonstrating its necessity."

B. Likelihood of Success on the Merits
1. Plaintiffs' Section 1983 Constitutional Privacy Claims

. . . . [44]

b. Analysis

In addressing whether the plaintiffs are likely to succeed on the merits of their constitutional invasion of privacy claim, the court must first address whether the plaintiffs are asserting a fundamental right as they claim and the precise contours of that right. To analyze whether the plaintiffs are asserting such a fundamental right and the contours of the right as defined by the facts of this case, the court is guided by the Third Circuit's decision in *Doe v. Luzerne County*, 660 F.3d 169 (2011).[45] In *Doe*, the Third Circuit described the law applicable to claims about pur-

---

44. The plaintiffs contend that "[a] policy that separates our privacy facilities on the basis of gender identity rather than sex also suffers from absolute unworkability." In support of this assertion, the plaintiffs refer to the spectrum of possible gender identities, such as genderqueer or third gender, that fall outside of individuals identifying with the binary constructs of "male" and "female." While it appears to be undeniable that sex-segregated privacy facilities such as restrooms and bathrooms appear to be incompatible with being able to accommodate the entire spectrum of possible gender identities (particularly for an individual that does not identify with either sex/gender), it is not as if dividing privacy facilities based on biological sex covers the entire spectrum of biological sex assignments. *See, e.g.,* Jennifer Rellis, *"Please Write 'E' in This Box" Toward Self-Identification and Recognition of a Third Gender: Approaches in the United States and India*, 14 Mich. J. Gender & L. 223 (2008) (explaining that "[o]ne to four percent of the world population is intersexed [sic—Eds.], not fully male or female."). Thus, one could argue that separating privacy facilities based on biological sex (which the plaintiffs define by a person's internal and external reproductive organs) is "absolute[ly] unworkabl[e]" as well. As such, certain groups of individuals could be excluded under either method of designating the use of restrooms, locker rooms, and other privacy facilities. For those individuals "for whom there is no safe, accessible restroom in public places," some commentators have suggested replacing sex-segregated public restrooms with "all-gender, multi-user facilities that protect the privacy and safety concerns of all patrons, while discriminating against no one." Terry S. Kogan, *Public Restrooms and the Distorting of Transgender Identity*, 95 N.C. L. Rev. 1205 (2017); *see also* Alanna M. Jereb, *The Bathroom Right for Transgender Students and How the Entire LGBT Community Can Align to Guarantee This*, 7 Wake Forest J.L. & Pol'y 585 (2017) (discussing two possible solutions to transgender students' bathroom issue, including the provision of unisex bathrooms).

Regardless, the court is not faced with having to determine the wisdom of the School District's practice or whether it is unworkable in this case. The facts of this case do not involve any of the potential scenarios contemplated by the plaintiffs as there is no evidence that any student at BASH who has received permission to use a facility corresponding to the student's gender identity falls into these other gender identities and, as the defendants have indicated that they do not necessarily have a plan in place for dealing with requests from students other than students identifying with the binary gender/sexes of male and female, it is unclear how the "workability" of the School District's practice as to students outside of the binary genders/sexes of male and female affect the plaintiffs in this case. . . . .

45. [The] court recognizes that the facts underlying the purported constitutional violation in that case are not remotely analogous to the facts in this case. *Doe* involved a female police officer plaintiff who was subjected to a flea infestation after entering a disarrayed and unsanitary residence while serving a bench warrant. During the flea decontamination process, Doe went to a hospital decontamination area and showered using chemical shampoo. After completing her shower,

ported violations of a constitutional right to privacy under the Fourteenth Amendment as follows:

> The United States Constitution does not mention an explicit right to privacy and the United States Supreme Court has never proclaimed that such a generalized right exists.". . . . *But see Sterling v. Borough of Minersville,* 232 F.3d 190 (3d Cir. 2000) (stating that the Supreme Court "acknowledged the individual's constitutional right to privacy" in *Griswold v. Connecticut,* 381 U.S. 479 (1965)). The Supreme Court, however, has found certain constitutional "zones of privacy." *C.N. v. Ridgewood Bd. of Educ.,* 430 F.3d 159 (3d Cir. 2005) (citing *Roe v. Wade,* 410 U.S. 113 (1973)). From these zones of privacy, we have articulated two types of privacy interests rooted in the Fourteenth Amendment. *Nunez v. Pachman,* 578 F.3d 228 (3d Cir. 2009). The first privacy interest is the "individual interest in avoiding disclosure of personal matters," and the second is the "interest in independence in making certain kinds of important decisions." The first privacy interest is at issue in this matter.
>
> "'The right not to have intimate facts concerning one's life disclosed without one's consent' is 'a venerable [right] whose constitutional significance we have recognized in the past.'" *C.N.* Justice Brandeis, in dissent, famously referred to this as "the right to be let alone." *Olmstead v. United States,* 277 U.S. 438 (1928) (Brandeis, J., dissenting).

Doe found that the decontamination area lacked towels and the only item that she could use to cover her naked body was "a roll of thin paper of the type that typically covers a doctor's examination table." Doe claimed that this paper was semi-transparent or at least became semi-transparent when she covered her wet body with it.

At the request of another female police officer who was assisting her with the decontamination, Doe covered her private areas with the paper and this other officer entered the room, closed the door behind her, and began inspecting Doe for any remaining fleas. While Doe's back was facing the door to the room, and with Doe having "most of her back, shoulders and legs . . . completely exposed . . . [with] the thin paper, which could have been semi-transparent, . . . wrapped around her buttocks and breasts[,]" two male police officers opened the door approximately a foot and observed Doe. One of the male officers had a video camera and was recording Doe. After a comment by one of the male officers, Doe turned her head toward the sound and noticed the male officers. Without turning around, Doe yelled at the male officers to leave the room. The parties disputed how much of Doe's body the two male officers observed in the decontamination area.

To make matters worse, the male officer who was filming Doe — he had also filmed portions of Doe's entire ordeal from the reporting of the contamination at the residence to Doe entering the hospital, purportedly for "training purposes" — uploaded pictures and video of Doe (and another officer that had also entered the residence with Doe) onto his work computer and apparently stored some of the pictures and video on a public computer folder accessible to anyone on the county network. This same male officer shared photos and videos of the incident with other members of the police department, although it was unknown who saw them and exactly what they saw. Nonetheless, apparently the files saved on the public computer contained a photo of Doe's bare back and a photo of Doe's bare back and bare shoulders, with both photos showing "the outline of Doe's buttocks — covered only by thin, wet hospital paper."

The touchstone of constitutional privacy protection is whether the information at issue is "within an individual's reasonable expectations of confidentiality." *Malleus v. George*, 641 F.3d 560 (3d Cir. 2011). The more intimate or personal the information, the more reasonable the expectation is that it will remain confidential. Indeed, the "federal constitution . . . protects against public disclosure [of] only highly personal matters representing the most intimate aspects of human affairs," thereby shielding from public scrutiny "only that information which involves deeply rooted notions of fundamental personal interests derived from the Constitution." *Nunez*.

We have found the following types of information to be protected: a private employee's medical information that was sought by the government; medical, financial and behavioral information relevant to a police investigator; a public employee's prescription record; a minor student's pregnancy status; sexual orientation; and an inmate's HIV-positive status. *Malleus* (citing cases and explaining that information encompassed by the constitutional right to privacy may be separated into categories reflecting sexual, medical and some financial information).

The Third Circuit went on to conclude that "Doe had a reasonable expectation of privacy while in the [d]econtamination [a]rea, particularly while in the presence of members of the opposite sex." In reaching this conclusion, the court also pointed out that "[p]rivacy claims under the Fourteenth Amendment necessarily require fact-intensive and context-specific analyses, and unfortunately, bright lines generally cannot be drawn." The court further explained that

> [t]he difficulty in drawing a bright line is evident as we are not aware of any court of appeals that has adopted either a requirement that certain anatomical areas of one's body, such as genitalia, must have been exposed for that person to maintain a privacy claim under the Fourteenth Amendment or a rule that a nonconsensual exposure of certain anatomical areas constitutes a *per se* violation.

The court also "refuse[d] to draw bright lines based on anatomical parts or regions," and explained that courts must "analyze the specific circumstances under which the alleged violation occurred."

The plaintiffs cite to *Doe* for the proposition that "[o]ne has a 'constitutionally protected privacy interest in his or her partially clothed body,'" and it appears that the other parties do not dispute that *Doe* recognized that particular constitutional privacy interest.[46] If this right is the end of the inquiry, there is no likelihood of the plaintiffs prevailing in this case.

_____

46. While the Third Circuit in *Doe* indicated that "[a]lthough the issue of whether one may have a constitutionally protected privacy interest in his or her partially clothed body is a matter of first impression in this circuit, other circuits—including the Second, Sixth and Ninth Circuits—have

... [T]he plaintiffs have yet to prove that the defendants violated their constitutionally protected privacy interest in their partially clothed bodies. Mary Smith [as a junior] entered a [girls'] bathroom [at the high school] and saw Student B [a transgender girl] while both students were fully clothed. As such, Mary Smith's constitutionally protected privacy interest in her partially clothed body was not violated.

Regarding Joel Doe, he [as a junior] was in his underwear and a t-shirt [in a boy's locker room changing for his mandatory physical education class] when he saw Student A[, a transgender boy], wearing only shorts and a bra, whereupon Doe quickly re-dressed and left]. [There] is conflicting evidence as to whether Student A saw Joel Doe in his underwear. There surely is not enough credible evidence that the court would conclude that Joel Doe was likely to prove that Student A saw him in his underwear.

Finally, Jack Jones testified that [as a junior] he was [in the locker room] in his underwear and initially had his back turned to [transgender boy] Student A. When he turned around, Student A was staring into Student A's locker and Jack Jones quickly moved away so Student A could not see him. While it appears that Student A was in close proximity to Jack Jones, the court cannot infer that Student A saw Jack Jones in his underwear and would not find that Jack Jones would be likely to succeed on such a claim if presented to a jury based solely on the evidence currently before the court. The court also notes that Jane Jones testified that when Jack Jones reported the incident to her, he did not tell her that Student A saw him in his underwear. Therefore, while it is unclear whether Joel Doe and Jack Jones are claiming that Student A saw them in their underwear because they inconsistently assert this point (which would seem to be extremely important to their claim), to the extent they are asserting as such, the court finds that they are not likely to succeed on any claim that involves them being wrongfully viewed while in a state of partial undress because of the conflicting evidence in the record.[48]

Nonetheless, [from] the plaintiffs' description of the fundamental right in this case—the fundamental right to bodily privacy from members of the opposite sex—[it appears] that the plaintiffs are seeking to include additional conduct as violating

---

held that such a right exists," the court did not explicitly state that such a privacy right existed. Nonetheless, in finding that Doe, who was partially clothed at the time of the purported initial violation, had a reasonable expectation of privacy while she was in the decontamination area, the court seemingly had to find that this privacy interest existed although it is apparent that the precise contours of that right are case determinative insofar as the Third Circuit remanded the case to the district court because of factual issues concerning the parts of Doe's body that the male officers actually viewed. In this regard, the Third Circuit found that there existed disputed issues of fact "as to which of Doe's body parts were exposed to members of the opposite sex and/or filmed while she was in the [d]econtamination [a]rea" insofar as "the issues of whether Doe's breasts or buttocks were exposed would affect the outcome of the suit."

48. Yet another example of this inconsistency is illustrated by the plaintiffs' statement in their reply brief that the defendants ... "conveniently ignore the fact that both Joel Doe and Jack Jones were already caught in the objectively offensive and embarrassing circumstance of standing in their underwear *when a classmate of the opposite sex was with them*." (emphasis added).

their right to privacy[:] (1) males being able to hear females when females are open-ing products to deal with menstruation issues or using the restrooms, (2) males being around females with the opportunity to view females where they could discern that the girls are having menstruation issues, (3) members of the opposite sex being in locker rooms or bathrooms with each other regardless of anyone being in a state of undress, and (4) having to view a transgender person in a state of undress since that student is actually a member of the opposite sex.

Generally, a fundamental right is "deeply rooted in this Nation's history and tra-dition" and "implicit in the concept of ordered liberty," such that "neither liberty nor justice would exist if they were sacrificed." *Washington v. Glucksberg*, 521 U.S. 702 (1997). The Supreme Court has "'always been reluctant to expand the concept of substantive due process because guideposts for responsible decisionmaking in this uncharted area are scarce and open-ended'" and because doing so "place[s] the matter outside the arena of public debate and legislative action." *Id.* Thus, "[t]he doctrine of judicial self-restraint requires [courts] to exercise the utmost care whenever [they] are asked to break new ground in this field." *Reno v. Flores*, 507 U.S. 292 (1993).

The plaintiffs have not identified and this court has not located any court that has recognized a constitutional right of privacy as broadly defined by the plaintiffs. The only court that seemingly has addressed a similar if not identical constitutional privacy claim was the United States District Court for the Northern District of Illi-nois in *Students and Parents for Privacy v. United States Dep't of Education*, 2016 WL 6134121 (N.D. Ill. Oct. 18, 2016) (hereinafter referred to as "*Students*"). . . .

[A]s in *Students*, the plaintiffs here have argued for the recognition of a very broad constitutional privacy right that has never been recognized by another court even though courts have recognized that sex-segregated bathrooms provide for pri-vacy protection from the opposite sex. In fact, if such a broad right was to exist, the Third Circuit in *Doe* would not have had to limit the right to one's partially clothed body, because the plaintiff would have had a general right to bodily privacy from the opposite sex. There would have been no need to remand the case to the district court to resolve the issue of whether the defendants actually violated the plaintiff's right to privacy . . . because the male officers would have violated her right to pri-vacy merely by entering the decontamination room while she was in there once the court determined that Doe had a reasonable expectation of privacy in the room. The plaintiffs' proposed right is so expansive that it would be a constitutional viola-tion for a female to be in the presence of a male inside of a locker room or bathroom and vice versa, and it would be a violation of one's constitutional right of privacy to view a member of the opposite sex in a state of undress even if the viewing party was fully clothed at the time. There is no support for such a broad right of privacy that has yet to be recognized.

The plaintiffs have also not demonstrated that such an expansive right of privacy is "deeply rooted in this Nation's history and tradition" and "implicit in the concept of ordered liberty. Even if this right was limited to a right to bodily privacy from the opposite sex in bathrooms and locker rooms, or even if the right was limited to a student's right of bodily privacy from the opposite sex in bathrooms and locker rooms at schools, these rights are not such that "neither liberty nor justice would exist if they were sacrificed." Despite these possible limitations to the broad right asserted by the plaintiffs, these are not the contours of the underlying right in this case because this case does not merely involve members of the opposite sex. Instead, although the plaintiffs refuse to refer to them as such, this case involves transgender students and whether it violates cisgender students' right to privacy for transgender students to be in the locker room or bathroom that does not correspond to the transgender student's biological sex at birth.

As in *Students*, the School District's practice here does not allow cisgender boys to go into the girls' bathrooms and locker rooms or allow cisgender girls to go into the boys' bathrooms and locker rooms. Instead, the School District permits students who indicate that they identify with a gender different than the sex assigned to them at birth to use the bathrooms and locker rooms which correspond to their gender identity. Despite the plaintiffs' concerns about gender fluidity, gender nonconformity, or other gender identity issues that fall along [a] spectrum . . . , there is no evidence in the record that any of the students that have requested and received permission from the School District have done anything other than live in a manner consistent with their gender identity. In this regard, Dr. Cooper[, the principal of Boyertown Area Senior High School,] indicated that all of the transgender students that have received permission to use the bathrooms and locker rooms corresponding to their gender identity have requested to have the School District refer to them as an initial or another name rather than their given name, and have asked to be referred to by the pronouns corresponding to their gender identity instead of their sex assigned at birth. There is also no evidence that these students do not also outwardly portray themselves in accordance with their gender identity or are not known by the community in the same regard. Furthermore, once the transgender students have received permission to go into the locker rooms and bathrooms consistent with their gender identity, the School District has prohibited them from going into the bathroom corresponding with their birth sex.

This court agrees with *Students* that high school students . . . have no constitutional right not to share restrooms and locker rooms with transgender students whose sex assigned at birth is different from theirs. Also, . . . there is no requirement at BASH that the plaintiffs (or any student for that matter) get changed in the locker room for gym class (although they do have to change depending on the gym activity and if they desire to try to obtain as high of a grade as possible) or use the multi-user restrooms. Thus, no cisgender student is compelled to use a restroom with a transgender student. If cisgender students decide to use the locker rooms, there are privacy stalls in the shower area with curtains and toilet stalls with doors and locks for students use if the student desires to not be viewed by a transgender student while changing. If cisgender students are uncomfortable even viewing a transgender student while they are changing for gym, the cisgender students could use the team room in the locker room that does not require them to go through the common area of the locker room, or the cisgender students could use a single-user facility to change. Similarly, any cisgender student concerned with running into a transgender student in a bathroom and who does not think that urinal dividers or toilet stalls provide the requisite protection of their privacy can access one of the single-user facilities. At bottom, no student at BASH is compelled to use a privacy facility in which he or she feels uncomfortable.

When discussing the need for students to be protected from exposure to the members of the opposite sex, the plaintiffs cite to numerous cases that simply have no application here. For example, the plaintiffs cite to *Fortner v. Thomas*, 983 F.2d 1024 (11th Cir. 1993), for the proposition that "[m]ost people have 'a special sense of privacy in their genitals, and involuntary exposure of them in the presence of other people of the other sex may be especially demeaning and humiliating.'" Pls.' Findings and Conclusions, ¶ 11. *Fortner* involves male inmates complaining about female correctional officers being assigned to locations that allow them to view inmates in the showers and on the toilet. Although unclear, the reference to the term "involuntary" appears to indicate that the inmates lacked the ability to prevent the female guards from seeing them naked. As already indicated, there is no requirement at BASH that would compel a student to involuntarily expose himself or herself to another student. . . .

Another example of citing to seemingly inapplicable cases is the plaintiffs' references to cases involving strip searches of students by members of the opposite sex, which is significantly more egregious than merely being in the presence of a transgender student. *See . . . Safford Unified Sch. Dist. No. 1 v. Redding*, 557 U.S. 364 (2009) (involving strip search of 13-year-old female student's bra and underpants) . . . .[54] A further example is cases involving bona fide occupational qualifications that would preclude individuals from one sex from being in an area that would violate the opposite sex's privacy interests. Although these cases reference having sex-segregated areas to accommodate privacy needs, none of the cases address whether the privacy interest mentioned is a constitutional right of privacy.

[E]ven if the right articulated by the plaintiff could be extended to support the existence of a constitutional right of bodily privacy from members of the opposite sex, the plaintiffs have not identified any basis for that right extending to a prohibition of seeing a member of the opposite sex in a state of undress such as Joel

---

54. The plaintiffs cite to *Safford* for two propositions: (1) that "adolescent vulnerability intensifies the . . . intrusiveness of the exposure," and (2) "[f]orcing minors to risk exposing their bodies to the opposite sex is an 'embarrassing, frightening, and humiliating' experience." Pls.' Mem. at 13 (quoting *Redding*). As for this second proposition, the plaintiffs' have mischaracterized *Redding* because the "opposite sex" was not involved in the strip search. Instead, the facts show that the school employees conducting the search of the 13-year-old girl student were an administrative assistant named "Helen Romero" and the school nurse named "Peggy Schwallier." While one's name is not automatically determinative of one's gender or sex (as the instant case makes clear), it appears that female school employees conducted the search of the female student.

Doe and Jack Jones experienced with Student A in October and November 2016. To recognize, for example, that a male's constitutional privacy rights are violated by merely viewing a female in a locker room or even by seeing a female in a state of undress in a locker room, would extend constitutional privacy rights beyond acceptable bounds. . . . [T]he plaintiffs reference a right to privacy by cisgender girls to not have transgender girls hear them when they are in the restroom (particularly when they are tending to menstruation issues). The plaintiffs cite to *Borse v. Piece Goods Shop, Inc.*, 963 F.2d 611 (3d Cir. 1992) in support of the proposition that an individual's use of their senses (which would presumably include hearing) to invade the seclusion of another is a privacy violation. The *Borse* case discussed this type of intrusion with respect to a common law intrusion upon seclusion tort claim and did not discuss it as if it was a constitutional invasion of privacy claim. Further, to the extent that it would even reach the status of a fundamental right of privacy, there is no indication that this would be extended to being heard by a member of the opposite sex when the student is in an area such as a locker room or multi-user bathroom where there is a limited amount of auditory privacy from anyone.

. . . . As a final issue, PYC and the plaintiffs disagree over the level of scrutiny to apply to the defendants' practice regarding transgender students' use of the bathrooms and locker rooms at BASH.[55] The plaintiffs argue that the practice is subject to strict scrutiny insofar as it infringes upon a fundamental constitutional right. PYC contends that strict scrutiny does not apply because the Third Circuit in *Doe* indicated that "'[a] person's right to avoid disclosure of personal matters is not absolute,' and '[d]isclosure may be required if the government interest in disclosure outweighs the individual's privacy interest.'" PYC's Mem. (quoting *Doe v. Luzerne Cty.*).

[T]he balancing test appears to be concerned with compelling disclosure of private information contained or sought to be included in records as the test repeatedly references "record[s]." Thus, it would not appear that this flexible balancing test is appropriate to examine the constitutionality of the School District's practice because the disclosure of private information in a record is not at issue here.

As such [*sic*], the court must determine, to the extent that the defendants' practice infringes upon the plaintiffs' privacy rights regarding the involuntary exposure of the intimate parts of the body (or even the possible disclosure of their partially clothed bodies), whether the infringement is narrowly tailored to serve a compelling state interest. *Reno.* . . . . [T]he defendants have a compelling state interest not to discriminate against transgender students. Even with the [Trump Administration's] revocation of the [Obama administration era joint Department of Education and Department of Justice] guidance that initiated the School District to change its practice for the 2016–17 school year [to allow transgender students to use facilities consistent with their gender identity], there have been recent cases determining that School Districts have violated the Equal Protection Clause and Title IX by

---

55. As far as the court can tell, the defendants do not address this issue.

precluding transgender students from using the restrooms. *See, e.g., Whitaker by Whitaker v. Kenosha Unified School Dist. No. 1 Bd. of Educ.*, 858 F.3d 1034 (7th Cir. 2017) (Title IX), and *Evancho v. Pine-Richland School District*, 2017 WL 770619 (W.D. Pa. Feb. 27, 2017) (Equal Protection Clause). While there have been other cases deciding to the contrary, *see, e.g., Johnston v. University of Pittsburgh of Commonwealth System of Higher Education*, 97 F. Supp. 3d 657 (W.D. Pa. 2015), this does not mean that the School District does not have a compelling state interest in not discriminating against transgender students with regard to the use of privacy facilities at BASH.

As for whether the practice is narrowly tailored, the School District's practice is narrowly tailored because the School District, *inter alia*, (1) does not coerce students to use the multi-user bathrooms and locker rooms, (2) requires students seeking to use the facilities corresponding to their gender identity to first consult with the counselor and administration and receive permission before gaining access, (3) provides privacy protections in the nature of areas in the locker rooms and bathrooms where students can go if those students are uncomfortable seeing or being seen by transgender students, and (4) provides alternative single-user facilities that would provide uncomfortable students with complete privacy and security for changing or taking care of bodily needs. The School District has attempted to provide transgender students with the opportunity to live their lives in a manner consistent with their gender identity, while attempting to minimize as much as possible any discomfort felt by other students by offering various forms of privacy protection and alternative arrangements for their use if they feel uncomfortable or need additional privacy.

Accordingly, the court finds that the plaintiffs have failed to establish that they are likely to succeed on the merits of their section 1983 action for invasion of privacy against the defendants.

2. Title IX

. . . .

b. Analysis

Title IX provides in pertinent part that "[n]o person in the United States shall, on the basis of sex, be excluded from participation in, be denied the benefits of, or be subject to discrimination under any education program or activity receiving Federal financial assistance[.]" 20 U.S.C. § 1681(a). "[A] public school student may bring suit against a school under Title IX for so-called 'hostile environment' harassment." *Saxe v. State Coll. Area Sch. Dist.*, 240 F.3d 200 (3d Cir. 2001) (citing *Davis v. Monroe Cty. Bd. of Educ.*, 526 U.S. 629 (1999); *Franklin v. Gwinnett Cty. Pub. Sch.*, 503 U.S. 60 (1992)). To prevail in a Title IX sexual harassment claim,

> a plaintiff must establish sexual harassment of students that is so severe, pervasive, and objectively offensive, and that so undermines and detracts from the victims' educational experience, that the victim students are effectively denied equal access to an institution's resources and opportunities.

[*Davis*. This determination "'depends on a constellation of surrounding circumstances, expectations, and relationships,' including, but not limited to, the ages of the harasser and the victim, and the number of individuals involved." *Id.*] The Court stressed that "[d]amages are not available for simple acts of teasing and name-calling among school children, even where these comments target differences in gender." Rather, private damages actions against the school are limited to cases in which the school "acts with deliberate indifference to known acts of harassment," and those acts have "a systemic effect on educational programs and activities." *Id.*

Saxe.

Although there have been a number of cases brought by transgender students claiming that school districts violate Title IX by maintaining separate privacy facilities based on biological sex and refusing to permit the transgender students to use the privacy facility corresponding to the student's gender identity, [*Students*,] is the only case similar to the instant case where cisgender students (and their parents) have sued a school district based in part on a Title IX sexual harassment hostile environment claim. In *Students*, Magistrate Judge Gilbert determined that the plaintiffs did not have a likelihood of success on the merits with respect to their Title IX sexual harassment hostile environment claim. The court again finds persuasive much of the rationale set forth by Magistrate Judge Gilbert in determining that the plaintiffs did not establish a likelihood of success on the merits of their Title IX claim.

In the first instance, as in *Students*, this court finds that the plaintiffs have failed to demonstrate a likelihood of success on the merits because they have not met the "threshold question," *i.e.* that they have suffered discrimination "on the basis of sex." . . . [T]he School District treats all students at school similarly. Under the current practice, the plaintiffs (and the other students at BASH) are not targeted on the basis of their sex because the School District treats both male and female students similarly. The practice applies to both the boys' and girls' locker rooms and bathrooms, meaning that cisgender boys potentially may use the boys' locker room and bathrooms with transgender boys and cisgender girls potentially may use the girls' locker room and bathrooms with transgender girls. In addition, with regard to the transgender students, both transgender boys and transgender girls are treated similarly insofar as they, upon receiving permission from the School District, may use the locker rooms and bathrooms corresponding with their gender identity. Moreover, the School District is not discriminating against students regarding the use of alternative facilities if students are uncomfortable with the current practice insofar as those facilities are open to all students who may be uncomfortable using the locker rooms or multi-user facilities at BASH. The School District's similar treatment of all students is fatal to the plaintiffs' Title IX claim. *See Moeck v. Pleasant Valley Sch. Dist.*, 179 F. Supp. 3d 442 (M.D. Pa. 2016) (concluding that plaintiff failed to support sexual harassment hostile educational environment action where even though "the actions of the coaching staff were vulgar and inappropriate," "[t]he record establishes that the coaching staff were not discriminatory—they 'harassed' everyone on the team, male and female. They did not harass because of sex but rather, harassed everyone regardless of their sex. . . . The coaches treated [the plaintiff] like everyone else, poorly and immaturely"); *see also Pasqua v. Metropolitan Life Ins. Co.*, 101 F.3d 514, 517 (7th Cir. 1996) ("Harassment that is inflicted without regard to gender, that is, where males and females in the same setting do not receive disparate treatment, is not actionable because the harassment is not based on sex.").

The plaintiffs have failed to cite to any case holding that a plaintiff can maintain a sexual harassment hostile environment claim when the allegedly sexually harassing party treats all individuals similarly and there is, as such, no evidence of gender/sex animus. Simply because the plaintiffs feel a particular way which they equate to their sex does not take away from the fact that the School District's practice is not targeting any group or individual because of their sex. Even if the court were to find that the practice is based on sex, the plaintiffs ignore that Title IX deals with "discrimination" based on sex and there can be no discrimination when everyone is treated the same.[61]

---

61. The court is compelled to address a few of the plaintiffs' additional arguments in support of the belief that the defendants discriminated on the basis of sex insofar as these arguments are somewhat overstated. These statements are (1) the female plaintiffs are concerned about males entering the girls' privacy facilities for lewd purposes, (2) the female plaintiffs cannot even question the presence of a biological male in their locker room, and (3) there are no methods for excluding males who have lewd intentions until after the damage is done. The court addresses this latter point first. Even in sex-segregated restrooms, the School District does not have a method of excluding males who have lewd intentions until after the damage is done. There is no evidence in the record that a police officer or gatekeeper is patrolling the students' privacy facilities and even if teachers or other school employees are near these areas, there is simply nothing stopping someone with truly lewd intentions from entering the privacy facilities. The School District's pre-2016–17 practice regarding the restrooms and locker rooms was dependent on the students following the rules and, if they did not, the School District using its surveillance systems and other tools of investigation to catch the perpetrators of any rule violations (all of which occur *after* the violation). At bottom, there is nothing to physically stop an individual with bad intentions no matter how the School District assigns bathroom and locker room usage.

Secondly, . . . all of the plaintiffs testified that they had no basis of knowing whether someone was designated a male or female at birth simply by looking at them. Their knowledge about the purported biological sex of Students A and B were based on having known the students for a period of time and their belief that the student was a girl or boy based on that prior knowledge but without any particular knowledge of the transgender student's anatomy. In addition, and as an example, Mary Smith will accept someone that looks like a stereotypical boy in the locker room or bathroom with her as long as that person has a female external and internal reproductive system. The court finds it more than reasonable to infer from her testimony that if she saw someone that she perceived to be a boy (but who was assigned female at birth), Mary Smith would have reacted the same way when she fled the 700s bathroom upon seeing Student B. Regardless, there is nothing in the record supporting the plaintiffs' statement that Mary Smith (or any other student at BASH) would not be able to go to school administration to report the presence of someone they perceive to be of the opposite biological sex as it is still the School District's policy that only students who receive permission to use the locker room and/or bathroom corresponding to their gender identity are permitted in those areas.

[Even if] they could show that the School District discriminated against them on the basis of their sex, the plaintiffs have still failed to show a likelihood of success on the merits of their Title IX claim because they have not shown that they can establish the elements of a hostile environment claim.... [W]hile the court has some doubts as to the level and reasonableness of the humiliation, fear, anxiety, stress, and dignity loss caused by the School District's practice, the court will presume for purposes of this opinion that the plaintiffs have shown that they subjectively viewed the School District's practice as harassment. The plaintiffs have nonetheless failed to show that they are likely to demonstrate that the School District's practice is so severe, pervasive, and objectively offensive that it undermined and detracted from their educational experience.

The "objective prong" of the hostile environment inquiry "must be evaluated by looking at the totality of the circumstances[] [which] ... may include ... the frequency of the discriminatory conduct; its severity; whether it is physically threatening or humiliating, or a mere offensive utterance; and whether it [so undermines and detracts from the victims' educational experience, that [he or she is] effectively denied equal access to an institution's resources and opportunities]." *Saxe*.... [E]ach plaintiff testified as to a single instance in which they viewed a transgender student in a locker room or bathroom.... To the best of her knowledge, Macy Roe[c] never saw any transgender student in a bathroom or locker room before she

---

As the final point, the plaintiffs use the fear of sexual assault as a basis to justify the continued separation of privacy facilities on the basis of biological sex and they cite to statistics by the Centers for Disease Control showing that nearly 12% of high school girls reported having been sexually assaulted. While is it highly alarming and troubling to know that such a high percentage of high school female students have reported being the victim of sexual assault, considering that the percentage does not reflect those students who do not report being assaulted, the plaintiffs provide no statistics as to how many of those sexual assaults have occurred in a locker room or bathroom at a school or how many of those sexual assaults have occurred in locker rooms and bathrooms in public places or schools that have decided to permit bathroom and locker room usage on the basis of gender identity. There is no evidence of any such horrendous misconduct occurring at BASH since the School District changed the policy there and the fear of harm is purely speculative.

c. Macy Roe graduated from BASH after the school adopted its trans-inclusive policy during her senior year, the 2016–2017 school year. She testified that after learning of the policy she reduced her restroom usage as much as she could, although she was unaware of any occasion when her gendered privacy was actually violated by anyone or encountered any transgender student in a locker room or restroom at BASH. She testified, as the court summarized it, that she "does not object to homosexual students using the girls' locker rooms, even if those students were sexually attracted to her, since they would have the same sex as her," that she "does not object to sharing a restroom or locker room with a student who has a different anatomy than her if, in her opinion, that student was 'born female[,]'" that she "would not object to sharing a locker room with a transgender boy who had surgery to construct a penis," but that if she "entered a public bathroom (outside of school) and noticed someone that looked like a male, she would leave the restroom. She would base this decision on whether the person was wearing stereotypical male clothing or had facial hair." "Although she alleges and asserts having suffered anxiety, stress, humiliation, embarrassment, apprehension, and distress, Macy Roe has not received any medical attention, counseling, or therapy since learning about the School District's practice. She has also not spoken to her guidance counselor, other administrators, or any teachers about transgender issues at BASH or about any graduated. Based on their testimony, none of these plaintiffs were subjected to pervasive sexual harassment in regard to their actual interaction with transgender students in the privacy facilities at BASH.

Nonetheless, the plaintiffs point to the impact of the School District's practice as establishing pervasive conduct because the practice permits transgender students who receive permission from the School District to use the privacy facilities corresponding to their gender identity. As a result of this practice Joel Doe has ceased using the locker room to change for gym class, has ceased changing for gym class, and uses the restrooms less frequently than he had previously. It does not appear that the other three plaintiffs have changed their usage of the locker room (except to the extent that Jack Jones indicated that he would conduct locker-room-wide searches for "girls" each time that he would change for gym class), but they all testified that their bathroom usage significantly diminished and, when they did use the multi-user bathrooms, they were uncomfortable and concerned about the potential presence of a transgender student. The plaintiffs have not cited to any case stating that the mere possibility of future exposure to the alleged harassment can render a single instance of harassment pervasive.

To the extent that the court could find that the School District's practice constituted pervasive harassment of the plaintiffs, the plaintiffs have still failed to show that it is likely that such harassment was severe or objectively offensive. Essentially, the plaintiffs' position is that the presence of "members of the opposite sex," meaning transgender students, creates a hostile environment for the plaintiffs and other cisgender students at BASH. Although the plaintiffs cite a number of cases to support their position that having members of the opposite sex in a privacy facility creates a hostile environment, none of the cited cases are applicable here. . . . *Lewis v. Triborough Bridge & Tunnel Authority*, 31 Fed. Appx. 746 (2d Cir. 2002) . . . purportedly held that an employer created a hostile work environment when it allowed a third-party cleaning company to have its male employees inside of the locker room while the female employee plaintiffs were undressed. *Lewis* is easily distinguishable from the facts of this case insofar as (1) the female plaintiffs complained to their employer for two years about the sexual harassment by the male cleaners, and (2) they alleged that the male cleaners "engaged in a variety of specific acts of sexual harassment, including entering the . . . women's locker room when female employees were undressed." Further, the "variety of specific acts of sexual harassment" not mentioned in the Second Circuit's opinion also included allegations from one of the female plaintiffs that the male cleaners were "leering at her and would crowd the entrance to the locker room, forcing her to 'run the gauntlet' and brush up against them." *Lewis v. Triborough Bridge and Tunnel Auth.*, 77 F. Supp. 2d 376 (S.D.N.Y. 1999). Additionally, the general manager of the plaintiffs' employer, during an inspection of the women's locker room, also referred to other female employees as

---

anxiety or stress she was experiencing at the time. The stress or anxiety did not affect her grades." [Footnote by Eds.]

"c[*]nts" and "fucking crybabies" and reportedly stated "'[b]oss man don't want no women with tiny hinnies [*sic*] on this job.'" [second alteration in *Boyertown*—Eds.] This conduct is not similar to the facts in this case.

The second case cited is *Schonauer v. DCR Entertainment, Inc.*, 905 P.2d 392 (Wash. Ct. App. 1995), which the plaintiffs reference to support the proposition that a hostile environment is created when a male employer at a nude dance club entered a dressing room while a female waitress was clothed and in a dressing room and restroom. . . . The court concluded that the plaintiff set forth enough facts to establish a claim for a hostile work environment insofar as, *inter alia*, (1) she was hired as a waitress and not as a dancer, (2) she wanted to be a waitress and not a dancer and informed her employer and management as such, and (3) the manager and the other employee "pressured her, repeatedly and intentionally, to provide fantasized sexual information and to dance on stage in sexually provocative ways." Regarding the manager's intrusions into the dressing room and bathroom, the court stated that "the hostile and offensive nature of th[e] environment [at the club] was arguably intensified by [the manager's] intrusions into the women's dressing room and bathroom." Thus, the allegations of sexual harassment went well beyond the manager's presence in the dressing room and bathroom.

[The plaintiffs cite] *People v. Grunau*, No. H015871, 2009 WL 5149857 (Cal. Ct. App. Dec. 29, 2009), for the proposition that girls should expect privacy in a girls' locker room and that a biological male staring at a girl in a locker room would shock or disturb the viewed-upon girl. This matter involved a criminal defendant charged with loitering on school grounds and violating a California law prohibiting individuals from annoying a child under 18. The victim, a 14-year-old girl who was wearing her swimsuit after swimming practice, was showering in the girls' locker room when she saw the defendant standing in the exit doorway. The defendant "made eye contact with [the victim], stared for about five seconds, closed the door, and left."

. . . . In concluding that the evidence was sufficient to convict the defendant, the California appellate court explained:

> Here, defendant blithely ignores an important fact: where his conduct took place. [The victim] was not simply rinsing off under an outdoor shower at a public pool. She was on a high school campus, out of general public view, and inside a girls' locker room, a place that by definition is to be used exclusively by girls and where males are not allowed. Unquestionably, a girls['] locker room is a place where a normal female should, and would, reasonably expect privacy, especially when she is performing quintessentially personal activities like undressing, changing clothes, and bathing. Under the circumstances, jurors reasonably could find that a normal female who was showering in a girls[*] locker room would unhesitatingly be shocked, irritated, and disturbed to see a man gazing at her, no matter how briefly he did so.

Grunau is also inapplicable because even though the court discussed that girls would expect privacy in a girls' locker room, *Grunau* involved an adult man who was actually leering at a 14-year-old girl while she was in a locker room. It is inconceivable how this case sheds light on a transgender student being present in the locker room, especially here where there are no allegations of any transgender student at BASH staring at another student (and, the court would be remiss if it was not pointed out that the defendant in *Grunau* had been convicted of prior sex offenses) or doing anything remotely improper. . . .

. . . *Norwood v. Dale Maintenance System, Inc.*, 590 F. Supp. 1410 (N.D. Ill. 1984) . . . . is clearly inapplicable here.[65] . . . *Norwood* involved a female employee's complaint that her employer violated Title VII when it refused to hire her to work as a day shift washroom attendant in a men's washroom. The employer claimed that it could base the decision on sex because it was a bona fide occupational qualification. The court concluded that . . . the employer produced sufficient evidence that the occupants of the building in which the washroom was located "would object to a member of the opposite sex entering their washrooms during the day to perform cleaning duties, and that if such a procedure were instituted the procedure would have a detrimental effect on the building." Thus, the court concluded "that the intrusion on personal privacy which would occur if opposite sex attendants were allowed access into the washrooms while in use is sufficiently substantial so as to constitute a factual basis for defendants['] sex-based policy."

Norwood does not involve a claim for hostile environment under Title IX. While it, and other cases throughout the United States have found bona fide occupational qualifications on the basis of sex permissible in certain circumstances, including those when privacy is an issue, they do not support a conclusion that the presence of transgender students in the BASH locker rooms and bathrooms is, in itself, a hostile environment under Title IX.

The . . . court has not found any case determining that the mere presence of transgender students in a high school locker room or bathroom, the viewing of a transgender student in a state of partial undress in a high school locker room or bathroom, or a transgender student viewing a cisgender student (which does not appear to have not happened in this case) in a high school locker rooms or bathroom constitutes severe, pervasive and objectively offensive conduct that would

---

65. The court notes that two of the plaintiffs' four citations to *Norwood* are actually not to statements by the court; instead, the court was summarizing the testimony of the employer's expert witness. . . . Similarly, the plaintiffs' reference . . . *Norwood* . . . because the court supposedly "not[ed] that many [individuals in the building] search for another restroom if an opposite-sex person is present." Yet, that portion of the court's opinion actually dealt with whether the employer closing the washrooms while opposite-sex employees serviced them was a reasonable alternative that would have allowed the employer to hire the plaintiff to work in the men's washroom. In discussing this alternative, the court noted that it was not feasible because during the closures "tenants would be forced to conduct an inconvenient, time consuming and sometimes difficult search for a washroom when the need to use a washroom may be acute." Thus, to the extent that the tenants would be searching for a different washroom, they were doing so because the washroom was closed.

state a cause of action under Title IX. In addition, the court does not find that the plaintiffs have shown that they are likely to prove that the School District's conduct is objectively offensive because a reasonable person would not find the practice of allowing transgender students to use the locker rooms and bathrooms corresponding to their gender identity to be hostile, threatening, or humiliating. There is no evidence that these students have committed any lewd acts in the locker room or bathrooms or that they have even interacted with the plaintiffs in any way whatsoever. There is no evidence that the transgender students have harassed the plaintiffs or any other student. All the evidence showed was that the transgender students were in the facilities for their intended purposes and they conducted themselves appropriately while in those areas.

The plaintiffs are clearly opposed to having themselves viewed by a transgender student in a state of undress or potentially viewing a transgender student in a state of undress. They are apparently opposed to the transgender student being in the locker room even if no one is getting dressed or undressed. They are opposed to transgender girls being in the girls' bathroom and locker room to the extent that female students are tending to menstruation-related issues and do not want those issues known to boys, even boys identifying as girls. As in *Students*, there are numerous privacy protections for students at the school that significantly reduce or eliminate any potential issues.

[The] School District has four shower stalls in each of the locker rooms that have curtains. While it is possible that a student could attempt to open those privacy curtains as happened with Mary Smith [who testified that she had been in the shower stall when other girls have opened the curtain to see if the shower stall was occupied], it is purely speculation that a transgender student is going to do so. Other than that speculative possibility, there is no indication that the privacy curtains do not provide the requisite privacy while in the locker room. In addition, the School District provided sufficient evidence to show that they are committed to providing all students with as comfortable of an environment as possible while at BASH and Dr. Cooper indicated that the locker rooms have team rooms that could be used by requesting students to change for this upcoming year.

. . . [T]he restrooms have stalls with locking doors that provide privacy even in the boys' bathrooms to the extent that those bathrooms lack dividers between urinals. The plaintiffs focus on some of the partitions not being high enough or low enough to provide for complete protection while in there. Despite the gaps, there is no indication that individuals while in the stalls cannot ensure that their privacy is maintained while inside of the stalls. Nonetheless, even with gaps along the edges of the doors and the gaps above and below the partitions, the plaintiffs have not shown that there is anything objectively offensive about the plaintiffs having to use the bathrooms with a transgender student, even to the extent that it is remotely possible that a transgender girl could potentially overhear a female student tending to menstruation issues while in the locker room. Further, once again, as with any student's use of the locker rooms or bathrooms at BASH, if the student is uncomfortable, the students can use a single-user facility to change or use the restroom and obtain the desired privacy there.[66]

Accordingly, for all of the above reasons, the plaintiffs have failed to establish a likelihood of success on their Title IX sexual harassment hostile environment claim.[67]

3. Pennsylvania Tort of Invasion of Privacy — Intrusion Upon Seclusion

. . . .

b. Analysis

With the common law tort of invasion of privacy, intrusion upon seclusion, Pennsylvania follows section 652B of the *Restatement (Second) of Torts*, which defines this tort as follows: "One who intentionally intrudes, physically or otherwise, upon the solitude or seclusion of another or his private affairs or concerns, is subject to liability to the other for invasion of his privacy, if the intrusion would be highly offensive to a reasonable person." . . . .

. . . [T]he plaintiffs do not cite to a case in which any court recognized a cause of action against a governmental entity for an intentional tort when third parties (and not agents or employees of the governmental entity) are the ones that commit the intentional tort. . . . The uncertainty as to whether the plaintiffs have a viable cause of action under Pennsylvania law for this type of invasion of privacy would alone

---

66. The court notes that the plaintiffs contend that the defendants cannot "escape liability by requiring victims to remove themselves from the environment." The plaintiffs cite to *Seiwert v. Spencer-Own Community School Corp.*, 497 F. Supp. 2d 942 (S.D. Ind. 2007) . . . . [That] court determined that a jury could conclude that a school district's actions in response to pervasive and serious bullying from other students was clearly unreasonable when (1) the school district did not even discipline one of the students even though that student had twice threatened to kill the bullied student, (2) the school district minimized the threats when discussing them with the bullied student, (3) the school district took action, but only in the nature of moving the bullied student to another classroom instead of dealing with the bullying itself, and (4) the school district disciplined both the bullied student and the bully when the bully decided to physically assault the bullied student.

. . . . Here, we are dealing with students' use of locker rooms and bathrooms. Providing the students with alternative places to get changed and use the restrooms should they be uncomfortable in the current arrangements (which may or may not actually involve a transgender student) is not even remotely comparable to the bullying situation in *Seiwert* and the school district's undeniably unreasonable response to the bullying in that case, which included removing the bullied student from the classroom.

67. Because of the court's resolution of the other elements to a hostile environment claim, the court has not addressed whether the plaintiffs were denied the benefits of any educational opportunity, class, or program as required by Title IX because the plaintiffs have not shown any actionable harassment. . . . It is unclear whether the plaintiffs' decision not to use the multi-user bathrooms as much (or at all) when they all indicated that they could still access bathrooms at BASH if they needed to do so (and that they did access the bathrooms albeit less often) would constitute a denial of an educational program or activity under Title IX.

serve as a basis for the court to find that the plaintiffs have failed to demonstrate a likelihood of success on the merits. Nonetheless, for sake of completeness the court will presume that such a cause of action exists and now determine whether the plaintiffs have established a likelihood of success on this claim.

The court does not deny that an individual seeks seclusion in a bathroom toilet stall from being viewed by other people outside of the stall. The cases cited by the plaintiff . . . in support of their contention that the transgender students invaded their privacy when they were in the common areas of the bathroom and locker room, involve alleged invasions of privacy in bathroom stalls. Here, there are no allegations and the plaintiffs presented no evidence that any transgender student invaded their seclusion while they were in a bathroom stall. . . .

The plaintiffs claim that

> [t]he objective offensiveness to the reasonable person [by having a member of the opposite sex, *i.e.* a transgender person, in the bathroom or locker room with them] is evident in the fact that we have long recognized the right to a private setting, free from persons of the opposite sex in restrooms and locker rooms, which are only made necessary since we often enter into a state of undress or perform private functions therein, which require a buffer from members of the opposite sex that we do not require from members of the same sex.

[alteration in *Boyertown*—Eds.] As indicated earlier, the plaintiffs then point to the School Code's requirement of separate facilities for the sexes as Pennsylvania's recognition of the need for privacy from the opposite sex in facilities.

The plaintiffs do not argue that by entering the multi-user bathrooms and the locker rooms at BASH that they attempted to seclude themselves from all students at BASH, nor could they insofar as those areas are shared common areas with other students. As for locker rooms generally, "[p]ublic school locker rooms . . . are not notable for the privacy they afford." *Vernonia Sch. Dist. 47J v. Acton*, 515 U.S. 646 (1995). Nonetheless, they believe that it is objectively reasonable to have their activities secluded from observation by members of the opposite sex when in the common areas of the locker rooms and bathrooms.

[The] court does not find that it is more likely than not (or even just likely) that Student A viewed either Jack Jones or Joel Doe while they were in their underwear based on the evidence currently before the court because both plaintiffs have made conflicting statements and it appears that the weight of evidence at this early stage shows that they saw Student A and reacted only to seeing Student A on one occasion (each). Regardless, the court does not find that a reasonable person would be offended by the presence of a transgender student in the bathroom or locker room with them, despite the possibility that the transgender student could possibly be in a state of undress more significant than Student A was in this case when the male plaintiffs saw him. In addition, the mere presence of a transgender student in the common area of the girls' bathroom washing hands, as experienced by Mary Smith, is also not objectively offensive to a reasonable person. Moreover, the fact that the Public School Code calls for sex-segregated water-closets and out-houses does not necessitate a finding that the presence of the transgender student is objectively offensive to a reasonable person because it is not determinative as to whether a reasonable person would object to the presence of a transgender student in the locker room or bathroom. Furthermore, even though Joel Doe, Mary Smith, and Jack Jones stated that their sole experiences with transgender students at BASH caused them embarrassment and humiliation, it is definitely not clear that the conduct they experienced or could experience at BASH in the future, especially considering the privacy protections and alternative arrangements available at BASH, would cause mental suffering, shame, or humiliation to a person of ordinary sensibilities. Accordingly, even if the plaintiffs could maintain this type of invasion of privacy claim against the defendants, even though they did not personally invade their seclusion while in any bathroom or locker room, the court does not find that they have demonstrated a likelihood of success on the merits.

C. Irreparable Harm

. . . .

2. Analysis

Concerning a showing of irreparable harm, "the plaintiff must demonstrate potential harm which cannot be redressed by a legal or equitable remedy following a trial.[. . . .]" Thus, to support the issuance of a preliminary injunction, a plaintiff must demonstrate a "clear showing of immediate irreparable injury . . . or a presently existing actual threat; (an injunction) may not be used simply to eliminate a possibility of a remote future injury, or a future invasion of rights, be those rights protected by statute or by the common law." The "risk of irreparable harm [also] must not be speculative." Further, if the threatened harm is compensable with money damages, a movant seeking preliminary injunctive relief has not demonstrated irreparable harm and the court should not issue a preliminary injunction.

The court has already determined that the plaintiffs have not shown a likelihood of success on the merits on any of their claims, so to the extent that they argue that the court should presume irreparable harm because of the existence of a constitutional invasion of privacy or a Title IX violation, this court need not consider this argument. . . .

[On] a practical level, the court finds that the privacy protections that are in place at BASH, which include the bathroom stalls and shower stalls in the locker rooms, the bathroom stalls in the multi-user bathrooms, the availability of a number of single-user bathrooms (a few of which will have lockers for storing items), the availability of students to store personal items in their locker or leave those items with the gym teacher, and the availability of the team rooms in the locker rooms (which would not involve students passing through the common area of the locker room), and the overall willingness of the defendants to work with the students and their families to assure that the students are comfortable at BASH, mitigates against a finding of irreparable harm. At this point in the litigation, the court is concerned with the privacy protections available at BASH for the upcoming school year and not whatever past protections were available to students and whether the students knew about all of the available options or were advised of them by the School District for the last completed school year.[74] The privacy protections available to students in 2017–18 are more than suitable to address any privacy concerns relating to the presence of transgender students in the locker rooms and bathrooms at BASH.

The court recognizes that during oral argument and as noted elsewhere in their submissions, the plaintiffs argue that the court cannot refuse to find irreparable harm based on these alternative arrangements because the "[g]overnment may not condition a benefit on someone waiving a constitutional right." (citing *Koontz v. St. Johns River Water Mgmt. Dist.*, 133 S. Ct. 2586 (2013). This is "known as the unconstitutional conditions doctrine, [which] vindicates the Constitution's enumerated rights by preventing the government from coercing people into giving them up." *Koontz*. This argument misses the mark.

There is no evidence that the School District is coercing the students to give up their constitutional right to privacy by providing them with additional facilities if they are uncomfortable in the locker room for any reason, including because of the presence of transgender students. The School District is also not denying any benefit to the plaintiffs because they are exercising a constitutional right. They may still use the locker rooms and multi-user bathrooms at BASH without limitation. In addition, the plaintiffs (at least the three that could be returning to BASH this year) may use the single-user facilities at BASH (to the extent there was an uncertainty about availability for use during the 2016–17 school year). This also is not a particular benefit conferred upon them because all students can use the single-user facilities, including the nurse's office with permission from the nurse. The only possible "benefit" being conferred is the use of the team rooms, but again, as with everything else, Dr. Cooper indicated that the use of the team rooms would be available to any student at BASH. There is no evidence supporting a conclusion that the School District is denying a benefit to the plaintiffs because they are attempting to exercise a constitutional right, and there is no evidence that the School District is attempting to coerce the plaintiffs into giving up such a right. As such, this argument lacks merit and the privacy protections available at BASH fully mitigate against any harm the plaintiffs could suffer here.

On the Title IX claim, only Joel Doe indicated that his grades suffered last year because of the defendants' practice insofar as he refused to dress for gym class because he believed that he did not have a suitable place to secure his belongings and he lost points toward his grade (although he did not fail the course). This concern appears to be resolved for the upcoming school year because at least a few of the

---

74. It does not appear that Jack Jones, Mary Smith, or Macy Roe inquired about alternative accommodations with the defendants. Macy Roe never even discussed any concerns with the defendants, and it is unclear that Mary Smith discussed the practice with the defendants other than reporting having seen Student B in the girls' bathroom.

single-user facilities, including the one in the nurse's office and the one near the gym, will have a locker for students to secure belongings and the defendants have indicated that Joel Doe can store his belongings in his hall locker or with the gym teacher if he decides to change in a single-user facility without a locker. Additionally, the plaintiffs know there are numerous alternatives for them to use the bathroom, so they should not have to refrain from using the restroom to the extent that they did so in 2016–17 without seeking out possibly available alternatives.

Accordingly, the court finds that the plaintiffs have not established that they would be irreparably harmed.[76]

D. Balance of Harm/Whether Non-Moving Party will Suffer Greater Harm

Because the court has determined that the plaintiffs have failed to establish a likelihood of success on the merits or irreparable harm, the court need not address the final two factors because the plaintiffs' failure "must necessarily result in the denial of a preliminary injunction." *In re Arthur Treacher's Franchisee Litig.*, 689 F.2d 1137 (3d Cir. 1982). . . .[77]

VI. Conclusion

The plaintiffs here are required to clearly show that they are entitled to the extraordinary remedy of a preliminary injunction. In addition, they have a

---

76. There is also an undercurrent of speculation that permeates this litigation. While BASH could have additional transgender students seek and receive approval to use the privacy facilities corresponding to their gender identity for the upcoming school year, the evidence in the record is that the School District is aware of three transgender students, including Student A, who are returning to BASH for 2017–18, with at least Student A having already received permission to use the boys' bathrooms and locker room. Nonetheless, it is unclear whether Student A will even have gym class with Jack Jones or Joel Doe, or whether a transgender female student will have gym class with Mary Smith (if she is even returning to BASH for her senior year). If there is not a transgender student in gym with them, there is no potential issue. To the extent that Jack Jones and Joel Doe used the multi-user bathrooms at BASH, there was no testimony that they interacted with a transgender male in the bathroom and it is possible that they will go the entirety of 2017–18 without doing so as well.

77. The court recognizes that in balancing the harms, the court must examine "the potential injury to the plaintiff if an injunction does not issue versus the potential injury to the defendant if the injunction is issued." *Novartis Consumer Health, Inc. v. Johnson & Johnson-Merck Consumer Pharm. Co.*, 290 F.3d 578 (3d Cir. 2002). As the plaintiffs have failed to establish a likelihood of success on the merits of those claims, . . . the balance of the harms would have favored the defendants because the effect of changing the current practice on the transgender students would be that they will be forced to use the bathroom of their birth sex, of which they do not identify, or end up being one of the limited number of students using the single-user facilities. Dr. Leibowitz credibly testified as to the negative effect on the transgender students if they are unable to use the facilities corresponding with their gender. As an additional note, . . . a preliminary injunction ceasing the current practice could presumably lead to litigation brought by the transgender students for a violation of the Equal Protection Clause or Title IX in light of the *Evancho* and *Whitaker* decisions. There is also precedent in this district that gender dysphoria can be a disability under the Americans with Disabilities Act, and there could be an issue with providing the requisite reasonable accommodations or the School District could be in violation of the Act. *See* [*Blatt*] *v. Cabela's Retail, Inc.*, 2017 WL 2178123 (E.D. Pa. May 18, 2017) [Ch. 14, *infra* at p. 1033].

particularly heavy burden because they are seeking to change the status quo insofar as the practice in place at BASH over the past year has been to allow transgender students to use the restrooms and locker rooms consistent with their gender identity. With regard to their section 1983 invasion of privacy claim brought under the Fourteenth Amendment, their sexual harassment hostile environment claim under Title IX, and their state law invasion of privacy claim, at this early juncture and upon the current record, the plaintiffs have not clearly shown that they are entitled to relief. In particular, they have not demonstrated that they are likely to succeed on the merits of these claims. Additionally, the plaintiffs have not demonstrated that they are likely to suffer irreparable injury if the court does not issue a preliminary injunction. Since the plaintiffs failed to satisfy either of these "gateway" factors, the court need not balance the parties' respective harms or consider whether a preliminary injunction is in the public interest. Accordingly, the court will deny the motion for a preliminary injunction. . . .

Discussion

1. Is the court overly dismissive of the plaintiffs' privacy concerns? After all, U.S. society does have widespread practices of sex-segregating locker rooms and other changing facilities. Or is the court overly credulous (for example, in proceeding to analyze certain claims under strict scrutiny rather than insisting that the plaintiffs didn't trigger strict scrutiny and stopping there)?

2. One female plaintiff professed to be unconcerned about the prospect of being seen naked by a student of the same biological sex who is sexually attracted to her and also about the possibility of someone with phalloplasty sharing the locker room with her. Why would genitalia at birth rather than at the time one shares a locker room possibly matter? And if sexual attraction is not the basis for sex-segregating locker rooms, what proper concern could justify this practice? If it is, then what locker rooms ought (cisgender) lesbigay students use? Note that concerns about gay people—primarily men—in communal showers were one argument voiced in defense of the former exclusion of lesbigay people from the U.S. military, *see generally, e.g.*, Kendall Thomas, *Shower/Closet*, 20 ASSEMBLAGE 80 (1993), and shared showers were earlier used to oppose racial integration of the military, Paul Siegel, *Second Hand Prejudice, Racial Analogies, and Shared Showers: Why "Don't Ask, Don't Tell" Won't Sell*, 9 NOTRE DAME J.L. ETHICS & PUB. POL'Y 185 (1995).

Note on Parents For Privacy, et al. v. William P. Barr, Attorney General, et al.

After a transgender boy enrolled at Dallas High School in Oregon, the school district, Dallas School District No. 2, adopted a "Student Safety Plan" that, among other things, allowed transgender students to use school restrooms, locker rooms, and showers consistent with their gender identity. After the district went forward despite some objections, a group of "current and former students and parents of current and former students in the District, as well as 'other concerned members of the District community,'" filed suit in federal court against the school district and, originally, federal defendants; the latter were ultimately dismissed from the suit after the Trump administration rescinded the Obama administration guidance regarding Title IX obligations toward transgender students. *See supra* at p. 891. The nonprofit LGBT rights organization Basic Rights Oregon (represented by the ACLU, the ACLU of Oregon, and local counsel) intervened to help defend the school district's policies. By the time the case made it to the U.S. Court of Appeals for the Ninth Circuit, the district was supported by numerous amici curiae including the Trans Youth Equality Foundation, Gender Spectrum, Gender Diversity, TransActive Gender Project, and the National Center for Transgender Equality. The U.S. District Court for the District of Oregon dismissed all counts of the complaint for failure to state a claim, and the court of appeals affirmed. *Parents for Privacy, et al. v. Barr, et al.*, 949 F.3d 1210 (9th Cir. 2020). Circuit Judge Tashima's opinion for the court held

> that there is no Fourteenth Amendment fundamental privacy right to avoid all risk of intimate exposure to or by a transgender person who was assigned the opposite biological sex at birth. We also hold that a policy that treats all students equally does not discriminate based on sex in violation of Title IX, and that the normal use of privacy facilities does not constitute actionable sexual harassment under Title IX just because a person is transgender. We hold further that the Fourteenth Amendment does not provide a fundamental parental right to determine the bathroom policies of the public schools to which parents may send their children, either independent of the parental right to direct the upbringing and education of their children or encompassed by it. Finally, we hold that the school district's policy is rationally related to a legitimate state purpose, and does not infringe Plaintiffs' First Amendment free exercise rights because it does not target religious conduct. . . .

After the court of appeals noted that the Supreme Court has held that the Fourteenth Amendment's Due Process Clause "specially protects those fundamental rights and liberties which are, objectively, deeply rooted in this Nation's history and tradition, and implicit in the concept of ordered liberty, such that neither liberty nor justice would exist if they were sacrificed," quoting *Washington v. Glucksberg*, 521 U.S. 702 (1997), the court agreed with the court below that there was no constitutional "'fundamental right to bodily privacy' that includes 'a right to privacy of one's fully or partially unclothed body and the right to be free from State-compelled risk of intimate exposure of oneself to the opposite sex.'" It judged all of the precedent plaintiffs invoked to be distinguishable, much of it because it involved egregious intrusions into personal privacy by state actors, such as police officers coercing a sexual assault victim into allowing, and then circulating, unnecessary nude photos of her. And it found its conclusion—that there was no constitutional privacy right such as the plaintiffs claimed—to be supported by the existence of alternative options and privacy protections for students who might not wish to share facilities with transgender students.

The court of appeals also agreed with the district court that the plaintiffs' hostile environment claim under Title IX of the Education Amendments of 1972 failed for multiple reasons. To make such a claim, the plaintiff would have had to allege facts amounting to discrimination on the basis of sex, but the courts ruled that there was none because the plan "'does not target any [students] because of their sex'" but rather "applies to all students regardless of their sex" and does not treat any students differently from others. The court specifically rejected the plaintiffs' argument that the district's plan "actually harasses both sexes on the basis of their sex by allowing students assigned the opposite sex at birth to enter privacy facilities," though the appeals court did not indicate any logical flaw in the argument but instead only observed that the plaintiffs provided "no authority to support the notion that 'equal harassment' against both sexes is cognizable under Title IX." (The court of appeals did opine that as an evidentiary matter, "treating both male and female students the same suggests an absence of gender/sex animus, while Title IX is aimed at addressing discrimination based on sex or gender stereotypes.") The court also held that the plaintiffs failed to allege that the supposed "harassment is both viewed subjectively as harassment by the victims and is, objectively, sufficiently severe or pervasive that a reasonable person would agree that it is harassment." The court pointed out that the plaintiffs did

> not allege that transgender students are making inappropriate comments, threatening them, deliberately flaunting nudity, or physically touching them. Rather, Plaintiffs allegedly feel harassed by the mere presence of transgender students in locker and bathroom facilities. This cannot be enough. The use of facilities for their intended purpose, without more, does not constitute an act of harassment simply because a person is transgender. *See Cruzan v. Special Sch. Dist., #1*, 294 F.3d 981 (8th Cir. 2002) (per curiam) (concluding that a transgender woman's "merely being present in the women's . . . restroom" did not constitute actionable sexual harassment of her female co-workers).

The court also rejected the parent-plaintiffs' constitutional parental rights claim. Although the court conceded that the parents may have a constitutional right to remove their children from the public schools, building on much case law rejecting parental rights to determine curriculum or other school policy the court of appeals ruled that the parent-plaintiffs "lack a fundamental right to direct Dallas High School's bathroom and locker room policy." The court of appeals reinforced its argument against the parental rights claim by noting "the practical issue . . . that accommodating the different 'personal, moral, or religious concerns of every parent' would be 'impossible' for public schools, because different parents would often likely, as in this case, prefer opposite and contradictory outcomes.'"

In addition, the court rejected the plaintiffs' free exercise of religion claim that the plan unconstitutionally interfered with the children's ability to practice "modesty" as required by their religious beliefs. The Free Exercise Clause does not provide special constitutional protection against "neutral laws of general applicability," which the court of appeals emphasized means "'neutral and generally applicable with respect to religion.'" The court saw no basis for holding that the plan's object was to suppress religious exercise or that it targeted conduct *because* of its religious motivation. Accordingly, the court looked only for a rational basis for the plan, which it found, with the court of appeals concluding that the plan "is rationally related to the legitimate purpose of protecting student safety and well-being," and eliminating discrimination on the basis of sex and transgender status.

Discussion

1. Note that, at least on the surface, the harms alleged by the plaintiff students— that the use of the boys' locker room by a transgender boy "caused several cisgender boys 'embarrassment, humiliation, anxiety, intimidation, fear, apprehension, and stress,' because they had to change clothes for their PE class and attend to their needs while someone who had been assigned the opposite sex at birth was present," and that "[a]s a consequence of their fear of exposure to [that transgender boy], some cisgender boys began using the restroom as little as possible while at school, and others risked tardiness by using distant restrooms during passing periods in order to try to find a restroom in which [that student] was unlikely to be present"—strongly echo the harms alleged in many lawsuits brought by transgender students excluded from sex-segregated restrooms consistent with their gender identity. Should observers conclude, as perhaps plaintiffs and their counsel intend, that while there may be subjective harms to transgender boys, for example, when they are excluded from boys' restrooms and locker rooms, there are also subjective harms to (some) cisgender boys when transgender boys are allowed to use those facilities? If that were true, would it necessarily follow that the "discomfort" of such cisgender boys should carry more weight than the "discomfort" of such transgender boys, perhaps because the latter are less numerous? Would there be ways to distinguish the causes or mechanisms of the two sorts of psychological harms the plaintiffs here seem to be contending exist?

2. The court of appeals rejected the plaintiffs' claim that the district's policy violated a fundamental constitutional right of privacy. The court primarily did so by drawing factual distinctions between the circumstances of this case and precedents finding violations of gendered, bodily privacy (or perhaps it is "bodily gendered privacy") by gratuitous or egregious conduct. But should we think, precedent aside, that gendered privacy is a fundamental constitutional right? Should we think female prisoners have a right not to be strip-searched by male guards, and male prisoners have a right not to be strip-searched by female guards? Should we be thought to have a constitutional right to insist that when the government provides

healthcare (*e.g.*, to senior citizens) it is constitutionally obligated to allow us to be examined only by doctors and nurses of the same sex as us? Why should gendered privacy be deemed fundamental? Why should male students have a privacy right not to be seen undressed (let alone partially undressed) by female students but no right against being seen undressed by male students? Is it a presumption of heterosexuality? And even if there is a fundamental right to gendered privacy, why should it be the genitalia of the people involved that determines the contours of the privacy right at issue? When so many societies have a greater acceptance of "co-ed" nudity than the U.S., might it be convention alone that makes gendered privacy fundamental? If so, ought convention be sufficient justification?

3. The court rejects the plaintiffs' Title IX claim because it concludes that the plaintiffs failed to establish that the district policy discriminated on the basis of sex. In the court's view, the plaintiffs' argument failed because they "cite no authority to support the notion that 'equal harassment' against both sexes is cognizable under Title IX." But why should precedent be necessary? Isn't the plaintiffs' argument that the district policy discriminates on the basis of sex because it subjects male cisgender students to potential privacy violations by transgender male students (whom plaintiffs consider female), *and also* because it subjects female cisgender students to potential privacy violations by transgender female students (whom plaintiffs consider male)? Is the court's argument rejecting that position logically (or in some other way) distinguishable from the position of some courts and commentators that limiting marriage to different-sex couples did not discriminate on the basis of sex, or from the position that there is no discrimination if an employer places different but allegedly "equal" burdens on both male and female employees? *See* David B. Cruz, *Making Up Women: Casinos, Cosmetics, and Title VII*, 5 Nev. L.J. 240, 246–47 (2004).

4. The court rejects the parent-plaintiffs' claim that the district's policy violates their constitutional right to direct the upbringing of their children, in significant part, it seems, due to the "practical issues" that would be involved if parents were able to dictate policy to public schools. Would such practical worries be implicated by a narrower parental rights claim, such as a right to keep their children enrolled in public school but have them exempted from PE (or from changing clothes for PE)? Even if such a constitutional right were recognized (should it be?), would it give the plaintiffs much of what they seek? (One could ask similar questions about the free exercise of religion claim—and, indeed, free exercise claims more commonly seek not invalidation of government rules but exemptions for the people whose religious exercise is burdened by the rule.)

Chapter 14

Medicalization and Disability

Transgender identity has long been understood through a medical lens, as a disorder or disability. The medical profession and popular culture long regarded trans people as being mentally ill, and this way of understanding transgender identity has far from wholly disappeared. In the United States, the mental health profession diagnoses mental illnesses using the *Diagnostic and Statistical Manual of Mental Disorders* (or "DSM™"), published by the American Psychiatric Association (in Washington, D.C.). Insurers use code numbers for mental ailments specified in the DSM. The fourth edition of the DSM (or "DSM-IV™") was published in 1994; a slightly revised version of that edition, DSM-IV-TR™ (for "Text Revision") was published in 2000, without changing the diagnostic criteria for Gender Identity Disorder ("GID"). The versions of DSM-IV™ generally were understood to consider trans people inherently disordered and were in place for almost two decades until they were superseded by the fifth edition, DSM-V™, in 2013.

Given this background, there have emerged strong critiques of medical frameworks for understanding trans people, as distinguished from a view of trans identities as simply additional forms of benign human variation. Similarly, people have specifically criticized resorting to use of laws against disability discrimination to redress anti-transgender discrimination, out of concerns regarding counterproductive perpetuation of stigma. This chapter examines these medical frameworks, critiques, and responses to such critiques. It also presents case law where litigants have invoked medical frameworks or disability laws, sometimes successfully, sometimes unsuccessfully.

Note on Gender Identity Disorder in DSM-IV™

The fourth edition of the American Psychiatric Association's *Diagnostic and Statistical Manual of Mental Disorders* contained the diagnosis "Gender Identity Disorder" (or "GID"), a condition estimated in this 1994 publication to involve 1 in 30,000 people assigned male at birth and 1 in 100,000 assigned female at birth seeking genitoplasty. To diagnosis a person with GID, a mental health professional had to find that the person had "a strong and persistent cross-gender identification," which DSM-IV™ defined to be "the desire to be, or the insistence that one is, of the other sex," as well as "persistent discomfort about one's assigned sex or a sense of inappropriateness in the gender role of that sex" and "distress or impairment in social, occupational, or other important areas of functioning." (DSM-IV™ excluded people with intersex conditions from the diagnosis.) For one court's detailed treatment of the diagnosis and its criteria, see *O'Donnabhain v. Commissioner of Internal Revenue*, Chapter 11, *supra* at p. 608.

Because conventionally gendered attire and activities differ for males and females (which is what makes them gendered) and the diagnosis of GID requires "cross-gender identification," the symptoms of GID vary for males and females, with boys preferring (or being "marked[ly] preoccup[ied]" in the DSM's phrasing) "traditionally feminine activities" and being uninterested in traditional boys' activities and toys. They may say they want to be a girl and insist "that they will grow up to be a woman," DSM-IV™ explains. Girls with GID, in contrast, eschew conventionally feminine attire and behaviors and "show little interest in dolls or any form of feminine dress up or role-play activity." In counterpart to boys with GID, a girl with that disorder "may assert that she will grow up to be a man." Such girls typically reveal marked cross-gender identification in role-play, dreams, and fantasies. Boys' and girls' gendered preferences usually manifest by age 2 to 4, though parents of some report that their children always had such cross-sex preferences. When it is an adult who has GID, they will be "preoccupied with their wish to live as a member of the other sex." To some extent they will wear clothes and engage in behaviors associated with "the other sex." Adolescents might follow either the children's pattern or the adults' pattern. The gender nonconformity of people with GID may precipitate teasing, ostracism, and isolation. But it also does not necessarily persist from childhood to late adolescence. DSM-IV™ reports that by late adolescence or adulthood, most children who were clinically referred no longer satisfy the GID diagnostic criteria, though three-fourths of boys with a history of GID are gay or bisexual (the data for girls' sexual orientation being unknown).

This diagnosis of Gender Identity Disorder was criticized and questioned from many quarters. *See, e.g..*, *In re Redacted* (Or. Cir. Ct. Feb. 5, 2013), Chapter 16, *infra* at p. 1116; *cf.* Phyllis Burke, Gender Shock: Exploding the Myths of Male & Female 60–66 (1996) (critiquing diagnosis of Gender Identity Disorder of Childhood, which appeared in DSM-III™). One notable critic is University of California, Berkeley professor and preeminent gender theorist Judith Butler. Consider her arguments in the following essay, published in the landmark 2006 book *Transgender Rights*. Paisley Currah et al., eds., Transgender Rights 274 (2006). (Note that Professor Butler refers to the DSM-IV™ diagnosis of "gender identity disorder" interchangeably as "gender identity disorder," "gender disorder," and "gender dysphoria" in this essay.)

Undiagnosing Gender[*]
Judith Butler

In recent years there have been debates about the status of the DSM diagnosis of gender identity disorder and, in particular, whether there are good reasons to keep the diagnosis on the books, or whether there are no longer very many good reasons. On the one hand, those within the GLBQTI community who want to keep the diagnosis argue that it offers certification for a condition and facilitates access to medical and technological means for transitioning. Moreover, some insurance companies will absorb some of the high costs of sex change only if they first can establish that the change is "medically necessitated." It's important, for these reasons, not to understand sex change surgery or hormonal usage as "elective surgery." . . . . The "diagnosis" can operate in several ways, but one way it can and does operate, especially in the hands of those who are transphobic, is as an instrument of pathologization. To be diagnosed with gender identity disorder is to be found, in some way, to be ill, sick, wrong, out of order, abnormal, and to suffer a certain stigmatization as a consequence of the diagnosis being given at all. As a result, some activist psychiatrists and trans people have argued that the diagnosis should be eliminated altogether, that transsexuality is not a disorder, and ought not to be conceived of as one, and that trans people ought to be understood as engaged in a practice of self-determination, an exercise of autonomy. Thus, on the one hand, the diagnosis continues to be valued because it facilitates an economically feasible way of transitioning. On the other hand, the diagnosis is adamantly opposed because it continues to pathologize as a mental disorder what ought to be understood instead as one among many human possibilities of determining one's gender for oneself.

[There] is a tension in this debate between those who are, for the purposes of the debate, trying to gain entitlement and financial assistance and those who seek to ground the practice of transsexuality in autonomy. We might well hesitate at once and ask whether these two views are actually in opposition to one another. . . . After all, if I want to transition, I may well need the diagnosis to help me achieve my goal, and achieving my goal is precisely an exercise of my autonomy. Indeed, we can argue that no one achieves autonomy without the assistance or support of a community, especially if one is making a brave and difficult choice such as transitioning. But then we have to ask whether the diagnosis is unambiguously part of the "support" that individuals need in order to exercise self-determination with respect to gender. After all, the diagnosis makes many assumptions that undercut trans-autonomy. It subscribes to forms of psychological assessment that assume that the diagnosed person is affected by forces he or she does not understand; it assumes that there is delusion or dysphoria in such people; it assumes that certain gender

---

[*] Excerpted from Judith Butler, *Undiagnosing Gender*, Chapter 14, *in* Paisley Currah, Richard M. Juang, & Shannon Price Minter, eds., Transgender Rights 274 (2006), © 2006 Judith Butler, with permission of the author.

norms have not been properly embodied and that an error and a failure have taken place; it makes assumptions about fathers and mothers, and what normal family life is and should have been; it assumes the language of correction, adaptation, and normalization; it seeks to uphold the gender norms of the world as it is currently constituted and tends to pathologize any effort to produce gender in ways that fail to conform to existing norms (or to a certain dominant fantasy of what existing norms actually are). It is also a diagnosis, we have to remember, that has been given to people against their will, and it is a diagnosis that has effectively broken the will of many people, especially queer and trans youth.

. . . . A "diagnosis" of gender disorder has to conform to the way that the DSM-IV defines gender dysphoria. The last revision to that set of definitions was instituted in 1994. . . . The 1994 definition is the result of several revisions, and probably needs to be understood as well in light of the American Psychiatric Association's decision in 1973 to get rid of the "diagnosis" of homosexuality as a disorder and its 1987 decision to delete "ego dystonic homosexuality," a remaining vestige from the earlier definition. Some have argued that the gender identity disorder diagnosis took over some of the work that the earlier homosexuality diagnosis performed, and that GID became an indirect way of diagnosing homosexuality as a gender identity problem. In this way, the GID continued the APA's tradition of homophobia, but in a less explicit way. In fact, conservative groups that seek to "correct" homosexuality, such as the National Association [for] Research and Therapy of Homosexuality, argue that if you can identify GID in a child, there's a 75 percent chance that you can predict homosexuality in that person as an adult, a result that, for them, is a clear abnormality and tragedy. Thus the diagnosis of GID is in most cases a diagnosis of homosexuality, and the disorder attached to the diagnosis implies that homosexuality remains a disorder as well.

. . . .

The diagnosis of gender dysphoria requires that a life takes on a more or less definite shape over time; a life can only be diagnosed if it meets the test of time. One has to show that one has wanted for a long time to live life as the other gender; it also requires that one prove that one has a practical plan to live life for a long time as the other gender. The diagnosis, in this way, wants to establish that gender is a relatively permanent phenomenon. It won't do, for instance, to walk into a clinic and say that it was only after you read a book by Kate Bornstein that you realized what you wanted to do, but that it wasn't really conscious for you until that time. It can't be that cultural life changed, that words were written and exchanged, that you went to events and to clubs, and saw that certain ways of living were really possible and desirable, and something about your own possibilities became clear to you in ways that they had not been before. . . . [You] cannot explicitly subscribe to a view that changes in gendered experience follow on changes in social norms, since that would not suffice to satisfy the Harry Benjamin standard rules [now, the World Professional Association for Transgender Health (WPATH) Standards of Care—Eds.] for the care of gender identity disorder. Indeed, those rules presume, as does the GID, that we all more or less "know" already what the norms for gender—"masculine" and "feminine"—are, and that all we really need to do is figure out whether they are being embodied in this instance or some other. . . .

Although there are strong criticisms to be made of the diagnosis . . . it would nevertheless be wrong to call for its eradication without first putting into place a set of structures through which transitioning can be paid for and legal status attained. In other words, if the diagnosis is now the instrument through which benefits and status can be achieved, it cannot be simply disposed of without finding other, durable ways to achieve those same results.

One obvious response to this dilemma is to argue that one should approach the diagnosis *strategically*. . . .

. . . [When] we ask who it is who would be able to sustain a purely instrumental relation to the diagnosis, it tends to be shrewd and savvy adults, ones who have other discourses available for understanding who they are and want to be. But are children and teens always capable of effecting the distance necessary to sustain a purely instrumental approach to being subjected to a diagnosis?

Richard Isay gives as the primary reason to get rid of the diagnosis altogether its effect on children. The diagnosis itself, he writes, "may cause emotional damage by injuring the self-esteem of a child who has no mental disorder." Isay, a doctor, accepts the claim that many young gay boys prefer so-called feminine behavior as children, playing with their mother's clothes, refusing rough-and-tumble activities, but he argues that the problem here is not with the traits but with "parental admonitions . . . aimed at modifying this behavior [which] deleteriously affect[s] these boys' self-regard." His solution is for parents to learn to be supportive of what he calls "gender atypical traits." Isay's contribution is important in many respects, but one clear contribution it makes is that it calls for reconceptualizing the phenomenon that refuses pathologizing language: he refuses to elevate typical gender attributes to a standard of psychological normality or to relegate atypical traits to abnormality. Instead, he substitutes the language of typicality for normality altogether. Physicians who argue against Isay not only insist that the disorder *is* a disorder, and that the presentation of persistently atypical gender traits in children is a "psychopathology," but they couch this insistence on pathologization with a paternalistic concern for the afflicted, citing how the diagnosis is necessary for insurance benefits and other entitlements. . . .

Some other solutions have been proposed that seek to ameliorate the pathological effects of the diagnosis by taking it out of the hands of the mental health profession altogether. Jacob Hale argues that psychologists and psychiatrists should not mediate this matter; the question of whether and how to gain access to medical and technological resources should be a matter between client and medical doctor exclusively. His view is that one goes to the doctor for other kinds of reconstructive surgeries or on other occasions where taking hormones may prove felicitous, and no one asks you a host of questions about your earliest fantasies or childhood practices of play. The certification of stable mental health is not required for breast reduction or menopausal ingestion of estrogen. The required intervention of a mental health professional on the occasion in which one wants to transition inserts a paternalistic structure into the process and undermines the very autonomy that is the basis for the claim of entitlement to begin with. . . .

. . . . The question remains, though, whether medical practitioners with no particular background in mental health will nevertheless use mental health criteria to make decisions that could be no less favorable than those made by mental health practitioners. If Hale is arguing, though, that it ought to be shifted to medical doctors as part of a drive to redefine the diagnosis so that it no longer contains mental health criteria in it, then he is also proposing a new diagnosis or no diagnosis, since the DSM-IV rendition cannot be voided of its mental health criteria. To answer the question of whether the shift to medical doctors would be propitious, we would have to ask whether the inclinations of medical practitioners are generally to be trusted with this responsibility, or whether the world of progressive therapists offers a better chance for humane and successful passage through the process of diagnosis. Although I do not have a sociologically grounded answer to this question, I consider that it has to be pursued before one can judge the appropriateness of Hale's recommendation. The great benefit of his view is that it treats the patient as a client who is exercising consumer autonomy within the medical domain. That autonomy is assumed, and it is also posited as the ultimate goal and meaning of transitioning itself.

But this raises the question of how autonomy ought to be conceived in this debate, and whether revisions in the diagnosis itself might provide a way around the apparent stand-off between those who wish to have the diagnosis deleted and those who wish to keep it for the instrumental value it provides, especially for those in financial need. There are two different conceptions of autonomy at work in this debate. The view that opposes the diagnosis altogether tends to be individualist, if not libertarian, and the views that argue in favor of keeping the diagnosis tend to acknowledge that there are material conditions for the exercise of liberty. . . .

. . . . Paradoxically, the insurance companies demean the notion of liberty when they distinguish, say, between mastectomies that are "medically necessitated" and those that constitute "elective surgery." The former are conceived as operations that no one readily chooses, that are imposed on individuals by medical circumstance, usually cancer. But even that conceptualization misrepresents the kinds of choices that informed patients make about how to approach cancer, where possible treatments include radiation, chemotherapy, arimidex, lumpectomy, partial and full mastectomy. Women will make different choices about treatment depending on how they feel about their breasts and the prospects of further cancer, and the range of choices made is significantly broad. Some women will struggle to keep their breasts no matter what; others let them go without much difficulty. Some choose reconstruction and make some choices about prospective breasts, and others choose not to. . . . .

[A] butch, nearly trans, person [Butler knew in San Francisco] who wanted her cancerous and non-cancerous breasts removed understood that the only way she could gain the benefits of a mastectomy was to get cancer in her other breast or to subject her own gender desires to medical and psychiatric review. Although she didn't consider herself trans, she understood that she could present as trans in order to qualify for the GID and insurance benefits. Sometimes reconstructive breast surgery is covered by medical insurance, even if done for elective reasons, but mastectomy is not included as elective surgeries covered by insurance. In the world of insurance, it appears to make sense that a woman might want less breast, but no sense that she would want no breast. Wanting no breast puts into question whether she still wants to be a woman. It is as if the butch's desire to have the breast removed is not quite plausible as a healthy option unless it is the sign of a gender disorder or some other medical urgency.

But why is it that we do accept these other choices as choices, regardless of what we take their social meanings to be? Society doesn't consider itself to have a right to stop a woman from enlarging or diminishing her breasts, and we don't consider penile enhancement to be a problem, unless it is being done by an illegitimate doctor who botches the results, as it sometimes sadly is. No one gets sent to a psychiatrist because they announce their plans to cut or grow their hair or to go on a diet, unless one is at risk for anorexia, and yet these practices are part of the daily habits of cultivating secondary-sex characteristics, if we expand that category to mean all the various bodily indicators or "cues" of sex. If the bodily traits "indicate" sex, then sex is not quite the same as the means by which it is indicated. Sex is made understandable through the signs that indicate how it should be read or understood. These bodily indicators are the cultural means by which the sexed body is read. They are themselves bodily, and they operate as signs, so there no easy way to distinguish between what is "materially" true and what is "culturally" true about a sexed body. I don't mean to suggest that purely cultural signs produce a material body, but only that the body does not become sexually readable without those signs, and that those signs are irreducibly cultural and material at once.

. . . . Those who claim that transsexuality is, and should be, a matter of choice, an exercise of freedom, are surely right, and they are right as well to point out that the various obstacles posed by the psychological and psychiatric professions are paternalistic forms of power by which a basic human freedom is being suppressed. . . . Richard Green, the president of the Harry Benjamin International Gender Dysphoria Association, and a strong advocate for transsexual rights . . . cites John Stuart Mill, arguing on behalf of this issue as a matter of personal freedom and of privacy. He writes that Mill "argued forcefully that adults should be able to do with their bodies as they wish providing it did not bring harm to another. Therefore, if the third gender, the transsexual, or the would-be limb amputee can continue to shoulder social responsibilities post-surgery, then the surgical requests are not society's business." Although Green makes this claim, one he himself calls "philosophical," he notes that it comes into conflict with the question of who will pay, and whether society has an obligation to pay for a procedure being defended as a matter of personal liberty.

 . . . . There are, surely, many psychiatrists and psychologists who insist on GID as a pathology. And there is a well-funded and impossibly prolific professor of neuropsychiatry and behavioral science at the University of South Carolina, George Rekers, who combines a polemical political conservatism with an effort to intensify and extend the use of this diagnosis. His main concern seems to be about boys, boys becoming men, and men becoming strong fathers in the context of heterosexual marriage. He also traces the rise of GID to the breakdown of the family, the loss of strong father figures for boys, and the subsequent "disturbance" that it is said to cause. His manifest concern about the emergence of homosexuality in boys is clear from his discussion as well, citing as he does the 1994 DSM conclusion that 75 percent of GID youth turn out to be homosexual as adults. Rekers has published loads of studies strewn with "data" presented within the context of empirical research protocols. Although intensely polemical, he understands himself as a scientist and an empiricist, and he attributes ideological bias to his opponents. He writes that "in a generation confused by radical ideologies on male and female roles, we need solid research on men and women who are well adjusted examples of a secure male identity and a secure female identity." His "solid research" is intended to show the benefits of distinguishing clearly between gender norms and their pathologies "for family life and the larger culture." In this vein, Rekers also notes that "preliminary findings have been published in the literature which report on the positive therapeutic effects of religious conversion for curing transsexualism . . . and on the positive therapeutic effect of a church ministry to repentant homosexuals." He seems to be relatively unconcerned with girls, which impresses me as entirely symptomatic of his preoccupation with patriarchal authority and his inability to see the threat that women of all kinds might pose to the presumptions he makes about male power. The fate of masculinity absorbs this study because masculinity, a fragile and fallible construct, needs the social support of marriage and stable family life in order to find its right path. Indeed, masculinity by itself tends to falter, in his view, and needs to be housed and propped up by various social supports, suggesting that masculinity is itself a function of social organizations and has no intrinsic meaning outside them. In any case, there are people like Rekers who make an adamant and highly polemical case, not only for retaining the diagnosis but for strengthening it, and give highly conservative political reasons for strengthening the diagnosis so that the structures that support normalcy can be strengthened.

Ironically, it is these very structures that support normalcy that compel the need for the diagnosis to begin with, including its benefits for those who need it in order to effect a transition. . . . The fact is, that under current conditions, a number of people have reason to worry about the consequences of having their diagnosis taken away or failing to establish eligibility for the diagnosis. Perhaps the rich will be able to shell out the tens of thousands of dollars that an FTM transformation entails, including double mastectomy and a very good phalloplasty, but most people, especially poor and working-class trannies, will not be able to foot the bill. At least in the United States where socialized medicine is largely understood as a communist plot, it won't be an option to have the state or insurance companies pay for these procedures without first establishing that there are serious and enduring medical and psychiatric reasons for doing so. . . . In other words, one must be subjected to a regulatory apparatus, as Foucault would have called it, in order to get to the point where something like an exercise in freedom becomes possible. One has to submit to labels and names, to incursions, to invasions, one has to be gauged against measures of normalcy, and one has to pass the test. So sometimes what this means is that one needs to become very savvy about these standards and know how to present oneself in such a way that one comes across as a plausible candidate. And sometimes therapists find themselves in a bind, being asked to supply a letter for someone they want to help, but abhorring the very fact that they have to write this letter, in the language of diagnosis, in order to help produce the life that their client wants to have. . . . Approaching the diagnosis strategically involves a series of individuals not quite believing what they say, signing on to language that does not represent the reality it is or should be. The price of using the diagnosis to get what one wants is that one cannot use language to say what one really thinks is true. One pays for one's freedom, as it were, by sacrificing one's claim to use language truthfully. In other words, one purchases one sort of freedom only by giving up another.

. . . .

If one comes out in favor of choice, and against diagnosis, it would seem that one has to deal with the enormous financial consequences of this decision for those who cannot pay for the resources at hand and whose insurance, if there is insurance, will not honor this choice as one that is to be included as a covered elective treatment. And even when local laws are passed, offering insurance to city workers who seek such treatments, as is the case now in San Francisco, there are still diagnostic tests to pass, so choice is clearly bought at a price, sometimes at the price of truth itself.

. . . . The call to have matters of gender identity depathologized and for elective surgery and hormone treatment to be covered as a legitimate set of elective procedures seems bound to fail, only because most medical, insurance, and legal practitioners are committed to supporting access to sex change technologies only if we are talking about a disorder. Arguments to the effect that there is an overwhelming legitimate human demand here are bound to prove inadequate. Examples of the kinds of justifications that ideally would make sense and should have a claim on insurance companies include: this transition will allow someone to realize certain human possibilities that will help this life to flourish, or this will allow someone to emerge from fear and shame and paralysis into a situation of enhanced self-esteem and the ability to form close ties with others, or this transition will help alleviate a source of enormous suffering or give reality to a fundamental human desire to assume a bodily form that expresses a fundamental sense of selfhood. Though some gender identity clinics, like the one at the University of Minnesota run by [Walter] Bockting, do make such arguments, and do provide supportive therapeutic contexts for people disposed to make a choice on this issue, whether it be to live as transgendered or transsexual, whether to be third sex, whether to consider the process as one of a becoming whose end is not in sight, and may never be. But even that clinic has to supply materials to insurance companies that comply with DSM-IV.[14]

. . . . Although the stated aim of the diagnosis is it wants to know whether an individual can successfully conform to living according to the norms of another gender, it seems that the real test that the GID poses is whether one can conform to the language of the diagnosis. . . .

Let's take a look at that language. The GID section of the DSM starts by making clear that there are two parts of this diagnosis. The first is that "there must be strong and persistent cross-gender identification." This would be difficult to ascertain, I would think, since identifications do not always appear as such: they can remain aspects of hidden fantasy, or parts of dreams, or inchoate structures of behavior. But the DSM asks us to be a bit more positivist in our approach to identification, assuming that we can read off of behavior what identifications are at work in any given person's psychic life. Cross-gender identification is defined as "the desire to be" the other sex, "or the insistence that one is." The "or" in this line is significant, since it implies that one might desire to be the other sex — and we have to suspend for the moment what "the other sex" is and, by the way, in my mind, it is not quite clear — without necessarily insisting on it. These are two separate criteria. They do not have to emerge in tandem. So if there is a way to determine that someone has this "desire to be" even though they do not insist on it, that would seem to be satisfactory grounds for concluding that cross-gender identification is happening. And if there is "an insistence that one is" the other sex, then that would function as a separate criterion which, if fulfilled, would warrant the conclusion that cross-gender identification is happening. In the second instance, an act of speech is required in which someone insists that one is the other sex, an insistence understood as a way of laying claim to the other sex in one's own speech and of attributing that other sex to oneself. So certain expressions of this "desire to be" and "insistence that I am" are precluded as viable evidence for the claim. "This must not merely be a desire for any perceived cultural advantages of being the other sex." Now, this is a moment for pause, since the diagnosis assumes that we can have an experience of sex without considering what the cultural advantages of being a given sex are. Is this, in fact, possible? If sex is experienced by us within a cultural matrix of meanings, if it comes to have its significance and meaning in reference to a wider social world, then can we separate the experience of "sex" from its social meanings, including the way

---

14. For an impressive account of how that clinic works to provide a supportive environment for its clients at the same time that it seeks to secure benefits through use of the diagnosis, see Walter O. Bockting, *The Assessment and Treatment of Gender Dysphoria, in* DIRECTIONS IN CLINICAL AND COUNSELING PSYCHOLOGY, VOL. 7 (1997), lesson 11, 3–22. For another impressive account, see Richard Green, *Reflections on 'Transsexualism and Sex Reassignment,' 1996–1999* (presidential address to the Harry Benjamin International Gender Dysphoria Association, London, Aug. 17–21, 1999), previously available at http://www.symposion.com/ijt/greenpresidential/green00.htm.

in which power functions throughout those meanings? Sex is a term that applies to people across the board, so that it is difficult to refer to my "sex" as if it were radically singular. If it is, generally speaking, then, never only "my sex" or "your sex" that is at issue, but a way in which the category of "sex" exceeds the personal appropriations of it, then it would seem to be impossible to perceive sex outside this cultural matrix and to understand this cultural matrix outside the possible advantages it may afford. Indeed, when we think about cultural advantages, whether we are doing something—anything—for the cultural advantage it affords, we have to ask whether what we do is advantageous for me, that is, whether it furthers or satisfies my desires and my aspirations. . . . I wonder whether it is possible to consider becoming one sex or the other without considering the cultural advantage it might afford, since the cultural advantage it might afford will be the advantage it affords to someone who has certain kinds of desires, who wants to be in a position to take advantage of certain cultural opportunities. If GID insists that the desire to be another sex or the insistence that one is the other sex has to be evaluated without reference to cultural advantage, it may be that GID misunderstands some of the cultural forces that go into making and sustaining certain desires of this sort. And then GID would also have to respond to the epistemological question of whether sex can be perceived *at all* outside the cultural matrix of power relations in which relative advantage and disadvantage would be part of that matrix.

The diagnosis also requires that there be "persistent discomfort" about one's assigned sex or "inappropriateness," and here is where the discourse of "not getting it right" comes in. The assumption is that there is an appropriate sense that people can and do have, a sense that this gender is appropriate for me, to me. And that there is a comfort that I would have, could have, and that it could be had if it were the right norm. In an important sense, the diagnosis assumes that gender norms are relatively fixed and that the problem is making sure that you find the right one, the one that will allow you to feel appropriate where you are, comfortable in the gender that you are. There must be evidence of "distress"—yes, certainly, distress. And if there is not "distress," then there should be "impairment." Here it makes sense to ask where all this comes from: the distress and the impairment, the not being able to function well at the workplace or in handling certain daily chores. The diagnosis presumes that one feels distress and discomfort and inappropriateness because one is in the wrong gender, and that conforming to a different gender norm, if viable for the person in question, will make one feel much better. But the diagnosis does not ask whether there is a problem with the gender norms that it takes as fixed and intransigent, whether these norms produce distress and discomfort, whether they impede one's ability to function. . . .

The diagnosis seeks to establish criteria by which a cross-gendered person might be identified, but the diagnosis, in articulating criteria, articulates a rigid version of gender norms. It offers the following account of gender norms (the emphases are mine) in the language of simple description: "In boys, cross-gendered identification is manifested by a marked preoccupation with traditionally feminine activities.

They may have a preference for dressing in girls' or women's clothes *or may improvise such items from available materials* when genuine materials are unavailable. Towels, aprons, and scarves are often used to represent long hair or skirts." . . . . Feminine clothing is called "genuine clothing," which leaves us to conclude that the materials with which these boys are improvising is less than genuine, other than genuine, if not ingenuine and "false." . . . . So there is a certain imaginary play, and a capacity to transfigure one item into another through improvisation and substitution. In other words, there is an art practice at work here, one that would be difficult to name, simply, as the simple act of conforming to a norm. . . .

    . . . .

The way you can tell that girls are having cross-gendered identification according to the DSM-IV is that they argue with their parents about wearing certain kinds of clothes. They prefer boys' clothing and short hair, apparently, and they have mainly boy friends, express a desire to become a boy, but also, oddly, "they are often misidentified by strangers as boys." I am trying to think through how it could be that evidence of one's cross-gendered identification is confirmed by being identified as a boy by a stranger. It would seem that random social assignment functions as evidence, as if the stranger knows something about the psychological makeup of that girl, or as if the girl has solicited that interpellation from the stranger. The DSM. . . . wants to be able to claim cross-gendered identification as part of gender identity disorder, and so as a psychological problem that can be addressed through treatment. It imagines that each individual has a relation to its "assigned sex" and that this relation is either one of discomfort and distress or a sense of comfort and being at peace. But even this notion of "assigned sex"—sex "assigned" at birth—implies that sex is socially produced and relayed, and that it comes to us not merely as a private reflection that each of us makes about ourselves but as a critical interrogation that each of us makes of a social category assigned to us, that exceeds us in its generality and power, but which also, consequentially, instances itself at the site of our bodies. It is interesting that the DSM seeks to establish gender as a set of more or less fixed and conventional norms, even as it keeps giving us evidence to the contrary, almost as if it is at cross-purposes with its own aims. . . . I'm not sure that the girl who seizes on this stray and felicitous interpellation is giving evidence to a preestablished "disorder" of any kind, but noting that the very means by which sex comes to be, through assignment, opens up possibilities for reassignment that excite her sense of agency, play, and possibility. . . .

    . . . . At the same time that the DSM understands itself as diagnosing a distress that then becomes a candidate for alleviation as a result of the diagnosis, it also understands that "social pressure" can lead to "extreme isolation for such a child." The DSM does not talk about suicide, even though we know that the cruelty of adolescent peer pressure on transgendered youth can lead to suicide. The DSM does not talk about risks of death, generally, or murder. . . . Apparently, the "distress" that comes from living in a world in which suicide and death by violence remain real issues is not part of the diagnosis of GID. . . . In a way, the fact of social violence against transgendered youth is euphemized as teasing and pressure, and then the distress caused by that is recast as an internal problem, a sign of preoccupation, self-involvement, which seems to follow from the wishes themselves. . . .

What is most worrisome, however, is how the diagnosis works as its own social pressure, causing distress, establishing wishes as pathological, intensifying the regulation and control of those who express them in institutional settings. Indeed, one has to ask whether the diagnosis of transgendered youth does not act precisely as peer pressure, as an elevated form of teasing, as a euphemized form of social violence. And if we conclude that it does act in such a way, standing for gender norms, seeking to produce adaptation to existing norms, then how do we return to the vexed issue of what the diagnosis also offers? If part of what the diagnosis offers is a form of social recognition, and if that is the form that social recognition takes, and if it is only through this kind of social recognition that third parties, including medical insurance, will be willing to pay for the medical and techno-logical changes that are sometimes desired, is it really possible to do away with the diagnosis altogether? . . . .

. . . . It is possible to say, necessary to say, that the diagnosis leads the way to the alleviation of suffering, and it is possible, necessary, to say that the diagnosis inten-sifies the very suffering that requires alleviation. Under present and entrenched social conditions in which gender norms are still articulated in conventional ways, and departures from the norm regarded as suspect, this is the paradox that auton-omy is in. Of course, it is possible to move to a country where the state will pay for sex reassignment surgery, to apply to a "transgender fund" that a broader commu-nity supplies to help those who cannot pay the high costs, or indeed to apply for a "grant" to individuals that covers "cosmetic surgery." And the movement for trans people to become the therapists and diagnosticians will surely help matters. These are all ways around the bind, until the bind goes away. But if the bind is to go away for the long run, the norms that govern how we understand the relation between gender identity and mental health would have to change radically, so that economic and legal institutions would recognize how essential becoming a gender is to one's very sense of personhood, one's sense of well-being, one's possibility to flourish as a bodily being. Until that time, freedom will require unfreedom, and autonomy is implicated in subjection. If the social world must change for autonomy to become possible, then individual choice will prove to have meaning only in the context of a more radical social change.

Discussion

1. Professor Butler asserts that "[a]lthough there are strong criticisms to be made of the diagnosis . . . it would nevertheless be wrong to call for its eradication with-out *first* putting into place a set of structures through which transitioning can be paid for and legal status attained." (emphasis added). What might her argument be presupposing on this point?

2. Butler suggests that to evaluate transgender scholar Jacob Hale's recommendation for depathologizing the process of gender transition, "we would have to ask whether the inclinations of medical practitioners are generally to be trusted with this responsibility, or whether the world of progressive therapists offers a better chance for humane and successful passage through the process of diagnosis." What do you think about that question?

3. Butler asserts that "[t]hose who claim that transsexuality is, and should be, a matter of choice, an exercise of freedom, are surely right," yet many who oppose letting transgender people use restrooms consistent with their gender identity rather than the sex they were assigned at birth insist that there are in nature just men and women, that a transgender woman is still a man, and a transgender man is still a woman.

4. Anti-gay, anti-trans Dr. George Rekers, whom Butler discusses, became embroiled in scandal in 2010 after *The Miami New Times* reported that Rekers hired a male prostitute from Rentboy.com to accompany him on a ten-day European vacation. Rekers professed not to have learned that the young man was a sex worker until half-way through the trip for which Rekers claimed he hired the man to carry his luggage as a travel companion. Penn Bullock & Brandon K. Thorp, *Christian Right leader George Rekers takes vacation with "rent boy,"* MIAMI NEW TIMES (May 6, 2010), https://www.miaminewtimes.com/news/christian-right-leader-george-rekers-takes-vacation-with-rent-boy-6377933. The sex worker subsequently publicly claimed to have given Rekers sexual massages. Anderson Cooper, *Sex Scandal Accusations and Denials,* AC-360, CNN (May 7, 2010), https://www.youtube.com/watch?v=sAiIXb9Aql0. Rekers called the article "slanderous" on his (since deleted) wordpress web site. Brian Montopoli, *George Rekers, Christian Right Leader, Denies Gay Prostitution Allegation*, CBS NEWS (May 6, 2010), https://www.cbsnews.com/news/george-rekers-christian-right-leader-denies-gayprostitution-allegation. Rekers subsequently resigned from the board of the National Association for Research and Therapy of Homosexuality (NARTH), ostensibly "to allow myself the time necessary to fight the false media reports that have been made against me." *George Rekers Resigns from Anti-Gay Group in Wake of "Rentboy" Scandal*, HUFFPOST (May 12, 2010), https://www.huffpost.com/entry/george-rekers-resigns-fro_n_573123.

5. Compare Butler's explanation of the collective character of "sex" (starting above with the observation that "[s]ex is a term that applies to people across the board") with David B. Cruz, *Sexual Judgments: Full Faith and Credit and the Relational Character of Legal Sex*, 46 HARV. C.R.-C.L. L. REV. 51, 63, 64 (2011):

> one might think that [in nature] there simply are males and females, that a person counts as either one or the other by virtue of certain inherent (non-relational) properties he or she possesses (even perhaps if these identity categories are criterially vague). . . . [However], that is not how law treats or uses identity categories like race or sex. Law treats these as social categories

and establishes social relationships; these relationships are marked by differential distributions [of] legal rights and obligations.

. . . . When a state dictates that a newborn person's sex be recorded officially on a birth certificate, it is not, contrary to some courts' representations, simply mirroring a historical "fact." Rather, the state is making a choice about how to divide its population into classes. . . .

Note on Controversy Over Use of Disability Laws to Reach Anti-Transgender Discrimination

As Professor Judith Butler's arguments, *supra*, might suggest, the characterization of transgender identity as a disorder has been controversial. So, too, has been the use of disability rights laws to try to secure protection against anti-transgender discrimination.

While Chapter 5 focused on the use of laws prohibiting sex discrimination in employment to protect workers from anti-transgender discrimination, that is not the only tactic people have pursued to try to secure protection from discrimination for transgender persons. Because the medical profession and popular culture long regarded many trans people as having a mental disorder, as the Gender Identity Disorder diagnosis discussed above reflects, trans workers and their attorneys have turned to laws forbidding discrimination on the basis of disabilities or "handicaps." The federal Rehabilitation Act of 1973, 29 U.S.C. § 701 *et seq.*, is one such early law that seemed promising, and, indeed, litigants secured some victories under that statute. *See Doe v. United States Postal Serv.*, 37 Fair Empl. Prac. Cas. (BNA) 1867, 1869 (D.D.C. 1985) (interpreting Rehabilitation Act to cover anti-"transsexual" discrimination); *Blackwell v. United States Department of the Treasury*, 639 F. Supp. 289 (D.D.C. 1986) (interpreting Rehabilitation Act to cover discrimination because of worker's transvestism).

In 1992, however, Congress amended the Rehabilitation Act to exclude from the various grounds for potentially covered disabilities the following: "transvestism, transsexualism, pedophilia, exhibitionism, voyeurism, gender identity disorders not resulting from physical impairments, or other sexual behavior disorders." Rehabilitation Act Amendments of 1992, Pub. L. 102-569, § 102, 106 Stat. 4344 (October 29, 1992) (codified at 29 U.S.C. § 706(8)(F)(I)). This exclusion brought the Rehabilitation Act into conformity with the identical exclusion written into the Americans with Disabilities Act ("ADA") when it was enacted in 1990. 42 U.S.C. § 12211(b)(1). These exclusions sharply limit the utility of the Rehabilitation Act and the ADA to protect against anti-transgender discrimination, though as discussed at the end of this section, litigants have begun to argue that the exclusions are unconstitutional or at a minimum must be construed very narrowly, leaving greater room for the basic protections of those statutes to operate. These federal exclusions also do not of their own force preclude trans people from protection under state laws forbidding disability discrimination.

Appealing to disability law to protect transgender persons has been a matter of some controversy. One concern is that it may reinforce a view that being transgender is inherently a mental illness, an undesirable state that should be cured if possible. A related concern is that it could be further stigmatizing to trans persons to strengthen the cultural link between their identities and mental illness or other disability. A third concern is that the availability of disability law to protect trans people could depend on access to care within the medical system in order to validate claims of disability, which could be differentially available to trans people depending on their class or socioeconomic status. Defenders of using disability law in this context argue that the first two stigma-related critiques misapprehend modern disability law, which treats people's disabilities not as shortcomings inherent in individual persons but as flowing from incompatibilities between societal arrangements and particular individuals' circumstances, with disability law aiming to transform social arrangements and ideally reduce the stigmatization of disability. They also argue that disability law does not require that the individual who has been the victim of discrimination be receiving any medical treatment or even have a medical diagnosis. For treatment of these concerns and counterarguments, see Jennifer L. Levi & Bennett H. Klein, *Pursuing Protection for Transgender People Through Disability Laws*, *in* Paisley Currah et al., eds., Transgender Rights 74 (2006).

Consider the following brief excerpts from articles addressing the medicalization of transgender identity and its interaction with legal protection for transgender persons.

Beyond a Medical Model: Advocating for a New Conception of Gender Identity in the Law[*]
Franklin H. Romeo

. . . . Two discourses have emerged in the legal examination of claims brought by transgender and other gender nonconforming people. [One] is a medical model, in which gender nonconformity is explained as a psychological condition most appropriately treated through medical services. While the medical model of gender provides a basis for legal redress for transgender people in some cases, this model is also limited. . . .

. . . . The medical model explains gender nonconformity through the psychiatric diagnosis of Gender Identity Disorder (GID) and relies upon medical evidence—both in the form of psychological diagnoses and physical treatments such as hormone therapy and gender-related surgeries—in order to establish gender transgressions as legitimate and therefore worthy of recognition and protection under the law. Like the biological model, the medical model assumes that two genders exist and enforces the norms typically associated with these genders. However,

---

[*] Excerpted from Franklin H. Romeo, *Beyond a Medical Model: Advocating for a New Conception of Gender Identity in the Law*, 36 Colum. Hum. Rts. L. Rev. 713 (2005).

the medical model is based upon the belief that some people suffer from a psychological condition (GID) that causes them to experience great discomfort regarding their assigned gender. The diagnostic criteria for GID generally include an ongoing desire since early childhood to be the "opposite" gender, a desire to physically modify one's body, and heterosexual desire in the gender with which one identifies. Under this model, gender nonconforming people who meet these criteria are eligible to transition from living as their birth gender to living as the gender with which they identify. This process is facilitated by a combination of psychological and physical care that both enables and requires transgender people to then conform to the expected norms of their lived gender.

. . . Increasingly, as the medical regulation of gender transitions has become more uniform and visible, courts have been willing to grant at least rudimentary legal protections to transgender litigants who are able to provide documentation of a GID diagnosis and related medical treatment. This has resulted in the expansion of transgender rights on two fronts: the ability of some transgender litigants to be legally recognized as the gender with which they identify, and the ability of some transgender litigants to access rights based upon a medical diagnosis of GID.

. . . .

The result of courts' reliance upon the medical model has been twofold. On one hand, use of the medical model has opened up a viable option for claims for transgender people whose experiences comport with the diagnostic criteria of GID. On the other hand, it sets up the medical establishment as a gatekeeping institution that regulates gender nonconformity and predicates legal rights on access to health care. Low-income transgender people who are unable to afford trans-friendly healthcare and gender transgressive people who do not fall within the narrative of GID prescribed by the medical establishment are unlikely to be able to avail themselves of legal protections that have emerged from the use of this model.

The medical model of gender privileges those who have the ability to access health care and choose to undergo all available medical procedures to modify their bodies, while providing very limited protection, if any, to those who do not. For example, it does not protect gender nonconforming people who are unable to access trans-friendly health care, intersex people who refuse "corrective" medical procedures, people who identify as genderqueer or otherwise express nontraditional gender identities, people who are unable to physically modify their bodies, and those who choose not to undergo surgical and hormonal treatments in order to express their gender. Because the experiences of many gender nonconforming people do not match the diagnostic criteria of GID, and because, for all except the most privileged few, accessing trans-friendly health care is extraordinarily difficult, the medical model of gender does not serve the vast majority of gender non-conforming people.

. . . .

The result of courts' reliance on the medical model of gender is that those instances of gender nonconformity recognized by the medical establishment are portrayed as real and legitimate—and therefore worthy of at least some legal protections—while other transgressive experiences of gender are viewed as unreal, fraudulent, or illegitimate. . . .

In addition, the medical model of gender has resulted in detailed and invasive examinations of gender transgressive bodies by courts. . . . [Even] for gender nonconforming people who intentionally invoke a medical model of gender to support their claim, the question considered by courts is not necessarily whether they and their doctor were able to establish a course of medical treatment consistent with their needs and health, but whether that treatment results in a body and behavior that sufficiently conform to normative gender standards so as to be considered legitimate in the eyes of the court.

Discussion

1. Do Franklin's class-based objections apply to that prong of many disability discrimination laws that prohibits discrimination on the basis of a perceived disability or handicap?

2. What social conditions might be likely to facilitate statutes' and judges' shifting away from a medical model? But note that such shifting might not necessarily take a form supportive of transgender autonomy projects. For example, Andrew Quigley has argued from cases involving transgender people seeking to deduct transition-related medical care, pursuing Medicaid assistance for medical transition procedures, or trying to secure transition care from a prison in which they're incarcerated that courts have become increasingly indifferent to gender and gender expression as distinct from anatomical sex. That is, "today, a medical diagnosis is a necessary but *in*sufficient condition for obtaining state funds to treat GID. Once a medical expert determines that GRS [the author's acronym for "gender reassignment surgery" (sic)] is 'medically necessary' to treat a gender-variant patient's severe distress, administrators and judges scrutinize the expert's determinations and make their own judgments as to the *actual* necessity of the prescribed surgery." D. Andrew Quigley, *Propagating Gender Stasis: Judicial Indifference and the Medical Assistance Model of Gender in Requests for State Medical Assistance*, 7 Mod. Am. 40, 40 (2011). Note that Quigley was writing before the American Psychiatric Association eliminated the diagnosis of gender identity and instituted the new diagnosis of gender dysphoria. *See* Diagnostic and Statistical Manual of Mental Disorders, 5th Edition, *infra* at p. 1017.

*Pursuing Protection for Transgender People Through Disability Laws**
Jennifer L. Levi & Bennett H. Klein

. . . .

Some transgender people (and allies) worry that using the legal category of disability to secure legal protections for transgender people will perpetuate social myths and stereotypes that transgender people are sick, abnormal, or inferior. This concern stems largely from the stigma still associated with the term *disability*, which in its colloquial sense is all too often misunderstood to mean physical infirmity, debilitation, or inability to work. What this concern fails to recognize, however, is that disability antidiscrimination laws do not use the term *disability* in its colloquial or popular sense. . . . Today, [disability civil rights laws] prohibit discrimination against individuals with a wide range of health conditions who are fully capable of working and participating in society. The barriers to equal opportunity that such individuals face are found not in physical incapacity or inferiority but in the prejudice, hostility, and misunderstanding of others about their health conditions. . . . Rather than discard an important source of legal protections, the transgender community must work with others both inside and outside the disability community to eliminate the stigma associated with disability and to ensure that state courts properly understand and apply disability antidiscrimination laws.

. . . .

. . . . One need not have obtained a medical diagnosis to demonstrate that one has a disability. . . . [One] need not demonstrate that one is receiving medical care or treatment in order to claim discrimination on the basis of disability. . . .

. . . .

. . . . According to the [medical] model [of disabilities], an individual's problem lies in his or her impairment; accordingly, the social response was to provide aid and assistance through medical intervention to "cure" the person's condition or rehabilitation programs to help a person approximate standards of "normalcy." The medical model perpetuated the stigma and social prejudice associated with disability because . . . "it treats the individual as deficient and inherently inferior. . . ."

. . . . [Under] the more modern view [of disabilities], the "disadvantaged status of persons with disabilities" is [viewed as] the product of a hostile (or at least inhospitable) social environment, not simply the product of bodily defects." . . . .

. . . .

_____

* Excerpted from Jennifer L. Levi & Bennett H. Klein, *Pursuing Protection for Transgender People Through Disability Laws, in* Paisley Currah et al., eds., Transgender Rights 74 (2006), by permission of the University of Minnesota Press.

This new understanding that social barriers, not individual inferiority, caused the disadvantaged status of individuals with disabilities led to the first antidiscrimination statutes in the 1970s. . . .

. . . .

One objection against bringing a disability claim on behalf of a transsexual person who has pursued medical care and treatment to transition from one sex to another is rooted in . . . rejection of a mental health diagnosis. . . . There need not .. [h]ave been an associated [*Diagnostic and Statistical Manual of Mental Disorders* 4th ed.] diagnosis for the individual to be covered by law. . . . [It] is enough that the impairment simply be acknowledged to be a health condition in order for an individual to come within the definition. . . .

. . . .

Despite the clear, intended coverage of the law, many transgender people object to pursuing disability discrimination cases because of the stigma associated with disability. . . . The answer to this objection is to address the stigma, not to enhance it by avoiding the law. . . .

Discussion

1. Does anything in Levi and Bennett's arguments presented above preclude decisions like those in *Sommers v. Iowa Civil Rights Commission*, 337 N.W.2d 470 (Iowa 1983), *infra* at p. 963; *Dobre v. National Railroad Passenger Corp. ("Amtrak")*, 850 F. Supp. 284 (E.D. Pa. 1993), *infra* at p. 974; or *Doe v. Boeing*, 846 P.2d 531 (Wash. 1993) (en banc), *infra* at p. 965.

2. Do Levi and Bennett's arguments about the understanding of disability *intended* by those who championed disability discrimination laws, one that sees disability as rooted in incompatibilities between individual functioning and social environments, engage fully with the processes by which stigma exists and may be ameliorated or exacerbated? If substantial segments of the U.S. population do not share that systemic understanding, might news or social media accounts of judicial decisions treating anti-trans discrimination as disability discrimination lead such persons to view transgender persons themselves as inherently disabled (along the lines of the views that Levi and Klein characterize as outdated)? Professor Jeannette Cox has argued that "disability discrimination law fails to live up to transgender advocates' expectations in significant ways. Most crucially, a person with gender dysphoria seeking to bring a claim under the ADA would have to characterize gender dysphoria as an 'impairment' and a 'disorder.'" Jeannette Cox, *Disability Law and Gender Identity Discrimination*, 81 U. Pitt. L. Rev. 315, 327 (2019).

3. Even if stigmatizing, might embracing disability arguments be worth it? For arguments that the answer can be "yes," with benefits outweighing costs, see, for example, Craig Konnoth, *Medicalization and the New Civil Rights*, 72 Stan. L. Rev. 1165 (2020) ("[I]t bears noting that for some groups, ADA protections have

sometimes proved more versatile than protections arising from other statutes. For transgender individuals in particular, attempts to use sex discrimination protections can be limited—for instance, sex discrimination claims generally do not apply to prisons."); Ali Szemanski, *When Trans Rights Are Disability Rights: The Promises and Perils of Seeking Gender Dysphoria Coverage Under the Americans With Disabilities Act*, 43 Harv. J.L. & Gender 137 (2020) ("A world without pathologization may indeed be ideal, but fighting for trans rights using the provisions of the ADA may provide necessary relief to individuals who live in the current world and not an idealized future world.").

————————

Professor David Cruz has sounded cautionary notes about reliance on medical authority to secure legal rights for transgender people:

Getting Sex "Right": Heteronormativity and Biologism in Trans and Intersex Marriage Litigation and Scholarship[*]
David B. Cruz

. . . .

As Sally Sheldon has written about the medicalization of abortion law in Britain, [Sally Sheldon, *Subject Only to the Attitude of the Surgeon Concerned: The Judicial Protection of Medical Discretion*, 5 Soc. & Legal Stud. 95, 96 (1996)], "[t]he doctors' power to define is accepted and reinforced, with other accounts pushed to the margins. This depoliticizes the judicial decision which can be legitimated with reference to scientific truth and is thus seen as uninfluenced by personal moral or political belief." This is as true of sex determination as it is of abortion. Now, Professor Sheldon found in her study that what "the courts did in these cases is actively to protect and entrench the monopoly of doctors, while policing those marginal cases which did not fall within the bounds of good medical practice." Again, my worry is that this can happen in the trans area, with those doctors whom I would consider more "progressive," the ones more willing to come close to saying that a person's sex ought to be determined by their gender identity regardless of surgical, hormonal, or other medical interventions, are likely to be the ones dismissed by law and marginalized.

Granted, there have been some practical benefits of medicalization in the abortion regulation context in Britain. As Sheldon found, "[i]n general, it seems that this largely acts to protect, rather than to impinge upon, women's reproductive autonomy." Likewise, medicalization can give a way for some courts to recognize some litigants' new legal sex identity, and a way for some number of persons to access medical care and gender confirming surgeries through insurance, as well as to make disability discrimination claims.

————————

[*] Excerpted from David B. Cruz, *Getting Sex "Right": Heteronormativity and Biologism in Trans and Intersex Marriage Litigation and Scholarship*, 18 Duke J. of Gender L. & Policy 203 (2010).

But Sheldon raises an important cautionary note that we should not overlook in this context:

> If the courts continue to adhere to the position of strong preference for medical self-regulation which has been so in evidence, then it seems that where the law has been effective in protecting the doctor-patient relationship from outside attacks, it is likely to be less useful at protecting reproductive autonomy within it. As such, while the alliance with medical interests may have had strategic advantages, it remains inadequate as a basis for building and protecting women's reproductive autonomy within the courts.

Similarly, it may be that medicalization might undermine the law's capacity to protect gender autonomy within doctor-patient relationships. By urging courts to defer to medicine where people have completed medical processes, courts could be more likely to side with a doctor over a trans client, particularly if the client exercises their constitutional right to refuse certain recommended treatments in cases where there is a dispute about whether law should recognize them as a different sex now. Moreover, "it is important to remember that the women in the front of the queue to be sacrificed in the strategy of 'playing it safe' are the most vulnerable — those who are unable to afford a termination outside of the [National Health Service] and who have least knowledge of how to play the system."

The same is likely to be true with respect to transgender issues, although this may to some extent be true of our legal system for any dispute: class and wealth matter. For example, as Dean Spade has observed, some jurisdictions rely on genital surgeries to determine when they will accept a gender reclassification, and this then "has an income-based impact, causing greater obstacles for middle- and low-income people who cannot afford to pay out of pocket for the procedure, if they even want or need it." [Dean Spade, *Trans Formation*, 31 L.A. LAW. 34, 37 (2008).]

. . . .

Discussion

1. Do these brief excerpts from Professor Cruz undervalue the potential benefits of viewing trans identity through a medical lens and according authority to legitimize sex identities to modern medicine? Those who treat gender dysphoria (and who formerly treated gender identity disorder) increasingly recognize that genitoplasty, for example, is not an appropriate treatment for all trans persons, a position that could prove influential with courts considering whether to treat a trans person in law as a member of the sex consistent with their gender identity.

2. Regardless of the force these concerns might have in a context where a court must rule on what sex the law regards a person as being, might they be less relevant in a setting where the legal issue is whether a person has discriminated against a transgender person on grounds of either sex or disability?

3. Jennifer Levi and Kevin Barry have reported that a group of "transgender rights and disability rights advocates and lawyers" who met to discuss the implications of *Blatt v. Cabela's Retail, Inc.*, No. 5:14-cv-04822, 2017 WL 2178123, 55 NDLR P 4 (E.D. Pa. May 18, 2017), *infra* at p. 1033, recognized that "that disability advocacy involves navigating contradictory disability models": "although *some* disability laws rely on a stigmatizing definition of 'disability' rooted in the medical model, laws like the ADA and Section 504 [of the Rehabilitation Act] do not; they are instead premised on the social model and are vital to securing rights for people who experience discrimination based on a medical condition." Kevin M. Barry & Jennifer L. Levi, *The Future of Disability Rights Protections for Transgender People*, 35 Touro L. Rev. 25, 49, 50, 51 (2019). As a consequence, "effective advocacy on behalf of people with gender dysphoria requires a thoughtful understanding of the promise and perils of both models of disability law." *Id.* at 52. Similarly, Eli Clare reports "find[ing]myself agreeing with parts of both arguments [about whether GID belongs in the DSM]" but calling for "question[ing] the fundamental relationship between trans people and the very idea of diagnosis." Eli Clare, *Body Shame, Body Pride: Lessons from the Disability Rights Movement*, in The Transgender Studies Reader 2 261, 265 (Susan Stryker and Aren Z. Aizura eds., 2013). Clare suggests that, "[w]ith a disability politics, we could learn to use diagnosis without being defined by it, all the while resisting the institutions that hold power over us. . . . [W]e could understand our lives and histories as *ordinary* from the inside, even as we're treated as curious, exotic, unbelievable, deceptive, sick, threatening from the outside. We could frame bodily difference as neither good nor bad, but as profoundly *familiar*." *Id.*

4. Keep in mind the arguments of Romeo, Bennett, Levi, Barry, Cruz, and Clare as you read the following materials.

Note on Sommers v. Iowa Civil Rights Commission

Transgender woman Audra Sommers was fired from her clerical job by Budget Marketing for "mispresenting" her sex as female after she was recognized by someone who knew her previously when she used to present as male. She lost a federal sex discrimination lawsuit she filed against Budget Marketing. *See Sommers v. Budget Marketing, Inc.*, 667 F.2d 748 (8th Cir. 1982), Chapter 5, *supra* at p. 138. In *Sommers v. Iowa Civil Rights Commission*, 337 N.W.2d 470 (Iowa 1983), the state supreme court affirmed the rejection of her sex and disability discrimination claims under the Iowa Civil Rights Act ("ICRA") by the Iowa Civil Rights Commission, whose decision had been upheld by a state trial judge. The Iowa Supreme Court affirmed the district court's conclusion that the commission did not act unreasonably, arbitrarily, or capriciously in denying jurisdiction because the "Iowa Civil Rights Act does not expressly include transsexuals as a protected class" and because the state legislature did not intend the ban on "sex" discrimination to reach discrimination against transsexual persons, in accord with numerous federal court decisions denying such an interpretation of Title VII's ban on sex discrimination. (Subsequently, in 2007, the state legislature amended the ICRA to include "gender identity" as a forbidden ground of discrimination. *See* 2007 Iowa Acts ch. 191, employment provision codified at Iowa Code § 216.6. And in 2020, the Supreme Court of the United States ruled that the primary federal law barring discrimination in employment, Title VII of the Civil Rights Act of 1964, forbids discrimination based on an employee's transgender status because that necessarily involves discrimination based on the employee's sex. *Bostock v. Clayton County, Georgia*, 140 S. Ct. 1731 (2020), Chapter 5, Section D, *supra*.

Regarding her disability discrimination claim, the state supreme court held "that in the context of employment transsexualism is not a disability" and so affirmed. The commission had adopted a regulation limiting the kinds of handicaps that would constitute covered "disabilities"; the regulation required either a physical impairment or a mental impairment. The court reasoned that "[n]o claim is made that a transsexual has an abnormal or unhealthy body. The commission could reasonably conclude that under its rule Sommers had no physical impairment." As for mental impairment, the statute at issue listed certain illustrative conditions, but the state supreme court ruled that gender identity disorder (or "transsexualism" as the court phrased it, consistently with the usage in the then-current third edition of the American Psychiatric Association's *Diagnostic and Statistical Manual of Mental Disorders*) was not like the specifically mentioned conditions:

> The delineated mental conditions are inherently likely to have a limiting effect on one or more major life activities. Transsexualism ordinarily should not affect a person's capacity to engage in those activities. Instead, transsexualism is more likely to have an adverse effect because of attitudes of others toward the condition. This does not mean, however, the condition meets the rule definition of impairment. The condition must independently come within the definition of impairment before attitudes of others can be said to make the condition a substantial handicap. Because transsexualism lacks the inherent propensity to limit major life activities of the listed examples of mental impairment, the commission could reasonably conclude it is not a mental impairment under the statute or rule.

> An adverse societal attitude does not mean that the transsexual is necessarily perceived as having a physical or mental impairment. Although a transsexual may have difficulty in obtaining and retaining employment, the commission could reasonably believe that difficulty is the result of discrimination based on societal beliefs that the transsexual is undesirable, rather than from beliefs that the transsexual is impaired physically or mentally as that term is used in the statute and defined in the rule. While we do not approve of such discrimination, we do not believe it is prohibited by the Iowa Civil Rights Act. . . .

How likely is it—as the court seems to suggest—in the United States in the 1980s, that people with negative attitudes toward transgender persons would *not* believe that trans people are mentally ill, disordered, or impaired? What is it about gender dysphoria that makes it *not* within "the class of psychological disorders delineated in the rule" (to wit, a mental impairment "such as mental retardation, organic brain syndrome, emotional or mental illness, and specific learning disabilities" 240 I.A.C. 6.1(2)(b))? Can you think of things that might reasonably be denominated "major life activities" with which "transsexualism" or gender dysphoria might interfere? What in the court's reasoning about transsexual people or its reasoning about the statute's applicability including its discussion of whether "transsexualism" is a mental illness either contributes to or doesn't contribute to the stigmatization of trans people?

Reading Guide for Doe v. Boeing Co.

1. For what conduct did Boeing fire its engineer Jane Doe, who was transgender? Why did it object to that conduct? Should that justification be considered sufficiently related to Doe's gender dysphoria that her firing should be judged "because of" her dysphoria?

2. To have a claim under Washington state law (contained in the Revised Code of Washington or RCW), Doe must have a "handicap" within the meaning of the statute. Where does the Supreme Court of Washington get a definition for that term? What two things does it require? Which, if either, does the court hold Doe satisfies?

3. What does the court say about the nature or breadth of Boeing's duty to accommodate Doe's gender dysphoria? Why does it conclude that Boeing's efforts were adequate? What did the court understand Boeing to be balancing in its treatment of Doe?

Jane Doe v. The Boeing Company

846 P.2d 531 (Wash. 1993) (en banc)

Opinion

GUY, Justice.

Jane Doe, a biological male who was planning to have sex reassignment surgery, sought damages for employment discrimination, alleging an unaccommodated handicap under RCW 49.60, Washington's Law Against Discrimination. She[1] was discharged by the Boeing Company for wearing "excessively" feminine attire in violation of company directives. The trial court ruled in favor of Boeing on the issue of liability. The Court of Appeals reversed and entered judgment for Doe. We granted Boeing's petition for review and reverse the Court of Appeals.

Facts

Jane Doe was hired as a Boeing engineer in 1978. At the time of hire, Doe was a biological male and presented herself as such on her application for employment. In 1984, after years of struggling with her sexual identity, Doe concluded that she was

---

1. Doe has completed sex reassignment surgery and will be referred to in this opinion with feminine pronouns.

a transsexual. . . . Dr. Timothy Smith, Doe's treating physician, confirmed Doe's self-assessment and diagnosed Doe as gender dysphoric. In April 1984, Doe began hormone treatments, as prescribed by Dr. Smith, as well as electrolysis treatments. In December 1984, Doe legally changed her masculine name to a feminine name.

In March 1985, Doe informed her supervisors, management and co-workers at Boeing of her transsexualism and of her intent to have sex reassignment surgery. Doe informed Boeing of her belief that in order to qualify for sex reassignment surgery, she would have to live full time, for 1 year, in the social role of a female. Doe based her belief on discussions with her treating psychologist and her physician about a treatment protocol for transsexuals known as the Harry Benjamin International Gender Dysphoria Standards ("Benjamin Standards"). Benjamin Standard 9 states: "Genital sex reassignment shall be preceded by a period of at least 12 months during which time the patient lived full-time in the social role of the genetically other sex."

[Boeing] informed Doe that while Doe was an anatomical male, she could not use the women's rest rooms or dress in "feminine" attire. Boeing informed Doe that she could dress as a woman at work and use the women's rest rooms upon completion of her sex reassignment surgery.

While Doe was an anatomical male, Boeing permitted Doe to wear either male clothing or unisex clothing. Unisex clothing included blouses, sweaters, slacks, flat shoes, nylon stockings, earrings, lipstick, foundation, and clear nail polish. Doe was instructed not to wear obviously feminine clothing such as dresses, skirts, or frilly blouses. Boeing applied its unwritten dress policy to all employees, which included 8 other transsexuals who had expressed a desire to have sex reassignment surgery while working for Boeing. Both Doe's psychologist and treating physician testified that what Doe was allowed to wear at Boeing was sufficiently feminine for Doe to qualify for sex reassignment surgery.

Between June and late September 1985, Boeing management received approximately a dozen anonymous complaints regarding Doe's attire and use of the women's rest rooms. On October 25, 1985, following the receipt of a complaint about Doe using the women's rest room, Boeing issued Doe a written disciplinary warning.[2] The warning reiterated Boeing's position on acceptable attire and rest room use and stated that Doe's failure to comply with Boeing's directives by November 1, 1985, would result in further corrective action, including termination. During this "grace" period, Doe's compliance with Boeing's "acceptable attire" directive was to be monitored each day by Doe's direct supervisor. Doe was told that her attire would be deemed unacceptable when, in the supervisor's opinion, her dress would be likely to cause a complaint were Doe to use a men's rest room at a Boeing facility.

---

2. After receiving the disciplinary warning, Doe limited her use of rest rooms to offsite women's rest rooms at lunchtime. The issue of rest room use does not alter our analysis since neither party contends this was a basis for her discharge.

No single article of clothing would be dispositive. Doe's overall appearance was to be assessed.

Doe's transsexualism did not interfere with her ability to perform her job duties as a software engineer at Boeing. There was no measurable decline in either her work group's performance or in Doe's own job performance. There was no testimony to indicate that Boeing's dress restrictions hindered Doe's professional development.

On November 4, 1985, the first day Doe worked after the grace period, Doe wore attire that her supervisor considered acceptable. Doe responded that she was disappointed that her attire was acceptable, and that she would "push it" the next day. By "push it", Doe testified that she meant she would wear more extreme feminine attire. The next day, Doe came to work wearing similar attire, but she included as part of her outfit a strand of pink pearls which she refused to remove. This outfit was similar to one she had been told during the grace period was unacceptable in that the addition of the pink pearls changed Doe's look from unisex to "excessively" feminine. Doe was subsequently terminated from her position at Boeing as a result of her willful violation of Boeing's directives.

Doe filed a handicap discrimination action against Boeing pursuant to RCW 49.60, Washington's Law Against Discrimination (hereafter "Act"). . . . The trial court held that Doe was "temporarily handicapped" under its construction of WAC 162-22-040. The trial court further concluded that Boeing's actions reasonably accommodated Doe's condition and, thus, ruled in favor of Boeing on liability.

On appeal, Doe challenged the trial court's determination that Boeing reasonably accommodated her gender dysphoria. Boeing cross-appealed the trial court's characterization of gender dysphoria as a handicap under RCW 49.60. Finding that Doe was handicapped and that Boeing failed to accommodate her condition, the Court of Appeals reversed the judgment, entered judgment for Doe on the issue of liability, and remanded the case for determination of Doe's damages and attorney fees on appeal. *Jane Doe v. Boeing Co.*, 823 P.2d 1159 (Wash. App. 1992). We reverse the Court of Appeals.

Issues

This case presents two issues for review. First, is Jane Doe's gender dysphoria a "handicap" under RCW 49.60.180? . . . .

Second, did Boeing have to provide Doe's preferred accommodation under RCW 49.60.180? . . . .

Analysis
I. Background

Washington's Law Against Discrimination provides that it is an unfair practice for any employer "[t]o discharge or bar any person from employment because of age, sex, marital status, race, creed, color, national origin, or the presence of any sensory, mental, or physical handicap." RCW 49.60.180(2). The statute does not define "handicap." The statute delegates the authority to the Washington State

Human Rights Commission . . . to adopt and promulgate rules and regulations to carry out the Act's provisions. Pursuant to this delegation, the Commission promulgated WAC 162-22-040, which defines handicap for the purpose of determining whether an unfair practice under RCW 49.60.180 has occurred. The regulation provides that:

> (a) A condition is a "sensory, mental, or physical handicap" if it is an abnormality and is a reason why the person having the condition did not get or keep the job in question . . . In other words, for enforcement purposes a person will be considered to be *handicapped* by a sensory, mental, or physical condition if he or she is *discriminated against because of the condition* and the condition is abnormal.
>
> (b) "The presence of a sensory, mental, or physical handicap" includes, but is not limited to, circumstances where a sensory, mental, or physical condition:
>
> > (i) Is medically cognizable or diagnosable;
> >
> > (ii) Exists as a record or history; or
> >
> > (iii) Is perceived to exist, whether or not it exists in fact.

WAC 162-22-040(1)(a), (b).

We adopted the Commission's definition of "handicap" in *Phillips v. Seattle*, 766 P.2d 1099 (Wash. 1989), which involved an unfair practice claim brought under RCW 49.60.180(2). We give the Commission's definition of "handicap" for unfair practice claims great weight since it is the construction of the statute by the administrative body whose duty it is to administer its terms.

Under WAC 162-22-040(1)(a), the question of whether a person is "handicapped" is a question of fact and not a question of law. As we stated in *Phillips*, the WAC definition requires both the "presence" of a handicapping condition and evidence that this condition was the reason for the discharge. The inquiry as to the "presence" of a handicapping condition under WAC 162-22-040(1)(b) is factual in nature because it depends upon expert medical testimony, relevant medical documentation, and state of mind. The question of whether a condition was the reason for a dismissal is also a factual inquiry because it depends upon documentation of the employer, testimony regarding the dismissal, and other relevant facts.

We acknowledge that the definition of "handicap" as defined by WAC 162-22-040 is problematic. The WAC definition requires a factual finding of discrimination because of the condition in order to determine whether the condition is a "handicap" in the first place. The trial court had difficulty applying the WAC definition[3]

---

3. The trial court read WAC 162-22-040 in the context of this case to define "handicap" as "an abnormality which has an effect on the individual's ability to perform his or her job such that the abnormality needs to be accommodated by the employer and that absent accommodation discrimination would result." Conclusion of Law 5.

and found that while Doe was "temporarily handicapped" by her gender dysphoria, she was reasonably accommodated by Boeing. Under the WAC definition, the trial court should have held that Doe was not "handicapped." The Court of Appeals also commented that the definition was problematic, but it rejected the trial court's narrow construction of the definition and declared gender dysphoria a "handicap" as a matter of law.

In upholding the Act to an earlier vagueness challenge, we pronounced that "[m]en of ordinary intelligence undoubtedly can understand what constitutes a 'handicap' within the context of RCW 49.60.180(1)." *Chicago, M., St. P., & Pac. R.R. v. State Human Rights Comm'n*, 557 P.2d 307 (Wash. 1976). Gender dysphoria is a medically cognizable and diagnosable condition. Those who suffer from the condition surely endure great mental and emotional agony. *See* Green, *Spelling "Relief" for Transsexuals: Employment Discrimination and the Criteria of Sex*, 4 Yale L. & Pol'y Rev. 125 (1985). However, unless a plaintiff can prove he or she was discriminated against because of the abnormal condition, his or her condition is not a "handicap" for purposes of the Act. WAC 162-22-040; *see also* Miller, *Hiring the Handicapped: An Analysis of Laws Prohibiting Discrimination Against the Handicapped in Employment*, 16 Gonz. L. Rev. 23, 31 (1980).

Despite the circular nature of the applicable regulation, we follow our holding in *Phillips* that the definition of "handicap" for enforcement purposes under RCW 49.60.180, as defined in WAC 162-22-040, requires factual findings of both (1) the presence of an abnormal condition, and (2) employer discrimination against the employee plaintiff because of that condition. One is not "handicapped" for purposes of enforcing an unfair practice claim unless both elements are satisfied.

II. Gender Dysphoria as a Handicap

We first address the question of whether Doe's gender dysphoria is a handicap under the Act. We conclude that Doe is not "handicapped" for the purposes of pursuing an unfair practice claim under RCW 49.60.180.

The first inquiry under the WAC definition is whether there is present an abnormal condition. It is uncontested that gender dysphoria is an abnormal, medically cognizable condition with a prescribed course of treatment. Assuming the presence of an abnormal condition, the next inquiry is whether the employer discriminated against the employee because of that condition. Under RCW 49.60, a finding of liability is dependent upon proof of discrimination. *See Dean v. Metropolitan Seattle*, 708 P.2d 393 (Wash. 1985) (en banc). In general, the nature of this inquiry is whether the employer took action against an employee because of the employee's condition, such as discharge, reassignment, or harassment, or whether the employer failed to take such steps as would be reasonably necessary to accommodate the employee's condition.[4] Failure to reasonably accommodate a "handicapped" employee consti-

---

4. Types of accommodations might be, for example, the construction of ramps to accommodate wheelchairs, installation of air filtering devices to accommodate respiratory ailments, permitting

tutes discrimination under the Act. *Dean*; *see also Holland v. Boeing Co.*, 583 P.2d 621 (Wash. 1978).

Boeing argues that Doe's condition of gender dysphoria is not a "handicap" under the Act because there is no evidence of discrimination. We agree. The record substantially supports the trial court's findings that Boeing did not discriminate against Doe because of her condition. Boeing discharged Doe because she violated Boeing's directives on acceptable attire, not because she was gender dysphoric. Doe was treated in a respectful way by both her peers and supervisors at Boeing. Doe's supervisor consistently rated her work as satisfactory on her performance evaluations. While complaints were filed with Boeing management about Doe's use of the women's rest room, the record is void of any evidence that Doe suffered harassment because of her use of the rest room or because of her attire.

Inasmuch as Boeing did not discharge Doe based on her abnormal condition but on her refusal to conform with directives on acceptable attire, we must turn our attention to whether Boeing discriminated against Doe by failing to reasonably accommodate her condition of gender dysphoria.

III. Scope of Duty to Accommodate

The Legislature intended the Act to prohibit discrimination in employment against individuals who suffer an abnormal physical, mental, or sensory "handicap." Laws of 1973, 1st Ex. Sess., ch. 214, § 1, p. 1648; *see generally* RCW 49.60.010, .030(1)(a). We recognize that employers have an affirmative obligation to reasonably accommodate the sensory, mental, or physical limitations of such employees unless the employer can demonstrate that the accommodation would impose an undue hardship on the conduct of the employer's business. WAC 162-22-080; *Dean*. The issue before us is whether Boeing had a duty to accommodate Doe's preferred manner of dress prior to her sex reassignment surgery. We hold that the scope of an employer's duty to accommodate an employee's condition is limited to those steps reasonably necessary to enable the employee to perform his or her job. *See generally* RCW 49.60.180(1); WAC 162-22-050(3); *Clarke v. Shoreline Sch. Dist. 412*, 720 P.2d 793 (Wash. 1986) (en banc).

Doe contends that Boeing's dress code failed to accommodate her condition and, thus, was discriminatory. We disagree. The record substantially supports the trial court's findings that Boeing reasonably accommodated Doe in the matter of dress by allowing her to wear unisex clothing at work. Despite this accommodation, Doe determined unilaterally, and without medical confirmation, that she needed to dress as a woman at her place of employment in order to qualify for sex reassignment surgery. Our review of the record is limited to determining whether substantial evidence exists to support the trial court's findings of fact. *Fred Hutchinson*

---

rest periods to accommodate a physical condition, changes to a work station to accommodate the medical needs of an employee, enhanced lighting or enhanced audio equipment. See also footnote 5.

Cancer Research Ctr. v. Holman, 732 P.2d 974 (Wash. 1987) (en banc). We find substantial support for the trial court's finding that Doe had no medical need to dress as a woman at work in order to qualify for her surgery.

> [P]laintiff's experts declined to state that any particular degree of feminine dress was required in order for plaintiff to fulfill any presurgical requirements. In fact, the evidence was uncontradicted that the unisex dress permitted by Boeing . . . would not have precluded plaintiff from meeting the Benjamin Standards presurgical requirement of living in the social role of a woman.

Finding of Fact 39. The trial court's findings are well supported by the testimony of Doe's own treating physician and psychologist, as well as other medical evidence. We treat findings of fact which are supported by substantial evidence as verities on appeal. *Beeson v. ARCO*, 563 P.2d 822 (Wash. 1977) (en banc). The Court of Appeals' contrary finding that Doe had a "medically documented need" to dress as a woman is error. "[A]n appellate court will not substitute its judgment for that of the trial court even though it might have resolved the factual dispute differently." *Beeson*.

Doe argues, however, that the trial court's findings on this point are irrelevant since Boeing did not have the benefit of such medical testimony prior to enforcing its dress policy. We disagree. The trial court found that Boeing's policy on accommodation of transsexuals was developed with input from Boeing's legal, medical, personnel and labor relations departments. The Boeing medical department consulted with outside experts in the field and reviewed the literature on transsexualism. The trial court also held that Boeing has a legitimate business purpose in defining what is acceptable attire and in balancing the needs of its work force as a whole with those of Doe. The record supports the trial court's findings of fact and conclusions of law that Boeing developed and reasonably enforced a dress policy which balanced its legitimate business needs with those of its employees.

Doe further argues that, as a gender dysphoric, her perceived needs should have been accommodated. We disagree. The Act does not require an employer to offer the employee the precise accommodation he or she requests. *Barron v. Safeway Stores, Inc.*, 704 F. Supp. 1555 (E.D. Wash. 1988). Her perceived need to dress more completely as a woman did not impact her job performance. Both the trial court and the Court of Appeals found that Doe's condition had no measurable effect on either Doe's job performance or her work group's performance. That is not to say that Doe did not have emotional turmoil over the changes that were taking place in her life, but that turmoil did not prevent her from performing her work satisfactorily. Based on the record, there was no need for any further action by Boeing to facilitate Doe in the performance of job-related tasks.

Doe also argues that Boeing failed to accommodate her unique condition because its dress policy was uniformly applied. The Court of Appeals agreed, stating that "identical treatment may be the source of discrimination in the case of a handicapped employee, while different treatment, necessary to accommodate a handicap, can eliminate discrimination." *Doe* (citing *Holland v. Boeing Co.*). We stated in *Holland*, however, that identical treatment *may be* a source of discrimination "*only when the work environment fails to take into account the unique characteristics of the handicapped person*." (Some italics ours.) While Boeing's dress code was uniformly applied, such generically-applied work rules are not discriminatory per se unless they affect an employee's ability to perform his or her job. In Doe's case, "different" treatment was not required to accommodate her condition because her condition did not affect her ability to perform her job.

In determining what is a reasonable accommodation, the evaluation must begin with the job specifications and how those tasks are impacted by the abnormal condition. *See Kimbro v. Atlantic Richfield Co.*, 889 F.2d 869 (9th Cir. 1989). In the case of trauma or physical deterioration, the answers are generally apparent and the issue becomes one of whether the accommodation is reasonable,[5] not what is the accommodation. In Doe's case, the analysis is not so simple. Doe's job performance was unchanged by reason of her condition. Based on the record, there was no accommodation that Boeing could have provided that would have aided Doe in the performance of her work. How she dressed or appeared had no impact on the physical or mental requirements of her employment responsibilities.

The concept of "reasonable" accommodation is linked to necessity. The employer's duty to accommodate is appropriately limited to removing sensory, mental or physical impediments to the employee's ability to perform his or her job. Doe's gender dysphoria did not impede her ability to perform her engineering duties. Therefore, Boeing had no duty to provide any further accommodation to Doe beyond what it provided for all employees.

Conclusion

The definition of "handicap" for enforcement purposes under RCW 49.60.180, as defined in WAC 162-22-040, requires factual findings of both (1) the presence of an abnormal condition, and (2) employer discrimination against the employee plaintiff because of that condition. We hold that under this definition Doe was not "handicapped" for purposes of RCW 49.60.180 because Boeing did not discriminate against her because of her condition. We further conclude that Boeing's actions were reasonable, and that no affirmative accommodation of Doe's condition was required because the scope of an employer's duty to accommodate an employee's

---

5. *See Dean* (employer could have accommodated an employee suffering from degenerative eye disease by informing him of job openings for which he might be qualified); *Holland* (employer could have accommodated an employee with cerebral palsy by transferring him from a position in which employee was unable to perform acceptably to a position in which he could perform); *Kimbro* (employer could have accommodated employee suffering from cluster migraines by offering him a leave of absence). It is a question of fact as to whether a particular accommodation is reasonable. *Phillips.*

condition is limited to those steps reasonably necessary to enable the employee to perform his or her job.

[The] Court of Appeals is reversed.

Andersen, C.J., Durham, Acting C.J., Utter, Brachtenbach, Smith and Johnson, JJ., concur.

———————

Discussion

1. What kind of interest does an employer such as Boeing have in the attire of its employees? In the appellate decision overruled by the state supreme court, the Court of Appeals of Washington had opined: "While the trial court held that Boeing had a legitimate business purpose in regulating the dress of its employees, there is nothing in the record or case law to suggest that Boeing's legitimate business concerns should extend beyond assuring the professionalism of an employee's dress. Boeing concedes that Doe's dress was at all times professional."

2. Presumably to present herself as a model employee asking for little from the courts other than the chance to live and work consistently with her gender identity, Ms. Doe through her lawyers emphasized that her transition did not impair her performance. Yet the court insists that the only accommodations employers must make are reasonable ones necessary to overcome an impairment to a person's work performance caused by her disability. Does that treatment of the duty of reasonable accommodation pose a Catch-22 for Doe?

Reading Guide for Dobre v. National Railroad Passenger Corp.

1. The court in *Dobre* rejects the transgender plaintiff's contention that she has a "mental impairment" within the meaning of Pennsylvania disability law. When the American Psychiatric Association recognized "transsexualism" as a mental disorder, what are the court's arguments for finding it insufficient for the state's statute?

2. Dobre also argued that she was discriminated against on the basis of a perceived handicap. For what reason does the court reject her argument?

Andria Adams Dobre v. National Railroad Passenger Corp. ("Amtrak")

850 F. Supp. 284 (E.D. Pa. 1993)

Memorandum and Order

HUTTON, District Judge.

. . . .

I. Factual Background

[Plaintiff Andria Adams] Dobre, a transsexual, was employed by [the defendant National Railroad Passenger Corporation ("AMTRAK")] from May, 1989, until March 28, 1990. When she[6] was hired by AMTRAK, Dobre presented herself as a man. After several months, she informed her supervisors that she was receiving hormone injections in order to begin the process of becoming female. However, she does not aver that she actually underwent sex-reassignment surgery during the period that she was employed by AMTRAK. Rather, plaintiff asserts that she was discriminated against because of her new gender while in the process of transforming her body to conform with her psychological sexual identity.

Dobre contends that after she informed her supervisors of the hormone treatments she was discriminated against in the following respects, among others: (1) she was told that a doctor's note was required in order to dress as a female; (2) she was required to dress as a male; (3) she was not permitted to use the women's restroom; (4) the plaintiff's supervisors referred to her by her male name; and (5) her desk was moved out of the view of the public. On June 30, 1993, she filed a complaint alleging in Count I that AMTRAK's actions constitute sex-based discrimination under Title VII of the Civil Rights Act of 1964, 42 U.S.C. § 2000e-2, and, in counts II and III respectively, that its actions constitute sex-based discrimination and handicap discrimination in violation of the Pennsylvania Human Relations Act ("PHRA"), 43 Pa. Cons. Stat. Ann. § 955(a). AMTRAK moves to dismiss the plaintiff's complaint.

II. Discussion

A. Standard

. . . . Defendant has moved to dismiss the complaint pursuant to Federal Rule of Civil Procedure 12(b)(6). When considering a motion to dismiss, this Court shall take all allegations contained in the complaint as true and construe them in the light most favorable to the plaintiff. The complaint shall only be dismissed if "'it is clear that no relief could be granted under any set of facts that could be proved consistent with the allegations.'"

---

6. Because the plaintiff refers to herself as a female in her written submissions, the Court will refer to her as "she" or "her" throughout this opinion.

B. Applying the Standard to Count I: The Title VII Claim

[Here the court follows cases including *Ulane v. Eastern Airlines, Inc.*, 742 F.2d 1081 (7th Cir. 1984); *Sommers v. Budget Marketing, Inc.*, 667 F.2d 748 (8th Cir. 1982), *see* Chapter 5, Section A, *supra*; and *Grossman v. Bernards Township Bd. of Educ.*, No. 74-1904, 1975 WL 302 (D.N.J. Sept. 10, 1975), *aff'd mem.*, 538 F.2d 319 (3d Cir. 1976), in holding that Title VII's ban on sex discrimination does not reach "discrimination based upon transsexualism" or "an employer from discriminating against a male because he wants to become a female."

[The court allows that "if AMTRAK considered Dobre to be female and discriminated against her on that basis (*i.e.*, treated her less favorably than male employees), then Dobre would be able to maintain a Title VII action as a female." Nonetheless, it concluded that "even when viewed in the most favorable light, the allegations in the complaint do not support a claim that the plaintiff was discriminated against as a female."]

C. Count II: Sex-Based Discrimination Under the PHRA

[Here the court followed another U.S. District Court for the Eastern District of Pennsylvania decision in rejecting the conclusion that Pennsylvania's provision forbidding sex discrimination in employment would reach "discrimination on the basis of transsexualism."]

D. Count III: Handicap Discrimination Under the PHRA

Section 5(a) [of the PHRA] also prohibits discrimination on the basis of an individual's non-job related handicap or disability. 43 PA. CONS. STAT. ANN. §955(a) (Purdon 1991 & Supp. 1993). A "non-job related handicap" is "a handicap or disability which does not substantially interfere with the ability to perform the essential functions of the employment which a handicapped person applies for, is engaged in, or has been engaged in." 16 PA. CODE §44.4 (1992). A "handicapped or disabled person" is one who has "a physical or mental impairment which substantially limits one or more major life activities; a record of an impairment; or who is regarded as having an impairment." *Id.* §44(i). The plaintiff argues that she has stated a claim in that her transsexualism constitutes a physical or mental impairment which substantially limits a major life activity. Alternatively, she argues that she is perceived as having such an impairment.

1. Transsexualism as a Physical or Mental Impairment

A "physical or mental impairment" means, inter alia, "a physiological disorder or condition . . . or a mental or psychological disorder, such as mental illness, and specific learning disabilities." *Id.* §44.4(ii)(A). [There] are no cases decided under the PHRA to support [Plaintiff's] position that transsexualism is a physical or mental impairment. Nevertheless, she argues that transsexualism is recognized as a disorder by the American Psychiatric Association.[7] Moreover, she argues that Pennsylva-

---

7. A transsexual is a person who has a sense of discomfort and inappropriateness about his or her anatomical sex and wishes to be rid of his or her genitals and live as a member of the opposite

nia's regulations are modeled after the regulations promulgated under the federal Rehabilitation Act, 29 U.S.C. § 701 *et seq.*, and caselaw under the Rehabilitation Act supports the conclusion that transsexualism is a "physical or mental impairment" under the Rehabilitation Act. *Id.* § 44.4 comment (noting that Pennsylvania's regulations are adopted verbatim from United States Dep't of H.E.W.'s section 504 regulations); *see also Blackwell v. U.S. Dep't of Treasury*, 639 F. Supp. 289 (D.D.C. 1986) (transvestitism is a protected handicap under Rehabilitation Act); *Doe v. United States Postal Serv.*, 37 Fair Empl. Prac. Cas. (BNA) 1867 (D.D.C. 1985) (transsexualism is a protected handicap under Rehabilitation Act).

[Not] every diagnosable disorder constitutes an "impairment" under § 44.4. *See, e.g.*, *School Dist. of Philadelphia v. Freidman*, 507 A.2d 882 (Pa. Commw. Ct. 1986) (holding that plaintiff's "neurotic compulsion for lateness" did not constitute a mental impairment under § 44.4). . . .

[In PHRA cases] Pennsylvania's courts have looked to cases decided under analogous statutory schemes in other states as persuasive authority. In *Sommers v. Iowa Civil Rights Comm'n*, 337 N.W.2d 470 (Iowa 1983), Iowa's Supreme Court rejected a claim that transsexualism was a "physical or mental impairment" under a regulatory framework modeled after the Rehabilitation Act and, therefore, identical to that employed in Pennsylvania. First, the court rejected the plaintiff's contention that transsexualism constituted a physical impairment. As to the plaintiff's claim that transsexualism constitutes a "mental impairment," the court concluded that transsexualism lacks the inherent propensity to limit major life activities of the specific enumerated examples of mental impairments in the regulation. Accordingly, the court held that the legislature did not intend to include transsexualism as a protected handicap.

As in *Sommers*, the plaintiff did not allege in the complaint that she suffers from any organic disorder of the body. Thus, she is not physically impaired. Further, the principle of ejusdem generis relied upon by the Court in Sommers applies with equal force under the PHRA. *See* 1 Pa. Cons. Stat. Ann. § 1903(b) (Purdon Supp. 1993) ("General words shall be construed to take their meanings from preceding words.").

In defining "mental impairment," the regulations specifically include such disorders as "mental or psychological disorder, such as mental illness, and specific learning disabilities." These disorders, unlike transsexualism, are inherently prone to limit major life activities. Indeed, the plaintiff avers in her complaint that her transsexualism "in no way interfered with [her] ability to perform her functions as an employee for AMTRAK." That transsexualism is distinguishable from the specifically enumerated mental impairments in § 44.4 in terms of its inherent effect on

---

sex. American Psychiatric Ass'n, Diagnostic and Statistical Manual of Mental Disorders § 302.50 (3d ed. rev. 1987). Transsexualism is also known as gender dysphoria. *See Doe v. Boeing Co.*, 846 P.2d 531 (Wash. 1993).

major life activities weighs heavily in favor of concluding that the legislature did not intend to include transsexualism to as a protected handicap.

Moreover, the express language of the Rehabilitation Act undercuts the plaintiff's claim. The plaintiff's reliance on *Doe* and *Blackwell*, which were decided under the Rehabilitation Act, overlooks the recent amendment to the Act, which unambiguously excludes transsexualism from the definition of the phrase "individual with a disability." Pub. L. 102-569 (1992) (codified at 29 U.S.C. § 706(8)(F)(i)). As the defendant correctly recognizes, this amendment did not effectuate a substantive change in the law, but rather, merely "clarifie[d] the original intent of Congress as to the parameters of the definition of disabled individual under [the Rehabilitation Act]." *Winston v. Maine Technical College Sys.*, 631 A.2d 70 (Maine 1993). Thus, Pub. L. 102-569 reveals that *Doe* and *Blackwell* were contrary to Congress' intent. For the foregoing reasons, the Court holds that the plaintiff has failed to state a claim upon which relief may be granted under the PHRA.

2. Transsexualism as a Perceived Handicap

The plaintiff's final argument is that she has stated a claim under the PHRA because she was regarded as having an impairment by AMTRAK. 16 Pa. Code § 44.4(i)(C) (1992). The phrase "is regarded as having an impairment" means that an individual

> has a physical or mental impairment that does not substantially limit major life activities but that is treated by an employer . . . as constituting a limitation; has a physical or mental impairment that substantially limits major life activities only as a result of the attitudes of others toward the impairment; or has none of the impairments defined in subparagraph (i)(A) but is treated by an employer . . . as having an impairment.

Id. § 44.4(ii)(D). The plaintiff's position is that she was "regarded as having an impairment" under the third prong of the definition in § 44.4(ii)(D), the so-called "perceived impairment" prong. More specifically, relying upon *Civil Service Comm'n v. Pennsylvania Human Relations Comm'n*, 556 A.2d 933 (Pa. Commw. Ct. 1989), the plaintiff asserts that she can state a claim under the "perceived impairment" prong even if her transsexualism does not constitute an actual physical or mental impairment under the PHRA and accompanying regulations.

The plaintiff's argument overlooks the fact that the Pennsylvania Supreme Court reversed the Commonwealth Court's decision in *Civil Service Comm'n* on this very issue. *Civil Service Comm'n v. Pennsylvania Human Relations Comm'n*, 591 A.2d 281, 284 (Pa. 1991). [In] *Civil Service Comm'n*, the Pennsylvania Supreme Court drastically narrowed the scope of the PHRA by interpreting the third prong of § 44.4(ii)(D) to require proof an actual impairment. The court's reasoning applies with equal force to claims based upon a mental impairment.

Whether the Pennsylvania Supreme Court's holding in *Civil Service Comm'n* comports with the intent of Pennsylvania's General Assembly is not for the Court to decide. The Court is bound to follow the instructions of Pennsylvania's Supreme

Court as to its interpretation of Pennsylvania law. Accordingly, having concluded that transsexualism is not an actual "physical or mental impairment" under §44.4, the Court must also conclude that the plaintiff cannot state a claim based upon §44.4(ii)(D).

An appropriate Order follows.

Final Judgment

AND NOW, this 30th day of November, 1993, upon consideration of the Defendant National Railroad Passenger Corporation's Motion to Dismiss pursuant to Fed. R. Civ. P. 12(b)(6), IT IS HEREBY ORDERED that the Defendant's Motion is GRANTED.

IT IS FURTHER ORDERED that:

   (1) the Plaintiff's Complaint is DISMISSED; and

   (2) the Defendant's Motion to Strike Certain Demands is DENIED as moot.

———————

Discussion

1. Note that the Pennsylvania Supreme Court's decision in *Civil Service Commission* means that in order for a plaintiff to prevail upon the ground of perceived disability discrimination, which is separate from the ground of actual disability discrimination, she must first establish that in fact she has a disability. Does that make sense as an interpretation of Pennsylvania law? Why might the state supreme court or the administrative commission to whose regulation it deferred have thought it important to limit the "perceived handicap" prong of the law?

2. Why should the presence of express exceptions in federal disability discrimination laws support interpreting Pennsylvania disability law as also excluding gender identity disorders? The *Dobre* court is correct that the Supreme Judicial Court of Maine had stated that "Section 706(8)(F) [amending the federal Rehabilitation Act to exclude "transsexualism" as a disability] . . . clarifies the original intent of Congress as to the parameters of the definition of a disabled individual under federal law." *Winston v. Maine Tech. Coll. Sys.*, 631 A.2d 70 (Me. 1993). *Winston* did *not*, however, further state that "this amendment did not effectuate a substantive change in the law," as *Dobre* says.

Moreover, *Winston*'s statement about the amendment's clarifying Congress's intent was accompanied by no citation to any authority whatsoever. One might be skeptical that Congress's intent in 1992 is necessarily an accurate reflection of the intent of the Congress that enacted the Rehabilitation Act in 1973, nearly two decades and 10 House elections earlier. A more natural inference from the text of the 1992 amendment might be that Congress then recognized that the extant statutory definition of "disability" in the Rehabilitation Act by its terms did apply to gender identity disorders ("transsexualism"), as the cases *Dobre* cites had held, and wished to change this coverage.

3. How does the *Dobre* court's discussion of the transgender plaintiff's contention that she had an "impairment" within the meaning of Pennsylvania law improve or contribute to the stigmatization of trans people? Does its treatment of the plaintiff's perceived handicap claim have any likely effect on such stigmatization?

Note on Conway v. City of Hartford

In *Conway v. City of Hartford*, No. CV95 0553003, 1997 WL 78585, 1997 Conn. Super. LEXIS 282 (Feb. 4, 1997), the Superior Court of Connecticut considered defendant City of Hartford, Connecticut's motion to strike the complaint and hence the discrimination suit by former employee Trevor Conway. Conway, a transgender man who had started working for the city before his transition, contended inter alia that he was fired because of his "transsexualism, or gender dysphoria," in violation of the bans in the Connecticut Fair Employment Practices Act ("CFEPA") on discrimination on the basis of a present or past history of mental disorder or physical disability.

The court here agreed to strike Conway's claims that he was discriminated against based on a physical disability. *Conway* found persuasive the arguments of *Sommers v. Iowa Civil Rights Commission*, 337 N.W.2d 470 (Iowa 1983), and *Dobre v. National R.R. Passenger Corp. (AMTRAK)*, 850 F. Supp. 284 (E.D. Pa. 1993), two decisions where courts held "transsexualism" not to be a physical disability for purposes of other states' disability discrimination statutes—even though the court recognized that Connecticut's statute used a different definition of "physical disability." The court also considered it "highly persuasive that the Rehabilitation Act of 1973 and the ADA explicitly exclude transsexualism as a physical disability." *Conway* did not explain why the lack of such explicit exclusion in CFEPA did not instead more strongly support the plaintiff. The third factor the court summarized to support its holding was that Conway failed "to plead sufficient facts to demonstrate that his condition falls within the Connecticut definition of physical disability." Thus, the court's ultimate holding on this point—"that the plaintiff's condition *as pleaded* could not be found to be a physical disability under Connecticut law" (emphasis added)—may be a fact- or lawyering-specific ruling rather than a broad pronouncement that gender dysphoria is never a physical disability under CFEPA.

In contrast to *Sommers* and *Dobre*, however, *Conway* rejected the city's argument that gender dysphoria is not a "mental disorder" within the meaning of CFEPA. Although CFEPA does not define "mental disorder," a different Connecticut law defining "[p]ersons with a mental illness" extended to people with mental disorders "as defined in the most recent edition of the American Psychiatric Association's *Diagnostic and Statistical Manual of Mental Disorders*" (DSM). *Conway* also relied on the facts that the DSM included gender dysphoria and that the U.S. Supreme Court had relied on the DSM as characterizing "a transsexual" as having "a rare psychiatric disorder." Accordingly, the court denied the motion to dismiss the counts of the complaint that relied on the city's having allegedly discriminated against Conway based on his having a (pre-transition) history of mental disorder. (The court did strike the elements of the complaint alleging sex discrimination "[g]iven the weight of outside authority holding that Title VII and similar state statutes do not prohibit discrimination against transsexuals and the absence of any Connecticut legislative intent to cover discrimination against transsexuals." Should that holding be revisited in light of the U.S. Supreme Court's decision in *Bostock v. Clayton County, Georgia*, 140 S. Ct. 1731 (2020), Chapter 5, Section D, *supra*, holding that discrimination based upon someone's transgender status is necessarily discrimination because of sex within the meaning of Title VII?)

Ultimately, however, Conway's lawsuit was dismissed for the plaintiff's repeated, intentional failure to comply with discovery orders, and the Appellate Court of Connecticut affirmed the dismissal. *Conway v. City of Hartford*, 760 A.2d 974 (Conn. Ct. App. 2000).

Note on Holt v. Northwest Pennsylvania Training Partnership Consortium

In *Holt v. Northwest Pennsylvania Training Partnership Consortium*, 694 A.2d 1134 (Pa. Commw. Ct. 1997), the Commonwealth Court of Pennsylvania by 6–1 vote affirmed the trial court's dismissal of transgender woman Kristine Holt's employment discrimination suit against her former employer, the Northwest Pennsylvania Training Partnership Consortium ("NPTPC") and other allegedly responsible parties. Holt had been hired by the NPTPC, "a social service agency administering publicly assisted job training to economically disadvantaged persons in a five-county area in Northwest Pennsylvania," in 1989 when she was still presenting as male. "Holt was assigned to the Venango Area Job Center in Oil City, Pennsylvania." Her "duties included conducting assessment interviews with potential participants to determine if they met eligibility requirements. The pool of potential participants for which Holt was responsible included inmates at the Venango County Jail."

In July 1992 Holt informed her supervisor that she was diagnosed as transsexual and would be transitioning, including presenting full-time as a woman. "Although NPTPC initially accepted Holt's transition, and directed its staff to treat Holt 'professionally, and with respect,' in September 1992, it informed Holt that he [*sic*] would be disciplined for violations of employer policy if he dressed as a woman." The next month she legally changed her name to Kristine, and the following month started dressing as a woman. A few weeks thereafter, "the Job Center manager ousted Holt from the workplace, whereupon Holt was then reassigned to NPTPC's main office. However, in December of 1992, Holt was dismissed for allegedly violating employer policy regarding the dress code after she began dressing in a unisex fashion at work. NPTPC was also advised by the warden at the Venango County Jail, Warden Britton, that because of safety concerns, Holt would no longer be permitted to enter the jail to conduct assessment interviews either as a male or a female." Holt sued, and the trial court granted the defendant's motion to dismiss the complaint on various grounds.

Some counts of her complaint alleged that the defendants had discriminated against her "based on a non-job-related handicap or disability in violation of Section 5(a) and (b)(5) of the Pennsylvania Human Relations Act (PHRA)," 43 P.S. § 955(a) and (b)(5). The trial court dismissed those counts because "transsexualism does not constitute a disability under the PHRA." The appellate court affirmed the dismissal. It observed that the Pennsylvania Supreme Court had ruled that for a handicap to count as a disability within the meaning of the PHRA on the ground that it was regarded as "a physical or mental impairment which substantially limits one or more major life activities," a plaintiff must establish that in fact they have such an impairment. But it then somewhat cursorily reasoned that this interpretation of the statute was correct "based upon the holding[]" of *Dobre v. National Railroad Passenger Corporation* (*"Amtrak"*), 850 F. Supp. 284 (E.D. Pa. 1993), *supra* at p. 974, which it took to hold in "a well reasoned and instructive opinion" that "transsexualism is not a physical or mental impairment [and] that a transsexual can [not] be regarded as having such an impairment."

Reading Guide for Smith v. City of Jacksonville Correctional Institution

1. In contrast to the preceding decisions in this section, some courts and administrative bodies have found disability discrimination laws to protect workers against anti-trans discrimination. *Smith v. City of Jacksonville Correctional Institution* is one such case. It was precipitated when a city fired a transitioning prison guard. For what reason or reasons did the city fire the plaintiff Smith?

2. The court appears to hold both that Smith has an actual handicap within the meaning of the Florida statute banning handicap discrimination in employment, and that she was also covered by the statute because she was perceived as having a handicap. What does the court require she prove to establish a prima facie case against her employer, defendant City of Jacksonville Correctional Institution ("the City")? What is the likely reasoning behind Florida courts treating proof of those things as raising the inference that the plaintiff's rights under the statute were violated?

3. To prove that she has a "handicap" within the meaning of the Florida statute, what does the court require Smith to show? On what "major life activities"—a phrase commonly used in federal and state disability discrimination laws, *cf. Sommers v. Iowa Civil Rights Commission*, *supra* at p. 963 does the court rely?

4. For what reasons does the court rejects the City's defense that *not* being transgender (today, one might say "being cisgender") is a bona fide occupational qualification ("BFOQ") for the position from which it terminated Smith?

Belinda Joelle Smith v. City of Jacksonville Correctional Institution, et al.

No. 88-5451, 1991 WL 833882 (Fla. Div. Admin. Hrgs. Oct. 2, 1991)
(Order Amending Recommended Order, Oct. 15, 1991)

. . . .

Statement of the Issues

The issue in this case is whether the Petitioner has been subjected to unlawful employment discrimination in violation of Chapter 760, Florida Statutes.

Preliminary Statement

... Petitioner, Belinda Joelle Smith ... filed a charge of discrimination based on sex and handicap against Respondent, City of Jacksonville/Jacksonville Correctional Institution, et al. [The] Florida Commission on Human Relations filed a determination of "No Cause/No Jurisdiction as to Sex" on Smith's charges of discrimination. ... Ms. Smith filed a Petition for Relief which was forwarded to the Division of Administrative Hearings.

. . . .

Petitioner and Respondent filed Proposed Recommended Orders. ... The parties Proposed Findings of Fact have been considered and utilized in the preparation of this Recommended Order, except where such proposals were not shown by the evidence, or were immaterial, irrelevant, cumulative or subordinate. ...

Findings of Fact [numbering omitted]

From 1972–1985, Petitioner was employed by the City of Jacksonville at the Jacksonville Correctional Institution. ... The facility housed approximately 300 male and 100 female inmates. ... During the entire time, Petitioner was employed at the Institution, Petitioner functioned as a male. ...[8]

The majority of people in this world are of the opinion that humankind is divided into males and females. That viewpoint is incorrect. Put simply, there is a certain percentage of humankind that are a mixture of male and female characteristics.

Sometimes the mixture consists of physical characteristics and sometimes the mixture consists of opposing physical, *i.e.* sexual, characteristics and mental, *i.e.* gender, characteristics. Transsexuality is the term of common parlance for the condition known to mental health professionals as gender dysphoria. Transsexuals essentially believe themselves to be opposite in gender to their anatomic characteristics and to have been born in the wrong body. Gender dysphoria is a persistent sense of discomfort and inappropriateness about one's anatomic sex accompanied by a persistent wish to be rid of one's genitals and to live as a member of the other sex.

---

8. In September, 1990, Smith underwent a gender change operation. After the operation, Smith was judicially determined to be a female. Therefore, Smith will be referred to in the feminine gender, even though at all times prior to September, 1990, Smith was a male.

. . . . Transsexualism is quite literally having the physical form of one sex and the mental form of the opposite sex.

Little is understood of how such halflings [*sic*] result. This lack of insight into the phenomena is in part due to psychology's very poor understanding of how personality and self-concepts are developed in human beings and how those traits interact with sexual orientation or sexual preference. However, it can be deduced that transsexualism is a result of a very fundamental or combination of fundamental physical and mental attributes. The desire of the transsexual to live and be recognized as the opposite sex begins at a young age. The desire is nonvolitional. The person so afflicted will progressively take steps to live in the opposite sex role on a full-time basis, often resulting in hormonal treatment and surgery to make the anatomy fit the mental form. The unaltered transsexual is a tormented person, beset with fundamental conflict and persistent rejection of self. Depending on the symptoms, transsexualism can result in a handicap. . . .

Ms. Smith first began to realize that she was a transsexual when she was around four years old. . . . In growing up, she. . . . cross-dressed in female clothes when home alone. All during her youth she experienced considerable personal confusion.

Around age eleven, she read a magazine article about transsexuality and discovered that there was a scientific basis for the feelings she was experiencing as a male child. The article discussed surgical gender reassignment. At that time, Petitioner realized that gender reassignment was what she needed and wanted. She dressed in her sister's clothes and went to her mother to explain her new awareness. When she approached her parents about what she had discovered about herself, the reaction was one of moral indignation and she was told never to talk about it again. . . . Thereafter, she kept her transsexualism hidden to the best of her ability. However, the struggle to unify the physical and mental aspects of her character was tremendous. Additionally, the struggle to maintain the outward appearance of a normal male was tremendous.

Upon discharge of Smith's father from the Navy, the family settled in Liberal, Missouri, a rural farm community. Petitioner attended high school in Liberal, graduating in 1966. While in high school, she felt guilty about her transsexual feelings and attempted to deny them by excelling at traditionally male endeavors. She competed actively in sports, lettering in basketball, baseball, and track. She felt constantly conflicted.

Petitioner began to date a girl while in high school. Petitioner told the girl of Petitioner's transsexuality, and she permitted Petitioner to cross-dress with her. Upon graduation, they married. However, the marriage lasted less than a year. Smith could function sexually only as long as she imagined herself as female and her partner as male. Petitioner's transsexuality was the reason for the breakup of the marriage.

. . . . While in the Navy, Smith consulted a Navy psychiatrist about her transsexuality. The psychiatrist diagnosed her as transsexual and explained that she might eventually have to get sexual reassignment to achieve any real sense of adjustment.

Smith was retained by the Navy despite the psychiatrist's diagnosis because she was not homosexual. Smith accordingly served out her full enlistment in the Navy and in 1970 or 1971 was honorably discharged.

. . . . In 1972, Petitioner began working for the correctional authority in Jacksonville. . . . She began with the City as an entry level corrections officer. . . .

Correctional officers are considered law enforcement personnel. Such law enforcement personnel work as part of a pari-military [*sic*] organization in which discipline, respect and cooperation are extremely important. Correctional officers are correctional officers twenty-four hours a day. They are accountable for their behavior during duty hours because poor behavior reflects on the individual officer and the officer's employment. However, there are some very real distinctions between law enforcement police officers and law enforcement correctional officers in their respective codes of ethics and the standards to which they are held when engaged in private conduct. One such distinction is that police officers have a higher standard of conduct in their private lives than correctional officers.

During the time relevant to Petitioner's complaint as well as currently, correctional officers wore unisex uniforms. Male and female officers had common restroom facilities. Both male and female officers patrolled all parts of the institution, including inmate bathing areas. Both male and female officers had direct contact with male and female prisoners.

Petitioner advanced rapidly. [Over the years she received numerous promotions, some over candidates with more seniority.—Eds.] Smith regularly received excellent performance evaluations. The evidence demonstrated that inmates are unpredictable as a group and that the ability of any person to gain respect and cooperation from them is a subtle quality often found in unlikely people. However, Petitioner through fourteen years of exemplary service demonstrated that she had such an ability. . . .

. . . . With the passage of years and the enforced male living [due to the need to care for his son for a period after his divorce], Smith found it increasingly difficult to deny her femaleness. She felt intense stress and internal conflict. She began to drink heavily. She developed a severe bleeding ulcer. Both of these problems progressively worsened. She . . . began to undergo a major depression and began to consider suicide. . . .

By July, 1985, Smith was feeling greater and greater stress. On July 8, while on vacation, she went out in the middle of the night to a very private, unpopulated, nearby beach wearing a woman's wig, makeup, a woman's burgundy French-cut bikini bathing suit with false breasts, a pink ladies' beach coat, and pink ladies' sandals. She was dressed this way as a manifestation of her transsexuality. While out, Smith had a flat tire. A passing patrolman stopped to help with the tire. Initially, Petitioner identified herself as Barbara Joe Smith. The officer who stopped to assist Smith ran Smith's tag and discovered that Smith's true name was William, not Barbara Joe. The officer filed a general offense report of the encounter with the City.

Once the report was filed, copies of this report were immediately circulated throughout the jail in sufficient quantity to "paper the walls." . . . . Smith did not participate or promote the circulation of the offense report and it was only the City's actions which caused the incident to become public.

. . . . Smith was summoned for a conference with the Director of Corrections and the Director of Police Services. . . . Smith explained that she was transsexual and that the event had been a manifestation of her transsexuality. The Directors asked Smith if she would be willing to accept counseling, but Smith explained to them that counseling would not "cure" her and that the only effective treatment would be sexual reassignment. Smith told McMillan that she was going to go ahead and pursue a sex change operation and would live as a female, including dressing as a female, for one year prior to the operation. The Directors thereupon decided that Smith could not be retained and the City's course of action would be to terminate her. They tried to persuade Smith to resign. . . . Petitioner ultimately refused to resign, and she resisted termination. Smith's eventual termination can only be considered involuntary since she sought to remain employed and was denied the right to do so.

. . . . The evidence did not demonstrate that any problem would have arisen from Petitioner's continued employment which would have been either dangerous or insurmountable.

. . . .

The events of July 8 did not result in an internal affairs investigation or a violation of law.

On July 19, 1985, the Sheriff served Smith with a "Notice of Proposed Immediate Suspension Without Pay With a Dismissal to Follow." The Notice outlined the charges against Petitioner as follows:

CHARGE I

Violation of Civil Service Rule 10.06(1), which reads as follows:

10.06(1): Cause shall include, but is not limited to. . . . inefficiency or inability to perform assigned duties . . . conduct unbecoming a public employee which would affect the employee's ability to perform the duties and responsibilities of the employee's job. . . .

CHARGE II

Violation of Civil Service Rule 561.01(1)(a), which reads as follows:

10.06(1)(a): The employee has violated any lawful official regulation or order or failed to obey any proper direction made and given by a superior officer.

and

10.06(4)(a)(5): The retention of the employee would be detrimental to the interests of the City Government.

This was the first time Petitioner had been charged with conduct unbecoming an officer and was the first offense on Smith's record which could be used against her in determining any punishment. The City's disciplinary guidelines recommended that an officer receive a written reprimand for the first offense of conduct unbecoming an officer. However, the Sheriff and City did not follow the guidelines since they considered transsexuality and its treatment prohibitive of Petitioner's continued employment.

[Smith] requested a hearing before the Jacksonville Civil Service Board. The hearing was held on October 8, 1985. Petitioner was present and was represented by counsel. Several coemployees testified on behalf of Smith at the civil service hearing. No employees testified in support of the City's position that they could no longer work with Smith and had lost respect for Smith. In fact, at the administrative hearing in this case, Sheriff McMillan acknowledged that he did not expect all of Smith's coemployees to be adverse to her. He said that he had not himself lost respect for Smith and that he could have continued to maintain a satisfactory working relationship with her. The Sheriff also testified that Sheriff's office employees are carefully screened for adaptability and flexibility. The Sheriff had no reason to suppose that his compassion and humanity were greater than that of other department employees. The fact that coemployees came forward to testify for Smith before the Civil Service Board tends to confirm the Sheriff's statements about Smith's coemployees.

The Board determined by a vote of four to one that the evidence at the hearing conclusively showed Smith had engaged in conduct unbecoming a public employee. Based on its findings of fact, the Board upheld the Sheriff's decision to dismiss Smith. . . .

The City's entire basis for terminating Smith was supposition that as a known transsexual she would not be able to command the respect of coemployees and inmates and would generally discredit the City. . . .

Importantly, at the time of Smith's termination in 1985, nothing had changed in Petitioner's abilities to perform her job. . . . No reasonable accommodation of Petitioner's handicap was explored or attempted by the City. [The facts described above] and Smith's experience in other jobs after her termination demonstrate that the City's apprehensions were unjustified and were not concerns which could not be reasonably accommodated as was done with female correctional officers and black correctional officers when those groups entered the correctional work force.

The evidence showed that inmate reaction to a transsexual is a "big unknown" and . . . may theoretically be disruptive. . . . However, there was no evidence which indicated that any inmates were aware of the July 8 incident or were cognizant of Petitioner's transsexuality. Additionally, the evidence demonstrated that an inmate's ability to discern a transsexual who is cross-dressing while at work may be difficult since correctional officers wear the same uniform and have strict rules regarding their appearance. No evidence was submitted as to what changes would have occurred in Petitioner's appearance had she been allowed to be female at work.[9] Moreover, all of the theoretical problems which may or may not occur could have been reasonably accommodated by restricting any overt appearance of Petitioner while at work.

Finally, the City had extensive general orders and personnel rules and regulations requiring that employees be respectful and courteous toward one another and forbidding disrespectful, mutinous, insolent, or abusive language towards a supervisory employee or any other employee. It also had prohibitions against speaking disparagingly about any coemployees or defaming or demeaning the nationality, creed, race, or sex of any person. Various punishments or administrative actions were prescribed for violations of these orders. Such respective behavior was demanded toward black and female correctional officers. The evidence did not demonstrate any legitimate reason for not demanding such behavior toward Petitioner.

After termination, Smith worked at a series of jobs. In almost each instance, her employers knew of her transsexuality and the fact that she was cross-dressing at work. Her experience at those jobs was basically what she had predicted she would have encountered if she had continued with the Sheriff's Office — that is, initial snickering and then general acceptance. For example, she worked as part of a clean-up crew at a construction site at which there were approximately (300) construction workers. . . . By the end of the construction site job, she had achieved general acceptance and had received apologies from various of the taunters. . . . The only exception to Petitioner's successful employment occurred when she was employed by Walmart as a sales manager. Apparently, the Walmart had segregated male and female restroom facilities and there was great concern over which restroom Petitioner would use.

 . . . .

Smith ultimately was accepted into a gender reassignment program. As part of that program, she was required to live as a female for a two (2) year adjustment and demonstration period. She successfully accomplished the adjustment. In 1990, she underwent her gender reassignment surgery. Since then, she has been living entirely as a female and has been judicially determined to be a female.

Since the gender reassignment surgery, Petitioner is now doing well. She feels much more at peace with herself and much happier than when she was a male. She has quit drinking altogether and no longer suffers from stomach ulcers. She no longer thinks about suicide. She has received acceptance by her brothers and sisters, and also by her son. She is working successfully as a salesperson for a retail tile company.

---

9. At the hearing, Petitioner's appearance was very conservative. She is of medium height and build for a woman, with blond hair and pale features. She did wear light makeup and fingernail polish. Her hair was pulled back. However, it is difficult to say whether in 1985 Petitioner would have worn makeup and fingernail polish around other people, given her empathy for other people's reactions and the fact that she still had male features such as a beard and a regulation short haircut. Jewelry was prohibited under the general orders.

Conclusions of Law

. . . .

Chapter 760, Florida Statutes prohibits discrimination in the work place and declares such discrimination to be an unlawful employment practice. Specifically, Section 760.10(1), Florida Statutes, in pertinent part, defines an unlawful employment practice as:

(a) To discharge or fail to or refuse to hire any individual, or otherwise to discriminate against any individual with respect to compensation, terms, conditions, or privileges of employment, because of such individual's race, color, religion, sex, national origin, age, handicap, or marital status.

As a general proposition, Petitioner bears the initial burden of demonstrating a prima facie case of discharge because of handicap. To establish a prima facie case, Smith must show (1) that she was handicapped, (2) that she was qualified for her position and that she satisfactorily performed her duties, and (3) that she was terminated despite satisfactory performance. *Green v. Mark III Industries*, 12 FALR 1988 (FCHR 1990). If a prima facie case is established, the burden then shifts to the employer to show that absence of the handicap is a bona fide occupational qualification. *Andrews v. Albertson's, Inc.*, 11 FALR 4874 (FCHR 1989). The employer's burden includes proof of a good faith attempt to accommodate the handicap and/or a showing of undue hardship in attempting a reasonable accommodation. *E.E.O.C. v. Townley Engineering and Mfg. Co.*, 859 F.2d 610 (9th Cir. 1988); *Andrews v. Albertson's, Inc.*, 11 FALR 4874 (FCHR 1989).

Smith indisputably established the second and third parts of the three part requirements of a prima facie case. She was a transsexual from the outset of her employment with the City. Her work during those years of transsexuality was outstanding. She continued to be the same person after her transsexuality became known. So far as her abilities were concerned, she remained as capable of performing as she previously had been. However, she nonetheless was terminated because of feared prejudicial perceptions of other people and the effect of that prejudice on Petitioner's ability to perform. Therefore, the only question left in regards to Petitioner's prima facie case is whether transsexualism constitutes a handicap under Chapter 760, Florida Statutes.

The Legislature provided no definition of the term "handicap" in the Human Rights Act as originally passed. The Act then was amended in 1989 to add the following definition:

'Handicap' means:

(a) A person who has a physical or mental impairment which substantially limits one or more major life activities, or who has a record of having, or is regarded as having, such physical or mental impairment;" Section 760.02, Florida Statutes (1989).

. . . .

Generally "handicap" connotes a condition that prevents normal functioning in some way: "A person with a handicap does not enjoy, in some manner, the full and normal use of his sensory, mental or physical faculties." *Chicago, Milwaukee, St. Paul and Pacific Railroad Co. v. Washington State Human Relations Commission*, 557 P.2d 307 (Wash. 1976). In this case, the record demonstrates that Smith was handicapped. Petitioner's transsexualism caused ongoing suicidal ideation, situational alcohol abuse, and poor health due to bleeding ulcers. By any view, these symptoms interfered with Petitioner's full and normal use of her mental and physical faculties and limited Petitioner's major life activities, *i.e.* life and health. The disparity between Smith's physicality and her feelings about herself caused her to be at odds with the rest of her world. That disparity, and her need to hide it, left her unable to merge the mental or physical aspects of her identity, manifesting in the loss of her health, depression and the will to live. Smith's day to day existence consequently was much more fundamentally burdened by handicap than if she had been subject to a multitude of conditions which would have been recognized beyond dispute as handicaps. Based upon the plain meaning of the term "handicap" and the medical evidence presented, an individual with gender dysphoria is within the coverage of the Human Rights Act of 1977 in that such individual "does not enjoy, in some manner, the full and normal use of his sensory, mental or physical [faculties"] and in this case has had at least two major life activities [impaired].

However, apart from actual handicap, Smith was handicapped because of the attitudes with which she was confronted by her employer. A handicap can result from the perception of others that a condition is handicapping, particularly if the perception is held by an employer. The City adamantly insists that Smith's condition impaired her ability to function effectively and continue in her chosen field of work. A person's inability to continue working in that person's chosen field is an impairment of a major life function regardless of whether it is caused by a physical or mental handicap, including a handicap caused by the perceptions of the employer. *See Blackwell v. United States Department of the Treasury*, 639 F. Supp. 289 (D.D.C. 1986). *See School Board of Nassau County v. Arline*, 480 U.S. 273, 283 (1987); *Doe v. U.S. Postal Service*, 37 FEP Cases 1867 (D.D.C. 1985) (a federal Rehabilitation Act case).

In this case, the City's main line of defense for terminating Smith is that an absence of transsexuality was a bona fide occupational qualification (BFOQ) for her position. Section 760.10(8), FLORIDA STATUTES, states:

(8) Notwithstanding any other provision of this section, it is not an unlawful employment practice under §§ 760.01-760.10 for an employer, employment agency, labor organization, or joint labor-management committee to:

(a) Take or fail to take any action on the basis of religion, sex, national origin, age, handicap, or marital status in those certain instances in which religion, sex, national origin, age, absence of a particular handicap, or marital status is a bona fide occupational qualification reasonably necessary for the performance of the particular employment to which such action or inaction is related.

The City contends that even if Smith could have performed the specific tasks of her position, she would not have been able as a known transsexual to command respect from coemployees, inmates, or members of the public and would consequently have been impaired as a corrections lieutenant.

Under the BFOQ defense, persons able to do a job may be denied employment by reason of religion, sex, nationality, or other protected status, because the protected status or condition itself precludes performance. Absence of the status or condition accordingly is a BFOQ and such absence must be required for satisfactory performance. For example, a Moslem cannot be a Baptist minister, and a male cannot be a ladies room attendant.

The BFOQ defense is a very narrow exception to the antidiscrimination purpose of Chapter 760, Florida Statutes, and can present exceedingly difficult questions involving a highly delicate balancing of values. *Dothard v. Rawlinson*, 433 U.S. 321, 334 (1977) (sex discrimination case). However, a BFOQ will not be recognized for mere employer convenience. *See Usery v. Tamiami Trail Tours, Inc.*, 531 F.2d 224 (5th Cir. 1976) (age discrimination).[10]

. . . . An employer may rely on a BFOQ defense only upon a showing that the handicapped employee cannot be accommodated in any reasonable way. *E.E.O.C. v. Townley Engineering and Mfg. Co.*, 859 F.2d 610 (9th Cir. 1988). Employers have an "affirmative obligation" to provide reasonable accommodation. *School Board of Nassau County v. Arline*, 480 U.S. 273 (1987). An employee who can perform "the essentials of the job if afforded reasonable accommodation" is entitled to relief. *Treadwell v. Alexander*, 707 F.2d 473 (11th Cir. 1983).

In this case, the City provided virtually no evidence to discharge its burden of proving a BFOQ. Its entire case consisted of the opinions of the Sheriff and his surmise and assumption about the responses of Petitioner's coemployees and inmates. . . . The City offered no witness—coemployee, inmate, or citizen—who testified on personal knowledge to any actual loss of respect for Smith or to any actual erosion of working relationships. The only evidence presented was that the general offense report was circulated in quantity. At best, this evidence only demonstrates that Petitioner's coemployees found the July 8 incident humorous.

There was no indication that the City attempted in any way to determine whether it really needed to terminate Smith. It simply terminated her out of hand after

---

10. Normally the BFOQ defense does not apply to handicap cases. Generally speaking, if a handicapped person can perform the job, there is ipso facto no BFOQ. However, this does not mean that there can never be a BFOQ defense in a handicap case. Obviously, a public restaurant would not be required to employ a typhoid carrier as a food handler. On the other hand, a person cannot automatically be denied employment because of having a communicable disease. *See School Board of Nassau County v. Arline*, 480 U.S. 273 (1987). In these cases, whether the handicap can be reasonably accommodated is the critical factor.

learning she was a transsexual. There was no checking, testing, or verification of any kind. Smith was given no chance to see if she could perform effectively. There was no inquiry, investigation, or interviewing to ascertain whether she would be rejected by coemployees, inmates, or other persons. . . . There was no attempt to become informed or educated in any way about transsexuality. There was no checking or inquiry to determine whether other transsexuals had successfully managed to preserve working relationships upon coming into the open. The City instead made a snap decision based on the personal predilections and perspectives of the Directors who met with Smith, without any effort then or later to assess the validity of their assumptions.

Moreover, the evidence demonstrated that there probably would not have been any significant impairment of working relationships with coemployees and if some individuals did have a prejudicial attitude toward Petitioner then appropriate discipline was in order for the holder of such an attitude.

Neither was there any showing of an adequate basis in fact for assuming that inmates would be adverse to Smith. The City expressly conceded that Smith had demonstrated a good record for relating to inmates. The person "Smith" had not changed. Moreover, there was no evidence indicating that the inmates knew or would have become aware of Smith's transsexuality.

Finally, the record is barren of any attempt to accommodate Smith. The City decided at the outset that there was no way to accommodate her and thereafter made no effort to do so. This represented a clear failure of its affirmative obligation to attempt reasonable accommodation. An employer which seeks to terminate an employee for handicap must provide the employee a reasonable opportunity to demonstrate ability to perform. *Bowe v. Colgate-Palmolive Company*, 416 F.2d 711 (7th Cir. 1969). If nothing else, the City's accommodation could have consisted of an effort to uphold and support Smith against such disrespect, if any, as might have materialized as is required under its own civil service rules. Yet the City made no attempt to apply or enforce any such rules with regard to Smith.

More important, even if the City had met its burden of showing an adverse reaction to Smith's transsexuality, it does not follow that the reaction would be entitled to the dignity of a BFOQ. Any adverse reaction to Smith solely because of her transsexuality would have been sheer prejudice. The very purpose of the Human Rights Act is to provide protection against that kind of intolerance. Smith's condition was wholly involuntary. There was nothing illegal, immoral, wrong, or bad about it. It was entirely personal to her and was harmful to no one else. She was as undeservedly afflicted as someone born with a physical deformity. Her condition accordingly was no less entitled to protection than any of the other protected conditions or status categories of the Human Rights Act.

As the Supreme Court stated in *School Board of Nassau County v. Arline*, 480 U.S. 273 (1987), the basic purpose of laws against handicap discrimination is "to ensure that handicapped individuals are not denied jobs or other benefits because of the prejudiced attitudes or the ignorance of others." The Supreme Court went on to point out in *Arline* that laws against handicap discrimination have been "carefully structured to replace such reflexive reactions to actual or perceived handicaps with actions based on reasoned and medically sound judgments." The Supreme Court additionally pointed out that "society's accumulated myths and fears about disability and disease are as handicapping as are the physical limitations that flow from actual impairment."

Simply put, prejudice cannot be a basis for a BFOQ. Permitting negative third party reactions—whether malignant bigotry or unthinking narrowmindedness and ignorance—to be elevated to a BFOQ would be to turn the Human Rights Act inside out and upside down. Not every adverse reaction can be honored, regardless of merit or worth. Third party reactions must be deserving of deference to receive it. Otherwise, bigotry and prejudice would need only to be entrenched to be upheld. Obviously that cannot be the law.[11] In order for an handicap to be considered a BFOQ some amount of evidence beyond mere speculation must be ascertained by the employer which would justify its conclusion of unemployability and that the handicap cannot be reasonably accommodated.

. . . . Respondent committed an unlawful employment practice against Petitioner when it fired her because of her handicap of transsexualism and Petitioner is entitled to reinstatement to a position similar in nature to the one she was terminated from or to a position employees in positions similar to Petitioners in 1985 were transferred to when the institution reorganized its employment classes, back pay through the date of reinstatement and attorney's fees and costs.

Jurisdiction is reserved for determination of reinstatement, back pay, appropriate attorneys' fee and costs in this proceeding if the parties cannot agree.

Recommendation

Based upon the foregoing Findings of Fact and Conclusions of Law, it is recommended that the Human Relations Commission enter a Final Order reinstating Petitioner, awarding back pay and attorneys' fees and costs and reserving jurisdiction should the parties fail to agree on appropriate reinstatement, back pay and attorney's fees and costs.

RECOMMENDED this 2nd day of October, 1991, in Tallahassee, Leon County, Florida.

DIANE CLEAVINGER

Hearing Officer

Division of Administrative Hearings

––––––––––

11. The only exception is if the City had demonstrated, with more than speculation, that Petitioner's transsexualism would have caused a dangerous situation involving inmates. *See, Dothard v. Rawlinson*, 433 U.S. 321 (1977). No such showing was made in this case. [relocated footnote—Eds.]

Discussion

1. Are the *Smith* court's discussions of Smith's transsexuality and/or why it qualifies as a handicap (actual or perceived) under the Florida statute likely to exacerbate or perpetuate stigma against transgender persons? Would a ruling *against* Smith have done more to foster anti-transgender stigma?

2. The court rejects the city's attempt to justify its discrimination as a BFOQ on the basis of a lack of respect for transgender persons. Its reasoning seems consistent with the Supreme Court's treatment of "private biases" in *Palmore v. Sidoti*, 466 U.S. 429 (1984), Chapter 8, *supra* at p. 472.

3. Is the *Smith* court's distinguishing of *Dothard v. Rawlinson*, 433 U.S. 321 (1977), persuasive? In *Dothard*, the court held that Alabama satisfied the BFOQ defense under Title VII of the Civil Rights Act of 1964, 42 U.S.C. § 2000e-2(e). Title VII, recall, generally prohibits sex discrimination in employment. In *Dothard*, the state had a regulation that prohibited women from working in most prison guard positions in men's prisons. Although agreeing "that the bfoq exception was, in fact, meant to be an extremely narrow exception to the general prohibition of discrimination on the basis of sex," the majority held that "[i]n the particular factual circumstances of this case," the state's regulation was lawful under the BFOQ provision. The majority reasoned that "[t]he likelihood that inmates would assault a woman because she was a woman would pose a real threat not only to the victim of the assault, but also to the basic control of the penitentiary and protection of its inmates and the other security personnel. The employee's very womanhood would thus directly undermine her capacity to provide the security that is the essence of a [prison guard's] responsibility." It believed this conclusion supported by "substantial testimony from experts on both sides of this litigation." Justice Marshall, joined by Justice Brennan, strenuously objected that "[t]here is simply no evidence in the record to show that women guards would create any danger to security in Alabama prisons significantly greater than that which already exists. All of the dangers — with one exception . . . — are inherent in a prison setting, whatever the gender of the guards." As for that one exception and attempting to make sense of the majority's invocation of female guards' "very womanhood," the dissenters observed:

> The Court refers to the large number of sex offenders in Alabama prisons, and to "[t]he likelihood that inmates would assault a woman because she was a woman." In short, the fundamental justification for the decision is that women, as guards, will generate sexual assaults. With all respect, this rationale regrettably perpetuates one of the most insidious of the old myths about women — that women, wittingly or not, are seductive sexual objects. The effect of the decision, made I am sure with the best of intentions, is to punish women because their very presence might provoke sexual assaults. It is women who are made to pay the price in lost job opportunities for the threat of depraved conduct by prison inmates.

Reading Guide for Enriquez v. West Jersey Health Systems

1. *Enriquez v. West Jersey Health Systems*, 777 A.2d 365 (N.J. Super. Ct. App. Div. 2001), is an appellate opinion that interprets state laws against sex discrimination and reads state laws against disability discrimination potentially to protect workers from anti-transgender discrimination. On what sources does the court rely for its conclusion that (forbidden) sex discrimination includes discrimination based on what it terms "gender" (which today, more commonly, might be referred to as "gender identity")?

2. How does the court characterize New Jersey's Law Against Discrimination ("LAD"), and, as a consequence, how does the court say the LAD should be interpreted? (The canon the court invokes is a common principle of statutory interpretation.) Why does the court not follow the lead of federal or other states' restrictive laws or judicial decisions?

3. The plaintiff Dr. Enriquez contends that the defendants discriminated against her on various forbidden grounds, including on the basis of handicap. On what branch of the statutory definition of "handicap" does she rely? What does the court say about whether that language encompasses "gender dysphoria or transsexualism"? What does it say about the proofs offered by plaintiff at the time the trial court granted summary judgment against her?

Carla Enriquez v. West Jersey Health Systems, et al.

777 A.2d 365 (N.J. Super. Ct. App. Div. 2001)

Before Judges KING, LEFELT and AXELRAD.

Opinion

The opinion of the court was delivered by

LEFELT, J.A.D.

These consolidated appeals arise from the summary judgment dismissal of two complaints filed by plaintiff Carla Enriquez, a male-to-female transsexual, for wrongful termination of her employment as medical director of a learning behavior center owned and managed by the various corporate and individual defendants. Most significantly, this appeal raises the novel issues of whether gender dysphoria or transsexualism is a handicap under the New Jersey Law Against Discrimination, N.J.S.A. 10:5-1 through -49 ("LAD"), and whether the LAD precludes an employer from discriminating on the basis of someone's sexual identity or gender. We answer both questions in the affirmative and reverse and remand for further proceedings.

I

. . . .

On November 20, 1995, defendant West Jersey Health Systems ("West Jersey") hired plaintiff as medical director of defendant outpatient treatment facility, West Jersey Center for Behavior, Learning and Attention ("Center"). Plaintiff and West

Jersey entered into a written Professional Services Agreement that could be terminated by either party upon ninety days' written notice.

In September 1996, less than a year after plaintiff's employment with West Jersey commenced, she began the external transformation from male to female. Plaintiff shaved her beard and eventually removed all vestiges of facial hair. She sculpted and waxed her eyebrows, pierced her ears, started wearing emerald stone earrings, and began growing breasts.

In the early months of 1997, plaintiff was confronted by defendants John Cossa, Maureen Miller, and Ellen Feinstein regarding their discomfort over her transformation. Cossa was West Jersey's vice president and president and chief executive officer of defendant West Jersey Clinical Association, also known as defendant West Jersey Physicians' Associates ("Physicians' Associates"), the entity which assumed control of the Center's professional staff in September 1997. Miller was vice president of outpatient services at West Jersey and Feinstein was her assistant.

By February 1997, plaintiff began manicuring and polishing her nails, growing long hair, and wearing a ponytail. On February 13, 1997, Cossa expressly questioned plaintiff about her appearance. According to plaintiff, Cossa asked if plaintiff would be willing to go back to her prior appearance if West Jersey asked her to. Cossa told plaintiff, "stop all this and go back to your previous appearance!"

In June 1997, plaintiff was diagnosed with gender dysphoria, which is a gender identity disorder listed in the *Diagnostic and Statistical Manual of Mental Disorders* (fourth ed., 1994) ("*DSM-IV*"), published by the American Psychiatric Association. This disorder is also known as transsexualism.

On July 22, . . . plaintiff received a letter from Miller stating that the hospital, pursuant to the professional services agreement, was terminating the agreement, without cause, effective in ninety days, on October 22 . . . . According to this letter, the Center's program was being assumed by Physicians' Associates as of the end of October. Plaintiff was advised that she would be contacted by Cossa to discuss a new contract with that entity.

From July 22 to September 29, 1997, plaintiff repeatedly tried to discuss a new contract with Cossa, without any success. Plaintiff claimed that as of September 1997, all of the other professional staff employed at the Center had become employees of Physicians' Associates.

On September 29, 1997, when plaintiff finally met with Cossa regarding a new contract for plaintiff, Cossa advised plaintiff that "[N]o one's going to sign this contract unless you stop this business that you're doing."

When Cossa and plaintiff next met, on October 13, plaintiff presented Cossa with a letter she had drafted to her family and patients, explaining her gender identity disorder and the treatment she was following. She had not yet sent the letter to anyone. Cossa asked plaintiff not to say anything yet and to let Cossa try to work things out.

On October 22, 1997, Cossa handed plaintiff a termination letter. According to this letter, Cossa and plaintiff had discussed the possibility of moving plaintiff to Physicians' Associates. However, defendants decided not to pursue that option and had made arrangements for other doctors to be available immediately to provide care to the Center's patients.

Cossa told plaintiff that the hospital would not allow plaintiff to send her proposed letter to the patients, and that the hospital had drafted a different letter. Plaintiff was also told not to return to the office for the rest of that day and that her patients had been canceled for the next three months.

In February 1998, plaintiff legally changed her name to Carla. In July 1998, approximately nine months after she was terminated, plaintiff underwent the surgical procedure to become a female. [Plaintiff] believes that the course of treatment she began, that ended with sex reassignment surgery, cured her gender dysphoria.

In December 1998, plaintiff filed her first complaint against defendants for disability discrimination under the LAD, gender or sexual orientation-affection discrimination under the LAD, breach of contract, and trade libel. The West Jersey defendants filed a motion for partial summary judgment, seeking dismissal of plaintiff's claim for disability discrimination. The motion judge granted defendant's motion, noting that other courts had concluded that transsexualism was not a recognized mental or physical disability under statutes very similar to ours.

II

. . . .

Though plaintiff is a physician, she did not diagnose herself [with gender dysphoria or transsexualism]. Dr. William Stayton from the University of Pennsylvania formally diagnosed plaintiff's condition. Plaintiff claims Dr. Stayton is an "internationally renowned expert in gender and sexual medicine." According to the letter plaintiff wanted to send her patients explaining her situation, there are "internationally accepted norms for treatment of this condition." These encompass the steps that plaintiff went through including "extensive psychological counseling, extended planning for 'transition,' the use of contrahormonal therapy, hair removal, living in the putative gender role full time (the so called 'Real Life Test') and finally, in some cases, sex reassignment surgery."

Also in the letter she planned to send her patients, plaintiff further explained gender dysphoria in this fashion:

> Current research tells us that early in fetal development, the infant's brain undergoes masculinization or feminization unrelated to chromosomal complement. Later, as we grow up, we identify with the 'cortical' or brain gender we were endowed with. Happily, for the majority of the population, the genetic (or chromosomal gender) and the cortical (or brain gender) are congruent. Later in development, we develop sexual preferences, sexual orientation, gender attribution, and gender function. Again, in the

majority of the population, all of these are congruent and society and the individual are happy.

> But some people do not have this harmony. We call these feelings "dysphoria" in medicine. Literally, this means "unhappy," but doctors have expanded its meaning to describe conditions that significantly effect [*sic* — Eds.] the individual. Gender Dysphoria describes a condition in which there is not this harmony. The physical and the inner selves are at odds.

Plaintiff argues that the court erred in dismissing her claim of discrimination based on either gender or sexual orientation/affection. The LAD provides in pertinent part that it is unlawful for an employer to terminate someone's employment based on that person's "affectional or sexual orientation, genetic information, sex or atypical hereditary cellular or blood trait," N.J.S.A. 10:5-12(a). . . .

. . . . [P]laintiff failed to establish a prima facie case for discrimination based on her affectional or sexual orientation because she was not a homosexual or bisexual or perceived to be homosexual or bisexual. . . . Plaintiff presented no evidence that she was discriminated against because of her "affectional, emotional or physical attraction" to others.

Plaintiff's complaint, however, also included a claim for gender discrimination. [Here, the court rejected the rationale of courts interpreting Title VII of the Civil Rights Act of 1964, 42 U.S.C.A. § 2000e-2(a)(1), or state laws against sex discrimination as not reaching anti-transgender discrimination, concluding that "[the] view of sex discrimination reflected in these decisions is too constricted."]

A generation ago, when Justice Handler served in the Appellate Division, he found that "[t]he evidence and authority which we have examined, however, show that a person's sex or sexuality embraces an individual's gender, that is, one's self-image, the deep psychological or emotional sense of sexual identity and character." *M.T. v. J.T.,* 355 A.2d 204 (N.J. Super. Ct. App. Div. 1976). We agree with Justice Handler that "sex" embraces an "individual's gender," and is broader than anatomical sex. "[S]ex is comprised of more than a person's genitalia at birth." Taylor Flynn, *Transforming the Debate: Why We Need to Include Transgender Rights in the Struggles for Sex and Sexual Orientation Equality,* 101 Colum. L. Rev. 392, 415 (2001). The word "sex" as used in the LAD should be interpreted to include gender, protecting from discrimination on the basis of sex or gender.

It is incomprehensible to us that our Legislature would ban discrimination against heterosexual men and women; against homosexual men and women; against bisexual men and women; against men and women who are perceived, presumed or identified by others as not conforming to the stereotypical notions of how men and women behave, but would condone discrimination against men or women who seek to change their anatomical sex because they suffer from a gender identity disorder. We conclude that sex discrimination under the LAD includes gender discrimination so as to protect plaintiff from gender stereotyping and discrimination for transforming herself from a man to a woman.

III

Plaintiff also contends that gender dysphoria is a handicap and a recognized disability under the LAD. It is unlawful to discriminate against an employee because of a handicap "unless the nature and extent of the handicap reasonably precludes the performance of the particular employment." N.J.S.A. 10:5-4.1. The LAD has defined "handicapped" as:

> suffering from physical disability, infirmity, malformation or disfigurement which is caused by bodily injury, birth defect or illness, . . . or from any mental, psychological or developmental disability resulting from anatomical, psychological, physiological or neurological conditions which prevents the normal exercise of any bodily or mental functions or is demonstrable, medically or psychologically, by accepted clinical or laboratory diagnostic techniques. . . .

In this case we are not dealing with any "physical disability, infirmity, malformation or disfigurement which is caused by bodily injury, birth defect or illness." We are dealing with the portion of the statute that provides that a person can be handicapped if they suffer from a "mental, psychological or developmental disability resulting from anatomical, psychological, physiological or neurological conditions which prevents the normal exercise of any bodily or mental functions or is demonstrable, medically or psychologically, by accepted clinical or laboratory diagnostic techniques."

Plaintiff is, however, relying exclusively on the clinical or laboratory diagnostic portion of the definition. She does not argue that transsexualism prevented the normal exercise of any bodily or mental functions. And, according to plaintiff, her condition did not interfere with the adequate performance of her work at the Center. Termination of a "handicapped" employee, whose condition does not prevent the employee from doing her job, is actionable under the LAD. *Gimello v. Agency Rent-A-Car Sys., Inc.,* 594 A.2d 264 (N.J. Super. Ct. App. Div. 1991).

Therefore, in this case plaintiff asks us to determine whether gender dysphoria is a handicap and protected by the LAD because it is a "mental, psychological or developmental disability resulting from anatomical, psychological, physiological or neurological conditions which . . . is demonstrable, medically or psychologically, by accepted clinical or laboratory diagnostic techniques."

As remedial social legislation, the LAD is deserving of a liberal construction, especially with regard to handicaps. *Clowes v. Terminix Int'l, Inc.,* 538 A.2d 794 (N.J. 1988); *Andersen v. Exxon Co., U.S.A.,* 446 A.2d 486 (N.J. 1982). The statutory definition of handicapped under N.J.S.A. 10:5-5(q) is very broad in its scope, and is not limited to "severe" disabilities. *Andersen v. Exxon.* Rather, it prohibits discrimination against those suffering from any disability. *Id.*

The parties agree that gender dysphoria is listed in the *DSM-IV* as a disorder. Defendants argue correctly, however, that this listing is not dispositive for classification as a disability under the LAD. Merely because a condition is a disorder listed in the *DSM-IV* does not mean it is also a handicap under the LAD. *A.B.C. v. XYZ Corp.*, 660 A.2d 1199 (N.J. Super. Ct. App. Div. 1995) (Petrella, J.A.D., concurring).

A disorder is not necessarily the equivalent of a disease, disability, illness, or defect, especially where these terms carry legal significance. *Id.* Moreover, the LAD itself does not preclude discrimination based on conduct. N.J.S.A. 10:5-2.1. In addition, the *DSM-IV* also cautions that categorization of conditions contained in the manual "may not be wholly relevant to legal judgments, for example, that take into account such issues as individual responsibility, disability determination, and competency."

The Americans with Disabilities Act (ADA) expressly excludes "transvestism, transsexualism, pedophilia, exhibitionism, voyeurism, gender identity disorders not resulting from physical impairments, other sexual behavior disorders." 42 U.S.C.A. § 12211(b)(1). That statute also contains a requirement that the impairment be one which substantially limits a major life activity. 42 U.S.C.A. § 12102(2)(A). Our own statute does not contain such a restriction. Moreover, our own Legislature has not considered or addressed similar exclusions. *A.B.C. v. XYZ* (Petrella, J.A.D., concurring).

Other state courts, however, appear to be split on this issue when construing their own statutes. For example, a Pennsylvania court has concluded that transsexualism is not a disability under the Pennsylvania Human Relations Act because that statute requires that the disability substantially limit a major life activity and because petitioner did not contend that transsexualism affected any bodily function. *Holt v. Northwest Pa. Training P'ship Consortium, Inc.*, 694 A.2d 1134 (Pa. Commw. Ct. 1997).

A Washington state court, however, has construed gender dysphoria as a handicap under the Washington Law Against Discrimination, finding that it is a medically cognizable and diagnosable condition, that those who suffer from it endure great mental and emotional agony, and that it has a prescribed course of treatment. *Doe v. Boeing Co.*, 846 P.2d 531 (Wash. 1993). [*Doe* is presented *supra* at p. 965. — Eds.]

An Iowa court reached the contrary conclusion construing its statute which also contains a "major life activity" restriction. *Sommers v. Iowa Civil Rights Comm'n*, 337 N.W.2d 470 (Iowa 1983). The court noted that a person who is anatomically of one sex but psychologically and emotionally of the other sex has a problem that does not necessarily constitute the kind of mental condition that the Legislature intended to be treated as a substantial handicap. Transsexualism should not ordinarily affect a person's capacity to engage in major life activities. [*Sommers* is presented *supra* at p. 963. — Eds.]

Our problem with the out-of-state cases concluding that gender dysphoria is not a disability is that our statute is very broad and does not require that a disability restrict any major life activities to any degree. In *Olson v. Gen. Elec. Astrospace*, 966 F. Supp. 312 (D.N.J. 1997), for example, the federal court found that plaintiff's conditions of depression and multiple personality disorder were recognized disabilities under the LAD because they were demonstrable, medically or psychologically, by accepted clinical or laboratory diagnostic techniques, because these ailments were generally understood by the medical profession as diseases, and because the plaintiff had sought legitimate treatment for them.

Our courts have held that the LAD recognizes as disabilities such conditions as alcoholism, *Clowes v. Terminix*; obesity, *Gimello v. Agency Rent-A-Car*; and substance abuse, *In re Cahill*, 585 A.2d 977 (N.J. Super. Ct. App. Div. 1991). The LAD has thus been broadly and liberally construed to include what otherwise might be termed emotional or mental disorders, in order to eradicate the evil of discrimination in New Jersey. "Employment discrimination due to sex or any other invidious classification is peculiarly repugnant in a society which prides itself on judging each individual by his or her merits." *Peper v. Princeton Univ. Bd. of Trs.*, 389 A.2d 465 (N.J. 1978).

Gender dysphoria is regarded medically as a "mental disorder occurring in an estimated frequency of 1:50,000 individuals." Cole, Emory, Huang, Meyer, *Treatment of Gender Dysphoria*, 90 TEX. MED. 68 (1994). Moreover, treatment for the disorder can now "be regarded as accepted medical practice." *Ibid. See also Farmer v. Brennan*, 511 U.S. 825 (1994) (transsexualism is a rare psychiatric disorder in which a person feels persistently uncomfortable about his or her anatomical sex and seeks medical treatment including hormonal therapy and surgery to bring about permanent sex change) (citations omitted).

The disorder is recognized within *DSM-IV*, thus confirming that the condition can be diagnosed by accepted clinical techniques. In fact, the *DSM-IV* lists four criteria necessary for diagnosing a gender identity disorder. Furthermore, gender dysphoria does not cause violations of the law as does exhibitionism, which was the *DSM-IV* disorder Judge Petrella struggled with in *A.B.C. v. XYZ*.

The *DSM-IV* also notes that each recognized disorder contained within the manual "is associated with present distress (*e.g.*, a painful symptom) or disability (*i.e.*, impairment in one or more important areas of functioning) or with a significantly increased risk of suffering death, pain, disability, or an important loss of freedom." With regard to gender dysphoria specifically, the manual notes that the "disturbance causes clinically significant distress or impairment in social, occupational, or other important areas of functioning." Transsexualism can be accompanied by a profound sense of loathing for an individual's primary and secondary sexual characteristics, which is overwhelming and unalterable. Dr. L. Gooren, *An Appraisal of Endocrine Theories of Homosexuality and Gender Dysphoria, in* HANDBOOK OF SEXOLOGY vol. 6, 410–24 (1988). Thus, gender dysphoria is a recognized mental or psychological disability that can be demonstrated psychologically by accepted clinical diagnostic techniques and qualifies as a handicap under the LAD.

To establish the first element of a discriminatory discharge case under the LAD, however, an employee must submit proof that he or she was handicapped. *Maher v.*

N.J. Transit Rail Operations, Inc., 593 A.2d 750 (N.J. 1991); *Clowes v. Terminix Int'l, Inc.* Here, the dismissal of plaintiff's complaint was based solely on the motion judge's conclusion that gender dysphoria was not a handicap under the LAD. While we have concluded that gender dysphoria can constitute a handicap, we have problems with the proofs submitted by plaintiff during the summary judgment proceedings.

We note that plaintiff's proofs are not clear regarding the quality and quantity of impairment plaintiff may have suffered from this disorder. While the LAD does not require proof that some major life activity was impaired, plaintiff must suffer a disability. There is some evidence that before the surgery plaintiff's stress increased and her "moods worsened." There is also evidence that before her surgery plaintiff was argumentative and had difficulty controlling her temper. Since the surgery, plaintiff acknowledged experiencing greater "humanity," with her patients noting "how much more open and able to talk to me they are, particularly the adolescents."

In addition, we recognize that as part of her treatment protocol, plaintiff underwent sexual reassignment surgery, a process that most persons would not undertake unless necessary to eliminate great stress or extreme discomfort. Solely from the circumstances of plaintiff's course of treatment, we can infer sufficient impairment of plaintiff's emotional and mental well being to constitute a disability under the LAD. Plaintiff's proofs were adequate to at least raise a factual issue for summary judgment purposes establishing that her condition was a disability under the LAD.

To constitute a handicap, however, the disability must also result "from anatomical, psychological, physiological or neurological conditions which . . . is demonstrable . . . psychologically, by accepted clinical . . . diagnostic techniques." The record is completely silent on this issue.

There is an absence of evidence from Dr. Stayton confirming that he diagnosed gender dysphoria in plaintiff, explaining the condition as it manifested itself in plaintiff, and detailing the methods the doctor utilized to diagnose plaintiff. While "[n]othing . . . prevents a medical doctor from testifying as an expert in [her] own case," *Carey v. Lovett*, A.2d 1279 (N.J. 1993), evidence of her specific disorder and its diagnosis appear to be beyond plaintiff's training and specialty.

While the *DSM-IV* does detail the elements necessary to diagnose a gender disorder, there has been some criticism of these elements. Dr. Herbert Bower contends, for example, that the classification "neglects a number of diagnostically significant symptoms and characteristics of classical transsexualism." The doctor argues that:

> The initially mentioned four criteria omit the overwhelming desire to have the genitalia altered. The symptomatology does not include important features such as masturbation with fantasy of intercourse with a person of the same anatomical gender, occasional arousal during cross-dressing in the initial phase, lack of sexual interest during adolescence, stressful puberty and an essentially normal child rearing process.

[Herbert Bower, *The Gender Identity Disorder in the DSM-IV Classification—
A Critical Evaluation*, at http://www.pfc.org.uk/ congress/abstract/abs–005.
html.]

Thus, to establish that she is handicapped under the LAD, plaintiff must prove
that she had gender dysphoria and that the disorder was diagnosed by "accepted
clinical or laboratory diagnostic techniques." The record is silent regarding whether
the diagnostic technique utilized by Dr. Stayton was "accepted."

The motion judge rejected plaintiff's complaint solely because he believed that
gender dysphoria could not be a handicap under the LAD. We disagree with this
assessment and reverse on that basis. Because the case must be remanded for trial on
plaintiff's gender discrimination claim, we leave plaintiff to her proofs on whether
she had gender dysphoria and whether her condition was diagnosed in a fashion
sufficient to qualify as a handicap under the LAD.

Affirmed in part, reversed in part and remanded.

Discussion

1. Note the importance to the *Enriquez* court of the specific details of the plaintiff's medical evidence behind or beyond the bare fact of her gender dysphoria diagnosis. Consider what burdens this approach could place on plaintiffs before they
are able to get to trial. At least for litigated cases, then, does this opinion's reasoning
have the negative sorts of class-based consequences about which critics of the medical model of transgender identity worry? Even if it seems likely to do so, should that
be outweighed by the prospect of protection afforded to Enriquez or other plaintiffs
in similar circumstances?

2. Related to the prior point, note how relatively modest the actual ruling is. The
court only rules out a categorical exclusion of gender dysphoria from the conditions
that *might* qualify as a handicap within the meaning of New Jersey's Law Against
Discrimination.

Reading Guide for Oiler v. Winn-Dixie

1. The plaintiff in this case, Peter Oiler, did not raise a disability discrimination claim, but reasoning about mental health diagnoses figures prominently in
the court's opinion. What reasons do the defendants give for firing employee Peter
Oiler? (What did they mean by reference to Oiler's "life-style"?)

2. How does the court understand Oiler's identity and behavior? What role do
the competing medical expert opinions play in the court's reasoning?

3. On what basis does the court distinguish *Price Waterhouse* when analyzing
Oiler's sex stereotyping claim?

4. What reason does the court give for rejecting Oiler's disparate treatment argument that the defendants tolerated female gender nonconformity while terminating him for his gender nonconformity?

Peter Oiler v. Winn-Dixie Louisiana, Inc.

No. 00-3114 SECTION: "I", 2002 WL 31098541 (E.D. La. Sept. 16, 2002)

Order and Reasons

Africk, J.

Plaintiff, Peter Oiler . . . filed this employment discrimination action to recover damages from his former employer, Winn-Dixie Louisiana, Inc. . . . , pursuant to Title VII of the Civil Rights Act of 1964, 42 U.S.C. § 2000e-2(a)(1), and the Louisiana antidiscrimination statute, La. R.S. 23:332(A)(1) (West 2002).[1]

At issue is whether discharging an employee because he is transgendered [*sic*] and a crossdresser is discrimination on the basis of "sex" in violation of Title VII. . . .

Facts

. . . . As a road truck driver, plaintiff delivered groceries from Winn-Dixie's grocery warehouse in Harahan, Louisiana, to grocery stores in southern and central Louisiana and Mississippi.

Plaintiff is a heterosexual man who has been married since 1977. The plaintiff is transgendered.[9] He is not a transsexual [*sic*] and he does not intend to become a woman. Plaintiff has been diagnosed as having transvestic fetishism with gender

---

1. . . . . In an April 15, 2002, status conference, . . . plaintiff's counsel agreed. . . . that plaintiff would waive any argument that state law provided broader protection or greater remedies than Title VII.

9. Plaintiff defines transgendered as meaning that his gender identity, *i.e.*, his sense of whether he is a male or female, is not consistently male.

Walter Bockting, Ph.D., a psychologist who describes himself as an expert on transgender issues, defines the term "transgendered" as:

> [A]n umbrella term used to refer to a diverse group of individuals who cross or transcend culturally-defined categories of gender. They include crossdressers or transvestites (who desire to wear clothing associated with another sex), male-to-female and female-to-male transsexuals (who pursue or have undergone hormone therapy or sex reassignment surgery), transgenderists (who live in the gender role associated with another sex without desiring sex reassignment surgery), bigender persons (who identify as both man and woman), drag queens and kings (usually gay men and lesbian women who do 'drag' and dress up in, respectively, women's and men's clothes), and female and male impersonators (males who impersonate women and females who impersonate men, usually for entertainment).

dysphoria[11] and a gender identity disorder.[12] He is a male crossdresser. The term crossdresser is used interchangeably with transvestite.

When he is not at work, plaintiff appears in public approximately one to three times per month wearing female clothing and accessories. In order to resemble a woman, plaintiff wears wigs and makeup, including concealer, eye shadow, foundation, and lipstick. Plaintiff also wears skirts, women's blouses, women's flat shoes, and nail polish. He shaves his face, arms, hands, and legs. He wears women's underwear and bras and he uses silicone prostheses to enlarge his breasts. When he is crossdressed as a woman, he adopts a female persona and he uses the name "Donna."

Prior to 1996, plaintiff only crossdressed at home. After 1996, assuming the identity of "Donna," plaintiff crossdressed as a woman in public. While crossdressed, he attended support group meetings, dined at a variety of restaurants in Kenner and Metairie, visited night clubs, went to shopping malls, and occasionally attended church services. He was often accompanied by his wife and other friends, some of whom were also crossdressed.

On October 29, 1999, plaintiff told Gregg Miles, a Winn-Dixie supervisor, that he was transgendered. He explained that he was not a transsexual and that he did not intend to become a woman. However, he told Miles that for a number of years

---

11. Dr. Bockting reports that:

Mr. Oiler's transgender identity can best be described as a male heterosexual crossdresser. While Mr. Oiler does report a history of some gender dysphoria (discomfort with the male sex assigned at birth), he is not transsexual; he does not want to take feminizing hormones or undergo sex reassignment surgery. . . . His motivation to crossdress appears two-fold: (1) to express a feminine side and (2) to relieve stress. In addition, he sometimes experiences sexual excitement in response to crossdressing. Associated distress includes emotional turmoil, agitation, and marital conflict. Therefore, a DSM-IV diagnosis of Transvestic Fetishism with gender dysphoria is warranted.

12. Dennis P. Sugrue, Ph.D., is also a psychologist who describes himself as an expert on transgendered issues. Dr. Sugrue does not agree with Dr. Bockting's diagnosis of transvestic fetishism, but he instead opines that plaintiff is transgendered with a gender identity disorder. He states in his report:

Mr. Oiler's cross-dressing behavior suggests that he is *transgendered*, a non-clinical term frequently used in recent years for individuals whose behavior falls outside commonly accepted norms for the person's biological gender. In clinical terms, *Gender Identity Disorder NOS (Not Otherwise Specified)* is the most appropriate diagnosis.

The [DSM-IV] provides three diagnostic options for individuals with gender disturbances: *Transvestic Fetishism*, *Gender Identity Disorder*, and *Gender Identity Disorder NOS*. Although cross-dressing can at times have an erotic quality for Mr. Oiler, his behavior does not meet the DSM-IV transvestic fetishism criteria. . . .

Mr. Oiler displays evidence suggestive of a *gender identity disorder* as defined by DSM-IV. For example, he frequently wishes to pass as the other sex, desires to be treated as the other sex, and is convinced that he has the typical feelings and reactions of the other sex. He does not, however, display a preoccupation with ridding himself of primary and secondary sex characteristics or the conviction that he was born the wrong sex — features necessary for the diagnosis of a *Gender Identity Disorder* (often referred to as *transsexualism*). Hence the diagnosis of *Gender Identity Disorder NOS*.

he had been appearing in public at restaurants and clubs while crossdressed. He told Miles that while he was crossdressed, he assumed the female role of "Donna." He asked whether he would be terminated if Michael Istre, the president of Winn-Dixie Louisiana, Inc., ever saw plaintiff crossdressed as a woman.

On the same day, Miles had a private meeting with Istre. Miles told Istre that plaintiff was transgendered. Miles explained that for several years the plaintiff had been appearing in public crossdressed as a woman. Istre contacted Winn-Dixie's counsel for legal advice.

Istre and Miles made the decision to terminate the plaintiff's employment with Winn-Dixie . . . [W]hen plaintiff did not resign voluntarily, Winn-Dixie discharged him. The reason plaintiff was terminated was because he publicly adopted a female persona and publicly crossdressed as a woman. Specifically, Istre and Miles, acting for Winn-Dixie, terminated Oiler because of his lifestyle, *i.e.*, plaintiff publicly crossdressed for several years by going to restaurants and clubs where he presented himself as "Donna," a woman.[38] Istre and Miles believed that if plaintiff were recognized by Winn-Dixie customers as a crossdresser, the customers, particularly those in Jefferson Parish where plaintiff worked, would disapprove of the plaintiff's lifestyle.[39] Istre and Miles thought that . . . they would shop elsewhere

---

38. Miles explained that by "lifestyle" he meant that the plaintiff "told me that he had been doing this for several years. He knew he was different from childhood. He . . . described what he did away from work. It wasn't that he did it at home. He went out into the public. He went out into the night life. He went out to dinner in a female persona and that was something he chose to do." In his deposition, Miles testified:

> Q: And so it was his off-the-job behavior over this period of time that you've referenced, is that what caused you to terminate him?
> A: You say behavior; I say life-style.
> Q: What do you mean by "life-style"?
> A: Mr. Oiler told me that he had been doing this for several years. . . . It wasn't that he did it at home. He went out into the public. He went out into the night life. He went to dinner in a female persona and that was something he chose to do.
> * * * *
> Q: So, what made it problematic for you such that you terminated him was the fact that he was taking this life-style out of his home into the public; is that correct?
> A: Yes, sir.
> Q: And, specifically, he was dressing in a certain way in full view of the public, going out to restaurants and clubs and things like that. Is that what made this something that you wanted to terminate him for?
> A: There's more to it than just that statement.
> Q: So what more? Just clarify for me.
> A: He had adopted a female persona. He called himself Donna when he went out. It wasn't just one or two things. It was the entire picture that he told.

39. Istre was concerned that plaintiff was "going out in public impersonating a woman, wearing the wig and the makeup and the jewelry and the dress and the shoes and the underwear and calling himself by name repeatedly." According to Istre, that "could have some effect on my business." Istre explained that, "I think with him doing all of these things, and when he is at work driving one of my trucks with a 45 or 50 foot trailer, whatever he is driving with Winn-Dixie, and walking through my stores and people recognizing him coming up to the front of the store or driving up

and Winn-Dixie would lose business. Plaintiff did not crossdress at work and he was not terminated because he violated any Winn-Dixie on-duty dress code. He was never told by any Winn-Dixie manager that he was being terminated for appearing or acting effeminate at work, *i.e.*, for having effeminate mannerisms or a high voice. Nor did any Winn-Dixie manager ever tell plaintiff that he did not fit a male stereotype or assign him work that stereotypically would be performed by a female.

. . . .

Issues Presented

Plaintiff alleges two grounds in support of his motion for summary judgment. First, plaintiff argues that Title VII prohibits employment discrimination on the basis of sexual stereotyping and that defendant's termination of him for his off-duty acts of crossdressing and impersonating a woman is a form of forbidden sexual stereotyping. Second, plaintiff contends that he is a victim of disparate treatment in violation of Title VII. He alleges that he was terminated because he cross-dressed while off-duty, although other similarly situated female employees were not discharged.

Defendant denies that plaintiff was fired for failing to conform to a male stereotype. It asserts that plaintiff's activities as a male who publicly pretended to be a female do not fall within Title VII's protection. As to plaintiff's disparate treatment claim, defendant contends that the there is no evidence in the record that any female employee of Winn-Dixie ever crossdressed and impersonated a male.

Title VII

Title VII, 42 U.S.C. §2000e-2(a) provides in part that "[i]t shall be an unlawful employment practice for an employer (1) to . . . discharge any individual . . . because of such individual's . . . sex . . ." The threshold determination with respect to plaintiff's first claim is whether a transgendered individual who is discharged because he publicly crossdresses and impersonates a person of the opposite sex has an actionable claim under Title VII.

In *Ulane v. Eastern Airlines, Inc.*, 742 F.2d 1081 (7th Cir. 1984), a male airline pilot was fired when, following sex reassignment surgery, she attempted to return to work as a woman. The court considered whether the word "sex" in Title VII meant not only biological sex, *i.e.*, male or female, but also "sexual preference" and

---

in the front of our stores, with the truck parked in the front of the parking lot or in the front of the building, walking in, going to the office and going through the back of the store, I think if my customers recognized him . . . I'd lose business."

Istre also considered the fact that plaintiff regularly worked in Jefferson Parish, stating that, "Well, Peter said . . . [cross-dressing] was unacceptable in Jefferson Parish, and when I looked at Jefferson Parish and the amount of stores that I have in Jefferson Parish, which is approximately 18 or so stores and I've got a large customer base there that have various beliefs, be it religion or a morality or family values or people that just don't want to associate with that type of behavior, those are the things that I took into consideration."

"sexual identity." The Seventh Circuit concluded, based upon the plain meaning of the word "sex" and the legislative history of Title VII, that sex meant "biological sex." The court recognized that it is a "maxim of statutory construction that, unless otherwise defined, words should be given their ordinary, common meaning." . . . .

Plaintiff argues that his termination by Winn-Dixie was not due to his cross-dressing as a result of his gender identity disorder, but because he did not conform to a gender stereotype. In support of his argument, plaintiff relies on the United States Supreme Court's decision in *Price Waterhouse v. Hopkins*, 490 U.S. 228 (1989). [*Price Waterhouse* is presented in Chapter 5 Section B, *supra* at p. 155.] In *Price Waterhouse*, the United States Supreme Court held that discrimination on the basis of sex or gender stereotyping was discrimination because of "sex" within the meaning of Title VII. In that case, the partnership candidacy of the plaintiff, a senior manager who was the only woman of eighty-eight candidates considered for partnership, was placed on hold for a year. The Supreme Court noted that the evidence suggested that "[t]here were clear signs . . . that some of the partners reacted negatively to Hopkins' personality *because she was a woman*." (italics added). Partners at the firm criticized her because she was "macho," "overcompensated for being a woman," and suggested that she needed "a course at charm school." The most damning evidence of sex discrimination was the advice Ms. Hopkins was given to improve her partnership chances. She was told she should "walk more femininely, talk more femininely, dress more femininely, wear makeup, have her hair styled, and wear jewelry."

The Supreme Court found that the plaintiff was discriminated against because of her gender, *i.e.*, because she was a woman, in violation of Title VII. The Court explained:

> In saying that gender played a motivating part in an employment decision, we mean that, if we asked the employer at the moment of the decision what its reasons were and if we received a truthful response, one of those reasons would be that the applicant or employee was a woman. In the specific context of sex stereotyping, an employer who acts on the basis of a belief that a woman cannot be aggressive, or that she must not be, has acted on the basis of gender. . . .
>
> As for the legal relevance of sex stereotyping, we are beyond the day when an employer could evaluate employees by assuming or insisting that they matched the stereotype associated with their group, for "'[in] forbidding employers to discriminate against individuals because of their sex, Congress intended to strike at the entire spectrum of disparate treatment of men and women resulting from sex stereotypes.'" *Los Angeles Dept. of Water and Power v. Manhart*, 435 U.S. 702 (1978). An employer who objects to aggressiveness in women but whose positions require this trait places women in an intolerable and impermissible catch 22: out of a job if they behave aggressively and out of a job if they do not. Title VII lifts women out of this bind.

. . . .

After much thought and consideration of the undisputed facts of this case, the Court finds that this is not a situation where the plaintiff failed to conform to a gender stereotype. Plaintiff was not discharged because he did not act sufficiently masculine or because he exhibited traits normally valued in a female employee, but disparaged in a male employee. Rather, the plaintiff disguised himself as a person of a different sex and presented himself as a female for stress relief and to express his gender identity. The plaintiff was terminated because he is a man with a sexual or gender identity disorder who, in order to publicly disguise himself as a woman, wears women's clothing, shoes, underwear, breast prostheses, wigs, make-up, and nail polish, pretends to be a woman, and publicly identifies himself as a woman named "Donna."

Plaintiff's actions are not akin to the behavior of plaintiff in *Price Waterhouse*. The plaintiff in that case may not have behaved as the partners thought a woman should have, but she never pretended to be a man or adopted a masculine persona.

This is not just a matter of an employee of one sex exhibiting characteristics associated with the opposite sex. This is a matter of a person of one sex assuming the role of a person of the opposite sex. After a review of the legislative history of Title VII and the authorities interpreting the statute, the Court agrees with *Ulane* and its progeny that Title VII prohibits employment discrimination on the basis of sex, *i.e.*, biological sex. While Title VII's prohibition of discrimination on the basis of sex includes sexual stereotypes, the phrase "sex" has not been interpreted to include sexual identity or gender identity disorders.

. . . .

. . . . By virtue of the many courts which have struggled for two decades with the issue of whether Title VII, in prohibiting discrimination on the basis of "sex," also proscribes discrimination on the basis of sexual identity disorders, sexual preference, orientation, or status, Congress has had an open invitation to clarify its intentions. The repeated failure of Congress to amend Title VII supports the argument that Congress did not intend Title VII to prohibit discrimination on the basis of a gender identity disorder. In reaching this decision, this Court defers to Congress who, as the author of Title VII, has defined the scope of its protection. . . .

Disparate Treatment

Plaintiff's second claim is that he, as a male crossdresser, was treated differently than three women employees whom he observed wearing male clothing and who were not fired for being crossdressers. . . .

. . . . [The] Fifth Circuit has stated:

> We have held that in order for a plaintiff to show disparate treatment, she must demonstrate "that the misconduct for which she was discharged was nearly identical to that engaged in by a[n] employee [not within her protected class] whom [the company] retained." Or put another way, the

conduct at issue is not nearly identical when the difference between the plaintiff's conduct and that of those alleged to be similarly situated accounts for the difference in treatment received from the employer. . . .

There is no evidence in the record establishing that any woman who worked for the defendant was a crossdresser, *i.e.*, a woman who adorned herself as a man in order to impersonate a man and who used a man's name. While there were women working for the defendant who wore jeans, plaid shirts, and work shoes while working in the warehouse or in refrigerated compartments, there is no evidence that they were transgendered or that they were crossdressers, *i.e.*, that they impersonated men and adopted masculine personas or that they had gender identity disorders.[65] Plaintiff's claim for disparate treatment fails because he has not demonstrated a genuine issue of material fact with respect to this claim and the defendant is entitled to judgment as a matter of law.

Conclusion

Accordingly, for the above and foregoing reasons,

IT IS ORDERED that the motion of defendant, Winn-Dixie, Louisiana, Inc., for summary judgment is GRANTED.

IT IS FURTHER ORDERED that the motion of plaintiff, Peter Oiler, for summary judgment is DENIED.

Discussion

1. Why do you suppose having a medical diagnosis—here, of transvestic fetishism with gender dysphoria, and a gender identity disorder—did not help Mr. Oiler persuade the court that the defendants had unlawfully discriminated against him on the basis of sex, when a formal diagnosis (of gender identity or gender dysphoria) has been emphasized in numerous judicial decisions finding sex discrimination against transgender persons viewed as transsexual?

2. How can one "disguise" oneself as a person of a different sex, "impersonate" a person of a different sex, or "present" oneself as a person of a different sex other than by engaging in conduct conventionally associated with that sex? If the defendants did not fire women who removed their body hair or went out in public in dresses but did fire Oiler for doing that, how is that *not* sex discrimination based on normative/prescriptive sex stereotyping? Can this aspect of *Oiler*'s reasoning be reconciled with the U.S. Supreme Court's analysis of why discrimination based on a person's transgender status necessarily involves discrimination on the basis of

---

65. Plaintiff acknowledged in his deposition that he did not know if the three female employees whom he alleged were similarly situated were crossdressers or transgendered. Nor did he know whether Winn-Dixie management perceived these female employees to be crossdressers or transgendered.

sex. *See Bostock v. Clayton County, Georgia*, 140 S. Ct. 1731 (2020), Chapter 5, Section D, *supra*.

3. If the basis for firing Oiler was the presumed disapproval by defendants' customers of Oiler's gender nonconformity, would that be "private biases" which "the law cannot, directly or indirectly, give . . . effect"? *Palmore v. Sidoti*, 466 U.S. 429, 433 (1984), Chapter 8, *supra* at p. 472.

4. The U.S. Court of Appeals for the Fifth Circuit, which encompasses Louisiana, where this U.S. district judge sat, has said that for a fired employee to show disparate treatment, a Title VII plaintiff must show that the defendant retained a co-worker whose conduct was "nearly identical" to that for which the plaintiff was fired. *Smith v. Wal-Mart Stores (No. 471)*, 891 F.2d 1177 (5th Cir. 1990) (per curiam), cited in *Oiler*. Here, the court seems to suggest that the gender nonconformity of Oiler's female co-workers was not as extensive (perhaps to the point of being different in kind) as Oiler's, and so would not support an inference that he was being treated less favorably because of his sex. The "nearly identical" test is a lower court doctrine, not one the Supreme Court has articulated. (Lower courts adopting it are glossing an evidentiary burden-shifting approach from *McDonnell Douglas Corp. v. Green*, 411 U.S. 792, 802–06 (1973).) Is its logic sound?

Suzanne Goldberg has argued that "in a mobile, knowledge-based economy, actual comparators are hard to come by, even for run-of-the-mill discrimination claims." Suzanne B. Goldberg, *Discrimination by Comparison*, 120 Yale L.J. 728 (2011). Moreover, Professor Goldberg argues, "[th]is methodological problem has spilled over, conceptually, to constrict the very idea of discrimination." In her view, "the demand for similarly situated, better-treated others underinclusively misses important forms of discrimination and forecloses many individuals from having even an opportunity to be heard because sufficiently close comparators so rarely exist." Thus, "by demanding that plaintiffs produce a comparator to have a viable case, courts have transformed the comparator methodology into the substantive law of discrimination." Might Oiler's be a case where "the individual bringing the claim . . . has a trait-related aspect of identity . . . that is treated as inherently not comparable to others outside the trait-bearing group"? If so, how should sex discrimination doctrine deal with it?

Reading Guide for Doe v. Yunits II

1. In a previous phase of this litigation, Massachusetts Superior Court Judge Linda Giles granted transgender girl Pat Doe a preliminary injunction to keep her school from disciplining her for wearing otherwise acceptable girls' attire to school. *See Doe v. Yunits (I)*, No. 00-1060-A, 2000 WL 33162199 (Mass. Super. Ct. Oct. 11, 2000), Chapter 13, *supra* at p. 824, *aff'd sub nom. Doe v. Brockton Sch. Comm.*, No. 2000-J-638, 2000 WL 33342399 (Mass. App. Ct. Nov. 30, 2000). The case was then transferred to a different Superior Court judge, Ralph D. Gants (who at the time of writing of this book is Chief Justice of the Supreme Judicial Court of

Massachusetts). In the next opinion, the court considers the defendants' motion to dismiss Doe's complaint. As she has framed it, does Pat Doe's argument against aspects of the school's dress code benefit only transgender students? Why does the court dismiss the school committee (*i.e.*, school board) defendants?

2. The court notes that the federal Rehabilitation Act contains an exclusion of (some) gender identity disorders from its ban on disability discrimination. For what reasons does the court conclude that Massachusetts law provides broader protection than the Rehabilitation Act? Following that determination, why does the court refuse to dismiss Count V (disability discrimination) of Doe's complaint?

Pat Doe, By Her Next Friend, Jane Doe v. John Yunits, et al. (Doe v. Yunits II)

No. 00-1060A, 2001 WL 664947 (Mass. Super. Ct. Feb. 26, 2001)

Memorandum of Decision and Order on Defendants' Partial Motion to Dismiss and Plaintiff's Motion for Leave to Amend

GANTS, Justice.

The plaintiff, Pat Doe, is a fifteen year old student now in the eighth grade at Brockton South Junior High School who has been diagnosed with gender identity disorder. Doe is biologically male but, as a result of the gender identity disorder, has a female gender identity and prefers to be referred to as a female. Phrased simply in non-medical terminology, Doe has the soul of a female in the body of a male.

Doe has filed an eight-count complaint against the defendants, seeking injunctive relief allowing her to wear clothing in School that is customarily worn by female teenagers, and damages for the School's earlier refusal to permit her to attend wearing such clothing. On October 11, 2000, Judge Linda Giles of this Court granted Doe a preliminary injunction barring the defendants from preventing Doe "from wearing any clothing or accessories that any other male or female student could wear to school without being disciplined." The defendants now seek to narrow the scope of the complaint by moving to dismiss certain defendants and certain counts. The plaintiff has moved to amend the complaint to add the City of Brockton as a defendant.

Defendant's Partial Motion to Dismiss

The defendants have moved to dismiss:

1. the members of the School Committee as to all counts;

2. the defendants Joseph Bage, the Superintendent of Schools, Kenneth Cardone, Principal of the School, and Dr. Kenneth Sennett, Senior Director for Pupil Services ("Sennett") in their individual capacities (allowing them to remain as defendants in their official capacities only);

. . . .

5. Count V of the complaint, alleging violation of Doe's right to be free from disability discrimination guaranteed by Article CXIV of the Declaration of Rights of the Massachusetts Constitution; . . . .

1. The School Committee Defendants

All that the plaintiff currently alleges with respect to the School Committee defendants is that they promulgated or are otherwise responsible for the Dress Code for the Brockton Schools. This Dress Code declares that certain types of clothing—mesh shirts, tank tops, short shorts, spandex shorts (unless covered), and cut-off jerseys or blouses—"will *not* be tolerated at any time." (Emphasis in original). In addition, the Dress Code declares that "[c]lothing which could be disruptive or distractive to the educational process or which could affect the safety of students" will also not be tolerated.

In the complaint, Doe does not challenge the facial validity of the Dress Code. Doe does not claim a right to wear mesh shirts, tank tops, short shorts, spandex shorts (unless covered), or cut-off jerseys or blouses. Nor does Doe contend that the School, within constitutional and statutory bounds, may not prohibit the wearing of clothing which is disruptive or distractive to the educational process. Indeed, in the complaint, Doe alleges that "to the best of Pat's knowledge, her appearance has never caused undue disruption, disorder, or distraction within the school."

Rather, Doe challenges the *application* of the Dress Code to her by the defendants Bage, Cardone, and Sennett. In short, Doe contends that she has a legal right to wear clothing typically worn by girls, and the unfavorable reaction to her dress by fellow students and teachers may not lawfully constitute the disruption or distraction that justifies the School to prevent her from wearing this clothing. In addition, Doe contends that this Dress Code may not lawfully be interpreted to permit a School policy barring any biological male from wearing female clothing for fear of such disruption. Plaintiff's attorney concedes that, as of now, there is no evidence that any member of the School Committee participated in applying the Dress Policy to Doe. . . . [L]iability requires proof that they caused the Dress Policy to be applied to Doe in the allegedly forbidden manner.

Therefore, this Court allows the motion to dismiss the School Committee defendants. . . . If in discovery the plaintiff uncovers evidence that all or some of these School Committee members participated in the decision to apply the Dress Policy to Doe, the plaintiff may seek leave to amend the complaint to return all or some of these dismissed defendants as parties in the case.

2. The Defendants Bage, Cardone, and Sennett In Their Individual Capacities

The defendants Bage, Cardone, and Sennett move to be dismissed in their individual capacities, recognizing that they may still be held liable in their official capacities. For all practical purposes, they move to be released from personal liability for their conduct, but acknowledge that the Brockton Public Schools or the City may remain liable in damages if their conduct is ultimately found to be wrongful.

. . . . Massachusetts law does recognize qualified immunity patterned after the federal qualified immunity under 42 U.S.C. § 1983, but that immunity applies only to discretionary functions, not ministerial acts. Discretionary functions are limited to "discretionary conduct that involves policy making or planning." *Harry Stoller & Co. v. Lowell,* 587 N.E.2d 780 (Mass. 1992). Consequently, many decisions made by public employees that we commonly recognize to involve the exercise of discretion, such as whether to remove a drunken motorist from the roadway, how to treat a patient in an emergency room, the implementation of state police disciplinary policies, and the monitoring of a probationer, have been deemed ministerial rather than discretionary for purposes of evaluating qualified immunity.

It is not yet clear from the record whether Bage, Cardone, and Sennett were performing a discretionary function or a ministerial act in barring Doe from School until she stopped wearing clothing commonly worn by teenage girls. [I]t is premature to determine whether they may enjoy the benefits of qualified immunity. Therefore, the motion to dismiss Bage, Cardone, and Sennett, which is premised on their eligibility for qualified immunity, must be denied.

. . . .

5. Count V of the Complaint

Count V alleges that the defendants have violated Article CXIV of the Declaration of Rights of the Massachusetts Constitution, which provides, "No otherwise qualified handicapped individual shall, solely by reason of his handicap, be excluded from the participation in, denied the benefits of, or be subject to discrimination under any program or activity within the commonwealth." The defendants contend that, as a matter of law, a person, like Doe, with a gender identity disorder is not a "qualified handicapped individual" within the meaning of Article CXIV.

The language of Article CXIV is similar to the language of Section 504 of the Rehabilitation Act of 1973, 29 U.S.C. § 794 ("Federal Rehabilitation Act" or "FRA"). It differs primarily in that Article CXIV speaks of a "qualified handicapped individual" while the FRA speaks of a "qualified individual with a disability," and the FRA refers to programs and activities administered by the federal government or receiving federal financial assistance rather than programs or activities "within the commonwealth." The difference in the terminology between a "qualified handicapped individual" and a "qualified individual with a disability" has no practical consequence because the FRA defines an "individual with a disability" as "any person who (i) has a physical or mental impairment which substantially limits one or more of such person's major life activities, (ii) has a record of such an impairment, or (iii) is regarded as having such an impairment." 29 U.S.C. § 705(20)(B). The Massachusetts Legislature, in G.L. ch. 151B, § 1(17), defines an individual with a "handicap" in nearly identical language. While the Massachusetts definition of an individual with a "handicap" formally applies only to the laws against handicap discrimination in G.L. ch. 151B, it would be foolhardy not to apply that same definition to Article CXIV. Consequently, for all practical purposes, in terms of their general definition, a "qualified handicapped individual" is also a "qualified individual with a disability."

Prior to 1992, at least two federal courts refused to dismiss a claim brought under the Federal Rehabilitation Act by persons suffering from gender identity disorders.[3] See *Blackwell v. U.S. Dep't of Treasury,* 639 F. Supp. 289 (D.D.C. 1986); *Doe v. United States Postal Service,* 1985 WL 9446 (D.D.C. 1985). Both courts examined the three alternative means by which a person may be **found** "handicapped" under the FRA, and concluded that the plaintiffs had stated a claim under the FRA, either because their gender identity disorder was a physical or mental impairment that substantially limited their ability to function, or because they were regarded as having such an impairment. *Blackwell; Doe.*

In 1992, perhaps in response to these court decisions, Congress amended the Federal Rehabilitation Act specifically to exclude from the protection of the statute individuals with "gender identity disorders not resulting from physical impairments." 29 U.S.C. §705(20)(F)(i). No such exclusion has been added to Article CXIV.

The defendants contend that, since Article CXIV derived from the Federal Rehabilitation Act, this Court should interpret CXIV to incorporate all subsequent amendments to the FRA, even when the Massachusetts Legislature has not itself enacted such amendments. The Supreme Judicial Court has made it clear that this Commonwealth has a proud and independent tradition in protecting the civil rights of its citizens, and will not follow in lock-step federal civil rights law. *See, e.g., Dartt v. Browning-Ferris Industries, Inc.,* 691 N.E.2d 526 (Mass. 1998) ("While we do on occasion consider judicial interpretations of Federal civil rights statutes instructive in our analyses of G.L. ch. 151B, we have not always done so."); *Labonte v. Hutchins & Wheeler,* 678 N.E.2d 853 (Mass. 1997) (Massachusetts courts will look to see how federal courts have interpreted federal civil rights law for guidance in interpreting state civil rights law, but have no obligation to follow federal case law in this area). Simply because the United States Congress chose, after enacting the Federal Rehabilitation Act, to exclude from the definition of an "individual with a disability" those persons with "gender identity disorders not resulting from physical impairments" does not mean that this Court must define a "handicapped individual" under Article CXIV to exclude persons with these disorders.

Indeed, the better view is that Massachusetts, in contrast with the federal government, chose in Article CXIV to protect all persons who meet the definition of "qualified handicapped individuals" from discrimination in state programs, regardless of the specific nature of their handicap. Massachusetts. . . . simply provided a generic definition of a "qualified handicapped individual" and allowed the courts to determine whether a plaintiff, based on that plaintiff's specific circumstances and the facts specific to his or her case, met that definition. There is wisdom to such an

---

3. One plaintiff was a transvestite [*sic*]; the other was a transsexual [*sic*].

approach. It recognizes that, as our knowledge of genetics, biology, psychiatry, and neurology develops, individuals who were not previously believed to be physically or mentally impaired may indeed turn out to be so, and may warrant protection from handicap discrimination.[4] [This] may mean that persons who were previously thought to be eccentric or iconoclastic (or worse) and who were vilified by many people in our society may turn out to have physical or mental impairments that grant them protection from discrimination. Stated differently, the traits that made them misunderstood and despised may make them persons enjoying special protection under our law.

Applying the generic definition of a "qualified handicapped individual," this Court cannot categorically say that Doe falls outside that definition. When evaluating the sufficiency of a complaint pursuant to Mass. R. Civ. P. 12(b)(6), the court must accept as true the factual allegations of the complaint and all reasonable inferences favorable to the plaintiff which can be drawn from those allegations. *Fairneny v. Savogran*, 664 N.E.2d 5 (Mass. 1996). "[The] complaint should not be dismissed unless it appears beyond a doubt that the plaintiff can prove no set of facts in support of his claim which would entitle him to relief." *Nader v. Citron*, 360 N.E.2d 870 (Mass. 1977). Genetic [*sic*; clearly should be "Gender"—Eds.] identity disorder is listed as a disorder in the *Diagnostic and Statistical Manual of Mental Disorders* (4th Ed.) and therefore arguably may be found to be "a physical or mental impairment." The plaintiff alleges that this impairment substantially limits several major life activities. In addition, plaintiff alleges that Doe, as a result of the clothing she wears and the manner she carries herself, is regarded as having such an impairment. This Court, on a motion to dismiss, must accept these allegations as true. In short, in view of the plaintiff's allegations, this Court cannot find that Doe is not a "qualified handicapped individual" entitled to the protections offered by Article CXIV. As a result, the defendants' motion to dismiss Count V must be denied.

. . . .

Plaintiff's Motion for Leave to Amend the Complaint

The plaintiff has moved for leave to amend the complaint to add the City of Brockton as a defendant. The plaintiff observes that, under G.L. ch. 76, § 16, "[a]ny pupil . . . who has been refused admission to or excluded from the public schools or from the advantages, privileges and courses of study of such public schools . . . , if the refusal to admit or exclusion was unlawful, . . . may recover from the town . . . in tort. . . ."

---

4. I note that, even under the FRA, an individual with a gender identity disorder "resulting from physical impairments" is not excluded from the definition of an "individual with a disability." 29 U.S.C.A. §705(20)(F)(i). In light of the remarkable growth in our understanding of the role of genetics in producing what were previously thought to be psychological disorders, this Court cannot eliminate the possibility that all or some gender identity disorders result "from physical impairments" in an individual's genome.

This Court has already denied the defendants' motion to dismiss Count VI, alleging constructive expulsion without due process, so it is appropriate in view of this statute to add the City of Brockton as a defendant if it is included within the statutory definition of a "town." G.L. ch. 4, § 7(34) declares that, "[i]n construing statutes the following words shall have the meanings herein given, unless a contrary intention clearly appears:... 'Town'... shall include city." Since no contrary intention clearly appears from G.L. c. 76, § 16, it is fair to infer that Doe, if she were to prevail on some or all of these claims, may be able to recover damages from the City of Brockton. Consequently, plaintiff's motion to amend must be allowed.

Order

For the reasons stated above, this Court ORDERS as follows with respect to the Defendants' Partial Motion to Dismiss:

1. The defendants' motion to dismiss the School Committee defendants ... is ALLOWED without prejudice.

2. The defendants' motion to dismiss Bage, Cardone, and Sennett in their individual capacities, premised on their eligibility for qualified immunity, is DENIED.

. . . .

5. The defendant's motion to dismiss Count V is DENIED.

. . . .

With respect to the Plaintiff's Motion for Leave to Amend the Complaint to Add the City of Brockton as a Defendant, the motion is ALLOWED.

Discussion

1. The court's opening paragraph purports to capture the essence of the case with the epigram "Doe has the soul of a female in the body of a male." What is the judge trying to convey here? To what extent is it illuminating? In what respects might this way of describing a transgender girl or woman be considered problematic? *See, e.g.,* Kimberly L. Yuracko, *Soul of a Woman: The Sex Stereotyping Prohibition at Work,* 161 U. PA. L. REV. 757, 799–803 (2013) (analyzing ways in which sex stereotyping jurisprudence might have negative consequences for views of masculinity and femininity).

2. Regarding Count 5 of Doe's complaint, why might it be "foolhardy" to interpret the state *constitution's* ban on disability discrimination as having different scope from the state's disability discrimination *statute*? *But cf.* Stephen M. Rich, *One Law of Race,* 100 IOWA L. REV. 201 (214) (arguing against judicial insistence that federal constitutional and statutory standards for assessing race discrimination be identical, or "converge").

3. With regard to persons with various disabilities, the court writes that "the traits that made them misunderstood and despised may make them persons enjoying special protection under our law." In what sense might the protection extended by laws against disability discrimination be considered "special"?

————————

DSM-V™

The fifth edition of the *Diagnostic and Statistical Manual of Mental Disorders* dramatically revised its diagnoses characteristic of transgender persons. As summarized by Kenneth J. Zucker, chair of the Sexual and Gender Identity Disorders Work Group formed by the American Psychiatric Association in 2008 and a controversial figure for some transgender people and allies, the pertinent DSM-IV-TR™ diagnoses were revised in numerous, substantial ways. Kenneth J. Zucker, *The DSM-5 Diagnostic Criteria for Gender Dysphoria*, in C. Trombetta et al., eds., Management of Gender Dysphoria: A Multidisciplinary Approach 33 (2015). The APA changed the "diagnostic label" from "Gender Identity Disorder" to "Gender Dysphoria," in part to emphasize the diagnosis's focus on distress (gender *dysphoria*) rather than identity (gender *identity* disorder). Gender Dysphoria was given its own chapter, no longer lumped together with sexual dysfunctions and paraphilias with which the "theoretical overlap" was limited and association with which was regarded by some as stigmatizing transgender persons. DSM-V™ shifted from describing "cross-gender identification" as central to the disorders—language the work group regarded as reflecting a "strictly binary gender identity concept [that] is no longer in line with the spectrum of gender identity variations that one sees clinically"—to describing Gender Dysphoria in terms of "an incongruence between, on the one hand, the identity that one experiences and/or expresses and, on the other hand, how one is expected to live based on one's assigned gender." The diagnostic criteria were adjusted, with the expectation that this would reduce false positives in children diagnosed with Gender Identity Disorder when they were merely displaying normative variation in gender expression. The criteria for Gender Dysphoria in adults and adolescents were made more specific than those for Gender Identity Disorder in DSM-IV™. The APA adopted a minimum six-month duration criterion to help ensure that people were not wrongly diagnosed on the basis of symptoms that might not prove enduring. In addition, DSM-V™ added a "posttransition" specifier, which would be of value with respect to, for example, ongoing hormone treatment of transgender people.

One thing that the revisions do not appear to have done is fully to depathologize the diagnosis of Gender Dysphoria. It is correct that, under DSM-V™, being transgender is not, on its own, a mental disorder. The diagnostic criteria for Gender Dysphoria clearly do not apply to all transgender people. The APA has not always exercised meticulous care in respecting that point. For example, the APA Fact Sheet on Gender Dysphoria said, in advance of the official DSM release, that in DSM-V™

"people whose gender at birth is contrary to the one they identify with will be diagnosed with gender dysphoria." But the Fact Sheet does go on to note more precisely that "gender nonconformity is not in itself a mental disorder" and that the "critical element" of the new diagnosis is "the presence of clinically significant distress associated with the condition."

One does, however, sometimes see activists or even scholars claim that Gender Dysphoria is not a mental disorder. *See, e.g.*, Caleb Lack, *Gender Dysphoria: New and Revised in DSM-5*, Great Plains Skeptic (May 3, 2014), https://www.skepticink.com/groups/2014/05/03/gender-dysphoria-new-and-revised-in-dsm-5/ ("Gender Dysphoria is no longer considered a mental illness per se. . . ."). *Cf.* Kevin M. Barry et al., *A Bare Desire to Harm: Transgender People and the Equal Protection Clause*, 57 B.C. L. Rev. 507, 538 n.199 (2016), excerpted *infra* (asserting that Gender Dysphoria "is not a 'disorder' at all"). For a more precise analysis, see, for example, Zinnia Jones, *"Being transgender is a mental illness": What does the DSM really say?*, Gender Analysis with Zinnia Jones (Aug. 29, 2017), https://genderanalysis.net/2017/08/beingtransgender-is-a-mental-illness-what-does-the-dsm-really-say/. Yet nothing in DSM-V™ says that Gender Dysphoria—unlike Gender Identity Disorder—is *not* a mental disorder or illness. Nor does anything in the introductory portions of DSM-V™ express that position. It remains the case that this is a manual "*of* Mental *Disorders*" (emphases added). Its introduction characterizes the manual as a "medical disease classification[]" and "a medical classification of disorders." And the criteria for diagnosing Gender Dysphoria involve distress or impairment, which have been the touchstones of the APA's approach to identifying mental illnesses. *See, e.g.*, David B. Cruz, *Controlling Desires: Sexual Orientation Conversion and the Limits of Knowledge and Law*, 72 S. Cal. L. Rev. 1297, 1313–16 (1999) (discussing definitions of mental illness including that in DSM-IV).

For a pre-DSM-V™ argument on principled and practical grounds for the retention of "the DSM diagnostic category for GID," see R. Nick Gorton, *Transgender as Mental Illness: Nosology, Social Justice, and the Tarnished Golden Mean*, in The Transgender Studies Reader 2 pp. 644–52 (Susan Stryker and Aren Z. Aizura eds., 2013). In contrast to DSM-V™, in its eleventh edition the International Classification of Diseases (ICD-11) promulgated by the World Health Organization in 2018, used by most of the world outside the United States, and discussed in Barry et al., *infra* at p. 1024, has removed its mental disorder classification of transgender status and placed a new sexual health condition of "gender incongruence" in a separate section not on "Diseases" or "Disorders" but on "Conditions related to sexual health."

The diagnostic criteria and the diagnostic features for Gender Dysphoria are presented next.

Diagnostic and Statistical Manual of Mental Disorders, 5th Edition (DSM-V™) [*]

Gender Dysphoria

. . . .

Diagnostic Criteria

Gender Dysphoria in Children   302.6 (F64.2)

A. A marked incongruence between one's experienced/expressed gender and assigned gender, of at least 6 months' duration, as manifested by at least six of the following (one of which must be Criterion A1):

> 1. A strong desire to be of the other gender or an insistence that one is the other gender (or some alternative gender different from one's assigned gender).
>
> 2. In boys (assigned gender), a strong preference for cross-dressing or simulating female attire; or in girls (assigned gender), a strong preference for wearing only typical masculine clothing and a strong resistance to the wearing of typical feminine clothing.
>
> 3. A strong preference for cross-gender roles in make-believe play or fantasy play.
>
> 4. A strong preference for the toys, games, or activities stereotypically used or engaged in by the other gender.
>
> 5. A strong preference for playmates of the other gender.
>
> 6. In boys (assigned gender), a strong rejection of typically masculine toys, games, and activities and a strong avoidance of rough-and-tumble play; or in girls (assigned gender), a strong rejection of typically feminine toys, games, and activities.
>
> 7., A strong dislike of, one's sexual anatomy.
>
> 8. A strong desire for the primary and/or secondary sex characteristics that match one's experienced gender.

B. The condition is associated with clinically significant distress or impairment in social, school, or other important areas of functioning.

Specify if:

With a disorder of sex development (*e.g.*, a congenital adrenogenital disorder such as 255.2 [E25.0] congenital adrenal hyperplasia or 259.50 [E34.50] androgen insensitivity syndrome).

Coding note: Code the disorder of sex development as well as gender dysphoria.

Gender Dysphoria in Adolescents and Adults   302.85 (F64.1)

A. A marked incongruence between one's experienced/expressed gender and assigned gender, of at least 6 months' duration, as manifested by at least two of the following:

1. A marked incongruence between one's experienced/expressed gender and primary and/or secondary sex characteristics (or in young adolescents, the anticipated secondary sex characteristics).

2. A strong desire to be rid of one's primary and/or secondary sex characteristics because of a marked incongruence with one's experienced/expressed gender (or in young adolescents, a desire to prevent the development of the anticipated secondary sex characteristics).

3. A strong desire for the primary and/or secondary sex characteristics of the other gender.

4. A strong desire to be of the other gender (or some alternative gender different from one's assigned gender).

5. A strong desire to be treated as the other gender (or some alternative gender different from one's assigned gender).

6. A strong conviction that one has the typical feelings and reactions of the other gender (or some alternative gender different from one's assigned gender).

B. The condition is associated with clinically significant distress or impairment in social, occupational, or other important areas of functioning.

Specify if:

With a disorder of sex development (*e.g.*, a congenital adrenogenital disorder such as 255.2 [E25.0] congenital adrenal hyperplasia or 259.50 [E34.50] androgen insensitivity syndrome).

Coding note: Code the disorder of sex development as well as gender dysphoria.

Specify if:

Posttransition: The individual has transitioned to full-time living in the desired gender (with or without legalization of gender change) and has undergone (or is preparing to have) at least one cross-sex medical procedure or treatment regimen—namely, regular cross-sex hormone treatment or gender reassignment surgery confirming the desired gender (*e.g.*, penectomy, vaginoplasty in a natal male; mastectomy or phalloplasty in a natal female).

. . . .

Diagnostic Features

Individuals with gender dysphoria have a marked incongruence between the gender they have been assigned (usually at birth, referred to as *natal gender*) and their experienced/expressed gender. This discrepancy is the core component of the diagnosis. There must also be evidence of distress about this incongruence. Experienced gender may include alternative gender identities beyond binary stereotypes.

Consequently, the distress is not limited to a desire to simply be of the other gender, but may include a desire to be of an alternative gender, provided that it differs from the individual's assigned gender.

Gender dysphoria manifests itself differently in different age groups. Prepubertal natal girls with gender dysphoria may express the wish to be a boy, assert they are a boy, or assert they will grow up to be a man. They prefer boys' clothing and hair-styles, are often perceived by strangers as boys, and may ask to be called by a boy's name. Usually, they display intense negative reactions to parental attempts to have them wear dresses or other feminine attire. Some may refuse to attend school or social events where such clothes are required. These girls may demonstrate marked cross-gender identification in role-playing, dreams, and fantasies. Contact sports, rough-and-tumble play, traditional boyhood games, and boys as playmates are most often preferred. They show little interest in stereotypically feminine toys (*e.g.*, dolls) or activities (*e.g.*, feminine dress-up or role-play). Occasionally, they refuse to uri-nate in a sitting position. Some natal girls may express a desire to have a penis or claim to have a penis or that they will grow one when older. They may also state that they do not want to develop breasts or menstruate.

Prepubertal natal boys with gender dysphoria may express the wish to be a girl or assert they are a girl or that they will grow up to be a woman. They have a preference for dressing in girls' or women's clothes or may improvise clothing from available materials (*e.g.*, using towels, aprons, and scarves for long hair or skirts). These chil-dren may role-play female figures (*e.g.*, playing "mother") and often are intensely interested in female fantasy figures. Traditional feminine activities, stereotypical games, and pastimes (*e.g.*, "playing house"; drawing feminine pictures; watching television or videos of favorite female characters) are most often preferred. Stereo-typical female-type dolls (*e.g.*, Barbie) are often favorite toys, and girls are their pre-ferred playmates. They avoid rough-and-tumble play and competitive sports and have little interest in stereotypically masculine toys (*e.g.*, cars, trucks). Some may pretend not to have a penis and insist on sitting to urinate. More rarely, they may state that they find their penis or testes disgusting, that they wish them removed, or that they have, or wish to have, a vagina.

In young adolescents with gender dysphoria, clinical features may resemble those of children or adults with the condition, depending on developmental level. As sec-ondary sex characteristics of young adolescents are not yet fully developed, these individuals may not state dislike of them, but they are concerned about imminent physical changes.

In adults with gender dysphoria, the discrepancy between experienced gender and physical sex characteristics is often, but not always, accompanied by a desire to be rid of primary and/or secondary sex characteristics and/or a strong desire to acquire some primary and/or secondary sex characteristics of the other gender. To varying degrees, adults with gender dysphoria may adopt the behavior, clothing, and mannerisms of the experienced gender. They feel uncomfortable being regarded by others, or functioning in society, as members of their assigned gender. Some adults may have a strong desire to be of a different gender and treated as such, and they may have an inner certainty to feel and respond as the experienced gender without seeking medical treatment to alter body characteristics. They may find other ways to resolve the incongruence between experienced/expressed and assigned gender by partially living in the desired role or by adopting a gender role neither conventionally male nor conventionally female.

———————

The American Psychiatric Association's elimination of the gender identity disorder diagnosis and adoption of an appreciably different gender dysphoria diagnosis is a signal achievement in the depathologization campaign by scholars and activists. The following article argues that it sets the stage for a shift in the understanding of the applicability of federal disability laws to anti-transgender discrimination.

Reading Guide for A Bare Desire to Harm

1. In what ways do the authors argue the gender dysphoria diagnosis in DSM-V™ differs from the gender identity disorder diagnosis in DSM-IV™, and why/how do they view these differences as significant?

2. What evidence do the authors present to support their conclusion that "transvestism, transsexualism . . . [and] gender identity disorders" were excluded from the Americans with Disabilities Act because of moral animus (roughly meaning moral hostility)? What argument do they offer for why these exclusions should be considered a transgender classification?

A Bare Desire to Harm: Transgender People and the Equal Protection Clause[*]

Kevin M. Barry, Brian Farrell, Jennifer L. Levi & Neelima Vanguri

Introduction

. . . .

"A prime part of the history of our Constitution . . . is the story of the extension of constitutional rights and protections to people once ignored or excluded." . . . .

. . . .

Like the LGB rights movement, the transgender rights movement has proceeded incrementally, successfully challenging cross-dressing laws, unfair workplace practices, public and private health insurance exclusions, and antiquated

———————

[*] Excerpted with permission from Kevin M. Barry (Professor of Law, Quinnipiac University School of Law), Brian Farrell (Associate, Sidney L. Gold & Associates, P.C), Jennifer L. Levi (Professor of Law, Western New England University School of Law), & Neelima Vanguri (Associate, Sidney L. Gold & Associates, P.C.), *A Bare Desire to Harm: Transgender People and the Equal Protection Clause*, 57 B.C. L. Rev. 507 (2016).

surgical requirements for obtaining changes to birth certificates and other official documents. [However], no transgender litigant has ever challenged—let alone succeeded in striking down—a facially discriminatory federal law under the Equal Protection Clause. . . . As a result, the constitutional rights of transgender people remain uncertain.

. . . . [The federal Americans with Disabilities Act] excludes from its definition of disability "homosexuality and bisexuality" because they "are not impairments and as such are not disabilities." . . . .

The ADA also excludes from coverage "transvestism," "gender identity disorders not resulting from physical impairments," and "transsexualism," but it does so for a very different reason. . . . [The] ADA excludes transvestism, transsexualism, and gender identity disorder ("GID") because of the moral opprobrium of two senior U.S. senators, conveyed in the eleventh hour of a marathon day-long floor debate, who believed that all were "sexual behavior disorders" undeserving of legal protection.

. . . . A successful ADA challenge would . . . be a crucial first step toward securing for transgender people . . . constitutional recognition of their equality, an affirmation of equality law's expansive embrace, and a firm rejection of moral animus as a justification for exclusion.

. . . .

I. Transgender People and Gender Dysphoria

. . . . A growing body of medical research suggests that the incongruence between a person's gender identity and assigned sex at birth is caused by "genetics and/or in utero exposure to the 'wrong' hormones during the development of the brain, such that the anatomic physical body and the brain develop in different gender paths."[46] . . . .

. . . . For a subset of transgender people, . . . the incongruence [between gender identity and assigned sex] results in gender dysphoria—*i.e.*, a feeling of stress and discomfort with one's assigned sex.[49] The national and international medical community widely regards such gender dysphoria, if clinically significant and persistent, as a serious medical condition in need of treatment. Many courts, legislatures, and agencies have accepted the consensus of the medical community and extended legal protections to people with gender dysphoria.

. . . .

---

46. Christine Michelle Duffy, *The Americans with Disabilities Act of 1990 and the Rehabilitation Act of 1973*, in Gender Identity and Sexual Orientation Discrimination in the Workplace: a Practical Guide 16-77 (Christine Michelle Duffy ed., 2014) (discussing recent medical studies).

49. Consistent with the DSM-5, this Article uses "gender dysphoria" (lowercase) as a general descriptive term to refer "to an individual's affective/cognitive discontent with the assigned gender," and "Gender Dysphoria" (uppercase) to refer "more specifically . . . [to] a diagnostic category." DSM-V.

A. Gender Dysphoria and the Medical Community

. . . .

In 2013, the American Psychiatric Association published the fifth edition of the [*Diagnostic and Statistical Manual of Mental Disorders*] ("DSM-5"), which removed the [gender identity disorder ("GID")] diagnosis entirely and added a new diagnosis, "Gender Dysphoria." According to the DSM-5, Gender Dysphoria is characterized by: (1) "a marked incongruence" between one's gender identity and one's assigned sex, which is often accompanied by "a strong desire to be rid of one's primary and secondary sex characteristics and/or to acquire primary/secondary "sex characteristics of the other gender"; and (2) intense emotional pain and suffering resulting from this incongruence. Among adolescents and adults, Gender Dysphoria often begins in early childhood, around the ages of two to three years ("Early-onset gender dysphoria"), but it may also occur around puberty or even later in life ("Late-onset gender dysphoria").

The international medical community's recognition of gender dysphoria as a serious medical condition has traced a similar path. The International Classification of Diseases ("ICD"), published by the World Health Organization pursuant to a consensus of 194 member states, has classified GID as a mental health condition since 1975. The eleventh revision of the ICD, expected in 2017, will rename "transsexualism"—the ICD's GID diagnosis for adolescents and adults—"Gender Incongruence," characterized by "a marked and persistent incongruence between an individual's experienced gender and the assigned sex."

1. From "Disorder" to "Dysphoria"

The DSM-5's deletion of GID and its addition of Gender Dysphoria reflects a major shift in the medical community's understanding of gender identity and impairment . . .

Gender Dysphoria differs from GID in four significant ways. First, and most obviously, unlike GID, Gender Dysphoria is not a "disorder." For well over thirty years, incongruence between one's identity and assigned sex was considered a "disorder" of identity, that is, something non-normative with the individual. This is no longer the case. Under the DSM-5, dysphoria, rather than incongruence, is the problem in need of treatment. The change from GID to Gender Dysphoria destigmatizes the diagnosis by shifting the focus of the clinical problem from identity to dysphoria. Simply put, having a gender identity different from one's assigned sex is no longer a "disorder"; it is perfectly healthy. What is not healthy, according to the DSM-5, and what therefore requires treatment, is the dysphoria that some transgender people experience.

Second, the diagnostic criteria for Gender Dysphoria are different than the GID criteria. Whereas the GID diagnosis required a "strong and persistent cross-gender identification" and a "persistent discomfort" with one's sex or "sense of inappropriateness" in the gender role of that sex, the criteria for Gender Dysphoria are more straightforward, requiring a "marked incongruence" between gender identity and assigned sex. Significantly, the criteria also include a "post-transition specifier for people who are living full-time as the desired gender. According to the DSM-5, this specifier was "modeled on the concept of full or partial remission," which acknowledges that hormone therapy and gender reassignment surgery may largely relieve the distress associated with the diagnosis, much as chemotherapy and radiation restore normal cell growth in people with cancer, and as anti-depressants restore healthy brain functioning in people with depression. Significantly, this specifier expands the diagnosis to those who may not formerly have been diagnosed with GID — *i.e.*, those without distress "who continue to undergo hormone therapy, related surgery, or psychotherapy or counseling to support their gender transition."

Third, the DSM-5 classifies Gender Dysphoria differently than previous versions classified GID. In every version of the DSM prior to 2013, GID was a subclass of some broader classification, such as "Disorders Usually First Evident in Infancy, Childhood, or Adolescence," alongside other subclasses, such as Developmental Disorders, Eating Disorders, and Tic Disorders. For the first time ever, the DSM categorizes the diagnosis separately from all other conditions. Under the DSM-5, Gender Dysphoria is now literally in a class all its own.

Lastly, the Gender Dysphoria diagnosis is strongly supported by recent advancements in the medical knowledge and treatment of gender identity issues. Unlike the earlier DSM's treatment of GID and transsexualism, the DSM-5 includes a section entitled "Genetics and Physiology," which explicitly discusses the genetic and, possibly, hormonal contributions to Gender Dysphoria. These findings, together with numerous recent medical studies, strongly suggest that physical impairments contribute to gender incongruence and, in turn, Gender Dysphoria. In sum, Gender Dysphoria has physical roots that the GID and transsexualism diagnoses do not expressly share.

2. A Treatable Medical Condition

If left medically untreated, Gender Dysphoria can result in depression, anxiety and, for some people, suicidality and death. Fortunately, medical treatment is available. There is no single course of medical treatment that is appropriate for every person with Gender Dysphoria. Instead, the World Professional Association For Transgender Health, Inc. ("WPATH") has established internationally accepted *Standards of Care* ("SOC") for the treatment of people with Gender Dysphoria. The SOC were originally approved in 1979 and have undergone seven revisions through 2012, reflecting the rapidly expanding body of medical research relating to gender identity.

. . . .

B. Gender Dysphoria and the Law

. . . [F]ederal and state courts have consistently recognized GID and, more recently, Gender Dysphoria, as serious medical conditions deserving of protection under disability antidiscrimination law, as well as other laws. Prior to the ADA's passage in 1990, federal disability antidiscrimination [case] law recognized GID as an impairment that may constitute a disability under the ADA's precursor, the Rehabilitation Act of 1973. . . .

Like federal disability antidiscrimination laws, state disability antidiscrimination laws historically protected people with GID. Prior to the ADA's passage, state disability antidiscrimination laws presented a diverse set of definitions for the term "disability" (or "handicap"). None of these laws explicitly excluded GID. Following the ADA's passage in 1990, many states amended their statutes to more closely track the ADA, which was widely "regarded as the 'state of the art' in disability discrimination." Today, approximately forty-three states have adopted antidiscrimination laws that track the ADA definition of disability virtually verbatim. Notably, only ten of these states have imported the ADA's exclusions. In the remaining forty states with no GID exclusion in their antidiscrimination statutes, a clear majority of courts and state agencies that have addressed the issue have held that GID and Gender Dysphoria are protected disabilities. . . .

II. Transgender People and the ADA

Although the ADA is not the only federal statute that facially discriminates against transgender people, the ADA's transgender classification is important because it perpetuates the very stigma the ADA seeks to dismantle. It is also the first federal transgender classification to be challenged under the Equal Protection Clause. . . .

The ADA excludes from coverage eleven medical conditions, including three associated with transgender people: "transvestism, transsexualism . . . [and] gender identity disorders." . . . . [Why] were they excluded from the ADA? The answer is straightforward: moral animus. The ADA's legislative history plainly demonstrates how two U.S. Senators excluded all medical conditions associated with transgender people in a feverish attempt to deny ADA coverage to mental conditions deemed morally unfit.

. . . .

A. The Civil Rights Restoration Act of 1987 and the Fair Housing Amendments Act of 1988

The first attempt at excluding transgender people from antidiscrimination laws came in May of 1988, during floor debate in the Senate over whether to override President Ronald Reagan's veto of the Civil Rights Restoration Act. Senator Jesse Helms of North Carolina argued unsuccessfully against an override on grounds that the Act would extend protection to "transvestites" under the Rehabilitation Act. His justification for excluding "transvestites" was overtly moral. "[H]andicaps," he argued, "are diseases which have no conceivable moral content and yet have been associated in the past with irrational fears—such as epilepsy—or else physical impairments. . . . Transvestism and other compulsions or addi[c]tions," by contrast, were considered by some to be "moral problems, not mental handicaps." Therefore, by extending protection to "transvestites," Congress wrongly "open[s] for the courts the opportunity to eliminate the entire concept of a moral qualification for any job, position, or privilege . . . by referring to the strong trend in psychiatry to classify almost all compulsive or destructive behavior patterns as discrete and medically treatable diseases." Senator Helms asked rhetorically,

> Do we really want private institutions, particularly schools and day care centers to be prohibited from refusing to hire a transvestite because some Federal court may find that this violates the transvestite's civil rights to wear a dress and to wear foam, that sort of thing? Do we really want to prohibit these private institutions from making employment decisions based on moral qualifications?

. . . . Senator Ted Kennedy of Massachusetts dismissed Senator Helms's argument as the fear-mongering of the "moral majority," which aimed to defeat passage of the Restoration Act by claiming that it would extend civil rights protections to gays and lesbians. Senator Helms's moral arguments failed, and Congress voted 73–24 to override the President's veto.

The second attempt at transgender exclusion came approximately five months later, on August 1, 1988, when the Senate considered amendments to the Fair Housing Act. Senator Helms again argued against civil rights protection for transgender people. . . . This time, Senator Helms succeeded, with the Senate voting 89–2 in favor of the amendment, making the Fair Housing Act the first antidiscrimination law to explicitly exclude transgender people. . . .

B. The Americans with Disabilities Act of 1990

On May 9, 1989, Senators Tom Harkin of Iowa and Ted Kennedy, along with thirty-two co-sponsors, introduced the Americans with Disabilities Act. . . .

1. Transgender Exclusions and the Senate

Support for an inclusive definition of disability abruptly changed during the Senate floor debate on the ADA on September 7, 1989, driven in large part by the moral animus of two senators. Late in the day, Senator William Armstrong of Colorado came to the floor and expressed his concerns with the ADA's definition of disability—specifically, its coverage of certain mental impairments that "might have a moral content to them or which in the opinion of some people have a moral content." According to Senator Armstrong, although "the ideals of our country certainly call upon the Senate to do whatever it can to be helpful to people in wheelchairs or who have some kind of a physical disability or handicap of some sort and who are trying to overcome it," the ADA wrongly extended coverage to "some things which by any ordinary definition we would not expect to be included." Noting that the ADA's coverage of mental impairments was "appealing to the heart" but ought to "give our heads some concern," Senator Armstrong added that he planned to introduce an amendment "that will take voyeurism and some other [mental impairments listed in the DSM-III-R] out."[144]

---

144. Senator Warren Rudman of New Hampshire likewise objected to the breadth of the ADA's definition of disability, particularly its coverage of alcoholism, drug addiction, compulsive gambling, pedophilia, kleptomania, and other "socially unacceptable, often illegal, behavior." Senator Rudman further stated,

Echoing Senator Armstrong's moral concerns, Senator Helms protested that the ADA "den[ied] the small businessman . . . the right to run his company as he sees fit." Specifically, the ADA deprived the employer of the right to make judgments about employees based on the employer's "own moral standards," with a particular emphasis on homosexuality and HIV status. Senator Helms elaborated:

> If this were a bill involving people in a wheelchair or those who have been injured in the war, that is one thing. But how in the world did you get to the place that you did not even [ex]clude transvestites? How did you get into this business of classifying people who are HIV positive, most of whom are drug addicts or homosexuals or bisexuals, as disabled? . . . What I get out of all of this is here comes the U.S. Government telling the employer that he cannot set up any moral standards for his business by asking someone if he is HIV positive, even though 85 percent of those people are engaged in activities that most Americans find abhorrent. That is one of the problems I find with this bill. . . . [H]e cannot say, look I feel very strongly about people who engage in sexually deviant behavior or unlawful sexual practices.

> . . . .

In contrast to the vigorous support of ADA coverage for people with HIV/AIDS, bipolar disorder ("manic depression"), schizophrenia, and related mental disorders, there was literally no support for coverage of medical conditions associated with transgender people. Indeed, in response to Senator Helms's objection to the ADA's coverage of "transvestites," Senator Harkin immediately accepted Senator Helms's Amendment 717 excluding "transvestites," citing Senator Helms's identical amendment excluding transvestites from the Fair Housing Act the previous year.

Late in the day, Senator Armstrong distributed his proposed amendment—a "long list of various kinds of conduct . . . extracted from the DSM III[-R]"—to Senators Harkin, Kennedy, Bob Dole of Kansas, and Orrin Hatch of Utah. . . . . [The] bill's sponsors' staff. . . . insisted that "homosexuality and bisexuality" be in the negotiated list of exclusions. Disability rights advocates reduced the list to approximately five conditions, which included homosexuality, bisexuality, and kleptomania but not any of the transgender exclusions. Dissatisfied with the meager list of exclusions, Senator Hatch entered the Senate antechamber and personally told disability rights advocates that he "needed some more." Advocates reluctantly obliged, selecting the three conditions associated with transgender people and six other conditions for exclusion from the ADA. . . .

A diagnosis of certain types of mental illness is frequently made on the basis of a pattern of socially unacceptable behavior and lacks any physiological basis. In short, we are talking about behavior that is immoral, improper, or illegal and which individuals are engaging in of their own volition, admittedly for reasons we do not fully understand. . . . [P]eople must bear some responsibility for the consequences of their own actions.

2. Transgender Exclusions in the House of Representatives

When the ADA moved to the House of Representatives for debate, coverage of HIV/AIDS was once again in controversy and, once again, prevailed. Nevertheless, the ADA's transgender exclusions once again met no opposition at all. . . .

While modest, the House's modifications underscore the moral animus that fueled the ADA's transgender exclusions. First, the House subdivided the list into two separate subsections, "Homosexuality and Bisexuality" and "Certain Conditions." Under the former, the House clarified that homosexuality and bisexuality were excluded from the ADA because they "are not impairments and as such are not disabilities." Under the latter, the House listed eleven impairments drawn from the DSM-III-R, including the three impairments associated with transgender people. In so doing, the House made abundantly clear that transvestism, GID, and transsexualism were excluded, not because they were not medical conditions, but rather because the people who had these conditions (transgender people) were deemed so depraved as to be unworthy of civil rights protection.

Second, the House version further clarified Congress's belief that GID and transsexualism were "sexual behavior disorders." But Congress was wrong. GID and transsexualism were never sexual behavior disorders; their exclusion was based on a mischaracterization of the medical literature, namely, the erroneous conflation of sexual behavior disorders with gender identity disorders. . . .

Finally, the House inserted the words "not resulting from physical impairments" after "gender identity disorders," presumably to cover [*i.e.*, let the ADA cover — Eds.] those whose gender identity disorder was attributable to a morally neutral physical impairment, not an "immoral, improper" mental disorder for which a person "should bear some responsibility."[200]

The House's version of excluded impairments was accepted at conference and became law when the ADA was signed on July 26, 1990. Two years later, on October 29, 1992, Congress passed an identical exclusion to the Rehabilitation Act.

III. Transgender People and the Equal Protection Clause

. . . .

A. Equal Protection Generally

. . . .

2. Rational Basis Review: Deferential and Demanding

For those classifications that do not merit heightened scrutiny, the burden is on the challenger of the law to show that the classification is not "rationally related to a legitimate government purpose." To complicate matters, the Supreme Court has

---

200. *See* 135 Cong. Rec. 19,896 (1989) (statement of Sen. Rudman), available at 1989 WL 183216 (supporting Senator Armstrong's amendment and stating that "people must bear some responsibility for the consequences of their own actions"). . . .

employed two distinct varieties of rational basis review—one deferential, the other considerably more demanding.

. . . . [U]nder the demanding version of rational basis review, the Court insists on evidence of an actual—not hypothetical—legitimate governmental interest, and a correlation in fact between the challenged classification and such purpose. As noted by many commentators, the Court's application of demanding over deferential rational basis review lacks coherence. . . .

The most that can be said of the extraordinarily few cases employing demanding rational basis is this: animus matters. . . . [W]hen it appears that the very goal of the legislature is to adversely impact a class—that is, disadvantage for disadvantage's sake—its impartiality is "suspect" and requires "careful consideration." As the Court famously stated in 1973, in *U.S. Department of Agriculture v. Moreno*, and as it has reiterated on multiple occasions since that time, "a bare . . . desire to harm a politically unpopular group cannot constitute a legitimate governmental interest." In short, evidence of animus can trigger demanding rational basis review. Once triggered, animus is an evidentiary trump card that discredits other "legitimate" governmental interests as pretextual.

Evidence of animus can be either direct or indirect. . . .

Direct evidence of animus (for example, in the statute's text or legislative history) is not required to trigger demanding rational basis review. The Court has inferred animus from the structure and practical effect of the challenged law. . . .

B. The ADA's Exclusion of Transvestism, Transsexualism, and GID Is a Transgender Classification

. . . . The ADA does not explicitly exclude "transgender" people. The ADA excludes people with GID, transsexualism, and transvestism. One might argue that the ADA exclusions are therefore not a "transgender" classification at all, but merely a classification of various medical impairments. This contention overlooks realities.

"Transgender" is an umbrella term that describes those whose gender identity does not conform to their assigned sex at birth. Because the defining feature of GID, transsexualism, and transvestism is nonconformity between gender identity and assigned sex at birth, everyone with these conditions is necessarily "transgender." Furthermore, because the ADA excludes not only those with these conditions, but also those who once had these conditions and all those perceived by others as having these conditions, the ADA in fact excludes a broad swath of the transgender community that does not have any of these conditions. . . .

Moreover, if there were any doubt as to the nature of the classification, it bears noting that the ADA does not simply exclude three medical conditions in the DSM associated with transgender people; it excludes the *only* three medical conditions in the DSM closely associated with transgender people. Congress's exclusion of all three DSM conditions associated with transgender people proves definitively that the ADA exclusions are a transgender classification.

C. What Level of Scrutiny for Transgender Classifications?

. . . [T]he next issue is what level of scrutiny to apply to the classification: "strict," "intermediate," or "rational basis." This section provides three alternatives. Subsection 1 proposes applying heightened scrutiny to transgender classifications because transgender people are a suspect/quasi-suspect class under the Supreme Court's four-factor test [—transgender people have suffered a history of discrimination, they have the ability to participate in and contribute to society, they exhibit immutable distinguishing characteristics, and they are a minority and lack political power.] Subsection 2 proposes applying heightened scrutiny to transgender classifications because such classifications are necessarily based on sex. Subsection 3 argues that such classifications fail even under rational basis review, because they are based on a bare desire to harm.

. . . .

2. A Sex-Based Classification: Heightened Scrutiny Based on Gender

Although the Supreme Court's four-factor test decidedly points toward heightened scrutiny of classifications based on transgender status, heightened scrutiny is warranted for another reason. Classifications based on transgender status are necessarily based on sex—a type of classification the Supreme Court has long subjected to intermediate scrutiny. This subsection argues that transgender classifications are sex-based classifications for two reasons: transgender people's nonconformance with sex stereotypes, and, more straightforwardly, transgender people's identification with a sex other than their birth sex.

. . . .

Conclusion

. . . .

A successful equal protection challenge to the ADA will extend disability rights protection to transgender people under a host of federal and state laws, and will inform the broader theoretical debate over the relationship between identity and impairment, and diagnosis and discrimination. A successful challenge will also reach far beyond disability rights to all laws that single out transgender people for disparate treatment, paving the way toward "equal dignity in the eyes of the law" for transgender people. In the words of Justice Kennedy, "The Constitution grants them that right."

Discussion

1. Should the evidence of moral animus behind the decisions of some Representatives and Senators to exclude transgender-related conditions from the ADA be sufficient to attribute that motive or purpose to the legislation and/or Congress as a whole and thereby "trigger demanding rational basis review" rather than the normal extremely deferential form of rational basis review? *See also, e.g.*, Katie Aber,

When Anti-Discrimination Law Discriminates: A Right to Transgender Dignity in Disability Law, 50 Colum. J.L. & Soc. Probs. 299 (2017) (arguing that ADA exclusion of gender identity disorders is based on animus and consequently unconstitutional).

2. This article was written before the explosion of litigation over transgender people's right to use common restrooms consistent with their gender identity (rather than the sex they were assigned at birth). A number of courts have subsequently ruled on the level of equal protection scrutiny to apply to anti-transgender discrimination. While an occasional decision has ruled rational basis review to be proper, *e.g., Johnston v. University of Pittsburgh*, 97 F. Supp. 3d 657 (W.D. Pa. 2015), the majority position as of the writing of this casebook appears to be that heightened scrutiny is required. *See, e.g., Glenn v. Brumby*, 663 F.3d 1312 (11th Cir. 2011); *Bd. of Educ. of the Highland Local Sch. Dist. v. U.S. Dep't of Educ.*, 208 F. Supp. 3d 850 (S.D. Ohio 2016); *Evancho v. Pine-Richland Sch. Dist.*, 237 F. Supp. 3d 267 (W.D. Pa. 2017); *Whitaker by Whitaker v. Kenosha Unified Sch. Dist. No. 1 Bd. of Educ.*, 858 F.3d 1034 (7th Cir. 2017). Separate from the animus argument, the authors of the article above argue that classifications based on transgender status should receive intermediate scrutiny because they "are necessarily based on sex." The Supreme Court adopted that reasoning (in the context of Title VII of the Civil Rights Act of 1964) in *Bostock v. Clayton County, Georgia*, 140 S. Ct. 1731 (2020), Chapter 5, Section D, *supra*.

3. The authors argue that "[a] growing body of medical research *suggests* that the incongruence between a person's gender identity and assigned sex at birth is caused by 'genetics and/or in utero exposure to the "wrong" hormones during the development of the brain . . .'" (emphasis added). Is that enough to meet a plaintiff's burden of proof in civil litigation (such as suits challenging statutes on constitutional grounds)?

4. The authors write: "Senator Helms protested that the ADA 'den[ied] the small businessman . . . the right to run his company as he sees fit.'" Note that Helms had a history as a segregationist, and that his lament echoed complaints some made when Congress was considering the Civil Rights Act of 1964. Does this comparison undermine the force of the "small businessman" objection to the ADA, or might the objection carry different force in the race and disability contexts?

Reading Guide for Blatt v. Cabela's Retail, Inc.

1. The following employment discrimination case develops the opportunity afforded by the move from gender identity disorder to gender dysphoria. What canon or principle of statutory interpretation does the court employ in construing the exclusion in the Americans with Disabilities Act for certain "gender identity disorders"? Note that this canon is fairly commonly invoked by courts. Why does the court conclude that the canon counsels in favor of a narrow interpretation of the ADA exclusion?

2. What exactly is the definition of "gender identity disorders" that the court embraces here? Why does the court think that it is a reasonable interpretation of the

statutory exclusion? (How does the court classify the various conditions enumerated in the statutory exclusion provision?)

Kate Lynn Blatt v. Cabela's Retail, Inc.

No. 5:14-cv-04822, 2017 WL 2178123, 55 NDLR P 41 (E.D. Pa. May 18, 2017)

[Ms. Blatt was represented by private counsel Brian Farrell, Neelima Vanguri, and Sidney L. Gold, as well as Kevin Barry, Professor of Law, Quinnipiac University School of Law.]

Opinion

Defendant Cabela's Retail, Inc.'s Partial Motion to Dismiss, ECF No. 13 — Denied

Joseph F. Leeson, Jr., United States District Judge

This action arises under Title VII of the Civil Rights Act of 1964 and the Americans with Disabilities Act of 1990 (ADA). Presently before the Court is Defendant Cabela's Retail, Inc.'s Partial Motion to Dismiss. Cabela's seeks dismissal of Count III (ADA — Disability Discrimination, Failure to Accommodate) and Count IV (ADA — Retaliation) of Plaintiff Kate Lynn Blatt's Amended Complaint because Blatt has failed to state a claim upon which relief can be granted. For the reasons set forth below, Cabela's motion is denied.

The defendant bears the burden of demonstrating that a plaintiff has failed to state a claim upon which relief can be granted. This Court must "accept all factual allegations as true, construe the complaint in the light most favorable to the plaintiff, and determine whether, under any reasonable reading of the complaint, the plaintiff may be entitled to relief."

. . . .

According to the Amended Complaint, in October 2005, Blatt was diagnosed with "Gender Dysphoria, also known as Gender Identity Disorder," which substantially limits one or more of Blatt's major life activities, including, but not limited to, interacting with others, reproducing, and social and occupational functioning. Blatt alleges that shortly after she was hired by Cabela's in September 2006, Cabela's began to discriminate against her on the basis of her sex and her disability, in violation of Title VII of the Civil Rights Act and the ADA, and that Cabela's retaliated against her for opposing this discrimination, also in violation of these statutes. Blatt further alleges that in February 2007, Cabela's terminated her employment based on her sex and disability.

The stated purpose of the ADA is to "provide a clear and comprehensive national mandate for the elimination of discrimination against individuals with disabilities." 42 U.S.C. § 12101(b)(1). In pursuit of this purpose, Congress opted to define the scope of the statute's coverage by means of a flexible and broad definition of "disability," namely, "a physical or mental impairment that substantially limits one or more major life activities of [an] individual." Id. § 12102(1)(A). Standing in contrast to this broad definition of disability, there are a few exceptions to the ADA's coverage. The provision at issue in this case, 42 U.S.C. § 12211, excludes from ADA coverage approximately one dozen conditions, including gender identity disorders.

Cabela's contends that § 12211's reference to gender identity disorders applies to Blatt's condition and that the provision therefore excludes her condition from the ADA's scope. Blatt responds that, if that is the case, then § 12211's exclusion of gender identity disorders violates her equal protection rights.

The constitutional-avoidance canon prescribes that "[w]hen the validity of an act of the Congress is drawn in question, and even if a serious doubt of constitutionality is raised, it is a cardinal principle that [the court] will first ascertain whether a construction of the statute is fairly possible by which the question may be avoided." *United States v. Witkovich*, 353 U.S. 194 (1957). Thus, if there is a "fairly possible" interpretation of § 12211 that permits the Court to avoid the constitutional question Blatt has raised, the Court must adopt that interpretation. As explained below, there is indeed such an interpretation, namely, one in which the term gender identity disorders is read narrowly to refer to only the condition of identifying with a different gender, not to encompass (and therefore exclude from ADA protection) a condition like Blatt's gender dysphoria, which goes beyond merely identifying with a different gender and is characterized by clinically significant stress and other impairments that may be disabling.[1]

Beginning with the text of the provision, the exceptions listed in § 12211 can be read as falling into two distinct categories: first, non-disabling conditions that concern sexual orientation or identity, and second, disabling conditions that are associated with harmful or illegal conduct.[2] If the term gender identity disorders were understood, as Cabela's suggests, to encompass disabling conditions such as Blatt's gender dysphoria, then the term would occupy an anomalous place in the statute,

---

1. By contrast, Cabela's suggested interpretation aligns with the term's definition in the revised third edition of the American Psychiatric Association's *Diagnostic and Statistical Manual of Mental Disorders* (the current edition at the time of the drafting of the ADA), where the term gender identity disorders is defined as broadly encompassing any disorder essentially marked by "an incongruence between assigned sex . . . and gender identity." *See* Diagnostic and Statistical Manual of Mental Disorders 71 (3d ed. revised 1987).

2. The first category includes homosexuality and bisexuality, *see* 42 U.S.C. § 12211(a), whereas the second category includes pedophilia, exhibitionism, voyeurism, compulsive gambling, kleptomania, pyromania, and "psychoactive substance use disorders resulting from current illegal use of drugs," *see* 42 U.S.C. § 12211(b).

The legislative history shows that Congress discussed the § 12211 exclusions in terms of these two distinct categories. First, there was a concern among some members of Congress that the bill would include "sexual preference as a disability or a protected class of individuals." *See The Americans with Disabilities Act of 1989: Hearing on H.R. 2273 Before the Subcomms. on Emp't Opportunities & Select Educ. of the H. Comm. on Educ. & Labor* 101 Cong. 14 (1989) (statement of Rep. Bartlett, Member, H. Comm. on Education and Labor). Second, there was a separate concern that the ADA "could protect individuals from discrimination on the basis of a variety of socially unacceptable, often illegal, behavior if such behavior is considered to be the result of a mental illness," including such conditions as "compulsive gambling, pedophilia, and kleptomania." 135 Cong. Rec. S10765-01, S10796 (daily ed. Sept. 7, 1989) (statement of Sen. Rudman), 1989 WL 183216.

as it would exclude from the ADA conditions that are actually disabling but that are not associated with harmful or illegal conduct. But under the alternative, narrower interpretation of the term, this anomaly would be resolved, as the term gender identity disorders would belong to the first category described above.

This narrower interpretation also comports with the mandate of the Court of Appeals for the Third Circuit that the ADA, as "a remedial statute, designed to eliminate discrimination against the disabled in all facets of society, . . . must be broadly construed to effectuate its purposes." *See Disabled in Action of Pa. v. Se. Pa. Transp. Auth.*, 539 F.3d 199 (3d Cir. 2008). Thus, any exceptions to the statute, such as those listed in § 12211, should be read narrowly in order to permit the statute to achieve a broad reach. *See Bonkowski v. Oberg Indus.*, 787 F.3d 190 (3d Cir. 2015) ("Following traditional canons of statutory interpretation, remedial statutes should be construed broadly to extend coverage and their exclusions or exceptions should be construed narrowly."). This interpretation is also consistent with the legislative history of § 12211, which reveals that Congress was careful to distinguish between excluding certain sexual identities from the ADA's definition of disability, on one hand, and not excluding disabling conditions that persons of those identities might have, on the other hand.[3]

In view of these considerations, it is fairly possible to interpret the term gender identity disorders narrowly to refer to simply the condition of identifying with a different gender, not to exclude from ADA coverage disabling conditions that persons who identify with a different gender may have—such as Blatt's gender dysphoria, which substantially limits her major life activities of interacting with others, reproducing, and social and occupational functioning. Because this interpretation allows the Court to avoid the constitutional questions raised in this case, it is the Court's duty to adopt it. Accordingly, Blatt's condition is not excluded by § 12211 of the ADA, and Cabela's motion to dismiss Blatt's ADA claims on this basis is denied.

Cabela's acknowledges that its motion to dismiss Blatt's disability discrimination claims rests on the Court's interpretation of § 12211. With respect to Blatt's ADA retaliation claim, however, Cabela's contends that even if Blatt has alleged a disability covered by the ADA, she has nevertheless failed to allege that she engaged in protected activity by opposing disability discrimination in her workplace. Specifically, Cabela's contends that "the Amended Complaint contains allegations that [Blatt]

---

3. For example, during the Senate debate, in response to inquiries about the proposed bill's coverage of homosexuality, HIV, and AIDS, Senator Thomas Harkin, a sponsor of the bill, clarified that although homosexuality itself would not meet the definition of a disability under the ADA, that would not prevent a person who is gay from receiving coverage under the statute if the person had a disability. *See* 135 Cong. Rec. S10765-01, S10767 (daily ed. Sept. 7, 1989), 1989 WL 183216. Similarly, the House Judiciary Committee commented that "[i]ndividuals who are homosexual or bisexual and are discriminated against because they have a disability, such as infection with the Human Immunodeficiency Virus, are protected under the ADA," and the Committee "specifically rejected amendments to exclude homosexuals with certain disabilities from coverage." H.R. Rep. 101-485, at 76 (1990), *reprinted in* 1990 U.S.C.C.A.N. 445, 499.

reported conduct that she alleges was discriminatory based on *her sex*, not any disability." Further, Cabela's contends that Blatt has failed to allege that she engaged in protected activity by asking for an accommodation for a disability or that Cabela's took an adverse employment action against her because of her alleged request for an accommodation.

Blatt responds that her Amended Complaint fairly alleges that she continually reported to her superior that she was subject to degrading and discriminatory comments on the basis of her disability, that she requested a female nametag and uniform and use of the female restroom as accommodations for her disability, and that as a result of requesting these accommodations she was subjected to a "pattern of antagonism" prior to her termination. Cabela's replies that Blatt's allegations that she was temporarily forced to wear an inaccurate name tag and was not allowed to use the female restroom do not amount to a "pattern of antagonism."

To state an ADA retaliation claim, Blatt must allege that: (1) she engaged in a protected activity; (2) she experienced an adverse employment action following the protected activity; and (3) there is a causal link between the protected activity and the adverse employment action. *See Krouse v. Am. Sterilizer Co.*, 126 F.3d 494 (3d Cir. 1997). Ordinarily, a causal connection may be shown by "(1) an unusually suggestive temporal proximity between the protected activity and the allegedly retaliatory action, or (2) a pattern of antagonism coupled with timing to establish a causal link." *Lauren W. ex rel. Jean W. v. DeFlaminis*, 480 F.3d 259 (3d Cir. 2007). A "pattern of antagonism" is a "consistent and continuous" pattern of conduct, which can include a "'constant barrage of written and verbal warnings'" as well as "'disciplinary action.'" *See Bartos v. MHM Corr. Servs., Inc.*, 454 Fed. Appx. 74 (3d Cir. 2011).

Here, Blatt has plausibly alleged that she engaged in protected activity by reporting discrimination and requesting accommodations for her disability. She has also plausibly alleged that she was subjected to a "pattern of antagonism" as a result of this activity, including Cabela's allegedly intentional and repeated refusal to provide her with a correct name tag.

The Court, accepting the allegations of the Amended Complaint as true, as it is required to do at this stage of the case, denies Cabela's request to dismiss Count III and Count IV of the Amended Complaint for the reasons set forth above. The case will be permitted to proceed to discovery, inter alia, on the facts that may or may not exist to support the claims and defenses set forth in the pleadings. A separate order follows.

Discussion

1. How, if at all, will the court's interpretation of the provision excluding (some) "gender identity disorders" from ADA coverage likely affect the stigmatization of transgender people?

2. The court gives a narrow interpretation of the ADA's gender identity disorder exclusion; how likely is this to protect trans people in practice? Kevin M. Barry, Brian Farrell, Jennifer L. Levi, & Neelima Vanguri, *A Bare Desire to Harm: Transgender People and the Equal Protection Clause*, 57 B.C. L. Rev. 507 (2016), *supra* at p. 1022, argues that Kate Lynn Blatt's employer's "negative reactions" were to her gender dysphoria. But how do we know that is the case, rather than simply being negative reactions to the difference between her gender identity and the sex she had been assigned at birth? How would a trans employee prove that? If employers fire trans employees before the employees have asked for an accommodation of their gender dysphoria, how would the employees establish that they were treated adversely because of their disability (the mental health condition "gender dysphoria" under the fifth edition of the *Diagnostic and Statistical Manual of Mental Disorders*) and *not* simply for their gender nonconformity? Or is it enough that in that case, the employer would have likely violated Title VII's ban on sex discrimination?

3. A potential advantage of relying on the Americans with Disabilities Act (or the federal Rehabilitation Act) as federal law protection against anti-transgender discrimination, and not simply on sex discrimination bans in statutes such as Title VII of the Civil Rights Act of 1964, is that "unlike [federal] sex discrimination law, [the ADA] applies to public accommodations and government services, and also mandates reasonable accommodations." Kevin Barry & Jennifer Levi, Blatt v. Cabela's Retail, Inc. *and A New Path for Transgender Rights*, 127 Yale L.J. Forum 373, 375 (2017). Whether for this reason or others, "[a]s a result of the *Blatt* litigation, transgender litigants have challenged discrimination under the ADA and Section 504 [of the Rehabilitation Act] in a broad range of settings. At the time of this writing, there are at least fifteen pending or recently decided cases under the ADA and Section 504 alleging discrimination based on gender dysphoria." Kevin M. Barry & Jennifer L. Levi, *The Future of Disability Rights Protections for Transgender People*, 35 Touro L. Rev. 25, 52 (2019). The cases Professor Barry and Professor Levi have identified span "employment, prisoner rights, and insurance and identity documents," *id.*, illustrating the breadth of these federal laws and their reach on the interpretation advanced in *Blatt*.

Reading Guide for McGowan, Reflections on *Schroer v. Billington*

1. The following article was written by Sharon McGowan (at the time of the ACLU LGBT Project, subsequently of the Civil Rights Division at the Department of Justice, and as of the date of this publication the Chief Strategy Officer and Legal Director of Lambda Legal), who served as counsel for Diane Schroer, a transgender woman who brought a successful employment discrimination suit against the Library of Congress. That litigation is discussed in Chapter 5, Section D, *supra* at p. 197; the sex discrimination aspects of the third major reported decision in the case are presented at p. 199; and related portions of McGowan's article are excerpted *supra* at p. 213.

2. What risks did McGowan identify that might be involved in arguing that anti-transgender discrimination violates laws against disability discrimination such as the Americans with Disabilities Act (ADA)? What benefits of making such an argument did she identify? Why did she ultimately not make an ADA argument on behalf of Ms. Schroer?

3. Instead, McGowan and the rest of Schroer's counsel made a substantive due process claim, that is, a claim that the Library's discrimination against Schroer unconstitutionally deprived her of liberty without due process of law, within the meaning of the Fifth Amendment's Due Process Clause. What are the "liberty interests" protected by that clause that they relied on? What was their argument as to how the Library violated Schroer's rights under the clause? What advantages did they believe their substantive due process argument afforded Schroer? What risks did they identify for this argument? In particular, why did they think the *Abigail Alliance* decision was a potential obstacle for the substantive due process claim? Why did the district court ultimately dismiss that claim?

Working with Clients to Develop Compatible Visions of What It Means to "Win" A Case: Reflections on Schroer v. Billington[*]
Sharon M. McGowan

. . . .

In this article, I recount my experience representing a transgender client, Diane Schroer, in her employment discrimination case against the Library [of Congress]. In doing so, I hope to illustrate practical and ethical questions and challenges that can arise in any kind of litigation. For example, ... [w]hen should an advocate bring a claim that has a high risk of producing bad law not only in her own case but also for future litigants based on her belief that, even in losing the claim, benefits might accrue to her client?

. . . .

Part II(B) discusses the second critical decision: how to best explain to the court the experience of transsexuality and the important interests at stake when an individual undertakes a gender transition. In thinking through this question, we were cognizant of the broader debate, outlined in Part II(B)(1), about whether it is appropriate for transsexuality to be considered a mental health disorder, and whether a mental health framework is appropriate for pursuing claims on behalf of transgender clients. Part II(B)(2) describes our attempt to reconcile these views with the views of our client on these various questions and the somewhat novel due process claim that we raised in our case to best account for the various interests and concerns at stake.

---

[*] Excerpted with permission from 45 Harvard Civil Rights-Civil Liberties Law Review 205 (2010). Copyright © 2010 the President and Fellows of Harvard College; Sharon M. McGowan.

. . . .

Part IV offers some post-litigation reflections. . . . In Part IV(B), I discuss our decision to continue pursuing our due process claim even after we knew that the court was open to considering our Title VII claim, a claim that would have been sufficient to make our client whole. Although our decision not to drop the claim resulted in a bad due process ruling with which we will need to contend in the future, I conclude that, on balance, the due process claim was a useful vehicle for presenting the important interests at stake for our client.

. . . .

II. Key Pre-Litigation Questions

As an impact litigation organization, the ACLU looks for cases that are factually "clean" and have a significant likelihood of producing a favorable ruling on an important legal issue. . . . [I]t appeared to be a straightforward case of discrimination due to the fact that Ms. Schroer was transgender. . . . We would need to address a number of important questions before we could agree to represent her.

. . . .

B. Beyond Sex Stereotyping: Weighing the Risks and Benefits of Raising Other Potential Legal Claims

Although sex stereotyping was a sound theory for our Title VII claim, we had lingering concerns that a court viewing transgender issues only through this lens might not gain a sufficient understanding of what it meant to be transgender. Consequently, we began considering other claims that might provide us with a better vehicle for describing the experience of being transgender to a court with little or no familiarity with the concepts of gender identity, gender transition, and transsexuality beyond the negative images that appear in mainstream media. As we explored other options, however, it was evident that they came with significant political baggage.

1. Litigating Transgender Discrimination Claims as Disability Discrimination

Some advocates for transgender litigants have used the clinical description of transsexuality, Gender Identity Disorder ("GID"), a recognized mental health condition in the American Psychiatric Association's *Diagnostic and Statistical Manual*, both as an explanation of the experience of being transgender and as a predicate for bringing disability discrimination claims, particularly in jurisdictions lacking clear protection against gender identity discrimination. Many of these cases have produced outstanding results for individual clients. However, the use of these arguments has been controversial.

In particular, critics have argued that the use of clinical terminology and the language of disability law contributes to the regulation of transgender people by "medicalizing" their identity, as this framework implies the need for a "cure."

Others have suggested that using a mental health diagnosis to explain the very identity of transgender people produces social stigma and discrimination. Specifically, transgender advocate Franklin Romeo has warned, "[b]ecause the experiences of many gender nonconforming people do not match the diagnostic criteria of GID, and because, for all except the most privileged few, accessing trans-friendly health care is extraordinarily difficult, the medical model of gender does not serve the vast majority of gender non[]conforming people." Likewise, Dean Spade has argued that the GID diagnosis is "misused by some mental health practitioners as a basis for involuntary psychiatric treatment for gender transgressive people."

The concerns expressed by these and other activists and scholars weighed heavily on my mind as we were deciding how we might explain Ms. Schroer's identity and experience as a transgender woman to a court. It struck me that any argument built upon the notion that transgender people's gender identity—an integral part of their overall identity—is itself a disorder, or that a desire to live according to one's gender identity is the manifestation of a mental disorder, might demean the experience of transgender people. Such arguments also had the potential to produce devastating consequences in terms of social stigma as well as the concomitant loss of autonomy and agency that is often associated with mental health diagnoses, which are viewed as limitations on an individual's capacity to make decisions for him or herself.

Nevertheless, I also found myself greatly influenced by the views of Jennifer Levi and Ben Klein, who have written persuasively about how disability discrimination claims on behalf of transgender people can be a powerful tool for explaining the experience of transsexuality.[57] While recognizing the limits associated with viewing the experience of transgender people through the lens of the mental health diagnosis of GID, Levi and Klein argue convincingly that the goal of disability nondiscrimination provisions is not to pathologize the individual with a particular health condition or need, but rather to recognize that society has an obligation to accommodate the needs of individuals with unique health conditions in order to maximize their ability to participate in society.

In a related article, Levi has described the benefits of using the disability framework—emphasizing in particular the duty of employers to accommodate those with health conditions—to help courts understand the ways in which seemingly neutral job requirements and social rules are impossible for transgender people to satisfy. [Citing Jennifer Levi, *Clothes Don't Make the Man (or Woman), but Gender Identity Might*, 15 Colum. J. Gender & L. 90 (2006).] The familiar disability discrimination framework gives judges a different way to understand how and why transgender people are unable to conform to the stereotypes and social norms associated with the sex assigned to them at birth:

---

57. Jennifer Levi & Bennett Klein, *Pursuing Protection for Transgender People Through Disability Laws*, *in* Transgender Rights 74, 80–83 (Paisley Currah et al. eds., 2006)[, excerpted *supra* at p. 959)].

A disability claim gives a court a construct for understanding why some-one cannot conform to a gender stereotype and does so in language a judge can understand. That is, different health conditions are widely under-stood to change the way an individual might respond to a particular job requirement, making the judge without the health condition a poor arbiter of the job requirement's effects. By incorporating a medical claim associ-ated with one's gender identity or gender expression, courts can distance themselves from the particular facts and circumstances of a case and take seriously the dysphoria experienced by a plaintiff's forced conformity to a gender norm. [*Id.*]

This analysis led us to consider bringing a disability discrimination claim as a companion to our sex discrimination claim. The problem was that, because Ms. Schroer suffered discrimination by a federal employer, we only had federal claims at our disposal, and the federal Americans with Disabilities Act contains an irratio-nal and discriminatory exclusion for any claims related to GID. Without a federal disability claim, we would have to find an alternative mechanism for explaining to the court how the decision to transition should be understood as equally important to an individual's well-being and personhood as the decision to address any other medical need. Finding a way to do so presented the second major challenge we faced in drafting our complaint.

2. Framing the Decision to Undertake a Gender Transition as an Exercise of Constitutionally Protected Liberty

. . . . Specifically, we looked to the liberty and autonomy guarantees encom-passed by the Due Process Clause in an attempt not only to explain to the court what it meant for an individual to be transgender, but also to convey the gravity of the decision to transition from living as the gender assigned to a person at birth to the gender that was consistent with the person's gender identity.

. . . . [W]e outlined the due process principles implicated by [the facts of Ms. Schroer's life history including her course of treatment of her gender identity dis-order]. First, we asserted that the Due Process Clause protects an individual's right to make certain private decisions without government penalty. Second, we alleged that among the private decisions protected by the Due Process Clause are deci-sions related to medical treatment and the determination of one's gender identity. We then stated that, at the time of the underlying events in this case, Ms. Schroer, with the assistance of medical professionals, was undertaking a course of medical treatment to address her gender dysphoria and to bring her body into conformity with her gender identity, but that the lack of consonance between her gender iden-tity and her body was unrelated to her ability to perform the duties of the job for which she applied. Finally, we alleged that, by rescinding its offer of employment and otherwise refusing to hire Ms. Schroer because of her decisions regarding her course of medical treatment for her gender dysphoria without constitutionally suf-ficient justification, the Library violated Ms. Schroer's rights guaranteed by the Due Process Clause.

3. Defending Our Substantive Due Process Claim

[T]he government moved to dismiss our due process claim. [T]he Library argued that Ms. Schroer could not establish that she had a protected liberty interest in her decision to undergo gender reassignment surgery, and that there was "no constitutional privacy interest implicated in a person's decision to undergo a medical procedure to change their sex."

From the outset, we insisted that the government had framed the due process question improperly. In making our argument, we took cues from the Supreme Court's 2003 decision in *Lawrence v. Texas*. In that case, the Court made clear that the proper question was not whether there was a "right to engage in homosexual sodomy," as the Court had erroneously stated in *Bowers v. Hardwick*. Rather, the question was whether there was a liberty interest in terms of choosing one's sexual relationships; if there was, then the right to form an intimate same-sex relationship would fall within that protected liberty. Likewise, in defending our due process claim, our first goal was to convince the court that the appropriate question was not whether there was a protected constitutional right to undertake a gender transition, but whether the Due Process Clause protected the right of an individual to exercise his or her liberty interest in making important medical decisions without undue interference from the government, with one of the decisions that a person might make being the decision to undertake a gender transition.

In order for this argument to work, however, we needed to establish that personal decisions about medical treatment fell within the privacy, autonomy and liberty interests protected by the Due Process Clause. To support this proposition, we relied principally on the Supreme Court's holding in *Whalen v. Roe* that the substantive due process guarantee protects against violations by the government of an individual's right to privacy, which has two components: (1) an "interest in avoiding disclosure of personal matters," and (2) an "interest in independence in making certain kinds of important decisions." Focusing on the second prong of *Whalen*, we asserted that medical decisions are among the most important decisions a person can make, and cited for support, among other cases, a series of Supreme Court decisions regarding the right to refuse forced medication, and the reproductive liberty cases.

Both because medical decisions are deeply personal choices and because they implicate beliefs about the meaning of life, death, pain, and suffering, courts have recognized that the "right of privacy" includes "the freedom to care for one's health and person" [quoting *Andrews v. Ballard*, 498 F. Supp. 1038 (S.D. Tex. 1980)]. Turning then to Ms. Schroer's case, we emphasized that her decision to undergo a medically indicated transition from male to female was fundamentally no different than other serious medical decisions, and therefore should be likewise entitled to the Due Process Clause's protection against undue burdens by the government.

[W]e then recited the case law establishing that the government was required to justify its decision to withdraw its offer of employment, a form of penalty, based solely on the fact that she had exercised her protected liberty. . . .

In each of these cases where the government, acting as employer, penalized an employee because of how he or she exercised a constitutionally protected liberty interest, courts demanded a showing by the government that the conduct triggering the penalty was related to the employee's ability to perform his or her job. Relying on this body of case law, we argued that the Constitution likewise restricted the right of the Library to refuse to employ Ms. Schroer because she, in consultation with her doctors, made the constitutionally protected decision to undertake a gender transition from male to female, a medically appropriate course of treatment for her health condition that in no way negatively affected her ability to perform the job.

There was some debate among members of our legal team whether presenting a due process claim in what was "really" a Title VII case was strategically unwise. Raising a due process claim might signal to the court that we did not believe our Title VII claim was viable. There was also recognition that the court might not adopt our framing of the due process question, and might instead apply the conventional *Washington v. Glucksberg*[, 521 U.S. 702 (1997)] analysis. A court using the *Glucksberg* test would likely find that there was no history and tradition of protecting decisions around gender transition and thus dismiss our due process claim without requiring the government to justify its actions. Creating negative due process case law in defense of what some viewed as a superfluous claim in the case could undermine our ability to use due process arguments in our future transgender advocacy.

While recognizing these legitimate concerns, a majority of us were convinced not only that our due process argument was correct, but also that its framework provided an opportunity to talk about how the decision to undertake a gender transition implicates liberty and autonomy, which are important constitutional values. In our view, this case was as much about Ms. Schroer's right to define herself without government penalty as it was about her right to be free of discrimination because of sex. While the Title VII claim would allow us to discuss the nondiscrimination principles at issue in the case, a due process claim would be a more effective way for us to talk about the autonomy and liberty concerns that were equally implicated by the Library's actions. As a result, we decided to stand by this claim in our complaint. The only compromise that we made in terms of our defense of this claim was that we presented the argument last in our brief in opposition to the government's motion to dismiss.

When the court issued its decision denying the government's first motion to dismiss, we could not tell what the court thought of our due process argument because the decision did not address the claim at all. By reading between the lines of the decision, it seemed to us that our discussion of gender dysphoria as a health condition, and our framing of the decision to transition as a medical one, had a positive effect in terms of the court's understanding of the important interests at stake in this case. In particular, we were heartened by the court's extensive recitation of our allegations about gender identity and gender dysphoria, and were optimistic that the court would ultimately recognize that our client's decision to transition involved important questions of self-definition and liberty.

In other ways, however, the court's recognition that Ms. Schroer's case involved her right to define herself as a woman, and live as a woman, appeared to present an obstacle in terms of our ability to convince the court that this case also involved impermissible sex stereotyping. As the court noted in its decision, Ms. Schroer was not someone who was simply looking to deviate from social stereotypes associated with masculinity. Rather, she identified as, and wished to live as, a woman. In many ways, she sought to embrace the social stereotypes associated with femininity. The court's recognition that Ms. Schroer was not simply a gender nonconforming man led to a dismissal without prejudice of our sex stereotyping claim. It appeared to us that the court believed that an employer's discomfort with someone who is transgender precluded an argument that the employer's actions were also motivated by impermissible considerations about proper behavior, conduct and appearance by men and women based on sex stereotypes.

Fortunately, in the course of discovery, we obtained statements from individuals involved in the Library's decision-making process that demonstrated how sex stereotyping influenced its decision, and therefore, we were able to amend our complaint to resuscitate those claims. . . .

IV. Post-Litigation Reflections

Even after securing an outstanding result for our client, there are always "what if?" moments at the end of litigation. . . .

B. Should We Have Dropped Our Due Process Claim?

After omitting any discussion of our due process claim from its ruling on the government's first motion to dismiss, the court dismissed the claim in its ruling on the government's renewed motion to dismiss. In considering our contention that Ms. Schroer had a liberty interest in making medical decisions about transition free from government penalty, the court began by noting that the constitutional right to privacy does not "'protect[] all choices made by patients and their physicians or subject[] to "strict scrutiny" all government interference with choice of medical treatment.'" Rather than adopting our framework, the court applied the substantive due process analysis articulated by the Supreme Court in *Washington v. Glucksberg*, and found that the right to undertake a gender transition was not "'objectively, deeply rooted in . . . history and tradition,'" and therefore was not entitled to constitutional protection. Consequently, the court ruled, Ms. Schroer had no claim that the Library had infringed upon liberty protected by the Due Process Clause.

Although we had remained hopeful that the court would accept our due process analysis, we were not completely taken by surprise when the court dismissed the claim. Between the time that we filed our complaint and when the court addressed our claim on the merits, the D.C. Circuit considered en banc, and rejected, a substantive due process claim regarding medical decision-making in a case called *Abigail Alliance for Better Access to Developmental Drugs v. Eschenbach*. In reaching its result, the *en banc* court overruled a panel decision that had approved the due process analysis that we had adopted in framing our due process claim. Specifically, the original panel considering the Abigail Alliance case found that the Supreme Court had approved "two distinct approaches when faced with a claim to a fundamental right," one of which was the "personal dignity and autonomy" approach articulated in [*Planned Parenthood v. Casey*, 505 U.S. 833 (1992)], which was our framework for presenting our due process claim. We had not relied on the panel decision in *Abigail Alliance* in our briefs, and the *en banc* court did not specifically address the panel's assertion that the Supreme Court had approved two alternative approaches to assessing due process claims. Nevertheless, we suspected that the *en banc* court's reversal of the panel's primary holding that the plaintiff's medical decision-making claim was cognizable using the "history and tradition" framework of *Glucksberg* would doom our due process claim.

Since the court's dismissal of our due process claim, there have been at least two appellate level decisions that have recognized [in the context of challenges to the "Don't Ask, Don't Tell" ban on military service by openly lesbigay persons] that the government must be able to justify adequately burdens on exercises of liberty that may not rise to the level of fundamental rights. These decisions reassure me about our chances of convincing courts to adopt our framing of the due process analysis in future cases. Although the *Abigail Alliance* decision greatly handicapped our chances of prevailing on this due process claim in courts within the D.C. Circuit, I continue to believe that it added an important dimension to the case by opening up an avenue for talking about highly personal decisions like undertaking a gender transition in a manner that affords the decision the constitutional respect that such decisions are due. With that said, I worry about how the due process ruling in our case will present an obstacle that we will need to overcome when litigating transgender cases down the road. Nevertheless, I am glad that we decided not to drop the claim, and hope that, in the future, other litigants will be able to develop these arguments further to produce a positive outcome for their clients.

Conclusion

Many lawyers go through an entire career without having the opportunity to represent a client like Diane Schroer. Even fewer are lucky enough to have an amazing client with a compelling story at a time when society and the law (in that order) are prepared to revisit an injustice that has been left unaddressed for many years. In our case, we attempted to breathe life into old claims that had been left for dead, and tried to think about transgender civil rights issues in new ways that would promote the equality, liberty, and dignity of a group of people whom society has all but stripped of their humanity and their hope. Overall, I believe that we succeeded, but not without experiencing a few bumps along the way. By describing the challenges that we encountered and by sharing our experience in grappling with these challenges, I hope that future advocates for transgender clients will be able to learn from and either avoid or successfully navigate the pitfalls that we encountered along the way. . . .

Discussion

1. McGowan writes approvingly of Jennifer Levi and Bennett Klein's argument about the goal of disability discrimination laws. Is that goal or purpose sufficient to overcome the possibility of unintended stigmatic *effects* of using such laws?

2. Given McGowan's basis for concluding that Diane Schroer did not have a viable ADA claim, should McGowan and the rest of Schroer's legal team have been spending any time thinking about the benefits of bringing a claim under the ADA in the first place?

3. Should counsel need to bring a substantive due process claim when a transgender person has been discriminated against by a federal governmental actor in order to convey to a court that a "client's decision to transition involved important questions of self-definition and liberty"? Are there other ways to help courts appreciate that?

Chapter 15

Name Changes and Naming Practices

Names matter. Names are signs or signifiers, markers of identity. Personal names identify unique individuals, and using or disregarding a person's name can be a way of respecting or dishonoring a person. Transgender scholar Katrina Rose has characterized names, for sexual minorities, as "one of the most basic aspects of their existence." Katrina C. Rose, *Three Names in Ohio:* In re Bicknell, In re Maloney *and Hope for Recognition That the Gay-Transgender Twain Has Met*, 25 T. Jefferson L. Rev. 89, 92 (2002). Moreover, because many names in the United States (and other societies) are gendered, "[f]or transgender people, the ability to choose and use a new name is a central concern because it is a claim to a self-authored identity and a refusal of a gender that feels externally and even violently imposed. . . ." Kris Franklin & Sara E. Chinn, *Transsexual, Transgender, Trans: Reading Judicial Nomenclature in Title VII Cases*, 32 Berkeley J. Gender L. & Just. 1, 2–3 (2017). Hence, Ms. Rose describes one transgender woman as having a "need not to be encumbered with a male first name during her pre-corrective genital reassignment surgery . . . period of gender transition."

This need is one that too often goes unmet. In the 2015 U.S. Transgender Survey ("USTS") (Sandy E. James et al., National Center for Transgender Equality, The Report of the 2015 U.S. Transgender Survey 4 (2016)), only 58% of respondents who were out as trans to their immediate family reported that anyone in their immediate family used their preferred name. *Id.* at 75. Forty-nine percent of respondents reported not having an ID or record with the name they preferred, and only 30% of respondents indicated they had completed a legal name change; 35% of those who did not try to change their name reported that they did not try because they could not afford it. *Id.* at 82. And even when transgender persons are ultimately able to secure judicial approval of their name change, it can sometimes come after degrading and humiliating examination of the details of their lives, their bodies, their sexualities. For one harrowing account by a transgender man, see Milo Primeaux, *What's in a Name? For Transgender People, Everything*, 91 N.Y. St. B.J. 40 (2019).

This chapter first sketches the trajectory of approaches to legal name changes by transgender persons in the United States. After exploring a New York decision that is one of the oldest cases in this textbook, the chapter traces Pennsylvania law on this issue from the early 1970s to the eve of the new millennium, showing the evolution of law on this topic in one hierarchical court system. The chapter then returns to New York to show more modern decisions and presents a basically contemporaneous case from Indiana (the state of origin of one of the early Pennsylvania petitioners). There follows a sample name-change petition illustrating the kind of court filing transgender persons might make to effectuate a name change. The chapter then closes with a case involving misnaming and misgendering as types of anti-trans harassment.

Over half a century ago, a New York court issued one of the earliest reported decisions considering a name change petition by a transgender person seeking to adopt a name conventionally associated with their gender identity rather than the sex they were assigned at birth.

Reading Guide for In the Matter of Anonymous

1. Although the petitioner in this case was a transgender woman, the court also discusses intersex conditions. (*See generally* Chapter 2, *supra*.) The term *hermaphrodite* appeared in the form *pseudo-hermaphrodite* in the court's opinion and has been used in medicine. Today, it is considered by many people with intersex conditions to be pejorative for a variety of reasons. Combining the names of a male and a female Greek god, it may connote that intersex conditions involve two sets of functioning genitals, a false, sensationalist depiction, or it may simplistically suggest that sex is based only upon gonads.

2. The court here rejects the petitioner's request for a change of birth certificate sex marker on the ground that it does not lie within the court's jurisdiction. That makes somewhat unmotivated (or undermotivated) its extensive discussion of sex identity. Be that as it may, what is the "simple formula" that the court adopts as the "test of gender"? (Note that the court's term "physiological orientation" is idiosyncratic and not clearly given precise meaning by the passages in which it appears.) Why does the petitioner satisfy that test and the court therefore grant the requested name change?

In the Matter of Anonymous

57 Misc. 2d 813, 293 N.Y.S.2d 834 (Civ. Ct. 1968)

Francis N. Pecora, J.

The petitioner, a transsexual, petitioned this court for an order (1) to permit petitioner to change his name from that appearing on his birth certificate to one assumed by petitioner, (2) to direct the Bureau of Records and Statistics of the Department of Health of the City of New York to change his birth certificate to reflect a change from male gender to female gender or, in the alternative, (3) to direct that a copy of an order forthcoming from this court be physically attached to his birth certificate now on file with the Department of Health.

Matters over which the Civil Court of the City of New York has jurisdiction are set forth in article 2 of the New York City Civil Court Act. The petitioner's application

for a direction by this court to the Department of Health to make a physical alteration of the birth certificate is in the nature of a writ of mandamus. Such relief can
only be obtained by a special proceeding in the Supreme Court of the State of New
York pursuant to CPLR article 78. Although the Civil Court has some incidental
equity jurisdiction, it is within well-defined statutory limitations and certainly does
not include matters seeking the relief sought herein. To this extent, the application
of the petitioner is denied.

The remainder of the petitioner's application demands much closer attention.
That an individual may assume any name, absent fraud or an interference with the
rights of others, is a right that existed at common law. This right is not restricted or
impaired by article 6 of the Civil Rights Law. As was stated by the court in *Matter of
"Shipley,"* 26 Misc. 2d 204, 205 N.Y.S.2d 581 (Sup. Ct. 1960): "The Civil Rights Law
provisions establishing judicial procedure for change of name are in addition to,
and not in substitution for, the common-law methods of change."

The court, after independent research, has concluded that the within application
is one of first impression. There have been many applications presented to this court
for a change of name under article 6 of the Civil Rights Law, but none wherein the
petitioner has sought a change of name from an obviously "male" name to an obviously "female" name, or vice versa.

The instant matter presents problems of immense proportions, not only from a
medico-legal viewpoint, but especially as it affects our society as a whole. Indeed,
with our present-day "enlightenment" toward those members of our society who,
for one reason or another, do not, or cannot, conform to the "norm," and with the
rapid strides of the medical profession made within the last few years, which have
brought a measure of understanding to the social problems of these so-called "non-
conformists," it is understandable that our courts will, more and more, be asked
to entertain petitions of this type. Perhaps the easiest method of disposing of this
application would be merely to deny the petition on the grounds that the instant
relief prayed for has never before been granted by this or any other court of this
State. To do so would, in effect, sweep the problem under the proverbial rug and
defer the determination until some time "in futuro." It is the court's opinion that
any difficulty presented herein is not so much in the nature of the problem itself,
but in trying to apply, perhaps inadequately, static rules of law to situations such as
that presented herein, which perhaps merit new rules and/or progressive legislation.

For purposes of clarification, the court, of necessity, was compelled to examine
not only into the "person" of the petitioner, but also into the nature of the operation
which "changed" said individual. The petitioner is a transsexual. The petitioner is
not a transvestite. "By definition, the transvestite is content to dress in the clothing of the opposite sex. The transsexual, on the other hand, will be satisfied only if
he can become converted into a sexually functioning person of the opposite sex."
See Wollman, *Surgery for the Transsexual*, 3 J. Sex Research 145–147 (1967). Sex-
reassignment operations have been performed by many surgeons in many cities,
including the United States. Dr. Leo Wollman, an acknowledged authority in the

field of transsexualism, testified at a closed hearing before this court. According to Dr. Wollman, the procedure used is to denude the penis by rolling back its epithelial cover and to use this invaginated sheath as a sensitive "vagina." The erotic sensation is retained, and vaginal orgasm is made possible.

The petitioner herein had a surgical corrective sex change (sex-reassignment) on September 14, 1966. The operation was performed in Casablanca. All male organs were removed. There is no chance that this petitioner will ever again function as a male either procreatively or sexually. The petitioner is now capable of having sexual relations as a woman although unable to procreate. "Her" physiological orientation is complete.

Among the many questions arising from this somewhat perplexing situation is one of fundamental importance. Is the gender of a given individual that which society says it is, or is it, rather, that which the individual claims it to be? The answer is not easily arrived at. It would be very simple to state that the gender of an individual has always been that which society says it to be. But to so state would be to disregard the enlightenment of our times. Let us examine the situation on a practical basis: A child is born. The doctor examines the child, perhaps carefully, perhaps only in a perfunctory manner. In any event, the doctor decides that the child is a "male." He fills out the birth certificate, which is duly recorded with the Department of Health, designating such child as a "male." For statistical purposes, and as far as society is concerned, this child is a "male." But, occasionally, a mother gives birth to a genetic female with a hypertrophied clitoris which, together with the gross appearance of the swollen labia, may lead to the erroneous diagnosis of a "male" newborn (pseudo-hermaphroditism). Of course, this physical sexual distinction may be corrected early in life by reparative surgery. But the point is that society, through the agency of this doctor, and absent reparative surgery, will continue to classify this individual as a "male," where, in fact, the true gender is "female." To go a step further, must this individual, in later life, again absent reparative surgery, conform to the dictates of society and comport himself as a "male," or should this individual rather be permitted to carry out her role in life as a true "female"?

The court is cognizant of the fact that the transsexual, anatomically, does not present the same problem as that of the pseudo-hermaphrodite. His social sex is determined by his anatomical sex. But again, by definition, his psychological sex, as distinguished from his anatomical sex, is that of the opposite sex. Absent surgical intervention, there is no question that his social sex must conform with his anatomical sex, his mental attitude notwithstanding. But once surgical intervention has taken place, whereby his anatomical sex is made to conform with his psychological sex, is not his position identical to that of the pseudo-hermaphrodite who has been surgically repaired? Should not society afford some measure of recognition to the altered situation and afford this individual the same relief as it does the pseudo-hermaphrodite?

It has been suggested that there is some middle ground between the sexes, a "no-man's land" for those individuals who are neither truly "male" nor truly "female."

Yet the standard is much too fixed for such far-out theories. Rather the application of a simple formula could and should be the test of gender, and that formula is as follows: Where there is disharmony between the psychological sex and the anatomical sex, the social sex or gender of the individual will be determined by the anatomical sex. Where, however, with or without medical intervention, the psychological sex and the anatomical sex are harmonized, then the social sex or gender of the individual should be made to conform to the harmonized status of the individual and, if such conformity requires changes of a statistical nature, then such changes should be made. Of course, such changes should be made only in those cases where physiological orientation is complete.

One of the conclusions reached by a committee of the New York Academy of Medicine was [that] "'the desire of concealment of a change of sex by the transsexual is outweighed by the public interest for protection against fraud.'" *Matter of Anonymous v. Weiner*, 50 Misc. 2d 380 (Sup. Ct. 1966). This court is in complete disagreement with the conclusion reached by the learned committee. A male transsexual who submits to a sex-reassignment is anatomically and psychologically a female in fact. This individual dresses, acts, and comports himself as a member of the opposite sex. The applicant appeared before this court and, were it not for the fact that petitioner's background was known to the court, the court would have found it impossible to distinguish this person from any other female. It would seem to this court that the probability of so-called fraud, if any, exists to a much greater extent when the birth certificate is permitted, without annotations of any type, to classify this individual as a "male" when, in fact, as aforesaid, the individual comports himself as a "female."

[The New York Academy of Medicine] further . . . stated that "'male to female transsexuals are still chromosomally males while ostensibly females.'" Nevertheless, should the question of a person's identity be limited by the results of mere histological section or biochemical analysis, with a complete disregard for the human brain, the organ responsible for most functions and reactions, many so exquisite in nature, including sex orientation? I think not.

Accordingly, the application of the petitioner for a change of name is granted, and the petitioner is further directed to file a copy of the order to be entered herein with the Department of Health, and said Department of Health is directed to attach a copy of said order to the birth certificate of the petitioner.

Discussion

1. The distinction between "transsexual," referring to one who medically transitions or desires gender transition, and "transvestite," referring to one who dresses in clothing typically worn by another sex, is sometimes used to create a distinction between "true" transsexuals and a sexual fetishist. The line is often drawn at genital surgery. Framed that way, the distinction has generally been repudiated by medical

professionals. Available data reflect that most transgender people do not have genital surgery. For example, of respondents to the USTS, the instrument with the largest sample size of its sort in the United States, only 11% of transgender women reported having had an orchiectomy, and 12% reported having had vaginoplasty or labiaplasty (with only 1% of nonbinary people assigned male at birth reporting having had each procedure). Of respondents assigned female at birth, only 2% reported having had any genital surgery (again with nonbinary persons reporting lower rates than transgender people, in this case, trans men). *See* SANDY E. JAMES ET AL., THE REPORT OF THE 2015 U.S. TRANSGENDER SURVEY 101–03. Reasons vary, but they include lack of access to medical care, medical contraindications, and comfort with current genital configurations. Older understandings were informed by a need to justify gender confirming surgery since early medical support centered on making the case for the medical necessity of genital surgery, and there was significant medical opposition to operating "on healthy tissue." It is thus no surprise that early cases, supported by medical testimony, focused on desire for genital surgery as the sine qua non of the condition then known as "transsexualism."

2. What do you suppose was the court's purpose in including a clinical description of genital reconstruction surgery to describe a transsexual person? What may have been the point of the court's specifying that the petitioner's genital surgery was performed in Casablanca?

3. In describing a newborn with clitoral hypertrophy (an enlarged clitoris, which might be taken as a penis), the court says that such "physical sexual distinction may be corrected early in life by reparative surgery." Note the slippage from language of descriptive variation ("distinction") to language of (normative) defect ("reparative"). For discussion of intersex conditions, which can include clitoral hypertrophy, and societal reactions to them, including the notion of "true gender" (as this court put it) or "true sex," see Chapter 2, *supra.*

The use of intersex individuals as a rhetorical device in an attempt to justify transgender identity is problematic because it conflates very different situations, tends to demean intersex people as abnormal in a normative rather than statistical sense, and ignores the complex reality of many different types of intersex conditions. While some intersex advocates feel that the intersex community should be seen as part of the transgender umbrella, and some intersex people identify also as transgender, more recently advocates tend to see "intersex" as describing a medical condition called DSD ("Disorders of Sex Development," or "Differences of Sex Development"), rather than an identity.

Many people with intersex conditions have a binary gender identity as male or female. Others, including people without medically diagnosed DSD, do not. What the *Anonymous* court in 1968 termed "far-out theories" are accepted by many today. Non-binary identity is now often understood to be within the umbrella of transgender and gender non-conforming identities. Jessica A. Clarke, *They, Them, and Theirs*, 132 HARV. L. REV. 894, 897–98 (2019). But as Professor Clarke notes, "not all nonbinary people identify as transgender, and many transgender people identify as men or women." *Id.* at 898. Beyond identification, some transsexual people resist nonbinary genders on the ground that the simple gender binary of male or female facilitates social acceptance for transsexual people. This understanding is, however, widely considered exclusionary by people in the transgender community today.

4. At the time of this decision, an intersex condition detected at birth was widely considered a medical emergency requiring surgery on infants, sometimes by pressuring distraught parents to worry about social ostracization and nonexistent risks of cancer. Such surgeries are frequently drastic, painful, sexually-numbing, and life-altering. What is your response to the possibility that the court imposed a surgical requirement for a transsexual person to be recognized as a member of the sex consistent with their gender identity because it was rhetorically easier to justify its socially controversial decision allowing a gendered name change?

5. Part of the New York Academy of Medicine's reasoning discussed by the court involves a notion of fraud, a frequent theme in cases addressing the legal rights of transgender people. What kind of fraud is contemplated here? Is it legal fraud, such as changing gender in order to avoid debts, or is it an unstated "social fraud" that the (overwhelmingly) male doctors found worrisome, perhaps in their potential personal relations with women?

6. The court's trope valorizing a transgender person who "passes," that is, who is indistinguishable from cisgender members of their gender, is considered problematic by many trans people and allies who today scorn the concept of passing as a certain gender as a necessary prerequisite for being a "real" member of the sex consistent with their gender identity. The valorization of passing reinforces traditional notions of a rigid dichotomy between biological males and females, casting transgender people who do not achieve full integration into the dichotomy as imposters engaged in gender fraud. Some transgender people at first appear more gender nonconforming and later appear more gender conforming.

———————

The next materials explore the evolution of name change law in cases brought by transgender petitioners in one jurisdiction, the state of Pennsylvania.

Early Pennsylvania Name Change Cases: *Dickinson* and *Dowdrick*

In the late 1970s, two different Pennsylvania trial courts considered name change petitions from transgender women seeking legal approval of the conventionally feminine names they had adopted as part of their process of transitioning to live as women. Although one decision granted the petition and the other denied it, they were united in making whether the petitioner had had gender confirmation surgery (or "sex reassignment surgery," as it was more universally called at the time) the touchstone of their analyses.

In mid-January 1978 in *In re Dickinson*, 4 Pa. D & C.3d 678 (C.P. 1978), Judge Gelfand of the Pennsylvania Court of Common Pleas in Philadelphia County entertained and granted a petition by a transgender woman who had been born in Indiana, in what the judge termed a case of first impression in the state. Her petition "pray[ed] for a decree changing her name to Roberta Dickinson and legally ruling that her sex has been changed from male to female," and it asked the judge to request the Indiana State Board of Health to amend her birth certificate to reflect her new name and change her sex marker, which apparently was a requirement for such amendments under Indiana law. Dickinson had previously secured a Social Security card and pieces of state ID with the name Roberta, which she had "nonfraudulently" been using for two years. She had also undergone "sex reassignment surgery, which operation was successful, resulting in her assuming the anatomic structures and sexual function of a female." It cited with approbation *Richards v. United States Tennis Assoc.*, 93 Misc. 2d 713 (N.Y. Sup. Ct. 1977), and *M.T. v. J.T.*, 355 A.2d 204 (N.J. Super. Ct. 1976), which treated transgender women as female for purposes of rights to participate in sex-segregated sports under New York state anti-discrimination law and of rights to marry under New Jersey state marriage law, respectively. Expressly following *M.T.*, Judge Gelfand believed granting the order simply gave effect to "a fait accompli," letting Ms. Dickinson "assum[e] legally the sex . . . she has already acquired surgically and to a medical certainty." (The court suggests that had the case involved a Pennsylvania birth certificate, it would have ordered amendment of the petitioner's birth certificate.) Accordingly, the court "ordered and decreed that: (1) The name of petitioner . . . be and is changed to Roberta Dickinson; (2) the sex of petitioner has been changed to and is legally recognized as female." Judge Gelfand also "requested" the Indiana State Board of Health "to change the name and sex of the petitioner on her birth record in conformity with this order"—presumably because Pennsylvania courts generally lack jurisdiction to order agencies of other states to take action in those states.

Fifteen days later in *In re Dowdrick*, 4 Pa. D. & C.3d 681 (C.P. 1978), Judge Sheely of the Pennsylvania Court of Common Pleas in Cumberland County rejected a different transgender woman's petition to change her name to Mary Ellen Dowdrick. She had recently opened credit accounts with two charge card companies and Blue Cross and Blue Shield when she filed the petition in November 1977, and she was undergoing psychological and hormone therapy with plans to have "sexual reassignment surgery" ("SRS") in October 1978—presumably marking the completion of one year living as a woman, which she was doing except at work where she had to present as male until she secured a court-ordered name change. The court's opinion hinged on Ms. Dowdrick's not having had SRS and on that basis distinguished earlier New York cases granting name changes to transgender women who had undergone SRS. The Pennsylvania Supreme Court had earlier interpreted the name change statute to grant trial courts discretion in name change proceedings not involving fraud to escape financial obligations, which they were to exercise "in such a way as to comport with good sense, common decency, and fairness to all concerned and to the public." Here, the court did not believe granting the petition would meet that standard:

Petitioner, by choice, has now adopted the life style of a woman, after having been married and being the father of two children. . . . With the exception of the bodily changes from the hormone injections, petitioner in all other aspects remains a man. There is nothing illegal in petitioner desiring to live and dress as a woman and the court's opinion today will not change this in any way. However, there is no guarantee that petitioner will have the surgical corrective sex change later this year. Until the sex reassignment surgery is completed, I decline to exercise the court's discretion in favor of the name change.

The reasoning of both decisions is somewhat legally questionable. Unlike some countries, the United States does not generally restrict the names that can be given to newborns, whether to insist upon conventional gendering or otherwise. (Celebrity child names as of the writing of this book have included Arrow, North, Future, and Moon Unit, to name a few.) So these courts seem to be policing gender through naming conventions more strongly than laws in the United States generally do.

Compare and contrast this pair of decisions from Pennsylvania's trial bench with the following ruling a few years later, with strikingly different rhetoric.

Reading Guide for In re Petition of Richardson to Change Name

1. The petitioner here is a transgender woman seeking to change her name to a more conventionally feminine first name (with an unusually repetitive last name). How does this judge react to her claim?

2. The judge recounts the standard the Pennsylvania Supreme Court had set for determining the lawfulness of name changes (not involving fraud to escape monetary obligations). Which element of that standard does the judge rule the petitioner failed to satisfy? What reason does the judge give for so ruling? Note that in the immediately following paragraph the opinion seems to shift ground to different sorts of concerns; what are those?

In re Petition of Percy Richardson to Change Name
23 Pa. D. & C.3d 199 (C.P. 1982)

Dowling, J.

Like the gargoyles of medieval architecture, with their distortion of human and animal figures, Percy wishes to fasten to his male body the female appellation of "Diane Diane."

In this Commonwealth, an individual cannot change his name without permission of the court acting upon a petition complying with certain statutory requirements. [Act of April 18, 1923, P.L. 75; 54 P.S. § 1 et seq.] Petitioner has fulfilled these requirements. He has advertised, given notice and presented testimony at a hearing that he was free of judgments. Mr. Richardson testified that he had no criminal record, was not engaged in criminal activity and was not attempting to avoid payment of any debts. The sole reason he advanced was "sexual preference." There was further testimony that Percy has had a boyfriend (male body and male name) for several years who is aware of his true identity. There was also introduced into evidence a letter from Dr. D.W. Spigner, Medical Director of the Hamilton Health Center, to the effect that he had been treating Percy for several years in the "female role gender with psychological testing . . . and ongoing maintenance of female hormones." It also stated that petitioner was enrolled in a gender transformation program at the Pennsylvania Hospital in Philadelphia. However, Mr. Richardson testified that he had not had any sex operations and was still physically a male. No one appeared in objection to the petition.

Even though all the statutory requirements have been complied with and no objection forthcoming, "in granting or refusing the petition . . . the Court has wide discretion . . . the petition may be granted . . . it will exercise that discretion in such a way as to comport with good sense, common decency and fairness to all concerned and to the public." *Falcucci Name Case*, 50 A.2d 200 (Pa. 1947).

Not surprisingly, there are few cases dealing with this bizarre situation. However, our neighboring county to the West, in a thoughtful and well reasoned opinion by Judge Sheely, held in an almost identical situation that in its judgment to permit a change of name where the individual's sex remained unchanged, "would not comport with good sense, common decency and fairness to all concerned, especially the public." *In re Dowdrick*, 4 Pa. D. & C.3d 681 (C.P. 1978). Judge Sheely distinguished the several other cases on this issue by noting that in those decisions, which permitted the change, sex reassignment surgery had been completed. [*See also In re Dickinson*, 4 Pa. D. & C.3d 678 (C.P. 1978).]

We can think of nothing which might be more deceptive to the public than to allow a male to use a female name. It is true, of course, that petitioner could have been given a female name at birth. One is reminded of the popular ballad of several years ago, "A Boy Named Sue," made famous by the legendary Johnny Cash. We also realize that defendant can call himself Diane and can request that others do so and probably, though unlawfully, go about in the world with that name using it to all intents and purposes; and if desired, have it engraved on his tombstone.

The point, however, as we see it is that we are being asked to lend the dignity of the court and the sanctity of the law to this freakish rechristening. To place a female name on a male is to combine incompatibles, and to do so legally is to pervert the judicial process, which is supposed to act in a rational manner.

Accordingly, we enter the following

ORDER

And now, September 24, 1982, the prayer of petitioner to change his name from Percy Richardson to Diane Diane is denied.

———————

Discussion

1. What language in the court's opinion might suggest the judge's view of transgender people? If particular judges holds such views, ought they recuse themselves pursuant to standard provisions in judicial ethics codes (and decisions under the Due Process Clause of the Fourteenth Amendment) requiring decisionmakers to be impartial and requiring recusal where there is even the appearance of bias? What about judges who hold the view that transgender people reflect natural human variation across times, places, and cultures, *cf.* Chapter 1, *supra*? For "a hard look at the dehumanizing rhetoric the law relies on to excuse doctrinally unsupportable denial of legal protection for transgender people," see Abigail W. Lloyd, *Defining the Human: Are Transgendered People Strangers to the Law*, 20 Berkeley J. Gender L. & Just. 150 (2005); *but cf.* Susan Stryker, *My Words to Victor Frankenstein above the Village of Chamounix: Performing Transgender Rage*, in The Transgender Studies Reader 244–56 (Susan Stryker & Stephen Whittle eds., 2006) (embracing and analyzing "transsexual monstrosity").

2. What test, standard, or definition is the court using to determine that petitioner is "male"?

3. What law would be violated by the petitioner's using the name Diane as the court suggests?

4. Despite characterizing the petitioner's preferred name usage in various negative ways including "unlawful[,]" the court's opinion can be read to imply that, after gender confirmation surgery, the name change would be permitted. Is this contradictory?

5. Is the judge's view of what courts do when they approve name change petitions accurate? Regardless, what would have been "irrational" about the court allowing the petitioner to choose her own name, a name which the judge conceded she could have been given at birth regardless of her natally assigned sex?

6. Fourteen years later, another Court of Common Pleas judge followed the reasoning of *Richardson* and denied another transgender woman's petition to change her name to one conventionally viewed as masculine. *See In re McIntyre*, 33 Pa. D. & C.4th 79 (C.P. 1996), *aff'd*, 687 A.2d 865 (Table) (Pa. Super. Ct. 1996), *rev'd sub nom. Matter of McIntyre*, 715 A.2d 400 (Pa. 1998). The trial judge's ruling is described in the Reading Guide for the state supreme court decision in *Matter of McIntyre, infra* at p. 1065.

Reading Guide for In re Harris

1. What would Judge Olszewski's lead opinion for the Superior Court hold about the lower court's interpretation of Pennsylvania case law about name change petitions by transgender persons, and why?

2. In the absence of more specific precedent from the Pennsylvania Supreme Court, what test does the lead opinion announce to govern, under certain

circumstances (which circumstances?), requests for name changes? What significance does genital reconstruction ("sex reassignment") surgery or lack thereof have under that test? What facts does Judge Olszewski address in applying that test?

In re Brian Harris, a/k/a Lisa Harris

707 A.2d 225 (Pa. Super. Ct. 1997)

Before Popovich, Saylor and Olszewski, JJ.

Olszewski, Judge:

As Tammy Wynette so aptly observed, sometimes it's hard to be a woman. This is especially true in the instant matter, which calls this Court to decide the case of Brian Harris, a thirty-nine-year-old man who, for the past twenty-two years, has lived as a woman. During this time, petitioner has consistently dressed and appeared in public as a female and has assumed the name "Lisa." In addition to his years of intensive psychological counseling, petitioner has undergone a number of medical procedures designed to make himself appear more feminine.[58] Specifically, petitioner receives routine estrogen hormone therapy and has had permanent reconstructive facial surgeries as well as breast implants. Although petitioner desires to have the sex reassignment surgery which involves the removal of the male genitalia and the construction of female genitalia, financial constraints have thus far made reassignment unavailable.

On April 30, 1996, petitioner filed an unopposed petition for name change in accordance with the statutory requirements of 54 Pa. C.S.A. § 701 *et seq.* Pursuant to this petition, a hearing was held on September 16, 1996, before the Honorable Gerard Long of the Court of Common Pleas of Cambria County. The first witness to testify was Dr. Constance Saunders, petitioner's counselor of twenty years. Dr. Saunders testified that, in her expert medical opinion, petitioner's desire to live as a woman was permanent and unassailable. In support of this opinion, Dr. Saunders relied upon petitioner's long history of living as a woman and the extensive surgical measures he had undergone in order to present himself more convincingly as a female. Additionally, Dr. Saunders testified that petitioner's hormonal makeup was naturally more female than male.

When asked whether the name change would benefit petitioner, Dr. Saunders testified that, both professionally and personally, the name change would be beneficial. Because of petitioner's outwardly feminine appearance, Dr. Saunders testified, he oftentimes encounters problems when required to present official identification. That is, the disparity between petitioner's female appearance and the male name on his license leads to confrontations and allegations of deceit. In fact, Dr. Saunders regularly accompanies petitioner to appointments in order to vouch that petitioner

---

58 Although there was testimony presented at the hearing in the instant matter that petitioner's hormonal makeup is more female than male, we will use masculine pronouns when referring to petitioner until such time that the name change is legally operative.

is, in fact, a man. Personally, Dr. Saunders testified that allowance of the name change would provide petitioner with a degree of dignity that is presently lacking in his life and, additionally, would afford an affirmance of petitioner's belief that he is genetically and hormonally more female than male.

Following Dr. Saunders testimony, petitioner briefly testified. In essence, petitioner stated that his desire to have his name legally changed was twofold. First, petitioner stated that he has used the name "Lisa" socially for over twenty years and that his gender identification is completely female. Additionally, petitioner swore that he desired additional surgeries, including reassignment, but that at present the costs of such procedures were prohibitive. Secondly, petitioner stated that the change of name would result in less confusion for those people requesting official identification from him in addition to eliminating the personal embarrassment that petitioner feels when he is forced to adamantly and repeatedly aver that he is a man.

. . . . [T]he court denied the petition for change of name. . . .

. . . . Preliminarily, we note that our Supreme Court long ago articulated the general standard to be applied to petitions requesting name changes. After determining that the petitioner has complied with the necessary statutory prerequisites, the court must hold a hearing after which the court may, at its discretion, grant or deny the petition. In making its determination, the court must act in such a way as to "comport with good sense, common decency and fairness to all concerned and to the public." *Petition of Falcucci*, 50 A.2d 200, 202 (Pa. 1947).

This standard has been applied with varying results by the three courts of common pleas which have addressed the instant issue. *In re Dickinson*, 4 D. & C.3d 678 (C.P. 1978), ... granted the petition.

Conversely, *In re Dowdrick*, 4 D & C.3d 681 (C.P.1978), and *In re Richardson*, 23 D. & C.3d 199 (C.P. 1982), both. . . . denied the petitioners' name change requests.[3]

After reviewing the above caselaw, the court in the instant matter held that "absent reassignment surgery it would not comport with common sense, common decency and fairness to all concerned, especially the public, to allow a change of name at this juncture." In essence, the court interpreted the caselaw from its sister courts as creating a bright-line test for determining when a transsexual may successfully petition for a name change.

The trial court's own interpretation is fundamentally flawed, however, for this petitioner has undergone permanent reconstructive surgeries whose only possible

---

3 In denying the name change petition, the *Richardson* court stated . . . :
  The point, however, as we see it is that we are being asked to lend the dignity of the court and the sanctity of the law to this freakish rechristening. To place a female name on a male is to combine incompatibles, and to do so legally is to pervert the judicial process, which is supposed to act in a rational manner.
In light of the above language, one must question whether, rather than applying the *Falcucci* standard, the *Richardson* court did not allow its personal beliefs and predilections to guide its decision.

benefit is to advance his stated desire to become a woman in all respects. Accordingly, we believe the trial court's reading to be unnecessarily narrow and decline to adopt it.

Instead, we believe that the better-reasoned approach is to require such a petitioner to demonstrate that he or she is permanently committed to living as a member of the opposite sex. While proof of reassignment surgery would undoubtedly fulfill this criteria [*sic*], the absence of such surgery does not automatically doom a petition to failure. Rather, the totality of each case's attendant circumstances must be evaluated in order to discern whether the petitioner is irretrievably committed to living as a person of the opposite gender. Therefore, we hold that, in cases in which a petitioner is seeking a change of name commensurate with a change of gender, each petition must be evaluated on a case-by-case basis to determine whether allowance of the name change would comport with good sense and fairness to all concerned.

In the instant matter, we are confronted with a factual scenario which is distinguishable from the three cases related above. It is true that petitioner has not undergone reassignment surgery; yet this fact alone cannot make this case analogous to *Dowdrick* and *Richardson*, for the instant petitioner has gone to much greater lengths than the *Dowdrick* and *Richardson* petitioners to permanently alter his gender and physical appearance. To-wit, in addition to hormone therapy, petitioner has had breast implants and facial reconstructive surgeries. These are irreversible and convince this Court that petitioner sincerely desires to live as a woman.

The standard that we enunciate today finds support in the decisions of our neighboring jurisdictions. In the name change petition *In re Anonymous*, 155 Misc. 2d 241, 587 N.Y.S.2d 548 (1992), the New York City Civil Court refused to change a pre-operative transsexual's name where the petitioner failed to present competent medical and psychiatric evidence of a commitment to living as a member of the opposite sex. The Civil Court, however, granted the name change when the same petitioner, still pre-operative, submitted appropriate medical and psychiatric affidavits upon reapplication. *In re Rivera*, 165 Misc. 2d 307, 627 N.Y.S.2d 241 (1995) [*infra*, at p. 1069].

New Jersey has adopted a standard even more permissive. In its opinion of *In re Eck*, 584 A.2d 859 (N.J. Super. Ct. App. Div. 1991), the New Jersey Superior Court, Appellate Division held:

> Absent fraud or other improper purpose a person has a right to a name change whether he or she has undergone or intends to undergo a sex change through surgery, has received hormonal injections to induce physical change, is a transvestite, or simply wants to change from a traditional "male" first name to one traditionally "female," or vice versa.

While we, like the courts of New York, require competent evidence of the petitioner's commitment to the new gender, we agree with the New Jersey Superior Court's holding that a transsexual's right to a name change does not depend upon the completion of any specific surgical process.

After careful review, we find that the facts of the instant matter plainly reveal that petitioner has made a permanent and unassailable decision to live his life as a woman. As such, the concerns of the *Dowdrick* and *Richardson* courts are not presently applicable; for should the instant petitioner discontinue his hormone therapy, the fact remains that his surgeries have permanently altered his physical appearance from that of a man to that of a woman. Additionally, we find petitioner's twenty-two-year commitment to living as a woman to be highly persuasive evidence that the petition to change his name was not made capriciously or without regard to future developments.

. . . . For twenty-two years, petitioner's visage has been such that, but for those times when he must present official identification, he convincingly passes among the general public as a woman. As such, we find that a legal name change would benefit both petitioner and the public at large and, in accordance with good sense and fairness to all concerned, should have been granted.

Order reversed; case remanded with instructions for the court to grant the petition seeking a legal name change from "Brian Harris" to "Lisa Harris"; jurisdiction relinquished.

POPOVICH, Judge, concurring:

While I join in the result offered by the majority [actually, the lead opinion, not for a majority—Eds.], I write separately to express my own reasons for granting appellant's petition for a legal name change. . . . The majority determined that appellant has a right to a name change because appellant made a permanent and invariable commitment to live his life as a woman. However, I am convinced that this determination is not necessary in order to avail appellant of his right to change his name.

In *Commonwealth v. Goodman*, 676 A.2d 234 (Pa. 1996), our supreme court set forth the legislative history of Pennsylvania's Judicial Change of Name statute, 54 Pa. C.S. § 701, as follows:

> The primary purpose of the Judicial Change of Name Statute . . . is to prohibit fraud by those trying to avoid financial obligations. This intent is reflected in the penalty provision of the statute, which applies only to "person[s] violating the provision of this chapter for the purpose of avoiding payment of taxes or other debts."

Further, the supreme court stated that the Judicial Change of Name statute is entirely procedural in nature and provides methods by which an individual may change his name on a permanent basis. *Goodman.*

This court must determine whether a petitioner has complied with the statutory requirements and to ensure that the person has no *fraudulent intentions* in changing his name. This is where the inquiry ends. . . . There is no evidence to suggest that appellant was attempting to change his name to avoid any financial obligation. In light of the statutory language and the legislature's intent, I believe that appellant's petition should be granted without probing into appellant's sex or his desire to express himself in the manner of his choosing.

In reaching this conclusion, I find the reasoning in *In re Eck*, 584 A.2d 859 (N.J. Super Ct. App. Div. 1991), very persuasive. A change of name statute "is to be construed consistently with and not in derogation of the common law." *Eck*. At common law, an individual is free at any time to adopt and use any name, if such name is used consistently, nonfraudulently and exclusively. *In the Matter of Montenegro*, 528 A.2d 1381 (Pa. Super. Ct. 1987); 54 Pa. C.S.A. § 701(b). "Absent fraud or other improper purpose a person has a right to a name change whether he or she has undergone or intends to undergo a sex change . . . or simply wants to change from a traditional "male" first name to one traditionally "female"[.]" *Eck*.

Moreover, if parents have an absolute right to choose to name their male child an obvious "female" name at birth, it is illogical that an adult does not have the same right to change his name in the future if he so desires, whatever the name shall be, provided that the person does not seek the change for fraudulent purposes.

SAYLOR, Judge, dissenting:

. . . . [A]lthough he possesses some of the outward physical characteristics of a female, his physical transformation to the opposite gender is not yet complete. To permit him to adopt an obviously female name would be to perpetuate a fiction, since the fact remains that petitioner is anatomically a male until he undergoes reassignment surgery. Only after such procedure would petitioner be a female, physically as well as psychologically. To judicially sanction a pre-operative male transsexual's adoption of an obviously female name would grant legal recognition to a physiological fiction.

Accordingly, I would affirm the trial court's denial of the petition for legal change of name.

Discussion

1. The opening humorous aside is from a song titled "Stand By Your Man." Does this initial sentence of the opinion send a signal to readers regarding the respect or lack thereof to be accorded to transgender people and their needs? Consider in this regard that the judge describes Lisa Harris as having "lived as a woman" for the past 22 years; given that, what would make it appropriate for the opinion to call Harris a "man" or to use male pronouns for Harris? Moreover, the majority's footnoted justification for its choice of masculine pronouns is questionable: There is no indication that the judge is authorized to include a gender change in the name change order, nor did the court defend the propriety of ignoring the petitioner's preferred pronoun because their name is one that is conventionally considered masculine. The pronoun usage effectively emphasizes majority skepticism about the petitioner's asserted gender.

2. By the way it distinguishes past decisions, does the court change its "case-by-case," "totality of the circumstances" standard into one requiring some kind of

surgery to permit one's name to be changed to one conventionally associated with another sex? (Does the court's statement that "a transsexual's [*sic*] right to a name change does not depend upon the completion of any specific surgical process" mean that some surgical process is required, or that none is required?) If so, that might valorize those who seek medical/physical gender transition over those who do not desire any medical/physical gender transition. Would that be appropriate in *name change* cases?

3. The court appears to be concerned about ensuring that the petitioner's name change petition not be made "capriciously or without regard to future developments." Why is the court concerned about this, and is it an appropriate concern? Moreover, to the extent that the court implies that the petitioner must demonstrate her ability to "pass as" a woman, what evidence would be required in order to meet such a standard, and it is appropriate to have this as a requirement for a court-ordered *name* change?

4. Every U.S. state has a statute or court ruling permitting a person to use any name non-deceptively without a court order (what *Harris* termed "consistently, non-fraudulently, and exclusively" used). It therefore appears that one need not obtain a court-ordered name change to use any name. It is likely incorrect to refer to one particular name as a "legal name," implying that it is the only correct name or the only name that a person is permitted to use. *See generally, e.g.*, Adam Candeub, *Privacy and Common Law Names: Sand in the Gears of Identification*, 68 Fla. L. Rev. 467 (2016).

5. Professor Heymann has argued that cases such as *In re Anonymous*, 587 N.Y.S.2d 548 (Civ. Ct. 1992), invoked by the *In re Harris* lead opinion, "adopted a descriptive theory of naming, identifying biological gender as the essential characteristic that gave a name its denotative validity." Laura A. Heymann, *Naming, Identity, and Trademark Law*, 86 Ind. L.J. 381, 430 (2011). She suggests that more recent decisions have properly "moved from a descriptive theory of naming to a causal theory of naming in that their focus is on whether the name is used to denote the individual rather than on whether it relates to any set of essential characteristics." *Id.* at 431. Names on her view thus must denote an individual — name the person — but may be changed without needing to preserve connotations associated with the person's former name, such as their sex/gender.

Reading Guide for Matter of McIntyre

1. The trial court in the following case twice denied the name change petition of the transgender woman seeking to be legally known as Katherine Marie McIntyre. *In re McIntyre*, 33 Pa. D. & C.4th 79 (C.P. 1996), *aff'd*, 687 A.2d 865 (Table) (Pa. Super. Ct. 1996), *rev'd sub nom. Matter of McIntyre*, 715 A.2d 400 (Pa. 1998). Exercising the discretion allowed it by state law doctrine regarding name changes, the court explained its choice:

> When an individual changes his name to one clearly accepted by society as female, in addition to his own personal considerations, there are

significant potential effects on the public. The implications for contorting basic and yet essential functions such as census taking are self-evident. Providers of public sanitation facilities need some clear-cut, decisive and well-accepted indicator of gender identity in order to be able to facilitate the health, sanitary and comfort needs of the public; the demands of their job would be increased many times over by court approval and therefore legal recognition of premature male-to-female name changes. The line must be drawn somewhere. When the courts are tasked with drawing that line, it must be based on a clear, reasonable and universally applicable standard. Some go so far as to assert that the differences between the sexes are superficial, perhaps manmade or even non-existent. This court disagrees.

Some of the trial court's reasoning seems primarily addressed to a change of name, and some seems primarily addressed to change of sex, the latter of which was not at issue in the petition. And, like *In re Richardson*, *supra* at p. 1055, the trial judge here—displaying a lofty notion of the judiciary's linguistic influence—denied Ms. McIntyre's name request because she had not changed her body through genital reconstruction surgery:

> The courts are the final arbitrators of disputes centered on the meaning of words. The quintessential and ever present duty of our court system is to attach fixed and meaningful definitions to the words and labels society uses and relies on to function. A rose is a rose. Remove one petal and it is still a rose. It is unnecessary to probe into the intricacies of biology and the absoluteness of genetic identity. But, one can go so far as to agree that at the point where one has removed every single petal from a rose, only then is it reasonable to say that it is a stem. The case for the assertion that it is still in essence and in fact a "rose" is self-evident, but we would concede that it may then properly be referred to as a "stem" and no longer in any meaningful way a "rose." Therefore, for these purposes here, in the same way that the complete and irreversible act of removing all of the petals from a "rose" renders it a "stem" and no longer a "rose," this court holds that the complete and irreversible act of sex reassignment surgery will legally change the person of Robert Henry McIntyre into Katherine Marie McIntyre. Only after petitioner undergoes his planned sex reassignment surgery will this court grant legal recognition to petitioner's name change.

The Superior Court affirmed the judgment of the Court of Common Pleas without opinion, but the state supreme court reversed in the decision presented next.

2. Relying on the *Falcucci Name Change* case, the Supreme Court of Pennsylvania majority articulates the legal standard that governs petitions for change of name. What is that test? What legal (as distinguished from factual) reason does the majority give for why the court of common pleas did not properly apply the correct test?

3. What does the majority identify as the primary purpose of Pennsylvania's Judicial Name Change Statute? What additional statutory purpose(s) does the concurrence identify?

4. Of what relevance does the majority say the petitioner's transgender status or medical transition details are?

In the Matter of Robert Henry McIntyre

715 A.2d 400 (Pa. 1998)

Before Flaherty, C.J., and Zappala, Cappy, Castille, Nigro and Newman, JJ.

Opinion

Zappala, Justice.

. . . .

Appellant, a fifty-three year old male, is a pre-operative transsexual who is undergoing hormonal therapy and psychotherapy in anticipation of sex-reassignment surgery. He has been struggling with personal gender identity issues since the age of ten. Appellant is the father of two adult sons and has been divorced since 1983.

In 1991, Appellant began dressing as a woman and held himself out to the community as a woman in all respects with the exception of his employment as a maintenance worker for the Harrisburg Parking Authority. He is generally known as Katherine Marie McIntyre, the name under which he leases his apartment, maintains various bank accounts and credit cards and is enrolled in membership in local organizations.

On August 25, 1995, Appellant filed a petition to change name . . . to Katherine Marie McIntyre pursuant to 54 Pa. C.S. §§ 701–705.[4] A hearing was held where Appellant presented testimony establishing that a pre-requisite to sex-reassignment surgery is that the patient undergo the "real-life test" whereby he lives for a minimum of one year in all aspects of his life in the gender he desires to be. Appellant argued that he is unable to satisfy this requirement because his employer will not recognize him as a female until it receives legal recognition of his name change.

---

4. Sections 701 and 702 provide as follows:
   § 701. Court approval required for change of name
   (a) General rule.—It shall be unlawful for any person to assume a different name by which such person is and has been known, unless such change in name is made pursuant to proceedings in court as provided by this chapter.
   (b) Informal change of name.—Notwithstanding subsection (a), a person may at any time adopt and use any name if such name is used consistently, nonfraudulently and exclusively.
   § 702. Change by order of court
   The court of common pleas of any county may by order change the name of any person resident in the county.
   Sections 703 (Effect on children), 704 (Divorced person may resume prior name) and 705 (Penalty for violation of chapter) are not relevant to the instant case.

The common pleas court denied the petition primarily on the ground that Appellant failed to present testimony or documentation of the statutory requirement that he be free of judgments. *See* Act of December 16, 1982, P.L. 1309, No. 295, §6(b). Appellant filed for reconsideration and submitted proof that he was, in fact, judgment free.

The common pleas court granted reconsideration but again denied the petition holding that it would not grant legal recognition of Appellant's name change until he undergoes sex-reassignment surgery. It found that granting the name change was premature and would be deceptive to the public and to Appellant's co-workers. . . .

Appellant contends that the trial court abused its discretion in denying his petition for name change absent a factual basis for doing so. . . . We agree.[5]

The trial court has wide discretion in ruling upon a petition to change name and should exercise its discretion in a way as to comport with good sense, common decency and fairness to all concerned and to the public. *Falcucci Name Change*, 50 A.2d 200 (Pa. 1947). Petitions for change of name may be denied upon lawful objection or if the petitioner seeks a name change in order to defraud the public. *Id.*

We must keep in mind, however, that the primary purpose of the Judicial Change of Name Statute, other than with regard to minor children, is to prohibit fraud by those attempting to avoid financial obligations. *Commonwealth v. Goodman*, 676 A.2d 234 (Pa. 1996). The penalty provision of the name change statute applies only to persons violating the act for the purpose of avoiding payment of taxes or other debts.

Here, it was undisputed that Appellant was judgment free and was not seeking a name change to avoid any financial obligations or commit fraud.[6] The fact that he

---

5. The Superior Court recently addressed the issue of whether a pre-operative transsexual may legally change his name to reflect the opposite sex in *In re: Brian Harris*, 707 A.2d 225 (1997), but a majority of the panel did not agree on the resolution. Judge Olszewski found that the petitioner must establish that he is permanently committed to living as a member of the opposite sex before the name change petition is granted.

Judge Popovich filed a concurring statement wherein he found that the petitioner's commitment to living as a woman was irrelevant to the determination of whether his petition to change name should be granted. He asserted that the court inquiry ends after it is determined that the petitioner has complied with the statutory requirements and that the petitioner has no fraudulent intentions in changing his name.

In his dissenting statement, Judge (now Justice) Saylor opined that a transsexual's name change petition should not be granted until sex reassignment surgery was completed.

6. In *Falcucci Name Change*, we observed that

if some medical practitioner petitioned for leave to change his name to that of an eminent and successful medical practitioner in the former's vicinity the court would properly deny the petition on the ground that a fraud on the public was intended. The same would be true if some member of the legal profession or some actor or a practitioner of some other profession would seek judicial authority to assume the name of an other person who gained renown in the petitioner's profession. When a petitioner for a change of name is a competitor of a highly successful person whose name he wishes to assume there is reasonable ground for suspicion that his motive in seeking a change of name is an unworthy one, and a due regard for both the public interest and for the person whose name is coveted would constrain a court to deny his petition. A court would also is a transsexual seeking a feminine name should not affect the disposition of his request.

The Superior Court of New Jersey espoused a similar view in *The Matter of William Eck*, 584 A.2d 859 (N.J. Super. Ct. App. Div. 1991). The petitioner in *Eck* was a transsexual who sought to change his name from William to Lisa. The lower court denied the request, concluding that it was inherently fraudulent for a male to assume an obviously female name for the purpose of representing himself to society as a female.

The Superior Court of New Jersey reversed, holding that

> [a]bsent fraud or other improper purpose a person has a right to a name change whether he or she has undergone or intends to undergo a sex change through surgery, has received hormonal injections to induce physical change, is a transvestite, or simply wants to change from a traditional "male" first name to one traditionally "female," or vice versa. Many first names are gender interchangeable ... and judges should be chary about interfering with a person's choice of a first name.
>
> Finally, we perceive that the judge was concerned about a male assuming a female identity in mannerism and dress. That is an accomplished fact in this case, a matter which is of no concern to the judiciary, and which has no bearing upon the outcome of a simple name change application.

Likewise, we find that there is no public interest being protected by the denial of Appellant's name change petition. The details surrounding Appellant's quest for sex-reassignment surgery are not a matter of governmental concern. As the name change statute and the procedures thereunder indicate a liberal policy regarding change of name requests, *In re: Grimes*, 609 A.2d 158 (Pa. 1992), we see no reason to impose restrictions which the legislature has not.

Accordingly, because Appellant has satisfied the statutory requirements, the trial court abused its discretion in denying his name change petition. The Order is reversed and the petition is granted.

Saylor, J., did not participate in the consideration or decision of this case.

Nigro, Justice, concurring.

.... I write separately ... to emphasize that deterrence against financial fraud may be the primary, but is not the only, purpose behind the Name Change Statute. Rather, there are other types of fraud, besides financial, that the Name Change Statute seeks to prevent.

---

properly refuse a request for a change in name if petitioner asked for the privilege of assuming a name that was bizarre or unduly lengthy or which would be difficult to pronounce or would have a ridiculous offensive connotation.

Appellant's request is not analogous to these circumstances where the public would be affected by the petitioner's choice of name.

Courts may face any number of situations, not financial in nature, where an individual is motivated to formally adopt a different name for improper reasons. For example, if evidence discloses that an individual is seeking to change his or her name in order to receive preference as a candidate on a university or employment application, the Statute would clearly compel the courts to deny that individual's name change petition.

However, under the circumstances of this case, I agree with the Majority that the record does not reflect that Appellant is seeking to change his name in order to perpetrate any type of fraud, financial or otherwise. Accordingly, I agree with the Majority's conclusion that Appellant's name change petition should be granted.

Discussion

1. It is common ground among the Pennsylvania Supreme Court justices as well as the Pennsylvania Court of Common Pleas judges that the state's name change statute bars courts from granting name changes for fraudulent purposes. The state supreme court and the court of common pleas disagreed about whether fraud or deception was implicated on the facts of McIntyre's petition. What might account for their differing views of the same litigated facts?

2. In seemingly interpreting the name change statute to allow courts to reject petitions *only* for failure to satisfy the requirements of the name change statute, the state supreme court appears to have limited the range of discretion implied by the language in the *Falcucci Name Change* case. In explaining its reasoning, does the state supreme court reject the doctrinal requirement emergent in the court of common pleas (also rejected by the superior court in the *Harris* case, *supra* this chapter) that trans persons have genital surgery in order to adopt names not conventionally associated with their natally assigned sex? (Does this case go even further than *Harris*, which rejected genital reconstruction surgery as a prerequisite for a gendered name change?) What language in *Matter of McIntyre* might support such a conclusion?

Other state court have often, though not invariably, been more hospitable to transgender name change applicants than the early decisions from the Pennsylvania courts of common pleas. Consider, in addition to *In re Anonymous*, *supra* this chapter, the following reported decisions from New York and Indiana.

Reading Guide for Matter of Rivera

1. Note that this was not petitioner's first name change petition; Rivera had previously filed in the Civil Court of Queens county, where it was twice denied. *Application of Anonymous*, 155 Misc. 2d 241, 242, 587 N.Y.S.2d 548, 549 (Civ. Ct. 1992); *see Matter of Rivera*, 165 Misc. 2d 307, 308, 627 N.Y.S.2d 241, 242 (Civ. Ct. 1995). The

court here in its full opinion exercises discretion to treat Rivera's application as a reapplication.

2. Regarding what factual issue does the court point to lack of evidence? What facts does the court use to support ruling in favor of the petitioner? What condition does the court purport to attach to its granting of the name change petition?

In the Matter of William R. Rivera

165 Misc. 2d 307, 627 N.Y.S.2d 241 (Civ. Ct. 1995)

LUCINDO SUAREZ, J.

Petitioner is a transsexual male who wishes to discard his male name and assume a female name. Petitioner states in his petition that he has undergone hormone therapy, breast augmentation and cosmetic surgery to further his female appearance, and that the use of his male name causes severe depression and the need for psychiatric help.

Upon due deliberation of the verified petition, and exhibits attached thereto, submitted in support thereof, and after conference with counsel for petitioner, the application to change the name of William Rodriguez Rivera to Veronica Rodriguez is granted to the extent discussed below. . . . .

While petitioner has the right at common law to adopt any name so long as fraud or misrepresentation is nonexistent, once he sought court approval his petition became subject to close scrutiny. It is this court's responsibility to ensure that the grant of name change will not mislead, confuse or deceive others in their dealing with petitioner. *In the Matter of the Application of Anonymous*, 155 Misc. 2d 241, 587 N.Y.S.2d 548 (Civ. Ct.1992); *In re Anonymous*, 153 Misc. 2d 893 (Civ. Ct. 1992); *Matter of Anonymous*, 57 Misc. 2d 813 (Civ. Ct. 1968). In support of his application, petitioner submitted one psychiatric report and numerous medical affirmations, including one from Dr. Alexander Tsynman, Medical Director of the Community Mental Health Center at St. John's Episcopal Hospital . . . , where petitioner has been in treatment since December 1991 for Gender Identity Disorder (transsexualism). Prior to 1991, Dr. Luba Chanin writes that petitioner was under her psychiatric care from 1982 until 1991. The prevailing psychiatric evaluation is that petitioner is a transsexual whose behavior, mannerisms and appearance are feminine, and that he is confident about his sexuality and choice of female gender. Dr. Benito B. Rish states that petitioner has undergone hormonal therapy for over 15 years, and that petitioner was born having both female and male characteristics. A psychotherapist states that petitioner is seen on a weekly basis and is under medication.

Although the documentation in support leads to the conclusion that petitioner's comportment and sex orientation is that of a female, there is no claim that petitioner has in fact undergone a sex operation. However, upon the review of the corroborating competent medical affidavits, and the totality of the circumstances herein, including petitioner's tenacity in the pursuit of this name change, it is ordered that petitioner's application to change his name from William Rodriguez Rivera to Veronica Rodriguez is granted solely upon the condition that petitioner may not use or rely upon this order as any evidence whatsoever or judicial determination that the sex of petitioner has in fact been changed anatomically. *Matter of Anonymous*, 64 Misc. 2d 309, 314 N.Y.S.2d 668 (Civ. Ct. 1970).

———————

Discussion

1. This ruling suggests that an order changing name is unrelated to an order changing sex. If so, then why did other cases require proof of surgical procedures? The court's stricture that this petitioner specifically may not rely on the order as a judicial determination of change of sex raises the question whether other petitioners receiving name change orders could so use their orders.

2. If they are not unrelated, then, although not unprecedented, what authority does Justice Suarez have to dictate to other courts how they must view his order or to dictate to this petitioner what she can or cannot do in litigation in other courts?

Reading Guide for In re A.L.

1. What legal rule does the appellate court hold governs court orders for birth certificate gender marker changes? What legal error does the appellate court hold the trial court made with respect to the rule? What is the court's order with respect to the petitioners' request to have their birth certificates amended to change their gender markers?

2. Petitioner L.S. sought not to have to publish his intended name change, which Indiana's name change statute generally requires (as do most or all states). What is the pertinent exception here allowed by Indiana Rules of Court Administrative Rule 9(G)? What evidence does the appellate court rely on in analyzing the applicability of this exception? Why does the court conclude that L.S.'s petition comes within the exception? What is the court's order with respect to L.S.'s request not to publish his intent to change his name?

In re the name Change of A.L. and in re the name Change of L.S.

81 N.E.3d 283 (Ind. Ct. App. 2017)

BAKER, Judge.

A.L. and L.S. are transgender men, who each filed a petition to change their legal gender marker. Additionally, L.S. filed petitions to change his name, to waive the publication requirement, and to seal the record pursuant to Administrative Rule 9. The trial court found that publication is required for changes of gender marker and name, and denied L.S.'s request to seal the record pursuant to Administrative Rule 9.

. . . .

Facts

A.L. and L.S. are transgender men.[7] Both men are currently working with counselors and medical professionals in their transition from female to male. A.L. has been living as a man for two years and has had medical procedures in line with his transition. L.S. has been living as a man for most of his life. He has been doing so full-time, in both his social and professional life, for approximately four years.

A.L.

On May 11, 2016, A.L. filed a pro se petition for a name change. He published his intent to change his name in a newspaper and, on July 13, 2016, the trial court granted the petition. At that same hearing, A.L. requested to have his gender marker changed on his birth certificate. The trial court directed A.L. to publish his intent to change his gender marker with a newspaper and set the matter for another hearing. A.L. subsequently obtained counsel. On August 23, 2016, A.L. filed a motion to correct error, asserting that the trial court's requirement that he publish notice of his intent to change his gender marker was contrary to Indiana law.

At an October 26, 2016, hearing, A.L. testified as to the good faith of his petition for change of gender marker and presented evidence of his medical transition. The trial court took the matter under advisement, later denying the petition because A.L. had not published his intent to change his gender marker with a newspaper. Following further litigation, on December 9, 2016, the trial court again denied A.L.'s request to avoid publication and ordered A.L. to provide proof of publication before the trial court would issue an order changing his gender marker. In relevant part, the trial court held as follows:

> 9. The Court specifically finds that Petitioner's requested gender change is being made in good faith without any fraudulent intent. . . .
>
> 10. The legislature [h]as provided no direct authority to the courts to specifically address gender marker changes and the Court of Appeals has provided only limited guidance thus far.
>
> . . . .
>
> 12. . . . . The Petitioner has made no showing that the Petitioner is personally at increased risk for violence (other than as a general member of the transgender[] community) or that this Petition would lead to an increased risk of violence for the Petitioner.
>
> . . . .
>
> 18. The Petitioner's arguments on this issue favor a general rule that would require no notice for any individual seeking to change their legal gender

---

7. A person who is "transgender" is "a person whose gender identity differs from the sex the person had or was identified as having at birth[.]" Merriam-Webster Dictionary, at https://www.merriamwebster.com/dictionary/transgender (last visited July 17, 2017).

and have their birth certificate amended. Without notice the potential for fraud greatly increases . . .

19. The court is understandably reluctant to force well-meaning and potentially vulnerable individuals to address intimate and personal issues central to their personal identity in the harsh public light of open court. However, such is the burden of a multitude of citizens who seek or are subjected to court intervention in the most personal areas of their lives. The judicial preference for open, transparent, and public court proceedings is well established in American jurisprudence. . . .

L.S.

. . . . With respect to L.S.'s request to waive publication of his intent to change his name and invocation of Administrative Rule 9, the trial court found as follows:

. . . Petitioner seeks sealing of these records under 9G(4) arguing that public access to these records will create a significant risk of substantial harm to the requestor. . . . [S]imilar to the request to proceed without publication, Petitioner's request, on these facts, would amount to a categorical ruling that in all instances for requested name change and gender marker change, transgender[] individuals would be entitled to proceed anonymously pursuant to the protections of Administrative Rule 9. The court declines to make such a categorical finding. Specifically, the court notes that Petitioner has made no showing that this Petitioner has been subject to any specific threats or violence as a result of Petitioner's transgender[] status. Further, and more to the point, Petitioner has made no showing that proceeding publicly with his petition would subject Petitioner to any increased risk of violence or harassment than that currently faced by Petitioner as a member of the transgender[] community. Moreover, there has been no evidence submitted that establishes that the public filing of such court cases has resulted in targeted violence against transgender[] individuals. . . .

Discussion and Decision

This appeal presents us with three issues to consider: (1) are transgender individuals who intend to seek a gender marker change required to provide notice by publication of that intention; (2) are transgender individuals who intend to seek a name change required to provide notice by publication of that intention; and (3) did the trial court err by finding that L.S. did not meet the burden of showing entitlement to relief under Administrative Rule 9?

I. Publication

Here, the trial court found that both A.L. and L.S. are required to publish notice of their intent to change their gender marker and that L.S. is required to publish notice of his intent to change his name.

A. Gender Marker

Authority for trial courts to issue orders requiring that the Indiana State Department of Health (ISDH) change an individual's gender marker on his birth certificate stems from a decision of this Court. *In re Pet'n for Change of Birth Certificate*, 22 N.E.3d 707 (Ind. Ct. App. 2014). In *Birth Certificate*, the trial court had denied the petition of a transgender man to change his gender marker, finding that it had no authority to grant the request. In considering the issue, we examined Indiana Code section 16-37-2-10(b), which provides that the ISDH "may make additions to or corrections in a certificate of birth on receipt of adequate documentary evidence. . . ." This Court reasoned as follows:

> Like name changes, the ISDH defers to the courts by requiring a court order to establish adequate documentary evidence for an amendment of gender on a birth certificate. Courts in our state have entered such orders. Further, the Indiana Bureau of Motor Vehicles expressly recognizes "certified amended birth certificate[s] showing a change in . . . gender" as proof of identity to obtain, renew, or amend an Indiana driver's license or identification card. See 140 IND. ADMIN. CODE 7-1.1-3(b)(1)(B) and (K).

> Though never addressed by this court, the amendment of a birth certificate with respect to gender is not novel. The vast majority of states, including Indiana, have allowed it in practice for some time.

> I.C. § 16-37-2-10 provides general authority for the amendment of birth certificates, without any express limitation (in the statute or elsewhere) regarding gender amendments. In light of this statute, as well as the inherent equity power of a court of general jurisdiction, we conclude that the trial court had authority to grant the petition at hand.

We noted the absence of legislative guidance regarding what evidence is required in support of a petition for a gender marker change, ultimately holding that "[w]ithout such guidance . . . it is our view that the ultimate focus should be on whether the petition is made in good faith and not for a fraudulent or unlawful purpose."

The relevant statutes have not been substantively amended since *Birth Certificate* was decided. There is no statute or rule requiring that an individual seeking a gender marker change publish notice of that intent. In this case, the trial court likened gender marker changes to name changes, but the statutory requirement for publication in name change cases does not apply to gender marker changes. It was erroneous to create a requirement where none exists.

Unless and until the General Assembly crafts specific requirements regarding gender marker changes, this Court's common sense standard in *Birth Certificate* is the bar that must be met. Thus, a gender marker change petitioner needs to establish that the petition is made in good faith and not for a fraudulent or unlawful purpose. If a trial court determines that the petitioner has met that standard, no further requirements need to be met and the petition should be granted. . . . We reverse on this issue and remand with instructions to grant both petitions and issue orders directing the ISDH to amend both birth certificates to reflect their male gender.

B. Name Change

. . . . As a general rule, upon filing a petition for a name change, a petitioner must, in relevant part, give notice of the petition by three weekly publications in a newspaper of general circulation published in the county where the petition was filed. Ind. Code § 34-28-2-3(a). . . .

II. Administrative Rule 9

A petition to change one's name under Indiana Code chapter 34-28-2 is, however, explicitly "subject to Indiana Rules of Court Administrative Rule 9." I.C. § 34-28-2-2.5(b). . . .

Administrative Rule 9 "governs public access to, and confidentiality of, Court Records." Ind. Administrative Rule 9(A). The rule seeks to balance, among other things, the risk of injury to individuals with the promotion of accessibility to court records as well as governmental transparency. The Commentary notes that the rule "attempts to balance competing interests and recognizes that unrestricted access to certain information in Court Records could result in an unwarranted invasion of personal privacy or unduly increase the risk of injury to individuals and businesses."

As a general rule, all court records are publicly accessible. Admin. R. 9(D)(1). There is, however, a list of exceptions to that general rule, which are found in Rule 9(G). Relevant to this appeal is an exception providing that a court record that would otherwise be publicly accessible may be excluded from public access upon a verified written request demonstrating that "[a]ccess or dissemination of the Court Record will create a significant risk of substantial harm to the requestor. . . ." Admin. R. 9(G)(4)(a)(ii).

In this case, L.S. presented the following evidence:

- Transgender individuals are disproportionately subject to violence and homicide.

- LGBT people are more likely than any other minority group to experience hate crimes in the United States.

- In 2016, twenty-six transgender individuals were murdered in the United States.

- A survey of transgender people in Indiana revealed that 74% of respondents experienced harassment or mistreatment on the job; 73% reported harassment in their elementary, middle, and high schools; and 27% reported physical assault.

- L.S. is "aware of the high rates of violence against transgender people in Indiana and nationwide" and fears that he "will experience threats and actual violence if the record of [his] Change of Name and Gender is public."

- L.S. has personally "witnessed a person, friend of mine, male to female transgender individual, a person get out of the car and come and grab her by her hair and shoved her face into the sidewalk, and uh, you know, hitting her. I mean blood. . . ."

- L.S. has experienced discrimination because of his transgender identity, testifying that he lost an internship opportunity because the interviewer discovered that the way in which L.S. was identified by Social Security did not "match" with how he appeared.

- L.S. testified that he believes that if information about his transgender status became public, he would be "at great risk for potential harm. . . . I mean it could be anything. I—I—I uh, violence, death, you know, it just depends on who—who gets a hold of me you know."

The trial court found, based on this evidence, that the transgender community is "disproportionately targeted for violence" as a result of gender identity. The trial court acknowledged "the demonstrable violence and harassment suffered by the transgender[] community as a whole." It also found, however, that L.S. did not establish that he had been subject to specific threats or violence; that publishing his petition would subject him to an increased risk of violence or harassment that exceeds what he already faces as a member of the transgender community; or that the public filing of such court cases has resulted in targeted violence against transgender individuals.

Initially, we return to the language of Administrative Rule 9(G)(4), which requires that L.S. establish that publication of notice of his petition would create "a significant risk of substantial harm" to him. Publication must occur multiple times in a newspaper of general circulation; among other things, it would reveal L.S.'s birth name and new desired name. I.C. § 34-28-2-3(b). Thus, to publish this notice would be to "out" L.S. as a transgender man to the general public.

L.S. provided evidence that, as an out member of the transgender community, he would face a significantly higher risk of violence, harassment, and homicide. He has personally witnessed a transgender friend being violently assaulted because of her gender identity. He has personally experienced discrimination in the workplace after a discrepancy between the way he looked and the way he was identified by Social Security outed him as a transgender individual. Publication of his birth name and new name would enable members of the general public to seek him out, placing him at a significant risk of harm. And in today's day and age, information that is published in a newspaper is likely to be published on the Internet, where it will remain in perpetuity, leaving L.S. at risk for the rest of his life. There was no evidence in opposition to L.S.'s evidence.

Under these circumstances, we find that L.S. established that publication of notice of his petition for a name change would create a significant risk of substantial harm to him. As a result, the trial court should have granted his requests to seal the record and waive publication pursuant to Administrative Rule 9. We remand with instructions to ensure that the record of this case remains sealed, and for consideration of L.S.'s petition for a name change.

The judgment of the trial court is reversed in part and remanded with instructions and for consideration of L.S.'s petition for a name change.

Discussion

1. It is unclear why the court assumes that ISDH cannot make its own decisions on amendment of birth certificates without court order, or that the court has power (exclusively or not) over ISDH to make such orders. Other states give the power directly to their departments of health to set rules and regulations for such amendments. Indeed, the Indiana statute cited above appears to provide for the amendment power to reside within ISDH.

2. The trial court viewed the same evidence and concluded that there was no specific evidence of threatened harm. Why might these courts reach opposing conclusions based on the same evidence?

3. It is true that in many areas, the public nature of litigation causes harm. For example, being publicly identified as having sued one's employer can make it difficult to find a new job at a time when many employers search for potential employee information online. Nonetheless, courts do not permit pseudonyms or sealing of files in most such cases. Is this different? *Cf. John Doe v. Blue Cross & Blue Shield*, 794 F. Supp. 72 (D.R.I. 1992), Chapter 11, Section A, *supra* at p. 584.

How does a person petition a court to change their name? "'The basic procedure requires that a petition be submitted with an original or certified copy of the birth certificate if born in [New York state]' . . . . 'A court date is then chosen and the applicant has to appear. If the name change is granted, the applicant then has to publish the name change and bring proof of publication to the court. After that, the name change order is finalized.'" Nico Lang, *For trans Americans, changing your name can still be a matter of life and death*, QUARTZ, Mar. 31, 2016, at https://qz.com/651310/for-trans-americans-changing-your-name-can-still-be-a-matter-of-life-or-death/.

The precise form one would use varies by state. Below is a sample petition from the state of New York on behalf of a fictitious client.*

Jacqueline Grant
The Law Office of Jacqueline Grant
325 7th Ave., Suite 1101
New York, NY 10018
jgrant@jgrantlaw.com

---

* Sample petition provided by and reprinted with the permission of the author, Noah E. Lewis.

(555) 123-3454
Attorney for Petitioner

CIVIL COURT OF THE CITY OF NEW YORK
COUNTY OF NEW YORK

In the Matter of the Application of
  Amy Lynn Smith
    a.k.a. **Amy L. Smith**
    a.k.a. **Amy Smith**
 	
For Leave to Assume the Name of
  Alexander John Adams Smith
	Index No.: _____
	
	PETITION FOR INDIVIDUAL
	ADULT CHANGE OF NAME

TO THE CIVIL COURT OF THE CITY OF NEW YORK:

Amy Lynn Smith, a.k.a. Amy L. Smith and Amy Smith, respectfully shows to this Court the following:

1. My present address is 2228 Adams Place, Bronx, NY 10458, in Bronx County.

2. I was born on June 12, 1977, in Philadelphia, PA, and I am now 39 years of age. A copy of my birth certificate, issued by the Pennsylvania Department of Health, number 0568519-1977, is annexed hereto as **Exhibit A**.

3. My present name is Amy Lynn Smith.

4. I wish to change my name to (first) Alexander (middle) John Adams (last) Smith.

5. I am single and have never been married.

6. I have never been convicted of a crime.

7. I am not currently confined as an inmate in a correctional facility or currently under the supervision of the State Division of Parole, or a County Probation Department as a result for a conviction for a violent felony offense or other felony as specified in Civil Rights Law.

8. I have declared bankruptcy. I filed for bankruptcy on June 20, 2006, in U.S. Bankruptcy Court for the Northern District of Georgia located at 121 Spring Street SE, Gainesville, GA 30501. The case number was 06-10436-reb. I received a notice dated July 2, 2006, signed by Judge Robert Brizendine that my debts were discharged. The case has been closed. A copy of this notice is attached hereto as **Exhibit B**.

9. There are no judgments or liens against me.

10. I do not have any children or support obligations to a child or children.

11. I am divorced. I am not responsible for spousal support. A copy of my judgment of divorce is attached hereto as **Exhibit C**.

12. I am a party to the following action: Harold Green v. Amy Smith, filed January 3, 2016, index number 16-000xxx before Hon. Lawrence, Supreme Court of the State of New York, County of Kings. Attached as **Exhibit D** is the Summons & Verified Complaint.

13. I wish to change my name for the following reason(s): I am a transgender man and I would like the name on my identity documents to reflect my male identity and appearance.

14. I respectfully request that the publication provisions of Civil Rights Law §§ 63–64 be waived and rendered inapplicable and that the records of this name change be sealed pursuant to Civil Rights Law § 64-a. I am concerned that publication of the name change would jeopardize my personal safety. I have experienced harassment when showing identity documents that convey my transgender status. Publication would publicize my transgender status to the general public and violence against transgender people permeates our society. Sealing the records of my name change is important to protect my medical privacy and safety. As the court in *Powell v. Schriver* noted, "transsexualism is the unusual condition that is likely to provoke both an intense desire to preserve one's medical confidentiality, as well as hostility and intolerance from others. The excrutiatingly [*sic*] private and intimate nature of transsexualism, for persons who wish to preserve privacy in the matter, is really beyond debate." 175 F.3d 107, 111 (2d Cir. 1999) (holding that disclosure of an inmate's transgender status by prison officials violated her constitutional right to privacy because "individuals who are transsexuals are among those who possess a constitutional right to maintain medical confidentiality"). The court in *In re E.P.L.*, 26 Misc. 3d 336 (N.Y. Sup. Ct. 2009), waived publication requirements and sealed the records for a transgender individual without a particularized history of violence or crime against him, finding that "there exist numerous documented instances of those targeted for violence based on their sexual orientation or gender identity," id. at 338, and that the petitioner "has a right to feel threatened for his personal safety in the event his transgender status is made public," id. at 339. The legislature recognized this threat and amended Civil Rights Law § 64-a in 2015 to support the holding in *In re E.P.L.* (See Assembly Bill A02242 (enacted)). The amended Civil Rights Law § 64-a specifically states that judges "shall not deny such waiver solely on the basis that the applicant lacks specific instances of or a personal history of threat to personal safety." (N.Y. Civ. Rights Law § 64-a (amended 2015)). The Supreme Court in Suffolk County has also affirmed in *Matter of J.A.L., Jr.*, 10138/2016 (N.Y.L.J. Dec. 6, 2016) that waiver based on the totality of the circumstances applies to transgender individuals even without a particular threat against them.

15. I have not made a previous application to change my name in this or any other court.

16. Should the Court find this petition deficient in any aspect, I respectfully request leave to renew the application with additional information as the Court may require.

WHEREFORE, Petitioner respectfully asks for an order granting permission to assume the name Alexander John Adams Smith.

Dated: _____

_____ Amy Lynn Smith

Dated: New York, New York Respectfully submitted,
January 8, 2020 The Law Office of Jacqueline Grant

By _____

Jacqueline Grant

3553 82nd St. #6D
Jackson Heights, NY 11372
nlewis@transcendlegal.org
(347) 612-4312
Attorneys for petitioner

VERIFICATION

Amy Lynn Smith, being duly sworn, deposes and says: I am the petitioner in the above-captioned action. I have read the petition and know the contents to be true to my own knowledge, except to those matters alleged on information and belief and as to those matters I believe them to be true.

_____ Amy Lynn Smith

Sworn to before me on the _____
day of _____, 2017

_____

Notary Public

CIVIL COURT OF THE CITY OF NEW YORK
COUNTY OF NEW YORK

_____

In the Matter of the Application of Index No.: _____
   Amy Lynn Smith

For Leave to Assume the Name of   ATTORNEY
Alexander John Adams Smith   AFFIRMATION

Jacqueline Grant, an attorney admitted to practice in the Courts of New York State, pursuant to CPLR § 2106 hereby affirms the following under penalty of perjury:

1. I am counsel for the petitioner, Amy Lynn Smith (the "Petitioner"). I respectfully submit this affirmation in support of Petitioner's Petition for Individual Adult Change of Name (the "Petition").

2. Annexed to the Petition as Exhibit A is a true copy, modified in size only, of Petitioner's certified Birth Certificate, number 0568519-1977, issued by the Pennsylvania Department of Health, of which I have examined the original.

3. Annexed to the Petition as Exhibit B is a true copy of Petitioner's bankruptcy discharge, which I retrieved from PACER.

4. Annexed to the Petition as Exhibit C is a true copy of Petitioner's divorce decree, of which I have examined a certified copy.

5. Annexed to the Petition as Exhibit D are true copies of the Summons, Verified Complaint and Compliance Conference Order in Green v. Smith that I retrieved from the New York State Unified Court System WebCivil Supreme eCourts website.

Dated: New York, New York   Respectfully submitted,
January 8, 2020   The Law Office of Jacqueline Grant

By _____

                                            Jacqueline Grant

                                            325 7th Ave., Suite 1101
                                            New York, NY 10018
                                            jgrant@jgrantlaw.com
                                            (555) 123-3454
                                            Attorneys for Petitioner

---

Petitions for court-ordered name changes are not the only instances where the names adopted by transgender people raise legal issues. Misnaming of trans people can be a form of misgendering that is legally actionable (or contributes to conditions that collectively are so actionable). *See, e.g.*, *Names and Pronouns*, MASS. DEP'T OF ELEMENTARY & SECONDARY EDUC., GUIDANCE FOR MASSACHUSETTS PUBLIC SCHOOLS: CREATING A SAFE AND SUPPORTIVE SCHOOL ENVIRONMENT: NONDISCRIMINATION ON THE BASIS OF GENDER IDENTITY (Feb. 15, 2015), available at http://www.doe.mass.edu/ssce/GenderIdentity.pdf (Chapter 13, *supra*). Consider in this regard the view of federal employment discrimination law banning sex discrimination—Title VII (of the Civil Rights Act of 1964)—adopted by the Equal Employment Opportunity Commission in the following ruling.

Reading Guide for Lusardi v. McHugh

1. Title VII of the Civil Rights Act of 1964, as amended, 42 U.S.C. § 2000e et seq., forbids employment discrimination on various grounds including sex. *See generally* Chapter 5, *supra*. By the time of the decision of the Equal Employment Opportunity Commission ("EEOC" or "Commission") in Tamara Lusardi's case, the EEOC had held that the sex prohibition includes a ban on discrimination based on transgender status or identity or transition. *See Macy v. Department of Justice* (a/k/a *Macy v. Holder*), No. 0120120821, 2012 WL 1435995 (E.E.O.C. April 20, 2012), Chapter 5, Section D, *supra* at p. 228. Title VII's ban on discrimination on specified grounds includes a ban on certain workplace harassment that in effect discriminates with respect to a term or condition of employment. *See Harris v. Forklift Systems*, 510 U.S. 17 (1993).

2. Of what conduct did federal employee Tamara Lusardi complain before the Commission? (Note that the restroom-usage aspects of Ms. Lusardi's complaints are primarily treated in Chapter 5, Section E, *supra* at p. 302.) What standard does *Lusardi* hold a plaintiff must show in order to establish unlawful sexual harassment (which includes gender identity harassment)? On what evidence does the Commission rely in concluding that Tamara Lusardi satisfied this standard?

3. What two liability standards does the Commission articulate for when a plaintiff can hold an agency (or company, in other cases) liable for the discriminatory actions of its employees? Which liability standard does the Commission hold Ms. Lusardi has satisfied? What evidence or reasoning does the court offer as to why she has satisfied that standard?

4. What relief does the U.S. Office of Special Counsel or the EEOC order for Lusardi?

Tamara Lusardi v. John J. McHugh, Secretary, Department of the Army

No. 0120133395, 2015 WL 1607756 (E.E.O.C. Apr. 1, 2015)

. . . .

Issue Presented

The issue presented is whether Complainant proved that she was subjected to disparate treatment and harassment based on sex when the Agency restricted her from using the common female restroom, and a team leader ([supervisor 3, hereinafter] S3) intentionally and repeatedly referred to her by male pronouns and made hostile remarks.

Background[1]

. . . . Complainant was employed at the [Army Aviation and Missile Research Development and Engineering Center ("AMRDEC")] Software Engineering Directorate ("SED") under the supervision of [supervisor 1, hereinafter] S1, the Quality Division Chief. During the relevant time period, . . . Complainant . . . worked as a Software Quality Assurance Lead under the direction of [supervisor 3, hereinafter] S3, the Software Engineering Lead, who was in turn supervised by [supervisor 2, hereinafter] S2, the Technical Chief. In August 2011, Complainant returned to her primary job at SED.

. . . .

[Transgender woman Tamara Lusardi discussed her gender identity with S1 as early as 2007 and began transitioning her gender presentation/expression in 2010. In April 2010, she secured an Alabama court order changing her name to a conventionally feminine one and requested that the government change her name and sex on all personnel records. The Office of Personnel Management ("OPM") did so on October 13, causing her work e-mail address to change to reflect her new name. On October 26, Lusardi met with S2 and S1 to discuss her transition; the three discussed how she would explain her transition to co-workers and her estimated timeline for any medical procedures. Lusardi initially agreed to use a single-user restroom—the "executive restroom" or the "single shot rest room"—rather than the multi-user "common women's restroom" until she had undergone an undefined surgery. The Deputy Program Manager testified that he made the final decision as to which bathroom she would use. Lusardi e-mailed the office staff on November 22, explaining her situation and indicating that for an initial period, she would use the executive restroom. She began presenting as a woman at work following the Thanksgiving holiday. She regularly used the executive restroom except on three occasions in early 2011. . . . After each incident, Complainant was confronted by S2 who told her she'd been observed using the common women's restroom, that she was making people uncomfortable, and that she had to use the executive restroom until she could show proof of having undergone the "final surgery." She testified that in January 2011 when S2 confronted her about using the common women's restroom, she responded, "I am legally female. I used it."]

Harassment

During the relevant time period, S3 repeatedly referred to Complainant by her former male name, by male pronouns, and as "sir." . . . . Complainant did not correct S3 because she did not want to question her supervisor in front of other people.

---

1. The factual background as laid out here is not exhaustive. Two comprehensive reports of the facts relevant to this case have already been compiled: the EEO Report of Investigation and the Agency's Final Agency Decision. We have considered those documents as well as the Complainant's Brief in Support of Appeal and the extensive transcript from the Fact-Finding Conference conducted [by the EEOC]. The facts pertinent to the legal analysis necessary are largely not in dispute.

Additionally, Complainant did not correct S3 in private because she felt she "was in enough hot water" and "anything else . . . would have gotten [her] kicked out of there."

. . . .

After Complainant's e-mail address changed to reflect her name, but before she began presenting as female, curious coworkers questioned Complainant about the situation. As a result of the questions S2 asked Complainant to "hold down the chatter with people that were inquiring" about her transition.

Complainant testified that, although she did not inform management that she felt she was being subjected to a hostile work environment, she did tell Colonel 2 that there were "some issues."

EEO Investigation and Final Agency Decision

Complainant initiated EEO counselor contact on September 6, 2011, and filed a formal complaint on March 14, 2012 . . . . The Agency accepted the complaint and conducted an investigation, including a fact-finding conference. . . .

In its final decision, the Agency concluded that Complainant failed to prove that the Agency subjected her to discrimination or harassment as alleged. . . .

The Agency further determined that, although S2 reminded Complainant about the bathroom access plan she had with management, the comments were not sufficiently severe or pervasive to constitute harassment.

With respect to Complainant's claim that S3 referred to her by male pronouns, names, and titles, the Agency concluded that these were isolated incidents that were not sufficiently severe or pervasive to constitute a hostile work environment.

On September 23, 2013, Complainant filed this appeal of the agency's final decision.

Contentions on Appeal

Complainant contends that the Agency erred when it found that she failed to show that she was subjected to sex discrimination and harassment. . . . Complainant also reiterates her claim that the Agency subjected her to a hostile work environment by allowing S3 to refer to her by a male name and pronouns. . . . Complainant maintains that "these daily humiliations and reminders that the Agency did not accept her gender identity created a hostile work environment."

. . . .

Analysis and Findings
Disparate Treatment: Restroom Facilities

. . . . In *Macy v. Department of Justice*, EEOC Appeal No. 0120120821 (April 20, 2012), the Commission held that discrimination against a transgender individual because that person is transgender is, by definition, discrimination "based on . . . sex," and such discrimination violates Title VII, absent a valid defense. . . .

Here, the Agency acknowledges that Complainant's transgender status was *the* motivation for its decision to prevent Complainant from using the common women's restroom. . . . This constitutes direct evidence of discrimination on the basis of sex.

. . . .

This case represents well the peril of conditioning access to facilities on any medical procedure. Nothing in Title VII makes any medical procedure a prerequisite for equal opportunity (for transgender individuals, or anyone else). An agency may not condition access to facilities—or to other terms, conditions, or privileges of employment—on the completion of certain medical steps that the agency itself has unilaterally determined will somehow prove the bona fides of the individual's gender identity.[3]

On this record, there is no cause to question that Complainant—who was assigned the sex of male at birth but identifies as female—*is* female. And certainly where, as here, a transgender female has notified her employer that she has begun living and working full-time as a woman, the agency must allow her access to the women's restrooms. This "real life experience" often is crucial to a transgender employee's transition. . . .

. . . . The decision to restrict Complainant to a "single shot" restroom isolated and segregated her from other persons of her gender. It perpetuated the sense that she was not worthy of equal treatment and respect. *Cf.* 42 U.S.C. § 2000e-2(a)(2) (making it unlawful to "segregate" employees in any way that deprives or tends to deprive them of equal employment opportunities). The Agency's actions deprived Complainant of equal status, respect, and dignity in the workplace, and, as a result, deprived her of equal employment opportunities. . . .

Harassment: Gender Pronouns, Titles, and Access to Facilities

To establish a claim of hostile work environment harassment, Complainant must show (1) that she was subjected to harassment in the form of unwelcome verbal or

---

3. Gender reassignment surgery is in no way a fundamental element of a transition. Transitions vary according to individual needs and many do not involve surgery at all. As the Office of Personnel Management has explained:

> Some individuals will find it necessary to transition from living and working as one gender to another. These individuals often seek some form of medical treatment such as counseling, hormone therapy, electrolysis, and reassignment surgery. Some individuals, however, will not pursue some (or any) forms of medical treatment because of their age, medical condition, lack of funds, or other personal circumstances. Managers and supervisors should be aware that not all transgender individuals will follow the same pattern, but they all are entitled to the same consideration as they undertake the transition steps deemed appropriate for them, and should all be treated with dignity and respect.

Office of Personnel Management (OPM), *Guidance Regarding the Employment of Transgender Individuals in the Federal Workplace* ("*OPM Transgender Guidance*"), available online at http://www.opm.gov/policy-data-oversight/diversity-and-inclusion/reference-materials/gender-identity-guidance/.

physical conduct because of a statutorily protected basis and (2) that the harassment had the purpose or effect of unreasonably interfering with the work environment and/or created an intimidating, hostile, or offensive work environment. *See Harris v. Forklift Systems*, 510 U.S. 17 (1993).

In this case, Complainant contends that she was subjected to a hostile work environment because management restricted her from using the common women's restroom even after Complainant made clear that she no longer agreed with the initial plan restricting her to the executive bathroom facility, and S3 engaged in demeaning behavior toward her by refusing to refer to her correct name and gender.

Complainant testified that S3 called her male names and "sir" in moments of anger or in group settings, and that his body language reflected a negative connotation and intentional conduct when he did so. [Complainant testified that she could tell S3 used male signifiers during heated discussions or moments of anger because "[h]is veins were popping out of his forehead, his face was red, and he was quite agitated." (Relocated text—Eds.)] Complainant testified that S3 called her "sir" on approximately seven occasions, including in an e-mail in which he engaged Complainant in a heated discussion about work matters. Complainant is not the only witness to testify that S3 intentionally referred to Complainant with male names. We note that one witness testified that he thought that S3 intentionally referred to Complainant as "sir" and by her former male name well after Complainant announced her transition to co-workers in November 2010. The witness further testified that S3 also smirked and giggled and said to her, "Oh well, do we call her [by her male or female name]?" Further, the record contains a copy of e-mail correspondence between Complainant and S3 on July 26, 2011. The e-mails reveal that, after Complainant wrote that S3 was on the side of other employees who do not treat her as an equal, S3 responded, "No Sir, not on anyone's side." The e-mails also reflect that this exchange occurred in the context of heated exchanges about work activities between Complainant and S3. S3 maintains that calling Complainant "sir" or referring to her with a male name was "just a slip of the tongue and only occurred twice.

After reviewing witness testimony and the e-mail exchanges between Complainant and S3, we are persuaded that S3's use of "sir" in this and several other situations was intentional. The e-mail exchanges reflect that S3 sometimes used male names and pronouns to insult Complainant or to convey sarcasm. Additionally, witness testimony indicates that S3 sometimes laughed and smiled when mentioning Complainant in groups and would say her feminine name with a smirk. Further, Complainant testified in detail about S3's agitated demeanor when referring to her with male pronouns and names and another witness spoke of S3's "general feeling of hostility" toward Complainant and the snide comments S3 made that pertained to Complainant's transition and clothing. Complainant also testified that S3 seemed to especially call her male names when in the presence of other employees as a way to reveal that Complainant is transgender, as well as to ridicule and embarrass her.

The Commission has held that supervisors and coworkers should use the name and gender pronoun that corresponds to the gender identity with which the employee identifies in employee records and in communications with and about the employee. See *Jameson v. U.S. Postal Serv.*, EEOC Appeal No. 0120130992 (May 21, 2013). Persistent failure to use the employee's correct name and pronoun may constitute unlawful, sex-based harassment if such conduct is either severe or pervasive enough to create a hostile work environment when judged from the perspective of a reasonable person in the employee's position. *See Oncale v. Sundowner Offshore Services*, 523 U.S. 75 (1998); see also *Jameson*; *OPM Transgender Guidance* ("Continued intentional misuse of the employee's new name and pronouns, and reference to the employee's former gender by managers, supervisors, or coworkers may undermine the employee's therapeutic treatment, and is contrary to the goal of treating transitioning employees with dignity and respect. Such misuse may also breach the employee's privacy, and may create a risk of harm to the employee.").

In this case, Complainant had clearly communicated to management and employees that her gender identity is female and her personnel records reflected the same. Yet S3 continued to frequently and repeatedly refer to Complainant by a male name and male pronouns. While inadvertent and isolated slips of the tongue likely would not constitute harassment, under the facts of this case, S3's actions and demeanor made clear that S3's use of a male name and male pronouns in referring to Complainant was not accidental, but instead was intended to humiliate and ridicule Complainant. As such, S3's repeated and intentional conduct was offensive and demeaning to Complainant and would have been so to a reasonable person in Complainant's position.

Moreover, in determining whether actionable harassment occurred, S3's actions must be considered in the context of the Agency's actions related to Complainant's restroom access. As we note above, even after Complainant indicated that she no longer wished to abide by her initial plan regarding bathroom use, the Agency refused to allow Complainant to use the restroom consistent with her gender identity. It publicly segregated and isolated Complainant from other employees of her gender and communicated that she was not equal to those other employees because she is transgender. S3's comments compounded that discrimination and sent the message that Complainant was unworthy of basic respect and dignity because she is a transgender individual. Additionally, S3 was a team leader and his actions sometimes occurred in the presence of other employees and during meetings, signaling that such conduct was endorsed by Agency leadership.

Considering all these circumstances as we must, we find that these actions were sufficiently severe or pervasive to subject Complainant to a hostile work environment based on her sex. Because Complainant established that she was subjected to a level of severe or pervasive sex-based harassment that meets the Title VII standard for liability, the final element of our analysis is whether the Agency itself is liable for that harassment.

An agency may be vicariously liable for unlawful harassment by an employee when the agency has empowered that employee to take tangible employment actions against the victim—*i.e.*, the harassing employee is a supervisor of the victim. *Vance v. Ball State University*, 133 S. Ct. 2434 (2013). In cases where the harassing employee (or employees) is a co-worker of the victim, an agency is responsible for acts of harassment in the workplace when the agency was "negligent in permitting the harassment to occur." Negligence in permitting harassment to occur can take many forms. An assessment of whether an Agency is liable under this standard depends on the facts and circumstances of each case and the unique context of each workplace.

In her appeal, the Complainant alleged that the Agency was liable under the negligence theory. We therefore analyze her claim under that standard.[10]

In this case, Complainant did not report S3's harassment to management. However, we note that S3's conduct sometimes occurred in groups or in the presence of other employees. For example, a witness testified that she witnessed S3 among a group of employees in which he would laugh and smile when Complainant's name was mentioned, and the group would laugh. Another witness testified that S3 would openly refer to Complainant by her former masculine name in the presence of other employees and smirk and giggle about it, well after he was aware of Complainant's gender identity as female. This witness testimony reflects that S3's conduct was pervasive, well-known, and openly practiced in the workplace. Consequently, we find that the Agency knew or should have known about S3's harassment. *See Mayer v. Dep't of Homeland Security*, EEOC Appeal No. 0120071846 (May 15, 2009) (Agency had constructive knowledge of sexual harassment because employees were aware that harasser was harassing Complainant); *Taylor v. Dep't of the Air Force*, EEOC Request No. 05920194 (July 8, 1992) (employers will generally be deemed to have constructive knowledge of harassment that is openly practiced in the workplace or is well-known among employees). There is no evidence that the Agency took prompt and effective corrective action to address the harassment. In fact, the only Agency actions we find in the record are when Complainant's supervisors chastised her for using a facility consistent with her gender and for discussing her transition with other employees. Consequently, we find that the Agency was negligent in permitting the harassment to occur and is therefore liable.

In summary, we find that Complainant proved that she was subjected to disparate treatment on the basis of sex when she was denied equal access to the

---

10. Given that the decision to restrict Complainant from the common restrooms consistent with her gender was instituted by management, there is an argument to be made that the supervisor liability standard is appropriate. We do not need to reach this issue, however, because Complainant has invoked the negligence liability standard and we find that she has met her burden under that analysis. See *Wilson v. Tulsa Junior College*, 164 F.3d 534, 540 n.4 (10th Cir. 1998) ("The Supreme Court recognized in [*Faragher*] and *Ellerth* the continuing validity of negligence as a separate basis for employer liability").

common female restroom facilities. We further find that the Agency is liable for subjecting Complainant to a hostile work environment based on sex by preventing her from using the common female restroom facilities and allowing a team leader intentionally and repeatedly to refer to her by male names and pronouns and make hostile remarks well after he was aware that Complainant's gender identity was female.

Decision of the Office of Special Counsel

Complainant filed a prohibited personnel practice complaint against the Agency with the U.S. Office of Special Counsel (OSC) based on the events described above. On August 29, 2014, OSC issued a report finding that the Agency had discriminated against Complainant based on conduct not adverse to work performance, in violation of 5 U.S.C. § 2302(b)(10). . . . OSC found that "the Agency unlawfully discriminated against [Complainant] on the basis of gender identity, including her gender transition from man to a woman—conduct which did not adversely affect her performance or the performance of others."

OSC recommended that the Agency provide appropriate lesbian, gay, bisexual, and transgender (LGBT) diversity and sensitivity training to AMRDEC employees at Redstone Arsenal. OSC further recommended that appropriate remedial training regarding prohibited personnel practices, especially as they relate to transgender employees, be given to AMRDEC supervisors at Redstone Arsenal. OSC also found that Complainant did not suffer any economic harm that would require back pay, and that Complainant was ineligible to collect compensatory damages because the facts of this case arose before Congress created a compensatory damages remedy under section 107(b) of the Whistleblower Protection Enhancement Act of 2012; that provision is not retroactive. OSC noted that it made no finding regarding Complainant's ability to recover damages under Title VII.[12]

The OSC report does not moot the claim before the Commission. OSC addressed whether the Agency's actions violated U.S. government personnel practices. The answer to that question was affected, but not settled, by Title VII principles. Our decision today addresses the Agency's actions in light of the sex discrimination provisions in Title VII. However, in the Order below, we take notice of the remedies already prescribed by OSC in order to avoid duplicative actions by the Agency.

Conclusion

Consequently, based on a thorough review of the record and the contentions on appeal, including those not specifically addressed herein, the Commission REVERSES the Agency's final decision. We REMAND this matter to the Agency to take remedial actions in accordance with this decision and the ORDER below.

---

12. We address the matter of compensatory damages under Title VII in our Order, below.

Order (E0610)

The Agency is ORDERED to undertake the following actions:

1. The Agency shall immediately grant Complainant equal and full access to the common female facilities.

2. The Agency shall immediately take meaningful and effective measures to ensure that coworkers and supervisors cease and desist from all discriminatory and harassing conduct directed at Complainant, and ensure that Complainant is not subjected to retaliation because of her EEO activity.

3. Within one hundred and twenty (120) calendar days from the date this decision becomes final, the Agency will conduct and complete a supplemental investigation on the issue of Complainant's entitlement to compensatory damages, and will afford her an opportunity to establish a causal relationship between the hostile work environment to which she was subjected and her pecuniary or non-pecuniary losses, if any. Complainant will cooperate in the Agency's efforts to compute the amount of compensatory damages, and will provide all relevant information requested by the Agency. The Agency will issue a final decision on the issue of compensatory damages. 29 C.F.R. § 1614.110. A copy of the final decision must be submitted to the Compliance Officer, as referenced below.

4. Within one hundred and twenty (120) calendar days from the date this decision becomes final, the Agency shall provide at least eight hours of EEO training to all civilian personnel and contractors working at its Aviation Missile Research Development Engineering Center at Redstone Arsenal, and the Huntsville Project Management Office. The training shall place special emphasis on sex discrimination, including issues of gender identity, harassment, and preventing and eliminating retaliation. Additionally, the training shall inform employees about the EEO process and how to report harassment in their workplace organization. The Agency may count the diversity and sensitivity training ordered by OSC towards the eight hours required by this Order

5. Within one hundred and twenty (120) calendar days from the date this decision becomes final, the Agency shall provide at least 16 hours of in-person EEO training to all management officials at its Aviation Missile Research Development Engineering Center at Redstone Arsenal, and the Huntsville Project Management Office, regarding their responsibilities to ensure equal employment opportunities and the elimination of discrimination in the federal workplace. The training shall place special emphasis on sex discrimination, including issues of gender identity, harassment, and preventing and eliminating retaliation. The Commission does not consider training to be disciplinary action. The Agency may count in-person diversity and sensitivity training ordered by OSC towards the sixteen hours required by this Order.

6. The Agency shall consider taking appropriate disciplinary action against S2 and S3 and report its decision. If the Agency decides to take disciplinary action, it shall identify the action taken. If the Agency decides not to take disciplinary action, it shall set forth the reason(s) for its decision not to impose discipline. If S2 or S3 have left the Agency's employ, the Agency shall furnish documentation of the departure date.

. . . .

8. The Agency is further directed to submit a report of compliance, as provided in the statement entitled "Implementation of the Commission's Decision." The report shall include supporting documentation and evidence that the corrective action has been implemented.

. . . .

If Complainant has been represented by an attorney . . . , she is entitled to an award of reasonable attorney's fees incurred in the processing of the complaint. 29 C.F.R. § 1614.501(e). The award of attorney's fees shall be paid by the Agency. . . .

———————

Discussion

1. The "severe or pervasive" standard is intended to identify when harassment is sufficiently serious as to amount to a change in the "terms" or "conditions" of a plaintiff's employment, discrimination with respect to which is forbidden by Title VII. Is the EEOC correct that the repeated use of male pronouns, honorifics ("Sir"), and names in this case rose (or sank) to that level? If a cisgender male employee were similarly repeatedly called by female pronouns, honorifics, and names, would that meet the standard? If a cisgender female employee were repeatedly called by male pronouns, honorifics, and names, would that meet the standard? Is either of these an appropriate comparison for use in helping to identify sex discrimination? (Is an affirmative answer to either of these questions necessary to show sex discrimination on the facts of Lusardi's case?) Or, to identify sex discrimination in circumstances such as Tamara Lusardi's, must factfinders ask whether the employer would or would not have used male pronouns, honorifics, and names to address an employee who was a transgender man? The latter seems to be the sort of comparison the United States argued is required in the employment discrimination suit brought by transgender woman Aimee Stephens. *See* Brief for the Federal Respondent Supporting Reversal, *R.G. & G.R. Harris Funeral Homes, Inc. v. E.E.O.C.*, No. 18-107, at 39–40 (U.S. Aug. 16, 2019). In affirming *Harris Funeral Homes* in *Bostock v. Clayton County, Georgia*, 140 S. Ct. 1731 (2020), the Supreme Court appears to have repudiated such double-flipping, rejecting the suggestion that to determine whether an employer who fires a man who is attracted to men engaged in sex discrimination, we would need to ask whether the employer also would have fired the employee if she were a woman attracted to women. *Id.* at 1747–48.

2. The EEOC reasoned: "An agency may not condition access to facilities . . . on the completion of certain medical steps that the agency itself has unilaterally determined will somehow prove the bona fides of the individual's gender identity." Could it be that an employer insists on genital reconstruction surgery not as a matter of *evidence* as to transgender employees' *gender identity*, but out of a belief about the *definition* of *sex*, of what *constitutes* someone as male or female? (If the latter were the case, would that necessarily mean that transgender employees barred from restrooms consistent with their gender identity were not discriminated against on the basis of sex?)

3. Similarly, the EEOC reasoned that, "[o]n this record, there is no cause to question that Complainant—who was assigned the sex of male at birth but identifies as female—*is* female." What *definition* of "female" might the Commission be adopting here? What in fact or in law might justify its adopting such a definition and precluding employers from adopting a different definition of the sexes? *Cf. M.T v. J.T.*, 355 A.2d 204 (N.J. 1976) (concluding a transgender person's "social sex or gender"—for purposes of gendered marriage law—is their "anatomical sex," seemingly referring to genitalia, but that a transsexual person who has had genital reconstruction, rendering their "psychological sex" (gender identity) and "anatomical sex" (genitalia) "harmonized," their sex for marriage law purposes will be that harmonized sex).

4. How likely to be helpful do the various remedial measures ordered by the U.S. Office of Special Counsel or the EEOC seem? Should Congress enact a "Gender Expression in Employment Act" as proposed by Erin Clawson? *See* Erin E. Clawson, *I Now Pronoun-ce You: A Proposal for Pronoun Protections for Transgender People*, 124 Penn St. L. Rev. 247 (2019). Lawson proposes that employers (rather than, for example, coworkers) be made liable for misgendering employees "not in isolated incidents or through petty slights," but where enduring the mistreatment becomes a condition of continued employment or is sufficiently severe or pervasive to be objectively "intimidating, hostile, or abusive." *Id.* at 274.

Legal Enforcement Guidance on Discrimination on the Basis of Gender Identity or Expression: Local Law No. 3 (2002); N.Y.C. Admin. Code § 8-102(23)

N.Y.C. Commission on Human Rights (Dec. 21, 2015)

The New York City Human Rights Law ("NYCHRL") prohibits discrimination in employment, public accommodations, and housing. It also prohibits discriminatory harassment and bias-based profiling by law enforcement. . . .

The NYCHRL prohibits unlawful discrimination in public accommodations, housing and employment on the basis of gender. Gender is defined as one's "actual or perceived sex and shall also include a person's gender identity, self-image, appearance, behavior or expression, whether or not that gender identity, self-image, appearance, behavior or expression is different from that traditionally associated with the legal sex assigned to that person at birth."[2] This document serves as the [New York City Commission on Human Rights]'s legal enforcement guidance of the NYCHRL's protections as they apply to discrimination based on gender, and gender identity and gender expression, which constitute gender discrimination under the NYCHRL. This document is not intended to serve as an exhaustive list of all forms of gender-based discrimination claims under the NYCHRL.

I. Legislative Intent

. . . .

The legislative history reflects that transgender people face frequent and severe discrimination such that protection from discrimination is "very often a matter of life and death."[5] Recognizing the profoundly debilitating impact of gender-based discrimination on transgender and other gender non-conforming individuals, the amendment makes clear that "gender-based discrimination—including, but not limited to, discrimination based on an individual's actual or perceived sex, and discrimination based on an individual's gender identity, self-image, appearance, behavior, or expression—constitutes a violation of the City's Human Rights Law."[6]

II. Definitions

These definitions are intended to help people understand the following guidance as well as their rights and responsibilities under the NYCHRL.

. . . .

Gender Expression:

the representation of gender as expressed through, for example, one's name, choice of pronouns, clothing, haircut, behavior, voice, or body character-istics. Gender expression may not be distinctively male or female and may not conform to traditional gender-based stereotypes assigned to specific gender identities.

. . . .

Gender Non-Conforming:

an adjective sometimes used to describe someone whose gender expres-sion differs from traditional gender-based stereotypes. Not all gender non-conforming people are transgender. Conversely, not all transgender people are gender nonconforming.

. . . .

Transgender:

an adjective used to describe someone whose gender identity or expression is not typically associated with the sex assigned at birth. It can be used to

---

2. Local Law No. 3 (2002); N.Y.C Admin. Code § 8-102(23).

5. *Id.*

6. *Id.*

describe people with a broad range of identity or expression. Someone who identifies their gender as androgynous, gender queer, non-binary, gender non-conforming, MTF (male to female), or FTM (female to male) may also consider themselves to be transgender.

III. Violations of the New York City Human Rights Law's Prohibitions on Gender Discrimination

Gender discrimination under the NYCHRL includes discrimination on the basis of gender identity, gender expression, and transgender status.[7] . . . . Under the NYCHRL, gender discrimination can be based on one's perceived or actual gender identity, which may or may not conform to one's sex assigned at birth, or on the ways in which one expresses gender, such as through appearance or communication style. Gender discrimination is prohibited in employment, housing, public accommodations, discriminatory harassment, and bias-based profiling by police and exists whenever there is disparate treatment of an individual on account of gender. When an individual is treated "less well than others on account of their gender,"[8] that is gender discrimination under the NYCHRL.

Harassment motivated by gender is a form of discrimination. Gender-based harassment can be a single or isolated incident of disparate treatment or repeated acts or behavior. Disparate treatment can manifest in harassment when the incident or behavior creates an environment or reflects or fosters a culture or atmosphere of sex stereotyping, degradation, humiliation, bias, or objectification. Under the NYCHRL, gender-based harassment covers a broad range of conduct and occurs generally when an individual is treated less well on account of their gender. While the severity or pervasiveness of the harassment is relevant to damages, the existence of differential treatment based on gender is sufficient under the NYCHRL to constitute a claim of harassment. . . . [R]efusal to use a transgender employee's preferred name, pronoun, or title may constitute unlawful gender-based harassment. . . .

Unlawful gender-based discrimination is prohibited in the following areas:

Employment:

> It is unlawful. . . . to set different terms and conditions of employment because of an employee's gender. Examples of terms and conditions of employment include work assignments, employee benefits, and keeping the workplace free from harassment.

Public Accommodations:

> It is unlawful for providers of public accommodations, their employees, or their agents to deny any person, or communicate intent to deny, the services, advantages, facilities or privileges of a public accommodation directly or indirectly because of their actual or perceived gender, including actual or

---

7. N.Y.C. Admin. Code § 8-102(23).
8. *Williams v. N.Y.C. Hous. Auth.*, 872 N.Y.S.2d 27, 39 (App. Div. 2009).

perceived status as a transgender person. Simply put, it is unlawful to deny any person full and equal enjoyment of a public accommodation because of gender.

Housing:

It is unlawful. . . . to withhold from any person full and equal enjoyment of a housing accommodation because of their gender.[9]

1. Failing to Use an Individual's Preferred Name or Pronoun

The NYCHRL requires employers and covered entities to use an individual's preferred name, pronoun and title (*e.g.*, Ms./Mrs.) regardless of the individual's sex assigned at birth, anatomy, gender, medical history, appearance, or the sex indicated on the individual's identification.

Most individuals and many transgender people use female or male pronouns and titles. Some transgender and gender non-conforming people prefer to use pronouns other than he/him/his or she/her/hers, such as they/them/theirs or ze/hir.[10] Many transgender and gender non-conforming people choose to use a different name than the one they were given at birth.

All people, including employees, tenants, customers, and participants in programs, have the right to use their preferred name regardless of whether they have identification in that name or have obtained a court-ordered name change, except in very limited circumstances where certain federal, state, or local laws require otherwise (*e.g.*, for purposes of employment eligibility verification with the federal government). Asking someone their preferred gender pronoun and preferred name is not a violation of the NYCHRL.

Examples of Violations

a. Intentional or repeated refusal to use an individual's preferred name, pronoun or title. For example, repeatedly calling a transgender woman "him" or "Mr." after she has made clear which pronouns and title she uses.

b. Refusal to use an individual's preferred name, pronoun, or title because they do not conform to gender stereotypes. For example, calling a woman "Mr." because her appearance is aligned with traditional gender-based stereotypes of masculinity.

c. Conditioning an individual's use of their preferred name on obtaining a court-ordered name change or providing identification in that name. For example, a covered entity may not refuse to call a transgender woman her

---

9. Protections on the basis of gender under the NYCHRL are subject to the same limitations as all other protected categories. *See* N.Y.C. Admin. Code §§ 8-102(5); 8-107(5)(a)(4)(1),(2); 8-107(4)(b).

10. *Ze* and *hir* are popular gender-free pronouns preferred by some transgender and/or gender nonconforming individuals.

preferred name, Jane, because her identification says that her first name is John.[11]

d. Requiring an individual to provide information about their medical history or proof of having undergone particular medical procedures in order to use their preferred name, pronoun, or title.

Covered entities may avoid violations of the NYCHRL by creating a policy of asking everyone what their preferred gender pronoun is so that no individual is singled out for such questions and by updating their systems to allow all individuals to self-identify their names and genders. They should not limit the options for identification to male and female only.

. . . .

————————

Discussion

1. The NYCHRL (also in Ch. 7, *supra* at p.425) adopts a broad definition of "gender," distinguishing between "actual" and "perceived" sex. What might this distinction imply? Does this language provide any insight into New York City's opinion on the "biological" nature of a transgender identity? Also, recall the concern in Sharon M. McGowan, *Working with Clients to Develop Compatible Visions of What It Means to "Win" A Case: Reflections on* Schroer v. Billington, 45 Harv. C.R.-C.L. L. Rev. 205 (2010), Chapter 5, Section D, *supra* at p. 227, Discussion note 3, over a line being drawn between "innocent" and "non-innocent" gender identities. Might this "actual or perceived" language allay the concerns that McGowan expressed, ensuring that not only "innocent" gender identities are protected from gender discrimination?

2. The statute's definition of "gender" also includes "gender identity, self-image, appearance, behavior, or expression." Notably, this guidance interprets gender expression to include "the representation of one's gender through one's name, choice of pronouns, clothing, haircut, behavior, voice, or body characteristics." What policy interests might justify such definitions? Can you imagine a scenario where it would be difficult to determine whether a person's clothing, haircut, or voice is a representation of their gender? Are these attributes *de facto* representations of one's gender? *Cf.* Kimberly L. Yuracko: *Soul of a Woman: The Sex Stereotyping Prohibition at Work*, 161 U. Pa. L. Rev. 757, 770–71 (2013). Professor Yuracko

————————

11. Where covered entities regularly request a form of identification from members of the public for a legitimate business reason, requesting a form of identification from transgender and/or gender nonconforming individuals is not unlawful. Just as is the case for many cisgender individuals, many transgender and/or gender non-conforming individuals' appearances may not appear the same as what is represented on their photo identification. Covered entities may use a form of identification to corroborate an individual's identification, but may not subject a transgender or gender non-conforming individual to a higher level of scrutiny than any other person presenting a form of identification.

argues that Title VII's ban on sex discrimination requires a "stable and workable definition of gender," and that one cannot therefore interpret its ban on sex stereo-typing discrimination to protect "all forms of gender expression — those that are stereotypical, atypical, and idiosyncratic; those that are persistent; and those that are transient." *Id.*

3. This guidance adopts a concise definition of gender discrimination: when an individual is treated "less well than others on account of their gender." The guidance also clarifies that "the existence of differential treatment" based on gender is suffi-cient to claim harassment, which is a form of prohibited discrimination. What are the positive and/or negative consequences of limiting people's ability to treat others differently based on gender in housing, public accommodations, and employment? Can you envision how opponents of this broad "differential treatment" standard might want to limit its applicability? (For example, what privacy concerns may be raised in response to the "differential treatment" standard?)

4. In legislation, there are many ways to avoid gendered pronouns, thus facilitat-ing application of law to people regardless of gender. *See* Donald L. Revell & Jessica Vapnik, *Gender-Silent Legislative Drafting in a Non-Binary World*, 48 Cap. U. L. Rev. 103 (2020). What pronoun and honorific (*e.g.*, "Mr.," "Ms.," "Mx.") practices in a school, workplace, or place of public accommodation, for example, can minimize misgendering and other forms of disrespect for trans and nonbinary persons?

Chapter 16

Identity Documents

In U.S. society, as in many others, our identities are routinely verified and gender is routinely included in the documents that attest to our identities. Dean Spade, now an Associate Professor of Law at Seattle University School of Law, notes

> the ubiquity of gender data collection in almost every imaginable government and commercial identity verification system. From birth to death, the "M" and "F" boxes are present on nearly every form we fill out: on the identity documents we show to prove ourselves and in the computer records kept by government agencies, banks, and nonprofit organizations. Additionally, gender classification often governs spaces such as bathrooms, homeless shelters, drug treatment programs, mental health services, and spaces of confinement like psychiatric hospitals, juvenile and adult prisons, and immigration prisons (often called "detention centers" despite the fact that the word "detention" misleadingly denotes a relatively short-term confinement, which is, time and again, not the case for people placed in these facilities). The consequences of misclassification or the inability to be fit into the existing classification system are extremely high. . . .

DEAN SPADE, NORMAL LIFE: ADMINISTRATIVE VIOLENCE, CRITICAL TRANS POLITICS, AND THE LIMITS OF LAW 77 (rev. ed. 2015). (For an earlier treatment of these issues by Professor Spade, see Dean Spade, *Documenting Gender*, 59 HASTINGS L.J. 731 (2008).) As Lisa Mottet has argued,

> the effect of not having government documentation that matches one's gender identity is tremendous. Although for many, lack of accurate documentation may trigger smaller problems caused by undesired disclosure of their transgender status, for others, the lack of government documentation can have dire effects. Policies that provide transgender people with identity documents that match their gender identity give them a better chance to live life in their gender, and avoid bias, discrimination, and violence in the areas most critical to quality of life, such as employment, housing, and education.

Lisa Mottet, *Modernizing State Vital Statistics Statutes and Policies to Ensure Accurate Gender Markers on Birth Certificates: A Good Government Approach to Recognizing the Lives of Transgender People*, 9 MICH. J. GENDER & L. 373, 379 (2013). Nonetheless, Heath Fogg Davis has argued that this "strategy of . . . mak[ing] it possible for transgender people to have the sex markers on our identity documents match our felt or lived sex identity," is a "strategy of assimmilation" that "does not solve the identity document problem for all transgender people." HEATH FOGG DAVIS, BEYOND TRANS: DOES GENDER MATTER? 25–26 (2017). Instead, he argues, we should "[e]radicat[e] sex markers from our birth certificates, passports, driver's licenses, and state identity cards." *Id.* at 53.

This chapter addresses some of the multiple strands of the complicated web of identity document law and policies regarding change of gender markers in the United States, with its federalist scheme of government, with federal and state governments exercising various regulatory jurisdiction. Section A addresses birth certificates. Section B turns to driver's licenses and state ID cards. Section C takes up passports, which are issued by the federal government.

A. Birth Certificates

Birth certificates are the first identity documents we are issued. Their sex/gender identifications are typically based on visual observation of a newborn's genitalia and not chromosomes, hormones, or any other components of sex including a person's gender identity, which is not discernable and may not even be set at birth. Attempting to change the sex/gender marker reflected on one's birth certificate can be burdensome in the case of states that require surgery or futile in the case of states that forbid amendments to reflect gender transition procedures.

As summarized by the National Center for Transgender Equality in 2020, 30 states,[a] the District of Columbia, Guam, and Puerto Rico allow people to change the "gender marker" on their birth certificates through an administrative process; 18 states[b] and the Northern Mariana Islands require a court order; American Samoa and the U.S. Virgin Islands lack a clear policy; and two states, Tennessee (by statute) and Ohio (by agency policy), forbid any change to the gender marker. Of those, 10 states[c] and New York City allow a non-binary or gender-neutral gender marker, most commonly "X." In terms of whether a jurisdiction requires medical evidence to support one's request for change to one's birth certificate gender markers, 9 states[d] and New York City do *not* require the signature of the person's medical provider; 13 states,[e] the District of Columbia, and Puerto Rico require evidence that the person has had "appropriate" treatment but do not require surgery; 11 states[f] and Guam by

---

a. AK, AZ, CA, CT, DE, FL, HI, ID, IL, IO, KS, KY, MD, MA, ME, MI, MN, MT, NE, NV, NJ, NM, NY, NC, ND, OR, PA, PR, RI, WA, and WV.

b. AL, AR, CO, GA, IN, LA, MO, MS, NH, OK, SC, SD, TX, UT, VA, VT, WI, and WY.

c. CA, CO, CT, NV, NJ, NM, OR, RI, UT, WA.

d. CA, CO, ID, MT, NV, NJ, NM, OR, and WA.

e. AK, CT, DE, FL, HI, IL, KS, MD, MA, MN, NY, PA, RI, and VT.

f. AL, AZ, AR, GA, KY, LA, MI, MO, NE, NC, and WI.

statute and 5 states[g] by agency practice or written policy require proof of surgery; and in 9 states,[h] American Samoa, the Northern Mariana Islands, and the U.S. Virgin Islands the judge or "policy official" decides due to lack of a specific policy or practice concerning necessary medical evidence. *See* National Center for Transgender Equality, *Summary of State Birth Certificate Gender Change Laws*, Jan. 2020, https:// transequality.org/sites/default/files/docs/resources/Summary%20of%20State%20 Birth%20Certificate%20Laws%20Jan%202020.pdf (last visited Feb. 29, 2020).

Birth certificates illustrate government power to label people in ways that do not conform with their own understanding of themselves. That power is a source of many problems faced by transgender people in obtaining identification documents that reflect who they are and do not expose them to practical difficulties. Whether a birth certificate should be regarded as a record of historical facts, a record of present facts, or both, is repeatedly contested when transgender people disagree with governmental authorities about whether the law allows them to amend the sex markers on their birth certificates.

Reading Guide for Anonymous v. Weiner

1. This action seeking an order compelling amendment of the name and the sex marker on the petitioner's birth certificate is one for mandamus (also known as Article 78 in New York state practice). Mandamus refers to an order commanding a person to perform a statutory or public duty. Thus, the court is not called upon to determine whether, in its judgment, the Director of the Bureau of Records and Statistics made the "right" judgment. Rather, the question is whether there was a statutory or public duty that the director violated. This is sometimes called the "clear duty" rule.

2. What reasons did the New York Academy of Medicine's Committee on Public Health give for concluding that transsexual persons (regardless of any transition-related surgeries they may have had) should not be permitted to amend the sex markers on their birth certificates?

3. Why does the court conclude that the defendant did not act unlawfully in refusing to change the petitioner's sex marker?

---

g. IA, ME, ND, WV, and VA.

h. IN, MS, NH, OK, SC, SD, TX, UT, and WY.

In the Matter of Anonymous v. Louis Weiner, as the Director of the Bureau of Records and Statistics of the Department of Health of the City of New York

50 Misc. 2d 380, 270 N.Y.S.2d 319 (Sup. Ct. 1966)

JOSEPH A. SARAFITE, J.

Petitioner instituted this article 78 CPLR proceeding, in the nature of mandamus, for an order directing respondent to change the sex designated on petitioner's birth certificate from "male" to "female" and, consonant therewith, to change the given name thereon to one assumed by petitioner subsequent to birth and to issue and substitute a new certificate.

. . . .

"The syndrome of transsexualism" involves "a truly untrodden, controversial and largely unexplored field of medicine." Harry Benjamin, *Clinical Aspects of Transsexualism in the Male and Female*, 18 AMER. J. PSYCHOTHERAPY 458 (1964). With appropriate hesitation because of the paucity of knowledge in this area of science, transsexualism has been described by a leading authority, Dr. Harry Benjamin, as "a striking disturbance of gender role and gender orientation . . . a disorder of the harmony and uniformity of the psychosexual personality . . . [a] split between the psychological and the morphological sex . . ." *Nature and Management of Transsexualism: With a Report on Thirty-One Operated Cases*, 72 WESTERN J. SURGERY, OBSTETRICS AND GYNECOLOGY 105, 106 (1964).

This petitioner has undergone "conversive" surgery [*sic*] and has assumed the name and role of a female in our society as a means of correcting the disharmony to which Dr. Benjamin refers. To consummate so far as possible this change in gender, an application for the issuance of a new birth certificate was submitted to the Director of the Bureau of Records and Statistics of the Department of Health of the City of New York. The request was held in abeyance pending the consideration and determination by the [New York City] Board of Health of the general subject of change of birth certificates of transsexuals. An earlier similar application had caused respondent's predecessor to seek the guidance of the Board of Health.

When confronted with this need for a formulation of policy and possible implementation by regulation, the Board of Health, in recognition of the serious consequences attendant upon a decision in the affirmative or in the negative, initiated an exhaustive inquiry into the subject and called upon the New York Academy of Medicine ["NYAM"] to study the problem and to submit its recommendations to the board. . . .

After detailed analysis of the many facets and ramifications of the change of sex on the birth certificate of a transsexual, including cognizance of the fact that at present 10 States have permitted such change . . . , the [NYAM Committee on Public Health] concluded that:

1. male-to-female transsexuals are still chromosomally males while ostensibly females;

2. it is questionable whether laws and records such as the birth certificate should be changed and thereby used as a means to help psychologically ill persons in their social adaptation.

The Committee is therefore opposed to a change of sex on birth certificates in transsexualism."

*** The desire of concealment of a change of sex by the transsexual is outweighed by the public interest for protection against fraud.

. . . . [R]espondent denied petitioner's application for amendment or issuance of a new birth certificate.

The proper scope of the judicial role . . . in reviewing the denial of petitioner's application is greatly restricted. Primary jurisdiction to formulate and implement the city's policy with regard to the records of "birth, fetal deaths and deaths" is vested in the Board of Health. New York City Charter § 567.

The prerequisite standards for amendment of a birth certificate are prescribed by the provisions of the New York City Health Code. These provisions—which have the force and effect of statutory law—represent and reflect the plenary jurisdiction of the Board of Health in this area.

Article 207 of the New York City Health Code provides, in pertinent part, for amendment of a birth certificate only if "the Commissioner or his designee is satisfied that the evidence submitted shows the true facts and that an error was made at the time of preparing and filing of the certificate, or that the name of a person named in a birth certificate has been changed pursuant to court order." . . . .

Thus, the critical issue before the court is whether the respondent acted in an arbitrary, capricious or otherwise illegal manner in deciding that the petitioner did not establish "that the evidence submitted shows the true facts and that an error was made at the time of preparing and filing of the certificate" and, accordingly, in denying the application for amendment and issuance of a new certificate.

The test of arbitrariness does not permit the court to substitute its views for those of the administrative body charged by law with the authority and responsibility of maintaining the records of births and deaths. In its role as ultimate arbiter of the legality of administrative action the judiciary may not arrogate to itself the power of a super-Board of Health to weigh the wisdom of respondent's acts.

Indeed, the nature of the problem posed initially to the Board of Health and now to the court requires a specialized training and skill for which the board is uniquely equipped. Judicial deference to the decision of those members of the Board of Health who are physicians or otherwise uniquely qualified appears mandatory in the singular circumstances here involved.

. . . . Implicit in this resolution is the board's interpretation of the Health Code to the effect that, as presently constituted, no authorization exists for the amendment requested by petitioner. As the Supreme Court of the United States declared recently under analogous circumstances:

> When faced with a problem of statutory construction . . . [the] court shows great deference to the interpretation given the statute by the officers or agency charged with its administration. "To sustain the . . . [Board's] application of this statutory term ['an error was made at the time of preparing and filing of the certificate'], we need not find that its construction is the only reasonable one, or even that it is the result we would have reached had the question arisen in the first instance in judicial proceedings." . . . . When the construction of an administrative regulation rather than a statute is in issue, deference is even more clearly in order.

Udall v. Tallman, 380 U.S. 1 (1965).

. . . .

Accordingly, the present application is denied and the petition dismissed.

The present proceeding has not been instituted nor has it been considered by the court as an application for a change in name in compliance with section 61 of the Civil Rights Law.

Discussion

1. Harry Benjamin's characterization of "transsexualism" reflects an understanding generally prevailing in early stages of research on gender identity. It embodies the idea that "morphological" sex, *i.e.*, anatomy, normally matches inherent, underlying psychological, social, and behavioral gendered traits. It is a step beyond Freud's (often misconstrued) 1912 statement that "anatomy is destiny," in that it recognizes that anatomy is not determinative of one's gender expression. At the same time, it sees differences between the two as a defect or developmental error, rather than as a natural variation of human experience. That view prevailed in the U.S. medical community until 2013, when the diagnosis of "gender identity disorder" in the fourth edition of the American Psychiatric Association's Diagnostic and Statistical Manual of Mental Disorders was replaced in the fifth edition with "gender dysphoria," rejecting the idea that having a gender identity different from the sex one was assigned at birth was a mental illness and instead focusing on the distress that can follow from incongruence between people's gender identity and sex assigned at birth as they live in society. The 11th edition of the *International Classification of Diseases* (ICD), promulgated by the World Health Organization and used by most of the world outside the United States, removed its mental disorder classification of transgender status and placed a new sexual health condition of "gender incongruence" in a separate section.

2. Contrast this court's approach with that used in *In re A.L.*, 81 N.E.3d 283 (Ind. Ct. App. 2017), Chapter 15, *supra* at p. 1070. In Indiana, the courts took the

responsibility to issue orders for gender changes on birth certificates, although there was no judicial authority statutorily designated expressly for that purpose. Here, the New York City Board of Health undertook an exhaustive study before deciding whether to allow birth certificate sex marker changes. A court would not likely be willing or able to engage in such study.

3. The court appears to have concluded that the defendant did not act unreasonably in following the NYAM's recommendation not to allow "transsexual" persons to change the sex marker on their birth certificate. What is the concern about "fraud" that appears to underlie the NYAM's and the court's conclusion? What does it presuppose about sex/gender?

Note on Hartin v. Director of Bureau of Records and Statistics

In *In the Matter of Deborah Hartin v. Director of the Bureau of Records and Statistics, Department of Health of the City of New York*, 75 Misc. 2d 229, 347 N.Y.S.2d 515 (Sup. Ct. 1973), transgender woman Deborah Hartin, after undergoing genital reconstruction surgery, filed an "article 78" proceeding, which is New York's name for a proceeding for mandamus to compel performance of a legally mandated duty. She sought to compel the respondent Director of the Bureau of Records and Statistics of the New York City Department of Health to issue her an amended birth certificate listing both her new first name Deborah and her sex as female. The bureau had issued a new certificate with "Deborah" but with no sex listed. Ms. Hartin argued that the omission of her sex marker was arbitrary and capricious and an abuse of discretion.

Ms. Hartin relied upon a regulation issued by the city Department of Health pursuant to Public Health Law § 4100 and the New York City Charter; the regulation provided: "A new birth certificate shall be filed when: . . . The name of the person has been changed pursuant to court order and proof satisfactory to the Department has been submitted that such person has undergone convertive [*sic*] surgery."

The court rejected her argument that the regulation obligated the bureau to issue her a new birth certificate marked "female." It read the regulation literally, observing that it "in no way dictates that a new certificate shall indicate the sex of the applicant." And it reasoned that it had to defer to the director. The nature of "the problem" the Board of Health was addressing, the court maintained, "requires a specialized training and skill for which the board, and not the court, is uniquely equipped." The board had concluded that however therapeutic genital reconstruction surgery, which it deemed "experimental," was for people like petitioner, it "does not change the body cells governing sexuality." And the court noted that one member of the board thought the government ought not "encourage[]" more people to undergo genital reconstruction surgery, which the board considered "mutilating." All this was enough justification for the court.

Reading Guide for Anonymous v. Mellon

1. By what does the court here regard human "sex" as being determined/defined?

2. What reasons does the court give for refusing to provide a declaratory judgment that the petitioner here, a "transsexual" woman in the parlance of the time, is female? (How does the court treat the fraud prevention rationale of earlier decisions that refused to treat a transsexual woman as female?) Why does the court think a writ of mandamus (ordering the defendant to act) would be equivalent to a declaratory judgment here?

3. By what standard does the court assess the government's policy here?

Anonymous v. Irving Mellon, as Director of Bureau of Vital Records, Department of Health of the City of New York

91 Misc. 2d 375, 398 N.Y.S.2d 99 (Sup. Ct. 1977)

EDWARD J. GREENFIELD, J.

Questions once regarded as simple are now recognized as matters of considerable complexity as we analyze more closely that which was once taken for granted. It used to be that one could make an instant determination of such matters as life or death—is a body living or not. Similarly, with respect to gender, a person was either male or female, and no three ways about it. These simplistic conclusions, under intensive examination have come to be challenged, and it is now recognized that there are a series of determinants which must be reviewed to answer these formerly simple questions.

. . . . [I]n 1975, after extensive psychological, psychiatric and endocrinological evaluation and workout, sex reassignment surgery was performed and petitioner became anatomically, as well as psychologically, a woman. Petitioner's name was changed by court order in Canada to a female name and a new passport was issued by the United States Department of State bearing the newly assumed female name and a photograph of an attractive young woman. On May 28, 1975, petitioner requested the respondent, who is charged by the Administrative Code of the City of New York with maintaining birth records and issuing certificates reflecting such change, to issue a corrected birth certificate to reflect petitioner's female name and sex. A new certificate was, in fact, issued on March 2, 1976 identifying petitioner by petitioner's female name, but in accordance with departmental practice, bearing no statement as to sex. In further correspondence, petitioner insisted that the birth certificate specify female sex, but these demands have been rejected.

An order is now sought in an article 78 proceeding directing Irving Mellon, the Director of the Bureau of Vital Records of the New York City Department of Health, to issue a birth certificate either showing petitioner's sex as female or showing the original sex and change of sex. In the alternative, petitioner seeks a declaratory judgment determining petitioner's sex to be female and directing that such a determination be attached to and filed with the birth records.

Insofar as petitioner seeks a declaratory judgment establishing female sexual identity, the application must be dismissed as presenting a nonjusticiable controversy. It is basic that courts will not make a declaratory judgment in a vacuum and that the question presented for determination must be determinative of an actual controversy between adverse parties. In fact, respondent takes no position on the request for declaratory relief, since it is not affected by that branch of the relief sought. The court, in effect, is being asked to render a judicial opinion in the absence of a genuine justiciable controversy which will determine the respective obligations of contesting parties. If the purpose of a declaratory judgment is to enable a party who is placed in an uncertain position to invoke the aid of the court to obtain a declaration of legal rights before being exposed to loss or damage and before any change of position, that purpose would not be served where petitioner has already irrevocably changed positions and there is no dispute as to obligations. Possible future controversies as to petitioner's sexual identity can be envisioned, but they are not here presented.

. . . . However fascinating the information presented by psychologists, surgeons, endocrinologists and clergymen may be, the court will not pick and choose one set of opinions over another if rational choices are equally available to the administrative body.

. . . . This court recognizes that sexual gender is not merely a matter of anatomy. Other determinants include psychological identity, acceptability by others, chromosomal makeup, reproductive capacity and endocrine levels. *See* Harry Benjamin, The Transsexual Phenomenon 3–10 (1966). Basing determination of gender upon any one indicator might well lead to an unwarranted conclusion. *See, e.g., Richards v United States Tennis Assn.*, 93 Misc. 2d 713 (Sup. Ct. 1977).

. . . . The court will today regard "protection of the public interest against fraud" as being of virtually no significance, since it is dubious that any one would go through such drastic procedures as sex reassignment surgery for the purpose of deceiving creditors or avoiding the draft. It has been judicially determined that chromosomal or genetic sex is not the determinative factor in deciding whether a person is male or female. *See Richards*. The fact is that no single characteristic is determinative.

. . . . The birth certificate is nothing in and of itself but a record, a statistic, a source. In cases such as those of transsexuals which are so beclouded by ambiguity, an administrative body such as the respondent may properly decline to take a position which will be used as evidence in other proceedings to establish jural relationships or rights and obligations. The fact of sex may be crucial in school admissions, in vocational or recreational opportunities, in military service, in connection with insurance and pensions, or upon an application for a marriage certificate. The Bureau of Vital Records can appropriately decline to make a determination which would have an effect upon possible future controversies. It is being asked to make a ruling ex parte. If the facts are susceptible to diverse interpretation however, it is not irrational to allow those facts to be contested and established adversarially in subsequent proceedings.

Petitioner requests that if respondent is unwilling to put down the word "female" on the birth certificate it should alternatively show the original sex as male and the present sex as female. There is no compelling reason why respondent should be required to do this. While petitioner may be willing to have those facts appear on the birth certificate, it is doubtful that other transsexuals would want to have that fact so advertised. In the promulgation of a general rule, respondent may properly consider the general good and refuse to make exceptions for individual cases.

It should be noted that a direction by the court to the respondent requiring it to enter the word "female" on the birth certificate, when respondent has declined to do so, would be tantamount to this court granting the application for a declaratory judgment. The determination would be the ex parte determination of this court alone, without a thorough airing of the facts. While respondent defends its own position in abstaining from choice, it does not in fact contest any of petitioner's contentions about the anatomic, endocrinological and genital changes which are alleged by petitioner. Respondent merely contends that its rule, taking no position, is reasonable under the circumstances.

The court concludes, as had earlier courts, that the respondent did not act arbitrarily, unreasonably or illegally in declining to designate petitioner's sex. Nothing done by the respondent will preclude petitioner under appropriate circumstances in attempting to establish female gender when legal obligations are to be decided. . . . The petition is denied and the proceeding is dismissed.

Discussion

1. The court recognizes here that it has no power to declare a person's sex absent such an issue being determinative in an actual dispute. It states that the purpose of declaratory relief (sought by the plaintiff) "would not be served where petitioner has already irrevocably changed positions and there is no dispute as to obligations." But was there really no dispute about legal obligations? If so, why didn't the defendant issue the petitioner a birth certificate with a gender marker as she sought? Could the court have reasonably ruled that a declaration as to sex would have been determinative in the case against the Bureau of Vital Statistics? (And what exactly does the court mean by "the petitioner has already irrevocably changed positions" and to what legal issue would that be relevant?) Is the court taking the position that the petitioner is not—without more—harmed by having a birth certificate that fails to list her sex while cisgender people do have birth certificates that list theirs?

2. The court recognizes, in its opening paragraph and elsewhere in the opinion, a multi-factorial analysis of sex, rather than the simple biological (ostensibly chromosomal) determinism of prior cases. While the court does not allow this to supplant the board's judgment, and its discussion is thus arguably dicta, it opens the door to future developments in legal analysis of the "sex" of transgender persons.

3. In emphasizing lack of fraud concerns about debts or military service, the court elides the fraud concern that motivated prior courts. The fraud implied there appears to have been that people would be deceived about the "true" sex of transgender women. One possible version of such concern about fraud might be that (cisgender) men would thereby be deceived into relations with transgender women, who "really" are men, compromising their heterosexuality as those men conceive it. That transformation could be anathema to such "deceived" men because homosexuality was then considered criminal, *see Bowers v. Hardwick*, 478 U.S. 186 (1986) (observing that having been the case in all 50 states and the District of Columbia up to 1961), and a mental illness with connections to pedophilia and dangerous sexual compulsions. Such concerns undergird the social trope that transgender people are deceptive, which thus depends upon biological determinism.

4. The court first declares that a birth certificate is merely a historical record that provides information about an instant in time, but then opines that it has importance as a determinant of sex-based social identification for purposes of education, employment, military service, insurance, and marriage. If it is merely a historical record, then why should it follow a person throughout their present and future life as a method of identification and determinant of social position? And if it is a method of identification and social determinant of the present, then why should a person not be able to provide for a change of the "record" upon gender transition? Now that the significance of sex for purposes of education, employment, military service, insurance, and marriage has been diminished or abandoned, is the court's reasoning still viable?

5. If only transsexual persons get birth certificates without sex markers, and this fact were or became known, what functional difference would there be between petitioner's fallback request and what the defendant provided her?

6. The court worries about the lack of adversarial factual contestation were the court to order the defendant to grant the petitioner the requested amendment to her birth certificate. Why should that matter? The court does not say that it would be improper for the defendant to adopt a rule allowing people such as petitioner to change the gender marker on their birth certificate, even though such changes would also result from ex parte decisionmaking. (And, technically, the director of the bureau is a party to this proceeding, so the court's characterization of this as "ex parte" depends upon its conclusion that there is no actual controversy between the petitioner and the defendant, only possible future disputes between the petitioner and other, not yet determined parties.)

7. For an analysis of a failed attempt from 2002–2006 to eliminate the genitoplasty requirement for changing a birth certificate sex marker in New York City law, drawing in part on one of the co-author's participant observation, see Paisley Currah & Lisa Jean Moore, *"We Won't Know Who You Are": Contesting Sex Designations in New York City Birth Certificates*, in The Transgender Studies Reader 2 pp. 607–622 (Susan Stryker and Aren Z. Aizura eds., 2013). In their view, "[a]s the concern about fraud fades from view, permanence emerges as a mechanism for the

state to reassert a biological imperative based on the 'natural attitude' [about sex, in contrast to a view of gender as a '"managed achievement"'].... Instead of changing the criteria for markers on identity documents, officials insist that individuals change their bodies to align with the 'natural attitude.'" *Id.* at 619. For an analysis of how Japan's adoption of a surgical sterilization requirement for change of sex in the national registry of citizens violates transgender people's rights, see Laura Norton, *Neutering the Transgendered: Human Rights and Japan's Law No. 111*, 7 Georgetown J. Gender & L. 187 (2006).

Reading Guide for K. v. Health Div., Department of Human Resources

1. Note that the court's language is dated. It is today widely considered improperly reductive if not pejorative to refer to a person as "a transsexual" or "a transgender." An appropriate reference would be to "a transgender person."

2. The state supreme court here reverses a lower court decision granting an order that the state issue a new birth certificate indicating the sex as male for the transgender man who had petitioned for a change of sex and name. In what sorts of situations does the court say the state's statutes would allow issuance of new birth certificates? How does the court describe the function of birth certificates such that it rejects the permissibility of changing them to comport with a transgender person's gender identity (even, as in this case, where the person has undergone genitoplasty)?

3. The Chief Judge concurs specially. He agrees with the majority that the lower court misinterpreted Oregon's laws governing birth certificates, so why does he write separately?

K. v. Health Division, Department of Human Resources of the State of Oregon

560 P.2d 1070 (Or. 1977) (en banc)

Before Denecke, C.J., and Holman, Tongue, Howell, Lent, Linde and Bradshaw, JJ.

Tongue, Justice.

The original petitioner, a transsexual person, filed in Multnomah County a petition for a certificate for change of sex from female to male and "that birth and school records should be changed in accordance with such certificate."

That court [ordered], over the objection on special appearance by the State Board of Health, that "a new birth certificate shall be issued to petitioner ... designating the sex as male and the name as" K.

The Court of Appeals affirmed....

Petitions for change of name are controlled by statutes, ORS 33.410-33.430. The only reference in those statutes to issuance of a "new birth certificate," is in the event of a change, by court order, of the name of the parents of any minor child. It is also provided, however, by ORS 109.310, 109.400 and 432.415, that when a child for whom an original birth certificate was filed has been adopted, a "supplemental [birth] certificate" shall be issued in the new name of the adopted parents and the original birth certificate shall be sealed, but remain on file. The only other statutory provision for preparation and issuance of a new birth certificate is in the event of the marriage of the parents of any child after its birth, as provided by ORS 432.425.

[The] Court of Appeals . . . held that "[w]e find . . . authority in ORS 432.135, which provides:

> "The acceptance for filing of any certificate by the State Registrar more than six months after the time prescribed for its filing, and any alterations of such certificate after it is filed with the State Registrar, shall be subject to regulations in which the division shall prescribe in detail the proofs to be submitted by any applicant for delayed filing or an alteration of a certificate, *or to the order of the county court or any other court of competent jurisdiction.*"

(Emphasis in Court of Appeals opinion)

[The] Court of Appeals quoted from decisions by this court to the effect that even when "seemingly unambiguous language," if applied literally, would reach a result "so at variance with the apparent policy of the legislation" as to be clearly unreasonable or absurd, the court must "look beyond the words" of the statute so as to "give effect to the intent" of the legislature, at least "[w]hen such an intent is manifest" . . . .

The difficulty with the application of such a rule in this case is that it has not been demonstrated, by legislative history or otherwise, that it would be "at variance with the apparent policy" of either the legislature or the State Board of Health to deny the issuance of a "new birth certificate" to a transsexual, thereby changing the designation of sex, as well as the original given name, from female to male. Much less has it been demonstrated that in the adoption of ORS 432.135 any such intent was 'manifest' by the Oregon legislature.

In our opinion, it is at least equally, if not more reasonable, to assume that in enacting these statutes it was the intent of the legislature of Oregon that a "birth certificate" is an historical record of the facts as they existed at the time of birth, subject to the specific exceptions provided by statute. This was also the view taken by the dissenting opinion of the Court of Appeals.

The majority of the Court of Appeals, however, appears to view a "birth certificate" as a record of facts as they presently exist, and thus as a record subject to change by order of a court by the issuance of a "new birth certificate" upon proof of any subsequent changes in the facts as recorded in the original birth certificate, including subsequent changes in sex.[5]

---

5. . . . . [It] appears from the record that the change in sex in this case was accomplished by surgery, as . . . this individual "had removal of all his internal female organs," together with "genitoplastic surgery to complete the surgical reconstruction."

In our opinion, it is not for this court to decide which view is preferable. On the contrary, we hold that this is a matter of public policy to be decided by the Oregon legislature. We also believe that it is by no means clear that it was the 'apparent' much less 'manifest' intent of the Oregon legislature in enacting ORS 432.135 to confer such broad powers upon the courts of this state.[6]

For these reasons the decision by the Court of Appeals is reversed.

DENECKE, Chief Justice, specially concurring.

I concur in the majority's opinion that the Court of Appeals erred. I specially concur to express my opinion that this is not the type of case in which we should grant a petition for review.

. . . .

I view this court, in considering petitions for review, to be primarily a law-announcing body, not an error-correcting court. I take this view not because of any exalted notions of the capabilities of this court, but because of judicial efficiency. . . .

I know, however, from experience that on occasion even a court which primarily considers itself a law-announcing court will grant a petition for review regardless of the lack of public importance of the case because of its opinion that error probably was committed. It will grant the petition because a party has suffered injury if there was error. . . . In my opinion such action is completely appropriate. Judicial efficiency must yield to the prevention of injustice.

Whether a person born in Oregon can have his or her birth certificate changed to reflect a sexual change does not in my opinion present any issue of importance. I am further of the opinion that there is no demand for a decision of this court delineating generally when a birth certificate can be changed. If I am mistaken in either of these opinions, the legislature can take corrective action. No party, neither "K" nor the state, has been injured by the [lower] court's decision.

I would dismiss the petition.

Discussion

1. Does the court majority opinion attach excessive weight to legislative intent, when the statutory language of ORS 432.135 explicitly allows the Oregon Board of Health to promulgate regulations regarding alteration of birth certificates? Today, statutory interpretation jurisprudence championed particularly by more conservative U.S. jurists de-emphasizes legislative intent in favor of giving effect to the meaning of statutory words. (For a dramatic example of this, see Justice Gorsuch's opinion for the Supreme Court in *Bostock v. Clayton County, Georgia*, 140 S. Ct.

---

6. No issue has been raised in this case whether a birth certificate may be "altered" or "corrected" by interlineation under the circumstances of this case, as distinguished from the issuance of a "new" birth certificate.

1731 (2020), Chapter 5, Section D, *supra*.) What should we think the words of ORS 432.135 fairly meant to the Oregon legislature or public? (Does applying them literally necessarily mean that K. loses?)

2. How plausible is the majority's assumption about the legislature's intent in enacting the statute? It limits its characterization of the assumed intent by qualifying it with the phrase "subject to the specific exceptions provided by statute." But if those exceptions undermine the supposed general principle or function of birth certificates in the state, why doesn't that call into question whether that really is the general principle?

3. Is this "historical facts" view of sex on birth certificates the problem here? If it is, is the solution to argue that the "facts" of sex are more complex, that medicine treats sex as involving more factors than just genitalia at birth? Addressing decisions that have refused to let transgender persons marry heterosexually (that is, marry someone of a sex different from that associated with their gender identity), Prof. Cruz has written:

> . . . . [Gender] non-recognition decisions have been met with stern criticism from other academics besides me. Yet ostensibly progressive critics sometimes argue as if the problem is that law does not accurately track a more complex underlying fact of gender. . . .

> . . . . [It is] the valorization of "nature" through notions of "medical science" and, thus, biology, and the attendant displacement of human responsibility, that I am concerned about. I worry that a . . . refusal of judgment may underlie the eager embrace of the medical profession and medical standards by pro-reform scholars and judges dealing with transsexual and intersex identity. The appeal to the self-evident normative authority of an autonomous and seemingly objective discipline such as medicine might seem to shield one from the perils or responsibility of taking a stand in making a recommendation or decision on what is, after all, a matter of law and a social issue. Whether or not there are Platonic forms, pure essences that exist independent of human recognition, those are not what law uses. Law is a human project, using human categories instrumentally for human purposes.

David B. Cruz, *Getting Sex "Right": Heteronormativity and Biologism in Trans and Intersex Marriage Litigation and Scholarship*, 18 Duke J. Gender L. & Pol'y 203, 211–12, 216–17 (2010).

Note on In re Heilig

In *In re Heilig*, 816 A.2d 68 (Md. 2003), the Court of Appeals of Maryland—the highest court in Maryland—held that the state's trial courts had jurisdiction "to determine and declare that a person has changed from one gender to another" even in the case of the petitioner, whose birth certificate was from Pennsylvania.

In particular, the Court of Appeals vacated the appellate decision below and directed that court to vacate the trial court's dismissal of transgender woman Janet

Heilig Wright's unopposed petition; the trial court was thereafter to consider competent evidence that Ms. Wright might put on. To establish that Wright was entitled to a judicial declaration recognizing a change of gender—by which the court seems to have meant what is frequently referred to as "sex," though the court's opinion notes that it uses "sex" and "gender" interchangeably—the court concluded that she would need "to present sufficient medical evidence of both the relevant criteria for determining gender and of the fact that, applying that [*sic*] criteria, he has completed a permanent and irreversible change from male to female." (The court explained that it was using the masculine pronoun because of its "conclusion that petitioner has not yet established an entitlement to a determination that his gender has been effectively changed from male to female," noting that petitioner's trial court filings referred to her with masculine pronouns as well. Before the court of appeals, petitioner was represented by two transgender women who are transgender scholars and activists, Alyson Dodi Meiselman and Phyllis Randolph Frye.)

After reviewing the medical literature on persons with intersex conditions and transsexual persons (Ch. 2, *supra* at pp.21–30), the Court of Appeals concluded that

> the current medical thinking does seem to support at least these relevant propositions: (1) that external genitalia are not the sole medically recognized determinant of gender; (2) that the medically recognized determinants of gender may sometimes be either ambiguous or incongruent; (3) that due to mistaken assumptions made by physicians of an infant's ambiguous external genitalia at or shortly after birth, some people are mislabeled at that time as male or female and thereafter carry an official gender status that is medically incorrect; (4) that at least some of the medically recognized determinants of gender are subject to being altered in such a way as to make them inconsistent with the individual's officially declared gender and consistent with the opposite gender; and (5) whether or not a person's psychological gender identity is physiologically based, it has received recognition as one of the determinants of gender and plays a powerful role in the person's psychic makeup and adaptation.

The court explained that

> the relevance of these propositions lies in the facts that (1) gender itself is a fact that may be established by medical and other evidence, (2) it may be, or possibly may become, other than what is recorded on the person's birth certificate, and (3) a person has a deep personal, social, and economic interest in having the official designation of his or her gender match what, in fact, it always was or possibly has become.

Because no party was opposing petitioner's claim that she "had successfully transitioned to become a woman and was entitled to be declared as such," the Court of Appeals determined that the relief she sought was inappropriate under the state's Declaratory Judgment Act ("DJA") (but not for lack of jurisdiction, as the intermediate appellate court had held). Nonetheless, petitioner had not filed under the DJA, and the Court of Appeals concluded that the "Circuit Court has Constitutionally-based [referring to the Maryland Constitution], and statutorily recognized, equitable jurisdiction to consider and rule upon the petition." "Obviously," the court of appeals recognized, "the [Maryland] Legislature cannot direct officials in other States to change birth certificates issued in those States but may deal only with birth certificates issued or issuable in Maryland," which it took to be "the thrust" of a Maryland statute authorizing amendments of the sex marker on Maryland birth certificates. That statute, the court reasoned, merely reflected the general equity jurisdiction of the Maryland courts. And, the court reasoned, there would be serious questions whether it would violate the Equal Protection Clause and/or the Privileges or Immunities Clause of the Fourteenth Amendment were Maryland law to allow persons born in the state to seek a declaration of change of gender but to close the state's courts to people born in other states seeking such declarations.

Turning to what Ms. Wright would have to show to secure a judicial declaration of change of gender, the court concluded that the question "depends upon and, to a large extent, must follow medical facts (medical facts, in this context, to include relevant psychological facts)." So it required competent medical evidence (and implied that expert testimony would be most helpful, if not required). Drawing upon various legal contexts in various jurisdictions that required surgery as a precondition for recognition of a change of gender,[i] the court embraced a substantive requirement that Ms. Wright show a "permanent and irreversible change from male to female."

Note on Somers, D.R.G., and Multi-State Circumstances in Birth Certificate Cases

In *Somers v. Superior Court*, 172 Cal. App. 4th 1407 (2009), the California Court of Appeal held that California's former statute governing issuance of new birth certificates "to reflect a change in gender" was unconstitutional insofar as its requirement that a petition be filed in one's county of residence, thus precluding relief for persons born in California who now reside outside the state. The court reversed the judgment against petitioner Gigi Marie Somers, a transgender woman, and remanded for the trial court to consider the merits of Ms. Somers's petition.

Somers had "undergone gender reassignment surgery," legally changed her name (in Kansas), and obtained a Kansas driver's license with her new name and female gender marker, but Kansas would not and could not change her California birth certificate. For that, she did meet the California statutory requirement at that time that she have "undergone surgical treatment for the purpose of altering his or her sexual characteristics to those of the opposite sex [*sic*]." However, the statutory impediment Somers faced was the residency requirement, which treated California-born persons differently depending on whether or not they had exercised their

---

i. "Hormonal therapy alone, which usually can be terminated or perhaps even reversed, has not, to our knowledge, been recognized as effecting either a sufficient change or a permanent one[,]" the court observed. If that ever was true, it is no longer universally true.

constitutional right to move to another state. The Court of Appeal could "discern no compelling state interest" and, indeed, "no rational basis for the disparate treatment." Thus, the court held that the denial of the opportunity to seek a change of gender marker to persons in Ms. Somers's position was unconstitutional. Its opinion appeared to rest primarily on the Equal Protection Clause of the U.S. Constitution's Fourteenth Amendment, although the opinion at points additionally invoked the Privilege or Immunities Clause of that Amendment, the Privileges and Immunities Clause of Article IV of the U.S. Constitution, and the California Constitution's equal protection guarantee.

California law regarding birth certificates has changed since *Somers*. In its current form, § 103425 of the California Health and Safety Code provides in pertinent part, with no residency requirement:

> (a) A person may file a petition with the superior court in any county seeking a judgment recognizing the change of gender to female, male, or nonbinary.

> (b) If requested, the judgment shall include an order that a new birth certificate be prepared for the person reflecting the change of gender and any change of name accomplished by an order of a court of this state, another state, the District of Columbia, or any territory of the United States.

Note how this newest version of the law also eases the burden of seeking a new birth certificate for California residents who no longer live in the county of their birth.

Note also that the *Somers* court's right to travel analysis depends crucially on the difference in treatment between people who live in California in the county of their birth, and people who do not including people living in other states. For a broader right-to-travel argument for a constitutional right to new or amended birth certificates for transgender persons, depending on the practical burdens faced by transgender people with gender markers inconsistent with their gender identity and presentation, see Julie A. Greenberg & Marybeth Herald, *You Can't Take It with You: Constitutional Consequences of Interstate Gender-Identity Rulings*, 80 Wash. L. Rev. 819 (2005). Be aware that the article's analysis rests on the notion of burdens on traveling, even from laws that, unlike the California statute in *Somers*, do not on their face discriminate against people who have moved to another state. If a state, say Ohio, refuses to grant new or amended birth certificates to transgender persons whether or not they remain in state or live out of state, it is not clear that such a state's law is at all treating recent travelers differently from people who have not traveled, or *penalizing* the right to travel, which is the focus of Supreme Court cases such as *Shapiro v. Thompson*, 394 U.S. 618 (1969). Although relatively modern cases such as *Attorney-General of New York v. Soto*, 457 U.S. 55 (1982), do recognize that sometimes a law's deterring travel might trigger heightened constitutional scrutiny, the cases *Soto* cites involved a law charging money to leave a state or imposing durational residency requirements treating newcomers to a state (who have thus recently exercised their right to travel) differently from people who have lived there longer.

And one of the Supreme Court's most recent "right to travel" cases found a constitutional violation based on state laws' *penalizing* people for exercising their right to travel. *Saenz v. Roe*, 526 U.S. 489, 505 (1999).

For a non-constitutional solution to an issue concerning a person living in a state other than where they were born, see *Matter of D.R.G. (E.R.F.)*, 55 Misc. 3d 457, 51 N.Y.S.3d 329 (Civ. Ct. 2016). In *Matter of D.R.G.*, a New York trial court previously ordered a name change for E.R.F. Now, after considering the infant's medical records, the court granted a petition for an order certifying that the sex of E.R.F., who'd been born in Colorado, had been "changed by surgical procedure." The court followed this procedure even though to change the sex on a birth certificate the law of New York, where E.R.F. resided, only requires a court-ordered name change and "an affirmation from a physician (MD or DO) licensed to practice medicine in the United States and who is in good standing." That affidavit simply had "to affirm that in keeping with contemporary expert standards regarding gender identity, the applicant's requested correction of sex designation of male or female more accurately reflects the applicant's sex or gender identity." 24 Rev. Code N.Y. § 207.05(a)(5). The court here followed this more demanding procedure so that Colorado would furnish E.R.F. an amended birth certificate with a changed gender marker. The New York court did not indicate whether it considered itself required to conduct such a hearing and make such an order, or whether New York law left it to the trial court's discretion whether to do so.

Reading Guide for In re Redacted

1. Prior to 2018, Oregon required a court order for people to change the name or sex marker on their birth certificate. When the judge made his opinion in this case public, he redacted the name of the petitioner, a transgender woman seeking to change the sex listed on her birth certificate from male to female. Oregon law at the time did not allow such changes unless one has had "sex reassignment surgery" (as state law names it), a requirement the petitioner and the amicus curiae in the case challenged as violating the Oregon constitution.

2. The court suggests that the class of transgender people is described by the mental health diagnosis of gender identity disorder (described more in Chapter 14, *supra*). On what grounds does he criticize that diagnosis?

3. What provision of the Oregon Constitution does the court apply? What does the court specify as "[t]he real question" or "issue" here? What is the unequal treatment the court identifies in Oregon law? What burdens or disadvantage for transgender people from Oregon law does the court discuss? How does the court describe the "classification" used by the challenged statutes, how does it characterize that classification, and what does it say justifies that characterization?

4. What is (or are) the doctrinal test(s) that the court uses for the petitioner's (state) constitutional claim? What reason(s) does the court give for holding that the state fails that test (or those tests)? What relief does it specify for the petitioner?

In re Redacted

(Or. Cir. Ct. Feb. 5, 2013)

Re: In the Matter ████████████

Linn County Case No. ███████

[JAMES C. EGAN, Circuit Judge]

████████████ brings to this court a question of the greatest significance. It is important in her life and it raises issues of constitutional law which test the separation of powers. In essence, ████ █████ is asking this court to overturn an act of the legislature based on the statute's failure to treat her equally with all of the other citizens of the State of Oregon. She also argues that the statute is irrational and vague.

This court issued a series of questions to ████████ ███ in order to ferret out the inconsistencies about which she complains. Some of those answers left the court wanting for information. Again, I reiterate that this is information necessary for the court to make a determination about one of its most significant powers—the power to overturn an act of the legislature. I take this very seriously.

In order to help me with these issues, I asked John Knight, Senior Staff Attorney for the American Civil Liberties Union, LGBT & AIDS Project to brief the issue. Mr. Knight informed me that the ACLU is briefing similar issues and he was willing to submit a brief, amicus curiae, on the issues.

I had a conversation with ████████████'s attorney and she has no objection to this plan. I accepted the amicus curiae brief from Mr. Knight on October 3, 2011, in order to help the court in the resolution of these issues. As a consequence of the ACLU's briefing, I believe that the Oregon Attorney General's Office took an interest in the case and they submitted their brief on May 24, 2012. Finally, ████████████'s counsel completed a reply brief filed June 29, 2012. I believe that all of the issues have been well vetted.

. . . .

Facts

████████, age 37, was born as a male child. Despite her biological gender, she has always felt that she was a female. At age 25 years, she began to live as a female in front of her family, friends, and her community. In 2004, she began hormone treatment to make the change from male to female. This treatment has been confirmed through the report of her health care provider. . . .

████████changed her status from male to female with the Department of Motor Vehicles in 2010. When she attempted to change her status with the Social Security Administration, the Government ruled her change in legal status would not be "complete" until she underwent a gender altering surgery or until she secured an order from a court of competent jurisdiction ordering a change in the status of her gender.

This refusal by the Government to recognize the fact that ██████████ is indeed now, for all practical purposes, a woman has led to a deprivation of Social Security benefits available only to women. In particular, there are medical treatments and procedures which are unavailable to ████ ████because the Social Security Administration simply will not yet recognize the change.

██████████ is a member of a class of citizens in Oregon commonly referred to as transgendered. Medical experts have developed the diagnosis of Gender Identity Disorder (GID) as a part of the process of understanding the transgender experience in an attempt to treat transgendered people. Whether it is a physical or a psychological condition is of no consequence here. Frankly, the title itself is somewhat discriminatory because it assumes that being transgendered somehow requires the classification of "disorder." Although scientists have determined that there is a "treatment" for the disorder," the "treatment" is simply a lesson in humane behavior: allow an individual to participate fully and comfortably in society in the gender role with which he or she identifies.

There is a growing body of literature, both medical and legal, dealing with the issues that arise out of the classification of a people as transgendered. This literature includes but is not limited to medical, psychological, sociological, political, religious, and legal articles, journals, books, treatises, and the like.

██████████petitioned this court for a General Judgment changing her sex from male to female on her birth certificate. She filed this petition on January 26, 2011. The hearing took place on February 28, 2011.██████████ filed her supplemental affidavit on April 11, 2011. The ACLU submitted its amicus brief on September 28, 2011, and the Attorney General submitted a brief on May 24, 2012. Petitioner's counsel submitted the reply brief on June 29, 2012.

Analysis

The reading of the plain text of ORS 33.460 and ORS 432.235 requires sexual reassignment surgery (SRS) before a person's legal gender and birth certificate gender marker will be changed. This is certainly a significant hurdle for transgendered people who are attempting to achieve change in status created by the state. This hurdle is financial, psychological, spiritual, and physical. It goes to the core values and fundamental rights of each individual in this situation.

The State makes a key concession in this case. In its brief the Senior Assistant Attorney General for the State of Oregon wrote:

> "There undoubtedly are advantages to having a birth certificate on which the designation of sex is congruent with one's gender identity, which is to say, on average, transgender persons who have not had surgery may well derive fewer benefits from birth certificates than everyone else (including transgendered persons who have had surgery)."

The State then goes on to argue that the real question is whether the state issues gender-identity congruent birth certificates to anyone.

Fortunately for this court, the State has answered its own question in this concession. Oregon issues its birth certificates "on average." In other words, state makes a calculated bet that an individual with a particular set of genitalia will fit neatly into the category of male or female.

Of course, the State does not want to take responsibility for this choice. Like much of the briefing in this case, it tries to reduce the question down to the observable, the categorical, and therefore, the deniable. In this effort, the argument follows a linear path:

> "The sex is congruent with the child's external anatomy, but is neither congruent nor incongruent with respect to the child's still non-existent gender identity. Congruence may or may not arise several years later depending on developments beyond the state's control."

In this argument, the Government necessarily buys into the position that gender identity is nonexistent at the time of birth. This trap is just as dangerous when a party argues that gender identity is already established at birth. The fact is that neither the Government nor the Petitioner has any real . . . way to figure this out.

The real question is not when gender identity is established or whether gender identity is acquired. The issue is who decides what is found on birth certificates and how does the designation of gender affect an individual's rights under the law. The answers are obvious but I will map them out for the sake of this legal decision. The Government decides what information is found on a birth certificate[] and the designation of gender made by the Government does affect an individual's rights under the law.

The State mistakenly believes that neither Petitioner nor the amicus party argues unequal treatment under the Oregon Constitution. As a matter of fact, Petitioner argues that the statute violates the Oregon Constitution and the ACLU makes the argument in its brief as well.

Article I, Section 20 of the Oregon Constitution forbids discrimination against any class of citizens. The Constitution reads:

> "No law shall be passed granting to any citizen or class of citizens privileges, or immunities, which, upon the same terms, shall not equally belong to all citizens."

The State cannot, in good conscience, argue that transgendered people do not meet the qualification of a legitimate "class" of people. Any such argument would be disingenuous as the ORS 33.460 and ORS 432.235 contemplate just such a class. *See State v. Borowski*, 231 Or. App. 511, 520 (2009), and *Tanner v. Oregon Health Science University*, 157 Or. App. 502, 521–22 (1998).

ORS 33.460 and ORS 432.235 purport to resolve the issue for the transgendered by offering up a solution—SRS surgery. In the case at hand, this court can clearly see the burden that is imposed on the transgendered community to acquire the same benefits as are allowed for all other citizens with correct gender identity on their birth certificates.███████ said that the surgery is out of her financial reach. That is a burden not imposed on most citizens.

Furthermore, the fact is that some transgendered do not want or seek an SRS surgery. For some, breast implantation or reduction is appropriate. For some, hormone treatment is sufficient. For others, no medical intervention is required at all. A rhetorical question comes to this court's mind. What would the Government argue if a non-surgical hermaphrodite were assigned the wrong gender identity? Would the State require a surgery for a person whose gender was obvious[ly] ambiguous at the time of birth and whose identity the State wrongly designated?

Viewed in this light, the surgical requirement itself is unconstitutional. Oregon Courts have repeatedly held that gender is a suspect classification because it is not within an individual's control and it is often associated with offensive social or political premises. More often than not, questions about gender identity are filled with discriminatory intent, stereotypes, and prejudice. *See State v. Borowski*, 231 Or. App. at 520; *Tanner v. Oregon Health Science University*, 157 Or. App. at 523; and *Hewitt v. SAIF*, 294 Or. 33, 43–46 (1982).

When statutes, such as these, fail[] to offer a privilege or immunity to members of a suspect class like the transgendered, then the law is inherently suspect and may be upheld only if the failure to make the privileges or immunities available to that class can be justified by a genuine difference between the disparately treated class and those to whom the privileges and immunities are granted. *Tanner*, 157 Or. App. at 523. As it stands, Oregon law prevents transgendered individuals who have not undergone surgery from the privileges and immunities that are allowed to the transgendered who have undergone surgery. The State has offered no[] compelling argument for this disparate treatment.

As a matter of fact, the evidence in this case tends to show that ████████ before surgery would be no different, than ████████ post surgery other than she would have fulfilled the Governments morbid and onerous requirement to amputate a particular digit. As the amicus party indicates in briefing, the growing body of medical evidence shows that surgical history is not an appropriate basis for distinguishing among transgendered people or in determining whether a transgendered person's request for revised identity documents is legitimate.

Some of the argument in this case hinges on the application of the strict scrutiny test. I note that the Court of Appeals stated that suspect classifications such as gender are subject to this test. *Gunn v. Lane County*, 173 Or. App. 97, 103 (2001). The theory here is that "a more demanding level of scrutiny" applies to disparate treatment of true classes under Article 1, Section 20 jurisprudence. *Morsman v. City of Madras*, 203 Or. App. 546, 555 (2006). From my perspective, we don't need to go that far. The bottom line is that the State cannot show a rational basis much less withstand[] strict scrutiny.

Conclusion and Order

For these reasons, I rule in favor of Petitioner,███████. The court will execute an order compelling the State to change the gender marker on her birth certificate. . . .

Discussion

1. The court concludes that the petitioner "is indeed now, for all practical purposes, a woman . . ." Is that literally true? If not, for what purposes might the petitioner not be a woman (purposes the court seems to treat as irrelevant to its analysis)? Is it right to ignore those purposes?

2. Is the court's discussion of the diagnosis of gender identity disorder relevant to its legal analysis? (If not, is its criticism of the diagnosis appropriately included in the opinion?) Note that the American Psychiatric Association subsequent to this decision eliminated that diagnosis from its *Diagnostic and Statistical Manual of Mental Disorders* and adopted a new diagnosis of gender dysphoria that is *not* applicable to all trans people simply because they are trans. For more discussion, see Chapter 14, *supra.*

3. The court qualifies its statement that the petitioner would be no different after SRS than before by granting "she would have . . . amputate[d] a particular digit." Does it make sense to think of a penis as a "digit"? Regardless, is that a fair characterization of vaginoplasty? One of this casebook's authors has criticized such framing by an anti-trans author. *See* David B. Cruz, *Gender and Objectivity* (Apr. 10, 2018, draft on file with author) (charging Paul McHugh with "simplistic[ally] mischaracteriz[ing] genital surgeries that fashion a vagina from a penis as 'amputat[ing] the genitals'" on the ground that it "'misrepresents the mechanics of male-to-female sex reassignment surgery'") (quoting first, Paul R. McHugh, *Psychiatric Misadventures*, 61 THE AMERICAN SCHOLAR 497, 503 (1992), and second, JAY PROSSER, SECOND SKINS: THE BODY NARRATIVES OF TRANSSEXUALITY 80 (1998)). And is the fact that a transgender woman has or has not had vaginoplasty (or penectomy) trivial or irrelevant, as the court may be read to imply at least in this context?

4. The court offers an analogy to a person with an intersex condition with genitalia/anatomy not clearly male or clearly female (the opinion uses the outdated terminology "nonsurgical hermaphrodite"). Even if the court is right in its implication that Oregon would not insist on surgery for them, is that enough to establish that the state is treating transgender people differently from others? For more discussion of intersex conditions, see Chapter 2, *supra.*

5. Kevin Barry has argued that states that require gender confirmation surgery for a transgender person to change the sex marker on their birth certificate are engaging in discrimination on the basis of gender dysphoria in violation of the

Americans with Disabilities Act. *See generally* Kevin M. Barry, *Challenging Inaccurate Sex Designations on Birth Certificates Through Disability Rights Law*, 26 Geo. J. on Poverty L. & Pol'y 313 (2019). On the use of disability rights laws to secure protections for transgender people, see generally Chapter 14, *supra*. Kyle Velte argues that any gender confirmation surgery requirement for amending birth certificate sex markers "should be invalided because (1) it is factually incorrect based on current medical and scientific understandings of sex and gender, (2) it is unconstitutional under the First, Fourteenth and Fifth Amendments, (3) it undermines the requirement of informed consent and principles of bioethics, (4) it contravenes the unconstitutional conditions doctrine, and (5) it violates state antidiscrimination law." Kyle C. Velte, *Mitigating the "LGBT Disconnect": Title IX's Protection of Transgender Students, Birth Certificate Correction Statutes, and the Transformative Potential of Connecting the Two*, 27 Am. U. J. Gender Soc. Pol'y & L. 29, 63–64 (2019).

Reading Guide for F.V. v. Barron

1. This suit challenged a state policy that categorically forbid trans people to change their birth certificate sex markers to accord with their gender identity. The plaintiffs sought "heightened scrutiny" (in the form also known as "intermediate scrutiny") referring to the extent of deference, or of presumption of constitutionality, that a court should provide to the government. Their request is thus to scrutinize the policy more carefully than a court would analyze ordinary economic legislation because it is based on sex, a constitutionally "quasi-suspect" form of classification. Under heightened scrutiny the challenged law is unconstitutional unless the defendants show that the law's use of sex classifications furthers an "important government interest" by means "substantially related" to that interest. *United States v. Virginia*, 518 U.S. 515 (1996).

2. How does the court frame the discrimination here—in what way are transgender people being treated differently from cisgender, *i.e.*, non-transgender, people? What reasons does the court give for concluding that Idaho's policy does not survive even rational basis review (the most deferential form of equal protection scrutiny)?

3. Why does the court decide to reach the issue of the level of equal protection scrutiny to apply to anti-transgender discrimination rather than accept the defendant's concession of unconstitutionality? What are the two different rationales the court gives for concluding that anti-transgender discrimination should be subject to heightened scrutiny? What reasons does the court give to support each of the two rationales? (Note that the full opinion does not bother to apply heightened scrutiny to the defendants' policy, presumably because if it is not even *rationally* related to a *legitimate* governmental interest, it necessarily cannot be *substantially* related to an *important* governmental interest.)

F.V. and Dani Martin v. Russell Barron, in his official Capacity as Director of the Idaho Department of Health and Welfare, et al.

286 F. Supp. 3d 1131 (D. Idaho 2018)

[The plaintiffs were represented by Lambda Legal and private counsel.]

Candy W. Dale, United States Magistrate Judge

Introduction

Transgender individuals born in Idaho cannot obtain a birth certificate with the listed sex matching their gender identity. The Idaho Department of Health and Welfare (IDHW) interprets state law to bar changes to the listed sex unless an applicant can show there was an error of identification at birth. Therefore, as a policy, IDHW categorically and automatically denies applications to change the listed sex for any other reason. The questions presented to the Court are whether IDHW's interpretation, as applied, violates the Equal Protection and Due Process clauses of the Fourteenth Amendment to the Constitution of the United States, and whether it impermissibly compels speech in violation of the First Amendment.

As a preliminary matter, the Court notes the rare posture of the case. Plaintiffs, two transgender women born in Idaho, [are] asking the Court for a declaration that IDHW's policy violates their constitutional rights and the rights of others similarly situated. Plaintiffs request that the Court apply heightened scrutiny review, and declare that IDHW's policy violates the Equal Protection Clause. . . .

In turn, Defendants do not defend the constitutionality of the policy. Instead, they admit it is unconstitutional. Specifically, that it violates the Equal Protection Clause, failing minimum scrutiny review because "a prohibition against changing the sex designation on the birth certificate of a transgender individual who has undergone clinically appropriate treatment to permanently change his or her sex" bears no rational relationship to a conceivable government interest. Defendants assert that, once they have an order from the Court in hand, they will create a new rule permitting transgender individuals to change the sex listed on their birth certificates. Defendants indicate also that the new rule will include a provision that any revision history related to changes to the listed sex or name changes will not be marked on the reissued birth certificates of transgender individuals. Defendants further indicate they cannot proceed to create a rule until they receive a court order.

Defendants assert that, because they have made these concessions, the Court should exercise judicial restraint and decide the Plaintiffs' motion on the narrowest ground—that the current policy, as applied, is not rationally related to a legitimate government interest, violates the Plaintiffs' equal protection rights, and is thus unconstitutional under minimum scrutiny review.

Plaintiffs counter that, in the face of pervasive government discrimination against transgender individuals, the Court has a constitutional duty and inherent authority to define the level of scrutiny that should be applied to their equal protection claim, and should determine favorable judgment is warranted on the basis of the other constitutional claims—in addition to fashioning a remedy mandating equal treatment.

Background

1. Idaho Vital Statistics Laws

. . . . The Idaho Vital Statistics Act (Act), Title 39, Chapter 2 of the Idaho Code, authorizes the Idaho Board of Health and Welfare (Board) to propose rules to carry out its provisions related to vital statistics—the Vital Statistics Rules (Rules). IDAPA 16.02.08.000. IDHW is the state agency responsible for enforcement of the Act and the Rules, (together, vital statistics laws) for providing the official interpretation of such laws, and for developing temporary and final proposed rules. State legislative approval is necessary to enact final proposed rules into law.

Idaho's vital statistics laws require that all amended birth certificates be marked as "amended," including a record of the nature of the change, unless the change is made under one of the following circumstances: (1) minor corrections made within one year after the date of the event necessitating the correction; (2) voluntary acknowledgements of paternity and non-paternity; and (3) for changes to name and paternal and maternal information in instances of adoption. In these circumstances, the vital statistics laws require the amendments not be marked or noted on the birth certificate.[3] A catch-all provision applies to any amendment not specifically provided for in the vital statistics laws. Notably, amendments made under the catch-all provision must be described on the birth certificate.

. . . .

As explained above, IDHW interprets Idaho vital statistics law to prohibit changes to the listed sex unless there was an error in recording the sex at birth. Notably, IDHW asserts that Idaho birth certificates reflect the "sex" of a person at birth and do not contain a "gender marker" designation. From this interpretation comes IDHW's policy of automatically and categorically denying applications made by transgender individuals for the purpose of changing the listed sex to reflect their gender identity.[4]

[The Court here reviews what it characterizes as the scientific consensus that "biological sex is determined by numerous elements"; the relation of biological sex to gender identity; the nature of gender dysphoria; the gender transition process; and statistics on discrimination against transgender individuals. The Court also

---

3. For example: Idaho Code § 7-1106 allows a biological father to establish paternity via an affidavit of paternity. The affidavit must be signed by both the father and the birth mother. If the child's birth certificate lists a different person as the father, a court order is required to change the father's name. The reissued, amended birth certificate must not be marked amended or include any record of the paternity change.

4. Idaho counts as one of only four remaining states that do not permit transgender individuals to change the sex listed on their birth certificate. The other three states are Kansas, Ohio, and Tennessee.

discusses the negative effects of the mismatch between the plaintiffs' gender identity and their sex assigned at birth.]

. . . .

Legal Framework
1. The Equal Protection Clause

. . . . An equal protection claim is established when plaintiffs show they were treated differently than other similarly situated people. *City of Cleburne v. Cleburne Living Ctr., Inc.*, 473 U.S. 432 (1985). Yet, states are given significant leeway to establish laws to effectively govern citizens and remedy societal ills. *Romer v. Evans*, 517 U.S. 620 (1996). Because of this, successful equal protection claims additionally require plaintiffs to show the difference in treatment was the result of intentional or purposeful discrimination. *Stone v. Trump*, 280 F. Supp. 3d 747 (D. Md. 2017).

In this matter, Plaintiffs, transgender individuals born in Idaho, have adequately alleged they were treated differently from non-transgender people born in Idaho. IDHW practices a policy of automatically and categorically denying applications made by transgender people to amend the birth-assigned sex on their birth certificates to align with their gender identity. . . . The IDHW Defendants provide no justification for the policy.

Yet, in turn, IDHW permits some classes of people, adoptive parents for instance, to make amendments to birth certificates without record of the amendment on the reissued certificate. IDHW has similar laws and policies related to the change of paternal information. These laws give certain people access to birth certificates that accurately reflect who they are, while denying transgender people, as a class, access to birth certificates that accurately reflect their gender identity. Therefore, as Defendants concede, Plaintiffs' equal protection claims are valid.

. . . .

The Court notes the importance and potential implications of restrictions and restraints IDHW may place on the ability of transgender people to apply for and receive approval of applications to change the sex listed on their birth certificates. Because the Court does not have a proposed rule before it, it will not extrapolate on the potential legal ramifications of such restrictions—such topics are not ripe for its consideration. However, any new rule must not subject one class of people to any more onerous burdens than the burdens placed on others without constitutionally-appropriate justification—for instance, to apply for a change in paternity information the applicant is not required to submit medical evidence, such as DNA confirmation, to prove paternity or non-paternity. Yet, all applicants for name changes are required to obtain a court order—regardless of the reason for the change.

The Court agrees there is no rational basis to support IDHW's policy. The following facts make this conclusion apparent: (1) IDHW already has a process in place for making amendments to birth certificates, as is evidenced by Idaho's vital statistics laws; (2) the vital statistics laws make certain that amendments or corrections are kept confidential when they pertain to sensitive personal and potentially private information, such as paternity or adoptive status; and (3) the laws make room for the amendment of any other information on the birth certificate with the proper form of application and evidence.

Thus, under an alternative, constitutionally-sound reading of Idaho's vital statistics laws, amendments to the listed sex are not only possible, but procedures are in place to facilitate such amendments—and the Act allows the Board to draft a rule that does just that. [IDAHO CODE §§ 39–241(3); 39–250.] As such, there is no rational basis for denying transgender individuals birth certificates that reflect their gender identity and IDHW's policy, as applied, violates the Equal Protection Clause.

Yet, as explained above, Plaintiffs ask the Court to take a step further to find that IDHW's policy similarly fails to withstand heightened scrutiny, which includes the mid-tier of equal protection review—intermediate scrutiny. Historically, intermediate scrutiny applies to quasi-suspect classifications based on sex and illegitimacy. *Clark v. Jeter*, 486 U.S. 456 (1988). For quasi-suspect classifications to be upheld, the state must show the classification is substantially related to an important governmental objective. "The purpose of this heightened level of scrutiny is to ensure quasi-suspect classifications do not perpetuate unfounded stereotypes or second-class treatment." *Latta v. Otter*, 19 F. Supp. 3d 1054 (D. Idaho), *aff'd*, 771 F.3d 456 (9th Cir. 2014).

Plaintiffs argue that IDHW's refusal to treat transgender people like others of the same sex, *i.e.* other males or females, requires intermediate review because such treatment discriminates on the basis of sex or otherwise employs another quasi-suspect classification—transgender status. In other words, Plaintiffs suggest two ways for the Court to conclude that heightened scrutiny applies to government classifications based on transgender status. The first—the Court could find that discrimination based on transgender status is discrimination based on sex or gender. The second—the Court could conclude that transgender status is a suspect classification in and of itself. In either case, Plaintiffs contend IDHW's policy is not substantially related to an important governmental objective and fails intermediate scrutiny review. . . .

A. Discrimination Based on Sex and Gender

. . . .

The Supreme Court's decision in *Price Waterhouse* is particularly important to the development of a more robust understanding of sex-based gender discrimination in the law. *Price Waterhouse*, 490 U.S. 228 (1989). There, the Court held that Title VII bars discrimination based on the fact that a person is a woman or a man, and based on the fact that a person fails to act like a woman or a man—*i.e.* it protects people from discrimination based on their failure to adhere to society's expectations of traditional gender roles.

. . . .

Of particular importance, significant changes in the medical understanding of gender identity call for a reexamination of its place in the equal protection context in relation to sex-based discrimination. . . .

Indeed, our medical understanding of biological sex and gender has advanced significantly in the forty-one years since *Holloway v. Arthur Andersen & Co.*, 566 F.2d 659 (9th Cir. 1977). For instance, it is universally acknowledged in leading medical guidance that not all individuals identify as the sex they are assigned at birth.[12] Despite . . . ongoing study to more fully understand the impact of differences in chromosomes, brain structure and chemistry, there is medical consensus that gender identity plays a role in an individual's determination of their own sex. Therefore, to conclude discrimination based on gender identity or transsexual status is not discrimination based on sex is to depart from advanced medical understanding in favor of archaic reasoning.

B. Defining New Suspect Qualifications—Transgender Status

In the equal protection context, the Supreme Court "has recognized that new insights and societal understandings can reveal unjustified inequality [. . .] that once passed unnoticed and unchallenged." *Obergefell v. Hodges*, 135 S. Ct. 2584 (2015). The Supreme Court employs a four-factor test to determine whether a class qualifies as suspect or quasi-suspect. Heightened scrutiny is warranted where the state discriminates against a class that (1) has been "historically subjected to discrimination," (2) has a defining characteristic bearing no "relation to ability to perform or contribute to society," (3) has "obvious, immutable, or distinguishing characteristics," and (4) is "a minority or is politically powerless." *United States v. Windsor*, 570 U.S. 744 (2013).

Courts have applied this test and have found that government discrimination based on transgender status is discrimination against a quasi-suspect class and thus is subject to intermediate scrutiny. *Adkins v. City of New York*, 143 F. Supp. 3d 134 (S.D.N.Y. 2015); . . . *Evancho v. Pine-Richland School District*, 237 F. Supp. 3d 267 (W.D. Pa. 2017).

The findings in *Adkins* and *Evancho* echo findings made regarding homosexual people as a class and recognized by this Court in *Latta*, the Ninth Circuit in

---

12. As set forth in [the World Professional Association for Transgender Health (WPATH)] *Standards of Care* protocols for the care of transgender and gender nonconforming people, including individuals with gender dysphoria. [sic] The WPATH protocols are endorsed by the following medical associations: The American Medical Association, the Endocrine Society, the American Psychological Association, the American Psychiatric Association, the World Health Organization, the American Academy of Family Physicians, the National Commission of Correctional Health Care, the American Public Health Association, the National Association of Social Workers, the American College of Obstetrics and Gynecology, the American Society of Plastic Surgeons, and The American Society of Gender Surgeons.

SmithKline Beecham Corp. v. Abbott Labs., 740 F.3d 471 (9th Cir. 2014), and the Supreme Court in *Windsor* and *Obergefell*. . . .

The pervasive and extensive similarities in the discrimination faced by transgender people and homosexual people are hard to ignore. . . . This is especially true in Idaho where transgender people have no state constitutional protections from discrimination based on their transgender status in relation to employment decisions, housing, and other services. Therefore, transgender people bear all of the characteristics of a quasi-suspect class and any rule developed and implemented by IDHW should withstand heightened scrutiny review to be constitutionally sound.

. . . .

Now therefore it is hereby ordered:

> . . . . The Court permanently enjoins the IDHW Defendants and their officers, employees, and agents from practicing or enforcing the policy of automatically rejecting applications from transgender people to change the sex listed on their birth certificates.

> . . . . IDHW Defendants and their officers, employees, and agents must begin accepting applications made by transgender people to change the sex listed on their birth certificates . . . ; such applications must be reviewed and considered through a constitutionally-sound approval process; upon approval, any reissued birth certificate must not include record of amendment to the listed sex; and where a concurrent application for a name change is submitted by a transgender individual, any reissued birth certificate must not include record of the name change.

It is so ordered.

———————

Discussion

1. The defendants, unusually, admit that the law does not further any permissible government interest. That "rational basis" standard is a very low bar. Why might they have conceded they could not survive it? Are there arguments that the policy is not constitutionally irrational? Consider the views of earlier judicial decisions upholding denials of birth certificate amendments to transgender people even when they have had genital reconstruction surgery. Although the court concludes that Idaho's policy treats transgender men and women differently from other men and women, is there an argument that, with respect to sex markers, the policy treats all men and all women equally?

2. Whether anti-transgender discrimination receives heightened scrutiny because it is a form of sex discrimination or because it is constitutionally quasi-suspect in its own right is important because it has relevance to the interpretation of the term "sex" used in many antidiscrimination statutes and constitutional doctrine,

as Justice Alito recognizes in his dissenting opinion in *Bostock v. Clayton County, Georgia*, 140 S. Ct. 1731, 1778–83 (2020), Chapter 5, Section D, *supra*. As the *F.V.* court suggests, it also could be relevant to the constitutionality of various possible conditions for a person to amend their birth certificate's sex marker. In *Bostock*, the Supreme Court held that, for purposes of Title VII of the Civil Rights Act of 1964, discrimination based on "transgender status" necessarily involves discrimination based on "sex." Although the opinion is framed as an interpretation and application of the meaning of that statute's words when it was enacted in 1964, its reasoning rests on largely conceptual discussion of what "sex" and "discrimination because of" sex mean, and the Court suggests that those words or phrases mean basically the same thing in 2020 that they meant in 1964. If so, then equal protection doctrine, which requires government to satisfy a heightened, "intermediate" scrutiny when it discriminates or classifies on the basis of sex, would likely require intermediate scrutiny of discrimination based on transgender status. This then heightens the significance of Discussion question 1, *supra*.

3. Note that the court's rendition of the four factors noted by *U.S. v. Windsor* for heightened equal protection scrutiny is technically accurate but potentially misleading. As the court words it here, it is sufficient for heightened scrutiny if a group satisfies all four factors. That is accurate, but the wording could be taken to imply that it is *necessary* to satisfy all four factors to secure heightened equal protection scrutiny—but the Supreme Court has not held the latter. Similarly, the court's discussion of *Obergefell*'s "recogni[tion]" of "homosexual people as a class" could be misconstrued. The Supreme Court in *Windsor* and *Obergefell* did not hold that sexual orientation is a suspect classification, though the Court made statements regarding the various equal protection level of scrutiny factors that could support such a ruling.

4. Presumably the court addresses *Price Waterhouse* and the "medical consensus that gender identity plays a role in an individual's determination of their own sex" as reasons not to follow *Holloway*'s pronouncement that anti-transgender discrimination is subject only to rational basis review under the Equal Protection Clause. *Accord Brown v. Zavaras*, 63 F.3d 967, 971 (10th Cir. 1995) ("Recent research concluding that sexual identity may be biological suggests reevaluating *Holloway*.") *Holloway* Ch. 5, Sec. 1, *supra* at p. 137, was a Title VII case, as was *Price Waterhouse*, but *Holloway* also reasoned that interpreting Title VII's ban on sex discrimination not to encompass discrimination because a person was transgender would not violate constitutional equal protection principles. Is the court's reasoning here enough to render *Holloway* nonbinding on a district court in the Ninth Circuit, were that necessary? Perhaps distinguishing or undermining *Holloway* is unnecessary; it has been suggested that *Holloway*'s equal protection pronouncement was dictum, and prior to *Barron* the Ninth Circuit (arguably in dictum) had said that the reasoning of *Holloway* was "overruled" by *Price Waterhouse*. *Schwenk v. Hartford*, 204 F.3d 1187, 1201 (9th Cir. 2000) ("The initial judicial approach taken in cases such as Holloway has been overruled by the logic and language of *Price Waterhouse*.").

Reading Guide for Arroyo Gonzalez v. Rossello Nevares

1. The Commonwealth of Puerto Rico, a U.S. territory to which the U.S. Constitution applies, has recently come to allow transgender people to amend their driver's licenses and other identity documents to indicate a sex consistent with their gender identity, but still does not allow them to amend their birth certificate sex marker. What might explain that difference?

2. What two types (or "clusters") of "privacy" rights does the court identify as protected by the Constitution? The court concludes in one paragraph that Puerto Rico's birth certificate sex marker policy violates the first kind of privacy right. What is the constitutionally protected activity the court identifies as violated by the policy? What is its explanation for why that activity is protected? What doctrinal limitation on government authority does the court articulate as protecting this privacy right?

3. Regarding the second type of constitutional privacy, what doctrinal test (concerning the fit of the policy to a sufficiently acceptable or powerful governmental purpose) does the court say the challenged policy fails? What harms does the court identify as flowing from the Commonwealth's policy?

4. What remedy does the court order? Where does the court get the evidentiary or eligibility requirements for a change of sex marker that it articulates?

Daniela Arroyo Gonzalez v. Ricardo Rossello Nevares

305 F. Supp. 3d 327 (D.P.R. 2018)

[The plaintiffs were represented by private counsel and Lambda Legal.]

Opinion and Order

Carmen Consuelo Cerezo, United States District Judge

This is an action for declaratory relief brought by three transgenders [*sic*] and an organization that advocates for the civil rights of LGBT people in the Commonwealth of Puerto Rico. They seek one common determination: that defendants be ordered to permit transgender persons born in Puerto Rico to correct their birth certificates to accurately reflect their true sex, consistent with their gender identity, in accordance with the practice delineated in 24 L.P.R.A. section 1136[1] and without adhering to the practice delineated in 24 L.P.R.A. section 1231 of using a strike-out line to change one's name, or otherwise including any information that

---

1. 24 L.P.R.A. section 1136 provides: "If the birth of an adoptee had previously been registered in the Vital Statistics Registry, *the registration certificate of such birth shall be substituted for another showing the new juridic status of the registered child,* as if he were a legitimate child of the adopters; Provided, that the original registration certificate of the birth of the adoptee, the decision of the court, and other documents shall be kept in the Registry in a sealed envelope and shall be confidential documents. In no registration certificate issued by the Registry shall the fact of the original registration be set forth, unless the petitioner of said certificate has expressly required the showing of such facts and a competent court has so ordered for justified causes; Provided, That such authorization shall not be required when the applicant be the adopter or the adoptee." (Emphasis ours [*sic*]).

would disclose a person's transgender status on the face of the birth certificate. A Motion to Dismiss filed on June 12, 2017 by defendants Ricardo Rossello Nevares, in his official capacity as Governor of the Commonwealth of Puerto Rico; Rafael Rodriguez Mercado, in his official capacity as Secretary of the Department of Health of the Commonwealth of Puerto Rico; and Wanda Llovet Díaz, in her official capacity as Director of the Division of Demographic Registry and Vital Statistics of the Commonwealth of Puerto Rico, was denied on August 29, 2017. Defendants have not filed an answer to the amended complaint. Plaintiffs filed a Motion for Summary Judgment on June 26, 2017, accompanied by a Statement of Material Facts.

Having considered the Motion for Summary Judgment, the declarations under penalty of perjury executed by the plaintiffs and other supporting materials, as well as defendants' opposition, the Court sets forth the following material facts that remain undisputed:

Findings of Fact

1. Plaintiffs are three transgender individuals and an organization [Puerto Rico Para Tod@s] with transgender members that seek to have their Puerto Rico birth certificates amended to accurately reflect their gender identity.

2. Ms. Daniela Arroyo's and Ms. Victoria Rodriguez's gender identity and expression is female.

3. Mr. J.G.'s gender identity and expression is male. His transgender status is not publicly known, nor known by his current employer or co-workers.

. . . .

6. All three plaintiffs wish to correct the gender marker on their birth certificates.

7. Ms. Arroyo and Ms. Rodriguez wish to correct the gender markers on their birth certificates to accurately reflect the identity of each as a woman, as determined by their gender identity.

8. Mr. J.G. wishes to correct the gender marker on his birth certificate to accurately reflect his identity as a man, as determined by his gender identity.

9. Ms. Arroyo's and Ms. Rodriguez' birth certificates do not reflect their true identity, are incongruent with their female identity and expression, and conflict with their other identification documents.

10. Mr. J.G.'s birth certificate does not reflect his true identity, is incongruent with his male identity and expression, and conflicts with his other identification documents.

11. Ms. Rodríguez changed her name and corrected the gender marker on her driver's license, U.S. Passport, and Social Security records.

12. Mr. J.G. changed his name on his birth certificate and has also changed his name and corrected the gender marker on his driver's license and Social Security records.

13. An individual's birth certificate is a primary identification document. In Puerto Rico, it is needed to obtain a driver's license, a marriage license, a U.S. passport, a Social Security card, a voting card, and generally as proof of identification to conduct banking transactions and other business.

14. Pursuant to its Birth Certificate Policy, Puerto Rico categorically requires that birth certificates reflect the sex assigned at birth and prohibits transgender persons from correcting the gender marker in their birth certificates so that these accurately reflect the persons' sex, as determined by their gender identity.

15. Birth certificates in Puerto Rico indicate a person's birth-assigned sex based on the appearancc of genitalia rather than their actual sex, as determined by their gender identity and lived experience.

16. Transgenderism is an immutable characteristic determined by the hormonal balance a person is born with. It is an innate trait caused by an individual's biological features and genetic makeup. Some scientists confirm that brain development is influenced by the prenatal environment, that is, to what hormones the fetus was exposed to in the uterus. . . .

17. Ms. Rodriguez is 28 years old, born in Puerto Rico, and currently a resident of the District of Columbia metropolitan area. . . . She is a transgender [*sic*] who was designated "male" in her birth certificate. . . . In 2007, by her sophomore year, she asked her professors and others to call her by her chosen name, Victoria. Calling her "Victoria" during the roll call prevented disclosure of her transgender status to other students. She was diagnosed that same year by her medical provider with gender dysphoria and underwent hormone therapy to relieve the condition. In 2011, while at law school, she legally changed her name and gender marker on all her identification documents, except for her birth certificate.

18. Ms. Arroyo is 18 years old, a high school graduate, transgender, [and] designated "male" in her birth certificate . . . [A]t the age 14 [she began] to socially and medically transition to align her life experience and body characteristics with her gender identity. She began hormone therapy in 2016 after having been diagnosed with gender dysphoria in 2013. . . . In February 2017, she legally changed her name to her current female name. In March 2017, she began the process to correct her name and gender marker in her identification documents to accurately reflect her gender identity as female but has been prohibited from correcting the gender marker in her birth certificate because of Puerto Rico's Birth Certificate Policy, thereby rendering her birth certificate incongruent with her other identification papers.

19. Mr. J.G. is 25 years old, born and raised in San Juan, Puerto Rico, and designated as female on his birth certificate. . . . In 2015, he commenced to medically transition to align his body characteristics and live his true self, as a man. That same year, having been diagnosed with gender dysphoria, he commenced hormone treatment.

20. The incongruence between a transgender person's gender identity and sex assigned at birth is associated with gender dysphoria. Gender dysphoria is a serious medical condition recognized in the American Psychiatric Association's *Diagnostic and Statistical Manual of Mental Disorders*, Fifth Ed. (2013) ("DSM-V").

21. Gender dysphoria refers to clinically significant distress that can result when a person's gender identity differs from the person's birth-assigned sex. If left untreated, gender dysphoria may result in psychological distress, anxiety, depression, suicidal ideation, or even self-inflicted harm.

22. Identity documents that are consistent with one's lived experience affirm and consolidate one's gender identity, mitigating distress and functional consequences. Changes in gender presentation and role to feminize or masculinize appearance as well as social acceptance and legal legitimacy are crucial components of treatment for gender dysphoria. Social transition involves dressing, grooming, and otherwise outwardly presenting oneself through social signifiers of a person's true sex as determined by their affirmed gender identity.

23. Not every person suffering from gender dysphoria undergoes the same treatment. From a medical and scientific perspective, there is no basis for refusing to acknowledge a transgender person's true sex based on whether that person has undergone surgery or any other medical treatment.

24. . . . . During [Ms. Arroyo's medical gender] transition [via hormone therapy], she brought her external appearance into alignment with her female identity.

. . . .

27. Ms. Arroyo and Mr. J.G. corrected their names on their respective birth certificates but pursuant to Puerto Rico's birth certificate policy, were prohibited from correcting the gender marker on their birth certificates.

. . . .

29. Ms. Arroyo asserts she feels stigmatized and harmed by Puerto Rico's birth certificate policy and claims her right to possess identity documents that accurately reflect who she is—a woman.

30. Ms. Rodriguez states she considers it futile to correct the name on her birth certificate since it is impossible to obtain a correction of the gender marker on her birth certificate. As a consequence, her birth certificate, which identifies her with a male name and sex, and her other identification documents, drivers' license and U.S. passport, are incongruent with each other. She asserts the need for her identity documents to be consistent with the woman that she is.

31. Mr. J.G. legally changed his name in 2016 to one traditionally associated with men. He updated his name and corrected the gender marker in his Puerto Rico driver's license. . . . He also corrected his Social Security records and updated his name in his birth certificate. . . . He attempted in April 2016 to correct the gender marker on his Puerto Rico voter identification card after the local Board of Registration staff requested his birth certificate. This was denied. As a result of this,

Mr. J.G. did not vote in the 2016 election because the presentation of his voter identification card disclosed his transgender status.

32. The forced disclosure of the transgender status of plaintiffs and other transgender persons by way of inaccurate birth certificates exposes them to prejudice, discrimination, distress, harassment, and violence.

33. On November 14, 2008, the Commonwealth of Puerto Rico (the "Commonwealth") issued Executive Order OE-2008-57 that established as a matter of public policy the prohibition of discrimination in the provision of public services. It applies to all public agencies and instrumentalities, including the Demographic Registry of Puerto Rico. Such sweeping [*sic*] outlawed discrimination in all forms, including gender identity.

34. Pursuant to this public policy, on August 10, 2015, the Commonwealth issued Executive Order OE-2015-029, permitting transgender individuals to change their gender marker in their driver's license. On June 19, 2014, the Department of Transportation and Public Works issued regulations implementing the Executive Order.

35. Pursuant to the aforementioned Executive Orders, on May 31, 2016, the Electoral Commission of the Commonwealth of Puerto Rico issued Resolution CEE-RS-16-9, permitting transgender individuals to change the gender marker on their voter identification cards.

36. The Department of Transportation and Public Works and the Electoral Commission of the Commonwealth of Puerto Rico both issue identification cards that reflect the applicant's correct gender marker in accordance with the public policy outlined in OE-2008-57, without disclosing the sex that was assigned at birth.

Based on these Findings of Fact, the Court states the following:

Conclusions of Law

The Supreme Court recognizes that "a constitutional right to privacy is now well established." *Daury v. Smith*, 842 F.2d 9 (1st Cir. 1988) (referring to *Roe v. Wade*, 410 U.S. 113 (1973); *Griswold v. Connecticut*, 381 U.S. 479 (1965). . . .

"The courts have identified two clusters of personal privacy rights recognized by the Fourteenth Amendment. One bundle of rights relates to ensuring autonomy in making certain kinds of significant personal decisions; the other relates to ensuring confidentiality of personal matters." *Vega-Rodriguez v. Puerto Rico Telephone Co.*, 110 F.3d 174 (1st Cir. D.P.R. 1997) (referring to *Whalen v. Roe*, 429 U.S. 589 (1977)).

"The autonomy branch of the Fourteenth Amendment right to privacy is limited to decisions arising in the personal sphere—matters relating to marriage, procreation, contraception, family relationships, child rearing, and the like." *Vega-Rodriguez*. The confidentiality branch, also referred to as 'informational privacy,' *see National Aeronautics and Space Administration v. Nelson*, 562 U.S. 134 (2011), "includes 'the individual interest in avoiding the disclosure of personal matters . . .'" *Daury* (citing *Whalen*). The Commonwealth's ban on changing the gender marker in plaintiffs' birth certificates implicates both.

The Commonwealth's forced disclosure of plaintiffs' transgender status violates their constitutional right to decisional privacy. Much like matters relating to marriage, procreation, contraception, family relationships, and child rearing, "there are few areas which more closely intimate facts of a personal nature" than one's transgender status. *Doe v. Town of Plymouth*, 825 F. Supp. 1102 (D. Mass. 1993) (finding the constitutional right to privacy encompasses nondisclosure of HIV status). "The decision of who to tell and when to relate such information is an emotionally sensitive area 'fraught with serious implications for that individual.'" *Id.* Disclosing that one is transgender involves a deep personal choice which the government cannot compel, unless disclosure furthers a valid public interest. "These matters, involving the most intimate and personal choices a person may make in a lifetime, choices central to personal dignity and autonomy, are central to the liberty protected by the Fourteenth Amendment. *At the heart of liberty is the right to define one's own concept of existence, of meaning, of the universe, and of the mystery of human life.* Beliefs about these matters could not define the attributes of personhood were they formed under compulsion of the State." *Planned Parenthood of Southeastern Pa. v. Casey*, 505 U.S. 833 (1992) (emphasis ours).

By permitting plaintiffs to change the name on their birth certificate, while prohibiting the change to their gender markers, the Commonwealth forces them to disclose their transgender status in violation of their constitutional right to informational privacy. Such forced disclosure of a transgender person's most private information is not justified by any legitimate government interest. It does not further public safety, such that it would amount to a valid exercise of police power. *See Whalen.* To the contrary, it exposes transgender individuals to a substantial risk of stigma, discrimination, intimidation, violence, and danger. Forcing disclosure of transgender identity chills speech and restrains engagement in the democratic process in order for transgenders to protect themselves from the real possibility of harm and humiliation. The Commonwealth's inconsistent policies not only harm the plaintiffs before the Court; it also hurts society as a whole by depriving all from the voices of the transgender community.

Having determined that the Commonwealth's Birth Certificate Policy violates transgender persons' decisional privacy and informational privacy, and further considering that: (1) the Commonwealth has adopted a public policy that prohibits discrimination by public agencies and instrumentalities in providing their services, including discrimination based on gender identity, and (2) the Department of Transportation and Motor Vehicles and the Election Commission of the Commonwealth have enabled transgender individuals to apply for new official identifications that display their true gender, without disclosing their transgender status, IT IS HEREBY ORDERED AND ADJUDGED that the Demographic Registry of the Commonwealth of Puerto Rico permit forthwith that transgender individuals change the gender marker in their birth certificates, as delineated in 24 L.P.R.A. section 1136, specifically, by issuing a new birth certificate with the applicant's true gender, without using a strike-out line or otherwise including any information that would disclose a person's transgender status on the face of the birth certificate, in compliance with this Opinion and Order.

The Demographic Registry of the Commonwealth of Puerto Rico SHALL ADOPT the criteria of the Department of Transportation and Public Work's "Request to Change Transgender Persons' Gender Marker," DTOP-DIS-324 Form, as the application form to be submitted by transgenders and which shall be accepted as the first step towards the issuance of their new birth certificates, in compliance with the Court's mandate. The transgender individual shall present the application accompanied by one of the following documents: (1) a passport that reflects a person's true gender, whether female or male, (2) a driver's license that reflects the person's true gender, whether female or male, or (3) a certification issued by a healthcare professional or mental health professional with whom the person has a doctor-patient relationship stating, based on his or her professional opinion, the true gender identity of the applicant, whether female or male, and that it is expected that this will continue to be the gender with which the applicant will identify him or herself in the future. If the applicant has not had any of the documents requested previously issued, a health care professional or mental health professional with whom the applicant has a doctor-patient relationship must certify based on his or her professional opinion that the true gender identity of the applicant is (__) female or (__) male and that it is expected that this will continue to be the gender with which the applicant will identify him or herself in the future.

Conclusion

The right to identify our own existence lies at the heart of one's humanity. And so, we must heed their voices: "the woman that I am," "the man that I am." Plaintiffs know they are not fodder for memoranda legalese. They have stepped up for those whose voices, debilitated by raw discrimination, have been hushed into silence. They cannot wait for another generation, hoping for a lawmaker to act. They, like Linda Brown, took the steps to the courthouse to demand what is due:

their right to exist, to live more and die less.

————————

Discussion

1. The decisional privacy interest the court identifies the plaintiffs as having (and the defendants as violating) is an interest in deciding whether to preserve their informational privacy regarding their transgender status. That raises a question whether we should think there is a separate, fundamental decisional autonomy right substantively protected by (the Due Process Clause of the Fourteenth Amendment to) the Constitution in play here or whether instead the only substantive due process right at issue is the plaintiffs' right to informational privacy, a right to keep the government from compromising their secrecy.

2. The opinion's legal analysis is fairly cursory. With respect to the decisional privacy claim, the opinion invokes some of the Supreme Court's language

characterizing the interests protected by the Due Process Clause; however, it does not examine whether the particular claimed right (to preserve the secrecy of one's transgender status) meets the Court's doctrinal tests (*e.g.*, is it deeply rooted in the nation's legal history and tradition or is it implicit in the concept of ordered liberty?). Nor does it expressly adopt strict scrutiny as the doctrinal test (is a challenged law narrowly tailored to a compelling governmental interest?), as opposed to (for example) the undue burden test that protects the decisional right to choose to have an abortion (does a challenged law have the purpose or effect of imposing a substantial obstacle in the path of the person seeking an abortion?), or any other substantive due process test, for that matter.

Likewise, the opinion does not clearly announce the doctrinal test it considers applicable to laws claimed to violate the right to informational privacy or to engage closely with the Supreme Court's reasoning in *Whalen v. Roe*. The court does argue that "[b]y permitting plaintiffs to change the name on their birth certificate, while prohibiting the change to their gender markers, the Commonwealth forces them to disclose their transgender status in violation of their constitutional right to informational privacy." What role does the first clause of that sentence play in the analysis? Would Puerto Rico's birth certificate policy be constitutional if it allowed neither sex marker changes nor birth certificate changes?

For a constitutional argument that transgender people have a right to amend their identity documents to change their sex markers, see, for example, Bryanna A. Jenkins, *Birth Certificate with a Benefit: Using LGBTQ Jurisprudence to Make the Argument for a Transgender Person's Constitutional Right to Amended Identity Documents*, 22 CUNY L. Rev. 78 (2019).

3. The court orders the defendants to furnish the plaintiffs with birth certificates with sex markers consistent with their gender identities that do not indicate that they are amended (which could disclose their transgender status). But, presumably because the plaintiffs are not the only three transgender people in Puerto Rico, the court also specifies a form with criteria for other applicants for a changed sex marker on their birth certificate. Is it proper for the court to remedy a constitutional violation by borrowing statutory criteria from another identity document context? Could the defendants move to be allowed to adopt other criteria (which the plaintiffs would meet) for future birth certificate sex marker change applicants?

4. *Arroyo Gonzalez* has been criticized in some quarters for adhering to a binary view of sex/gender. Consider in particular the language in the remedy paragraph immediately preceding the court's "Conclusion" header. Should the court have formulated its remedy to require states to allow a third, nonbinary gender marker as an option for people amending their birth certificates, as a small number of states have done (as a result of judicial compulsion or legislative choice)? *Cf. Zzyym v. Pompeo*, 958 F.3d 1014 (10th Cir. 2020), Section C, *infra* at p. 1159 (constitutional litigation

seeking the right for person with intersex condition to have nonbinary sex marker on passport). Should we think such a nonbinary option is constitutionally required?

5. The following factual assertions by the *Arroyo Gonzalez* plaintiffs were not contested by the defendants. Are they reasonably contestable?

* "Plaintiffs are three transgender individuals . . . that seek to have their Puerto Rico birth certificates amended to accurately reflect their gender identity." "All three plaintiffs wish to correct the gender marker on their birth certificates." (Could the defendants have argued that Puerto Rico birth certificates neither "reflect [one's] gender identity" nor contain "gender" markers rather than sex markers?)

* Arroyo and Rodriguez "wish to correct the gender markers on their birth certificates to accurately reflect the identity of each as a woman, as determined by their gender identity." (Could the defendants argue that birth certificate sex markers do not reflect anyone's identity as determined by their gender identity and/or that identity as a woman is not determined by gender identity?)

* The plaintiffs asserted that their birth certificates "do not reflect their true identity" or their "actual sex, as determined by their gender identity and lived experience." "From a medical and scientific perspective, there is no basis for refusing to acknowledge a transgender person's true sex based on whether that person has undergone surgery or any other medical treatment." (Could the defendants have argued that "true identity" and "true sex" are not concepts used in law, or at least not in Puerto Rico birth certificate law, that "actual sex as determined by gender identity and lived experience" is not what Puerto Rico birth certificates are intended to record, and/or that a person's "actual sex" or "true sex" is not determined by gender identity or lived identity?)

* The plaintiffs asserted that, "pursuant to Puerto Rico's birth certificate policy, [they] were prohibited from correcting the gender marker on their birth certificates." (Could the defendants have argued that, as plaintiffs contended, "Birth certificates in Puerto Rico indicate a person's birth-assigned sex based on the appearance of genitalia" and are thus historical records, as a number of courts have ruled in birth certificate disputes, so changing them when someone manifested a gender identity inconsistent with that sex is not a "correction"?)

6. Although primarily targeting courts that have refused to treat transgender persons in law as members of the sex consistent with their gender identity, David Cruz has argued that legal sex is an instrumental category that can be used for various purposes, and that the quest for some Platonic essence of sex is misguided:

> It misdirects our focus, to someone's political detriment, to appeal to the natural or to "the facts" of sex (as proclaimed by medical practitioners) as the basis for what are really political judgments about what identities and relationships to recognize. This happens in articles and opinions that repeatedly invoke "reality" or "biological reality"; birth attendants that succeed or fail to record "accurate gender"; supposed "historical facts" in birth registries that all seem to presume there is some objective "truth"

of sex or gender, discernable if only we try harder to set aside old ways of thinking and turn to the "experts." Indeed, even many transsexual persons' "discovery narratives" (which we certainly must recognize are favored by clinicians and reform-minded courts) invoke some true essence of sex, a truth recognizable by legal systems if only they could get past simplistic measures of sex like the natal concordance of gonads, genitals, and chromosomes promulgated in [*Corbett v. Corbett* (*see* Chapter 17, *infra*)].

David B. Cruz, *Getting Sex "Right": Heteronormativity and Biologism in Trans and Intersex Marriage Litigation and Scholarship*, 18 Duke J. Gender L. & Pol'y 203 (2010). Might such criticisms have force against appeals to "true identity," "true sex," and "actual sex" by the *Arroyo Gonzalez* plaintiffs and court? Do Prof. Cruz's arguments improperly deny legal recognition of the realities of transgender people's lives even though this essay may be read as agnostic regarding the existence in nature of human "true sex"?

7. As a bookend to birth certificates, identifying people with reference to the beginning of our lives, consider death certificates. Those are a site where transgender people are vulnerable to being identified as a member of a sex inconsistent with their gender identity. For a rare exploration of the issues, including a relatively new California law requiring that death certificates reflect decedents' gender identity, see Delaney Naumann, *A Woman in Life, but a Man After Death: Protecting the Postmortem Identities of Transgender Individuals*, 10 Est. Plan. & Community Prop. L.J. 181 (2017).

B. Driver's Licenses and State Identification Cards

Driver's licenses (or state ID cards) are one of the most common ways for adults in the United States to authenticate their identity. One's license may be required to cash a check, to pay for items by check or credit card, to gain admission to events for which one has registered, to verify one's eligibility to work, to establish one's entitlement to use a purchased ticket to board a flight, or to allow police to check one's insurance coverage or search for outstanding warrants. Most driver's licenses include a sex/gender marker—as indeed they must to satisfy the standards of federal regulations issued to implement the REAL ID Act of 2005 and, for example, allow someone to board a flight. *See* 6 C.F.R. § 37.17 (2018) ("To be accepted by a Federal agency for official purposes, REAL ID driver's licenses and identification cards must include on the front of the card (unless otherwise specified below) the following information: . . . (c) Gender, as determined by the State."). In any of these transactions, a transgender person's sex/gender may become an issue if their appearance or gender presentation does not match the gendered expectations of the person checking their ID.

Consider, for example, self-declared "stone butch" Leslie Feinberg's account of the perils of having to indicate a sex/gender on identity documents from her book

Leslie Feinberg, Transgender Warriors: Making History from Joan of Arc to RuPaul 61–62 (1996):*

When I say I am a gender outlaw in modern society, it's not rhetoric. I have been dragged out of bars by police who claimed I broke the law when I dressed myself that evening. I've heard the rap of a cop's club on the stall door when I've used a public women's toilet. And then there's the question of my identity papers.

My driver's license reads *Male*. The application form only offered me two choices: *M* or *F*. In this society, where women are assumed to be feminine and men are assumed to be masculine, my sex and gender expression appear to be at odds. But the very fact that I could be issued a license as a male demonstrates that many strangers "read me" as a man, rather than a masculine woman.

In almost thirty years of driving I've heard the whine of police sirens behind my car on only three occasions. But each time. a trooper sauntered up to my car window and demanded, "Your license and registration — sir." Imagine the nightmare I'd face if I handed the trooper a license that says I am female. The alleged traffic infraction should be the issue, not my genitals. I shouldn't have to prove my sex to any police officer who has stopped me for a moving violation, and my body should not be the focus of investigation. But in order to avoid these dangers, I broke the law when I filled out my driver's license application. As a result, I could face a fine, a suspension of my license, and up to six months in jail merely for having put an *M* in the box marked sex.

And then there's the problem of my passport. I don't feel safe traveling with a passport that reads *Female*. However, if I apply for a passport as *Male*, I am subject to even more serious felony charges. Therefore, I don't have a passport, which restricts my freedom to travel. I could have my birth certificate changed to read *Male* in order to circumvent these problems, but I don't see why I should have to legally align my sex with my gender expression, especially when this policy needs to be fought.

Why am I forced to check off an *F* or an *M* on these documents in the first place? For identification? Both a driver's license and a passport include photographs! Most cops and passport agents would feel insulted to think they needed an *M* or an *F* to determine if a person is a man or a woman. It's only those of us who cross the boundaries of sex or gender, or live ambiguously between those borders, who are harassed by this legal requirement.

Many of my transsexual sisters and brothers are required legally to amend their birth certificates before they can change their other identification papers to conform to their lives. But states have different policies on changing birth

---

certificates—some simple, some grueling. Why should transsexual men and women be harassed, or denied the right to travel, merely based on which state they were unlucky enough to have been born in? I am told I must check off *M* or *F* because it is a legal necessity. But when I was a child, I was required to check off race on all legal records. It took mighty, militant battles against institutionalized racist discrimination to remove that mandatory question on documents. The women's liberation movement won some important legal victories against sex discrimination too, like ending the policy of listing jobs in "female " and "male" categories. So why do we still have to check off male or female on all records? Why is the categorization of sex a legal question at all? And why are those categories policed?

Why *do* driver's licenses and passports in the U.S. contain sex markers? Why are those sex markers allowed in most states and on passports binary, either *M* or *F*? For an argument for governments to issue genderless identity documentation, see, for example, Anna James Neuman Wipfler, *Identity Crisis: The Limitations of Expanding Government Recognition of Gender Identity and the Possibility of Genderless Identity Documents*, 39 Harv. J.L. & Gender 491 (2016). Challenges to the rules for changing sex markers on driver's licenses raise fundamental questions about the identification purposes of such documents and precisely how the information they contain does, or does not, serve those purposes.

In addition, because driver's licenses are issued by state governments in the federal system in the United States, there is widespread variation in the rules governing change of sex/gender markers on them. Some states provide a gender-neutral option; the majority do not. A minority of states do not require a certification from a medical provider of applicants seeking to change their sex/gender marker; states vary in the range of licensed professionals whose certifications are acceptable. A significant minority of states require an amended birth certificate or proof of surgery. For a scoring of state and territorial policies based on their trans-friendliness, see National Center for Transgender Equality, *Driver's license policy grades, 2020*, available at https://transequality.org/sites/default/files/docs/resources/Drivers%20 License%20Grades%20Jan%202020.pdf (last visited Feb. 29, 2020), linked from National Center for Transgender Equality, *ID Documents Center* (last updated Jan. 2020), https://transequality.org/documents (last visited Feb. 29, 2020).

Reading Guide for K.L. v. State of Alaska, Division of Motor Vehicles

1. Language usage can evolve quickly, and the court's use of "transgendered" was largely outdated even in 2012. The preferred nomenclature was that used by the plaintiff: "transgender."

2. What was Alaska's policy regarding changing the sex marker on one's driver's license or state ID card? What constitutional challenges did the plaintiff make to that policy? Which constitutional challenge does the court address?

3. On what provision of Alaska law does the court rely? What kinds of individual interests does that provision protect, and which such interest does the court hold is implicated here?

4. How does Alaska's policy threaten that interest? What doctrinal test does the court apply to Alaska's policy as a result of that threat? What governmental interests does the defendant argue the policy serves? How does the court view the strength of those interests in this context? In what ways does the court suggest that the challenged policy is counterproductive with respect to those interests? Which part of the applicable doctrinal test does the court rule the policy fails? What permanent relief does the court order, and what transitional relief does it require?

K.L. v. State of Alaska, Department of Administration, Division of Motor Vehicles

No. 3AN-11-05431, 2012 WL 2685183 (Alaska Super. Ct. Mar. 12, 2012)

Michael Spaan, Superior Judge.

. . . .

I. Facts and Proceedings

K.L. is a male-to-female transgendered person who lives her life as a female. K.L.'s United States passport identifies her as female, as does her medical certificate to operate as a pilot, her airman certificate, and her work identification.

. . . . K.L. completed an application for a renewed Alaska driver's license, in which she submitted a Certificate of Name Change to change her name from D.L. to K.L. On this application K.L. indicated her sex as female. On June 12, 2010 the DMV accepted the Certificate of Name Change and issued a new license to K.L. with a female sex identifier.

The DMV's Standard Operating Procedure ("SOP") D-24 sets forth the procedures used by the DMV when an applicant seeks to change information on his or her driver's license. While the DMV merely accepts the applicant's word for changes in weight, height, hair color, and eye color, a medical certification of a sex change was required before the DMV would change the sex code on an individual's license.

The DMV employee processing K.L.'s initial application was apparently new to the DMV, and it is unknown whether proof of sex change surgery was requested from K.L. Once the DMV realized that there was no documentation reflecting a surgical change of male-to-female, an Order of Cancellation notice was sent to K.L. This notice, sent by the DMV on July 9, 2010, indicated that K.L. could avoid cancellation by presenting verification from a doctor that a surgical change was performed.

K.L. disputed the cancellation of her license and requested an administrative hearing. . . .

The Administrative Hearing Officer ("AHO") . . . . concluded that SOP D-24 is a regulation that was not promulgated in accordance with the Administrative Procedure Act ("APA") of AS 44.62. . . .

Thus, the AHO held that the DMV cannot rely on SOP D-24, and therefore has no authority to change the sex on a license until such time that a regulation is adopted that complies with the Administrative Procedure Act. The AHO then found that any licenses issued under that policy were done so in error and would be deemed invalid. . . .

II. Issues for Consideration

[Not challenging the invalidity of SOP D-24, K.L. argues instead that her license marked female did not contain an "error" within the meaning of the state law providing for cancellation of issued licenses; that disallowing sex marker changes or requiring proof of surgery for them "violates fundamental liberty and privacy rights" and "violates the right of equal protection," both under the Alaska constitution; and that the proper remedy is a new regulation "which does away with proof of surgical treatment, focusing instead on gender identity and expression."]

III. Discussion

. . . . [T]he absence of any regulation allowing licensees to change the sex designation on their driver's license impermissibly infringes on a constitutionally-protected zone of privacy.[10]

[The court starts its analysis by affirming the AHO's conclusions that the former regulation was invalid, that in the absence of such regulation the DMV had no authority to change the sex marker on K.L.'s license, and that the amended license indicating her as female without her having submitted proof of surgery did contain an "error" and so was properly canceled.]

. . . [B]ecause the DMV now has no procedure for changing the sex designation on a driver's license, the issue before this Court . . . [16] . . . is whether the Alaska Constitution affirmatively requires the DMV to have a procedure in place for licensees to change the sex designation on their license.

Unlike the federal Constitution, Alaska's constitution provides an explicit right to privacy. [Article 1, section 22 of the Alaska Constitution provides: "The right of the people to privacy is recognized and shall not be infringed."] "Because this right to privacy is explicit, its protections are necessarily more robust and 'broader in scope' than those of the implied federal right to privacy." However, "'the rights to privacy and liberty are neither absolute nor comprehensive . . . their limits depend

---

10. Because the Court's decision is based on the right to privacy, the Court will not reach the issue of whether K.L.'s equal protection rights have also been violated.

16. At oral argument on February 6, 2012, the DMV informed the Court that it currently has no intention of adopting any new policy concerning changes of sex designation on licenses.

on a balance of interests' that will vary depending on the importance of the rights infringed."

When the state burdens or interferes with a fundamental aspect of the right to privacy, it must demonstrate a "compelling governmental interest and the absence of a less restrictive means to advance that interest." On the other hand, when state action interferes with non-fundamental aspects of privacy, "the state must show a legitimate interest and a close and substantial relationship between its interest and its chosen means of advancing that interest." Thus, this Court must consider both the nature and extent of the privacy invasion and the strength of the state interest in not having a procedure in place allowing licensees to change the sex designation on their license.

1. The Nature and Extent of the Privacy Invasion

Cases interpreting the right to privacy have recognized at least two interests protected by the right. One is an individual's interest in personal autonomy and independence in decision-making. Another is an individual's interest in protecting sensitive personal information from public disclosure. With respect to this latter interest, the Alaska Supreme Court has explained that, "[i]n short, ... the right of privacy embodied in the Alaska Constitution is implicated by the disclosure of *personal* information about oneself." *Doe v. Alaska Superior Court*, 721 P.2d 617 (Alaska 1986).

A common thread woven into our decisions is that privacy protection extends to the communication of "private matters," or, phrased differently, "sensitive personal information," or "a person's more intimate concerns[.]" This is the type of personal information which, if disclosed even to a friend, could cause embarrassment or anxiety.

For example, in *Falcon v. Alaska Pub. Offices Comm'n*, 570 P.2d 469 (Alaska 1977), a physician challenged the constitutionality of a statute that required him to disclose the names of his patients in order to serve on a school board. The court noted "that where applicable rules or regulations insure that [potentially stigmatizing personal] information will be available only to authorized personnel in the context of a valid governmental program, no constitutional violation has occurred." However, because the statute in *Falcon* made the disclosures available to the public, and because the disclosures could potentially reveal the nature of a patient's ailment, the court held that the statute posed an impermissible threat to protected privacy rights. To prevent an infringement of these rights, the court enjoined the State from applying the law to physician-patient situations until it adopted appropriate curative regulations.

In *Rollins v. Ulmer*, 15 P.3d 749 (Alaska 2001), the court considered a challenge to a law requiring medical marijuana users to register with the Department of Health and Social Services. The court noted that "[i]t can hardly be disputed that the medical marijuana registry requires disclosure of sensitive information: mere presence in the registry identifies a person as suffering from a 'debilitating medical condition' and as being a marijuana user." The court agreed that "the general publication of this information could be stigmatizing and invasive of the right to privacy." Nevertheless, because the law explicitly required the department to keep the registry confidential, the court found no violation of the constitutional right to privacy.

In *Alaska Wildlife Alliance v. Rue*, 948 P.2d 976 (Alaska 1997), a wildlife group sought disclosure of the names and time sheets of public employees and private contractors involved in a state wolf control program. The Alaska Department of Fish and Game provided the group with the records, but redacted the names of select employees involved in the program. Although one's name and status as a public employee or private contractor tells little about the individual's personal life, the court found that the disclosure of such information implicated the right to privacy because various state offices had received letters and phone calls which threatened the lives and property of individuals involved in the program. Thus, the court concluded that "where there are credible threats against the lives of public employees and private contractors, their expectation that the state will protect them by not disclosing their names is legitimate." The court further concluded that the wildlife group's interest in "verifying accountability of public funds" did not justify putting the Department's employees and private contractors at risk of harm. Therefore, the court upheld the Department's redaction of the names.

The Alaska courts have yet to consider the right to privacy in the context of one's status as a transgender or transsexual. However, the Second Circuit has recognized that "[t]he excrutiatingly [*sic*—Eds.] private and intimate nature of transsexualism, for persons who wish to preserve privacy in the matter, is really beyond debate." *Powell v. Schriver*, 175 F.3d 107 (2d Cir. 1999). Like HIV, "transsexualism is the unusual condition that is likely to provoke both an intense desire to preserve one's medical confidentiality, as well as hostility and intolerance from others." *Id.* Therefore, "individuals who are transsexuals are among those who possess a constitutional right to maintain medical confidentiality." *Id.*

Here, K.L. asserts that one's status as being transgendered is private, sensitive personal information. K.L. asserts that a driver's license that does not match a person's expressed gender identity forces disclosure of one's transgendered status. This, in turn, can also result in disclosure of a sensitive medical condition known as Gender Identity Disorder. K.L. argues that the disclosure of this information can not only cause severe embarrassment and anxiety, but can also result in an individual being placed at risk of harm, harassment, or subject to discrimination.

The Court agrees that one's transgendered status is private, sensitive personal information. Here, however, the fact that the DMV currently has no procedure allowing licensees to change the sex designation does not directly threaten the disclosure of this personal information. Nevertheless, the Court finds that such a threat is imposed indirectly. While Alaska law does not require anyone to obtain a driver's license, such a license is necessary to enjoy the benefits of operating a motor vehicle in the state. Furthermore, individuals are often required to furnish their driver's license to third parties as a form of identification. When a person such as K.L. furnishes a driver's license bearing a male sex designation, the discrepancy between the license and their physical appearance can lead to the forced disclosure of the person's transgendered status. Thus, while the DMV is not the entity requiring disclosure or the entity actually disclosing this information, the threat of disclosure is nonetheless real. The situation is somewhat analogous to the court's observation in *Falcon* that, in particular situations, "disclosure of the mere fact that an individual has visited a certain physician may have the effect of making public certain confidential or sensitive information." For example, where a physician engages in a specialized area of practice (such as treating sexual problems or venereal disease), the disclosure of a patient's identity can also reveal the nature of the treatment.

Therefore, the Court finds that K.L.'s privacy expectation in this regard is entitled to protection. However, the Court does not find it necessary to determine at this time whether this expectation implicates fundamental aspects of the right to privacy. The Court is not now suggesting that K.L. has a fundamental right to have the gender designation changed on her driver's license. K.L.'s expectation that the routine disclosure of her driver's license will not expose her transgendered status to the public at least implicates non-fundamental aspects of the privacy right. Therefore, the State must show that not allowing anyone to change the sex designation on their driver's license bears a close and substantial relationship to the furtherance of a legitimate state interest.

2. The Strength of the State Interest

The DMV essentially puts forth the state's interests in having accurate documentation and identification and preventing fraud or falsification of identity documents. The DMV argues that the ability to change weight, height, hair color, and eye color, but not gender, bears a fair and substantial relation to the clear legislative goal of having driver's licenses that do not contain errors, misinformation, or inaccuracies that can be used to perpetuate identification theft, fraud, or other malfeasance. According to the DMV, the current scheme substantially furthers the legitimate state goal of issuing accurate and fixed forms of identification that cannot be readily changed or manipulated, and of dealing with the licensure of drivers in a comprehensive and uniform manner. As discussed below, however, the Court finds that the DMV's current licensing scheme regarding sex designations does not bear a close and substantial relationship to the furtherance of these interests.

As to the state's interest in having accurate documentation and identification, the Court agrees with K.L. that a licensing policy based on the appearance of one's physical features concealed from public view can undermine the accuracy of identification of individuals based on driver's licenses. With respect to the DMV's policy on weight, height, hair color, and eye color, this policy is reasonable as it concerns those physical features which are visibly expressed to the public. Thus, allowing [licensees] to change the description of such features will allow for more accurate identification of individuals based on driver's licenses. On the other hand, one's sex designation concerns physical features which are concealed from and not apparently discernable to the public. By not allowing transgendered individuals to change their sex designation, their license will inaccurately describe the discernable appearance of the license holder by not reflecting the holder's lived gender expression of identity. Thus, when such individuals furnish their license to third-persons for purposes of identification, the third-person is likely to conclude that the furnisher is not the person described on the license.

In addition, the Court agrees with K.L. that the absence of any procedure for changing the sex designation on an individual's license can create discrepancies and inaccuracies between Alaska driver's licenses other forms of government issued identification. For example, persons such as K.L. can obtain a United States passport with a female sex designation by providing a physician's medical certification declaring that the applicant has had appropriate clinical treatment for gender transition. Therefore, as is the case with K.L., this can lead to discrepancies between an individual's Alaska driver's license and United States passport.

Likewise, the current DMV scheme can even create discrepancies among Alaska driver's licenses with respect to current license holders and new license applicants. For example, if an individual such as K.L.—who holds both a United States passport and a secondary form of identification with a female sex designation (*e.g.*, a pilot's license)—were to apply for an Alaska driver's license for the first time, it is possible that the DMV would issue her a license describing her sex as female. On the other hand, where such a person has already obtained an Alaska license, any subsequent license is required to have the original sex designation. Therefore, some transgendered licensees may hold an Alaska driver's license reflecting their lived gender identity, while others may not.

Thus, for the reasons above, the Court finds that the DMV's absence of any procedure for changing the sex designation on an individual's license does not bear a close and substantial relationship to the furtherance of the state's interest in accurate documentation and identification. Indeed, the absence of any such policy can actually result in inaccurate and inconsistent identification documents.

As to the state's interest in preventing fraud or falsification of identity documents, the DMV admits that it has seen no evidence of fraud resulting from the sex designation on one's license. Because it is conceivable that such fraud could be accomplished, the Court finds that some regulation concerning the procedure for changing the sex designation on a license is necessary. However, the DMV's outright refusal to allow anyone to change the sex designation on their license does not bear a close and substantial relationship to the prevention of such fraud.

. . . . [T]he DMV is hereby ordered to adopt a new regulation—in accordance with the safeguards provided by the APA—providing a procedure allowing licensees to change the sex designation on their driver's license.[48] The DMV shall have 180 days to comply with this order.

---

48. This Court does not suggest the form or scope of such regulation, so long as it provides a procedure by which individual's may change the sex designation on their license. Indeed, certain

While the DMV's current scheme will remain in effect until a new regulation becomes effective, K.L.'s privacy interests must be protected in the interim. Therefore, the stay of K.L.'s license cancellation will continue to remain in effect until the new regulation becomes effective, at which point K.L. shall have the opportunity to comply with the new regulation. If the DMV determines that K.L. is again unable to comply with the regulation, any new constitutional questions arising from the details of the regulation must be asserted by future challenge in separate proceedings.

It is so ordered.

_____

Discussion

1. In *Yonaty v. Mincolla*, 97 A.D.3d 141 (N.Y. App Div. 2012), New York State's highest court ruled that falsely describing a person as lesbian, gay, or bisexual did not constitute slander per se because of the state's well-defined public policy of protection and respect for the civil rights of people who are lesbian, gay, or bisexual. Is that correct, and if so, can that be harmonized with this case's reasoning about negative views of transgender people?

2. The court distinguishes sex from eye color apparently on the ground that allowing driver's license amendments to change eye color improves their identification function because eye color is a trait generally visible to the public. What is visible to the public about sex, though, is not generally a person's genitalia but their gender expression or presentation. But one cannot actually change one's eye color; one can only mask it with colored contact lenses, for example. One could also wear a wig, or padding to make one's weight greater. But until you strip someone down, you cannot verify their actual weight. And sex is similar if one believes sex generally to be determined by genitalia. Do these observations support or undermine the rationality or persuasiveness of the challenged policy?

3. The court concludes that the challenged policy "can create discrepancies and inaccuracies between Alaska driver's licenses and other forms of government issued identification." Of what legal relevance are such discrepancies?

Reading Guide for Love v. Johnson

1. To change the sex marker on a driver's license in Michigan under the policy challenged in this case, a person must present a certified birth certificate showing the desired sex. Michigan will not accept other government documents that identify a person and indicate sex, such as a passport or another state's driver's license. What constitutional violations did the plaintiffs allege here? The defendants moved

_____

restrictions on the procedure may be both reasonable and necessary. However, the Court does advise the DMV to take into consideration the constitutional implications that such a regulation may have on the right to privacy and the protection of sensitive personal information.

to dismiss the complaint for failure to state a claim. Which alleged violation does the court hold the plaintiffs adequately alleged? Why doesn't the court analyze the other constitutional claims?

2. What constitutional liberty interest (protected by the Due Process Clause) does the court agree the plaintiffs adequately alleged is violated by Michigan's policy? How does the policy allegedly violate that interest?

3. What kind of judicial scrutiny does the court apply to the challenged policy? What government interests or objectives does the defendant argue justify the policy's alleged infringement of a constitutionally protected liberty interest? Why does the court conclude the defendants do not satisfy the applicable level of scrutiny?

Emani Love, et al. v. Ruth Johnson

146 F. Supp. 3d 848 (E.D. Mich. 2015)

Opinion and Order Denying Defendant's Motion to Dismiss

NANCY G. EDMUNDS, United States District Judge

Plaintiffs, a group of [six] transgender individuals, filed this civil rights lawsuit against the Michigan Secretary of State seeking a declaration that the department's policy for changing the sex on a state-issued ID [including a driver's license] is unconstitutional. According to the complaint, the policy has made it unduly burdensome—and in some cases impossible—for Plaintiffs and others like them to obtain a state ID that accurately reflects their gender. In this way, Plaintiffs are forced to rely on an official ID that does not conform with their physical appearance. This, they maintain, indirectly divulges their transgender status to complete strangers and places them at serious risk of harm.

. . . .

I. Background

. . . . Plaintiffs' complaint focuses on the Michigan Secretary of State's alleged role in impeding the gender transition process by establishing unduly burdensome requirements for transgender individuals to alter the gender designation on their state IDs.

In 2011, Michigan Secretary of State Ruth Johnson ("Johnson" or "Defendant") implemented a new policy (the "Policy") for "changing sex" on a state ID. The Policy provides as follows:

> An applicant may request to change the sex on their driver license or [personal identification card]. The individual must provide a certified birth certificate showing the sex of the applicant. A birth certificate is the *only* document accepted as proof to change an individual's sex. A U.S. passport cannot be accepted as proof of a sex change.

(emphasis in original). Under the Policy, then, transgender individuals must procure an amended birth certificate in order to obtain a new state ID.[2] Plaintiffs maintain that this requirement places "onerous and in some cases insurmountable obstacles to prevent transgender persons from correcting the gender on driver's licenses and state IDs . . . [and] stands in contrast with the decisions of the federal government and numerous states to ease restrictions on changing gender on identity documents. . . ." Indeed, according to Plaintiffs, the U.S. Department of State only requires a doctor's certification that a person "has had appropriate clinical treatment for gender transition" to change the gender on his or her passport. Likewise, "[a]t least 25 of the States and the District of Columbia do not require a transgender person to undergo surgery to change the gender" on their state ID.

Because state laws differ in terms of whether and how an individual can amend the gender on their birth certificate, the practical effect of the Policy varies. Under Michigan law, Plaintiffs Emani Love and A.M. are required to undergo sex-reassignment surgery to procure an amended birth certificate. By contrast, Plaintiffs Tina Seitz, Codie Stone, and E.B. "cannot obtain an accurate [Michigan] driver's license under any circumstances because their state of birth does not allow them to amend the gender on their birth certificate." In this way, the Policy creates various subclasses based solely on an individual's state of birth.

. . . . Plaintiffs now seek a declaration that the Policy is unconstitutional on the basis that it impermissibly interferes with their right to free speech, substantive due process, and equal protection under the law. Plaintiffs further allege that the Policy implicates their right to travel and autonomy in medical decision-making. Defendant, for her part, maintains that each of Plaintiffs' five claims are substantively devoid of merit and should be dismissed on the pleadings.

. . . .

III. Analysis

. . . .

A. Substantive Due Process-Fundamental Right to Privacy

According to Plaintiffs, the State's Identification Policy (the "Policy") violates their right to privacy under the Due Process Clause of the Fourteenth Amendment because it forces them to reveal their transgender status to complete strangers. This disclosure of highly personal and intimate information, Plaintiffs maintain, is both embarrassing and places them at great risk of bodily harm.

The Supreme Court has long recognized that the Due Process Clause "bar[s] certain government actions regardless of the fairness of the procedures used to

---

2. Interestingly, Plaintiffs assert that "Michigan residents obtaining a new driver's license or state ID for the first time are not required to present a birth certificate at all in order to obtain a driver's license or state ID listing the correct gender."

implement them. . . ." *Daniels v. Williams*, 474 U.S. 327 (1986). . . . Two types of interests have been identified as protected "by the right to privacy that is rooted in [] substantive due process"—the interest in "independence in making certain kinds of important decisions," and the "interest in avoiding disclosure of personal matters." *Lambert v. Hartman*, 517 F.3d 433 (6th Cir. 2008) (quoting *Whalen v. Roe*, 429 U.S. 589 (1977); *Nixon v. Adm'r of Gen. Servs.*, 433 U.S. 425 (1977)). Plaintiffs' claim implicates the latter interest, which the Sixth Circuit has described as the right to "informational privacy." *Id.* (quoting *Bloch v. Ribar*, 156 F.3d 673 (6th Cir. 1998). A plaintiff alleging a violation of her right to informational privacy must demonstrate that the interest at stake relates to a "fundamental liberty interest." *Id.* "Only after a fundamental right is identified should the court proceed to the next step of the analysis—the balancing of the government's interest in disseminating the information against the individual's interest in keeping the information private." *Id.*

The Sixth Circuit has "recognized an informational-privacy interest of constitutional dimension in only two instances: (1) where the release of personal information could lead to bodily harm (*Kallstrom v. City of Columbus*, 136 F.3d 1055 (6th Cir. 1998)), and (2) where the information released was of a sexual, personal, and humiliating nature (*Bloch*)." *Id.* Here, Plaintiffs maintain that the Policy endangers "their personal security and bodily integrity. . . ." In other words, Plaintiffs assert that the disclosure of their transgender status implicates the liberty interests identified under *Kallstrom* and *Bloch*.

In *Kallstrom*, the plaintiffs were three undercover police officers who were actively involved in a drug conspiracy investigation of the Short North Posse; a violent gang in the Columbus, Ohio area. The Government indicted 41 members of the gang and the plaintiffs testified at the trial of eight of the defendants. During the trial, the city released the personnel records of the undercover officers to defense counsel, who then shared the information with the defendants. . . . The officers later filed suit against the city contending that the release of their personnel files infringed upon their right to privacy under the Fourteenth Amendment.

On appeal, the Sixth Circuit had little trouble concluding that the officers' privacy interests were of "constitutional dimension" because they implicated a fundamental interest in "preserving their lives and the lives of . . . their family members, as well as preserving their personal security and bodily integrity." This interest, according to the court, is implicated "where the release of private information places an individual at substantial risk of bodily harm . . . from a perceived likely threat. . . ." . . . .

The Sixth Circuit has also recognized the constitutional right to informational privacy in the context of "personal sexual matters." In *Bloch v. Ribar*, the court considered whether the plaintiff had a fundamental right "to prevent the dissemination of confidential and intimate details of a rape. . . ." The plaintiff's claim was triggered by a press conference in which the county sheriff released "highly personal and extremely humiliating details of the rape suffered by Ms. Bloch . . . [including] details of the acts perpetrated against her that were so embarrassing she had not even told her husband." The court, relying on the same logic employed in *Kallstrom*, explained that "sexuality and choices about sex, in turn, are interests of an intimate nature which define significant portions of our personhood. Publically [*sic*—Eds.] revealing information regarding these interests exposes an aspect of our lives that we regard as highly personal and private." Against this backdrop, the court concluded that "information regarding private sexual matters warrants constitutional protection against public dissemination."

According to Plaintiffs, "because the Policy requires [them] to carry an ID with a sex that conflicts with their lived sex, Defendant forces them to reveal their transgender status to complete strangers." This disclosure, Plaintiffs maintain, "places them at serious risk of physical harm, endangering their personal security and bodily integrity and thereby rising to constitutional dimensions." Defendant, for her part, argues that, "in contrast to the 'very real threat' in *Kallstrom* posted by a violent gang against the undercover officers who . . . testified against them, Plaintiffs cite to statistics about the risks to transgender individuals in general, and allege hypothetical risks. . . .'"

The Court is not persuaded by Defendant's logic for a number of reasons. First, the *Kallstrom* court unambiguously identified the right to personal security and bodily integrity "from *a perceived likely threat* . . ." (emphasis added). In other words, contrary to Defendant's suggestion, "hypothetical risk" plays an important role in determining whether Plaintiffs' privacy claim implicates a fundamental liberty interest. Here, Plaintiffs have offered a plethora of evidence which, accepted as true, suggests that the Policy poses a real threat to their "personal security and bodily integrity." Indeed, in addition to general statistics "regarding the high incidence of hate crimes among transgender individuals . . . when their transgender status is revealed," . . . Plaintiffs point to first-hand experience of "harassing conduct that transgender persons often live through when forced to produce an ID document that fails to match their lived gender." *See* Compl. ("Emani Love was publicly embarrassed when she went to vote and the precinct worker outed her as transgender after looking at her state I.D. which incorrectly lists her gender as male"); *id.* ("E.B. felt awkward and embarrassed when he was asked for an I.D. to order a a drink at a bar and after seeing the ID, the server started calling him 'ma'am'"); *id.* ("When Tina Seitz had to show her driver's license at a retail store . . . the clerk looked at her license and said 'that's not you.'"); *id.* ("Codie Stone had a hostile experience at a hardware store where the clerk was extremely friendly to him before he produced his license after which the clerk's tone and demeanor changed completely when he provided his license listing the incorrect gender."). These allegations cut at the "very essence of personhood" protected under the substantive component of the Due Process Clause. *Kallstrom*.

The Second Circuit, in *Powell v. Schriver*, specifically recognized the "hostility and intolerance" toward transsexuals in support of its conclusion that "the Constitution does indeed protect the right to maintain the confidentiality of one's transsexualism." 175 F.3d 107 (2d Cir. 1999). . . .

. . . . Similar to *Kallstrom*, the Court finds "no reason to doubt that where disclosure of this [highly intimate] information may fall into the hands of persons" harboring such negative feelings, the Policy creates a very real threat to Plaintiffs' personal security and bodily integrity. *Kallstrom*. Accordingly, the Court finds that by requiring Plaintiffs to disclose their transgender status, the Policy directly implicates their fundamental right of privacy.

Where, as here, state action infringes upon a fundamental right, "such action will be upheld under the substantive due process component of the Fourteenth Amendment only where the governmental action furthers a compelling state interest, and is narrowly drawn to further that state interest." *Kallstrom*. Defendant vaguely identifies two purported interests—albeit not in the context of a fundamental right—in support of the Policy: (1) "maintaining accurate state identification documents" to "promote effective law enforcement" and, (2) ensuring "that the information on the license is consistent with other state records describing the individual." Whether the Policy is narrowly tailored to further these interests "will turn on whether it is the least restrictive and least harmful means of satisfying the government's goal. . . ." *United States v. Brandon*, 158 F.3d 947 (6th Cir.1998).

The Policy bears little, if any, connection to Defendant's purported interests, and even assuming it did, there is no question that requiring an amended birth certificate to change the sex on one's license is far from the least restrictive means of accomplishing the state's goals. Indeed, as Plaintiffs point out "[b]ecause of the Policy, the sex listed on [their] licences [*sic*—Eds.] fails to match their appearance and the sex associated with their names." In this way, the Policy undermines Defendant's interest in accurately identifying Plaintiffs to "promote law enforcement." As the court reasoned in *K.L. v. State, Dep't of Admin., Div. of Motor Vehicles*,

> [b]y not allowing transgendered individuals to change their sex designation, their license will inaccurately describe the discernable appearance of the license holder by not reflecting the holder's lived gender expression of identity. Thus, when such individuals furnish their license to third-persons for purposes of identification, the third-person is likely to conclude that the furnisher is not the person described on the license.

No. 3AN-11-05431, 2012 WL 2685183 (Alaska Super. Ct. Mar. 12, 2012) [*supra* at p. 1141]. Moreover, Defendant's Policy only applies to individuals who are seeking to renew or change an existing license. *See Applying for a License or ID? Applicant Checklist*, available at http://michigan.gov/sos/0,4670,7-127-1627_8669_9040_9043-312849—,00.html. In other words, a first-time transgender applicant may present a "[c]ertified birth certificate . . . [or a] valid, unexpired U.S. passport or passport card" for identity verification purposes. *Id.* This is significant, Plaintiffs maintain, because the U.S. Department of State only requires a doctor's certification that an individual has "had appropriate *clinical* treatment for gender transition to the new gender" to change the gender designation on a passport. *See* Compl. (emphasis added); U.S. Dep't of State, *Gender Reassignment Applicants*, available at http://travel.state.gov/content/passports/en/passports/information/gender.html. Defendant fails to articulate how this two-tiered system promotes the state's purported interest in ensuring "that the information on the license is consistent with other state records describing the individual. . . ." Def.'s Br.

Finally, the Court need not spill a considerable amount of ink on the narrow tailoring requirement. As Plaintiffs point out "[a]t least 25 of the states and the District of Columbia do not require a transgender person to undergo surgery to change the gender on his or her driver's license or state ID card." The Court seriously doubts that these states have any less interest in ensuring an accurate record-keeping system. Moreover, as discussed, the U.S. Department of State, and, according to Plaintiffs, "at least 13 [other] states[,] have implemented policies only requiring a medical provider's certification" in order for an individual to change the gender on their state ID. Accordingly, the Court is unable to conclude at this juncture that the Policy narrowly serves the state's interest in maintaining "accurate" identification documents or promoting effective law enforcement.

In light of the Court's finding that Plaintiffs have raised a cognizable privacy claim . . . , the longstanding principle of judicial restraint cautions against adjudicating the remaining four constitutional claims. . . .

Accordingly, for the reasons thus stated, the Court DENIES Defendant's motion to dismiss.

So ORDERED.

Discussion

1. How much support do the plaintiff's allegations of "awkard[ness]," "embarrass[ment]," and lack of "friendl[iness]" support their contention that Michigan's policy exposes them to "serious risk of harm"?

2. If by "transgender status" the plaintiffs mean having a gender *identity* different from the sex one is assigned at birth, does having one's state ID indicate a sex different from that conventionally associated with a person's name and attire necessarily disclose transgender status? Might not a person presenting as female with a driver's license with a male sex marker be either (1) a transgender woman or (2) a cisgender man who chooses to wear feminine clothing and make-up? If so, then isn't the information that is being disclosed by Michigan ID card sex markers not a person's gender identity (and so cisgender/transgender status) but the person's sex assigned at birth? Is there a constitutional privacy right to keep one's sex private? Is it unconstitutional for government identity documents to include a sex marker at all?

3. Is it true that "the Policy creates various subclasses based *solely* on an individual's state of birth" (emphasis added)? Even if not, does treating people differently based on the laws of their state of birth advance the alleged state interests supporting the challenged policy?

4. Given the limited purposes the defendant advances to support its ID policy, would a final judgment against the state driver's license/identification card policy in this litigation necessarily mean that transgender people must constitutionally be allowed to change the sex markers on their birth certificates?

C. Passports

State Department Policies

In early 2001, the U.S. Department of State adopted a written policy permitting transgender persons to change the sex marker on their passport, as well as on birth certificates maintained by the Department issued for children of U.S. citizens born abroad. This required an affidavit from a surgeon with specific reference to the surgical procedures that had been performed. Transgender people who could provide documentation of intent to obtain gender confirmation surgery within one year were permitted to obtain a "limited" passport good for one year.

In 2010, the State Department changed its policy to allow transgender people to update their gender marker without needing to undergo surgery. *See* U.S. Department of State—Bureau of Consular Affairs, *Change of Sex Marker*, https://travel .state.gov/content/travel/en/passports/need-passport/change-of-sex-marker.html (last visited Jan. 28, 2020). An applicant must provide certification of clinical treatment determined by a physician to be appropriate to facilitate the individual's gender transition. No specific details are necessary about the particular type of treatment. A State Department template for such a physician letter includes statements sworn under penalty of perjury that the physician had a doctor-patient relationship with the applicant, that they had either treated the person or reviewed their medical records, and that the applicant had appropriate clinical treatment for transition to either male or female. The letter must be from a U.S.-licensed physician and not a psychologist. A court-ordered gender change or amended birth certificate is not accepted in place of the required physician's letter because the requirements of state laws for sex marker changes on these documents vary. If a person is "in the process of transition" to "male or female," the physician letter may so state, and the applicant will be issued a "limited" two-year passport. The photo used for the passport must "resemble" the applicant's current appearance.

The Department's Foreign Affairs Manual ("FAM"), the authoritative source for the Department's policies and procedures, contains the specifics of the current policy at 8 FAM 403 (formerly 7 FAM 1300 Appendix M). It notes that the policy is based on standards and recommendations of the World Professional Association for Transgender Health (WPATH), recognized as the authority in this field by the American Medical Association (AMA). *See also Change of Sex Marker*. Sex reassignment surgery is not a prerequisite for passport issuance based on gender change.

The Manual explicitly states that "[m]edical certification of gender transition from a licensed physician as described in 8 FAM 403.3-2 is the only documentation of gender change required. Other medical records must not be requested."

To verify the applicant's identity, primary or secondary ID reflecting the sex desired on the passport is required. Primary ID includes documents such as a valid passport or certificate of naturalization. Secondary ID refers to documents such as a driver's license with or without photo, social security card, work or student ID, or a school yearbook with a photograph. If primary ID reflecting the sex desired on the passport is not available, then primary ID in the "birth gender" is acceptable if it readily identifies the applicant. The manual permits evidence of either a court ordered name change or customary usage. The same policy applies to both adults and minors. However, all passport applications for minors are also subject to parental consent requirements. The FAM specifically instructs officers to refer to the applicant by the pronoun appropriate to "her/his new gender even if the transition is not complete." The officer may ask only "appropriate questions regarding information necessary to determine citizenship and identity." 8 FAM 403.3–4

As is clear from the references to "transition" in conjunction with the use of "male or female," the policy springs from a binary conception of sex that was dominant at the time the policy was being formulated. Since that time, however, recognition that gender identity may be non-binary has been growing. As of the writing of this case book, there is no provision in the policy for a sex marker reflecting non-binary or intersex identity. The FAM has a section on "Intersex Conditions (Disorders of Sex Development)." 8 FAM 402-3.6. Even that, however, requires that the sex be listed as either male or female. In the cases of *Zzyym v. Kerry* and *Zzyym v. Pompeo*, *infra*, the United States District Court repeatedly ruled that the intersex plaintiff should be permitted to obtain a passport with a gender neutral marker, such as "X." (That decision was, however, ultimately vacated by the United States Court of Appeals for the Tenth Circuit. *Zzyym v. Pompeo*, 958 F.3d 1014 (10th Cir. 2020), *infra*.) Several countries issue such passports. This procedure is authorized by the United Nations International Civil Aviation Organization (ICAO), which sets forth international travel document standards.

Note on Zzyym v. Kerry *and* Zzyym v. Pompeo Trial Court Decisions

In a first round of litigation with the U.S. Department of State, Dana Alix Zzyym sued then-Secretary of State John Kerry of the Obama administration and then-Director of the Colorado Passport Agency for the U.S. Department of State Sherman Portell in their official capacities for denying Zzyym a passport. *Zzyym v. Kerry*, 220 F. Supp. 3d 1106 (D. Colo. 2016). Zzyym, who uses singular "they" form pronouns, is an intersex person who identifies as nonbinary, that is, neither entirely male nor entirely female, although at the time the sex marker on Zzyym's Colorado driver's license listed female. Accordingly, Zzyym would not check either the Male or the Female box on a passport application; instead Zzyym wrote "intersex" on the application and submitted a separate letter explaining that they were intersex and requesting X in the sex field of a passport, which would be consistent with passport standards established by International Civil Aviation Organization ("ICAO"). Citing the Department's binary-only gender policy, the Department denied Zzyym's request and administrative appeals.

Zzyym then sued on Oct. 25, 2015. Zzyym's complaint maintained

> (1) that the Department's conduct was in violation of the [federal Administrative Procedure Act ("APA")] because it was "arbitrary and capricious;" (2) that the conduct also violated the APA because it exceeded the Department's Congressionally-delegated authority; (3) that such action deprived plaintiff of due process in violation of the Fifth Amendment; (4) that it similarly deprived plaintiff of equal protection in violation of the Fifth Amendment; and (5) that the Court should issue a writ of mandamus to compel the Department to issue a passport accurately reflecting plaintiff's self-described sex.

On March 18, 2016, the Department then "filed a motion seeking judgment on the administrative record on plaintiff's APA claims and dismissal of the claims contained within the remainder of plaintiff's Complaint" under Federal Rule of Civil Procedure 12(b)(6) for failure to state a complaint on which relief could be granted. On November 22, the district court issued an opinion ruling that the administrative record, even supplemented by a statement the defendants submitted, revealed the agency's decisionmaking to be arbitrary and capricious under the APA.

The court understood the Department to be contending essentially that "the government decided to issue passports only marked 'M' or 'F' because the proper documentation needed to prove a passport applicant's sex necessarily took that form." Yet, the court noted, the Department accepts evidence in the form of "third-party affidavits" to support someone's sex when they are claiming a binary sex, but rejects such evidence to support an asserted nonbinary sex. Hence, the form of evidence does not explain the *substantive* insistence that travelers must claim a binary sex.

The court also rejected the suggestion that the inclusion of binary sex data in passport RFID chips supports the policy. Not only did that not explain adoption of the binary-sex-only policy in 1976, but the government also did not argue that its refusal to reprogram software and hardware to accommodate a nonbinary gender for a small group of nonbinary intersex persons justified its contemporary adherence to the policy.

The court did not accept "the importance of enabling U.S. passport information to sync with law enforcement databases that exclusively use binary gender systems" as providing a non-arbitrary, non-capricious basis for the policy because not all law enforcement records include a completed sex marker field and because the

Department lets transgender and intersex persons adopt a binary sex marker that is contrary to what their "state identification documents (and perhaps law enforcement database records?)" specify.

Finally, the court was unconvinced by the defendants' assertion that, "'because only a few countries recognize a third sex marker in their issuance of passports and visas'" as allowed by the ICAO standards, the Department was concerned about possible "inconvenience or uncertainty" if a traveler with a nonbinary sex marker were to visit "countries that do not yet recognize a third gender marker." The court concluded that questions this rationale raised—whether this rationale is purely speculative, whether other countries simply seek to validate passports rather than the information they contain, and whether any attendant difficulties should be understood as the problem of the person who chooses a nonbinary sex marker for a passport—left the administrative record unable to "explain why these factors rationally support the policy in place."

As a result, the court remanded the matter to the State Department for reconsideration. Subsequently, the Department reconsidered but decided to adhere to its policy. Zzyym then reopened the lawsuit, leading to the next opinion in this litigation. (At the time of this decision, Dana Zzyym was represented by private counsel, Lambda Legal, and an attorney from the United States Army Corp of Engineers.)

In *Zzyym v. Pompeo*, 341 F. Supp. 3d 1248 (D. Colo. 2018), the district court reached only Zzyym's claims under the APA (counts I and II of the supplemental complaint) and not Zzyym's constitutional claims. It did so because its APA ruling afforded Zzyym the relief they personally sought. This was thus an example of the doctrine of constitutional avoidance, whereby courts prefer non-constitutional grounds for decision if such grounds are reasonably available.

In assessing the challenge to the Department's binary-sex-only policy, the court observed in passing that the term "policy" is a bit of a misnomer. The policy which the Department claims requires it to issue passports only marked "M" for male or "F" for female is really a collection of rules pertaining to gender contained within the Foreign Affairs Manual. These rules do not explicitly state that the Department cannot issue a passport containing an alternative gender marking, and also do not contemplate the existence of a gender other than male or female.

On the APA claim that the State Department acted arbitrarily and capriciously, the court rejected all five of the rationales the Department proffered for its refusal to grant Zzyym a policy without an M or F sex marker. In the court's view, the Department's reasons were insufficient to show that its action was "the product of a rational decision-making process" as required by the APA. The court thought the defendants' arguments on the first three reasons added nothing to what the court had rejected in its previous ruling; the fourth argument, about lack of medical consensus about defining who is intersex, the court thought riddled with inconsistency in how the Department treated Zzyym; and the fifth argument about the time and cost of adjusting systems to accommodate a non-binary sex marker the court rejected as based on rank speculation.

In addition, the court concluded that the federal Passport Act of 1926 did not authorize the State Department to deny a passport to an intersex person such as Dana for failure to pick either an inaccurate "male" designation or an inaccurate "female" designation on the passport application. The court read relevant precedent to require both that the Department have a reason to deny someone a passport on grounds not listed in the statute but also that it be "a good" reason. Because it saw no such reason, and because "adherence to a series of internal policies that do not contemplate the existence of intersex people is not good reason," the court concluded that "the Department has acted in excess of its statutory jurisdiction."

Accordingly, the district court "grant[ed] Dana's request for injunctive relief and enjoin[ed] the Department from relying upon its binary-only gender marker policy to withhold the requested passport from Dana."

Reading Guide for Zzyym v. Pompeo

1. As confirmed by Supreme Court precedent, the federal Passport Act does not authorize the State Department to deny passports for any reason whatsoever. By what reasoning does the Court of Appeals conclude that the Act did give the Secretary of State the authority to deny passports to any individual who fails to self-identify as male or female on a passport application?

2. Pursuant to the federal Administrative Procedure Act, the court must conclude that the Agency (here, the State Department or the Secretary of State) did not exercise its statutory authority in an arbitrary or capricious way in denying non-binary intersex person Dana Zzyym a passport. How does the court describe the deferential character of its review under this standard?

3. Which two of the Department's reasons for its binary-only passport policy does the court of appeals conclude were supported by the administrative record at the time at which it made the decision Zzyym's lawsuit challenged? What reasons does the court give for so concluding? What reasons does it give for rejecting Zzyym's objections to those rationales?

4. Which three of the Department's reasons for denying Zzyym's passport did the court rule were not supported by the administrative record? What reasons did the court give for rejecting these rationales of the Department?

5. Given that the court of appeals holds that the administrative record supported three of the Department's rationales for denying Zzyym's passport, why does it vacate and remand the case to the district court rather than simply reverse the court and uphold the Department's actions?

Zzyym v. Pompeo

958 F.3d 1014 (10th Cir. 2020)

[Dana Zzyym was represented by Lambda Legal and private counsel.]

Before Bacharach, Seymour, and McHugh, Circuit Judges.

Bacharach, Circuit Judge.

United States citizens ordinarily need a passport to leave or reenter the country. The passport serves a dual function, proving both identity and allegiance to the United States.

For decades, the State Department has identified applicants based on characteristics like an individual's sex. In identifying an applicant's sex, the State Department has taken a binary approach, considering everyone as either male or female.

This approach has thwarted Dana Zzyym's ability to get a passport. Zzyym applied for a U.S. passport, but was intersex and could not accurately identify as either male or female. Because neither option applied, Zzyym requested a passport with an "X" designation for the sex. The State Department refused and denied Zzyym's application. Zzyym sued, alleging that reliance on the binary sex policy [exceeded] the State Department's statutory authority, [was] arbitrary and capricious under the Administrative Procedure Act, and [violated] the U.S. Constitution.

The district court concluded as a matter of law that the State Department had violated the Administrative Procedure Act because [adherence] to the binary sex policy exceeded the State Department's statutory authority and [application] of the policy to Zzyym was arbitrary and capricious. [The] court thus did not reach Zzyym's constitutional claims.

. . . .

The State Department defines an intersex individual as "someone 'born with reproductive or sexual anatomy and/or chromosomal pattern that does not fit typical definitions of male or female.'" This definition fits Zzyym, who was born with both male and female genitalia. Given the presence of genitalia for both sexes, Zzyym's birth certificate was initially left blank for the sex designation. But Zzyym's parents decided to raise Zzyym as a male, so the original birth certificate's blank for sex was filled in as "male." The State Department has treated this birth certificate as the original.

Zzyym lived as a male until adulthood. As an adult, Zzyym explored living as a woman and obtained a driver's license identifying as female. But Zzyym grew increasingly uncomfortable living as a woman and eventually identified as a non-binary intersex person. While identifying as intersex, Zzyym obtained an amended birth certificate identifying the sex as "UnKnown." [*sic*—Eds.]

When applying for a passport, Zzyym understood the need for accuracy. So rather than check the box for male or female, Zzyym wrote "intersex." To support the identification as intersex, Zzyym supplied [a] letter requesting an "X" sex designation and [a] letter from a physician stating that Zzyym is intersex. [Zzyym] also provided the State Department with the amended birth certificate identifying the sex as "UnKnown" and a Colorado driver's license identifying the sex as female.[3]

[The] State Department denied Zzyym's request to designate the sex as "X," explaining that every applicant needed to check the box for either male or female. The State Department offered Zzyym three options:

1. Zzyym could obtain a passport identifying the sex as female, consistent with the driver's license.

2. Zzyym could obtain a passport identifying the sex as male if a physician attested that Zzyym had transitioned to become a male.

3. Zzyym could withdraw the application.

Zzyym declined these options and requested reconsideration, providing two more physicians' letters stating that Zzyym is intersex. The State Department declined to reconsider and again denied Zzyym's application based on the binary consideration [*sic*] of everyone as either male or female.

[Zzyym] sued and the district court ordered a remand, concluding that the State Department's denial of Zzyym's application was arbitrary and capricious. On remand, the State Department decided to retain its policy and again denied Zzyym's application for a passport with an "X" sex designation. The district court again concluded that the State Department had violated the Administrative Procedure Act, and the government appeals.

IV. The State Department acted within its statutory authority

The district court concluded that the State Department had exceeded its statutory authority by enforcing its binary sex policy against Zzyym. . . .

[We] conduct de novo review of the district court's determination of the State Department's statutory authority. If the State Department lacked statutory authority, its decision must be set aside [under the Administrative Procedure Act — Eds,] 5 U.S.C. § 706(2)(C).

[The] Passport Act allows the Secretary of State to "grant and issue passports, and cause passports to be granted, issued, and verified in foreign countries . . . under such rules as the President shall designate and prescribe for and on behalf of the United States and no other person shall grant, issue, or verify such passports." 22 U.S.C. § 211a. In turn, the President has delegated the authority to prescribe rules to the Secretary of State. . . .

The statutory language is permissive, authorizing the State Department to deny passports for reasons not listed in the Act. *Haig v. Agee*, 453 U.S. 280 (1981). For example, the Act does not say whether the State Department can deny passports to

---

3. After applying for an intersex passport, Zzyym obtained a driver's license identifying the sex as "X."

applicants unwilling to state their birth dates or Social Security numbers. Despite the absence of an express statutory provision, few would question the State Department's authority to deny passports when applicants withhold their birth dates or Social Security numbers. *See* 22 C.F.R. § 51.20(b) (requiring applicants to answer all questions pertaining to eligibility for a passport).

The Passport Act is silent about the State Department's authority to deny a passport to applicants who do not identify as male or female. Given this silence, Zzyym disputes the State Department's statutory authority to deny a passport to an applicant unwilling to check the box for either male or female.

The Supreme Court has addressed other challenges to the State Department's authority to deny passports for reasons that are not listed in the Passport Act. In these cases, the Supreme Court has analyzed the State Department's statutory authority by considering past administrative practice and congressional acquiescence. *See, e.g., Kent v. Dulles*, 357 U.S. 116 (1958); *Zemel v. Rusk*, 381 U.S. 1 (1965); *Haig v. Agee*.

The Supreme Court first relied on past administrative practice in *Kent v. Dulles*, 357 U.S. 116 (1958). There the government insisted that applicants disclaim membership in the Communist Party in order to qualify for passports. When some applicants refused, the State Department declined to consider their applications.

The Supreme Court held that the State Department had exceeded its statutory authority. In reaching this holding, the Court observed that the State Department had previously denied passports based on citizenship, allegiance to the United States, or unlawful conduct. By contrast, the State Department had inconsistently denied passports based on belief or association. This inconsistency made it unlikely that Congress had acquiesced in denying passports based on an applicant's membership in the Communist Party.

But when the State Department has consistently restricted passports, courts assume that Congress has acquiesced if it has not legislated on the subject. For example, in *Zemel v. Rusk*, the Supreme Court held that the State Department could refuse to validate passports for travel to Cuba. The Court reasoned that the Passport Act's language was broad enough to permit restrictions on where the applicant could go, emphasizing the State Department's history of restricting destinations.

But the State Department must sometimes confront novel challenges. Without past opportunities to enforce a policy, the State Department's open assertion of authority implies congressional acquiescence. *Haig v. Agee*.

The Supreme Court inferred such congressional acquiescence in *Haig v. Agee*. There the State Department revoked the passport of a former CIA officer who had exposed undercover CIA operatives while travelling abroad. In the past, the State Department had rarely encountered the need to revoke a passport based on national security or foreign policy. But the infrequency of previous challenges didn't matter; the Court reasoned that the State Department had "openly asserted" its power to revoke a passport for reasons involving national security and foreign policy and

Congress had not stepped in. The Court thus concluded that Congress had implicitly approved the State Department's exercise of statutory power. So the Court upheld the State Department's revocation of the passport.

Agee's logic fits here. Prior to Zzyym's application, the State Department had never denied a passport based on an applicant's unwillingness to identify as male or female. But under *Agee*, the infrequency of enforcement does not strip the State Department of statutory authority. In denying a passport to Zzyym, the State Department followed a binary sex policy that had been in place for roughly 39 years.

Zzyym argues that the passport application itself did not alert Congress to the State Department's policy. But the binary sex policy was hardly a secret, for the State Department had enacted regulations requiring every applicant to use particular forms and to answer all of the questions on those forms. Congress could have said if it wanted to allow applicants to bypass certain questions. Given the longevity of the State Department's policy and Congress's apparent acquiescence, we conclude that the binary sex policy fell within the State Department's statutory authority.[4]

. . . Zzyym contends that the State Department can deny passports only for the reasons identified in *Kent*, *Zemel*, and *Agee*: citizenship, allegiance, unlawful conduct, foreign policy, and national security. We disagree. Though the Supreme Court has crystallized some lawful and unlawful justifications for denying a passport, these justifications are illustrative — not exhaustive. The Supreme Court addressed them only because they were at issue in the three cases. *See, e.g.*, *Kent* (focusing only on established reasons for denying a passport that are "material here"). The Supreme Court didn't suggest that these were the only reasons that could justify denial of a passport. We thus conclude that the State Department had statutory authority to deny a passport to Zzyym for failing to identify as a male or female.

V. The State Department's reliance on its binary sex policy was arbitrary and capricious

The resulting issue is whether this application of the binary sex policy was arbitrary and capricious based on the existing administrative record. *See* 5 U.S.C. §706(2)(A) (arbitrary-and-capricious standard); *Copar Pumice Co. v. Tidwell*, 603 F.3d 780 (10th Cir. 2010) (existing administrative record). For this inquiry, we presume that the policy was valid and place the burden of proof on Zzyym. *W. Watersheds Project v. Bureau of Land Mgmt.*, 721 F.3d 1264 (10th Cir. 2013).

Our review is "narrow," and we are "not to substitute [our] judgment" for the State Department's. *Motor Vehicle Mfrs. Ass'n of U.S., Inc. v. State Farm Mut. Auto.*

---

4. The district court concluded that the State Department had exceeded its authority because federal law does not permit denial of a passport application "without good reason." We view the quality of the reasons as pertinent to Zzyym's claim that the State Department's reasoning was arbitrary and capricious. *See* Part V, below. The issue of statutory authority turns on past administrative practice and congressional acquiescence — not the quality of the State Department's reasoning.

Ins. Co., 463 U.S. 29 (1983). Given the narrowness of our review, we will disturb the administrative action only if the State Department relied on improper factors, disregarded an important aspect of the problem, provided an explanation that was implausible or inconsistent with the evidence, or failed to consider an appropriate alternative.

On appeal, the government defends its reasons for requiring Zzyym to identify as a male or female.

A. Only two of the State Department's five reasons are supported by the administrative record

The State Department gave five reasons for relying on the binary sex policy:

1. The policy ensured the accuracy and reliability of U.S. passports.

2. The policy helped identify individuals ineligible for passports.

3. The policy helped make passport data useful for other agencies.

4. No medical consensus existed on how to determine whether someone was intersex.

5. Creating a third designation for sex ("X") was not feasible.

We conclude that the first, fourth, and fifth reasons lack record support, but the second and third reasons are supported.

1. The State Department's first reason . . . lacks support in the record

The State Department justified the binary sex policy in part as a way to promote accuracy and reliability, reasoning that every U.S. jurisdiction had identified all citizens as either male or female. For this justification, the State Department focused on how it determines eligibility for passports. This determination ordinarily requires the State Department to verify an applicant's identity through identification documents issued by other U.S. jurisdictions. So the State Department considered how those jurisdictions identify characteristics such as an individual's sex.

The State Department noted that many U.S. jurisdictions allow amendment of identification documents, but differ on when to allow an amendment. For example, if a male transitions to a female, different jurisdictions may vary in [whether] to allow amendment of a birth certificate to reflect the new sex and [what] evidence is required to obtain the amendment. Given these differences, the State Department focuses only on original identification documents.[5]

We thus consider how U.S. jurisdictions have treated a citizen's sex in original identification documents. For this inquiry, we use May 2017 as the applicable time frame because that is when the State Department denied Zzyym's request.

---

5. Zzyym has not challenged the State Department's policy of relying only on original identification documents when evaluating passport applications.

In May 2017, every U.S. jurisdiction used a binary sex policy in a citizen's original identification documents, always listing the sex as either male or female.[6] Given the prevalence of binary sex policies, the State Department reasoned that listing a sex other than male or female would hamper verification of an applicant's identity.

Zzyym argues that requiring consistency between inaccurate identification documents does not render them more accurate or reliable. We agree. And for intersex individuals like Zzyym, treating every applicant as male or female would necessarily create inaccuracies.

The State Department acknowledges that some individuals are born neither male nor female. Forcing these individuals to pick a gender thus injects inaccuracy into the data. A chef might label a jar of salt a jar of sugar, but the label does not make the salt any sweeter. Nor does requiring intersex people to mark "male" or "female" on an application make the passport any more accurate.

But the State Department prizes accuracy. To promote accuracy, the State Department requires applicants to submit original birth certificates and establish identity with corroborating identification documents. If the designated sex does not match the identification documents, the applicant must obtain medical certification by a licensed physician.

Given these requirements, an intersex applicant like Zzyym could not accurately complete the passport application in May 2017. If the applicant was intersex, the original identification documents would not accurately identify the applicant's sex. So the State Department's reliance on original identification documents would prevent intersex applicants from accurately identifying their sex.

At oral argument, the State Department. . . . noted that it had offered to produce a passport with an "F" (matching Zzyym's original Colorado driver's license) or an "M" (matching the original birth certificate). But when asked what an applicant like Zzyym should do to ensure the accuracy of the passport, counsel for the State Department acknowledged that (1) "it may be difficult when one is confronted with a form with limited options that may not track one's best answer to a question" and (2) applicants "have to choose what fits best, and that may not be the most accurate answer that they would like to provide, but it is the answer that is available."

---

6. Zzyym argues that the agency failed to consider recent efforts by some states to authorize amended documents recognizing a third sex, characterizing these efforts as a trend toward allowing a third sex designation. But the State Department did consider this development, acknowledging that by 2017 a handful of jurisdictions had "issued amended birth certificates in a third sex, and . . . a very few number of state courts [had] issued court orders recognizing a sex change to a sex other than male or female." Despite these developments, the State Department continued to rely on original documents and resist acceptance of amended documents.

Zzyym also points out that state policies have evolved since May 2017. For example, Zzyym says that [twelve] states and the District of Columbia now authorize sex designations other than "M" or "F" on identification documents and [seven] states allow a gender-neutral category on birth certificates. But we cannot consider this information because we are limited to the administrative record as of May 2017.

In many cases, however, the "best" available answer may not conform to the applicant's original identity documents. States issue most original identification documents; and when the State Department denied Zzyym's application, most state identification documents pigeonholed everyone as male or female even though some people are neither. So reliance on the original identification documents would sometimes create inaccurate information.

Zzyym's experience illustrates the inevitable inaccuracies of a binary sex policy. Zzyym had two original identification documents that would ordinarily establish the sex: The original birth certificate identified Zzyym as male, and the driver's license said female. With conflicting identification documents, the State Department instructed Zzyym to either identify as female or obtain a medical certification showing transition to male. But this instruction didn't make sense because Zzyym hadn't transitioned from female to male, and Zzyym's original birth certificate said that Zzyym was male.

The State Department's policy effectively allowed Zzyym to obtain a passport by claiming to be either male or female. But the State Department's binary sex policy assumes that Zzyym must be one or the other. How could Zzyym be neither male nor female and accurately identify as either sex?

Given the State Department's willingness to allow Zzyym to identify as either male or female, the binary sex policy sunders the accuracy and reliability of information on Zzyym's passport application.

* * *

 The State Department lacks record support for its asserted interest in accuracy and reliability. The State Department mirrored how every U.S. jurisdiction was treating gender in May 2017, but these jurisdictions shoehorned everyone into a binary sex classification ill-suited for intersex applicants. The State Department thus relied on information that didn't accurately describe intersex applicants like Zzyym.

2. The State Department's second reason (that the binary sex policy helped the State Department identify individuals ineligible for passports) is supported by the record

The State Department also explained that the binary sex policy helpfully matches how other federal agencies record someone's sex. This explanation is supported by the record.

The State Department denies passport applications for various reasons. To evaluate these applications, the State Department must gather a broad range of information from federal, state, and local authorities. For example, the State Department may need to collect information from other federal agencies to decide whether an applicant has defaulted on a federal loan, has committed a sex offense, or has obtained a conviction for drug trafficking.

The State Department thus underscored two facts bearing on the need for consistency in data recorded by different federal agencies:

1. "Sex is one of the primary data points used by these agencies in record-keeping. . . ." Appellants' App'x vol. 1, at 85; *see id.* at 45–46 ("Sex is a key component of the 'biometric identity' that the Department uses to verify the identity of the applicant and distinguish individuals.").

2. "[A]ll such agencies recognize only two sexes." *Id.* at 85.

In May 2017, the State Department's system required an applicant's data to match many other federal agencies. And every federal database identified each person as either male or female. So if the State Department searched for Zzyym with an "X" designation for sex, the search would yield mismatches for the applicant's sex. To uncover the reason for the mismatches, an employee in the State Department would need to manually override the "X" designation of sex.

The State Department could thus rationally insist on identifying the applicant's sex in a way that matched other federal databases.[7] To minimize confusion, the State Department reasonably concluded that a binary sex policy could enhance the ability to verify identity.[8]

Of course, the State Department also searches state and local databases in order to assess eligibility for a passport. . . . Though some state agencies did accommodate a third sex designation in 2017, the State Department reasonably concluded that inaccuracies could still arise when contrasting an "X" sex designation with the more common methods of designating someone's sex.

Zzyym points out that the State Department could obtain useable information from other agencies despite differences in the ways that they identified an individual's sex. For example, if an applicant's sex didn't match a federal agency's records, the State Department could verify an applicant's social security number, date of birth, and name. But manually overriding the mismatches would require additional resources.

Zzyym also points out that the State Department was apparently willing to tolerate mismatches for transgender individuals. For these individuals, the State Department used a process allowing an applicant to identify a sex differing from the one on the driver's license or birth certificate. Zzyym questions why the State

---

7. Zzyym contends that the State Department failed to consider the federal government's permission for foreign individuals to enter the United States with passports bearing an "X" designation for sex. But the State Department could reasonably distinguish between the difficulties in accepting a foreign passport and issuing a U.S. passport. Accepting a foreign passport may not implicate the depth of communication with other federal databases that is needed to ensure eligibility for a U.S. passport. And we must defer to an agency's "reasonable conclusions regarding 'technical or scientific matters within the agency's area of expertise.'" *Utah Envtl. Cong. v. Richmond*, 483 F.3d 1127 (10th Cir. 2007).

8. Zzyym argues that mismatches "may in fact aid" the State Department because "[a]ny mismatch is flagged—whether an M/F or X/M/F disparity—ensuring that the underlying application receives more scrutiny." But Zzyym cites no authority or evidence for this proposition. Without any authority or evidence, we decline to speculate on the possibility that more mismatches could aid the State Department.

Department was willing to accept mismatches for transgender applicants but not intersex applicants.

This argument proves that the State Department could accommodate discrepancies—not that it had to do so. In adopting the transgender policy, the State Department needed to evaluate all pertinent factors. *Citizens to Pres. Overton Park, Inc. v. Volpe*, 401 U.S. 402 (1971). But we have little information on the mix of factors contributing to the State Department's policy for transgender applicants. For example, nothing in the record suggests whether the State Department considered the possibility of mismatches with state databases as a factor weighing against the transgender policy.

Regardless of what the pertinent factors were, we know that the State Department was ultimately willing to tolerate some mismatches between transgender applicants' passport applications and the original identification documents. But we don't know how the State Department weighed the inevitability of these mismatches. Given the absence of information on how the State Department weighed this factor for transgender applicants, we cannot speculate. So the State Department's apparent tolerance for mismatches among transgender applicants does not bear on the reasonableness of this factor for intersex applicants.

Transgender applicants aside, Zzyym points out that mismatches may emerge whenever the State Department and a particular state use different methods to identify an individual's sex. For example, Zzyym points to the instruction to identify as either male or female, which may or may not correspond to states' underlying databases. So under either approach, mismatches will arise.

But the State Department has reasonably tried to limit unnecessary mismatches. Under arbitrary-and-capricious review, the agency need not select a perfect solution—just a rational one. Because the State Department could rationally try to reduce unnecessary mismatches, we conclude that the administrative record supports the State Department's second reason to rely on the binary sex policy.

3. The State Department's third reason (that the binary sex policy helped make passport data useful for other agencies) is supported by the record

The State Department also reasoned that using a third sex designation could burden other state and federal agencies when they use the State Department's data. Again, the State Department noted that (1) most agencies' systems accommodate only two sexes and (2) allowing a third sex designation could complicate searches. These complications, the State Department reasoned, would burden other agencies that use passport data. For example, the State Department pointed to law enforcement, which often uses passport data to identify victims and to locate criminal suspects.

Zzyym argues that the State Department's rationale lacks record support and relies on "sweeping assumptions about technical specifications of third-party computer systems." We disagree. The State Department could reasonably conclude that use of a third sex designation would impede at least some other systems that classify everyone as either male or female. We thus conclude that the administrative record supported the State Department's third reason to rely on the binary sex policy.

4. The State Department's fourth reason . . . is unsupported by the record.

The State Department also concluded that the medical community lacks a consensus on how to determine whether someone is intersex, rendering an "X" designation "unreliable as a component of identity." But this reasoning lacks support in the administrative record and does not apply to unquestionably intersex individuals like Zzyym.

According to the State Department, medical experts vary on whether to base intersexuality solely on somatic characteristics, self-identification as intersex, or both. But the State Department cites no scientific evidence of this disagreement about the medical definition of intersexuality.

[Indeed,] the State Department's appellate brief defines intersexuality based on somatic characteristics, stating that an intersex person is "someone 'born with reproductive or sexual anatomy and/or chromosomal pattern that does not fit typical definitions of male or female.'" This definition appears consistent with the academic literature on intersexuality.[8]

In district court, the State Department pointed out that three physicians had given three different reasons for classifying Zzyym as intersex:

1. Zzyym "was born with ambiguous genitalia."

2. Zzyym "has had the appropriate clinical treatment for transition to intersex."

3. Zzyym "was born intersex," "identifies as intersex," and "has had surgery for transition to female genitalia."

These differences, the State Department argued, illustrated the lack of medical consensus about the meaning of intersexuality.

[Even] if the medical community disagreed on whether some individuals are intersex, the State Department would need to explain why the lack of a consensus would justify denying Zzyym's application. *See Burlington Truck Lines, Inc. v. United States*, 371 U.S. 156 (1962) (stating that administrative decisions must rationally connect the factual findings to the decision being made).

The State Department didn't provide such an explanation, assuming instead that disagreement about whether some applicants were intersex would prevent

---

8. *See* [four medical sources omitted by Eds.]; *see also* Jessica A. Clarke, *They, Them, and Theirs*, 132 Harv. L. Rev. 894 (2019) (stating that intersex individuals are "people who are born with any of a range of sex characteristics that may not fit a doctor's notions of binary 'male' or 'female' bodies" (quoting *Intersex Definitions*, Interact, https://interactadvocates.org/intersex-definitions/)); Aileen Kennedy, *Fixed at Birth: Medical and Legal Erasures of Intersex Variations*, 39 Univ. New S. Wales L.J. 813, 813 (2016) ("The term 'intersex' describes variations in sex development whereby a person's biological sex traits are not exclusively male or female.").

classification of anyone as intersex. Why? The State Department has never questioned whether Zzyym is intersex. Given Zzyym's undebatable intersexuality, the State Department failed to explain why a lack of consensus about other individuals would justify forcing intersex individuals like Zzyym to inaccurately identify themselves as male or female. Without such an explanation, we conclude that the State Department lacked record support for its fourth reason to rely on a binary sex classification.[9]

5. The State Department's fifth reason . . . lacks support in the record

Finally, the State Department reasoned that a third sex designation would be infeasible because of the required time and expense. But the State Department did not estimate the additional time or expense. The State Department said only that it anticipated "considerable" challenges to [alter] various systems, [update] systems within the Bureau of Consular Affairs, [update] internal State Department systems, and [update] systems within other federal agencies that rely on passport data.

After the district court granted judgment to Zzyym, the State Department moved to stay the court's order. With this motion, the State Department attached a declaration quantifying the time and expense to alter the passport system. The declarant [noted] that standard U.S. passports are electronic and contain chips with a secure digitized image and biographic data, [described] many information technology systems that would require modification, and [estimated] that changing existing software systems would take 24 months and cost $11 million. We decline to consider these estimates because "review of agency action 'generally focuses on the administrative record in existence at the time of the agency's decision.'" *Copar Pumice Co. v. Tidwell*, 603 F.3d 780 (10th Cir. 2010).[10]

---

9. Zzyym also argues that the State Department could have adopted the conclusions of the World Professional Association for Transgender Health (WPATH). After all, WPATH's conclusions had spurred the State Department to revise its policy for transgender passport applications.

[In] our view, the State Department was not required to use the WPATH standards for intersex individuals despite using these standards for transgender applicants. WPATH is a private nonprofit health organization that makes recommendations, not a public entity creating international standards for passports. And the State Department's Foreign Affairs Manual has not established WPATH standards as official government standards or required the government to defer to WPATH standards in future policymaking. The Foreign Affairs Manual states only that the government chose to use the WPATH standards for individuals transitioning from one sex to another. Adopting WPATH's recommendation for transgender individuals does not require adoption of the recommendation for intersex individuals.

10. The State Department also submitted a second declaration that discussed consideration of a "one-off" passport. This declarant acknowledged the possibility of incorporating "'one-time' modifications to certain systems to change the sex marker in the issuance system's database, to an 'X.'" Despite this possibility, the State Department ultimately decided not to produce a one-off passport because it would undermine the validity of U.S. passports and compromise national security and foreign policy objectives. But the administrative record contains no mention of concerns involving national security or foreign policy, so we decline to consider this argument.

[To] assess the government's allegation of an obvious increase in cost, we must engage in a searching, careful inquiry. *City of Colorado Springs v. Solis*, 589 F.3d 1121 (10th Cir. 2009). In doing so, we cannot accept conclusory statements in lieu of a meaningful explanation. *See Zen Magnets, LLC v. Consumer Prod. Safety Comm'n*, 841 F.3d 1141 (10th Cir. 2016).

The expense is not obvious. Indeed, nine states (California, Colorado, Maine, Minnesota, Nevada, New Jersey, Oregon, Vermont, and Washington) insist that "adding non-binary gender designation in accord with national and international standards has required negligible administrative effort—the kind that accompanies routine changes to government documents." Br. of Amici Curiae States. One of these states (Colorado) represents that it incurred no cost in adopting a third sex designation. Given the conflicting information and the absence of any cost evidence in the administrative record, we do not regard the additional expense as obvious.

In the absence of any meaningful explanation, the State Department lacks record support for its reliance on additional time and expense.

B. The State Department did not fail to consider alternatives

Zzyym insists that the State Department had to consider the alternative of a third sex designation before deviating from international standards. *See Motor Vehicle Mfrs. Ass'n of U.S., Inc. v. State Farm Mut. Auto. Ins. Co.*, 463 U.S. 29 (1983). But the State Department did consider those standards, and reliance on the binary sex policy conformed to those standards.

The International Civil Aviation Organization (ICAO) sets standards to ensure that every country's passports are machine-readable. The State Department followed that policy, making every U.S. passport machine-readable.

[The] binary sex policy conforms to the ICAO standard. The ICAO allowed use of a third sex designation but did not require it. The State Department simply decided not to use the ICAO's option,[11] reasoning that it would not have matched how any U.S. jurisdiction was treating the designation of sex in original identification documents. The State Department thus considered the alternative of using a third sex designation.

VI. Given the existence of two reasons that are supported and three others that are unsupported, the State Department must reconsider its denial of Zzyym's application

We have concluded that (1) the State Department's first, fourth, and fifth reasons are unsupported and (2) the second and third reasons are supported. We have no

---

11. Only a few countries use the ICAO's "X/<" option even though it has been standardized for roughly 20 years. *See* Appellee's Supp. App'x at 57 (listing Australia, Bangladesh, Denmark, India, Malta, Nepal, and New Zealand as the only countries issuing passports in 2017 with a third sex designation).

way of knowing whether the State Department would still have relied on the binary sex policy if limited to the second and third reasons.

When an administrative decision rests on multiple grounds—some supported and some not—we must determine what the agency would have done had it recognized its errors. When an agency has indicated that its reasons were independent and one of the reasons was flawed, we have upheld the agency action. *Am. Fed'n of Gov't Emps. AFL-CIO, Local 2263 v. Fed. Labor Relations Auth.*, 454 F.3d 1101 (10th Cir. 2006). But we have never encountered a situation where we cannot tell whether the agency would have taken the same action if it had known that some justifications were unsupported.

. . . . [W]hen we review administrative decisions[,] we lack the power to "guess at the theory underlying the agency's action." *SEC v. Chenery Corp.*, 332 U.S. 194 (1947). If we can't determine whether the agency necessarily relied on deficient reasons, it would make little sense to uphold the agency's action. . . .

. . . . The State Department never said [whether] the State Department's five reasons were independent or [what] the State Department would have decided if it had not considered the inevitability of inaccuracies, surmised a lack of medical consensus, and assumed the infeasibility of a third sex designation.

It certainly appears that concern for accuracy was key to the State Department's decision. Congress has criminalized false information in a passport application, and the State Department separately requires applicants to truthfully answer every question on the application. In the face of a criminal penalty and regulatory requirement, we cannot simply assume that the State Department would have relied on the binary sex policy even after learning that it would create inaccuracies in passports.

These inaccuracies are inevitable because some people, like Zzyym, are indisputably intersex. But the State Department has not acknowledged the inherent inaccuracies that arise when applying the binary sex policy to these individuals.

Without this acknowledgment or an explanation for forcing indisputably intersex applicants to apply as either male or female, the State Department undermined the accuracy of Zzyym's identifying information and assumed without any evidence that an intersex designation would be too costly and lack a medical consensus.

At the same time, we differ with the district court as to the disposition. The district court concluded that the State Department lacked any supportable reasons to rely on the binary sex policy. We disagree. In our view, the State Department reasonably concluded that its policy matched how most jurisdictions identified an individual's sex, facilitating the State Department's assessment of eligibility for passports and other agencies' use of passport data. We thus [vacate] the district court's entry of judgment for Zzyym and the court's issuance of a permanent injunction against enforcement of the binary sex policy as to Zzyym and [remand] with instructions to vacate the State Department's decision and reconsider Zzyym's application for an intersex passport.[12]

Discussion

1. As alluded to earlier, Zzyym's supplemental complaint challenging the renewed denial of their passport application contains two counts alleging constitutional violations. *Zzyym v. Tillerson & Portell*, Supplemental Complaint for Declaratory, Injunctive and Other Relief, No. 1:15-cv-02362-RBJ (D. Colo. July 3, 2017).

Count VI of Zzyym's supplemental complaint alleges that the defendants violated Zzyym's substantive rights under the Fifth Amendment's Due Process Clause in two ways. First, Zzyym asserts that the "State Department's Decision and Binary-Only Gender Policy impermissibly infringe upon Plaintiff's fundamental right to movement, including Plaintiff's fundamental right to travel abroad." Second, Zzyym asserts that the "State Department's Decision and Binary-Only Gender Policy impermissibly interferes with the most intimate choices a person may make in a lifetime, including Plaintiff's right to existence and self-expression as a person who is neither male nor female." The government's actions must satisfy at least intermediate scrutiny and possibly strict scrutiny, Zzyym contends, but the actions in Zzyym's view "fail to serve even a legitimate governmental interest."

Count VII of the supplemental complaint charges that the government violated Zzyym's equal protection rights guaranteed against federal violation by the Fifth Amendment. In particular, Zzyym asserts that the defendants unconstitutionally discriminated in at least three ways. First, Zzyym asserts, "Defendants' Decision and Binary-Only Gender Policy discriminate against Plaintiff on the basis of sex, both facially and as applied, by barring Plaintiff from obtaining an accurate U.S. passport with a gender marker other than 'M' (male) or 'F' (female)," which Zzyym argues is sex discrimination both because it relies on sex-based considerations and because it is premised upon sex stereotyping. Second, Zzyym asserts, the defendants discriminated "based on their status as [a person] who cannot identify as male or female or their status as intersex with nonbinary gender," forms of discrimination for which the Supreme Court has not identified the proper level of equal protection scrutiny, though Zzyym argues that the defendants' actions cannot pass even rational basis review, the most lenient possible scrutiny. Third, relying on the same allegedly fundamental liberty interests invoked in Count VI of the complaint to trigger heightened equal protection scrutiny, Zzyym also asserts in Count VII that "Defendants discriminate against Plaintiff with respect to Plaintiff's access to the fundamental right to travel and freedom of movement without undue government

---

12. We express no opinion on whether the State Department's second and third reasons—in themselves—would justify the State Department's decision to require Zzyym to check either the male or female box on the application. The ultimate evaluation would require assessment of a different set of findings. Those findings would necessarily be based on the administrative record in existence when the State Department reconsiders its decision. *See* n.4, above.

restriction and fundamental liberty interests in individual dignity and autonomy, including Plaintiff's right to self-definition and privacy." Again, Zzyym argues that the defendants cannot pass strict or even intermediate scrutiny.

Are any or all of Zzyym's constitutional contentions persuasive? Consider to what extend the Supreme Court's reasoning about why discrimination based on transgender status necessarily involves discrimination on the basis of sex, *see Bostock v. Clayton County, Georgia*, 140 S. Ct. 1731 (2020), Chapter 5, Section D, *supra*, might lend support to Zzyym's equal protection challenge.

2. Jessica Clarke has suggested that "new" arguments on behalf of nonbinary people today "emphasize the liberty and autonomy of each individual with respect to gender," and "authenticity." Jessica A. Clarke, *They, Them, and Theirs*, 132 Harv. L. Rev. 894, 918 (2019). After discussing the trial court opinion in *Zzyym v. Pompeo*, she notes

> potential areas of divergence between feminist and nonbinary gender advocacy. Some feminists may be concerned that expanding the space outside binary gender will trade off with efforts to expand what it means to be a woman. Others may believe sex discrimination law should challenge only the most egregious forms of subordination of women, rather than pursuing the libertarian project of releasing all people from the straightjacket of gender. And others have criticized moves toward gender neutrality on the ground that, due to the unique forms of subordination experienced by people who were socialized as women, certain spaces or opportunities should be reserved for only those who were assigned female at birth.

Id. at 919. Are there ways to argue in favor of Dana Zzyym that would avoid these ostensible pitfalls? And are these criticisms all well taken, identifying things the law should indeed make effort to avoid?

Chapter 17

Marriage

For many people in the modern world, meeting a compatible partner, falling in love, and marrying is an important life goal. Society may indeed expect this in some countries, such as the United States. All countries allow couples to marry when they comprise a man and a woman—or, rather, when they comprise persons the country deems to be a man and a woman. For transgender people in many countries, the failure of the marriage laws to treat them as the sex consistent with their gender identity has barred them from what the couples understand as marrying heterosexually; that is, the law says that a transgender woman is in law male (as she was assigned at birth) and so cannot marry a man, and a transgender man is legally female (as he was assigned at birth) and so cannot marry a woman.

Although some religious denominations have allowed same-sex couples to marry for some time, modern nations did not begin allowing two people they regarded as being of the same sex to contract marriage until 2001, when the Netherlands allowed same-sex couples to marry civilly starting in April of that year. As of the writing of this book, close to 30 countries have eliminated the mixed-sex requirement for civil marriage nationwide. Prior to a country's so doing, and in the majority of countries in the world that have not made this change, whether a couple with one transgender member could marry depended on what sex that country's law (or the law of the relevant jurisdiction, be it a sub-unit such as a state in the United States or a super-unit such as the European Union) determined the transgender person's sex to be.

Marriage, thus, has been and still widely is a key site where law has had to grapple with its understanding of sex. Legal rights for (heterosexually identified) transgender people have in many cases depended on that. This has been acutely true in the United States, where the legal consequences of civil marriage are numerous (in contrast to many other Western nations that have deemphasized the differences in legal treatment between married and unmarried conjugal couples). A report of the General Accounting Office as it was then known determined that some 1,138 federal statutes made legal rights, privileges, or immunities turn upon a couple's status as civilly married or not. U.S. Gen. Accounting Office, Defense of Marriage Act: Update to Prior Report GAO-04-353R (Jan. 23, 2004). When transgender people's lived sex has been denied and their natally assigned sex declared governing, their seemingly heterosexual marriages have been declared invalid (as same-sex couplings outside the scope of civil marriage), with devastating consequences.

Transgender people have been denied the right to get married in the first place, or to seek alimony after what they thought was their marriage ended. They have been denied the right to sue for the wrongful death of their spouse on the grounds that they were never really legally married. They have had all their parental rights terminated in cases where children (in what they thought was their marriage) were born through assisted reproductive techniques.

Now in the United States, mixed-sex requirements for civil marriage imposed by the state or federal governments were ruled unconstitutional by the Supreme Court in *Obergefell v. Hodges*, 135 S. Ct. 2584 (2015); although the Court relied primarily on the substantive constitutional right to marry in *Obergefell*, its recent broad, "but-for causation" view of sex discrimination in the Title VII case *Bostock v. Clayton County, Georgia*, 140 S. Ct. 1731 (2020), Chapter 5, Section D, *supra*, would also support the sex discrimination challenge to the mixed-sex requirement for civil marriage that some of the *Obergefell* plaintiffs raised.[a] Yet until the advent of U.S. marriage equality, and in the many jurisdictions around the world where a mixed-sex requirement is still in place, marriage and marriage law have been and will remain important arenas for legal contestation over the meaning of sex, transgender identities, and the sphere of legal possibilities for transgender people.

This chapter proceeds historically, starting with *Corbett v. Corbett*, 2 All E.R. 33 (1970) (Eng.), a landmark English case denying the validity of a marriage between a transgender woman and a man whose sex went unquestioned, a case whose impact on marriage law has been widespread. It presents cases from many U.S. states, most of which have denied the validity of marriages involving transgender persons, though one early case involving marriage dissolution and post-divorce support obligations was a notable exception to the pattern (*see M.T v. J.T.*, 355 A.2d 204 (N.J. Super. Ct. App. Div. 1976), *infra* at p. 1190), as well as a 2002 decision from the European Court of Human Rights overruling several of its earlier non-recognition decisions and requiring the UK to let a transsexual woman marry a man (*see Goodwin v. United Kingdom*, 2002-VI Eur. Ct. H.R. 1. [ECHR 28957/95 (July 11, 2002)], *infra* at p. 1202). The chapter discusses some of the legal and practical problems for a jurisdiction like the United States, where the laws governing identification of a transgender person's sex vary among the states, and it highlights concerns (resonant

---

a. Indian tribes or nations in the United States are not directly governed by the U.S. Constitution and so there still remains variation in marriage eligibility under tribal laws. There is also some question whether a trans woman, for example, who prior to nationwide marriage equality in the U.S. married a cis man in a jurisdiction that did not regard the woman as legally female for marriage law purposes and that did not allow same-sex couples to marry, would have her marriage adjudged lawful, *see, e.g.,*, Julian N. Larry, *The Transgender Marriage Dilemma*, 33 Wis. J.L. GENDER & Soc'y 23 (2018), although the authors of this case book are of the view that the unconstitutionality of the state's laws at the time of the marriage ceremony is not vitiated simply because the Supreme Court had not yet decided *Obergefell*.

with some of the discussion in Chapter 14, *supra*) about the use of medical authority as the solution to state's insisting that people's sex is eternally whatever it was designated at birth.

Reading Guide for Corbett v. Corbett

1. The English decision in *Corbett v. Corbett* was decided by Sir Roger Fray Greenwood Ormrod, at the time a Judge of the Probate, Divorce and Admiralty Division, and later a British Lord Justice of Appeal on the Court of Appeals of England and Wales. Judge Ormrod had trained as a doctor prior to taking the bench, and his full opinion in *Corbett* lavished praise upon the medical experts who testified.

2. *Corbett* is a path-breaking decision regarding whether transsexual persons can legally marry as members of the sex consistent with their gender identity or only as members of their natally assigned sex, which matters in jurisdictions that limit civil marriage to different-sex couples. It has been expressly relied on in other cases denying transgender people the right to marry a person of the sex to which they had been identified as belonging at birth, including *Littleton v. Prange*, 9 S.W.3d 223 (Tex. App. 1999), *infra* at p. 1200, and *In re Estate of Gardiner*, 42 P.3d 120 (Kan. 2002) *infra* at p. 1215. As Alex Sharpe has insisted, "[i]t is important to consider *Corbett* not only because of its considerable impact on judicial thinking, but because it provides a context in which to both understand and gauge subsequent reform jurisprudence. . . ." Alex Sharpe, Transgender Jurisprudence: Dysphoric Bodies of Law 39 (2002).

3. Judge Ormrod rules that the marriage of Arthur Cameron Corbett and April Corbett née Ashley was void *ab initio*, granting the annulment sought by Arthur, because April was not legally female and England only allowed different-sex couples to marry at that time. What is the legal test he adopts for determining a person's sex for purposes of marriage? What reasons does he give for adopting that test? What is the factual basis for his concluding that April was not a woman under that test?

4. In an alternative holding, Judge Ormrod assumes for sake of argument that April and Arthur were lawfully married but treats the marriage as voidable (here, at Arthur's behest) for failure to "consummate" the marriage by engaging in penile-vaginal intercourse. (At common law, an unconsummated marriage was not void, and thus was valid as to third parties, but was voidable at the instance of either party.) He also indicates, in what may be dicta, that had he not accepted Arthur's account of the facts, wherein he and April did not consummate their marriage, he would be prepared to rule that intercourse between them would be legally ineffective to count as consummation. On what basis would he so rule?

Corbett v. Corbett (Otherwise Ashley)

[1971] P 83, [1970] 2 All ER 33, [1970] 2 WLR 1306, (48 MLR 82) (P.D.A.)

. . . .

Ormrod J. read the following judgment.

The petitioner in this case, Mr. Arthur Cameron Corbett, prays, in the first place, for a declaration that a ceremony of marriage which took place in Gibraltar on 10th September 1963 between himself and the respondent, then known as April Ashley, is null and void and of no effect because the respondent, at the time of the ceremony, was a person of the male sex. In the alternative, he alleges that the marriage was never consummated owing to the incapacity or wilful refusal of the respondent to consummate it, and asks for a decree of nullity. . . . [The] respondent pleaded that the petitioner was estopped from alleging that the marriage was void and of no effect or, alternatively, that in the exercise of its discretionary jurisdiction to make declaratory orders, the court, in all the circumstances of this case, ought to refuse to grant the petitioner the declaration prayed for in the prayer to the petition.

. . . .

The case resolves itself into the primary issue of the validity of the marriage, which depends on the true sex of the respondent; and the secondary issue of the incapacity of the parties, or their respective willingness or unwillingness, to consummate the marriage, if there was a marriage to consummate. . . .

. . . . The respondent was born on 29th April 1935 in Liverpool and registered at birth as a boy . . . , and brought up as a boy. It has not been suggested at any time in this case that there was any mistake over the sex of the child. In 1951, at the age of 16 years, he joined the Merchant Navy. Before being accepted, the respondent had what she (I shall use "he" and "she" and "his" and "her" throughout this judgment as seems convenient in the context) described in cross-examination as a "vague medical examination," and was accepted. . . . [Respondent] did one and a half voyages as a merchant seaman before . . . [h]e was subsequently returned to this country and became a patient at Ormskirk Hospital. . . . [In] January 1953, at the age of 17, he was referred by his general practitioner to the psychiatric department of the Walton Hospital, Liverpool, where he came under the care of Dr. Vaillant, the consultant psychiatrist. . . . Dr. Vaillant gave evidence under a subpoena issued on behalf of the petitioner, and produced the hospital records which showed that the respondent had been physically examined by one of Dr. Vaillant's assistants and that no abnormality had been observed other than that he presented a "womanish appearance" and had "little bodily and facial hair." . . . . After some six months' treatment, the doctor who had been treating the respondent under Dr. Vaillant's supervision reported his conclusions to the general practitioner in a letter dated 5th June 1953, which reads in part as follows:

> This boy is a constitutional homosexual who says he wants to become a
> woman. He has had numerous homosexual experiences and his homo-

sexuality is at the root of his depression. On examination, apart from his womanish appearance, there was no abnormal finding.

. . . .

. . . [I]n 1956, he went to the south of France, where he met the members of a well-known troupe of male female impersonators, normally based at the Carousel night club in Paris, and later himself became a member of the troupe. By this time, on any view of the evidence, the respondent was taking the female sex hormone, oestrogen, regularly, to encourage the development of the breasts and of a feminine type of physique. At that stage he was known as "Toni/April."

. . . . After about four years at the Carousel night club, he was introduced to a certain Dr. Burou who practised at Casablanca, and, on 11th May 1960, he underwent, at Dr. Burou's hands, a so called "sex-change operation," which consisted in the amputation of the testicles and most of the scrotum, and the construction of a so-called "artificial vagina," by making an opening in front of the anus, and turning in the skin of the penis after removing the muscle and other tissues from it, to form a pouch or cavity occupying approximately the position of the vagina in a female, that is between the bladder and the rectum. Parts of the scrotum were used to produce an approximation in appearance to female external genitalia. I have been at some pains to avoid the use of emotive expressions such as "castration" and "artificial vagina" without the qualification "so-called," because the association of ideas connected with these words or phrases are so powerful that they tend to cloud clear thinking. It is, I think, preferable to use the terminology of Miss Josephine Barnes, who examined the respondent as one of the medical inspectors in this case. She described the respondent as having a "cavity which opened on to the perineum." . . . .

Following the operation, the respondent returned to London, now calling herself April Ashley, and dressing and living as a female. In evidence she stated that, after the operation, she had had sexual relations with at least one man, using the artificial cavity quite successfully. In November 1960, about six months after the operation, the petitioner and the respondent met for the first time. . . . He said [in court] that he had had sexual relations with a large number of women before his first marriage, and with others, both during it, and after it was dissolved in 1962. He also described his sexual deviations. From a comparatively early age, he had experienced a desire to dress up in female clothes. In the early stages of his marriage he had done so in the presence of his wife on a few occasions. Subsequently, he had dressed as a woman four or five times a year, keeping it from his wife, but the urge to do so continued. With considerable insight he said "I didn't like what I saw. You want the fantasy to appear right. It utterly failed to appear right in my eyes." These remarks are highly relevant to the understanding of the human aspects of this unusual case. From about 1948 onwards his interest in transvestism increased; . . . gradually he began to make contact with people of similar tendencies and associated with them from time to time in London. This led to frequent homosexual behaviour with numerous men, stopping short of anal intercourse. As time went on he became more and more involved in the society of sexual deviants, and interested in sexual deviations of all kinds. In this world he became familiar with its ramifications and its personalities, amongst whom he heard of Toni/April as a female impersonator at the Carousel, which he described as "the Mecca of every female impersonator in the world." Eventually, through an American transvestite known as "Louise," he got in touch with the respondent and they met for the first time on 19th November 1960 at his invitation for lunch at the Caprice restaurant. The petitioner's description of this first meeting contains the key to the rest of this essentially pathetic, but almost incredible story. By this time he was aware that April Ashley, as she was now calling herself, had been a man and had undergone a so-called "sex-change operation." When he first saw her he could not believe it. He said he was mesmerised by her. "This was so much more than I could ever hope to be. The reality was far greater than my fantasy." In cross-examination he put the same thought in these words, "It far outstripped any fantasy for myself. I could never have contemplated it for myself."

. . . . After the meeting in November 1960 they saw more and more of each other, meeting daily and sometimes twice a day. He had originally introduced himself to her under an assumed name but soon disclosed his real identity. . . . According to the petitioner, his original motive in seeking an introduction to the respondent was essentially transvestite in character, but quite soon he developed for her the interest of a man for a woman. He said that she looked like a woman, dressed like a woman and acted like a woman. He disclosed his true identity to the respondent to show that his feelings had become those of a full man in love with a girl, not those of a transvestite in love with a transsexual. He repeatedly said that he looked on the respondent as a woman and was attracted to her as a woman. On the other hand, it is common ground that, before the ceremony of marriage, nearly three years later, there was no sexual activity in a physical sense between them at all of any kind, although there was the most ample opportunity. At the most, their relationship went no further than kissing and some very mild petting. At no time did the respondent permit the petitioner to handle her naked breasts or any part of her body. . . . Listening to each party describing this strange relationship, my principal impression was that it had little or nothing in common with any heterosexual relationship which I could recall hearing about in a fairly extensive experience of this court. I also think that it would be very unwise to attempt to assess the respondent's feminine characteristics by the impression which the petitioner says she made on him. While I accept his account of his sexual experience from a qualitative point of view, I am sceptical [sic] about the quantity of it, but I have no difficulty in concluding that he is a man who is extremely prone to all kinds of sexual fantasies and practices. . . .

By September 1961, the situation between the petitioner and his wife had become impossible owing to his obsession with the respondent, and a separation was arranged. In the meanwhile, with his assistance, she had changed her name to April Ashley . . . and obtained a passport in that name. Attempts . . . to change her birth certificate, however, failed. At some stage after the operation, the Ministry of

National Insurance issued her with a woman's insurance card, and now treat her as a woman for national insurance purposes. During 1961, she worked successfully as a female model, until the press got hold of the story and gave it wide publicity. Later that year the petitioner decided to live in Spain and bought a villa and a night club . . . at Marbella. . . . After his wife obtained a decree absolute in June 1962, ... [i]n July 1963, the petitioner took the first steps about a marriage. He consulted a lawyer in Gilbraltar about it and discussed financial arrangements with the respondent.

. . .

After the ceremony, they returned to the villa at Marbella where some sexual approach was made by the petitioner. It is, however, common ground that the respondent then said that she was suffering from 'abscesses' in her so-called vagina and the subject was dropped, and they continued to sleep apart . . . for the next three or four nights. She then left for London as had been previously arranged. . . . [H]e went to London on about 4th October 1963 and stayed about a week in a flat with her. There is a direct conflict of evidence as to what happened sexually between them at this period. He says that she continued to complain of the abscesses. She says that they had cleared up and that they slept together, and that on several occasions he succeeded in penetrating her fully, but immediately gave up, saying "I can't, I can't" and withdrew without ejaculation, and burst into tears. On 12th October, the petitioner returned to Spain; the respondent . . . remained in London until early December, when she joined him at the villa. . . . After about three days, the respondent suddenly packed her suitcases and, immediately and without warning, left for London. This was the end of their relationship. They had been together for no more than 14 days in all since the so-called marriage. . . .

. . . . [O]n 16th February 1966, the respondent's solicitors issued an originating summons under §22 of the Matrimonial Causes Act 1965 claiming maintenance. . . . The . . . proceedings reached the stage of filing affidavits of means but got no further. The petitioner did not challenge the validity of the marriage in his affidavit but eventually, on 15th May 1967, filed his petition in this suit.

I now turn to the medical evidence and will begin by reading the report and the supplementary report of the medical inspectors to the court, Mr Leslie Williams, FRCS, FRCOG, and Miss Josephine Barnes, DM, FRCS, FRCOG:

> "We, the undersigned, appointed by the High Court Medical Inspectors in the above cause, have . . . examined the sexual organs of April Corbett (otherwise Ashley) the respondent. We find that the breasts are well developed though the nipples are of masculine type. The voice is rather low pitched. There are almost no penile remains and there is a normally placed urethal [*sic*] orifice. The vagina is of ample size to admit a normal and erect penis. The walls are skin covered and moist. There is no impediment on "her part" to sexual intercourse. Rectal examination does not reveal any uterus or ovaries or testicles. There is no scar on the thigh indicating where

a skin graft might have been taken. We strongly suggest. . . . that an investigation into "her" chromosomal sex be carried out by some expert such as Prof. Paul Polani, Dept. of Paediatric Research, Guys Hospital, London.

. . . .

"Supplementary Report

"April Corbett the respondent was examined . . . by Miss Josephine Barnes and Mr. Leslie Williams. April Corbett had had an operation for the construction of an artificial vagina and the surgical result was remarkably good. It may be noted that the normal vagina is lined by skin which is moistened by mucoid secretion from the cervix uteri. The artificial vagina in this case also appeared to be lined with skin and it was moist presumably owing to the presence of sweat glands in the skin used to line the artificial vagina. The suggestion in the first report that a chromosome test should be done was because the result of such a test would be one means of making our factual information about the case more complete."

. . . .

The suggested investigation into the respondent's "chromosomal sex" . . . . was carried out by Professor [Hayhoe] of Cambridge who reported, on 31st October 1968, that all the cells which he examined were of the male type.

The expert witnesses called by the petitioner were Professor C J Dewhurst, FRCSE, FRCOG, Professor of Obstetrics and Gynaecology at Queen Charlotte's Hospital; Professor Dent, MD, FRS, FRCP, Professor of Human Metabolism at University College Hospital; and Dr. J B Randell, MD, FRCP, DPM, consultant psychiatrist at Charing Cross Hospital. Professor Dewhurst is the co-author of a book called *The Intersexual Disorders*; and is particularly interested in cases which exhibit anomalies in the development of the sex organs. Dr. Randell has made a special study of individuals with abnormal psychological attitudes in sexual matters, particularly transvestites and transsexuals. He and Professor Dewhurst are working together with a plastic surgeon in a team which is studying the treatment of transsexuals by operations similar in character to that which was performed on the respondent by Dr. Burou. The experts called by the respondent were Dr. Armstrong, MD, FRCP, consultant physician at Newcastle Royal Infirmary; Professor Ivor Mills, FRCP, Professor of Medicine at Cambridge; and Professor Roth who is Professor of Psychiatry in the University of Newcastle-on-Tyne. Dr. Armstrong has written a number of papers on sex and gender problems and is co-editor of a well-known book *Intersexuality in Vertebrates including Man*. Professor Mills is particularly interested in endocrinology as applied to cases showing various kinds of sex anomalies, that is, in the study of the chemical substances produced by the sex organs and other tissues in the body, and of their effects in the individual patient. Professor Roth has considerable experience of the psychological aspects of such cases.

. . . .

There was general agreement among all the doctors on the basic principles and the fundamental scientific facts. . . . Two kinds of psychological abnormality are recognised, the transvestite and the transsexual. The transvestite is an individual (nearly, if not always a man) who has an intense desire to dress up in the clothes of the opposite sex. This is intermittent in character and is not accompanied by a corresponding urge to live as or pass as a member of the opposite sex at all times. Transvestite males are usually heterosexual, often married, and have no wish to cease to play the male role in sexual activity. The transsexual, on the other hand, has an extremely powerful urge to become a member of the opposite sex to the fullest extent which is possible. . . . As a result of the publicity which has been given from time to time to so-called "sex-change operations," many of them go to extreme lengths to importune doctors to perform such operations on them. . . . [S]ome serious-minded and responsible doctors are inclining to the view that such operations may provide the only way of relieving the psychological distress. . . . The purpose of these operations is, of course, to help to relieve the patient's symptoms and to assist in the management of their disorder; it is not to change their patient's sex, and, in fact, they require their patients before operation to sign a form of consent which is in these terms:

> "I ___ of ___ do consent to undergo the removal of the male genital organs and fashioning of an artificial vagina as explained to me by ___ (surgeon). I understand it will not alter my male sex and that it is being done to prevent deterioration in my mental health."

. . . .

. . . . On this part of the evidence my conclusion is that the respondent is correctly described as a male transsexual, possibly with some comparatively minor physical abnormality.

I must now deal with the anatomical and physiological anomalies of the sex organs, although I think that this part of the evidence is of marginal significance only in the present case. In other cases, it may be of cardinal importance. All the medical witnesses accept that there are, at least, four criteria for assessing the sexual condition of an individual. These are—

> (i) Chromosomal factors.

> (ii) Gonadal factors (*i.e.* presence or absence of testes or ovaries).

> (iii) Genital factors (including internal sex organs).

> (iv) Psychological factors.

Some of the witnesses would add—

> (v) Hormonal factors or secondary sexual characteristics (such as distribution of hair, breast development, physique etc. which are thought to reflect the balance between the male and female sex hormones in the body).

It is important to note that these criteria have been evolved by doctors for the purpose of systematising medical knowledge, and assisting in the difficult task of deciding the best way of managing the unfortunate patients who suffer, either physically or psychologically, from sexual abnormalities. As Professor Dewhurst observed "We do not determine sex — in medicine we determine the sex in which it is best for the individual to live." These criteria are, of course, relevant to, but do not necessarily decide, the legal basis of sex determination.

. . . .

My conclusions of fact on this part of the case can be summarised . . . as follows. The respondent has been shown to have XY chromosomes and, therefore, to be of male chromosomal sex; to have had testicles prior to the operation and, therefore, to be of male gonadal sex; to have had male external genitalia without any evidence of internal or external female sex organs and, therefore, to be of male genital sex; and psychologically to be a transsexual. The evidence does not establish that she is a case of Klinefelter's syndrome or some similar [intersex] condition of partial testicular failure, although the possibility of some abnormality in androgenisation at puberty cannot be excluded. Socially, by which I mean the manner in which the respondent is living in the community, she is living as, and passing as, a woman more or less successfully. Her outward appearance, at first sight, was convincingly feminine, but on closer and longer examination in the witness box it was much less so. The voice, manner, gestures and attitude became increasingly reminiscent of the accomplished female impersonator. The evidence of the medical inspectors, and of the other doctors who had an opportunity during the trial of examining the respondent clinically, is that the body, in its post-operative condition, looks more like a female than a male as a result of very skilful [sic] surgery. Professor Dewhurst, after this examination, put his opinion in these words — "the pastiche of feminity [sic] was convincing." That, in my judgment, is an accurate description of the respondent. It is common ground between all the medical witnesses that the biological sexual constitution of an individual is fixed at birth (at the latest), and cannot be changed, either by the natural development of organs of the opposite sex, or by medical or surgical means. The respondent's operation, therefore, cannot affect her true sex. The only cases where the term "change of sex" is appropriate are those in which a mistake as to sex is made at birth and subsequently revealed by further medical investigation.

. . . . Counsel for the respondent. . . . submitted . . . that "assignment" was a matter for the individual and his doctor, and that the law ought to accept it as determining his sex. The word "assign," although it is used by doctors in this context, is apt to mislead since, in fact, it means no more than that the doctors decide the gender, rather than the sex, in which such patients can best be managed and advise accordingly. It was also suggested that it was illogical to treat the respondent as a woman for many social purposes, such as nursing her in a female ward in hospital, or national insurance, and not to regard her as a woman for the purpose of marriage. These submissions are very far-reaching and would lead to some surprising results in practice but, before examining them in detail, I must consider the problems of law which arise in this case on a broader basis.

It appears to be the first occasion on which a court in England has been called on to decide the sex of an individual and, consequently, there is no authority which is directly in point. This absence of authority is, at first sight, surprising, but is explained, I think, by two fairly recent events, the development of the technique of the operation for vagino-plasty, and its application to the treatment of male transsexuals; and the decision of the Court of Appeal in *S v S (otherwise W) (No 2)*, [1962] 3 All ER 55, [1963] P 37, in which it was held that a woman, suffering from a congenital defect of the vagina, was not incapable of consummating her marriage because the length of the vagina could be increased surgically so as to permit full penetration. There are passages in the judgments which seem to go so far as holding that an individual, born without a vagina at all, could be rendered capable of consummating a marriage by the construction of an entirely artificial one. But for this decision, the respondent would have had no defence to the prayer for a decree of nullity on the ground of incapacity. Until this decision, all matrimonial cases arising out of developmental abnormalities of the reproductive system could be dealt with as cases of incapacity, and, therefore, it has not been necessary to call in question the true sex of the respondents, assuming that it had occurred to any pleader to raise this issue. Now that it has been raised, this case is unlikely to be the last in which the courts will be called on to investigate and decide it. I must, therefore, approach the matter as one of principle.

The fundamental purpose of law is the regulation of the relations between persons, and between persons and the State or community. For the limited purposes of this case, legal relations can be classified into those in which the sex of the individuals concerned is either irrelevant, relevant or an essential determinant of the nature of the relationship. Over a very large area the law is indifferent to sex. It is irrelevant to most of the relationships which give rise to contractual or tortious rights and obligations, and to the greater part of the criminal law. In some contractual relationships, *e.g.* life assurance and pensions schemes, sex is a relevant factor in determining the rate of premium or contributions. It is relevant also to some aspects of the law regulating conditions of employment, and to various State-run schemes such as national insurance, or to such fiscal matters as selective employment tax. It is not an essential determinant of the relationship in these cases because there is nothing to prevent the parties to a contract of insurance or a pension scheme from agreeing that the person concerned should be treated as a man or as a woman, as the case may be. Similarly, the authorities, if they think fit, can agree with the individual that he shall be treated as a woman for national insurance purposes, as in this case. On the other hand, sex is clearly an essential determinant of the relationship called marriage, because it is and always has been recognised as the union of man and woman. It is the institution on which the family is built, and in which the capacity for natural heterosexual intercourse is an essential element. It has, of course, many other characteristics, of which companionship and mutual support is an important one, but the characteristics which distinguish it from all other relationships can only be met by two persons of opposite sex. There are some other relationships such as adultery, rape and gross indecency in which, by definition, the sex of the participants is an essential determinant: see *Rayden on Divorce*, *Dennis v Dennis*, and the Sexual Offences Act 1956, §§ 1 and 13.

Since marriage is essentially a relationship between man and woman, the validity of the marriage in this case depends, in my judgment, on whether the respondent is or is not a woman. . . . The question then becomes what is meant by the word "woman" in the context of a marriage, for I am not concerned to determine the "legal sex" of the respondent at large. Having regard to the essentially heterosexual character of the relationship which is called marriage, the criteria must, in my judgment, be biological, for even the most extreme degree of transsexualism in a male or the most severe hormonal imbalance which can exist in a person with male chromosomes, male gonads and male genitalia cannot reproduce a person who is naturally capable of performing the essential role of a woman in marriage. In other words, the law should adopt, in the first place, the first three of the doctors' criteria, *i.e.* the chromosomal, gonadal and genital tests, and, if all three are congruent, determine the sex for the purpose of marriage accordingly, and ignore any operative intervention. The real difficulties, of course, will occur if these three criteria are not congruent. This question does not arise in the present case and I must not anticipate, but it would seem to me to follow from what I have said that greater weight would probably be given to the genital criteria than to the other two. This problem and, in particular, the question of the effect of surgical operations in such cases of physical inter-sex, must be left until it comes for decision. My conclusion, therefore, is that the respondent is not a woman for the purposes of marriage but is a biological male and has been so since birth. It follows that the so-called marriage of 10th September 1963 is void.

. . . . If the law were to recognise the "assignment" of the respondent to the female sex, the question which would have to be answered is, what was the respondent's sex immediately before the operation? If the answer is that it depends on "assignment" then, if the decision at that time was female, the respondent would be a female with male sex organs and no female ones. If the assignment to the female sex is made after the operation, then the operation has changed the sex. From this it would follow that if a 50 year old male transsexual, married and the father of children, underwent the operation, he would then have to be regarded in law as a female, and capable of "marrying" a man! The results would be nothing if not bizarre. I have dealt, by implication, with the submission that, because the respondent is treated by society for many purposes as a woman, it is illogical to refuse to treat her as a woman for the purpose of marriage. The illogicality would only arise if marriage were substantially similar in character to national insurance and other social situations, but the differences are obviously fundamental. These submissions, in effect, confuse sex with gender. Marriage is a relationship which depends on sex and not on gender.

I now turn to the secondary issue of incapacity or wilful refusal to consummate the marriage, assuming for this purpose that the marriage is valid and that the respondent is to be treated as, or deemed to be, a woman. . . . I was . . . impressed by the petitioner's frankness in dealing with his letter written on 26th October 1964. . . .

I . . . accept his evidence that the respondent evaded the issue of sexual relations, and that he did not press it believing that this aspect of the marriage would come right in the end. . . . In any event, however, I would, if necessary, be prepared to hold that the respondent was physically incapable of consummating a marriage because I do not think that sexual intercourse, using the completely artificial cavity constructed by Dr. Burou, can possibly be described in the words of Dr. Lushington in *D.E. v A.G. (falsely calling herself D.E.),* (1845) 1 Rob Eccl 279, as "ordinary and complete intercourse" or as "vera copula" — of the natural. When such a cavity has been constructed in a male, the difference between sexual intercourse using it, and anal or intra-crural intercourse is, in my judgment, to be measured in centimetres.

I am aware that this view is not in accordance with some of the observations of the Court of Appeal in *S v S (otherwise W) (No 2),* but, in my respectful opinion, those parts of the judgments which refer to a wholly artificial vagina, go beyond what was necessary for the decision in that case and should be regarded as *obiter.* The respondent in that case was assumed to be a woman, with functioning ovaries, but with a congenital abnormality of the vagina, which was only about two inches long and small in diameter, according to the report of the medical inspectors. This is a very different situation from the one which confronts me. There are, I think, certain dangers in attempting to analyse too meticulously the essentials of normal sexual intercourse. . . .

The mischief is that, by over-refining and over-defining the limits of "normal," one may, in the end, produce a situation in which consummation may come to mean something altogether different from normal sexual intercourse. . . .

. . . I hold that it has been established that the respondent is not, and was not, a woman at the date of the ceremony of marriage, but was, at all times, a male. The marriage is, accordingly, void, and it only remains to consider the pleas raised by the reamended answer of estoppel or, alternatively, that the court should, in its discretion, withhold a declaration; and the proper form of the order in which my judgment should be recorded. . . . Here the alleged estoppel is an estoppel *in pais* or by conduct. I am content to follow the decision of Phillimore J in *Hayward v Hayward,* in which he held that the doctrine of estoppel was not applicable in proceedings for a declaration that a marriage was void, and that, in any event, no estoppel *in pais* could arise in that case, as in this, because the relevant facts were known equally to both parties. The suggestion that a ceremony, which is wholly ineffectual and void in law, can be rendered effectual between the actual parties by some species of estoppel, would produce the anomalous result that any third party, whose interests are affected by this "marriage," could at any time successfully challenge its validity, relying on the admissions in the evidence given before me. This defence accordingly fails. . . .

The petitioner, is therefore, entitled, in my judgment, to a decree of nullity declaring that the marriage in fact celebrated on 10th September 1963 between himself and the respondent was void *ab initio.*

Disposition:

Decree of nullity to petitioner.

Discussion

1. What untoward consequence(s) does Judge Ormrod fear would follow if he ruled that a transsexual woman such as April were legally female for purposes of marriage law? Can you identify any similar untoward consequences that might follow from ruling that such a transsexual woman is *not* legally female for marriage law purposes?

2. Judge Ormrod's opinion might be read to suggest that the sex of intersex persons who wish to marry should be primarily determined by their genitals, but that the sex for marriage purposes of a transsexual person without an intersex condition (likely such as April) who wishes to marry cannot depend upon her having a vagina rather than a penis. He also seems to countenance that a person with an intersex condition might be able to consummate a marriage using a surgically extended or perhaps surgically created vagina, but a transgender person cannot. Are those distinctions justified?

3. Note that Judge Ormrod seems to endorse a notion that David B. Cruz in teaching and lecturing has termed "variable sex"—that the sex of a person for purposes of a law that turns on sex depends on the purposes of the particular law at issue, so that a person might be of one sex for one purpose (such as a national health insurance card) and a different sex for a different legal purpose (such as different-sex-only marriage). Thus, at the macro level, Ormrod might be understood to embrace "law's consequentialist nature and the instrumental ways in which laws deploy identity." David B. Cruz, *Sexual Judgments: Full Faith and Credit and the Relational Character of Legal Sex*, 46 Harv. C.R.-C.L. L. Rev. 51, 62 (2011). But if this is so, what could it be about civil marriage that makes inappropriate a more thoroughly instrumentalist focus on the functions of (different-sex) marriage, the functions of legal "sex" for different-sex marriage, and the actual effects on real people's lives of deeming a transsexual woman to be male for marriage law?

4. Ormrod insists that "sex," as distinguished from "gender," is essential to marriage. But since the marriage of a sterile person who is incapable of reproducing is not void but only voidable, and hence valid so long as the parties wish to remain valid, it would seem odd to say "sex" for procreative purposes is *essential* to marriage. Is there any other sense in which sex, in the sense of "the biological sexual constitution" of a person, might be judged "essential" to marriage?

5. *Corbett* has long been subject to great scholarly criticism. One of the authors of this casebook has lamented its "unfortunate biologism," David B. Cruz, *Getting Sex "Right": Heteronormativity and Biologism in Trans and Intersex Marriage Litigation and Scholarship*, 18 Duke J. Gender L. & Pol'y 203, 204 (2010), and describes some of the many other critiques of the decision, *see id.* at 211 n.8 (citing as examples

and providing specific critical pages in Richard F. Storrow, *Naming the Grotesque Body in the "Nascent Jurisprudence of Transsexualism,"* 4 MICH. J. GENDER & L. 275 (1997); Mary Coombs, *Sexual Dis-Orientation: Transgendered People and Same-Sex Marriage*, 8 UCLA WOMEN'S L.J. 219 (1998); Leslie I. Lax, Note, *Is the United States Falling Behind? The Legal Recognition of Post-Operative Transsexuals' Acquired Sex in the United States and Abroad*, 7 QUINNIPIAC HEALTH L.J. 123 (2003); Helen G. Berrigan, *Transsexual Marriage: A Trans-Atlantic Judicial Dialogue*, 12 L. & SEXUALITY REV.: LESBIAN, GAY, BISEXUAL, & TRANSGENDER LEGAL ISSUES 87 (2003); Mark Strasser, *Harvesting the Fruits of* Gardiner: *On Marriage, Public Policy, and Fundamental Interests*, 71 GEO. WASH. L. REV. 179 (2003); Terry S. Kogan, *Transsexuals, Intersexuals, and Same-Sex Marriage*, 18 BYU J. PUB. L. 371 (2004); Briana Lynn Morgan, Note, *The Use of Rules and Standards to Define a Transsexual's Sex for the Purpose of Marriage: An Argument for a Hybrid Approach*, 55 HASTINGS L.J. 1329 (2004); Katrina C. Rose, *A History of Gender Variance in Pre-20th Century Anglo-American Law*, 14 TEX. J. WOMEN & L. 77 (2004); Marybeth Herald, *Transgender Theory: Reprogramming Our Automated Settings*, 28 T. JEFFERSON L. REV. 167 (2005).

Reading Guide for M.T. v. J.T.

1. New York courts in the early 1970s were not particularly receptive to claims that a transgender person had civilly married as a member of the sex consistent with their gender identity. *Anonymous v. Anonymous*, 67 Misc. 2d 982, 325 N.Y.S.2d 499 (Sup. Ct. 1971), and *B v. B*, 78 Misc. 2d 112 (Sup. Ct. 1974), denied the validity of one putative marriage involving a transgender woman and one involving a transgender man. In *Anonymous v. Anonymous*, the transgender woman had not had genitoplasty at the time of her putative marriage to a presumably cisgender man, which the court held to be a void attempted marriage between a same-sex couple. In *B. v. B.*, the court declared void the purported marriage of a transgender man who had not had phalloplasty to a presumably cisgender woman, seemingly in reliance on *Anonymous*.

Not all courts were so willing to invalidate seemingly heterosexual marriages of transgender persons. The following mid-1970s decision by a New Jersey court provides a contrast to *Anonymous* and *B*. How does the court frame the controlling legal issue in the case?

2. The appellate court in this case recounts numerous facts, including medical opinions, about transgender woman M.T.'s identity and anatomy. Which, if any, of them appear to play a direct role in the court's legal analysis of the issue of the validity of her marriage to J.T.?

3. What reasons does the court give for choosing not to follow *Corbett v. Corbett*? Are they persuasive?

4. What test should we understand the court to adopt for determining the sex of a transgender person for purposes of New Jersey marriage law (which limited marriage at the time to different-sex couples)?

M.T. v. J.T.

355 A.2d 204 (N.J. Super. Ct. App. Div. 1976)

Before Judges CARTON, CRAHAY and HANDLER.

Opinion

The opinion of the court was delivered by HANDLER, J.A.D.

This appeal presents the portentous problem of how to tell the sex of a person for marital purposes. Involved is a postoperative transsexual, born a male but now claiming to be a female.

The case started inauspiciously enough when plaintiff M.T. filed a simple complaint in the Juvenile and Domestic Relations Court for support and maintenance. The legal issue sharpened dramatically when defendant J.T. interposed the defense that M.T. was a male and that their marriage was void. Following a hearing the trial judge determined that plaintiff was a female and that defendant was her husband, and there being no fraud, ordered defendant to pay plaintiff $50 a week support. Notice of appeal was then filed by defendant.

. . . . M.T. testified that she was born a male. While she knew that she had male sexual organs she did not know whether she also had female organs. As a youngster she did not participate in sports and at an early age became very interested in boys. At the age of 14 she began dressing in a feminine manner and later began dating men. She had no real adjustment to make because throughout her life she had always felt that she was a female.

Plaintiff first met defendant in 1964 and told him about her feelings about being a woman. Sometime after that she began to live with defendant. In 1970 she started to go to Dr. Charles L. Ihlenfeld to discuss the possibility of having an operation so that she could "be physically a woman." In 1971, upon the doctor's advice, she went to a surgeon who agreed to operate. In May of that year she underwent surgery for the removal of male sex organs and construction of a vagina. Defendant paid for the operation. Plaintiff then applied to the State of New York to have her birth certificate changed.

On August 11, 1972, over a year after the operation, plaintiff and defendant went through a ceremonial marriage in New York State and then moved to Hackensack. They lived as husband and wife and had intercourse. Defendant supported plaintiff for over two years when, in October 1974, he left their home. He has not supported plaintiff since.

Dr. Ihlenfeld, plaintiff's medical doctor with a specialty in gender identity, was accepted as an expert in the field of medicine and transsexualism. A transsexual, in the opinion of this expert, was "a person who discovers sometime, usually very early in life, that there is a great discrepancy between the physical genital anatomy and the person's sense of self-identity as a male or as a female. * * * [T]he transsexual is one who has a conflict between physical anatomy and psychological identity or psychological sex." Usually sexual anatomy was "normal" but for some reason transsexuals did not see themselves as members of the sex their anatomy seemed to indicate. According to Dr. Ihlenfeld, there are different theories to explain the origin of that conflict. There was, however, "very little disagreement" on the fact that gender identity generally is established "very, very firmly, almost immediately, by the age of 3 to 4 years." . . . .

. . . . [M.T.] wanted sex reassignment surgery as well as treatments and hormones so that she could end the conflict she was feeling, "confronted with a male body," in order to live her life completely as the woman she thought herself to be. Dr. Ihlenfeld diagnosed her as a transsexual. He knew of no way to alter her sense of her own feminine gender identity in order to agree with her male body, and the only treatment available to her was to alter the body to conform with her sense of psyche [sic] gender identity. That regimen consisted of hormone treatment and sex reassignment surgery. Dr. Ihlenfeld recommended such an operation and treated plaintiff both before and after it.

The examination of plaintiff before the operation showed that she had a penis, scrotum and testicles. After the operation she did not have those organs but had a vagina and labia which were "adequate for sexual intercourse" and could function as any female vagina, that is, for "traditional penile/vaginal intercourse." . . . . Plaintiff had no uterus or cervix, but her vagina had a "good cosmetic appearance" and was "the same as a normal female vagina after a hysterectomy." . . . . So far as [the doctor] knew, no one had tested plaintiff to find out what chromosomes she had. He knew that plaintiff had had silicone injections in her breasts; he had treated her continuously with female hormones to demasculinize her body and to feminize it at the same time. In the doctor's opinion plaintiff was a female; he no longer considered plaintiff to be a male since she could not function as a male sexually either for purposes of "recreation or procreation."

Plaintiff also produced Charles Annicello, a psychologist who worked at the gender identity clinic of the Johns Hopkins University Hospital. He was qualified as an expert in transsexualism. . . . The witness said that transsexualism represented only one sexual variant although it was not known whether its cause was chromosomal, gonadal, or hormonal. Annicello expressed the opinion that if a person had a female psychic gender and underwent a sex reassignment operation, that person would be considered female although no person is "absolutely" male or female.

Dr. Richard M. Samuels, a Ph.D. with a specialty in behavioral therapy and sexual dysfunctions, testified as an expert in psychology as it related to transsexualism. . . . Some psychological changes are noted following a sex reassignment operation. Thus, a transsexual was often depressed preoperatively, but after the operation he or she lived a "fuller and richer life" and was better able to overcome obstacles in employment, housing, social security and welfare benefits; a sense of satisfaction and relief was felt since the body was now in line with the psyche. For Dr. Samuels the most important factor in determining whether a person should have a sex reassignment operation was how consistently the patient lived in the chosen gender role.

A sex reassignment operation did not determine a person's gender. After a transsexual underwent a sex reassignment operation to remove male organs, Dr. Samuels would characterize that person as a female.

Defendant called as an expert witness Dr. T, a medical doctor who was defendant's adoptive father. Over plaintiff's objection he was allowed to testify as an expert. Dr. T classified sex at birth according to sexual anatomy. . . . The witness had heard all of the prior testimony and he said that in his opinion plaintiff was still a male because she did not have female organs. . . . On cross-examination Dr. T reiterated that it was the anatomy alone which determined the real sex of an individual and that gender in contrast to sex was not a significant factor. . . .

The trial judge. . . . noted that defendant knew of [M.T.'s] condition and cooperated in her sex reassignment surgery. The parties married in New York and subsequently consummated their marriage by engaging in sexual intercourse. The judge also found that defendant later deserted plaintiff and failed to support her.

. . . . The judge. . . . stated:

> It is the opinion of the court that if the psychological choice of a person is medically sound, not a mere whim, and irreversible sex reassignment surgery has been performed, society has no right to prohibit the transsexual from leading a normal life. Are we to look upon this person as an exhibit in a circus side show? What harm has said person done to society? The entire area of transsexualism is repugnant to the nature of many persons within our society. However, this should not govern the legal acceptance of a fact.
> * * *

. . . .

The issue must then be confronted whether the marriage between a male and a postoperative transsexual, who has surgically changed her external sexual anatomy from male to female, is to be regarded as a lawful marriage between a man and a woman.

An English case, *Corbett v. Corbett*, 2 W.L.R. 1306, 2 All E.R. 33 (P.D.A. 1970) [*supra* at p. 1178] appears to be the only reported decision involving the validity of marriage of a true post operative transsexual and a male person. . . . The court subscribed to the opinion of the medical witnesses that "the biological sexual constitution of an individual is fixed at birth (at the latest), and cannot be changed, either by the natural development of organs of the opposite sex, or by medical or surgical means. . . ." . . . . He concluded on alternative grounds that the marriage had not been, and indeed could not be, consummated.

We cannot join the reasoning of the *Corbett* case. The evidence before this court teaches that there are several criteria or standards which may be relevant in determining the sex of an individual. It is true that the anatomical test, the genitalia of an individual, is unquestionably significant and probably in most instances indispensable. For example, sex classification of an individual at birth may as a practical matter rely upon this test. For other purposes, however, where sex differentiation is required or accepted, such as for public records, service in the branches of the armed forces, participation in certain regulated sports activities, eligibility for types of employment and the like, other tests in addition to genitalia may also be important. Comment, *Transsexualism, Sex Reassignment Surgery, and the Law*, 56 CORNELL L. REV. 963, 992–1002 (1971).

[We] must disagree with . . . *Corbett* that for purposes of marriage sex is somehow irrevocably cast at the moment of birth, and that for adjudging the capacity to enter marriage, sex in its biological sense should be the exclusive standard. . . .

Our departure from the *Corbett* thesis. . . . stems from a fundamentally different understanding of what is meant by "sex" for marital purposes. The English court apparently felt that sex and gender were disparate phenomena. In a given case there may, of course, be such a difference. A preoperative transsexual is an example of that kind of disharmony, and most experts would be satisfied that the individual should be classified according to biological criteria. The evidence and authority which we have examined, however, show that a person's sex or sexuality embraces an individual's gender, that is, one's self-image, the deep psychological or emotional sense of sexual identity and character. Indeed, it has been observed that the "psychological sex of an individual," while not serviceable for all purposes, is "practical, realistic and humane." Comment, *supra*; *cf. In re Anonymous*, 57 Misc. 2d 813, 293 N.Y.S.2d 834, 837 (Civ. Ct. 1968).

The English court believed. . . . that "true sex" was required to be ascertained even for marital purposes by biological criteria. In the case of a transsexual following surgery, however, according to the expert testimony presented here, the dual tests of anatomy and gender are more significant. On this evidential demonstration, therefore, we are impelled to the conclusion that for marital purposes if the anatomical or genital features of a genuine transsexual are made to conform to the person's gender, psyche or psychological sex, then identity by sex must be governed by the congruence of these standards.

Implicit in the reasoning underpinning our determination is the tacit but valid assumption . . . that for purposes of marriage under the circumstances of this case, it is the sexual capacity of the individual which must be scrutinized. Sexual capacity or sexuality in this frame of reference requires the coalescence of both the physical ability and the psychological and emotional orientation to engage in sexual intercourse as either a male or a female.

. . . . The potential for fraud . . . is effectively countered by the apt observation of the trial judge here: "The transsexual is not committing a fraud upon the public. In actuality she is doing her utmost to remove any false facade."

. . . . If . . . sex reassignment surgery is successful and the postoperative transsexual is, by virtue of medical treatment, thereby possessed of the full capacity to function sexually as a male or female, as the case may be, we perceive no legal barrier, cognizable social taboo, or reason grounded in public policy to prevent that person's identification at least for purposes of marriage to the sex finally indicated.

In this case the transsexual's gender and genitalia are no longer discordant; they have been harmonized through medical treatment. Plaintiff has become physically and psychologically unified and fully capable of sexual activity consistent with her reconciled sexual attributes of gender and anatomy. Consequently, plaintiff should be considered a member of the female sex for marital purposes. It follows that such an individual would have the capacity to enter into a valid marriage relationship with a person of the opposite sex and did do so here. In so ruling we do no more than give legal effect to a Fait accompli [*sic*], based upon medical judgment and action which are irreversible. Such recognition will promote the individual's quest for inner peace and personal happiness, while in no way disserving any societal interest, principle of public order or precept of morality.

Accordingly, the court below correctly determined that plaintiff at the time of her marriage was a female and that defendant, a man, became her lawful husband, obligated to support her as his wife. The judgment of the court is therefore affirmed.

Discussion

1. To what extent do you think that the defendant's conduct toward M.T. might have influenced the court in reaching its decision? To what extent did the expert testimony seem important? Is the court right that it is making no controversial normative judgments but merely "giv[ing] legal effect to a fait accompli"?

2. What advantages or disadvantages can you identify of *M.T.*'s test of harmonization of "psychological sex" (gender identity) and "anatomical sex" (apparently, genitalia)?

3. Despite its progressivism in recognizing a transgender woman's sex and the validity of her marriage to a man, *M.T.* has met with criticism from progressive quarters. Professor Flynn, for example, has argued that "[c]ourts that adopt an essentialized sex-gender binary are uniform in their insistence on a 'missionary' model of heterosexual sexuality—one in which the man's role is distilled to penetration and the woman's role to passive receptivity." Taylor Flynn, *Instant (Gender) Messaging: Expression-Based Challenges to State Enforcement of Gender Norms*, 18 Temp. Pol. & Civ. Rts. L. Rev. 465, 481 (2009). She has specifically quoted and criticized *M.T.*: "For trans women, the focus, as framed by one court, is whether she has a 'normal' vagina that could 'function as any female vagina,' which the court defined as being for the purpose of 'traditional penile/vaginal intercourse.'" *Id.* at 482.

4. An Ohio Probate Court judge declined to follow *M.T.*, instead expressly embracing the reasoning of *Corbett v. Corbett*, *supra* at p. 1178, in denying a marriage license for a transgender woman and a presumably cisgender man in *In re Declaratory Relief for Ladrach* (or, *In re Ladrach*), 513 N.E.2d 828 (Ohio Prob. Ct. 1987). The state of Ohio does not provide for amendment of the sex marker on birth certificates for transgender persons who have undergone medical transition procedures. Although Elaine Ladrach had had vaginoplasty, Judge Clunk concluded (with

no independent examination of the Ohio marriage statute, which does not define "male" or "female"):

> After reviewing the reported cases, law review articles and the posthearing brief of the applicant, this court concludes that there is no authority in Ohio for the issuance of a marriage license to consummate a marriage between a post-operative male to female transsexual person and a male person.

> . . . . [It] is this court's opinion that the legislature should change the statutes, if it is to be the public policy of the state of Ohio to issue marriage licenses to post-operative transsexuals.

Does this mean that a transsexual woman in Ohio may not marry a cisgender man, or that she may not marry anyone?

Note on Marriage Eligibility in Australasia

Since 2014, the marriage laws of New Zealand have allowed couples to marry without regard to sex in New Zealand and the Ross Dependency, though not in the territories of the Cook Islands, Niue, or Tokelau, in which the New Zealand Parliament lacks authority over marriage. Since the end of 2017, Australia has likewise eliminated the mixed-sex requirement for civil marriage, thus obviating the question of the sexes of a couple wishing to marry. Prior to that time, however, courts in each country had issued rulings supporting transgender persons' right to marry consistent with their gender identity.

In *Attorney General v Otahuhu Family Court*, (1995) 1 NZLR 603 (HC), the High Court of New Zealand (Wellington) entertained an application by the Attorney-General

> on behalf of the Registrar of Births, Deaths and Marriages for a declaration as to whether two persons of the same sex genetically determined may by the law of New Zealand enter into a valid marriage where one of the parties to the proposed marriage has adopted the sex opposite to that of the proposed marriage partner through sexual reassignment by means of surgery or hormone administration or both or by any other medical means.

In answering that question, Justice Ellis of the High Court (or, "Ellis J" as that court would write) declined to follow *Corbett v. Corbett, supra* at p. 1178, concluding that *Corbett*

> has been the subject of criticisms which in my view are difficult, indeed impossible, to answer satisfactorily. They are directed to the essential role of a man and a woman in marriage. It has to be conceded that the ability to procreate is not essential, nor is the ability to have sexual intercourse. Neither the common law nor ecclesiastical law ever required the first. On the other hand, it used to be the case that a marriage which had not been consummated was voidable. That is no longer the law. In my view the law of New Zealand has changed to recognise a shift away from sexual activity

and more emphasis being placed on psychological and social aspects of sex, sometimes referred to as gender issues.

The court found more persuasive the reasoning of cases such as *M.T. v. J.T.*, *supra* at p. 1190.

Focusing on the question of transgender persons' sex status as it bears on their ability to marry, and reserving questions that might arise in other areas of law, Ellis reasoned:

> Some persons have a compelling desire to be recognised and be able to behave as persons of the opposite sex. If society allows such persons to undergo therapy and surgery in order to fulfil that desire, then it ought also to allow such persons to function as fully as possible in their reassigned sex, and this must include the capacity to marry. Where two persons present themselves as having the apparent genitals of a man or a woman, they should not have to establish that each can function sexually.

> Once a transsexual has undergone surgery, he or she is no longer able to operate in his or her original sex. A male to female transsexual will have had the penis and testes removed, and have had a vagina-like cavity constructed, and possibly breast implants, and can never appear unclothed as a male, or enter into a sexual relationship as a male, or procreate. A female to male transsexual will have had the uterus and ovaries and breasts removed, have a beard growth, a deeper voice, and possibly a constructed penis and can no longer appear unclothed as a woman, or enter into a sexual relationship as a woman, or procreate. There is no social advantage in the law not recognising the validity of the marriage of a transsexual in the sex of reassignment. It would merely confirm the factual reality.

(Note the echo of *M.T. v. J.T.* in that last sentence.) The court could discern "no socially adverse effects from allowing such transsexuals to marry in their adopted sex[.] I cannot see any harm to others, children in particular, that is not properly proscribed and manageable in accordance with the existing framework of the law."

All that remained was to determine when a transgender person should be treated as a member of the sex consistent with their gender identity for purposes of civil marriage. The court thought that a "somatic test" asking whether a trans person has conformed their body to those of the sex consistent with their gender identity "is an adequate test. It is formulated on the basis of the undisputed evidence that persons who have undertaken such procedures will have already had the social and psychological disposition of the chosen sex." Accordingly, the court declared

> that for the purposes of § 23 of the Marriage Act 1955[,] where a person has undergone surgical and medical procedures that have effectively given that person the physical conformation of a person of a specified sex, there is no lawful impediment to that person marrying as a person of that sex.

Does this formulation differ from that of the question the court posed at the outset? For what transgender persons would this declaration not protect their right to marry heterosexually? What advantages or disadvantages might there be to a requirement of genital surgery as a prerequisite for a transgender person to marry as a member of the sex consistent with their gender identity (whether or not *Otahuhu Family Court* should be interpreted as endorsing such requirement)?

* * *

About eight years later across the Tasman Sea, the Family Court of Australia in *Attorney General for the Commonwealth v. Kevin,* (2003) 172 F.L.R. 300 (Austl.), agreed to an extent in the case of a transgender man whose medical transition (without genitoplasty) it treated as sufficient to allow him to marry a woman.

This case arose when transgender man Kevin and presumably cisgender woman Jennifer (both pseudonyms) married and subsequently filed a judicial application seeking a declaration that their marriage was valid under the Australian marriage statute. The Attorney General intervened in those proceedings to argue that Kevin was not a man for purposes of the marriage law. As summarized by the Family Court on Appeal, family law Justice Richard Chisholm

> concluded that, for the purpose of ascertaining the validity of a marriage under Australian law, the question of whether a person is a man or a woman is to be determined as at the date of the marriage and that in the context of the rule that the parties to a valid marriage must be a man or a woman, the word "man" has its ordinary current meaning according to Australian usage. The trial judge further concluded in the light of the evidence that Kevin was a man for the purpose of the law of marriage at the date of the marriage.

The Attorney General appealed the 2001 judgment of Chisholm J, which was affirmed by the Full Court of Family Court of Australia, consisting of Chief Justice Nicholas and Justices Ellis and Brown.

The Full Court agreed with Chisholm J that *Corbett v. Corbett* (*supra* at p. 1178) should not be followed. According to the Australian judges, Lord Justice Ormrod's judgment in *Corbett* "adopted an 'essentialist view' of sexual identity that excluded matters other than biology." Whether or not *Corbett* was right when it was decided, at the time of *Kevin*, the full Family Court ruled, "Ormrod J's test is far too limited and we do not think that it represents the law in this country." The court reached this conclusion in part because it saw "a considerable shift in our community away from the purely sexual aspects of marriage in the direction of defining it in terms of companionship." Rather than embrace Ormrod's "proposition that the capacity for genital intercourse is the essential role of the woman or the man in marriage[,]" the appellate judgment recounted Chisholm J's reasoning that "the task of the law was not to search for some mysterious entity, the person's 'true sex,' but to give an answer to a practical human problem, that is, 'to determine the sex in which it is best for the individual to live.'"

Based on the evidence before Chisholm, he had concluded, "at least on the balance of probabilities, that the characteristics of transsexual people were as much biological as those of intersex people." (This was significant because of case law protecting intersex people's right to marry as a member of the sex with which they identified.) The appellate justices sustained this conclusion: "Dealing first with brain sex, we think that it was open to the trial judge, on the evidence before him, to find as a matter of probability that there was a biological basis for transsexualism."

But biology was not dispositive for the full Family Court, which regarded "cultural and social factors" as "clearly relevant to the issue of the meaning of 'marriage' and 'man' for the purpose of the marriage law." Because the Full Court agreed with Justice Chisholm that the proper question was what Kevin's sex was at the time of his marriage to Jennifer, not at the moment of his birth, the "cultural and social factors" invoked probably include "the extensive non-medical evidence from some 39 witnesses, 23 of whom were family and friends of Kevin and 16 of whom were work colleagues and acquaintances. That evidence was to the effect that Kevin had always regarded himself as a male and had always been treated as such." The Full Court quoted Chisholm on the testimony's significance:

> The cumulative impact of the evidence of these 39 witnesses is striking. It shows the husband as perceived by those involved with him and his family, at work, and in the community. It shows him as a person: not an object of anatomical curiosity but a human being living a life, as we do, among others, as a part of society. It shows him living a life that those around him perceive as a man's life. They see him and think of him as a man, doing what men do. They do not see him as a woman pretending to be a man. They do not pretend that he is a man, while believing he is not.

"Like the trial judge," the Full Court "reject[ed] the argument that one of the principal purposes of marriage is procreation." Prefiguring U.S. Justice Scalia's dissent four months later in *Lawrence v. Texas*, 593 U.S. 558, 605 (2003) (Scalia, J., dissenting), the Full Court wrote:

> Many people procreate outside marriage and many people who are married neither procreate, nor contemplate doing so. A significant number of married persons cannot procreate either at the time of the marriage or subsequently—an obvious example being a post-menopausal woman. Similarly, it is inappropriate and incorrect to suggest that consummation is in any way a requirement to the creation of a valid marriage.

Because it regarded Kevin as "post-operative" even though he had not had phalloplasty for several reasons the appellate judgment seemed to regard as good, the Full Court affirmed Justice Chisholm's declaration that Jennifer and Kevin's marriage was legally valid.

> It may be that parliament would not have had this in contemplation in 1961 (although we are not satisfied as to this), but the question is whether the parliament intended that the meaning of the words should be confined to their meaning in 1961.

The Full Court answered in the negative, reasoning that "the court should be slow to adopt a restrictive interpretation of the Marriage Act which has such a discriminatory effect, in circumstances where there is no clear expression of a legislative intention to adopt such a restrictive approach."

It should be noted that the Full Court was obviously concerned about the implications of its reasoning (relying on Kevin's gender affirmation surgeries) for transgender people who have not had such surgeries but may wish to marry heterosexually:

> This leaves the more difficult question of the position of pre-operative transsexual persons. As we have said, this case does not require us to determine this question. In all of the decided cases to which we have referred their position has been distinguished from post-operative transsexual persons and comments have been made to the effect that this is a matter for parliament to determine. In this country at least, there have been no signs that the Federal parliament has any interest in these questions. The solution is not, of course, solely in the hands of the Federal parliament. There has been greater interest within most of the states and territories and for many purposes it is the law of the states and territories that most affect transsexual persons.

The Full Court justices reassured readers — or perhaps themselves — that the court's judgment at least was advancing the situation of trans people, "post-operative" or otherwise:

> Our decision like that of Chisholm J in this case, is in our view, the correct interpretation of the law. We would add, however, that we believe that the recognition of the position of post-operative transsexual persons is at least a step in the direction of the recognition of the plight of such persons and hopefully a step that will enable them to lead a more normal and fulfilling life. A question arises as to whether the courts can logically maintain that the position of post-operative transsexual persons is a matter for them but that of pre-operative transsexual persons is one for parliament. This has the effect of leaving such persons as the only persons in the community who are prevented from marrying a person who they legitimately regard as a person of the opposite sex, while remaining free to marry a person of their own sex.

The court did not resolve that question, though the very posing of it might indicate its inclinations.

Was the Full Court right to reject any possible specific intent of the Parliament in 1961 as controlling the interpretation of the marriage statute in 2003? Were the Australian Justices right to have treated "sex" as referring less to an abstract biological issue and more to a situated social issue? Was Justice Chisholm right to have found as a fact, because of Kevin's pre-marriage medical gender affirmation procedures, which included hormone treatment, breast reduction surgery, and a total hysterectomy with bilateral oophorectomy (removal of the ovaries) — but *not* a phalloplasty, and thus presumably Kevin still had a vagina and labia — that "Kevin's body was no longer able to function as that of a female, particularly for the purposes of repro-duction *and sexual intercourse*" (emphasis added)?

Note on Littleton v. Prange

An intermediate appellate court showed the fragility of the separation of religion and government in the United States in the context of disputes over transgender persons' marriage rights in *Littleton v. Prange*, 9 S.W.3d 223 (Ct. App. Tex. 1999).

Littleton arose after transgender woman Christie Lee Littleton lost her husband of about seven years, Jonathan Littleton. Ms. Littleton sued Jonathan's doctor Mark Prange for medical malpractice under the Texas Wrongful Death and Survival Stat-ute in her capacity as Jonathon's surviving spouse. Upon receiving Christie's answer to a discovery question about any prior names, Prange learned that Ms. Littleton had been identified at birth as male. The doctor then moved for summary judgment on the ground that Christie could not recover as a surviving spouse under the stat-ute because she was legally still male and Texas (like all other U.S. states at the time) did not allow two males to marry civilly. The trial court agreed, and the Court of Appeals of Texas affirmed the dismissal of Ms. Littleton's suit.

The lead opinion was written by Chief Justice Phil Hardberger, with Justice Karen Angelini concurring in the judgment. Much as the first reported decision rejecting a same-sex couple's claimed constitutional right to marry invoked "the book of Gen-esis," *see Baker v. Nelson*, 191 N.W.2d 185, 186 (Minn. 1971), Hardberger's framing of the issue in *Littleton* reflects a sectarian religious bias at work:

> This case involves the most basic of questions. When is a man a man, and when is a woman a woman? . . . .
>
> The deeper philosophical (and now legal) question is: can a physician change the gender of a person with a scalpel, drugs and counseling, or is a person's gender immutably fixed by our Creator at birth? The answer to that question has definite legal implications that present themselves in this case involving a person named Christie Lee Littleton.

In answering the question at issue, the lead opinion noted the opinions of Ms. Littleton's doctors that after her course of treatment including vaginoplasty, she was medically a woman, but insisted that "the question remains: is a transsexual still the same sex after a sex-reassignment operation as before the operation?" After review-ing case law from various jurisdictions on birth certificate sex marker amendment and marriage validity, the lead opinion reasoned that because the Texas legislature had not specified guidelines on when a transgender person might be able to marry as a member of the sex consistent with their gender identity, the issue of when some-one has legally changed sex could not be submitted to a jury (or, presumably, any factfinder).

"Based on the facts of this case, and the law and studies of previous cases," the lead opinion observed, "[t]ranssexual medical treatment . . . does not create the internal sexual organs of a women [*sic*] (except for the vaginal canal). There is no womb, cervix, or ovaries in the post-operative transsexual female," and "[t]he male chromosomes do not change with either hormonal treatment or sex reassignment surgery. Biologically a post-operative female transsexual is still a male." Noting medical disagreement over whether Ms. Littleton should at the time of the marriage (or the suit) be considered "a female," the lead opinion emphasized that "[h]er female anatomy, however, is all man-made. The body that Christie inhabits is a male body in all aspects other than what the physicians have supplied."

While the litigation was ongoing, several months before the trial court granted summary judgment to Prange, Ms. Littleton had amended her Texas birth certificate to indicate that she was female. The lead opinion deemed this irrelevant on the facts of the case, alluding to its opening religious framing of the issue by insisting that "Christie *was created* and born a male" (emphasis added). The lead opinion reasoned that the amending court had engaged only in what the majority characterized as "ministerial" action. The opinion insisted that the amending court had incorrectly interpreted the birth certificate amendment statute to allow correction if a certificate did not "[]accurately" reflect the facts about petitioners at the time they seek amendment; instead, it was only misstatement of the facts at birth that could be corrected; and there was no contention that Ms. Littleton had been listed as male at birth through fraud or error. Hence, Ms. Littleton was male, hence unable to marry Mark, hence not his surviving "spouse," and thus unauthorized to sue for wrongful death under the state statute.

Justice Angelini concurred in the judgment, insisting that the Court of Appeals properly acted to interpret state law in the absence of specific guidance from the relevant statutes. Citing Julie A. Greenberg, *Defining Male and Female: Intersexuality and the Collision Between Law and Biology*, 41 ARIZ. L. REV. 265 (1999), she argued that the lead opinion's reliance on the *Corbett v. Corbett* factors for marital sex—chromosomal, gonadal, and genital—could be problematic in the case of a claimed marriage involving intersex persons. But she insisted that the court need not resolve such concerns now because Christie Littleton's chromosomes, gonads, and genitals were concordant at birth. (Incidentally, there was no direct evidence of Ms. Littleton's chromosomal configuration in the record of the case.)

Justice Alma L. Lopez dissented. Noting that Christie Littleton's original birth certificate produced by Dr. Prange was the only evidence that she was not female, whereas Littleton "presented significant controverting evidence that indicated she was female," Justice Lopez argued that this created a genuine issue of material fact as to whether Christie was Mark's surviving spouse sufficient to defeat Prange's summary judgment motion. She accused the majority of "assum[ing] that gender is accurately determined at birth" even though "the traditional method of determining gender"—visual examination of genitals at birth—"does not always result in an accurate record of gender." She argued, by analogy to civil procedure rules' treatment of amended pleadings, that because the original birth certificate was substituted with the amended one, the original certificate was "a nullity."

Should state, local, and federal judges in the United States be allowed to invoke religious reasoning in support of their exercise of governmental authority, even despite the Constitution's prohibition on establishments of religion? Was the Texas Court of Appeals majority right to conclude that there was not even a genuine issue of fact whether Christie Lee Littleton was a woman within the meaning of Texas's marriage and wrongful death statutes, which did not define the sexes? Is the situation of intersex individuals sufficiently infrequent and marginal that they need not be considered by courts deciding how to interpret "sex" for purposes of civil marriage?

Reading Guide for Goodwin v. U.K.

1. Note that in the following case, a Grand Chamber of the European Court of Human Rights, rather than a smaller panel of the court, rules in favor of the transgender woman plaintiff after a string of earlier cases before that court had rejected challenges to England's refusal to treat the legal sex of a transgender person as consistent with their gender identity (rather than the sex to which they were assigned at birth). In each case the ratio of dissenting to majority votes narrowed, and the Court increasingly strongly emphasized the need for the U.K. to reassess its treatment of transsexual persons. *See Rees v. United Kingdom*, 107 Eur. Ct. H.R. (ser. A) at 15 (1986) (rejecting by 12–3 vote right to private life challenge to refusal to change legal sex of transsexual plaintiff); *Cossey v. United Kingdom*, 184 Eur. Ct. H.R. (ser. A) at 18 (1990) (rejecting by 10–8 vote private life challenge); *Sheffield & Horsham v. United Kingdom*, 1998-V Eur. Ct. H.R. 2011 (rejecting by 11–9 vote private life challenge).

2. The court's analysis is not rigidly doctrinal, seeming to involve a more totality-of-the-circumstances balancing. What considerations does the court identify that weight in favor of concluding that UK law infringes the plaintiff's right to respect for her private life? What potentially countervailing governmental interests does the court consider in one fashion or other, and, to the extent you can tell, why does the court conclude that these do not outweigh the plaintiff's interests?

Case of Christine Goodwin v. The United Kingdom

Application no. 28957/95, Council of Europe: European Court of
Human Rights, July 11, 2002, https://www.refworld.org/cases,ECHR,
4dad9f762.html [accessed 2 June 2020]

Judgment

Strasbourg

11 July 2002

In the case of Christine Goodwin v. the United Kingdom,

The European Court of Human Rights, sitting as a Grand Chamber composed of the following judges:

Mr. L. Wildhaber, President, Mr. J.-P. Costa, Sir Nicolas Bratza, Mrs. E. Palm, Mr. L. Caflisch, Mr. R. Türmen, Mrs. F. Tulkens, Mr. K. Jungwiert, Mr. M. Fischbach, Mr. V. Butkevych, Mrs. N. Vajic, Mr. J. Hedigan, Mrs. H.S. Greve,

Mr. A.B. Baka, Mr. K. Traja, Mr. M. Ugrekhelidze, Mrs. A. Mularoni, judges, and also of Mr. P.J. Mahoney, Registrar,

Having deliberated in private on 20 March and 3 July 2002,

Delivers the following judgment, which was adopted on the last mentioned date:

Procedure

1. The case originated in an application against the United Kingdom of Great Britain and Northern Ireland lodged with the European Commission of Human Rights under former Article 25 of the Convention for the Protection of Human Rights and Fundamental Freedoms by a United Kingdom national, Ms. Christine Goodwin ("the applicant"), on 5 June 1995.

. . . .

3. The applicant alleged violations of arts 8, 12, 13 and 14 of the Convention in respect of the legal status of transsexuals in the United Kingdom and particularly their treatment in the sphere of employment, social security, pensions and marriage.

. . . .

The Facts

I. The Circumstances of the Case

12. The applicant is a United Kingdom citizen born in 1937 and is a post-operative male to female transsexual.

. . . .

15. The applicant claims that between 1990 and 1992 she was sexually harassed by colleagues at work. She attempted to pursue a case of sexual harassment in the Industrial Tribunal but claimed that she was unsuccessful because she was considered in law to be a man. She did not challenge this decision by appealing to the Employment Appeal Tribunal. The applicant was subsequently dismissed from her employment for reasons connected with her health, but alleges that the real reason was that she was a transsexual.

16. In 1996, the applicant started work with a new employer and was required to provide her National Insurance ("NI") number. She was concerned that the new employer would be in a position to trace her details as once in the possession of the number it would have been possible to find out about her previous employers and obtain information from them. Although she requested the allocation of a new NI number from the Department of Social Security ("DSS"), this was rejected and she eventually gave the new employer her NI number. The applicant claims that the new employer has now traced back her identity as she began experiencing problems at work. Colleagues stopped speaking to her and she was told that everyone was talking about her behind her back.

17. The DSS Contributions Agency informed the applicant that she would be ineligible for a State pension at the age of 60, the age of entitlement for women in the United Kingdom. In April 1997, the DSS informed the applicant that her pension

contributions would have to be continued until the date at which she reached the age of 65, being the age of entitlement for men, namely April 2002. On 23 April 1997, she therefore entered into an undertaking with the DSS to pay direct the NI contributions which would otherwise be deducted by her employer as for all male employees. In the light of this undertaking, on 2 May 1997, the DSS Contributions Agency issued the applicant with a Form CF 384 Age Exemption Certificate. . . .

18. The applicant's files at the DSS were marked "sensitive" to ensure that only an employee of a particular grade had access to her files. This meant in practice that the applicant had to make special appointments for even the most trivial matters and could not deal directly with the local office or deal with queries over the telephone. Her record continues to state her sex as male and despite the "special procedures" she has received letters from the DSS addressed to the male name which she was given at birth.

19. In a number of instances, the applicant stated that she has had to choose between revealing her birth certificate and foregoing certain advantages which were conditional upon her producing her birth certificate. In particular, she has not followed through a loan conditional upon life insurance, a re-mortgage offer and an entitlement to winter fuel allowance from the DSS. Similarly, the applicant remains obliged to pay the higher motor insurance premiums applicable to men. Nor did she feel able to report a theft of 200 pounds sterling to the police, for fear that the investigation would require her to reveal her identity.

II. Relevant Domestic Law and Practice

[Here the court observes that, inter alia, English law allows people to adopt new first and last names that are then legally valid including used for identity documents; that pursuant to *Corbett v. Corbett (Otherwise Ashley)*, 2 All E.R. 33 (1970) (Eng.), opinion by Mr. Justice Ormrod, *supra* at p. 1178, sex for the purpose of marriage is determined by the non- or pre-surgical state of a person's chromosomes, gonads, and genitalia, so that genitoplasty cannot transform a legal male into a legal female; that birth certificates count as records of facts at the time of a person's birth rather than of current identity, with sex determined exclusively by the biological criteria (chromosomal, gonadal and genital) as specified in *Corbett*; that transgender women are only eligible for pensions after satisfying criteria for greater years as males must in contrast to females; and that transsexual persons might be legally liable if they do not provide full disclosure of their previous names to an employer.]

G. Current Developments

1. Review of the Situation of Transsexuals in the United Kingdom

49. On 14 April 1999, the Secretary of State for the Home Department announced the establishment of an Interdepartmental Working Group on Transsexual People. . . .

50. The Working Group produced a report in April 2000 in which it examined the current position of transsexuals in the United Kingdom, with particular

reference to their status under national law and the changes which might be made. It concluded:

". . . .

5.3. [Official] documents will often be issued in the acquired gender where the issue is identifying the individual rather than legal status. Thus, a transsexual person may obtain a passport, driving licence, medical card etc, in their new gender. . . .

5.4. Notwithstanding such provisions, transsexual people are conscious of certain problems which do not have to be faced by the majority of the population. Submissions to the Group suggested that the principal areas where the transsexual community is seeking change are birth certificates, the right to marry and full recognition of their new gender for all legal purposes.

5.5. We have identified three options for the future;

- to leave the current situation unchanged;

- to issue birth certificates showing the new name and, possibly, the new gender;

- to grant full legal recognition of the new gender subject to certain criteria and procedures.

We suggest that before taking a view on these options the Government may wish to put the issues out to public consultation."

51. The report was [publicized in various ways].

2. Recent Domestic Case-Law

52. In the case of *Bellinger v. Bellinger* [2002] 1 All ER 311, the appellant who had been classified at birth as a man had undergone gender re-assignment surgery and in 1981 had gone through a form of marriage with a man who was aware of her background. She sought a declaration under the Family Law Act 1986 that the marriage was valid. The Court of Appeal held, by a majority, that the appellant's marriage was invalid as the parties were not respectively male and female, which terms were to be determined by biological criteria as set out in the decision of *Corbett*. . . . Dame Elizabeth Butler-Sloss, President of the Family Division noted . . . :

"[95.] . . . We inquired of Mr Moylan on behalf of the Attorney-General, what steps were being taken by any government department, to take forward any of the recommendations of the [intergovernmental working group] Report, or to prepare a consultation paper for public discussion.

[96.] To our dismay, we were informed that no steps whatsoever have been, or to the knowledge of Mr Moylan, were intended to be, taken to carry this matter forward. . . . That would seem to us to be a failure to recognise the increasing concerns and changing attitudes across western Europe which have been set out so clearly and strongly in judgments of Members of the European Court at Strasbourg, and which in our view need to be addressed by the UK. . . ."

53. In his dissenting judgment, Lord Justice Thorpe considered that the foundations of the judgment in *Corbett* were no longer secure, taking the view that an approach restricted to biological criteria was no longer permissible in the light of scientific, medical and social change.

. . . .

He also noted the lack of progress in domestic reforms. . . .

The Law
I. Alleged Violation of Article 8 of the Convention

59. The applicant claims a violation of Article 8 of the Convention, the relevant part of which provides as follows:

"1. Everyone has the right to respect for his private . . . life . . .

2. There shall be no interference by a public authority with the exercise of this right except such as is in accordance with the law and is necessary in a democratic society in the interests of national security, public safety or the economic well-being of the country, for the prevention of disorder or crime, for the protection of health or morals, or for the protection of the rights and freedoms of others."

B. The Court's Assessment
1. Preliminary Considerations

71. This case raises the issue whether or not the respondent State has failed to comply with a positive obligation to ensure the right of the applicant, a post-operative male to female transsexual, to respect for her private life, in particular through the lack of legal recognition given to her gender re-assignment.

72. The Court recalls that the notion of "respect" as understood in Article 8 is not clear cut, especially as far as the positive obligations inherent in that concept are concerned: having regard to the diversity of practices followed and the situations obtaining in the Contracting States, the notion's requirements will vary considerably from case to case and the margin of appreciation to be accorded to the authorities may be wider than that applied in other areas under the Convention. In determining whether or not a positive obligation exists, regard must also be had to the fair balance that has to be struck between the general interest of the community and the interests of the individual, the search for which balance is inherent in the whole of the Convention (*Cossey v. UK* [1990] ECHR 10843/84 at para. 37).

73. The Court recalls that it has already examined complaints about the position of transsexuals in the United Kingdom (see *Rees v. UK* [1986] ECHR 9532/81, *Cossey v. UK*; *X, Y and Z v. UK* [1997] ECHR 21830/93, and *Sheffield and Horsham v. UK*). In those cases, it held that the refusal of the United Kingdom Government to alter the register of births or to issue birth certificates whose contents and nature differed from those of the original entries concerning the recorded gender of the individual

could not be considered as an interference with the right to respect for private life (*Rees v. UK*, and *Cossey v. UK*). It also held that there was no positive obligation on the Government to alter their existing system for the registration of births by establishing a new system or type of documentation to provide proof of current civil status. Similarly, there was no duty on the Government to permit annotations to the existing register of births, or to keep any such annotation secret from third parties (*Rees v. UK* [1986], and *Cossey v UK*). It was found in those cases that the authorities had taken steps to minimise intrusive enquiries (for example, by allowing transsexuals to be issued with driving licences, passports and other types of documents in their new name and gender). Nor had it been shown that the failure to accord general legal recognition of the change of gender had given rise in the applicants' own case histories to detriment of sufficient seriousness to override the respondent State's margin of appreciation in this area (*Sheffield and Horsham v UK*).

74. [Since] the Convention is first and foremost a system for the protection of human rights, the Court must have regard to the changing conditions within the respondent State and within Contracting States generally and respond, for example, to any evolving convergence as to the standards to be achieved. It is of crucial importance that the Convention is interpreted and applied in a manner which renders its rights practical and effective, not theoretical and illusory. . . . In the present context the Court has, on several occasions since 1986, signalled its consciousness of the serious problems facing transsexuals and stressed the importance of keeping the need for appropriate legal measures in this area under review.

75. The Court proposes therefore to look at the situation within and outside the Contracting State to assess "in the light of present-day conditions" what is now the appropriate interpretation and application of the Convention (see the *Tyrer v the United Kingdom* judgment of 25 April 1978, Series A no. 26, and subsequent case-law).

2. The Applicant's Situation as a Transsexual

76. The Court observes that the applicant, registered at birth as male, has undergone gender re-assignment surgery and lives in society as a female. Nonetheless, the applicant remains, for legal purposes, a male. This has had, and continues to have, effects on the applicant's life where sex is of legal relevance and distinctions are made between men and women, as, *inter alia*, in the area of pensions and retirement age. . . . Though the Government submitted that [it] made due allowance for the difficulties of her position, the Court would note that she nonetheless has to make use of a special procedure that might in itself call attention to her status.

77. It must also be recognised that serious interference with private life can arise where the state of domestic law conflicts with an important aspect of personal identity (see, *mutatis mutandis*, *Dudgeon v. UK* [1981] ECHR 7525/76 at para. 41). The stress and alienation arising from a discordance between the position in society assumed by a post-operative transsexual and the status imposed by law which refuses to recognise the change of gender cannot, in the Court's view, be regarded

as a minor inconvenience arising from a formality. A conflict between social reality and law arises which places the transsexual in an anomalous position, in which he or she may experience feelings of vulnerability, humiliation and anxiety.

78. In this case, as in many others, the applicant's gender re-assignment was carried out by the national health service, which recognises the condition of gender dysphoria and provides, *inter alia*, re-assignment by surgery, with a view to achieving as one of its principal purposes as close an assimilation as possible to the gender in which the transsexual perceives that he or she properly belongs. The Court is struck by the fact that nonetheless the gender re-assignment which is lawfully provided is not met with full recognition in law, which might be regarded as the final and culminating step in the long and difficult process of transformation which the transsexual has undergone. The coherence of the administrative and legal practices within the domestic system must be regarded as an important factor in the assessment carried out under Article 8 of the Convention. Where a State has authorised the treatment and surgery alleviating the condition of a transsexual, financed or assisted in financing the operations and indeed permits the artificial insemination of a woman living with a female-to-male transsexual (as demonstrated in the case of *X, Y and Z v. UK* [1997] ECHR 21830/93), it appears illogical to refuse to recognise the legal implications of the result to which the treatment leads.

79. The Court notes that the unsatisfactory nature of the current position and plight of transsexuals in the United Kingdom has been acknowledged in the domestic courts (see *Bellinger v. Bellinger* at para. 52) and by the Interdepartmental Working Group which surveyed the situation in the United Kingdom and concluded that, notwithstanding the accommodations reached in practice, transsexual people were conscious of certain problems which did not have to be faced by the majority of the population (para. 50 above).

80. Against these considerations, the Court has examined the countervailing arguments of a public interest nature put forward as justifying the continuation of the present situation. It observes that in the previous United Kingdom cases weight was given to medical and scientific considerations, the state of any European and international consensus and the impact of any changes to the current birth register system.

3. Medical and Scientific Considerations

81. It remains the case that there are no conclusive findings as to the cause of transsexualism and, in particular, whether it is wholly psychological or associated with physical differentiation in the brain. The expert evidence in the domestic case of *Bellinger v. Bellinger* was found to indicate a growing acceptance of findings of sexual differences in the brain that are determined pre-natally, though scientific proof for the theory was far from complete. The Court considers it more significant however that transsexualism has wide international recognition as a medical condition for which treatment is provided in order to afford relief (for example, the *Diagnostic and Statistical Manual* [*of Mental Disorders*] fourth edition (DSM-IV) replaced the diagnosis of transsexualism with "gender identity disorder"; *see also*

the International Classification of Diseases, tenth edition (ICD-10)). The United Kingdom national health service, in common with the vast majority of Contracting States, acknowledges the existence of the condition and provides or permits treatment, including irreversible surgery. The medical and surgical acts which in this case rendered the gender re-assignment possible were indeed carried out under the supervision of the national health authorities. Nor, given the numerous and painful interventions involved in such surgery and the level of commitment and conviction required to achieve a change in social gender role, can it be suggested that there is anything arbitrary or capricious in the decision taken by a person to undergo gender re-assignment. In those circumstances, the ongoing scientific and medical debate as to the exact causes of the condition is of diminished relevance.

82. While it also remains the case that a transsexual cannot acquire all the biological characteristics of the assigned sex, the Court notes that with increasingly sophisticated surgery and types of hormonal treatments, the principal unchanging biological aspect of gender identity is the chromosomal element. [Chromosomal] anomalies may arise naturally (for example, in cases of intersex conditions where the biological criteria at birth are not congruent) and in those cases, some persons have to be assigned to one sex or the other as seems most appropriate in the circumstances of the individual case. It is not apparent to the Court that the chromosomal element, amongst all the others, must inevitably take on decisive significance for the purposes of legal attribution of gender identity for transsexuals (see the dissenting opinion of Thorpe LJ in *Bellinger v Bellinger* cited in para. 52 above; and the judgment of Chisholm J in the Australian case, *Re Kevin* [(2001) 165 F.L.R. 404 (Austl.) (Chisholm, J.), aff'd sub nom., Attorney-Gen. for The Commonwealth v. "Kevin and Jennifer" and Human Rights and Equal Opportunity Comm'n* (2003) 172 F.L.R. 300]).

83. The Court is not persuaded therefore that the state of medical science or scientific knowledge provides any determining argument as regards the legal recognition of transsexuals.

4. The State of Any European and International Consensus

84. Already at the time of the *Sheffield and Horsham v. UK* (1998) case, there was an emerging consensus within Contracting States in the Council of Europe on providing legal recognition following gender re-assignment. The latest survey submitted by Liberty in the present case shows a continuing international trend towards legal recognition. In Australia and New Zealand, it appears that the courts are moving away from the biological birth view of sex (as set out in the United Kingdom case of *Corbett v. Corbett*) and taking the view that sex, in the context of a transsexual wishing to marry, should depend on a multitude of factors to be assessed at the time of the marriage.

85. The Court observes that in the case of *Rees v UK* in 1986 it had noted that little common ground existed between States, some of which did permit change of gender and some of which did not and that generally speaking the law seemed to be in a state of transition. In the later case of *Sheffield and Horsham v. UK*, the Court's judgment laid emphasis on the lack of a common European approach as

to how to address the repercussions which the legal recognition of a change of sex may entail for other areas of law such as marriage, filiation, privacy or data protection. While this would appear to remain the case, the lack of such a common approach among forty-three Contracting States with widely diverse legal systems and traditions is hardly surprising. In accordance with the principle of subsidiarity, it is indeed primarily for the Contracting States to decide on the measures necessary to secure Convention rights within their jurisdiction and, in resolving within their domestic legal systems the practical problems created by the legal recognition of post-operative gender status, the Contracting States must enjoy a wide margin of appreciation. The Court accordingly attaches less importance to the lack of evidence of a common European approach to the resolution of the legal and practical problems posed, than to the clear and uncontested evidence of a continuing international trend in favour not only of increased social acceptance of transsexuals but of legal recognition of the new sexual identity of post-operative transsexuals.

5. Impact on the Birth Register System

86. In the *Rees v. UK* case, the Court allowed that great importance could be placed by the Government on the historical nature of the birth record system. The argument that allowing exceptions to this system would undermine its function weighed heavily in the assessment.

87. It may be noted however that exceptions are already made to the historic basis of the birth register system, namely, in the case of legitimisation or adoptions, where there is a possibility of issuing updated certificates to reflect a change in status after birth. To make a further exception in the case of transsexuals (a category estimated as including some 2,000–5,000 persons in the United Kingdom according to the Interdepartmental Working Group Report) would not, in the Court's view, pose the threat of overturning the entire system. Though previous reference has been made to detriment suffered by third parties who might be unable to obtain access to the original entries and to complications occurring in the field of family and succession law, these assertions are framed in general terms and the Court does not find, on the basis of the material before it at this time, that any real prospect of prejudice has been identified as likely to arise if changes were made to the current system.

88. Furthermore, the Court notes that the Government have recently issued proposals for reform which would allow ongoing amendment to civil status data. It is not convinced therefore that the need to uphold rigidly the integrity of the historic basis of the birth registration system takes on the same importance in the current climate as it did in 1986.

6. Striking a Balance in the Present Case

89. . . . . It must be acknowledged . . . that on certain points the risk of difficulties or embarrassment faced by the present applicant may be avoided or minimised by the practices adopted by the authorities.

90. Nonetheless, the very essence of the Convention is respect for human dignity and human freedom. Under Article 8 of the Convention in particular, where the

notion of personal autonomy is an important principle underlying the interpretation of its guarantees, protection is given to the personal sphere of each individual, including the right to establish details of their identity as individual human beings. In the twenty first century the right of transsexuals to personal development and to physical and moral security in the full sense enjoyed by others in society cannot be regarded as a matter of controversy requiring the lapse of time to cast clearer light on the issues involved. In short, the unsatisfactory situation in which post-operative transsexuals live in an intermediate zone as not quite one gender or the other is no longer sustainable. Domestic recognition of this evaluation may be found in the report of the Interdepartmental Working Group and the Court of Appeal's judgment of *Bellinger v. Bellinger*.

91. The Court does not underestimate the difficulties posed or the important repercussions which any major change in the system will inevitably have, not only in the field of birth registration, but also in the areas of access to records, family law, affiliation, inheritance, criminal justice, employment, social security and insurance. However, as is made clear by the report of the Interdepartmental Working Group, these problems are far from insuperable, to the extent that the Working Group felt able to propose as one of the options full legal recognition of the new gender, subject to certain criteria and procedures. As Lord Justice Thorpe observed in the *Bellinger* case, any "spectral difficulties," particularly in the field of family law, are both manageable and acceptable if confined to the case of fully achieved and post-operative transsexuals. Nor is the Court convinced by arguments that allowing the applicant to fall under the rules applicable to women, which would also change the date of eligibility for her state pension, would cause any injustice to others in the national insurance and state pension systems as alleged by the Government. No concrete or substantial hardship or detriment to the public interest has indeed been demonstrated as likely to flow from any change to the status of transsexuals and, as regards other possible consequences, the Court considers that society may reasonably be expected to tolerate a certain inconvenience to enable individuals to live in dignity and worth in accordance with the sexual identity chosen by them at great personal cost.

92. [This] Court has since 1986 emphasised the importance of keeping the need for appropriate legal measures under review having regard to scientific and societal developments. Most recently in the *Sheffield and Horsham v UK* case in 1998, it observed that the respondent State had not yet taken any steps to do so despite an increase in the social acceptance of the phenomenon of transsexualism and a growing recognition of the problems with which transsexuals are confronted. [T]he need to keep this area under review was expressly re-iterated. Since then, a report has been issued in April 2000 by the Interdepartmental Working Group which . . . identified various options for reform. Nothing has effectively been done to further these proposals and in July 2001 the [England and Wales] Court of Appeal noted that there were no plans to do so. It may be observed that the only legislative reform of note, applying certain non-discrimination provisions to transsexuals, flowed from a decision of the European Court of Justice of 30 April 1996 which held that

discrimination based on a change of gender was equivalent to discrimination on grounds of sex.

93. [The] Court finds that the respondent Government can no longer claim that the matter falls within their margin of appreciation, save as regards the appropriate means of achieving recognition of the right protected under the Convention. Since there are no significant factors of public interest to weigh against the interest of this individual applicant in obtaining legal recognition of her gender re-assignment, it reaches the conclusion that the fair balance that is inherent in the Convention now tilts decisively in favour of the applicant. There has, accordingly, been a failure to respect her right to private life in breach of Article 8 of the Convention.

II. Alleged Violation of Article 12 of the Convention

94. The applicant also claimed a violation of Article 12 of the Convention, which provides as follows:

> "Men and women of marriageable age have the right to marry and to found a family, according to the national laws governing the exercise of this right."

. . . .

B. The Court's assessment

97. [In] the cases of *Rees v. UK*, *Cossey v. UK* and *Sheffield and Horsham v. UK* the inability of the transsexuals in those cases to marry a person of the sex opposite to their re-assigned gender was not found in breach of Article 12 of the Convention. These findings were based variously on the reasoning that the right to marry referred to traditional marriage between persons of opposite biological sex (*Rees v. UK*), the view that continued adoption of biological criteria in domestic law for determining a person's sex for the purpose of marriage was encompassed within the power of Contracting States to regulate by national law the exercise of the right to marry and the conclusion that national laws in that respect could not be regarded as restricting or reducing the right of a transsexual to marry in such a way or to such an extent that the very essence of the right was impaired (*Cossey v. UK, Sheffield and Horsham v UK*). Reference was also made to the wording of Article 12 as protecting marriage as the basis of the family (*Rees v. UK*).

98. Reviewing the situation in 2002, the Court observes that Article 12 secures the fundamental right of a man and woman to marry and to found a family. The second aspect is not however a condition of the first and the inability of any couple to conceive or parent a child cannot be regarded as per se removing their right to enjoy the first limb of this provision.

99. The exercise of the right to marry gives rise to social, personal and legal consequences. It is subject to the national laws of the Contracting States but the limitations thereby introduced must not restrict or reduce the right in such a way or to such an extent that the very essence of the right is impaired (*see Rees v. UK*).

100. [The] first sentence refers in express terms to the right of a man and woman to marry. The Court is not persuaded that at the date of this case it can still be

assumed that these terms must refer to a determination of gender by purely biological criteria. . . . There have been major social changes in the institution of marriage since the adoption of the Convention as well as dramatic changes brought about by developments in medicine and science in the field of transsexuality. The Court has found above, under Article 8 of the Convention, that a test of congruent biological factors can no longer be decisive in denying legal recognition to the change of gender of a post-operative transsexual. There are other important factors—the acceptance of the condition of gender identity disorder by the medical professions and health authorities within Contracting States, the provision of treatment including surgery to assimilate the individual as closely as possible to the gender in which they perceive that they properly belong and the assumption by the transsexual of the social role of the assigned gender. The Court would also note that Article 9 of the recently adopted Charter of Fundamental Rights of the European Union departs, no doubt deliberately, from the wording of Article 12 of the Convention in removing the reference to men and women.

101. The right under Article 8 to respect for private life does not however subsume all the issues under Article 12, where conditions imposed by national laws are accorded a specific mention. The Court has therefore considered whether the allocation of sex in national law to that registered at birth is a limitation impairing the very essence of the right to marry in this case. [It] is artificial to assert that post-operative transsexuals have not been deprived of the right to marry as, according to law, they remain able to marry a person of their former opposite sex. The applicant in this case lives as a woman, is in a relationship with a man and would only wish to marry a man. She has no possibility of doing so. In the Court's view, she may therefore claim that the very essence of her right to marry has been infringed.

102. The Court has not identified any other reason which would prevent it from reaching this conclusion. The Government have argued that in this sensitive area eligibility for marriage under national law should be left to the domestic courts within the State's margin of appreciation, adverting to the potential impact on already existing marriages in which a transsexual is a partner. It appears however from the opinions of the majority of the Court of Appeal judgment in *Bellinger v Bellinger* that the domestic courts tend to the view that the matter is best handled by the legislature, while the Government have no present intention to introduce legislation.

103. [Though] there is widespread acceptance of the marriage of transsexuals, fewer countries permit the marriage of transsexuals in their assigned gender than recognise the change of gender itself. The Court is not persuaded however that this supports an argument for leaving the matter entirely to the Contracting States as being within their margin of appreciation. This would be tantamount to finding that the range of options open to a Contracting State included an effective bar on any exercise of the right to marry. The margin of appreciation cannot extend so far. While it is for the Contracting State to determine inter alia the conditions under which a person claiming legal recognition as a transsexual establishes that gender re-assignment has been properly effected or under which past marriages cease to

be valid and the formalities applicable to future marriages (including, for example, the information to be furnished to intended spouses), the Court finds no justification for barring the transsexual from enjoying the right to marry under any circumstances.

104. The Court concludes that there has been a breach of Article 12 of the Convention in the present case.

. . . .

FOR THESE REASONS, THE COURT

1. Holds unanimously that there has been a violation of Article 8 of the Convention;

2. Holds unanimously that there has been a violation of Article 12 of the Convention;

. . . .

———————

Discussion

1. "Where a State has authorised the treatment and surgery alleviating the condition of a transsexual, financed or assisted in financing the operations and indeed permits the artificial insemination of a woman living with a female-to-male transsexual (as demonstrated in the case of *X, Y and Z v. UK* [1997] ECHR 21830/93)," the Court reasons, "it appears illogical to refuse to recognise the legal implications of the result to which the treatment leads." Does this suggest that a European country wishing to continue to treat a transgender person as a member of the sex to which they were assigned at birth would be well advised to deny surgical (and perhaps other medical) transition procedures through their national health systems and to deny assisted reproductive techniques to a cisgender woman cohabiting with a transgender male? The court's opinion also might be read to limit its judgment, "confined to the case of fully achieved and post-operative transsexuals." If that is the case, how should that phrase, undefined in the opinion, be understood?

2. Is the court's reasoning in paragraph 101 about the denial of the essence of a transsexual person's right to marry predicated upon the illegality of civil marriages between persons of the same sex? Would the reasoning there apply to a cisgender gay man who wishes to marry another cisgender man? As of the writing of this casebook, the European Court of Human Rights has adhered to the position that member nations do not violate the European Convention on Human Rights by limiting marriage to different-sex couples.

3. In paragraph 103 the court states: "While it is for the Contracting State to determine inter alia the conditions under which a person claiming legal recognition as a transsexual establishes that gender re-assignment has been properly effected or under which past marriages cease to be valid. . . ." Does this mean states could force the divorce of a couple assigned different sexes at birth if one of them transitions?

Reading Guide for In re Estate of Gardiner

1. This case concerns a challenge to the validity of the marriage of J'Noel Gardiner, a transgender woman, and her putative legal husband Marshall Gardiner, a presumably cisgender man who died intestate (without a will), by the man's estranged son. If J'Noel were not a surviving wife, the man's son would inherit his estate instead of the woman who believed herself married to the man. Some of its language is dated: Even when accurate as a descriptor, *transsexual* is best used as an adjective and not in the totalizing noun phrase "a transsexual"; "post-operative transsexual" is disfavored today because it is ambiguous as to what surgery or surgeries have been performed and, to the extent it is taken to refer to genital reconstruction surgeries, might inaccurately connote that all transgender people (or even just all transgender people who seek medical treatment to reconfigure their bodies) desire genitoplasty.

2. The heart of the Kansas Supreme Court's opinion is a lengthy quotation of the lengthy survey in the opinion of the appellate court of case law determining the sex of transgender persons for various purposes. What does the state supreme court say is the chief difference between the two approaches (two "line[s] of cases") it sees, and what does it mean by that? How does it deal with what might be understood as the complexity of physical sex as evidenced in the varying physiologies ("anomalies and conditions") of people with intersex conditions?

3. How does the state supreme court deal (less than fully explicitly) with J'Noel's full faith and credit argument that Kansas was obliged to accept her sex as reflected in her (amended) Wisconsin birth certificate?

4. What principles of statutory interpretation does the court avow for interpreting Kansas's marriage statute with its limitation of marriage to "opposite-sex" couples? Why does the court conclude that the statute renders J'Noel's marriage unlawful? What in the legislative history does the court contend supports its conclusion?

5. Some critics have charged that the reasoning of the court's opinion does not seem to allow transgender people to marry *anyone* under Kansas law. *See, e.g.,* Karly A. Grossman, *Transsexuals and the Legal Determination of Sex*, 39 Fam. L.Q. 821, 830 (2005) (explaining this "insinuation" in reasoning of *Gardiner*); Mark Strasser, *Marriage, Transsexuals, and the Meaning of Sex: On DOMA, Full Faith and Credit, and Statutory Interpretation*, 3 Hous. J. Health L. & Pol'y 301, 320 (2003). What language might support that reading of the court's opinion? What language might suggest that the court did *not* hold that J'Noel could not marry anyone?

In the Matter of the Estate of
Marshall G. Gardiner, Deceased
42 P.3d 120 (Kan. 2002)

[J'Noel Gardiner and Joe Gardiner were both represented by private counsel. J'Noel was supported by amici the ACLU of Kansas and Western Missouri; the ACLU of Illinois; Lambda Legal; and the Gender Public Advocacy Coalition (GenderPAC). Joe was supported by amicus the Thomas Moore Center for Law & Justice.]

The opinion of the court was delivered by ALLEGRUCCI, J.

J'Noel Gardiner appealed from the district court's entry of summary judgment in favor of Joseph M. Gardiner, III, (Joe) in the probate proceeding of Marshall G. Gardiner. The district court had concluded that the marriage between Joe's father, Marshall, and J'Noel, a post-operative male-to-female transsexual, was void under Kansas law.

The Court of Appeals reversed and remanded for the district court's determination whether J'Noel was male or female at the time the marriage license was issued. The Court of Appeals directed the district court to consider a number of factors in addition to chromosomes. Joe's petition for review of the decision of the Court of Appeals was granted by this court.

[As described by the Court of Appeals, J'Noel's birth certificate in Wisconsin indicated her sex as male; following "sex reassignment surgery" it was there amended to indicate her sex as female pursuant to a Wisconsin court directing the state's Department of Health and Social Services to prepare a new birth record. Kansas businessman Marshall Gardiner, estranged from his sole son Joe, met J'Noel in Kansas; Marshall "was told about J'Noel's prior history as a male," and "[t]he two were married in Kansas" in 1998. "Both parties agree that J'Noel has gender dysphoria or is a transsexual [sic—Eds.]." J'Noel underwent numerous gender confirming treatments including "sex reassignment surgery." "Eugene Schrang, M.D., J'Noel's doctor, ... in a letter dated October 1994, stated that J'Noel has a 'fully functional vagina' and should be considered 'a functioning, anatomical female.'"]

. . . . Marshall died intestate in August 1999. This legal journey started with Joe filing a petition. . . . alleging that he was the sole heir in that the marriage between J'Noel and Marshall was void since J'Noel was born a man. J'Noel argues that she is a biological female and was at the time of her marriage to Marshall. There is no dispute that J'Noel is a transsexual.

[Joe] opposed J'Noel's receiving a spousal share of Marshall's estate on several grounds—waiver, fraud, and void marriage in that J'Noel remained a male for the purpose of the "opposite sex" requirement of K.S.A.2001 Supp. 23-101.

On cross-motions for summary judgment, the district court denied J'Noel's motion by declining to give full faith and credit to J'Noel's Wisconsin birth certificate. . . . Joe's waiver argument was based on a writing that purports to waive J'Noel's interests in Marshall's property. The district court declined to conclude as a matter of law that the writing constituted a waiver. The factual issue of fraud was not decided on summary judgment. The district court granted Joe's motion with regard to the validity of the marriage on the ground that J'Noel is a male.

. . . . The sole issue for review is whether the district court erroneously entered summary judgment in favor of Joe on the ground that J'Noel's marriage to Marshall was void.

On the question of validity of the marriage of a post-operative transsexual, there are two distinct "lines" of cases. One judges validity of the marriage according to the sexual classification assigned to the transsexual at birth. The other views medical and surgical procedures as a means of unifying a divided sexual identity and determines the transsexual's sexual classification for the purpose of marriage at the time of marriage. The essential difference between the two approaches is the latter's crediting a mental component, as well as an anatomical component, to each person's sexual identity.

. . . .

Joe's principal argument is that the statutory phrase ["opposite sex"] is plain and unambiguous. . . . The plain and unambiguous meaning of K.S.A.2001 Supp. 23-101, according to Joe, is that a valid marriage must be between two persons who are of opposite sex at the time of birth.

Applying the statute as Joe advocates, a male-to-female transsexual whose sexual preference is for women may marry a woman within the advocated reading of K.S.A.2001 Supp. 23-101 because, at the time of birth, one marriage partner was male and one was female. Thus, in spite of the outward appearance of femaleness in both marriage partners at the time of the marriage, it would not be a void marriage. . . . As the Court of Appeals stated in regard to J'Noel's argument that K.S.A.2001 Supp. 23-101, as applied by the district court, denied her right to marry: "When J'Noel was found by the district court to be a male for purposes of Kansas law, she was denied the right to marry a male. It logically follows, therefore, that the court did not forbid J'Noel from marrying a female."

Joe's fallback argument is that the legislature's intent was to uphold "traditional marriage," interpreting K.S.A.2001 Supp. 23-101 so that it invalidates a marriage between persons who are not of the opposite sex; *i.e.*, a biological male and a biological female.

Joe also contends that the legislature did not intend for the phrase "opposite sex" in K.S.A.2001 Supp. 23-101 to allow for a change from the sexual classification assigned at birth.

The other facet of Joe's argument is that policy questions are for the legislature rather than the courts. In K.S.A.2001 Supp. 23-101 and K.S.A.2001 Supp. 23-115, the legislature declared the public policy of recognizing only marriages between a man and a woman. . . .

The Court of Appeals extensively reviewed cases involving transsexuals from other states and countries. [The] Court of Appeals' discussion of cases is, in part, quoted here:

> "The cases generally fall into three categories: cases dealing with the amendment of identification records, usually birth certificate name and/ or sex changes; cases dealing with discrimination, most pointedly in the workplace; and cases dealing with marriage between a transsexual and a nontranssexual. . . .

"In 1984, the United States Court of Appeals, Seventh Circuit, analyzed an issue concerning transsexualism and workplace discrimination. In *Ulane v. Eastern Airlines, Inc.*, 742 F.2d 1081 (7th Cir.1984) [*see* Chapter 5, Section A, *supra*], a post-operative male-to-female transsexual who was a pilot for Eastern Airlines was fired . . . shortly after sex reassignment surgery. The transsexual sued the airline, alleging that the employer violated Title VII by discharging her from her position as a pilot. A federal district court agreed with the transsexual, finding discrimination against this person as both a female and a transsexual, and the airline appealed.

". . . . First, the court stated: 'It is a maxim of statutory construction that, unless otherwise defined, words should be given their ordinary, common meaning.' The court explained that the words of Title VII do not outlaw discrimination against a person who has a sexual identity disorder. It noted that the law clearly prohibits discrimination against women because they are women or men because they are men; it does not protect a person born with a male body who believes himself to be female or a person born with a female body who believes herself to be male.

"After noting that nothing was said in the legislative history about transsexuals, the court stated that it appears clear that Congress did not intend the legislation to apply to anything other than 'the traditional concept of sex.' Had Congress intended it to apply, surely it would have said so, the court explained. Thus, the court declined to expand the definition of 'sex' as used in Title VII beyond its 'common and traditional interpretation,' stating: 'We agree with the Eighth and Ninth Circuits that if the term "sex" as it is used in Title VII is to mean more than biological male or biological female, the new definition must come from Congress.'"

. . . .

J'Noel submitted a supplemental brief to this court in order to bring to the court's attention a decision of the Family Court of Australia, which is dated October 12, 2001. J'Noel refers to the new decision as *In re Kevin*. . . .

The record in the Australian case was richly and comprehensively developed, in sharp contrast with the record in the case before us. . . .

Here, the district court's conclusion of law, based on its findings of fact, was that "J'Noel is a male." In other words, the district court concluded as a matter of law that J'Noel is a male and granted summary judgment on that basis.

The district court stated that it had considered conflicting medical opinions on whether J'Noel was male or female. This is not the sort of factual dispute that would preclude summary judgment because what the district court actually took into account was the medical experts' opinions on the ultimate question. The district court did not take into account the factors on which the scientific experts based their opinions on the ultimate question. The district court relied entirely on the Texas court's opinion in *Littleton* for the "facts" on which it based its conclusion of law. There were no expert witnesses or medical testimony as to whether J'Noel was a male or female. The only medical evidence was the medical report as to the reassignment surgery attached to J'Noel's memorandum in support of her motion for partial summary judgment. There was included a "To Whom It May Concern" notarized letter signed by Dr. Schrang in which the doctor wrote: "She should now be considered a functioning, anatomical female."

[The] Court of Appeals included in its opinion a review of some scientific literature. As courts typically do, the Court of Appeals also turned to a law journal article that reported on scientific matters relevant to legal issues. The Court of Appeals quoted extensively from [Julie A.] Greenberg, *Defining Male and Female: Intersexuality and the Collision between Law and Biology*, 41 Ariz. L. Rev. 265 (1992). Professor Greenberg's thesis is that sexual identification is not simply a matter of anatomy, as demonstrated by a number of intersex conditions—chromosomal sex disorders, gonadal sex disorders, internal organ anomalies, external organ anomalies, hormonal disorders, gender identity disorder, and unintentioned [*sic*] amputation.

Thus, the essential difference between the line of cases, including *Corbett* and *Littleton*, that would invalidate the Gardiner marriage and the line of cases, including *M.T.* and *In re Kevin*, that would validate it is that the former treats a person's sex as a matter of law and the latter treats a person's sex as a matter of fact. In *Littleton*, the thread running throughout the majority's opinion was that a person's gender was immutably fixed by our Creator at birth [quoting *Littleton* without quotation marks—Eds.]. Summing up its view of Christie's mission to be accepted as a male, the court stated: "There are some things we cannot will into being. They just are." *Corbett* was approvingly described by the Texas majority as holding, "once a man, always a man." The Texas court decided that there was nothing for a jury to decide, and "[t]here are no significant facts that need to be decided." Because " Christie was created and born a male," the Texas court "h[e]ld, *as a matter of law*, that Christie Littleton is a male." (Emphasis added.)

In contrast, the Australian court stated:

> "It will be necessary to identify whether particular propositions in the reasoning are statements of fact or of law. I take it to be a question of law what criteria should be applied in determining whether a person is a man or a woman for the purpose of the law of marriage, and a question of fact whether the criteria exist in a particular case." *In re Kevin*.

The Australian court's analytical approach echoes that of our Court of Appeals. Indeed, *Gardiner* is cited and discussed by the Australian court.

. . . .

The district court concluded as a matter of law that J'Noel was a male because she had been identified on the basis of her external genitalia at birth as a male. The Court of Appeals held that other criteria should be applied in determining whether J'Noel is a man or a woman for the purpose of the law of marriage and remanded in order for the district court to apply the criteria to the facts of this case. In this case of first impression, the Court of Appeals adopted the criteria set forth by Professor Greenberg in addition to chromosomes: "gonadal sex, internal morphologic sex, external morphologic sex, hormonal sex, phenotypic sex, assigned sex and gender of rearing, and sexual identity," as well as other criteria that may emerge with scientific advances.

The harmonizing of psychological and anatomical sex was the touchstone for the New Jersey court. It also was the touchstone for the Australian court. . . .

On appeal, J'Noel argues that the marriage is valid under Kansas law. However, in the district court, J'Noel's sole argument was that the marriage was valid under Wisconsin law and Kansas must give full faith and credit to Wisconsin law. In fact, J'Noel argued that the validity of the marriage under Kansas law was not an issue in this case and intimated the marriage would be prohibited under K.S.A. 2001 Supp. 23-101. She argued, in part:

> "The way that counsel for Joe Gardiner portrayed this issue, I think, is perhaps very clever and it's probably something that I would have done if I were in his shoes. He said, can someone change their sex? Does a medical doctor or a judge have the right to change somebody's sex?

> "And the answer to that may, in fact, be no, but I think the more interesting question, and the question that's really before the Court is one which I think was addressed by Counsel, and that is—perhaps that is an issue for the State legislature to deal with. In Wisconsin the State legislature has clearly held this issue. The statute in Wisconsin is clear, and this statute has been cited in the brief.

>   . . . .

> "However, we would urge the Court to rule on our motion favorably with respect to the sexual identity of Miss Gardiner and we would urge the Court to rule that as a matter of summary judgment she is, in fact, a female entitled, under the listed very narrow interpretation of Wisconsin law.

>   . . . .

> ". . . Does this, in fact, make J'Noel Gardiner a man—from a man to a woman?

> "I think the answer is, well, no, not technically speaking, but we're not talking about technically. We're talking about that as a matter of law, not technically, not talking scientifically. . . .

> "In this case, the Wisconsin legislature clearly contemplated a person who had sexual reassignment surgery is allowed to change her sexual identity in conformance with the surgery that transpired.

>   . . . .

> "Going onto the sexual identity question, I think that counsel for Joe Gardiner have very cleverly tried to posture the questions differently than

it actually exists. This is really a very simple, straightforward matter. The question is, does Kansas need to give full faith and credit to the Wisconsin statute and court order and the birth certificate that order created under Wisconsin law?

"I think the answer to that is clearly yes. This Court is not being asked to determine whether or not J'Noel Gardiner is, in fact, a male or female. That is simply not a matter that is before this Court on this motion for summary judgment, and we would submit even at the time of trial. Surgeons may testify as to certain scientific facts and they may disagree as to whether or not that Miss Gardiner is, in fact, a male or a female.

. . . .

"There is no need for this Court to make a decision of whether or not Miss Gardiner is in fact, a man or a woman. That's simply not a matter before this Court. The issue is whether or not Wisconsin is allowed to create their own laws and whether those laws and those decisions made by a Wisconsin tribunal and the administrative acts that follow that court order are in fact something that this Court is bound to follow.

. . . .

"[W]e're not asking the Court to approve or disapprove of issues that relate to transsexuals marrying. We really encourage the Court to look at the very, very narrow issue here.

"Clearly, there's issues for the Kansas legislature to look at, and I don't think this Court or any other Court in Kansas should impose its own opinions on the legislature, but I think this Court does have a responsibility to enforce the law as it applies in other states to Kansas and give those other states full faith and credit."

The district court granted summary judgment, finding the marriage void under K.S.A. 2001 Supp. 23-101. Summary judgment is appropriate when there is no genuine issue of material fact. Here, the parties have supplied and agreed to the material facts necessary to resolve this issue. There are no disputed material facts. We disagree with the decision reached by the Court of Appeals. We view the issue in this appeal to be one of law and not fact. The resolution of this issue involves the interpretation of K.S.A. 2001 Supp. 23-101. The interpretation of a statute is a question of law, and this court has unlimited appellate review.

The fundamental rule of statutory construction is that the intent of the legislature governs. In determining legislative intent, courts are not limited to consideration of the language used in the statute, but may look to the historical background of the enactment, the circumstances attending its passage, the purpose to be accomplished, and the effect the statute may have under the various constructions suggested. Words in common usage are to be given their natural and ordinary meaning. When a statute is plain and unambiguous, the court must give effect to the intention of the legislature as expressed, rather than determine what the law should or should not be.

The words "sex," "male," and "female" are words in common usage and understood by the general population. *Black's Law Dictionary* (6th ed. 1999) defines "sex" as "[t]he sum of the peculiarities of structure and function that distinguish a male from a female organism; the character of being male or female." *Webster's New Twentieth Century Dictionary* (2d ed. 1970) states the initial definition of sex as "either of the two divisions of organisms distinguished as male or female; males or females (especially men or women) collectively." "Male" is defined as "designating or of the sex that fertilizes the ovum and begets offspring: opposed to *female*." "Female" is defined as "designating or of the sex that produces ova and bears offspring: opposed to *male*." [Emphasis added.] According to *Black's Law Dictionary*, a marriage "is the legal status, condition, or relation of one man and one woman united in law for life, or until divorced, for the discharge to each other and the community of the duties legally incumbent on those whose association is founded on the distinction of sex."

The words "sex," "male," and "female" in everyday understanding do not encompass transsexuals. The plain, ordinary meaning of "persons of the opposite sex" contemplates a biological man and a biological woman and not persons who are experiencing gender dysphoria. A male-to-female post-operative transsexual does not fit the definition of a female. The male organs have been removed, but the ability to "produce ova and bear offspring" does not and never did exist. There is no womb, cervix, or ovaries, nor is there any change in his chromosomes. As the *Littleton* court noted, the transsexual still "inhabits . . . a male body in all aspects other than what the physicians have supplied." J'Noel does not fit the common meaning of female.

That interpretation of K.S.A.2001 Supp. 23-101 is supported by the legislative history of the statute. That legislative history is set out in the Court of Appeals decision:

> "The amendment to 23-101 limiting marriage to two parties of the opposite sex began its legislative history in 1975. The minutes of the Senate Committee on Judiciary for January 21, 1976, state that the amendment would 'affirm the traditional view of marriage.' . . . .

> "K.S.A. 23-101 was again amended in 1996, when language was added, stating: 'All other marriages are declared to be contrary to the public policy of this state and are void.' This sentence was inserted immediately after the sentence limiting marriage to two parties of the opposite sex.

> "In 1996, K.S.A. 23-115 was amended, with language added stating: 'It is the strong public policy of this state only to recognize as valid marriages from other states that are between a man and a woman.'"

The Court of Appeals then noted:

> "The legislative history contains discussions about gays and lesbians, but nowhere is there any testimony that specifically states that marriage should

be prohibited by two parties if one is a post-operative male-to-female or female-to-male transsexual. Thus, the question remains: Was J'Noel a female at the time the license was issued for the purpose of the statute?"

We do not agree that the question remains. We view the legislative silence to indicate that transsexuals are not included. If the legislature intended to include transsexuals, it could have been a simple matter to have done so. We apply the rules of statutory construction to ascertain the legislative intent as expressed in the statute. We do not read into a statute something that does not come within the wording of the statute.

In *Ulane v. Eastern Airlines, Inc.*, 742 F.2d 1081 (7th Cir. 1984), the federal district court, like the Court of Appeals here, held sex identity was not just a matter of chromosomes at birth, but was in part a psychological, self-perception, and social question. In reversing the district court, the Seventh Circuit stated:

> "In our view, to include transsexuals within the reach of Title VII far exceeds mere statutory interpretation. Congress had a narrow view of sex in mind when it passed the Civil Rights Act, and it has rejected subsequent attempts to broaden the scope of its original interpretation. For us to now hold that Title VII protects transsexuals would take us out of the realm of interpreting and reviewing and into the realm of legislating. . . . This we must not and will not do."

. . . .

We agree with the Seventh Circuit's analysis in *Ulane*. It is well reasoned and logical. Although *Ulane* involves sex discrimination against Ulane as a transsexual and as a female under Title VII, the similarity of the basic issue and facts to the present case make it both instructive and persuasive. As we have previously noted, the legislature clearly viewed "opposite sex" in the narrow traditional sense. The legislature has declared that the public policy of this state is to recognize only the traditional marriage between "two parties who are of the opposite sex," and all other marriages are against public policy and void. We cannot ignore what the legislature has declared to be the public policy of this state. Our responsibility is to interpret K.S.A. 2001 Supp. 23-101 and not to rewrite it. That is for the legislature to do if it so desires. If the legislature wishes to change public policy, it is free to do so; we are not. To conclude that J'Noel is of the opposite sex of Marshall would require that we rewrite K.S.A. 2001 Supp. 23-101.

Finally, we recognize that J'Noel has traveled a long and difficult road. J'Noel has undergone electrolysis, thermolysis, tracheal shave, hormone injections, extensive counseling, and reassignment surgery. Unfortunately, after all that, J'Noel remains a transsexual, and a male for purposes of marriage under K.S.A. 2001 Supp. 23-101. We are not blind to the stress and pain experienced by one who is born a male but perceives oneself as a female. We recognize that there are people who do not fit neatly into the commonly recognized category of male or female, and to many life becomes an ordeal. However, the validity of J'Noel's marriage to Marshall is a question of public policy to be addressed by the legislature and not by this court.

The Court of Appeals is affirmed in part and reversed in part; the district court is affirmed.

DAVIS, J., not participating.

BRAZIL, S.J., assigned.

———————

Dicussion

1. Although the court of appeals said that the point of a tracheal shave is to affect the voice, it may have confused that procedure with vocal surgery to affect the pitch of one's voice (presumably, for a transgender woman, to try to produce a higher voice). Trans women who undergo a tracheal shave do so to reduce the size/prominence of one's Adam's apple, a male-linked secondary sex trait.

2. The Kansas Supreme court claims that "[t]o conclude that J'Noel is of the opposite sex of Marshall would require that we rewrite K.S.A. 2001 Supp. 23-101." Is that plausible? With what specific language in Kansas's (anti-gay) marriage statute would such a holding conflict?

3. The 2002 holding in *Gardiner*, ousting J'Noel from her status as Marshall's widow and from her inheritance, was only possible because Kansas law, as was common, excluded same-sex couples from civil marriage. (The first U.S. state to eliminate the mixed-sex requirement for civil marriage was Massachusetts as a result of the decision of that state's highest court in *Goodridge v. Department of Public Health*, 798 N.E.2d 941 (Mass. 2003), rendered November 18, 2003 and effective on May 17, 2004 — the 50th anniversary of the U.S. Supreme Court's decision in *Brown v. Board of Education*, 347 U.S. 483 (1954).) Consider the following critique of how *Gardiner* was litigated by J'Noel:

> . . . . Many of the arguments made on J'Noel's behalf might be classified as part of an "Oppress Them, Not Me" strategy of playing to judicial heterosexism. Thus, . . . J'Noel's briefs frequently attempt to draw an unbridgeable gulf between gay and lesbian persons and transpersons, even in patently false ways. For example, J'Noel's brief repeatedly beat the reader over the head with the assertion that "a transsexual is not a homosexual." While this refrain might have tried to make the mere point that there is no necessary connection between transsexuality and homosexuality, J'Noel goes further, avowing that "[a] homosexual engages in sexual relations with a member of his or her same sex. A transsexual does not." According to J'Noel, transsexuals "desire the removal of [the wrong sexual] apparatus and further surgical assistance in order that they may enter into normal heterosexual relationships." However much transsexuality and homosexuality are erroneously conflated in society, J'Noel's claim is plainly not true of all transsexual persons, many of whom do identify as lesbian or gay. Moreover, as Judith Halberstam has observed, "the simple opposition of transsexual versus gay and lesbian masks many other lines

of affiliation and coalition that already exist within multiple queer communities [. . . .]"

There was no need for J'Noel's attorneys to make such claims simply to distance her from homosexuality. . . .

David B. Cruz, *Getting Sex "Right": Heteronormativity and Biologism in Trans and Intersex Marriage Litigation and Scholarship*, 18 Duke J. Gender L. & Pol'y 203 (2010).

What were lawyers representing heterosexually identified transgender persons wishing to marry to do in advocating zealously for their clients?

Note on Gebhardt, Full Faith and Credit for Status Records

Building upon analyses in Julie A. Greenberg & Marybeth Herald, *You Can't Take It with You: Constitutional Consequences of Interstate Gender-Identity Rulings*, 80 Wash. L. Rev. 819 (2005), Shawn Gebhardt has argued in *Full Faith and Credit for Status Records: A Reconsideration of* Gardiner, 97 Calif. L. Rev. 1419 (2009), that the Kansas intermediate appellate and state supreme court decisions in *In re Estate of Gardiner* failed to appreciate that (in his view) the primary question in the litigation was whether Kansas was required under the Full Faith and Credit Clause of the Constitution to treat J'Noel Gardiner's sex for the purpose of deciding whether her marriage in Kansas was valid as determined by the earlier Wisconsin amendment of her Wisconsin birth certificate. He argues that Kansas was so required, premising his argument on a characterization of birth certificates as "status records."

The Full Faith and Credit Clause provides: "Full Faith and Credit shall be given in each State to the public Acts, Records, and judicial Proceedings of every other State. And the Congress may by general Laws prescribe the Manner in which such Acts, Records and Proceedings shall be proved, and the Effect thereof." U.S. Const., Art. IV, Sec. 1. Gebhardt correctly notes that the Supreme Court has held that states' obligations under this clause are very strong when it comes to judgments rendered by other states ("judicial Proceedings"), which they have a virtually unflagging obligation to enforce, but reasonably weak when it comes to other states' legislation ("public Acts"), where states can generally prefer their own laws if they have a "strong public policy" that another state's law would violate. Yet the Supreme Court has not specified what kind of obligations states have to give effect to "Records" from other states.

Gebhardt thoughtfully argues in part that

there are several reasons why some executive actions, embodied in records, deserve the same level of full faith and credit. First, the consequences of indeterminacy can be quite severe. Second, personal status records are intensely personal to the individual to whom they pertain, and therefore, the ability of others to obtain standing to contest the effectiveness of otherwise legitimate records should be limited. Third, many of the policies underlying res judicata doctrines similarly counsel against permitting chronic attacks on an established precedent. . . .

A key piece of his reasoning is that "by issuing status records, the executive branch of government is responsible for a great variety of rights—obligations between private parties, between private parties and the state, and between public entities." He views the Full Faith and Credit Clause as intended to "create[] an economical and streamlined way to enforce rights acquired in sister fora." He also argues that "the faith and credit rule provides stability, so that all actors can predict how other states will treat their various legal statuses." In his view, "[b]ecause personal status conflicts often arise in the family law or wills and estates context, permitting repetitive or harassing litigation poses real threats, financially and emotionally, to family stability." And he argues that "the Constitution, which protects human dignity, requires that status determinations be respected, and that where possible, the individual should be the driving force behind initiating changes in his or her own status."

Moreover, Gebhardt relies on a generalization that, in his view, "[d]isputes involving a legal status—or involving rights, obligations, or other legal statuses stemming from a legal status—established by a record issued or amended in a sister state will almost always be wholly local to that sister state." In particular, he argued:

> a dispute that, at bottom, is a dispute over the sex of one of the partners, when that question has been decided in a sister forum, is not one that is local—or even partly local—to Kansas. It is wholly local to Wisconsin, the state in which the legislature passed statutes detailing the amendment procedures governing Wisconsin-issued birth certificates, in which a judge issued an order to change a record in accord with those statutes, and in which an amended certificate was issued and a legal status was changed. Thus, this is an area in which a sister state is competent to legislate but the forum state is not. A Wisconsin birth certificate will forever be a Wisconsin birth certificate. It will never be a Kansas birth certificate, and therefore Kansas has no interest in either the regulation of Wisconsin birth certificate or the status that arises from such regulation.

Gebhardt's theorizing is not limited to birth certificates, but it also does not clear to apply to every possible kind of "Record" of another state. Rather, there is something special for him about "status" records: "Executive records that pertain to the creation or modification of status present one of the strongest cases in favor of robust faith and credit for executive records."

> Because such status records [as corporate charters or birth certificates] cement an individual's, or individual entity's, standing in the eyes of the law, they are normally issued in a nonadversarial context. This is [in part] because the rights and obligations that status records establish are unique to the person to whom the record pertains. Third parties normally have no interest in the status of another, and therefore have no standing to challenge

that status. Moreover, status records create a relationship between an individual and the state, not among multiple individuals. At the same time, individual interests are at their peak when the government determines an individual's status.

He extrapolates from the U.S. Supreme Court's decision in the divorce case *Williams v. North Carolina* (*Williams II*), 325 U.S. 226 (1945). Gebhardt insists that "status is a unique jurisprudential concept. There are powerful policy reasons for allowing only one, definitive pronouncement of status to which all other jurisdictions must defer. First, everyone — the individual, the state, and the public — has an interest in treating status issues as final and subject to uniform recognition."

Gebhardt subsidiarily deploys a parallel to a common law rule of recognition by one state of marriage entered into in another state, "the 'place of celebration' rule, upholds the validity of a marriage that was valid where it was celebrated (*i.e.*, performed)." To overcome that rule, under the broadly adopted doctrine, a forum state would have to satisfy a strong version of a public policy exemption. Gebhardt argues that is appropriate because "the individual rights at stake are among the most precious that exist. 'The right "to marry, establish a home, and bring up children" is a central part of the liberty protected by the Due Process Clause. . . .'" And he analogizes to res judicata: "although administrative awards are not usually accorded the same preclusive effects as are judicial decisions, the factual findings of administrative bodies are entitled to extraterritorial recognition. Because some types of records are closely related to the facts they establish, at times even being one and the same, it does not seem too great a stretch to apply these preclusion principles to records as well. Records embody and evidence factual findings. . . ."

Note on Cruz, Sexual Judgments

David B. Cruz disagrees with the analyses of Julie Greenberg and Marybeth Herald and of Shawn Gebhardt. In *Sexual Judgments: Full Faith and Credit and the Relational Character of Legal Sex*, 46 Harv. C.R.-C.L. L. Rev. 51 (2011), Professor Cruz argues that a conceptual flaw underlies their position: Although these claims maintain that sex is a "status" the determination of which in one state should be binding on other states, the supporting arguments wrongly conceive of sex in law as a simple fact, a property of an individual person, that can be adjudicated finally by a single state, rather than a regulatory tool that partitions a population for prospective regulatory purposes.

Reviewing Supreme Court case law and scholarship on the Full Faith and Credit Clause, Cruz argues that "the effect that the Full Faith and Credit Clause will have in one state with respect to another state's rules for sex determinations varies according to whether the rendering state has reduced a past application of its rules to an enforceable judgment (through judicial proceedings) or whether, instead, they remain more prospective rules of statutory, common, or state constitutional law (public acts) or evidentiary administrative actions (records of facts)." Moreover, "even where court-ordered judgments about a person's sex identity are at issue, it would be incorrect to conclude that these are necessarily or even frequently binding upon other states. One cannot understand the constitutional effect of the Full Faith and Credit Clause, and the nature of any claim or issue preclusion it might mandate, without an appreciation of what issue or issues a judgment of legal identity properly decides. . . ."

Cruz contends "that . . . law treats or uses identity categories like race or sex[. . . .] as social categories and establishes social relationships; these relationships are marked by differential distributions [of] legal rights and obligations." He offers age and adulthood as an illustration: age is by and large a simple fact, but just because one state may treat a person as having reached adulthood, the legal age of majority, for some purpose at a specified age doesn't mean that other states have to treat people of that age as adults for those others states' regulatory purposes.

Similarly with sex: "When a state dictates that a newborn person's sex be recorded officially on a birth certificate, it is not, contrary to some courts' representations, simply mirroring a historical 'fact.' Rather, the state is making a choice about how to divide its population into classes." States' laws treating a transgender person as being a member of different sexes—and note how that locution itself ("a member") suggests that sexes are classes, that is, sets of humans related in certain ways—are not necessarily disagreeing about physical properties of humans, but about what definitions to use for sex and what ways to group people for things like access to sex-segregated facilities.

To add a specific illustration not in Cruz's article, one state that treated 18-year-olds as "adults" able to purchases alcohol and another state that insisted one must be 21 to be an "adult" able to buy alcohol don't disagree about the fact of the age of a 20-year-old; they are disagreeing about how to exercise their own legislative powers to restrict those who may purchase alcohol.

Cruz contends in *Sexual Judgments* that this is the same form of situation that obtains when states disagree about the sex of a transgender person, such as in *Gardiner* (*supra* this chapter):

> The disagreement between Kansas [which treated transgender woman J'Noel Gardiner as male] and Wisconsin [where she amended her birth certificate to indicate that she was female] stemmed not from any difference in knowledge concerning J'Noel's physiology, psychology, or medical treatments, but rather from a difference in legal definitions. What Wisconsin "definitively" resolved was J'Noel's legal sex identity [for Wisconsin law], that is, where J'Noel lies in the state of Wisconsin's scheme of sex relationships (partitioning the state population into classes of legally male and legally female persons). Kansas adopted a different definition of male and female, a different partition of its population.

For this reason, Cruz argues, the Full Faith and Credit Clause "does not compel Kansas to apply Wisconsin law to every dispute in Kansas involving J'Noel's sex. The Wisconsin sexual judgment could not have decided all those issues in advance, for Wisconsin has no general legislative or adjudicative jurisdiction or competence to declare authoritatively what sex relationships obtain among the people of Kansas." To expand on the article's arguments, Cruz would add that Gebhardt is therefore misguided in claiming of *Gardiner* that "a dispute that, at bottom, is a dispute over the sex of one of the partners, when that question has been decided in a sister forum, is not one that is local — or even partly local — to Kansas. It is wholly local to Wisconsin. . . ." Legal *sex* simply means different things in Wisconsin and Kansas, so it is not the case that J'Noel Gardiner's sex-for-purposes-of-Kansas-marriage-law was "decided" when Wisconsin ruled on her sex-for-purposes-of-Wisconsin-birth-certificates (and presumably many other issues of Wisconsin law).

And it is not just a matter of what Wisconsin has or hasn't decided, but what it can or cannot decide. *Sexual Judgments* observes that under the U.S. scheme of federalism, a state's authority to regulate is limited. Wisconsin, for example,

> as a general matter [may] only . . . legislate directly for or directly regulate those within its territory. At most, then, Kansas would have to credit the sex change judgment of Wisconsin and treat J'Noel as female for purposes of Wisconsin law including retrospective matters already decided by Wisconsin courts. But if Kansas remains constitutionally free to prefer its own substantive law (say, of marriage and intestacy), then Wisconsin law — and the Wisconsin court judgment declaring J'Noel to be female — are legally irrelevant, or at least generally impose no binding strictures on Kansas.

Thus, to expand on the article's argument, when Gebhardt declares that the Full Faith and Credit Clause is supposed to protect "rights acquired in sister fora," that is insufficient, because Wisconsin is extremely limited in the rights it can impose against another state like Kansas in favor of people born in Wisconsin but now living in Kansas.

In *Sexual Judgments*, Cruz does offer an example of where Wisconsin's sex determination might well control:

> Matters would be somewhat different had J'Noel married a man in Wisconsin, divorced there, and obtained real property in Wisconsin during the divorce pursuant to a judicial divorce decree. Then, the Wisconsin court would properly have adjudicated relationships between two of its citizens and property within its jurisdictional authority. In that case, the content of the judgment would be an authoritative declaration of the ownership or non-ownership relationships among the two parties and the properties. Hence, a state such as Kansas would have to give full faith and credit to the divorce decree and its allocation of that real estate, even if Kansas would not have regarded the parties as ever married in the first place because it would not have recognized the woman's legal change of sex in Wisconsin.

Cruz argues that it does not save the Full Faith and Credit Clause argument for interstate recognition of sex determinations to appeal, as Greenberg & Herald and Gebhardt do, to notions of sex as a "status." First, that move ignores the Supreme

Court's emphasis in *Baker v. General Motors Corporation*, 522 U.S. 222 (1998), that the force of one state's judgment in another state depends upon whether the issue in the second state involves matters that one state has no authority to resolve. Wisconsin has no general authority to tell Kansas whom Kansas has to let contract marriage in Kansas. Second, the appeal to status "too casually transforms conflict of laws doctrines into Full Faith and Credit Clause rules. It would be a mistake to take common law rules and, without more, enshrine them as constitutional commands." Third, the argument for mandatory interstate recognition of sex determinations would raise the problem (too quickly dismissed by Gebhardt, in Cruz's view then and now) that if the first court judgment determining the sex of a transgender person who had received gender confirmation surgeries ("sex reassignment surgery" in somewhat older parlance) classified her (in J'Noel Gardiner's case) as a member of her natally assigned sex (male, in her case), she would be stuck that way for all time in all states under that view of full faith and credit.

Fourth and most foundationally, the status-based argument gives inadequate weight to the relational nature of the statuses it draws upon to prime its analogy pump. Adoption and filiation establish parent-child relationships (or non-relationships in the cases of unsuccessful suits to establish paternity) between a putative parent and a putative adoptee or filiatee; divorce decrees change the marital relationship of the previously married couple involved. In any of these cases, the court rendering judgment and issuing the decree has personal jurisdiction over a constitutionally sufficient number of those involved in the status determination—the putative parent and child or the member of the couple who wishes to be divorced—and the state involved has legislative jurisdiction over them. A decree that the people involved (putative parent and child, or soon to be sundered spouses) are or are not in a specified relation to each other is fully within the rendering state's territorially allocated authority.

But in a sex determination, the state of Wisconsin (to continue with the Wisconsin-Kansas example discussed by Professors Greenberg and Herald) has legislative jurisdiction over the petitioner (the trans or intersex person who wants to set the record straight, so to speak), as well as over the classes of male and female citizens of (and, generally, persons present in) Wisconsin. But it does not have legislative jurisdiction over the classes of male and female citizens of Kansas. A Wisconsin judgment, then, necessarily cannot be one that generally binds the people of Kansas into a set of sexed relationships with the petitioner.

In addition to the jurisdiction-over-persons issue, an individual's legal sex is somewhat like a civil marriage. Both are, at their core, prospectively regulatory. Being civilly married is a condition that is an input to hundreds of state and federal laws. When a state marries a couple, the "act of sovereign authority" in which it engaged, as Tobias Barrington Wolff has put it, is to establish how its marriage-dependent laws will treat that couple in the future. When a state determines one of its resident's sex (or the sex of a person present in the state), the state is establishing how its sex-dependent laws will treat that person in the future. Neither of these (marriage or sex) is subject to mandatory enforcement as a judgment due full faith and credit in another state.

(Note also that Judith Butler has observed that "[s]ex is a term that applies to people across the board, so that it is difficult to refer to my 'sex' as if it were radically singular[]" and has suggested that, "generally speaking," it is "never only 'my sex' or 'your sex' that is at issue, but a way in which the category of 'sex' exceeds the personal appropriations of it. . . ." Judith Butler, *Undiagnosing Gender, in* Paisley Currah, Richard M. Juang, & Shannon Price Minter, eds., Transgender Rights 274, 290 (2006).)

For all the foregoing reasons, Professor Cruz argues in *Sexual Judgments* that the Full Faith and Credit Clause cannot provide a federalism "fix" for transgender people who may have their sex declared consistent with their gender identity in one state but face another state's refusal to treat them as having legally shifted from the sex they were assigned at birth. The hope for a constitutional solution lies instead in the guarantees of equality and autonomy protected by the Equal Protection and Due Process Clauses (and the equal protection component of the Fifth Amendment's Due Process Clause where federal governmental action is concerned).

Discussion

1. Should one regard Cruz's "trapped in your birth sex" concern as compelling? What if one approaches the question from a utilitarian perspective and believes that most transgender people will be able to secure a favorable amendment to their birth certificate or judicial declaration of their sex consistent with their gender identity, and that of those who cannot, some of them will be able to undergo further medical transition procedures and then return to a court to try to get a new sex determination predicated on new facts? If that were true (and it seems hard to predict empirically), would that be good cause to set aside the objection?

2. Does Prof. Cruz's objection to the status-ification of "sex" lose force if one concludes that the state legislatures (for example) that enacted laws concerning birth certificate amendments believed, rightly or wrongly, that sex really just *is* an inherent property of individuals? (What then if two state legislatures both acted on such a belief but sharply disagreed about the proper understandings, and hence legal definitions, of "male" and "female"?)

Reading Guide for In re Marriage License for Nash

1. What is the basis for the plaintiff couple's constitutional equal protection challenge to the denial of the marriage license they sought? What level of equal protection scrutiny does the court apply, and why? What is the majority's reasoning for why the denial satisfies that level of scrutiny?

2. What is the couple's argument based primarily on the Full Faith and Credit Clause of the U.S. Constitution? The majority gives alternative grounds for rejecting that argument; what are they?

3. What is the dissenting judge's basic argument? What analogies does she draw? Does she ever specify the precise *legal* basis for her dissent?

In the Matter of the Application for a Marriage License for Jacob B. Nash and Erin A. Barr

Nos. 2002-T- 0149, 2002-T-0179, 2003 WL 23097095
(Ohio Ct. App. Dec. 31, 2003)

[Jacob Nash and Erin Barr were represented by private counsel Randi A. Barnabee and Deborah A. Smith; Ms. Barnabee is a trans woman attorney specializing in transgender legal issues and also represented the plaintiff in, *inter alia*, *Smith v. City of Salem*, 378 F.3d 566 (6th Cir. 2004), superseding 369 F.3d 912 (June 1, 2004), *supra* Chapter 5, Section C. Citizens for Community Values, a right-leaning Christian organization, filed an amicus brief opposing Nash and Barr, as did The Trumbull County Prosecutor's Office.]

DIANE V. GRENDELL, J.

[Transgender man Jacob Nash was identified as female upon birth in Massachusetts, married and divorced a man there, and moved to Ohio the following year. He applied to the Trumbull County, Ohio Court of Common Pleas to change his name from a conventionally female name to Jacob Benjamin Nash in December 1999, attaching a copy of his Massachusetts birth certificate which still designated him as female; the court granted the name change petition in July 2000. Thereafter, he applied to the City Clerk of Fitchburg, Massachusetts, to amend his birth certificate to change his sex marker; an amended certificate with his new name and male sex designation was issued in April 2002. Nash subsequently obtained an amended Ohio driver's license changing the sex designation from female to male. In August 2002, he and presumably cisgender woman Erin Barr applied to the Trumbull County Court of Common Pleas for a marriage license.]

. . . . In the application, the applicants failed to declare Nash's former marriage. Upon a search of the court's records, the court noticed the previous court entry granting Nash's name change. . . . Nash was informed that the license would not issue. [The matter was set for an evidentiary hearing, prior to which he and Barr] submitted an unsigned amended application for a marriage license to the court indicating that Nash was previously married. [They] testified . . . that the failure to indicate Nash's previous marriage was a mere oversight. The trial court, however, found that [their explanation] ". . . lacks credibility[]" [and their action was] "intentional and made with the purpose of misleading the court." [The court denied the license because it falsely listed no prior marriage.]

. . . . On October 2, 2002, and during the pendency of [Nash and Barr's] appeal, [they] submitted a second application . . . properly disclosing Nash's previous marriage. An evidentiary hearing was set for November 5, 2002. Nash claims to be a post-operative female-to-male transsexual. Upon the advice of counsel, however, Nash refused to answer any of the trial court's questions pertaining to Nash's sex reassignment surgeries. Nash's attorney argued that these questions were irrelevant because of Nash's designation as male on the amended Massachusetts birth certificate. [The] trial court found that "the refusal of Jacob B. Nash to permit the Court to make reasonable inquiry permitted by R.C. 3101.05 prevents the court from determining if the requirements for a marriage license have been met under the Ohio statutes." Thus, the trial court denied the applicant's second application. . . . [They again] timely appealed the trial court's decision. The two separate appeals were consolidated. . . .

In their first assignment of error, [they] argue that the trial court violated their Fourteenth Amendment guarantee of equal protection by requiring from Nash more than a driver's license, which the applicants claim "is usually dispositive proof of a person's identity, age and sex." . . . .

. . . . "[E]qual protection analysis requires strict scrutiny of legislative classification only when the classification impermissibly interferes with the exercise of a fundamental right or operates to the peculiar disadvantage of a suspect class." *Massachusetts Bd. of Retirement v. Murgia*, 427 U.S. 307 (1976). Otherwise, the classification is subject to rational basis analysis, *i.e.* whether there exists some rational relationship to a legitimate governmental interest. *Graham v. Richardson*, 403 U.S. 365 (1971).

Although transsexuals do not constitute a suspect class, *Holloway v. Arthur Andersen & Co.*, 566 F.2d 659, 663 (9th Cir. 1977) [*see* Note, Chapter 5, Section A, *supra*], the right to marry has long been recognized as a fundamental right. *See Zablocki v. Redhail*, 434 U.S. 374 (1978). "[N]ot * * * every state regulation which relates in any way to the incidents of or prerequisites for marriage[, however,] must be subject to rigorous scrutiny." *Id.* "[R]easonable regulations that do not significantly interfere with decisions to enter into the marital relationship may legitimately be imposed." *Id.*

R.C. 3101.05 is a reasonable regulation that does not significantly interfere with decisions to enter into the marital relationship and, thus, for purposes of equal protection analysis, the statute is entitled to examination under the rational basis standard. States possess a legitimate interest in protecting the institute of marriage within its borders. *See* [the federal Defense of Marriage Act,] 28 U.S. Code § 1738C. R.C. 3101.05's requirements are, at least, rationally related to further that legitimate interest by insuring that no legal impediments to a proposed marriage exist.

Moreover, the statute, as applied to the applicants, does not violate their equal protection rights. . . .

The probate court has exclusive jurisdiction to grant marriage licenses, R.C. 2101.24(A)(1)(f), and possesses "plenary power * * * to dispose fully of any matter that is properly before the court * * *." R.C. 2101.24(C). When processing a marriage license application, "[i]f the probate judge is satisfied that there is no legal impediment and if one or both of the parties are present, the probate judge shall grant the marriage license." R.C. 3101.05(A). Thus, although a marriage license will normally issue based upon the sworn license application and submission of proper identification, when evidence arises that indicates the possible existence of a legal impediment to the marriage or raises a question regarding an applicant's identification, the court can do what is reasonable and necessary under the circumstances to quell the court's concerns and properly dispose of the matter.

In this case, the court, through a cursory search of its records, discovered evidence that raised a question about the identification and sexual designation of Nash. Thus, when the court required further information from Nash and conducted an evidentiary hearing on the matter, it violated neither of the applicants' equal protection rights. Rather, it was treating like cases alike and unlike cases accordingly. The court cannot be expected to turn a blind eye to evidence that comes before it that could possibly foreclose the issuance of a marriage license. Rather, the court is permitted to proceed with the case accordingly, including requiring additional information or conducting an evidentiary hearing on the matter.

Moreover, in the face of the evidence before the court, the court was not only permitted to require additional information from Nash, as well as conduct an evidentiary hearing on the matter, it was required to do what was necessary to insure that the issuance of the marriage license was proper and valid. In other words, this case was not the usual case and the court was required to treat this case accordingly. In doing so, the applicants' equal protection rights were not violated.

The applicants' first assignment of error is, therefore, overruled.

In their second assignment of error, the applicants argue that Nash's amended Massachusetts birth certificate designating Nash a male was entitled to full faith and credit as a public act or record of another state. The applicants further argue that there is no public policy in Ohio prohibiting a transsexual from changing the sex designation on his or her birth certificate or from marrying a member of his or her biological sex.

"Full Faith and Credit shall be given in each State to the public Acts, Records, and judicial Proceedings of every other State. And the Congress may by general Laws prescribe the Manner in which such Acts, Records, and Proceedings shall be proved, and the Effect thereof." Section 1, Article IV, U.S. CONST. Congress has prescribed that another state's records "shall have the same full faith and credit in every court and office within the United States * * * *as they have by law or usage in the courts or offices of the State * * * from which they are taken.*" 28 U.S.C. §§ 1738, 1739 (emphasis added). Thus, Ohio courts must give the same effect to records from Massachusetts as that record would be given by Massachusetts courts themselves.

Although Massachusetts permits a post-operative transsexual to amend his or her original birth certificate to "reflect the newly acquired sex," "[t]he record * * * relative to birth * * * shall be prima facie evidence of the facts recorded * * *." Mass. Gen. Laws, Chapter 46, Section 19. A birth certificate submitted as evidence in a Massachusetts court is, therefore, not conclusive proof of the facts recorded therein, but is only prima facie evidence of those facts. *Miles v. Edward O. Tabor, M.D., Inc.*, 443 N.E.2d 1302 (Mass. 1982).

"'*Prima facie* evidence means evidence which not only remains evidence throughout the trial but also has up to a certain point an artificial legal force which compels the conclusion [by the trier of fact] that the evidence is true,' *Cook v. Farm Serv. Stores*, 17 N.E.2d 890 (Mass. 1938), until it is rebutted. Once evidence is introduced contradicting the prima facie evidence, the prima facie evidence need be given 'only the weight that . . . [it] deserve[s] in the estimation of the [trier of fact].' *Id.*" *Miles.*

In this case, the amended birth certificate submitted by Nash as evidence of his sex was rebutted by the evidence already in possession of the trial court, to wit, Nash's original birth certificate designating Nash's sex as female. Thus, the trial court gave Nash's amended Massachusetts birth certificate the proper full faith and credit, prima facie evidence of the facts contained therein.

Moreover, since each state retains some attributes of sovereignty and, thus, may enact its own laws and, in effect, define its own public policy, *see Pacific Emp. Ins. Co. v. Indus. Accident Comm.*, 306 U.S. 493, 501 (1939), the full faith and credit clause is not violated when granting full faith and credit to another state's records would violate the public policy of the state applying the other state's records. *See Nevada v. Hall*, 440 U.S. 410 (1979); [string cite omitted].

Ohio, like most states, has a clear public policy that authorizes and recognizes marriages only between members of the opposite sex. [Citing, *inter alia*, state statutes and *In re Ladrach*, 513 N.E.2d 828 (Ohio Prob. Ct. 1987).]

In addition, public policy in Ohio concerning changes to birth certificates is to allow a court to "correct[] **Errors/Mistakes Only** on the original birth record," and not changes in the sexual designation when the original designation was correct. *See* http://www.odh.state.oh.us/VitStats/la-correct.htm (visited Sept. 4, 2003) (emphasis sic) (the official website of Ohio Department of Health, which pursuant to R.C. 3705.02 has the authority to "adopt rules as necessary to insure that this state shall have a complete and accurate registration of vital statistics"). Even if Ohio permitted changes to the sexual designation as noted on the original birth certificate, this would not affect the clear public policy authorizing and recognizing only marriages between members of the opposite sex.

"[W]hen words are not defined in a statute they are to be given their common and ordinary meaning absent a contrary legislative intent." *Moore Personnel Serv., Inc. v. Zaino*, 784 N.E.2d 1178 (Ohio 2003). A female is defined as "the sex that produces ova or bears young," while a male is defined as "the sex that has organs to produce spermatozoa for fertilizing ova." *Webster's II New College Dictionary* (1999). Thus, the "words * * * 'male,' and 'female' in everyday understanding do not encompass transsexuals." *In re Estate of Gardiner*, 42 P.3d 120 (Kan. 2002). Further, since "words [that] are employed in a statute which had at the time a well-known meaning * * * are presumed to have been used in that sense unless the context compels to the contrary," *Standard Oil Co. v. United States*, 221 U.S. 1 (1911), and since the statutory language in question was enacted in the early 1900s, without change, it cannot be argued that the term "male," as used at that time, included a female-to-male post-operative transsexual.

Thus, this court agrees with the court in *Ladrach* that "if it is to be the public policy of the state of Ohio to issue marriage licenses to post-operative transsexuals" to marry someone who has the same biological sex as the transsexual, it is the responsibility of the legislature to make the necessary statutory changes to reflect this change in public policy. Moreover, as Justice Lundberg Stratton expressed concern about in her dissent in *In re Bicknell*, 771 N.E.2d 846 (Ohio 2002) [(approving name change for same-sex couple to have same last name)—Eds.], courts should not, by judicial legislation, place a "stamp of state approval" on any act that "is directly contrary to the state's position against same-sex * * * marriages." Justice Lundberg Stratton's concern in *Bicknell* is amplified in this case because, in permitting this marriage to proceed, we would be placing our "stamp of state approval" on an actual marriage that is directly contrary to Ohio's public policy on same-sex marriages, rather than approving a name change that only would give the intimation of a same-sex marriage, as was the case in *Bicknell*. Thus, this would start us down the slippery slope to judicially legislating same-sex marriages, an area within the purview of the legislature alone.

Further, it has been over 15 years since the decision in *Ladrach* was announced and over 12 years since the decision in *Gajovski v. Gajovski*, 610 N.E.2d 431 (Ohio Ct. App. 1991) [(holding that a man could not terminate support for his ex-wife because she began romantically cohabiting with another woman, as that did not count as "concubinage" because "homosexuals" "can never marry")—Eds.], was announced. In that time, the legislature amended R.C. 3101.01 four times without changing the relevant language designating that only "male persons * * * and female persons * * * may be joined in marriage." "A reenactment of legislation, without modification after judicial interpretation, is further indication of []implied legislative approval of such interpretation." Since the legislature has not changed the pertinent wording of R.C. 3101.01, even in light of the *Gajovski* and *Ladrach* decisions, and has remained silent regarding the issue of sexual designation of a post-operative transsexual, this court is loath to expand the statutory designation of individuals who may marry through judicial legislation. *See Hancock Mut. Life Ins. Co. v. Warren*, 181 U.S. 73 (1901) ("It [is] for the legislature of Ohio to define the public policy of that State"); *Bicknell* (Lundberg Stratton, J., dissenting) ("This is a social policy decision that should clearly be made by the General Assembly after full public debate and discourse, not by judicial legislation."); *Gardiner* ("We view the legislative silence to indicate that transsexuals are not included. If the legislature intended to include transsexuals, it could have been a simple matter to have done so.").

After an extensive review of the case law throughout the country, other courts faced with the issue of a transsexual's sex designation have come to similar conclusions. [The court proceeds to discuss *Gardiner* and *Littleton*, *supra* this section, and *Ulane v. Eastern Airlines, Inc.*, 742 F.2d 1081 (7th Cir. 1984), Chapter 5, Section A, *supra*.]

. . . . Since the Ohio legislature clearly has neither changed the public policy regarding marriages and transsexuals, as expressed in R.C. 3101.01 and interpreted in *Gajovski* and *Ladrach*, nor expanded the definition of male or female beyond their common and traditional interpretations, a marriage between a post-operative female-to-male transsexual and a biological female is void as against public policy. . . . Thus, the trial court was not required to grant full faith and credit to Nash's amended Massachusetts birth certificate because to do so would infringe on clear Ohio public policy against same-sex marriages.

For these reasons, the applicants' second assignment of error is without merit.

. . . . Regardless of whether the failure to declare Nash's prior marriage was sufficient to deny the first application, any marriage license issued by the court would have been void as against public policy.

. . . . The decision of the Trumbull County Court of Common Pleas, Probate Division, is affirmed.

[Presiding Judge Donald R. Ford's brief concurring opinion is omitted.]

JUDITH A. CHRISTLEY, J., dissenting.

Establishing public policy is complicated business. Throughout this country's history, federal and state governments have passed various laws grounded in concerns over what should be done to save people from themselves.

For example, we have a plethora of paternalistic legislation and judicial decision making based on "indisputable" natural law and thinly veiled religious dogma that portrays women and other folk as fragile and somewhat moronic creatures incapable of protecting or thinking for themselves. *Radice v. New York*, 264 U.S. 292 (1924) (upholding a conviction for a violation of a law that prohibited the employment of women in restaurants between the hours of 10:00 p.m. and 6:00 a.m. based on the legislature's finding that "night work is substantially and especially detrimental to the health of women.").

[Similar discussion of *Muller v. Oregon*, 208 U.S. 412 (1908), omitted.]

Laws against miscegenation were judicially supported as efforts to preserve racial integrity and to "prevent the corruption of blood[.]" *Loving v. Virginia*, 388 U.S. 1 (1967). Slavery and other civil inequities were defended on the basis that "negroes" were inferior to whites. *See, generally, Scott v. Sanford*, 60 U.S. 393 (1857) (observing that because African-Americans had "been regarded as beings of an inferior order, and altogether unfit to associate with the white race, either in social or political relations; and so far inferior, that they had no rights which the white man was bound to respect; * * * the negro might justly and lawfully be reduced to slavery for his benefit."); *Plessy v. Ferguson*, 163 U.S. 537 (1896) (upholding the "separate but equal" doctrine).

The establishment of our current civil rights legislation required that we rethink the long established history and origins of our prejudices. Without exception, the continuation of those prejudices was defended in the name of natural law, the God-given order of things, and because it had always been that way. Then, as today, the defenders of the status quo always seemed to have God's lips to their ears.

Not all of these decisions are a hundred years old or older. It was only recently that the Supreme Court of Ohio invalidated the criminal statute that prohibited homosexual, but not heterosexual, importuning. Moreover, it was only in the last thirty years that the United States Supreme Court held that a requirement forcing pregnant teachers in the Cleveland school system to take maternity leave without pay beginning five months before the expected birth of the child was unconstitutional. *Cleveland Bd. of Edn. v. LaFleur*, 414 U.S. 632 (1974) (also noting that some of the considerations underlying the leave policy were to save pregnant teachers from embarrassment of giggling schoolchildren, women "began to show" at the end of the fourth month of pregnancy, and to insulate schoolchildren from the sight of conspicuously pregnant women).

I understand that it is not always appropriate to apply modern sensibilities to prior decisions. That being said, certain questions are so obvious, and certain results are so clearly wrong, that we must look back and, like Dr. Phil, wonder "What were they thinking?"

A person reading the above examples of legislation and judicial decision making would be appalled at the generalizations and outright ignorance used by courts and legislatures to justify obviously unconstitutional laws. Today, however, the majority holds that, in an effort to protect the institution of marriage, a transgender person may not marry someone belonging to that person's original gender classification. In doing so, it claims to be protecting the sanctity of marriage. My question to them is "What is the danger?" How is anything harmed by allowing those, who by accident of birth do not fit neatly into the category of male or female, from enjoying the same civil rights that "correct sex" citizens enjoy? The state's "interest" in protecting the sanctity of marriage in this manner is totally suspect. I would hope that the General Assembly and the courts would have better things to do with their time than to manufacture ways to polarize and alienate significant portions of our citizenry when there is no need.

For these reasons, and as a matter of public policy, I respectfully dissent.

Discussion

1. Is it question-begging, or not, to assume that a policy against marriages of same-sex couples usefully illuminates the circumstances under which two people should be deemed *to be* a "same-sex" couple? In what sense would a holding that a transgender man is a man for purposes of a different-sex-only marriage law start

the court down a slippery slope to judicial approval of same-sex couples' marrying when that would be in direct contravention of the different-sex-couples-only marriage statute?

2. How persuasive is the inference that the state legislature approved of the decisions of one probate court judge when it enacted subsequent changes to the statute involved in that trial court's decision? If the court gave credit to Mr. Nash's amended Massachusetts birth certificate, wouldn't it be holding as a matter of law that he is male, and so his marriage to Ms. Barr wouldn't have been (legally) a same-sex marriage (in violation of Ohio public policy)?

3. What language in the court's opinion might be read to suggest that transsexual persons could not marry anyone whatsoever?

4. Are the dissenter's comparisons apt? If the majority had tried to give a less positivistic ("the legislature said so"), more functional ("here are the good consequences of our decision/bad consequences of contrary decision") justification for their holding, what might they have argued? Would that have been more persuasive?

Reading Guide for Kantaras v. Kantaras

1. The operative legal reasoning of the Florida Court of Appeal in this case challenging the validity of a marriage between a transgender man and a cisgender woman is rather short (primarily, the antepenultimate paragraph of the opinion). What is the court's conclusion about the meaning of "a male" and "a female" in the Florida marriage statutes? Since the court engages in no independent examination of the meaning of the statutory terms, upon what does it base its conclusion?

2. What reason(s) (if any) does the court give for concluding that the ability of a transgender person to marry a person of the sex they were assigned at birth is an issue that should be addressed by the state legislature?

Linda G. Kantaras v. Michael J. Kantaras
884 So. 2d 155 (Fla. Ct. App. 2004)

[Linda Kantaras was represented by the Christian Right legal advocacy organization Liberty Counsel. Michael Kantaras was represented by private counsel and Karen Doering, then a Florida-based attorney from the National Center for Lesbian Rights.]

FULMER, Judge.

Linda Kantaras appeals from a final judgment dissolving her marriage to Michael Kantaras. This appeal presents an issue of first impression in Florida: whether a postoperative female-to-male transsexual person can validly marry a female under the current law of this state. We hold that the law of this state does not provide for or allow such a marriage; therefore, we reverse the final judgment and remand for the trial court to declare the marriage of the parties void ab initio.

[After undergoing "sex reassignment," Michael Kantaras] met Linda, and Linda learned of Michael's surgeries. Linda, who was pregnant by a former boyfriend, gave birth to a son in June 1989. Linda and Michael applied for a marriage license with Michael representing that he was male. The two married in July 1989 in Florida. In September 1989, Michael applied to adopt Linda's son, with Michael representing to the court that he was Linda's husband. Linda gave birth to a daughter in 1992 after Linda underwent artificial insemination with the sperm of Michael's brother.

In 1998 Michael filed a petition for dissolution of marriage seeking to dissolve his marriage to Linda and to obtain custody of both children. Linda answered and counterpetitioned for dissolution and/or annulment claiming that the marriage was void ab initio because it violated Florida law that bans same-sex marriage. Linda claimed that the adoption of her son was void because it violated Florida's ban on homosexual adoption, and she claimed that Michael was not the biological or legal father of her daughter. After a lengthy trial, the trial court entered an [809 page!— Eds.] order finding that Michael was legally a male at the time of the marriage, and thus, the trial court concluded that the marriage was valid. The trial court also concluded that Michael was entitled to primary residential custody of the two children.

In outlining its reasons for determining that Michael was male at the time of the marriage, the trial court stated, in part:

24. Michael at the date of marriage was a male based on the persuasive weight of all the medical evidence and the testimony of lay witnesses in this case, including the following:

(a) As a child, while born female, Michael's parents and siblings observed his male characteristics and agreed he should have been born a "boy."

(b) Michael always has perceived himself as a male and assumed the male role doing house chores growing up, played male sports, refused to wear female clothing at home or in school and had his high school picture taken in male clothing.

(c) Prior to marriage he successfully completed the full process of trans-sexual reassignment, involving hormone treatment, irreversible medical surgery that removed all of his female organs inside of his body, including having a male reconstructed chest, a male voice, a male configured body and hair with beard and moustache, and a naturally developed penis.

(d) At the time of the marriage his bride, Linda was fully informed about his sex reassignment status, she accepted along with his friends, family and wor[k] colleagues that Michael in his appearance, characteristics and behavior was perceived as a man. At the time of the marriage he could not assume the role of a woman.

(e) Before and after the marriage he has been accepted as a man in a variety of social and legal ways, such as having a male driving license;

male passport; male name change; male modification of his birth certificate by legal ruling; male participation in legal adoption proceedings
in court; and as a male in an artificial insemination program, and participating for years in school activities with the children of this marriage
as their father. All of this, was no different than what Michael presented
himself as at the date of marriage.

25. Michael was born a heterosexual transsexual female. That condition
[which] is now called "Gender Identity Dysphoria," was diagnosed for
Michael in adulthood some twenty (20) years after birth. Today and at the
date of marriage, Michael had no secondary female identifying characteristics and all reproductive female organs were absent, such as ovaries, fallopian tubes, cervix, womb, and breasts. The only feature left is a vagina
which Dr. Cole testified was not typically female because it now had a penis
or enlarged, elongate[d] clitoris.

26. Michael after sex reassignment or triatic [*sic*—Eds.] treatments would
still have a chromosomal [pattern] (XX) of a woman but that is a presumption. No chromosomal tests were performed on Michael during the course
of his treatment at the Rosenberg Clinic.

27. Chromosomes are only one factor in the determination of sex and they
do not overrule gender or self identity, which is the true test or identifying
mark of sex. Michael has always, for a lifetime, had a self-identity of a male.
Dr. Walter Bockting, Dr. Ted Huang and Dr. Collier Cole, all testified that
Michael Kantaras is now and at the date of marriage was medically and
legally "male."

28. Under the marriage statute of Florida, Michael is deemed to be male,
and the marriage ceremony performed in the Sandford [*sic*] County Court
house on July 18, 1989, was legal.

. . . .

The Florida Legislature has expressly banned same-sex marriage. . . . In 1997,
the legislature enacted the Florida Defense of Marriage Act, prohibiting marriage
between persons of the same sex. . . .

Courts in Ohio [*In re Ladrach*, 513 N.E.2d 828 (Ohio Prob. Ct. 1987), and *In
re Marriage License for Nash*, Nos. 2002-T- 0149, 2002-T-0179, 2003 WL 23097095
(Ohio Ct. App. Dec. 31, 2003), *supra* this chapter], Kansas [*In re Estate of Gardiner*,
42 P.3d 120 (Kan. 2002), *supra* this chapter], Texas [*Littleton v. Prange*, 9 S.W.3d
223 (Ct. App. Tex. 1999), *supra* Note this chapter], and New York [*Anonymous v.
Anonymous*, 67 Misc. 2d 982, 325 N.Y.S. 2d 499 (1971); *B. v. B.*, 78 Misc. 2d 112,
355 N.Y.S. 2d 712 (1974), both *supra* Note this chapter] have addressed issues involving the marriage of a postoperative transsexual person, and in all cases the courts
have invalidated or refused to allow the marriage on the grounds that it violated
state statutes or public policy. . . . .

There is one case in the United States that has permitted transsexual marriage. In *M.T. v. J.T.*, 355 A.2d 204 (N.J. Super. 1976), the husband sought an annulment on the ground that his wife was a male-to-female transsexual. The New Jersey court rejected the husband's argument, upheld the validity of the marriage, and affirmed a judgment of the lower court obligating the husband to support the transsexual as his wife. . . .

In the case before us, the trial court relied heavily on the approach taken by an Australian family court in *In re Kevin*, (2001) 28 Fam. L.R. 158, *aff'd*, 30 Fam. L.R. 1 (Austl. Fam. Ct. 2003), which the trial court believed "correctly states the law in modern society's approach to transsexualism." In that case, the Australian court took the view that courts must recognize advances in medical knowledge and practice and found that a female-to-male transsexual should be considered a man for purposes of marriage. . . . [T]he Family Court of Australia stated in its conclusion: . . . . "Unless the context requires a different interpretation, the words 'man' and 'woman' when used in legislation have their ordinary contemporary meaning according to Australian usage. That meaning includes post-operative transsexuals as men or women in accordance with their sexual reassignment. . . ."

[The] controlling issue in this case is whether, as a matter of law, the Florida statutes governing marriage authorize a postoperative transsexual to marry in the reassigned sex. We conclude they do not. We agree with the Kansas, Ohio, and Texas courts in their understanding of the common meaning of male and female, as those terms are used statutorily, to refer to immutable traits determined at birth. Therefore, we also conclude that the trial court erred by declaring that Michael is male for the purpose of the marriage statutes. Whether advances in medical science support a change in the meaning commonly attributed to the terms male and female as they are used in the Florida marriage statutes is a question that raises issues of public policy that should be addressed by the legislature. Thus, the question of whether a postoperative transsexual is authorized to marry a member of their birth sex is a matter for the Florida legislature and not the Florida courts to decide. Until the Florida legislature recognizes sex-reassignment procedures and amends the marriage statutes to clarify the marital rights of a postoperative transsexual person, we must adhere to the common meaning of the statutory terms and invalidate any marriage that is not between persons of the opposite sex determined by their biological sex at birth. Therefore, we hold that the marriage in this case is void ab initio.

Our holding that the marriage is void ab initio does not take into consideration the best interests of the children involved in this case. While we recognize that the trial judge went to great lengths to determine the best interests of the children, the issue of deciding primary residential custody was dependent on the trial court's conclusion that the marriage was valid. We do not attempt to undertake a determination of the legal status of the children resulting from our conclusion that the marriage is void. The legal status of the children and the parties' property rights will be issues for the trial court to examine in the first instance on remand.

Reversed and remanded with directions to grant the counterpetition for annulment declaring the marriage between the parties void ab initio.

Discussion

1. The Court of Appeal notes that the trial court found that "[a]t the time of the marriage [Michael] could not assume the role of a woman." What might this mean? After all, the trial court also found (as specified in its full opinion) "Michael still has a vagina." True, Michael also had an "elongated," "enlarged" clitoris that resembled and had the same tissue structure as a small penis. But cisgender women's clitorises vary in size.

2. Given the ostensible linguistic basis for the court's primary conclusion (in the antepenultimate paragraph of the opinion), why might the judges have gone into all the detail about Michael's sex/gender that they described (even more in the full opinion than in this edited version)?

3. After the case was remanded, Michael and Linda went to mediation, resulting in "a settlement in which Michael retain[ed] all of his parental rights and responsibilities and [continued] to share legal custody with the children's mother." National Center for Lesbian Rights, Case Summary & History: *Kantaras v. Kantaras*, , http://www.nclrights.org/cases-and-policy/cases-and-advocacy/kantaras-v-kantaras/ (last visited July 10, 2020).

Getting Sex "Right": Heteronormativity and Biologism in Trans and Intersex Marriage Litigation and Scholarship[*]
David B. Cruz

. . . . [C]ritiques of the non-recognition decisions and arguments in favor of recognition [of trans people's lived sex for different-sex-only civil marriage] have too often been framed . . . as if the only problem has been the law's failure to follow some medical practitioners in embracing a more nuanced version of biological sex. While this approach, which I call "getting sex right," could have some positive results, . . . it rests on a mistaken—and dangerous—view of legal sex as a mirror of natural fact.

[I]t is precisely the valorization of "nature" through notions of "medical science" and, thus, biology, and the attendant displacement of human responsibility, that I am concerned about. I worry that a similar refusal of judgment may underlie the eager embrace of the medical profession and medical standards by pro-reform scholars and judges dealing with transsexual and intersex identity. The appeal to the self-evident normative authority of an autonomous and seemingly objective discipline such as medicine might seem to shield one from the perils or responsibility

---

[*] Excerpted from David B. Cruz, *Getting Sex "Right": Heteronormativity and Biologism in Trans and Intersex Marriage Litigation and Scholarship*, 18 Duke J. of Gender L. & Pol'y 203, 204, 211–12, 216–19, 221–22 (2010).

of taking a stand in making a recommendation or decision on what is, after all, a matter of law and a social issue. Whether or not there are Platonic forms, pure essences that exist independent of human recognition, those are not what law uses. Law is a human project, using human categories instrumentally for human purposes.

It misdirects our focus, to someone's political detriment, to appeal to the natural or to "the facts" of sex (as proclaimed by medical practitioners) as the basis for what are really political judgments about what identities and relationships to recognize. This happens in articles and opinions that repeatedly invoke "reality" or "biological reality"; birth attendants that succeed or fail to record "accurate gender"; supposed "historical facts" in birth registries that all seem to presume there is some objective "truth" of sex or gender, discernable if only we try harder to set aside old ways of thinking and turn to the "experts." Indeed, even many transsexual persons' "discovery narratives" (which we certainly must recognize are favored by clinicians and reform-minded courts) invoke some true essence of sex, a truth recognizable by legal systems if only they could get past simplistic measures of sex like the natal concordance of gonads, genitals, and chromosomes promulgated in *Corbett* [*v. Corbett*, [1971] P 83, [1970] 2 All ER 33, [1970] 2 WLR 1306, (48 MLR 82), *supra* this chapter].

As Sally Sheldon has written about the medicalization of abortion law in Britain, "[t]he doctors' power to define is accepted and reinforced, with other accounts pushed to the margins. This depoliticizes the judicial decision which can be legitimated with reference to scientific truth and is thus seen as uninfluenced by personal moral or political belief." [Sally Sheldon, *Subject Only to the Attitude of the Surgeon Concerned: The Judicial Protection of Medical Discretion*, 5 Soc. & Legal Stud. 95 (1996).] This is as true of sex determination as it is of abortion. Now, Professor Sheldon found in her study that what "the courts did in these cases is actively to protect and entrench the monopoly of doctors, while policing those marginal cases which did not fall within the bounds of good medical practice." Again, my worry is that this can happen in the trans area, with those doctors whom I would consider more "progressive," the ones more willing to come close to saying that a person's sex ought to be determined by their gender identity regardless of surgical, hormonal, or other medical interventions, are likely to be the ones dismissed by law and marginalized.

Granted, there have been some practical benefits of medicalization in the abortion regulation context in Britain. As Sheldon found, "[i]n general, it seems that this largely acts to protect, rather than to impinge upon, women's reproductive autonomy." Likewise, medicalization can give a way for some courts to recognize some litigants' new legal sex identity, and a way for some number of persons to access medical care and gender confirming surgeries through insurance, as well as to make disability discrimination claims.

But Sheldon raises an important cautionary note that we should not overlook in this context:

If the courts continue to adhere to the position of strong preference for medical self-regulation which has been so in evidence, then it seems that where the law has been effective in protecting the doctor-patient relationship from outside attacks, it is likely to be less useful at protecting reproductive autonomy within it. As such, while the alliance with medical interests may have had strategic advantages, it remains inadequate as a basis for building and protecting women's reproductive autonomy within the courts.

Similarly, it may be that medicalization might undermine the law's capacity to protect gender autonomy within doctor-patient relationships. By urging courts to defer to medicine where people have completed medical processes, courts could be more likely to side with a doctor over a trans client, particularly if the client exercises their constitutional right to refuse certain recommended treatments in cases where there is a dispute about whether law should recognize them as a different sex now. . . .

[A]rguments grounded in, for example, rights of medical privacy and autonomy [are] far more normatively appropriate, at least in the U.S. context, than attempts to "get sex right," and illuminate the supposedly objective "truth" of sex. It better avoids a positivistic flight from normativity.

      . . . .

My fear about instead relying on medicine alone is that it might not give courts the resources to start building a true doctrine of gender autonomy. Medicalization encourages a delegation of authority over gender not to individuals, but to medical professionals, a class that has largely maintained itself as gatekeepers over, hence deniers of, access to various gender confirming treatments. Gender autonomy would instead vest primary authority for determining the gendered directions of our lives to us individually—something I think many people working and living in this area believe the law should do. Indeed, I would go further. Under a view such as the disestablishment of sex and gender, [David B. Cruz, *Disestablishing Sex and Gender*, 90 Calif. L. Rev. 997 (2002),] almost all sex distinctions in law would be unconstitutional, and we thus would not need to fight these definitional legal battles day in and day out on as many fronts; to the extent that sex ceases to matter in law, getting sex "right" will seem less imperative. I recognize the likely challenges in getting courts to accept such arguments, but I believe those challenges must be confronted and, eventually, overcome so that scholars and attorneys can support trans people without bolstering the regulatory power of psychiatry and medicine. . . .

Discussion

Does Professor Cruz overestimate the risks of reliance on medical authority to achieve rights protections for trans people? (*But cf.* Alex Sharpe, Transgender Jurisprudence 4 (2002) ("[M]edico-legal discourse has deployed transgender people in furtherance of much wider regulatory strategies around sexual practice and gender performance.")) Is Cruz's analogy to the medicalization of abortion access (in Britain) appropriate? Does he underestimate the value of the gains for trans people possible with invocations of medical authority? Do the developments in the years since publication of *Disestablishing Sex and Gender* shed any light on the relative likelihoods of the negative and/or positive effects of medicalization in the gender recognition context?

Index